Inside 3D Studio, Release 4

Steven D. Elliott

Phillip L. Miller

Contributions by:
Alan DeVore
Gregory Pyros
Jonas Riukis
John Slater

Texture maps on *Inside 3D Studio* CD-ROM created by:
Tim Forcade

Cover art by:
Greg Phillips

NRP
NEW RIDERS PUBLISHING

New Riders Publishing, Indianapolis, Indiana

Inside 3D Studio, Release 4

By Steven Elliott and Phillip Miller

Published by:
New Riders Publishing
201 West 103rd Street
Indianapolis, IN 46290 USA

Printed in the United States of America   3 4 5 6 7 8 9 0

Library of Congress Cataloging-in-Publication Data

Elliott, Steven D., 1960-
    Inside 3D studio, release 4 / Steven D. Elliott, Phillip L. Miller.
      p.   cm.
    Rev. ed. of: Inside 3D studio / Steven D. Elliott... [et al.].
c.1994.
    Includes index.
    ISBN 1-56205-415-5 : $55.00
    1. Computer animation. 2. Autodesk 3D studio. 3. Computer graphics. I. Miller,
Phillip L. II. Title.
TR897.7.I54   1995   94-48226
006.6–dc20   CIP

Warning and Disclaimer

Publisher	Don Fowley
Associate Publisher	Tim Huddleston
Product Development Manager	Rob Tidrow
Marketing Manager	Ray Robinson
Director of Special Projects	Cheri Robinson
Managing Editor	Tad Ringo

About the Authors

Steven D. Elliott recently accepted the position of lead writer for 3D Studio documentation at Autodesk, Inc. Prior to that, he was an independent consultant specializing in computer graphics training and production. He has consulted with Autodesk on education issues for both AutoCAD and 3D Studio, and he taught AutoCAD and multimedia applications at the Authorized Training Center at Moraine Valley Community College in Palos Hills, Illinois.

Mr. Elliott is a registered architect and holds advanced degrees in architecture and computer science from the University of Illinois.

Phillip L. Miller is Autodesk's Senior Multimedia Instructor and is located at their San Rafael, California campus. His duties include curriculum creation, dealer training, and assistance in multimedia product development. His instruction covers the full range of Autodesk software and brings him in contact with 3D Studio users from around the world.

Mr. Miller is a registered architect who before joining Autodesk was a project architect and visualization specialist for a full-service architectural and engineering firm in northern Illinois. He graduated from the University of Illinois with a Masters of Architecture and additional concentrations in fine arts and computer science.

Mr. Miller and Mr. Elliott are *Inside 3D Studio*'s original authors. Both are contributors to *3D Studio Special Effects* (from New Riders Publishing) and have contributed numerous articles to *CADENCE* magazine.

Trademark Acknowledgments

All terms mentioned in this book that are known to be trademarks or service marks have been appropriately capitalized. New Riders Publishing cannot attest to the accuracy of this information. Use of a term in this book should not be regarded as affecting the validity of any trademark or service mark.

3D Studio is a registered trademark of Autodesk, Inc.

AutoCAD is a registered trademark of Autodesk, Inc.

Autodesk Animator Pro is a trademark of Autodesk, Inc.

Acknowledgments

Mr. Elliott wishes to thank his wife, Jean, and daughter, Mary. Their love, support, and, most of all, patience made this book possible. He also thanks J.C. Malitzke and Don McIntyre of Moraine Valley Community College, and Wayne Hodgins of Autodesk for their professional support and encouragement over the years.

Mr. Miller congratulates his wife, Karen, on her tolerance and assures her that, yes, it is finally done—again.

Product Director
Kevin Coleman

Senior Acquisitions Editor
Jim LeValley

Production Editor
Sarah Kearns

Editors
Amy Bezek
Laura Frey
Stacia Mellinger
Cliff Shubs
John Sleeva
Lillian Yates

Editorial Assistant
Karen Opal

Book Designer
Kim Scott

Production Team Supervisor
Katy Bodenmiller

Graphics Image Specialists
Dennis Sheehan
Clint Lahnen

Production Analysts
Angela D. Bannan
Dennis Clay Hager

Production Team
Mona Brown
Michael Brumitt
Charlotte Clapp
Rob Falco
Donna Haigerty
Kimberly K. Hannel
Michael Henry
Ayanna Lacey
Cheryl Moore
Chad Presser
Brian-Kent Proffitt
Erich Richter
Hillary Smith
Tim Taylor
Jill Thompson
Jeff Weissenberger
Holly Wittenberg
Michelle Worthington

Indexers
Gregg Eldred
Michael Hughes

Contents at a Glance

Table of Contents

INTRODUCTION

Introduction

When 3D Studio appeared in 1990, it was a breakthrough product. Until then, the few rendering or animation programs available on the PC were either extremely limited, very expensive, or both. 3D Studio opened the door to affordable, professional, and productive desktop rendering and animation on the PC.

Inside 3D Studio Release 4 is a companion to the excellent reference and tutorial manuals that ship with 3D Studio. It explains in detail the more difficult or less frequently used commands that give many users trouble. It also demonstrates techniques and strategies for accomplishing effects that will help you to be more productive and produce better results.

If you are a beginner at using 3D Studio, you will still find this book to be a valuable next step on the learning curve after you have worked through the original manuals. If you are an intermediate or advanced user of 3D Studio, you will find that this book provides many fresh insights and tips that you can add to your professional toolkit.

Getting the Most from Inside 3D Studio Release 4

As previously stated, *Inside 3D Studio Release 4* is a companion to the manuals that ship with the 3D Studio program, not a replacement. The best approach is to make sure that you have at least browsed the *Reference Manual* and carefully read the *Tutorials Manual*. The 3D Studio manuals provide the foundation upon which *Inside 3D Studio Release 4* is built.

Two approaches are available for using *Inside 3D Studio Release 4*. One is to just sit down and read it. Many figures have been included to illustrate techniques and discussions in the book. In addition, you will find figures for the major steps in the exercises so that you can simply read the exercises and pick up the important concepts.

A better method, however, is to work through the exercises at your computer. It is not realistic to expect you to sit at your computer while reading the sections between the exercises, so here is one possible strategy. Read one or two chapters at your leisure, away from the computer. While reading, mark the exercise steps or techniques that you have trouble visualizing. After completing one or two chapters, go to your computer and try the exercises for those chapters. Refer to the marks you made while reading, and manually work through those techniques. Using this method, you can maximize your comfort while reading in your favorite chair and maximize your productivity at the computer.

Using the 3D Studio Manuals with This Book

To save time and maximize the value that you receive from this book, a strong effort was made to avoid repeating information that you could get from the 3D Studio manuals. While it was not possible to avoid repetition completely, you will find that the majority of the information *Inside 3D Studio Release 4* presents is either a completely new strategy for using 3D Studio, or builds upon commands that were only introduced or covered lightly in the manuals.

This approach assumes that you are partially familiar with the information in the 3D Studio reference and tutorial manuals. Sometimes you will encounter a reference to a command description or a tutorial in the 3D Studio manuals. It is not required that you be familiar with the referenced information to proceed, but it will help. You can use references from *Inside 3D Studio Release 4* to help identify portions of the manuals that you missed or forgot about, and then return to the 3D Studio manuals and review the appropriate sections.

Organization of the Book

Inside 3D Studio Release 4 is organized around five parts and appendixes. These sections are as follows:

✔ "Getting Started," Chapters 1 through 3

✔ "Basic Modeling," Chapters 4 through 8

✔ "Advanced Modeling," Chapters 9 through 14

✔ "Basic Animation Techniques," Chapters 15 through 19

✔ "Advanced Animation," Chapters 20 through 23

✔ "Appendixes," A through F

Part One covers issues of setting up and configuring 3D Studio, system and file management techniques, concepts of perspective, color, and motion, and some universal modeling techniques that are common to multiple modules in 3D Studio. The chapters in this section provide a framework for using 3D Studio. Think of it as setting up your workshop—by the end of this section, you will have arranged all of your tools and prepared them for use. The remaining chapters provide information on how to use those tools.

Parts Two through Five cover basic and advanced modeling and animation. Each part begins with chapters about modeling or animation, and then progresses through materials, lighting, cameras, and output. The chapters in the middle of each part vary according to the information and topics appropriate to a specific section.

Inside 3D Studio Release 4 finishes with six useful appendixes. In general, Appendix A discusses system hardware requirements that you need to consider for your workstation. Appendix B provides information on the various types of output devices with which you should be familiar, even if you rely on service bureaus. Appendix C briefly describes some stand-alone programs that can be used to support 3D Studio production or enhance its output. Appendix F provides instructions for installing files from the CD-ROM.

How to Read the Tutorials

The tutorials for *Inside 3D Studio Release 4* follow a two-column format. The column on the left describes the actions that you are to perform. The column on the right describes what you should see when you perform the actions in the left column. The following is an example of an exercise. Do not try to work this exercise—it is only presented as an example.

Most exercises will begin with some explanatory text such as this. The text tells you what the exercise should accomplish and sets the context for the exercise.

Sample Exercise Format

You might encounter text such as this in the middle of an exercise when one or more actions require an extended explanation.

Start or reset 3D Studio	Puts all modules of 3D Studio into their default state
Choose Load *from the* File *pull-down menu, select the file* CHEVY.3DS, *and then click on* OK	Loads the mesh model of a 1957 Chevrolet 210

continues

continued

Choose Renderer/Render View *and click in the* Camera *viewport, accept the defaults in the Render dialog box, and then click on* Render

Starts the rendering process and displays the Render Progress dialog box, as shown in figure I.1

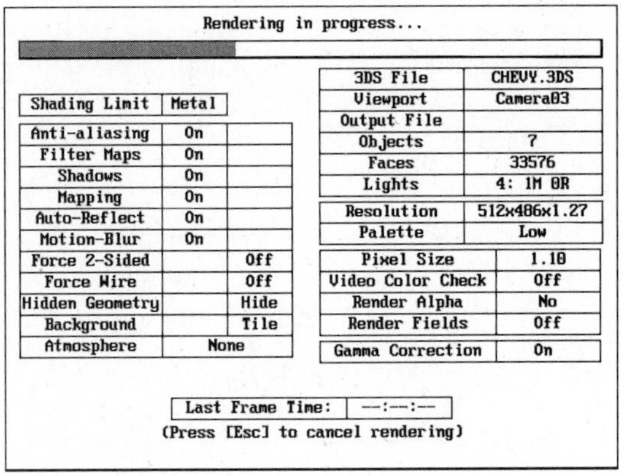

Figure I.1
A sample exercise figure.

The word *Choose* in an exercise always indicates a menu selection. If the selection involves a pull-down menu, you will be told explicitly where to find the menu item. If the selection is from the side screen menu, the menu branches will be separated by slashes, as in the 3D Studio documentation. Setting the values for an LSphere object, for example, requires choosing Create/LSphere/Values. The word *Select* always refers to selecting one or more objects, elements, faces, or vertices. It never refers to menus or icons.

Because this book is designed for people who already have some experience with 3D Studio, some exercise steps are implied rather than explicitly stated. You might, for example, find yourself instructed to "Create a smooth, 20-segment LSphere with a radius of 100 units," rather than forced to read all of the steps required to create the sphere.

Exercises and the CD-ROM

Many of the exercises use files that are either included on the *Inside 3D Studio* CD-ROM or shipped with 3D Studio, or they show you how to create the necessary geometry yourself. Exercise files are located in the \I3D subdirectory on the CD-ROM. Instructions on how to use the files on the CD-ROM or to install them on your hard drive are described later in this introduction.

Other Programs Used with 3D Studio

3D Studio is an excellent program all by itself, but the addition of a few other programs to your toolbox can greatly increase your capabilities. Three types of programs that are directly referenced in the book are described in the following sections.

Animator Pro

Animator Pro is a 2D paint-and-animation program that also is published by Autodesk. While it has been criticized for being only an 8-bit program (256 colors maximum), it still is a valuable addition to 3D Studio. Parts of the chapters concerning mapped materials, and 8-bit rendering and animation, refer to this program.

A few exercises also show you how to create simple material maps using Animator Pro. If you do not own this program, you still can work the exercises with almost any 8-bit or 24-bit paint program that has similar features.

AutoCAD, AutoVision, and AutoCAD Release 13

Chapter 11, "Integrating AutoCAD with 3D Studio," discusses the use of AutoCAD with 3D Studio. AutoCAD is the most popular drafting and design program available—because of that, 3D Studio users need to understand what is involved with bringing 3D AutoCAD models into 3D Studio. If you do not own AutoCAD, this chapter will help you to understand and possibly avoid the difficulties involved with importing AutoCAD DXF files into 3D Studio. If you do own AutoCAD, this chapter will prove valuable in helping you to plan and build 3D models that can be successfully exported to 3D Studio.

AutoCAD Release 13 includes many modeling enhancements and the ability to read and write 3D Studio files. Chapter 11 covers the differences between the various methods of transferring modeling information and the abilities gained by each. Release 13 also ships with AutoVision "in the box" and brings with it additional issues that are important to the 3D Studio user.

True-Color Paint and Image-Processing Programs

Creating high-quality images for use as material maps in 3D Studio requires the use of a 24-bit paint or image-processing program. Chapter 12, "Materials and Mapping," presents true-color map editing, but does not specifically call out the commands or features of any single program.

Using the Inside 3D Studio CD-ROM

Inside 3D Studio Release 4 comes with a CD-ROM packed with many megabytes of programs, meshes, maps, scripts, and other sample software. If you do not yet own a CD-ROM drive, you seriously should consider getting one. With prices for a respectably fast CD reader dropping to around $200, you can't afford not to have one. The value of the files on the CD-ROM that ships with 3D Studio and the CD-ROM that comes with *Inside 3D Studio Release 4* easily justify the cost of purchasing a CD-ROM drive.

The exercise files can be used directly from the *Inside 3D Studio* CD-Rom, so "installing" them is not really necessary. You might want to copy other files on the CD-ROM onto your hard drive or another storage device. In that case, you can either use the install routines found with some of the sample programs or copy the files directly to a directory on your hard disk.

For information about installing the files from the *Inside 3D Studio* CD-ROM, see Appendix F.

Installing the Exercise Files

All of the exercise files that are not included with 3D Studio are contained in a single directory on the *Inside 3D Studio* CD-ROM: \I3DS. You can access these files directly from the CD-ROM when you execute the exercises, or you can create a directory called \I3DS on your hard drive and copy the files there. Some of the exercise files require maps from the World Creating Toolkit CD-ROM that ships with 3D Studio. You will need to copy these files to a subdirectory that is referenced in 3D Studio's Map-Paths parameter. See Chapter 1, "Configuring and Preparation," for details on setting your map paths.

3D Studio automatically looks for map files in the directory from which a 3DS file was loaded. If you copy the exercise files to your hard drive, make sure that you keep the mesh files and map files together, or at least put the map files in a directory where 3D Studio can find them at rendering time. Details about organizing and managing map files are presented in Chapter 2, "Concepts and Theories."

Using the Sample Meshes

A number of sample meshes are provided on the *Inside 3D Studio* CD-ROM for your use. These meshes are licensed free for use in your animations. You cannot, however, resell or otherwise distribute the files.

Using Material Maps

Over 200 MB of maps are provided on the CD-ROM for your use. These maps are licensed free for use in your animations. You cannot, however, resell or otherwise distribute the files.

Viewing the Sample Flics

The sample flic files are provided for your viewing pleasure and to help spark your imagination. These files are copyrighted by their original artists, and you cannot sell or reuse these files without the permission of the artist.

Registering Shareware

Most of the sample programs on the *Inside 3D Studio* CD-ROM are either demonstration programs or shareware programs. Shareware programs are fully functioning products that you can try out prior to purchasing—they are not free. If you find a shareware program useful, you must pay a registration fee to the program's author. Each shareware program provides information about how to contact the author and register the program.

Using CompuServe

Just as you cannot afford to go without a CD-ROM reader, you cannot afford to go without CompuServe. The CompuServe Information Service is an online, interactive network that you can access with a modem and any telecommunications software. The most important feature of this service (at least as far as this book is concerned) is the ASOFT forum.

The ASOFT forum is an area of CompuServe that is maintained by Autodesk for the direct support of 3D Studio and Animator Pro. Hundreds of people from all over the world visit this forum to share ideas, ask and answer questions, and generally promote the use of 3D Studio. If you ask a question on the forum, you are as likely to receive an answer from one of the original programmers as you are to receive an answer from any number of other 3D Studio users. And every question, from the most basic to the most mind-bending puzzler, receives the same quick and courteous treatment.

Examining 3D Studio Release 4

Autodesk and the Yost Group have taken their commitment to component technology to heart and created this release's new features as 3D Studio Plug-Ins.

Release 4—The Plug-In Release

3D Studio Release 4 is essentially a Plug-In release inside and out. On the inside, the core executable was enhanced to allow Plug-In developers substantially more freedom in manipulating the 3D Studio database and user interface. On the outside, the new abilities provided with Release 4 are themselves varieties of 3D Studio Plug-Ins, whose creation was made possible by Release 4's core enhancements. This component development strategy allowed faster development of the top wish-list items, while not creating a learning curve for a new user interface to the core program.

New capabilities of 3D Studio Release 4 include the following:

✔ Inverse Kinematics (provided by the IK_I.KXP Plug-In) gives you the ability to manipulate hierarchies from child to parent rather than the conventional method of parent to child. IK also gives you the powerful ability to have a child follow the motion and rotation of another object and solve the animation for the rest of its hierarchy.

✔ Keyframer Scripting Language (provided by the SCRIPT_I.KXP Plug-In) provides the capability to write and use custom scripts to manipulate entities within the Keyframer environment. With Keyscript, you can do nearly anything a KXP Plug-In can.

✔ Encapsulated Postscript file output (provided by the EPS_I.BXP and EPS_I.PXP Plug-Ins) enables you to output an EPS file of your rendered 3D Studio images.

✔ Camera Control and Perspective Match (provided by the FPREVIEW.VLM Plug-In) gives you finite camera manipulation within an interactive, rendered viewport. It also enables you to display a color background image inside of 3D Studio's 3D Editor and Keyframer modules, and provides very accurate controls to make proper alignment of the camera and background image possible.

✔ Keyframer Fast Preview (also provided by the FPREVIEW.VLM Plug-In) provides interactive playing of the Keyframer's current animation and creates color FLC files relatively quickly.

Although the first three Plug-Ins can be manually loaded within 3D Studio, the last two functions are provided through a VLM program that must be included in your User-Program list in order to be used.

You cannot "upgrade" 3D Studio Release 3 by simply adding the preceding Plug-Ins to a current install. These Plug-Ins require the IPAS enhancements internal to 3DS.EXE and will not load without the Release 4 executable being present because they depend on its new, internal abilities.

While the core code included many enhancements for developers, it also corrected many minor bugs and anomalies. The true number and type of adjustments are considered confidential by Autodesk; however, it has been said publicly that well over 100 situations have been corrected. This makes this release of 3D Studio the most stable in its history.

Plug-In: The New Term for IPAS

The IPAS programming language was introduced with Release 2 to provide third-party developers with a method of writing applications for use within 3D Studio. A program written with this language was termed an *IPAS external process,* of which there were four types: Image, Procedural, Animation, and Surface. These titles provided the letters for the acronym *IPAS,* and also served to identify their file name extensions: IXP, PXP, AXP, and SXP.

Release 3 introduced two more external process formats: Bitmap (BXP) and Keyframer (KXP). At that time, it was felt that keeping the term IPAS was better than expanding the existing acronym into a tongue twister and that all external processes would still be referred to as IPAS routines.

Although Release 4 does not provide another external process type, it was found that the name "IPAS" was confusing to the public and most often needed explaining. As a result, what was formerly known as an IPAS routine is now referred to as a 3D Studio *Plug-In.* This is an official renaming by Autodesk, and most developers (now called 3D Studio *Plug-In Partners*) will be renaming their products and literature accordingly. Although this new term may take some veteran users quite a while to get accustomed to, *Inside 3D Studio Release 4* refers to external process utilities by their new title of Plug-In.

Release 4 Quick Start for Previous Inside 3D Studio Readers

If you are a veteran 3D Studio user who has previously read *Inside 3D Studio,* then you may want to concentrate on the following sections of this edition to get quickly up to speed with Release 4's new features:

- ✔ Chapter 1—User Program Configuration
- ✔ Chapter 1—EPS Output
- ✔ Chapter 11—Integrating with AutoCAD Release 13
- ✔ Chapter 13—Interactive Camera Control
- ✔ Chapter 15—Fast Preview Rendering
- ✔ Chapter 20—Animating with Inverse Kinematics
- ✔ Chapter 22—Keyframer Scripting

Although these sections target the new features of Release 4, several sections of *Inside 3D Studio Release 4* have been enhanced to give you further insight into this in-depth program. After becoming comfortable with 3D Studio's new features, veteran 3D Studio users will probably want to browse through the other sections of *Inside 3D Studio Release 4* to reinforce their growing understanding of the program and computer animation in general.

New Riders Publishing

The staff of New Riders Publishing is committed to bringing you the very best in computer reference material. Each New Riders book is the result of months of work by authors and staff who research and refine the information contained within its covers.

As part of this commitment to you, the NRP reader, New Riders invites your input. Please let us know if you enjoy this book, if you have trouble with the information and examples presented, or if you have a suggestion for the next edition.

Please note, though: New Riders staff cannot serve as a technical resource for 3D Studio or for questions about software- or hardware-related problems. Please refer to the documentation that accompanies 3D Studio or to the application's Help systems.

If you have a question or comment about any New Riders book, there are several ways to contact New Riders Publishing. We will respond to as many readers as we can. Your name, address, or phone number will never become part of a mailing list or be used for any purpose other than to help us continue to bring you the best books possible. You can write us at the following address:

New Riders Publishing
Attn: Associate Publisher
201 W. 103rd Street
Indianapolis, IN 46290

If you prefer, you can fax New Riders Publishing at (317)581-4670.

You can send electronic mail to New Riders from a variety of sources. NRP maintains several mailboxes, organized by topic area. Mail in these mailboxes will be forwarded to the staff member who is best able to address your concerns. Substitute the appropriate mailbox name from the following list when addressing your e-mail. The mailboxes are as follows:

ADMIN	Comments and complaints for NRP's Publisher
APPS	Word, Excel, WordPerfect, and other office applications
ACQ	Book proposals and inquiries by potential authors
CAD	AutoCAD, 3D Studio, AutoSketch, and CAD products
DATABASE	Access, dBASE, Paradox, and other database products
GRAPHICS	CorelDRAW!, Photoshop, and other graphics products
INTERNET	Internet
NETWORK	NetWare, LANtastic, and other network-related topics
OS	MS-DOS, OS/2, and all other operating systems except UNIX and Windows

UNIX	UNIX
WINDOWS	Microsoft Windows (all versions)
OTHER	Anything that doesn't fit into the preceding categories

If you use an MHS e-mail system that routes through CompuServe, send your messages to the following:

mailbox @ NEWRIDER

To send NRP mail from CompuServe, use the following address:

MHS: *mailbox* @ NEWRIDER

To send mail from the Internet, use the following address format:

mailbox @newrider.mhs.compuserve.com

NRP is an imprint of Macmillan Computer Publishing. To obtain a catalog of information, or to purchase any Macmillan Computer Publishing book, call (800) 428-5331.

Thank you for selecting *Inside 3D Studio Release 4!*

Part I

Getting Started

Chapter Snapshot

Many factors that influence the success of your animations are decided before you ever sit down in front of your workstation. Without good planning and organization, even simple jobs turn into a terrible mess. This chapter discusses the basic steps involved in getting ready to start an animation project. The following topics are presented:

✔ Configuring your preferences in 3D Studio

✔ Understanding and setting gamma correction

✔ Running 3D Studio under Windows 3.1

✔ Running other programs from the 3D Studio shell

✔ Exploring strategies for modeling complex scenes

✔ Using other modelers with 3D Studio

✔ Examining file management techniques

✔ Archiving your work

✔ Creating and using story boards

CHAPTER

Configuring and Preparation

Before you start, you should read the *Installation and Performance Guide* that ships with 3D Studio. You also need to have information about your graphics cards and any third-party video drivers close at hand. Finally, for the section on story boards, consider having a small pad of paper and a pencil handy. You might want to try sketching techniques as you read the story board section.

Installing 3D Studio

A few steps are required before you can run 3D Studio for the first time. Even before you install the software, you should think about how your system is set up and whether or not you want to make any changes.

Once you properly install 3D Studio's hardware lock and examine your system's memory and disk configuration, you can proceed with installing 3D Studio.

The Hardware Lock

The first step in installing 3D Studio is to plug the hardware lock into your computer's parallel port. 3D Studio uses the same lock for all releases of the program, so if you are upgrading from an older version of 3D Studio, a new lock is not included in your upgrade package.

3D Studio's hardware lock must be plugged into one of your available parallel ports before you start 3D Studio. You should turn off your computer and all attached peripherals before you plug in the hardware lock to prevent any chance of damaging the lock due to electrical discharge. If 3D Studio fails to see the lock, you will receive the error message Sentinel Pro Not Found when you attempt to start the program. There are a number of solutions to this problem. A few of the most common solutions are the following:

- ✔ **The hardware lock is loose.** Check the connection with the parallel port.

- ✔ **The parallel port is configured wrong.** Newer computer systems use enhanced parallel ports that are often incompatible with the lock. Check your system manuals to see if there is a way to set your parallel port for an AT compatible mode or otherwise disable any advanced features.

- ✔ **The parallel port does not have enough power to drive the lock circuitry.** Try attaching your printer to the lock and turn the printer on. Sometimes this will draw enough power through the lock to initialize it.

- ✔ **If all else fails, buy a separate parallel port card for the lock.** These cards are cheap (about $20), and Autodesk technical support claims this will work when all else fails.

There are a few other techniques and special conditions that Autodesk has described in a file named HWLOCK.TXT. This file is available for downloading from the ASOFT forum on CompuServe.

Memory Concerns

3D Studio is a *virtual memory* program. This means that if 3D Studio uses all of the available system memory (RAM) on your system, it then uses part of your hard drive as if it were RAM. The part of your hard drive that 3D Studio uses as RAM is called the *swap file.*

The advantage of this technique is that 3D Studio can keep working even though it has run out of RAM. Without the ability to use the swap file on your hard drive, 3D Studio would crash when a rendering job ran out of RAM. In fact, 3D Studio will crash with an Out of RAM error message if it uses all of the available RAM and all available space on your hard drive.

The downside to using virtual memory is that access to the swap file on your hard drive is incredibly slow when compared to accessing RAM. A rendering can take two to three times as long if swapping is required. This might not be a concern for rendering a single frame, but for an animation, even a few extra seconds per frame quickly add up. Imagine that you are rendering a one minute animation of 1,800 frames. If swapping to your hard drive adds just an extra one minute per frame, that equals 30 extra hours of rendering time!

Another problem associated with swapping is that once the swap file is created, it can never decrease in size and is used even if your next render could easily fit into RAM. This slows down operations considerably. The only way to clear the swap space is to quit 3D Studio and start it again.

Once you have 3D Studio installed and configured, you can check whether or not a swap file has been created by choosing the Current Status command from the File pull-down menu. This command displays the Current Status dialog box, as shown in figure 1.1. You are primarily interested in the Memory (Kbytes) portion of the dialog box.

```
        Current Status
     ┌──────────────────────┐
     │      3D Lofter        │
     │  Shapes:        0     │
     │  Vertices:      0     │
     ├──────────────────────┤
     │      3D Editor        │
     │  Objects:       0     │
     │  Vertices:      0     │
     │  Faces:         0     │
     │  Lights:        0     │
     │  Cameras:       0     │
     ├──────────────────────┤
     │    Memory (KBytes)    │
     │  Available:   14484   │
     │  Used:         3360   │
     │  Swap file:       0   │
     │  Page faults:     0   │
     ├──────────────────────┤
     │  Last Render:  --:--:-- │
     │       ┌────────┐      │
     │       │   OK   │      │
     │       └────────┘      │
     └──────────────────────┘
```

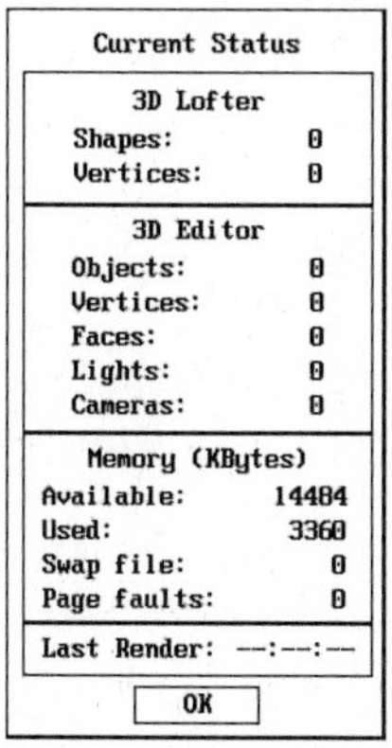

Figure 1.1
Checking memory use with the Current Status dialog box.

The memory portion of the dialog box contains four entries that tell you how memory is being used, as follows:

✔ **Available:** Indicates how much RAM 3D Studio found when it was started. This number should be reasonably close to the amount of extended memory you have installed in your system. The available memory will probably not be exactly equal to the amount of extended memory because it may be affected by various device drivers, memory managers, or other programs.

✔ **Used:** Tells you how much memory 3D Studio has accessed so far. You want this value to be less than, or equal to, the available memory.

✔ **Swap file:** If the amount of memory used exceeds the amount available, then a swap file is created to provide the extra virtual memory. The moment this value exceeds zero, 3D Studio's performance drops through the floor.

✔ **Page faults:** Indicates how many times 3D Studio has accessed the swap file.

As you can see, the use of virtual memory helps 3D Studio avoid crashing, but you pay a heavy price in reduced performance. If you render many projects that create a swap file, you should seriously consider adding more RAM to your system.

Disk Concerns

A full installation of 3D Studio requires a minimum of 23 MB of disk space to hold all of the program executable, support, and sample files. Do not make the mistake of thinking that you can shoehorn 3D Studio onto a system with 30 MB of free disk space and do anything useful. Productive use of 3D Studio requires a lot of disk space.

As you read previously, 3D Studio creates a swap file on your hard drive when it runs out of memory. If there is insufficient room on the hard drive to create the swap file, 3D Studio crashes with an Out of memory error. The amount of disk space that you want to keep free varies with the amount of RAM that you have installed and the type of projects that you render. As you add more RAM to your system, your requirements for swap file space go down because it is more likely that your entire rendering job will fit into available RAM. Setting aside 16 MB or even 32 MB of disk space for a swap file provides a good margin of safety.

Where should you locate the swap file? The default location for 3D Studio's swap file is the root directory of the drive where 3D Studio is installed. This is usually less than optimal for two reasons. First, if you access 3D Studio over a network, the network drive will become the swap file location and suffer from performance lags due to network bottlenecks. Secondly, placing the swap file on a general use drive makes it susceptible to fragmentation. *Fragmentation* is the effect where files and empty space on a heavily used drive tend to get broken into many small chunks and scattered about the disk. This effect can greatly reduce the performance of disk accesses to the swap file.

A good solution is to partition your hard drive into smaller logical drives and set up a dedicated drive to hold only the swap file. For example, assume that you have a 540 MB hard drive and you partition it into a 500 MB drive C and a 40 MB drive D. You could then specify that the 3D Studio swap file is always placed on drive D. As long as you do not store other files on drive D, 3D Studio will always have a clean, non-fragmented, 40 MB chunk of disk space for use as a swap file. The drawback is that 3D Studio is now limited to no more than 40 MB of virtual memory.

During the installation process, you are asked to specify a drive for the location of the virtual memory swap file. The default will be the same drive that you specified for the location of the 3D Studio program files. If you have set up a special petition to hold the swap file, you should identify that drive.

You can also change the location of the swap file after installation by editing the PharLap switches within 3D Studio. You use the provided program CFIG386.EXE to make these changes directly to the 3DS.EXE file. The switch that you need to change is the -swapdir setting. Because you are directly modifying the 3DS.EXE file, you need to be very careful about the changes that you make. Check the "Performance and Memory Management" chapter of the *Installation Guide* for details on this and other PharLap switches.

Finally, some people have reported problems with running 3D Studio on compressed drives (such as those using Doublespace or Stacker). The problem seems to occur when the swap file is located on a compressed drive. If you are using a disk compression program, you should seriously consider setting aside an uncompressed portion of the drive for the swap file. Use the technique described previously to direct the swap file to your uncompressed drive.

Starting the Install Program

After the hardware lock is installed and you have decided onto what drive you want to install 3D Studio, place the first disk into your floppy drive, log in to the drive, and enter **INSTALL** to load 3D Studio onto your computer's hard disk. Follow the instructions displayed by the installation program.

Setting System Configuration

Now that 3D Studio has been installed on your computer, it should be configured for optimum performance. This is where you tell 3D Studio what computer hardware you have, what videotape equipment you will be using, and the answers to a few other questions that the program needs to know.

The following paragraphs discuss fine-tuning the configuration of 3D Studio through the use of the 3DS.SET file. 3D Studio will work quite well, right out of the box, with its default 3DS.SET file. If you are eager to get started, jump ahead to the section "Configuring the Vibrant Options."

The 3DS.SET File

The primary configuration file for 3D Studio's setting is the file 3DS.SET. This is a simple text file that can be edited with any ASCII mode text editor. As you read the following sections in this chapter, you will soon realize that most of the settings stored in the 3DS.SET file can be changed from within 3D Studio. The reason for studying the 3DS.SET file is that it provides the most complete and permanent control over 3D Studio.

You should not edit the 3DS.SET file with any editor that inserts formatting codes or non-ASCII information into the file. To stay on the safe side, avoid using word processors like MS Word or WordPerfect, even in their DOS Text mode. Your best choice for editing the 3DS.SET file is either the DOS utility EDIT.COM, or better yet, use 3D Studio's own internal text editor.

3D Studio looks for the 3DS.SET file as soon as you start the program, and reads all the information immediately. After the program starts, it never looks at 3DS.SET again. If you make changes to the file from within 3D Studio, you will need to exit and restart the program for them to take effect.

If you need different configurations of the 3DS.SET file, you can save them with different names, and tell 3D Studio to use other configurations by using a command-line option. They must be kept in the same directory as the main 3D Studio executable. Starting the program by typing **3DS** ↵, for example, will start 3D Studio with the settings in your 3DS.SET file. If you type **3DS SET=3DS-BIG.SET** ↵, the program loads the configurations in the 3DS-BIG.SET file. Make sure that you don't have spaces around the equal sign, or the program will not accept the alternate SET file.

Having alternate SET files is a very powerful time-saving feature of the program that many users neglect to use. If, for example, you are working on a project that requires 256-color animations for playback on a computer screen, your required configuration would be very different from one in which you were rendering full-color, high-resolution images that eventually will be recorded on videotape one frame at a time. Instead of editing the configuration file numerous times, just create a separate one for each type of project that you work on.

Editing the 3DS.SET file is an easy procedure. The file is very well-documented to help you make decisions during editing. Any line that starts with a semicolon is considered a comment and is ignored by the program. The headers for each area have been designed to organize related settings into groups for ease of customizing. The order that the parameters appear in the file is not important.

The file consists of a series of parameter names on the left, followed by an equal sign and a value (sometimes called an argument) on the right side. The values YES and ON are interchangeable, as are NO and OFF.

Approximately the first 36 lines control your display hardware. These settings are controlled by the Vibrant Graphics Display Driver within 3D Studio. You should leave the display settings alone and let the Vibrant configuration program adjust the values. This is the only section of the 3DS.SET file that has its own separate editor.

The section "Configuring the Vibrant Options" describes how to change the display settings.

Following the Vibrant section are three sections dedicated to new parameters added for 3D Studio Release 4, with the remaining sections based upon various 3D Studio functions and program modules. The following sections describe the 3DS.SET parameters as they appear in the file.

New R4 General Parameters

This section covers various new parameters that would normally be scattered throughout the various sections of the 3DS.SET file. Grouping these new parameters at the top of the file simplifies the process of updating customized SET file from the previous version of 3D Studio. You can simply check these parameters, set them to your desired values, and then paste them as a block into your existing SET files.

An important point to note about these parameters is that, by default, they are commented out with a semicolon placed at the beginning of each line. This causes the new parameters to be ignored and lets 3D Studio operate as it normally did in Release 3. You must make a conscious effort to enable these parameters and then set them to your desired values.

```
;-----------------------------------------------------------------
;   NEW RELEASE 4 PARAMETERS
;-----------------------------------------------------------------
;FIELD-NO-DOUBLE = YES
;BATCH-RENDER-PAUSE = YES
;MAX-PIXEL-SIZE = 1.5
;TEXTURE-SHARPEN = .6
;MAX-SHADOW-LEVELS = 7
;SORT-CASE-SENSITIVE = YES
;KEEP-ALPHA-255=NO
;VPOST-ZBUFFER = YES
;SET-IPAS-RDONLY = YES
;-----------------------------------------------------------------
```

The FIELD-NO-DOUBLE parameter controls how frames are interpreted in the Keyframer for rendering with field mode turned on. If the parameter is set to YES, rendering in field mode treats each frame in the Keyframer as a field rather than as a full frame. This means that frames 1 and 2 in the Keyframer would be rendered as fields 1 and 2, and they would be combined as a single frame. This gives you the ability to place keys on each field. See Chapter 23, "Animation for Field/Frame-Accurate Recording," for more information on fields.

BATCH-RENDER-PAUSE affects the execution of command-line rendering with batch files. When set at its default value of YES, 3D Studio will pause during rendering and wait for user input for any render warning dialogs. An example is the dialog that an object needs mapping coordinates. If the parameter is set to NO, then 3D Studio ignores any dialogs needing user input and proceeds with the rendering. The advantage to setting this parameter to NO is that one bad file will not hold up a large batch rendering job. The drawback is that you will get unexpected results from the bad files that are rendered.

Early versions of 3D Studio Release 4 had the BATCH-RENDER-PAUSE parameter listed twice in the 3DS.SET file—once in this New Release 4 section and once in the Render Parameters section. You should delete one of these entries from your file to avoid confusion and conflicting settings.

The MAX-PIXEL-SIZE parameter is used to smooth edges of high contrast lines in an animation. The default maximum value for this parameter is 1.5, as described in the *Installation Guide.* Certain, rare rendering jobs may need this value set even higher than the maximum of 1.5. You can achieve this by activating this parameter with a value of 2.0. Activating this parameter does not automatically use a pixel size of 2.0; it simply enables you to set the pixel size that high. It is recommended that you not use such a high setting unless you really need very smooth edges and you are willing to pay a considerable price in increased rendering time.

The TEXTURE-SHARPEN parameter adjusts the effect of the Blur slider in the Mapping Parameters dialog box of the Materials Editor. Sometimes even the lowest setting of texture blur in the Mapping Parameters dialog box does not produce sharp enough maps, but turning FILTER-MAPS completely off is also undesirable. In these cases, you can activate the TEXTURE-SHARPEN parameter. The default value is 0.6 and values of 1.0 to 1.6 help to sharpen the maps while still taking advantage of map filtering. If you sharpen your texture maps, all maps in the scene are sharpened and you increase the likelihood of scintillation problems. You should not set the TEXTURE-SHARPEN parameter any higher than 1.6.

MAX-SHADOW-LEVELS controls memory consumption for ray-traced shadows. The default setting is 7—lowering this value (to 5 or 6) causes 3D Studio to use less memory when calculating shadow information at the expense of longer calculation time. You only want to use this option when you have ray-traced shadow casting lights and you suspect that memory consumed for the shadows is causing you to page to disk.

The SORT-CASE-SENSITIVE feature enables you to alter the object name sorting for dialog boxes. By default, 3D Studio is case-insensitive when it displays objects names, mixing capitalized names with uncapitalized names. You can force case-sensitive listing by activating this option set to YES. As mentioned in the SET file, case-sensitive sorting is helpful for AutoCAD import since AutoCAD entities always use all capital letters.

KEEP-ALPHA-255 is a special-purpose parameter that can be ignored by most people. Normally, 3D Studio ignores an Alpha channel where all of the pixels have a value of 255 (white). The reason for this is that an all-white Alpha channel represents a transparency map with no transparency. There may be special situations where you will need to keep an all white Alpha channel, and in those cases you can set this parameter to YES.

VPOST-ZBUFFER creates a depth map that can be used by certain Plug-In programs. Your Plug-In documentation should tell you whether or not you need to activate this parameter.

SET-IPAS-RDONLY is a network-rendering parameter for Plug-Ins. Check your Plug-In manuals for instructions on whether you need to change this parameter from its default.

New R4 Text Editor Parameters

These parameters control how the built-in text editor functions. These parameters work with the text editor color parameters mentioned later in this chapter.

```
;---------------------------------------------------------------------
;      NEW RELEASE 4 TEXT EDITOR PARAMETERS
;---------------------------------------------------------------------
;ED-JOIN-LINES = YES
;ED-AUTO-INDENT = YES
;ED-SPLIT-LINES = YES
;ED-TRANSLATE-TABS = NO
;ED-TAB-LENGTH = 8
;ED-CTRL-CLIP-KEYS = Yes
;---------------------------------------------------------------------
```

ED-JOIN-LINES set to YES causes two lines to be joined together as one if you backspace from the start of the lower line. When set to NO, backspacing from the start of a line will move the cursor up one line, but will not join the two lines together.

ED-SPLIT-LINES defaults to YES and causes a line to be split into two lines when you press ⏎Enter in the middle of the line. When set to NO, pressing ⏎Enter in the middle of a line will move the cursor down one line, but will not split the line into two lines.

ED-AUTO-INDENT, when set to YES, causes all lines created after an indented line to use the same level of indentation. This is very handy for writing program code. When set to NO, new lines always start all the way to the left regardless of the indentation of the previous line.

ED-TRANSLATE-TABS allows 3D Studio to insert true tab characters when you press the Tab↹ key, if set to YES. When set to NO, 3D Studio inserts the specified number of spaces when a Tab↹ key is pressed.

ED-TAB-LENGTH specifies the length of a tab character or the number of spaces to insert when ED-TRANSLATE-TABS is set to NO. The value must be in the range of 2–24.

New R4 Fast Preview Parameters

These settings control the default operation of the Fast Preview and Camera Control Plug-In.

```
;---------------------------------------------------------------------
;      NEW RELEASE 4 PARAMETERS FOR FAST PREVIEW AND CAMERA CONTROL
;---------------------------------------------------------------------
;FPREVIEW-PLAY-MODE = SKIP
;FPREVIEW-TARGET-FRATE = 30
;FPREVIEW-TWOSIDED = YES
;FPREVIEW-SHADE-LIMIT = WIRE
```

continues

```
;FPREVIEW-TEXTURED-COLOR = 128,128,128
;FPREVIEW-BACKGROUND-BITMAP = <path/filename>
;FPREVIEW-BACKGROUND-COLOR = 0,0,0
;FPREVIEW-DISTANCE-STEP = <float-value>
;FPREVIEW-ANGLE-STEP = 10
;------------------------------------------------------------------
```

Most of these parameters merely set the defaults for the buttons and fields found under the Control Panels of Camera Control and Fast Preview. If you find yourself regularly resetting the control panel options, consider changing their defaults with these parameters.

There are two parameters in this list that are not set by any control in the Camera Control or Fast Preview user interface. These parameters are FPREVIEW-PLAY-MODE and FPREVIEW-TEXTURED-COLOR.

FPREVIEW-PLAY-MODE controls how 3D Studio attempts to achieve the target playback frame rate. The default method is to drop the shading limit from its specified setting to a lower value (say Flat or Wire) to allow faster playback. On many systems, even dropping to Wire mode rendering will not achieve the target playback rate. Many users will want to activate this parameter and set it to SKIP. This setting tells 3D Studio to hold the specified rendering mode and to drop frames in an attempt to reach the desired playback. This will result in jerkier playback, but it will come closer to giving you an accurate sense of the animations timing.

FPREVIEW-TEXTURED-COLOR sets the color used to represent mapped materials. If the parameter is commented out (the default), 3D Studio uses the material's diffuse color instead of the map. If this parameter is activated, you must specify a color to be used for all mapped materials. It is preferable that you always specify a diffuse color for your mapped materials and leave this parameter commented out. See Chapter 6, "Introduction to the Materials Editor," for a discussion of material colors and mapping.

The Output Devices Options

The next area of the 3DS.SET file sets the output devices. The output device parameters tell 3D Studio what printer and video tape controller you are using, as follows:

```
;------------------------------------
;     OUTPUT DEVICES
;
DEFAULT-HARDCOPY = RHPADI
VTR-DEVICE = DIAQUEST
VTR-PRE-STOP = OFF
;
;------------------------------------
```

When specifying these devices, you can choose between two types of drivers. The first type is an internal driver built into 3D Studio. To use this type of driver, simply type its name in the value side of the statement.

The second type of driver is an external *Autodesk Device Interface* (ADI) driver. The ADI specification was designed by Autodesk as a standard method of communication between Autodesk programs and external devices. The manufacturer of the hardware, or an independent company, writes an ADI driver to communicate with their hardware. By telling 3D Studio to use the ADI driver, it knows how to communicate with the external device.

An ADI driver for 3D Studio might not function properly as an ADI driver for another Autodesk program, such as AutoCAD. Also, ADI environment variables such as RCPADI and RDPADI will override the display settings in the 3DS.SET file. If you use multiple Autodesk programs, you should reset all ADI environment variable whenever you start the program.

3D Studio can use ADI drivers for display graphics boards, rendering graphics boards, video tape recorders, and other single frame output devices, digitizers, and printers.

The way that 3D Studio knows the name of the external driver program is through a DOS environment variable that holds the drive, path, and file name of the driver. For example, the default 3DS.SET file uses an ADI driver for the hardcopy device that is accessed through the variable RHPADI. The sample hardcopy ADI driver provided with 3D Studio is the file RDPPJET.EXP for the Hewlett-Packard Paintjet printer. To use this device, you must execute the following DOS command:

```
SET RHPADI=C:\3DS3\DRIVERS\RDPPJET.EXP
```

assuming, of course, a standard 3D Studio installation on drive C. Most people execute this command as part of their AUTOEXEC.BAT file or a batch file to start 3D Studio. The next time you run 3D Studio, the external driver will automatically be called to enable you to configure it by answering a few questions; the answers will be stored in a file in the main 3D Studio directory, called 3DADI.CFG. If you need to reconfigure the external drivers, delete this file and the program will ask you the questions again.

The first line identifies your printing device. There are no internal printer drivers for 3D Studio, so you must use an external ADI driver identified by the RHPADI variable, as described previously. Very few printer drivers are available for 3D Studio. The best method of printing rendered files is to render to a file, and then output the file through a printing utility or desktop publishing program. This method is advantageous because external programs usually have more control over the printer and can adjust the contrast, brightness, and other parameters of the image before sending it to the device. In addition, having the file on disk enables you to save it for future use, or to print it again without waiting for a second render if there is a problem with the printer.

The next line identifies your video tape recorder controller. There is an internal driver available for the DiaQuest family of controllers. If you are using the internal driver, type **DIAQUEST** after the equal sign. If you are using an external driver, such as the Sony recordable laser disk (LVR3000N) or Sony Hi-8 (EVO-9650), which are included with the program, you must type **VTPADI**, and set the variable to point to the appropriate driver, as discussed previously.

The line labeled VTR-PRE-STOP controls whether a STOP command is automatically sent to the VTR device before commands such as Rewind, Play, Fast Forward, and so on are issued. The proper answer to this depends on your VTR controller and tape deck. Some controllers issue this command themselves. With controllers that continue working after control is returned to 3D Studio, receiving a Stop command while in another process can cause problems with the driver. If the controller's documentation does not have this information, set it to NO first. If you then have problems, switch it to YES.

Disk Paths

The disk path section is mostly self-explanatory. It controls where 3D Studio looks for its support files. If no parameters are given, all the files are assumed to be in the main 3D Studio directory where the executables are located. If a full path name is not given, the files are assumed to be in a subdirectory under the main 3D Studio directory.

```
;---------------------------------
;    DISK PATHS
;---------------------------------
SHAPER-PATH = "shapes"
LOFTER-PATH = "lofts"
MESH-PATH = "meshes"
FONT-PATH = "fonts"
MAT-PATH = "matlibs"
MAP-PATH = "maps"
PROJECT-PATH = "projects"
DRIVER-PATH = "drivers"
PROCESS-PATH = "process"
IMAGE-PATH = "images"
FLIC-PATH = "images"
PREVIEW-PATH = "flics"
VPOST-PATH = "vpost"
TEMP-PATH = "temp"
;
;---------------------------------
```

If you run 3D Studio on a network, you might want to have several of the data files and maps located on a central file server for access by other machines. However, you should keep all of your temporary files, drivers, process files, and previews on your local disk. This increases the speed of your renderings and prevents temporary files created by other machines on the network from writing over each other.

Some of these path settings are more critical than others. The paths for data files such as SHP, LFT, 3DS, PRJ, and MLI only tell 3D Studio where to look first. You can easily override these paths using the file selector dialog box. Other paths cannot be overridden at all. A good example is the process path; you can only access Plug-In routines that are stored in the directory identified in the process path parameter. Plug-Ins located anywhere else will not be seen by 3D Studio.

You can also have up to 250 map path directories set. You should try to keep the number of directories as low as you can because 3D Studio has to search through each path in the order listed until it finds the maps it needs. See the section, "Managing Maps and Libraries," later in this chapter for more information on setting up map paths.

General Configuration Parameters

The general configuration area covers global configuration issues. This is where you tell 3D Studio if you have a Microsoft mouse or Summagraphics digitizer internal driver, or possibly an external ADI driver and the COM port to which the device is attached. You also can switch the mouse buttons for left-handed people and control the size of the cursor pick box.

```
;---------------------------------
;    GENERAL CONFIGURATION PARAMETERS
;---------------------------------
;
INPUT-DEVICE = mouse
COM-PORT = 1
MOUSE-SPEED = 1
MOUSE-BUTTON-SWITCH = OFF
PICK-BOX = 5
GAMMA-CORRECT = ON
DISPLAY-GAMMA = 1.80
FRAMEBUFFER-GAMMA = 1.80
FILE-INPUT-GAMMA = 1.80
USE-TGA-GAMMA = ON
FILE-OUTPUT-GAMMA = 1.80
VIEW-PRESERVE-RATIO = ON
BGND-PRESERVE-RATIO = ON
VIEW-SCALE-UP = OFF
AAP-TIFFLOAD = OFF
REGION-TOGGLE = OFF
SELECTED-RESET = ON
PRINTER-NUMBER = 1
BACKUP-FILE = ON
H-LABEL = Y
W-LABEL = X
D-LABEL = Z
CONST-H = 0.0
CONST-W = 0.0
```

continues

```
CONST-D = 0.0
EQUATE-TGA = "pic"
EQUATE-TGA = "win"
EQUATE-TGA = "vst"
ZIP-COMMAND = "pkzip -a"
;
;----------------------------------
```

There are six questions relating to Gamma values. The default settings that ship with 3D Studio are listed in the preceding sample parameters. The section, "Setting Gamma Correction," later in this chapter, provides further discussion of how to determine which settings will work for you.

There are two related questions on image scaling—VIEW-PRESERVE-RATIO and BGNDPRESERVE-RATIO. These variables control what happens to the aspect ratio whenever you use an image as a proxy background or load an image file within 3D Studio to view it. If the image is not the same size as your display, 3D Studio will shrink or expand it to fit. If the answer to either of these parameters is NO, the images will be stretched to fit the screen in both dimensions. If you answer YES, 3D Studio will keep the aspect ratio the same as the image and leave an equal-sized black border on two sides of the image. This will look like a letter-box television image if it is wider than your screen. You will have to determine which format is better for each project you work on.

The axis labeling questions determine which way is up on your image. If you are creating all of your geometry within 3D Studio, keep the default values. If you are bringing in geometry from any other program that has a different axis labeling system, you might want to change the labeling system to be consistent with your other program. If you have AutoCAD files, for example, you may want to change the W-LABEL (width) to Z and the D-LABEL (depth) to X to be consistent with the conventions of that program.

The EQUATE parameters can be utilized if you have a program or series of files that do not have a standard three-letter extension, but are otherwise equivalent to a file format utilized by 3D Studio. Some programs that utilize the Truevision AT-Vista framebuffer, for example, save their files in a TARGA file that is 756×486 pixels with an extension of VST. Other programs save standard TARGA files with a PIC or WIN extension. If you want to use these files without renaming them, this is where you identify them for 3D Studio.

ZIP-COMMAND is a parameter that can be used by the program to take the mesh file and all the associated maps and compress them into a single file. This is the only way to gather all these into one group without extensively searching and verifying that they are together.

One of the more popular compression programs is PKZIP, stemming from a company named PKWARE. After the files are gathered and compressed into one, they have a ZIP extension, which is where the name originated. These files often are referred to as *zipped files*. If you have another archive program that you prefer, you can put the name in the ZIP-COMMAND parameter.

2D Shaper Parameters

The parameters in the 3DS.SET file for the 2D Shaper control the defaults for the number of interpolations between vertices and the maximum number of spline segments and vertices.

```
;-----------------------------------
;    2D SHAPER PARAMETERS
;-----------------------------------
;
SPLINE-MAX = 100
SHAPE-MAX = 500
SHAPE-STEPS = 5
;
;-----------------------------------
```

The parameter for the maximum number of vertices, SHAPE-MAX, uses a memory buffer for each vertex. Setting this much higher than you need unnecessarily wastes memory. If you try to import a complicated file from another program and run out of memory, however, this is the parameter that needs to be increased before trying again.

Set this parameter to the minimum number of 2 to gain some memory for a rendering-only station. If, however, you are saving a project file on another machine from the pull-down menu or from the Network Rendering option, and there is a shape with more vertices than your SHAPE-MAX can handle, the program will not load the project file. This has been a source of confusion many times as people will not understand why a certain machine does not render.

3D Lofter Parameters

The Lofter parameters are similar to the controls for the 2D Shaper, enabling you to set the maximum number of shapes and vertices. Both the PATH-MAX and DEFORM-MAX parameters use memory buffers, so the same tips for conserving memory apply to them as to the 2D Shaper parameters in the previous section that take up memory buffers.

```
;-----------------------------------
;    3D LOFTER PARAMETERS
;-----------------------------------
;
MOD-MAX = 32
PATH-MAX = 100
PATH-STEPS = 5
DEFORM-MAX = 50
LOFT-BANKING = ON
;
;-----------------------------------
```

The LOFT-BANKING parameter controls whether the object being lofted is twisted in 3D Studio with the path as it lofts or lofts flat, such as you would need for a flat road. This parameter can be used to great advantage when modeling if you remember to set it properly for a particular project.

3D Editor Parameters

Most of the parameters in the 3D Editor portion of the file should be left in their default state. All the parameters that need to be adjusted are easily available from within 3D Studio while it is running. The parameters found here include defaults for the lights, shadow settings, vertex welding threshold, and controls for bringing in DXF files from other programs.

```
;---------------------------------
;    3D EDITOR PARAMETERS
;---------------------------------
;
DEFAULT-AMBIENT = 10,10,10
DEFAULT-OMNI = 180,180,180
DEFAULT-SPOT = 180,180,180
SHADOW-EXCLUSION = ON
SHADOW-MAP-SIZE = 512
SHADOW-MAP-BIAS = 1.0
SHADOW-SAMPLE-RANGE = 3
RAYTRACE-BIAS = 1.0
SHADOW-BIAS-ABSOLUTE = OFF
WELD-THRESHOLD = 0.01
REMOVE-DOUBLE-FACES = ON
FILL-PLINES = ON
DXF-ARC-DEGREES = 10.0
SAFE-FRAME = 10
;
;---------------------------------
```

External Programs

You can have up to 14 external programs listed on a pull-down menu for access from within 3D Studio. They could be batch files, EXE files, PXP, or KXP programs (if you choose not to load them from the PXP or KXP Loader dialog box).

```
;---------------------------------
;    EXTERNAL PROGRAMS
;---------------------------------
;
USER-PROG1 = "c:\ani\ani.exe","Ani Pro"
USER-PROG2 = "c:\3ds3\process\SunPath_i.pxp","SunPath"
;USER-PROG3 = "",""
;
;---------------------------------
```

You should run 3D Studio with the 3DSHELL command to allow these programs enough memory to run. There are two parameters required here, both in double quotes and separated by a comma, as follows:

```
USER-PROG5 = "C:\VISTA\TIPS.EXE","Vista TIPS"
```

The first parameter in quotes is the exact path and file name needed to run the program from the DOS command line. The second parameter will appear in your pull-down menu. This example will load and run the *Truevision Image Processing System* (TIPS). Using this program, you can create maps, modify images, and save them to disk while still inside 3D Studio. If you want to shell out to another PharLap program, such as Animator Pro, you might need to have some of your settings changed with respect to how much memory 3D Studio reserves when it starts. You can change your settings by using the CFIG386 program that ships with 3D Studio.

See the *3D Studio Information Guide* for detailed information on using CFIG386.

If you have any batch files, COMMAND.COM must be either in your main 3D Studio directory or specified in the DOS environment variable COMSPEC. This usually is automatically set by later versions of DOS. You can check your COMSPEC variable by entering SET at the DOS command line.

Keyframer Parameters

The following group of parameters controls the Keyframer module of the program:

```
;-----------------------------------
;     KEYFRAMER PARAMETERS
;-----------------------------------
;
MODAL-KFBUTTONS = OFF
NTH-SERIAL = OFF
DTV-SCALE-UP = OFF
KF-SPEEDLIMIT = 30
;
;-----------------------------------
```

One of the variables that might need to be modified is NTH-SERIAL, which may not make sense the first few times you look at the explanation in the file. This parameter controls those times when you do not want to render every frame, but render some other sequence, such as every other frame, or every fifth frame as a test or for a special effect. If you want to have the file name sequence named TEST0000.TGA, TEST0001.TGA, TEST0002.TGA even if you were rendering frames 0, 5, and 10, set NTH-SERIAL to ON. If you prefer to have the files saved as TEST0000.TGA, TEST0005.TGA, and TEST0010.TGA, leave it OFF. Leaving NTH-SERIAL ON has the advantage of being able to record the frames through a disk-to-tape operation, which requires sequentially numbered frames. Leaving it OFF, however, allows you to reference the frames in the file quickly, knowing that frame TEST0756.TGA relates to frame 756 in the full animation.

The DTV-SCALE-UP parameter determines whether a disk image is scaled to fill the screen in a disk-to-tape operation or is centered in the framebuffer.

KF-SPEEDLIMIT was added to 3D Studio 3 due to the increases in speed in computers and graphics boards. This parameter limits the playback speed of wireframes in the Keyframer, in frames per second. If you are rendering for NTSC, it is commonly left to 30, for PAL it is 25, and for film it is 24.

Materials Editor Parameters

The following parameters control the Materials Editor module. They can usually be left at their defaults. After the tutorials are completed, however, change the BACKLIGHT-MATERIAL to ON. This positions a light behind the rendered sample spheres in the Materials Editor, down and to the right. It gives the effect of a light glancing at an angle to your material. This setting is especially valuable with metals.

```
;----------------------------------
;     MATERIALS EDITOR PARAMETERS
;----------------------------------
;
MATERIAL-LIBRARY = "3ds.mli"
BACKLIGHT-MATERIAL = ON
ANTIALIAS-MATERIAL = OFF
MEDIT-AMBIENT = 20,20,20
TEXTURE-BLUR-DEFAULT = 7
;
;----------------------------------
```

ANTIALIAS-MATERIAL should be left OFF. Turning it ON makes the rendered spheres look better, but it increases sample rendering time.

Renderer Parameters

The following parameters determine all your defaults for rendering images. Almost all of them are configurable in the program at render time, but it is a good idea to set them to your most common configuration.

```
;----------------------------------
;     RENDERER PARAMETERS
;----------------------------------
;
SHADING-MODE = METAL
FORCE-WIRE-THICKNESS = 1.0
ANTIALIASING = ON
```

```
Z-CLIP-NEAR = 1.0
CLEAR-BUFFER = OFF
PIXEL-SIZE = 1.1
FILTER-MAPS = ON
AA-FILTER-KERNEL = 0
RES1 = 320,200,0.82
RES2 = 256,243,1.23
RES3 = 512,486,1.23
RES4 = 640,480,1.0
DEFAULT-NULLRES = 640,480,1.0
REFLECT-FLIP = OFF
MIRROR-CLIP-ANY = OFF
NONFLAT-AUTOREFLECT-LEVELS = 1
COPLANAR-FACE-THRESHOLD = 0.001
RENDER-BAND-HEIGHT = 10
RENDER-WARN-UV = ON
RENDER-FIELDS = OFF
FIELD-ORDER = 1
NEW-SUBTRACTIVE-TRANSPARENCY = OFF
OUTPUT-RENDER-COORDS = ON
SAVE-LAST-IMAGE = OFF
LAST-IMAGE-FILE = "lastrend.img"
IMAGE-TYPE = TARGA
IMAGE-COMPRESSION = ON
JPEG-COMPRESSION = 100
RENDER-ALPHA = OFF
ALPHA-SPLIT = OFF
TGA-DEPTH = 24
DITHER-TRUECOLOR = ON
ANIM-TYPE = FLIC
DITHER-256 = ON
FLIC-COLORS = 256
FLOYD-DITHER-FLICS = OFF
FLOYD-DITHER-STILLS = ON
VISTA-MODE = NTSC
VIDEO = NTSC
VIDEO-COLOR-CHECK = ON
METHOD = CORRECT
SUPER-BLACK = 15
MOTION-BLUR-NUMBER = 7
MOTION-BLUR-SAMPLES = 4
MOTION-BLUR-DURATION = 1.0
SCENE-BLUR-DITHER = 50
BATCH-RENDER-PAUSE = YES
;
;---------------------------------
```

CLEAR-BUFFER is only used if you have a framebuffer installed in your system. It determines whether the framebuffer screen is cleared before a new rendering is begun.

The resolution button settings (RES1 through RES4) should be set to your most common rendering sizes. It also is a good idea to set one of them to exactly half of your normal screen size in each direction, keeping the aspect ratio the same. This enables you to create test renderings in 25 percent of the time it normally takes.

DEFAULT-NULLRES should be set to whatever your normal rendering size would be: for example, $756 \times 486 \times 0.857$ for the Truevision AT-Vista, or $512 \times 486 \times 1.266$ for Truevision TARGA or TARGA Plus. This parameter determines the default resolution and aspect ratio whenever you render to NULL or NO DISPLAY.

The FIELD-ORDER is extremely important in single frame output. It controls which field is rendered first while field rendering. On almost all systems, the default of 1 should be kept. If you are sending your files to a service bureau, however, you should probably do a quick test for them, unless they commonly use 3D Studio files for output and know what the setting is.

For more information on field rendering, see Chapter 23, "Animation for Field/Frame-Accurate Recording."

There are two settings for the default output file type—one for stills and the other for animations. IMAGE-TYPE is the setting for stills, and can be set for TARGA, GIF, JPEG, Color or Monochrome TIFF, or BMP. ANIM-TYPE controls the default for animation files. This can be set to either FLIC for 256-color animations that will play back on a computer, or any of the still file types previously mentioned. The program will automatically append four digits if you choose to render an animation with a still file type, such as FILE0000.TGA, FILE0001.TGA, and so on.

In 3D Studio Release 3, there was an error in the 3DS.SET file concerning the internal driver for the Truevision AT-VISTA. The variable was listed in the file as VISTA; 3D Studio, however, is looking for VISTA-MODE. The variable defaults to a value of NTSC if it is missing from the SDS.SET file so that users with the NTSC standard will have no problems. If you render to a PAL mode, 3D Studio Release 4 accepts the parameter as either VISTA or VISTA-MODE.

Color Register Parameters

These parameters control the colors of the 3D Studio interface. They have no effect on the output and are purely a personal preference. If you have multiple versions of 3DS.SET, it is a good idea to change the default colors so that you always know which settings are current. Some users like to change the menu bar with every revision of the program to remind themselves which version they are currently using.

```
;-----------------------------------
;    COLOR REGISTER PARAMETERS
;-----------------------------------
;
PALETTE-1 = 0,0,0
PALETTE-2 = 0,114,162
PALETTE-3 = 0,168,0
PALETTE-4 = 129,187,202
PALETTE-5 = 168,0,0
PALETTE-6 = 232,232,232
PALETTE-7 = 115,115,115
PALETTE-8 = 141,141,141
PALETTE-9 = 192,192,192
PALETTE-10 = 84,84,255
PALETTE-11 = 84,255,84
PALETTE-12 = 84,255,255
PALETTE-13 = 255,84,84
PALETTE-14 = 192,148,0
PALETTE-15 = 255,255,0
PALETTE-16 = 255,255,255
;
;-----------------------------------
```

Text Editor Color Register Parameters

These settings are undocumented in the manual and control the colors of the text and the color of the selected text in the built-in text editor accessed with the F11 key. This is the end of the 3DS.SET file.

```
;-----------------------------------------------------
;    TEXT EDITOR COLOR REGISTER PARAMETERS
;-----------------------------------------------------
ED-TEXT-COLOR = 9
ED-SEL-TEXT-COLOR = 4
END
;
;-----------------------------------------------------
```

Configuring for Network Rendering

A major feature introduced with 3D Studio Release 3 was the addition of network rendering capabilities. Even if you do not have a network, these features will save you a tremendous amount of time. To take advantage of all of these new features, your computer needs to be configured properly for network rendering. Make a sketch of your office showing the location of each rendering station and assign a number to each one. This will make the configuration much easier and prevent errors.

The Theory of Network Rendering

Beginning with 3D Studio Release 3, you can prepare a file to be rendered on one machine and automatically have all the other machines on your network assist in the rendering process while you continue working on another file. 3D Studio handles all the procedures, file organization, and control, and after it is properly installed, network rendering is totally transparent as you work.

Every machine has both the capability of being a rendering slave and a master network controller at the same time. The advantages of this method of operation are far-reaching. If the machine that started the rendering is powered down, for example, every other machine can calculate which frames still need to be rendered, and continue operation. In addition, the entire process is controlled by writing files to a directory common to all machines, and makes no specific network BIOS calls so that it will run across any network that can share directories and perform some basic file-locking.

Benefits of Network Rendering

Network rendering provides a tremendous time-savings over the manual method of starting each machine separately, and guessing how many frames each machine could render in the same time period. Using the manual method, each computer had to be given a range of frames to render, for example, frames 200 to 299. If that particular machine stopped rendering for any reason, even though all the other machines were finished with their frames, there was no intelligence to tell the other machines to go back and pick up the missed frames. Network rendering can detect the error and assign the other machines on the network to finish the job.

Another benefit of network rendering is that the projects to be rendered are automatically entered into a rendering queue, which enables you to enter a series of different projects to be rendered. Before Release 3, each machine was given a particular project and could not be told to start another project until after the first project had finished.

The license agreement with 3D Studio enables you to configure as many rendering stations as you want, with no additional charge. This leads to the concept of a *rendering farm*, a collection of stations networked together, some even using a switch box to avoid having to purchase more than one monitor and keyboard. No fancy framebuffers are required for a rendering station, only a plain VGA graphics card, network card, and small (200 MB) hard disk. All the money saved from this configuration can be put into memory and fast processors to maximize rendering performance.

Various 3D Studio resellers and system integrators have recently stepped in to offer preconfigured rendering networks. These systems are usually multiple rack mounted PCs with all of the networking, cabling, configuration, and even installation of 3D Studio preset and ready to go. Some systems even offer proprietary performance enhancements and software utilities to improve network rendering. If you do not like to worry about setting up hardware and configuring networks, then one of these systems might be worth a look.

Another method of configuring a rendering farm is to set up every computer in the office as a rendering station. Whenever anyone leaves, they are instructed to start 3D Studio in render slave mode, and the computer then becomes part of the rendering network. This has many advantages. Everybody in the office, from the receptionist to the president, uses their computer for day-to-day activities, and the animation department has the use of the systems all night. The drawback is that in many offices, politics, work schedules, and the varying capacities of the computer systems can cause more headaches than help for the animation department. This technique requires the full and conscientious cooperation of every one involved if it is going to work.

Network Rendering on a Single Machine

Even if you do not have a network, the network rendering functions will help you in your operations. You can prepare a series of files to render, set them in the Network Queue, and they will render while you are gone. You can change the order for rendering while the files are working, and start and stop different processes as you desire.

Configuring the Network

The configuration for network rendering is extremely fast. The most important part of the process is the planning phase. Have your network administrator prepare a few common directories that all machines can access. If you have the luxury, spread them over a few physical hard disks to speed up the rendering process. Have one common directory for all the network control files, for example, H:\3DS3INFO; one for the rendering output, G:\3DS3REND; another for maps common to all projects, K:\MAPS; and another working directory where the 3DS files, project-specific maps, shapes, and lofts are stored.

The purpose of putting these directories on separate drives is to speed up network performance by reducing the likelihood of multiple slave stations accessing the same drive at the same time. If you have partitioned one large drive into a number of smaller logical drives, this technique will be of little benefit.

If your network has optional file locking for different drives, it is very important to turn it on for the drive where the network information files are kept—in this case, H:\3DS3INFO.

One of the single largest problems in network rendering stems from not having all of the machines on the network time-synchronized with the server. Almost all networks have some facility to automatically accomplish this by running a small program. This program should be run in your AUTOEXEC.BAT file each time you start your computer, and also as a part of the batch file you use to start 3D Studio, both in standard workstation mode and in render-slave mode. If you do not have access to a program such as this, you will get better results by turning off the network crash detection for all machines. To do so, change the parameter NET-TIMEOUT-CHECK to NO in the 3DSNET.SET file. It is not recommended to run your network this way unless you absolutely must.

Configuring the 3DSNET.SET File

The 3DSNET.SET file, like the 3DS.SET file, must be edited with a text editor that does not embed control and formatting codes in the file. The editor that comes with later versions of DOS, called EDIT, works well for this purpose.

Any line that starts with a semicolon is considered a comment. A few comment lines have been added to make the editing easier when copied to different stations. The comment lines under the NET-OWNER and NET-NAME lines are there to make sure that NET-OWNER and NET-NAME are the proper length. If they are too long, the program considers them an error. If they are too short, the columns in the network log files and data files will not line up and are much more difficult to read.

Network Version of 3DSNET.SET

Here is a sample 3DSNET.SET file for a network. The order of the parameters is of no significance. You should move the parameters that will change to the front of the file. Copy the default 3DSNET.SET file to all machines, into the 3DS3 executables directory, and then change the first three parameters for that particular machine. If your network is configured as previously outlined, the following settings will work for you unaltered.

You should set the NET-OWNER variable to the name of the person who sits at the desk where the machine is located. The NET-NAME is the name of the machine. You will find it easier to keep track of the machines by using a consistent naming scheme for all machines. The following list shows an example of a network naming system. The first two characters are the number of the machine on the network, followed by a hyphen, followed by the person's name in the NET-OWNER parameter. There is a variable amount of spaces until you reach the machine type field and speed start field in column 12, with a hyphen and the amount of memory after that.

If you know that you will never need to render to a local disk, you should set the NET-LOCAL-PATH to the server. This helps avoid problems if someone accidentally hits the wrong button when sending a file to render.

If this file is for a rendering-only station, the only change is in the NET-MACHINE-TYPE parameter, which would be set to SLAVE. Nothing else needs to be adjusted.

```
;---- NETWORK 3DSNET.SET -----------
NET-OWNER = "Greg Pyros   "
;            "<-12 exact->"
NET-NAME =  "16-GregP    486/66-48"
;            "<-20 spaces exactly>"
NET-MACHINE-ID = 16
;
;-- make no changes below this line --;
NET-MACHINE-TYPE = OFF
NET-DISPLAY = NULL
NET-REZ-WARNING = YES
NET-BOX-MODE = YES
NET-PATH = "H:\3DS3INFO"
NET-DESTINATION = SERVER
NET-LOCAL-PATH ="G:\3DS3REND"
NET-SERVER-PATH = "G:\3DS3REND"
NET-SQUAWK = 2
NET-POLL-TIME = 5
NET-TIMEOUT-CHECK = YES
NET-TIMEOUT = 10
NET-VERBOSE = YES
NET-DAT-FILE = YES
NET-FILE-RDONLY = YES
END
;------------------------------------
```

Stand-Alone Version of 3DSNET.SET

The non-networked version of the 3DSNET.SET file needs some of the parameters changed.
The owner and name have no significance, and the machine ID can always be the same. The
major functional changes are the NET-DESTINATION set to LOCAL, and the NET-PATH
parameter for all the rendering control files set to the TEMP directory under the main 3DS
directory. You should set the NET-SERVER-PATH the same as the NET-LOCAL-PATH to
avoid problems if someone accidentally sends the file to the nonexistent network.

```
;------ STANDALONE 3DSNET.SET --------
NET-OWNER = "Greg Pyros   "
;            "<-12 exact->"
NET-NAME =  "01-GregP    486/66-48"
;            "<-20 spaces exactly>"
NET-MACHINE-ID = 1
NET-MACHINE-TYPE = OFF
NET-DISPLAY = NULL
NET-REZ-WARNING = NO
NET-BOX-MODE = YES
```

continues

```
NET-PATH = "TEMP"
NET-DESTINATION = LOCAL
NET-LOCAL-PATH ="IMAGES"
NET-SERVER-PATH = "IMAGES"
NET-SQUAWK = 2
NET-POLL-TIME = 5 NET-TIMEOUT-CHECK = NO
NET-TIMEOUT = 10
NET-VERBOSE = YES
NET-DAT-FILE = YES
NET-FILE-RDONLY = YES
END ;-------------------------------------
```

Configuring the Vibrant Options

You now have configured all of the options available to you outside 3D Studio. The next portion of the configuration takes place on the way into 3D Studio, within the Vibrant configuration menu. Vibrant Graphics is a company that developed many fast drivers for graphics cards used with 3D Studio. Autodesk licensed their driver technology and included it with 3D Studio. This is by far the easiest method of configuring the graphics drivers for 3D Studio, and includes support for over 250 graphics boards.

To tell the program you want to configure the graphics cards, type **3DSHELL VIBCFG** to start the process. The program's sign-on screen appears, as shown in figure 1.2, and you are in the configuration menu.

Figure 1.2
The Vibrant configuration screen.

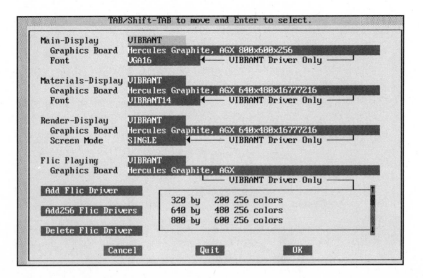

There are four sections of the configuration, each relating to a portion of the 3D Studio program. The process is similar for each section. Use [Tab⇄] to move forward and [⇧Shift]+[Tab⇄] to move backward.

Main Display

Three options are available in the Main Display section: the Driver, Graphics Board, and Font. The Driver selection enables you to choose between the VIBRANT, RCPADI, VGA, or VESA drivers. You should always choose the VIBRANT driver unless there is no option listed for your particular graphics board. If you are choosing the VESA option, make sure that any VESA drivers for your graphics board are loaded prior to starting 3D Studio. If you are using the RCPADI driver, ensure that your driver is loaded on the system and that the environment variable is properly set before starting 3D Studio. Refer to your driver documentation and your DOS manual for information on setting these variables.

If you chose VIBRANT for the main display driver, highlight the Graphics Board options and press Return. You will be presented with an alphabetized list of hundreds of graphics boards and major graphics chip manufacturers in case your board is not listed, but utilizes one of the chip sets (see fig. 1.3).

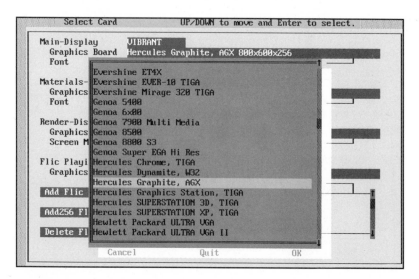

Figure 1.3
The choices of graphics cards.

To move quickly through the list, type the first letter of the name of the graphics board manufacturer.

After you choose a graphics card, another dialog box appears, from which you choose available resolutions and supported color modes (see fig. 1.4).

Figure 1.4
The choices of
▾ resolutions
and colors.

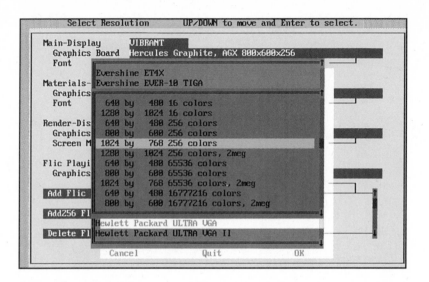

Choose a mode that will enable you to display 256 colors at the highest resolution supported by your monitor and card. If you select a mode that does not support 256 colors, you will not be able to utilize the object colors features of 3D Studio.

After the resolution and color mode are chosen, a pop-up screen appears that gives you an opportunity to test the graphics mode. The default is NO, but it is a good idea to test it for compatibility at this time.

A color graphic appears at the selected resolution when you test the video mode (see fig. 1.5). Press any key to return to the previous screen, or wait 10 seconds to return automatically. You then have the option of keeping the selected mode or trying a different one.

Figure 1.5
Testing the
video mode.

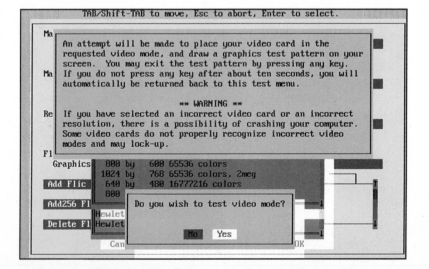

The program selects a font that works well at the selected resolution. If you prefer a different font, select it from the Font options.

Materials Display

The options for the Materials Display configuration are identical to the Main Display. If there is a 16.7 million color mode available at 640 × 480 resolution, you should choose it at this time. It is not recommended to have a higher resolution than this because it will only slow you down. If you do not have a 16.7 million (24-bit) color mode, try 65,000 (16-bit) or 32,000 (15-bit) mode in this order. With any of these modes, you will be able to display all your material samples simultaneously. If your graphics card will only support 256 colors at this resolution, all of the samples will display in grayscale, except for the sample on which you are currently working. If your graphics card does not have the capability of 640 × 480 resolution with 256 colors, you will not be able to use the Materials Editor.

Render Display

Setting up the Render Display is similar to the other options. Instead of selecting a font, however, you can select either single- or dual-screen mode if you have a two screen configuration and are using the Vibrant drivers for the rendering output. If you are not using a Vibrant rendering driver, the screen mode option makes no difference.

Flic Playing

The Flic Playing options are similar to the other options. First select the driver, either VIBRANT or ADESK-FLCLIB. Again, if your card is supported by Vibrant, this would be the preferred choice. After choosing your graphics board, the easiest method to configure the Vibrant driver is to click on the Add 256 Flic Drivers button. This automatically inserts every mode for your card that will play a flic. If there are some modes that you would not want to use, such as a 1280 × 1024 mode that is not supported by your monitor, highlight that mode and select Delete Flic Driver.

You now must make one of the three choices along the bottom of the Vibrant screen. Select Cancel to exit from the configuration program and enter 3D Studio with your previous values. Select Quit to return to DOS without saving your current values. Choose OK to save your values and enter 3D Studio.

Adjusting System Options Within 3D Studio

Most of the controls for the overall program configuration are available from the Info pull-down menu. This also is where you can find information about the current status, exactly how many objects and vertices there are in your scene, and many other features. You can find your serial number by selecting the About 3D Studio menu item. Select the Current Status Menu item when you want to determine the maximum amount of memory you have used, the amount you have available, the amount of swap size you have used, if any, and the length of time it took for your last render.

The Program Configuration Dialog Box

The Configure menu item brings up the Program Configuration dialog box, which enables you to set many of the basic parameters for your work session (see fig. 1.6). This is where you select whether to use a mouse or a tablet, and to control relative mouse speed and the size in pixels of your pick box.

The Program Configuration dialog box also enables you to define the defaults for common disk paths used by the program, such as shapes for the Shaper and the directory where rendered images are placed. Clicking on the Map Paths button brings up the Specify Map Paths dialog box, which enables you to add and delete map paths from the automatic search path (see fig. 1.7).

Figure 1.6
The Program
Configuration
dialog box.

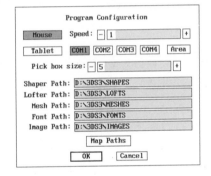

Figure 1.7
The Specify Map
Paths dialog box.

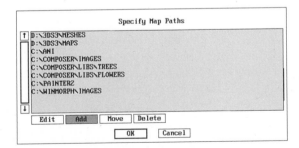

The Specify Map Paths Dialog Box

You can specify up to 250 map paths in the Specify Map Paths dialog box. *Map paths* are the directories where bitmap images are stored to be used by the Materials Editor, the Renderer,

and Video Post. A map path can point to a local hard disk, a network drive, a CD-ROM player, or any other mass storage device.

The program first searches the top map path for a file, then the second, and so on. You should always have the most often used map paths at the top of your list for maximum search speed and keep the list as short as possible. You don't want to wait five minutes to find out that the file you chose as a bitmap is not on your system.

By selecting one of the four buttons below the map paths list box, you can modify the list of map paths by changing, adding, moving, or deleting map paths from the list. Selecting Add, and then clicking in the map paths list, brings up the standard 3D Studio file selector dialog box where you can choose a directory and verify that your file is in it. After clicking on OK, your path will be added to the map paths list.

Selecting Edit requires that you then click on an exiting path in the map paths list—the file selector dialog appears again. The difference between Edit and Add is that Edit replaces the selected map path with the path you choose in the file selector.

The System Options Dialog Box

Another location for adjusting the configuration of general parameters while inside 3D Studio is the System Options dialog box, which also is found as a menu item under the Info pull-down menu (see fig. 1.8). All of the On/Off button parameters (described in detail earlier in this chapter) can have their defaults controlled in the 3DS.SET file.

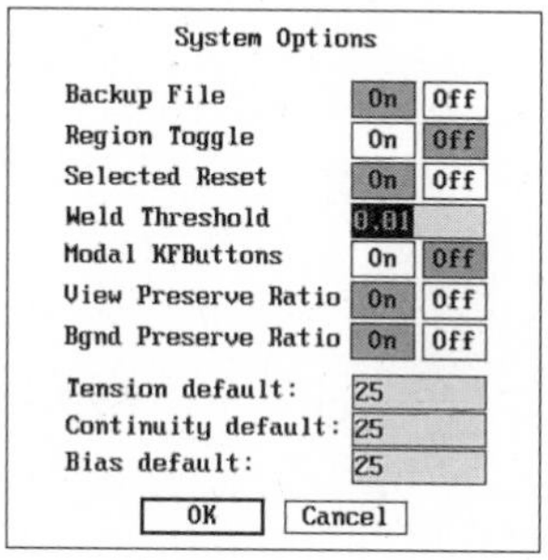

Figure 1.8
The System Options dialog box.

The Backup File parameter controls whether to automatically save to a backup file when you save a file with the same name as a previously saved file.

The Region Toggle parameter determines the method for adding to selection sets. This parameter controls whether an object is deselected if chosen twice when using Crossing or Window selection method, or if it remains a part of the selection set.

The Selected Reset parameter controls whether the Selected button is turned off automatically when a new command is chosen from the menu, or if it remains in effect until a command is chosen that does not utilize selection sets, or is manually turned off.

The Weld Threshold determines the maximum distance, in units, that two vertices can be from each other and still be welded together with the Weld command, or welded automatically when a DXF file is loaded.

The Modal KFButtons setting controls whether the Track Info and Scene Info buttons in the Keyframer remain active or are turned off when exiting the dialog box.

View Preserve Ratio and Bgnd Preserve Ratio establish whether bitmaps automatically fill the screen when viewing, when used as a background in the 3D Editor or Keyframer, or whether the aspect ratio is maintained. A black border will be on two sides of the image if the bitmap aspect ratio does not match the object exactly. These buttons do not control the aspect ratio of a rendered background image.

The *Tension, Continuity,* and *Bias* (TCB) boxes control the Keyframer's defaults for these settings. Changes to the defaults only affect new animation adjustments and do not change any animation that has already been completed.

Configuring the Renderer

All the defaults for the Renderer are determined in the 3DS.SET file in the Renderer Parameters section. While in 3D Editor, choose Renderer/Render View, and then select a viewport to display the Render Still Image dialog box (see fig. 1.9). The controls on the left side and bottom are adjustable from this dialog box, while the right side consists of status information and is changed from other menus.

Figure 1.9
The Render Still Image dialog box.

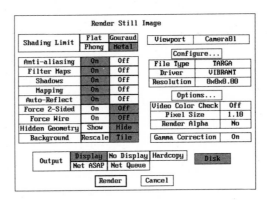

Shading Limits

The Shading Limit radio buttons determine the highest shading method used for rendering. The methods are, from lowest to highest: Flat, Gouraud, Phong, and Metal.

If a material for an object is designed as a Phong material, and the Metal Shading limit is chosen, the material will still be rendered as Phong. The shading limit cannot force a material to render higher than its designed value. However, if a material is Phong, and the Shading Limit is Gouraud, the material will be rendered as Gouraud.

Shading Limits in the Renderer dialog box are handy for test renderings when you want the speed of a Flat or Gouraud method, and are willing to sacrifice the quality of Phong or Metal.

Anti-Aliasing

3D Studio uses analytical anti-aliasing, instead of the oversampling method used by many other 3D animation packages. With this high-quality method of anti-aliasing, the only option is ON or OFF. A related control is the Pixel Size, which is covered later in this chapter.

Other Options

Filter Maps controls whether any texture maps are smoothed and blended as they recede into the distance. Turn this off for testing, and back on for final rendering.

The Shadows setting enables you to control whether shadow calculations will occur while rendering. Turn off this setting for quick tests.

If Mapping is turned off, the renderer does not load any bitmaps when rendering. This setting does not affect auto-reflection maps.

Auto-Reflect determines whether any automatic reflections are calculated for the rendering. If there are no auto-reflecting materials, this button is ignored.

Force 2-Sided establishes if both sides of each face are rendered, or only those with the normals facing the camera. Some geometry might require that Force 2-Sided be turned on to render properly. Turning it on, though, can greatly increase your rendering time. Models imported from other programs may need this option enabled to render properly.

Force Wire renders all geometry with a single-pixel line, no matter what material is actually set to be used. Anti-aliasing must be turned on to use this option.

Hidden Geometry determines how the renderer treats objects that are hidden in the 3D Editor or Keyframer. If Show is selected, all objects are rendered. If Hide is selected, hidden objects remain hidden. This can be used to speed up redraws while working on a project and still allow rendering the entire scene. If morphing is used, however, hidden geometry must remain hidden.

Background controls whether a bitmap smaller than your rendering display is enlarged to fill the screen (Rescale), or whether the bitmap remains at the original size and is repeated to cover the background (Tile).

Viewport is informational only and tells you which viewport is about to be rendered.

Device Configuration

The File Type, Driver, and Resolution boxes cannot be adjusted from the main Render dialog box. To change any of them, select the Configure button and the Device Configuration dialog box appears (see fig. 1.10). This is the same dialog box that can be displayed by choosing Renderer/Setup/Configure.

Figure 1.10
The Device
Configuration
dialog box.

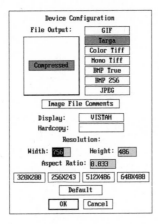

The File Output portion of the Device Configuration dialog box enables you to select the type of rendered file to write, and whether it is compressed. If the Image File Comments button is selected and TARGA files are being output, another dialog box appears before rendering in which you can type any information that you want saved inside the file. This information can be accessed through the File Info command.

The Display and Hardcopy boxes bring up a dialog box where any of the configured displays or hardcopy devices can be chosen. If you will be rendering to a larger size than your display, NULL should be chosen or the rendering size will automatically be brought down to the size of your display device.

The Resolution controls the width, height, and aspect ratio of the rendered image. Default means that the configuration in the 3DS.SET will be used. If NULL and Default are both selected, the 3DS.SET variable DEFAULT-NULLRES in the 3D.SET file will determine the rendering size.

Render Options

As shown in figure 1.11, the Render Options dialog box can be displayed by two different methods—through the Options button in the Render dialog box or by choosing the Renderer/Setup/Options from the command columns.

The defaults for these parameters are stored in the 3DS.SET file. The motion blur section deals both with object motion blur and scene motion blur. See Chapter 21, "Special Keyframer Techniques," for further discussion of motion blur.

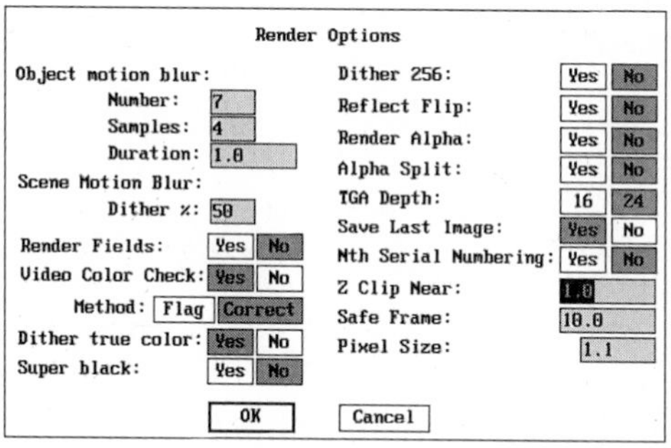

```
                    Render Options
Object motion blur:        Dither 256:        Yes  No
        Number:  7         Reflect Flip:      Yes  No
       Samples:  4         Render Alpha:      Yes  No
      Duration: 1.0        Alpha Split:       Yes  No
Scene Motion Blur:         TGA Depth:         16   24
        Dither x: 50       Save Last Image:   Yes  No
                           Nth Serial Numbering: Yes No
Render Fields:    Yes  No  Z Clip Near:       1.0
Video Color Check: Yes No  Safe Frame:        10.0
       Method:  Flag Correct Pixel Size:       1.1
Dither true color: Yes No
Super black:      Yes  No
            OK        Cancel
```

Figure 1.11
The Render
Options
dialog box.

Render Fields should be activated when rendering frame-by-frame to videotape for smoother animation, and should never be used for rendering stills or flics.

Video Color Check will have the program verify that all your rendered colors, especially the highlights and intense colors, are legal for NTSC video. You also have an option of flagging the offending colors. Flagging, however, replaces the colors with black, and might not be easily visible against a black background. You might want to temporarily have a solid color background that contrasts with your geometry so that the black is more apparent.

Dither True Color should almost always be set to Yes. It controls how the colors from the 48-bit color space of 3D Studio get reduced to 24-bits.

Super Black determines just how dark the darkest portions of your image become. If this parameter is set to Yes, the program uses the SUPER-BLACK setting in the 3DS.SET file to determine the lowest level of the colors. This is only used when doing video compositing.

Dither 256 is only checked when rendering a 256-color image. It determines if gradients are banded or dithered. Dithered gradients usually look better, but they greatly increase the size of flics and slow the playback speed. See Chapter 8, "8-Bit Still Imaging," for a discussion about using Dither 256.

Reflect Flip controls whether reflection maps are flipped horizontally. If your map contains text, it usually will be more realistic if Reflect Flip is Yes.

Render Alpha determines whether 3D Studio will render out a 24-bit TARGA file or a 32-bit file, the last eight bits being the transparency, or Alpha channel. The Alpha channel can be used in video compositing. Unless you plan to do a later process with your files using alpha, do not turn it on. The extra information increases the file size and storage requirements. If TGA Depth is set to 16 (as discussed later in this section), the program will not render alpha information.

Alpha Split is only checked when both TGA depth (discussed later in this section) is set for 24-bit and Render Alpha is turned on. Instead of creating a 32-bit TARGA file, this option causes the program to write out two files—one a 24-bit color file, and the other an 8-bit grayscale alpha mask file. The alpha file is named beginning with an "A_" and then the name of the file. If you are rendering an animation, the last four characters are numbers, so this gives you only two characters for differentiating your animations.

TGA Depth determines whether the files that are written to disk are 24- or 16-bit dithered files. This decreases the amount of storage space required for the images, and depending on their final use, may be adequate for many purposes. Alpha data is not rendered if this parameter is set to 16.

Save Last Image controls whether the last image buffer is written to disk and saved. If you are rendering large images, you should turn off this parameter for disk space conservation. Most users with a dual monitor system also prefer to leave this parameter off. If you leave it on, you can greatly increase the speed of saving the file by pointing it to a RAM-disk with the parameter LAST-IMAGE-FILE in your 3DS.SET file. This parameter stores the full 32-bit image if Render Alpha is on.

Nth Serial Numbering controls whether the file names of animations rendered with a step other than one are numbered sequentially or numbered per the actual frame number.

Z Clip Near determines at what point objects near the camera are clipped. This can be used to create a cut-away of an object. Any objects or parts of objects between your camera and the Z Clip Near distance will not be shown.

Safe Frame is a percentage of the screen that is shown by the green rectangle when you press Alt+E. It is the approximate size seen on a normal television monitor. This is very useful in determining the area that the viewer can see for titles, and to make sure that all important portions of your animations are seen by the viewer.

The Pixel Size parameter controls the smoothness of the edges of objects. For any tests and low-resolution renderings, set this to 1.0. Higher settings take more time to render, and depending on the image, might appear to soften the edges. For titles and highly detailed logos, keep this in the 1.2 to 1.3 range. For architectural work and other projects with many straight edges, a setting near 1.5 might prove beneficial.

As mentioned earlier, it is possible to adjust the 3DS.SET file to allow settings as high as 2.0. Such high settings should only be used when absolutely necessary.

Configuring the Network Renderer

Most of the work in configuring the network rendering functions is completed by editing the 3DSNET.SET file. See the previous discussion in this chapter for more information on setting up the 3DSNET.SET file. Some of these settings can be adjusted within the program, but it should not be necessary to change them often.

In the Renderer dialog box, select Net Queue or Net ASAP (*As Soon As Possible*) and another dialog box appears. At the same time, the driver automatically changes to either Net Queue or Network. The network setting overrides whatever you have set in the individual station's 3DSNET.SET file.

I

Note The Disk button is irrelevant because network rendering always renders to a file.

The differences between Net Queue and Net ASAP are not immediately obvious. If there are no other jobs in the network queue, there is no difference between them. If there are other jobs, Net Queue adds the current job to the end of the list, while Net ASAP places the current job at the top of the list and puts any other jobs on hold until it is completed.

Network Queue Entry

The Network Queue Entry dialog box lists all machines on the network that are currently available as network slaves (see fig. 1.12). You can choose any of the available machines, or choose All to select all of them. If you are rendering a single frame or a flic, your project will be assigned to a single machine.

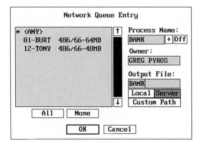

Figure 1.12

The Network Queue Entry dialog box.

Selecting machines with all or individual selections will only let those particular machines that are currently available render that project. If more machines become available (even the machine you currently are working on), they will not be utilized. The Any selection, which is always first on the list, solves this problem. It allows any machine, whether currently available or not, to be used for rendering the project.

If you have a machine that you do not want to utilize, such as a machine with too little memory for this particular rendering, select that machine to exclude it from the queue for that job, and put a "–" in the first column.

The machines appear in alphabetical order, which is why it is recommended to number the machines in the NET-NAME parameter in the 3DSNET.SET file as previously discussed. It is much easier to remember which machine is which when listed with the machine number, location, type, and amount of memory available.

The Process Name parameter must be different for each process currently on the queue. If a name is already in use, either type a different name or select "+," which will append an "01" to the end of the name. If the Off button is selected, the process can be defined and entered into the queue, but it will be put on hold until released for rendering.

The Owner box defaults to the OWNER-NAME in the 3DSNET.SET file. If you are starting a job from someone else's workstation and want to mark it as yours, you can change this parameter. It is used for record keeping only and has no effect on the process.

The Output File box holds the name of the files after they are rendered. If the file is a still, you can use eight characters to define it. If the file is an animation, any characters after the first four are overwritten by the frame number.

The Local/Server buttons control whether the process is to render to the path defined as NET-LOCAL-PATH or NET-SERVER-PATH in your 3DSNET.SET file. Custom Path enables you to directly specify where the files are to be stored.

Network Queue Management

After selecting OK in the Network Queue Entry dialog box, the Network Queue Control dialog box appears (see fig. 1.13). This is the same dialog box that is accessed through the Network/Edit Queue pull-down menu.

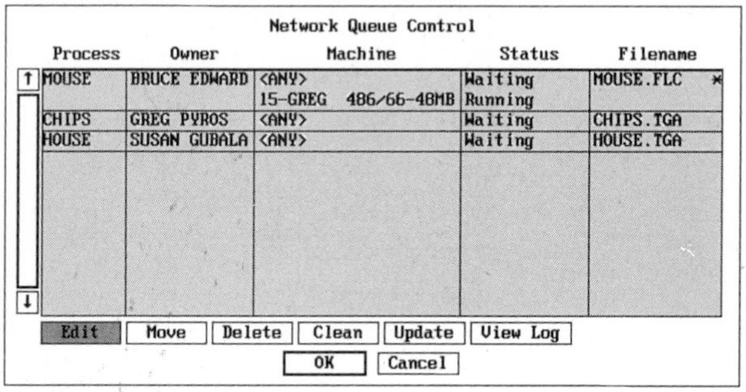

Figure 1.13
The Network Queue Control dialog box.

	Process	Owner	Machine	Status	Filename
↑	HOUSE	BRUCE EDWARD	\<ANY\>	Waiting	HOUSE.FLC ✕
			15-GREG 486/66-48MB	Running	
	CHIPS	GREG PYROS	\<ANY\>	Waiting	CHIPS.TGA
	HOUSE	SUSAN GUBALA	\<ANY\>	Waiting	HOUSE.TGA

Network Queue Control

Edit | Move | Delete | Clean | Update | View Log

OK | Cancel

One of the most important features to remember about the Network Queue Control dialog box is that while it is open, the file is locked and no other machine on the network can start its next frame, or even exit the rendering process. Close it as soon as you are finished with it.

The Network Queue Control dialog box enables you to reorder processes in the queue before they are rendered, edit parameters, view the log files, delete processes, and most importantly, clean failed processes from the active file. If a machine was rendering a frame and the owner needed to do some word processing, for example, he could press (Alt)+(Esc) to exit the rendering and use the machine. The machine is then marked as failed, and the frame is reassigned to another machine. If the user then finishes the word processing and returns the machine to slave mode, because the machine is marked as failed, it is not assigned any more frames in the process. If a machine fails because it does not have access to one of the maps required, it is not assigned the next frame because it would then only fail again. The Network Queue Control dialog box must be called up again and the Clean button selected. This is the only way to restart a slave machine after it has crashed or is marked as failed for any reason.

If a process is failing and you are not sure why, select View Log. The entire rendering history will be called up and any failed machines will be plainly marked, and the reason for the failure will be listed.

Network Parameters Configuration

The Network Parameters dialog box, as shown in figure 1.14, is accessed by choosing Network/Configure from the pull-down menu. The parameters that can be temporarily changed include the machine's ID number, the rendered file output paths, and the network information path. The local machine's display device can be changed here as well.

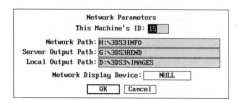

Figure 1.14
The Network Parameters dialog box.

Usually there is no reason to change any of this information, and doing so could cause problems for you later. For this reason, you should only make changes to the 3DSNET.SET file and copy it throughout the network. If the machine's ID was inadvertently changed to the same as another machine on the network, for example, the entire network rendering process could fail. In addition, if the Network Display Device was changed from NULL to VIBRANT, for example, and you are currently rendering to a $756 \times 486 \times 0.833$ file, and the graphics card is only capable of 640×480 pixels, this machine would have its files saved at $640 \times 480 \times 0.857$. All the files from the incorrectly set up machine would have to be rerendered. Likewise, if the Network Path was changed, the machine would have no idea what to work on and would sit idle.

Setting Gamma Correction

Gamma correction is one of the most important image quality features of 3D Studio and one of the least understood. If you have not done so, take a minute and read pages 4 through 7 of the 3D Studio *Advanced User's Guide*. It has an excellent description of what gamma is, and how it can be used to your advantage.

Never gamma-correct an image twice, or it will wash out. If you have an output device that gamma corrects automatically, and you have no way to turn off this feature, you must turn off the gamma correction in 3D Studio.

The controls for gamma correction are accessed by choosing Info, then Gamma from the pull-down menu. All five settings in the Gamma Control dialog box are defaulted to whatever is in your 3DS.SET file (see fig. 1.15). If you are network rendering, it is extremely important that all the individual machines have all these parameters set exactly the same, with the exception of Display Gamma. If you do not have this set properly, there is a strong possibility that different machines will use different settings, and your animation will flash with different colors when played back. 3D Studio does not read gamma correction information from a mesh file or a project file, so even if it is set properly on your main workstation, it will render incorrectly on other stations.

Figure 1.15
The Gamma
Control
dialog box.

```
               Gamma Control
Display gamma:      1.8      Set
Framebuffer gamma:  2.2      Set
Input file gamma:   2.2
Output file gamma:  2.2
    Gamma correction:  On  Off
         OK      Cancel
```

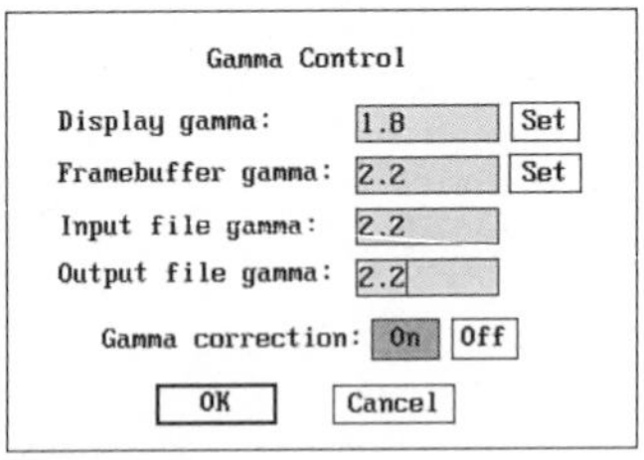

If you are not sure of the proper settings for the gamma parameters, there are some rules of thumb that will help you. Turn on gamma correction, and set your Display gamma to 1.8 and the Framebuffer gamma between 1.8 to 2.2. The Output File Gamma for print depends on the hardcopy device, but most operate at 1.0 gamma. For video, set Output File Gamma to the same as your Framebuffer Gamma. Your Input File Gamma should be the same as your Output File Gamma.

Display Gamma

3D Studio includes a few tools to assist you in determining what the proper gamma settings are for your system. While you are in the Gamma Control dialog, select Set next to the Display gamma input box. This brings up the Display Gamma dialog box with a single slider along the bottom, and an image with two gray boxes, one inside the other (see fig. 1.16). Move the slider until both boxes appear to be the same color gray. You might have to squint to get them close. The number shown is the proper Display gamma for your system. Materials developed in the Materials Editor will look the same as the rendered materials with this setting.

Framebuffer Gamma

The Framebuffer setting is only used if you have a separate framebuffer, such as a TrueVision Targa or Matrox Illuminator graphics boards, installed in your system. Using the Set button for Framebuffer Gamma has been known to give false readings with some equipment, especially if the board is set to provide its own gamma correction or if output is set to NTSC video rather than an RGB signal. You might have to do some experimentation with these settings to get a true reading. These numbers are only a guide. You will have to experiment to find the gamma numbers that work best with your system.

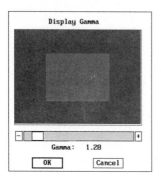

Figure 1.16
The Display
Gamma
dialog box.

Your goal is to get the image in the Materials Editor (controlled by Display Gamma) and the image in your framebuffer to look the same, and to have your framebuffer correctly show what you will get from your output device.

If you have a dual monitor setup, a useful technique is to enter the Materials Editor and set output for both the Display and Framebuffer in the control panel. Getting a material and clicking on the Render Sample button will render the sample sphere on both the main display and your framebuffer display. If the monitors are properly adjusted and gamma is properly set, the two images should look the same.

File Output Gamma

The gamma settings for the display and framebuffer only control what you see on your screens. They do not affect your final output if you are rendering to disk. File Output gamma sets the gamma correction for files that are written to disk.

If you are rendering files for recording to video tape, the File Output Gamma should be set at the same value as your framebuffer gamma. Again, the most common video settings are between 1.8 and 2.2, with a gamma of 2.2 being the theoretically correct value for video.

If you are rendering file for print output, you will often set the File Output Gamma for 1.0. This is because many printers are digital linear devices, while service bureaus handle their own gamma correction.

The end result of all of this is that if you have your own output devices, you should set File Output Gamma to whatever you believe gives you the best output. If you use a service bureau, then you should work with the service provider to agree upon the best gamma setting.

Keep in mind that if you regularly output to both video and print, you will likely use different File Output Gamma settings for each type of output.

Lastly is the issue of rendering images for use as texture maps. In this case, your File Output Gamma should match your File Input Gamma. The question then becomes what should these two settings be? See the following discussion of File Input Gamma for this information.

File Input Gamma

File Input Gamma applies a reverse gamma correction to a file used as a background or material map to prevent that image from being gamma corrected twice.

Imagine that File Input Gamma did not exist. If you rendered an image with File Output Gamma set at 1.8 and then proceeded to use that image as a texture map, the texture map would end up being gamma corrected a second time when the scene was rendered. The result of this is that the texture map would appear too bright and washed out. File Input Gamma compensates for this effect.

The problem is that to be effective, File Input Gamma must be set to the same value as was used to create the texture map image in the first place. This is not a problem if you never use anyone else's images, buy CDs of image libraries, and always render your own images for use as texture maps. In that rare case, you always have direct control of the gamma setting used to create the maps.

Gamma Summary

When gamma correction was first introduced to 3D Studio, it spawned a number of long discussions on the 3D Studio support forum on CompuServe. You may want to download the files from library 3 named GAMMA.ZIP and GAMMA2.ZIP. Unfortunately, gamma correction varies for every single machine, and the results are highly susceptible to esthetics and personal interpretation.

In general, you should experiment with various gamma settings and determine what works best for your way of doing business. If you like the result, and your clients like the result, then stick with what you've got.

Saving Custom Configurations

It is easy to edit your 3DS.SET file and create multiple versions, but there are some parameters that are not stored in the 3DS.SET file. The active area on a digitizing tablet or some of the settings in the Render dialog, for example, cannot be recorded in your 3DS.SET file. You can save the settings in projects files, however, and you can have multiple project files for multiple choices.

Saving Empty Project Files

After you have your 3D Studio configuration set exactly how you like it, you can save it and call it up again later. First, customize all the parameters in every module of the program. Next, before creating any geometry, save a project file, such as TABLET.PRJ, if you have configured a digitizing tablet the way you like it. You can save another project file configured for video resolution, or configured to start 3D Studio in box mode. Save as many configurations as you want. All of the settings that you can access through dialog boxes, except the gamma control settings, are stored in the project file.

The 3DS.PRJ File

The 3DS.PRJ file is a special type of 3D Studio project file. Settings stored in this file are automatically used as defaults when the program starts, similar to an AUTOEXEC.BAT file in DOS or an ACAD.DWG file in AutoCAD. This is the only file that passes gamma information to 3D Studio. Save a file with this name to your default project directory to use its default settings for the project.

You cannot fully configure 3D Studio through only the 3DS.SET file or the use of project files. While the default settings will work fine for many users, a fully custom configured setup of 3D Studio will use matched pairs of SET and PRJ files.

Setting Up 3D Studio to Work with Other Programs

When you are inside 3D Studio, you have the ability to shell out to other programs and return without exiting and reloading the program and your current file. When you shell out, you are running a second copy of COMMAND.COM, and your standard programs and utilities that do not need additional extended or expanded memory will work as usual.

Many programs require more free memory than 3D Studio's standard shell allows. To make shell more useful, you need to make 3D Studio leave as much room as possible in your conventional memory area for other programs to run. 3D Studio includes a utility, called 3DSHELL.COM, which enables you to do this easily.

3DSHELL.COM

The 3DSHELL.COM utility is totally transparent to the user and does everything automatically for you. Instead of entering 3DS to start 3D Studio, enter 3DSHELL. That's all there is to it. Now you will have much more room for a shell. If you need to pass command-line parameters to 3D Studio, just type them as usual—for example, **3DSHELL VIBCFG**.

The Program Pull-Down Menu

3D Studio accesses other programs in two ways. One is by shelling out to the DOS command line and running the other programs as usual. To do this, either press F10 or choose Program/DOS Window from the pull-down menu.

After you are at the DOS prompt, you can run most of your favorite programs. While 3D Studio is still in memory and still has open disk files, do not run any disk utilities, such as CHKDSK, that will close open files, or alter memory. You do not want to do anything that will prevent you from getting back to 3D Studio.

The other method of running an external program from within 3D Studio involves putting commonly used programs directly on the Program pull-down menu (see fig. 1.17). These programs are entered in your 3DS.SET file in the External Programs section. Refer to the discussion of the 3DS.SET file earlier in this chapter for the procedure to add programs. You can run EXE, BAT, and PXP or KXP programs from the menu, but not COM programs.

Figure 1.17
The Program pull-down menu.

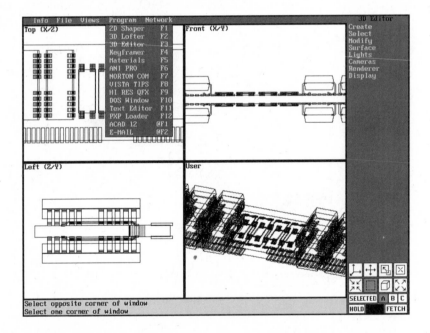

The only problems you will likely have with running external programs from within 3D Studio are memory-related. If you want to run an external program which uses extended or expanded memory, you might have to limit the amount of memory 3D Studio itself uses. This is accomplished by running a program called CFIG386.EXE, which comes with 3D Studio. 3D Studio defaults to using all the EMS memory in your computer. To allow other programs to use this memory, you must reserve some of your memory for other programs. Remember, however, that this memory will no longer be available for use by 3D Studio. The settings you will need to adjust to shell out to a program like Animator Pro are -extlow, -exthigh, and

-maxvcpi. The actual numbers you need to insert depend on your configuration. See pages 108 to 111 of the *Installation Guide* for further information on using CFIG386.EXE.

Setting Up 3D Studio under Windows 3.1

You can run 3D Studio under Windows 3.1 if you need to. Though this is not recommended due to memory constraints and speed loss, however, it does have some advantages. You can test map files quickly, and create documents while having 3D Studio accessible. Configuring 3D Studio to run under Windows is a fairly straightforward process.

Installing the PharLap Device Driver

To run 3D Studio from within Windows, first copy the PHARLAP.386 device driver from your main 3D Studio directory to your Windows directory. The following example shows the COPY command line to use if you installed 3D Studio and Windows in their respective default directories.

```
COPY C:\3ds3\pharlap.386 c:\windows
```

The next step is to tell Windows to use the driver. Edit your SYSTEM.INI file and add the line device=pharlap.386 to the [386Enh] section of the file.

Configuring the Windows PIF File

Next, you need to create a Windows PIF file with the Windows PIF Editor. The settings for the PIF file are shown in figures 1.18 and 1.19. You might want to have a second 3DS.SET configuration file for Windows. If so, place the name under Optional Parameters, as shown in figure 1.18.

Installing Graphics Board Drivers

Try using your normal 3D Studio graphics driver under Windows first. If your graphics board will not support running at high resolution under Windows, try configuring 3D Studio to run in a VESA or a VGA mode under Windows. Again, it may be beneficial to run with two separate 3DS.SET files with two different graphics drivers, one for use within Windows, and one for DOS.

Using Online Help

3D Studio comes with a standard online help facility. The help file may be easily modified to add any information that is custom to your facility. The help text is contained in a series of text files with HLP extensions.

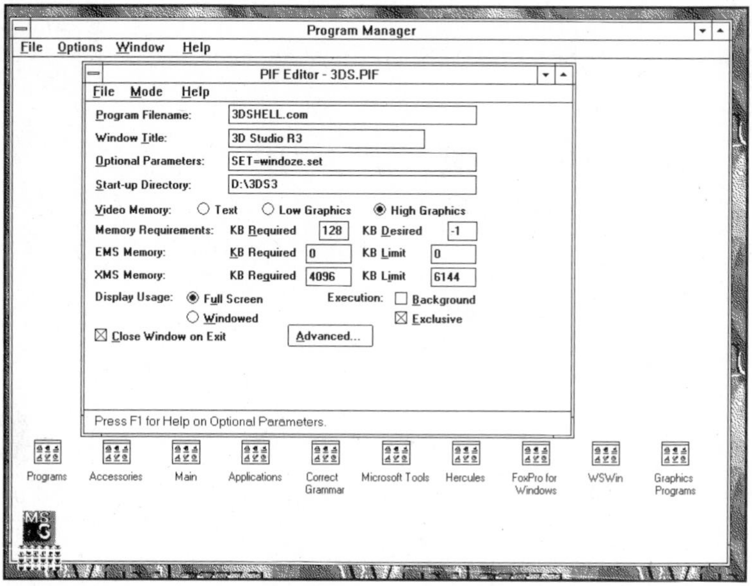

Figure 1.18
Editing 3DS.PIF.

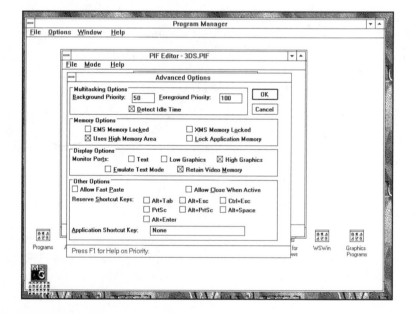

Figure 1.19
The PIF Editor
Advanced Options
dialog box.

Accessing Online Help

To access the online help, press and hold Alt, and move your mouse over any of the menus. The cursor changes and has a question mark next to it. If you click on a menu item, a help screen appears (see fig. 1.20).

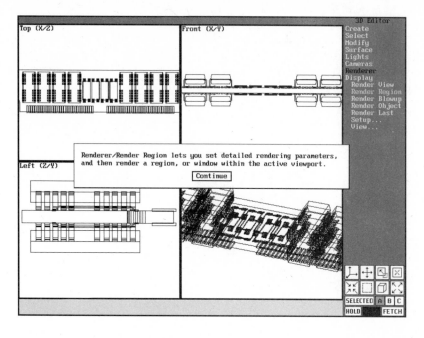

Figure 1.20
3D Studio
online help.

The help is available for any menu item in any module and any item in the Materials Editor. If a menu item leads to another menu, you must go to the submenu to get help on one of the items.

Using Custom Function Keys

3D Studio Release 4 enables you to create custom function keys. A custom function key executes a series of command column menu picks as if you had used your mouse to pick the items. You can program up to 12 custom function keys. Custom function keys are accessed by holding down the [Ctrl] key and a function key ([F1] through [F12]).

The 3DS.KEY File

When the 3D Studio is loading, it looks for a file in the main 3D Studio directory called 3DS.KEY. If this program is there, it loads your stored custom function key values into memory. The custom function keys are immediately available after 3D Studio starts.

Programming the Custom Function Keys

To program a custom function key, hold down the [Ctrl] key and move your mouse to the command that you want to store in the command column. The cursor changes and a K is added to it. This signifies that the program is ready to store commands as a custom function key.

When you click on a menu item with the Ctrl key pressed, the Custom Function Keys dialog box appears, and you can choose in which function key to store the command (see fig. 1.21). After you store your new custom function key, you can print a copy of the custom function key list to post by your computer. The Custom Function Keys dialog box can be accessed by choosing Info, then Key Assignments from the pull-down menu.

Figure 1.21
The Custom
Function Keys
dialog box.

```
                    Custom Function Keys

        CTRL-F1   Renderer/Render View
        CTRL-F2   Renderer/Render Region
        CTRL-F3   Renderer/Render Object
        CTRL-F4   Select/Object/Single
        CTRL-F5   Select/Object/Quad
        CTRL-F6   Modify/Object/Move
        CTRL-F7   Modify/Object/Rotate
        CTRL-F8   Surface/Material/Choose
        CTRL-F9   Surface/Material/Assign/Object
        CTRL-F10  Surface/Mapping/Adjust/Find
        CTRL-F11  Display/Hide/By Name
        CTRL-F12  Display/Unhide/By Name

                     Exit    Print
```

Organizing a Project

Creating animation with 3D Studio is so much fun that it's tempting to jump right into the program and start modeling. Nothing could be more detrimental to the success of your project. Before beginning any production work, you must plan out the animation in detail, just as you would for any construction or engineering job.

Organizing your animation files focuses on the following main subjects:

✔ Models, including SHP, LFT, 3DS, and PRJ files

✔ Materials and maps

✔ Output files

✔ Backups and archives

Properly planning for the management of these files increases your chances for a successful and smooth-running project.

Building a Scene from Multiple Files

The first organizational technique involves the construction of the scene and all of its supporting models. If your subject is simple, you can model the whole scene in a single 3DS file. It is more likely, however, that your scene consists of many objects and that modeling these objects separately is an easier approach. Assuming that you have decided to model each object independently, you must concern yourself with how all of the objects come together for the final rendering.

Strategies

Just like layering strategies with CAD systems, probably no one ever will agree on the best strategy for building a 3D model. It appears, however, that modeling strategies fall into two basic techniques.

With one technique, you model each object separately and independently from the other. After all of the objects are modeled, you bring them together into a single file and arrange them as necessary. Such a technique works extremely well in two situations. One situation in which this technique works well is when the scene is relatively simple and composed of common, well-known objects. You know what a coffee mug or a light bulb looks like, for example, so it is easy to start a new file and make them from scratch.

The other situation arises when you already have an appropriate model on file. The model was used in an earlier project, was included on the 3D Studio CD-ROM, or was purchased from a third-party vendor. If you needed a detailed model of a table fan, for example, you could use the model provided on the 3D Studio CD-ROM rather than build one yourself (see fig. 1.22). In this case, make a copy of the file, edit it as needed, and merge it into your main scene.

Figure 1.22
The FAN.3DS file from the 3D Studio CD-ROM.

The second modeling technique requires you to set up the main scene first. You represent the objects in the scene by using simplified geometry or stand-in objects. The stand-in objects are copied out of the scene to serve as guides for the creation of detailed models. The detailed models eventually replace the stand-ins in the main scene. This approach offers the advantage of determining the basic shape, volume, and position of each object before you spend much time on modeling. A common mistake is to model an object in great detail only to have it end up far away in the background or, worse yet, completely obscured by a foreground object. This second approach is a necessity for almost any type of large, complicated scene.

As you may have guessed, most projects require a blending of these two techniques. Starting with a simplified scene usually results in a better, more efficient model.

Scale and Position Concerns

A common concern among 3D Studio users that have come from a more traditional CAD background is, "How do you adjust objects to the proper scale?" The issues of scale and precision placement are not as critical in 3D Studio as in a program used for manufacturing or construction, such as AutoCAD. You must remember that 3D Studio is a visualization tool and if the size, proportion, and arrangement of the scene appears correct, then it *is* correct. Do not become too concerned about the exact unit size or position of a model. You should be more concerned with correct proportions and relationships between objects.

That said, you do need to know how to initially adjust the relative scale of your objects and then maintain that relationship throughout the project. If you begin by blocking out the scene with stand-in objects, you then can use the stand-ins as guides for creating detailed models.

Assume, for example, that you plan to use the model MARBVASE.3DS that ships with 3D Studio as part of a still-life scene. If you blocked out the scene first, you can use the following steps to set up the scene:

1. Use the Save Selected command from the File pull-down menu to save the vase stand-in object to a file named VASE.3DS.

2. Load the file VASE.3DS.

3. Use the Merge command from the File pull-down menu to import only the mesh objects from the file MARBVASE.3DS.

4. Scale and move the marble vase to match the size and position of the stand-in object, then delete the stand-in object.

5. Save the file.

After completing the previous steps, the vase would be properly sized and positioned relative to the stand-in object in the main scene. It is easier to apply materials and make small modifications to the vase while it is in its own file. Later, when you import the vase into the main scene, it is already at the proper size and location.

Replacing

One technique for importing detail models into a scene is to use the Replace command from the File pull-down menu. The Replace command is quick, preserves position relationships in the scene, and automatically deletes the stand-in object as the detailed model is imported. One of the drawbacks to this method is that the Replace command requires that the imported objects have the exact same name as objects already in the scene. If there is not a perfect name match, the unmatched objects are ignored.

Use the marble vase again as an example. You have a single stand-in object in your scene called vase. The detail model of the marble vase is made up of multiple objects representing a wooden stand, granite trim rings, and the vase. The Replace command will only import the single object that has the same name as the stand-in object. All other objects with different names are ignored. You can get around this restriction by using the Create/Object/Attach command to combine all of the objects into a single object with the same name as the stand-in. This works well if you have no need to individually animate the separate parts of the detailed model.

Merging

Another technique uses the Merge command from the File pull-down menu. This command has the advantage of selectively bringing in all of the objects from the detailed model regardless of whether a stand-in object with the same name exists. The Merge command also gives you the option of renaming, skipping, or replacing any imported objects that have the same name as existing objects. This makes the Replace command appear to be a subset of the Merge command.

Merge also has the added benefit of importing lights, cameras, and animation keys with the imported mesh objects. So, you ask, why would anyone bother to use the Replace command? The answer is that Replace is faster. If all you need is to replace stand-in objects with their detailed counterparts, use Replace.

Coordination with Other Modeling Programs

While 3D Studio is one of the most powerful surface modelers around, you sometimes must resort to another program to get the job done. A common secondary modeler for 3D Studio users is AutoCAD, but the following techniques will work for any CAD program that writes valid DXF files.

File Conversions

After choosing a modeling strategy, either creating all objects in one file or multiple files of individual objects, you must convert the file from its native format into the 3DS format. Because most CAD and modeling programs write DXF files, you can use 3D Studio's built-in DXF reader to handle the conversion. The steps for loading a DXF file are as follows:

1. Within your CAD program, write a DXF file of your model.

2. Exit the CAD program and start 3D Studio.

3. Choose the Load command from the File pull-down menu. The load file dialog box appears (see fig. 1.23).

4. Activate the *.DXF button in the load dialog box and select the DXF file that you just created.

New Riders Publishing
INSIDE
SERIES

Figure 1.23
Loading DXF files
with the load
dialog box.

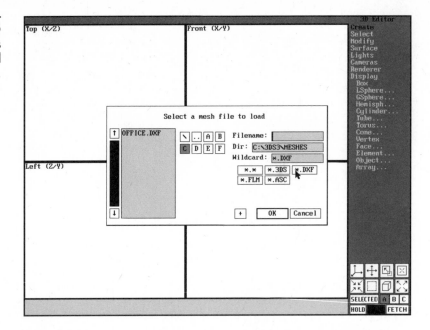

At this point, 3D Studio displays the Loading DXF File dialog box, asking you to choose how to derive objects from the DXF file (see fig. 1.24). Most of the time, the appropriate choice will be by layer. Detailed information on strategies for organizing your layers prior to creating the DXF file is presented in Chapter 11, "Integrating AutoCAD with 3D Studio."

Figure 1.24
The Loading DXF
File dialog box.

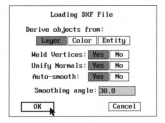

Another useful alternative to DXF translation is the InterChange Plus program by Syndesis Corporation. This program directly reads the file formats of many 3D design and CAD programs and translates them into the formats of other programs, including 3D Studio.

Maintaining Coordination

A primary concern of using external modelers with 3D Studio is how to maintain coordination between the modeling program and the 3DS file. If all of the design work in the external modeler is complete, then this is a non-issue. Simply treat the converted 3DS files as your master models and begin building the scene. If, however, the models are part of an on-going design process, you must take steps to ensure that your 3DS model stays in synchronization with the design model in the other program.

The solution lies in always making design changes in the master file of the external modeler. Using the external modeler, you first identify discreet components of the overall project and write them out as independent DXF files. These DXF files are then converted to 3DS files and are maintained as separate models. When design changes occur, you first change the master design file of the external modeler. After the change is complete, you write out only those components that were affected as DXF files and convert them to replace the corresponding 3DS models. The key lies with the component models. If you converted the entire design model every time a change occurred you would spend all of your time converting models and no time rendering and animating. Maintaining the component models enables you to convert only those components that have changed, and thus preserve the work that you have completed on the rest of the model. Details on this technique are also presented in Chapter 11.

Managing Maps and Material Libraries

Another organizational issue concerns where to store all of the bitmaps and libraries of materials that you apply to the surfaces of your model. The definitions of the materials are stored both in the 3DS file and in a library that uses the extension of MLI. The material definitions contain the settings of all of the attributes that control color, shininess, transparency, and so on, as well as references to image files applied as maps. When 3D Studio renders a model, it reads the reference to the image file and searches specific directories on the hard disk to find the requested image. If the image is not found, a warning dialog box appears, as shown in figure 1.25. You must either cancel the rendering or proceed without properly rendering that material.

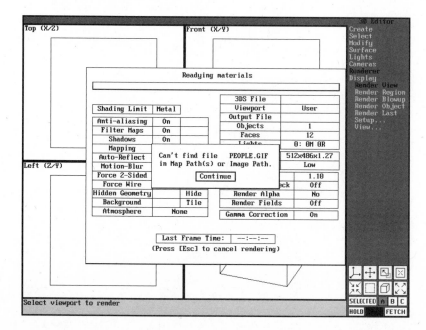

Figure 1.25
Map not found warning.

3D Studio Release 2 enabled you to specify only nine different directories to search for image files; the current release allows up to 250 directories. Depending upon your opinion, the 250 directory list in the current release is either a blessing or a curse. In one sense, you never have to suffer the frustration of 3D Studio failing to find a needed image file. On the other hand, it is now possible to create an incredible mess of directories where your models pull image files from all over your hard disk. The paragraphs below describe techniques for how to make sense of these options.

Global Libraries

This first technique is to create global libraries accessed by any project or model. These libraries consist of a global materials library directory, where the master MLI files are stored, and a series of master image directories for all of the image files.

The most logical place for your global materials library directory is the \MATLIBS directory created automatically when you install 3D Studio. The default location of the \MATLIBS directory is shown in figure 1.26. Separate MLI files can be stored in this directory, with each file addressing a certain type of material. Examples of such library files include the following:

✔ METALS.MLI for metal materials

✔ FOLIAGE.MLI for grasses, leaves, and vines

✔ BLOCKS.MLI for bricks, blocks, and tile

Figure 1.26
3D Studio's
MATLIBS
directory.

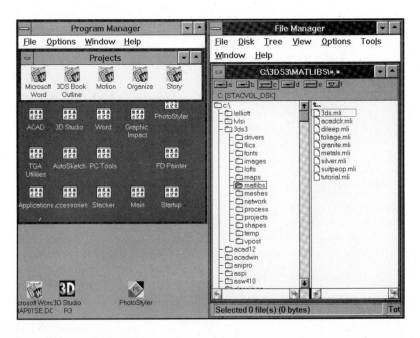

Global image directories are most frequently organized with one of two strategies. The first strategy divides the files by type: GIF, TGA, JPG, TIF, and so on. This strategy has the advantage of minimizing the number of directories required, and it worked moderately well under Release 2 with its limitation of nine map directories. The drawback appears when you try to locate a particular image. You probably remember what it looks like—wood, rock, metal—but you probably can't remember what file type it was.

A preferable strategy organizes images by subject and allows the file types to be mixed. This results in directories named WOOD, MARBLE, SKIES, BACKGRND, and so on. Such an organization makes it easier for you find images of a specific subject. Because 3D Studio allows 250 directories, you can organize your images into very precise topics. A good example of this strategy can be seen in the arrangement of the map directories provided on the 3D Studio CD-ROM (see fig. 1.27).

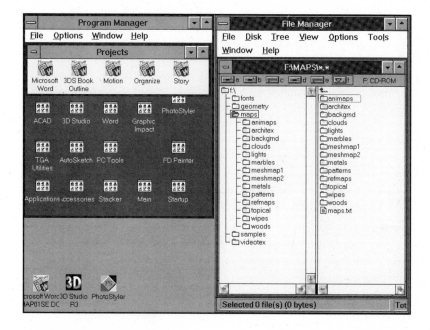

Figure 1.27
The map directories on the 3D Studio CD-ROM.

Project Libraries

Global libraries are great when you first put together a project, but what about later? It is terribly frustrating to restore an old project from backups, load it into 3D Studio, and find out at render time that needed map files are missing for critical materials. This is particularly troublesome when custom maps are created for a specific project.

The solution is to create private libraries for each project. Each project should have its own directory for related models, shapes, lofts, and image files. Right from the start, you should create an MLI file unique to that project and save it in the project directory. As materials are created and applied to the model, you store their definitions in the project MLI file.

When you create an image file as a custom map for the project, store it in the project directory and not in one of the global directories. Later, if you feel that a custom map might be useful to other projects, copy the image file into the appropriate global directory. Also, after the final material definitions are set, copy all image files used by those materials from the global directory into the project directory. This might sound like a terrible waste of disk space, but this technique ensures that the images your materials rely on won't be deleted or altered in the global directories. Besides, unless you place no value on your time, the cost of disk space is always cheaper than the cost to rebuild lost map files.

Managing Output Files

After you have built your model, set up the cameras and lights, and applied materials, you are ready to render an image or an animation. The question now becomes an issue of what file format to use and where to place the files. One location for your output files is the project directory. Another, possibly better, solution is to create an output subdirectory below the project directory, on a separate removable drive, or on a large network drive. Two concerns drive this decision to create a separate output subdirectory. First, rendering still images and animations creates several large files. Handling all of these files is easier if they are separate from everything else. The second reason is closely related in that you want to avoid mixing rendered images in the same directory as your map images and model files. Unless your file-naming strategies are very well-planned, you might find it difficult to tell the difference between renderings and maps by looking at the file name alone.

Files for Different Types of Output

3D Studio is very flexible when it comes to choosing an output format for renderings and animations. The choice of what file format to use has very little to do with 3D Studio, and is solely based upon what you plan to do with the file once out of 3D Studio. The file formats supported by 3D Studio are described in the following:

✔ **GIF.** An 8-bit, 256-color format developed for CompuServe. This format is supported by some paint programs and is also the native picture format for Animator Pro. Definitely use this format if you intend to bring the images into Animator Pro.

✔ **TARGA.** A 24-bit, 16.7 million color format developed by Truevision for their TARGA series of graphics cards. This format is supported by most high-end image processing programs and is currently the preferred format for output to video tape. The TARGA format is a good choice for general purpose 24-bit color files and is the de facto standard for files output to video.

✔ **TIFF.** Another 24-bit format based on an international standard. Most image processing programs also support the TIFF standard, making it an alternative to TARGA. Because the TIFF standard has many different variations, there are some compatibility problems between programs that offer TIFF support. TIFF is, however, the primary image format in the print and desktop publishing industry, as well as on the Macintosh platform. If you plan to send the images to a print service bureau, page layout program, or a Macintosh user, then consider the TIFF format. The Color TIFF button creates a 24-bit color image, while the Mono TIFF button creates an 8-bit gray-scale image.

✔ **BMP.** This format was new for 3D Studio Release 3 and represents the image file standard for Windows. The BMP file can be created as a true-color file (24-bit) or a 256-color file (8-bit). Choose this format if you intend to use an image with a Windows-based presentation program.

✔ **JPEG.** Also another new format beginning with Release 3. The JPEG format provides a variable quality compression scheme that degrades the quality of the image as the compression level increases. Fortunately, JPEG allows for extreme levels of compression before most people can detect the loss of image quality. The JPEG format might be a good choice for storage of map images, and is also supported by most high-end image processing programs. JPEG technology is relatively new, but is already having an impact on methods of storing image files and recording images to videotape.

You are well-advised to stay informed about future JPEG developments.

✔ **FLIC.** This format was developed by Autodesk for the Animator and Animator Pro programs. It is an 8-bit (256-color) format that supports multiple frames for animation. This output format is only available in the Keyframer. Microsoft recently announced that the FLIC format would be supported as the standard 8-bit animation format in Windows. This format should be used to create animations for use with Animator Pro or Windows-based presentation programs.

File Conversions

What if the file format that you need is not one of the options previously listed? At present, your best choice is to use one of the many available file conversion programs on the market. Many high-end image processing programs can read and write files of many different formats, although it is a bit of overkill to use a program like Photostyler for format conversion. One simple choice is the AniConvert program included with Animator Pro. AniConvert supports many formats on the PC, Amiga, and Macintosh. Another choice is included on the CD-ROM with this book. It is a shareware program called Graphics Workshop that enables you to view, print, convert, and transform image files of many formats.

Finally, 3D Studio has introduced a new Plug-In format for BXP functions. The BXP support enables developers to create bitmap translation functions that work within 3D Studio. You soon might be able to read and write many image file formats using BXPs. See the next section for a Postscript BXP included in the current Release of 3D Studio.

Postscript Output

Along with all of the output option described previously, you can now output your images in Postscript format thanks to a BXP provided with Release 4 of 3D Studio. You use this BXP by including the extension of EPS in the file name when saving a still image or animation to disk. Including the extension overrides the selected file format button and instructs 3D Studio to save the image as an encapsulated postscript file.

The settings used for the creation of the EPS file are specified by activating the EPS file output options from the PXP Loader under the Program pull-down menu. Details about these settings are presented in the New Features manual of 3D Studio Release 4.

The following paragraphs describe a couple of issues that you may want to consider when configuring EPS output.

Page Size: You should set these fields to the calculated image size rather than a physical paper size. The image size is the dimension of your image in pixels divided by the output resolution described in the following. You do not want to specify the exact paper size for two reasons:

1. The actual printable area for most printers is smaller than the physical paper size. For example, a laser printer using 8.5×11.0-inch paper may only be able to print to an area of 8.1×10.5 inches. You can determine the printable area by checking your printer manual.

2. Specifying the actual paper size for a small image causes large border areas of blank space surrounding the image to be included as part of the EPS file. If you use another program to print the image (such as a desktop publishing or image processing program), these empty borders will cause you extra work to crop and scale the image. It is preferable to set the Page Size to fit tight around the edges of your image and use your printing program to set borders and page position.

Resolution: This setting refers to your output print resolution, but it should not necessarily be set to the same resolution as your printer.

If you are creating a color file and printing to a true color device (such as a dye-sublimation printer), then the resolution setting should be equal to the resolution of your printer. This is because each pixel in your image will print directly to a dot on the page.

If instead you are printing to a non-true color device (inkjet or thermal wax) or a monochrome printer, you should use a resolution setting much lower than the printer resolution. The reason for this is that the printer must approximate colors and grayscales through the use of dither patterns and halftone screens. These patterns and screens often reduce the effective image resolution to one-half, or even one-quarter for the printer resolution. If you render the image to the full printer resolution, you are wasting time and disk space.

For more information about halftone screens and printing resolutions, see Chapter 14, "24-Bit High Resolution Imaging," and Appendix B, "Rendering and Output Equipment."

The settings that you specify in the EPS File Output Options dialog box are stored in the file EPS.CFG. If you use EPS output during network rendering, you need to ensure that all slave rendering stations have an identical EPS.CFG file.

Archiving and Backing Up Your Files

You have heard this before, but it is worth repeating—back up your data files! Nothing is more frustrating than turning on your computer and finding that the hard drive quietly passed to digital heaven sometime during the night. Your emotion quickly turns to panic when you realize that your last backup set of 500 floppy disks is dated months before you started the project that is due next week. If you want to kill your chances as a professional animator, try explaining to a client that their presentation is not ready because you lost all of the files when your disk drive failed.

Buy a good, high-capacity backup device and use it regularly. Appendix A, "System Requirements," discusses various types of hardware, including backup devices, that you will want to consider purchasing. Some devices are more versatile than others and can be used for more than just backing up your data. For now, the most important feature of a good backup device is that it is removable. It does no good to have your backup on a second internal hard drive when your office catches fire and the whole system melts. Remove your backup media and store it someplace far away from your office.

3DS Archive Command

3D Studio Release 3 introduced a convenient menu pick to group a PRJ project file with all of the referenced image maps into one compressed archive. 3D Studio uses the PKZIP program, version 2.04g, as its default. You control the type of archive created and the program used to create it by editing the 3DS.SET file.

Modifying the ARCHIVE Statement in 3DS.SET

The following exercise shows you how to modify the 3DS.SET file for maximum compression when archiving with the PKZIP program. This exercise uses the built-in text editor in 3D Studio, but you can use any text editor that you prefer.

Choose Text Editor *from the pull-down menu*	Loads the internal 3D Program Studio text editor
Choose Load *from the* File *pull-down menu and select* 3DS.SET	Loads the 3DS.SET file
Choose Search *from the* Cursor *pull-down menu*	Displays the Search for Text dialog box

continues

continued

Type **PKZIP** *in the edit field and click on the* Search *button*	Finds the first instance of PKZIP and displays the following line: `ZIP-COMMAND = "pkzip -a"`
Position the cursor after the -a and type **ex**	Tells PKZIP to sacrifice some speed for the maximum possible compression
Choose Save *from the* File *pull-down menu and save the file to 3DS.SET*	
Choose Exit *from the* File *pull-down menu*	
Exit 3D Studio and restart	The changes take effect after you restart 3D Studio

You can replace the PKZIP command within the quotes with any archive program and its appropriate command-line parameters.

A drawback to the built-in Archive command is that it only saves 3D Studio as a PRJ file with all of its related image maps. The PRJ format saves the current state of all of the modules in 3D Studio. This means that anything currently in the 2D Shaper, 3D Lofter, 3D Editor, or Keyframer is saved in the single PRJ file. Unfortunately, most projects use many Shape, Loft, and Mesh files and these are left behind by the Archive command. Also, any procedural materials (SXPs), or animated processes (AXPs) are not included in the archive. The best use of the Archive command is as a fast and convenient way to pack up your current work while you are still in 3D Studio. Do not rely on it as a complete archive of your whole project.

Manual Archiving

If you want to archive all of the various Shape, Loft, and Mesh files associated with a project, you still must do it manually. Use your favorite archiving program to compress all of the files in your project directory into a single file. If you have created separate map or output subdirectories under the project directory, be sure to tell the archive program to recurse subdirectories and store the path names. This enables you to restore the project files back into the same directory structure later on.

A handy trick is to use 3D Studio's built-in Archive command as a map collector. It quickly pulls copies of all the referenced image maps into your project directory. Unzip the 3DS created archive to restore the maps. You then can archive the whole directory into one big file.

Using Story Boards

What is a story board? Many people imagine story boards as the slick pictures advertising executives create on TV. Unfortunately, this leaves the impression that story boards are only something used to sell an idea. In reality, story boards are an important part of designing any presentation.

Story boards were developed in the 1930s as directors and animators came to realize that the traditional written script did not quite work for describing how to shoot an animated film. Live-action drama relies heavily on dialogue and less on complex action. Animations, on the other hand, try to minimize dialogue and tell the story primarily through the action. In some ways, animation has more in common with pantomime than with live-action drama. The result of recognizing the inherent weakness of the written script for animation was the development of the story board.

Originally, the story writers sketched each major scene or important action and tacked the images to a board for review. The sketches contained a minimum amount of text to describe dialog or camera effects. If the scene didn't work graphically, it was discarded. This technique proved so beneficial that today nearly all films and professional presentation rely on story boards during the design phase.

One final but very important side benefit of using story boards involves their use as a contract document. You should create the story board for an animation and get the client to approve it before any work on building models and scenes begins. Both you and the client should sign the story board or a letter confirming its approval. Then if a dispute arises over changes to the animation, you can refer back to the story board as the original source of the agreement.

The Process

So what is the process for creating a story board? Before you can create a story board, you must have a story to tell. Too many animators jump into the program expecting the story and sequence of actions to reveal themselves as the animation develops. Nothing could be further from reality. You must have three things in hand before you sit down in front of your computer, as follows:

- ✔ A story to tell
- ✔ A story board of the important scenes
- ✔ A script for the action and any sound effects

These three things are not always separate physical documents. Often the story board and the script are combined; maybe the story is only in your head. Regardless of the form that they take, you must fully plan and develop all three components before you begin animating.

Getting Started

Storytelling

What story are you going to tell with this animation? How will you hold the audience's attention? How will the story start? How will it end? How much time will the story take to tell? You must consider all of these things. Sometimes you have the complete story handed to you for animation. More often you just receive the seed of a story idea and a requirement for a certain amount of running time.

A client says, "Produce an animation of our proposed new building to help attract tenants." That is a story idea, but it is not detailed enough to move into the story board phase. Issues to consider for this story begin with the questions, "What are the main selling features of the building?" and "Is proximity to transportation hubs being promoted?" Then consider a bird's-eye view pointing out major transportation centers. How do you show the entry sequence leading to the lobby and public reception area? How do you show the office suites? How do you get to the office suites? Computer graphics and demo tapes are littered with lifeless, boring, architectural walk-throughs that seem to be filmed by real estate zombies wandering through the building. As the animator, it is your job to come up with an interesting way to tell even the most boring story and do it within the time constraints set by the client.

Story Board

Now you have a story to tell, and hopefully you've written it down and read it back a few times. Make sure that you're comfortable with it. How do you know whether this story will translate well into an animation? That is the job of the story board.

Take the story and break it down into the major scenes, important sequences of action, and transitions between scenes. If you are not sure if a scene or action is important enough, include it any way. It is easier to weed out and discard scenes than it is to begin animation and discover that you left an important issue unresolved. After the story is broken down, draw quick, conceptual sketches of each scene or action. This is where many of you are saying, "Wait! I got into computer graphics because I don't like drawing by hand!" Remember that these sketches are for no one's eyes but your own. The story board sketches should be quick and rough, and if they look a little childish, so much the better. If you spend any time trying to make the story board sketches look good, you'll lose the flow of the action and miss the purpose of creating the story board.

With all of the sketches complete, tack them on a board or spread them out on a table and review the story. Does the action flow from one scene to the next? Is there any awkwardness in the way the story unfolds? Does anything seem to be missing? Can all of these scenes be animated in the time allowed? These questions are much easier to answer with the sketches laid out in front of you than when the story is just written down. Analyze the story board and change any of the sketches as needed. If you have to read the notes next to a sketch to figure out what is happening at that point of the story, you have a problem. The scene or action in question is too weak. You either need to give the scene more emphasis or discard it. The text next to a sketch exists only for detail information and to describe how the scene is put together. Don't expect the text to make up for weak action or a poorly planned scene.

Script

With the story board approved, it is now time to write the script. In live action film, the script tells the actors what to say, what to do, and when to say and do it. The typical 3D Studio animation script doesn't need to be quite so elaborate. Your script will focus on identifying key frames and defining what happens on those frames. If you plan to include sound effects, then you must synchronize the sound with the key frames as well.

One useful approach to the script is to take a copy of the story board and begin adding frame numbers next to the sketches. This also provides a convenient place to note what sound effects belong with each scene. At this point your assumptions about timing and the overall length of the animation are put to the test. You will work through the story board and script many times until you find the right timing for the animation.

Types of Story Boards

You can use a couple of different types of story boards in the course of creating an animation. The first type follows closely what was described earlier. That is, a quick, rough sketch of the relevant scenes with notations to the side for timing, camera effects, and sound. This is by far the most important version of the story board and is the one from which you work while creating the animation.

The other type of story board is as a presentation device. Remember the advice that both the animator and the client sign off on the final story board as part of the contract requirements? Many times you might not be comfortable presenting the rough working version of the story board for client signature. In that case, you can buy commercially available story board forms that include small blank screens with lined blocks for your notes. A sample story board sheet is shown in figure 1.28. Redraw the story board cleanly on these forms for presentation and client approval.

Creating this type of story board should only occur after you have completed the working story board and are satisfied with its contents. Trying to draw a presentation story board and work out the animation at the same time just does not work.

Creating a Story Board

The process of creating a story board has been described in the preceding section. A few technical issues, however, must be addressed here. First, the drawing technique used should be fast and rough—anything that slows the flow of ideas will kill the creative process. Many people make the mistake of using the preprinted story board forms that contain multiple scenes on a single large sheet. Many problems are associated with that approach. The preprinted frames have a tendency to inhibit the drawing process, you try too hard to keep things in the lines and the sharp edges of the frames are not compatible with a fast drawing technique. Also, if multiple frames are on a single sheet, it is difficult to discard or replace frames as you make changes. Every scene should be on a separate sheet of paper, and if that scene does not work out, discard it and try a new approach.

Figure 1.28
A typical
preprinted story
board sheet.

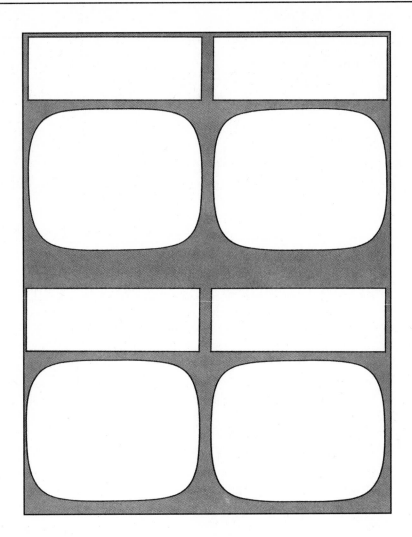

A second technique concerns the size of the story board. The drawings of each scene should be kept small to promote fast, conceptual drawing. If the paper is too big, you will have the uncontrollable urge to fill in unnecessary detail and background to make the drawing more "finished." The small, gummed back sketch pads, or even cheap notepads, make great story board sheets. They are cheap, the pages are easy to tear out, and they are available in small sizes. After all of the scenes are drawn, the individual sketches are easy to lay out on a board and can be torn off, replaced, or rearranged with minimal effort.

After the client has signed off on the story board and you begin the animation, keep referring to it to guide your work. If multiple people are working on the project, give each of them a copy of the story board for reference. A Hollywood director does not go on location to shoot without taking the script along, and you should not sit in front of the workstation without having the story board close at hand.

Creating the Big Bounce Story Board

The following example gives you a chance to create a quick story board for a simple animation. Remember that the sketches for a story board should be very loose and rough. You also should keep the sketches small and use a separate page for each scene or action that you sketch.

If you do not have a small format sketch book, make your own sketch sheets by tearing a standard 8-$\frac{1}{2}$ × 11-inch page into four quarters 4-$\frac{1}{4}$ × 5-$\frac{1}{2}$ inches.

✔ **The Story.** The story board that you are going to create is for a story titled, "The Big Bounce." The final animation runs about 20 seconds.

You are looking at a beautiful landscape at the edge of a cliff when a red ball rolls up to the edge of the cliff and stops. The ball seems to look over the edge and then after a brief pause, it bounces twice and jumps over the edge.

You follow the ball down, gaining speed as you go, just inches away from the face of the cliff. Suddenly, the ball strikes the ground with great force and rebounds out of view.

You are left standing at the base of the cliff, wondering what just happened, when you notice three more balls in the background. Slowly, the balls rotate, one by one, revealing scores of 9.5, 9.6, and 9.4. A near perfect bounce.

✔ **Drawing the Story Board.** The first step is to divide the story into its major scenes and action sequences. Consider the following scenes:

1. Opening shot. Cliff with landscape beyond.

2. Ball rolls out to edge of the cliff.

3. Ball looks over edge.

4. Ball bounces.

5. Ball goes over the edge.

6. Falling.

7. Ball hits the ground.

8. Ball bounces out of view.

9. Shot of balls in the background.

10. Balls roll over revealing numbers.

11. Zoom in on middle ball.

12. Ball fades to black with just numbers on the screen.

You may have ideas for a slightly different division of scenes. If so, feel free to draw them. Figure 1.29 shows an example of what part of the story board might look like.

Figure 1.29
Sample story
board frames.

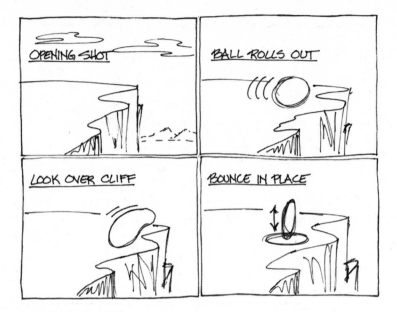

✔ **Adding Frame Numbers.** Now that you have a story board, it is time to consider timing and on which frame each action occurs. Add frame numbers and camera descriptions to each story board sketch. Here is a suggestion of how the timing could work out, assuming a play back rate of 15 frames per second.

1. Opening shot. Pause on scene of the cliff.
   (3 seconds, frames 1-45)

2. Ball rolls out to edge of the cliff.
   (2 seconds, frames 46-75)

3. Ball pauses and looks over edge.
   (2 seconds, frames 76-105)

4. Ball bounces two times, quickly, in place.
   (3 seconds, frames 106-150)

5. Ball goes over the edge.
   (0.5 second, frames 151-158)

6. Falling. See cliff flashing by. Ball stretches during fall.
   (2.5 seconds, frames 159-195)

7. Ball hits the ground. Squashes flat. Ground shakes.
   (0.5 seconds, frames 196-203)

8. Ball bounces out of view.
   (0.5 seconds, frames 204-210)

9. Shot of balls in the background. Pan and zoom in on balls.
   (1 second, frames 211-225)

10. Balls roll over, one at time, revealing numbers. Pause.
    (3 seconds, frames 226-270)

11. Zoom in on middle ball.
    (1 second, frame 271-285)

12. Ball fades to black with just numbers on the screen.
    (1 second, frames 286-300)

You have just worked through the process of devising a story, drawing a story board, and producing a script for a simple animation. Even for a simple animation such as this, working out the timing and the key frames for all the scenes is quite involved. Imagine trying to create a sophisticated animation without first working out the story board and the script.

Summary

Preparing to create animations involves much more than just installing the 3D Studio software. You must understand how to get the most out of your equipment, decide how to organize your files, and plan out the story and script of your animation.

Jumping into an animation project without proper preparation results in sloppy work and wasted effort. You do not have to completely agree with everything presented in this chapter, but if you think through the issues presented and decide what works for you, you can save yourself a lot of work.

Chapter Snapshot

Many skills must come together before you can create successful renderings and animations with 3D Studio. When using the various modules in 3D Studio, you will realize that many disciplines are represented in the program. The arts of modeling, lighting, photography, theater, painting, and storytelling are all important skills for the professional animator. This chapter introduces you to the following concepts as they pertain to 3D Studio:

✔ Understanding perspective and how your choice of camera lens affects the composition of your scene

✔ Exploring the nature of color and the differences between colored pigment and colored lights

✔ Understanding the laws of natural motion and how they can add life and interest to your animations

Concepts and Theories

3 D Studio has many tools you can use to control perspective and view composition in your scenes. If you don't explore and try to understand the various options you have, you are like a professional photographer trying to get by with one 50mm camera lens. Your choices of camera lens and camera placement go a long way toward making the difference between a merely interesting model and a truly professional-looking image composition.

Understanding Human Vision

People relate to perspective in different ways. You are probably familiar with the example of straight railroad tracks extending on flat ground to the horizon. The tracks appear to converge in the distance at a single point, as shown in figure 2.1. The convergence of these lines is a basic trait of perspective. The tracks are an extreme example, as few observations are so distinct and separable. It is possible that your mind does not see things in that way.

Figure 2.1
Train tracks
converging to a
vanishing point on
the horizon.

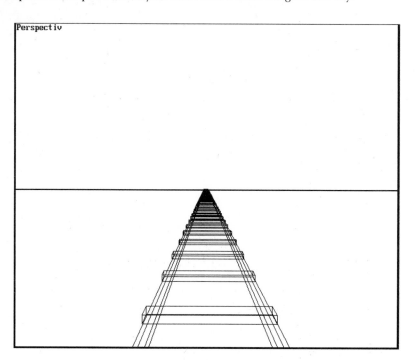

Your eye takes in many images, very rapidly, which your mind then composes to form an overall picture of the scene from which it makes conclusions. The brain organizes shapes and forms according to spatial relationships. If you analyze a snapshot of the scene, you see that all lines are "slanting" or converging. But the mind's eye tends to correct the real world view and understands these lines as being parallel rather than converging. This is an interpretation of reality—after all, the objects really are parallel. It also is much easier to navigate through a world that your mind spatially understands. Imagine a world where you would need to constantly judge the effects of perspective before walking across the room to pick up a glass! The ability to not see the world in perspective is thus quite useful and by far the norm. Your mind does this spatial transformation automatically. You don't need to think about it.

To truly understand perspective, you must learn how to see the world not as it appears, but how it really is. Perspective is learned; it is not readily apparent. Artists learn to find converging lines and vanishing points when they draw a scene and keep its rules in the back of their mind when they sketch objects. It was not until the Renaissance that a full understanding of perspective was made, so don't feel bad if it isn't immediately obvious to you.

Even though your mind may not interpret what it sees according to the rules of perspective, it does know them. A drawing or illustration that has perspective flaws looks "off" to anyone. You might not be able to identify what is wrong, but you know intuitively that something is not right.

Perspective also has a great influence on the perceived mood and action of an image. A scene portrayed with *flat* perspective appears to be stable and at a distance, in contrast to an extremely *flared* perspective, which makes the scene appear in motion, chaotic, and very close. Figure 2.2 shows two similar views of OLDCITY3.3DS—one with a flat perspective and one with a flared perspective. Perspective is an important contribution to composition. Learning the basic rules of perspective help you compose scenes to get the desired effects.

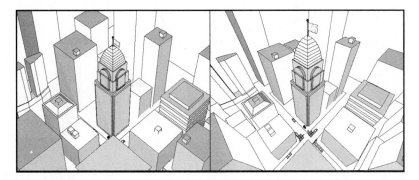

a) flat perspective   b) flared perspective

Figure 2.2
Two views of the old city: a) flat perspective. b) flared perspective.

You can much more readily understand the rules and effects of perspective by analyzing photographs. These frozen images, made from a stationary vantage point, prevent you from assembling a mind's eye view of them. Each perspective view that 3D Studio gives you is in essence such a photograph.

3D Studio's Camera Analogy

Excellent perspective capabilities are built into the 3D Studio environment. You can use these to learn quite a bit about how perspective affects the perception and drama of a view as you experiment with them in your scenes.

3D Studio relates the rules of perspective in photographic terms. The basis for descriptions is the 35mm *single lens reflex* (SLR) camera, by far the most common camera available with interchangeable lenses. All the lens terminology that 3D Studio relates corresponds directly to the 35mm camera.

The camera is a good analogy because you can pick up any 35mm camera and reproduce the effects that 3D Studio creates. Of course, using 3D Studio enables you to "photograph" scenes that are impossible to capture with a camera. The compositional effects, however, are the same. If you can view it through a Camera viewport, then you can re-create it with a 35mm camera.

Traditional Perspective

Several empirical, mechanical, and construction-based methods for drawing perspectives have been created and are in use daily. These methods employ very specific steps and procedures for creating a hand-drawn perspective. Luckily, 3D Studio does all this for you within its Camera viewport with greater accuracy than most delineators even come close to achieving. The following discussion relates the perspective terms that artists traditionally use to 3D Studio's camera analogy.

Traditional perspective theory places the observer's eye at a station point and looks at a point in the distance termed the *center of vision*. This is equivalent to the placement of the *camera* and the camera's *target* in 3D Studio. A correlation between the two models can be seen in figure 2.3.

Figure 2.3

Traditional perspective terminology in comparison to 3D Studio's camera analogy.

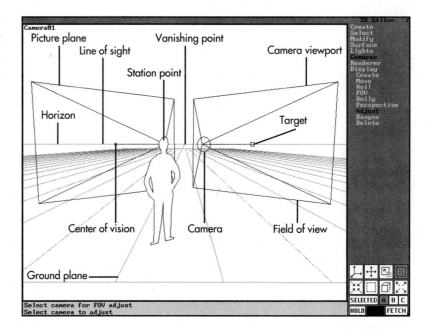

A line struck between your eye and your center of vision is often termed the *line of sight*. 3D Studio draws this line visually to connect the camera and target. This vector traces your eyes center of vision and in so doing shows what your eye is capable of seeing. If an object is blocking this line, then you cannot see past it. It's a useful technique to use this line of sight for reference when viewing the scene from above to position your cameras and targets.

Lines of sight can be traced between your eye and each object in the scene. These lines are plotted on a theoretical plane suspended between you and the scene and termed the *picture plane*. For an artist, this is equivalent to the piece of paper on which a scene is drawn. For 3D Studio, it's the frame of the final image, and so is actually the Camera viewport.

Note The concept of a picture plane is actually how perspective was first discovered. A sheet of glass was used to frame a scene with the lines of sight between the artist and objects "traced" onto the glass.

The plane upon which the observer stands while regarding a scene is described as the *ground plane*—the floor or land on which the majority of objects in the scene are resting. The ground plane is located at your eye height's distance below you—that is, the height of the horizon (between five and six feet for most people).

The height of your eye (*station point*), or camera location, also is the height of the scene's horizon. The *horizon line* is drawn through the station point, or camera, parallel to the ground plane. All lines parallel to the ground converge to points on the horizon. You can think of the horizon as an infinitely large plane extending into the distance while always maintaining a constant height from the ground plane. As items recede into the distance, they come closer and closer to appear to lie on the horizon.

The horizon is important because all horizontal lines (lines that lay on planes parallel to the ground plane) visually converge to vanishing points located on it. Lines on planes below your eye converge upward to the line of the horizon, while lines above your eye converge downward. Lines in the scene directly at eye level are coincidental with the horizon and read as one "line." 3D Studio has no term for vanishing points because it doesn't require their use. By understanding the existence of vanishing points, you can better place objects within a scene and determine the best point from which to view them.

An angle you can view from side-to-side is termed the *cone of vision* or *angle of view*, equivalent to 3D Studio's Field of View, as shown in figure 2.4. In traditional perspective, the angle of view is often considered to be 30 degrees to either side of the line of sight. This is actually more from the convenience of using a 30–60 degree triangle than physical truth. The angle upon which the human eye can focus is closer to 48 degrees—the Field of View provided by 3D Studio's default 48.24mm lens.

One-Point Perspective

The world in which you live is based primarily on right angles. You write on rectangular paper, create objects composed of square corners, build most buildings perpendicular to the ground, and place them "square to the world" on an orthogonal grid of streets and blocks. Perspective has the most impact on parallel lines and right angles. Because of this, it is quite common to talk of perspective in relation to a simple cube.

The following exercises refer to figures of a toy block that demonstrate various principles of perspective. You can load the file TOYBLOCK.3DS into the 3D Editor if you want to experiment with the views yourself.

Figure 2.4
The default Field of View displayed in 3D Studio.

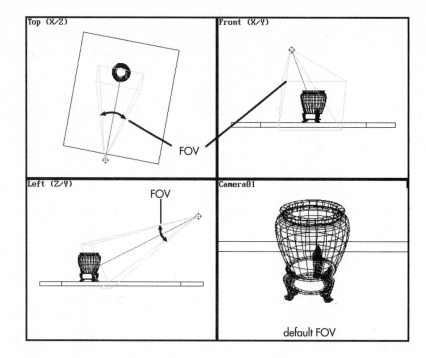

Figure 2.5
The Toy Block model in one-point perspective.

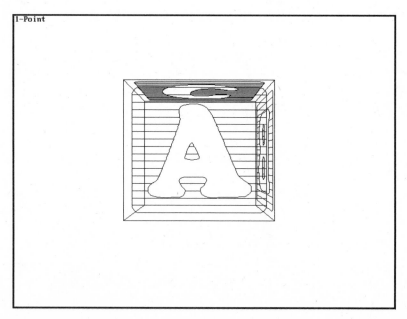

Loading the Toy Block

Choose Reset *from the File pull-down menu and press* (F3)	Resets the 3D Studio environment and enters the 3D Editor
Choose Load from the File pull-down menu	Displays the Load File dialog box
Select TOYBLOCK.3DS *from the CD-ROM and click on OK*	Loads the file and displays the view in figure 2.5

When you are "square" to the side of the cube, only the lines perpendicular to you converge on the horizon. You can see the effect in the 1-Point Camera viewport, as shown in figure 2.5. The vanishing point lies on the horizon line and coincides with the center of vision. The block's other lines have a vanishing point of infinite distance to either side—thus no vanishing point at all. These lines do not converge and are parallel to you and your horizon. Because there is only one vanishing point, such a view is termed a *one-point perspective*.

Two-Point Perspective

If you are not square to the block, there is a vanishing point for each of the two visible sides. These are located off-camera, on the horizon line, to the left and right. You can see the result in the 2-Point Camera viewport shown in figure 2.6. Because there are now two vanishing points, such a view is called a *two-point perspective*. Whereas a one-point view must be perpendicular to one of the block's faces, a two-point view can be from anywhere. Keep in mind that you must maintain a level line of sight (the target and camera must be level with the ground plane) to ensure that vertical lines remain vertical. Because these vertical planes remain constant, it is quite easy for delineators to determine distances using a two-point perspective, which is one reason two-point perspective is the most common hand-drawn perspective model. The effect of two-point perspective can be seen in the current model, as shown in the following exercise.

Changing to a Two-Point Perspective

Click in the 1-Point *viewport*	Makes the 1-Point camera viewport active
Press (C) *on the keyboard*	Displays the Camera Selector dialog box
Select the camera named 2-Point *and click on the* OK *button*	Displays the view in figure 2.6

Figure 2.6
The Toy Block
model in two-point
perspective.

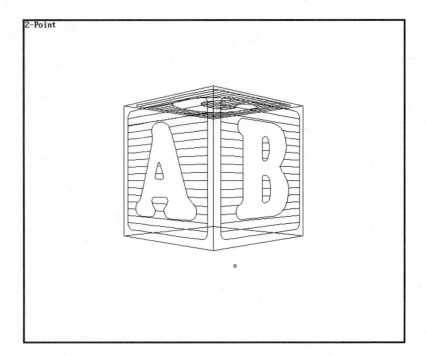

Three-Point Perspective

When you are no longer looking at the block along a level line of sight (that is, you are looking up or down), vertical lines also converge to a vanishing point. You can see this result in the 3-Point Camera viewport, as shown in figure 2.7. All three of the block's planes now have vanishing points, and such a view is predictably termed a *three-point perspective*. The cube's vertical lines visually converge to a vanishing point on a line drawn vertically from the center of vision. If you are looking down at a point below the horizon, the block's vertical lines converge downward. These lines converge upward if you're looking above the horizon. If you are looking level with the horizon, you have a two-point perspective. A three-point perspective is easily seen in the current model, as follows.

Changing to a Three-Point Perspective

Click in the 2-Point *viewport*	Makes the 2-Point camera viewport active
Press C *on the keyboard*	Displays the Camera Selector dialog box
Select the camera named 3-Point *and click on the* OK *button*	Displays the view in figure 2.7

Figure 2.7
The Toy Block model in three-point perspective.

All lines have vanishing points. The block has only three, one for each of its groups of parallel planes. In a scene that you construct, there might be hundreds. Delineators and artists usually concern themselves with the basic three and make approximations as to the rest. You can determine each of these points. Each line that is parallel with the ground plane, or resting evenly on the floor, has a vanishing point on the horizon. If lines are vertically skewed, slanted, or leaning from the ground plane, they converge to vanishing points located directly above or below the horizon. As you can see, a full three-point perspective can be a complex ordeal. This complexity is one reason that artists prefer to avoid them. That said, don't worry about it—3D Studio takes care of the calculations and enables you to spend your time in composition.

The Importance of Horizons

Remember that your eye level determines the horizon. Because most people are within a foot of being the same height, their eyes share the same horizon as yours if they stand on the same ground plane. The eyes of a crowd are thus collinear and align with the horizon, as illustrated in figure 2.8. If you see a head above the horizon, you know the person is taller than you are or is standing on higher ground.

Figure 2.8
Peoples' eye levels
aligning along
the horizon.

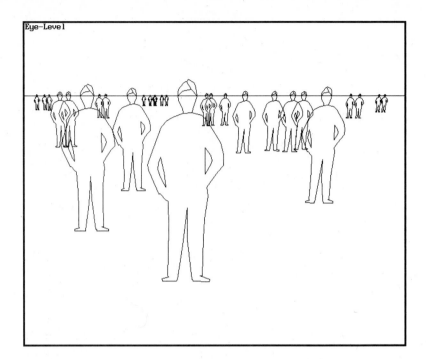

Obviously, a horizon line exists in 3D Studio only if sufficient objects exist in the distance to define it. Most models do not have geometry extensive enough to diminish to a natural horizon. An exterior scene commonly uses a background to create depth and establish a horizon. Pay careful attention to the real horizon line (the height of your camera) and the background's illustrated horizon line. If the horizons are not close, the corresponding scene looks as if it has either been sunk in a valley or perched on a hill. If neither of these effects are desirable, then you should move your camera to the background's horizon level or adjust the background image. Figure 2.9 demonstrates two distinct background horizon effects.

3D Studio Release 4 now includes the ability to see a camera's horizon line with the new Camera Control command (described at the end of Chapter 13, "Lighting and Camera Special Effects").

It is all too easy to place a stock image as a background only to find that it does not align with the height of the camera, the true definition of where a horizon line is. Objects and lines in the scene diminish in perspective correctly, but the vanishing points do not fall upon the horizon. This might seem somewhat trivial, and sometimes subtle, but most people realize that something is not quite right with the image.

35mm Camera Lens Types

You should become familiar with how the lens sizes of a 35mm camera affect vision because they are the terms 3D Studio uses to describe the Camera viewport.

a) high horizon   b) low horizon

Figure 2.9
Background horizon effects:
a) high horizon
b) low horizon.

The correlation between lens size and field of view is only valid as long as you are referring to the same camera type. Other film dimension standards (for example, 4"×5" or 70mm motion picture) have different ranges of lens sizes to associate with field of view.

3D Studio's default lens is 48.24mm, which delivers a field of view equivalent to your natural eyesight. This is a slightly wider lens than most 35mm camera users are accustomed to because the 50mm lens is usually (and inaccurately) equated to be that of standard vision.

The smaller the lens size, the wider the field of view becomes. Try this out yourself by calling up the Camera/Adjust dialog box for one of the cameras in the Toy Block model. As you select smaller lens sizes, the field of view increases. Manipulating a camera should make this relationship obvious, as is done in the following exercise.

Changing Lens Sizes

This exercise assumes that you still have the file TOYBLOCK.3DS loaded from the previous exercise. If not, load the TOYBLOCK.3DS file.

Click in the 3-Point *viewport of the* TOYBLOCK *model*	Makes the viewport active
Press C *on the keyboard*	Displays the Camera Selector dialog box
Select the camera named My-Cam *on the* OK *button and click*	Makes My-Cam the active camera for the viewport
Choose Cameras/Adjust *and click in the* My-Cam *viewport*	Displays the Camera Definition dialog box (see fig. 2.10)
Click on the Show Cone: ON *button*	
Click on the 28mm *button and click on* OK	

continues

continued

Notice the change in the My-Cam viewport and the size of the displayed field of view cone in the orthogonal viewports. The cone represents the field of view for the 28mm lens.

Choose Cameras/Adjust *and click in the*
My-Cam *viewport*

Click on the 15mm *button, then click on* OK

Notice the new changes in the My-Cam viewport and the field of view cone. Now try the same steps, but choose larger lenses, such as 85mm and 135mm.

Figure 2.10
3D Studio's
selection of stock
35mm lenses.

```
                    Camera Definition
      Camera: My-Cam
                                Stock Lenses
      Lens  28.0      mm      15mm   28mm   85mm
      FOV   76.36364  deg     20mm   35mm   135mm
           Calculate          24mm   50mm   200mm
      Roll: 0.0       deg
      Show Cone: On  Off        OK       Cancel
```

Wide-Angle Lenses

Lens sizes below 50mm (or more appropriately, below 48.24mm) take in more of a field of view than is normally possible by the human cone of vision. These are considered to be *wide-angle lenses,* and their views often are referred to as *wide-angle views.* The effects of perspective viewed through such lenses are exaggerated. The stock lenses provided by Camera/Adjust correspond to stock lenses in a camera store.

Selecting a lens below the standard 35mm and 28mm wide-angle lenses can cause excessive perspective distortion, which can produce dramatic effects, or confusing ones, depending on how you compose the final scene. The very small lenses, 10–15mm are often called *fish-eye* lenses because the actual lens begins to appear spherical. Geometry viewed through fish-eye lenses' corners appear "bent" as you look from side-to-side. 3D Studio's smallest lens, a 9.8mm fish-eye, delivers a 178 degree field of view, which has the effect of almost seeing behind yourself! You should reserve such lenses for extremely special effects.

An important human perception concerning three-point perspective is that the more an object flares, the larger the object (or the smaller the observer) appears to be. This effect stems from daily observations. If a building is quite tall and you are near, it is obvious that its vertical lines converge upward from you. The closer you are, the more the building fills the scene. As you strain your neck to see it, the more distorted the view becomes. The flaring of a three-point perspective, as shown in figure 2.11, can reinforce these effects.

Telephoto Lenses

Camera lenses that are over 50mm in length are known as *telephoto lenses.* These zoom-in to the scene closer than your eye can, acting similar to a telescope. Large telephoto lenses, which you can often see on sport sidelines, actually are the size of small telescopes. The amount of the scene they can take in is proportionally smaller and their effect is to flatten out

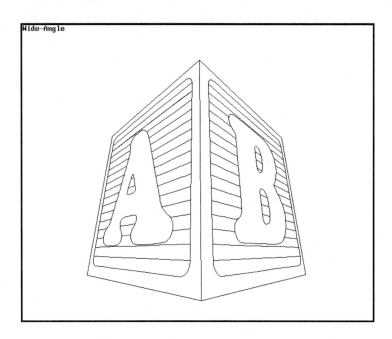

Figure 2.11
Flaring perspective resulting from a wide angle lens.

perspective. The perspective flare is minimized because only a small angle of the scene is viewed. You can simulate this effect on a photograph by cropping a small region and analyzing the lack of con-verging lines. The larger the lens, the smaller this cropped view becomes, and the flatter the perspective appears. Sometimes you might prefer a flattened perspective, as seen in figure 2.12.

Figure 2.12
Flattened perspective from a telephoto lens.

The 85mm lens is nicknamed a *portrait lens* because it slightly flattens the features of the subject and results in a more flattering image. If you use a wide angle lens for a portrait, it distorts your subject's features, and you will probably lose your commission.

You should never run out of the high range in camera lens selections. 3D Studio has an unbelievably high 10,000,000mm lens limit! Such a lens is the equivalent of a large observatory telescope or highly powerful electron microscope. A lens of this size effectively eliminates perspective and makes the view appear as a planer projection or a true elevation.

Parallax

Many artists and delineators prefer to confine their illustrations to a two-point perspective because of human perception and ease of use. Human perception tends to "correct" the splaying of a scene's vertical lines. Seeing an image in three-point perspective makes many people question its correctness. This is typical in interior views, when wide angle lenses are required to get enough of the view. The vertical lines near the edge of the view begin to splay somewhat nervously because everyone knows that walls are straight up and down.

The convergence of vertical lines in photography is termed *parallax*. Whenever you aim your camera up or down so that it is not level with ground plane, your view becomes a three-point perspective and begins to show signs of parallax. These effects are most apparent at the edges of a view and they exaggerate more and more as the field of view widens. Figure 2.13 shows an interior view with parallax.

Figure 2.13
An interior
perspective
with parallax
distortion.

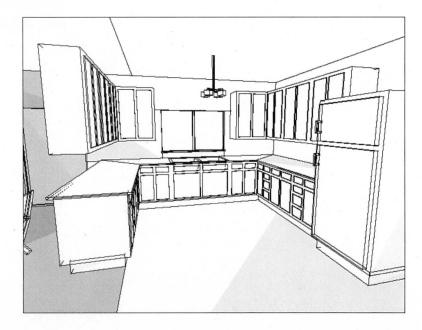

Perspective Correction

In traditional illustration, especially architectural and interior photography, parallax is an effect to be avoided and photographers go to great lengths to correct it. You can avoid this effect completely by always keeping your camera level to the ground. This can lead to less than exciting compositions, however, and is likely to force you to crop a scene or move your camera to an unreasonable height.

View finder cameras, also known as *large format, variable plane,* or *4×5's,* enable a photographer to correct the effects of parallax by manipulating their internal mirrors. The same capability is available with 35mm cameras that have special *perspective control* (PC) lenses. Thankfully, much of the same capability is now available to the 3D Studio camera since Release 3's new Renderer/Render Blowup feature (see fig. 2.14).

Figure 2.14
The same interior view with perspective correction.

See Chapter 13, "Lighting and Camera Special Effects," for more information on using the new Renderer/Render Blowup feature for correcting parallax.

Scene Composition

The arrangement of objects in a scene, the relationship to their surroundings, and the way they are viewed combine to form what is commonly referred to as *composition,* or the final picture. Composition can be extremely subjective and thus very confusing for those trying to learn it. Very few artists agree on its definition, yet the majority agree on whether a particular piece of art has or lacks good composition. It is a feel, or intuition, learned over time. The key is that you can learn to recognize whether a particular composition is good.

3D Studio is fantastic for creating beautifully rendered objects. It's all too easy to fall into the trap of seeing this as an end. A photo-realistic image can be perfect in lighting, form, and texture while all the time being static, uninteresting, and kitsch. Just because you have one of the ultimate artistic tools does not mean you can stop thinking like an artist!

Underlying principles exist that many regard as rules of thumb, or at least items for consideration, when organizing a composition. Consider the following principles when you create compositions, but do not feel as though you need to live by them:

✔ **Scenes should be organized around a center of interest.** The center does not have to be the geographic center of the images, but rather the thematic focus of the scene. Scenes that lack a center of interest look cluttered, noneventful, or just plain boring. A center of interest need not be an object—it could be a vanishing point in a one-point perspective, for example.

✔ **Scenes should not be perfectly symmetrical about either axis.** Scenes that are perfectly centered on a symmetrical axis look stagnant, pat, and extremely formal. When the horizon is centered, the scene appears to be split and it can be difficult to create a center of interest.

✔ **Scenes should have balance.** *Balance* refers to the overall visual "weight" that compositional pieces have. This can refer to the color, darkness, or visual complexity, as well as the size of the objects.

✔ **Without some overlap of form, elements within compositions may appear to float, and may not seem firmly rooted to the scene.** Overlapping objects within a scene provide a greater definition of depth.

✔ **Compositional issues are not limited to an object's geometry.** Textures assigned to objects, the shadows they cast, reflections of other objects, and the use of background images are all compositional elements to be considered.

As with all rules, these are made to be broken. It's possible to create a good composition that betrays the basic "rules." It is not uncommon for artists to see another's work, scratch their heads, and say, "I can't believe it works!"

Figure Ground

Artists sometimes reduce a scene's components to their silhouettes as an aid to develop and confirm their compositions. This technique makes all of a scene's objects entirely black against a white background, which has the effect of viewing the scene with a powerful white

light cast from behind. Only the total, overall form is present. The internal edges and overlaps of objects are obscured. The scene reads as one quick gesture. This technique is referred to as *figure ground.*

You can actually use this figure ground in 3D Studio by rendering with Split Alpha turned on. Render your view to disk and then use Render/View/Image to look at the separate alpha file. Your scene is presented in reverse figure ground with all of the objects silhouetted in white against a black background. (This was not the reason Split Alpha was included in the program, just a different way of using it.)

The following exercise shows you how to create a figure ground study of the file STILLIFE.3DS. You can save time when making your own figure ground studies by rendering with flat shading and turning off mapping.

Rendering a Figure Ground

Choose Reset *from the* File *pull-down menu and press* F3

Reset 3D Studio and enter the 3D Editor	Choose Load from the File pull-down menu
Select the file STILLIFE.3DS *from the* MESHES *directory*	Loads the file STILLIFE.3DS (see fig. 2.15)
Choose Renderer/Render View *and click in the* Camera *viewport*	Displays the Render Still Image dialog box
Click on the Options *button*	Displays the Render Option dialog box
Click on the buttons Render Alpha: Yes, Split Alpha: Yes, *and then click on* OK	Instructs 3D Studio to render the alpha channel and place it in a separate file
Click on the Disk *button and click on* Render	
Click on the OK *button in the* Save Image *dialog box*	Accepts the default name of STILLIFE.TGA and the default directory of IMAGES
Choose Render/View/Image	
Select the file A_STLIFE.TGA *and click on* OK	Displays the alpha file as a figure ground (see fig. 2.16)

Figure 2.15
The file
STILLIFE.3DS.

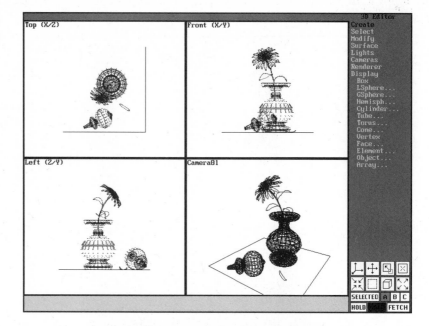

Figure 2.16
The figure ground
image of
STILLIFE.3DS.

Thumbnail Sketches

Artists and filmmakers often use small, quick thumbnail sketches to develop and refine compositions (see fig. 2.17). These do not need to be detailed or even very accurate. The term *thumbnail* refers to size. A thumbnail sketch should only be big enough to capture the overall composition of a scene. This could be a figure ground study, stick figures, overlapping box "stand-ins," or whatever best represents the elements in the composition. Many who use thumbnail sketches do them quickly and often. It is not uncommon to do five or six per minute, trying different combinations. The advantage is that they give you a reference of what you've tried and where you are going.

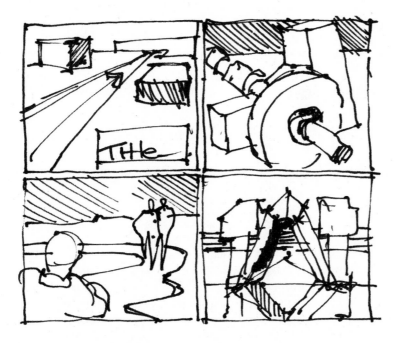

Figure 2.17
Typical thumbnail sketches of a composition.

Camera and Object Dragging

3D Studio's cameras are extremely powerful compositional tools. They enable you to analyze unlimited viewing angles and proportions from any point. The key is to not lose your work, especially if it already involves animation. You also need to compare your different solutions. One useful technique for experimenting with composition is to clone the original camera by pressing ⟨Shift⟩ as you modify it. Keep the other Camera viewport active for comparison and experiment. After you arrive at a satisfactory view, clone again and again until you are convinced of your final composition. At this point, you can keep the other cameras for reference, save them to their own .3DS file for future use, delete them, or keep the original and inherit the tracks of the keeper in the Keyframer.

You can compose the placement of objects by cloning and manipulating them in much the same way as cameras. Again, the key is not to lose work. Save or Hold often and be sure not to affect the original objects unless that is the intent. Freezing original objects will keep them around for reference while eliminating the chance that you might accidentally move them.

Understanding Color Theory

Color affects everything that you see and do. Seeing the color red can make you stop, and the color of a room affects your mood. You make important purchasing decisions based upon an object's color. Understanding the effects of color and how to exploit color to produce a desired effect are valuable tools.

Experiencing Color

Color is the surface characteristic of an object. When a stop sign appears red to your eye, you make the conclusion that the stop sign is "red." You accept this as a tangible fact and describe it as a red sign or that it is painted red. But in reality, it is not the object that is red, but rather the light reflected from it. The pigment with which the sign is painted absorbs all the light spectrum except for red, so it is the red part of the spectrum that reflects back to your eye. Your eye senses the reflected red light, and your brain concludes that the sign is indeed red.

Daily life and experience betray the effect of light to most people. As a rule, you do not interact with colors of light. You do not specify it, you rarely mix or play with it, and you are in few situations where the majority of the spectrum isn't present. You are accustomed to the effects of white, or near-white, light during most of your life. For the most part, you interact with color by dealing with substances that reflect light predictably. These substances are called *pigments*. Even if you do not use traditional artistic pigments, such as paints or ink, you experience the color mixing of pigments whenever you cook, mix drinks, spill liquids, or even have laundry disasters. Color is an important component of your life—you coordinate and match colors whenever you design, decorate, or dress.

Now, however, you are using a device that communicates with light (your computer monitor) and a tool to create and manipulate light (3D Studio). You must realize that the color of light, which pigments reflect, actually is the "color" that your eyes see. This is a leap in perception and it might take a while to become fully comfortable with it. Before you can jump into learning the intricacies and effects of light, you must first understand the colors of pigment.

The RYB Color Model

The color model you learned as a child and have used since is based on pigment. Yellow paint mixed with blue paint forms swirls of green paint. These are the color rules that pigments, paints, and even crayons follow. You were taught that there are three primary colors: red, yellow, and blue. These colors are pure. They are not mixed from any others, and they are used to mix all other colors. When these primary colors are mixed in equal strength, the secondary colors—orange, green, and purple—are formed. The infinite number of gradations possible between these colors often is referred to as being harmonious or analogous. Because color models are based on their primaries, this model is referred to as the *Red-Yellow-Blue* (RYB) color model.

The color wheel is the traditional tool for demonstrating the RYB model. (Refer to the first color plate in the middle of this book for a depiction of the RYB color wheel.) The primaries are placed on an equilateral triangle that has the secondaries forming an inverse triangle. Colors actually proceed around the circle in the order of the light spectrum, or rainbow. Many artists organize their palette in a color-wheel sort of fashion so that they can quickly and easily mix colors. (It is somewhat ironic that although the palette is organized according to the light spectrum, it is primarily used to discuss the mixing of pigments.)

Describing Color with HLS

"What type of green was that green awning?" "It was a deep, teal-green, but I'm not sure how blue of a teal, or really how dark it was." Color is elusive. It is difficult for anyone to recall colors accurately from memory. Even when you concentrate on understanding an object's color, it changes as the character of the light that illuminates it shifts position and tone. "Oh, but that awning looked greener later in the day." For clarity, the color of a pigment is often described by three of its properties. Although most agree on the basis for these descriptions, there are several schools of thought as to what these terms are actually called.

The part of the color wheel that a color is based upon is known as the *hue*. When people refer to the color of an object, they actually are referring to its hue. The term hue has fairly universal acceptance. In the case of the awning described previously, the hue is blue-green.

Each hue can range from very dark to very light, often referred to as the color's *value, depth,* or as in 3D Studio, its *luminance*. As a color approaches white, it has a high luminance; as it deepens and approaches black, it has a low luminance. The color is pure when it has middle luminance because it is not being washed out or darkened. A monochrome painting is a good example of one hue being used with all of its luminance or values. You can relate to the term luminance easier if you think of it as "illumination," where an intense light washes out a color to white and minimal light causes a color to be very dark. The previously mentioned awning was deep in color, and so had a lower luminance.

Finally, the purity of a color is referred to as its *chroma, intensity, strength,* or as in 3D Studio, its *saturation*. You also can think of saturation as the degree to which a color has been mixed with other colors. A pure color is fully saturated because it has not been mixed with any other, in contrast to a gray color that has been mixed substantially and thus has a low or zero saturation. To finish with the awning, the color was definitely teal, so it could not have been mixed with much red; it had a fairly high saturation.

Together, these descriptions of color are known as the *HLS model*—for hue, luminance, and saturation—and can be used together to describe all colors. For traditional artists, these correspond directly to the Munsell System's hue, value, and chroma scales. 3D Studio provides HLS color sliders as an option whenever you choose colors.

3D Studio's Materials Editor is a great environment to learn color mixing. The following exercise helps you explore the meaning of the HLS color sliders and how they affect each other. (As you do this, you will notice that the RGB sliders to the left are changing position as well. You can disregard this for now. The manipulation of the RGB sliders is discussed later in this chapter under "Lighting Theory.")

Using the Material Editor To Explore HLS Color

Choose Materials *from the* Program *pull-down menu*	Enters the Materials Editor (see fig. 2.18)
Click on the Diffuse *button*	Sets Diffuse as the active color swatch
Click on any color in the Hue slider	Sets the hue value; there is no change in the color swatch
Drag the Luminance slider to the middle of the range, or a value of 128	The color swatch turns medium gray
Drag the Saturation slider all the way to the right, or a value of 255	The color swatch becomes a bright color

You now have a pure *spectral*, or color wheel-based, color hue displayed in the Diffuse color swatch.

Drag the Hue slider left and right	Changes the color in the color swatch

As you increase and decrease the Hue value with the slider, you will see the color shift smoothly across the spectrum within the swatch.

Drag the Luminance slider to the right	The color swatch becomes white
Drag the Luminance slider to the left	The color swatch becomes black

Increasing the Luminance lightens the color causing it to be washed out, and it eventually becomes white. Decreasing the Luminance deepens the color until it approaches, and finally becomes black.

Drag the Luminance slider back to the middle, or a value of 128	The color swatch returns to full color
Drag the Saturation slider all the way to the left	The color swatch turns gray

So far, the colors have been fully saturated, at full intensity. Now, as you decrease the saturation, the color becomes less distinct and finally becomes true gray. As the saturation approaches zero, it is eliminating color and all that remains is the luminance. The hue now has been completely neutralized, and you can prove it by sliding it across the spectrum. The gray is constant, has no color, and is controlled completely by its luminance. Moving the luminance up and down produces an even ramp between black and white.

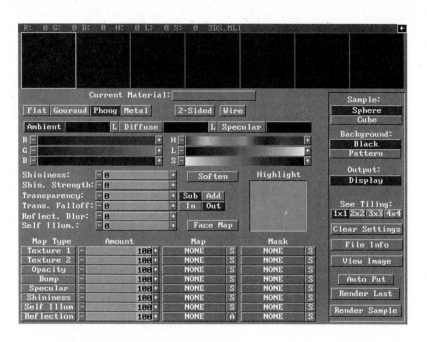

Figure 2.18
The Materials
Editor interface.

Blending Pigment Color

Three overlapping circles of primary colored "paint" serve to show the basics of pigment blending (see the first color plate). In the plate, the three circles mix with each other to form the secondaries. Brown is formed as the three blend together in the middle. This also is the result if you mix complimentary colors. Because these are across from each other on the RYB color wheel, they are composed of the three primaries. White is represented by the absence of color because it actually is the canvas or paper on which pigment is applied.

The Characteristics of Black

The color missing from the color wheel is black. As a child, you were taught to create black by mixing all the other colors, but that usually results in mud, not black. Because of this difficulty, many people regard black as a primary, purchasing it as a separate pigment. As you further understand the properties of color, however, you realize that the absence of black is a weakness in the color model and the availability of pigments, not in your color-mixing skill.

Many artists never use true black, but rather mix their own very dark and deep color blends. When mixed in full saturation, some adjacent colors on the RYB color wheel (Indigo and Crimson, or Ultramarine and Hooker's Green are common combinations) can produce deep colors that approach black. The reason for this mixing choice is that black "out-of-the-tube" gives a flat, unnatural appearance. These dark, rich colors are preferred because they appear to the eye to have more depth, and actually appear darker than colors mixed with black. Artists have learned to reserve black for creating burnt and stained effects because it tends to neutralize hues and create "dirty" colors.

Black also is reserved to mix extremely cold and unnatural true grays. Very little in the real world is actually absent of color or truly gray, let alone black. Nearly all of the colors that you see around you have some red, yellow, or blue. Because this reflects human perception, it is an important concept to remember when you assign and mix colors in 3D Studio.

The CYM Color Model

Although the RYB model is extremely old and was used by most of the masters, it is not a true color model. Mixing true, intense colors of violet, magenta, and cyan from the RYB primaries seems to be impossible. Confronted with this dilemma, many students are told that these colors are simply difficult to mix and that it is best to purchase them directly in tube form, which is a misunderstanding of color because these colors can never be mixed from red, yellow, and blue. Not to say that traditional artists do not know what they are doing; they are using a color model that they can relate to the world around them.

Pigment Primaries

White light also is formed from three primary colors: red, green, and blue. The complimentary colors of light's primaries are cyan, yellow, and magenta—the true primary colors of pigment. It is from these primaries that all pigments (or subtractive substances) are formed. These primary colors make this the *CYM* color model. In the CYM model, red is a mixture of magenta and yellow, blue is a blend of cyan and magenta, and what most people regard as yellow tends to be yellow with a tint of magenta. One reason the CYM color model is not extensively taught is that these intense, primary colors are unnatural and difficult to relate to. A true primary in nature is rare, as is its day-to-day use.

If nature abhors a vacuum, then it at least hates a pigment primary. This difficulty of creating true cyan, magenta, and yellow pigments is one strong reason why the RYB model has been used for so long. Pure yellows weren't actually available until the 1800s, and a true magenta wasn't developed until the 1850s. Artists through the ages have been forced to use pigments whose colors have already been subtracted, or mixed. A good example is to look at old color plates that used the RYB model. They look flat and possibly muddy because they rely heavily on black for darkening. This lack of intense primaries also is one reason that the old masters' paintings have a certain mood and color theme common to them—the intense primaries simply weren't available. You should consider this a testament to the skill and observations of earlier artists, rather than a reflection of their unfamiliarity with the CYM or RGB model.

Four-Color Printing and CYMK

An important difference with CYM is that mixing the primaries together results in black, not brown. This is why artists can create a near black by mixing intense, adjacent colors of the RYB. These colors happen to have the roots of the CYM primaries.

> When you create colors with the CYM model, and thus mix pigments, the ingredients often are expressed in terms of percentages of the mix (for example, 50-percent yellow, 45-percent cyan, and 5-percent magenta make a certain shade of green). These form the recipes for a painter's sundries.

Color printing is a pigment-based media that requires black and uses the CYM model globally. Because of this, CYM often is referred to as an *ink color model*, where cyan, yellow, and magenta are the primaries and black is created by mixing them. Three overlapping circles of "ink" serve to show this basic model (refer again to the first color plate). In reality, the mixed black is a very deep and intense blue or purple, but is perceived as black. Although you can mix all printed black after this fashion, the printing industry uses black ink in addition to CYM, reducing the alignment nightmare that would be required of the three primaries to produce the black you see in most text and graphics. Printing is thus referred to as a four-color process, where black is an added color—the K in CYMK.

The following exercise illustrates the CYM (subtractive, pigment) model through the use of three spotlights. The model is made up of three spotlights and one omni light shining down on a matte white square. The omni light is full intensity white and provides the general illumination for the square. The spotlights represent pigments and use a new feature of 3D Studio to cast negative light.

The CYM.3DS Model

Choose Reset from the File *pull-down menu and press* F3	Resets 3DS to default settings
Load the file CYM.3DS *from the CD-ROM*	CYM.3DS loads
Press Alt+L	Lights in the scene appear (see fig. 2.19)
Choose Lights/Spot/Adjust *and select the light named* Cyan-Ink	The Spotlight Definition dialog box appears
Examine the light settings, and then click on OK *(see fig. 2.20)*	

The light named Cyan-Ink actually is a full-intensity red light with a multiplier of –1.0. The result of this setting is that red light is subtracted from whatever surface the Cyan-Ink light strikes. This effect is exactly the way that cyan ink behaves; it absorbs red light and reflects blue and green.

Select the light named Yellow-Ink

Examine the light settings and click on OK *(see fig. 2.21)*

continues

continued

The Yellow-Ink light is full intensity blue with a multiplier of –1.0. This subtracts blue light and leaves red and green, just like yellow ink.

Select the light named Magent-Ink

Examine the light settings and click on OK *(see fig. 2.22)*

The Magent-Ink light is full intensity green with a multiplier of negative one. This subtracts green and leaves red and blue, just like magenta ink.

Choose Renderer/Render View and *select the* Top *viewport*

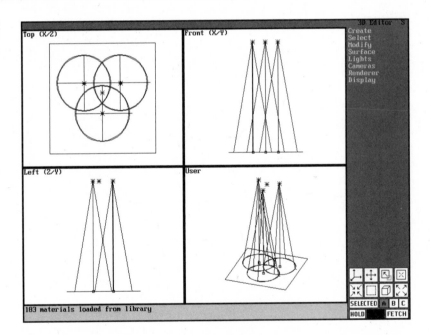

Figure 2.19
The CYM.3DS
model.

The rendered image shows three circles of cyan, yellow, and magenta on a white background. These circles represent the pigment primaries. Where only two of the circles overlap, you see the light primaries of green, red, and blue. Where all three circles overlap, you see the mixture of all pigment (black), which is equal to the absence of all light.

I

Getting Started

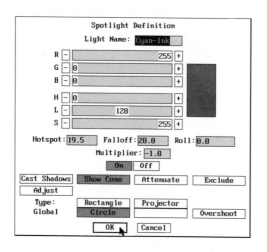

Figure 2.20
Spotlight definition for the Cyan-Ink spotlight.

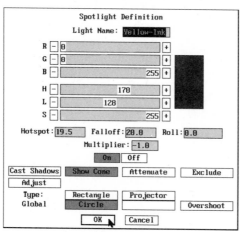

Figure 2.21
Spotlight definition for the Yellow-Ink spotlight.

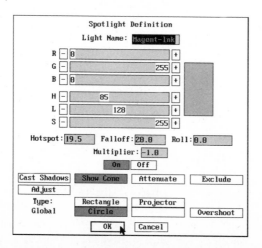

Figure 2.22
Spotlight definition for the Magent-Ink spotlight.

Color Composition

Color composition refers to the choices that you make for the colors in a scene. Good color choices can set a mood and lend a sense of unity to a scene. Bad color choices make a scene look unrealistic, garish, or cartoonish. This section discusses various subjective properties of color and how to use them.

Complimentary Colors

Colors opposite one another on the color wheel represent each other's compliment color. For the basic RYB model, the primary color compliments are red and green, yellow and purple, and blue and orange. Complimentary colors can be derived from any location on the wheel, as a reddish-orange would compliment a greenish-blue.

Complimentary colors have several important features. Used side-by-side, a complimentary color brings out the intensity in its associated color and creates the maximum visual contrast to it. This also creates the most visual strain because the compliments compete for one another's color—that which is missing from themselves. This can create an undesirable "jumping" or "buzzing" effect when stared at by the human eye. Blended together, compliments create shades of brown and gray, acting to neutralize the intensity of the parent's hue and usually avoided in traditional color mixing. When a colored object casts a shadow, it is shifted toward the object's compliment color. This effect extends to colored light sources that have the effect of casting shadows that have a complimentary color shift.

Warm Versus Cool Colors

The type and extent of hue present is commonly referred to as the color's *temperature*. Warm colors contain more red, orange, and yellow, whereas cool colors have more blue. Warm violets are thus red-based and cool greens are blue-based. Neutral browns and grays also are distinguished by temperature and thus the amount of red or blue they have.

Temperature is an important concept when you assigning colors to share across an object. You should decide if an object is "cool" or "warm," then maintain consistency with your color assignments. Animals, for example, tend to share families of warm colors, whereas plants tend to be cool.

Advancing and Receding Colors

Warm and cool colors also have the psychological effect of advancing or receding, an effect of the human eye's interpretation of the spectrum order, where red is first and violet last. Warm colors, especially red, appear to advance and come closer, while cool colors appear to recede and move away—one reason the majority of store signage is red.

Your experience with distance serves to reinforce this perception because the atmosphere cools colors by reflecting blue onto them as they extend to the horizon. Distant objects lose their color intensity and approach gray while their hues shift toward the blue spectrum. Keep this in mind when you create and edit background images. As the scene recedes into the horizon, it should lose intensity and become cooler. 3D Studio has no mechanism to do this automatically. Doing this manually by using a paint program should be regarded as a subtle but essential step in creating realistic backgrounds.

Restrictions on the Use of Gray

Because it is very rare for a gray to be truly absent of color, you should use true grays carefully. Objects based on true grays and lit with "gray" lights look unnatural and computer-generated. The reason is simple—creating this effect in the real world is very difficult. In general, a slight warm or cool color shift in lights as well as materials appears much more realistic.

Color as Reflected Light

Pigment color actually is the light reflected from an object. Colored light, the light reflected off objects, is what makes up our visible world. An object is red because it absorbs the blue and green spectrum and reflects the remaining red light.

Each pigment absorbs a particular portion of the spectrum and reflects the light with which it is associated. Mixed pigments actually subtract the various colors of the spectrum from the blend to form the new "color." Blue (which does not reflect red or yellow) mixed with yellow (which does not reflect red or blue) forms green by completely subtracting the capability of the blend to reflect red. Pigments are subtractive and are what 3D Studio is referring to when it talks about a transparent material in the Materials Editor being "SUB."

Exploring Lighting Theory

Color is only perceived by the light reflected from a pigment. If all light were always pure white, then the previous discussions of pigment colors would be all that was necessary. But light is not always pure white, and colored light combines with pigments to produce many different effects. This section compares the differences between the pigment and light color models and explores how colored light is used to achieve various effects.

The RGB Model

When white light refracts through a prism, its color components separate to create a rainbow. This is the spectrum particular to white light and the color range that the human eye can perceive. The colors proceed across the spectrum in the order red, orange, yellow, green, blue, indigo, and violet to form the acronym ROYGBIV (it seems as if indigo is included primarily to make the abbreviation pronounceable). Of these spectral colors, the primaries are red, green, and blue, and the color model for light is referred to as the *RGB model*, as discussed previously.

Note

Non-white lights each refract their own spectrum because part of the total spectrum must be missing for them to be "colored."

Whereas white is the absence of pigment in the CYM model (represented by the white of the canvas), black is the absence of light in the RGB model (and can be thought of as true darkness). The three primaries of light blend to form white light. As they blend with each other, they form the secondaries of cyan, magenta, and yellow, the primaries of the CMY pigment model.

The dichotomy between light and pigment is an important concept to grasp to fully understand how materials appear in varying lighting conditions. They are opposites, yet compliments to one another. One model's primaries are the other model's compliments. RGB emits light, whereas CYM reflects it. An object's pigment cannot be seen without light striking it, while colored light needs an opaque surface to strike to be seen. Combining all light colors results in white, whereas combining all pigment colors results in black. Finally, RGB mixes its colors by adding them and CYM by subtracting them.

Mixing Colors of Light

Three overlapping "spotlights" of light demonstrate this basic model (refer once again to the first color plate). Here, black is represented by the absence of color, and white is created by the mixing of the three primaries red, green, and blue. As the pools of light mix, they form the secondaries cyan, magenta, and yellow. Viewing the two models side-by-side, it is suddenly obvious that the RGB model is truly the inverse of the CMY model, as each one's primaries are the other's secondaries.

The example model RGB.3DS uses three spotlights to demonstrate the additive RGB light color model. The model is made up of three spotlights shining down on a matte white square. The spotlights represent pure colored light on a white surface with no other light or pigment affecting them.

The RGB.3DS Model

Load the file RGB.3DS *from the CD-ROM*

Press [Alt]+[L]

Lights in the scene appear (see fig. 2.23)

Choose Lights/Spot/Adjust *and select the light named* Red-Lite

The Spotlight Definition dialog box appears

Examine the light settings, and then click on OK *(see fig. 2.24)*

The light named Red-Lite is a full-intensity red light. Because it contains only red, and no green or blue, the white surface can only reflect back red.

Select the light named Green-Lite

Examine the light settings and click on OK *(see fig. 2.25)*

The light named Green-Lite is a full-intensity green light. Because it contains only green, and no red or blue, the white surface can only reflect back green.

Select the light named Blue-Lite

Examine the light settings and click on OK *(see fig. 2.26)*

The light named Blue-Lite is a full-intensity blue light. Because it contains only blue, and no green or red, the white surface can only reflect back blue.

Choose Renderer/Render View *and select the* Top *viewport*

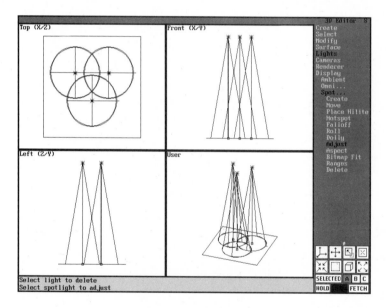

Figure 2.23
The RGB.3DS model.

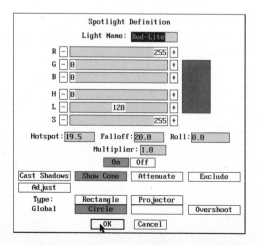

Figure 2.24
Spotlight definition for the Red-Lite spotlight.

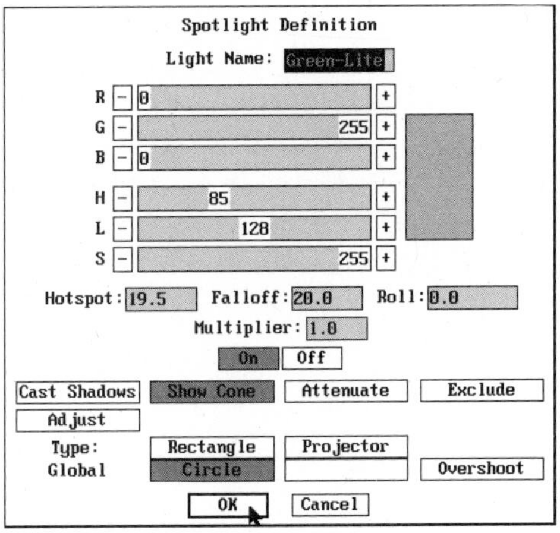

Figure 2.25
Spotlight definition for the Green-Lite spotlight.

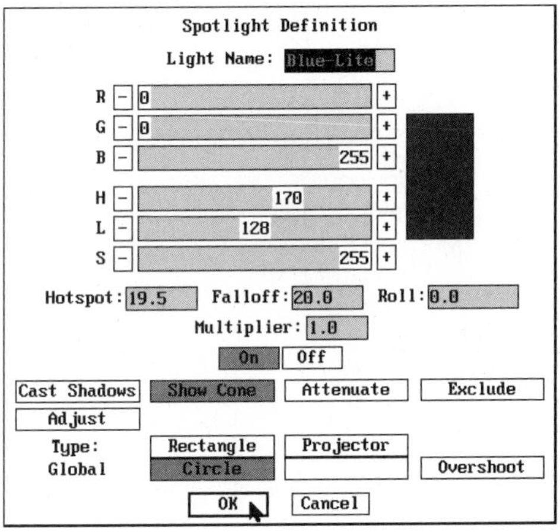

Spotlight Definition

Light Name: Green-Lite

R	–	0	+
G	–	255	+
B	–	0	+
H	–	85	+
L	–	128	+
S	–	255	+

Hotspot: 19.5   Falloff: 20.0   Roll: 0.0
Multiplier: 1.0
On   Off

Cast Shadows   Show Cone   Attenuate   Exclude
Adjust
Type: Rectangle   Projector
Global   Circle   Overshoot
OK   Cancel

Figure 2.26
Spotlight definition for the Blue-Lite spotlight.

Spotlight Definition

Light Name: Blue-Lite

R	–	0	+
G	–	0	+
B	–	255	+
H	–	170	+
L	–	128	+
S	–	255	+

Hotspot: 19.5   Falloff: 20.0   Roll: 0.0
Multiplier: 1.0
On   Off

Cast Shadows   Show Cone   Attenuate   Exclude
Adjust
Type: Rectangle   Projector
Global   Circle   Overshoot
OK   Cancel

The rendered image shows three circles of red, green, and blue. These circles represent the light primaries. Where only two of the circles overlap, you see the pigment primaries of yellow, cyan, and magenta. Where all three circles overlap, you see the mixture of all light (white), which is equal to the absence of all pigment.

What you have to get used to is that light color is *additive* and pigments are *subtractive*. With additive colors, the more color you add, the whiter the hue; with pigments, the more color you add, the darker the hue. Most people outside the theater or lighting industry have little to no experience or opportunity to mix colors of light. The concept is understandably a bit foreign. But you are in the presence of the RGB model every day because all color televisions and computer monitors display their color through separate red, green, and blue channels. A thorough understanding of the RGB model is worth mastering because nearly all

computer-based color applications are based on it. Luckily, 3D Studio's color sliders provide an excellent method for mastering the concept. The following exercise uses the Materials Editor to explore the RGB color model.

Using the Materials Editor to Explore RGB

Enter the Materials Editor

Click on the Diffuse *button*

Click on a color in the Hue slider, then set Luminance at 128, and Saturation at 255	Creates a fully saturated color in the Diffuse color swatch
Move the Hue slider back and forth while watching the RGB sliders	The RGB sliders move while you manipulate the hue

As you move the slider across the Hue spectrum, pay attention to the RGB sliders to the left. Notice that only one channel of the RGB sliders moves at one time. As you cycle through the spectrum, you are exploring the maximums and minimums of each red, green, and blue light component.

Drag the Saturation slider all the way to the left	The color swatch turns gray and the RGB sliders line up

As you decrease the color's saturation, notice that the RGB components slide toward one another until they align. Because the RGB values now are in balance, the light has no color and the swatch is gray. Remember that this is a shortcut to create gray. Notice that the hue and luminance values are still intact, and if you increase the saturation, the original color is restored.

Manipulate all three RGB sliders so that they are not aligned and are not at either end of the slider	
Drag any one of the RGB sliders to 0	The Saturation slider moves to the right and the color swatch becomes fully saturated
Drag the same RGB slider back to the right	The Saturation slider moves to the left and color swatch "grays"

Any color that has one or two of the RGB sliders at 0 is always a fully saturated color. This is evident as you drag one of the RGB sliders to the left. As you do this, the saturation slider moves to the right and reaches full saturation at the same time that the color slider reaches 0.

Drag the Luminance slider to the right, and then back to the left	All three RGB sliders move to the right and then to the left simultaneously

continues

continued

As you increase the color's luminance, all three of the RGB channels increase to the right until white is created. This means all of the light's spectrum is being reflected. Decreasing the luminance slides the RGB sliders to the left until black is formed; no light is being reflected. You can create the same effect by sliding the RGB channels all the way to the right or left with one important difference; the hue value is constantly changing and is effectively eliminated at the extremes because there is no color.

If you want to explore the values of a color, it's best to use luminance because its extremes of white or black do not change the hue value.

Complimentary Colors in Light

If you are in an environment illuminated with colored light, your eye adapts to the environment by becoming very sensitive to the compliment color of the light source—the color required to restore white light. This phenomena is known as *color constancy* and has the effect of placing the compliment color in the nonilluminated or shadowed areas in the mind's eye. The most typical example of this would be the purple-to-blue based shadows evident in a scene lit by the yellow-to-orange based light of an incandescent light. The more color-intense the light source, the more shift is perceived in the shadows.

Artists, scene painters, and set designers recognize this effect and maximize the perceived depth of their shadows by color shifting them toward the compliment color of the light. Most light, whether natural or man-made, has a yellow-to-orange hue that produces complements of violet to deep blue. As this is more of human perception of light than actual pigment, it is important to "help" 3D Studio make this slight color shift because viewers look at an image rather than participate in the scene.

3D Studio uses ambient light to simulate the total accumulated reflected light present in a scene. It contributes light to all objects uniformly, regardless of additional light sources, and is the light present in nonilluminated objects and shadows. For added realism, a color shift in the ambient light to the compliment of the dominant light source produces the effect of color constancy and deeper, richer darks and shadows throughout the scene. The techniques for producing this effect are explained in Chapter 7, "Lights, Cameras, and Basic Rendering Options."

Bounce and Inherited Light

Light that strikes an object is absorbed or reflected. Red objects absorb green and blue light, reflecting the red light back to our eyes. This is why these objects are perceived as being "red." Besides reflecting to our eyes, the reflected light affects nearby objects with reflected, or *bounce light*. Placing a matte red object against a matte white wall and illuminating the scene with a white light source creates a red tint on areas of the "white" wall. The wall is said to have *inherited* the bounced color.

This effect of bounce and inherited light is known as *radiosity* and is only available in true ray-tracing programs, or more appropriately, a radiosity program. Ray-tracing traces rays from a source to a surface, continually reflecting off surfaces and striking others until they are no longer within the scene. Ray-tracing is used by 3D Studio to calculate its ray-traced shadows. Rays are traced from the light source to the surfaces to determine the resulting shadow edges. Ray-traced renderers concern themselves with repeating reflections from mirror-like surfaces, tracing the rays of reflection bouncing between shiny, reflective surfaces. Radiosity renderers trace the light energy from the source and the reflected energy and color from *every* surface in the scene. The rendered effects of radiosity are stunning, but the calculations and computer time are extremely intense. While a ray-trace renderer will eventually have its reflection rays bounce from the scene, the rays of reflected energy in the radiosity model theoretically bounce within the scene forever, constantly becoming weaker.

While 3D Studio provides several methods to isolate or approximate ray-tracing, the effects of radiosity are not directly built-in. This does not mean that you should disregard this effect, because you can simulate some of its effects within 3D Studio by the careful placement of lights and even material definitions. Radiosity is a perceivable, real-world phenomenon and if your goal involves photo-realism, some effort should be expended to approximate its effects. This is especially true if the final product is to be a still image where the eye has time to evaluate the scene.

 See Chapter 13, "Lighting and Camera Special Effects," for more information about radiosity.

The Color of Light

A perceived correlation exists between the color of a light source and the level of illumination. Bright illumination usually is associated with a blue sky and cool colors, while low illumination is associated with candlelight, fire, and warm colors. Keep this in mind when you select the color of a primary light source.

Natural Light

The light that nature provides during the day is primarily white. Experience teaches you that bright sunlight is true white light and it's natural to believe that the colors of an object are truest when viewed under direct sunlight. In actuality, the color of sunlight varies considerably.

You might be aware of the absence of sunlight's color rendering capabilities. Think of the number of times you have been in a store and been unconvinced of a material's color. The man-made light that illuminates the store doesn't provide the entire visible spectrum to correctly see the color. Your eye knows it, and is trying to compensate for the lost color. You might even have taken the item near a window, or out the door, to view it in natural light and confirm the true color.

Sunlight

Sunlight is not easy to quantify because it expresses itself in many flavors, tones, and hues. Early morning sun can be a warm gray light on a clear day or a cool gray light on a foggy day. Late afternoon sun can produce a very warm, yellow tone, while a sunset might range from brilliant red to a mauve purple. High-noon sun can easily be near white, while the ambient light casting through a north facing skylight at the same time might just as easily be cool. There are no formulas to calculate all the qualities of sunlight. You must learn to observe the world around you and apply your observations to the scene you create. Learn to look deeply into a photograph or a horizon and analyze the quality of light.

Atmosphere

The earth's atmosphere has much to do with the quality and color of the sunlight. The more atmosphere, the more color effect. That is why we have spectacular sunrises and sunsets. When the sun is perpendicular at midday, it penetrates the smallest amount of atmosphere and is at its whitest.

Sunlight also has varying properties according to longitude and time of year. The sun is directly overhead at the equator, low in the sky at the poles, high in the summer, and low in the winter. The sunlight found in the equatorial dessert is some of the whitest that strikes the earth.

In addition, the atmosphere has a magnifying effect on the sun and moon when they are close to the horizon. The bodies are visually larger during this time and their color influence is magnified as well.

You need to consider the condition of the atmosphere because it also affects the light quality. An industrial polluted sky creates a warm brown light, whereas the water-laden air of fog, rain, or snow creates a cool light. An overcast sky causes most light to be of a reflected nature and notably grayer.

Light in Outer Space

If you observe a scene that has no atmosphere, there is no filtering of the light, and there is very little, if any, reflected or ambient light to illuminate other portions of the environment. Scenes on the moon or in space should have extremely white light and nearly no ambient light, resulting in very crisp, black shadows characteristic of NASA photographs. Only areas of an object that can trace a line of sight to the sun are visible. The rest of the object is as black as the surrounding void. The shadow the earth casts on the moon is such an example. The outline of the new moon actually is the reflected light of the earth illuminating it.

Moonlight

Moonlight is nature's other contribution with which to illuminate the world. Most of us tend to think of it as a yellow-based "light," but doing so is too simple. The moon is just reflecting the sun. As the sun's light filters through the atmosphere, so too does the moon's. The moon changes color as it moves in the night sky, much as the sun does. The moon's light is a characteristically warm yellow as it sits low in the sky, and becomes whiter as it climbs higher. Because it is such a weak source, the illumination available is low and the amount of light reflected off surfaces is minimized. The ambient light of a scene that portrays moonlight should be quite low and have a strong color shift to the moon's compliment color.

Artificial Light

Much of your time is spent indoors in environments illuminated by artificial light. If you are to render and animate interior scenes correctly, you must understand the various colors of artificial light and how your eye perceives them.

Light Temperature

Man has created many forms of light. Their color characteristics are often described in terms of Kelvin temperature (not to be confused with warm and cool colors). This term is analogous to a piece of metal being heated: it begins with a deep red glow, warms to a brilliant red, heats to orange, then yellow, and on through the spectrum until it becomes "white hot." As a guideline, a sunrise is about 2,000 degrees Kelvin, the noon sun 5,000 degrees, an overcast sky 7,000 degrees, and a blue sky 10,000 degrees. This book does not go into the specifics of each light source temperature. They are presented here primarily as a comparative tool and as a bit of background information for readers new to the subject.

Kelvin temperature is equivalent to the hue and saturation. The brightness or intensity of light really is a function of its luminance. Lights in a scene that are supposed to be of the same type can be given different intensities, but should share close to the same hue and saturation values.

Incandescent Light

The oldest and most common artificial lamp is the *incandescent*, or humble light bulb. Incandescent lamps are point sources and their intensity is limited only to how many watts you provide at that point. The color cast from an incandescent lamp definitely is warm and orange based with their color temperatures close to that of a sunrise. Halogen lamps also are of the incandescent family. These tend to be a significantly brighter light source and cast a whiter, warm light.

Fluorescent Light

Fluorescent lamps cast a much whiter, blue-to-green based colored light than incandescent lamps. The lower-temperature fluorescents are probably at fault if you can't tell the color of an item in a store. Even though these lamps are "whiter," their light causes many colors— especially the compliment colors of red, orange, and skin tones—to wash out. The amount of light a fluorescent lamp produces actually is a fixed quantity. If you need more illumination, you increase the linear footage of lamp. Although fluorescent lamps are a linear light source, they are most commonly grouped together or are folded back unto themselves to create sufficient illumination levels. In daily use, they act more as a "point" source. This observation is quite good to know because 3D Studio does not yet support true linear light sources.

Colored Lights

Some artificial lamps are quite a bit worse at color rendition than fluorescent ones. *Sodium-based* lamps often are found in use as street lights and in factories. These lamps are some of the brightest and most energy efficient available, but also cast a very saturated orange-to-yellow light. *Mercury* lamps are an older lamp type, common to street lamps, that cast a saturated blue-green light.

Man-made light can be colored. Incandescent lamps are available in a wide range of tints. You can put colored, translucent lenses on lamps to cast any imaginable color. Stoplights are an example of colored lenses that you see every day.

 3D Studio's light sources currently are not capable of reproducing the effect of a colored lens by shining through a transparent "lens" object. This is easily accomplished by tinting the color of the light source, however— Chapter 13 explores ways to simulate this effect.

The most dramatic colored lights you experience daily are *neon.* These emit very saturated colors and can illuminate a scene in a most fascinating way. Re-creating their effects in 3D Studio is tricky, but can be well worth it. Chapter 13 explores creating neon effects in-depth.

Although the color quality of artificial lamps varies greatly, you should be aware that this variation is not generally considered favorable. Lighting manufacturers do their best to produce lamps that come the closest to creating white light. Understanding how artificial light affects the overall quality of a scene is important for when you analyze the world around you. As an artist and animator, your goal is to portray moods, not to perfectly simulate a lighting condition.

Considerations of Colored Light

Having said all that about artificial light, you probably don't need to use much of it directly. Your primary goal in 3D Studio is to create a believable scene, artistic expression, or simply a pleasing image. The way you manipulate light to achieve your results is completely up to you. You are probably best off using the information about particular lamps as a mental reference as you analyze the world around you.

What you see in your 3D Studio world depends on how you light it—it literally is what you light it. The colors you choose for light sources have a dramatic effect on the scene's mood and the color rendition of your objects.

Use highly saturated lights with caution when you illuminate entire scenes. Reproducing the characteristics of sodium lamps, for instance, has the effect of not illuminating blue-to-purple based objects and making white objects appear the same as orange objects. Re-creating the color of poor, man-made lights can portray your scene as sterile or color-washed. This might be exactly what you want if you are demonstrating the effects of different lighting choices. For the most part, however, you want to make a scene as alive as possible.

Photographers that are forced to take pictures under these conditions commonly use colored filters to minimize the effect that the colored lights have on the scene.

Intensely colored lights can have fantastic effects if you use them with care. If you look at theater lighting from the stage's point of view, you don't see white light but entire batteries of colored light. These mix on stage, giving some areas and many shadows more richness and vibrancy than could ever be achieved from even, white illumination. Colored lights can have impressive effects when used on completely white objects as well. The white surfaces reflect all the light spectrum and display the mixing hues and intensity of the various lights cast on them.

Color and Light Summary

There is no right or wrong way to mix color, as long as you achieve the result you want. But understanding how these two color models interact can speed your color-making decisions and make sense of certain lighting situations. Remember that 3D Studio enables you to use the HLS or RGB color model every time you define a color. You can use them in any combination that you want to arrive at the exact color.

Examining Motion Theory

Many people approach computer animation solely from the standpoint of building the model. They assume that if you build a sufficiently good-looking model, it will come to life by itself. Unfortunately, they assume wrong. Demo tapes and even some critically acclaimed animations suffer from objects that move in an awkward and unrealistic manner. You can avoid this trap by realizing that in any animation, motion is an important part of the overall product. You must design your motion with as much care as you give to building the model and applying materials. Understanding how objects move and how to simulate that movement in computer animation requires becoming familiar with the concepts of motion theory.

Motion as a Design Element

Effective motion is as important to the success of your animation as any other element of the design. Motion might even be the most important element. You readily accept animations of unreal or fantastic objects, such as talking animals and scrubbing bubbles, because they move in a life-like manner. You also have seen animations where the subject is modeled in great detail and painstakingly rendered, but for some reason it just does not hold your attention. An analysis of unsuccessful animations usually reveals too little motion or motion that is not life-like. In other words, your imagination often quietly fills in the missing detail in a model, but it does not forgive crude and unrealistic motion.

So how does motion become part of your overall design? Planning for motion must begin immediately—even before you begin to build the model. Examine your story board. How are objects moving and where are they going?

The Physics of Motion

You understand the importance of believable motion and the need to design that motion. It is now time to study physics. You know that the theory states, "Every action causes an equal and opposite reaction," but do you really understand how that translates into believable motion?

Imagine a standing figure about to perform a broad jump. Does the figure just suddenly pop across space? Of course not! First, the figure crouches down as the hips move back and the torso leans forward to maintain balance. As the crouch begins, the arms swing back until everything comes to a stop with the body in a full crouch, leaning forward, and arms extended fully back. After the most brief pause, the figure rises up on its toes and the arms begin to swing forward. Next, the legs drive the body forward as the arms swing out and the figure leaves the ground. Finally, as the figure flies across space, the arms reach fully forward and the legs start to swing forward to prepare to land. Figure 2.27 illustrates this sequence.

Figure 2.27
The motion of a
broad jump.

The previous jumping sequence uses nearly all the important elements of animating believable motion, as follows:

✔ Anticipation

✔ Squash and stretch

✔ Overlapping action

✔ Follow-through

✔ Exaggeration

✔ Secondary action

These elements are covered soon enough, but first try to imagine the landing sequence of the jumping figure.

Motion Exercise

Sketch the actions of a broad jump as a story board, and then play the flic JUMP.FLC to compare it with your sequence.

If you are in 3D Studio, choose Renderer/View/Flic

Select JUMP.FLC *from the CD-ROM*	Plays the jumping sequence
Press Esc	Returns to 3D Studio

Otherwise, if you are at the DOS prompt, start the AAPLAYHI.EXE program from the CD-ROM

Choose Load Flic *from the* File *pull-down menu*

Select JUMP.FLC

Click on the play icon >>	Plays the jumping sequence
Press Esc	Stops playback

Choose Quit *from the* ANI *pull-down menu*

Anticipation

Anticipation is a preliminary action that sets up a primary action. This setup action serves many useful purposes in animation. One use of anticipation is to simulate real motion. If an object is at rest, some preliminary action that transfers energy to the object must occur so that it can use that energy to execute the primary action. Before the figure can jump, it has to crouch down and swing its arms for counter-balance. Just try to jump without bending your knees or swinging your arms.

The other use of anticipation prepares the audience for what is about to happen, or directs their attention to where it is going to happen. Imagine a rope snapping under a heavy load. You have experienced this when a shoelace breaks or an overloaded clothesline snaps. The action is abrupt and without warning. If you animated such a sequence true-to-life, the audience would miss the actual breaking of the rope and would probably miss other important points of the animation while they were figuring out what happened. The traditional solution to this scenario uses an extreme case of anticipation to prepare for the primary action. A close-up of the rope shows it stretching, a few strands snap, then suddenly, POW! The rope breaks and you accept that the heavy safe is about to land on Porky's head. The anticipation of the close-up prepares you for the breaking of the rope. You have seen this sequence a hundred times and you probably never stopped to think, "Gee, ropes really don't break that way!"

One final example of using anticipation to direct audience attention involves camera movement. This time imagine an architectural walk-through of a house. You are in the family room and slowly pan around the space. Next, you want to see the kitchen on the right; turning and walking to the kitchen is boring and suddenly jumping to the kitchen in a quick cut is too abrupt and confusing. You employ anticipation by finishing the pan of the family room with the camera looking at an open passage into the kitchen. A brief pause on the still image of the kitchen anticipates the cut (technically, a transition effect rather than an actual motion, but the same principle), and the audience makes the mental jump to the kitchen before the animation actually cuts to that scene.

Squash and Stretch

A property of living tissue and many other common materials is that they are soft and deform under the stress of motion. Think of the last time you watched the slow-motion replay of a hard-hitting football tackle. The body of the ball carrier probably stretched and deformed in ways that didn't seem humanly possible (or at least not survivable), and then suddenly the player was whole again and getting up off the field. This is an example of *squash and stretch*. All objects, unless they are very dense and very hard, exhibit some form of squash and stretch.

Remember the story board of the bouncing ball from Chapter 1? The elongation of the ball as it fell and the flattening of the ball when it hit the ground also demonstrated the principle of squash and stretch. Imagine how a bowling ball and a rubber ball bounce. The bowling ball, being heavy and hard, bounces very little and does not deform at all when it hits the ground, as shown in figure 2.28. You might even consider making the ground deform when the bowling ball lands. A rubber ball, however, is much softer and lighter, so it deforms more than the bowling ball and bounces higher, as shown in figure 2.29.

You must never violate the law that states: "No matter how much an object deforms, it must always maintain the same apparent volume." Consider a water balloon that deforms as you handle it. You aren't adding or removing any water as it deforms, so the volume remains constant. The squash command in the Keyframer properly employs this technique. When an object squashes along one axis, it automatically expands along the other two. The squash command is too simple for sophisticated animation, however. It is up to you, the animator, to ensure that any deformation along one axis is offset by an opposite deformation along other axes maintaining a constant volume.

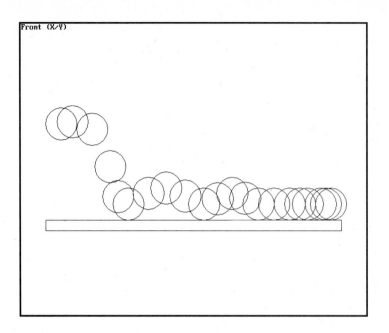

Figure 2.28
A bowling ball bouncing on the ground.

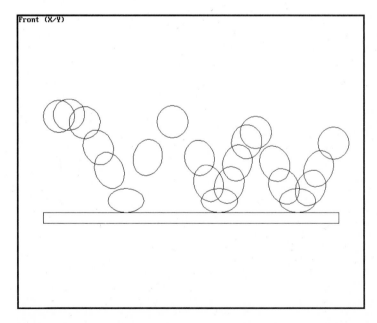

Figure 2.29
A rubber ball bouncing on the ground.

Overlapping Action

Another important element of believable motion is the concept of *overlapping action*. Not everything happens all at the same time. Overlapping action is seen in safety films that show crash dummies in a car that slams into a wall. A novice animator would position the car model at the point of impact and start adjusting the positions of all the objects in the car. Look closely at the film and see what really happens. The first few frames after impact, the front of the car crumples and crushes all the way back to the front wheels, yet the car's interior and the dummies haven't moved. They have yet to experience the impact. The situation rapidly changes in the next few frames as the dummies lunge forward against their safety belts, the windshield explodes, and so on. All this action is the result of a single event—the crash—yet each action begins at a different time. If you watch the rest of the crash, you notice that everything stops at different times as well.

You employ this same technique for other motion effects in your animations. Take the example of moving a figure's arm from a position of rest to pick up a glass on a table. A common mistake is to advance a few frames from the at-rest position, then move all the arm objects to the final position, resulting in a very lifeless motion because everything starts and stops moving at the same time. The proper sequence requires that the upper arm begin to rise first. Then the forearm pivots out, followed by the wrist bending back. Finally the fingers curl around the glass. Each of these motions begins before the preceding motion is complete, providing the realistic overlap that your audience subconsciously expects. Traditional animators often refer to this technique as "The Successive Breaking of Joints," because the motion is visualized by the joints breaking free from the at-rest position in a successive order. The motion begins at the shoulder and works its way down to the knuckles in the fingers.

Follow-Through

Follow-through is a companion to overlapping action and it means the same thing for animation as it does for throwing a ball or swinging a bat. An action almost never comes to a complete and sudden stop. Instead, inertia carries the object beyond the termination point, often causing the object to slowly reverse direction and settle back to the intended stop location.

3D Studio provides *tension, continuity,* and *bias* (TCB) controls in the Keyframer to help you control natural motion and follow-through. Although these controls are useful, you must not rely on them too much. Most of the time, you need to manually specify the appropriate follow-...d then use the TCB controls to fine-tune the motion.

Note For more information about the TCB sliders, see Chapter 16, "Manipulating Tracks and Keys."

New Riders Publishing
INSIDE SERIES

Staging

Staging actually has more to do with composition than motion. The idea behind staging is that objects in motion should be positioned in a way that the motion is quickly detected and clearly understood. A common mistake involves placing an action where it cannot be noticed or in front of a more interesting object that divides the audience's attention. If your audience cannot detect an action, why use it?

Try to visualize the primary objects in your scene as silhouettes. If an action occurs within the silhouette of another object, it is hard to detect. If you move the action to one side, where it is not masked by another object, it stands out much better. Look at figure 2.30. The rendered view of the robot arm shows it picking up a box. When you view the scene in silhouette, you cannot easily discern what is happening. Compare figure 2.30 with figure 2.31. The scene in the second figure is easier to understand in both the rendered and silhouette views. The only difference is that the action is staged to the side of the robot arm.

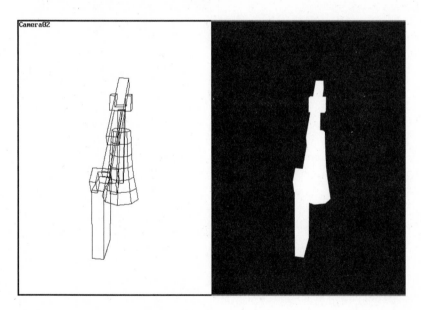

Camera02

Figure 2.30
A rendered and silhouette view of the robot arm.

Figure 2.31
A better view of
the robot arm.

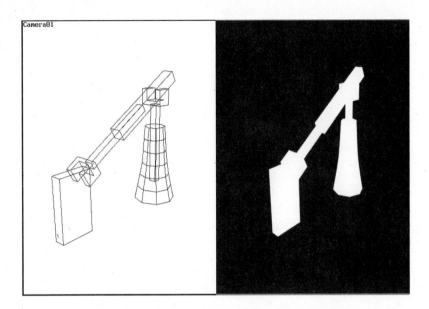

Tip

Here is a good test for proper staging. Turn off all the lights in the scene. Go to the Keyframer and hide any unimportant or distant background objects. Keep only the primary object in the scene, along with any nearby secondary or background objects. Make a preview flic with only the faces rendered. The result is a preview flic of the main objects in your scene, rendered as black silhouettes on a blue background. If the motion that you want to convey is visible in silhouette, then it is easy to recognize in the final animation.

Exaggerated Motion

After all the effort you put into making your animations "realistic," it seems counter-productive to speak of exaggerating anything. You often must exaggerate a motion or effect, however, to ensure that the audience catches it. In no way does the proper use of exaggeration invalidate or harm the believability of an animation. The possible exception is animation produced for courtroom presentations where strict adherence to precise motion is more important than good presentation.

Exaggeration works in conjunction with anticipation and staging to direct the audience's attention to the action that you want them to see. Anticipation sets up the action, staging ensures that the action occurs where it can be seen, and exaggeration makes sure that the action is not so subtle that the audience fails to notice.

You can see good examples of exaggeration if you watch a TV sitcom and then a drama show. Sitcoms are full of gross exaggeration, the double-takes, stumbles, and sweeping motions used to accomplish mundane tasks. Those exaggerations are employed for comedic effect. Now watch a drama with the same critical eye. The exaggeration is still there, just toned down.

Notice the extra flourishes when an actor reaches for the phone or pulls out some keys. Notice how facial expressions are more pronounced than in real life. Such exaggeration does not detract from the reality of the scene, rather it enhances reality by making sure the audience catches what is happening. Employ these same techniques in your animations.

Secondary Action

Secondary action is what happens as a result of another action. It is easy to forget about secondary action because you take such side effects for granted in real life. Even though you might not consciously notice secondary action in real life, you need to include it if your animations are to be interesting and realistic.

A common error of omission regarding secondary motion involves bouncing balls. Consider an animation that shows a basketball bouncing off the rim of the goal. Many animators fail to show the rim deflecting from the force of the bounce. The deflection of the rim is a secondary motion and its absence makes the animation look fake and mechanical. Figure 2.32 shows the sequence of a rim deflecting from the bounce of a ball.

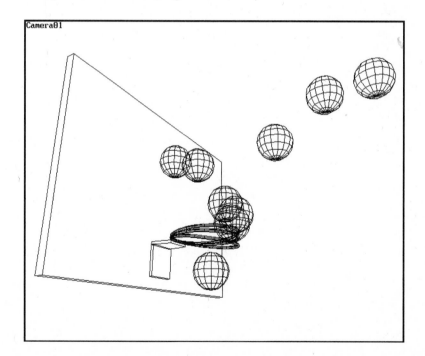

Figure 2.32
Rim deflection.

In the following exercise, you play a flic that demonstrates secondary action. Notice that the rim of the goal deflects downward as the ball strikes and springs up when the ball leaves.

Bouncing Example

Load and play the flic named BBALL.FLC to see the result of applying secondary action to the rim of a basketball hoop.

Start the AAPLAYHI.EXE *program*

Choose Load Flic *from the* File *pull-down menu*

Select BBALL.FLC

Click on the play icon >>   Plays the bouncing sequence

Press Esc   Stops playback

Choose QUIT *from the* ANI *pull-down menu*

Studies of Animal Motion

The recognized prime reference on both animal and human motion is the collected work of Eadweard Muybridge, the photographer who took high-speed photographs of animals and people while they were performing various tasks. His book, *Complete Human and Animal Motion*, is a required reference for anyone who wants to animate living creatures.

Studying the photographs of Muybridge does not automatically make you ready to bring your animals to life. It is difficult to hold an audience's attention if you just duplicate the typical walk of an animal. Instead, you must give the creature a personality. Refer back to the paragraphs on anticipation and exaggeration and think about how you can employ those techniques to impart personality and life to your models. A few examples are adding an extra bounce to the walk of a puppy, frantic scrambling to the legs of a small running mouse, or causing a duck to rear back in preparation of take off.

Studies of Human Motion

Everything stated about animal motion applies to human motion, except that you must be more careful with exaggerated effects. You are much more aware of how your own body moves. Because of that, you are less forgiving of exaggeration or movement that goes too far beyond what is really possible. The best way to get a feel for what is possible is to observe how the people around you move. Consider this an official license for people-watching.

Chapter 15, "Introduction to the Keyframer," shows you the technical steps for animating a walking human figure. For now, you need to concentrate on two properties of human motion that often are overlooked: balance and curved motion.

Balance

With the exception of falling, the body is always balanced. If you extend your right arm, your left arm, shoulder, and torso all pivot and move back. This action balances the extended mass of your right arm. Likewise, few people stand perfectly ram-rod straight. Instead, they shift their weight to one leg, causing the hips and torso to twist as they shift over to balance on one leg. The other leg carries little weight and acts as an outrigger to compensate for small changes in balance.

> Walking and running are special cases of falling. When you walk, you constantly cycle through a process of falling forward, restoring balance, and falling forward again. Running works the same way except that you spend most of your time falling forward.

Figure 2.33 demonstrates the difference between an unnatural straight pose and a realistic-looking balanced pose. Remember that every motion in the body is offset by a balancing motion in another part of the body.

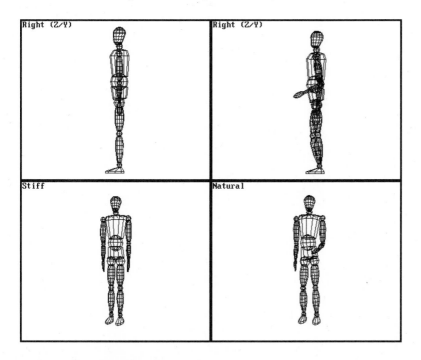

Figure 2.33
An unnatural pose versus a natural pose.

Curved Motion

No straight lines exist in nature. This statement also applies to natural motion. 3D Studio provides TCB sliders to control curved motion, but remember that you use these to fine-tune a motion that you design manually. Two examples where curved motion often is missed are arm-swings and head-turns.

Watch a person as they swing their arm up for a hand shake. Does the arm simply swing straight up? Usually the arm not only swings up, but it also swings out from the side and back in again. This subtle motion makes all the difference between an unnatural, robotic move and something that appears life-like. See figures 2.34 and 2.35 for examples of two head-turns. Many people make the mistake of animating the turn as it appears in figure 2.34. The features of the face follow a straight line as the head turns from side to side. Figure 2.35 demonstrates a more realistic head motion. Notice that the head dips down and back up as it turns. The features of the face now follow a curved path from one side to the other. The greater the amount of dip, the more emotion conveyed by the turn.

Figure 2.34
An unnatural head turn.

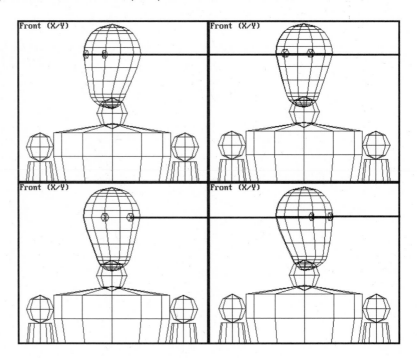

Figure 2.35
A natural
head turn.

Summary

This chapter has introduced some of the important concepts that form the foundation of good animation. Color, as it relates to pigment and light, is how you paint your scene in 3D Studio. Manipulating cameras, and understanding perspective, is how you compose your image. Finally, the concepts of motion theory provide the tools for bringing your models to life. As you read the following chapters, which are more technical, keep the concepts from this chapter in mind.

Chapter Snapshot

This chapter introduces some techniques and strategies that help with the various modeling tasks in 3D Studio. The issues presented are common to two or more of the modules in 3D Studio. The following issues are discussed:

✔ Determining the level of accuracy and detail required for various modeling tasks

✔ Reducing model complexity for faster rendering

✔ Understanding basic modeling tools

✔ Enhancing productivity through the use of keyboard shortcuts and command modifiers

✔ Setting up and manipulating model viewports

✔ Creating and using selection sets

✔ Protecting your work from unexpected disaster

✔ Archiving your work

CHAPTER

Universal Modeling Techniques

Certain modeling techniques are universal to any type of project or task. This chapter introduces some techniques and strategies that help with various modeling tasks in 3D Studio.

Modeling Decisions

Whenever building a model, one of the primary considerations should concern the precision and amount of detail needed to effectively portray the subject. Too much detail is a waste of effort, slows down rendering speed, and can lead to problems with the application of maps and materials. Too little detail causes the scene to appear cartoonish and incomplete, and may not convey the story or issues that the scene is intended to tell.

Accuracy

How accurate does the model need to be? Unlike CAD systems in which accuracy is slavishly adhered to, 3D Studio is much looser and more flexible. A good rule of thumb is, "If it looks right, it is right." This is not to imply that you can "fudge" dimensions in your models or ignore accuracy altogether. What it does mean is that you must be aware of the fact that 3D Studio is, above all else, a visualization tool.

Most of the time, you can achieve appropriate accuracy by trusting your own sensibilities. What makes a model appear accurate often has very little to do with exact dimensions. The human visual system is lousy at distinguishing exact distances, lengths, and spacing; what it excels at is comparing proportions and relationships. If you are comfortable with the proportions and relationships between the objects in your scene, then your audience will be comfortable, too.

Sometimes, you simply must concern yourself with dimensional accuracy. Good examples are scientific animations, forensic presentations, and certain types of architectural presentations. You must realize, however, that even for projects demanding extreme accuracy, there exists a threshold beyond which any extra precision is a waste of time.

One way to evaluate your threshold for precision is to examine your intended output media. Measure the visible width and height of your scene, and divide those values by the width and height of your output resolution. The resulting number is the model dimension covered by one pixel. You waste effort by modeling to a precision that is less than one-half of a single pixel's dimension.

In an animation, the visible width and height of your scene vary depending upon camera position and *field-of-view* (FOV). Calculate your precision requirements from the most critical scene in the animation.

The following exercise measures the precision threshold in a scene. You plan to create a rendering of a low-rise office building to display on-screen at a resolution of 640 × 480 pixels. You want to know how precise to make the model.

Measuring Precision Threshold in a Scene

Your first step is to create a simple stand-in model and place the camera. Figure 3.1 shows a stand-in for an office building 180' wide, 130' deep, and 34' tall.

Choose Reset *from the* File *pull-down menu*	Resets 3D Studio
Choose Load Project *from the* File *pull-down menu and select* PRECISE.PRJ	Loads the project file and displays the screen in figure 3.1
Press Alt+C, *and then press* Alt+E	Displays the camera location in all viewports and displays the Safe Frame rendering area
Click in the camera01 *viewport, type* U, *and then press* Enter *without moving the cursor*	Makes the camera viewport active and converts it to an equivalent User viewport
Click on the Full Screen *icon*	Displays the User viewport full-screen
Choose Display/Tape/Show, *then* Display/Tape/Find, *and click in the new* User *viewport*	Displays the Tape Measure and scales it to the User viewport

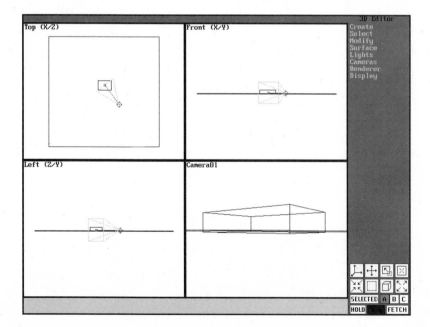

Figure 3.1

A stand-in scene of an office building.

continues

continued

Choose Tape/Move *and move one end of*
the tape to the left edge of the outer Safe Frame
rectangle and the other edge to the right
of the Safe Frame *rectangle*

Measures the width of the field of view
cone. The reported distance should be
about 284' wide (see fig. 3.2)

Figure 3.2
Measuring the
height and width
of the field-of-view
cone.

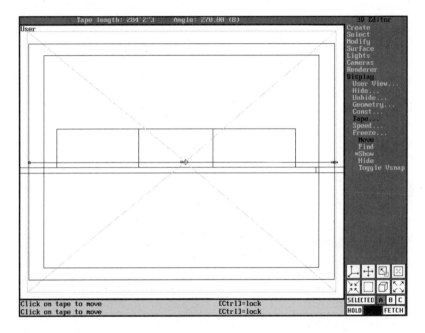

Use the same procedure to measure the height of the outer Safe Frame rectangle. The
measured height should be about 213'. Divide the measured width by the configured render
width and the measured height by the render height. The results should be as follows:

$$284 \div 640 = 0.44$$

$$213 \div 480 = 0.44$$

The result of 0.44', or about 5", means that each pixel in the image covers about 5" in the
scene. If you assume that an object is centered on a pixel, then that object can move up to 2.5"
to either side and is still within the same pixel. This model and camera view have a precision
threshold of plus or minus 2.5".

In the preceding exercise, you calculated the same value of 0.44' for both the height and the width of the image. These values are equal only when the aspect ratio for your rendering device is set to 1.

When you configure the rendering device for your video setup, the aspect ratio reported in the Render Configure dialog box is not always 1. Configuring for a TARGA card with a video resolution of 512 × 486 yields an aspect ratio of 1.23. When this occurs, you get a different value for the distance covered by one pixel when measuring horizontally than when measuring vertically.

You must decide which value governs the most critical details in your scene.

You can employ a similar technique for projects in which precision is not that critical. Make some rough estimates about the size of primary views, and divide those sizes by the output resolution. This provides an estimate of the precision threshold suitable for many projects.

Detail

The issue of appropriate detail is closely related to precision. In the previous example, one pixel equaled a distance of 5" in the scene. Any detail smaller than 5" loses definition in the final rendering.

You also want to consider appropriate visual detail for your scenes. Many situations exist in which a detail is large enough to appear in a scene, yet you leave it out. Why? Because some details are not appropriate to the message that you are trying to convey. Take the example of the office building described previously. You have created the model of the building and located it on the site. Now you intend to add some people and cars in the foreground. You calculate the precision threshold for the cars and realize that details, such as windshield wipers and hood ornaments, are all visible. Do not model them—the details on the cars would detract from the main subject of your rendering: the building. In this case, concerns about composition and focus overrule exact attention to detail.

You also can consider employing an artist's technique in your models. Often, an artist represents a detail with just a suggestion of a shape or a shadow where something belongs. The viewer then subconsciously fills in the details. You might be surprised at how little detail you actually need to model.

Another situation in which you should leave out detail is when creating animations for courtroom presentation. Detail and realism often cloud the issue at hand. Renderings that are too realistic can prejudice the jury and are often rejected as evidence. You must work closely with your client to determine the appropriate level of detail for such a project. Usually you will use the minimum amount of detail necessary to get the point across.

Complexity

Model complexity refers to the number of faces used to build your models. The rule of thumb is to use as few faces as possible to achieve the required level of realism. This is because rendering speed is directly tied to the number of faces in the scene. The more faces in a scene, the longer that scene takes to render.

You can summarize the many different techniques for reducing model complexity into the following two basic strategies:

✔ First, you control the creation of faces through the various settings for shape and path steps, Lofter optimization, and 3D Editor settings for segments and number of sides. These settings directly control the number of faces used to create an object.

You can also try using various Plug-In (IPAS) programs, such as OPTIMIZE from the Yost Group or 3DTURBO from Schrieber Instruments. These programs enable you to interactively reduce the number of faces in a finished model.

✔ The second strategy involves using maps instead of actual geometry. You can represent many details in a model by applying a map, or picture, of the detail, rather than actually modeling the detail with faces. Figures 3.3a and 3.3b show an example of this technique using a model of a calculator. The extremely simple geometry produces a complex rendering through the careful use of maps. A color image of this model and its map is provided in the color plates at the center of the book. The rule here is, "Never model in geometry what can be represented with a map."

Figure 3.3a
The wireframe
model for a
calculator.

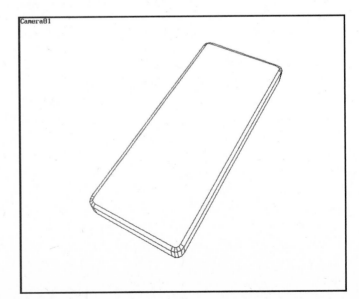

Figure 3.3b
Rendering of the calculator with detail applied as a texture map.

Exploring Accuracy Techniques

3D Studio provides many tools to assist you in the accurate production of your models. Some of these tools span more than one module, although their precise function may change slightly. This section takes a look at tools and techniques for accurate modeling that appear in more than one module.

Units Setup

The units setup dialog box is primarily intended as a user interface control. It enables you to specify how units are interpreted and displayed. It also causes some interesting side effects if you are not careful when you set it.

The dialog box has two functional parts, as shown in figure 3.4. The first part controls display format and uses the three buttons down the left side. You can choose decimal, metric, or architectural.

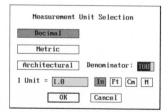

Figure 3.4
The units setup dialog box.

The following list describes the three format buttons and how they affect the display of units in your model:

✔ Decimal units are fixed at two decimal places for a precision to 1/100th of a unit.

✔ Metric units display as meters with a fixed precision of three decimal places. Three decimal places of precision means that the display reads in meters and millimeters.

✔ Architectural displays in feet and inches and is the only choice that enables you to control display precision. The denominator field to the left of the architectural button sets the number of divisions per inch.

The denominator field for architectural units must be a whole number within the range of 1–100. No other restrictions are imposed on this; you could set architectural read-out to the nearest 13th of an inch. Always check the value in the denominator field when you choose architectural units.

The second part of the dialog box is the row of buttons along the bottom. Here is where you set exactly what one unit equals. The four buttons determine what a unit represents—inches, feet, centimeters, or meters. The field to the left of the buttons determines how many of these items are equal to a single unit. It is very important for you to make sure that all of your choices in the units setup dialog box work together.

3D Studio does not check for uniformity in your units settings. It is possible to set architectural units for display in feet and inches, where one unit equals two meters. With such a setup, you could draw a line 10 units long that would equal 20 meters and have a display length of 65' 7".

3D Studio also preserves the unit settings when it saves files. When a file is merged into a current 3D Studio module, its stored units settings are compared and scaled to match the current settings. Try the following exercise to illustrate the point.

In this exercise, you will create and save a shape using the default units of 1 unit=1.0". When you reload the shape after changing the units setting, you discover that 3D Studio remembers an object's original units and automatically rescales for merging at a different scale.

Changing Units in the 2D Shaper

Choose 2D Shaper *from the* Program
pull-down menu

Enters the 2D Shaper

Choose Create/Quad *and draw a 100-unit*
square

Choose Save *from the* File *pull-down menu, click on the* All Polys *button, and then enter a file name of* SQ100IN.SHP

Saves the shape file and the current default units setting of 1 unit = 1.0 in

Choose Units Setup *from the pull-down menu and change the units settings to* 1 unit = 1.0 cm

Choose Merge *from the* File *pull-down menu and select the file* SQ100IN.SHP

Merges the saved shape with the current shape (see fig. 3.5)

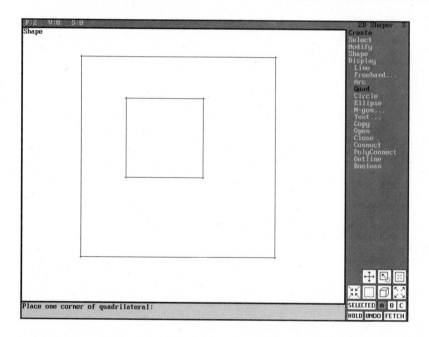

Figure 3.5
The result of merging the shape after changing the units setup.

The dimensions of the new square are about 2.5 times larger. Why? 3D Studio saved the square as 100 inches to a side. When the square was merged back into the file, 3D Studio checked the new units settings of 1 unit = 1.0 cm. The square then was converted from 100 inches to the equivalent number of centimeters, or 254 cm to a side.

AutoCAD users might find 3D Studio's method of saving units confusing. In AutoCAD, a unit is a unit and has no inherent meaning. When 3D Studio loads an AutoCAD DXF file, it recognizes the generic nature of AutoCAD units and sets one AutoCAD unit equal to one of whatever is set for 3D Studio units.

Drawing Aids

The drawing aids dialog box is selected either from the Views pull-down menu or by pressing Ctrl+A. This dialog box, as seen in figure 3.6, enables you to set the position and spacing of the grid display, the spacing of the grid snap, and the increment for angle snap. The careful setting and use of the angle and grid snaps in 3D Studio is imperative for accurate modeling.

Using Grids

3D Studio has a displayable grid for visual reference. A major feature of the 3D Studio grid is that it is displayed within a three-dimensional volume rather than being fixed to a two-dimensional plane. 3D Studio maintains grid spacings for all three axes and displays a grid using the two axes appropriate for each of the six orthogonal viewports. No grid is displayed in any user or perspective viewport, however.

The grid does not affect geometry in any way and is only used as a visual reference. You set the grid to whatever value is appropriate for the model that you are constructing.

Figure 3.6
The drawing aids
dialog box.

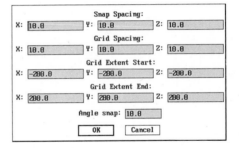

Using the Snap Grid

The Snap grid constrains cursor movement to fixed increments when a create or modify command is active. You can set a different Snap spacing along each of the three axes. The X, Y, and Z Snap spacings also are independent of the X, Y, and Z Grid spacings. Even though the Snap is independent from the grid, it is always a good idea to have the Snap and Grid work together. Set the Snap spacing as an even division of the Grid spacing. A Snap spacing of 2 or 5 units, for example, is a good choice for a Grid spacing of 10 units.

3D Studio does not support geometric Object Snaps or relative coordinate input as AutoCAD does. Your primary tool for accurate placement in the 3D Editor is Snap. You need to use Snap whenever creating or modifying items when precision is important.

Two characteristics of 3D Studio's Snap might confuse you. First, Snap is only in effect when a Create or Modify command is active. In the case of the Modify commands, Snap does not activate until after you select an item to modify, and the effect of Snap is different based upon whether you selected the item on an edge or on a vertex. If you select the item on a vertex, the item is automatically moved to the nearest snap location. This is an efficient way to quickly align items to snap points, but it might not be the effect that you want. You can tell that this has occurred by looking at the status line after selecting an object to modify. If the coordinate display is not an even snap increment, right-click to cancel the command and try again, making sure to select on an edge. You also can turn on Box mode to perform the modify, which makes it much easier to select an edge.

The second characteristic that might confuse some users is that Snap is switched on and off independently in each viewport. Many users expect that after Snap is turned on in any viewport, it is turned on everywhere. This is not the case, however. Always check the status of Snap when you make a viewport active.

Angle Snaps

The Angle Snap field enables you to specify a constraint for any command that requires an angle value. This Snap setting is extremely useful for just about any type of rotation or bend command. The default setting is 10 degrees, but you might consider 5 or 15 degrees to be a more useful value. An Angle Snap of 15 degrees enables you to easily specify the major angles common to architecture and manufacturing: 15, 30, 45, 60, and 90 degrees.

The Tape Measure

The tape measure is a handy graphical device used for measuring distances and angles (see fig. 3.7). Activate the tape measure by choosing the Display/Tape/Show command. After locating the tape in the active viewport, you can move either end to place it between the points that you want to measure. The length of the tape and its angle relative to the current viewport are displayed in the status line at the top of the screen.

Keep in mind that the displayed length of the tape is a three-dimensional distance. This can lead to inaccurate results if you concentrate on placing the tape in only a single viewport. Figure 3.8 shows an example of measuring the width of a box. If you were concentrating on only the Front viewport, you might think that you were properly measuring the box width without realizing that the tape also ran back along the Z axis, as evident in the Top viewport. In this case, you are not measuring the width of the box, but rather the diagonal distance across the top.

Figure 3.9 shows the proper placement of the tape to measure the width of the box. You should always check the placement of the tape in at least two viewports. If the distance that you are trying to measure is parallel to a viewport, you also can use the command Display/ Tape/Find to set the tape parallel with the current viewport.

Figure 3.7
The tape measure.

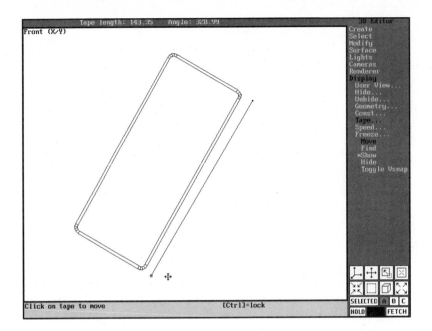

Figure 3.8
Inaccurate measurement of an object's width.

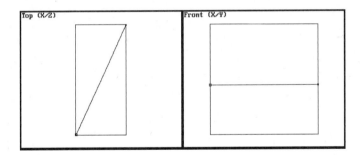

Figure 3.9
Proper measurement of an object's width.

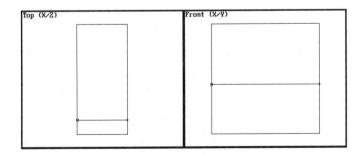

Axis Manipulation

3D Studio bases many of its Modify commands on a defined reference axis. This axis can be placed and set for use by many operations, or it can be the centroid of what is currently being manipulated. The axis is the point around which items are rotated, scaled, and skewed. 3D Studio uses one of two possible axis systems. These axes are referred to as the *global axis* and the *local axis*.

In AutoCAD, a reference axis is referred to as a *base point*, and you are prompted for it every time you execute a rotate or scale command. 3D Studio does not prompt for a base point; instead, it uses the global or local axis.

Global Axis

If you need to modify multiple items around a specific point, or use the same point repeatedly, then consider modifying the global axis. The *global axis* is the central axis system for all of the items in the module. You can display the location of the global axis by choosing Modify/Axis/Show (see fig. 3.10). The axis appears as a black X, with its default position at the global coordinate origin of 0,0,0. For the 2D Shaper, a single global axis runs perpendicular to the screen.

The 3D Editor uses three global axes, one parallel to each of the X, Y, and Z coordinate axes. Modify commands in the 3D Editor use the axis that is perpendicular to the active viewport.

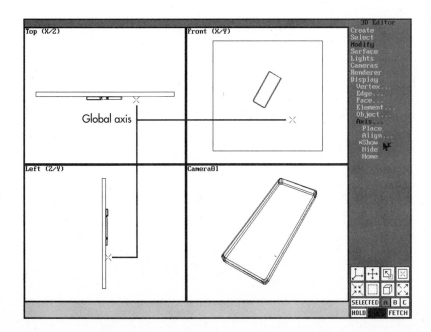

Figure 3.10
The global axis.

Repositioning the Global Axis

Fortunately, the global axis does not have to remain at the coordinate origin. You can place the axis anywhere you want by selecting the Modify/Axis/Place command. When using Modify/Axis/Place, you must specify the new axis location in at least two viewports to establish a point in 3D space.

For accurate placement, the Axis/Align branch provides several options. Align/Vertex will snap the axis to a selected vertex, while Align/Element or Align/Object enables you to place the axis with respect to the center or sides of an item. Align calculations are only valid for the current orthogonal viewport. They are not three-dimensional placements. You still must execute the Axis/Align commands in at least two viewports for accurate three-dimensional placement. You reset the global axis to its default position by choosing Modify/Axis/Home.

Local Axis

The local axis is defined by the centroid of a 2D or 3D box that encloses the selected item or items. This box is referred to as the *bounding box*. 3D Studio defines a bounding box for each object when it is created and calculates a temporary bounding box for selection sets. Using the local axis option is handy if you want to scale or rotate a selection about its own center.

Remember that the local axis is defined as the centroid of a box surrounding a selection and does not take into consideration the shape of any items in the selection. This can confuse you if you mistakenly expect the local axis to coincide with a selection's apparent center of mass. Figure 3.11 demonstrates the difference between the apparent center of mass and the local axis in the 2D Shaper.

Figure 3.11
The location of the local axis relative to the center of mass.

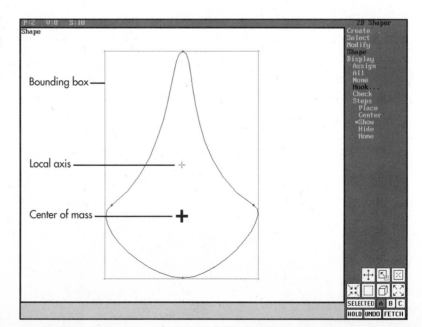

Manipulating Views

3D Studio provides a fast and efficient way to manipulate views of your model. The viewing tools range from controlling only the screen layout in the Shaper to full control of layout and view orientation in the 3D Editor and Keyframer.

Viewport Arrangement

You can adjust the screen viewport layout in all modules except the Lofter and the Materials Editor. Pressing Ctrl+V in any of the other modules displays the viewports dialog box for choosing your desired screen layout.

Figure 3.12 shows the dialog box with the 12 standard viewport layouts at the top of the screen. Select the layout you want to use by clicking on the appropriate arrangement, and then clicking on the OK button.

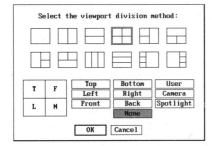

Figure 3.12
The viewports dialog box.

View Orientations

More important than setting the viewport layout is setting the various viewport orientations. Because the Shaper is a two-dimensional module, it has only one view orientation—the plan view. The other three modeling modules—the Lofter, 3D Editor, and Keyframer—all enable you to quickly and easily set up many view orientations.

Refer to the viewports dialog box shown in figure 3.12. The buttons at the bottom of the dialog box represent the 10 standard view orientations in 3D Studio. You can set a viewport to use one of these view orientations by clicking on the view button that you want, and then clicking in the appropriate viewport icon to the left of the buttons. The first letter of the view orientation then is displayed in the viewport to confirm your selection.

Of the 10 view orientations, the Camera view and the Spotlight view are not available in the Lofter. Because the Lofter cannot contain cameras or lights, these views are not allowed. Also, the None view is rarely used because it just prevents that portion of the screen from displaying anything. It seems that the primary reason for the existence of the None view is to support the deletion of cameras. When you delete a camera, any viewport assigned to that camera reverts to the None view.

Using the viewports dialog box is an excellent way for you to learn the various view orientations that are available. There is, however, a much faster way to set view orientations than with the viewports dialog box. You can use the following single-letter shortcuts to assign a view to the active viewport:

✔ ⊤ Displays the Top view.

✔ ⒡ Displays the Front view.

✔ ⓛ Displays the Left view.

✔ ⓡ Displays the Right view.

✔ ⓚ Displays the Back view.

✔ Ⓑ Displays the Bottom view.

✔ ⓤ Displays the User-defined axonometric view. The User view tripod appears, and you adjust the view angle with the cursor.

✔ ⓒ Displays a Camera perspective view. If you have more than one camera, a dialog box appears in which you select a camera by its name.

✔ ⓢ Displays a perspective view from a spotlight. If you have more than one spotlight, a dialog box appears in which you select a spotlight by its name.

✔ ⓓ Disables the viewport. A disabled viewport prevents the display of any geometry similar to the None option in the viewports dialog box. The difference between Disabled and None is that pressing ⓓ in a disabled viewport restores the previous view orientation.

No shortcut key is available for the None view.

The User View

The User view is a versatile and powerful tool in 3D Studio. There are two primary ways to adjust the viewing angle of the User view. The first method uses the User view tripod, and the second method uses the keyboard arrow keys.

Understanding the User Tripod

When you press ⓤ to activate the User view or click on the User view icon in the lower right corner of the screen, the User view tripod appears in the active viewport. This tripod spins all three axes as you move the cursor. The tripod represents the current viewing angle. When you click on the cursor, the tripod disappears and the view is drawn from that angle.

Figure 3.13 shows a viewport with the User view tripod displayed. The three axes represent the positive direction of the global coordinate axes. When you move the cursor left or right, the X and Z axes rotate around the Y axis. Viewing from positive Y, left rotates counterclockwise and right rotates clockwise. Moving the cursor up and down rotates the Y axis about an imaginary axis that is parallel and horizontal to the screen. The Y axis is always vertical.

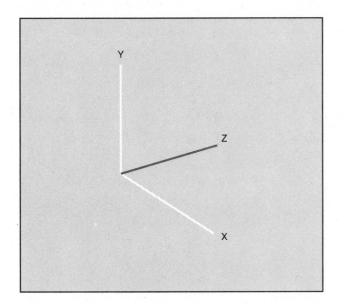

Figure 3.13
The User axis tripod.

As they rotate, these axes change from white to gray. A white axis indicates that your viewing position is located along the positive range for that axis. Gray indicates that your viewing position is along the negative range for that axis. Examine the default User view tripod, where the Y and X axes are white and the Z axis is gray. This orientation means that your view is from a point to the right, above, and in front of the scene (+X, +Y, and -Z). Figure 3.14 shows a cube with its top, front, and right faces labeled with the corresponding User view axis. In 3D Studio, positive Z points into the screen, or toward the back view.

Pressing ⓇR when the User view tripod is displayed resets the tripod to its default rotation.

Adjusting the View with Arrow Keys

After a User view is displayed in a viewport, you can adjust the view rotation with the keyboard arrow keys. Pressing the left or right arrow keys rotates the view about the Y axis. Pressing the up and down arrow keys rotates the Y axis about an imaginary axis parallel and horizontal to the screen.

The amount of rotation for each arrow key press is determined by the following three conditions:

✔ If angle snap is not active, each arrow key press rotates the view 10 degrees.

✔ If angle snap is active, each arrow key press rotates the view an amount equal to the angle snap setting.

✔ If you press and hold the `⇧Shift` key, each arrow key press rotates the view 1 degree.

Figure 3.14
How views
correspond to the
User view axes.

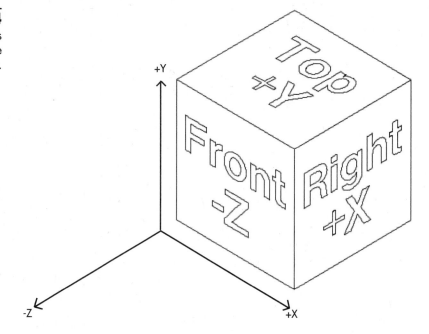

Adjusting the User View Center

All adjustments to the User view are performed with respect to the User view center. The User view center is automatically reset whenever you execute a Zoom command in the User viewport.

You also can adjust the center of the User view manually. First, display the User view plane by using the Display/User View/Choose command. Then set the center of the User view plane with the Place command. Placing the User view center requires that you perform the Place command in at least two orthogonal views to specify a 3D point.

Manually setting the User view center is useful when you want a User view rotation centered on an object. Just remember that if you perform any Zoom command in that viewport, the User view center is reset.

Converting Other Views to a User View

You can convert any standard orthogonal view or Camera view to a User view by pressing Ⓤ, and then ↵Enter. This is extremely useful when you want a view that starts out aligned with an orthogonal view, but can be rotated with the arrow keys.

Using Selection Sets

Many commands in 3D Studio prompt you to select a single object as the subject of that command. Often, what you really want to do is apply the command to a group of objects. 3D Studio provides this capability through the creation of selection sets.

A *selection set* is a temporary group of items that you can manipulate as a single item. You can define up to three different selection sets and recall them at any time you want. 3D Studio stores your three selection sets under the names A, B, and C. To activate a selection set for use, click on the appropriate letter icon at the lower right of the screen, and then click on the Selected button. Figure 3.15 shows the icons with selection set B active and the selected button turned on.

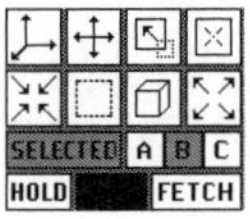

Figure 3.15
Selection set buttons.

Selection sets can contain a mixture of items. The 3D Editor enables you to build selection sets of objects, elements, faces, or vertices. The 2D Shaper only allows selection sets of vertices or polygons. A modify command may affect some, all, or none of the items in a selection set, depending upon which branch of the Modify menu is active. The basic rule is that high-level items are affected by low-level commands and low-level items are ignored by high-level commands. Here are three examples based upon a selection set containing a few each of vertices, faces, elements, and objects:

Example 1: If you execute the Modify/Vertex/Move command, all of the selected vertices and the vertices within any selected elements and objects are affected. The vertices of any faces selected through a Select/Face command are ignored.

Example 2: If you execute the Modify/Face/Move command, all of the selected faces and the faces within any selected elements and objects are affected. The vertices selected through a Select/Vertex command are ignored.

Example 3: If you execute the Modify/Object/Move command, only the selected objects are affected. All selected vertices, faces, and elements are ignored.

An exception to the preceding examples occurs when an entire object is selected with one of the low-level commands. Selecting all of the elements of an object with Select/Element is the same as selecting the object with Select/Object. Likewise, selecting all of an object's faces with Select/Face and all of its vertices with Select/Vertex is the same as selecting the object with Select/Object.

 Selection sets do not work with any command that affects elements. You can, however, select elements and then use that selection set with a command that affects faces or vertices.

Building Selection Sets

The primary method for building selection sets is through the use of the Select screen menu branch. First, click on the desired selection set icon, either A, B, or C, and then choose the type of item that you want to select. You must select elements one at a time. The remaining items, objects, faces, and vertices are selected using one of the following options:

✔ **Single.** Selects items one at a time by picking them.

✔ **Quad.** Selects items by drawing a rectangle on the screen.

✔ **Fence.** Selects items by drawing an irregular closed polygon on the screen.

✔ **Circle.** Selects items by drawing a circle on the screen.

Vertices, by their very nature, must be completely inside a quad, fence, or circle to be selected. Selection of faces, objects, and polygons is controlled by two additional selection settings, as follows:

✔ **Window.** Selects only those items completely within the quad, fence, or circle.

✔ **Crossing.** Selects items within or crossing the boundary of the quad, fence, or circle.

The Select/Object branch also contains two additional selection methods. These are Select by Name and Select by Color. Select by Name displays the dialog box shown in figure 3.16. You can select object names in the name list or select groups of objects by typing a wild-card pattern in the edit field to the right and clicking on the Tag button.

 Anyone who has used earlier versions of 3D Studio will immediately notice that deselect commands are no longer available under the Select branch. You now deselect items by pressing and holding Alt while performing a regular Select command.

New Riders Publishing
INSIDE
SERIES

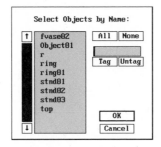

Figure 3.16
The Select Objects
by Name
dialog box.

Selection Shortcuts

The following keyboard shortcuts can be used to build selection sets:

- ✔ Alt+A Selects everything visible.

- ✔ Alt+N Deselects everything visible.

- ✔ Ctrl+N Displays the Select by Name dialog box.

- ✔ Ctrl+**pick** Whenever you are prompted to select an item you can press and hold Ctrl while picking, and those items are added to the current selection set.

- ✔ Spacebar Turns the Selected button on and off.

Maintaining Multiple Selection Sets

You are not limited to just three selection sets. 3D Studio enables you to build selection sets based upon the properties of items. This feature enables you to store more selection sets through the careful use of color, material, and smoothing groups.

Selections Based on Smoothing Groups

Later chapters describe how 3D Studio uses smoothing groups to render smooth surfaces from faceted face meshes. You also can use some of the 32 available smoothing groups to store selection sets.

The command Surface/Smoothing/Show displays the dialog box shown in figure 3.17. This dialog box contains buttons for all of the numbered smoothing groups currently assigned in the model; those numbers not appearing in the dialog box are not being used and are available for grouping items into selection sets. Clicking on one or more of these buttons puts all of the faces using the selected smoothing groups into the current selection set.

The following exercise shows you how to use a smoothing group to store a selection of faces.

Figure 3.17
The Show
Smoothing
Groups dialog
box.

```
        Show Smoothing Groups
  [1] [2] [3] [4] [5] [6] [7] [8]
  [9] [10] [11] [12]
  [17]


       [   OK   ]  [ Cancel ]
```

Storing Selections as Smoothing Groups

Choose Reset *from the* File *pull-down menu and make sure that you are in the 3D Editor*	Resets 3D Studio
Choose Load *from the* File *pull-down menu and select the file* SMOOTH.3DS	Loads the sample file
Choose Select/Object/Single *and pick the sphere and torus objects*	Adds these objects to the current selection set
Choose Surface/Smoothing/Show *and note which smoothing groups are not being used, then click on* Cancel	Displays a dialog box listing all of the smoothing groups used in the model
Choose Surface/Smoothing/Group *and click on button* 32	Makes unused smoothing group number 32 the current smoothing group
Choose Surface/Smoothing/Assign, *then turn on the* Selected *button and pick anywhere in the active viewport*	Assigns smoothing group 32 to the selected faces

Whenever you want to reuse the selected faces, you only need to use the Surface/Smoothing/ Show command and select the appropriate smoothing group. Keep in mind that you might need to clear this smoothing group from the faces before the final render. If the smoothing group is not cleared, the Renderer will smooth across all of these faces. You can clear the smoothing group by making the group active, choosing the Surface/Smoothing/Face/Clear Group command, and applying the command to the selected faces.

The current release of 3D Studio makes this technique more difficult by randomly applying smoothing groups to faceted objects. This has the side effect of using up all of the available smoothing groups. You can get around this problem by clearing some smoothing groups for use as selection sets, or by using other selection strategies such as selecting by color, described next.

Selections Based on Color

Another feature in the 3D Editor enables you to assign color to objects. This is an organizational strategy similar to layer colors in AutoCAD. When selecting objects, you can add objects to the selection set based upon their color. Because 3D Studio allows for a palette of up to 64 object colors, you can define up to 64 color-based selection sets.

Selection Based on Materials

The Surface/Materials/Show command functions much the same as Smoothing/Show. Materials/Show displays the dialog box shown in figure 3.18. Select the materials that you want to use to determine a selection set from the list, and 3D Studio adds all of the faces using the selected materials to the current selection set.

Figure 3.18
The Show Materials dialog box.

Cautions

Selection sets are a powerful technique for storing and manipulating items in your model. As with any powerful tool, however, there are some cautions regarding its use. Here are a few things to watch for:

✔ Low-level selections are ignored by high-level commands. A Modify/Object/Move command will only move selected objects and leave selected faces behind. It usually is a good idea to create selection sets of a single item type, such as a selection set of only faces or only objects.

✔ Selection sets are not automatically cleared when you create a new set. You should choose the Select/None command or press Alt+N to deselect all currently selected items before creating a new selection set.

✔ If items are hidden or frozen, they are not affected by any command, even if they are part of the current selection set.

✔ Even though a selection set is defined and visible on-screen, it is not used unless the Selected button is on. If you plan to use a selection set, always check the status of the Selected button.

Understanding Keyboard Entry

With the exception of coordinate entry, 3D Studio provides fast and powerful capabilities through the keyboard. Watching an experienced 3D Studio user, you are quickly struck by how often they use the keyboard. This is especially surprising for a program as graphically oriented as 3D Studio. An important feature of 3D Studio's keyboard support is that almost every keyboard function is activated by only one or two keys. This makes keyboard entry very fast.

This section introduces generic keyboard techniques that are useful in more than one module. Other keyboard techniques that are specific to a single command or task are defined in other parts of this book.

Command Shortcuts

Nearly every command present on a pull-down menu has a one- or two-character symbol to its right. Entering that key combination is the quick way to activate the command. Other commands and functions in 3D Studio also have keyboard alternatives that are only mentioned in the 3D Studio reference manual. Some command shortcuts are more useful than others.

The following are a few of the handiest command alternatives that you should use frequently:

✔ Ctrl+L Loads a file for the current module from the disk.

✔ Ctrl+S Saves the data in the current module to disk.

✔ Ctrl+J Loads a .PRJ project file into the 2D Shaper, 3D Lofter, 3D Editor, and Keyframer.

✔ Ctrl+P Saves a .PRJ file to disk.

✔ Esc Cancels almost anything.

✔ N Opens a new file.

✔ Ctrl+H Saves your work to the temporary Hold buffer.

✔ Ctrl+F Retrieves your last held work.

✔ ⓢ Turns on/off Snap.

✔ Ⓖ Turns on/off Grid.

✔ Ⓐ Turns on/off Angle Snap.

✔ Ⓧ Turns on/off local axis.

✔ Ⓦ Turns on/off full screen viewport.

✔ ⓘ (left apostrophe) Redraws active viewport.

✔ ˜ (tilde) Redraws all viewports.

✔ Ⓐⓛⓣ+˜ Redraws entire screen, including menu and prompt areas (useful under Windows).

✔ Ⓒ Saves current view.

✔ Ⓘ Restores saved view.

✔ Ⓐⓛⓣ+Ⓡ Renders active viewport.

✔ Ⓕ①① Activates the 2D Shaper.

✔ Ⓕ②② Activates the 3D Lofter.

✔ Ⓕ③③ Activates the 3D Editor.

✔ Ⓕ④④ Activates the Keyframer.

✔ Ⓕ⑤⑤ Activates the Materials Editor.

✔ Ⓕ⑥⑥ Activates the Image Browser.

✔ Ⓕ⑦⑦ Activates Camera Control/Fast Preview.

✔ Ⓕ⑧⑧ Activates Inverse Kinematics.

✔ Ⓕ⑨⑨ Activates Keyscripting.

✔ Ⓕ①⓪① Shells to DOS.

✔ Ⓕ①①① Activates the Text Editor.

✔ Ⓕ①②① Activates the Plug-In Loader.

✔ Ⓠ Quits 3D Studio.

Many other keyboard alternatives are available in 3D Studio. Check the 3D Studio Reference Manual and the keyboard alternatives reference card for a comprehensive list.

Note If you are a Windows user, the keyboard combination to switch from 3D Studio to any other active Windows application is ⟨Alt⟩+⟨Tab⟩.

Hit Lists

Many commands in the 3D Editor and the Keyframer require you to select an object. When you see a prompt in the command line that begins with Select Object, you have the option to select an object by its name. Pressing ⟨H⟩ displays the dialog box shown in figure 3.19. This dialog box often is referred to as the "hit list" because the result of selecting an object's name from the list is the same as hitting or picking the object graphically.

Figure 3.19
The Click on Object by name dialog box.

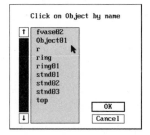

If you name your objects with clear, easy-to-understand names, the hit list becomes a powerful method for object selection.

Modifier Keys

Most modern programs make use of modifier keys, and 3D Studio is no exception. Modifier keys extend the functionality of a command by enabling you to alter how the command works. You alter a command by pressing a modifier key either at the beginning of the command or by holding the key down continuously throughout the command.

Few commands require that you hold the key down continuously. Most commands only require that you press the modifier key for the first pick or selection; after that, you can release the key. 3D Studio also does a fairly good job of telling you when a modifier key is available. Modifier key options for most commands are listed on the right side of the command line while the command is active.

The following is a list of some of the more useful modifier keys. If you must hold down a modifier key during the entire command, it is noted. Otherwise, assume that the key is released immediately after picking a point or selecting an item.

✔ **Cloning.** Pressing ⌈⇧Shift⌉ as you select an item for many Modify commands manipulates a copy of the selected item, rather than affecting the original. This feature makes the Copy command virtually obsolete.

✔ **Direction Constraints.** Pressing ⌈Tab⌴⌉ after selecting objects for many Modify commands cycles through various directional constraints. This is somewhat similar to Ortho mode in AutoCAD, but much more flexible. Depending upon the command and the current module, the ⌈Tab⌴⌉ key alters motion, rotational axis, scaling axis, mirror plane, and bend and taper orientation.

✔ **Cube.** Pressing ⌈Ctrl⌉ while picking the first point of a box command in the 3D Editor creates a cube, rather than a rectangular solid.

✔ **Square.** Pressing ⌈Ctrl⌉ while picking the first point of a Quad command in the Shaper creates a square, rather than a rectangle.

✔ **Correct Aspect Text.** Pressing ⌈Ctrl⌉ as the first point of a Text/Place command in the Shaper forces the font to respect its original aspect ratio. You define only the text height.

✔ **Spline Vertex Move.** Pressing and holding ⌈Ctrl⌉ while adjusting a vertex in the Shaper or Lofter moves the vertex, rather than adjusting the curvature. Any motion constraint set by the ⌈Tab⌴⌉ key is ignored.

✔ **Spline Vertex Unlock.** Pressing and holding ⌈Alt⌉ while adjusting a vertex in the 2D Shaper unlocks the outgoing (yellow) direction arrow. You then can adjust the angle and size of the outgoing direction arrow independently of the incoming (red) direction arrow.

The following modifier keys do not actually affect modeling commands. They are important, however, and deserve mention:

✔ **Camera/Target Lock.** Pressing ⌈Ctrl⌉ when selecting a camera for the Move or Dolly command locks the camera and target together. The command then affects both equally.

✔ **Light/Target Lock.** Pressing ⌈Ctrl⌉ when selecting a spotlight for the Move or Dolly command locks the light and target together.

✔ **Hotspot/Falloff Lock.** Pressing ⌈Ctrl⌉ when selecting a spotlight for either Hotspot or Falloff adjustment locks the hotspot and falloff together. The command then maintains the ratio between them.

✔ **Path Move.** Pressing ⌈Alt⌉ when selecting a key for a Paths/Move Key command in the Keyframer moves all keys on the path, rather than just the selected key.

✔ **Global TCB Adjust.** Pressing ⌈Alt⌉ when selecting a key for a Paths/Adjust TCB command in the Keyframer adjusts the TCB for all keys on the path.

Coordinate Input

Keyboard entry of coordinates, distances, angles, and scales in 3D Studio is weak to nonexistent. If you have any CAD experience at all, 3D Studio's coordinate input will frustrate you to no end. The best strategy is to remember that 3D Studio is a visualization tool and is therefore used in a looser manner than a CAD program. If you require exact values, use the snap settings wherever possible.

Preventing Disaster

No matter how fast you can build models or how many productivity techniques you know, it is all worthless if you lose your work. A program as powerful as 3D Studio gives you an almost unlimited opportunity to mess up. The following paragraphs describe some strategies for protecting yourself from disaster.

Saving Files

As with any program, you should save your files often. 3D Studio is unique in the number and flexibility of its various file saving strategies. There are three separate commands for saving your work, and each command includes an option for saving incrementally numbered files. Figure 3.20 shows a standard save file dialog box identifying the file name field, the file format buttons, and the file increment button.

Figure 3.20
The save file
dialog box.

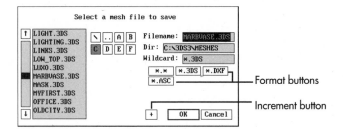

You can enter any valid file name in the file name field. 3D Studio puts the current file name in the field as a default for convenience. You can also choose different file formats for your save command by clicking on any of the supported format buttons below the file name field. Finally, if you click on the file increment button, 3D Studio appends a two-digit number to the first six characters of the name in the file name field. This is a fast way to create incrementally numbered files as a history of your progress.

The following items are definitions of the three types of file save commands available in the File pull-down menu:

✔ **Save.** Saves only the work in the current module using the native file format for that module. In the Materials Editor, this command is under the Library pull-down menu and is called Save Library.

✔ **Save Project.** Saves the work in all of the modeling modules in a single project file. The library in the Materials Editor is ignored.

✔ **Archive.** Saves a project file and compresses it with all of the map files used by materials assigned in the scene. The library in the Materials Editor is ignored.

Backup Files

When you save a file to the same name as an existing file, 3D Studio can create a backup file as well. The *backup file* is a copy of the original file that uses the extension of the original file as its file name and has an extension of BAK. The resulting files will have the names SHP.BAK, LFT.BAK, 3DS.BAK, MLI.BAK, and PRJ.BAK.

You can tell that the names of the backup files certainly are not appropriate for long term storage, and they were never intended for that purpose. The purpose for the backup files is to provide you with an escape route if you accidentally save a file to an existing name. If you realize the mistake soon enough, you can shell to DOS and rename the *.BAK file back to an appropriate 3D Studio file.

Undoing a Mistake

The single most important development in the history of computing is the Undo command— or so it would seem. Most software users have come to rely heavily on the use of the Undo command, even to the extent of using Undo instead of regularly saving their work. If you have fallen into this trap, be warned. Relying on the Undo command can be an extremely painful mistake.

3D Studio provides an Undo command in only two of its five modules. The preferred method is to use the Hold and Fetch commands, combined with frequent file saving.

Undo

Figure 3.21 shows the location of the UNDO button in the lower right corner of the screen. This button only appears in the 2D Shaper and 3D Lofter. Many 3D Studio users have been burned by expecting to use the UNDO button in the 3D Editor or the Keyframer. It is not there!

Figure 3.21
The location of the
UNDO button in
the 2D Shaper.

Another drawback is that the UNDO button provides only a single step Undo. You can reverse the effect of the last command only. More often than not, you do not realize your mistake until after you execute another few commands—by then it is too late. A good rule of thumb is to pretend that Undo does not exist.

Hold and Fetch

The preferred method for reversing the effects of a command is to use the HOLD and FETCH buttons at the bottom right corner of the screen. Clicking on the HOLD button saves the state of the current module in memory. You can then perform any number of commands and still return to the held state by clicking on the FETCH button.

You should get into the habit of clicking on the HOLD button frequently, especially if you are about to perform a command with which you are unfamiliar. The HOLD and FETCH buttons are not as flexible as a multilevel Undo, but they come close.

Also, if your system should crash, preventing you from exiting 3D Studio normally, you can still retrieve the contents of the hold buffers. Whenever you click on the HOLD button, 3D Studio writes a temporary file to the TEMP directory. These temporary files are regular 3D Studio files with special names; you can directly load these files by renaming them with standard file names, as follows:

✔ **MODSH$$$.TMP** The name of the 2D Shaper Hold file. Rename to *filename*.SHP.

✔ **MODLH$$$.TMP** The name of the 3D Lofter Hold file. Rename to *filename*.LFT.

✔ **MODEH$$$.TMP** The name of the 3D Editor and Keyframer Hold file. Rename to *filename*.3DS.

You should rename these files immediately after recovering from a crash and before starting 3D Studio again.

Summary

Remembering these universal modeling techniques will save you considerable time and effort in various modules of 3D Studio. Of these techniques, selection sets are probably the most flexible and useful available; they also are one of the most underutilized. As you are creating and manipulating items in 3D Studio, always consider whether you will need to select the same items again for another purpose. If so, consider finding a way to store that selection set for later use.

Chapter Snapshot

The 2D Shaper and 3D Lofter are really two parts of the same tool. There are a few situations when you might use one without the other, but those are rare. Most of the time, you will find yourself moving from the 2D Shaper to the 3D Lofter to the 3D Editor. This is a natural and powerful progression that provides you with many modeling options. Unfortunately, many users are intimidated by the 3D Lofter and spend considerable time trying to force the 3D Editor to do everything. This chapter discusses the following:

✔ Understanding the Shaper and Lofter, and their terminology

✔ Exploring how to create and edit polygons in the Shaper

✔ Exploring how to edit vertices and adjust spline curves in both the Shaper and the Lofter

✔ Understanding Shape Steps and Path Steps and how to use them to make efficient models

✔ Exploring how to import Shapes into the Lofter and place them on the path

✔ Examining how to edit the Lofter path

✔ Understanding lofting controls

Part II

Basic Modeling

4

CHAPTER

2D to 3D: The 2D Shaper and 3D Lofter Combination

The 2D Shaper is a two-dimensional drawing environment with special features unique to 3D Studio. One of these features is that everything you create is a segmented spline curve. Straight lines in the 2D Shaper actually are a type of curve and you can easily curve and straighten shapes with many editing commands.

The primary purpose of the 2D Shaper is to provide the 3D Lofter with geometry, called *shapes*. Other uses of the 2D Shaper include creating two-dimensional geometry for export directly to the 3D Editor and for creating paths for use in the 3D Lofter and the Keyframer.

Understanding 2D Shaper Terminology

For the most part, the terminology used in the 2D Shaper is the same as that used in other modules of 3D Studio. Chapter 3, "Universal Modeling Techniques," discussed the nature of drawing aids, global versus local axes, and selection sets. All these concepts function in the 2D Shaper as previously described. A few terms, however, are different or unique to the 2D Shaper.

Vertices

Vertices in the 2D Shaper serve two purposes. As with most drawing and modeling programs, *vertices* serve as the start and end points between segments. In the 2D Shaper, however, vertices also store the curvature information for the ends of any segments attached to them. You adjust a curve by manipulating the curvature information at one or more vertices.

Segments

Segments connect two vertices. They can be linear or curved—if they are curved, their smoothness is controlled by the number of divisions or steps that exist between the vertices.

Steps

The Shape Steps setting controls the number of segment divisions between each vertex. The Steps setting affects all polygons in the 2D Shaper globally. The higher the steps setting, the smoother the curved segments appear. The trade-off is that steps translate directly into faces in the 3D Editor, so the higher the steps setting, the higher the face count in the final mesh.

Polygons

A *polygon* is any collection of one or more segments. The 2D Shaper imposes no restrictions on the polygons that you create. A polygon is the highest-level item in the 2D Shaper and is roughly similar to an object in the 3D Editor.

Shapes

A *shape* is a collection of one or more polygons. It is not so much a graphic item as a technique for moving polygons from the 2D Shaper into another module of 3D Studio. Depending upon which module the shape is sent to, it may have certain restrictions imposed upon it. These restrictions are discussed later in this chapter.

Creating Polygons

All the commands under the Create branch create polygons. Essentially, everything that you create must be a polygon. Vertices and segments only exist in their capacity for defining polygons.

Basic Polygons

The basic polygons make up a collection of simple geometric shapes. Creating these shapes requires only a few picks to complete the commands. A list of the basic polygon commands follows:

- ✔ Line
- ✔ Arc
- ✔ Quad
- ✔ Circle
- ✔ Ellipse

Of these, only the Line and Quad commands employ any special modifiers or techniques.

Lines

Creating lines involves more than just picking points on the screen. You should remember three features. First, *lines* in the 2D Shaper are continuous, linked segments. All the segments created in a single command belong to a single polygon. If you want to create individual line segments, you must right-click to end the Line command after each segment and then pick a new start point for the next segment. If you begin the next segment too close to the end vertex of another segment, 3D Studio automatically assumes that you want to add to the end of that segment.

Tip
AutoCAD users understand the 2D Shaper better when they realize that lines and polygons in the 2D Shaper are like AutoCAD's Polyline entity.

If you have a heavy hand while creating lines in the 2D Shaper, you quickly discover another feature of the Line command. When you press and hold the Pick button while specifying vertex locations, you drop into the vertex spline adjust command. This command displays the vertex *direction arrows* that enable you to adjust the curvature of the segment at that vertex. Figure 4.1 shows these arrows as they appear during a Create/Line command. If you are a little slow on releasing the Pick button, 3D Studio thinks that you are trying to adjust the curve and briefly displays the direction arrows. The result is a brief flash at the vertex location and then curved line segments! The only solution is to exercise your index finger so that you develop rapid-fire clicking—this way you will not move the mouse as you pick points.

Figure 4.1
Curve direction arrows appearing during the Line command.

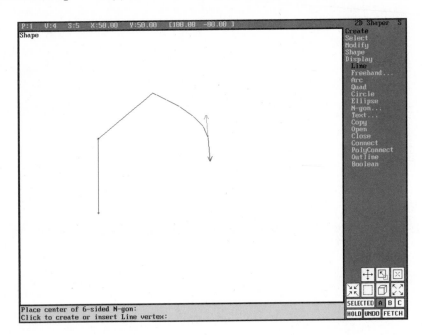

The final feature to remember is that the Line command doubles as an insert vertex command. Picking on a segment for the first point of a Line command inserts a new vertex between the ends of that segment.

Quads

A quick way to create squares is to hold down Ç while picking the first vertex of a quad, then release it. The 2D Shaper now enables you to drag out a square for the second vertex pick.

N-Gons

The N-Gon command enables you to create regular polygons with from 3 to 100 sides. Choosing the # Sides command under the N-Gon branch enables you to manipulate a slider that sets the number of sides used for subsequent polygons. After you set the number of sides, choose whether to create a flat-sided polygon or a circular polygon, as shown in figure 4.2.

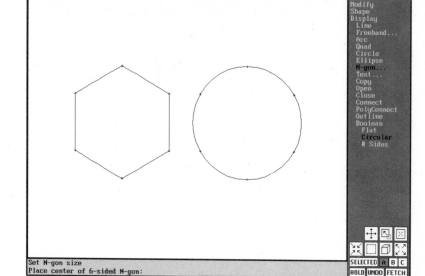

Figure 4.2

Flat and circular N-Gons.

Tip Why have a circular polygon command when you already have a Circle command? The Circle command creates circles with only four vertices. When you need circles with more than four vertices, use the circular N-Gon command.

Text and Fonts

The most important issue to remember about text in 3D Studio is that when you place text, it is no longer text. The purpose of placing text in the 2D Shaper is to create letter-shaped polygons. Because 3D Studio is creating polygons and not text, be sure to check your spelling carefully before placing text in the 2D Shaper.

Tip AutoCAD users frequently have trouble with text in the 2D Shaper. Remember, there is no DDEDIT or CHANGE command for fixing typos in 3D Studio.

To create text, follow these steps:

1. Choose the font that you want to use. 3D Studio can read its own FNT file format, Adobe Illustrator AI format, or Postscript Type 1 PFB format.

2. Type your desired text into a field in the Enter Text dialog box, checking for misspellings and other errors.

3. Indicate the height and width of the text string.

You cannot type text and see it appear on-screen as you can with many other drawing programs because 3D Studio enables such flexibility in the size and shape of your text. You have these two choices for controlling the size of text that you place in the 2D Shaper:

✔ Pick two points that define a rectangle. The text is scaled both vertically and horizontally to fit inside the rectangle. Depending upon the amount of text entered and the size of the rectangle you specify, the text might be radically distorted using this method (see the top two text strings in fig. 4.3).

✔ Press and hold Ctrl as you pick the first point. 3D Studio now reads only the vertical distance between the points that you pick to define the text height. This method preserves the original spacing and aspect ratio of the font, shown in the bottom text string of figure 4.3.

Figure 4.3
Text placed with wide and narrow bounding boxes, and with the Ctrl key.

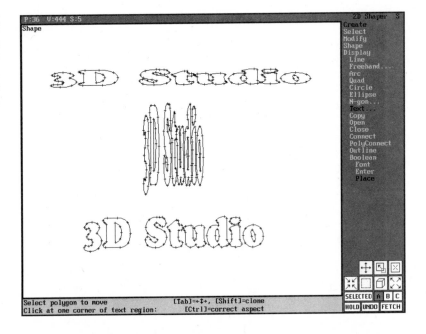

3D Studio does pose a problem, however, because of the way it calculates text height. Most programs that handle text read the text height ratio from the font definition, and that ratio remains constant for all letters of a specified size. 3D Studio calculates text height as the height of a box that encloses the entered text string. This means that individual letter heights vary depending upon whether there are upper- or lowercase letters with descenders in the text string. Figure 4.4 shows various text strings placed using Ctrl and a text height of 50 units.

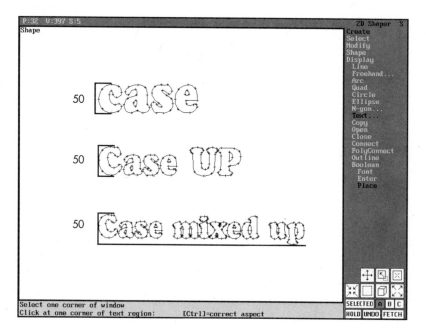

Figure 4.4

Inconsistent text heights.

This problem is annoying when you need to place multiple strings of text at a consistent height. Getting around this flaw requires a simple trick. Always enter your text with two dummy letters at the end of the string. Make one letter uppercase and the other lowercase with a descender, such as g or j. This technique forces 3D Studio to consider the full range of the font for every string entered. You can delete the extra letters after you place the text. Of course, if your desired string already includes uppercase and lowercase-descended letters, this step is unnecessary.

Outlines

The Outline command could belong in the Modify branch. The Outline command cannot create anything on its own—it must have a polygon to modify. Nonetheless, outlines are a fast and convenient way to produce multiple, concentric copies of a polygon. These concentric copies are quite handy when creating outline text, hollow logos, and other similar shapes.

You must take care when using the Outline command because it always deletes your source polygon. After you specify an outline width, 3D Studio deletes the source polygon and creates concentric copies one-half the width distance to either side of the source polygon. Figure 4.5 shows the before and after conditions of using the Outline command.

Figure 4.5
A polygon before and after using Outline.

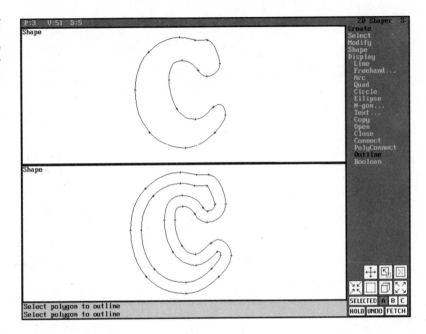

It is easy to make the mistake of assuming that the original polygon will be available after the command is complete—it is not. If you need to keep the source polygon after an Outline command, try the following technique:

✔ Make a copy of the polygon and place it exactly on top of the original polygon. (This is easiest to do with Snap turned ON.)

✔ Use the Outline command as usual. The selected polygon will be destroyed by the Outline command, but the copy will remain unscathed.

✔ Redraw the screen to see all of the polygons.

This technique leaves you with the two outlined polygons and a copy of the original polygon.

Boolean Operations

The Boolean command is another that arguably belongs under the Modify branch. The Boolean command requires two source polygons, and it always deletes both sources in the process of creating the Boolean polygon. 3D Studio places the following three restrictions on the source polygons:

✔ The polygons must be closed.

✔ The polygons cannot self-intersect.

✔ The polygons must overlap. A polygon that is completely enclosed within another is not considered an overlapping polygon.

Beyond those restrictions, the Boolean command is a very easy and stable tool. Figure 4.6 shows examples of invalid polygons for Boolean operations.

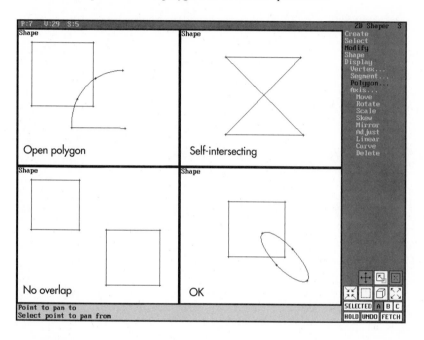

Figure 4.6

Three invalid Boolean conditions and one valid condition.

Boolean operations in 3D Studio are much different from 2D and 3D Boolean operations in AutoCAD. 3D Studio provides no commands for editing primitives or exploding the solid.

Connecting Polygons

The Create branch in the 2D Shaper has the following three separate commands for connecting open polygons:

✔ Line

✔ Connect

✔ PolyConnect

Each command has different capabilities. The Line command enables you to connect any number of polygons manually with any number of line segments. If you start the Line command by picking the first vertex of an open polygon, 3D Studio assumes that you want to add vertices between the first vertex and the second vertex in the segment you picked, as shown in figure 4.7. You then must right-click to cancel the command and try again from another direction. The advantage of using the Line command is that you can use more than one segment to connect the polygons.

Figure 4.7
Picking the first vertex of a polygon with the Line command.

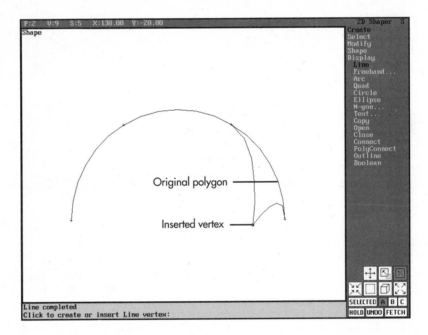

The Connect command is forgiving about whether you pick on the first or last vertex of a polygon. All that Connect requires is that you pick on the end vertices. Connect then dutifully connects the vertices with a single line segment. Connect is faster than Line, but it allows only single-segment connections. It has the advantage of enabling you to chain multiple open polygons quickly into a single complex polygon.

PolyConnect is the fastest method of the three, but it also is the least flexible. PolyConnect prompts you to select two polygons, then it connects both ends of one polygon to the opposite ends of the other. In other words, it connects the first vertex of the first polygon to the last vertex of the second polygon and vice versa. If this results in a crossed connection, as shown in figure 4.8, you can undo the command and try again. Press and hold Alt while selecting both polygons, and the command now connects the first vertex of the first polygon to the first vertex of the second polygon and the last vertex of one to the last vertex of the other. PolyConnect is very fast, but can be used only to connect two polygons with single-segment connections.

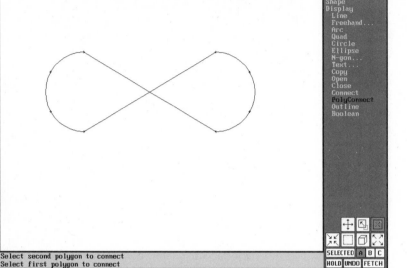

Figure 4.8
Crossed connections with PolyConnect.

Selecting Polygons

After you create your polygons, everything else you do with them involves selections. Remember that all the Modify/Polygon commands ask you to select a polygon. Selection sets are just 3D Studio's method of enabling you to select more than one item at a time.

Selection sets in the 2D Shaper are much less involved than they are in the 3D Editor. There are no fancy techniques, such as selecting by name, smoothing, or color. Just point and click. You also have the options of Quad, Circle, and Fence combined with the modifiers of Window and Crossing.

Editing Polygons

The Modify/Polygon branch of the 2D Shaper screen menu contains the various commands for editing polygons. Commands such as Move, Rotate, Scale, and Skew all involve picking a selection and specifying a new value. All Modify commands have these three useful features:

✔ The base point for rotation and scaling commands is toggled between the global and local axes by clicking on the Local Axis icon or by pressing X.

✔ Directional constraints are controlled by the Tab⁺ key. Each time you press Tab⁺, the directional constraints change from free motion to vertical constraint to horizontal constraint.

✔ Cloning a selection is enabled by pressing ⬆Shift as you pick the selection.

Mirroring Polygons

The behavior of directional constraint with respect to the Mirror command deserves a little more scrutiny. The direction of the arrows displayed with the pick box determines the direction of the "flip," and the location of the pick box determines the position of the mirror line. Figure 4.9 shows how the directional constraints affect mirroring a polygon.

Figure 4.9
Effects of directional constraints on mirroring.

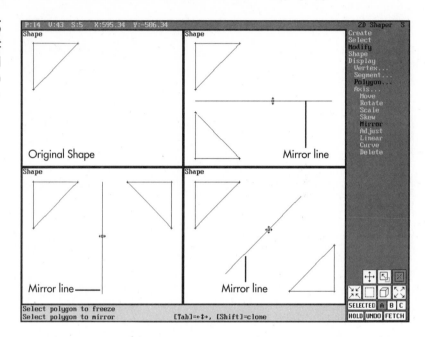

Use arrows to interpret the directional constraints as follows:

✔ Vertical arrows flip the selection vertically about a horizontal mirror line.

✔ Horizontal arrows flip the selection horizontally about a vertical mirror line.

✔ Four arrows flip the selection diagonally about a 45-degree mirror line.

Opening and Closing Polygons

There are a few commands that seem sorely out of place with their location under the Create branch. Two of these are Open and Close. As stated earlier, the purpose of the 2D Shaper is to create shapes for other modules in 3D Studio. Polygons may be required to be Open or Closed, depending upon which module a shape is headed for and its intended use. Two commands under the Create branch enable you to Open or Close a polygon quickly.

The Open command is really the Modify/Segment/Delete command in disguise. The tip-off to this fact is that the prompt in the command line reads `Select Polygon Segment to`

Delete when you choose the Open command. The Open command does not check to see whether a polygon is already open; it obediently deletes whatever segment you select. You can perform the Open command on the same polygon as many times as you want or until you run out of segments to delete.

AutoCAD users who are familiar with polyline editing might have trouble with the Open command. You expect the Open command to delete only the single segment between the last and the first vertices of the polygon, and that a polygon that is open already cannot be opened again. Remember, in 3D Studio, the Open command really is a segment-delete command.

The Close command works exactly as you expect. After choosing Close, you are prompted to select a polygon to close. The command then draws a single segment between the last and first vertices of the selected polygon.

Selecting Vertices

The real power of many of the Modify/Vertex commands appears when they are applied to a selection set of vertices. You can create selections of vertices by picking them singly or by using the Quad, Circle, or Fence options of the Select/Vertex branch. If you select all the vertices in a polygon, the entire polygon is highlighted, including the segments between the vertices. Selecting all the vertices in a polygon is equal to selecting the entire polygon from the Select/Polygon branch.

Editing Vertices

Editing vertices is the most common way of manipulating geometry in the 2D Shaper. With the exception of the Mirror command, you can duplicate all the Modify/Polygon commands by selecting all the vertices of a polygon and performing the corresponding Modify/Vertex command.

Inserting Vertices

No command is available to insert vertices in the Modify/Vertex branch. The 2D Shaper, however, provides the following three commands that have the effect of inserting vertices into an existing polygon:

✔ **Create/Line.** If you pick the first vertex of a line command on a polygon segment, a new vertex is inserted between the vertices at the ends of that segment. All following picks insert more vertices into the same segment until you right-click to end the command.

Right-clicking to place the first vertex of a Create/Line command forces 3D Studio to insert the first vertex into an existing polygon. If no polygon is selected, the command cancels. This is a handy way to avoid creating new polygons accidentally when you really want to insert vertices into an existing polygon.

✔ **Modify/Segment/Break.** When you select a segment, this command inserts two vertices at the location you pick and divides the segment into two parts. If the segment is part of an open polygon, the result is two separate polygons. If the segment is part of a closed polygon, the result is an open polygon, even though no gap in the polygon is visible.

✔ **Modify/Segment/Refine.** This command inserts a single vertex into a segment at the point you pick. It also analyzes the curvature of the segment at that point and adjusts the curvature at the new vertex to maintain the original curve. This command is handy for adjusting the complexity of a polygon.

Modifying Single Vertices

You can perform all the Modify/ Vertex commands on a single vertex, although some of the commands work best with selection sets. Also, with the exception of the Rotate command, you cannot use Local Axis when modifying a single vertex.

The Move and Delete commands work as you would expect. The only caveat concerning Move is similar to the caution about slow clicking when creating lines. If you hold the mouse button too long when clicking on the new location during a Move command, you drop into the spline curve adjustment function. Adjusting spline curves is discussed later in this chapter.

The Scale and Skew commands move the vertex with special motion constraints. Skewing a single vertex is similar to moving it with horizontal or vertical constraints. Scaling a single vertex provides an interesting variation on the Move command. With a free-motion cursor enabled, Scale moves a single vertex along a line that passes through the original vertex location and the global axis. This is useful if you center the global axis or place it at a significant reference point.

Rotating a single vertex about the global axis works exactly as you would expect. Rotating a single vertex with Local Axis turned on, however, is a different story. If the vertex is linear, rotating it has no effect. If you rotate a single curved vertex about the local axis, however, there is a noticeable effect on the curved segments passing through the vertex. This is a special case of spline adjustment and is discussed in the section of this chapter on adjusting spline curves.

Modifying Selected Vertices

All the Modify/ Vertex commands work with selection sets of vertices and enable the use of the local axis. Remember that the location of the local axis is calculated as the center of a rectangular bounding box that surrounds the selected vertices. You will find the greatest modeling opportunities by selecting only a few vertices in a polygon and then experimenting with various Modify/Vertex commands, using both the global and local axes.

Use caution when skewing selections of vertices that are collinear. 3D Studio checks whether a collinear selection of vertices is parallel to the skew direction when you start the command. If the selection is parallel to the skew direction, an invalid Skew dialog box is presented and the command is canceled automatically. Unfortunately, 3D Studio does not make this check if you change the skew direction after you begin the command. In this case, pressing Tab⇥ might cause the skew direction to become invalid, and the selected vertices will disappear into the upper left corner of your screen. Your only recourse is to cancel the command by right-clicking and then clicking on the Undo button to restore the vertices.

This exercise demonstrates a simple vertex-editing technique that relies on a vertex selection set. This technique can also be used with flat polygons to create a variety of star shapes.

Making a Starfish

Choose Reset *from the* File *pull-down menu*	Resets all modules in 3D Studio
Choose Create/N-Gon/# Sides	Displays the Set N-Gon Sides dialog box
Set the sides slider to 10	
Choose Circular *from the* N-Gon *branch*	
Pick a center point and drag the radius out to 160 units	
Choose Select/Vertex/Single	
Click on selection button A	Specifies the use of selection set A
Select every other vertex starting with the vertex at 1 o'clock (see fig. 4.10)	Adds vertices to selection set A; as vertices are selected, they turn red
Choose Modify/ Vertex/Scale	
Turn on the Selected *button*	Instructs 3D Studio to use the current selection set
Turn on the local axis by clicking on the Local Axis *button or pressing* X	
Pick anywhere on the screen and drag the selected vertices to a scale of 45 percent	Moves the selected vertices together to form a starfish shape (see fig. 4.11)
Choose Select/None	Deselects the vertices

Figure 4.10
Selected vertices.

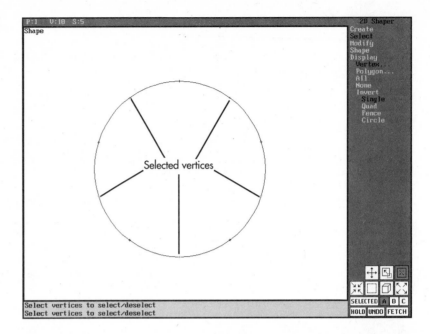

Figure 4.11
The finished
starfish shape.

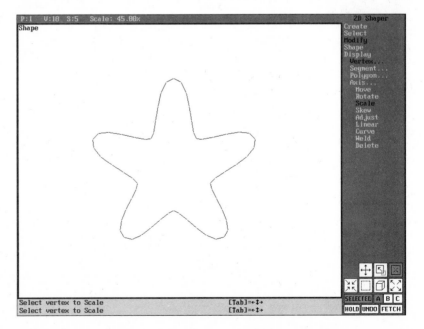

Adjusting Spline Curves

It is now time to look at the most powerful feature of the 2D Shaper: adjusting spline curves. You might have noticed that the Modify branches contain commands called Curve, Linear, and Adjust for both polygons and vertices. Everything created in the 2D Shaper is based on spline curves, and these commands give you control over the amount of curvature displayed.

Spline curve information is stored in each vertex of a polygon. The information is displayed and set through the manipulation of direction arrows. Each vertex carries two direction arrows, and each direction arrow carries three properties that define the curve at that vertex as follows:

✔ **Order.** The colors of the arrows indicate the order in which the vertices progress around the polygon. The red direction arrow points toward the segment coming into the vertex. The yellow arrow points toward the segment leaving the vertex. Therefore, the red arrow points along the segment leading to the previous vertex, and the yellow arrow points along the segment leading to the next vertex.

✔ **Tangent direction.** Each segment is tangent to its direction arrow at the vertex location. If the direction arrows are parallel, forming a straight line, the curve passes smoothly through the vertex. If the direction arrows do not form a straight line, the curve contains a kink, or sharp point, at the vertex location. Figure 4.12 shows direction arrows for both a smooth curve and a kinked curve.

✔ **Degree of curvature.** The length of a direction arrow sets the degree of curvature for its corresponding segment. The longer the arrow, the greater the curvature of the segment. Figure 4.13 shows curves demonstrating both long and short direction arrows. If you drag the direction arrows down to a length of zero, all curvature is canceled and the segment becomes linear at that vertex.

Although technically incorrect, you might find it helpful to think of the length of the direction arrow as the radius of an arc. A long direction arrow creates an arc with a large radius as the segment leaves the vertex. It takes an extreme amount of curvature to bend the segment back around to the direction of the next vertex.

The order of the direction arrows is determined by the order in which the polygon vertices were created. You cannot change the vertex order without opening, reconnecting, or otherwise redefining the polygon. You can, however, adjust the other two properties: tangent direction and degree of curvature.

Figure 4.12
Direction arrows
for smooth and
kinked curves.

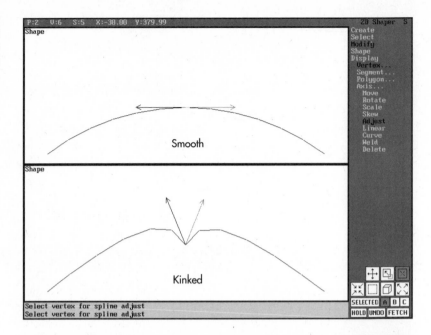

Figure 4.13
The effect of
direction arrow
length on a curve.

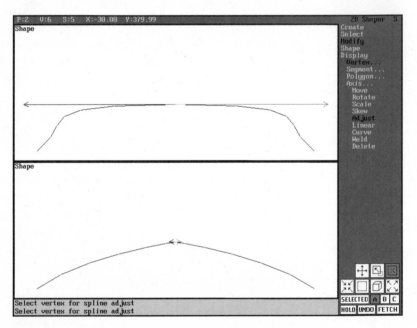

Vertex Adjustments

The following three primary commands are used to adjust curvature at a vertex:

- ✔ Linear
- ✔ Curve
- ✔ Adjust

These commands can be applied to either a single vertex or a selection set of vertices.

Linear

The Vertex/Linear command causes all selected vertices to release their curvature information. Both segments entering and leaving the vertex become linear at that location. The affected segments still might appear curved because of curved vertices at their opposite ends.

Curve

The Vertex/Curve command applies a default curve value to all the selected vertices. The 3D Studio Reference Manual describes this default value as the same value as if the vertex were part of a circular polygon. That statement is oversimplified.

Each of the two direction arrows at a vertex is calculated independently. The circle value that the direction arrow receives is based upon the distance to the adjacent vertex and whether the selected vertex is an end vertex of an open polygon. The net result is that the direction arrows at the vertex rarely are of equal length, and the effect is difficult to predict. The only time a predictable result occurs is when the selected vertex is part of a square polygon. Curving a square always creates a circle.

Tip

If you make a vertex linear and then use the Adjust command to apply curvature manually, you can achieve more predictable results. The Adjust command begins by pulling out the curve direction arrows equally so that they are identical. Details on using the Adjust command are presented in the following section.

Adjust

The Vertex/Adjust command enables you to adjust the curvature of selected vertices manually. The prompt `Select Vertex for Spline Adjust` requires you to press and hold the mouse Pick button over a single vertex, even when you are adjusting a selection set of multiple vertices. As long as you hold the button down, you can manipulate the direction arrows in the following manner:

✔ Moving the cursor parallel to the outgoing (yellow) direction arrow changes the length of both arrows equally.

✔ Moving the cursor perpendicular to the outgoing (yellow) direction arrow rotates both of them about the vertex.

✔ Pressing and holding Ctrl locks both arrows and enables you to move the vertex rather than adjust the curve. While moving the vertex in this manner, the current settings for the directional constraints and snap grid are ignored. Releasing Ctrl puts you back into curve adjusting mode.

✔ Pressing and holding Alt locks the incoming (red) direction arrow and enables you to adjust the outgoing (yellow) arrow independently. Releasing Alt unlocks the red arrow.

If you are adjusting a selection set of vertices, the adjustments you make are applied to all the vertices in the selection set—with one exception. Any linear vertices in the selection set are unaffected by any adjustments, other than pressing Ctrl to move the selection.

Line and Move

With both the Create/Line command and Modify/Vertex/Move command, if you press and hold the mouse Pick button while placing a vertex, you enter the Vertex/Adjust command. Adjusting the vertex works as described previously, and when you release the Pick button, you return to the original command. With the Move command, this occurs only when moving single vertices.

Rotate

Sometimes you want to adjust the rotational value of the curve direction arrows but you do not want to change their length. This can be hard to do with the regular Vertex/Adjust command, but you can use a technique with the Modify/Vertex/Rotate command to accomplish the task. If you rotate a single vertex with Local Axis active, only the angle of the direction arrows is affected. You cannot see the direction arrows while doing this, and the technique has no effect on a linear vertex.

Segment Adjustments

Segment adjustments work on both vertices at each end of the segment simultaneously. These commands are unique because they manipulate curves in ways that would be very difficult to duplicate with any other command.

Linear and Curved

Both these commands are similar to the corresponding commands under Modify/ Vertex. The difference is that they affect only one of the two direction arrows at each vertex. The direction arrows that point toward the middle of the selected segment are either curved or removed by these commands, but the companion direction arrow on the opposite side of the vertex is left unchanged. These commands are good for rounding the side of a box or flattening part of a circle.

Adjust

Adjusting the curvature of a segment is like no other Adjust command in the 2D Shaper. The reference manual states that Modify/Segment/Adjust "alters, equally, the spline values of vertices at each end of a selected segment." This statement does not hold true for all situations. It is possible, during segment adjustment, to get the direction arrows to react equally but opposite to each other. In other words, one set of arrows grows and the other expands, or one set rotates clockwise and the other set rotates counterclockwise.

Another way of looking at segment adjustment might make it a little clearer. When you select a segment to adjust, imagine that you are picking up the midpoint of the segment. As you drag the segment midpoint around the screen, both sets of direction arrows point toward the midpoint and are adjusted to maintain a smooth curve through the midpoint. Figure 4.14 shows some examples of adjusting a segment.

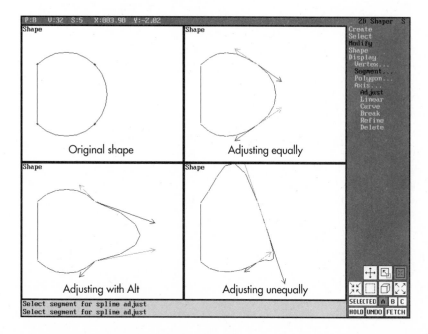

Figure 4.14
Adjusting segment curvature.

The modifier keys of Ctrl and Alt work the same for segment adjustment as they do for vertex adjustment—with one exception. Pressing and holding (Alt) locks the two direction arrows that point away from the segment.

II

Basic Modeling

Polygon Adjustments

The curvature adjustments under the Modify/Polygon branch are really a shortcut for the same commands under Modify/Vertex. Selecting all the vertices in a polygon and then using a Modify/Vertex command is exactly the same as using a Modify/Polygon command.

Controlling Shape Complexity

The issue of managing the complexity of your models is a recurrent theme throughout this book. You constantly are making trade-offs between precise modeling and fast rendering. The goal is to use full precision only where necessary and to keep the model as simple as possible.

Decisions about managing complexity begin in the 2D Shaper. You control complexity in the 2D Shaper through careful vertex placement, curve adjustment, and the setting of shape steps.

Vertices and Curves

A common mistake made by many new 3D Studio users is to use more vertices than necessary. The temptation is to place many closely spaced vertices around a curve. This is a throwback to traditional drafting and CAD techniques in which you were taught to approximate a curve with many short line segments.

The 2D Shaper works with true spline-based curves, so you can specify very complex curves by placing a few vertices and then adjusting the curvature at each vertex. Figure 4.15 shows an example of two nearly identical polygons. One was created with many vertices and minimal curve adjustment, and the other was created with a few vertices and careful curve adjustment.

A comparison of these two polygons shows that the top one contains 18 vertices and the bottom polygon contains only 10. Complexity of a shape is determined by the number of segments between two vertices times one greater than the number of shape steps. The result of this calculation is similar to determining the number of sides or facets in the 3D Editor. The example in Figure 4.15 uses the default step setting of 5, so the calculations are as follows:

Top polygon: 18 segments $\times$ (5 Steps + 1) = 108 facets

Bottom polygon: 10 segments $\times$ (5 Steps + 1) = 60 facets

The polygon with fewer facets lofts into a more efficient model and renders faster. The bottom polygon is 44 percent more efficient than the top polygon, yet maintains about the same quality and precision.

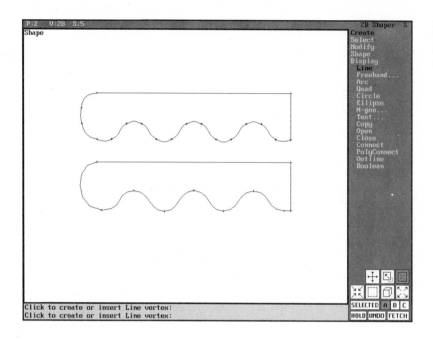

Figure 4.15
Modeling with spline curves.

Setting Shape Steps

Shape steps refers to the number of intermediate divisions between vertices. You set the step number by choosing the command Shape/Steps and adjusting the slider in the Set Steps dialog box. You can set the slider to any number between 0 and 10. Shape steps are necessary for the display of curves. If you set shape steps to 0, there are no divisions between vertices and everything is connected with straight lines. If you set shape steps to 10, curves appear very smooth due to the greater number of divisions. You want to set the shape steps as low as possible while retaining acceptably smooth curves.

Try the following exercise to get a better grasp of the effect of shape steps.

Setting Shape Steps

Choose Reset *from the* File *pull-down menu*

Create a circle of any size

Choose Shape/Steps *and move the slider to 10*

Notice that the circle appears smoother—but not much.

Change the step setting again, this time to 0

continues

continued

The circle now looks like a square. Remember that the curve information that defines the circle is still present, but curves do not display well at low step settings.

Choose Modify/Vertex/Adjust *and select any vertex*

*Hold down the Pick button and adjust the direction
arrows (fig. 4.16 shows the direction arrows as
they are adjusted)*

You can see the direction arrows, but no visible change occurs in the shape of the polygon.

Change the shape steps back to 5

Notice that you can now see the adjusted curve. Figure 4.17 shows the result of adjustments in figure 4.16.

It is important to remember that curve information is not lost when shape steps are reduced. You first can define your polygons with a high step setting, making it easier to lay out your curves. After the polygon is created, you can experiment with different step settings to find the appropriate trade-off between curve detail and model efficiency.

Figure 4.16
Adjusting a
vertex with shape
steps at 0.

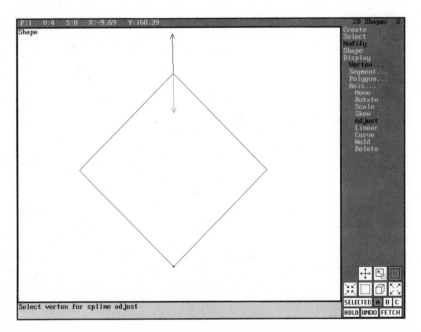

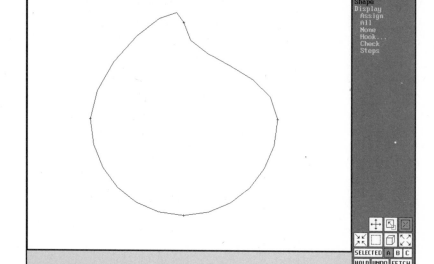

II

Basic Modeling

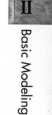

Figure 4.17
The adjusted circle with shape steps set at 5.

 Do not fall into the trap of setting shape steps once and then forgetting them. You should consider resetting the shape steps often. The best step setting for a rectangular shape (probably 0) is much lower than the appropriate setting for a shape with a lot of curves.

Refining Segments

There are times when adding vertices to a polygon, in order to reduce the shape step setting, is a valid technique for reducing overall complexity. Remember that the step setting increases the number of divisions between all vertices, straight and curved alike. Because a linear segment with 0 divisions looks just as good as a linear segment with 10 divisions, you want to use low step settings and concentrate more vertices around the curves. This technique results in the most efficient model possible.

 You do not want to reduce shape steps too far if you plan to bend or squash the three-dimensional object created from the shape. Many 3D Editor modifications and Keyframer effects work better with meshes that contain multiple, evenly spaced segments.

The command Modify/Segment/Refine makes the technique of inserting extra vertices along curves an easy process. You use the Segment/Refine command by picking any segment at the location where you desire a vertex. 3D Studio inserts a vertex at that location and automatically adjusts the curve information to maintain the original curve of the segment.

The best way to use this command is to design your polygon using a minimum number of vertices and a high step setting. Then use Segment/Refine to add extra vertices to the curved segments. Most curves need only a few additional vertices. Small, short curves usually need only one intermediate vertex, and large, sweeping curves may require three or more extra vertices. After you have added the extra vertices, reduce the step setting and check the appearance of your polygon. You often can reduce the step setting to one-half or even one-third of its original value with no apparent loss of quality. This technique can improve the efficiency of your models dramatically.

The following exercise demonstrates how you can reduce the number of facets in your shapes through the use of the Segment/Refine command.

Segment Refining

Choose Reset *from the* File *pull-down menu*

Choose Load *from the* File *pull-down menu and select the .SHP file* REFINE.SHP

Your screen should look like figure 4.18. It shows an efficient model with 10 vertices. At the default step setting of 5, it contains 60 facets.

Figure 4.18
The original shape.

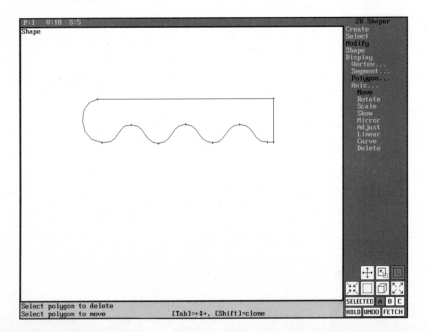

Choose Modify/Polygon/Move	
Use ⟨⇧Shift⟩ *to move a copy of the polygon directly below the original*	Clones the polygon during the Move command
Choose Modify/Segment/Refine	
Pick the points indicated in figure 4.19 to add the necessary vertices to the copied polygon	Adds vertices to the curves
Choose Shape/Steps *and adjust the step slider to 1*	Changes the display to look like figure 4.20

Compare the two polygons at the new step setting. The original polygon looks quite crude at this setting and would be unacceptable for almost any job. The polygon that you modified looks much better. It looks almost as good as the first polygon did at a step setting of 5. The difference is that the second polygon with 19 vertices and a step setting of 1 contains only 38 facets. The second polygon is 47 percent more efficient than the first one.

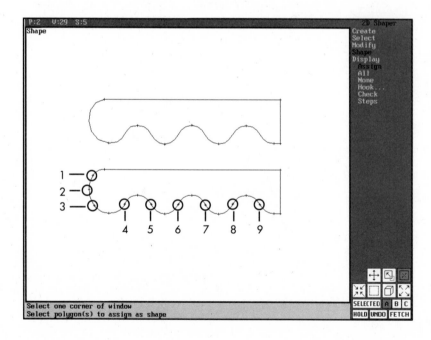

Figure 4.19
Pick points for the Modify/Segment/Refine command.

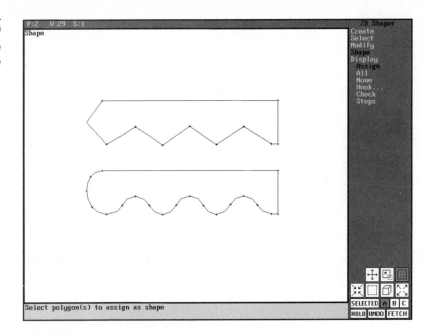

Figure 4.20
The result of the Segment/Refine operation.

Understanding Shapes

A shape is a collection of one or more polygons in the 2D Shaper. You do not manipulate shapes directly. Shapes are merely one of the methods for exporting polygons from the 2D Shaper to other modules of 3D Studio.

Shapes can be exported to other modules for the following uses:

✔ Both the loft path and loft shape in the 3D Lofter

✔ Two-dimensional mesh objects in the 3D Editor

✔ Motion paths in the Keyframer

The requirements vary depending upon which module and for what purpose the shape is destined.

Closed Versus Open Shapes

The concept of closed shapes and open shapes is pretty clear. A *closed shape* is one where the last vertex of the shape is connected to the first vertex with a segment. What might not be clear is that shapes do not have to be closed to be useful. Both the 3D Lofter and the Keyframer can accept open shapes as paths. Shapes must be closed only when they are exported to the 3D Editor as a 2D object, or the 3D Lofter as a loft shape.

Valid Versus Invalid Shapes

The decision to term a shape "valid" or "invalid" was an unfortunate choice. Just as with open shapes, Keyframer and 3D Lofter paths have no problems with most "invalid" shapes. An *invalid shape* is one that is open or crosses over itself. A shape can cross over itself in two ways. It can be a single polygon with self-intersecting segments or it can be two or more polygons whose edges overlap.

Virtually any shape, valid or invalid, is acceptable as a path for the 3D Lofter or Keyframer as long as it consists of a single polygon. Only valid shapes, which may include multiple polygons as long as they do not overlap, can be used in the 3D Editor or as a loft shape in the 3D Lofter.

Lofting Simple Objects

The 3D Lofter is an extremely powerful tool for creating three-dimensional geometry. The 3D Lofter accepts complex shapes from the 2D Shaper and sweeps them through a path to generate a mesh object. This section focuses on basic uses of the 3D Lofter and beginning path manipulation. Issues such as deformation grids, fit deformation, and helical paths are presented in Chapter 9, " Lofting Complex Objects."

Understanding 3D Lofter Terminology

The 3D Lofter carries over much of the same terminology from the 2D Shaper. Some of the terms are applied a little differently, and there are a few new terms as well. Figure 4.21 identifies some of the 3D Lofter components described in the following sections.

Shapes

Valid shapes are imported from the 2D Shaper and placed on any level of the 3D Lofter path. You can think of shapes as a sort of extrusion template. The three-dimensional object that the 3D Lofter creates will be forced to conform to each shape that it encounters along the path.

Path

The *path* serves as an armature that holds the shapes and describes the spine of the lofted object. The path is a spline curve that can be manipulated the same as splines in the 2D Shaper. The difference is that the loft path is fully three-dimensional, whereas the 2D Shaper splines are only two-dimensional.

You also can specify path steps in the same way you specify shape steps in the 2D Shaper. The 3D Lofter actually provides separate controls for both shape steps and path steps. The important difference between shape steps and path steps is that the path steps are also levels.

Levels

A *level* is a division along the path that can hold a shape. Both vertices and path steps are considered levels, and both can hold a shape. The levels in your path have a significant impact on the complexity of your geometry. Every level represents a segment in the final 3D mesh object. The more levels you have on the path, the more segments and faces you have in your 3D mesh object.

Your decisions regarding path steps and vertices are similar to the decisions about shape steps and vertices in the 2D Shaper. In the 3D Lofter, your decisions are complicated by the need to have a level, either a path step or a vertex, at each location where you have a significant feature in your geometry. In general, you should place path vertices for features of geometry and rely on path steps for smoothing curves.

Figure 4.21
A 3D Lofter
path and its
components.

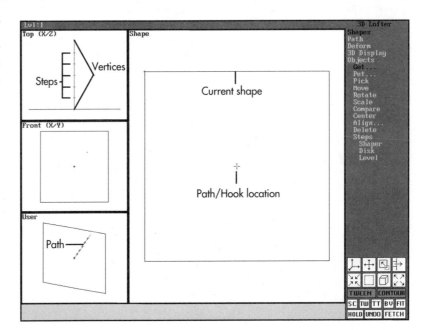

Examining 2D Shaper Interaction

The 2D Shaper and the 3D Lofter are closely related. You often will find yourself switching between the 2D Shaper and the 3D Lofter in the process of lofting a single object. Understanding how the 2D Shaper and the 3D Lofter interact is the key to lofting objects effectively.

Assigning Shapes

Before you can send anything from the 2D Shaper to the 3D Lofter, you first must assign one or more polygons as the current shape. The commands to do this are under the Shape branch of the 2D Shaper. The Assign (for single pick selection), All, and None commands are used to assign and unassign polygons to the current shape.

A good rule of thumb is to choose Shape/None before proceeding with the definition of a new shape. This technique clears out any previously assigned polygons and enables you to assign a new shape from scratch.

A common mistake is assigning polygons to the current shape without realizing that there are other polygons already in the shape. These other polygons might be off-screen or simply overlooked, but they lead to unpredictable results when you try to bring the shape into the 3D Lofter.

The 2D Shaper has no command for assigning shapes through a quad or fence. Such an assign technique would be useful for assigning text strings to loft as a single object. You can, however, assign all the polygons in the current selection set easily. First, select all polygons with a command such as Select/ Polygon/Quad. Then choose Shape/Assign and click on the selected button. Clicking anywhere on the screen assigns all the selected polygons to the current shape.

Shape Hook

The *shape hook* determines where the shape is placed in relation to the path when it is brought into the 3D Lofter. By default, the shape hook is located at the 0,0 coordinate. Most of the time, you can ignore the location of the shape hook because the 3D Lofter provides handy commands to center and align the shape on the path.

Specifying the location of the shape hook in the 2D Shaper is useful when you plan to assign several shapes, one at a time, and place them on different levels of the path. In that case, you can arrange the polygons and locate the shape hook more efficiently in the 2D Shaper. Choose Shape/Hook to display the following commands used for manipulating the visibility and location of the shape hook:

✔ Show/Hide controls visibility of the shape hook.

✔ Place enables manual location of the hook.

✔ Center automatically locates the shape hook at the center of the current assigned shape's bounding box. This command is exactly the same as Shape/Center in the 3D Lofter. Figures 4.22a and 4.22b identify the shape hook after it has been centered on a polygon and shows how it relates to the path in the 3D Lofter.

✔ Home automatically locates the shape hook at the 0,0 coordinate location.

Figure 4.22a
A centered shape hook in the 2D Shaper.

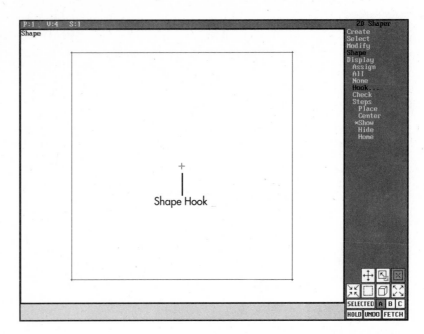

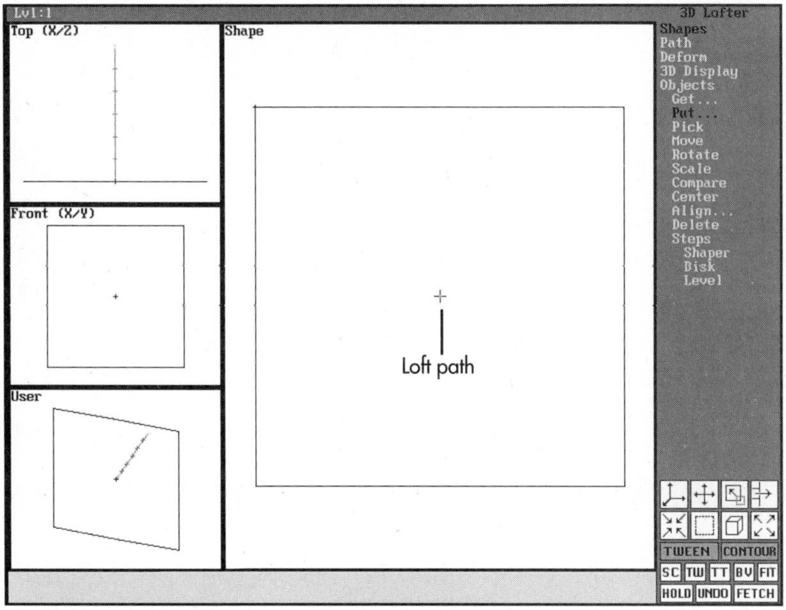

Figure 4.22b
The Path in the 3D Lofter corresponds with the Shape Hook in the Shaper.

First Vertex

Unless you are lofting a single polygon as the only shape on the path, you need to be concerned about the location of the first vertex. Every polygon maintains a list of its vertices. The vertex at the head of that list is called the first vertex. The first vertex location has great significance when the shape is brought into the 3D Lofter.

The first vertex of an open shape must be one of the two endpoints. An open shape can be brought into the 3D Lofter only as a path. The first vertex determines which end is considered the beginning of the path.

The first vertex for closed shapes is important because nested polygons within a shape and shapes along the path are linked together at their first vertices. Figure 4.23 shows the result of misaligned first vertices on the end faces of a lofted shape. As the object is lofted and placed into the 3D Editor, the first edge of the first face is defined as the edge linking the first vertex of each shape on the path. If the first vertices do not have approximately the same orientation, the faces of the object will be twisted. Figure 4.24 shows the result of misaligned first vertices on the side faces of a lofted shape.

You can avoid the problem of misaligned first vertices by always displaying them in the 2D Shaper. The first vertex of each polygon is displayed in black when you select Display/First/Show in the 2D Shaper. You now can tell easily when shapes made of multiple polygons contain first vertices that are out of alignment.

Figure 4.23
Misaligned first vertices for nested polygons.

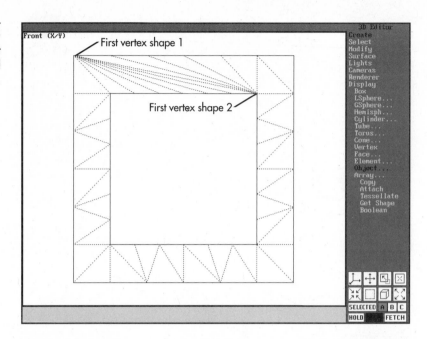

Figure 4.24
Misaligned first vertices for lofted polygons.

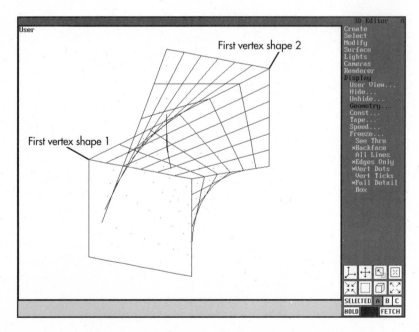

Editing Polygons to Align First Vertices

You can align the first vertex of multiple polygons by editing the polygon with the Modify commands in the 2D Shaper. Sometimes the first vertices can be aligned by merely rotating or moving a polygon to the appropriate position. These techniques work well when you are dealing with regular polygons that share a common center.

Specifying the First Vertex

Often you have complex polygons that you cannot easily modify, and yet you need to align their first vertices. This situation can occur when lofting outlined shapes. More often than not, the first vertices of the outlined polygons are not at the same vertex. You can fix this by choosing the command Display/First/Choose and selecting the vertex that you want designated as the first vertex.

Getting and Putting Shapes

You bring shapes into the 3D Lofter using the commands under the branch Shapes/Get. The three commands in this branch are 2D Shaper, Disk, and Level. As you can imagine, 2D Shaper gets the current shape assigned in the 2D Shaper and puts it on the current path level. The commands Disk and Level get a shape from a file on disk or copy a shape from another level on the path.

Putting shapes works the same way as getting shapes—only in reverse. The command Shapes/Put also has the option of 2D Shaper, Disk, and Level except that now the shape on the current path level is copied to the selected destination.

Getting Paths

As mentioned earlier, you can import a shape from the 2D Shaper as a Path in the 3D Lofter. The only restriction is that the current shape contains just one polygon. The advantage to creating paths in the 2D Shaper is that you have many more powerful editing tools available. The 2D Shaper is useful for generating paths of regular polygons or complex shapes.

The following exercise demonstrates the power of getting shapes from the 2D Shaper. You will create both the loft path and the loft shape in the 2D Shaper to create a mitered picture frame.

Creating a Mitered Frame

Choose Reset *from the* File *pull-down menu*

Turn Snap on

Choose Create/Quad

continues

continued

*Pick a point near the upper left corner of the screen, and
drag a quad down and to the right 200 units wide and 300
units tall*

Choose Create, *then* Line

*Define a cross section similar to the one in figure 4.25; make
sure that the polygon is no more than 40 units wide and 30
units tall*

Figure 4.25
Picture frame
shapes in the
2D Shaper.

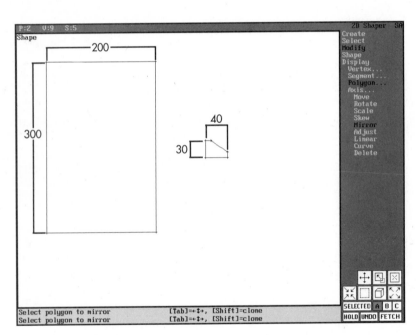

Set shape steps to 0

Choose Shape, *then* Assign, *and select the quad*

Assigns the quad as a shape; the
quad turns yellow to indicate that it
is the assigned shape

Press F2 *to enter the 3D Lofter*

Choose Path/Get/Shaper *and then click on the* OK
button in the warning dialog box

Imports the quad as the current
path

Press F1 *to return to the 2D Shaper*

Select the quad, then select the cross section polygon	Deselects the quad and assigns the cross section polygon as the current shape
Press F2 *to return to the 3D Lofter*	
Choose Shapes/Get/Shaper	Imports the cross section as the current shape on the path
Choose Center *from the* Shapes *branch*	Centers the cross section on the path (see fig. 4.26)

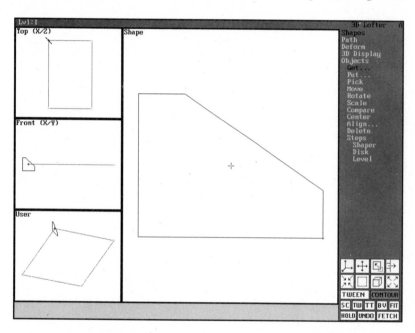

Figure 4.26
The 3D Lofter path and loft shape for the picture frame.

Choose Objects, *then* Make	Displays the Object Lofting Controls dialog box
Type **Frame** *in the* Object Name *field*	Specifies the name that the 3D Editor object will have
Check that the Contour *button is on and click on the* Create *button*	Creates the 3D object named Frame and places it in the 3D Editor
Press F3 *to enter the 3D Editor*	Displays the 3D Frame in the 3D Editor (see fig. 2.27)

continues

continued

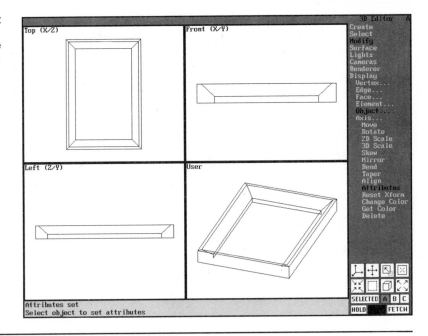

Figure 4.27
The picture frame
in the 3D Editor.

Exploring the Path

The default path in the 3D Lofter is a straight spline that is 100 units long. Rarely will you leave the path in this configuration. Most of the time you will add vertices, curve the path, and, as described in Chapter 9, perform deformations along the path. Think of this default path as a convenient reference point and nothing more.

Adjusting Curved Paths

The 3D Lofter provides many commands for adjusting the form of the path. Two of the most frequently used commands are Insert Vertex and Move Vertex. Insert Vertex enables you to add a vertex anywhere along the path, either between two existing vertices or on the end of the path. The Insert Vertex command works the same way as Create/Line command in the 2D Shaper, except that you cannot start a new path; you only can add to the existing one.

The Move Vertex command in the 3D Lofter works the way Modify/Vertex/Move does in the 2D Shaper. You select a vertex to move and then pick its new location. If you hold the mouse Pick button down while placing the second point, the direction arrows appear and behave the same as they do in the 2D Shaper.

New Riders Publishing
INSIDE SERIES

Path Steps and Refine

The issue of path complexity and the definition of curves is an important issue in the 3D Lofter, just as shape complexity is critical in the 2D Shaper. The Path commands of Path/Refine and Path/Steps in the 3D Lofter are similar to the commands Modify/Segment/Refine and Shape/Steps in the 2D Shaper. Review the previous paragraphs on shape complexity and the Refine command, and apply the same techniques to creating paths in the 3D Lofter.

The following exercise demonstrates how to refine a complex path to reduce the number of path steps required. The resulting mesh object also uses far fewer faces than a similar object lofted with default settings.

You also learn how to use the Refine command to round off a vertex causing a sharp corner. This same technique can be used in the 2D Shaper to fillet segments.

Creating a Neon 3D

Choose Reset *from the* File *pull-down menu, press* F1 *to enter the 2D Shaper, then choose* Create/Text/Font   Displays the Font File dialog box

Select the file BARREL.FNT *as the current font file*

Choose Enter *from the* Text *branch*

Type **3D** *in the text field and click on the* OK *button*

Choose Place *from the* Text *branch*

Press Ctrl *while picking a point near the upper left corner of the screen, and drag down to specify a text height of 300 units*   Creates text-shaped polygons in the 2D Sharper (see fig. 4.28)

Create a circle with a radius of 10 units

Choose Modify/Polygon/Delete *and delete the center hole from the "D" polygon*

Assign the "3" polygon as the current shape

Press F2 *to enter the* 3D Lofter

Choose Path/Get/Shaper   Imports the "3" shape as the current path

Click in the top viewport and then click on the Full Screen *icon*   Fills the entire screen with only the top viewport for easier editing of the path

Choose Refine *from the* Paths *branch*

continues

continued

Figure 4.28
Text polygons.

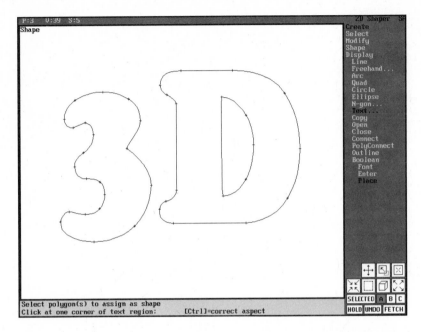

Next, you will delete the sharp kink in the back of the 3. Your mesh object will look better if there is a smooth curve on the back of the 3 rather than the sharp kink. The following steps show you how fillet the kink:

*Pick a point on either side of the middle vertex
on the back of the "3" path (see fig. 4.29)*

Choose Delete Vertex *from the* Paths *branch*

Select the vertex between the two vertices you just inserted	Deletes the vertex; the path is filleted between the new vertices
Choose Refine *again*	
Click on the locations shown in figure 4.30 to add vertices	Adds extra vertices to critical curves so that path steps can be reduced

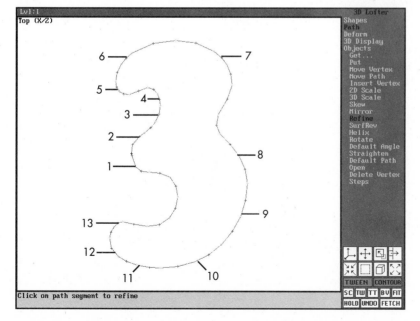

Figure 4.29
The location of two picks for the Refine command.

Figure 4.30
Multiple pick locations for the Refine command.

continues

continued

Choose Steps *from the* Paths *branch and drag the slider to 1*	Displays the Path Steps dialog box and reduces the number of steps in the path
Press [F1] *to return to the* 2D Shaper	
Pick the "3" polygon and then the circle polygon	Unassigns the "3" polygon and assigns the circle as the current shape
Press [F2] *to return to the* 3D Lofter	
Click on the Full Screen *icon*	Restores the standard four-view screen
Choose Shapes/Get/Shaper	Brings in the circle as the current shape on the path
Choose Center *from the* Shapes *branch*	Centers the circle on the "3" path
Choose Steps *from the* Shapes *branch and drag the slider to 2*	
Choose Objects/Make	Displays the Object Lofting Controls dialog box
Name the object Neon-3, *make sure that both* Contour *and* Tween *are on, and click on the* Create *button*	Makes an object named Neon-3 and places it in the 3D Editor
Press [F3] *to enter the* 3D Editor	Displays the new object in the 3D Editor (see fig. 4.31)
Choose Modify/Object/Attributes *and select the* Neon-3 *mesh object*	Displays the Object Attributes dialog box

Note the information near the middle of the dialog box. This object contains about 1,700 faces.

Click on the OK *button*	Clears the dialog box from the screen

Now that you have created the Neon-3 object, try using the same technique to loft the letter D.

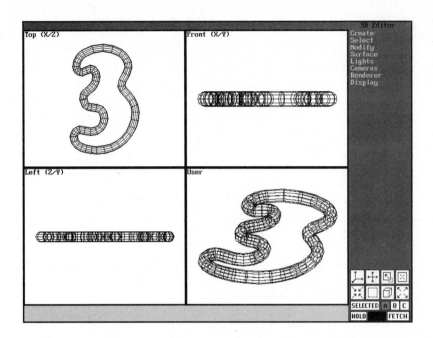

Figure 4.31
The Neon-3
mesh object.

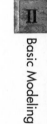

Look at the Neon-3 mesh object that you just created. It looks good, and its surfaces are fairly smooth. This object is suitable for any rendered view except, perhaps, an extreme close-up.

Many users of 3D Studio would have lofted the Neon-3 mesh object without refining the path and without altering the shape steps and path steps from the default setting of 5. Such an object would contain almost 6,100 faces. Your object with about 1,700 faces is 72 percent more efficient, renders faster, and looks just as good from most viewing angles.

Examining Shape Manipulation in the 3D Lofter

You have many tools to manipulate shapes after they are imported into the 3D Lofter. Although the commands are not as extensive as those available in the 2D Shaper, they can take care of many small refinements and prevent you from making an extra trip back to the 2D Shaper. All the commands for editing shapes are located under the Shapes branch.

Editing Shapes on the Path

The following five primary edit commands are available under the Shapes branch:

- ✔ Move
- ✔ Rotate
- ✔ Scale
- ✔ Delete
- ✔ Center

The first four commands work as their counterparts do in the 2D Shaper. One difference is that there is no global or local axis toggle in the 3D Lofter. The Rotate and Scale commands always use the path as their base point. Also, no selection sets are in the 3D Lofter because there can be only one shape on each level and the commands affect all the polygons within the shape. This last point is particularly important in regard to the Delete command. The Delete command is used to remove the current shape from the path completely, not to delete a polygon from within the shape.

The Center command relocates the shape so that the path passes through its center. If you take the time to specify the shape hook in the 2D Shaper explicitly, the shape is already located properly in regard to the path. Many people, however, prefer to ignore the shape hook while in the 2D Shaper and then center the shape on the path in the 3D Lofter. This technique works well because most real-world objects are manufactured with a central axis of symmetry. The Center command takes on added significance with the RevSurf and Helix paths, discussed in Chapter 9, "Lofting Complex Objects."

Using Multiple Shapes

You can create many useful and realistic models by lofting a single shape along a path. The 3D Lofter, however, is capable of much more. The real power of the 3D Lofter is evident when you begin to put multiple shapes along the path.

As mentioned earlier, shapes serve as templates for the lofted mesh object. If the shape changes from one level to the next, it causes the mesh object to transform gradually to match the new shape as well. At first, you might think that this is a rather specialized feature of the 3D Lofter. Upon closer examination, you find that many everyday objects make a transition from one shape to another—bolts, turned table legs, and tool handles, to name a few. The capability to change from one shape to another is an important feature of the 3D Lofter.

Vertex Restrictions

A few restrictions to lofting multiple shapes in the 3D Lofter exist. One of these restrictions is that all the shapes must have the same number of vertices. This restriction is not as limiting as it first might seem. The Modify/Segment/Refine command in the 2D Shaper enables you to insert extra vertices into a segment without changing the segment's shape. This command is the number one tool for matching up the number of vertices.

Aligning First Points

Another consideration is whether the first vertices of each shape are aligned. If the vertices are not aligned, the mesh will twist as it transforms from one shape to another. Usually, you do not want this to happen, so you use one of the techniques described earlier to align the first vertex.

If you have created a loft definition but you are not sure whether the first vertices are aligned properly, what can you do? You can save yourself a trip back to the 2D Shaper by using the command Shapes/Compare. This command prompts you to select a level on the path, and then displays the shape on that level superimposed on the current level's shape, as shown in figure 4.32. The first vertex of the selected level's shape is highlighted in green, and you can compare its location to the first vertex of the current level's shape. After viewing both shapes, you can decide whether to align the vertices with a 3D Lofter command, such as Shapes/Rotate, or to return to the 2D Shaper to modify the shapes there.

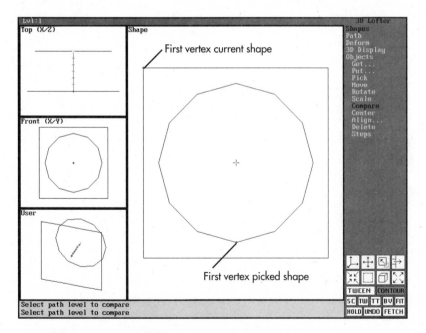

Figure 4.32
Using Shapes/ Compare in the 3D Lofter.

Understanding Tween

Tween is a button located in the lower right corner of the screen, and it appears in the Objects/Preview and Objects/Make dialog boxes. The Tween button has a great impact on the overall complexity of your model and is directly related to your path steps setting. If

Tween is turned on, a cross-sectional shape, or segment, is generated at each vertex and each path step. This can result in many extra segments added to your object. If Tween is off, a cross-sectional shape is generated only at vertex locations. Figure 4.33 shows the neon number lofted with Tween on and with Tween off.

Figure 4.33
Lofting with Tween on (A) and with Tween off (B).

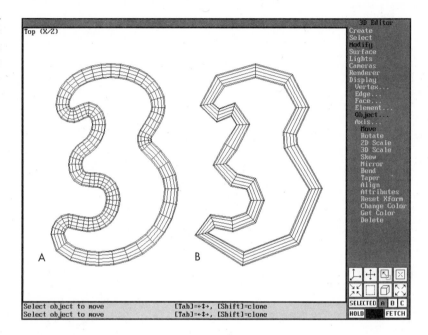

The result of turning off Tween is exactly the same as setting the path steps to 0. Either technique works well for paths consisting of only straight segments. Many users pay too little attention to the setting of path steps and the refining of curves. You will have greater success at creating efficient, fast-rendering objects if you learn to work aggressively with the Path/Refine and Path/Steps commands. Your goal is to create a path with enough vertices to define the curves properly while using as few steps as possible. If you do this, you almost always will have Tween turned on because the only steps left in your paths will be steps that you absolutely need.

Understanding Contour

The Contour button is always beside the Tween button. Contour controls whether the shapes on your path turn to follow curves. In many ways, Contour is like the difference between Skew

and Bend in the 3D Editor. If Contour is on, your shapes turn as they follow curves in the path. Contour forces the shapes to stay perpendicular to the path, resulting in smooth bends where the path curves. If Contour is off, the shapes remain parallel to the front viewport, regardless of how the path curves. This produces an object that is skewed from side to side rather than bent. Figure 4.34 demonstrates the difference between the neon number lofted with Contour on and with Contour off. Usually, if you design a path with a curve, you want your object to bend. In that case, leave Contour on.

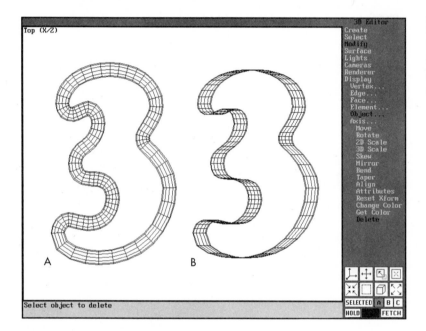

Figure 4.34
Lofting with Contour on (A) and with Contour off (B).

II

Basic Modeling

Making Objects

The Objects/Make dialog box is rather intimidating the first few times you encounter it. In reality, most of the choices in the dialog box are fairly straightforward and easy to understand after you have been through them a few times. This section looks at all the settings in the dialog box except lofted Mapping coordinates and the Weld Vertices button. These two issues are covered in Chapter 9.

Naming

The Name field is highlighted automatically as soon as the dialog box appears. This is a fairly good tip-off to the importance of naming your objects. Never accept the default name; always enter a meaningful name for the object in the name field. The only time you can ignore entering a name is if you are lofting a sequence of similar objects and want to name them sequentially. You name the first object and include the numbers 01 at the end of the name. As you loft the remaining objects, you can save time by clicking on the + button at the bottom of the dialog box. The + button adds 1 to the name in the name field and creates the object using the current settings.

Capping

The two capping buttons determine whether 3D Studio covers the ends of your lofted object. Because 3D Studio is a surface modeler, everything that you create is hollow. The illusion of solidity is created by capping the ends of objects. If you want your object to appear open and hollow, instruct the 3D Lofter to leave one or both of the ends uncapped.

If you do not cap your objects, the side walls will appear thin and unrealistic. You also might have to reassign normals manually for the object to render properly. Manipulating normals is covered in Chapter 5, " Building Models in the 3D Editor."

 If you are lofting an object on a closed path, 3D Studio ignores the Cap Start and Cap End buttons. Examples of closed paths are closed polygons imported as paths from the 2D Shaper or fully circular paths created with SurfRev. A closed path has no ends, so the settings of the Cap buttons are ignored.

Smoothing

The two smoothing buttons determine whether your object appears as a smooth or faceted surface. This is similar to choosing a smoothed or faceted sphere in the 3D Editor. The big difference is that you have control over whether the length, the width, or both are smoothed.

Turning on the Smooth Length button instructs 3D Studio to smooth the object along the length of the path. This produces smooth bends as the object follows a curved path, but it renders the cross-sectional shape as faceted.

Turning on Smooth Width smoothes the perimeter of the shape. This setting produces smoothly curved cross sections but renders curves in the path as faceted.

Turning on both buttons renders a fully smoothed object. Figure 4.35 shows three 90-degree bends rendered as fully smoothed, smooth length only, and smooth width only.

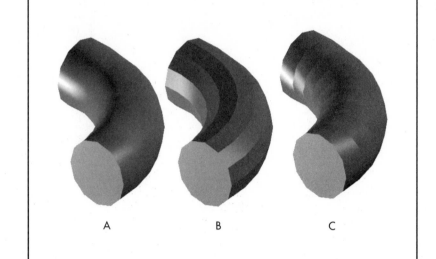

Figure 4.35
The effects of smoothing: fully smoothed (A), smooth length (B), and smooth width (C).

Optimizing

The Optimization button is a tool to help you minimize the complexity of the objects that you loft. Optimization analyzes the shape and removes unnecessary shape steps wherever possible. Shapes that combine flat segments with curved segments benefit the most from optimizing because step detail is retained for the curved sections and removed from the flat segments that do not need it, as shown in figure 4.36. If your entire shape is curved, optimizing provides no extra benefit.

A useful side effect of optimizing is that it also reduces the number of faces used to cap the ends of shapes. Because of this advantage, you always should loft geometry in the 2D Shaper, even if you want only a two-dimensional object in the 3D Editor. The 3D Editor can import shapes from the 2D Shaper as two-dimensional objects, but it cannot take advantage of optimization. Figure 4.37 shows two two-dimensional letters in the 3D Editor. The letter on the left was imported directly from the 2D Shaper. Notice all the faces revealed with Display/ Geometry/All Lines. The letter on the right was lofted with Optimization on and then had the side and back faces deleted. The lofted letter contains 32 percent fewer faces via the optimizing process.

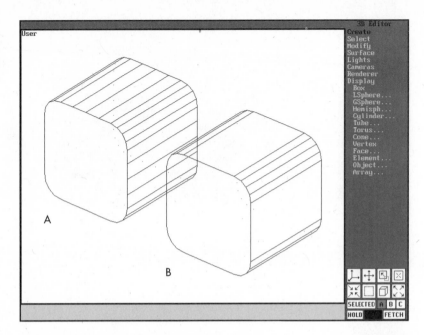

Figure 4.36
3D Optimization:
not optimized (A)
and optimized (B).

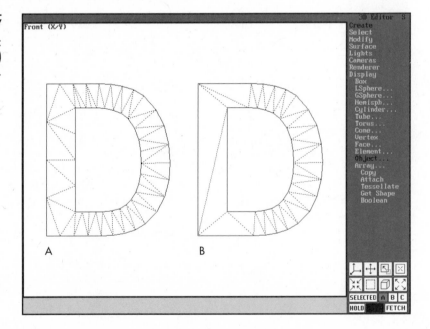

Figure 4.37
2D Optimization:
not optimized (A)
and optimized (B).

Three notable situations exist where optimizing cannot or should not be used. The first is when the shapes on the path are not the same. In this case, 3D Studio presents you with an error message and refuses to loft the object until you turn off Optimization. You can loft between a circle and a square if they have the same number of vertices, but you cannot optimize them. The number and order of flat and curved segments between shapes must be the same for optimizing to work.

Finally, you usually do not want to turn on Optimization for lofted mapping coordinates or for lofting morph objects. Both of these situations are discussed in Chapter 9.

Path and Shape Detail

The Path and Shape Detail buttons enable you to alter the step settings for the path and all shapes immediately before lofting. These buttons are used only when the Tween button is also on. When Tween is off, steps are not used and these buttons have no meaning. Clicking on the High Detail button uses the step settings exactly as you set them. Clicking on Medium Detail reduces the steps setting by half and then rounds up to the nearest whole number. Clicking on Low Detail is the same as having the step settings set at 0.

The Path and Step Detail buttons are crutches, but they are moderately handy when testing lofts for the appropriate step settings. Good modeling technique requires you to analyze your needs, and then set the path and shape steps appropriately before lofting an object. Assuming you have thought out the proper step values for your object, it should be lofted with Tween on and both the Path and Shape Detail buttons on High.

Storing and Reusing Lofts

Many people are conscientious about saving their final 3DS mesh files. This is a good habit because it helps build a collection of models that you can reuse at any time. What is often overlooked is that Loft files can serve as an equally valuable resource—if you remember to save them.

Imagine that you have created a loft for a nice-looking lamp base. This lamp base uses a circle shape on an intricate path. If you saved only the 3DS file, you have the mesh of this object but not the loft that created it. If you decide later that you want this same object but with a hexagonal cross section, the mesh file does you no good. If you had the loft file, however, you could swap the circle shape for a hexagon shape and make a new object. You always should consider saving your loft files if there is any chance that you will need a similar object with a different cross section.

Summary

You now have completed the introduction to the 2D Shaper and 3D Lofter combination. One of the most important issues presented in this chapter is the concept of reducing model complexity. Understanding how to refine shapes and paths and manipulate their step settings can save you considerable time when rendering your projects. In addition, understanding how to manipulate spline curves and place objects on the path will help you build more sophisticated models than is possible with the 3D Editor alone.

Chapter Snapshot

This chapter reviews the fundamental aspects of the 3D Editor, including the following:

✔ Understanding the 3D Editor terms, conventions, and construction

✔ Understanding considerations when creating the Editor's geometric primitives

✔ Exploring techniques for complex selection set manipulation

✔ Examining the nuances of the Modify command branch

✔ Sculpting, modeling, and scooping geometry with 3D Studio's Boolean engine

CHAPTER

5

Building Models in the 3D Editor

The 3D Editor is the working stage for the 3D Studio environment. It is here that objects are put into position, assigned materials, illuminated, viewed, and composed.

This chapter covers the basic environment of the 3D Editor—its terminology, methods, and characteristics of operation. The commands are explained in terms of daily use, rather than their specific syntax of execution. Much of what follows will provide insight into different approaches to the same situation.

Very few hard-and-fast rules exist for modeling in 3D Studio. If a technique works, use it. The following is not meant to tell you how to model, but rather to spur you to think about techniques that you in turn might use for a variety of applications or situations.

Understanding the 3D Editor Environment

The 3D Editor is the primary workplace within 3D Studio. It combines a model shop, a paint booth, a light lab, and a photography studio. Because of all its capabilities, it has by far the most command branch options of 3D Studio's five modules. Learning to use these options to their full potential in the 3D Editor is important because you'll use many of the same commands in the Keyframer.

3D Editor Terminology

The complexity of geometry possible in the 3D Editor is staggering. When you browse through the World Creating Toolkit CD-ROM and pull up a highly detailed sample mesh, such as CADDILAC.3DS, you'll likely be taken aback by its complexity. As you look closely at the mesh, however, you'll notice that it's made of simple, discrete pieces that have been knitted together. In fact, the 3D Editor uses only two very basic geometric types to create and edit all of its complex geometry.

Geometrical Components

The basic geometry of 3D Studio is organized by and into the following entity types:

✔ The *vertex* defines a point in three-dimensional space and is the most basic of entities. As shown in figure 5.1, a vertex defines no geometry except the location of a point in space. It has no surface or properties of its own, and so cannot be seen in a rendering. A vertex that is not connected to other vertices to form a mesh is known as an *isolated vertex*.

Note   A vertex is equivalent to an AutoCAD polyline or polyface mesh vertex.

✔ A *face* is a triangular mesh that is formed by connecting three vertices (see fig. 5.2). Because each face has only three points, each defines a geometric plane. Faces are flat by definition. They are what "skin" a model, give it form, and allow it to have materials and reflect light.

3D Studio's face is equivalent to an AutoCAD 3DFace with only three sides. A conventional four-sided 3DFace is the equivalent of two 3D Studio faces.

As you assemble faces, they begin to define identifiable forms. 3D Studio organizes collections of these forms as mesh entities that can be manipulated and organized.

✔ Adjacent faces that are created from the same set of vertices are said to have *shared* or *welded* vertices. When groups of faces share vertices, they are no longer separate entities. They define a surface and begin to form a *mesh*, which may be any combination of flat, curved, or bent surfaces, as long as they are continuously connected by faces that share vertices. The term *mesh* is used by 3D Studio to refer generically to geometry and is not a specific entity type.

 A mesh is equivalent to an AutoCAD PFace or polyface mesh.

✔ The mesh's extent defines a 3D Studio *element*—the smallest piece of geometry to which mapping coordinates can be applied. Although an element can be as small as an isolated vertex, there must be at least one face to apply mapping coordinates.

✔ One or more elements combine to form a 3D Studio *object*. Objects actually are a "selection" of elements. An object does not need to be a continuous mesh as an element does. It is very common for an object to be made up of widely separated elements, and it might contain isolated vertices (which are in turn individual elements). Objects also are your basic organizational tool: they have names for identification, can be assigned controlling attributes, and most importantly, they are the only mesh items that can be manipulated and animated within the Keyframer.

 Objects can be thought of as analogous to AutoCAD Layers.

II

Basic Modeling

Figure 5.1
Unconnected (isolated) vertices shown in the Ticks display mode.

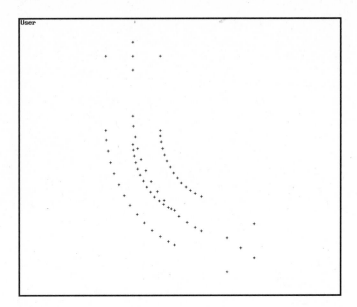

Figure 5.2
The same vertices connected with faces, shown in All Lines and Edges Only display modes.

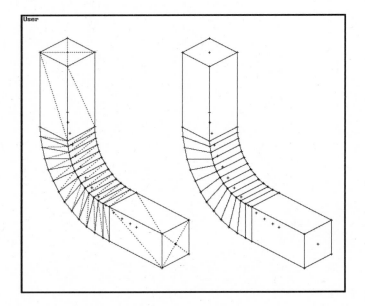

There is thus a geometrical hierarchy within 3D Studio that has the following order (from lowest to highest):

1. The vertex (which can be isolated).

2. The face (which must contain three vertices).

3. The element (which contains vertices that are continuously connected with faces or is an isolated vertex).

4. The object (which contains elements that in turn have vertices that may be connected with faces).

Graphical Components

The following terms describe several physical characteristics common to meshes (see fig. 5.3). These forms define the basic components of the rendered mesh, also shown in figure 5.3.

✔ An *edge* is the line that connects two vertices across a face. Each face thus has three edges. Adjacent faces that share two vertices also share an edge. Faces are the result of vertices; they cannot be created on their own. You can use edges to delete or modify the faces that form them and to create other faces based on their location. An edge can be either visible or invisible. This is solely for visual clarity as you manipulate your meshes; it has no effect on the mesh's geometry or its rendering characteristics (except in the Renderer's Wireframe mode).

✔ An *end* is the set of faces that forms the coplanar *cap* of an element. When you loft objects, ends are formed as the object is capped.

✔ A *side* usually is associated with the steps that form an arc—one side for each step. Sides also usually refer to two coplanar faces which share an edge; many people call these facets.

✔ A *segment* is a cross-sectional division along the length of an element. Each segment provides an opportunity to deform the element at that section. When you loft objects, you create a segment for each step in its path. You should base an element's need for segments on your need to bend or twist the mesh.

Manipulation Components

When you manipulate an object or a selection, several components can aid, guide, and control the outcome of the process. The following components do not actually exist per se, but are used temporarily for commands (see fig. 5.4):

✔ A *bounding box* is a rectangular box whose size is defined by the extent of the object or the current, temporary, selection set. 3D Studio uses a bounding box as a stand-in when dragging selections during commands. Its extent and orientation can influence the effects of various Modify commands, materials, and Keyframer transformations.

✔ The *transformation matrix* is a table of numbers maintained by 3D Studio to keep track of changes to the location and shape of objects. The location of an object is determined by the intersection of three planes in the center of the bounding box. Its use is completely transparent to the user, but can influence the effect of certain materials and Keyframer transformations.

Figure 5.3
Graphical components and the rendered mesh.

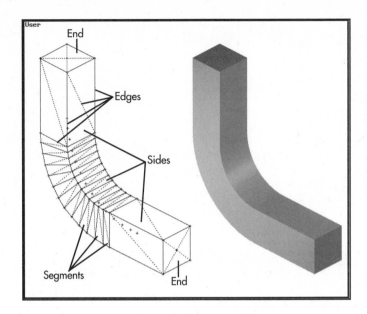

✔ The *local axis* is the intersection of the three axes defined by the transformation matrix and is thus the bounding box's center. You can use the local axis as a reference point for selections during most Modify commands within the 3D Editor.

Figure 5.4
Components used by 3D Studio for manipulating objects and/or selections.

The Importance of Naming Objects

Names are the major tool for organizing objects within 3D Studio. The name you choose for an object is important for efficient selection and quick manipulation. You should name objects so that you can easily identify them in select-by-name dialog boxes.

Unlike AutoCAD or DOS, 3D Studio enables you to use nearly any ASCII character in a name (function keys are not recognized). These are searched according to their numeric ASCII value and can be used to organize groups of objects. Using a standard keyboard, you can start a name with an exclamation point (!) to put the object first, while a tilde (~) will put it last. You also can use Ctrl to create some of the more obscure characters, with Ctrl+A being the very first and Ctrl+Backspace being the very last characters.

Giving 3D Studio objects names containing unconventional characters will make them ineligible for DXF import into AutoCAD.

Objects can be created in several ways, each having its own advantages. You can loft them, detach them, copy them, clone them, get them from the 2D Shaper, import them from disk, or create primitives directly. Regardless of which method you use to create an object, you will always be required to assign a new, unique name to it. Object names can have from 1 to 10 characters and are allowed to contain spaces. Because 3D Studio is case-sensitive, object names that might "read" the same could still distinguish different objects.

Wild Cards

The long-awaited capability of 3D Studio to recognize the standard DOS wild-card conventions was finally included in Release 3. This is called *tagging*, and can be used whenever multiple selections are permitted in a select-by-name dialog box.

You can use Ctrl+N to access the select-by-name dialog box from within any command that affects objects.

The standard wild-card key characters—the question mark (?) and the asterisk (*)—are available within 3D Studio and perform exactly as in DOS except that they recognize the case of the string. If you are accustomed to using DOS, it may take some time to get used to this case-sensitivity. After you're comfortable with case-sensitivity, you might find that you miss it at the DOS prompt.

Name your objects with easily identifiable character strings to speed up making selections.

As a quick review, the question mark (?) replaces any single character, and the asterisk (*) replaces all characters from that point onward. Note that the tag *m* does not mean *any* occurrence of *m*, but anything at all, as the asterisk recognizes only characters placed before it and ignores anything after it.

This is unlike the asterisk used in AutoCAD Release 11 and higher. The wide variety of wild-card matches available to AutoCAD are not currently available with 3D Studio Release 4.

You can use the Tag feature whenever 3D Studio allows multiple names for a selection. Type the search string in the tag field, and then click on the Tag or Untag button to select or deselect the object names that match your string, as shown in figure 5.5. Your wild-card string remains, so you can edit and apply it again in the same selection or in future selections with different commands.

Figure 5.5
The Select Objects
by Name dialog
box using the
Tag Feature.

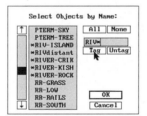

To navigate quickly through long lists of names, press (Alt) plus the first letter of the object name you want. You will then jump to that area in the list. This shortcut is available within any type of named list within 3D Studio (object names, material names, file names, etc.).

Subsequent Object Naming

As you create objects within 3D Studio, the default name suggested by the various Create dialog boxes is based on the name of the last object you created. 3D Studio assumes that you might be creating a series of objects that relate to one other. The last name is appended with 01, with any characters above eight being truncated (for example, Wall becomes Wall01). If there is already a number at the name's end, it is increased incrementally (for example, Box01 becomes Box02). The names of cloned objects are based on their parent, not the last object created from the Create branch.

The number appended is based on the lowest available for that prefix name. 3D Studio prefers to keep the name lists orderly, filling in the numerical gaps that might exist as you delete or change earlier numbers or supply numbers that are higher than the next one available.

Giving sequential names to families of objects makes them easier to select in the future because you can use wild cards to tag and isolate them.

The default incremental naming can lead to some confusion for meshes that are brought into 3D Studio by DXF import. See Chapter 11, "Integrating AutoCAD with 3D Studio," for details on this possible problem.

Setting Up Views

The ability to establish the desired appropriate views quickly is very important for efficient work. The shortcut keys for establishing views—**T**op and **B**ottom, **L**eft and **R**ight, **F**ront and bac**k**, **U**ser, **C**amera, and **S**potlight—should be memorized and used often.

As you will see in this chapter, the results of the Create and Modify branch commands depend a great deal on which viewport is active when you use them.

The User View

You will probably find the User view particularly useful while modeling. This view is similar to a traditional axonometric or isometric drawing, and might actually fulfill the final image needs for technical models where perspective is not necessarily desirable.

II

Basic Modeling

For AutoCAD users, the User view's operation is very similar to that of the VPoint command.

You can quickly access the User view's diagrammatic tripod by pressing ⒰. This icon is a good tool for quickly viewing your model from various positions. The key to determining your angle of view to the model, or "which way is up," lies in the color of your tripod axes—an axis is light when it is pointing in the positive direction, and dark when it is pointing in the negative direction. So, if your upward axis is light, you are looking down on the model. Adjust the tripod with your mouse, and then click to set the view.

The keyboard's arrow keys are particularly useful when the User view is active. Press an arrow key to rotate the view in 10-degree increments (the default). If you hold down an arrow key, the view is continually rotated, an effect similar to spinning a model stand. This is a convenient method for checking your model. If your keyboard has 45 degree arrow keys, the view will rotate in both directions when you hold one down. Holding down ⓢShift and pressing an arrow key rotates the view in 1-degree increments.

Beginning with Release 3, User views recognize the current Angle Snap toggle option. When you turn on Angle Snap, both the User view tripod and keyboard arrows will rotate in increments equal to the current angle snap. Holding ⓢShift will rotate the view in 10-percent increments of the angle snap. This can be very useful for setting up precise angles, such as 45 degrees.

Using Drawing Aids in the 3D Editor

The drawing aids common to the 2D Shaper and 3D Lofter are available in the 3D Editor, and as in all modules, you can quickly access their controlling dialog box with ⒞trl+Ⓐ. The consistent use of these aids is extremely important for maintaining accuracy during the life of the model.

Using Snap

The primary tool for accurate placement in the 3D Editor is Snap. You can quickly turn on Snap by pressing Ⓢ; Snap is independent for each viewport. The use of Snap is critical whenever creating or modifying items where precision is important. The Snap settings themselves will, of course, vary during the course of your modeling. You can activate Snap anytime, even during a command, but you should usually turn it on before you begin a Create or Modify operation.

When you select an item for a Modify command, Snap is temporarily suspended so that you can pick the mesh. The first point returned by Snap might seem to be off-grid, while other times it is correctly on the Snap increment. This is not a bug, but an underlying selection process. When you select a mesh at an edge, the pick point is snapped on grid and your second pick point respects your Snap increment. When you select a mesh at a vertex, the pick point is snapped to the nearest snap point and the resulting Snap increment will be off by the initial displaced distance. If you are working in Box mode, or with a selection set, you are incapable of selecting a vertex, so the Snap increment is always respected.

Knowing how Snap actually works can help you align an object's vertex to the Snap increment. If you select an object at a vertex, the mesh will move to the closest Snap location, which will be used as the basis for other operations, such as creating or moving objects about it.

Moving a mesh by selecting one of its vertices for the first pick point and then clicking again, without moving your cursor, will align the mesh on the current Snap grid.

Using Angle Snap

Angle Snap can be turned off and on quickly by using Ⓐ. Like Snap, Angle Snap is independent for each viewport. Unlike Snap, you can activate Angle Snap during a command, and it will affect your chosen angle correctly.

Using Grid

The question of whether to use Grid is an individual one. Grid display is strictly for reference and affords no additional accuracy. For some modelers, this visual cue is important, while others rely completely on Snap settings and the coordinate display. If the Grid works for you, then by all means, use it. But remember that setting up the grid at an appropriate position takes time, and you might want to try modeling without it.

Controlling Display Speed

As your model increases in complexity and face count, it becomes increasingly important to minimize the time spent waiting for your graphics card to finish redrawing. Because 3D Studio is designed as a production tool, there are several methods to increase the screen redraw speed. Just remember the simple concept that the more information drawn on-screen, the slower the redraw.

The built-in Vibrant Drivers since Release 3 have increased the overall display speed from that of earlier releases. Depending on your graphics card, these allow for a wide range of color and display resolutions. The Vibrant setup within Release 4 correctly warns that selecting a color depth greater than 256 colors for the general display will impair redraw speed. Resolutions higher than 640×480 provide clarity at the cost of redraw speed as well.

Using Box Mode

Box mode displays the least information and is the fastest display option. Only the bounding boxes of objects are displayed. This option is extremely useful with large models.

It is often quicker to press Alt+B to switch to Box mode, perform several display changes (such as deselecting all entities, changing ticks to dots, displaying lines only, and so on), and press Alt+B again to switch back to Full Draw mode, than to perform the same display changes while staying in full draw mode.

Another advantage of Box mode is that by defining the object's extents, it helps you position complex objects by their extreme edges.

Use Box mode to align complex meshes accurately. This is both faster and more precise when you need objects to sit on the same plane. Remember this technique, particularly for aligning rows of text in the 3D Editor and Keyframer.

Point and Tick Displays

Because it does not impact display speed, displaying vertices with the Geometry/Point option is the standard display option. Each vertex is represented by a single display pixel. This mode, however, can make it somewhat difficult to identify vertices—especially isolated ones. The Geometry/Tick option replaces the dots with crosses and is often used when locating or editing vertices. Since this option does impact redraw speed, it is often reset to Point once the need for vertex information is finished.

You can interrupt an extensive redraw by pressing Esc or by right-clicking for each viewport currently redrawing. Using Esc four times in succession is usually quicker than using the mouse.

Edge Display

The Geometry/Edges Only option should also be the default display mode, unless you are editing vertices or invisible edges (see Chapter 10), in which case use Geometry/All Lines to show the edges of every face, hidden or unhidden. For most meshes created within 3D Studio, only the hard edges and corners are visible. Imported DXF files can easily have an abundance of visible faces, and you might want to change this for clarity and redraw speed. You can manually change the display of individual edges with Modify/Edge/Visible or Invisible.

You can change the edge display of entire objects through the use of Modify/Edge/AutoEdge in a procedure nearly identical to the Auto Smooth function. See Chapter 10, "Creating and Editing Faces and Vertices in the 3D Editor," for more information.

Fastdraw and Fastview

Fastdraw reduces the number of edges displayed according to the parameter you set with Display/Speed/Set Speed. You can press [V] to put a single viewport into Fastdraw mode, or choose Display/Speed/Fastview to put all viewports into Fastdraw mode. You can assign Fastdraw to objects by name, by color, or by object (where you can select them individually or by a selection set).

Hiding and Displaying Geometry

By limiting the number of objects on-screen with Display/Hide or Unhide, you not only reduce the amount of lines redrawn, but also the number of vertices and faces considered when you create selections. An organized approach to naming with careful use of key character strings is the greatest aid for quickly displaying or hiding selections of names. (You also can hide with object selection sets—unfortunately, they cannot be used to unhide.)

You can hide individual elements of an object or faces of an element with Display/Hide as well. These items still belong to the object or element and can be redisplayed by selecting the parent in Display/Unhide. In this case, selection sets are valid for unhiding even if all of an object's geometry is hidden because the object's name and definition are still active (they have not been "hidden").

Use the Hide/Element and Hide/Face options carefully when you need to isolate portions of an object for clarity, or when you want to affect only a portion of the object without detaching a portion of it. The vertices of hidden elements and faces are *not* affected by future modifications to the parent object. If the parent object or element is moved, its hidden vertices with their faces remain behind. It's good practice to unhide the items after you have finished a task, because this can lead to confusing situations in the future.

Understanding Normals

3D Studio is built for speed; with this goal in mind, 3D Studio is built around the concept of face normals. In technical terms, a *normal* is a vector perpendicular to the plane defined by the face. It is these vectors that 3D Studio uses to determine face visibility. In use, this means that as each face defines a plane, it also defines a hemisphere from which its surface can be viewed (see fig. 5.6). If you are viewing a face from an angle that is behind its normal, and are thus "behind" the face, 3D Studio does not waste the time to calculate it for display.

Figure 5.6
Viewing angles for viewing a face normal.

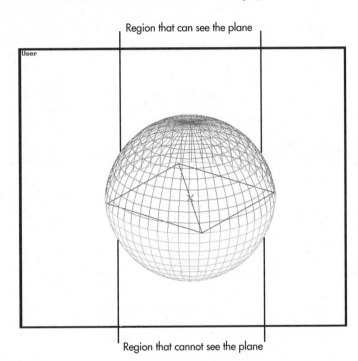

Backface and See Thru

The display of normals as relevant to the viewports' angle of view is controlled by the Display/Geometry/Backface and See Thru options. When Backface is on, you can see only the faces that are presenting normals to the view (this includes hidden edges shown by the All Lines option). When See Thru is on, all edges are displayed regardless of normals. These differences are shown in figure 5.7. Another advantage to viewing the model with Backface is that it displays faster since there are fewer lines to draw.

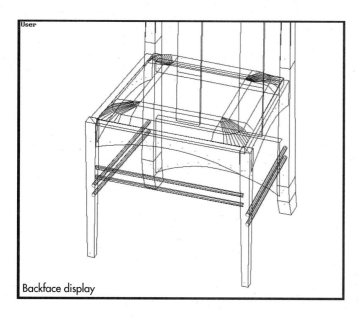

Backface display

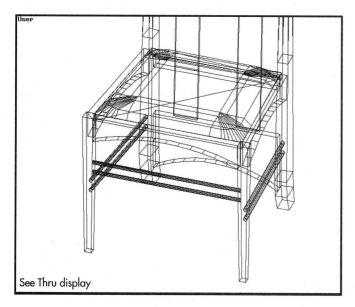

See Thru display

Figure 5.7
Backface display
versus See Thru
display modes.

Normals in Use

With normals, if a face can be seen with Backface on, then it will be rendered from that vantage point. If the face cannot be seen, it will be ignored in the Renderer's calculations. Manipulating a cube is a good way to quickly understand 3D Studio's concept of normals.

Face Normals for a Cube

Choose Display/Geometry/Backface | Backface is switched on

Press and hold Ctrl *while* *choosing the* Create/Box *command* | A cube is created with equal sides (the backsides of the cube are not visible)

The cube's normals are facing out—the default for all objects created within 3D Studio. The cube looks correct from all angles within the User or Camera view, as shown in figure 5.8.

Select the faces of one side of the cube and delete them

Enter User *view and rotate the view by holding down an arrow key* | The cube appears to spin in place

When viewed through the open side, the inside edges of the cube are not visible, and you can see directly through the cube, as shown in figure 5.9. The normals of these sides face out, so the faces cannot be seen from within.

Choose Display/Geometry/See Thru | All of the cube's lines are displayed

With all edges visible, it is impossible to tell that a side has been deleted.

Switch back to Backface *display, choose* Surface/Normals/Object Flip, *and* *select the cube* | The cube's normals are flipped and the inside faces of the cube are now visible through the transparent outside faces

Flipping the normals changes the direction they face, as shown in figure 5.10.

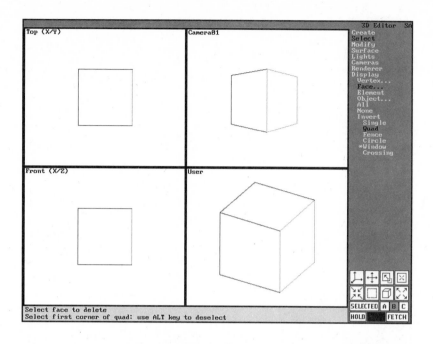

Figure 5.8
The complete cube, as seen from various angles.

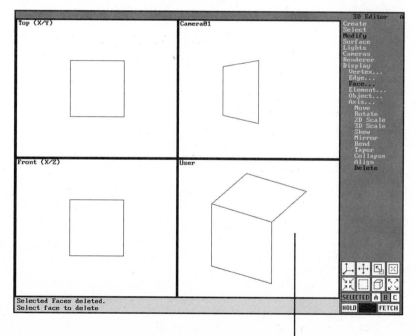

Figure 5.9
The face normals of an "opened" cube.

Deleted side (inside of cube cannot be seen)

Figure 5.10
The opened cube with flipped normals.

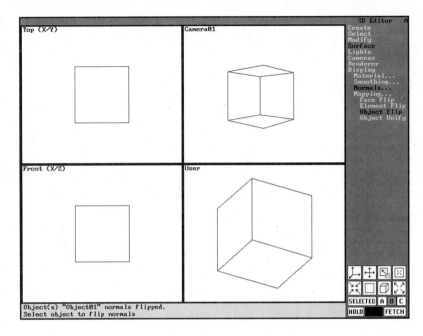

You can override 3D Studio's use of normals by assigning faces a 2-sided material, or forcing 3D Studio to render both sides of all faces by selecting the 2-Sided option in the Rendering dialog box. You must weigh the time gained by modeling only one side of an object against the speed lost by rendering many more faces (see Chapter 10 for more detail).

 3D Studio bases its Boolean calculations on the orientation of an object's normals. Boolean operations will *not* work correctly on sloppily created or oddly edited objects containing non-uniform normals.

For efficient modeling, you should take advantage of 3D Studio's use of normals to save rendering time. When doing so, it's best to view the model in Backface mode most of the time. This is somewhat like a hidden-line view (on the element level) where only the part of the mesh with normals facing the observer can be seen. Note that all vertices are still displayed for reference.

Pitfalls with Infinitely Thin Objects

When you're modeling, remember that nothing in "real life" is without thickness, unlike a mesh, which is a single face "thick." You should seriously consider modeling an object with three dimensions if the observer is going to see its edge (unless, of course, the effect of an infinitely thin plane is your objective). When this knife-edge thinness is rendered, as in figure 5.11, the effect, even within an animation, can be somewhat disturbing.

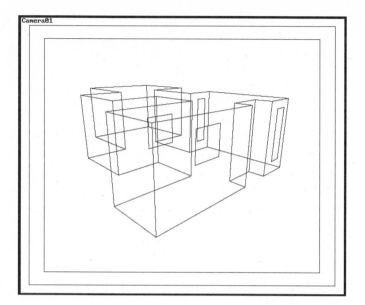

Figure 5.11
The paper-thin appearance of modeling with coplanar meshes that depend on 2-sided rendering.

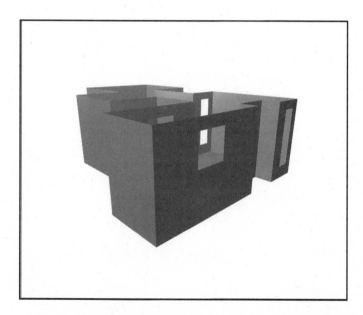

For an open box then, the most effective model has all of its sides defined. For the cube exercise, the sides need thickness for the cube to appear correct. This modeling concept holds especially true for architectural models where you can often see through windows and doors, and wall thicknesses are essential to the model's believability.

The effects of normals can give rise to surprising results. 3D Studio calculates shadows by "looking" from the spotlight's position at the scene and taking into account the faces that it can "see"—those whose normals face the light source. Because of this, faces the observer cannot see might cast a shadow, and those that can be seen might not cast a shadow. Automatic reflections behave the same way, building their interpretation of the scene from the reflecting surface's angle of view. As with shadows, reflections can reflect what cannot be seen and not reflect what can. This might lead to either very strange and unwanted effects, or—with careful planning—very clever, engineered effects. It's best to thoroughly understand these principles, be aware of the consequences, and plan for them appropriately.

Understanding Smoothing

Circles, arcs, and splines are not directly supported by the 3D Editor, but rather are approximated with segments, which in turn are made up of faces. The smoother the curve, the more segments and faces are required. Objects that need to appear very round and curvilinear require a high number of segments and faces to be convincing.

To minimize this modeling overhead and maintain speed, 3D Studio includes the concept of *smoothing*. Smoothing affects an object by rendering it as if the geometry were actually spherical. Edges that exist between the smoothed faces essentially are ignored by the rendering engine as the boundary mesh is smoothed. Figure 5.12 shows the effects of smoothing while using Flat, Gouraud, Phong, or Metal rendering options. As figure 5.12 shows, Flat shading ignores smoothing, Gouraud smoothes well but has angular highlights, Phong smoothes very evenly and has rounded highlights, while Metal smoothes just as evenly but maintains more contrast between color and highlight.

Figure 5.12
The effects of smoothing on the four shading limits.

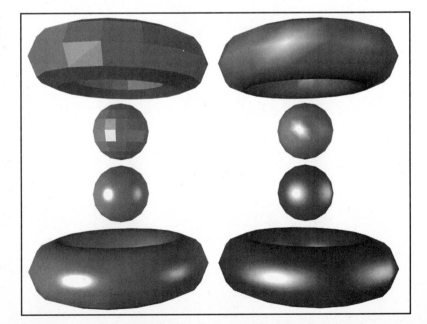

Smoothing creates this illusion of roundness by assigning *smoothing groups* at the face, element, or object level. All faces that belong to a smoothing group are smoothed across edges between adjacent faces. You must keep in mind that smoothing can work only between welded faces. So, while an element might have several smoothing groups assigned to it, the effect of smoothing cannot extend to other elements within the same object—even if they are assigned the same smoothing group.

The effect of smoothing is most dramatic on spherical meshes—the form that the smoothing function approximates. Although spheres created with dramatically different face counts have centers that render amazingly alike, the extra detail becomes important at the sphere's profile. Figure 5.13 shows how the apparent "roundness" of any curved form's perimeter is always determined by the number of faces that go into making it. As a modeler, you must balance the number of faces in a scene against the amount of detail you need. Remember that smoothing does not affect an object's true geometry—only the way its surface is rendered.

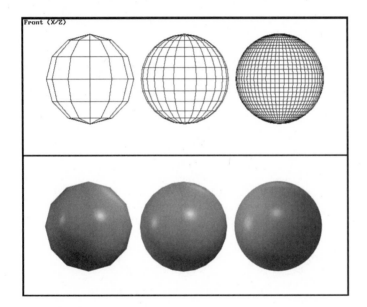

Figure 5.13
Comparing the edge clarity and rendered smoothness of 12-, 24-, and 60-sided LSpheres.

Tip

One effect of the improved anti-alias capability that came about with Release 3 is that segments are more crisply defined than before. As a result, you might need to boost the face count of curves somewhat because 3D Studio is not rendering the geometry quite as "fuzzily" as it did before.

Smooth and Faceted Creation Choices

When you create objects with approximated curves, such as cylinders and spheres, you must select whether you want the object faceted or smoothed. This choice does not affect the object's geometry, but rather the assignment of its smoothing groups. A smooth sphere is created with one common smoothing group, while a faceted one has a different group assigned to each side (up to the maximum number of smoothing groups available). Figure 5.14 shows a smooth cylinder, which has one group assigned to the faces of the shaft and one to its ends, and a faceted cylinder, which has a different group assigned to each side segment and end.

Figure 5.14

Default smoothing groups for faceted and smooth cylinders.

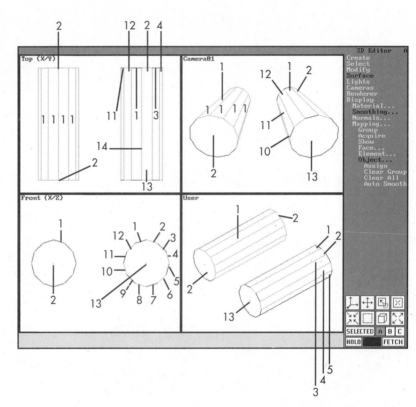

When you create an object in Release 3 or 4, 3D Studio assigns a smoothing group to every face within it. Flat or faceted ends that are coplanar are assigned to the same group. This does not have an immediate effect on rendering, but it does affect the display when faces on these sides are later distorted to be non-coplanar. Instead of appearing as a crease or a bend, the fold renders smooth. This can be either exactly what you want or an unwanted surprise—just keep in mind that this is the default.

New Riders Publishing
INSIDE
SERIES

Auto Smooth

Elements and objects can be quickly assigned smoothing groups with the Auto Smooth command. This command assigns smoothing based on the angles formed between the element's or object's faces. See Chapter 10, "Creating and Editing Faces and Vertices in the 3D Editor," for more detail.

The 3D Construction Planes

3D Studio determines the placement of all newly created objects, lights, and cameras by using construction planes. These are three orthogonal planes, each parallel to one of the world axes, as well as User planes that can positioned anywhere. The orthogonal planes are defined by their common point of intersection, which begins by default at (0,0,0). You can redefine this point at any time, but you cannot rotate the planes—the planes always respect the true X, Y, and Z axes.

Use the User view when you need to define a rotated construction plane or one that is not parallel to the world axes.

As you work on a mathematical grid or even a canvas, you might think of the Z axis as coming out at you or receding back past the page. This is 3D Studio's default definition. People who work with built objects rather than drawn objects relate to the Z axis as meaning up or down. A building's plan is drawn in the X and Y axes, and its walls project up in the Z axis while the foundations go down. This is AutoCAD's default and is often referred to as the *right-hand rule*. These two concepts are shown in figure 5.15. To change 3D Studio's default, edit the 3DS.SET file and change the H-LABEL (height) setting from X to Z, and the D-LABEL (depth) from Z to X.

When you create an object in an Orthogonal viewport, you are determining the placement of two of the pick point's three coordinates. The third is determined by the remaining construction plane (for example, when you create objects in a top or bottom view, you are defining the X and Y positions with the Z position being determined by the current placement of the Z construction plane).

II

Basic Modeling

Figure 5.15
Default
construction plane
labeling versus the
right hand rule
method.

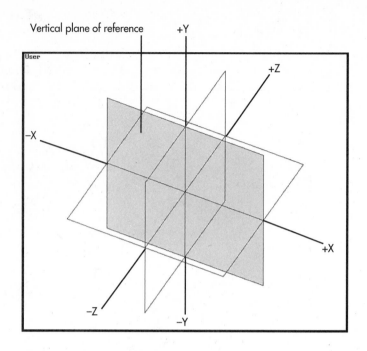

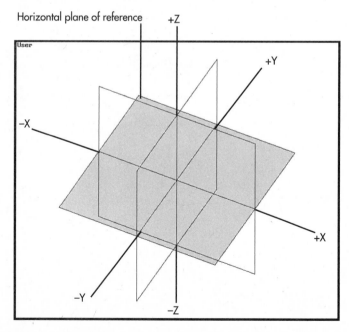

In any Orthogonal viewport, the available axes are shown in the status line.

If you create an object in a User view, the object is created parallel to the construction plane defined by that view, and its height is projected back perpendicularly.

Remember that 3D Studio always maintains the model's "true" home origin at (0,0,0), regardless of where or how often the global axis or construction planes are moved, or whether a User view construction plane is defined. This is extremely significant for DXF files because the imported mesh's origin will always align with that of 3D Studio.

The orthogonal planes are made visible by activating them with the Display/Const/Show option. To place them, simply point in an Orthogonal viewport to determine two planes. If the third plane is important, you must select it in a viewport that is at a right angle to the first (for example, if you are in the Right viewport, you must select another Orthogonal viewport other than Left). Throughout this book, these are referred to as *perpendicular viewports*.

You must select the second point carefully because one of the other two coordinates values of the center point is always redetermined (unfortunately, the directional-tab settings and the many align options available for axis determination are unavailable when you're placing construction planes). If you know the exact location where you want to place the construction center, you can enter the Cartesian coordinates manually by typing all three. The true origin can be restored quickly with the Const/Home option.

See Chapter 5 of the 3D Studio *Advanced User's Guide* for more information.

User View Construction Planes

As mentioned earlier, the User view also determines a plane in which you can create and modify objects. This construction plane can be placed at varying depths relative to the User view.

It is sometimes beneficial to see the actual position of this plane; to do so, choose Display/User/Show—the trick is that you must first choose the User view to display it, even if only one User view exists. After you choose the view, the plane's position can be further refined by placing its center in any nonperspective viewport.

In Orthogonal viewports, the extent of the User view is displayed with a rectangular icon. The icon's size will grow and shrink as you zoom in and out within the User view. The User/Place command moves the User plane's center to a point picked in an Orthogonal viewport. This changes what the User view shows, but does not change its angle or orientation.

You also can align the User view to an existing face by choosing User/Align. This can be a great help when you're working on obliquely angled geometry, or even orthogonal geometry that is not square to the construction planes.

Using Construction Planes Efficiently

Remember that construction planes are in effect only when you're constructing objects with the Create branch. In practice, you'll gain the most benefit from construction planes when you need to create several objects that rest on the same plane. If you're relocating the plane for the creation of a single object, it usually is quicker simply to create the object and then move it.

Because the planes determine even the location of created cameras and lights, it proves inconvenient when the planes are dramatically distant from the model's location. For modeling expediency, the construction planes should be placed reasonably close to the area being modeled.

Global and Local Axis

When you modify geometry in the 3D Editor, you usually have the choice of basing the command's effects on either the global axis or the selection's local axis. The lower right icon controls which axis is current, and you can quickly switch axes by pressing $\boxed{X}$ at any time.

Accuracy

Two approaches predominate among 3D Studio modelers. The first is to carefully arrange the construction planes to create the object, whether a primitive or loft, in precisely the spot needed. Although the argument for "doing it right the first time" might have some nostalgic merit, it might not be appropriate for 3D Studio. For all of its capabilities, the program is fairly weak when it comes to defining specific locations easily (whether by keyboard entry or snapping to existing geometry). You can spend significant time and frustration needlessly striving for accuracy.

The second method is a more cavalier approach in which the time is spent creating the object correctly, and not caring too much about where it initially appears. Once created, the object is simply moved into position. This is more of an artist's approach than an engineer's, since the time is spent analyzing the composition of the final placement rather than the construction location itself. Of course, you need to use the approach that is best for you and the given application. If you've always used one technique, try the other to discover its merits or reinforce your original conclusions.

Creating Objects and Elements

Of all the modules, the 3D Editor is the primary workplace. It is here that objects are manipulated, placed into final positions, assigned materials, illuminated, and viewed. This section discusses the objects you can create using the commands under the Create branch. It is assumed that you already know the basics of these commands. The following is additional information you should consider when creating these geometric basic forms.

Determining When to Loft or Create

Whether you create a primitive in the 2D Shaper, 3D Lofter, or 3D Editor really comes down to personal preference and what works fastest for you. A square drawn in the Shaper and lofted to the Editor will be identical to a cube created with Create/Box in the Editor, except that the latter method is probably much quicker. The 2D Shaper and 3D Lofter's primary use is for creating complex geometry—not geometric primitives. Unless you are creating iterations of a basic form for morphing, the 3D Editor is almost always your best choice.

3D Editor's Basic Building Blocks

The 3D Editor's geometric primitives form the building blocks from which many other forms can be made. They also serve as sculpting or modeling tools when used with the Create/Boolean operations.

The geometric primitives available within the 3D Editor include the following:

- ✔ Box (as a cube or rectangle)
- ✔ Sphere (based on quadrilateral or triangular facets)
- ✔ Hemisphere (quadrilateral facets only)
- ✔ Cylinder (in solid or hollow form)
- ✔ Torus (a donut)
- ✔ Cone

All of these primitives, except for Box, have value sliders to control the number of sides (arc steps) and segments (cross sections), and the complexity of the mesh. Each time you create an object, you should examine these value settings and consider how much detail will be required of the object in the scene.

Note   You can create a box with segments by using the GRID.SXP routine.

Creating geometric primitives in the 3D Editor is a straightforward procedure, once you select whether the object is to be smoothed or faceted (assigned one smoothing group or one for each side) and confirm its values, you simply pick the base point and drag for its total size. For accuracy, you need to either pay careful attention to the coordinate display as you drag, or set the Snap settings to an appropriate increment.

You can use the keyboard to define a new object, but you'll probably find it cumbersome; you must enter all coordinates for both the start and finish points of each command segment.

For the Box, Cylinder, Tube, and Cone commands, you can specify height with the keyboard even if the previous values were set with the mouse.

Box

Box objects are convenient and ideal for many one-shot uses. They can form quick stand-ins, simple sculpting tools for Boolean operations, and basic backdrops or floors. To create a perfect cube, hold down Ctrl while you select the first point, and thus save a step when you make forms quickly (see fig. 5.16).

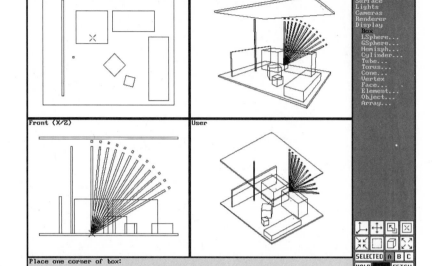

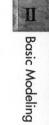

II

Basic Modeling

Figure 5.16
Rectangles, walls, and cubes created with the Box command.

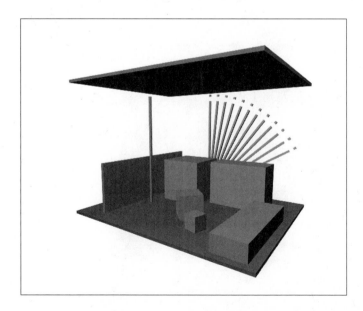

Spheres and Domes

Which sphere type you use (LSphere, Hemisphere, or GSphere) really depends on what you plan to do with it. Figure 5.17 shows the three options as both faceted and smoothed objects.

Figure 5.17
The different sphere types with and without smoothing.

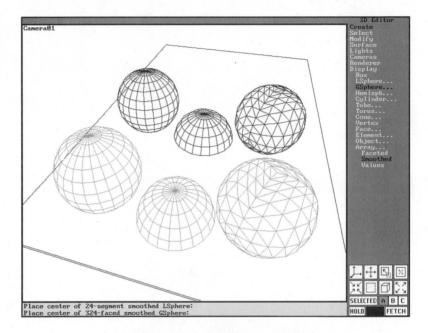

GSpheres, which are constructed of triangles, have smoother profiles for a given number of faces than do the quadrilateral-based LSpheres. They also do a better job of deforming because none of their faces are coplanar and each can be manipulated. GSpheres do have problems relating to orthogonal geometry because they cannot be separated evenly along a given plane. This is something that LSpheres do naturally, and this is also why there is no GHemisphere option. If you need the sides of the sphere to interact with orthogonal geometry (as in Boolean operations), the LSphere should be your first choice.

Hemispheres are quite predictable. After you pick the center and drag the radius, the object sits on the remaining construction plane. You create spheres the same way, but their placement takes some getting use to. Unlike hemispheres, spheres do not sit on the construction plane. The center of the sphere lies at the intersection of the construction planes.

Do not confuse GSpheres with true geodesic domes. Geodesic domes (made popular by Buckminster Fuller) are formed from equilateral triangles, which are all very close in size. GSpheres, however, are made out of isosceles triangles that can vary in size considerably. Although the geodesic dome can be cut evenly across a latitude, it would require more triangles than 3D Studio's GSphere, and this is the primary reason it is not included as an option.

Cylinders

You can create both solid cylinders and tubes (hollow cylinders). The side values required for these objects (if smoothed) will vary according to how closely you intend to view their ends. If the ends cannot be seen, you can create a minimum of sides. Figure 5.18 shows that the shafts of an eight-sided cylinder and tube render much like a 100-sided cylinder and tube, yet the profiles of their edges are dramatically different. Note the impact that smoothing has compared to the rear, unsmoothed objects; also, the 100-sided faceted objects have so many faces that they appear nearly smooth.

If you can see the ends, you'll probably find that tubes require more sides than cylinders because there will be a definite contrast along the tube's inside diameter.

 If you find that a 100-sided cylinder is not smooth enough for your needs (which is quite possible for high-resolution images or very large objects that arc through the scene), you'll need to loft circles that contain more arc steps.

Segmented cylinders have only one real purpose: to bend. If you do not intend to bend a cylinder, then it should be created with only one segment to save faces. Remember, the number of sides determines the overall smoothness of a circle. Segments only affect the rendering quality of the cylinder (or any extruded, curved object for that matter) if it is later deformed.

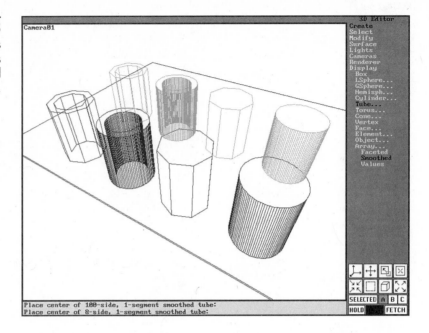

Figure 5.18
The various segment values for Cylinder and Tube objects.

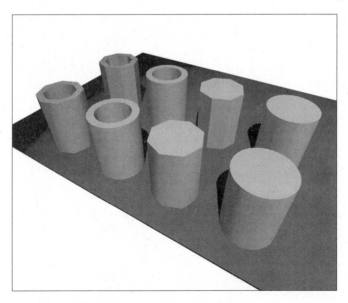

Torus

The *torus*, or donut, is a unique shape that has correspondingly unique uses. Toruses are commonly used for tires and rings, or for the circular trough to be subtracted by a Boolean operation. When toruses are created, the center point of the torus is at the intersection of the

construction planes, similar to spheres. Figure 5.19 shows that increasing the values dramatically affects the roundness of the torus, and that different viewing angles require different optimum settings for the number of segments and sides.

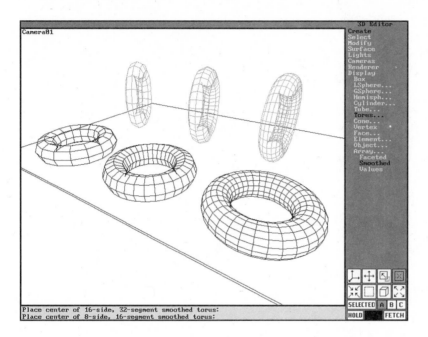

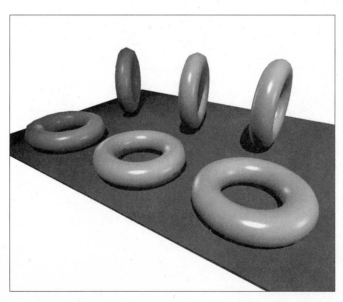

Figure 5.19
The various segmentation values for Torus objects.

Cones

Release 3 improved cones by adding a value slider for the number of steps along the cone's height, in addition to the segments of its circle (previous versions required you to loft a circle with a scale deformation to create a bendable cone). Cones appear straightforward enough, but you need to understand some things in order to predict their renderability. The first surprise is that you cannot create a cone that sharpens to a single point. Creating a cone with a second radius of zero results in a small, flat, circular tip, as shown in figure 5.20. Lofting a circle with a zero scale creates the same effect. This is not a bug, but rather a modeling enhancement. If the sides of a cone were to meet at a single vertex, all faces would be shared faces, and they would be affected by an assigned smoothing group. As the left cones of figure 5.21 show, this has the effect of smoothing over the tip of the cone as if it were a sphere.

Figure 5.20
A detailed view of the minimum size a cone tip radius can be.

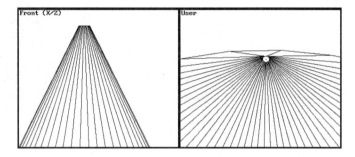

A four-sided "cone" is most easily formed by creating a four-sided GSphere. Such an object is very useful for animated "skinning" Plug-Ins such as TUBER.SXP.

You can create a single-vertex cone only if you scale in the vertices and weld them into one, or create them in another modeling program such as AutoCAD.

In reality, a cone reflects light linearly from its base to its tip. The smoother the cone, the less striping is apparent. To increase the rendered smoothness of a cone, you need to increase its values. Because a cone is not spherical, the standard rule (fewer faces smooth equivalently to many faces) does not apply. In the cone's case, the higher the segment and side values, the smoother the cone will render (see fig. 5.21). If you don't intend to bend or deform the cone, you'll be better off using your faces for higher sides than for additional segments.

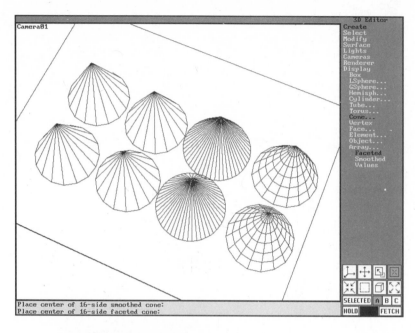

Figure 5.21
Cone objects with varying values and their rendered smoothness.

II

Basic Modeling

You can minimize the size of a cone's tip by applying 2D scaling to the point's vertices about the local axis. This sharpens the tip without affecting the smoothing characteristics. Do not reduce the scale of the vertices past 3D Studio's minimum accuracy—the vertices will begin to coincide, and you won't be able to return them to a circular formation. This will have a "pinching" effect on the smoothing.

Objects Direct from the 2D Shaper

You can bring closed shapes that exist in the 2D Shaper directly into the 3D Editor by using Create/Object/Get Shape. The shape will be imported as a completely flat object, coplanar to the construction plane of the current nonperspective viewport.

The Shape Detail options correspond to the number of vertices per segment (see fig. 5.22). The High option will create all of the vertices in the current Step setting, the Medium option will create half of them, and Low will ignore steps, connecting only the defined vertices. If you turn off the Cap Shape option, only vertices will be imported into the 3D Editor.

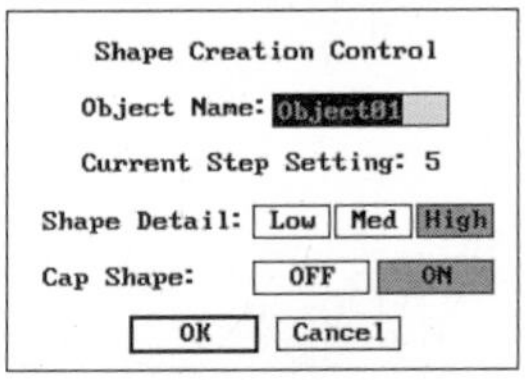

Figure 5.22

Creating an object directly from the 2D Shaper with Create/Object/Get Shape.

```
┌──────────────────────────────────┐
│     Shape Creation Control        │
│  Object Name: Object01            │
│  Current Step Setting: 5          │
│  Shape Detail: [ Low ][ Med ][High]│
│  Cap Shape:      [ OFF ][  ON  ]  │
│        [  OK  ][ Cancel ]          │
└──────────────────────────────────┘
```

Although Get Shape can save a step by bypassing the 3D Lofter, you will not be able to take advantage of the 3D Lofter's Optimization option. This is especially important for text objects, which require a high number of steps for their arcs, but contain many straight segments that will not be optimized.

Building Objects with Elements

Elements can be separated from and added to objects constantly throughout the modeling process. It's good to think of any element as a potential building block that can be broken off, reattached, cloned, modified, and used in a Boolean operation.

Attaching Objects

Lofted objects and the 3D Editor's geometric primitives can be used to form more complex geometry by attaching them with Create/Object/Attach. Only objects can be attached. If you need to attach an element, you must detach it as an object first and then attach it. The surface properties of the original mesh (materials, smoothing, and mapping) are maintained, but the object attributes (object color, matte object, shadow casting, and external processes) are inherited from the parent.

You cannot retrieve the original mapping coordinates of a mesh attached to another object using Mapping/Acquire. Only the mapping information of the parent object can be acquired—even if the mesh is later detached. See Chapter 6, "Introduction to the Materials Editor," for more information on mapping coordinates.

Detaching Elements

You can break elements off an object with Create/Element/Detach, after which the elements become an independent object. The term detach is somewhat misleading: anything—not just an element, face, or vertex—that you detach from an object becomes an independent object. After you detach an object, you are free to attach it to another object or manipulate it by itself.

Copying and Cloning

The Create command branch contains Copy commands for elements and objects. The Copy command obviously copies the item that you select, and copies of elements become new objects. If you need the objects created by Copy to be additional elements of the original object, you will need to use Create/Object/Attach after you copy them. When you copy a selection of objects, you are given the option to create a single object from the selection or copy the selected objects to individual objects.

In practice, however, you'll frequently pass over the Create/Copy command in favor of cloning. You can make a copy of an object or selection during any Modify branch command by holding down ⬧Shift while you select the command's first reference point. This point occurs when you are selecting a single entity for modification or the base point when you're working with a selection. Cloning creates a copy of the mesh just as Copy would, except that a clone might be modified in the process.

The result of any ⬧Shift+Modify command is a new, cloned object. ⬧Shift+Modify thus is identical to Create/Copy. Most modelers will use Copy and Clone interchangeably, choosing the one that happens to be closest to the branch in which they currently are working.

When you copy elements and objects, they take with them all of the information of their parent. The material, mapping coordinates, and attributes remain the same. These copied meshes also maintain the original bounding box orientation.

Use ⬧Shift+Modify/Face to clone a mesh when you do not want to inherit the parent's bounding box. This will give the new object a bounding box that corresponds to the global axes.

Creating Objects with Array

Release 3 introduced the Array command to quickly create multiple copies of an object at a prescribed distance or angle. This capability has been a standard feature in CAD programs for some time, and it was a welcome addition to 3D Studio's Create branch. 3D Studio includes two linear array options (Linear and Move) and two radial array options (Radial and Rotate).

AutoCAD users will find Radial/Array to be very similar to a Polar Array, and that Linear/Array is much like a Rectangular Array limited to a single row.

If you array a selection set of objects, each object created becomes a new object. The Array commands do not give you the option to "copy" to a single object from many. Each new object becomes a numbered iteration of its parent's name.

Arrays must be conducted in a nonperspective viewport. The Array commands behave like multiple executions of either the Create/Copy, ⟨Shift⟩+Move, or ⟨Shift⟩+Rotate commands, and place their copies according to the current viewport's plane.

You can create very intricate arrays with successive array operations in a series of User views.

Array/Move

The option Create/Array/Move is quite straightforward and might be the most useful Array option. With it, you simply move the object selection the displacement you want arrayed. The distance and direction of this move becomes the repeated distance and angle of a one-row, linear array, as shown in figure 5.23. Your ⟨Tab⟩-controlled, multidirectional arrows control the pick points as normal and allow for arrays at any angle. For accurate arrays, set and use Snap accordingly. There are no restrictions on object overlap or distance. The number of copies (including the original) is specified after you move the distance. The default is 10, but as with most commands, 3D Studio displays your most recent choice.

To create a traditional rectangular array, array the object in one direction, select the results, and array the selection in the other direction. Though this might seem cumbersome at first, you might soon appreciate the capability to array freely at any angle.

Figure 5.23
Examples of using Create/Array/Move.

Array/Linear

The Linear option is for those who need to be very precise about their arrays. It limits you to the four directions selectable with Tab↕. The direction for the array must be selected before you begin your array. Angled arrays are not possible unless you perform them in a rotated User view. The Linear Array dialog box, shown in figure 5.24, displays several methods for determining your distance increment.

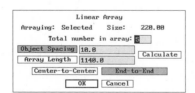

Figure 5.24
The Linear Array dialog box.

The distance of your array is based on the corresponding length of the bounding box side. You can specify either the incremental distance for the objects (with the Object Spacing field), or the overall length that the array must fit within (with the Array Length field). The values of the fields in the Linear Array dialog box are interrelated—if one field changes, it affects the others. The Calculate button in the Linear Array dialog box is used to update the values in the other fields when the value in one field is changed.

You can specify two methods for measuring these distances. The Center to Center option measures the total distance between the center points of the objects, while the End to End option specifies the gap between the objects (see fig. 5.25). This command assumes that you do not want the arrayed objects to overlap and will issue warning messages to that effect. If you intend objects to overlap, you can safely ignore the messages.

Figure 5.25
Distance specification methods for linear arrays.

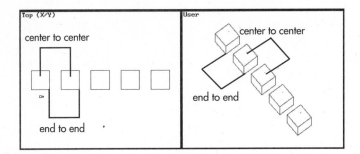

 AutoCAD users will find that the Center to Center option behaves the way a Rectangular Array calculates distance.

You can flip between any of the options and make changes to all the parameters freely. The results will be recalculated and displayed correctly. The method that is the easiest for you to relate to is, as always, the one you should choose to work with.

Array/Rotate

The Rotate option of Create/Array behaves much like the Modify/Rotate command. Because of this, it is the only command in the Create branch whose result depends on whether you use the global or local axis. With it, you simply rotate the selection to the angle you want each copy to be arrayed. The angle and direction of this "rotate" becomes the repeated angle for the radial array, as shown in figure 5.26. You can achieve accuracy for this angle by using an appropriate angle snap. The center of the rotation is the active axis. The number of times the item is to be copied about the axis is specified after you rotate the selection.

You also have the option of whether to rotate the arrayed objects created by the array. With Rotate Objects on, the arrayed objects are rotated with respect to the center, much like the petals of a flower (see fig. 5.27). With Rotate Objects off, the objects maintain their parent's original orientation, somewhat like houses built over a hill.

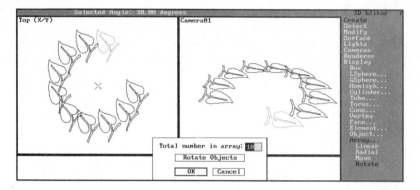

Figure 5.26
A rotated array using the global axis with Rotate Objects off.

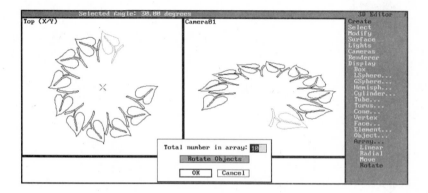

Figure 5.27
A rotated array using the global axis with Rotate Objects on.

II

Basic Modeling

Using Array/Rotate about the local axis creates a pinwheel or spinner effect, as shown in figure 5.28. This command will most often be used with the global axis at a point that will become the center of the arrayed objects.

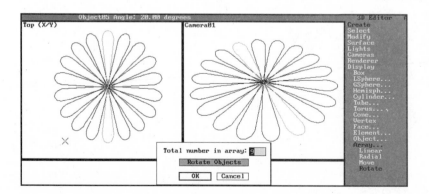

Figure 5.28
A rotated array using the local axis with Rotate Objects on.

If you are arraying a selection about its local axis, you must have Rotate Objects turned on, or all the objects will be arrayed in place, unrotated, and identical to the first.

Array/Radial

The Array/Radial command is the dialog box cousin to Array/Rotate. Like Rotate, it bases itself on the use of the global or local axis. Unlike Rotate, you must first determine the direction around the circle the array will proceed. This is done by using Tab⇌ to switch between the unique clockwise and counterclockwise icons. Once selected, you enter the Radial Array dialog box, as shown in figure 5.29.

Figure 5.29
The Radial Array
dialog box.

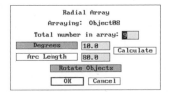

As with Array/Linear, after you decide the number of objects to be created, you have several options. You can specify the exact degree increment between each object with the Degree field. Alternatively, you can specify the total rotation angle for the array in the Arc Length field, and the command will calculate the Degree value required. You are free to try different combinations, calculate the results, change the number to be arrayed, and so on before you create objects. Unlike Array/Linear, the command does not alert you if your arrayed objects will overlap.

Modifying Objects

After you create objects, you can, of course, modify them. It is under the Modify branch that you usually will perform the most critical operations in the stages of creating models.

Object Attributes

The most common reason to access the Modify/Object/Attributes command is to change the object's name. The Object Attributes dialog box, shown in figure 5.30, also provides access to some subtle modeling tools that you can use to good effect. It is here you can define whether an object casts shadows, receives shadows, or acts as a matte object. These attributes help perfect several mapping and modeling techniques, as well as increase the model's rendering speed.

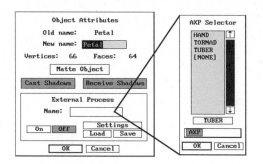

Figure 5.30
The Object
Attributes dialog
box and the AXP
Selector.

With wild-card strings now supported, you might consider renaming objects in existing models to aid in selections.

The Object Attributes dialog box is also where *Animated eXternal Processes* (AXPs) are defined and adjusted. When an object is assigned an AXP Plug-In, its entire identity changes—the Plug-In now uses that object to create the effect it was designed for. Some of the newer AXPs include SKIN (procedural meshing between sliced objects), FLAME (realistic flame effects using stand-in objects), and VAPOR (realistic atmospheric effects using stand-in objects), and are becoming common tools for animators and modelers alike.

Object Color

Since Release 3, 3D Studio has enabled you to assign a display color to an object as an organizational tool. This is useful for both modeling clarification and selection purposes. Separate objects can now be given any one of 64 colors; this is a welcome aid in distinguishing the objects in a complex model. (For AutoCAD users, this is much like assigning layer colors.) An object's color also is a selection criterion. You thus can organize objects under visible colors for later selection sets.

You must use a 256-color (or more) display to see object colors. If you use a 16-color display, all objects are displayed in white.

You can assign colors only to entire objects. Attached objects assume the color of their parent. Colors are assigned to objects with the Modify/Object/Change Color command from which the palette of 64 colors is presented. You can acquire a previously assigned color by using Modify/Object/Get Color. After this, you may assign the acquired color to a selection or set it as the default creation color for future objects.

II

Basic Modeling

The internal object color palette used with the standard 3D Studio display colors unfortunately creates poor contrast for many of the object color choices. Included on the Inside 3D Studio CD-ROM are additional 3DSOBJ.COL palettes (PASTEL.COL and BRIGHT.COL) that provide additional options for color choices. There is also an alternative 3DSBLACK.SET file that contains the Color Register Parameters to transform the 3D Studio display environment to a black screen for maximum color contrast.

The default colors are built into the program, but you can create custom colors from any Animator or Animator Pro color palette, which is saved as the 3DSOBJ.COL file in your 3DS3 directory. You may consider creating your own palette to accommodate the colors that you are the most comfortable with. This is especially true if you have taken the time to customize 3D Studio's display colors to your preferences.

The color you assign an object actually is only a reference number that indicates the color's location within the program's palette. It will not correlate to the same color in a second palette, unless it happens to appear in the same location on the palette.

Object Shadow Control

The Cast Shadows and Receive Shadows options influence how the Renderer interprets the object. These options have the special effect of keeping the object from casting shadows or letting shadows be cast on them. Although this capability is essential to create certain situations, it also has the benefit of reducing rendering time when cast shadows are being calculated.

If you've positioned objects in a scene where they will never cast shadows, turning off their shadow parameters will improve both rendering time and overall shadow quality. This is a common situation for objects that define the floor, ground, or base of a scene.

The object's shadow attributes can be coupled with the exclusion capabilities of omni and spotlights to create or reinforce certain lighting effects. You will commonly need to exclude an object from one light source while allowing it to be lit by another. See Chapter 7, "Lights, Cameras, and Basic Rendering Options," and Chapter 13, "Lighting and Camera Special Effects," for techniques for using both capabilities.

Excluding objects from a shadow-casting spotlight will prevent those objects from casting shadows as well, but only if the 3DS.SET's SHADOW-EXCLUSION parameter is set to ON.

Matte Object

When the Matte Object option is on, an object's profile is calculated but its faces are not rendered. Instead, the object acts as a cutout to the background color or background bitmap image. This attribute is useful for placing objects in the scene that allow other objects to slip behind and seemingly disappear.

External Process Control

You also can use the Object Attributes dialog box to assign the powerful AXP routines and determine their properties. These processes are selected with the Name option and edited with the Settings option. Figure 5.30 shows the AXP Selector dialog box. You can save settings that you have found work well for your purposes with the Save option; you also can load previously saved settings with the Load option. Note that you must name a process before you can load parameters for it.

> AXP parameters are saved to PRM files that can be assigned any name. Several safeguards exist to ensure that one AXP's settings cannot be loaded into another's.

AXPs are 3D Studio Animated Plug-Ins that generally use simple geometry to define the boundaries of a much more complex process. This simple geometry is used for all modeling and scene set-up, and the complex process is calculated only at rendering time. This can be an animated feature (such as TORNADO.AXP), one that actually changes the geometry (for example, TUBER.AXP and HAND.AXP), or a combination of both. As for all external processes, the possibilities are limited only by the imagination and programming skill of the people who create them.

While the difficulty in finding a process for particular needs has definitely lessened in the last year, you will probably find many uses for processes you already have. Many users get Plug-Ins to do things that their creators never imagined. Other Plug-Ins fill very specific needs and previously impossible animations become almost easy. Some of the newer AXPs include FLAME and VAPOR, which create realistic flame and atmospheric effects using stand-in objects.

> A good example of an AXP is the Yost Groups animated Plug-In SKIN. This Plug-In uses slices of an original mesh (created by the PXP Plug-In SLICE) to determine control points for Bézier Spline or Catmull patch surfaces. At rendering time, SKIN joins the assemblage of slices with a seamless mesh. This provides you with a perfectly smooth model without joints, and enables you to animate the slices at will without worrying about awkward connections.

Selection Manipulation

The two real keys to being productive with 3D Studio are learning all of the possible transformations and keeping them at your fingertips, and mastering all the ways of creating selection sets so that you can quickly perform those transformations.

So far, each version of 3D Studio has introduced new methods for selecting. Release 3 was no different, but the enhancements are well worth the time spent relearning the terminology. Although elements are still limited to one-by-one selections, the Selection branch provides you the additional options of selecting objects with Quad (the traditional, rectangular method), Fence (an irregular, closed polygon), or Circle. For each of these selection methods, you also might choose Window mode (the entire item must be within the boundary) or Crossing mode (any vertex within the boundary selects the entire item).

3D Studio no longer has direct deselect options. To deselect previously selected geometry, hold down [Alt] in combination with any selection method. This is a big speed enhancer because you don't have to jump back and forth between the menu items.

Combining Selection Options

It is important to become familiar with all of your selection options and use them interchangeably for whatever best fits your purposes. Additional object selection options include the following:

✔ By Name is the most common and has become much easier thanks to wild-card tagging. Objects that need to be edited together or organized for display purposes should be given names that can be easily tagged. Remember the keyboard shortcut [Ctrl]+[N] to access the Select/Object/By Name dialog box.

✔ By Color is the newest option and works well as long as you have assigned useful color groupings. Assigning colors to objects not only makes them display clearer, but in effect creates a permanent selection set that doesn't alter any other properties. With 64 colors at hand, you could organize up to 64 object-based selection sets.

✔ Hide Object and Hide Element isolate the objects that need manipulation. By hiding objects that belong to an existing selection set, you can segregate those that you do not want to affect without deselecting them.

✔ Freeze Object isolates and restores objects from selections. This is a subtle method for building more complex selections.

✔ Invert is best used in conjunction with other selection methods. To select objects that are not assigned the material GOLD, for example, choose Material/Show GOLD and then choose Invert.

✔ The keyboard alternates (Alt)+(A), to select all objects, and (Alt)+(N), to select none (deselect all), are quick selection techniques. Or choose Select All or Select None from the Select branch.

✔ Holding (Ctrl) while touching elements and objects when using Modify commands is a helpful shortcut to select or deselect.

✔ Pressing (Alt)+(W) puts you into a Quad selection mode when using Modify commands as well (the current Selection branch setting determines whether the Quad is in Crossing or Window mode).

✔ The **H**it option (activated with the (H) key) is useful to select a single object by name, regardless of which command branch you're currently in.

Although **H**it is an available option for Modify commands, you probably will find it less than useful because it requires you to select the object's name rather than its location, and thus does not give you a base reference point. For Modify commands, the **H**it option is best used to help you build selections with Selection branch commands.

Objects and elements that are selected twice by single selection or by name become deselected, regardless of the Region Toggle setting. This can prove very helpful; you can select an entire object and deselect one of its elements by selecting that element. Always remember that you can use the (Spacebar) to toggle the use of selection sets.

3D Studio currently supports three selection sets: A, B, and C. Each set is independent, and you can save various selection sets by switching among the three sets. Items selected are kept in the selection set until they are deselected—regardless of whether the item is displayed. This can lead to surprises as a new selection set is built, and some previously selected items are unhidden and become part of the current selection set.

Freezing Geometry

The Display/Freeze option enables you to specify objects that are not to be edited, yet are displayed for reference. This is useful when objects overlap each other in complex arrangements, and you need to modify some objects based upon the placement of the others.

For AutoCAD users, the Freeze option is equivalent to a Locked Layer, except that the object's color is grayed-out when frozen in 3D Studio.

Although the Freeze option is intended to isolate objects from modification, it is valuable when used to build complex selection sets. You can use Freeze to exclude an object from an overlapping set of selections, and then unfreeze it for the last part of the selection or when the modify command is completed.

Selection Limitations of Elements

Elements can be looked upon as being solitary by nature—they can be selected only one by one, never in multiples, and can be modified only one at a time when you use the Modify/Element command branch. So, although a selection might contain several elements, you can modify only one at any given time. If you need to manipulate multiple elements, build your selection and consider using the Modify/Face branch instead. You also might consider detaching the elements to a new object with Create/Face/Detach if you plan on manipulating the group of elements often.

Understanding Edit Commands for Objects and Elements

The Modify branch tends to be your primary workplace within the 3D Editor. All of the commands used to manipulate existing meshes or create them with cloning are under the Modify branch.

Several operating procedures are typical to the Modify branch, including the following:

✔ You must select all of a command's displacement points within the same viewport.

✔ You can use multiple viewports when building a selection set, but after the command has been initiated, you are constrained to a single viewport.

✔ You must work in a viewport that defines a plane; you cannot be in a perspective viewport.

✔ The viewport you choose to work in defines the plane in which the command's modifications are made.

✔ Many commands base their effects on whether the selection's global or local axis is being used. The construction planes of the Create branch have no effect.

✔ All Modify commands specify their effects by dragging. Unfortunately, keyboard entry is not supported for Modify commands.

✔ Distance and Angle Snap are your primary tools for accuracy. It is best to use drawing aids ($\boxed{\text{Ctrl}}$+$\boxed{\text{A}}$) to change these values to suit your needs often.

In many of the following command discussions, elements and objects are referred to collectively as selections. This is to reinforce the point that all Modify/Object commands can work on selections and are not limited to single objects. When you modify elements, the term *selection* refers to a single element, because elements may never be modified as selections per se.

Cloning With Modify Commands

Cloning is a powerful concept to remember when using any Modify command within 3D Studio. Holding down ⟨⇧Shift⟩ when performing any command will create a copy of the selection being modified. This creates a new object, which the program will prompt you to name. If you're modifying a selection of multiple objects or pieces from them, you also have the option of copying them to a single or multiple object. Cloning with the Move command copies the items to the location(s) you specify.

If you are cloning a selection set, you can continue to clone as long as you continue to hold ⟨⇧Shift⟩ and pick points for the command.

Move

The Modify/Move option is about as straightforward a command as anyone would expect. It moves the selection by a displacement defined by two pick points. ⟨⇧Shift⟩+Move clones a selection identical to one created with Create/Copy. It is a good command for you to experiment with to become completely familiar with the effects you are creating in three dimensions.

Each nonperspective viewport defines a two-dimensional plane in which you work. The third dimension is determined by the item's current position. You can always constrain yourself to one-dimensional movement by cycling through the Vertical, Horizontal, and Free-move options accessed with ⟨Tab ⇄⟩.

Remember that the User view defines a plane parallel to your viewing angle, and items will move across it accordingly. This is best understood by setting up concurrent Top, Front, and Side viewports to see the impact your User view modifications have. This also is a good time to become comfortable with using the ⟨Spacebar⟩ to turn on and off the use of selection sets.

The following exercise creates a series of cubes to keep track of three-dimensional displacement when you use the Move command.

Modifications in Three Dimensions

Create a viewport arrangement containing Top, Right, Front, *and* User *views*	
Choose Create/Box *and create a box in the* Top *viewport while holding* Ctrl	Creates a box with three equal sides—in other words, a cube
Select the cube using any method *Press the* Spacebar	Makes the selection active and activates the Select button
Create a series of five cubes by using Array/Move *in the* Top *viewport; use* Tab *to control the direction*	

The space between the cubes is determined by the distance moved between them.

Choose Array/Move *and move the selected cube vertically a distance twice as far from the first array*	Creates 4 cubes that complete an L pattern of nine cubes
Switch to the Right *viewport, then choose* Array/Move *to move the cube up vertically an even greater distance than before*	Creates 4 cubes that complete a "tripod" of cubes similar to the User view icon, as shown in figure 5.31
Right-click on the Zoom Extent *icon*	Zooms out in all viewports

By using the selection set of the original cube, you do not need to select it for the last array. This would have been difficult without a selection set because there are five cubes in the same place for the Right viewport.

Enter the Top *viewport, choose* Modify/Move, *and move the cube to various positions*	Moves the cube along the Top viewport's plane

In the Right and Front viewports, the cube stays in the same plane as the lower row of cubes. As you move the cube in the Top viewport, you are defining only two components of the three-dimensional point. The third is always constant to the plane of the viewport. Notice also that the axes of the active Orthogonal viewport are always shown in the status line.

Enter the Right *viewport and continue to move the cube*	The cube moves in a vertical line in the Right viewport and a horizontal line in the Top viewport
Enter the Front *viewport and move the cube*	The cube moves in a vertical line relative to the Front and Top viewports

This reinforces that you always work in a two-dimensional mode relative to your current viewport.

Enter the User view and move the cube	The cube is displaced in all three of the other viewports, as well as the User view

The User view defines its own plane, which might not align with Orthogonal viewports. You might find it difficult to see that the cube is moving in respect to a plane without a reference.

Choose Display/User/Choose *and select the* User *view for display*	The User view's title changes color to show that it is chosen
Choose User/Show	Displays the User view's construction plane in the other viewports
Move the cube; use Tab⁓ *to constrain movement vertically or horizontally*	The cube stays parallel to the user view icon as it moves (see fig 5.32)

The distance offsets chosen in the User view fall within the same plane of the User view.

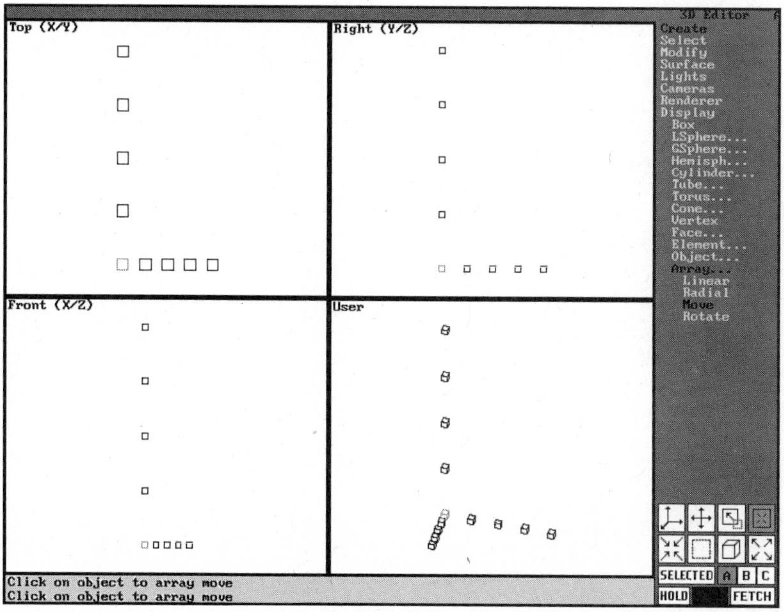

Figure 5.31
A tripod of cubes defining the three axes.

II

Basic Modeling

Figure 5.32
The User views construction plane, and the User view itself.

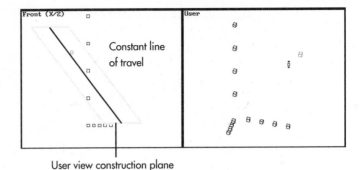

User view construction plane

Using the Rotate Command

The Modify/Rotate command bases its results on the location of the currently used axis, whether it is the defined global axis or the selection's local axis. Figure 5.33 shows the different results depending on the axis chosen. Remember that pressing ⓧ is a quick method to make the local axis active or inactive.

Figure 5.33
Examples of the Rotate command using the local and global axes.

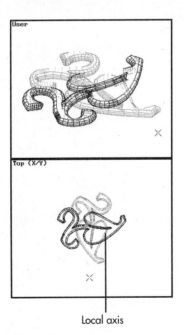

Local axis

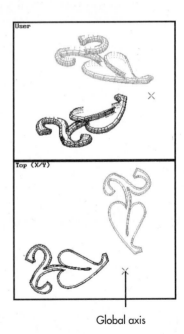

Global axis

Angle Snap (accessed quickly by pressing Ⓐ) can be very effective when you use Rotate. You can set the incremental angle value by accessing the Drawing Aids dialog box (accessed with Ctrl+Ⓐ). The value, like all drawing aid settings, is stored in the 3DS.PRJ or the current project file.

The default for the Angle Snap setting is usually 10 degrees, but you might find that 5 degrees or 15 degrees is more useful because it enables you to snap to 45 degree increments.

Another good reference technique for this command is to locate the global axis at a geometric point, especially a vertex or object/element base point. When you clone with ⇧Shift+Rotate, you can create "pinwheels" or "fans" of objects that might be attached as one object.

Although the 3D Editor limits your rotation accuracy to 0.25 degree, you can rotate objects very accurately by adjusting their Frame 0 rotation key in the Keyframer with Key Info.

Scale

The 2D Modify/Scale and 3D Modify/Scale options use similar methods, but differ greatly in results. As with Rotate, Scale depends on the current axis location, as this is the point about which the selection is scaled.

Scale's effect is expressed in percentages and so does not recognize definable snap increments. Because keyboard input is unavailable for Scale, you must use the mouse to drag the selection to the desired ratio, keeping an observant eye on the resulting percentages in the coordinate display. You can define percentages only in increments of 0.25 percent (for example, 10.25 percent, 10.50 percent, 10.75 percent).

If you need a smaller percentage increment than 0.25 percent, you'll need to calculate the result, possibly with a calculator, and perform the Scale twice (for example, to get a 99.99 percent scale you would scale up by 101.00 percent and then down by 99.00 percent: $1.01 \times 0.99 = .9999$).

There is a maximum scale of 400 percent and a minimum of 1 percent. If a greater or smaller scale is needed, you must perform the Scale multiple times. If you need to arrive at a specific scale that is beyond either limit, you should calculate the scale steps beforehand. For example:

600 percent = 400 percent × 150 percent

and

0.25 percent = 1 percent × 25 percent

Tip

An alternative method for making very accurate, large, or minute scale adjustments for objects is to adjust their Frame 0 scale key in the Keyframer with Key Info. This provides you with eight decimal places of accuracy for the scale in each axis.

Scale is often useful if you use it with the local axis (accessed with the $\boxed{X}$ key) because it determines the three-dimensional centroid of the selection. With the local axis activated, the selection appears to inflate and deflate with Scale. When you are using the global axis, Scale will appear to "move" the selection toward the axis when scaling up, and away from the axis when scaling down.

When you clone with $\boxed{\text{Shift}}$+Scale about the local axis, the result is similar to a volumetric offset. You can use this to create new "insides" or "outsides" for a selection. If you are not using the local axis, you will notice that the overall position of your cloned geometry appears to "move" in a linear fashion toward or away from the global axis as you drag the scale up or down.

The 3D Scale command scales the geometry proportionally up or down about all three axes. The result of a 3D Scale is thus identical in any valid viewport you choose. Figure 5.34 shows this universal scaling as performed in relation to the global axis.

Figure 5.34
The 3D Scale command using the global axis.

Global axis ———

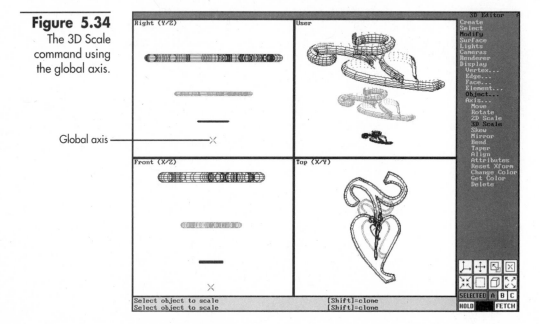

With 2D Scale, the geometry is scaled proportionally only in the axes that are coplanar to your current viewport—the remaining axis' proportion remains constant. The effects of 2D Scale when performed on geometry in different viewports are shown in figure 5.35. It is thus very important to pay careful attention in which viewport you are performing this operation. Using 2D Scale in a User viewport has the effect of scaling the selection according to the User plane, distorting it in all three of the orthogonal construction planes (unless the User view is parallel to the global axes, of course). You can create some very tricky modeling changes by doing this if you carefully prepare the User view. In most cases, you'll probably want to work with 2D Scale in an Orthogonal viewport.

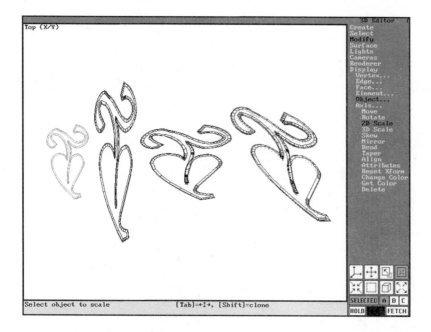

Figure 5.35
The results of a free-move 2D Scale command when performed in the Front, Right, and User viewports.

Skew

Skew affects a selection's geometry by "stretching" or "sliding" the locations of the mesh's vertices along one axis. The direction of the skew is controlled with Tab↕ and is dependent on the axis in use. If you use the local axis, the selection is skewed equally about its middle, pulling to the right and to the left or up and down, as shown in figure 5.36.

Figure 5.36
The effects of the
Skew command
using the objects'
local axes.

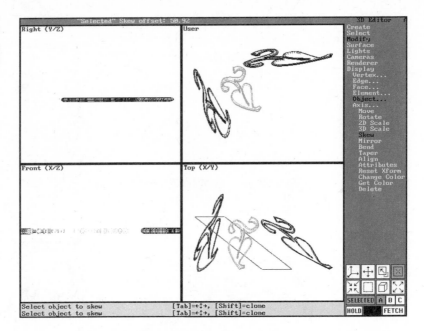

To restrict Skew to flare to only one side, you must use the global axis. You may find it useful to control Skew's influence by placing the global axis at the selection's edge, thus anchoring that one side (see fig. 5.37). Moving the global axis off-center will give more "weight" to that side during the skew.

You can clone objects by using ⇧Shift +Skew to create a series of intersecting "bent" objects, or to use tools for Boolean operations. A series of skewed objects also can be used for "waving" and "tilting" morphing effects.

Mirror

Modify/Mirror creates a mirror image of the selection about a selected point. The direction of the mirror is determined by the viewport you are working in and the directional arrow you've selected. The multidirectional arrow "points" in the direction of the mirror rather than showing the mirror line as in many CAD packages. When the dual-directional Tab arrow is active, the selection is mirrored about a 45-degree line, as shown in figure 5.38.

Remember that because your pick point determines the mirror line, it is the midway point between the extents of the old and new object. If you need an angle that is not orthogonal, say 30 degrees, you must either establish a User view at that angle or mirror the selection and then rotate it.

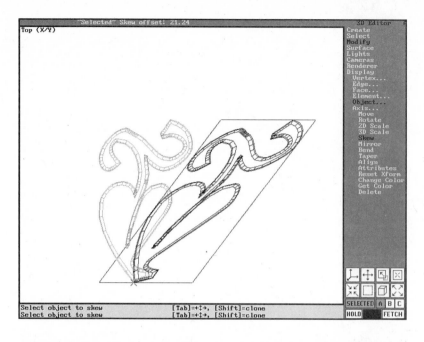

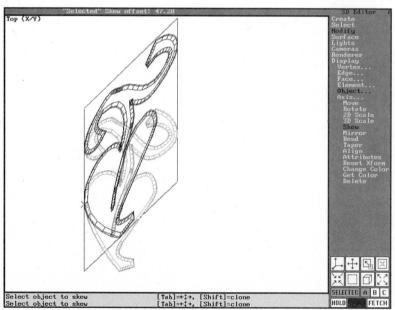

Figure 5.37
The effects of the
Skew command
with the global
axis placed at the
objects extremity.

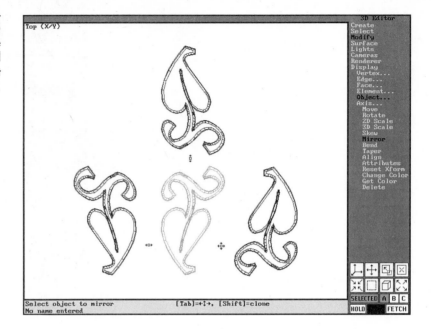

Bend

Modify/Bend rotates the location of the selection's vertices about an angle that has its base at one side of the selection's bounding box. This has the effect of bending the object much like an antenna or flagpole, where one edge is firmly planted and the other can be bent through 180 degrees, all the way to the "ground," as shown in figure 5.39. Using Bend repeatedly can create twisting effects and is often used to clone objects for morphing targets.

Because Bend uses the selection's bounding box for its reference, neither the global nor local axis position have any effect. The direction of the bend is determined by the directional Tab arrow. You might find it useful to think of the arrow as pointing "up" from the bounding box side that is acting as the "ground."

Bending an object more than once can easily distort an object's geometry far past the point of being recalled. This is because Bend uses the bounding box for its calculations. A bent object will have a different bounding box, and a future bend will result in still different geometry, as shown in figure 5.40.

This is important to remember when you create morph targets that are intended to bend smoothly back and forth. To ensure consistent proportions, you should always ⇧Shift+Bend the original object instead of later iterations (unless, of course, the additional distortion is desirable).

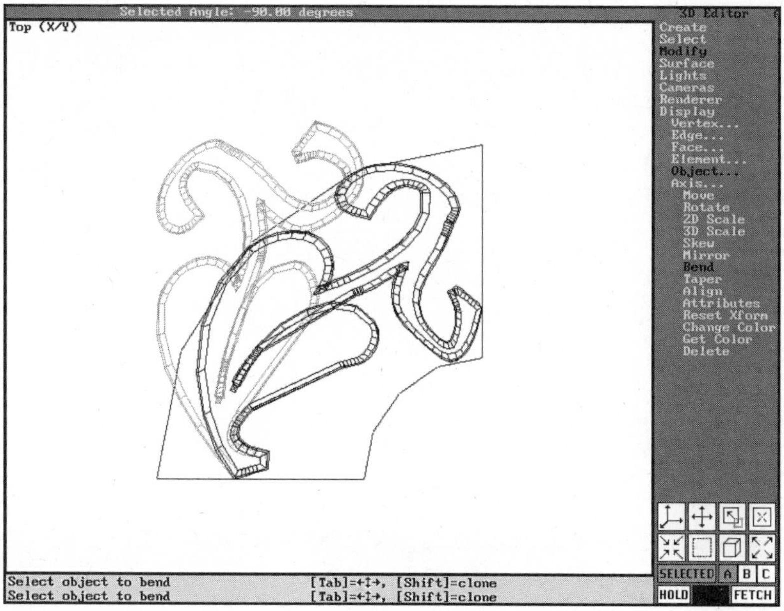

II

Basic Modeling

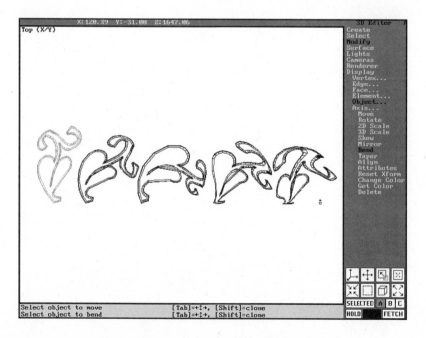

Figure 5.39
An example of the Bend command (in progress).

Figure 5.40
The effect of repeated bends on the same object.

Taper

The Taper command acts something like a cross between Skew and 2D Scale by tapering one side of a selection, thus "skewing" from both directions or "scaling" the side. Taper, like Bend, bases its result on the selection's bounding box, and its effect is not necessarily reversible with a taper in the opposite direction. Taper's effect is controlled by the viewport in which you are working and the directional cursor you choose, as shown in figure 5.41.

Taper affects only the two dimensions of your current viewport's construction plane, while the third stays constant. If you require a taper in three dimensions (as in creating a cone), you must use Taper in two perpendicular viewports, with the same percentage. Taper's deformation is expressed as a percentage and is limited to a whole value from 1—400 percent, manipulating this percentage limitation.

As with the Skew command, you will use Taper mostly with Orthogonal viewports. Using Taper predictably within a User view can be very useful, but will take careful preparation of the view.

Figure 5.41
Examples of the
Taper command.

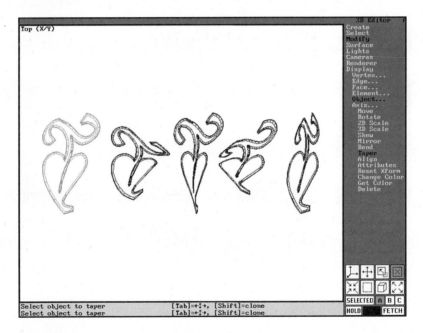

Align

The Modify/Align command is a tool to move and rotate a single object or element into alignment with the plane of the active viewport, based upon the selection of a single face. This does not alter the item's geometry whatsoever—only its orientation to the world. 3D Studio prompts you whether to align the item as Facing Toward or Facing Away, based on the selected face's normal.

Although Align's transformation is quite accurate, the resulting position can be a little unpredictable. Align tries to base the item's new location on that of the selected face, but might center it in the viewport instead, especially if the active viewport is a User view. Just be prepared to move the item into its final position after it is aligned.

If you need to align the side of one object with the odd angle of another, first align a User view to the face of the base object and then align the desired object to that view.

If you need to align a selection and maintain the positions of the items in respect to one another, consider making a single object of that selection before performing the alignment, and detach the selection again if needed. This can be done very easily with Create/Face/Detach.

You can more easily separate the new Boolean object into its originals if you assign each a unique material or arbitrary smoothing group before the operation. Surface/Material/Show or Surface/Smoothing/Show can be used to subsequently isolate those faces for detachment.

Delete

Using Modify/Delete effectively is a matter of working carefully. If you are deleting a selection, be sure that you haven't unhidden a previously selected item recently and thus made it part of the current selection. When deleting, keep in mind that there is no Undo in the 3D Editor, and that it always pays to save the file (using Ctrl+S) and hold it (using Ctrl+H) often.

Creating Boolean Objects

The 3D Editor's Create/Boolean function is a powerful modeling tool well worth mastering. Of all the 3D Editor's tools, this one comes closest to simulating traditional sculpting and modeling techniques. With it, you can combine objects. Like in modeling (with Union), use one object to carve out another as in sculpting (with Subtraction), or create what would have been sculpted out (with Intersection). These three functions are shown in figure 5.42.

The Boolean engine introduced with Release 3 is far superior to that of Release 2's, resulting in a minimum of faces. So if you are an earlier user that has bad Boolean memories, relax and relearn this useful capability.

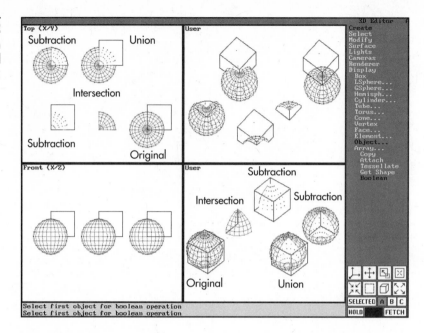

Figure 5.42
Boolean operation options and their results.

The object resulting from a Boolean operation maintains the material assigned to the faces of the original objects. This enables you to select the remnants of the two original objects with Surface/Material/Show.

Using Boolean's Weld option will remove all mapping coordinates from both objects. If you do not use the Weld option, the original mapping coordinates are somewhat maintained (any faces that have been changed by the operation now have distorted mapping).

If you plan to restore the object's original mapping information, you should make a clone of each object before performing the Boolean operation and do not choose Weld option; then acquire and apply it to the new elements. This procedure, however, will not work for objects having lofted mapping coordinates.

In practice, the Boolean command is used more like a Modify command than its Create branch location might suggest. After all, a new object is not really being created, an existing one is being modified.

Cautions and Adjustments for Boolean operations

The Hold button on the Boolean operation dialog box is there for a very good reason—the results can be surprising and might be unwanted. It's always good practice to hold before performing a Boolean operation.

Another good practice is to create clones of objects to be used in Boolean operations. Besides providing a backup of the deleted objects, you also retain any mapping information that might exist. This can then be assigned to the respective portions of the new object.

Consider the following rules of thumb in conducting successful Boolean operations:

✔ It is critical to ensure that the normals of the object are correctly faced. This is a strong reason to take the time to keep face normals correctly turned because Boolean operations are based on normal orientation.

✔ If you are performing multiple Boolean operations on the same object, you must examine the normals of the newly created object each time. If they prove incorrect, you'll need to select the object, apply the Modify/Vertex/Weld command to the selection, and finish with Surface/Normals/Unify Object before trying another operation.

✔ Always try to keep the intersection of the objects one geometric feature "deep," or rather, do not try to extend the walls of one object past more than one wall of the other object.

✔ If the Boolean operation is not successful, see whether ignoring the last face cleanup portion of the operation helps. This is accomplished by holding down [Alt] until the faces are created. This will more than likely result in a higher face count, but might solve a troublesome operation.

✔ If the operation is not successful and you do not want more faces, realign one of the objects slightly and try again.

✔ If realigning does not work or is not desired, add additional faces to the objects by tessellating faces (Create/Face/Tessellate), dividing edges (Modify/Edge/Divide), or possibly turning edges (Modify/Edge/Turn).

Do not let this checklist scare you into avoiding Boolean operations. They work on the first try most of the time, especially if you adhere to the first three steps.

The Boolean calculations of Release 3 and 4 can correctly handle much more variation between the selected objects than did Release 2. It normally is not necessary to increase the complexity of simple objects before performing a Boolean operation.

Carving with Boolean Subtraction

The order in which you select objects for a Boolean operation is important only when you're performing a subtraction. In this case, the second object selected is the geometry that is subtracted from the first. You can think of this as "taking a bite from," "sculpting," "carving," "removing from," "drilling," "punching," or whatever analogy makes the most sense to you.

Successful sculpting with Boolean subtractions comes down to carefully studying the form you are using to subtract with. The second object can be thought of as a "chisel" or "router bit" that creates a particular "groove" in the first object. The following exercise uses the Boolean command to create a quick, open box.

You might find it useful to maintain a selection of "carving tools" as shapes that you can Loft for Boolean subtractions. More complex Boolean forms can be saved as meshes and merged when needed.

Creating an Open Cube with a Boolean Subtraction

Create a cube using Ctrl +Create/Box	Creates a box with three equal sides
Press X	Activates the local axis (the local axis icon button is highlighted)
Use Shift +2D Scale *to clone a cube at 80 percent of the original*	Creates the inside wall of the cube

Switch to a perpendicular viewport and move the inside cube upward so that it intersects the top plane of the first cube (make sure your Tab arrow is one-directional).

Choose Boolean/Subtract, *select the outer cube first, and then the inner cube*	Subtracts the inner cube from the outer cube, as shown in figure 5.43

The resulting object is an open cube with capped walls, even thicknesses, and a minimum of faces.

There are times when selecting an object created by a Boolean operation and welding its vertices (with Modify/Vertex/Weld) will further refine the mesh and reduce the face and vertex count.

Boolean/Subtract also is a good method for creating chamfers and fillets on existing objects. The following exercise uses the open cube you created in the previous exercise.

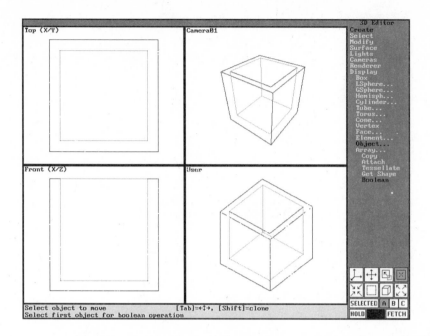

Figure 5.43
Creating an open cube with Boolean/Subtract.

Chamfering with Boolean Subtraction

Create a box in a side viewport that is at least as long as the cube	Creates a box to be used as the chamfering tool
Rotate the box 45 degrees	Sets the box to create an even, outside chamfer
Move the box to one of the cube's top corners; the box should cut through the outside wall, but not the inside wall (see fig. 5.44)	

The intent is to create an even chamfer on all four sides of the cube. It would be difficult and time-consuming to create four different chamfering boxes and position them at the same angle to the sides, so using the cloning function is a time server, while being more accurate.

Choose Modify/Axis/Align/Object, *select the cube in the* Top *viewport, and choose the* Center *option*	Centers the global axis on the cube
Press X *to turn off the local axis*	Verify this with the local axis icon
Enter the Top *viewport and press* S *to turn on Angle Snap*	Displays an S in the display's upper-right corner

continues

continued

Choose ⌗Shift+Rotate; *rotate the box 90 degrees about the cube to clone the next chamfering box*	Forms a new box at the same angle to the cube's side as the first
Select both boxes and activate the selection with the Spacebar	

You will not need to leave the Rotate command if you select with Ctrl.

Choose ⌗Shift+Rotate *and rotate the selection 180 degrees*	Creates the remaining two chamfer boxes, as shown in figure 5.45

All four of the cube's sides now have chamfering boxes at equal distances and angles, and are in position to create the outside chamfer.

Choose Boolean/Subtract, *select the cube, and then select a chamfer box (you may want to Hold at this point)*	A 45-degree chamfer is formed on one of the cube's sides
Repeat the Boolean subtraction three more times with the remaining chamfer boxes	A chamfer is made with each operation until the cube has four chamfered sides, as shown in figure 5.46

Figure 5.44

Positioning for the first chamfering box.

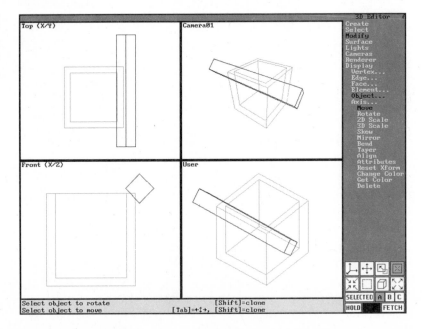

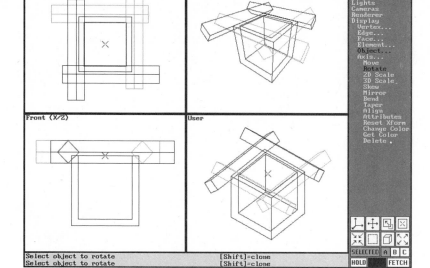

Figure 5.45
Final positions for the chamfering boxes.

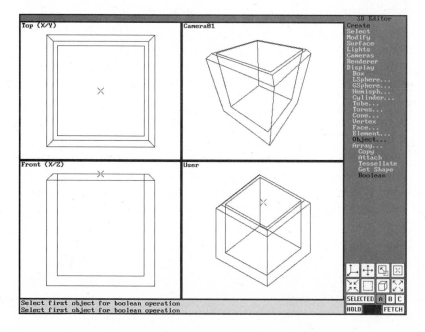

Figure 5.46
The completed chamfered cube.

To create a radiused fillet instead of a chamfer, simply use an object that contains an inside curve and duplicate the preceding exercise. The shape shown in figure 5.47 is especially useful as a filleting tool.

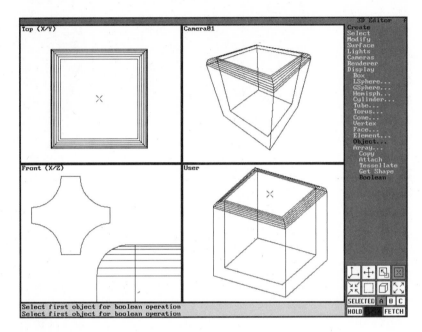

Figure 5.47
Creating fillets with Boolean/Subtract operations.

Modeling with Boolean Union

The Boolean/Union command combines the two selected objects and removes any overlapping geometry. Before performing a Boolean union, you should consider carefully whether it is actually needed. Ask yourself whether the underlying intersection will be able to be seen. If it can, the Boolean option is a good choice. If it cannot, consider allowing the objects to intersect naturally. If the combined object needs to share smoothing groups, act upon a reflection the same way, or share an SXP or AXP process, you will need to use Boolean/Union to the objects and use the weld option, regardless of the underside/inside's visibility.

A Boolean union is most commonly used with "solid" objects—that is, objects that do not have a wall thickness, or rather an inside and an outside. The reason for this is that union replaces only the areas that overlap. Joining objects with walls has very little effect because all of the Boolean work is hidden within the wall thicknesses. The intersecting tubes in figure 5.48 look very similar before and after a Boolean union.

You also can use a Boolean union to create two elements that could be separated for other uses with Create/Element/Detach. Note that you should not use the Weld option when detaching is the goal. The following exercise shows how the Boolean command can easily accomplish what would be difficult to model directly.

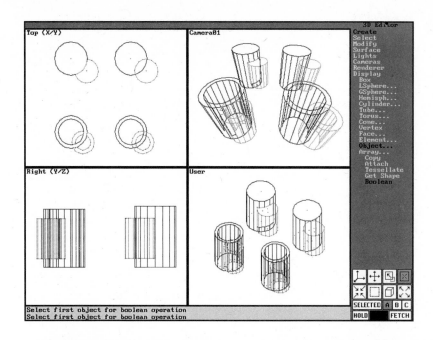

Figure 5.48
Examples of
Boolean union
operations.

Creating Two Objects with a Boolean Union

Create two overlapping GSpheres
of slightly different sizes

Choose the Boolean *command and*
select the spheres

In the Boolean *dialog box, choose* Union—*do not weld*	The union of the two spheres is formed by deleting the overlapping geometry
Move one of the sphere elements to the side and detach it, if you like	Equal open circles are cut into the sides of the spheres

When you use a Boolean union operation to edit objects, no mesh is formed where the geometry once overlapped. As the resulting elements are pushed apart, there is a hole in the mesh where the two objects were joined.

Scooping New Objects with Boolean Intersection

The Boolean/Intersection command creates the object that would have otherwise been "carved out" with a Boolean subtraction. This is sometimes difficult to visualize, but can create geometry that would have otherwise been very difficult to model.

The following exercise chamfers the six sides of a sphere in one Boolean/Intersection operation. This exercise uses an LSphere instead of a GSphere because its geometry relates much better to the eventual "sliced" sides.

Creating a Chamfered Sphere

Press Ctrl+A *and set the Snap increment to 10 units*	Accesses the Drawing Aids dialog box
Set the Snap increment to 10	
Press S	Activates Snap
Choose Create/Box *and create a 200-unit cube by holding* Ctrl *while dragging*	
Create a 32-sided L sphere, centered in the cube, with a 120 degree radius	
Switch to a perpendicular viewport, and move the sphere up 100 units by selecting one of its sides	Centers the sphere in the cube, as shown in figure 5.49

It is often convenient to recall the part of the geometry left over from one of the original objects. The easiest way to do this is to use Material/Show to select the material originally assigned.

Assign any material to the cube	Enables you to select the cube from the finished object
Choose Create/Object/Boolean *and select the cube and sphere*	
Perform a Hold, then select Intersection *from the* Boolean Operation *dialog box*	

Draws six circles in the highlight color on the sphere and deletes those areas.

Choose Surface/Materials/Show *to select the material you assigned the original cube*	Highlights the new, flat sides of the object, as shown in figure 5.50

One of the primary uses for a Boolean intersection is to retrieve what was taken out in a Boolean subtraction. It is often necessary to have the piece that "fell on the floor" to use in an animation. You might want to show the piece that is punched out from a metal die, for example. To do this, copy the original objects and perform two Boolean operations, thus creating the "cut" object and what was "cut out."

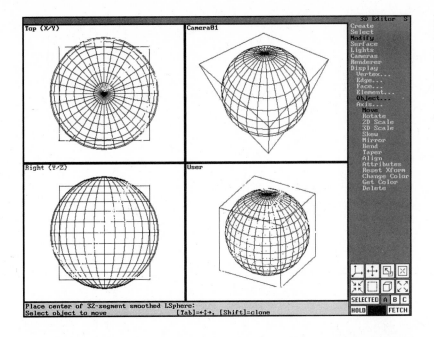

Figure 5.49
The sphere is centered in the cube to ensure six equal partitions with the Boolean operation.

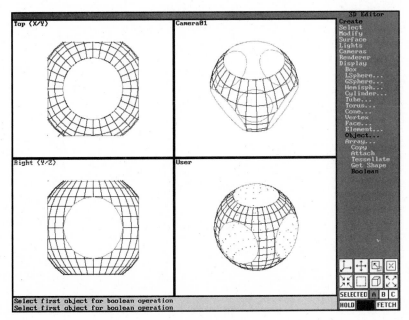

Figure 5.50
The chamfered sphere following a Boolean intersection, showing the selected sides of the original intersecting cubes.

The following exercise produces a series of objects that can be used together to animate the effects of a square rod punching through a cylinder and pushing that section of the cylinder out onto the floor.

Using Two Boolean Operations

Create a 60-sided cylinder in the Top *viewport and name it* Can01

The large side count is to ensure a definite curved edge on the resulting pieces.

Switch to a perpendicular viewport, create a long squashed box that is off-center of the cylinder, and name it Rod01

Move the box so it intersects the cylinder (see fig. 5.51)

Now that you have created the basic elements, create enough copies of the originals to create all the desired pieces.

Press `Alt`+`A` *(Select All)*	Selects both Can01 and Rod01
Choose Object/Move, *ensure that Snap is on and the selection is active, hold* `⇧Shift`, *and select the same point twice*	Displays a dialog box, asking whether you want to copy to single or multiple objects
Choose Multiple Objects *and accept the default names (*Rod02 *and* Can02)	Creates a clone of each object
Choose Hide/Objects *and click in the viewport*	Hides the originally selected objects
Choose the Boolean *command, select* Rod02, *and then select* Can02	

Note that the object you select first will have the final object name.

Choose Intersection *from the Boolean dialog box*	Creates the intersecting wedge bar with curved ends named Rod02
Move Rod02 *in a straight line away from the operation and Unhide All*	The new piece is to fly out the side in the animation
Move Rod01 *from the cylinder in the opposite direction while holding* `⇧Shift`	Makes a clone of Rod01 that you can simply name Rod
Choose the Boolean *command; select* Can01 *and then* Rod01	Rod01 carves a hole from Can01; the three objects are ready to be animated, as shown in figure 5.52

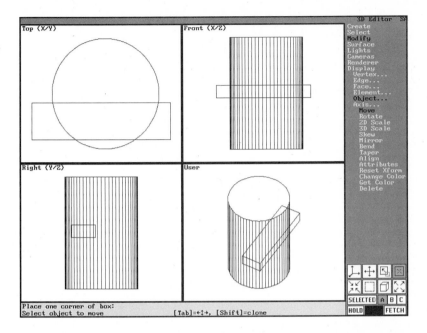

Figure 5.51
Object positions for future Boolean operations.

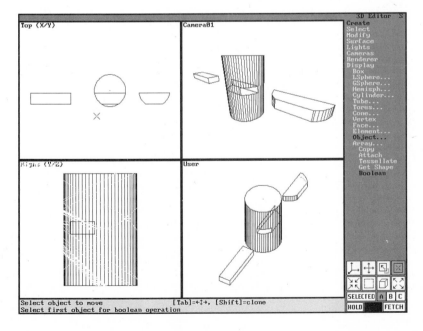

Figure 5.52
The resulting objects in place and ready to be animated in the Keyframer.

II

Basic Modeling

Summary

This chapter represents only the basic creation and manipulation procedures and techniques available within the 3D Editor. Chapter 10, "Creating and Editing Faces and Vertices in the 3D Editor," investigates the more detailed techniques of vertex and face manipulation. The command essentials you have learned in this chapter will be built upon and expanded when manipulating the true building blocks of meshes—faces and vertices.

After you form your basic meshes, you will soon need to give them color, texture, illuminate them with appropriate light, and view them in perspective. These form the critical material, lighting, and camera portions of the modeling process, and are introduced in the next two chapters.

Chapter Snapshot

In this chapter, you will learn about one of 3D Studio's most influential modules for single images. The Materials Editor will help you create realistic images and illusions. To master the Materials Editor, you'll need to become familiar with the following:

✔ Understanding procedures within the Materials Editor

✔ Understanding material color components, properties, and shading modes

✔ Understanding basic map types and how bitmaps are interpreted by them

✔ Maximizing the use of mapping parameters

✔ Mapping coordinate types, their applications, and techniques for application and correction

✔ Using Animator Pro for creating and manipulating bitmaps

Besides being able to create objects with many useful materials, you'll find it a simple task with Release 4's expanded display and high color support. You can to view up to seven material samples at the same time, eliminating the aggravating task of jumping from one window to another.

CHAPTER

Introduction to the Materials Editor

The Materials Editor is arguably the most influential of 3D Studio's modules for single images. It is in the Materials Editor that materials are created and illusions perfected to form the essential ingredients of photo-realistic images. The Materials Editor enables you to explore and experiment. Think of it as an artist's palette, theater scene shop, and alchemist's lab all rolled into one.

3D Studio Release 3 improved the Materials Editor's environment considerably by expanding it to a 640 × 480 display and supporting high color. All seven of the sample windows can be shown at the same time if you configure the Materials Editor for a 16- or 24-bit color display. This also means you don't have to "jump" back and forth between samples to view differences between your adjustments or compare materials side by side. Configuring the display for a resolution higher than 640 × 480 increases the resolution of the sample windows, but at the expense of speed. The text area itself is fixed at 640 × 480 and will be centered at higher display resolutions. For most purposes, 640 × 480 24-bit color is the optimum display choice.

Although the Materials Editor has many capabilities, it interacts heavily with the 3D Editor. Materials are created and perfected in the Materials Editor, but are assigned, updated, and positioned by using the 3D Editor. As you create and assign materials, you jump back and forth between these modules extensively. As always, the keyboard alternatives of F3 (for the 3D Editor) and F5 (for the Materials Editor) are great time-savers.

Understanding Basic and Simple Materials

The Materials Editor has always been capable of creating believable and complex combinations of color and mapping. 3D Studio Release 3 brought a much higher level of sophistication and the capability to create extensive permutations with comprehensive, tricky, and stunning mapping effect combinations.

So what is a "simple" or "basic" material when simple surfaces can be difficult to simulate while complex surfaces quite easy? The following classifications of material characteristics are used for discussion in this book:

- ✔ **Simple Material.** Materials that have only the base color and shininess properties defined. Simple materials are the fastest to render and require no additional memory.

- ✔ **Basic Material.** Materials that have additional property determinations, but no mapping information. Basic materials can be slower to render than simple materials, but require no additional memory.

- ✔ **Basic Mapped Material.** Materials that have one or more Release 2 maps applied to them, and access one or more bitmaps, including Texture, Opacity, Reflection, and bump maps. Most mapped materials require mapping coordinates, and all mapped materials require additional memory to render.

- ✔ **Fully Mapped Material.** Materials that incorporate the family of map types and masks first available with Release 3. These do not require more memory than basic mapped material—only more forethought and sophistication. See Chapter 12, "Materials and Mapping," for extensive discussion of fully mapped materials.

- ✔ **Complex Material.** Materials that require independent calculations at rendering time or cubic maps. Complex materials include automatic, flat mirror, and cubic reflections, box mapping, and all SXP procedural materials. These materials can require more memory and time to render and are discussed in Chapter 12.

Any discussion of the appearance and qualities of materials nearly always includes speed of rendering and memory requirements—the material's *cost*. A cheap material renders quickly and requires little or no additional memory, whereas an expensive material renders slowly and requires a substantial amount of memory. The qualities of materials in terms of memory and speed cost have the following ascending order:

Simple materials

2-sided materials

Transparent materials

Mapped materials (other than bump and automatic reflection)

Bump-mapped materials

Reflection as a flat mirror

Reflection as a cubic mirror

In addition, the cost of mapped materials depends entirely on the size and number of different bitmaps used.

Every modeler's goal is to create the material that delivers the most convincing illusion that the object and scene need for the given output. The second consideration is rendering cost. A material that looks great, but requires 6 MB of RAM, might not be appropriate. You need to strike a balance between the appearance and cost. This chapter looks carefully at how to do this.

Materials Editor Overview

The Materials Editor is comprehensive and can feel overwhelming. The process, however, is basic, as each material is based on the same principles with more complex materials simply building on previous decisions. The Materials Editor is organized into a few basic areas, as shown in figure 6.1. You can think of each material as a recipe that has four types of ingredients, as follows:

✔ *Shading mode* to which the material is limited

✔ *Base color* of the object

✔ *Properties* of the material, such as shininess and transparency

✔ *Mapping* that you can apply to the material

The corresponding areas of the Materials Editor have the tools to enable you to make certain adjustments to the material's appearance. The shading mode area has two attribute buttons; the base color has sample color swatches and RGB and HLS color sliders; the properties have property sliders, property buttons, and a highlight curve; mapping has amount sliders, map file slots, and parameter (settings) buttons.

Figure 6.1
The Materials
Editor display
components.

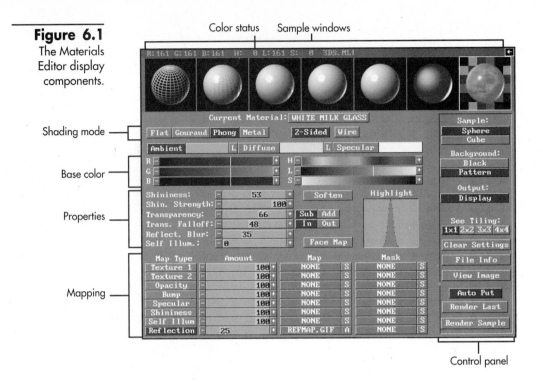

Color status   Sample windows

Shading mode

Base color

Properties

Mapping

Control panel

Setup Options

The Materials Editor has several options that affect the display of its material samples. You can control these options by using buttons on the Control Panel and toggles in the Options pulldown menu. When options are changed, they affect the display of future rendering samples, leaving previous samples unchanged.

You can display the sample as a sphere or a cube. Spheres show the full effects of highlight and shade, and they are your best default unless you manipulate face maps.

Starting with Release 3, 3D Studio includes a display option called *Backlight* that shines a glancing light at the sample's rear to create an outlining crescent. This outlining crescent provides a stronger insight into the effects of Specular settings, and is also a good default setting.

You can permanently set the Materials Editor's Backlight option to ON by changing BACKLIGHT-MATERIAL to ON in the 3DS.SET file.

The sample's background can be black or have a colored and checkered pattern. Unless the material is at least partially transparent, it should be black. There also is an anti-alias feature

New Riders Publishing
INSIDE
SERIES

that you can turn on, which makes for better-looking samples, but takes longer and adds no actual insight as to the effects of your material.

3D Studio gives you control of the ambient light color used to render your samples. You can control this in the 3DS.SET file by changing the MEDIT-AMBIENT setting. You can set this value to match your scene's ambient light level when an exact correlation is critical.

Seeing a Material's Effect

Each parameter you change in a material's definition effects its appearance when rendered. The only way to see this effect prior to Release 3 was to click on Render Sample, which of course rendered the sample sphere or cube (see fig. 6.2). You now can use Spacebar or ↵Enter.

Figure 6.2
Rendering options on the Control Panel.

Beginning with Release 3, 3D Studio provided a more sophisticated method of seeing material changes with the Render Last and Auto Put options. These options enable you to isolate a material's effect specific to an object and location in the scene. The next exercise demonstrates this frequently used procedure.

Using Auto Put and Last Render

Load a model in the 3D Editor

Locate an object whose material you want to edit; you can use Acquire *to identify an object's material*

Render the desired scene in a method that best views the object (for speed and clarity)

This should be the most appropriate view with the best lighting. To see a material's effect as applied to an object, use the Render Object option. If you want to see the effect as they pertain to a small portion of the scene, use Render Region. If you want to carefully examine the same area, use Render Blowup on the same area.

continues

continued

Press Alt+R, *and then press* Esc *quickly to begin the rendering (if you are not interested in seeing the results right now)*	The parameters for the Renderer are now "set," and rendering the scene is optional
Press F5	Switches back to the Materials Editor
Press F	Gets the material in question
Edit the material and press T	Puts the edited material to the scene
Click on Render Last	The object is rendered in the scene with the changed material

You can continue to edit the material and see its effects as long as you put it to the scene before the rendering. The Auto Put option makes this procedure even easier.

Click on Auto Put	
Make more changes to the material and click on Render Last *without putting it to the scene first*	Automatically puts material to the scene

AutoPut modifies the materials in a scene in the 3D Editor. Be sure that you have saved the scene before experimenting with materials using AutoPut.

Configuring your rendering display for a smaller resolution, or rendering a smaller portion of the screen or a specific object, considerably speeds the rendering for material checking.

Assigning Materials

After you create or modify a material, you must assign it to a mesh before it can have effect. This can only be done in the 3D Editor, by assigning the material under the Surface/Material branch. Although you can assign materials to faces, elements, or objects, the material information actually is stored at the face level. You might want to think of the object and element assignment options as convenient methods for assigning groups of faces.

Whenever you create faces (or elements or objects) from scratch (not copied, cloned, or subdivided), they are assigned a material named *Default.* The standard Default material is actually a shiny, white Phong material similar to white plastic and is sufficient to understand the mass and shape of the mesh until more detail is required. Under normal circumstances, you cannot change or rename the default material definition.

You can redefine the Default material by putting a material with the magic name ~DEFAULT in the current library.

Assigning Materials to Meshes

Before you can assign a material to a mesh, it must first be the current material. This is done by choosing the material from the current Materials Library (Surface/Material/Choose), acquiring it from a mesh to which it already has been assigned (Surface/Material/Acquire), or putting it to the scene as the current material while in the Materials Editor.

The Put to Current option, accessed by pressing Ⓒ, was new with Release 3. It is a refinement of the original Put to Scene option in that it not only updates the material definition in the scene, but makes it the current material, ready for assignment, and gives you the option of renaming it on the way to the 3D Editor.

After you assign a material in the 3D Editor, you can import its definition to the Materials Editor by using the Get From Scene option, accessed by pressing Ⓕ. As changes are made to a material, they must be put to the scene for them to have an effect in the rendered model. Putting the material to the current library (by pressing Ⓟ) is optional because a mesh in the scene does not require it to accept the updated material updated in the library. All of the Materials Editor functions have corresponding hot keys, as shown in table 6.1, which should be learned to make working within it as fast as possible.

II

Basic Modeling

Table 6.1
Option Shortcut Keys

Option	Key
Put Material to Scene as **C**urrent	C
Get **F**rom Scene	F
Get Material from Library	G
Render **L**ast	L
Load Library	Ctrl+L
Merge Libraries	Ctrl+M
Put Material **T**o Scene	T
Put Material to Library	P
Remove Material from Library	R
Save Library	Ctrl+S
Navigation Keys for Samples	← or [,], and → or [.]
Configure to Add Map Paths	*
Render Sample Window	Spacebar

The relationship the Materials Editor has with the current Materials Library, the library on disk, the 3D Editor, and assigned materials can be somewhat confusing. Figure 6.3 graphically shows the commands and procedures the Materials Editor uses to exchange and store material definitions between the scene and libraries. While reading this chapter and learning material creation procedures, figure 6.3 should be referenced often. While it may seem somewhat complex at first, an understanding of the various relationships is essential—once learned, it becomes second nature.

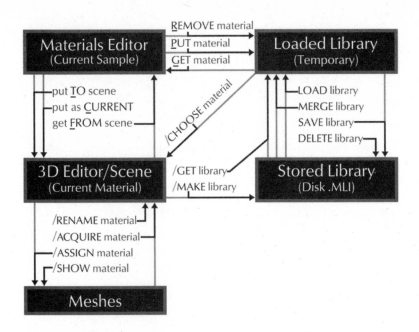

Figure 6.3
The overall Materials Editor relationship.

Using Libraries

Material definitions are stored in Material Library files that you can think of as recipe books for materials (these files have an MLI extension and are stored in the MATLIBS subdirectory). When you start 3D Studio, the 3DS.MLI loads into memory by default.

You can define which library is initially loaded by changing the MATERIAL-LIBRARY parameter in the 3DS.SET file.

The current library becomes a scratch pad of sorts during your material experiments. New materials definitions are saved and existing ones changed in this temporary library using Put Material. You can delete materials with Remove and combine the definitions of different libraries with Merge Library. Feel free to experiment, save, and merge because all these actions only update the temporary MLI. Your changes are not saved to disk unless you specifically do so with Save Library.

Libraries are a good method for organizing extensive lists of materials or materials particular to a certain project. Each time you save a library you are given the opportunity to change its name or overwrite the existing definition. Considering the relatively small size (3DS.MLI starts out as 46 KB) and the time it takes to create them, you should consider keeping the original libraries for future reference. Use the Delete Library function only after careful consideration.

A library's materials are a good starting point for creating new libraries. The definitions point to color combinations, map manipulations, and subtle property changes that make them work. Because of this, starting libraries from scratch with the New option is rare.

The material definitions currently in the scene can act as the basis for new libraries, which actually is the easiest method for creating custom libraries. You can draw on the materials stored in a current library (such as 3DS.MLI) as the starting points for these new materials. After putting these to the scene, use the Surface/Material/Make Library command in the 3D Editor to create a new Materials Library. This library only has the definitions from the model. After you make a library, you must load it (from the Materials Editor using [Ctrl]+[L] or in the 3D Editor using Material/Get Library) before you can use it.

Showing/Selecting Assigned Materials

In the 3D Editor, you can display the current assignment of materials by selecting the assigned faces with Surface/Material/Show, which displays a list of all materials assigned within the model, not just those present in unhidden geometry (as is the case if you use Smoothing/Show). This selection option is useful for isolating faces already assigned a material and especially for displaying unassigned faces that still possess the default material. The faces are selected, not just "shown." This does not select the face's vertices or the object's definition.

Examining Questions You Should Ask About Materials

You should ask questions about every material, no matter how complex or mundane the material is. The following is an approximate order of questions to ask yourself when you create a basic material:

- ✔ What is the material to represent?

- ✔ What is the material's overall color? What color do you see in its highlights and shadows?

- ✔ Does it resemble a plastic or metal surface?

- ✔ How shiny is it? How strong is the highlight?

- ✔ Is the material transparent? If so, how much? Does it glow? Can you see through all parts of the mesh? If not, what opacity map would you like?

- ✔ Does it cast a light or glow? If so, how much?

- ✔ Is it a wire frame? If so, how big are the wires?

- ✔ Is there an applied texture? If so, which one? How prominent? How should it be manipulated? Does it happen once or repeat?

✔ Are the surfaces smooth? If not, how bumpy is it? Which bump map do you want to use? How should it be manipulated? Does it happen once or repeat?

✔ Does the surface reflect an image? If so, which one? How strong is it? How should it be manipulated? Does it happen once or repeat?

✔ Can you see through parts of the mesh? If so, what opacity map do you want to use? How much can you see through? How should it be manipulated? Does it happen once or repeat?

✔ Do you need to see both sides of the mesh?

You actually answer all these questions in the Materials Editor for each material, using value sliders, button choices, file selections, and parameter values. These answers are stored as the definition for each material.

Material Color and Using the RGB and HLS Sliders

The ambient, diffuse, and specular colors make up the dominant property of most materials. If there are no maps, then this is your primary control of the material's appearance. This chapter refers to these settings as the material's *base color*.

Texture maps blend with the base colors ambient and diffuse values according to the strength of the map. If these maps are at 100 percent, the ambient and diffuse base colors are completely replaced by those of the replaced texture map. The bitmaps used by other maps, such as reflection maps, have their colors affected by the material's base color, while others, such as bump maps, play on variations of the material colors directly.

It is advisable to assign a color to all materials, even if their maps make the color obsolete. This enables you to make quick rendering studies that still enable you to distinguish shape and location while Mapping is off. Most of the stock materials in 3DS.MLI do not have base color properties. When you use these, you might want to add an appropriate base color to make test renders faster and more useful (the added color information does not have an effect on the material when rendered with Mapping on).

You can determine colors by mixing the primary colors of light (*red, green, and blue*—RGB), using pigment definitions (*hue, luminance, and saturation*—HLS), or a combination of both. The sliders that you use to control these values are shown in figure 6.4. Each slider determines a value from 0 to 255, or 8 bits of color. Each system has three channels, so the total color depth is 24-bit color (3 channels × 8 bits). This color depth is commonly called *true color* and is usually more than adequate for the human eye.

Figure 6.4
Material base
color sliders.

Color status of the current
color swatch

RGB channels

HLS channels

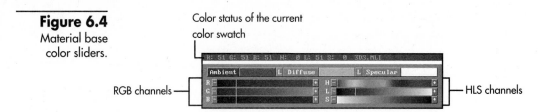

The value for each slider is visible in the color status area at the top of the display. Although the color in the color swatch is your primary cue, you need to refer to the exact slider value in the color status area for fine tuning adjustments.

RGB colors are *additive*—they get brighter and approach white as their values increase. HLS colors vary according to channel. *Hue* specifies a color within the spectrum. *Luminance* tells how dark or light the hue is. A mid-level luminance of 127 is the true hue, increasing to 255 makes white and decreasing to 0 forms black. Saturation determines how deep, strong, or pure the hue is. A value of 255 is the pure hue, while reducing it mixes more of the missing color channels with it until gray is formed at 0. See Chapter 2, "Concepts and Theories," for a full discussion of defining color using the Materials Editor.

Material Color Components

A material's base color is broken into the three qualities: *ambient* (the color shown in shade), *diffuse* (the color shown in light), and *specular* (the color of highlights). Choosing these colors for realistic effect takes practice. Begin by looking at real-world objects that share your material's qualities. Look deep into their color, their shade, and their highlights. Is the highlight's color similar to the light source's or is it tinting it? How is the shaded color affected by what it is placed on?

Specular highlights are seen on a mesh when the observer's angle of incidence to a face equals that of the light source to that face. The mesh displays the material's diffuse color when fully illuminated, and not within the specular highlight. As the illumination decreases, the diffuse color mixes with that of the ambient. Where there is no light, only the ambient color is rendered (and then only by the scenes ambient light)

Diffuse

Of the three base color qualities, Diffuse has the most impact on the materials appearance and is the easiest to determine. The diffuse color is the one you refer to when you describe a material in real life. Refer as often as possible to the world around you and analyze its colors. Very few objects have fully saturated hues. Those that do tend to be signs (signage, packaging, advertisements), toys, and cartoons. Others have much more complex blends.

When you analyze real-world colors, you need to flood at least an area of it with white light, eliminating any surface shading. This light is ideally quartz or xenon (the highest temperature lamps readily available), but halogen works well enough. You can isolate the diffuse color by holding a pocket halogen flashlight very close to the surface.

Specular

The specular color mixes with the illuminating light's color. This varies between materials, but is usually based either on the diffuse color or has no color (zero saturation). A good starting point for materials is to copy the diffuse color to the specular color and increase the Luminance towards white. Swatches are copied between properties by clicking on the color swatch and dragging it to the new position. By using Luminance to adjust the specular color, you ensure that it always correlates to the original, diffuse color.

Beginning with Release 3, 3D Studio enabled you to copy color swatches and map information between materials by dragging the swatch or tile and using the left- and right-arrow (or comma and period) keys to cycle through the current seven materials.

The influence that specular color has on a material is directly related to its shininess and shininess strength values. Materials that have no shine cannot form a specular highlight. If the material has shine and a highlight is formed on a material, the material's diffuse color mixes with the specular in an additive, or light-like, manner.

A material's specular color is not rendered unless a light's angle of incidence reflects back to your rendered viewing position, as shown in figure 6.5. (Note that this angle to see a highlight is the same angle for seeing the reflection of an object placed at the spotlight's source.)

Figure 6.5
Specular
highlights created
from light sources.

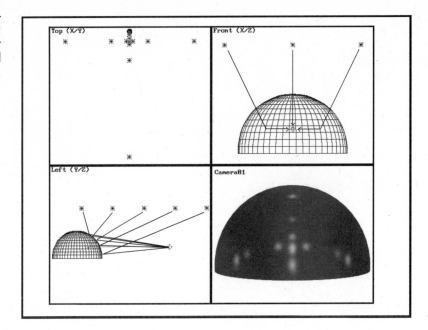

Ambient

Although the ambient value represents a material's shaded portion, it has an effect across most of an object because usually only a small proportion is in direct light at any given time. Most objects are illuminated with glancing light that is shaded across their surfaces. As they are shaded, the ambient value mixes with the diffuse value in a *subtractive*, or pigment-like, manner. Once in complete shadow, the ambient color is used exclusively. This color is usually still quite dark because its only illumination is from your ambient light value.

Darkening the ambient value is often beneficial to achieve deep material colors. You can do this easily by copying the diffuse color swatch to the ambient color swatch and lowering its luminance.

In reality, few materials have different ambient and diffuse values. (Some that do are those materials that glow or are naturally iridescent.) The shading that occurs across most surfaces is the simple reduction of illumination, which is why the manuals suggest that you start by keeping the ambient and diffuse values constant.

You can simulate materials that have a very rich quality to them, such as lacquered woods, by bringing their ambient color to mid luminance and full saturation. A chestnut brown diffuse material given a bright red ambient value forms a very warm, rich brown.

The Materials Editor also has the capability of locking the three color components together so that any change you make to one is made in the other. The use for locking is limited, considering the ease with which you can copy color swatches. But if you tend to use many materials that have the same ambient and diffuse or diffuse and specular colors, you might consider locking them for editing convenience.

When a scene is illuminated solely with ambient light, a mesh's rendered appearance is controlled entirely by its material's ambient base color. This effect of color "switching" is important to realize when using a pure white ambient light to illuminate the scene—a common situation when creating flat work for two-dimensional prints .

Simulating Radiosity with Ambient Color

The color shift that you observe across real-world surfaces usually is from the color reflected off nearby objects. Place a stack of white paper on a larger piece of red paper and you see the red in the white paper's shading. Paper is matte, so it has no mirror-like properties. The color you see is being reflected from the red papers surface. The more you illuminate the red paper, the more of its color is reflected, or "bounced," onto the white.

The red reflection from the preceding example is known as *bounced* or *inherited color*, and is simulated by ray-tracing software in a capability termed *radiosity*. You can use 3D Studio to approximate this effect without a memory cost by varying the material's ambient color or by strategically placing omni lights (see Chapter 13, "Lighting and Camera Special Effects," for the latter technique).

Experiment with this effect by copying the material across the seven slots and adjusting the ambient values. You might be surprised by the subtle effects that even dramatic color shifts have on the sample spheres. Remember that the ambient color is subtractive and it is the CYM color model's "rules" that are in effect. (See Chapter 2, "Concepts and Theories," for more information on the rules of the CYM color model.)

As you complete a scene, look for objects placed close to objects with saturated colors, especially those in direct light. Shifting their material's ambient values to the rendered color of the nearby objects simulates inherited color. This is a very subtle touch, but can lead to more photo-realistic effects.

Shading Modes

The four shading modes (from quickest to slowest) are Flat, Gouraud, Phong, and Metal. Each of these shading modes tells 3D Studio which shading algorithm to use to create the appearance of that material. It is important, however, to remember the difference between shading modes and shading limits. A shading limit is set in the Renderer and sets the maximum overall quality for the scene. If you have only flat materials in a scene, it won't matter which shading limit you choose—all materials will be rendered as flat. But if you have, say, Phong and Metal materials in a scene, and just want to see the relative masses of the objects in it, you can set the shading limit to flat, and all objects—no matter what the shading modes of their materials—will be rendered as flat-shaded.

> To accurately render materials, you must set the shading limit as high as the highest-quality material in the scene.

Each mode brings certain rendering capabilities that you need to remember to avoid confusion in later renderings. The Flat shading mode, although the fastest, cannot receive or cast shadows and ignores smoothing information—it is always flat. Neither Flat nor Gouraud-shaded materials can use bump maps or are affected by atmosphere definitions, and only metal materials can create metallic gleam and shine characteristics.

Shading Smoothed Objects

The Materials Editor is a good place to see the effects of the various shading modes side-by-side. The following exercise uses its sample spheres as a tool in understanding the various shading modes.

Shading Modes in the Materials Editor

This chapter assumes that the Backlight option is always in use. Make sure that Options/Backlight is on so that the differences between shading modes are more clearly illustrated. At the completion of this exercise, the sample windows will appear as shown in figure 6.6.

Figure 6.6
The sample spheres rendered with the five shading modes.

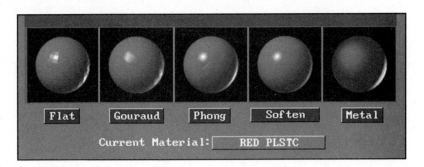

Click in the far left sample window   Makes the slot active

Press G to bring up the library's
list of materials and get a simple material,
such as WHITE or RED PLASTIC

Copy this material to the adjacent by pointing in the sample window and dragging it to the next window while holding down the mouse button	The Phong-shaded material is now displayed in the next window identically
Copy the material to the next three windows	There are now five copies of the material
Enter the first sample window, click on the Flat *shading mode, and press* (Spacebar)	Renders the sample sphere as a faceted sphere

Rendering the first material as flat-shaded makes the sample sphere resemble a mirrored ball, with each facet being identifiable. Notice how the Backlight defines a definite ridge line of facets across the right hand side.

Enter the second window, click on the Gouraud *shading mode, and press* (Spacebar)	Renders the sample as a smooth sphere

Rendering the second material as Gouraud-shaded creates a smooth sphere, but the Backlight points to this mode's limitations—it only averages between faces. For curvilinear geometry, such as the sphere, highlights can be caught at slightly different angles and render the facets at rates different enough to destroy the effects of smoothing. The specular highlight also is fuzzier than the sharp round highlight of the Phong sphere to its right.

Enter the third window, click on the Phong *shading mode, and press* (Spacebar)	Reinforces the fact that this is the Phong option

Rendering the third material as Phong-shaded creates a sphere that has a smoothed center, much like the Gouraud's. This sphere's highlight is much rounder and less scattered than that created with Gouraud shading. The Backlight creates a smooth crescent of light that is somewhat harsher than the Gouraud-shaded sphere.

Enter the fourth window, click on the Soften parameter *button, and press* (Spacebar)	Renders the sphere as before, but the harsh crescent of backlight has been considerably softened

Rendering the fourth material as Phong with Softness on shows a sphere identical to the previous, except its backlit crescent is closer in color to the diffuse rather than the specular, and so appears more like the Gouraud shading mode.

Enter the fifth window, click on the Metal *shading mode, and press* (Spacebar)	The sphere renders smoothly, but much different than the previous three samples

Rendering the fifth material as metal will show a smooth sphere that has qualities different from the previous three smooth samples. The sphere has more contrast between its areas, its highlight is more diffuse, and its backlit highlight is more striking.

II

Basic Modeling

This exercise points to two features that were introduced with Release 3—Soften/Phong and Metal shading. The Soften attribute is only available on Phong-shaded materials and the Soften button appears only when the Phong shading mode is selected. When turned on, Soften reduces the bright highlight effect of glancing light that is unrealistic for many real-world materials.

Soften does not add additional rendering time and it should be standard for materials that are not highly reflective. The standard Phong quality is most appropriate for plastic, high-gloss paint, lacquers, glass, and other glossy materials that can have a harsh glancing highlight. For most other materials, Soften should be the default.

The Metal shading mode (introduced in Release 3) does away with the Specular color swatch and value. Metal materials derive their highlight color directly from their Diffuse color values and the shape of their highlight curve. Metal materials shade and create highlights in a very different manner than do the other modes, so Metal is not so much a shading mode refinement as it is a different material type. This is how Metal derives its name, and not by its calculation technique of using the Cook/Torrance algorithm (as opposed to the Phong and Gouraud modes that directly name their algorithm). Metal is the highest of the rendering modes and has all the capabilities of Phong.

Shading Non-Smoothed Objects

For rectilinear geometry, the effects of the different shading modes are not as pronounced. You can examine these qualities by doing the next exercise.

Rendering Flat Objects

For this exercise, you might want to turn on anti-aliasing to ensure a clear comparison. At the completion of this exercise, the sample windows appear (see fig. 6.7).

Figure 6.7
The sample cubes rendered with the five shading modes.

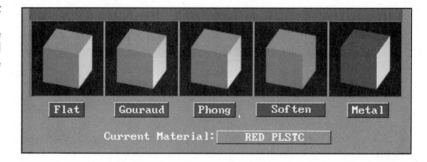

Return to the five samples from the previous exercise

Choose the Cube display option, click in the first window, and press `Spacebar`	Renders a Flat-shaded cube in place of the sphere
Click in the second window and press `Spacebar`	Renders a Gouraud-shaded cube because the Cube display option is still in effect

These first two sample cubes, Flat and Gouraud, appear to be identical. Actually, the sides of the flat cube are the same color, whereas the sides of the Gouraud cube shade slightly across their faces. This is the primary difference with Flat shading—each plane is given a uniform color.

Rerender the third and fourth windows by pressing `Spacebar`	Renders the Phong-shaded cubes

The Phong (third) cube seems nearly identical to the second cube. If you were to examine it closely, you would find that it is shaded a bit more evenly across the surface, and in smaller steps. This is because Phong is averaging the color of each pixel, whereas Gouraud was averaging between the two faces of each side. The Softened Phong (fourth) cube has reduced the backlight's highlight to make the right side appear much darker than the previous three cubes.

Click in the fifth window and press `Spacebar`	Renders a Metal-shaded cube much different from the rest

The Metal-shaded (fifth) cube renders quite dark when compared to the previous four. The sample cube is not presenting faces at an angle to catch a highlight and so renders quite dark. This is in contrast to the vibrantly backlit right side. This points to the fact that Metal-shaded materials can be a poor choice for rectilinear objects since they will render very differently.

This points to an important fact about rendering modes. If an object's surface is not smoothed, its rendered appearance is nearly identical between Gouraud and Phong shading (Flat-shaded materials can have the effect of rendering various faces at slightly different rates). Of these modes, however, only Phong materials can use bump maps and react with atmospheres. If your model is rectilinear and you do not need a bumped material, you can save a little rendering time by assigning it a Gouraud material. Flat-shaded materials might work if you don't plan to cast shadows on the object assigned them, and rendering speed is more important than quality.

2-Sided

The 2-Sided property should be used for geometry that you can see through, such as glass, some wire frames, or areas of the model that have troublesome normals. This is an expensive option causing the program to render many more faces then usual (see the discussion on face normals in Chapter 10, "Creating and Editing Faces and Vertices in the 3D Editor," for more information).

Wire Frame

3D Studio Release 3 changed Wire Frame from a shading mode to a shading attribute, and in doing so expanded its capabilities considerably. Activating the Wire attribute button brings up the Wire Frame Mode dialog box, shown in figure 6.8.

Figure 6.8
The Wire Frame
Mode dialog box.

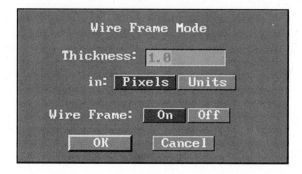

When the Wire Frame attribute is on, the visible edges of a mesh are rendered according to the size that you specify. Think of this as the wire's gauge and specify it according to resolution pixels or actual units. The effects of these choices are similar unless you are rendering a perspective viewport. Here, wire-frame materials that have pixel definitions are rendered uniformly, much as if you trace a photograph with a single-width pen. When specified as units, the wire frame edges obey the rules of perspective and recede accordingly. This can create dramatic effects. Close up, each line of the wire frame resembles a creased piece of paper—the crease lying on the mesh's edge and the paper extending along the plane of the face. The next exercise will investigate these variations.

Wire frame materials render in the scene only if anti-aliasing is on. While you are in the Materials Editor, the wire-frame materials are always anti-aliased and there is no need to change the Material Editor's display setting on your own. When rendering with the Renderer, the material appears to be solid if anti-aliasing is not enabled.

Investigating Wire Frame Mode

Return to the five cubes, choose the Phong *material, and activate the* Wire *button*

The Wire Frame Mode dialog box appears

Leave the Thickness value at 1.0, choose the Pixels *option, click on* OK, *and render the sample*

Renders only the edges of the cube

Copy this material to the side, activate the 2-Sided attribute, and render the sample

Renders the cube as a transparent wireframe

Copy both of these materials to the side, switch back to the Sphere display option, and render the two new materials

Outlines each facet of the spheres in Wire Frame mode, as seen in figure 6.9

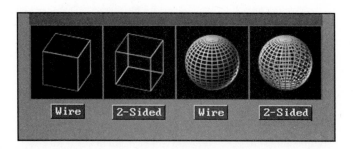

Figure 6.9
Wire Frame mode within the Materials Editor.

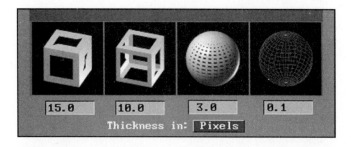

Figure 6.10
Wire Frame with different pixel thickness.

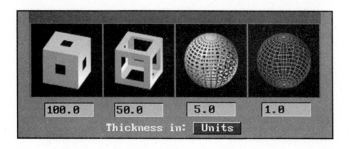

Figure 6.11
Wire Frame with different unit thickness.

continues

II

Basic Modeling

continued

*Switch to the 2-sided cube, change its
Wire Frame attribute to Units, increase
the Thickness to 50.0, and render*

The sides are wide and have no artifacts at the corners.

*Change the display back to Sphere, give
the spheres thicknesses of 3.0 and 1.0,
and render*

Renders the spheres very well, with clearly
defined wires

The effect that these materials have in the scene vary according to how large the objects are
that receive them. You specify actual units and might need several similar materials that have
varying wire thicknesses for different sized objects.

Unit-defined thicknesses can require some forethought as to values, but they do give you two
advantages over pixel determinations: they render correctly at their corners, and most
importantly, they diminish in perspective.

Wire Frame mode renders all visible edges, so it is important to make invisible those edges you
do not want to render. The AutoEdge command makes this assignment fairly easy. Wireframe
materials behave exactly as the Backface viewing option. It renders all of a mesh's currently
displayed edges and hides correctly on the element level only. Wire frames do not block the
view of other meshes. See the discussion on Face Maps at the end of this chapter for creating a
true hidden line drawing that simulates Wire Frame mode.

The Renderer provides a Force Wire option that makes materials in the scene
render as if they were one-pixel Wire Materials. This is a Global setting, and
activating it will cause materials in the Materials Editor to render one pixel
wide, regardless of their settings.

Because Wire Frame is now a shading attribute, its effect can be combined with any other
materials properties. If a material is smooth, Metal-shaded, semi-transparent with mapping, so
is its wire frame. Although capable of fascinating results, the Wire Frame property is not
perfect. If edges are invisible, they take their portion of a welded intersection with them.
Figure 6.12 shows how these locations might thus appear dog-toothed or serrated because of
the absent triangle. The only recourse is to reduce the wire's size to make it less noticeable or
display those edges.

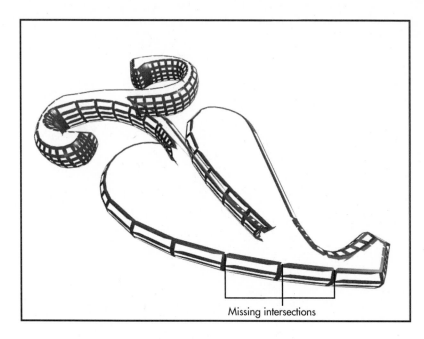

Figure 6.12
Large wire thickness causing some problems at intersections.

Missing intersections

Material Properties

Each material has a set of properties that are controlled by strength sliders with ranges from 1 to 100. The combinations of these properties impact the character of the material, no matter how many maps you might apply.

Properties of Shininess

The amount of polish, gleam, or gloss a material has is determined by its shininess and shininess strength. The combined effect that these two values have is graphically shown in the resulting highlight curve. As you increase the values, a bell curve forms. As the curve approaches the top, the highlight's color becomes that of the specular's. As the curve broadens, the highlight is distributed and its color mixes with the diffuse. A sharp curve creates a narrow point of specular color, whereas a low, broad curve creates a large, soft highlight that is not as much a departure in color. Many real-world materials (such as leather, oiled wood, or a matte balloon) have an even, low sheen that you can simulate by using zero shininess and increasing shininess strength levels.

Note

As the area of the highlight curve increases, so does the angle from which a specular highlight can be viewed. The higher the highlight curve, the more the highlight is composed of the specular base color. The lower the curve, the more it mixes with that of the diffuse base color.

The specular highlight qualities represented by the highlight curve are the same for flat, Gouraud, and Phong materials (depending on the limits of their mode). They are, however, very different for Metal materials. As figure 6.13 shows, the same shininess and shininess strength values produce very different curves and rendered results.

Figure 6.13
The highlight curves and rendered effects of various shininess settings on Phong and Metal materials.

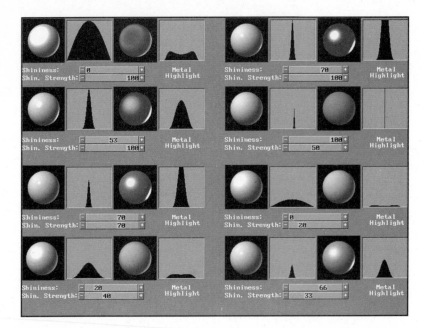

The shininess controls have the greatest effect on Metal materials because their mixture determines the specular color. The highlight curve display reacts differently with metal, creating a two-peaked curve at low settings and a tall, thick vertical line when high—the shinier a Metal material, the greater its contrast. It is in these dark areas that reflections are seen.

Properties of Transparency

The capability to look through a material is determined by the values of its Transparency and Transparency Falloff properties. To fully witness this effect, always use the Patterned Background display option. This pattern might seem a bit garish, but it has key primary colors with which you can compare.

The Transparency value dictates the percentage that the entire material is transparent. The Add and Sub property buttons to Transparency's right control whether things seen through the material are darker (as in a glass bottle or balloon) or lighter (as in a light bulb or beam of light). Transparency Falloff effect is controlled by the In and Out buttons to its right. The Falloff value dictates the transparency of the material's center with the In option, or its edge's with the Out option.

If a material is transparent, you can see through to its inside. Due to the thinness of many transparent materials, it is more common to give them a 2-sided property rather than to model their inside surface and edges. The edges of most transparent materials seem denser to your eye as you look through more material along the edges. To create this illusion of material depth, you need to enter an Inside Falloff value or the object has uniform transparency and appears to be the infinitely thin vessel it really is. If you model both sides, you should try a zero Falloff value first, and then adjust Inside Falloff upward until the desired effect is achieved. The use of Outside Falloff is fairly rare, as few materials are denser in their center than at their ends (examples include translucent solids and light beams). The variations of these settings are investigated in the following exercise.

 3D Studio includes an alternative transparency algorithm that you can access by changing the 3DS.SET parameter NEWSUBTRACTIVE-TRANSPARENCY to ON. When this parameter is on, transparent materials produce a rendering anomaly by removing color seen through them inversely of their transparency (for example, 100 percent-transparent red glass blocks all green and blue channels). Because of this very unnatural characteristic, it is highly recommended that you do *not* use the new algorithm—even though the documentation encourages you to do so. The program ships with this option off, so it shouldn't be a problem unless you personally change the setting.

Investigating Transparency

Begin by setting the background to Pattern *and selecting* CYAN PLASTIC

Increase the Transparency slider to 50, and render

Renders the Phong-shaded Cyan sample sphere

The sphere renders with an even 50-percent transparency, as seen in the first window of figure 6.14

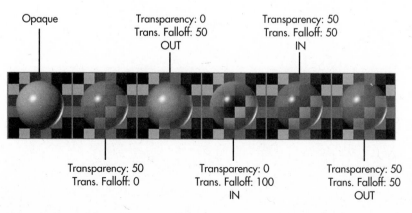

Figure 6.14
Differences in transparency with various slider values.

continues

continued

*Copy this material to the right, reduce
the Transparency to 0, increase the
Transparency Falloff to 100, and render*

Because the material began with an Outside Falloff parameter, the outside of the sphere is completely transparent, whereas the center is opaque.

*Copy this material to the right, click
on the In Falloff parameter, and render*

The center of the sphere is now transparent and the outside edge is opaque.

This effect points to a common misunderstanding between the two transparency parameters. The Transparency and Falloff values are cumulative, yet independent, and can affect the material without the other being active.

Copy this material to right, give it a 50% Transparency and Falloff value, and render	The sphere renders as transparent as the first window, but has more opaque edges
Copy this material to the right and change it to have Outside Falloff by clicking on Out	The sphere is now opaque in the center and more transparent at the edges

As can be seen, most transparent materials should have Inside Falloff. So far, the material has been treated as one-sided, much as if the object was a hemisphere and not a sphere. If the object in your scene is situated so that you can see through to its inside, the material should be made 2-sided.

Click on the 2-Sided Shading Attribute *button for the first material, and render*	The sphere becomes more opaque than it was before, but is still uniformly transparent
Click on the 2-Sided *button in each material, and render them each in turn*	The spheres all become more opaque and the influence of Falloff is more apparent, as seen in figure 6.15

Figure 6.15
The same
transparency
values with
2-Sided materials.

Although the two transparency values work together, they do not need each other to define a material's transparency. The Transparency value defines the overall level, whereas the Falloff determines its location and nature.

You also can define the overall transparency of a material by using an assigned opacity map. Whenever an opacity map is active, it overrides the Transparency parameter because the map defines the strength and location of the material's transparency. The nature of the transparency is still determined by the Falloff value and In/Out designation (no map defines Falloff).

Materials that have transparent properties do not require more memory, but do have an effect on rendering speed. As more transparent materials are added to a scene, the overall rendering times increase, especially if the transparent objects overlap one another.

Properties of Self-Illumination

Materials can simulate the emission of light by being given a Self-Illumination (Self Illum) parameter value. As this value is increased, the effect of the ambient color is reduced. If a material is fully self-illuminated with a value of 100, there is no shade and the diffuse color is used everywhere but at the highlights. Figure 6.16 shows the effect of a material as it increases from 0 to 100-percent self-illumination. Even a low value in the Self Illum slider has a noticeable impact, whereas the higher values are very similar.

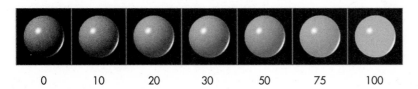

| 0 | 10 | 20 | 30 | 50 | 75 | 100 |

Figure 6.16
The effects of various levels of self-illumination on a Phong material.

Because a fully self-illuminated material cannot be shaded, it cannot receive a cast shadow.

A self-illuminated material does not cast any light of its own, giving the appearance that it is lit internally and refuses to be affected by shade and shadow. This means that it has uses other than simulating a glowing object. There are times when you might want an object to appear cartoon-like—bold in color and unshaded (this works best if the object is coplanar). Objects that are being used as background "billboards" are often assigned a self-illuminated material so that their image remains consistent throughout the scene. Other objects are self-illuminated, such as televisions, projection screens, signs, and lamps. Don't worry if a material is not casting light on its own because you can simulate and control this effect. (See Chapter 13, "Lighting and Camera Special Effects," for simulating light-casting objects.)

You can combine the Self Illum with an Additive Transparent property to create a convincing material for lamps or light beams (Using In and Out Falloff directions, respectively).

3D Studio includes the capability to specify which area of a material is self-illuminated with a self-illuminated map. Because the map also determines the intensity of the self-illumination, the value slider is ignored. (See Chapter 12, "Materials and Mapping," for more information about using self-illuminated maps.)

Understanding Basic Maps

Maps are your primary tool for creating illusion within 3D Studio. You can combine maps in numerous ways to make even the simplest mesh appear rich and complex. Careful use can make models extremely efficient and realistic. Because of their impact, it is important to have a strong working knowledge of their makeup and use.

Bitmap Formats

Many formats of bitmap file types are now supported by the Materials Editor. Any bitmap that is written in one of these formats is a valid map candidate.

Although Release 4 provides the ability to write EPS files, it *cannot* read them—thus, they are not a valid option for material definitions. This is due to the wide variety of EPS formats and related libraries.

Of the seven map types now available in the Materials Editor, only three actually use the bitmap's color information. Texture, reflection, and specular maps all use the bitmap's color information and convert it to 24-bit color for rendering. These are referred to as *color maps.*

All other maps within the Materials Editor use only the luminance values of a bitmap. The bitmap is thus treated as a grayscale, regardless of any color information it may contain. Although these are actually luminance maps, they are referred to by 3D Studio as *intensity maps* because they respond to the sum of the color intensity of the bitmap.

Confusion can arise when using colored bitmaps for intensity maps—the visual contrast between colors might not relate at all to the corresponding contrast in luminance. Fully saturated 255 values of Red, Green, and Blue, for instance, will read as the same intensity values. When using colored bitmaps, it often helps to examine them within a paint program as a grayscale image if the result you are getting is not what you expected.

Bitmap Interpretation

Whenever 3D Studio reads a bitmap (be it in 1-, 8-, 16-, 24-, or even 32-bit color), it converts it to 24-bit color, which requires three bytes of memory for each pixel of the bitmap. Other than the concern for file size, there is no advantage to using lower color bitmaps for color maps.

Intensity maps perform the same 24-bit conversion and take the same amount of memory per pixel even though they are only using the 256 levels of luminance. It is thus common to use grayscale bitmaps for intensity maps to save on disk space and to make their effect more obvious while viewing and editing them.

Note If an intensity map is strictly black-and-white, you can save additional disk space by converting it to a 1-bit, black-and-white format.

Using the same map file for different map uses does not require extra memory. You "pay" in memory only for the first use of a bitmap—regardless of how many times you use them. If the bitmaps have already been loaded, and thus paid for, additional map usage takes only additional time, not memory.

Tip A bitmap is loaded into memory only once by the Renderer. This is true even if the same bitmap file is used several times with different parameters for varying map types and within different materials. You can save a considerable amount of memory by reusing bitmaps for materials. This is especially useful for random maps that are used to give grit and texture to many different materials within a scene. The key is to create quality bitmaps and use them often.

The memory requirements of maps can become a problem if many maps are used or if they are quite large (for example, a 320 × 200 GIF or TGA requires 192 KB, and a 640 × 480 GIF or TGA requires nearly 922 KB). When you create and use maps, it should be your goal to create and use the smallest map that does the job properly.

File Types and File Info Capabilities

When selecting and coordinating bitmaps, you need to know their size, proportions, color depth, and the image contained. The View Image and File Info options, provided in 3D Studio Release 3 and later, give you this insight.

The File Info option brings up a file dialog box from which you can select any file for information. If this is not a recognized image format, the file's size and date are returned. Figure 6.17 shows that when the selected file is a recognized bitmap, its format, pixel width and height, aspect ratio, gamma, and frames are displayed as well. Note that the Type contains the color depth of the bitmap and that only TGA files have a recorded Gamma and Ratio value.

Figure 6.17
Typical file
info reports.

```
                    Image File Information
        File: BULLET.TIF           Type: TIFF-8 Compressed
               Path:          C:\3DSR3\IMAGES
          Date: 11/14/1993   Time: 17:18:44   Size:    858
   Width: 70   Height: 70   Aspect Ratio: Undef  Gamma: Undef  Frames:  1
                       Comments:



                           [   OK   ]



                    Image File Information
        File: 727ALPHA.TGA         Type: TARGA 32 Compressed
               Path:          C:\3DSR3\IMAGES
          Date: 11/14/1993    Time: 06:39:02   Size:  34248
   Width: 320  Height: 200  Aspect Ratio: 1.0000  Gamma: 1.0000  Frames:  1
                       Comments:



                           [   OK   ]
```

 In the Materials Editor, you can drag a map's file slot over to the View File or the File Info tile to activate that command with the dragged file.

The View Image option enables you to view any loadable bitmap while within the Materials Editor. The image appears according to its correct size and aspect ratio. If the image is larger than your display, you are asked if you want to resize or chop it. If the image is large and your time is valuable, you are better off chopping the image because resizing it can take a considerable amount of time and memory as the program proportionally resizes both of the image's axes.

 Avoid bitmaps that have the same name but are located in different areas on the disk. A bitmap's name can only be referenced once and subsequent calls to the same name continue to produce the original bitmap, regardless of how you identify subsequent files. Bitmaps are called in the order specified by the map paths. The first map found with the specified name is used.

Using File Slots

The file slots for each map type display the bitmap's name and also contain the directory path from which the file was selected, as well as all its parameter settings. When you copy a file slot, you copy this information too, which can be very convenient for maintaining the same parameters across several map types. You can copy file slots between materials by using ⬅ and ➡.

You also can use ⬚ (comma) and ⬚ (period) to navigate. These are easy to remember because they are the lowercase keys of ⬚ and ⬚. Many users find them less of a finger stretch than the arrow keys.

File slots also are useful to store different map types and parameter variations. Simply copy the file slot to a map type that is not being used and refer to it or copy it back later. If you try numerous combinations, or your material is complicated, remember that you can always copy file slots to another material and store them there.

You can copy file slots to and from any map slot, except to that of the reflection map. Because reflection maps do not use any parameters, it discards all the parameters carried along by a copied file slot. Copying the slot back from one copied to the reflection map slot results in default parameter values that can be useful to reset a single file slot.

Mapping Parameters

After you select a bitmap as a map, you can manipulate it in many ways. The image can be offset, rotated, scaled, tinted, reversed, repeated, and blurred all unto itself. The Map Settings button, shown in figure 6.18, gives you access to the Mapping Parameters dialog box (see fig. 6.19).

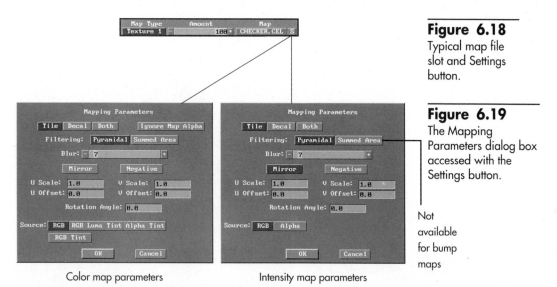

Color map parameters

Intensity map parameters

Figure 6.18
Typical map file slot and Settings button.

Figure 6.19
The Mapping Parameters dialog box accessed with the Settings button.

Not available for bump maps

II

Basic Modeling

The mapping parameters introduced with Release 3 made many habits and routines learned in earlier releases obsolete. When you combine bitmaps, you no longer have to match the true bitmap size and ratios. You also find yourself creating far fewer custom maps—in Release 3 or later, you can individually manipulate them. You also can combine maps in ways never before possible.

Tiling and Decal Parameters

Each bitmap can be applied once with the Decal option or repeated across the entire surface with the Tile option. When tiled, the bitmap is used exactly as if it is made with copies laid side-by-side. When decaled, it is as if the bitmap has a central image surrounded by a solid background.

The Decal option makes its background invisible by taking the pixel in the upper left hand corner of the map as its key color and making all pixels that share it transparent, allowing decals to show the material's base color and any other maps that might be active. Care needs to be taken to ensure that the color of the upper left pixel is not duplicated within the field of the image (for very effective decals, see the section on Alpha channels in Chapter 12).

Decals of images are applied only once, regardless of the bitmap's Scale parameters or mapping coordinate's Tile repeats. Adjusting either of these parameters only changes the size and proportion of the single decal image.

The Both option enables you to tile the bitmap with the transparency of a decal. This option was introduced with Release 3 and has great potential. Figure 6.20 shows the effects of the same image applied as a 100-percent texture map with the three settings.

Figure 6.20
Examples of the Tiling, Decals, and Both parameter options.

A bitmap that repeats its pattern seamlessly is said to be a *tileable bitmap*. Tileable maps can repeat in one direction as in wood planking, or in both directions, as in wood veneer. These maps are very useful because they can be small and still give a convincing effect. (See Chapter 12 for creating tileable maps.)

Using the same bitmap in both tile and decal mode causes a `Conflicting use of alpha` error message to be delivered each time you render the material. This message is somewhat confusing because it refers to Decal mode as alpha information. This is not necessarily a fatal error because the materials can still render correctly (especially if the two definitions are for different materials). The error message appears each time you render the sample or scene, however, because 3D Studio is warning you that the bitmap you are using may not be the one you want. Unfortunately, the only way to get around this dilemma is to copy the bitmap as a different file (which requires you to load it into memory twice) and reference it again.

The Ignore Alpha option appears only for color maps and is fully described in Chapter 12. For files that are not 32-bit color (that is, they do not have an Alpha channel), this option has no effect and can be ignored.

Blur, Filter Type, Negative, and Mirror Parameters

As an introductory discussion, this chapter simply refers to map filtering as *blur*. In broad terms, blur smoothes out a bitmap's rough edges and only impacts a bitmap when the Filter Maps option is on during a rendering (it is always on in the Materials Editor).

The differences in filtering types and the effects of blur are discussed in Chapter 12.

The Negative parameter reverses the colors of a bitmap, making the equivalent of a color or a black-and-white photographic negative. The primary use for Negative is to reverse the effects of intensity maps, as shown in figure 6.21. Notice how the rear bump map material reverses the direction of the dents as the bitmap is made negative. The use of Negative on color maps is primarily for rare special effects.

Figure 6.21
The use of
Negative to
reverse the
effects of an
intensity map.

The Mirror parameter flips the bitmap in both the U and V directions, resulting in four half-size images in an area that originally contained one. As figure 6.22 shows, it does not flip and mirror the image as the 3D Editor's Mirror commands flips a mesh (see below for how to do a traditional mirror). The materials and mapping coordinates shown in figure 6.22 are the same as those in figure 6.19, with only the Mirror parameter being activated. Mirror can be used to give more variation to a tiled map or to double the effects of face maps.

Figure 6.22
The use of Mirror
to randomize
and increase a
bitmap's repeat.

 The Mirror parameter also makes any bitmap "tileable" since the bitmap images meet evenly as they are flipped. This can produce a very noticeable pattern if the bitmap is not substantially random—a quality that for some materials, such as parquet wood, is exactly the desired effect.

UV Coordinates for Scale, Offset, and Rotation

You can manipulate a bitmap much the way you would a rectangular polygon in the 2D Shaper about its local axis. What are regarded as the X and Y axes in the 2D Shaper have the labels U and V in the Mapping Parameters dialog box. As figure 6.23 shows, the U and V axes cross in the bitmap's center to define the UV origin. The valid range for all the UV parameters is a plus or minus value from 10 million to one 1-millionth. This gives you far more control over the placement, scale, and rotation of bitmaps than any equivalent command for modifying meshes.

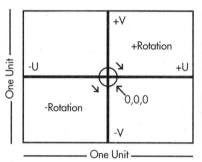

Figure 6.23
The UV coordinate system for bitmaps.

The bitmap can be scaled in either direction and to nearly any value. The image is scaled about its UV origin, equal in the positive and negative directions, similar to the 2D Shaper's Scale command.

To truly mirror a bitmap about either of its axes, enter a negative scale factor (for example, a V scale factor of -1.0 mirrors the map upside down).

The bitmap can be given an Offset distance in the U and V directions. The standard coordinate rules apply with one unit being equal to the overall U-width or V-height respectively. If you modify the map's scale parameter, then the relative offset is scaled as well.

The bitmap also can be rotated about the UV origin to nearly any degree with positive values going clockwise. Rotating the map more than 360 degrees does not have any additional effect.

AutoCAD users can relate a bitmap's UV settings to that of blocks. Scale and rotation will behave exactly as they would for a block having a central insertion point.

You can use mapping parameter values for several purposes besides scaling, moving, or rotating the Mapping icon in the 3D Editor. The scale and offset parameters are always proportional to the bitmaps, they can be aligned with other maps within the same material, and you have much more control over their accuracy. As a model nears completion, it is much easier to make final tweaks and adjustments in the Mapping Parameters dialog box than with the corresponding Mapping icon in the 3D Editor (especially if the mapped mesh has lost the capability to have its mapping acquired).

Source and Tinting Options

The method by which a bitmap's color is read is termed its *source*. Intensity maps have only one option—whether to use the RGB, value of the image, or its Alpha channel. The only valid choice for this option is RGB, unless the file is a 32-bit color image with an Alpha channel. Color maps have several more options as their color information can be tinted before they are applied to the material. Although there are only two such maps (texture and specular), texture maps are used to such a high degree that becoming familiar with this capability is very useful.

The standard method used by color maps to interpret a bitmap's color is to read its RGB information. This is the color map's source, and for most materials it usually is the RGB option. Next to the RGB are two different ways to tint the map in an even fashion. RGB Luma Tint and Alpha Tint each produce a pair of color swatches as shown in figure 6.24. (See Chapter 12 for Alpha Tint usage.) Clicking on a color swatch produces the color selector shown to the right. Changing these color values is somewhat similar to using the map with a lower slider value and letting the material's base color show through, but gives you more control.

Figure 6.24
Tinting options available to color maps by changing the source.

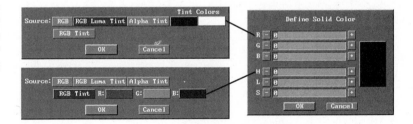

Selecting RGB Luma Tint as the source ramps the bitmap's values between two colors; it does not just tint it. The two color swatches to the right represent the top and bottom of the color ramp. Black is replaced by the left swatch, white by the right, with all other colors as shades based on their luminance (for example, a Luminance of 127 is replaced by the 50/50 mixture of the two swatches). This very important ability is explored in the following exercise.

Luma and tint can have unexpected results when the input File Gamma is on. Because the image is being gamma corrected, the tint might not behave exactly as you expect—especially for the dark end of the spectrum. This is not an error, but can lead to some confusion.

Exploring Luma Tint

Begin by creating a Phong material with a 100-strength texture map of CLDSMAP.JPG, and render the sample	Renders the sample sphere with a cloud pattern
Click on the file slot's S button	The Mapping Parameters dialog box appears
Click on the RGB Luma Tint *source button*	Two-tint color swatches (black-and-white) appear
Click on OK *and render the sample*	Turns the cloud image to a grayscale
Adjust the Luma Tint's black swatch to white and the white swatch to black, and then render	The cloud's luminance values are reversed, as if the Negative option had been used
Adjust the Luma Tint's right swatch back to white and give the left swatch a deep blue value	The clouds become monochrome blue to white image
Adjust the white swatch to be a chrome yellow value and render	The clouds become yellow against a blue sky
Adjust the yellow swatch to be a light cream white and the blue swatch to be a dark brown, and then render	Renders the sky as if it were a sepia tint image, reminiscent of old photographs

Selecting RGB Tint as the source displays three color swatches that color-shift the original Red, Green, and Blue channels accordingly. Understanding the rules of RGB color mixing is very important for achieving good results. Remember that white depends on three full RGB channels. If the combined color value of the three channels is less than 255 for each, then white is tinted. If the combined value is greater, then white becomes "brighter than white" and other colors begin to make extreme color shifts. Adjusting RGB tinting is shown in the next exercise.

Exploring RGB Tint

Return to the preceding material's parameter dialog box and click on the RGB Tint *button*	Replaces the two color swatches with red, green, and blue swatches
Click on OK *and render*	Renders the sky as normal

continues

continued

Unlike Luma Tint, there is no effect with RGB Tint until the color channels have been altered.

Copy the material to the side

Return to RGB swatches, enter the blue swatch, reduce it to 155, and render	The sky becomes more teal and the clouds become a little green

Reducing the Blue channel has lowered the blue within white to create the green shift. To restore white to the cloud, the missing blue value must be included in the other channels.

Copy this material to the side

Increase the red and green swatches' Blue channel to 50, and then render	The sky is still teal, but the clouds return to white

White has been restored because it now contains a full 255 value of blue. Note that this did not "cancel" the tint, but rather shifted the color balance of the image. If the goal is to make the surface more blue, then you need to starve the other colors to let the Blue channel dominate.

Copy the original material to a new slot window	Provides a fresh palette to start with
Leave the Blue channel at 255, but decrease the Green channel to 55, and then render	The sphere is somewhat bluer, but the clouds are now magenta

White has been deprived of 200 levels of green and the resulting Blue and Red channels' mix of magenta fills the void.

Increase the Green channel to 155, decrease the Red channel to 155, and render	The sphere is a very rich deep blue and the clouds seem correct

Notice that as the sphere has been tinted blue, so have the white clouds. White has still been reduced by the 200 levels, but the appearance seems "right." The reason is that the equal missing Red and Blue channels actually form yellow—the compliment to blue. This is an important concept to grasp when tinting images. For an unequal (that is, the channels do not combine to form 255,255,255 white) tinted image to appear "right," the missing or additional color must be the compliment to the dominant or starved color value.

Extensive color shifts also can transform the appearance of a bitmap. If you use a spring green leaf as a texture map and switch its Red and Green channels, the leaf renders a fall brown. Likewise, if you start with a fall leaf, it is now a bright green leaf. This can be very useful in cutting down your bitmap library, while increasing its consistency.

Types of Basic Maps

The basic maps are texture (Texture 1 and Texture 2), opacity, bump, and reflection. All affect the material based on their Amount sliders and their parameter settings. If a map is not used with a value of 100, it is mixing with the values in the base color and material parameters.

The question of which map to use is based on effect and size. A bitmap's effect is the image. Whether this image can be tiled without showing seams in one or both directions can be important. A bitmap needs to be large enough to fill close to the portion of the scene that contains it. This directly relates to output size and the prominence of the material in the scene. As a material's image becomes larger than its bitmaps, it begins to become fuzzy, blurred, and possibly pixelated. The extent of this effect depends on your angle of view to the material and the bitmap's color depth and contrast.

You can make a map only so small and still have it render effectively. The Renderer always creates a slight blur across a bitmap's pixels when they are larger than the pixels in the rendered image. This usually goes unnoticed, but as figure 6.25 shows, it can be very obvious if the rendered texture's image is several times larger than the map that created it. This is also true of very thin pieces within a map seen very close up. In both cases, the edges appear very blurred. The higher the contrast, the greater the apparent blur.

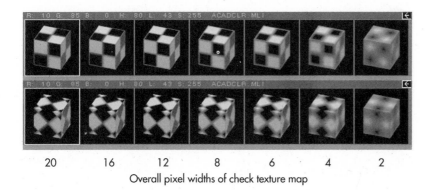

20   16   12   8   6   4   2

Overall pixel widths of check texture map

Figure 6.25
The effects of using bitmaps of varying pixel sizes.

To avoid this effect, don't use a map rendered more than two or three times its original size, and try to avoid one- or two pixel-wide details whenever possible. Avoiding this effect usually is not a problem, but can be if modelers get a little too stingy with their bitmap sizes.

This shortcoming of small bitmaps points out an important concept. If the map is going to be tileable, you should make it a single repeat of a reasonable size, enabling you to increase the map's detail and tile it as necessary with the various mapping parameters. A 200 × 200 bitmap that has four checker squares renders much sharper than a 200 × 200 bitmap that has 100 checkers. With the advent of mapping parameters, there is no reason for a bitmap of 100 checkers to even exist in your library except for use as a reflection map (which cannot use mapping parameters).

Texture Maps

Texture maps are the easiest to relate to. They apply their bitmap to the material much like wallpaper, if tiled, or a stamp, if decaled. 3D Studio enables you to specify two separate textures with the Texture 1 and Texture 2 map types. The effects of texture mapping are the same as long as only one of these maps is active at the same time. For basic mapped materials, it is assumed that only one is active. (For information on using both texture maps, see Chapter 12.)

The use of a texture map with a 100 value was described in the Source Tinting exercise. A similar tinting can be done by simply lowering the slider value. Many of the texture options are explored in the next exercise.

Exploring Texture Maps

Begin by getting the MARBLE-PALE *material from the 3DS.MLI*	Renders gray marble with pink veining
Copy the material to the side (this is for reference)	
Increase the diffuse and ambient colors to 255 Red, and then render	
Reduce these values back to black, increase the specular color to 255 Red, and render	The sphere has an intense red highlight
Reduce the shininess to 0 and the shininess strength to 100	Maximizes the highlight curve
Render the sample	The red highlight washes out about a third of the marble texture

This emphasizes the fact that the texture map is completely replacing the Ambient and Diffuse values, but is still fully affected by the Specular value.

Copy the original MARBLE-PALE back to reset the sample	
Make the diffuse color a medium blue, copy it to the ambient swatch, and reduce the luminance a bit	
Reduce the Texture slider to 80, and render	The marble becomes a purple tone
Reduce the Texture slider to 50, and render	The marble becomes very blue and the red veins lose prominence

Reduce the diffuse and ambient's Saturation to 0	The swatches become gray
Render the sample	The marble becomes a medium gray with subtle veins

You can go on and on. Giving drastically different ambient and diffuse values will have even different effects (try a pure red ambient with a blue diffuse, for example).

You can completely change the effect of a texture map by mixing its values with that of the base color. When this is coupled with Luma or RGB tinting, the result can be even more diverse.

Opacity Maps

Opacity maps replace the Transparency slider value by setting what parts and to what degree a material is opaque or transparent. Opacity uses intensity maps, with white being completely opaque and black completely transparent. The 253 values of gray (or luminance) in between deliver varying degrees of opacity. The Transparency Falloff values are still observed and combined with the opacity map's values.

The way an opacity map works is actually modeled after an Alpha channel, which is discussed in Chapter 12.

It is important the realize that once an opacity map is activated, the material is considered 100-percent transparent except for the areas that are non-black in the opacity map's bitmap. The corresponding opacity map slider tells how opaque to make the material in relation to the bitmap—the property transparency slider is inactive whenever an opacity map is defined. This means that an opacity map slider value of 50 reduces normally opaque white bitmap pixels to 50-percent transparency and a value of 0 makes the entire material transparent, regardless of the bitmap's values. This is why it is an opacity map rather than a transparency map. This means that an opacity map can never have black areas of its bitmap be anything other than 100-percent transparent. The next exercise demonstrates the basics of opacity.

Since opacity maps cannot be made more opaque within the Materials Editor—only more transparent—they often require custom editing within a paint package to achieve the desired luminance and resulting opacity.

Exploring Opacity Maps

Begin by getting CYAN MATTE *from the 3DS.MLI*	Renders cyan colored material
Click on the opacity map's file slot and choose CHECKER.CEL	
Change the See Tiling to 3 × 3, the background to Pattern, and render the sample	Renders the sphere as a cyan ball with square holes
Click on the 2-sided parameter and render	Repeats the hollow checker pattern on the reverse side
Copy the material to the side, activate the map's Negative parameter, and render	The opposite squares are now opaque
Reduce the map's value slider to 50, and render	The opaque squares are now 50-percent transparent
Increase the Transparency Falloff value to 100, click on the In option, and render	The checker pattern is now transparent in the center

---

Opacity maps only make an object transparent, not hollow. The transparent areas in a material are like clear glass or plastic, not holes. Because of this, they still catch highlights (as in the preceding exercise). See the "Shininess Maps" section in Chapter 12 for ways to negate this effect.

Opacity maps are extremely useful when combined with ray-traced shadows, replacing a significant amount of geometry with what could be a very simple, tiled bitmap. Note, however, that Shadow map shadows do not respect opacity and will cast solid shadows.

Bump Maps

Bump maps give a simulated texture to Phong and Metal materials by indicating areas to pull out, project, or "bump" out. The Renderer creates this illusion by altering the light values across the mapped surface as if there were "bumps" to cast shadows and receive highlights. Bump maps do not affect geometry. The raised edges are an illusion that don't bump or dent a mesh's surface—they only simulate the effect of highlight and shade.

Bump maps are still very useful and essential for creating convincing textures. Bump maps use intensity maps opposite of the way opacity maps use them. Black areas are unaffected and white areas are "bumped out" to the maximum effect. The remaining 254 values of gray (or luminance) deliver increasing degrees of "bumpiness" as they approach white.

Bump maps are most effective when they begin at the lowest, black values and work forward. You get more realistic effects if you have a black field and work towards mid-gray than if you start with mid-gray and work to white. You can make this change in a paint program by sliding the image's overall luminance down, using contrast and brightness controls, or by ramping up the grayscale. There unfortunately is no Luma Tint capability for intensity maps at this time.

Each pixel on a bump map projects forward square-like. These squares project like terraces and do not slope to one another. A good visualization for how bump maps work is to take a framed grid of pins (or square pegs) and push them against an object. The elevations of the resulting pin head profile relates to the shades of gray that would make up the surface's bump map. The "recipes" for common bump map types are listed in the following, with their effects illustrated in figure 6.26.

- ✔ Grooves, grout lines, ridges, and panels are all based on simple linework. The addition of a thin transition gray at the edge is often used to simulate a subtle bevel and soften the possible scintillation common with thin lines.

- ✔ To simulate a sloped surface, you need to create a ramp of gray values (easy with Animator Pro's VGRAD or HGRAD ink).

- ✔ If the simulated slope is rounded like a cone, you need to use a gradation in a circular pattern (easily done with Animator Pro's RGRAD ink). This can be seen in the third example of figure 6.24.

- ✔ To simulate a round surface, you need to create a "weighted ramp" that resembles the curvature. Notice that this is different than an even ramp because the falloff is shallow in the center and greater at the edges.

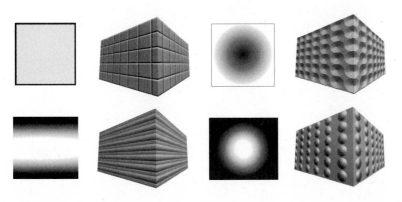

Figure 6.26
Typical bump map bitmaps and their resulting effects.

To simulate a dent, groove, or something else going into the surface, start by making the entire surface white, thus "out." The gray-to-black portions of the bitmap are then less projected, thus "in." To create a groove, you make the field white, the bottom line of the groove black, and the walls gray. This is actually a very simple procedure with the Negative mapping parameter. To simulate an ice-cream scoop dent, for example, you reverse what you create for a round bump.

One method for creating evenly shaded bump maps for slopes, bevels, and curves is to model their basic geometry in 3D Studio and use the rendered images as the basis for bitmaps. A spherical bump map can be made by modeling a smooth sphere, assigning it a matte white material and placing one spotlight dead center to it. Render the Spotlight viewport and you have a perfectly shaded, and dithered, image—perfect for a bump map.

The important thing to realize (and one that is often overlooked) is that mapping coordinates are projected completely through a material and thus have direction. Viewed from the opposite side, the map is reversed, which is not a problem with any map type other than bump maps because reversing their effect means what used to push out now pushes in. This effect is clearly shown in figure 6.27, as the same boxes in figure 6.24 were rotated 90 degrees to show the rear side of the planar projection. You need to be careful where you assign bump-mapped materials and how you position their mapping. If you are not careful, the bricks that have struck grout lines on one side of building have their grout oozing out when you turn the corner.

Figure 6.27
Bump map effects
projecting through
an object.

To have the correct bump effect on both sides of an object, create a second version of the same material and use Negative for its bump map. By assigning this material to the object's back or inside, you do not have to detach and reapply mapping coordinates. This keeps the object intact and eligible for smoothing. There is no memory penalty for this technique because both materials use the same bitmaps.

Bump maps do much to the rendered surface, but they do have the limitation of showing scintillation and aliasing for thin lines, harsh angles with great contrast, and tight parallel lines. If you encounter this problem, the first thing to try is to increase the Blur settings. In general, you have to blur bump maps far more than other maps. Make sure that Filter Maps is on in the Renderer.

The second thing to try when perfecting bump bitmaps is to enlarge the original bitmap and add an intermediate degree of gray to the enlarged edges. Remember, a bitmap's effectiveness is a product of its size. Small maps rendered far beyond their original size are overly blurred by the Renderer's inherent sampling mechanism.

It is often helpful to maintain a suite of similar maps that are identical but vary in resolution because you can use the minimum size map, and thus the least RAM, for any given application. In the case of a tile bump map, the lowest resolution might have the grout lines one pixel wide, the next 3 to 5 pixels, and the largest 7 to perhaps 15 pixels.

Creating Bump Maps with the Z-Buffer

Release 4 provides the ability for Image Plug-Ins (IXPs) to access the Renderer's internal z-buffer. The *z-buffer* gauges the distance of meshes from your viewing point, and records the depth as intensity levels of gray pixels. The result is a grayscale bitmap with white being very close, black very distant, and shades of gray forming the intermediate distances. A z-buffer image is somewhat analogous to conventional sonar—it only concerns itself with mass and the distance to it. Light and material definitions are simply ignored. This process creates an intensity bitmap that is ideal for use as a bump map.

Figure 6.28 shows the steps of this process. The original scene mesh can be seen in the upper left. Although complex in appearance, it was created in one step with the RIPPLE PXP. The corresponding Top view to the right betrays the mesh's simple beginning as a grid. This is the view that was rendered in Video Post to create the z-buffer image seen in the lower left. This bitmap was then used as a bump map to achieve the rendered effect shown on the cube in the lower right.

Figure 6.28
Original scene geometry, the resulting z-buffer image, and the result of using the z-buffer bitmap as a bump map.

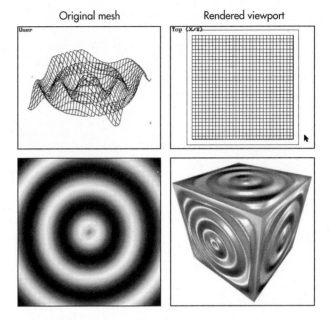

Resulting z-buffer image   z-buffer image used as a bump map

The CD-ROM includes a shareware program from the Yost Group that enables you to render a z-buffer image of your scene to disk. The Plug-In is named SEEZ_I.IXP (for "See z-buffer") and includes a .TXT file for additional reference. As with all IXP Plug-Ins, the program must be located in your PROCESS directory to be used. To use SEEZ, you need to enter the Keyframer's Video Post program and include two lines, as shown in figure 6.29. (See Chapter 21, "Special Keyframer Techniques," for detailed information on using Video Post.) The first line tells Video Post to render the scene, and the second line says to apply the SEEZ_I Image Process Plug-In to what was just rendered.

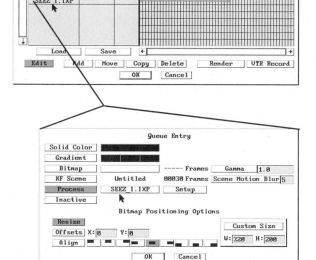

Figure 6.29
Video Post setup for using SEEZ_I.IXP.

II

Basic Modeling

Reflection Maps

There are several methods for creating reflections in 3D Studio, and all are accessed through the reflection map slot. Reflections can be used as an end in themselves, such as a mirror, or as a subtle touch to make a shiny or reflective object appear more realistic.

A reflection's effect is different from a texture's. Textures are fixed in location whereas reflections move across a stationary object as you move around it, or stay constant as the object is revolved and your eye is stationary.

The effect of reflections depends much on your angle of view to them, and so are only calculated properly when viewed in camera viewports. Remember this when you make quick previews of your scene for material judgments.

A reflection's color is directly affected by the material's base color. The material's diffuse and specular colors are effectively flipped and the ambient value minimized with reflections. The bitmap respects the material's specular color and is mapped in all diffuse and ambient areas. Reflections are destroyed by direct light, so what would have been rendered as the specular color now uses the diffuse color (that is, what is not capable of reflecting is showing the base, diffuse color). Because the highlight curve affects the amount of highlight, it affects how much of a reflection cannot be seen. Keep the following points in mind to maximize a reflection's impact (or do the reverse to minimize it):

✔ If you want a material to be as reflective as possible, minimize the area of the highlight curve

✔ If you do not want the reflection's color to have a tint, use a white specular color and a black ambient color

✔ If you want to minimize the color present in highlights, use a black diffuse color

 Because Metal materials create their specular highlight from their Diffuse and Shininess settings, they react very differently with reflections than Phong and Gouraud materials. This is especially true of materials that combine texture and reflections maps.

Unlike other maps, there is only one parameter that you can set for reflection bitmaps— Reflection Blur. This is controlled by the *Reflect Blur* property slider rather than a parameter dialog box, and it is not a filter map as other maps are. Blur is used for several reasons, as follows:

✔ The rendered image shows a degraded reflection because the bitmap used is not large enough. Blurring the reflection smoothes across the enlarged pixels and helps disguise this problem.

✔ The surface is not highly polished and is not supposed to be exactly like a mirror. Surfaces such as plastic and apples do not show reflections as pure as a chrome or glass surface.

✔ The bitmap's image is not what is actually around the reflecting object. Blurring the image disguises this fact.

 Beginning with Release 3, reflections are more accurate and usually require less blur than previously necessary. Older models might need their Reflection Blur values adjusted accordingly.

One thing to realize about reflection-mapped materials is that they can appear to be self-illuminated. This is because the reflection map replaces the material's diffuse and ambient color areas and reacts minimally to shade. The material can thus be seen independent of a light source. The premise is that the map represents a reflection and so there must be something in the scene that is illuminated and being reflected back to the material. This effect can be disturbing if the reflection's light level does not approach that of the scene. This can be especially disconcerting when very dark environments have materials containing bright reflection maps. In such cases, you need to reduce either the material's specular luminance or the map's strength to reduce the impact of the unshaded reflection. You have complete control over a reflection map's effect. If you need to reflect the scene's true lighting conditions, you should use another form of reflection (see Chapter 12, "Materials and Mapping," for more information).

Spherical Reflections

When a single bitmap is assigned to be a reflection, it is termed a *spherical reflection map*, deriving from the way the program "wraps" it around the inside of an imaginary "sphere" that bounds the scene. Lines of sight are traced back from an object's center to see the image on the sphere (done for each plane within a mesh). By using this technique, reflection maps do not require any mapping coordinates.

Some considerations are required for this wrapping technique to work realistically. As the map looks back for each plane, it is seeing only a small part of the mapping sphere, and so only a small portion is mapped to any one plane—regardless of the mesh's physical size. Thus, the results are poor for rectilinear geometry that does not have many planes to look back from. Spherical reflections are best for curvilinear geometry because their many faces catch more of the bitmap and read convincingly.

The choice and size of which bitmap to use for a spherical reflection is very important for its believability. To make the object appear reflective, you need to ask yourself if this reflection is going to be realistic or semi-realistic.

If your goal is realism, you need to base the map on the scene. If you use a background bitmap, it is a good candidate for the reflection map because its inclusion in the object's reflection is a natural. If there is no background, an image of the current scene might work for the illusion, but remember that it is being wrapped. For either case, the map works best if it is at least the output size (which the background image should be anyway).

If you want the reflection to occur only in the highlight (such as a window in the gleam of a balloon), you can now use a specular map instead of a reflection for the effect (see Chapter 12 for details).

Spherical mapping's primary purpose is to make objects appear to be reflective, which falls somewhere between a trick and an illusion. The reflection might not even be identifiable— you just know that it is reflecting "something." These bitmaps work best if they are busy, abstract, and have colors present in your scene. The REFMAP.GIF, GOLD.GIF, and METAL7.JPG sample bitmaps that ship with 3D Studio are good examples of this.

The complexity of the reflecting geometry has an impact on the reflection as well. The bitmap's size needs to accommodate the largest reflecting plane (meaning the largest visual plane, not necessarily the largest physical plane) in the finished scene. The portion of the map reflected should be as large as the rendered plane. Thus, if a reflecting plane is prominent, the bitmap needs to be quite large to reflect a portion that has enough pixels, otherwise, it delivers a "chunky" image, especially for rectilinear meshes that have few planes with which to reflect.

You should also take care when you use highly saturated and flat bitmaps for reflections. Because the effect of the ambient color is all but replaced, a fully reflective material is very similar to one that is self-illuminated. If the bitmap does not vary in color, the reflecting mesh appears to "glow" because it has a minimal capability for shade, and this fact is not disguised by variations in the reflection.

As the map is wrapped around the sphere, it pinches or swirls at its poles and a seam appears vertically when the ends meet. You can eliminate the latter effect if the bitmap is tileable from right to left (this is a very good quality for generic background bitmaps as well). The kinking effect is best controlled if the top (and bottom) of the bitmap's image is more random, such as clouds and grass, and does not include a vertical element to emphasize the swirl.

As explained later in this chapter in "Spherical Mapping Techniques," the optimum proportions for a spherical bitmap are 2 to 1. This means that to minimize distortion, reflection bitmaps should be twice as wide as they are tall.

Using Mapped Materials

To render a mapped material, the objects that use them must first be given mapping coordinates so that the program knows what type of map to use, where, how big, and at what angle to place it.

You can assign mapping coordinates only to objects or their independent elements. Unlike smoothing, the effects of mapping can be continued across meshes if they are assigned the same coordinates and materials.

Materials that only use reflection maps, SXPs, face maps, and/or Box-assigned materials do not require mapping coordinates and, moreover, ignore any that are assigned.

The final effect of a material is dependent upon the mapping coordinates assigned to the surface. Proper positioning and scaling require time, and the techniques and procedures to do them correctly are not the easiest to learn. Luckily, Release 4 provides several tools that make this task much easier and the use of mapping parameters has made many mapping coordinate adjustments unnecessary.

Mapping Types

There are several methods for assigning mapping coordinates. The best technique depends upon both the object's geometry and tiling characteristics of the bitmaps.

The three methods available for manually assigning the mapping projection are Planar, Cylindrical, and Spherical. The type can be chosen with Surface/Mapping/Type or by acquiring one that has already been assigned. Each projection method displays an appropriate icon (as shown in figure 6.30) that aids and placement and represents the true position, angle, size, and proportion for the material's bitmaps.

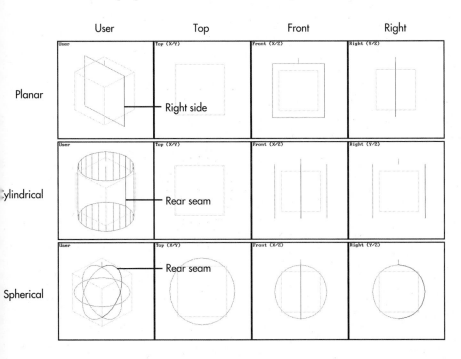

Figure 6.30
The three mapping icons, as seen from their different sides.

The icons use several visual keys to clarify which way is up and facing you. The small vertical line points up for all the icons. The Planar icon's dark line is always its right hand side. The dark line for Cylindrical and the dark arc for Spherical indicate the icons' backside. The direction these cues face controls the orientation of your bitmaps.

This is an important concept to understand and one that has been made a little more confusing with Release 3's mapping parameters. If a bitmap has default parameters (1.0 scale, 0.0 offset, and 0.0 rotation), the location, rotation, size, and proportion of the bitmap corresponds exactly to the mapping coordinates displayed by the icon. When you adjust a bitmap's parameters, you are always doing so in relation to the mapping icon (for example, if you change the U and V scale to 0.5, the bitmap fits in the mapping icon's border twice in each direction).

Mapping coordinates are applied through an entire object. If a mesh's side is perpendicular to the projecting map's angle, it catches the edge of the bitmap, causing the "caught" pixels to streak through those sides of the mesh.

Planar Mapping Considerations

Planar projection is the most common form of mapping and the easiest to understand. The rectangular icon simply represents the extents of your bitmap. As you change the shape of the icon, you stretch the picture. Planar mapping is projected infinitely through the object, as shown in figure 6.31. It does not matter how close the icon is to the mesh, only the icon's size and angle to the mesh matter.

Figure 6.31
Planar projection.

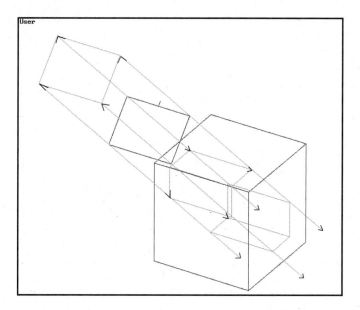

Because the bitmap stretches to fit the mapping coordinates, the icon needs to be the same proportions as your bitmap if you want your material to be undistorted. In previous releases (and in many other programs), this was a chore. You had to keep a record of every bitmap's resolution, and then had to scale the mapping icon to meet the correct proportions (usually with a calculator in hand). Mapping parameters makes matching bitmap and coordinate proportions much easier.

Applying Planar Maps

There are several basic methods for sizing icons. The first is Adjust/Scale and works much like the standard Modify/Scale command by scaling the icon about its center. As normal, the choice of which axis to scale is controlled by Tab⇆.

This command was greatly improved in Release 3 by enabling you to size the icon to the exact extents of an object by pressing Alt as you select the object. The size of the icon is based on the object's temporary bounding box, and so is always parallel to the world axes or square to your User view. The icon's vertical location is centered on the object's local axis and the icon is always facing you with its top always up. This Alt+Scale combination still uses the current directional Tab setting, so you can keep one side's length constant.

When Alt+Scale is used in a User view, it scales to enclose the object's three-dimensional bounding as is seen in that view. This is a quick way to align and scale a map at an odd angle such as from "above and to the right."

The Adjust option choices help you to place, find, view, draw, or rotate an icon within your viewport:

✔ The Adjust/Center option centers the current icon about the local axis of a selected object. This is similar to Alt+Scale, except that the icon's current rotation and proportion are maintained.

✔ The Adjust/Rotate option always rotates the icon about its center and makes no reference to any other axis.

✔ The Adjust/Find option's only use is to locate an icon that is too small, very far away, or out of the field of the current view. This command simply scales the existing icon up to fill about three-quarters of your viewport, while preserving the aspect ratio and rotation angle.

✔ The Adjust/View Align option is commonly used to quickly orient the icon to your viewport. The icon is rotated about its center so its position stays relatively the same. Unlike the Alt+Scale option, View Align keeps the map's scale constant.

✔ The Adjust/Face Align option rotates the current icon to be parallel with a selected face. The icon is spun in place about its center and does not move to the face.

✔ The Adjust/Region Fit option enables you to draw the Planar icon in a nonperspective viewport. The icon is then drawn on the viewport's construction plane to the size and proportion dragged (pressing Ctrl first constrains your drag to a square). The only trick is that the first corner you pick is always the upper left corner of the icon (drawing a rectangle from lower right to upper left results in an inverted icon).

II

Basic Modeling

Note Region Fit is the only mapping option that enables you to relate to drawing units and thus uses Snap. All other options rely on percentages of the icon's size.

3D Studio includes the Adjust/Bitmap Fit to accurately and instantly proportion the icon to a selected bitmap. If you select a 320 × 200 GIF, the icon resets to a 1:1.6 ratio. The bitmap is selected from a file-select dialog box and uses the current File Info Path (as of today, there is no way to narrow the search to a given material's maps). The icon uses its width as the controlling dimension. Using Bitmap Fit or Reset/Scale scales the icon vertically only.

Finally, the Adjust/Reset option is available as a tool for returning the mapping icon's default square proportion. As with Bitmap Scale, the Reset/Aspect Ratio keeps the current width constant and resizes the vertical. The Reset/Rotation option does more than you might think because it always makes the icon face the Front view, pointing up.

Planar Mapping Techniques

Planar maps are meant to be applied square to a mesh's face. Although this is correct, it is not convenient. Most objects turn corners, and require matching mapping coordinates on adjacent sides as well. You can detach the face to become a separate object, rotate the map and apply it again, but this degrades the usability of your model, prevents smoothing across the adjacent faces, and might cause problems in alignment. The key is to apply planar maps at an angle, as shown in the following exercise

Investigating Planar Mapping

Begin by creating a material that uses CHECKER.CEL from the Meshes directory as a 100-percent texture map, and put it current to the scene with C with the name "CHECK"

The example is also using a 50-percent gray Luma Tint.

Switch to the 3D Editor and create a box with varying side lengths

The different proportions will help see future mapping assignments.

Choose Surface/Mapping/Type *and make sure that it is planar*

Displays the Planar icon if within view

In the Front *viewport, choose* Mapping/Adjust/Scale, *and select the box while holding* Alt

Scales the Planar icon to the exact size of the box's side (see the left of fig. 6.32)

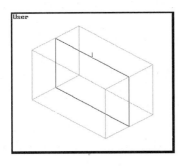

Figure 6.32
Scaling the icon to fit a side, and the possible effect when the icon is the exact size of the object.

Choose Mapping/Apply Object, *and apply the map to the box*	Applies the mapping coordinates to the box
Choose Material/Assign/Object, *and assign the current CHECK material*	Assigns the CHECK material to the box's faces
Switch to a User *or* Camera *view, and render the view (or object)*	Applies the check pattern to the front of the box, but its sides are gray with white streaks (see the right of fig 6.32)

The effect points to an odd occurrence. Because the icon was the exact size of the face, the slight blur that occurs within maps is projected back, instead of either color. Scaling the map slightly will change this.

Choose Adjust/Scale *and scale the icon to about 101 percent in both axes while in the* Front *viewport*	Scales the icon up from its center
Reapply the coordinates, and render the User *view again*	Streaks the colors of the check through the sides, as shown in the left cube of figure 6.33

The square checks have been stretched to fit the box's side. Restoring them to the proper aspect ratio requires a couple of adjustments.

Switch to the Front *viewport and choose* Mapping/Adjust/Bitmap Fit	A file dialog box appears
Select CHECKER.CEL and click on OK	Scales the icon's height about its center to meet the new ratio

The icon's height now exceeds that of the box and would result in only a partial repeat of the map.

Choose Adjust/Scale *and scale the size of the bitmap in both directions until it is close to the height of the box*

continues

II

Basic Modeling

continued

Figure 6.33

Planar mapping projecting through the object, and mapping with the correct aspect ratio.

The icon's aspect ratio will remain the same, as long as you adjust it in a perpendicular viewport.

Apply the new mapping and render User view

Tiles the correctly proportioned map across the front, as in the right cube of figure 6.33

The map is correct, but only on one side.

Switch to the Top viewport, choose Adjust/Rotate, and rotate the icon 45 degrees (use Angle Snap with a 15-degree increment for an accurate rotation)

Move the center of the icon to the corner of the box (see fig. 6.34), apply it, and then render the User view

The checkers are now on both faces and cast through the box's top, as in figure 6.34

Figure 6.34

The rotated mapping icon in position, and the resulting checker pattern.

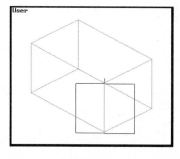

The checkers are repeating around the sides, but are no longer square. As the map was projected at an angle, the length of the bitmap's U direction was stretched. The width must shrink for the map to tile proportionally.

Press F5 *to switch to the Materials Editor
and access the material's mapping parameters*

Change the U Scale to 0.707 and click on OK

This is the cosine of the rotation angle.

Click on Auto Put *and then* Render Last

Proportions the checkers correctly,
as in the left cube of figure 6.35

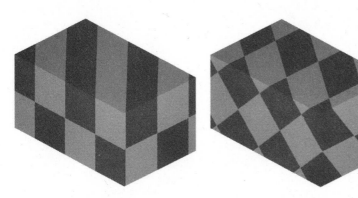

Figure 6.35
The correctly proportioned wrapping checkers, and mapping at an oblique angle to all surfaces.

The streaks are still occurring through the top of the box. Correcting this with planar mapping is easy. Keeping the bitmap's proportions true is impossible, however.

Press F3 *to switch back to 3D Editor and
enter the* Right *or* Left *viewport*

*Rotate the icon 45 degrees, apply the
mapping, and render the* User *view*

Applies a checker pattern over
the entire surface of the box, as in
the right cube of figure 6.35

Although the checkers are now everywhere, they are no longer a square proportion, except on the box's front side. You can continue to readjust the mapping parameters, but will never be able to get more than one side to have the correct aspect. This is because the angle of inclination for the U and V axis is now different for each plane. Correcting one will distort the others.

Correcting planar distortion is a common situation, and one that will probably need to be done for every model. Remember that you need to reduce the mapping scale by an amount inverse to which it was scaled up by striking the surface at an angle. As it turns out, the correcting ratio is a simple expression of the mapping icon's angle to the receiving surface, as follows:

Correcting Ratio = Cosine (icon's angle of approach)

As figure 6.36 shows, the icon's angle of approach should be equal to either side of the mesh (thus being one-half the included angle of adjacent mesh sides). Remember also that the mapping icon needs to have the same aspect ratio as the material's dominant texture map for the correcting ratio to be relevant (an adjustment easily made with Surface/Mapping/Adjust/Bitmap Fit).

Figure 6.36
The correcting ratios for various angled meshes.

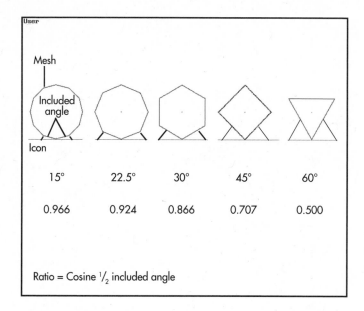

You can adjust the mapping scale by changing the material's mapping parameters, the icon's tiling values, or the width of the mapping icon itself. Whichever method you choose to use, you should remain consistent to make future editing a clearer process. You should note, however, that scaling the mapping icon is not nearly as accurate as adjusting mapping parameters. Readjusting a scaled mapping icon is also difficult—there is no reference to your previous increase as there is when adjusting its tiling values or material mapping parameters.

The key to correctly angled planar mapping is to ensure an equal angle of the mapping icon to each side of the mesh. If the object is hexagonal or octagonal, you need to apply separate coordinates to adjacent pairs of faces. In this case, you have to detach the object into two individual objects and apply the coordinates separately.

Cylindrical Mapping Considerations

Cylindrical mapping projects its coordinate from a center point outward to infinity, much like the ripples in a pond (see fig. 6.37). The cylinder's height determines the size of the bitmap's height, or V scale. Because of this, the size of the radius is not important, only the location of its center. The cylinder's main purposes are to help you find the map's center and to show which way is up and back. The front of this icon is the line opposite the dark line, and not the circle. This needs to be kept in mind when you use Adjust/Align commands.

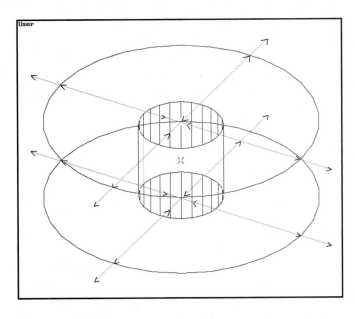

Figure 6.37
Cylindrical projection from the cylindrical mapping icon.

The icon's back edge indicates where the bitmap's edges meet. This is where a seam appears when rendering if the material's bitmap is not tileable in its U direction. Parts of a mesh that are parallel to the top and bottom of the icon experience swirls or streaks (as in the cylinders of fig. 6.38), of which every row of pixels is being "sliced through" at that point. This can also occur to faces that are near parallel as the bitmap's pixels are projected outward.

Figure 6.38
Cylindrical mapping intersecting a flat top and a tessellated top.

The (Alt)+Scale option is very useful for snapping the cylinder to the exact size of the object and thus centering it. Remember that the diameter does not matter—it is only an aid in locating the center and seeing the projection. This option does scale the vertical size to meet the object's size, and that dimension is important.

The Adjust/Center option is equally useful because it centers the icon on the object's local axis and does not change the map's rotation or vertical scale when doing it.

The Face Align and View Align methods spin the map about its center to the correct alignment, as with Planar mapping.

Because the bitmap is projected outward radially from the cylinder centerline, there is no aspect ratio that can be adjusted. The Region Fit and Bitmap Fit commands thus do not apply and cannot be accessed for cylindrical mapping.

Cylindrical Mapping Techniques

Often you need a cylindrical-mapped bitmap to render undistorted—especially bitmaps that have text, logos, or portraits. To ensure an undistorted map, you must balance the bitmap's ratio with the icon's projected radius to arrive at the required icon height. As the map wraps around the cylinder, its width is stretched to the length of the circumference ($2 \times radius$). Multiplying this distance by the bitmap's ratio produce the required height of the cylindrical icon ($ratio \times 2 r$) in real units. The bitmap's ratio is simply its height divided by its width. Correcting for this ratio is demonstrated in the following exercise.

Correcting Cylindrical Projection with Icon Height

Begin by creating a material that uses ADESK2.TGA as a decaled texture map at 100 percent and render the sample	Displays the bitmap's logo over the material's base color
Put this material to the scene by pressing (C), *name it* TEXT, *and return to the 3D Editor by pressing* (F3)	
Create a smooth 32-sided cylinder can that has a radius of 20" and a height of 200" in the Top *viewport*	

Inches will designate units for this exercise.

Choose Mapping/Type/Cylindrical	Displays the Cylindrical Mapping icon
Switch to the Front *viewport, choose* Adjust/Scale, *and click on the can while pressing* (Alt)	Scales the icon to the exact size of the can
Apply the mapping and the current material and render in a Camera *or* User *view*	Stretches the text around the can (upper can of fig. 6.39)

Figure 6.39
Distorted and correctly proportioned cylindrical mapping.

Because the map cannot get any wider, the height of the bitmap needs to be adjusted for the can's height.

Return to the Materials Editor and drag the map's file slot over to the File Info *button*	Reports that the map is 512×482 in size and so has a 0.9414 height to width ratio

The correcting ratio for the icon's height can now be calculated. The circumference of the can is $20" \times 2 \times$, which is close to 125.66". The required height for the icon is thus $125.66 \times 0.9414 = 118.3"$. Because the icon is currently the full height of 200", it needs to be reduced to $118.3 \div 200 = 59$ percent of its current height.

Return to the 3D Editor and scale the icon down to 59 percent by using Adjust/Scale

Apply this new mapping to the can and render	The decal now appears in the center of the can with the correct proportions (lower can of fig. 6.39)

This technique works fine as long as you can adjust the icon's height. More often than not, however, you are stuck with the cylinder's height and forced to use a correcting ratio to make the image appear undistorted. You can use the preceding procedure in reverse to arrive at the required bitmap ratio, as demonstrated in the following exercise.

Correcting Cylindrical Projection with Bitmap Scale

Select the can used previously and 2D scale it in the Front viewport down to 10 percent of its current height

The can is now 20" tall

Render the can for reference

Acquire the mapping from the can with Adjust/Acquire

The icon is much taller than the can. This responds to the original mapping that was applied, but because the can was scaled, it is no longer of any use.

Use Adjust/Alt+Scale *in the* Front *viewport to reset the scale*

Scales the icon to fit the can's new size

Apply the mapping and render

The logo still appears very squat, as seen in the upper left can of figure 6.40

Figure 6.40
Distorted and correctly proportioned cylindrical mapped decals.

Return to the Materials Editor and click on the texture map's S button to access the texture map's parameter dialog box

Displays the Mapping Parameters dialog box

The original icon height of 118.3" will always be correct for a 20" cylinder of this radius and a bitmap with a 0.9414 height to width ratio. Because the radius is fixed, the only option is to change the bitmap's proportion. Currently, the icon is 20"/118.3"=0.169 of what it is supposed to be. Changing the U scale will correct this.

Change the bitmap's U Scale value to 0.169 and click on OK

Changes the material's map ratio

Click on Auto Put *and choose* Render Last	Renders the can with a correctly proportioned logo (see fig. 6.40, upper right)
Reenter the map's parameter box, then choose the Both *option and* Render Last *again*	Tiles the logo around the can with the correct proportions (see fig. 6.40)

For every bitmap proportion, there is only *one* corresponding cylinder map proportion that creates an undistorted map. If you create a special map for a specifically sized cylinder, you must proportion the bitmap to match the geometry. Sizing the geometry or its mapping proportion either distorts the map or makes it the incorrect size to fit the geometry. The most common need for accurate Cylindrical Mapping is in packaging design. The height and radius of a wine bottle or pop can are fixed, and it is usually very important for their labels to appear correctly. The required map proportion is as follows:

Bitmap Label's Height/Width = Can's Circumference/Height

Spherical Mapping Considerations

Spherical mapping projects its coordinates from a center point outward to infinity in all directions, much like an omni light's illumination, (see fig. 6.41). The size of the icon has absolutely no effect on the size of the bitmap. The location of its center in relation to the applied object is the sole determination for how large the bitmap ends up. The icon's purpose is to aid you in locating the correct center point and showing you which way is up and back.

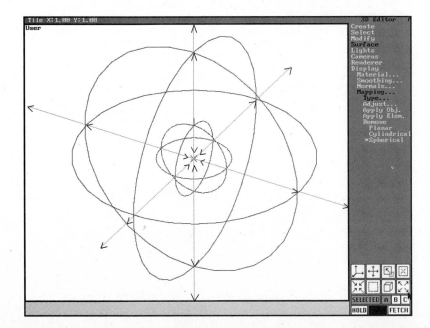

Figure 6.41

Spherical projection from the spherical mapping icon.

II

Basic Modeling

The Adjust/Center and [Alt]+Scale options are the most useful for snapping the spherical icon to an object's center. Because center location and rotation are your only concern, it does not matter that [Alt]+Scale also resizes the icon.

Rotation and orientation have a great effect on spherical mapping's results. The icon's poles are points of convergence for the bitmap and can cause pinching and swirls. The back latitude shows the map's critical seam point, which is apparent if the bitmap used is not tileable in its U direction (see "Spherical Reflections" for more information). Rotating the icon correctly is important. Because the Adjust/Rotate command spins the icon on its center, you can rotate its projection without disturbing the location.

Spherical Mapping Techniques

Spherical mapping begins by stretching the bitmap vertically from pole to pole. It then wraps it horizontally starting at the back meridian all the way around. The map is then projected back onto the coordinate's sphere. As any cartographer knows, there is no way to make a rectangular map fit on a sphere without distortion. The only area you do have some control of is on the mapping coordinate's equator. Here the map has been wrapped the full circumference, whereas the height has been wrapped around only one-half of the circumference. This means that a bitmap should have a width to height ratio of 2:1 for it to appear undistorted at the equator.

Bitmaps that do not have an original 2:1 ratio must have their U or V dimensions scaled. The formula is simply U/V=2.0.

You now can choose which axis to scale. Most bitmaps are too narrow for their height. If the vertical dimension is to be full height, then the width must be scaled down. A 640 × 480 bitmap requires its U value to be scaled by 640/(2 × 480)=0.6667. If the horizontal dimension must be constant, then the V value would need to be scaled up by 480/(640/2)=1.5. Adjusting for these values is demonstrated in the following exercise.

Exploring Spherical Mapping

Begin by creating a material that uses
CHECKOP.CEL *as a 100-percent texture map,*
and put it to the scene as current by pressing [C]

The squares will enable you to determine distortion at the equator.

Create a smooth G-Sphere with 576 faces

Choose Surface/Mapping/Type/Spherical	The Mapping icon becomes the Spherical icon
Choose Mapping/Adjust/Scale *and select the sphere while pressing* [Alt]	Positions the icon in the sphere's center and extends to it edges

The size of the icon does not matter because the mapping is projected evenly from the icon's center. The size of the icon is only an aid in determining its top and rear meridian.

Assign the current material to the sphere and render	Renders the sphere, but the checks along the equator are too wide (see the left ball in fig. 6.42)

Figure 6.42
The effect of bitmap scale on the proportions of spherical projection.

Press F3 *to return to the Materials Editor and drag the map's file slot over to* File Info	Reports that the CEL is 392 × 390 in size
Change the bitmap's U Scale to 0.5026 and click on OK—*this is equal to 392/(390×2)*	
Click on Auto Put *and choose* Last Render	Renders the sphere in the scene with smaller, but proportioned squares (see the middle ball in fig. 6.42
Return the bitmap's U Scale to 1.0, change its V Scale to 1.9898, and click on OK—*this is equal to 390/(392/2)*	
Choose Last Render	Renders the sphere in the scene with larger, but proportioned squares (see the right ball in fig. 6.42)

You could have changed the mapping coordinate's Tile settings to modify the checks' appearance as well, but this would not have given you nearly the same flexibility.

Modifying Mapping Coordinates

Assigning mapping coordinates is the first step toward perfecting a material's appearance for a particular surface. As the model progresses, it is usually the case that those coordinates need to be fine-tuned, repositioned, rotated, radically changed, or reapplied.

Acquiring Mapping Coordinates

The Adjust/Acquire option is your primary tool when readjusting mapping coordinates that have already been assigned to objects. Once acquired, the mapping icon can be adjusted and its coordinates applied to that and/or other objects. Although this ability is very useful, you should note that it can *only* be done at the object level.

When you assign mapping coordinates to an element within an object you have no chance of reacquiring them from that mesh—even if you detach the element as its own object. Each object carries a reference to its first mapping. It is this icon that is acquired no matter how many elements are assigned their own icons. When objects are attached to one another, the first mapping of the parent object takes precedence. The child object, now an element, loses the capability to have its icon acquired forever.

Mapping coordinates can be very important and are time-consuming to duplicate. It usually pays to create more objects in your scene in order to retain the capability to acquire their coordinates, rather than to create fewer objects with several elements and have to develop mapping icons from scratch whenever you need to adjust them. You can link objects together in the Keyframer to act as one.

A useful method for keeping the mapping information for attached objects, or elements, is to use simple stand-in objects (Box cubes work well for this). Before attaching objects, acquire the child's mapping icon, create the stand-in and assign the mapping to it. When you assign mapping to an element, create another stand-in and map to it as well. You can assign these stand-ins the same color for easy reference or store them as their own 3DS files. If you assign them the corresponding material as well, you are on your way to creating an "acquirable materials library," which you can merge into any model as needed.

Adjust Map Scale with Tile

The Adjust/Tile option controls the X and Y repeat values for the mapping coordinates, as shown in figure 6.43. In earlier releases, this was the only tool available for defining mapping repeats that are different than the icon's boundary. There is no extra capability gained by using this option because the effect of Tile settings is equivalent to scaling the icon (although it is quite a bit more accurate). An X Repeat of 4 is equivalent to scaling the icon to 25 percent along the X axis. By defining the number of repetitions, this command is actually the inverse of the UV Scale parameter available for bitmaps.

Figure 6.43
The 3D Editor's Map Tiling dialog box with the correction for a 45-degree angle.

What Adjust/Tile does afford you is the ability to affect the scale of all the bitmaps present within all the materials assigned to the object. This can be convenient if the material has numerous bitmaps, or if several materials are assigned within the same object and they all need the same scale adjustment.

Using map tiling in combination with material parameters can lead to confusion, however. After all, the material's mapping parameters are combining with those of the tile values, and the effect may not be immediately obvious. In general, adjusting bitmap scale works best within the Materials Editor, where you can visualize, reference, copy, and save the various scaling iterations. Using Tile values does enable you to keep one material definition that is shared among objects having varying tiling repeats, but those variations will be restricted to the object level due to mapping coordinates.

Remember that tile information is stored within the mapping coordinates and can be lost, while the UV scales of a material's maps are always editable. Reserve the Adjust/Tile option for making final adjustments of mapping coordinates that are difficult to resize manually or have several materials using numerous bitmaps that all require similar scaling.

Material Parameters—The Great Work Around

The capability to modify the rotation, scale, and offset of a material's maps by adjusting their Mapping Parameters has changed many of the previous "rules" for refining mapping coordinates. All of these abilities are accessed by clicking on the Settings button belonging to any map file slot active within a material (refer back to fig. 6.18).

As a model nears completion, you might want to consider fine-tuning the placement of bitmaps within the Materials Editor rather than the 3D Editor. As anyone who has scaled icons knows, they are not the most graceful things for making small refinements. You are limited to adjustments in increments of 1/4 degree of rotation and a 1/4 percent of scale and can only do it with your mouse. There are many times when this is simply too crude. The higher precision available with parameters can definitely help. The other reason to consider using parameters is that you can save your experiments and backtrack if necessary.

Release 4 now allows the mapping icons to respect the first point returned while in Snap mode, thus making Snap a valuable tool in making mapping adjustments.

After refining a material's mapping parameters, simply put it back to the scene. If the material is used by more than one object and you only want to affect the appearance of some of the objects, put it to the scene as current and rename it on the way over. Applying this new version of the material to the object that needs final adjustment isolates the results. There is no memory penalty for doing this because the copied materials use the same bitmaps.

Face Maps—The New Mapping Shortcut

Release 3 introduced *face maps* as a new form of automatic mapping. This method stretches the bitmap to fit across the quadrilateral formed by each pair of faces that share an edge. If the program does not find a pair with which to match a face, it renders half of the map cut across the diagonal.

Any mapped material can be made into a face map by simply clicking on the Face Map parameter button located just above the mapping file slots. Once a face map, the material ignores any mapping coordinates that exist for a mesh and relies on the mesh's face structure entirely for its effect.

The program searches the mesh for face pairs in the order they are created for that element. This works fine for segments and facets on objects created "whole" through the Lofter or Create branch but can lead to problems for those with built or tessellated faces, those that have been edited by a Boolean operation, and those created in external programs (such as AutoCAD). These meshes, in all probability, lack orderly face-matching and have split face maps. You can correct this by using Modify/Edge/Turn to flip the orientation of the faces on an edge-by-edge basis.

A face map's orientation is completely controlled by the order in which the face's vertices are found. You can change this ordering by the edge visibility between adjacent faces. In general, a face tries to "mate" with another that shares an invisible edge. If none, or more than one exists, the face is matched with the oldest face created. This is obviously not an exact science. Figure 6.44 shows two arrangements of faces for the same star and two ways of assigning invisible edges. Figure 6.45 shows the resulting face map assignments. The face maps want to match with faces that share invisible edges. This may not result in an even match, as one half is oriented differently than the other half.

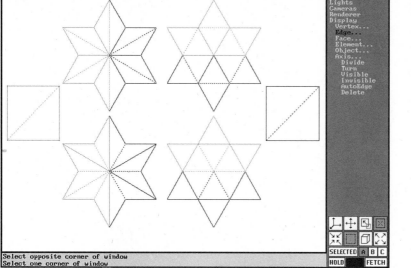

Figure 6.44
Various face arrangements and edge visibilities for the same geometry.

Figure 6.45
The resulting face map rendering as assigned to figure 6.44's mesh.

One very useful option to use with face maps is the bitmap's Mirror parameter. This affects a face map by repeating it four times with each face. Because each iteration is mirrored, the complete image appears without being diagonally sliced. Figure 6.46 shows these effects.

Figure 6.46
The same face mapped material with its Mirror parameter activated.

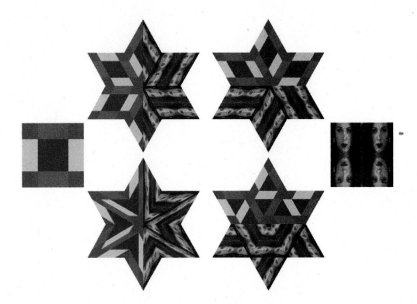

The only method for correcting the orientation within the mesh is to Turn faces and change edge visibilities. If a map is tiling correctly but is facing the wrong direction, you can control the overall orientation through the bitmap's Rotation parameter defined in the material.

Face maps also reference the face's normal for orienting which corner is which. If the mesh has erratic normals and you resort to using a 2-Sided material, the face maps do not align properly. If the face map's orientation is important, then the mesh's normals should always be unified and faced appropriately.

Tiling has no effect on face maps because it is not a product of mapping coordinates. You can create additional repetitions within each face by adjusting the bitmap's Scaling and Offset parameters.

Tip

A traditional hidden line image can be achieved by using a black bitmap that has a white border and applying it as a face map material (an example of this is HIDDEN1.CEL used by the FACEMAP HIDN LIN material in the 3DS.MLI). Unlike Wire frame materials, this hides geometry that is behind the mesh and ignores Edge visibility. Remember that you can use Luma Tint to make this generic map any color and reverse its colors by using Negative.

Face maps are especially useful for bitmaps that are tileable in both directions. These materials wrap seamlessly around an object and can be very convincing. This effect is extremely difficult to reproduce with manually assigned mapping. Materials that are random in nature and do not depend on scale, such as granite, sand, and stucco, are good candidates for this type of application. This is not a good choice for materials that depend on scale for their effect, such as tile or brick, unless the mesh has very uniformly sized faces.

The following exercise investigates the use of object tessellation as a means to add texture to a mesh. The tessellation commands themselves are described in Chapter 10, "Creating and Editing Faces and Vertices in the 3D Editor."

Object Tessellation and Face Maps

Begin by making the CHECK texture material a face map by clicking on the Face Map *parameter button and rendering the sample*

The sample sphere is very densely covered with checkers

Switch to the cube display and render again

The checker pattern occurs once on each side of the sample cube

Put this material to the scene and enter the 3D Editor

Create a series of objects with varying face counts

An example arrangement is shown in figure 6.47.

Choose Material/Assign/By Name *and assign all of the objects the current CHECK material*

Render the scene for a reference image

Each facet has a checker map, as seen in figure 6.47.

Notice that each side and facet has a perfectly repeated checker map. This is because all the faces were created in order and share consecutive edges.

Press Alt+A *to select all and clone the selection into a new object*

Hide the original objects for future use and reference

Choose Create/Object/Tessellate *and select the object*

The Tessellation Controls dialog box appears

Choose the standard Face *option and place the Tension value at 0*

Tessellates the object's mesh, as in figure 6.48

continues

continued

Figure 6.55
The result of spraying with cycle draw.

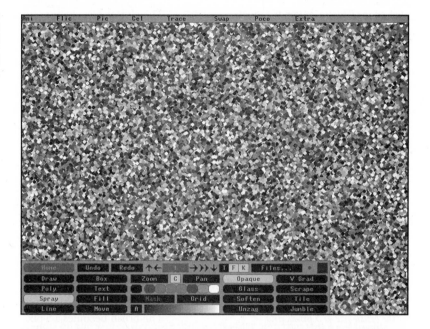

Figure 6.56
A rendered object, using the cycle-drawn spray map as a texture and bump map.

The following exercise demonstrates how to use Animator Pro to create a label to be applied as a decal map.

Creating a Decal Label

Start or reset Animator Pro

Click on a medium red color in the cluster box

Makes red the active color

Using Opaque ink, click on the Box *tool and draw a box about 300 pixels wide by 200 pixels high in the middle of the screen*

Draws a rectangle filled with red

Click on the Brush Size *icon and specify a square brush with a width of 10 pixels*

Displays the brush menu for adjusting brush size (see fig. 6.57)

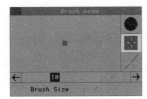

Figure 6.57
Setting the brush size and shape.

Press (Spacebar) *after adjusting the brush*

Right-click on the Box *tool and click on the* Filled *button to turn it off*

Displays the Tools panel and instructs Animator Pro to draw hollow boxes

Press (Spacebar)

Click on a Cyan *color in the cluster box*

Position the cursor about 10 pixels below and to the right of the upper-left corner of the red box, then drag out a rectangle about 280 × 180 pixels

Draws a Cyan border just inside the edges of the red box

Right-click on the Text *tool, and then click on the* Font *button*

Displays the Tools palette, and then displays the Font selection palette

Select the font BARREL10.FNT, *and then click on the* Load *button*

Makes BARREL10 the current font

Click on the Justify *button, and then click on* Center

Sets the text tool for center-justified text

Press (Spacebar)

continues

continued

Right-click on any ink slot other than Opaque, and then choose Dark ink from the list to occupy that slot	Makes Dark ink available in the Home panel and makes it the active ink as well
Press (Spacebar)	
Click on the Text *tool and pick two points to specify a text rectangle just inside the Cyan border*	
Type **Inside 3D Studio** ⏎	The words "Inside 3D Studio" appear center-justified on two lines inside the box
Click inside the text box, position the text in the center of the box, and click again to release it	
Click inside the text box again, move the text 5 pixels down and 5 pixels to the right, and then click again	
Right-click to paint the text onto the screen	The text is painted in the box using Dark ink
Click on the White *slot in the mini-palette*	Makes White the current color
Click on the Opaque *ink slot*	Makes Opaque the current ink
Right-click on the Text *tool, and then click on the* Reuse *button*	The text "Inside 3D Studio" reappears on the screen in white ink
Click inside the box and move the text 5 pixels up and 5 pixels to the left of its current location	
Right-click to paint the text on the screen and press (Spacebar)	You now see white text with a drop shadow (see fig. 6.58)
Choose Get *from the* CEL *pull-down menu*	
Pick two points defining a rectangle around the image with at least a 1-pixel black border	The 1-pixel black border ensures that the transparent color of the decal is black and not red
Choose Files *from the* CEL *pull-down menu and click on the* Save *button*	
Save the file in the 3D Studio \MAPS *directory as* I3D-ANI.CEL	

You now have an image suitable for use as a decal in 3D Studio. The key to this technique is making the black border around the image. 3D Studio uses the first pixel in the upper-left corner of the image as the transparent color when a map is applied as a decal. If you had clipped the CEL tight to the image, then red would have been the transparent color. Figure 6.59 shows a vase with the decal applied.

Figure 6.58
The completed image.

Figure 6.59
A vase with decal applied.

The following exercise shows you how to save modeling and rendering time by using maps rather than geometry to represent detail. Many items that you model have details such as buttons, logos, engraving, and vents that would be extremely difficult to model as true geometry. Details should usually be represented by maps, the exception being if your view will be so close to the object that true 3D geometry is needed to maintain realism.

Creating a Geometry Map

Start or reset 3D Studio

Load the file CALC.3DS

The mesh file of a thin rounded rectangle sitting on a large flat floor appears (see fig. 6.60)

Figure 6.60
A thin rounded rectangle ready for manipulation.

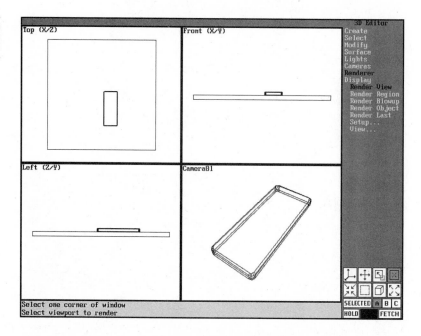

Choose Lights/Ambient *and adjust the Luminance slider to 255*

Fills the scene with full intensity light that will wash out any shading effects

Choose Renderer/Setup/Configure, *and then click on the* GIF *button and the* 640 × 480 *button*

Configures 3D Studio to output 256 color files

Choose Renderer/Setup/Options *and click on* Dither 256: No

Turns off dithering of GIF files

Choose Display/Hide/Object *and select the large object named* Floor

Click in the Top *viewport, then click on the* Zoom Extents *button*

Fills the Top viewport with only the calculator object

Choose Renderer/Render View *and click in the* Top *viewport, click on the* Flat Shading *mode button, click on* Anti-Aliasing Off, *and then click on the* Disk *button to save the rendering to a file*

Renders the calculator with flat shading against a black background

Type **CALCFACE** *in the Filename field and click on* OK

Quit 3D Studio—do not worry about saving the 3DS file

Start Animator Pro

Choose Files *from the* Pic *menu and click on the* Load *button*

Select the GIF file CALCFACE *and click on the* Load *button*

The flat white silhouette of the calculator appears on the screen (see fig. 6.61)

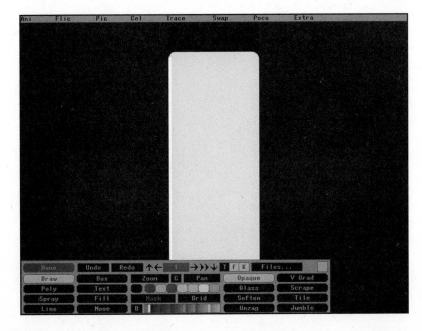

Figure 6.61
The calculator's silhouette.

continues

continued

Right-click on the cluster box in the lower-middle of the Home panel	Displays the Palette panel
Click on the All *button in the upper right of the palette panel, and then choose* Default *from the* Value *pull-down menu*	Resets Animator Pro to its default color palette
Click on the A *cluster button to activate cluster A, and then press* (Spacebar)	Makes cluster A the active cluster and returns to the Home panel
Click on a medium gray from the middle of the cluster box, click on Opaque *ink and the* Fill *tool, and then pick anywhere in the black background of the image*	Fills the screen background with medium gray opaque ink
Click on the Arrow *icon to the right of the current frame indicator in the upper-middle of the Home panel*	Saves the changes made to the current frame
Right-click on the Fill *tool, select* Fill To *from the tool list, and then press* (Spacebar)	Replaces the Fill tool with Fill To
Click on the black slot at the far left of the mini-palette, then pick one point in the gray background and one point in the white silhouette of the calculator	Fills the calculator shape with black ink
Draw buttons, numeric display, and other features as you desire to represent the calculator face, only within the black shape of the calculator (see fig. 6.62 for one possible arrangement)	
Choose Clip Changes *from the* Traces *pull-down menu*	A scrolling box appears briefly around the calculator, defining it as the current CEL
Choose Files *from the* CEL *pull-down menu, and click on the* Save *button*	
Save the CEL as CALCFACE.CEL *in the 3D Studio \MAPS directory*	
Quit Animator Pro, restart 3D Studio, and reload the file CALC.3DS	
Press (F5) *to enter the Materials Editor*	

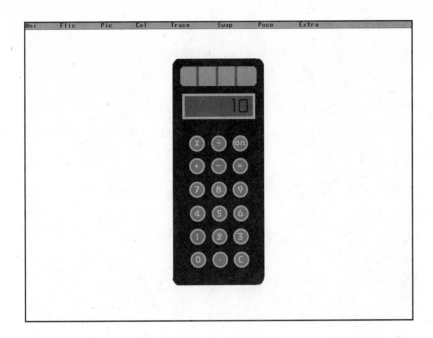

Figure 6.62
One possible calculator configuration.

Click on the center sample window at the top of the screen and adjust the Shininess slider to 53 and the Shininess Strength slider to 100	Specifies the shininess values for your new material
Click on the None map slot to the right of the Texture 1 button, select the file CALCFACE.CEL, and then click on OK	Specifies CALCFACE.CEL as texture map number 1
Render a sample cube against a background pattern, press C, *type* **CALCULATOR FACE**, *and then click on* OK	Renders a sample of the material and sets it as the current material in the 3D Editor (see fig. 6.63)
Press F3 *to enter the 3D Editor*	
Choose Surface/Material/Assign/Object *and select the calculator, then click on* OK	Assigns the Calculator Face material to the Calculator object
Choose Surface/Mapping/Adjust/Scale *and hold down* Alt *while selecting the calculator in the* Top *viewport*	Assigns and scales the Planar Mapping icon to fit the extents of the Calculator in the Top viewport
Choose Mapping/Apply Obj *and select the Calculator, then click on* OK	Applies the mapping coordinates to the Calculator

continues

continued

Figure 6.63

Choosing a material for the calculator in 3D Editor.

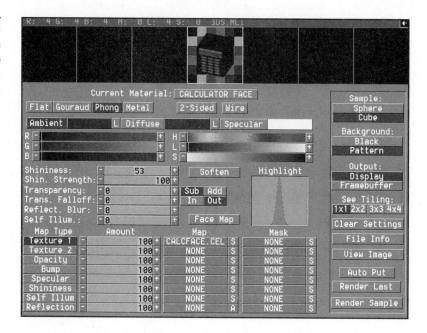

Choose Renderer/Render View *and click in the* Camera01 *viewport (figure 6.64 shows an example of how the calculator might look)*

Consider the amount of work required if you were to model all of the buttons and the numeric display as mesh geometry, rather than apply them as a map. You can also increase the realism of mapped geometry by combining it with an appropriate bump map.

The following exercise demonstrates how to create bump maps through rendering and through the use of gradient inks in Animator Pro. You will render a rounded bump map in 3D Studio and compare it with a linear ramp in Animator Pro.

You begin this exercise by loading a file with geometry ready to render. It is worth your while to investigate the way that this file is set up because the generic setup can be used to render bump maps from almost any geometry. The keys to the geometry are as follows:

✔ The geometry uses the flat white material.

✔ A spotlight is placed straight on the center of the rendered view.

✔ The spotlight is placed as close as possible to the object, while still providing even illumination.

✔ The spotlight has a pure white color with a luminance no greater than 180.

Figure 6.64
The finished product.

The last two points are interesting. If you move the spotlight farther away from the object, the rays of light that strike the object come closer and closer to being parallel. The near-parallel light rays flatten the shading and create a less effective bump map. Placing the light close to the object renders with a fuller gradation from black to white and produces a more effective bump map.

Details about setting the light at no more than a luminance of 180 are presented in Chapter 7, "Lights, Cameras, and Basic Rendering Options." The concern for creating bumps maps is that as the luminance goes beyond 180, the specular highlight begins to wash out the shading and reduce the effectiveness of the bump map.

Creating a Bump Map

Start or reset 3D Studio

Load the file CYLINDER.3DS, *and then press* Alt+L	Loads the model in figure 6.65 and displays the lights
Choose Gamma Control *from the* Info *pull-down menu and click on the* OFF *button*	Turns off gamma correction
Choose Renderer/Setup/Configure, *and then set the configure parameter for Mono Tiff, no Compression, resolution of Width: 640, Height: 480, and Aspect Ratio: 1.0; then click on* OK	Configures for rendering a monochrome TIFF file for use as a bump map (see fig. 6.66)

continues

continued

Figure 6.65
The
CYLINDER.3DS
model.

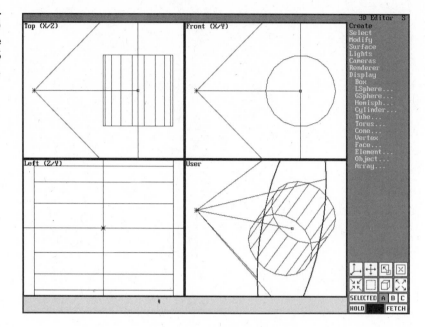

Figure 6.66
The Device
Configuration
dialog box.

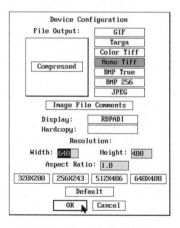

Choose Renderer/Render View *and click in
the* Left *viewport*

*Click on the buttons to turn off anti-aliasing
and turn on saving to disk, then click on* Render

Save the file directory as
CYLINDER.TIF *and click on* OK

Quit 3D Studio

Turning off gamma correction and anti-aliasing is vitally important for creating bump maps. If you gamma correct the output file, 3D Studio alters the values of the gradation, producing a flatter bump map. Gamma correction is great for high-quality color output, but leave it off for rendering grayscale bump maps.

Anti-aliasing is turned off because you do not want to anti-alias between the gray object and the black background. Anti-aliasing produces gray values at the edges of the geometry that do not accurately represent bump map values. This can cause strange ridges at the edges of your bump map.

Finally, you want to render to a monochrome TIFF file because this gives you a palette with 256 levels of gray when you import the file into Animator Pro. Rendering to any other format includes color in the palette, even though no color is used in the geometry. This causes dithering of the shading on the geometry and reduces the effectiveness of the bump map.

Start Animator Pro

Choose NumPic *from the* Poco *pull-down menu, then choose* Load Single (RGB) Pic *from the* Convert *dialog box*	Starts the Poco program that loads and converts other image types into Animator Pro
Select the TIF file CYLINDER.TIF *and click on the* Load *button, then choose* Exit	Loads the TIFF file and completes the Poco program (see fig. 6.67)

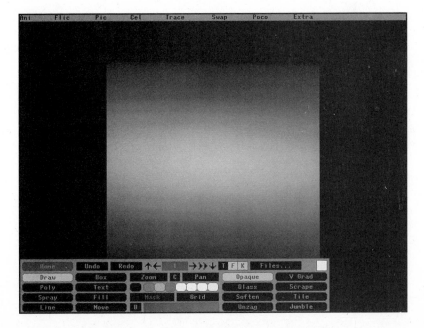

Figure 6.67
The imported grayscale TIF file in Animator Pro.

II

Basic Modeling

continues

continued

Choose Clip *from the* CEL *pull-down menu*	The rendered portion of the image is clipped as the current CEL
Choose Files *from the* CEL *pull-down and save the CEL to the 3D Studio* \MAPS *directory as* ROUND.CEL	Saves the CEL to a file without any background
Right-click on the cluster box to display the Palette panel, then click on cluster button A to make it active	
Choose Get Cluster *from the* Cluster *pull-down menu and click on color slot 0 in the upper left corner of the palette, then click on color slot 255 in the lower right corner of the palette*	Defines cluster A as containing all of the colors in the palette arranged as a grayscale ramp
Click on B Cluster *button, then choose* Get Cluster *again and click twice on the white color slot 255 in the lower right corner of the palette*	Defines cluster B as a single color (white) cluster
Press (Spacebar) *to return to the Home panel and choose* V Grad *from the inks slots, then click on the* K *(key color) button to the left of the* Files *button in the Home panel*	Makes V Grad the current ink and turns off transparency for the black key color
Choose Paste *from the* Cel *pull-down menu and right-click to paste the CEL back on the screen*	

VGRAD ink uses the colors in the active cluster. Cluster B contained only white, so the CEL was pasted as a solid white square.

Click on the B Cluster *button to switch it to cluster A*	The grayscale ramp of cluster A appears in the cluster box
Choose the Box *tool from the Tools slots, then draw a box that covers the top half of the white square*	Creates a box that ramps from black at the top to white at the bottom
Right-click on the cluster box to return to the Palette panel, and then choose Reverse *from the* Cluster *pull-down menu*	Cluster A ramps from white to black

Press (Spacebar) *to return to the*
Home panel and draw a box that covers
the remaining bottom half of the white
square

The V Grad ink and Box tools are still active, and you draw a box that ramps from white at the top to black at the bottom.

Choose Clip *from the* CEL *pull-down menu,*
then save the CEL as SHARP.CEL *in the*
3D Studio \MAPS directory

Figure 6.68 shows the ROUND.CEL on the left and SHARP.CEL on the right.

Quit Animator Pro

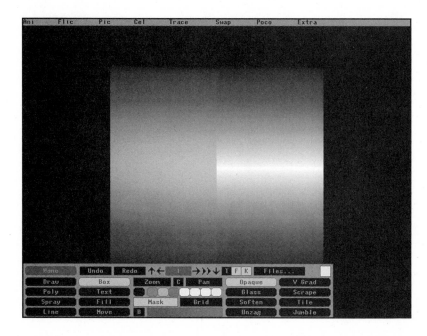

Figure 6.68
A comparison
of the two
bump maps.

Note the difference between the two images. The plain vertical gradient on the right is a linear progression from black to white and back to black again. 3D Studio accurately renders this bump map as a straight sloped surface that rises up and falls back. You were taught that this type of shading represents a cylinder, but 3D Studio knows better. Compare that image to the shading of a true cylinder on the left. The lighter white values occupy much more of the center of the image and then quickly fall off to black at the edges. This is an accurate bump map for a curved surface.

continues

continued

Now you create materials using these bump maps and apply them to geometry.

Start 3D Studio and load the file BUMPWALL.3DS	Loads the file shown in figure 6.69—the geometry already has mapping coordinates applied

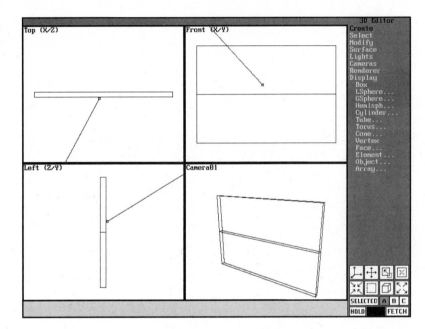

Figure 6.69
The BUMPWALL.3DS geometry.

Press F5 *to enter the Materials Editor*	
Choose Get Material *from the* Material *pull-down menu and select* White Matte	Renders a sample of the White Matte material in the first sample window
Click on the map slot for bump map and select the file ROUND.CEL	
Click on the S *button to the right of the map slot and set the V Scale to 0.2, then click on* OK	Specifies that the bump map will repeat five times across the height of the mapping icon
Choose Put Material *from the* Material *pull-down menu, type the name* **ROUND BUMP**, *and then click on* OK	Stores the material in the current library

Repeat the last four steps to create
a material in the second sample
window named SHARP BUMP, *use the*
map file SHARP.CEL, *and then press*
F3 *to return to the 3D Editor*

Assign the material ROUND BUMP *to*
the bottom object, then assign the material
SHARP BUMP *to the top object*

Choose Renderer/Render View *and*   Renders the view in figure 6.70
click in the Front *viewport*

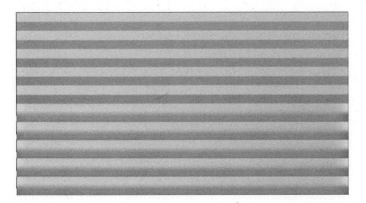

Figure 6.70
The geometry
rendered with
bump maps.

It is a common mistake to apply linear gradients as bump maps for circular geometry. Remember that a straight ramp in Animator Pro always produces a bump map for flat sloped bumps. Rounded bump maps are best created by rendering rounded white geometry to a grayscale image.

Note

If you find that you need a grayscale cluster in Animator Pro to create rounded bump maps, you can create it by using the following procedure:

1. Create a cluster of 91 color slots and set them all to black. Each slot represents a one-degree increment from 0 to 90.

2. The luminance value of each slot is equal to (COS A) × 255, where A represents the degree or slot number.

This produces a cluster that you can use with any of the gradient inks to create rounded bump maps. A sample GIF with this cluster is included on the CD-ROM as ROUND.GIF.

These exercises show that even though Animator Pro does not have some of the sophisticated tools and 24-bit color depth of other image processing programs, it is still a valuable tool for work with 3D Studio. Not all maps require 24-bit color, and bump maps can only use 8 bits of grayscale.

Summary

This chapter has only covered the basics of materials and mapping. These basics form a solid foundation on which to build complex and evolving materials. As your scene's need for realism increases, so will its material's. Chapter 12 will explore many of the abilities introduced with Release 3, but the basics of color mixing and mapping will remain the same.

Chapter Snapshot

This chapter discusses the following topics relating to lights, cameras, and basic rendering options:

✔ Examining basic lighting setups

✔ Understanding how 3D Studio actually illuminates

✔ Exploring the capabilities of lights and issues concerning their use

✔ Creating accurate and appropriate shadows

✔ Examining issues of placing cameras, framing compositions, and working with perspective

✔ Making the best use of the basic rendering options

Lights, Cameras, and Basic Rendering Options

The final impression of your 3D Studio world is controlled by the way it is illuminated and viewed. All too easily, users neglect these critical components after investing considerable time modeling the scene's meshes and defining its materials. A scene's lighting, however, has considerable impact on the overall mood and atmosphere. Similarly, the composition framed by a camera can define importance, imply movement, and create drama.

Understanding Standard Lighting Setups

The number, position, color, and intensity of lights within a scene combine to form a scene's lighting setup. These components can vary considerably between models according to mesh complexity and the overall mood that needs to be created. Lighting forms a major part of an image's final composition by accenting geometry, reinforcing color, and casting shadows—all of which can be considered compositional elements in their own right.

Initial Lighting Setups

A model's final lighting needs are, of course, very individual. In the beginning stages of modeling and composition, the lighting setup's purpose is to illuminate the model adequately enough to make modeling and material decisions visible. For these conceptual stages, the lighting setup can be thought of as "house lights" for the construction of the model's props and scenery.

Roles of Lights

Lights often are referred to by the role they play in the scene. A *key* (or *primary*) *light* is the brightest and often casts shadows. This light often represents the sun, a flood/spotlight, or the light cast from average ceiling fixtures. Lights placed in the background to provide even illumination from various sides are referred to as *fill lights*. A spotlight with a very narrow falloff aimed at a specific area is known as an *accent light*. Lights placed to the rear or below to cast a rim or halo of light color are known as *back lights*. Finally, a light that projects an image, whether it be a shadow silhouette cutout or a 35mm slide, is called a *projector light*. When a light is placed very close to a surface and allowed to cast its light down across this surface, it is called *grazed lighting*. Grazed lighting is most often used with heavily textured surfaces and has the effect of highlighting all the ins and outs of a surface. Light cast down a brick wall, catching the mortar joints is a good example of grazed lighting.

The essential component of effective lighting is *contrast*—without contrast, an object has no form. The effect of an overly illuminated scene is of totally washed out and undefined forms. If light levels do not vary as they envelop the scene, the objects contained within the scene appear flat. Placement of the primary light source directly behind the camera should be avoided because doing so may illuminate each side of the model too evenly. Moving the same light somewhat to either side (the effect of light coming over one's shoulder) can make for superior lighting, since contrast is created by the shifted source.

Basic Illumination

The point at which you first need to see parts of the model rendered is when you must place your first lights. Of course, 3D Studio will enable you to render without lights, illuminating the scene entirely with ambient light, but such a rendering is without depth or contrast. (Note that illuminating the scene with only white ambient light is often used for rendering flat art work.)

3D Studio bases its illumination on the angle the light source is to the mesh, and *not* its distance to it. When a light source is square to a plane and far away, the angles of the light's rays that fall on the plane's surface are nearly parallel, and the resulting illumination is very even. If the same light is placed quite close, the angles of the light's rays that strike the surface vary considerably and produce a pronounced hotspot. It usually is desirable to shade objects gradually across their faces and not to create such hotspots. To do this, you must place the light sources at an angle to the object (to create gradations) and at a significant distance (to minimize hotspots). The resulting basic setup is thus composed of two omni lights placed at a diagonal to the model (see fig. 7.1), with one higher and the other lower than the ground plane (see fig. 7.2).

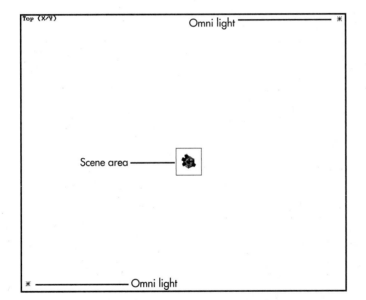

Figure 7.1
Horizontal placement of initial omni lights.

These initial omni lights begin as your principal light sources and should have luminance values of between 120 and 180. As your scene grows in lighting complexity and more specific lights are added, these lights are dimmed to become fill lights with luminance values of 20 to 60. It is important that the omni lights' distances be at least as great as they are illustrated in figures 7.1 and 7.2. Placing lights close does not make them brighter—only the angles of the rays more diverse.

This basic setup can be enhanced by adding a spotlight in the corner of the scene between the two omni lights. This now becomes the primary light and should receive the default light value (which has a luminance of approximately 180). Whenever a primary light is created, it is important to lower other existing light levels to allow it to dominate. One of the most important qualities of an image is contrast, and this is not achievable with consistently bright light sources.

Figure 7.2

Vertical placement of initial omni lights.

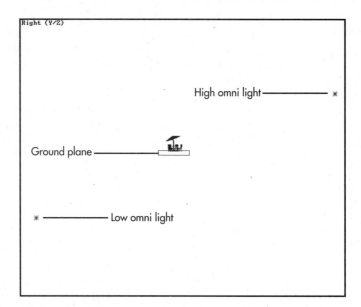

Understanding 3D Studio Lighting Concepts

Each type of light brings with it certain characteristics and capabilities. This section explores the effects achievable by each source and compares their common traits.

Types of Light

3D Studio provides three types of lights for illuminating a model. These are the ever-present *ambient light*, the point source *omni light*, and the directional, shadow-casting *spotlight*. Each type of light has its own sub-branch below the Lights command branch. Although many of the commands are similar between lights, each type can only be controlled from its respective command branch.

All light within 3D Studio respects the color laws of RGB additive illumination. The selection and assignment of light color is consistent between all forms of light. These colors can be mixed using any combination of *Red, Green, Blue* (RGB) and *Hue, Luminance, Saturation* (HLS) channels and values. See Chapter 2, "Concepts and Theories," for more information on color, illumination, and color mixing.

Characteristics of Light Entities

Lights are named just as objects are named. You can control them in the Keyframer and access them with the Hit option by knowing and using their names. When lights are created, they are given a generic default name starting with Light01.

It is often useful to give a more descriptive name to a light, such as Spot01, Omni01, Sun, or perhaps Backlight. By using a naming system that identifies omni lights from spotlights, you can select them by name with confidence when using the Hit option or with tracks in the Keyframer.

Lights are similar to objects in other regards as well. They can be cloned with the ⟨⇧Shift⟩ key and are placed on the construction planes at the time of creation.

The screen display of light icons is controlled with ⟨Alt⟩+⟨L⟩, although lights do not need to be displayed to cast light. Lights that are On have a yellow color, and those that are Off are blackened.

Ambient Light

Ambient light is 3D Studio's method for simulating the bounced and inherited light that fills a room, scene, or environment. Because ambient light is universally applied, increasing its level will reduce contrast and "flatten" the scene. A scene illuminated solely by ambient light has no contrast or shading—all sides and faces are rendered with the same intensity. When a mesh is not illuminated by any spotlights or omni lights, it is still illuminated by ambient light.

When a mesh is illuminated only by ambient light, the resulting material color is a product of the materials' ambient base color. Illuminating a scene with pure white ambient light will render all meshes according to their materials' ambient color values. Additional light sources in such a situation would shift the rendered colors slowly to the materials' diffuse base color.

Ambient light is not an entity that can be positioned or aimed, but rather a level. It has no focus or location and affects the entire model in the same manner. Because of this, it might be easier to think of ambient light as a system parameter rather than a light source. This light level dictates the lowest illumination of any mesh in the scene. Only one option controls ambient light—the Lights/Ambient command—which produces a color selecting dialog box, as shown in figure 7.3.

The illumination produced by the ambient light is always present and can never be reduced (except by an atmosphere described in Chapter 13, "Lighting and Camera Special Effects"). A very common mistake is to make this light too bright. Although an ambient light level of 30 to 50 might be useful for seeing the effects of initial modeling, a level of 7 to 15 is more common and appropriate for finished scenes.

Figure 7.3
Adjusting ambient
light to the
compliment of a
dominant yellow-
orange light.

Figure 7.3
Adjusting ambient
light to the
compliment of a
dominant yellow-
orange light.

```
                    Ambient Light Definition
       R  −      14                            +
       G  −      18                            +
       B  −      12                            +

       H  −                             234    +
       L  −      12                            +
       S  −      42                            +
                        OK        Cancel
```

Because ambient light is always present, its light and color are what you see in cast shadows. If you want to make the colors of your scene look especially deep, you should tint the ambient light's color slightly to be the compliment of the dominant shadow-casting lights. If the light is the yellowish cast of the moon, then an ambient light level of deep purple would intensify the moonlight's effect, as shown by the color definition in figure 7.3.

At times, a full-intensity ambient light is very useful. If you do not want any shading to occur across a scene, a white ambient light does the trick. This often is used for rendering "flat" art such as text, logos, and designs. Because the scene's total light level is white, no effects from any other light sources exist *if* the scene's materials have identical ambient and diffuse base colors (as in 100-strength texture mapped materials). If differences exist between the ambient and diffuse values, the objects will shift toward their diffuse values as the illumination increases across their surfaces. With pure white ambient light, only the ambient component of materials will be rendered. To create flat illumination for such a case, the additional light sources will need to be turned off.

Omni Lights

Omni lights are point light sources very similar to a naked bulb hanging on a wire, or the sun viewed by itself in outer space. An omni light traces its illumination from its position to all faces that are oriented toward them. Because omni lights are not designed to cast shadows, their rays cannot be blocked by any mesh and, therefore, decrease the darkness of any shadows on which they cast light.

Omni lights have several options, discussed later in this section. When you create an omni light, and each time you adjust it with Lights/Omni/Adjust, the dialog box shown in figure 7.4 appears. You can adjust an omni light at any time and even vary it over time in the Keyframer.

The primary purpose of omni lights in most scenes is to act as fill lights. It is quite common to have numerous omni lights at great distances, in varying colors, and with low levels to cast shades of light and mix them on the model. This is a technique borrowed from theatrical lighting, but one that is quite applicable to 3D Studio.

In being omni-directional, omni lights are quite predictable in their resulting illumination, and have a variety of secondary uses as well. Placing omni lights very close to meshes creates bright specular highlights. Placing omni lights at strategic angles behind or below meshes can create subtle glows and give the effect of bounced color. Omni lights given negative multipliers (see later in this chapter) are often placed in areas of the scene to create pools of shade.

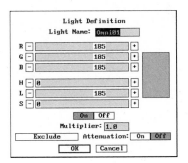

Figure 7.4
The omni
Light Definition
dialog box.

Spotlights

Spotlights are the primary lighting control within 3D Studio. Spotlights cast directional, aimed light in a manner similar to a flashlight, floodlight, or even a laser beam. Spotlights are the most commonly used lights because they give you the most control over the location and effect of illumination within your scene.

Spotlights have many options, several of which transform them into completely different lighting forms. When you create a spotlight, each time you adjust it with Lights/Spotlight/ Adjust, the dialog box shown in figure 7.5 appears. As with an omni light, you can adjust a spotlight at any time and vary it over time in the Keyframer.

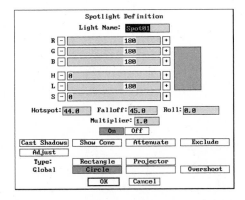

Figure 7.5
The Spotlight
Definition
dialog box.

Characteristics Common to Lights

The two positionable lights—omni and spotlights—share many characteristics of illuminating the scene. The characteristics discussed in this section apply to both types of lights and do not differ just because they happen to be in different command branches.

In addition, 3D Studio Release 3 introduced several new capabilities for lights. These options are available for both omni lights and spotlights, and the concepts concerning their effects are applicable to both types of sources.

II

Basic Modeling

Light Color as Illumination

A light's color actually is an indication of how much illumination it will cast. Light is additive, so the RGB values of lights accumulate to illuminate a surface. The closer to white this color is, the "brighter" the light is. As a light's color progresses to black, it dims. A light's hue is always relevant—regardless of how dim it is. A light with an RGB color of 6,2,4 is still purple, and one with 2,6,2 is still green, even though both of their color swatches look black. These dark colors still emit light, even though they do not appear to do so.

The amount of light emitted is determined by the HLS luminance value. Although this is not programmatically correct (because all calculations are really done with RGB values), it is visually correct for that color's hue and saturation. In this regard, it might help you to think of a light's luminance value as being its "illumination" level.

When determining a light's color definition, it is important to concentrate on the color—its hue and intensity—and not worry about how bright or dark it is. After the desired color is mixed, you can use the luminance slider to play with its illumination level. This gives you a full light-to-dark range for that color without disturbing its hue and saturation settings.

 You can create a family of lights that share the same color values by creating the first light and cloning it. By varying the luminance settings of the new lights, you change their intensity or "wattage" while maintaining the same "color" of illuminated light.

Users often do not realize that they do not need a white light (of 255 luminance) to cast a pure white light. The actual level needed by any of the RGB channels to achieve a 255 level effect is only 180. This is why an RGB of 180,180,180 is 3D Studio's default value for lights. As a light's color is darkened below 180, it loses its maximum lighting capability in a linear fashion—about 14 steps for every 10 color channel levels. A light with an RGB color of 180,0,0 still can produce a 255,0,0 color on a surface (if its material can reflect red, that is), whereas a 100,0,0 colored light can produce a red of only 141 or so. As a light is increased above 180, the angle at which it creates a 255 color level decreases.

Illumination and Angle of Incidence

The amount a surface is illuminated from a light depends completely on the light's angle to the surface and not on the light's proximity. This is the light's *angle of incidence* to the surface. If the surface is at a right angle to the light, it is illuminated at full effect. As the surface tilts away from the light source, this angle is lowered and the illumination received diminishes. This means that as a light is placed farther away, it illuminates the scene more and more evenly—each mesh's angle to the light source is slowly approaching 90 degrees. The effects of this form of illumination will be explored in the following exercise.

Investigating the Effect of a Light's Angle of Incidence

Although this exercise uses an omni light, note that a spotlight aimed perpendicularly at the same spot has the same effect.

Begin by creating a box in the Top *viewport*	The box has the white, default material
Choose Lights/Omni/Create *and place the new light in the center of the box just above the surface*	Accept the default light RGB color of 180,180,180, and the placement should look similar to figure 7.6

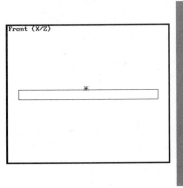

Figure 7.6
The omni light's initial placement and the illumination of a very close omni light.

Choose Lights/Ambient *and make it black by moving the Luminance slider to 0*	Isolates the effects of the light
Choose Renderer/Setup/Background *and make it a solid mid-gray by making the* Saturation 0 *and the* Luminance 127	Gives a basis to judge the light's effect
Click in the Top *viewport and render*	There is a pinpoint hotspot

The point directly below the light is illuminated at full strength, whereas the corners of the box are nearly black because of their very low angle of incidence to the omni light.

Click in a side viewport and move the light up until it has about a 30 degree angle to the corners (see fig. 7.7 for the appropriate distance)

continues

continued

Figure 7.7
The second placement of the omni light and the illumination of a close omni light.

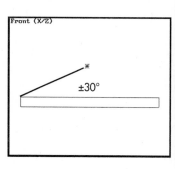

Render the Top *viewport*

The effect of the light is still a circular point of light, but is more spread out.

As the light is raised higher, its angle to the surface becomes greater. The corner areas that previously had a 1 degree angle of incidence now have a 30 degree angle and are that much brighter than before. The difference in gray levels between the center and the edge is about 200.

Move the light up until it has about a 60 degree angle to the corners

The light completes an equilateral triangle, as shown in figure 7.8

Render the Top *viewport*

The entire surface is illuminated, and the circle grows to that shown in figure 7.8

Figure 7.8
The third placement of the omni light and the resulting level of illumination.

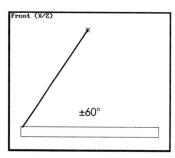

Again, as the light is placed farther away, the angle to the surface increases. The closer this angle gets to 90 degrees, the closer to white the surface is rendered. There are now 150 levels of difference in gray from the source to the edge.

Move the light far up, close to a 5 degree angle to the corners

The light moves far above the surface, as shown in figure 7.9

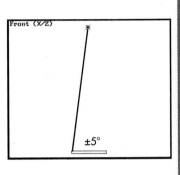

Figure 7.9
The placement of the omni light at a far distance and the resulting near-even illumination of the surface.

II

Basic Modeling

Render the Top *viewport*

The entire surface is very white, and it is difficult to even see the gradiated light circle.

The light is now far enough away from the surface that the angle of area varies only a little. A variation still exists across the surface of about 50 levels of gray.

Move the omni light very, very far up

The box should be so small as to barely be seen at the viewport's bottom.

Render the Top *viewport*   Renders the box as a solid white square

The light is close enough that the entire surface is between 89–90 degrees from the light. Because of this, the surface no longer has a gradation—everything is white.

A material's specular color is displayed when a light's angle of incidence to the viewing angle is quite high—between about 85–90 degrees. The specular color is used even if the light level is far below 180. To see the effect of a material's specular color, repeat the previous exercise with a material that has a distinctly different and saturated specular color. See figure 6.5 in Chapter 6, "Introduction to the Materials Editor," for a description of this interaction between material colors and light.

Multiplying Light Intensities

The Multiplier definition introduced in Release 3 can be thought of as a dimmer switch for a very bright light. Changing its values is the same as changing the color's luminance. A white light (255 luminance and 0 saturation) given a 0.5 multiplier emits the same light as a gray light (127 luminance and 0 saturation). The reverse, of course, is also true—a 127 gray light with a 2.0 multiplier becomes pure white.

The luminance (or, more properly, the RGB value) of a light's color used to be the sole determining factor as to how bright or intense the light source was. This meant that a light with a dark brown color was actually emitting a dim, orange light. For many, this concept is somewhat difficult to understand. After all, dark-colored lights do not "look like" they are emitting light. For many people, it is easier to gauge a light's color family and eventual lighting effect when its color is "bright."

Multiplier values enable you to keep the light's color swatches at a bright color to which you can relate, while still emitting a much dimmer or brighter light. This is useful if you feel more comfortable always seeing the "true" color sense of the cast light.

The family of lights mentioned earlier in the "Light Color as Illumination" section could have maintained the same luminance and had their multiplier adjusted instead. This is a convenient alternative because the color swatch in each light's definition box is the same and visually points to the fact that they all share the same color value.

As lights are made brighter and brighter by increasing their multipliers, their color qualities can change. As the three RGB color channels are increased, their limit is always 255. When a channel reaches 255, it stays at this limit as the other channels continue to approach it. The following exercise helps to visualize the changing qualities of multiplied light.

Investigating Light Multipliers

Return to the scene in the preceding exercise

Place the omni light as shown in figure 7.10, above and to the side of the default white box

Adjust the omni light's color values to Red 255, Green 32, and Blue 32, and leave attenuation off

The light's color swatch turns a bright, deep pink

Render a User or Camera view that shows the top and sides

A red glow is cast evenly over the top of the box, as shown in figure 7.11

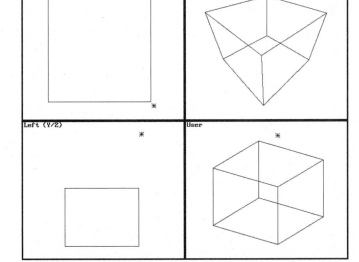

Figure 7.10
Light set up to demonstrate multipliers.

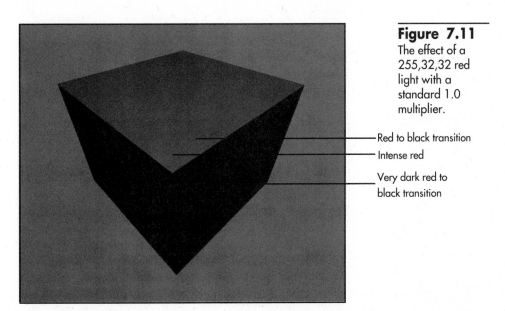

Figure 7.11
The effect of a 255,32,32 red light with a standard 1.0 multiplier.

— Red to black transition
— Intense red

Very dark red to black transition

The red is most intense at the corner, near the omni light, and falls off across the surface. Also notice that the box's sides are very dim. This points to the fact that illumination is calculated according to the incidence of the striking light. The omni light is at a shallow glancing angle to the sides, and thus the illumination is very low. The top is at a much steeper angle and receives more light, but as the surface recedes, its angle to the point source decreases and the top's light level is diminished. This is how faces are shaded in 3D Studio.

continues

continued

Choose Lights/Omni/Adjust, *increase the omni light's multiplier to* 8.0, *and render again*

The center area of the box's top becomes white and falls off to red on the sides (see fig. 7.12)

Figure 7.12
The same red light with an 8.0 multiplier.

Bright pink transition ——

White corner ——

Very dark red ——

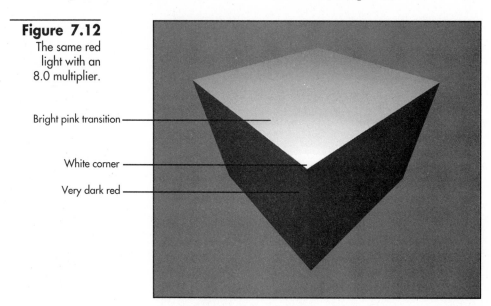

As the light's color was multiplied, all 3 channels reached 255 (32×8.0 = 256), and so the light became white in the corner area nearest the omni light. As the light diminishes over the box's surface, its light level reduces and returns to red. The increase of light gives the sides a much redder color, although their sharp angle to the omni light cuts off enough light that there is no chance of white being calculated.

Increase the omni light's multiplier to 16.0 *and render again*

The top of the box becomes almost completely white, whereas the sides become almost an even red (see fig 7.13)

This increase makes the top's diminishing angle less and less influential as only the extreme edges show a tint of red. The sides are now very red, although nowhere close to white. (To achieve a white area at this angle requires a multiplier of at least 60 or 100.)

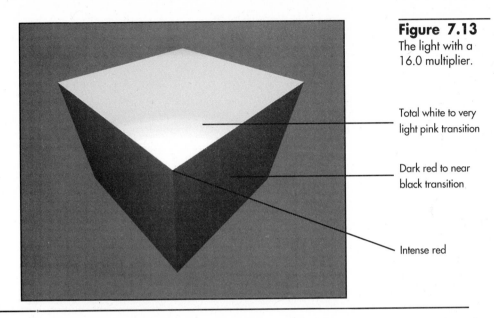

Figure 7.13
The light with a 16.0 multiplier.

Total white to very light pink transition

Dark red to near black transition

Intense red

The preceding example demonstrates how a light can change color as areas become more shaded. This is a capability impossible without the use of light multipliers. Without multipliers, a light made a very white pink could shade to a dark gray pink, not red—and a red light could never become whiter. The other rule of light to remember when using multipliers is that a light never can increase a color channel it does not have initially.

If you repeat the preceding example but lower the Blue channel to zero, the light increases to pure yellow and never arrives at white. The falloff color proceeds through shades of orange until it becomes red again. If the Green channel is reduced to zero as well, the light always remains pure red (although its purest intensity would be spread farther). Understanding how these colors mix can lead to very stunning lighting effects or give the impression of unique materials.

Multipliers also have the novel capability to remove illumination cast on objects. If a light is given a negative multiplier value, it subtracts its color from the illumination of other lights and thus darkens the area. This unique ability, and light multipliers in general, will be demonstrated in the next exercise.

Using Negative Multipliers

Enter the Top *viewport in the preceding example and press* ⇧Shift+Move *to move the omni light to the side*

Creates a clone of the first omni light

Increase the luminance of the new light to 255 and return its multiplier to 1.0

Makes it a "standard" or "traditional" white light

continues

continued

Change the original omni light's multiplier to -1.0 and make sure its Attenuation is on (note that this omni light should still have an RGB color of 255,32,32)	The original omni light now subtracts illumination
Render the viewport as before	Shades the cube from cyan to light gray

The original omni light is subtracting its primarily red color. The cyan is created because the pure Red channel completely reduces the white's, with the remaining channels creating cyan—the compliment color of red.

Decrease the original omni light's multiplier value to -8.0	Subtracts more light color
Render the viewport	Shades the cube from black to cyan to light gray

The original omni light used to produce white light at the center and diminish to shades of red. This lowers all the white's channels to zero within the first range and replaces the red, forming cyan over the second range.

When removing a light color, you actually are shifting the hue of other lights to the compliment of the negative light. If you only want to reduce the illumination of an area in the scene, make sure that the light with the negative multiplier has a zero saturation—in other words, it is gray. This way, all the color channels of other lights are reduced at the same rate and no color shift occurs. If you want to reduce the illumination and shift the scene's color toward red, use a light that does not have much, if any, of a Red channel. This allows the Red channel in the positive lights to remain in effect while reducing the Green and Blue channels, thus making them more red.

Note The ambient light value always is in effect and cannot be reduced by lights with negative multiplier values.

For accurate interior lighting, there is an additional factor to keep in mind when dimming lights that share the same values. As man-made lights grow dimmer, the lamp's temperature reduces as well. This results in a warm color shift as the intensity is lowered. A normally near-white halogen, for example, dims to a deep orange.

Attenuating Illumination

As light travels from its source to surfaces in the world around us, its light level diminishes over distance. If you hold a flashlight directly over a table, it's quite bright. Aim it across the room and its illumination is much dimmer. Point it across the street and it might barely have an influence on the neighboring home. This diminishing, decay, or watering down of light is termed *attenuation* and is a simple result of physics.

In real life, light attenuates at an inverse square ratio (if a lamp had X illumination at 10 feet, it would have 1/4X at 20 feet for example). While correct, this level of decay is usually considered far too great in computer graphics. The reason is that light bounces off of surfaces and illuminates the world from all angles, even though it's attenuating. Only radiosity rendering programs have the ability to reproduce this inherited light (see Chapter 2, "Concepts and Theories"). Thus, by convention, most computer programs that include attenuation abilities for lights do so in a linear fashion (the same lamp that had X illumination at 10 feet would now have 1/2X at 20 feet). In this regard, 3D Studio follows suit—its attenuation decays in a linear fashion.

The Attenuation parameter within the Light Definition dialog boxes is simply an on-and-off button that indicates whether or not the selected light is currently using the ranges that have been assigned it. The actual distance for the light drop-off is controlled by the Omni/Ranges and Spot/Ranges commands.

All lights begin with a default set of ranges having radii of 100 units. Turning Attenuation on affects a light, even though you have not used a Ranges command to specifically define its distance.

The Ranges commands produce a concentric set of circles, as seen in figure 7.14. These circles define the inner and outer extents for the light's illumination. The inner circle defines the limit to which the light illuminates as normal. The outer circle defines the limit at which any light is cast. The level of illumination thus goes from normal intensity to zero between these two circles. The order in which you select the inner and outer ranges makes no difference— the larger radius always is interpreted as the outer cutoff. It is important to realize that the range circles actually represent a sphere of projected light. Because the range circles are only displayed in the active viewport, you might need to adjust them in perpendicular viewports to ensure correct distances.

When adjusting ranges, you must set both radii at that time. Setting only one and exiting the Ranges command cancels the command and the first range you input.

Figure 7.14
Attenuation circles for omni and spotlights.

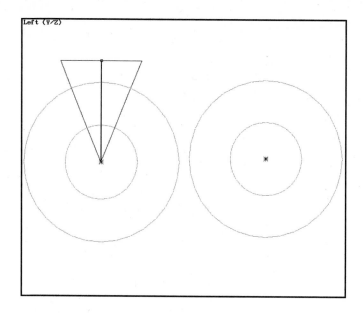

The range circles illustrate how an omni light emits light because it does so in all directions from its center point source. The circle analogy is somewhat weaker when applied to spotlights because their light is actually focused in a cone or beam of light. When adjusting spotlight ranges, it is very useful to have their cones showing to relate the two ranges together.

 Because the Ranges command uses the light source as its center, you cannot select the spotlight's target to adjust the spotlight.

If you are simulating lighting effects within a space, pay special attention to the lights' ranges. All lights of a given intensity (wattage, lumen output, and so on) placed within the same atmosphere should have the same ranges. This is especially important when the light sources are in a regular pattern, such as a grid, and their effects can easily be compared. For these lights, it often is best to create one correctly and clone it to maintain the same ranges—adjusting individual ranges is fairly inaccurate. The concept of attenuation and defining their ranges is explored in the following exercise.

Simple Use of Attenuation

Return to the preceding exercise's model and turn the white omni light off.

Choose Lights/Omni/Range *and select the red omni light*

Two concentric circles appear, with the omni light as their center

*Using a side viewport, drag the inner circle's radius
to midway in the box, and the outer circle to the
outside edge of the cube (see fig. 7.15)*

*Enter the omni light's definition box
and turn on Attenuation*

The ranges specified take effect

Render the scene again

The omni light now has a range and
illuminates only the corner, as shown in
figure 7.16, and can be seen in the
color plate section.

By setting the ranges, you clearly can see the multiplier's effect. The top corner is affected by
the omni light's inner circle range and is in full effect—making the top white. As the illumination continues to the outer circle, it diminishes to black, lowering the intensity and thus the
multiplier along the way. The area close to the outer ring that is at only six percent illumination is actually the light's color with a standard 1.0 multiplier.

II

Basic Modeling

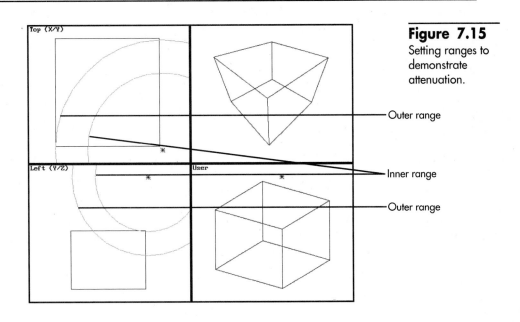

Figure 7.15
Setting ranges to
demonstrate
attenuation.

Outer range

Inner range

Outer range

Figure 7.16
An intense omni light using attenuation.

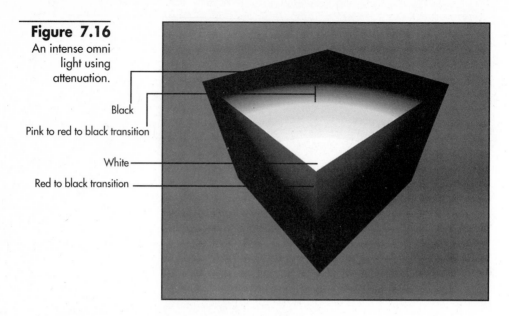

Black

Pink to red to black transition

White

Red to black transition

Excluding Objects from Light

The Exclude option in the Light definition dialog boxes enables you to specify objects in the scene that are not to receive that light's illumination. This is a capability not available in the real world, but one that professional photographers and set designers would love to have. The capabilities and effects of this option are remarkable.

To exclude objects from a light, simply click on the light's Exclude button, and a list of objects appears in an Exclude Objects dialog box (see fig. 7.17). Objects are chosen by name, and excluded objects are marked with an asterisk. The Exclude button remains unhighlighted until at least one object is excluded and remains highlighted as long as one is selected.

Figure 7.17
The Exclude Objects dialog box.

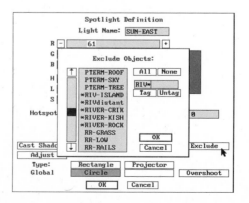

Although the original intent of the Exclude capability was to exclude specific objects from a light's illumination, it is much more dramatic when used to isolate the light's illumination on an object—in other words, exclude all other objects but the one you want to illuminate.

Shadow-casting spotlights that exclude objects still cast shadows for them unless the SHADOW-EXCLUSION parameter in the 3DS.SET file is set to ON. The default setting for this is off, which can lead to confusing situations and does not improve rendering speed.

The capability to exclude objects is different from changing the objects' Cast Shadows attribute. An object that does not cast shadows is still illuminated, whereas an excluded object does not receive illumination from that light.

Highlight Considerations

A specular highlight is created when the angle of the light striking a surface is equal to the viewing angle of the same surface. In other words, *the light is reflecting back to your eye.* This area of equal viewing and light striking incidence is the center of the light's highlight for that plane. The extent of the highlight is dictated by the shininess of the material—the more area under the materials highlight curve, the broader the highlight; the taller the curve, the more the highlight color approaches the materials specular color.

A material must have some degree of shine *and* have a non-black specular color for a highlight to be produced on its surface from any light.

Highlights are formed whenever a light source can trace an equal angle of incidence from itself to the mesh, and then back to your viewing position—your eye. Highlights will always result from omni lights (and spotlights with overshoot) in such positions and with spotlights that include the mesh within their falloff cone. As shown in figure 7.18, the light is placed so that it bounces light back to your viewing position by making the light's angle of incidence to the surface equal to your eyes.

The highlight will occur regardless of how dim the light happens to be or in what direction a spotlight is aimed (as long as its cone includes the mesh). Dim lights simply create dimmer highlights on the mesh. It is currently not possible to create a light that does not create a highlight on a shiny surface.

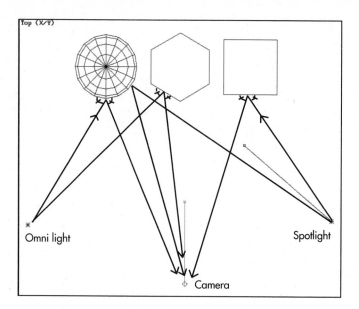

Figure 7.18
Highlight angles
for various lights.

Placing Highlights

The Place Highlight commands for spotlights and omni lights give you some control over where their specular shine will be for a given view. This does nothing to the object itself, but rather moves the light source in relation to the view from which you pick it.

 You cannot clone lights when using Place Highlight.

Omni lights and spotlights are moved differently when using Place Highlight. Omni lights keep their relative distance to the highlighted face during the translation so that they illuminate with the same intensity before and after. Spotlights, however, keep a constant light to target distance, but move the target to the highlighted face. This changes the spotlight's distance to the surface and will alter the spotlight's illumination if the target did not begin at the selected face.

Considering the resulting light movement, this command might be better remembered as the "Move Light to Create Highlight" option. The light's radical change of position can make this command a poor choice for adjusting the scene's principal light sources, especially if these happen to be spotlights.

The highlight is placed on the object you select in any viewport, although a camera viewport is the most common. Unlike other commands, you are expected to pick the field of the face rather than an edge or vertex. This is because the light's placement is based on the point within the face picked and not on the face itself. As objects overlap in a viewport, the program

bases its selection on sorting the objects in the order of creation. The face selected also might be the one for the opposite side of the object. The positioned angle of the spotlight also is influenced by the angle at which the viewport is viewing the face.

For materials that have specular maps, the Place Highlight command is extremely useful when trying to place or control the appearance of the resulting specular "reflection."

The Place Highlight command's primary purpose then is to customize the highlight of a particular face as it is seen from a particular view. Such lights often are called *accent lights* and have a very narrow falloff. Within 3D Studio, it can be very effective to make these lights exclude other objects so that the effect on the aligned face is even more dramatic.

Another use for Place Highlight is to move a light so it is perpendicular to a face and illuminates it at full effect. This is accomplished by first aligning a view perpendicular to the face (Display/User View/Align is very convenient for this), and then using Place Highlight on the same face.

Omni Light Considerations

Before 3D Studio Release 3, you had very little control over the illumination given by omni lights. You simply placed them in the scene with the desired light color, and the program did the rest. Light strength was simply a measure of the color's luminance. The distance the light was cast was infinite, and you just selected the source. If you so choose, omni lights can continue to work this way, but attenuation gives you more alternatives.

Omni Light Attenuation

With attenuation, omni lights now can be limited as to their range settings, and their light can diminish over distance—they are no longer like the sun. This is important to remember, because unattenuated omni lights have an additive effect on the light level of all objects within the scene (their light rays cannot be blocked).

Omni light ranges are extremely useful for controlling the effects of fill, back, or accent lights. If an area of the scene requires a touch of orange, such as the "light" emitted from a texture-mapped fireplace, then placing an omni light and limiting its ranges gives a localized orange cast.

A common mistake is to believe that "hanging" an omni light in a room creates a glow in the air about it as it would in real life. This cannot happen. Lights in 3D Studio can cast light only upon the faces that they strike, and this actually is quite correct. A light placed in outer space does not emit a glow because there is nothing to illuminate. The streaks of laser light so common in the movies are actually a fallacy; in reality, nothing is seen. The street lamp outside your house creates a glow, or halo, because it strikes millions of airborne particles floating about it. (See Chapter 13, "Lighting and Camera Special Effects," for methods to model a light's halo.)

Glows around omni lights can be created by using IPAS routines.

Omni Lights and Radiosity

When omni lights are used with exclusion and ranges, they are ideal sources for simulating radiosity and inherited color. This approach slows the rendering process more than adjusting the material's ambient color value (as described in Chapter 6), but creates a very realistic effect. Chapter 13 includes several exercises that incorporate this technique to create convincing illusions.

Limiting lights to a small number of objects over a small range will minimize the rendering calculation time. The addition of such lights is much less of a rendering hindrance than you may be used to when adding lights.

Spotlight Capabilities

The many capabilities of spotlights make them the primary lighting tool within the 3D Studio environment. Unlike omni lights, the direction of their light can be controlled, they can cast shadows, can be rectangular in shape, and can even project a bitmap image.

Spotlight Shapes

Spotlights can be projected in the shape of a cone (the default) or a rectangle, as seen in figure 7.19. The illumination effects of the light's center circular hotspot are the same—only the defining edges are different. A light can be switched between the two types of projection by choosing the Spotlight Definition dialog box's Circle or Rectangle option buttons at any time.

The distance between the spotlight and its target has no influence on its illumination—it is included solely as a convenient tool with which to aim the spotlight.

New Riders Publishing
INSIDE
SERIES

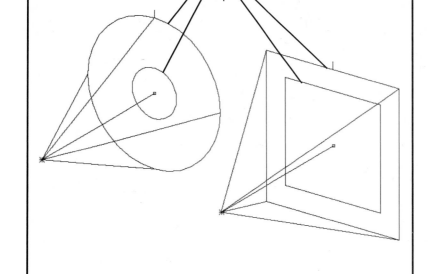

Figure 7.19
Spotlight shape
options.

Hotspot and Falloff

The most commonly adjusted aspects of spotlights are their falloff and hotspot values. These are graphically shown by the circle or rectangle cone when adjusting them with the Spot/Highlight and Spot/Falloff commands. Most modelers find that it is easiest to display these aids constantly by setting the Show Cone option in the light's definition box.

The hotspot and falloff values have an effect similar to the inner and outer ranges of an attenuated omni light. The *hotspot* defines the extents of the spotlight's full illumination—it does not increase the values as the name might imply. The *falloff* defines the range over which the spotlight intensity fades to black. This fade, or *decay*, is not linear as with omni ranges, but actually is a cubic spline interpolation. This means that most of the transition occurs close to the falloff's outer edge.

 If a broad gradation over a spotlight's pool is needed, you can use attenuation to create the effect by setting the spotlight's inner range circle so that it just intersects the mesh's surface.

The size difference between the hotspot and falloff defines the softness or fuzziness of the light pool's edge. A narrow hotspot and broad falloff creates a very soft edge, whereas a hotspot close to the same size as the falloff makes the light pool's edge very crisp.

continued

Make the spotlight the same color as the omni light (255,32,32) and increase its multiplier to 8.0	Dramatizes the effects of the spotlight's falloff
Delete the omni light and render the scene	Renders the box similar to how the omni light did in the previous exercise (see fig. 7.21)

Figure 7.21
The resulting illumination.

The line traced by the spotlight's target recreates the angle of incidence found with the original omni light. The falloff of the light creates a colored transition across the top to the rear corner, however.

Move the spotlight's target to the middle of the box's top (this should be similar to fig. 7.22)

Render the scene

The box's top is almost an even color with very little falloff, as shown in figure 7.23.

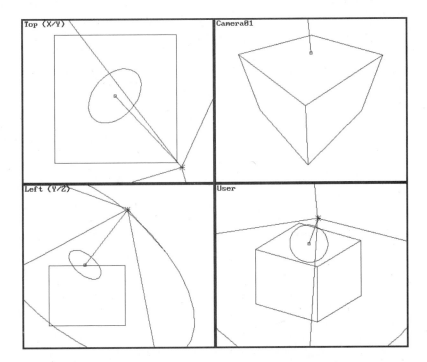

Figure 7.22
The spotlight targeting the center of the box's top.

II

Basic Modeling

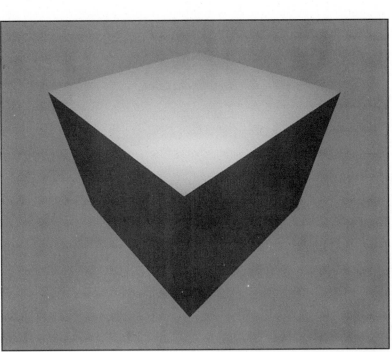

Figure 7.23
The resulting even illumination of the top and darker hue of the sides.

Figure 7.24
Aiming the spotlight of the rear corner.

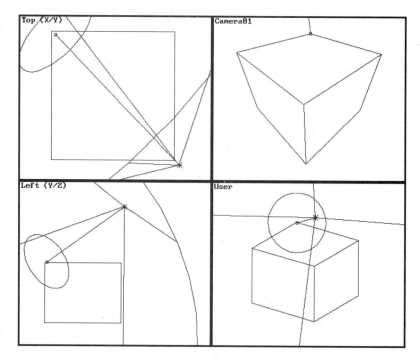

Figure 7.25
The resulting illumination.

Because the target is aimed at the center, the calculated angle is averaged across the entire top, resulting in a fairly even color distribution.

Move the spotlight's target to the rear corner
of the box (similar to fig. 7.24)

Render the scene

The front of the cube is now black as the falloff begins in the front and proceeds to white in the back, as shown in figure 7.25.

The front areas of the cube are now dark because they have fallen below the illuminated angle of incidence. This front black corner proceeds to red and then pink across the top surface.

Overshoot

The spotlight's light pool can be eliminated by using the Overshoot option within the definition box. This, in effect, eliminates the constraints set by falloff and hotspot. The illumination produced is equivalent to what would have been produced only within the hotspot. This option basically turns the spotlight into an "aimed omni light," yet retains the rest of the spotlight capabilities. Because of these qualities, this capability is sometimes referred to as *infinite overshoot*. The important thing to realize is that overshot spotlights are no longer restricted to a cone of light, and illuminate in all directions similar to an omni light.

When Overshoot is active, the spotlight still respects Ranges if Attenuation is on.

The light produced by an overshot spotlight is still the same as an omni light's and will still shade according to its angle of incidence to the surface. You can prove this by changing the spotlight used in the last exercise to Overshoot. The resulting illumination still leaves black spots at the extreme corners where the striking light is still shallower than the minimum lighting angle.

Overshoot is useful when general illumination is needed, but you still need the spotlight's shadow and/or projector options. These capabilities still observe the spotlight's falloff cone. A spotlight with overshoot should be thought of as an omni light that has shadow casting and projector capabilities constrained to its falloff.

Attenuation

The distance a spotlight's illumination travels can be set with Spot/Ranges and controlled by the light's Attenuation option in much the same manner as omni lights. The illumination decay between the two ranges is analogous to that between the spotlight's falloff and hotspot cones. An attenuated spotlight is thus decaying between two sets of parameters—its hotspot and falloff cones, and its range circles.

Do not mistake the spotlight's target for its range, or even initial range. The target's purpose is solely for aiming and has no effect on Range distances.

Projector

Spotlights can now project images in a slide/film projector fashion and, in doing so, open up many special-effect possibilities. The colors of the projected image blend with the spotlight's and reduce the amount of light according to the bitmap colors' luminance values. Black completely blocks light, whereas white will not stop any light.

A projector light is the only method for casting patterns of colored light because transparent objects do not transfer their color values through their ray-cast shadows. A projected image can cast the colors of a stained glass window, whereas the mesh of the transparent material only casts the color of the light behind it.

The process of creating a projected image is very simple, though a little deceiving. Notice a blank button below the Projector option button in the Spotlight Definition dialog box. Activating this button brings up a bitmap file dialog box from which you can select the image to be projected (see fig. 7.26).

Figure 7.26
The Select projector image dialog box.

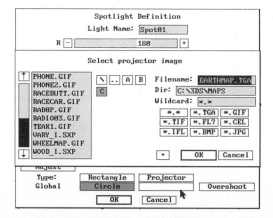

If an animation is chosen as the projector image (a FLI, FLC, animated CEL, IFL, or sequence of bitmap files), each frame is shown in sequence when a range of frames is rendered in the Keyframer. The slide projector is thus turned into a movie projector.

After selecting the bitmap, you must activate the Projector button for it to take effect. The placement of this button next to the Rectangle option implies that projection only modifies it when actually either type of spotlight can project an image.

The projected bitmap is stretched to fit the limits of the spotlight's falloff. For a circular spotlight, the bitmap is stretched to the boundary square that encloses the circle, and the image is clipped by the circle.

When the Projector option is used in conjunction with Overshoot, the image is still constrained to the size of the falloff. This edge, however, will be aliased if the projected image's edge color (that is, background) blocks the spotlight's color. Because white never mixes additively, it should be the first choice for an image's background as long as the light has a positive multiplier.

Including a one-pixel-wide white perimeter on projected bitmaps will eliminate the harsh aliasing that occurs when the projecting spotlight is employing overshoot.

Projector lights actually have a strong tradition of use in the theater and interior/lighting design. One of the most traditional effects is when the image is opaque (black on white) and casts a shadow rather than an image. When used in this manner, a projector light is often called a *gobo light*. Implying cast shadows with this technique can create dramatic and memory efficient effects within 3D Studio.

The bitmap chosen as a projector must be exactly what you want projected. Unfortunately, projector lights have no parameter options available to tint, make negative, tile, or change proportions and rotations, as are available with texture maps. Projector lights also have no way to access an imbedded Alpha channel for use as a gobo.

Adjusting Spotlight Projections

A spotlight's graphic rectangle should really be thought of as a Planar Projection icon because it acts in exactly the same way. The proportions and rotation of the bitmap are dictated by the placement of the rectangle. Both spotlight types have small vertical lines to indicate the top of a projection, but no dark right side because it is obvious which way is front.

The projected image can be rotated with the Spot/Roll command. This command acts exactly like the Rotate or Camera/Roll command. The Roll parameter is displayed in the light's definition and can be changed there as well.

II

Basic Modeling

The proportions of a circular spotlight are obviously fixed, but those of a rectangular one can be adjusted with either the Spot/Aspect or the Spot/Bitmap Fit commands.

When projecting an image, the Bitmap Fit option should be your first choice because it is easiest, most accurate, and most relevant. Accessing the command and selecting a rectangular spotlight brings up the Select Bitmap for Aspect Ratio Fit dialog box. After selecting the desired bitmap, which more than likely is the projected image, the rectangle's width is changed to meet the respective ratio.

The Aspect option only needs to be used if you need to distort the projected image. This might be the case if a spotlight is projecting on an angled plane. If it is important for the image to be undistorted and you cannot move the spotlight to be perpendicular, you need to adjust its aspect ratio. The Spot/Aspect command only works by dragging and thus can be a bit tricky to get right. The correcting ratio can be determined in the same manner as for planar projection (described in Chapter 6, "Introduction to the Materials Editor"). The correcting ratio (the COSINE of the included angle or, more appropriately, the SIN of the angle of incidence) must be applied to the correct bitmap ratio. This procedure is shown in figure 7.27.

Figure 7.27
Correcting
planar projection
distortion.

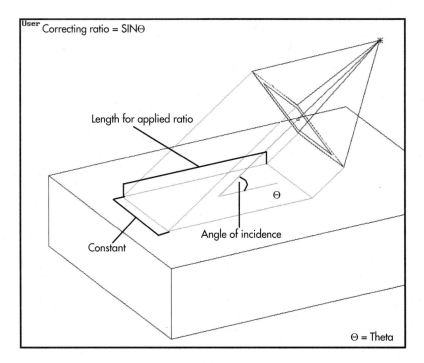

The obvious difficulty is in calculating the correct angle, or its distances, and keeping the combined bitmap and correcting ratio straight. If you do not need to have the light shining from that exact spot, moving it perpendicular to the surface is a much easier solution to correct the distortion.

The Aspect command also is used quite often without projecting an image. An approximation of linear light sources can be made by elongating the limits of a rectangular spotlight to their maximum. See Chapter 13, "Lighting and Camera Special Effects," for examples of this technique.

Spotlight Viewports

You can view what a spotlight sees in much the same manner as a camera does. The Spotlight View was the latest viewport option and can be accessed by the keyboard alternate of $ to activate a list of existing spotlights from which you can choose. The view is down the barrel of the spotlight cone and is shown in perspective with a constant level of flare. This is the only type of view other than a camera that displays the scene in perspective. The boundary of the view is a fixed value based on the spotlight's distance to the target. This also defines the limits for a rectangular spotlight's aspect ratio.

A Spotlight View's border is always yellow, or active, even when the spotlight is turned off.

The Spotlight View is a good visualization tool when you need to accurately place the spotlight's light pool. A projector spotlight view is a commonly used tool in making final adjustments to the proportions and location of the protected image. Whenever you click in a Spotlight View, the respective spotlight is selected. This can be very convenient while you adjust aspect ratios.

Understanding Light and Its Shadows

In the 3D Studio world, lights illuminate every face that is oriented toward them (i.e., presents a normal to them) until they are stopped by their respective ranges or falloffs. This light transmits through the front and back of meshes unless the light is told to cast shadows. Because only spotlights can cast shadows, omni lights will continue to penetrate the scene and devalue the darkness of a cast shadow.

You can create the effect of a shadow-casting omni light when a shadow-casting spotlight is used with an Overshoot attribute.

Creating lighting effects can be somewhat difficult if shadows are not used. The light coming from the left is blending from that of the right and with the fill lights. It can be very difficult to create contrasts and drama in a model without employing shadows.

3D Studio supplies two forms of shadows with very different properties. The choice of which to use comes down to the basic questions of should the shadow edge be crisp or soft, and does the shadow need to respect the object's transparency?

Casting shadows is an expensive option, but one that adds tremendous realism to the finished scene. Ray-trace shadows consume rendering time, whereas Shadow Maps require memory resources in addition to some rendering time. Limiting the spotlight's falloff to just the area that requires shadows saves rendering time for both types. Excluding objects from shadows, either within the spotlight or through the object's attribute, also aids in reducing rendering overhead.

Shadow Parameters

Each light's shadow can be set individually or globally. Because each light affects a different area of the scene and has different requirements, you more than likely will be adjusting the shadow parameters of each light. Each spotlight contains a Local Shadow Control dialog box accessed with the Adjust button in the Spotlight Definition dialog box, as shown in figure 7.28.

Figure 7.28
The Local Shadow Control dialog box.

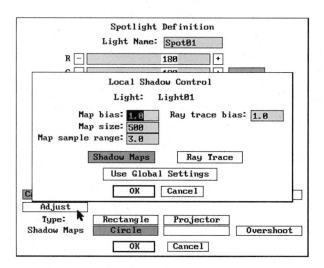

The global shadow values are located, oddly enough, under the Renderer branch as Setup/Shadows. This controls the parameters of all shadow-casting lights that have the Use Global Settings button activated (the default). The effects of these parameters are the same—they just are not tailored to each light's needs. The global values are used as the default values in newly created lights and those not using local shadow control.

Ray-Traced Shadows

The inclusion of ray-traced shadows with Release 4 delivers the capability to create crisp, accurate shadows while eliminating many headaches involved with using the previous standard shadow maps. Although this is a new option, it might be considered as the first choice because ray-traced shadows have more capabilities and are easier to use.

Ray-traced shadows are very accurate, with crisp edges, and nearly always engage the object that casts them (an annoying trait that shadow maps must fight to overcome). As figure 7.29 shows, ray-traced shadows also take into account a material's opacity. (The color of the transparent material is not taken into account for the cast shadows, however.)

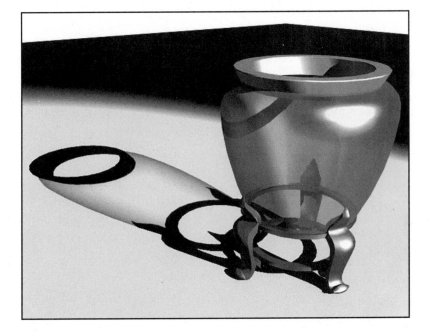

Figure 7.29
Ray-traced shadows on an object with transparency.

Ray-traced shadows take into account any opacity information contained within a material. This can come in the form of an opacity map and its mask, and the material's Transparency parameter sliders and In/Out options. These are the only aspects that define transparency. Additional maps defining textures or bumps have no effect on the cast shadow. To simulate these surface markings requires that you copy the appropriate bitmap to be an opacity map or mask for the material.

Tip

If you need to cast shadows that include the colors of transparent plastics and glassware, you need to use a non-shadow-casting projector spotlight. This spotlight needs to exclude the transparent objects so the projected image will cast past it and act as its "shadow." If the object is struck by a shadow-casting light, the illusion will fail because duplicate shadows will exist. The bitmap image should be the color of the transparent material and may even approximate its opacity.

Ray-traced shadows are ideal for simulating bright light sources, especially sunlight. The only drawback is that these shadows require extensive calculations during a rendering. Because the area calculated for each spotlight is based on its falloff, constraining their radii to smaller, specific areas can save considerable rendering time.

Spotlights that use ray-traced shadows treat all opacity in terms of luminance or intensity. Material cutouts can be very convincing when illuminated by these lights. These materials have matching texture and opacity maps and are often are used for entourage objects, such as trees, people, and cars, but also can be the individual leaves of a tree or the mullion bar pattern in a window.

Ray Trace Bias

The only parameter to control the effects of ray-traced shadows is the Ray Trace Bias setting. This is not immediately obvious within the Shadow Control dialog box because the three shadow map parameters remain editable when the Ray Cast option is selected.

Unlike shadow map parameters, this value rarely needs to be adjusted. A value of 1.0 forms no bias, whereas large values begin to pull the shadow away from the casting object and lower values try to pull it closer. This value will need to be adjusted if the objects casting shadows contain self-intersecting elements. An example of this is the color plate image of "AutoCAD Created Columns." This model was composed principally of self-intersecting forms and required a Ray Trace Bias of 0.02 for the shadows to engage properly. Ray-traced shadows that contain holes when they should be solid or do not engage the shadow-casting mesh have bias values that are too high and need to be reduced.

Shadow Maps

Creating shadows with shadow maps is the traditional 3D Studio method available in previous releases. The characteristics of shadow maps have not changed since Release 2, but the capability to exclude objects and use overshoot makes them much more useful.

The primary capability of a shadow map is to create soft shadows. This is a more realistic effect, but can be difficult to achieve because its control is a critical balance of its three parameters. Casting shadows with shadow maps requires memory, but renders faster than ray-traced shadows—especially within a complex model. The trade-off, however, is that shadow maps take preparation time and constant testing to ensure their accuracy and appropriateness.

In real life, the crispness of a shadow is a product of the object's proximity to the surface on which it is casting a shadow. A window that casts a shadow of its mullions across the room is very soft, whereas the chair that sits in the same light casts a very crisp shadow. Because of this duality, you might consider using multiple shadow-casting lights having different shadow effects for scenes that require extreme realism.

You might find that the realistic effect of soft shadows is lost on many people who view your work. To the majority of lay people, the definition of a shadow is a crisp, definite shape cast from the object. If the shadow will not have the opportunity to be examined, such as in an animation, the sophisticated effects gained from soft shadows are nearly always lost.

Shadow Map Size and Shadow Quality

The shadow map's size is the most critical—and expensive—factor in getting a shadow "right." The Renderer creates a square bitmap to the size specified in the Map Size parameter. The memory cost for this map is 4 bytes per map pixel, so a 500-line shadow map costs $500 \times 500 \times 4 = 1$ MB of RAM. This map is then stretched to the size of all shadow-casting objects with the spotlight's falloff cone and projected back onto the receiving surfaces.

Because the shadow map is actually a bitmap, the shadow begins to pixelate and form jagged edges if it is not at least the size of the rendered area. The larger the shadow casting objects' extents, the more the shadow map is stretched and the higher its resolution needs to be to maintain an unaliased edge. You can limit the mapped areas size, and thus the size of the required shadow map, by constraining the spotlight's falloff. You can also decrease the shadow map's extents by turning off the cast shadows attribute of distant objects.

Note Overshoot is extremely useful with shadow maps because their effect can be localized without creating pools of light.

Maps larger than the output size form shadows with sharper defined edges. The effects of various shadow maps sizes can be seen in figure 7.30. This figure shows a sharp shadow twice the size of the shadow area and a squarish and inaccurate result of a map one-fifth the size of the shadowed area. The shadow shown in the lefthand side of the figure actually is casting a map the same size as the light's falloff area, but is still somewhat pixelated at the base.

Figure 7.30
A correct shadow map size for the given resolution and scene, and a shadow map far too small for the scene.

Map Bias and Engagement Accuracy

The Map Bias value is basically used to fix the inherent inaccuracy shadow maps have in engaging the objects that cast them. The lower the bias value, the more the shadow is pulled to the object.

The manual recommends Map Bias values of 1.0 for architectural models, and 3.0 for broadcast-design work. It is very important not to use these values blindly without first experimenting with them in your scene. Each model's, and possibly each spotlight's, needs vary according to the light's angle and distance and the final output resolution. In addition, the size of the scene casting shadows plays an important factor in the engagement accuracy of shadow maps. This fact is not described in the manuals, but is one that can be very frustrating to track down. Figure 7.31 shows the cast shadow when only the vase is casting shadows, and how the same shadow parameters severely detach the shadow as soon as the ground plane's Cast Shadows parameter is turned on.

Figure 7.31
Shadow quality of a single shadow-casting vase object, and shadow quality when the ground plane casts shadows.

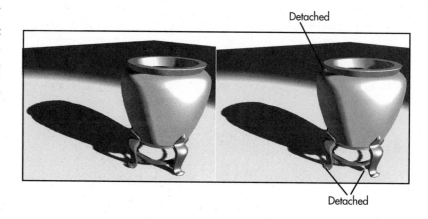

Detached

Detached

The 3DS.SET file contains the parameter SHADOW-BIAS-ABSOLUTE, which controls how the program places shadows. The Renderer usually bases a shadow's bias on its relationship to the screen. You can change this so that it bases its output on units within the scene instead by setting this value to ON. This option should be used cautiously, with the knowledge that it will change the way all lights in all models cast shadows. It should also be noted that because this is a 3DS.SET parameter, this option cannot be transported with the saved 3DS or PRJ file to another system.

When you are using absolute shadow bias, the values change considerably. The standard bias values are based on a scene that is approximately 100 units in depth. As your scene grows, the respective shadow bias grows as well in a linear fashion. A scene 500 feet in depth is actually 6000 units and requires a bias 60 times as large. This can obviously be very confusing, and the rules of thumb regarding shadow map values you may have learned are now dramatically changed.

Map Sample Range and Edge Softness

The Map Sample Range value controls the softness of the shadow's edge. The higher this value is, the softer the shadow edge will be. The key word in this parameter is "sample" because the program actually is creating many samples of the shadow and averaging their edges together to create the soft edge. The quality and accuracy of this edge is, as always, a balance of three shadow map parameters. The shadow on the left in figure 7.32 has a sample value of 1.0 and shows exactly how coarse the shadow map really is. The shadow on the right shows the first step of sampling as the value of 2.0 barely produces a soft edge on the coarse shadow.

Figure 7.32
The shadow with a sample range of 1.0, and the shadow with a sample range of 2.0.

As the sample values increase, so does the shadow's softness. The time it takes to render these soft shadows increases as well because the program is calculating that many more edges for the average. The shadow on the left in figure 7.33 shows a sample range of 5.0, whereas the shadow on the right shows a sample range of 7.0. Examine the shadows cast by the vase's legs and you can see that as the shadow gets softer, it also gets thinner.

Figure 7.33
The shadow with a sample range of 5.0, and the shadow with a sample range of 7.0.

Note that these values are specific to the given resolution, bias map size, spotlight distance, and size of the scene; differing values will vary proportionately.

Some observers might be disturbed because the shadow does not get softer as it falls away from the object. In real life, the shadow is sharpest where the object touches the shadow-receiving surface and softest at its far tip. 3D Studio does not do this naturally, however. For high resolution images that will have time to be scrutinized, this could be a problem and should be thought of when choosing between ray-traced and shadow-map shadows.

Object Shadow Attributes

Each object has shadow exclusion capabilities built into its attribute definitions. Choosing Modify/Object/Attributes displays the dialog box shown in figure 7.34. When these attributes are combined with the exclusion capabilities of lights, the capability to create special lighting effects is considerable. (Chapter 13, "Lighting and Camera Special Effects," investigates these possibilities in detail.)

Figure 7.34
The Object
Attributes
dialog box.

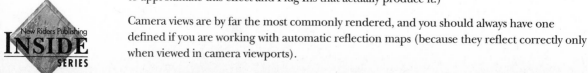

As can be discerned from the option buttons, you can control whether objects cast or receive shadows. The use of these attributes will be unique for every model, but realize that using them does save in rendering time. This is especially true for objects that take up a great deal of the scene, such as ground planes, walls, and ceilings. Most of the time, these objects do not need to cast shadows, and ceilings do not need to receive them. Turning off the appropriate attributes saves considerable rendering time and makes shadow maps much more accurate.

Understanding Cameras and Perspective

Cameras are 3D Studio's principal method for defining perspective. As described in Chapter 2, "Concepts and Theories," 3D Studio cameras are based on a 35mm *Single Lens Reflex* (SLR) with what could be considered the world's ultimate zoom lens attachment. The only aspect that does not correlate in this analogy is that the 3D Studio camera always maintains a sharp focus through the entire scene, regardless of depth. In this respect, the 3D Studio camera is like a minute pin-hole camera. 3D Studio cameras do not have *depth of field* (also known as *racked focus*) as a standard feature. (See Chapter 18, "Animating Lights and Cameras," for ways to approximate this effect and Plug-Ins that actually produce it.)

Camera views are by far the most commonly rendered, and you should always have one defined if you are working with automatic reflection maps (because they reflect correctly only when viewed in camera viewports).

When creating cameras, many people find it advantageous to give them names that relate to their view and/or lens, rather than the generic CAMERA01 label given by default. By using names such as Front, Wide, or North, you can select the cameras in the Hit and Keyframer dialog boxes with more clarity.

Creating and Placing Cameras

Cameras are created and moved in much the same manner as spotlights. The use of the Ctrl key enables you to move both the camera and its target at the same time when performing any command that moves the camera. This is important because it keeps the angle of view consistent. You can adjust a camera by selecting it or its target, much like a spotlight. As with other entities, you can clone cameras during most commands while holding down Shift. Cameras can be universally displayed or hidden with the Alt+C key alternative.

As with spotlights, a camera's target is included strictly for aiming—its distance to the camera has no impact on the resulting view.

It is often convenient to adjust cameras from within a Camera view. Clicking in a Camera viewport automatically selects that camera while you are using a Camera branch command. All the Camera branch commands can be used within a Camera viewport, except for Ranges. When using the Move command, you are moving only the Camera's target. This is the same as standing in place and panning around with a hand-held camera. If you use the Ctrl key, both the camera and target move. Note, however, that unlike other viewports, you are not constrained by your directional Tab arrow when you use the Ctrl key within a camera viewport.

The standard viewport Zoom command works within a Camera viewport by "zooming" the lens, as the name implies. Zoom extents, on the other hand, has no effect. The camera position remains constant as the *Field of View* (FOV) is halved or doubled with each full zoom increment. The remaining viewport commands are not options within a Camera view.

Release 4 includes the new function *Camera Control*, which enables you to adjust cameras within a rendered viewport and gives you greater control while doing it. See the end of Chapter 13 for information on using this new command.

Making Camera Adjustments

A camera's parameters can be adjusted manually by using the Camera/Adjust command to access the Camera Definition dialog box, as shown in figure 7.35.

Figure 7.35

The Camera
Definition
dialog box.

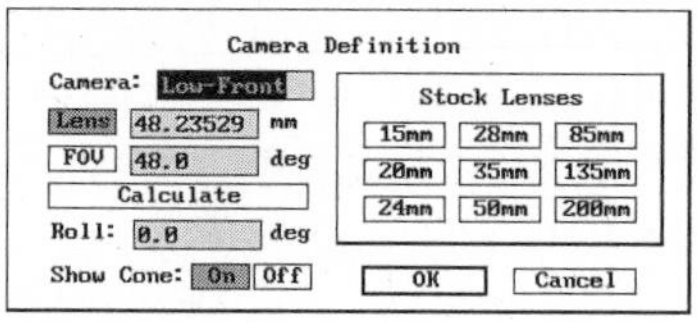

The values for lens size and FOV angle are inversely related to one another and are basically two ways to describe the same thing. This relationship is actually only of use if you are already familiar and comfortable with 35mm lens sizes. You can enter either value to define the camera's lens, but only by changing the FOV value do you affect the definition. The Calculate button transposes one field's value into the correlating setting and must be used to enter lens sizes in millimeters. If you choose a Stock Lens size, both values are changed at the same time.

> **Note** When manually setting the lens size, you must use Calculate to establish the FOV angle or the camera's definition does not change. You do not have to do this after adjusting the FOV setting unless you want to see the resulting lens size.

For those readers that are doing very technically accurate re-creations, it should be noted that the lens sizes provided by 3D Studio are only close approximations of the real-world lens FOVs. The FOV values themselves are extremely accurate and should be used when high precision is required.

Camera Views and Output Size

What might not be initially obvious is that the view captured by your camera depends on the width-to-height ratio of your output image or rendered file. As your ratio becomes horizontal, the camera has the appearance of being zoomed in. When the ratio becomes taller, the camera appears to zoom out. Figure 7.36 shows the view framed with a 3:2 ratio (the standard ratio for 35mm slides), and the dollying effect when this ratio is made square. The dramatic difference of making it a 2:3 ratio is shown in figure 7.37. Note that the view's perspective has not changed—only the amount of the scene taken in.

These figures also show the use of a *safe frame*. A safe frame is an invaluable feature that shows the final cropped image. The outer rectangle shows the absolute outer edge of the final bitmap image, while the inner rectangle is an approximation of the cutoff point that occurs with video overscan. Because the safe frame rectangle is proportional, the output sizes of 600×400 and 3000×2000, for example, will have the same safe frame ratio. The size of the inner border can be tailored to your system's needs, with the Safe Frame value located within the Render Options dialog box. This is accessed from Renderer/Setup/Options or from within the Rendering dialog box.

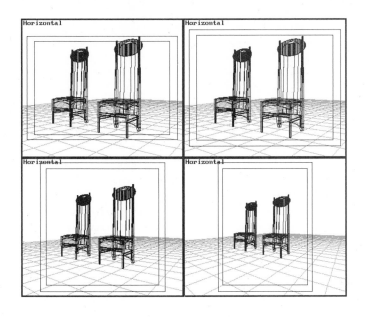

Figure 7.36
The camera view with a 3:2 width-to-height output ratio and a 1:1 square output ratio.

II

Basic Modeling

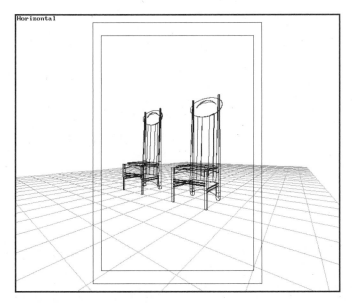

Figure 7.37
The same camera with a 2:3 width-to-height output ratio.

The safe frame display can be turned on from within any viewport with Alt+E.

The inner safe frame is important if your destination is video or tape, whereas the outer frame is important if you are making a hard copy or print. Without safe frame, you have no idea of what your final composition will be. Because of this, it is strongly recommended that you always have safe frame activated when adjusting the composition of *any* view that is intended for rendering.

Lens Size and Field of View

The 35mm lens sizes relate to how much perspective flare there is in the view. The normal field of view, and resulting perspective flare, that most people experience in daily vision is 48 degrees. This is a little wider than the 50mm lens the camera industry accepts as the equivalent to the human eye, but is used by 3D Studio as the default FOV. Below this point (using wide-angled and fish-eyed lenses), more of the scene is taken in, and the effects of perspective are exaggerated. Above this size (with telephoto lenses), the scene comes forward and the effects of perspective are reduced and flattened. See Chapter 2, "Concepts and Theories," for a more detailed discussion of perspective and cameras.

The FOV can be changed dynamically with the Cameras/FOV command. The camera and target positions stay constant as the lens sizes and resulting field of view are adjusted. Adjusting this effect while in a Camera viewport is very similar to adjusting a 35mm zoom lens. Displaying the camera's cone of vision by activating the camera definition's Show Cone option is often helpful for seeing what is visible from non-camera viewports.

Cameras and Perspective Flare

As described in Chapter 2, the size of the camera lens and the resulting field of view determine how much perspective flare is in the view. The lower the lens size, the larger the field of view and the more flared the perspective. As most 35mm camera lenses do not go below 28mm, neither should their 3D Studio counterparts, unless you want a very flared view of your scene. Figure 7.38 shows the scene viewed through a 28mm lens and the same scene through a 200mm lens.

Figure 7.38
The view through a wide-angled 28mm lens, and the scene viewed through a 200mm telephoto lens.

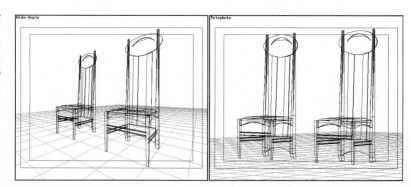

Perspective flare also connotes distance and size. A flared image gives the impression that you are very close to the subject. A flat perspective makes the scene appear farther away and possibly much larger.

The perspective flare of the camera can be dynamically adjusted with the Camera/Perspective command. When this is used, the camera's picture plane stays constant as the camera's position is dollied and the lens size changes. This effect is not easy to relate to and is, in fact, somewhat dizzying. This is precisely why it has been used as a special effect in notable films. When used in the 3D Editor, it is a good tool to get the "look" and drama you want from the camera without having to adjust the FOV and then reposition the camera.

You might want to Hold before using the Camera/Perspective command because it is easy to lose track of exactly how far the camera has dollied.

Do not confuse the Perspective command with the capabilities of a 35mm *perspective control* (PC) lens or a large-format, variable-plane camera. With these lenses, the camera is stationary and the perspective is "corrected," whereas the Perspective command moves the camera location. For creating a view that simulates a PC lens, see "Render Blowup" in Chapter 13.

Issues of Moving Cameras

A camera's target is only an aid for positioning, and the target's distance from the camera has no effect on the composition. The line connecting the camera and target visually shows the center line of sight. You can move the camera and target together by pressing [Ctrl] at the beginning of the operation.

When cameras and their targets are moved, they keep a constant field of view. As you move the target away from the camera, the displayed field-of-view cone grows but keeps the same angle. This is equivalent to moving about the scene with a fixed 35mm lens—the composition is constantly changing, but the lens size and resulting field of view are not. To change the field of view, and thus switch lenses, you must either change it in the Camera Definition dialog box, zoom with the FOV command, or dolly and zoom with the Perspective command.

Dollying a Camera's Position

You can move the camera along the line of sight vector defined by it and its target with the Cameras/Dolly command. This is not the same as a real-world camera dolly, where the camera stays tracked on the ground, regardless of the angle it is pointing. The Dolly command in 3D Studio is more like a helicopter-mounted camera because it is not constrained by land-based tracks and will follow the vector faithfully.

It is a very common need to keep the camera at a constant height above the ground plane, with walk-throughs being a typical example. You can do this by always moving the camera in the Top viewport and never using Dolly unless the camera and targets' height above the ground plane are exactly the same.

Rolling a Camera's Composition

The angle the camera views the scene is controlled by its Roll parameter angle. This is equivalent to how you might hold a 35mm camera in your hand. Rolling the camera by 90 degrees is the same as shooting the scene vertically with your hand camera sideways.

If the camera is not at a convenient angle for manual entry in the Camera Definition dialog box, you can dynamically roll it with the Cameras/Roll command.

The Roll command often is used to place the image of the view on its side for a vertical composition. This can allow your graphics card to display the full image while outputting a "taller" image than normally possible. A standard horizontal composition and a vertical composition created by rolling the camera 90 degrees are shown in figure 7.39.

Figure 7.39
A traditional horizontal composition and a vertical composition achieved with the Roll command.

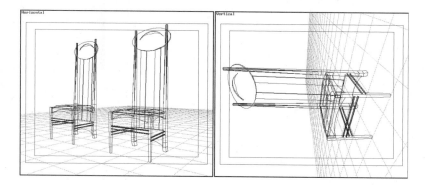

Exploring Rendering Options

The Renderer branch commands provide you with numerous options with which to control the look and composition of your final image. It is here that the size and color depth of the image are determined, and the extent to which 3D Studio renders the scene.

Specifying How Much to Render

3D Studio provides you with several options to control how much of the scene is to be rendered. With previous releases, and most other programs, you are limited to rendering whatever is displayed in the active viewport. With speed as the primary goal, several options are included: View, Region, Blowup, and Object.

Accessing the Renderer with any option from within the 3D Editor produces the dialog box shown in figure 7.40. The specific options available for the Renderer's configuration are discussed thoroughly in Chapter 1, "Configuring and Preparation."

```
                    Render Still Image
              ┌─────┬───────┐        ┌──────────┬──────────┐
Shading Limit │ Flat│Gouraud│        │ Viewport │ Vertical │
              │ Phong│ Metal │        └──────────┴──────────┘
              └─────┴───────┘            Configure...
Anti-aliasing  │ On │  Off  │        File Type    TARGA
Filter Maps    │ On │  Off  │        Driver       VIBRANT
Shadows        │ On │  Off  │        Resolution  640x480x1.00
Mapping        │ On │  Off  │            Options...
Auto-Reflect   │ On │  Off  │        Video Color Check   Off
Force 2-Sided  │ On │  Off  │        Pixel Size        1.10
Force Wire     │ On │  Off  │        Render Alpha       No
Hidden Geometry│Show│  Hide │
Background     │Rescale│Tile │        Gamma Correction   On

          ┌───────┬────────────┬──────────┬─────────┐
Output    │Display│ No Display │ Hardcopy │  Disk   │
          │Net ASAP│ Net Queue │          │         │
          └───────┴────────────┴──────────┴─────────┘
                   Render      Cancel
```

Figure 7.40
The Render Still Image dialog box accessed from the 3D Editor.

The Standard Render View

The Render View option is the standard way most renders are made—that is, everything that can be seen in that viewport is rendered. This can be accessed quickly by pressing Alt+R for any active viewport while in the 3D Editor or Keyframer.

Your only control of rendering speed is how much can be seen from the active viewport and to what extent the model fills the image. The same model viewed in different viewports can render with very different times, depending on what is visible in each.

Isolating an Object with Render Object

The capability to render a single object is primarily an aid to see the effects of material modifications for that object. You must physically select the object because the use of selection sets is not valid for this option.

When used with Auto Put and Render Last in the Materials Editor, this rendering option basically replaces the sample sphere or cube with the object as it is illuminated within the scene. The drawback is for any material that contains an automatic or flat mirror reflection or objects that have shadows cast across them. Neither of these effects can be shown with Render Object because only the selected object is being considered.

Capturing a Window with Render Region

The Render Region option enables you to render just a section of the scene. This is particularly useful when you are fine-tuning shadow map parameters, altering reflective materials, or coordinating the material and mapping placement of various objects. Objects that cast shadows or are reflected in another object's surface are still calculated, even though they might not be within the Render Region's cropping window.

Using Render Last

After an object is selected or a region defined, it can be recalled with the Render Last option. This enables you to define what you want to render once and quickly access it while still in the 3D Editor or, better yet, from the Materials Editor. Unfortunately, no keyboard alternate is available for this very useful feature, and you should assign it to your set of custom hot keys for quick access.

Setup Options for Rendering

Numerous options are available within the Renderer/Setup branch, but several of these are available from within other commands.

Options and Configurations

The Renderer/Configure and Renderer/Options commands produce dialog boxes that can be accessed from the standard Rendering dialog box at rendering time. (Descriptions for these settings can be found in Chapter 1.) The Configure option is convenient for changing your output resolution and seeing its effects on camera views.

The Shadows command produces the Global Shadow Control dialog box, which acts as the default for all initial lighting settings. Each spotlight can, and probably should, have its own settings, so this basically sets the starting point for their shadow control.

Background Color and Images

The Renderer/Background produces the dialog box shown in figure 7.41, and is the sole control for the model's background display. Within the Background Method control box are options for Solid Color, Gradient, and Bitmap that produce their own defining dialog boxes, as shown in the cascading portions of figure 7.41.

Figure 7.41
Background
dialog options.

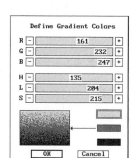

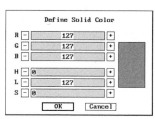

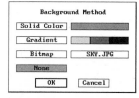

The Solid Color option is fairly obvious. Most rendering is done by default against a black background, but you might want to switch this to a white background for print work. Anti-aliasing is done directly against the background color(s); when Alpha channels are created, backgrounds are always ignored in their composition.

The gradients created with Release 3 and later are extremely good and incur nearly no banding as long as you have the Renderer's "Dither true color" option set to Yes. Turning this option off can easily lead to banded colors for soft gradients. An often-overlooked option is the ability to adjust where the transition point occurs for the gradient background. By clicking on the arrow's tip, you can slide the division point up and down to any vertical position (see fig. 7.42). Moving it all the way to the top or bottom defines a traditional two-color gradient.

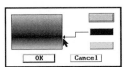

Figure 7.42
Adjusting the gradient background division height.

The Bitmap option enables you to choose any supported image file. The memory cost for this is three bytes per pixel, regardless of the image's true color depth. If the image needs to be resized, an additional three bytes per pixel for the output resolution is needed as well. The bitmap used for a background always is paid for and cannot be reused as a material's bitmap without paying in memory for it again.

No alignment or scale options are available for background bitmaps. If the image needs to be repositioned, stretched, rotated, or rescaled, it needs to be done in an external paint program first. (See Chapter 12, "Materials and Mapping," for details on editing background images.)

Summary

This chapter described all the commands essential to illumination and camera viewing. With these commands, you can create extremely convincing 8-bit images and animations, as described in more detail in the next chapter.

Realistic and attention-grabbing images require a well-rounded composite of all techniques, tools, and procedures. As in the real world, very little worth achieving in 3D Studio can be done with a single command or an isolated mesh, no matter how well-crafted. The object needs to be thoughtfully illuminated to accentuate its qualities and viewed in a manner that forms a solid and interesting composition.

Chapter Snapshot

This chapter takes many of the techniques presented earlier and discusses how to use them for effective 8-bit still imaging. This chapter discusses some problems and techniques involved in creating 8-bit images, but is mainly a large exercise. This exercise uses much of what you have learned in previous chapters to create an 8-bit image that rivals the quality of a full-color 24-bit image. Rendering in 8-bit color does not mean that you must settle for low-quality output. This chapter presents the following topics:

✔ Using 8-bit files

✔ Examining problems associated with 8-bit color and how to overcome them

✔ Understanding the implications that 8-bit color and its lower resolution have on the level of detail used when building your geometry

✔ Editing 8-bit images in a paint program, such as Animator Pro

✔ Creating on-screen presentations from your 8-bit images with another program (in this chapter, the scripting capabilities of AAPLAYHI are used)

CHAPTER

8-Bit Still Imaging

Much of the focus in magazines and in Autodesk's marketing of 3D Studio is on 24-bit images and high-end output devices. These 24-bit images have a range of 16.7 million colors and usually are rendered at high resolutions. Many people are intimidated by this emphasis and fail to realize that 3D Studio is an excellent tool for the creation of 8-bit images and Animator Pro-style flic files. 8-bit images are limited to only 256 colors and usually are rendered at screen resolutions such as 640×480.

You are not going to get your work on a major television network using 8-bit technology, but many independent local television stations, multimedia producers, disk-based presentations, and information kiosks rely primarily on 8-bit technology. This chapter discusses how and when to use 8-bit files.

Using 8-Bit Images

Many markets exist for 8-bit images and animation. Using 8-bit color does not mean that your images are inferior or nonprofessional. It only means that for one reason or another you have chosen to use this file format. The 8-bit file format also has some advantages that justify its use, such as the following:

- ✔ **Small file size.** Small files are a necessity for *disk-based presentations*, or presentations that must run on limited hardware.

- ✔ **Fast loading and display.** The small file size helps speed up the time it takes to load 8-bit images into memory and display 8-bit images on-screen.

- ✔ **Wide software compatibility.** 8-bit file formats, such as GIF and the 8-bit versions of BMP and PCX, are supported by many paint and presentation programs.

- ✔ **Low video hardware requirements.** The low-end VGA standard that supports 8-bit color at 320×200 resolution is still used on many systems. SVGA support of 8-bit color at a resolution of 640×480 also is very popular, while higher resolutions and 24-bit color support are much less common.

If you are creating images for display on a client's system, portable presentations, or disk-based marketing, then you may need to work with 8-bit images.

Examining 8-Bit Color Restrictions

Working in 8-bit color imposes some restrictions on what you can do, but these restrictions are not as onerous as they might at first seem. The limit of 256 colors requires that you exercise care when you plan the use of color in your images. You also must compromise between minimizing file size or minimizing the side effects of the color restrictions. These restrictions are summed up as banding, dithering, and color palette control. They are discussed in the following sections.

Banding

Banding is what happens when there are not enough colors available to represent a smooth transition from one color to the next. These transitions are called *color ramps* or *gradients* and are used for shading geometry or when you choose the Gradient Background option in 3D Studio. Because not enough colors exist to represent the gradient smoothly, it is divided into a few broad bands of color that approximate the gradient. Figure 8.1 shows a sphere rendered against a gradient background. Both the sphere and the background exhibit severe banding.

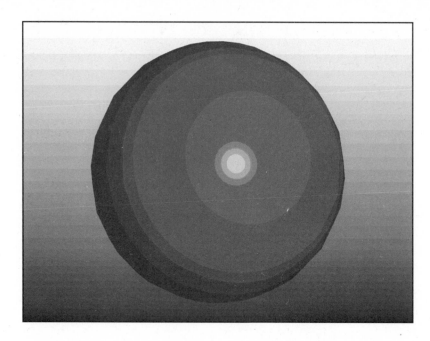

Figure 8.1
Color banding in
an 8-bit image.

The two main techniques used to avoid banding are careful color selection and the avoidance of gradients. Color selection focuses on the fact that you have only 256 colors with which to work. If you choose colors for your scene that are widely different, such as multiple primaries or fully saturated hues, each color receives only a few palette slots for its shading colors, and banding is inevitable. If instead you choose most of your colors from one color family with a complementary color thrown-in for contrast, the colors can share many of the same shades and you reduce banding.

Avoiding gradients requires breaking up the surface of your geometry. Smooth solid-color objects suffer the most from banding effects. The only way to represent shading on the surface of a smooth object is to use a gradient as the color changes from light to dark. One way to break up the surface and avoid banding is to use mapped materials. Look at the objects around you right now. How many have smooth, solid color surfaces? Painted metal usually has a smooth solid surface but almost everything else has bumps, grooves, and patterns. Not only do bump maps, texture maps, and reflections add to the realism of your scene but they also break up the surface to reduce banding.

Figure 8.2a shows a rendering using solid colors of widely different hues. The vase is green, the sphere is blue, the table top is brown, and the whole scene is banded. Figure 8.2b is the same scene with only the materials changed. The vase is now a tan marble, the sphere is shiny copper, and the table has a wood grain texture. Banding is hardly noticeable. The key to this rendering is that the textures break up the surfaces and the materials share a similar color range.

Figure 8.2a
A scene with
banding caused
by poor material
selection.

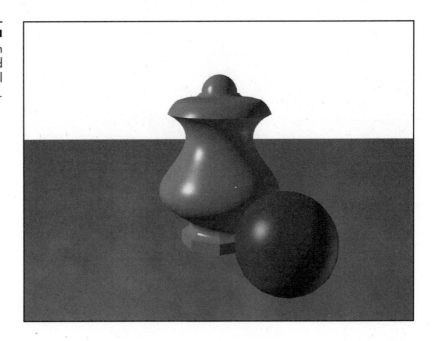

Figure 8.2b
The same scene
using mapped
materials to avoid
banding.

Dithering

Sometimes banding cannot be avoided. You need to model smooth-painted surfaces where textures and bumps are not acceptable. In such a case, 3D Studio provides a setting in the Render Options dialog box called Dither 256. The default for this setting is on, but you might want to change it or at least consider whether you want to use dithering when you prepare to render. Dither 256 does nothing to eliminate banding. What it does do is make banding less noticeable by scattering pixels at the edges of color bands. Dithering blurs the edges between bands, which helps your eye ignore the edges and accept the illusion of a smooth color gradient.

The drawback to dithering is that it can greatly increase file size. Most 8-bit image formats use a compression technique that identifies and compresses areas of contiguous color. A side effect of dithering is that it eliminates many areas of contiguous color causing file size to increase. The rendered file size of the simple sphere in figure 8.1 increased by 50 percent when Dither 256 was turned on. More importantly, the image in figure 8.2b increased in size by 30 percent with dithering turned on, even though dithering provided almost no improvement in the quality of the image. In general, you should try to achieve your desired level of quality through mapping techniques with Dither 256 turned off. You then must decide whether dithering is necessary for the image quality that you require, and balance that decision against the need for smaller file sizes.

Palette Control

Another method for controlling quality in 8-bit images is to adjust the color palette for the image manually. 3D Studio provides an option for rendering 8-bit animations, but it also is useful for single frame images. If you access the Renderer/Setup/Configure command while in the Keyframer, you are presented with an option to choose a color palette (see fig. 8.3). The Low, Medium, and High options are used only when rendering animations; however, the Custom option also affects single images rendered in the 3D Editor. The Custom Palette option enables you to specify which 256-color palette to use at rendering time. This file can be an Animator Pro COL file or any GIF, FLC, or CEL.

The advantage of choosing a custom palette for single-image rendering is that you can adjust the palette to give priority to important colors in your scene. When 3D Studio saves a scene to an 8-bit file format, it first renders the scene with 48 bits of color and then reduces it down to 8 bits. Because 3D Studio lacks subjective aesthetics, composition, or focus, it can only estimate which colors are important for the scene. The result might be too many shades for unimportant background objects and not enough shades for your main subject. The solution is to design your own custom color palette with several shades for the most important colors in your scene and allow the background colors to suffer greater banding.

Figure 8.3

Setting a custom palette in the Keyframer.

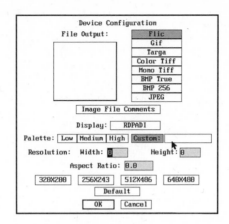

Understanding Model Complexity

Another issue concerning 8-bit imaging is rendering resolution and model complexity. Typically, 8-bit images are rendered for display on a standard computer screen, often at a rendering resolution of 640×480. Compare that to typical 24-bit resolutions for video at 756×512 or for film printing at 2048×1536. You quickly realize that the detail necessary for high-color, high-resolution rendering is overkill for 8-bit rendering. Save yourself rendering time and build your models with the realization that low color and low resolution do not require as much detail.

In the following exercise, you employ some of the modeling and rendering techniques from the last few chapters. You create a scene for 8-bit, on-screen display that involves lofting, creating geometry in the 3D Editor, merging geometry from other files, and creating lights and materials. The subject of this exercise is an artist's desk with a blank pad waiting for paint.

Modeling and Rendering a Scene

First, create some simple geometry on the 3D Editor to represent the desk, a water can to wash out the brush, and the block of art paper.

Start or reset 3D Studio

Press Ctrl+A, *then set the* Snap *and* Grid Spacing, *as shown in figure 8.4*	Sets the snap, grid, and grid extents
Right-click on the Zoom Extents *icon, then click in the* Top *viewport and click on the* Full Screen *icon*	Zooms all viewports to the new grid extents, and then zooms the Top view to fill the screen

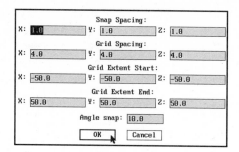

Figure 8.4
The drawing aids settings.

II

Basic Modeling

Press S *to turn on Snap, choose* Create/Box *and create a box 50 units wide by 30 units deep with a length of 3 units, and then name the object* Table-Top	Creates the table top for the scene
Create another box 18 units wide by 24 units deep with a length of 1 unit, and name it Pad	Creates an object to represent the pad of artist's paper
Choose Create/Tube/Values *and set the Sides slider at 24, then choose* Create/Tube/Smoothed	
Create a tube with Radius 1 set at 2 units, then press S *to turn off Snap; set Radius 2 at about 1.8 units, then press* S *to turn Snap back on; specify a length of 5 units, then name the object* Can	Creates a hollow tube to represent the water can
Click on the Full Screen *icon*	Displays all four viewports on the screen

All of the objects that you have created are lying on the same horizontal plane (see fig. 8.5). This is most noticeable in the Front and Left viewports where the bottoms of all three objects match up. Now you need to move the Can and Pad objects up so that they rest on the table.

After positioning the Can and the Pad, merge a lamp into your scene.

Choose Modify/Object/Move, *and then move the Can and the Pad up 3 units*	Places the objects on the table top
Press Alt+A *to select all of the objects in the scene*	All the objects turn red, indicating that they are selected
Choose Merge *from the* File *pull-down menu, turn off the* Cameras, Lights, *and* Animation *buttons, and then select the file LUXO.3DS from the 3D Studio \MESHES directory*	Selects a model of a lamp that ships with 3D Studio and merges only the mesh objects with your model
Click on the All *button in the* Select Objects to Merge *dialog box, and then click on* OK	After a pause, the Luxo lamp appears on the screen, as shown in figure 8.6

continues

continued

Figure 8.5
The table top, pad, and can.

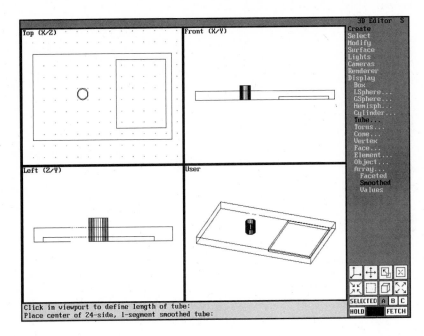

Choose Surface/Normals/Object Flip
and select the base of the lamp

At the time this exercise was written, the normals of Luxo lamp base were oriented the wrong way. This command flips them for proper rendering.

Often you have little control over where a stock object appears when you merge it into your model. The object might be way off to one side or the other, or worse yet, it might appear right in the middle of other objects in your scene. That is why you selected everything in the scene before merging the Luxo lamp. It is now an easy process to invert the selection set and move the lamp into position.

Choose Select/Invert

All the previously selected objects are unselected and all the parts of the lamp turn red, indicating that they are selected

Choose Modify/Object/Move *and press* (Spacebar)
to activate the current selection set, then move the lamp to the back left corner of the table top

The lamp is placed on the table

Click on selection button B *and then press* (Alt)+(A)

Activates selection set B, and puts all objects into the selection

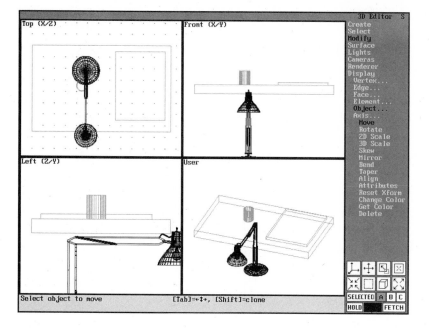

Figure 8.6

The Luxo lamp merged into your model.

II

Basic Modeling

Choose Merge *from the* File *pull-down menu (all buttons except Mesh Objects should still be off), click on* OK, *and select the file* BRUSH.3DS *from the CD-ROM*

Click on the All *button in the* Select Objects to Merge *dialog box, and click on* OK

A small paintbrush appears in the scene

Choose Select/Invert *and then choose* Modify/Object/Move, *press* (Spacebar), *and move the brush so that it lies on top of the pad*

Puts the brush into the current selection and removes all other objects

Right-click on the Zoom Extents *icon*

Your screen should appear similar to figure 8.7.

You need one more object to complete the scene—the painter's palette. Create a palette shape in the 2D Shaper and then loft it in the 3D Lofter. If, however, you have not saved your work, do so now.

Choose Save *from the* File *pull-down menu, save the file with the name* PAINTING, *then click on* Save

Press (F1)

Enters the 2D Shaper

continues

continued

Figure 8.7
The lamp and
brush merged and
positioned in
your scene.

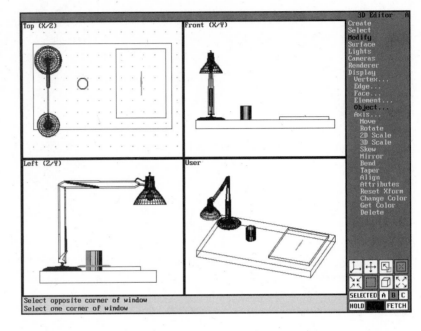

With Snap turned on, choose Create/Ellipse and specify an ellipse with a vertical radius of 5 units and a horizontal radius of 4 units	Creates the basic shape for the palette
Turn off Snap and specify another ellipse for the thumb slot	

Figure 8.8 shows an example of how you might place the second ellipse.

Choose Create/Boolean, select the large ellipse first and then the small ellipse, click on the Subtraction button, and then click on OK	Subtracts the small ellipse from the large ellipse, creating a thumb slot
Choose Modify/Segment/Refine and pick points 1, 2, and 3 (shown in fig. 8.9), then choose Modify/Vertex/Delete, and delete vertices A and B (shown in fig. 8.9)	Fillets the sharp points created by the Boolean subtraction
Choose Modify/Vertex/Adjust and adjust the curvature at the top of the thumb slot to be a little flatter, then create a circle with a radius of about 0.4 units just above the thumb slot	Your palette shape is almost complete (refer to fig. 8.10 for the circle location)

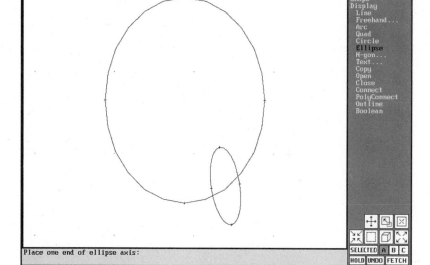

Figure 8.8

The ellipses for the basic palette and thumb slot.

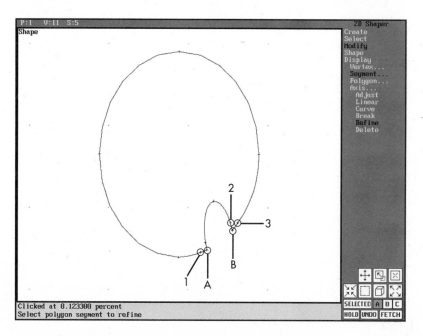

Figure 8.9

The pick points for Segment/Refine and Vertex/Delete.

continues

continued

Choose Shape/Steps *and set the slider at 2, then choose*
Modify/Segment/Refine, *and pick the 8 points
shown in figure 8.10 (if you have trouble, you can load
the shape file,* PALETTE.SHP)

Optimizes the palette shape in
preparation for lofting

Figure 8.10
Segment refine
points for the
palette shape.

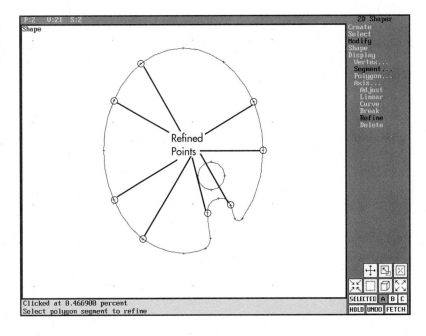

Choose Shape/All *and then press* F2

Assigns all the polygons as the current
Shape and enters the 3D Lofter

Click in the Top *viewport to make it active and then
click on the* Full Screen *icon*

Fills the screen with only the Top
viewport

Choose Path/Move Vertex, *press* Tab⇄ *until the vertical
constraint arrows appear, and select the top vertex on the
path, then move the vertex down until the path length at
the top of the screen reads 1.00 unit*

Shortens the path to one unit long

Click on the Zoom Extents *icon, check that Snap is
turned off, and move the top vertex again until the path
is about 0.3 units long (if a "Close Path" message
appears, click on* No)

Sets the path for lofting the thick
palette at 0.3 units

Choose Path/Steps *and set the slider at 0, then
click on the* Full Screen *icon*

Removes unneeded steps from
the path, and restores all four viewports

Choose Shapes/Get/Shaper, *then choose* Shapes/Center	Gets the palette shape from the 2D Shaper and centers it on the path
Choose Objects/Make *and enter the parameters shown in figure 8.11, then click on* Create	Makes the Palette object and puts it in the 3D Editor

```
Object Lofting Controls

Object Name:  Palette

Cap Start:     Off   On
Cap End:       Off   On
Smooth Length: Off   On
Smooth Width:  Off   On
Mapping:       Off   On
Optimization:  Off   On
Weld Vertices: Off   On
Path Detail:   Low  Med  High
Shape Detail:  Low  Med  High

     Tween     Contour
  +     Create     Cancel
```

Figure 8.11
Lofting parameters for the Palette object.

Press F3	Enters the 3D Editor—the Palette object is standing on edge and floating above the table

Turn on the local axis, and use Modify/Object/Rotate *and* Move *to place the Palette object flat on the table top*

Your scene should look like figure 8.12.

The banding problems caused by 8-bit rendering can be alleviated by using mapped materials. You are going to use texture, reflection, and bump maps on almost every object in this scene. Now is a good time to apply mapping coordinates to your objects while they are still square to the standard viewports.

A common mistake is to carefully position all the objects, only to discover that applying mapping coordinates involves considerable extra effort. Whenever possible, decide on a mapping strategy while objects are still square to the standard viewports. Put objects in their final position after mapping.

Choose Surface/Mapping/Type/Planar	Sets the mapping type to planar
Choose Surface/Mapping/Adjust/Scale, *then hold down* Alt *while selecting the table top in the* Top *viewport*	Positions and scales the mapping icon to fit the table top

continues

continued

Figure 8.12
All the objects
ready for final
positioning.

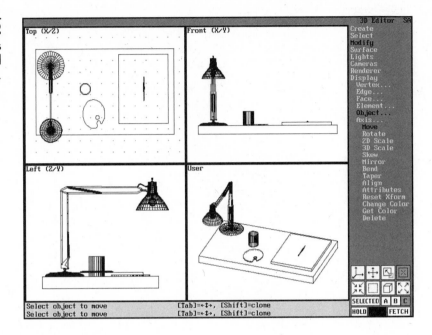

Choose Surface/Mapping/Apply Obj. *and select the table top*	Applies the mapping coordinates to the table top
Repeat the last two steps to apply planar mapping coordinates to the pad and palette in the Top *viewport*	Applies planar mapping coordinates to the pad and palette
Choose Surface/Mapping/Type/Cylindrical *and use the* Alt+Scale *technique while selecting the can in the* Front *viewport, then apply the coordinates to the can*	Positions, scales, and applies cylindrical mapping coordinates to the can

Now arrange the objects in your scene to form a pleasing composition. If you are building a model from engineering drawings, floor plans, or a map, you have detailed instructions on where each object belongs. When you model an artistic scene such as this one, you have much more freedom regarding the placement of objects. In this situation, it is best to place your camera first and then compose your scene while referring to an active camera view. What looks good in an orthogonal view might not look so good in a camera view. It only makes sense to have the view you are rendering visible as you compose your scene.

The viewports in 3D Studio are probably nowhere close to the same aspect ratio as your output resolution. It is always a good idea to turn on Safe Frame when you compose a camera view because it displays a yellow frame around the limits of the configured rendering resolution.

New Riders Publishing
INSIDE SERIES

Press Alt+B, *right-click on the* Zoom Extents *icon, right-click on the* Zoom Out *icon three times, and press* Alt+B *again*

Turns on Box mode for quick redraw and zooms out all four viewports for easy camera placement; full draw then is restored for accurate viewing

Choose Camera/Create *and pick points for the camera and its target in the* Top *viewport, then click in the* User *viewport and press* C, Alt+E

Places a camera and displays its view in the former User viewport, then displays the Safe Frame in Camera viewport

Choose Camera/Move *and adjust the camera position to a view similar to that in figure 8.13*

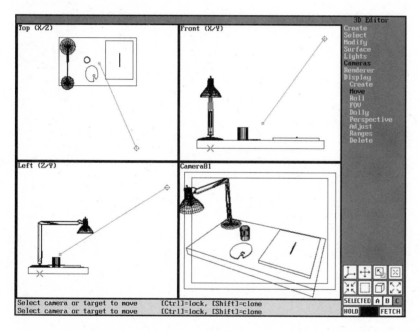

Figure 8.13
The placement of the camera.

Press Alt+C *and then right-click on the* Zoom Extents *icon*

Hides the camera icon and zooms in on the three remaining Orthogonal viewports

Using any Modify commands, compose the objects into a pleasing arrangement (see fig. 8.14 for an example)

If you have been following the exercise closely, selection set A contains only the objects for the lamp, while selection set B contains only the objects for the brush. Use the Selected button with the Modify commands to position these objects easily. If you lose the selection sets, you can rebuild them quickly by using Select/Object/Quad or Select/Object/By Name.

continues

continued

Figure 8.14
The final
composition
of the scene.

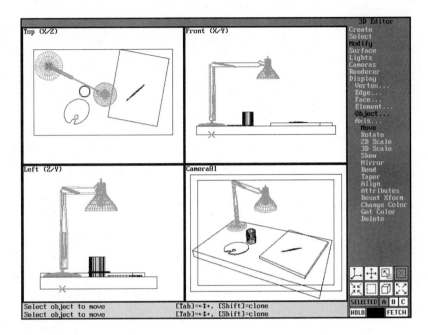

The last steps left in this exercise are to set up lights and assign materials. The discussions on color and lighting theory in Chapter 2 point out that it is nearly impossible to get true white light in the real world, so you don't want to use white light for your renderings either. This scene is being illuminated by a standard tungsten lamp in a swing arm fixture. You will simulate this illumination with a yellow spotlight and a bluish ambient light.

Click in the Left *viewport and click on the* Full
Screen *icon*

Choose Lights/Spot/Create *and place the spotlight in*   Locates a spotlight inside the Luxo
the center of the bulb, place the target directly beneath it   lamp (Cast Shadows and Show Cone
on the table top, then set the Spotlight Definition as   are on)
shown in figure 8.15

Choose Lights/Spot/Hotspot *and select the new*
spotlight, then adjust the hotspot angle so that
it just touches the edge of the lamp shade
(about 120 degrees)

Click on the Full Screen *icon and choose*
Lights/Spot/Move, *hold down* Ctrl *while*
selecting either end of the spotlight in the Top *viewport,*
then move the spotlight until it is centered in the Bulb
again

New Riders Publishing
INSIDE
SERIES

Creating the spotlight in the Left viewport only centered the light on two axes, so you must move the light in another viewport to center it on the other axis.

Choose Modify/Object/Delete *and select the Bulb object*	The mesh object Bulb is not seen in this rendering and interferes with the shadow casting spotlight

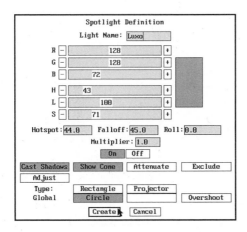

Figure 8.15
The settings for placement of the spotlight.

II

Basic Modeling

Right-click twice on the Zoom Extents *icon, then choose* Lights/Omni/Create *and place an omni light in the location shown in figure 8.16*	Places an omni light for fill-in illumination
Specify the settings for the omni light at R:38, G:38, and B:22	
Choose Lights/Ambient *and specify settings of R:0, G:0, and B:15*	Sets the ambient light to be a dim complement to the main light in the scene

Most of the objects in your scene are going to use standard materials in the 3DS.MLI library. You now will create two special materials for two of the objects using map files from the *Inside 3D Studio* CD-ROM.

Press F5	Enters the Materials Editor
Click on the first sample window, then click in the Current Material *field and type* **PAINT**	Defines a material definition called PAINT
Set the sliders for the ambient and diffuse colors at R:169, G:143, and B:100, then set the Specular Luminance slider at 255	Sets the color specifications for the base material

continues

continued

Figure 8.16
Placement of the
omni light.

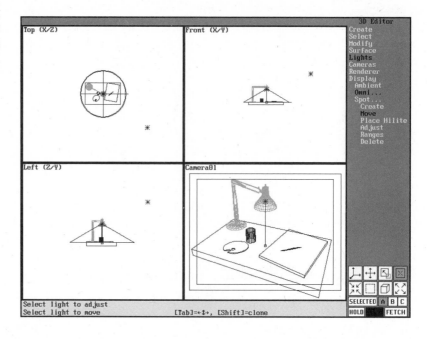

Set the Shininess slider at 50 and the Shininess Strength at 100	Sets the material shininess values
Click on the Map *slot for Texture 1, choose the file* PAINT.CEL *from the CD-ROM, set the amount slider at 100, click on* S, *and turn on the* Decal *button*	Applies a decal for the color of paint blobs on the palette
Click on the Map *slot for Bump and select the file* PAINT-B.CEL *from the CD-ROM, then set the amount slider at 40*	Specifies a bumpy texture for the areas of the paint blobs
Click on the Map *slot for Shininess and select the file* PAINT-B.CEL, *set the amount slider to 100, click on* S, *and turn on the* Negative *button in the* Mapping Parameters *dialog box*	Uses the same file as the bump map, but is reversed to block shininess from all areas except the paint blobs
Click on the Render Sample *button, then choose* Put Material *from the* Material *pull-down menu and click on* OK	Displays the material on a sample sphere and stores the material in the materials library (see fig. 8.17 for the material settings)

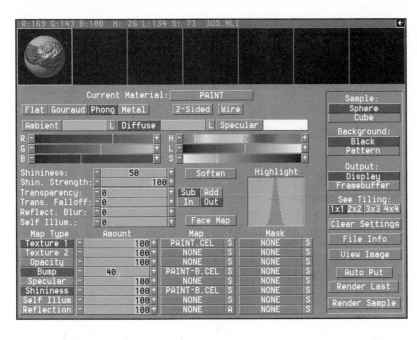

Figure 8.17
The settings for the PAINT material.

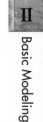

Click in the second sample material window, then choose Get Material *from the* Material *pull-down menu, and select the material* WHITE MATTE

Loads the standard material WHITE MATTE from the materials library

Click in the Current Material *field and change the name to* WHITE PAPER, *then click on the* Map *slot for Bump, select the file* FABRIC.JPG *from the* \MAPS *directory, and set the amount slider at 6*

Add a bump map to an existing texture to create a new material

Click on Render Sample, *then choose* Put Material *from the* Material *pull-down menu, and click on* OK

Stores the material in the materials library

Press F3, *then choose* Surface/Material/Choose, *and select the material* WHITE PLSTC REF

Choose Surface/Material/Assign/Object, *click on selection button A, press* Spacebar *to activate the selection set, and click in the active viewport, then click on* OK

Assigns the material WHITE PLSTC REF to all of the objects that make up the Luxo lamp

Choose the material WOOD-ASH *and assign it to the object table top*

continues

continued

Choose the material BRUSHED METAL *and assign
it to the object Can*

Choose the material PAINT *and assign it to the object
Palette*

Choose the material WHITE PAPER *and assign it to
the object Pad*

The brush that you merged at the beginning of this exercise already has materials assigned to it. Now you are ready to render your scene. The purpose of this exercise is to show you how well 8-bit rendering can work when applied properly. If you have upgraded your display system for 24-bit display, you have two choices for the completion of this exercise, as follows:

Option 1:

Choose Renderer/Setup Configure, *then choose one
of the VESA modes as your rendering device*

VESA modes support only 8-bit color.

Choose Renderer/Setup/Options *and turn off the*   Turns off 8-bit dithering
Dither 256 button

Choose Renderer/Render View, *click in the* Camera
viewport, and accept the default rendering parameters

When rendering is complete, the image is displayed on your main screen in 8-bit color. See figure 8.18 for an example of the rendered image.

Option 2:

Choose Renderer/Setup/Configure *and click on*   Specifies 8-bit GIF file output
the GIF *button for file output*

Choose Renderer/Setup/Options *and turn off the*   Turns off 8-bit dithering
Dither 256 button

Choose Renderer/Render View, *and click in the*   Renders the view, but the image is first
Camera *viewport, then turn on the* Disk *button, accept*   displayed in your display's 24-bit
all of the other default rendering parameters, and specify   format
an output file name of PAINTING.GIF

Press (Esc) *when rendering is complete, then choose*   Displays the 8-bit GIF image (see
Renderer/View/Image *and select*   fig. 8.18)
PAINTING.GIF

If you view the final 8-bit image, you notice that almost no banding is visible. The use of the various texture maps, reflection maps, and bump maps serve to break up the surfaces and prevent banding.

Figure 8.18
The final rendered image.

II

Basic Modeling

Editing 8-Bit Images

After you render your 8-bit images, chances are you will eventually edit them using a paint package. You can perform such tasks as applying titling, image touch-up, and creative processing with 8-bit paint programs. Animator Pro is a handy program for many of these tasks.

Text Overlay

One common use for Animator Pro is the application of title effects to images rendered in 3D Studio. When using high-resolution and 24-bit color, it is best to apply text effects within 3D Studio, but for 8-bit work at typical screen resolution, Animator Pro is hard to beat.

Figure 8.19 shows an example of text overlay on an image rendered in 3D Studio. Using techniques similar to the decal map exercise in Chapter 6, drop-shadow text was overlaid on an image of the painter's palette. This could then be used as the opening screen on a disk-based presentation.

Touch-Up

Paint programs also can be used to touch up images after they are rendered in 3D Studio. Sometimes, no matter how hard you try, some banding effects or artifacts are left in an undesirable part of the image. Animator Pro tools, such as Spray and Sep, are useful for touching up these areas.

You can use other inks, such as Light, Dark, and Glass, to affect the overall contrast and brightness of the final image. Grays Only is very useful for preparing images for output to a monochrome laser printer.

Figure 8.19 was touched up using Animator Pro. The paint blobs were touched up and moved to a different part of the palette. Contrast was enhanced through the application of dark ink to everything but the palette. Finally, the whole image was converted to grayscale for printing through the Grays Only command.

Exploring Presentation Techniques

After you render your 8-bit images and touch them up in Animator Pro, what do you do with them? Obviously, if you went to the trouble of modeling and rendering something, you want to show it to someone. You can use 3D Studio to display images manually for coworkers, but this is not a good technique for professional business presentations. What you need to consider is some way to display your work in a scripted or interactive fashion.

ANIPLAY Scripts

Animator Pro comes with a scriptable player named ANIPLAY.EXE (a similar program is provided on the *Inside 3D Studio* CD-ROM called AAPLAYHI.EXE). These programs enable you to display animations in the FLI and FLC format, as well as still images in the GIF format. The display of these images is controlled by a script file that you can program as either a stand-alone self-running presentation or as an interactive program that requests user input.

Authoring Programs

Many other multimedia authoring programs exist on the market that enable you to produce interactive presentations using one or more of the file types that 3D Studio supports. These programs range from the highly sophisticated programming language GRASP to author-friendly presentation programs, such as HSC Interactive and PowerPoint.

The following exercise shows you how to take various images created in 3D Studio and Animator Pro and turn them into an interactive presentation. Use the program AAPLAYHI.EXE to display the presentation and any text editor to write the script.

The exercise simulates a small disk-based presentation that you could distribute on a single high-density disk. The images are close-ups of various objects from the preceding exercise, and are as follows:

✔ **TITLE.GIF.** Close-up of the palette with the art shop name

✔ **INTRO.GIF.** Overall shot of the scene with introductory message

✔ **LAMP.GIF.** Close-up of the lamp

✔ **PAPER.GIF.** Close-up of the pad of paper

✔ **PAINT.GIF.** Close-up of the palette, paint brush, and can

✔ **END.GIF.** Close-up of the palette with choices to repeat or end the presentation

The exercise shows how you can combine 3D Studio 8-bit images and Animator Pro image editing to produce useful presentations. The lure of 24-bit imaging is strong, but don't forget that a lot of valuable and profitable work can still be accomplished by using 8-bit imaging.

A Scripted Presentation

*Start any text editor that saves
in text-only format*

Enter the following script file:

```
    title.gif -p 2
    loop (forever)
     intro.gif -p 2 -t fadein .1
     lamp.gif  -p 2 -t fadein .1
     paper.gif -p 2 -t fadein .1
     paint.gif -p 2 -t fadein .1
     end.gif -t fadein .1
     keychoice
      choice escape
        title.gif -p 1 -t fadein .1 fadeout 2
        exittodos
      choice C
        title.gif    -p 2 -t fadein .1
      endchoice
    endloop
```

Creates a script file that employs pauses (-p),
transitions (-t) fadein, looping loop
(forever), and user interaction key choice.
Details on programming the player are
found in the file AAPLAYHI.DOC

Save the file as ART-SHOP.SCR

Start the program AAPLAYHI *and configure for
640×480 screen resolution*

Sets up the player AA.CFG file for the correct
screen resolution

Choose Play Script *from the* File *pull-down
menu, and select the file* ART-SHOP

Plays the script once and exits to DOS

You also can run the script by entering AAPLAYHI ART-SHOP.SCR -A at the DOS command
prompt.

Summary

In this chapter, you explored various techniques for creating and using 8-bit images. While
full-color, 24-bit imaging is required for most high-quality video and print productions, there
is still a valid market for 8-bit work. Such markets as game development, interactive CDs,
educational programs, and disk-based presentations still rely heavily on 8-bit images. It will be
some time before 8-bit images are completely replaced by full-color formats.

Part III

Advanced Modeling

Chapter Snapshot

This chapter continues the investigation of the 2D Shaper and 3D Lofter that began in Chapter 4, "2D to 3D: The 2D Shaper and 3D Lofter Combination." This chapter discusses the following topics:

✔ Editing complex paths

✔ Creating back-tracking paths

✔ Creating surfaces of revolution

✔ Creating and using helical paths

✔ Using deformation grids

✔ Understanding Fit deformation

✔ Applying lofted mapping coordinates

CHAPTER

Lofting Complex Objects

C hapter 4 showed you the basics of using the 2D Shaper and 3D Lofter combination. At that time, you were introduced to the possibilities of importing a path from the 2D Shaper and for curving the path through the Move Vertex command. This chapter delves much deeper into two advanced topics.

First is the exploration of complex paths. Many users try out the built-in paths for surfaces of revolution and helical shapes; therefore, those techniques are discussed. 3D Studio also provides many other advanced tools for the manipulation of the 3D Lofter path, including the capability for the path to double back on itself and to contain multiple levels at the same point in space.

The second topic is a discussion of the various deformation grids and how they interact. *Fit deformation* is a very popular technique, and this chapter shows you how to expand your use of deformations through the combination of the deformation grids with path manipulation.

Understanding Paths

The Paths branch in the 3D Lofter can be functionally divided into three sections: path editing commands, special paths, and restoration of various path defaults.

Editing Paths

Many path editing commands work just like the polygon editing commands in the 2D Shaper or the modify object commands in the 3D Editor. Chapter 4 discussed this when the commands Insert Vertex, Move Vertex, Delete Vertex, and Refine were compared to their counterparts in the 2D Shaper. The remaining commands are much the same. If you know them in the 2D Shaper, you know them in the 3D Lofter. The primary difference for the 3D Lofter commands is that these commands do not have the option to choose either a global or local axis. All but two of the remaining path edit commands treat the first vertex of the path as the global axis.

Some path edit commands might seem of little value until you consider combining them with 3D Display. The 3D Display command enables you to see objects in the 3D Editor as you work with the path in the 3D Lofter. This is where the real value of path edit commands, such as Move Path and Rotate, become evident. These commands are extremely useful for placing the path in exactly the right location before you loft an object. This can save you time later on when you go to the 3D Editor to manipulate these objects.

Move Path

The Path/Move Path command moves the path to a new location in 3D space. With 3D Display turned on, this command enables you to place the path accurately so that lofted objects arrive in the 3D Editor at precisely the right location.

2D and 3D Scaling

The Path/2D Scale and Path/3D Scale commands work just like scaling an object in the 3D Editor. The base point of the scaling operation is always the first vertex on the path.

Skew

Again, the Path/Skew command is similar to the Polygon/Skew command in the 2D Shaper. The vertex positions are only affected along the two axes parallel to the current viewport. The first vertex on the path serves as the base point for the command.

Note If the path appears as a straight line in the current viewport, avoid setting the directional cursor (Tab key) parallel to the path. This is an unpredictable situation that can strangely affect the orientation of the shape at the first vertex.

Mirror

The Path/Mirror command works as usual and obeys all three directional cursors. Unlike the mirror commands in other modules, you cannot simultaneously move and mirror the path. The first vertex of the path remains fixed in its original position.

Rotate

The Path/Rotate command spins the path about any axis with the first vertex of the path used as the center of rotation. This is another command that suddenly takes on great value when you consider how it interacts with the 3D Editor.

Some users are frustrated when they import DXF files from AutoCAD into the 2D Shaper, and then loft them. The lofted object appears in the 3D Editor "on its side" and must be rotated into the proper position. Many people consider an AutoCAD drawing, or even a 2D Shaper polygon, to be the plan view or "top" of an object. The default orientation for the 3D Lofter places the shape parallel to the Front view and lofts it back along 3D Studio's Z axis. The solution is simple—rotate the path.

The following short exercise demonstrates how rotating the path enables you to loft an object parallel to any desired viewport. The example is a floor plan that you loft parallel to the Top viewport, rather than the default orientation parallel to the Front viewport.

Rotating the Path

Start or reset 3D Studio

Press F1 *to enter the 2D Shaper*

Press Ctrl+U *to display the* Units Setup *dialog box, and then set units to* Architectural *and one unit equal to one inch*	Defines architectural units for this exercise; the fraction denominator is not important for this task
Choose Load *from the* File *pull-down menu and select the file* PLAN.SHP	Loads a shape of a simple floor plan (see fig. 9.1)

continues

continued

Figure 9.1
The floor plan
shape in the
2D Shaper.

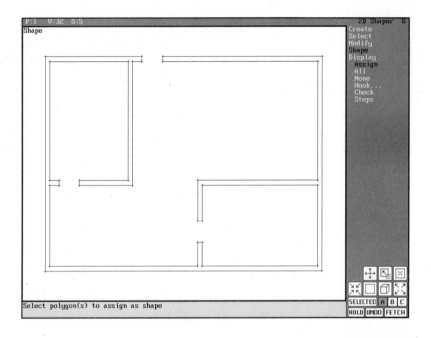

Figure 9.2
The floor plan in
the 3D Lofter.

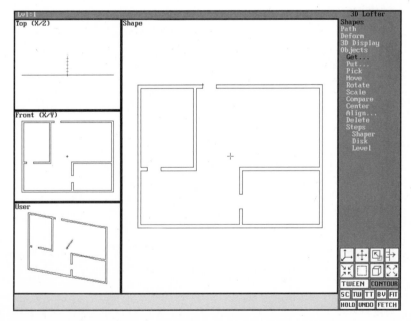

Choose Shape/All, *and then press* F2 *to enter the 3D Lofter*	Assigns the floor plan as the current shape and enters the 3D Lofter
Choose Shapes/Get/Shaper, *choose* Shapes/Center, *and then right-click on the* Zoom Extents *icon*	Brings the floor plan into the 3D Lofter, centers the shape on the path, and zooms out to display the shape in all viewports (see fig. 9.2)
Choose Objects/Make, *enter an object name of* Plan01, *accept all the defaults by clicking on the* Create *button, and then press* F3 *to enter the 3D Editor and right-click on the* Zoom Extents *icon*	Lofts the object into the 3D Editor with the name Plan01; you then enter the 3D Editor and zoom out to see the entire object (see fig. 9.3)

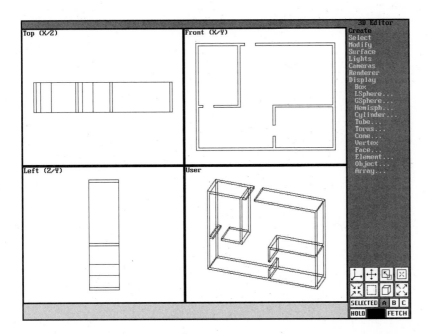

Figure 9.3
The object Plan01 in the 3D Editor.

At this point, many users grumble about 3D Studio not lofting floor plans properly, and then set about rotating the object Plan01 into position. The problem lies in not understanding the default orientation of the 3D Lofter and how to use the many options available for manipulating the path. You now move and rotate the path to loft a second copy of the floor plan right beside the first one and in the preferred orientation.

continues

continued

Press F2 *to return to the 3D Lofter*	
Choose 3D Display/On *then* 3D Display/Choose, *click on the* All *button, and then click on* OK	The 3D object Plan01 in the 3D Editor appears in the 3D Lofter
Choose Path/Move Path *and select the path in the* Top *viewport, then move the path approximately 50' to the right*	Moves the path and the shape to the right of Plan01
Click in the Front *viewport and type* **R**	Converts the Front viewport to a Right viewport
Choose Path/Rotate *and click anywhere in the* Right *viewport, specify a rotation of 90 degrees, and then right-click on the* Zoom Extents *icon*	Automatically selects the path, and also orients the path with the Shape parallel to the Top viewport (see fig. 9.4)

Figure 9.4
The rotated path and shape in the 3D Lofter.

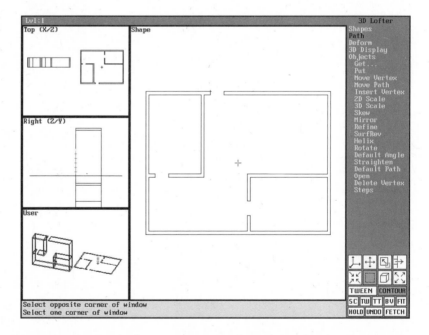

Choose Objects/Make *and click on the* + *button*	Creates a new object in the 3D Editor with the name Plan02
Press F3 *to enter the 3D Editor and right-click on the* Zoom Extents *icon*	Enters the 3D Editor and zooms out to view both objects (see fig. 9.5)

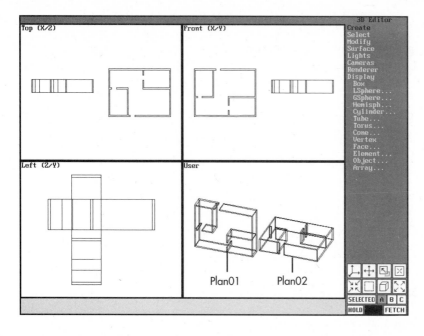

Figure 9.5
The object Plan02 lofted next to object Plan01.

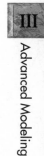

As you can see in the preceding exercise, the object Plan02 was lofted into the 3D Editor in the proper orientation. You even were able to reposition Plan02 prior to lofting to prevent it from occupying the same space as the object Plan01. For many objects, the decision to rotate and move the path rather than a lofted object is one of personal preference; sometimes, however, manipulating the path is the faster and easier way to properly orient an object.

Open

The Path/Open command is much like the Create/Open command in the 2D Shaper (see Chapter 4, "2D to 3D: The 2D Shaper and 3D Lofter Combination"). The only difference is that the Path/Open command "knows" whether a path is closed and refuses to try to open an already open path.

Path Defaults

Three commands under the Path branch restore one or more of the default properties of the path. The advantage these commands have over New from the File pull-down menu is that they never remove the shape assigned to the first vertex and often preserve other properties of the path.

Default Angle

The Path/Default Angle command restores the path to its default orientation perpendicular to the Front viewport. This command does not alter the number of vertices or curvature of the path, nor does it affect the shapes at any level.

Straighten

The Path/Straighten command removes all curvature information from the path vertices, and arranges the vertices in a straight line. The total path length, number of vertices, and spacing between the vertices are all preserved.

Default Path

The Path/Default Path command replaces the current path with the default path. The default path is a straight line with two vertices and a step setting of five. Any vertices on the path beyond the second vertex and any shapes on the path beyond level 7 are discarded.

Closed Paths

A closed path is any path in which the first and last vertices are welded together. You can create a path that appears closed, but does not have its first and last vertices welded. As far as 3D Studio is concerned, such a path is open.

Closed paths exhibit two important traits, as follows:

✔ They are not capped because they have no beginning and no end.

✔ If they are smoothed along their length, they show no seam where the first and last vertex meet.

Closed paths were used in Chapter 4 to create the picture frame exercise and the neon letter exercise.

Back-Tracking Paths

An extremely powerful but seldom discussed option is the capability of a path to back-track over itself. The best way to demonstrate this is to examine the file 3DSOCKET.LFT that ships with 3D Studio. Figure 9.6 shows the file as it appears when you load it into the 3D Lofter.

At first glance, this loft seems to use a straight path. It is only when you examine the mesh object that this loft creates, or manipulate the vertices on the path, that you suspect the truth. Figure 9.7 shows a close-up of the same path after some of its vertices are moved to the right.

What you discover is that what originally seems to be a simple straight path actually is a complex closed path that doubles back on itself. Table 9.1 describes what is happening with 3DSOCKET.LFT.

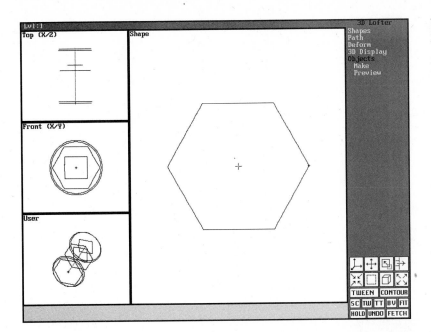

Figure 9.6
The file
3DSOCKET.LFT
in the Lofter.

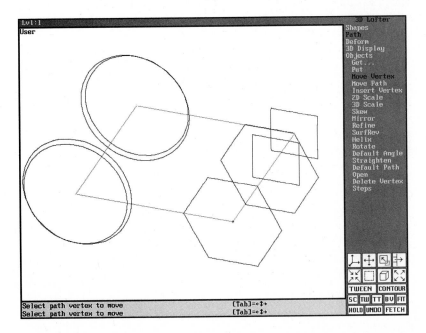

Figure 9.7
The altered
path for
3DSOCKET.LFT.

III

Advanced Modeling

Table 9.1
Analysis of the 3DSOCKET.LFT Path

Lvl	Inside Description	Lvl	Outside Description
1	Hexagon hole	5	Coincident with Lvl 4 and changes direction back toward Lvl 1, transitions from square hole to a circle solid
2	Hexagon hole	6	Circle solid
3	Square hole	7	Circle solid
4	Square hole	8	Coincident with Lvl 1, transitions from circle solid to a hexagon hole

A convenient way to visualize this type of path is to think of an athletic tube sock. Stretch the sock out, and the path runs down its center—the fabric represents the surface created by shapes on the path. If you roll the open end of the sock back on itself, the path doubles back as well; what was once the inside of the sock becomes the outside. Closing the path is like snipping off the toe of the sock and stitching the ends together.

3DSOCKET.LFT is an example of a closed back-tracking path. The following exercise shows you how to make an open back-tracking path. Here you create a drive extension for the 3D socket. The path doubles back on itself at the end to form the square drive socket for the ratchet handle.

Creating an Open Back-Tracking Path

Start or reset 3D Studio

Press F1 *to enter the 2D Shaper, press* Ctrl+A, *and then set the snap increment to 1.0*

Choose Create/Quad *and create a 30 unit square*

Choose Create/Circle *and create a circle centered on the square and touching the square's corners (radius about 21.21 units)*

Create another circle centered on the square with a radius of 30 units

New Riders Publishing
INSIDE SERIES

Choose Select/Polygon/Single *and select both circles, then choose* Modify/Polygon/Rotate, *press the* (Spacebar), *press* (X), *and rotate the circles 45 degrees*

Selects both circles and rotates them about their local axis so that their vertices line up with the square

Choose Display/First/On *and examine the first vertex of each polygon—you want them to match up. If they do not match, choose* Display/First/Choose *and select a first vertex for all three polygons so that they align with the same corner of the square*

Aligns the first vertices for proper lofting; the arrangement of the shapes should appear like figure 9.8

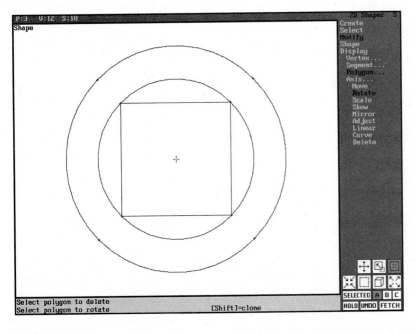

Figure 9.8
Shapes in the 2D Shaper.

III

Advanced Modeling

Press (Alt)+(N), *choose* Shape/Assign, *and select the square*

Deselects the circles and assigns the square as the current shape

Choose Shape/Hook/Center

Places the shape hook at the center of the square

Press (F2) *to enter the 3D Lofter, click in the* Top *viewport and then click on the* Full Screen *icon*

Fills the screen with the 3D Lofter Top viewport

continues

continued

Turn on Snap *and choose* Path/Move Vertex, *press* [Tab⁝] *until vertical constraints appear, then select the top vertex and move it up until the path length display reads 200 units*	Lengthens the path
Choose Path/Steps *and set the steps at 0*	Removes steps between vertices
Click on the Zoom Extents *icon and choose* Path/Insert Vertex, *then insert vertices along the path at 30, 35, 100, 110, 150, and 170 units (keep the path straight); choose* Path/Straighten	Adds extra vertices to the path (see fig. 9.9) and straightens it if you inadvertently caused it to curve

Figure 9.9
The 3D Lofter path with added vertices.

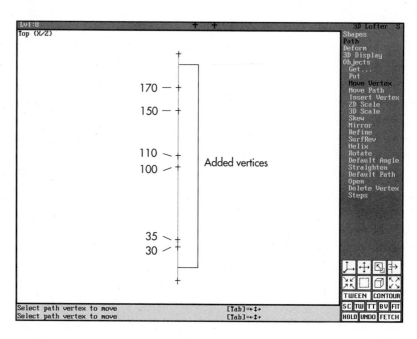

Choose Shapes/Steps *and set the shape step setting to 3*	
Choose Shapes/Get/Shaper	Imports the square shape from the 2D Shaper

Choose Shapes/Put/Level *and click on the path vertices at locations 30, 170, and 200*	Copies the square shape to the specified vertices
Press [F1] *and choose* Shape/None, *then choose* Shape/Assign, *select the small circle, and press* [F2]	Enters the 2D Shaper and assigns the small circle as the current shape, and then reenters the 3D Lofter
Choose Shapes/Pick *and select the path vertex at location 35, then choose* Shapes/Get/Shaper	Makes the vertex at location 35 the current level and puts the small circle shape at that level
Choose Shapes/Put/Level *and select the vertex at location 100*	Copies the small circle shape to the vertex at location 100
Press [F1] *and choose* Shape/None, *then choose* Shape/Assign, *select the large circle, and press* [F2]	Enters the 2D Shaper and assigns the large circle as the current shape, and then reenters the 3D Lofter
Choose Shapes/Pick *and select the path vertex at location 110, then choose* Shapes/Get/Shaper	Makes the vertex at location 110 the current level and puts the large circle shape at that level

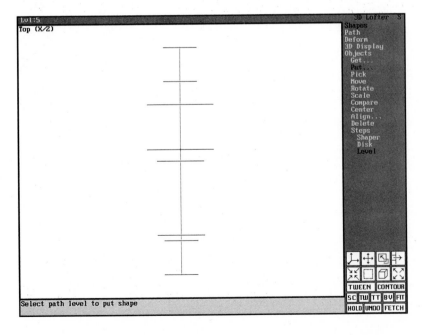

Figure 9.10
The path with all shapes imported.

III

Advanced Modeling

continues

continued

Choose Shapes/Put/Level *and select the vertex at location 150*

Copies the large circle shape to the vertex at location 150; the path should now look like figure 9.10

Make sure that Contour is off (click on the Contour button if necessary)

Choose Path/Move Vertex *and select the vertex at location 170, then move the vertex straight down until it matches up with the vertex at location 150*

The two vertices become coincident

While Path/Move Vertex *is still active, select the end vertex at location 200 and move it straight down until it is at location 120*

The end of the path doubles back past the two vertices at location 150

Click on the Full Screen *icon, and then right-click on the* Zoom Extents *icon*

Displays all four viewports and zooms out to show the entire path (see fig. 9.11)

Figure 9.11
The completed path and shapes ready for lofting.

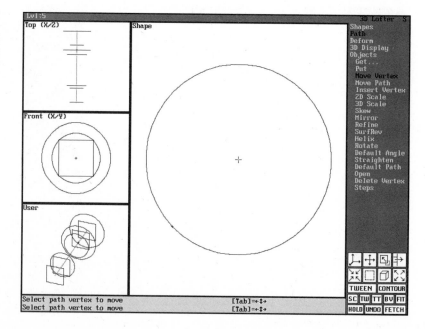

Choose Objects/Make, *specify the object name* Drive, *turn off* Optimization, *and then click on* Create	Creates the object and places it in the 3D Editor
Press F3 *and right-click on the icon*	Displays the Drive object, Zoom Extents, as seen in figure 9.12

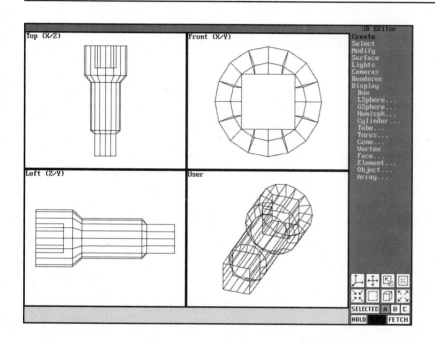

Figure 9.12
The lofted drive object.

Examining the path that you created in the preceding exercise, you can see that at the location where the vertices double up and head back along the path, the shapes on the path become holes drilled back into the object. Many people might use Booleans to create such forms. The preceding technique with the 3D Lofter can create more efficient and predictable objects.

An interesting side-effect of back-tracking paths is their effect on smoothing. If you render the object created in the previous exercise, you will find that 3D Studio tries to smooth around the flat end where the path doubles back on itself. This is because the face angle becomes indeterminate when two path vertices occupy the same point in space. The result is that the face angle drops to zero and the faces are smoothed. When lofting back-tracking paths, you should either set the Smooth Length option to Off and manually smooth the object, or use the Auto Smooth option in the 3D Editor. See Chapter 10, "Creating and Editing Faces and Vertices in the 3D Editor," for more information on smoothing.

SurfRev Paths

The path command SurfRev creates arcs and circular paths. This command typically is used to create surfaces of revolution where you create a profile in the 2D Shaper and sweep it around the circular path. Essentially, two types of surfaces of revolution are as follows:

- ✔ **Surfaces that have a hole through the center.** Rings are an example of such a surface.

- ✔ **Surfaces closed about a central core.** Examples of these types of surfaces are vases, pots, and doorknobs.

Each type of surface requires a different path treatment.

Ring Objects

Ring objects rely on the proper setting of the path diameter, with the shapes often centered on the path. The path diameter directly controls the size of the lofted object. The shape does not have to be centered on the path, but you must manually place the shape if you want any position other than centered.

Closed Objects

Closed objects require more care to create than ring objects. The most important rule for a closed object is that the defining shape contains a perfectly straight segment that matches up with the axis of rotation. If the segment is not straight, you end up with a mess of extra faces at the center of your mesh object. At best, these faces make the model less efficient and slower to render; at worst, the faces wreak havoc on smoothing groups and lofted mapping coordinates. Figure 9.13 shows examples of poorly designed SurfRev shapes versus a properly designed shape, and figure 9.14 shows the mesh objects that they create.

As you can see in figure 9.14, the first two mesh objects have extra faces hidden inside their cores. The third mesh object has no extra core faces. When lofting a closed surface of revolution, you can turn on the Weld Vertices button in the Objects/Make dialog box and have 3D Studio remove these unneeded core faces. This technique works only if the core faces are all within the weld threshold distance—the best way to ensure that is to have a straight core segment.

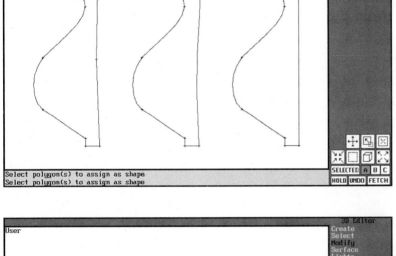

Figure 9.13
Various SurfRev shapes.

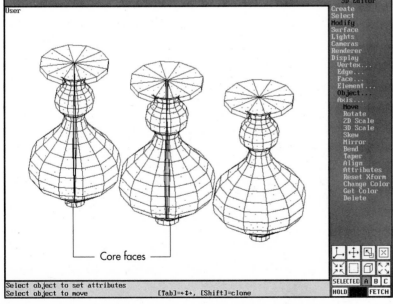

Figure 9.14
Mesh objects created from the shapes in figure 9.13.

Another aspect to consider when lofting closed surfaces of revolution concerns the alignment of the surface to the path. The side of the shape that becomes the core side is determined by the Shapes/Align commands. The shape can be positioned so that either its left side or its right side is placed at the center (core) of the SurfRev path. Alignment combines with the clockwise versus counterclockwise setting for the path to determine which way the normals of the mesh object point. Usually, you want the normals to point out from the center of the object. You can ensure this by always using a clockwise path for left-aligned shapes and always using a counterclockwise path for right-aligned shapes.

It is easy to forget to consider the clockwise versus counterclockwise orientation of the path when lofting surfaces of revolution. Many people simply disregard this issue, and then check the normal orientation in the 3D Editor. If you turn on Display/Geometry/Backface, it becomes readily apparent which way the normals of an object are pointing. If the normals are pointing in the wrong direction, the command Surface/Normals/Object Flip quickly corrects the situation.

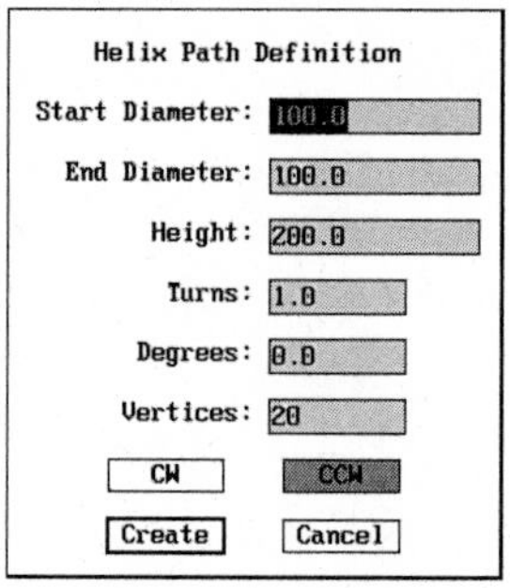

Figure 9.15
The Helix Path
Definition
dialog box.

```
         Helix Path Definition
  Start Diameter: [100.0        ]
    End Diameter: [100.0        ]
          Height: [200.0        ]
           Turns: [1.0          ]
         Degrees: [0.0          ]
        Vertices: [20           ]
        [   CW   ]    [   CCW   ]
        [ Create ]    [ Cancel  ]
```

Helix Paths

The command Path/Helix creates a spiral path of as many turns and vertices as you want. The dialog box for creating a helical path is shown in figure 9.15. The proper values for each field depend upon the shape you are lofting and what you intend to do with it.

The fields of the Helix Path Definition dialog box are as follows:

✔ **Start Diameter.** This is the diameter of the first turn at the bottom of the helix. The minimum value for this field should be equal to the width of the loft shape. If the value is less than the shape's width, the mesh intersects itself.

✔ **End Diameter.** This is the diameter of the last turn at the top of the helix. If the helix rises vertically, then the minimum value for this field also is equal to the width of the loft shape. If, however, you are lofting a flat helix (such as an electric heating coil), then the minimum value is equal to the start diameter plus the product of two times the width of the loft shape, times the number of turns.

✔ **Height.** If the helix is flat, this value is zero. If the helix rises and the start and end diameters are equal, the minimum value for this field is the height of the loft shape times the number of turns.

✔ **Turns.** The number of full 360 degree turns that the path makes.

✔ **Degrees.** Turns in the path expressed as the total number of degrees. If a value is entered in both of these fields, they are added together. For example, entering 4 in the turns field and 90 in the degrees field, adds the values together for a total of 4.25 turns or 1530 degrees.

✔ **Vertices.** Total number of vertices in the path. The minimum value for this field is three times the number of turns plus one. A good rule of thumb is that the number of vertices is always equal to the number of vertices needed to define one full circle, times the number of turns, plus one.

Keep in mind the issues of complexity and path steps discussed in Chapter 4, "2D to 3D: The 2D Shaper and 3D Lofter Combination." Good default values for a circular path are four vertices with a step setting of two or three. If the number of turns in a helix is equal to T, then a good value for vertices is 4T+1.

You can use the helical path to loft many common objects. Figure 9.16 shows a spring and a heating coil both lofted using a ten-unit diameter circle as the shape. The values used to create the helical paths are listed in table 9.2.

Table 9.2
Helix Path Values for Objects in Figure 9.16

Field	Spring Object	Coil Object
Start Diameter	30	10
End Diameter	30	100
Height	75	0
Turns	5	5

Table 9.2, Continued
Helix Path Values for Objects in Figure 9.16

Field	Spring Object	Coil Object
Degrees	0	0
Vertices	21	21
CCW	Yes	Yes

Figure 9.16
Objects created with a helix path.

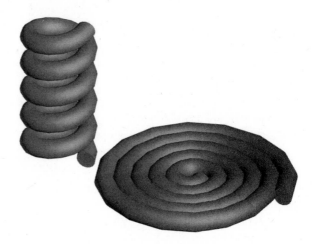

Loft Banking Control

The models demonstrated in the preceding section work extremely well because the loft shape is a circle. Anyone who tried to loft a rectangular shape using 3D Studio Release 2 discovered that the Contour button not only enabled the shape to turn as it followed the path, but also bank as it climbed. This is a desirable effect for most organic shapes, but does not serve well for objects such as highway ramps or machine screws.

3D Studio Release 4 gives you control over this effect through the LOFT-BANKING variable in the 3DS.SET file. The default value of LOFT-BANKING is on. If you edit the 3DS.SET file and specify LOFT-BANKING = OFF, shapes on your loft path do not bank. Figure 9.17 shows two objects lofted with exactly the same parameters, except that the first used the default LOFT-BANKING = ON, and the second was lofted with LOFT-BANKING = OFF.

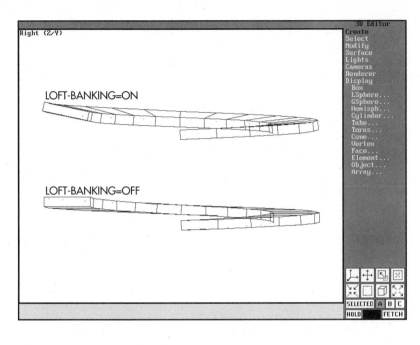

Figure 9.17
LOFT-BANKING
ON versus OFF.

Using Deformation Grids

You can accomplish only so much by manipulating the path or by placing different shapes along the path. A vital tool in getting the most out of the 3D Lofter is using the Deformations branch. This section looks at the first four deformations of Scale, Twist, Teeter, and Bevel. The last deformation option, Fit, is discussed in its own section later in this chapter.

Before moving on to specific deformation commands, you should review the general aspects shared by all the deformation grids. Figure 9.18 shows a typical deformation grid. In general, the horizontal lines represent the levels (cyan for vertices and ochre for steps) on the path, whereas the vertical lines represent values on the deformation grid. The single blue vertical line is the deformation control curve, and deformation values are set wherever the curve crosses a horizontal level.

The following list points out a few general rules to keep in mind when working with deformation grids:

✔ **Set the limits of the grid appropriately.** The Limits command enables you to establish the range of values that the grid presents. If you are working with scale deformation and all your values fall between 0 and 100 percent, you do not need to stare at a grid that goes all the way to 400.

✔ **Snap works with the horizontal grid values.** If your snap spacing is set at 10 units and Snap is on, you are constrained to increments of 10 percent in the Scale grids and increments of 10 degrees in the Twist and Teeter grids. Snap has no effect on vertical position in the graph.

III

Advanced Modeling

✔ **Always check the symmetry settings.** Scale and Teeter both have a symmetry setting. Always decide whether you want your adjustments to be independent or symmetrical about the X and Y axes, and check the symmetry setting before you begin making adjustments.

✔ **Remember that the deformation curve is not the path.** It is easy to fall into the assumption that the deformation curve is the same as the path. The shape and vertex spacing of the deformation curve are completely independent of the path. Though the shape of the deformation curve controls the shape of the lofted object, it does not necessarily look anything like the final lofted object.

✔ **Set the path steps to zero.** Complicated paths with high step settings can make the deformation grids very hard to read. Setting the path steps to zero while you make your preliminary adjustments often helps. Make sure that you set the path steps back to their final value and check the deformation grid before you loft the object (see the next point).

✔ **Realize that changes in the deformation curve that occur between horizontal levels are ignored.** The value of the deformation curve is applied only where it crosses a horizontal level line on the grid. If the curve makes a sharp change in direction between levels, it is not apparent in the lofted shape. You can visualize the effect of a deformation grid by imagining straight segments connecting all the points where the curve crosses a horizontal level. Figure 9.19 displays this effect.

As figure 9.19 illustrates, if the deformation curve makes important changes between levels, you must either change the curve or add more vertices or steps to the path.

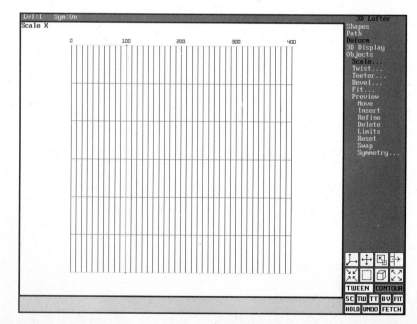

Figure 9.18
A typical
deformation grid.

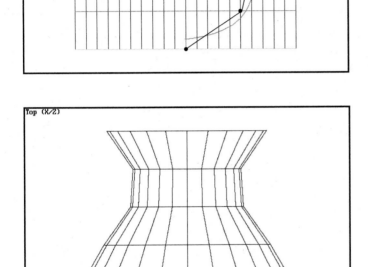

Figure 9.19
A comparison of the deformation curve with the final lofted object.

III

Advanced Modeling

Scale

The Scale deformation grid enables you to alter the X and Y scale factor of the shape. The scale base point is always on the path. A powerful modeling option is to use scale deformation on shapes not centered on the path. Figure 9.20 shows an appliance handle lofted by scaling a shape with its edge aligned to the path.

Figure 9.20
The 3D Lofter setup and mesh object for an appliance handle.

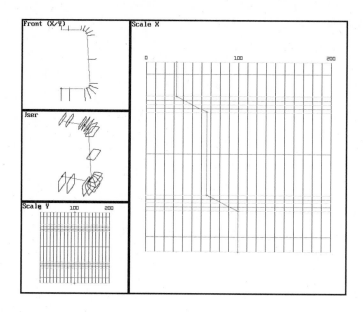

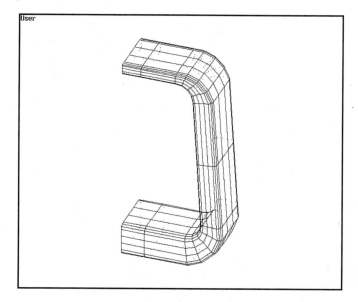

Twist

The Twist deformation grid controls rotation of the shape about the path. You can create similar effects by placing multiple shapes on the path and using the Shapes/Rotate command, but the deformation grid usually is easier to control.

Teeter

Teeter enables you to rotate the shape about the X and Y axes perpendicular to the path. Often you can use teeter with a shape offset from the path to generate objects difficult to create by other means. Figure 9.21 shows the 3D Lofter setup and mesh object for an arch created with an X-axis Teeter.

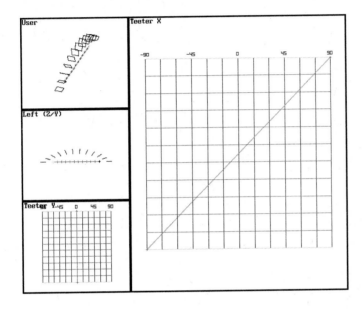

Figure 9.21
The 3D Lofter setup and mesh object for an arch.

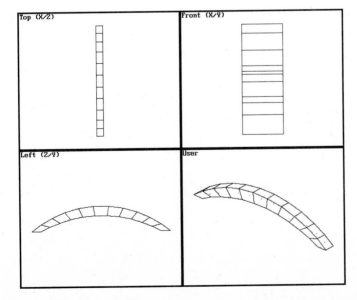

Bevel

The Bevel deformation grid performs a function similar to the manufacturing process of chamfering. You use the grid to specify the exact units to cut back or push out a shape from its original size. Bevels work best with large blocky shapes. Thin shapes or shapes with sharp points are difficult to bevel, and you are better off modeling the effect through other methods.

Sometimes your attempted bevel causes the shape to self-intersect, and 3D Studio presents the error dialog box in figure 9.22. Remember that the Bevel deformation grid enables you to add size to a shape, as well as cut it back. Frequently, changing the direction of a bevel allows the operation to succeed.

Figure 9.22
The invalid bevel warning.

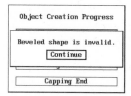

Figure 9.23 shows two different Bevel deformation grids. Both create an object with 10 units of inward bevel. The first grid begins by cutting the shape inward 10 units and allowing it to expand back out to its original size. The second grid starts with the shape at its original size, and then expands out an additional 10 units. The resulting mesh objects are very similar, yet one bevel might succeed where the other one fails.

Figure 9.23
Two different bevel grids that produce similar objects.

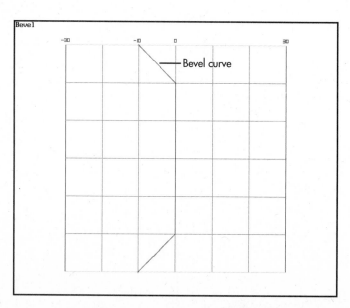

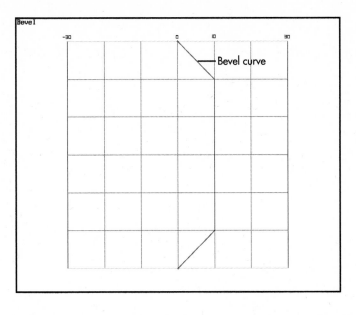

The following exercise shows you how to create a typical logo treatment by lofting beveled text. This technique works best on thick blocky letters, such as BARREL and SWISS.

Lofting Beveled Text

Start or reset 3D Studio, and then press
F1 *to enter the 2D Shaper*

Choose Create/Text/Font *and select*
BARREL.FNT

Choose Create/Text/Enter *and type*
I3D, *then click on* OK

Choose Create/Text/Place, *hold down*   Creates text in the 2D Shaper similar
Ctrl, *and specify a text height*   to figure 9.24
of 200 units

The large shapes of the BARREL font work well for creating beveled text; a few problem areas exist, however. Beveling does not work well with sharp points, and three such areas are in the I3D shape. These problem areas are the point in the center-back part of the 3, and the top and bottom left-side corners of the hole in the D. Use the Segment/Refine technique described in Chapter 4 to round off these points.

continues

continued

Figure 9.24
Logo text in
the Shaper.

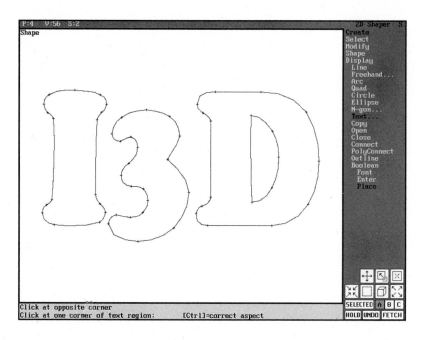

Choose Modify/Segment/Refine *and pick
the points in figure 9.25, then choose* Modify/
Vertex/Delete *to delete the pointed vertices*

Rounds off the pointed vertices

Figure 9.25
Refining the
text shapes.

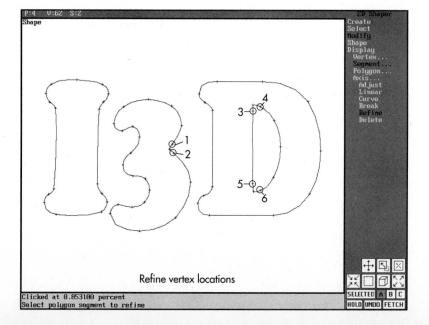

Choose Shape/All, *then press* [F2]
to enter the 3D Lofter

Assigns all the text as the
current shape

Choose Shapes/Get/Shaper, *then choose*
Shapes/Center

Imports the text into the Lofter
and centers it on the path

Right click on the Zoom Extents *icon*

Choose Path/Move Vertex *and move the top
of the path down to 60 units*

Choose Path/Insert Vertex *and insert two
vertices at 20 units and 40 units, then
set path steps to 0*

Choose Deform/Bevel/Limits *and set the
new limit to 10*

Choose Deform/Bevel/Insert *and place a vertex
at each horizontal cyan line, then move the top
and bottom vertices to -10 (see fig. 9.26)*

Click on Preview *to check the outcome of the bevel*

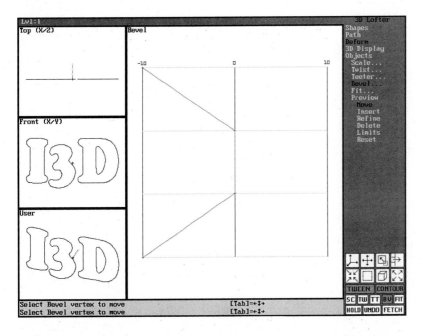

Figure 9.26
The Bevel
deformation grid.

III

Advanced Modeling

continues

continued

Even though the preview seems to be all right, an attempt to create this object results in the invalid bevel error. Bevel errors can sometimes be very difficult to track down. The problem here occurs at the top left corner of the number 3. Zooming in on that location in the Front viewport and performing another preview reveals the problem. Figure 9.27 shows that the beveled shape is self-intersecting.

Figure 9.27
The self-intersecting bevel shape.

Bevel shape
self-intersects

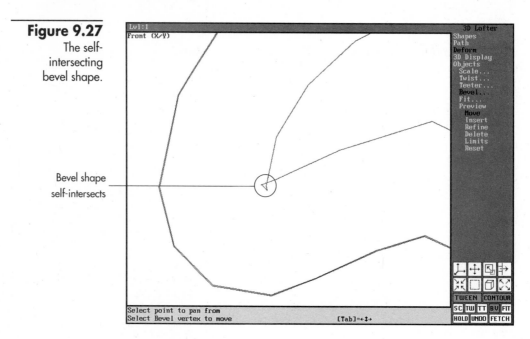

You can correct this problem by using a smaller bevel, or in this case, you can correct it by keeping the same bevel distance, but altering where the bevel occurs.

Choose Deform/Bevel/Move, *move the bottom vertex to –6, move the next two vertices to +4, and then move the top vertex to –6 (see fig. 9.28)*

Choose Objects/Make *and name the object* Logo

Press F3 *and right-click on the*   Displays objects in the 3D Editor, as
Zoom Extents *icon*   shown in figure 9.29

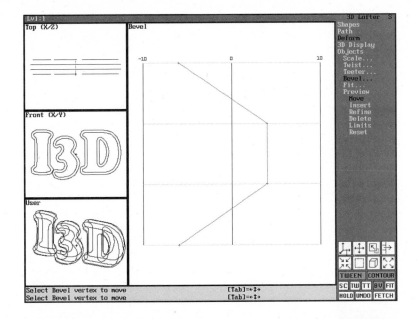

Figure 9.28
The revised
deformation grid.

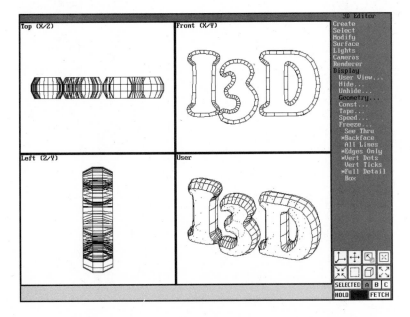

Figure 9.29
The lofted object.

III

Advanced Modeling

The next exercise demonstrates a second technique you can use to produce beveled and engraved text. This technique requires you to create and edit the bevel shape manually. You do this with the Create/Outline command in the 2D Shaper.

Lofting Engraved Text

Reset 3D Studio and press F1	Starts you in the 2D Shaper
Choose Create/Text/Font *and choose the file* SERIFBLD	
Enter the text **3DS** *and place with a height of 200 units while holding down* Ctrl	Places the text with correct aspect ratio and a height of 200 units
Choose Create/Outline *and pick each polygon one at a time to specify an outline width of 10 units*	Outlines all the letters; do not forget to also outline the inside hole of the D (see fig. 9.30)

Figure 9.30
The outlined text.

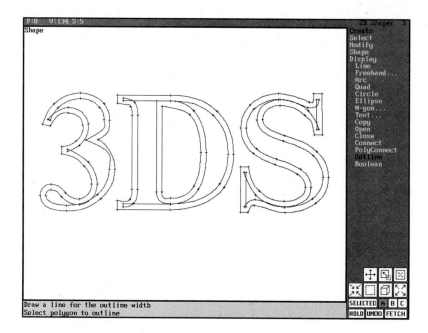

The next step requires that you modify the vertices of the interior polygons to form the bottom of the engraved letters. This process is slow and time-consuming, and requires careful use of the Modify/Vertex/Adjust command. The two rules that you must observe while editing the vertices are as follows:

✔ The inner polygons must never cross over themselves or another polygon.

✔ You must not delete or add any vertices to the inner polygons that you do not also delete or add to the outer polygons.

Continuing To Loft Engraved Text

Choose Modify/Vertex/Adjust *and manipulate the vertices of the inner polygons (see fig. 9.31)*

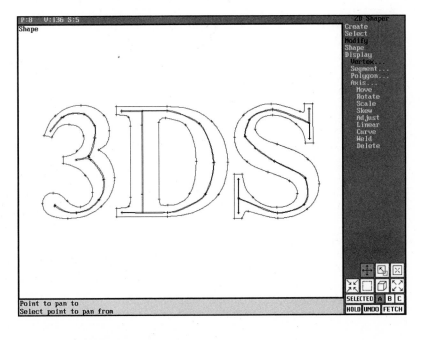

Figure 9.31
The edited inner polygons.

If you find it difficult to edit the vertices, you can load a completed set of letters from the CD-ROM. Load file ENGRAVE.SHP

continues

continued

Choose Display/First/Choose *and select the first vertex location for each polygon*	Enables you to ensure that the first vertices of all polygons align
Choose Create/Quad *and draw a rectangle that surrounds the text*	Represents the slab from which the text will be carved
Choose Shape/Assign *and select the quad and all the outer text polygons, including the hole of the D*	Assigns the selected polygons as the current shape
Press (F2), *and then choose* Shapes/Get/Lofter	Imports the shape into the 2D Shaper
Choose Path/Move Vertex *and shorten the path to 50 units*	
Press (F1) *and choose* Shape/None, *then choose* Shape/Assign *and select the quad and all the inner text polygons*	Reenters the Shaper and assigns the quad and the bottom text polygons as the current shape
Press (F2), *choose* Shapes/Pick *and select the back vertex on the path, then choose* Shapes/Get/Shaper	Imports the current shape at the opposite end of the path
Choose Objects/Make, *name the object* Engrave *and turn off the* Optimize *button, then click on* Create	Lofts the object into the 3D Editor
Press (F3) *and click on the* Zoom Extents *icon*	Displays the object in the 3D Editor (see fig. 9.32)

Depending upon your requirements, you might need to create a box object in the 3D Editor to cover the thin hole left at the bottom of the engraved letters. As an alternative, you also can weld the vertices at the bottom of the letters to permanently close the seam. Finally, a nice effect is to apply one material to the overall slab, and then apply a contrasting material to the engraved faces of the letters. Figure 9.33 shows the slab rendered with a marble slab face and gold metal letters.

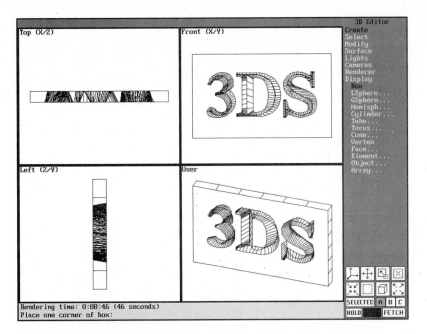

Figure 9.32
The engraved text in the 3D Editor.

Figure 9.33
The rendered engraving with a marble slab and gold letters.

Understanding Fit Deformation

The final deformation is the Fit deformation. This command provides the capability to create three-dimensional objects by specifying the profile of the top, side, and front view of the object. This command has a few restrictions, but it is still an extremely fast and powerful technique for generating complex geometry.

Shapes

The Fit deformation relies on you specifying three shapes that serve as the profiles of the three-dimensional object. 3D Studio refers to these three shapes as Fit X, Fit Y, and the Loft Shape. *Fit X* and *Fit Y* represent the top and side views of the object and actually serve as scaling limits for the Loft Shape. The *Loft Shape* can be thought of as the front or cross-sectional view of the object, and it is the shape actually passed along the path.

When you create these shapes in the 2D Shaper, it is usually best to arrange the shapes in the way a draftsman would draw them by hand. That is, draw the top view first, project the side view out to the right or left, and then project the front view down. This technique makes it easy to check that the top view and side are the same length. Figure 9.34 shows an example layout of shapes ready for import into the 3D Lofter.

Figure 9.34

Three fit shapes for an aircraft wing in the 2D Shaper.

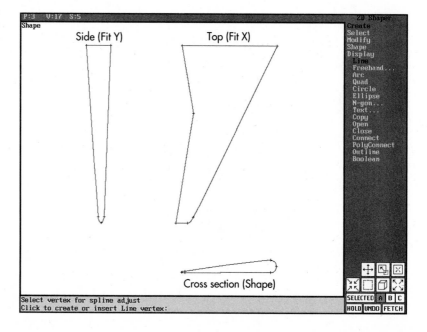

Setting up the Fit deformation in the 3D Lofter requires frequent moving back and forth between the 3D Lofter and the 2D Shaper. The steps involved are as follows:

1. Create the shapes in the 2D Shaper and assign the front view shape as the current shape.

2. Use Shapes/Get/Shaper to place that shape on the path.

3. Under the Deform/Fit branch, choose Reset and check your desired status for symmetry. Most often, you have separate fit shapes for the top and side of the object; therefore, symmetry should be off.

4. Return to the 2D Shaper and assign the top view shape as the current shape.

5. In the 3D Lofter, make the Fit X viewport active and use Deform/Fit/Get/Shaper to import the top view shape.

6. Return to the 2D Shaper and assign the side view as the current shape.

7. Repeat step 5 for the Fit Y viewport.

8. Choose Deform/Fit/Gen Path to allow 3D Studio to process the fit shapes and generate a lofting path for the object.

 Gen Path rotates the path back to default angle and moves the path origin back to 0,0".

9. Choose Objects/Make to create the object. Figure 9.35 shows the Lofter set up and the mesh object created from the shapes in figure 9.34.

The preceding process requires three trips between the 2D Shaper and the 3D Lofter. You can change between these modules quickly by pressing (F2) to go to the 3D Lofter and (F1) to go to the 2D Shaper. Clicking on the module name in the upper right corner of the screen also quickly moves you back and forth between modules.

The next section discusses the restrictions placed on the design of your fit shapes, but there are a few other issues of which you should be aware. You can improve your chances for a successful Fit deformation by adhering to the following rules of thumb:

✔ Always choose Deform/Fit/Reset when starting a new Fit deformation. The length of the path 3D Studio generates is set by the first fit shape imported after a reset. Although you can replace both fit shapes many times, the length of the path remains fixed until you issue a Fit/Reset command.

Figure 9.35
The lofted
aircraft wing.

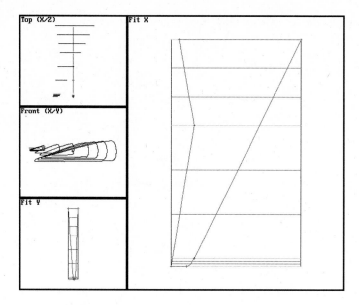

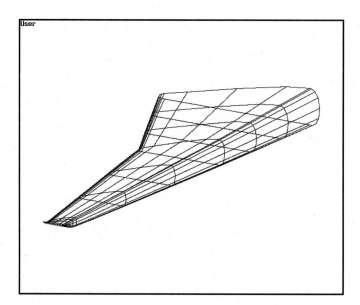

✔ The top view shape (Fit X) and the side view shape (Fit Y) should be the same length. This is not an explicit requirement, but if the two shapes are of unequal length, 3D Studio scales the second Fit Shape that is imported to match the length of the first Fit Shape.

✔ A vertex is placed on the path for every vertex in both the top view (Fit X) and side view (Fit Y) shapes. You can greatly reduce the complexity of your final object by making the vertices in the two shapes line up.

✔ You can place multiple front view or cross-sectional shapes on the path. If the cross section of your object changes along the path, then import another shape at that level. Many users overlook this capability. See the exercise on lofting a rowboat later in this chapter for an example of this technique.

✔ You can edit the path after the Deform/Fit/Gen Path command is performed. In fact, you can ignore the Deform/Fit/Gen Path command altogether and use the fit shapes on any path that you manually create. This technique works well for generating morph targets by manipulating the path created by Deform/Fit/Gen Path or for placing multiple shapes on the generated path. The rowboat exercise also demonstrates editing the path after the Deform/Fit/Gen Path command.

Shape Restrictions

Four basic restrictions for the Fit X and Fit Y shapes are outlined in the 3D Studio manual. They are reviewed in the following list:

✔ The fit shapes must be a single, closed polygon. No outlines or nested shapes allowed.

✔ The fit shapes must have at least one and no more than two vertices at both their top and bottom. This roughly translates into requiring that the shapes end in either a point or a flat segment.

✔ No curved segment can extend above the top vertex or below the bottom vertex. The required top and bottom vertices described in the preceding point must represent the maximum limits of the shapes.

✔ The fit shapes cannot contain undercuts. An easy way to check for undercuts is to imagine a horizontal line passing through the shapes. If you can place the horizontal line in a position where it cuts through the shape in more than two places, you have an undercut. Figure 9.36 shows undercuts revealed by this technique.

Figure 9.36
Undercuts in an invalid fit shape.

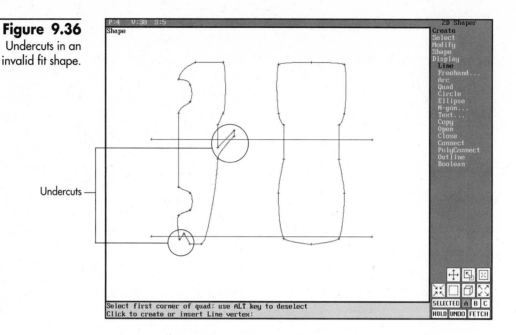

The following exercise shows you how to use Fit deformation to loft the hull of a rowboat. An important variation is the use of multiple shapes on the path to allow for carving out the seating area.

Lofting a Row Boat

Start or reset 3D Studio, then press F1   Enters the 2D Shaper

*Draw top view and side view polygons of
a rowboat hull; make both shapes 240 units long*

*Draw two cross section shapes for the rowboat—
one shape is solid and the other is hollowed out
(see fig. 9.37)*

It is critical that you use the same number of vertices for both the solid and hollowed out versions of the cross section shape. If the two shapes do not have the same number of vertices, 3D Studio refuses to perform the loft. Notice that the solid cross-section shape has extra vertices across its top to give it the same number of vertices as the hollowed out shape.

Choose Shape/Assign *and select the top view
polygon as the current shape, then enter the
3D Lofter and choose* Deform/Fit/Get/Shaper
to place the polygon as the Fit X shape

New Riders Publishing
INSIDE
SERIES

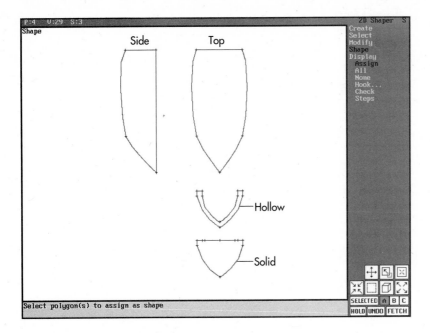

Figure 9.37
The four rowboat shapes.

Choose **Deform/Fit/Symmetry/Off**, *return to the 2D Shaper and assign the side view polygon, and import it as the Fit Y shape in the 3D Lofter*

Choose **Deform/Fit/Gen Path** *(see fig. 9.38)*

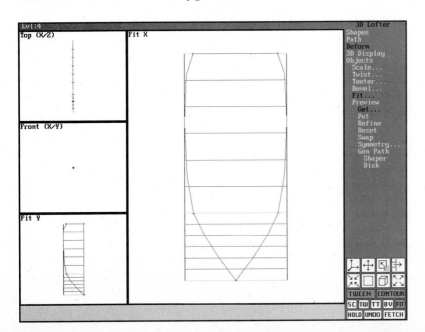

Figure 9.38
The rowboat fit shapes and generated path.

continued

The next step involves placing the two cross-section shapes on the path. The solid shape is placed at the bow and the stern to form the bulkheads. Then add extra vertices to the path to hold the shapes transitioning from solid to hollowed out.

Choose Path/Steps *and set the steps to 0, then choose* Path/Insert Vertex *and insert four vertices at locations 30, 40, 220, and 230*	Adds extra vertices to the path
In the 2D Shaper, assign the solid cross section as the current shape; then in the 3D Lofter, choose Shapes/Get/Shaper *to place the shape at the first vertex*	Imports the solid shape at the first vertex on the path
Choose Shapes/Center, *then choose* Shapes/Put/Level *and select the path vertices at locations 30, 230, and 240*	Copies the solid shape to other path vertices
In the 2D Shaper, assign the hollowed out cross section as the current shape	
In the 3D Lofter, choose Shapes/Pick *and select the vertex at location 40, then choose* Shapes/Get/Shaper	Imports the hollowed out shape
Choose Shapes/Center, *then choose* Shapes/Put/Level *and select the vertex at location 220*	Copies the shape to the vertex at location 220; your screen should now look like figure 9.39
Make sure that the Contour *button is off and choose* Path/Move Vertex, *then select at location 40 and move it down to match up with the vertex at location 30*	Makes the shapes at vertex locations 30 and 40 occupy the same space on the path
Select the vertex at location 220 and move it up to match the vertex at location 230	Makes the shapes at vertex locations 220 and 230 occupy the same space on the path
Choose Objects/Make, *name the object* Row Boat, *turn off* Optimize, *and click on* Create	Creates the Row Boat object
Press F3 *to enter the 3D Editor and right-click on the* Zoom Extents *icon*	Enters the 3D Editor and displays the new object (see fig. 9.40)

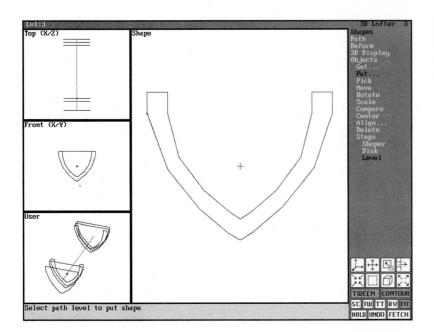

Figure 9.39
The multiple
shapes on
the path.

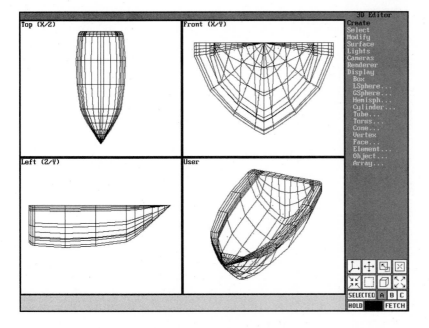

Figure 9.40
The lofted
rowboat.

III

Advanced Modeling

Editing the path after performing the Gen Path command does not harm the Fit deformation in any way. You should try to preserve the overall length of the path, but even that is not an absolute requirement. Adding the extra vertices and placing the solid and hollowed out shapes at the same location allows the bulkheads to drop straight down in their transition from solid to hollow. If this technique is unclear, go back and review the section on back-tracking paths earlier in this chapter.

Examining Lofted Mapping Coordinates

Many of the objects that you create in the 3D Lofter are rendered with mapped materials. Chances are that all but the simplest objects defy the capabilities of the three standard mapping types of Planar, Cylindrical, and Spherical. 3D Studio provides the capability to apply mapping coordinates at the time you loft an object.

When you choose Objects/Make, you have the option to turn on the Mapping button. If the Mapping button is on when you click on Create, the mapping coordinates dialog box in figure 9.41 appears. In 3D Studio Release 2, to provide meaningful values to the options in the dialog box, you had to have a good idea of what material you planned to use with the object. The current version of 3D Studio makes the options in the Mapping dialog box virtually obsolete. The meanings of the various options in this dialog box are discussed in the following sections.

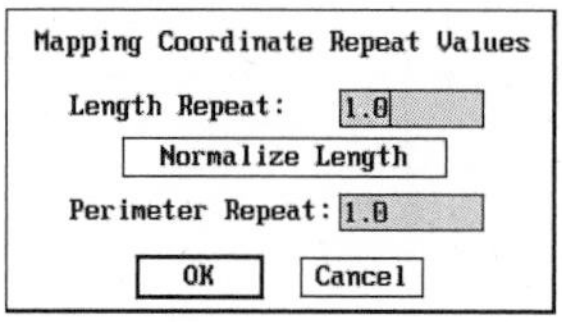

Figure 9.41
The mapping coordinates dialog box in the 3D Lofter.

```
Mapping Coordinate Repeat Values

 Length Repeat:    [1.0   ]
          [   Normalize Length   ]
 Perimeter Repeat: [1.0 ]

        [  OK  ]   [ Cancel ]
```

Length Repeat

The Length Repeat field tells 3D Studio how many times to repeat the map along the length of the path. If the path is closed, a restriction requires that the number of cross sections on the path be at least 1.5 times greater than the Length Repeat number. The number of cross sections is equal to the number of vertices if Tween is off, or the number of levels if Tween is on.

A modifier to the Length Repeat field is the Normalize Length button. If this button is on, the map is scaled evenly along the length of the path. If the button is off, the map is scaled unevenly based upon the spacing of the path vertices. Most of the time, you will want the Normalize Length button to be on.

Perimeter Repeat

The Perimeter Repeat field determines the number of times the map repeats around the shape on the path. The lofted mesh object must have twice as many vertices around its perimeter as the value in the Perimeter Repeat field. The number of vertices is equal to the following equation:

V = Number of vertices in the shape

S = The Shape Step setting

Object perimeter vertices = V + (S × V)

With the current version of 3D Studio, these map settings become almost obsolete. Consider always setting both Repeat Fields to 1.0 and turning on the Normalize Length button. You then can use the U-V scale fields in the Map Settings dialog box of the Materials Editor to control the number of map repetitions. This technique has no restrictions on the number of cross sections or vertices.

The next exercise demonstrates the use of lofted mapping coordinates and the technique discussed in the preceding Tip. Imagine lofting a candy cane and then trying to apply the spiraling candy stripe with a mapped material. It would be nearly impossible to do this without lofted mapping coordinates.

Using Lofted Mapping Coordinates

Start or reset 3D Studio, and then press F2   Enters the 3D Lofter

Load the file CCANE.LFT *(see fig. 9.42)*

Choose Objects/Make *and name the object* Candy-Cane, *turn off* Optimization, *and turn on* Mapping, Contour, *and* Tween, *then click on* Create.

When the Mapping *dialog box appears, set 1.0 for both of the repeat fields and turn on the* Normalize Length *button*

Press F3 *and right-click on the*   Displays the lofted candy cane
Zoom Extents *icon*   (see fig. 9.43)

Press F5 *to enter the Materials Editor*

Click on the map slot for Texture 1 and   Sets CCANE.CEL as the map for Texture 1
select the file CCANE.CEL, *then drag the*   and displays the image of red and green
file over to the View Image *button to*   stripes on a white background
display the CEL file

continues

continued

Figure 9.42
The candy cane
loft.

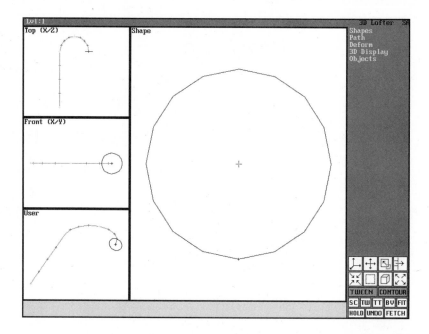

Figure 9.43
The candy cane
mesh object.

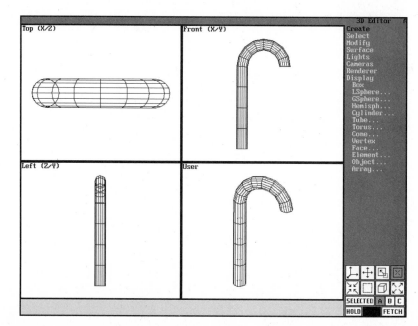

Click on the S button to the right of the map slot and specify a V Scale value of 0.2

Causes the map to repeat 5 times along the vertical direction

Specify a specular color of L:255, a shininess of 60, and a shininess strength of 100, then click on Render Sample

A sample sphere with red and green swirls appears in the materials sample slot

Press C *and specify the current material name as* CANDY CANE

Names the material and makes it the current material in the 3D Editor

Return to the 3D Editor and assign the CANDY CANE material to the Candy-Cane object

Set up lights and a camera at your discretion and render the camera view (see fig. 9.44)

Figure 9.44
The rendered candy cane.

III

Advanced Modeling

The advantage of specifying map repeat in the Materials Editor rather than in the lofted Mapping Coordinates dialog box is that you easily can change the repeat values in the Materials Editor. The only way to change the repeat values with lofted coordinates is to re-loft the object and reassign the material.

Summary

This chapter demonstrated some of the powerful tasks you can accomplish with the 3D Lofter. The 3D Lofter is possibly the most underused module in 3D Studio because it appears rather cryptic, and is used only to provide source material for the 3D Editor and the Keyframer. You will be well-rewarded if you take the time to learn the powerful modeling capabilities of the 3D Lofter.

Chapter Snapshot

Many of the subtleties of realistic and efficient modeling are at the vertex and face level. After an entity is created, you might need to stretch vertices, turn or align faces, or build additional faces. Smoothing groups are perfected and face normals are truly analyzed at this level as well.

It is very common for modelers to spend the majority of time working at the face and vertex level. It is here that the meshes are truly defined and their qualities perfected. This chapter analyzes the commands that manipulate these finite elements and give specific character to models by exploring the following topics:

✔ Understanding and manipulating the global axis and bounding box definitions

✔ Exploring model editing at the vertex level

✔ Examining model editing at the face level

✔ Using the Modify/Vertex branch commands

✔ Understanding face creation alternatives

✔ Examining issues concerning the use of the Modify/Face branch commands

✔ Modeling effects with smoothing groups

✔ Unifying face normals

✔ Introducing IPAS modeling possibilities

Creating and Editing Faces and Vertices in the 3D Editor

Many subtleties of realistic and efficient modeling are at the vertex and face level. When a mesh is created, it might need to have its vertices stretched, faces turned or aligned, or additional faces built. The vertex and face level is also where smoothing group assignments are perfected and face normals analyzed. Modelers commonly spend the majority of time working at the face and vertex level when perfecting their models. This chapter analyzes the commands that manipulate these finite elements and give specific character to models.

Using Global and Local Axes

3D Studio bases many of its Modify commands on a defined reference point called the axis. This point can be placed and set for use by many operations, as the *global axis*; or it can be the centroid of what is currently being manipulated, as the *local axis*. The *axis* is the point about which items are rotated, scaled, and skewed, and vertices are tapered.

For AutoCAD users, the global axis is equivalent to the base point requested from commands (such as in ROTATE: "About which point"). The difference with 3D Studio is that you specify this point before, not after, the command by choosing and possibly placing axes.

The two axes act exactly the same—they just define two different reference points. The difference is that you have complete control of the global axis' placement, whereas the local axis is determined for you. You can quickly switch between using the two axes with the X key or by selecting the local axis icon.

Aligning the Global Axis

The global axis is the only positionable point that you have with many Modify branch commands. It takes a little time to align to the correct spot, and you must decide whether this accuracy is indeed needed. Many modelers prefer to modify the selection quickly and worry about its placement later. At the vertex and face level, this approach does not usually work because elements of the mesh are being stretched and twisted—you cannot go back and readjust. The careful placement of the global axis thus becomes a major issue when manipulating vertices and faces.

To place the global axis, you must first display it by selecting Modify/Axis/Show. The Axis/Place option enables you simply to pick the point in the two-dimensional space of a non-perspective viewport. As in placing construction planes, you need to pick points in two viewports to specify the global axis location for all three-dimensional coordinates.

For accurate placement, the Axis/Align command gives you several options not available with construction planes. Align/Vertex snaps the axis to a selected vertex, and Align/Element or Object enables you to place the vertex according to the item's bounding box. The Align/Element and Align/Object options provide nine locations that can be convenient for many modify commands. Align calculations are valid only for the current orthogonal viewport—they are not three-dimensional placements. For a true vertex snap, you still need to use Align/Vertex in two perpendicular viewports. Similarly, to place the global axis at the true center of an object, you must use Align/Object/Center in two perpendicular viewports.

New Riders Publishing
INSIDE
SERIES

Understanding Bounding Boxes

The *bounding box* is more than a tool for display speed; it is used by 3D Studio as a quick stand-in to represent your selection when using Modify commands. The orientation and extents of the bounding box become your guide for positioning your selection and thus is an important concept to understand.

As figure 10.1 shows, the bounding box displays as a rectangular solid, with its edges defined by the extents of the object or selection. For objects, the bounding box's orientation is defined when the object is created. The three planes of the box are constructed parallel to the respective global axes. Lines drawn through the centers of these planes define a set of internal axes unique to that object. This is the object's *transformation matrix* and is what 3D Studio uses internally when calculating changes in the position, scale, and rotation of the object. The intersection of the three axes defines the object's centroid and is used as the permanent location of the object's local axis.

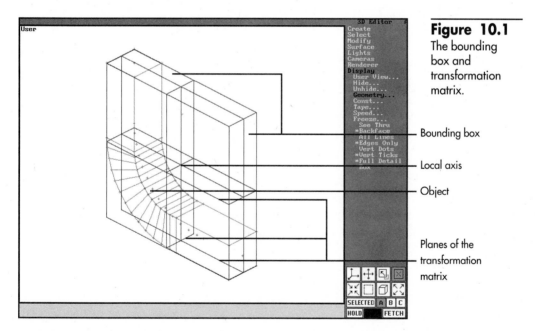

Figure 10.1
The bounding box and transformation matrix.

Bounding box

Local axis

Object

Planes of the transformation matrix

An object's bounding box (and thus its transformation matrix) is fixed when the object is created. The bounding box grows and shrinks as an object's extents change, but does not change in its orientation respective to the object. As you rotate an object, its bounding box rotates as well and is no longer square to world axes.

Only operations that actually create new objects at the face level can modify the bounding box defined for that mesh. When elements or objects are detached, cloned, copied, or attached, they become new objects with bounding boxes that still correspond to the parent. Using Faces/Detach resets the faces' bounding box according to the world axes.

You can reset an object's bounding box, and thus its transformation matrix orientation, with the Modify/Object/Reset Xform command.

In general, the bounding box affects only the way the object is displayed during a modification or box mode. 3D Studio's use of the matrix is completely transparent while in the 3D Editor. The only time it is of particular consequence is when you assign an SXP process that uses the object's transformation matrix for its placement. (See Chapter 12, "Materials and Mapping," for more information.)

Resetting an Object's Bounding Box

An object's transformation matrix, and thus its bounding box, is set upon creation. As objects are rotated and manipulated, their bounding boxes no longer relate to the world axis. To realign the sides of the bounding box so that they again correspond to the world axis, use the Modify/Object/Reset Xform command.

The Reset Xform command was a new and welcome addition to Release 3. In previous releases, the only way to reset an object's bounding box was to detach all its faces into a new object (which could seriously affect the mesh in the Keyframer). With the Reset Xform command, you simply select the object, and its transformation matrix is realigned square to the world axes.

An object's transformation matrix is very important when animating objects because its orientation dictates the axes about which the object rotates. The Keyframer bases all rotation and scale operations according to the object's bounding box (and thus transformation matrix). Changing an object's transformation matrix has a significant effect on how that object will react in the Keyframer.

You will need to become acutely aware of bounding box orientations as you begin to work with Release 4's *inverse kinematics* (IK) and Keyscript. With IK, you set the extents to which an object can rotate and move in relation to its three internal axes. With Keyscript, the data returned to you from an object always relates to the object's transformation matrix. It thus may become common for you to use Reset Xform to get objects to perform predictably in these new modules.

Temporary Bounding Boxes

Whenever you modify a selection set, 3D Studio calculates a temporary bounding box defined by the selection's extents with respect to the world axes. This selection bounding box also determines a temporary local axis at its centroid. As the extents of the selection change, so does the position of the local axis. Figure 10.2 shows the bounding box inherent to various objects. Figure 10.3 shows how a new bounding box—square to the world axis—is created when these objects are modified as a selection.

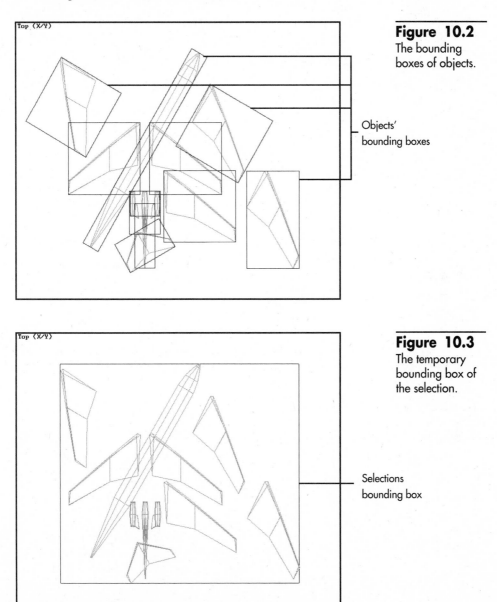

Figure 10.2
The bounding boxes of objects.

Objects' bounding boxes

Figure 10.3
The temporary bounding box of the selection.

Selections bounding box

III

Advanced Modeling

> **Tip**
>
> If you are modifying an object that has a rotated bounding box but need to see its boundary with respect to the world axes, use Modify/Face rather than Modify/Object. You are then affecting a selection rather than an object, and the bounding box will be a temporary one that is square to the world axes.

Using the Local Axis

The local axis is automatically determined for you, based on the centroid of the selection's bounding box. Because of this, the local axis can be convenient and relevant to use. If the exact location of a Modify command is not critical (very common with a Rotate command in which you are going to move the items later anyway), you do not need to waste time placing the global axis and can use the local axis instead.

Other commands work best when the local axis is used. It is very common, for example, to scale vertices and faces about their local axes so that the effects are uniform. Remember that you can quickly turn on and off the local axis with the $\boxed{X}$ key.

Creating a Bounding Box Object

3D Studio includes a very simple PXP program (see the section on IPAS modeling tools later in this chapter) called BOX.PXP that creates a box object to enclose the extents of an object—much like a bounding box. This routine is sometimes useful for encasing an oddly shaped object, and then applying a material to it or using it as a basis for Keyframer operations.

When using BOX.IXP, a bounding box mesh is created that represents the object as if it were a selection or if Reset Xform had just been performed on it; boxes thus created always are aligned with the world axes.

Manipulating Vertices in the 3D Editor

Most of the time, you do not create vertices outright as independent entities. Every time a mesh is created or cloned, you create vertices because they define faces. When you work with vertices, you literally are working with nothing—they are only points in space.

You will find most of the Modify/Vertex commands to be very similar to those designed for objects and elements. The reason for this similarity is that all Modify branch commands actually affect vertex locations. 3D Studio actually manipulates vertices—not faces, elements, or objects. When you scale an object, you are scaling the location of its vertices. When you move, skew, or taper an object, you are moving its vertices. The faces that make up the mesh simply follow along to the new positions dictated by the vertices. Thinking of this when you perform any Modify command might make the results more predictable and obvious.

Creating Vertices

Isolated and solitary vertices should exist only for one reason: to build faces upon. They really have no other purpose. Vertices never define a mesh by themselves and cannot be independently rendered. When faces are deleted, 3D Studio prompts you, asking whether you want to delete the vertices at the same time. Unless you plan to build the faces off the vertices again, this answer should always be yes.

Vertex Visibility

Vertices of unhidden geometry always are displayed when not in Box mode. This is true even if you are using the Backface and Fastdraw options. You cannot select or edit vertices while using Box mode, even if you already made a selection of vertices before entering Box mode. When Box mode is active, the entire Modify/Vertex branch is ignored.

Just because vertices are displayed, however, does not mean that you can see them clearly. With the standard Dots mode, vertices are a single pixel on your screen and can be very difficult to see, especially at high display resolutions. Whenever you select or manipulate vertices, consider switching from Display/Geometry/Vert Dots to Vert Ticks for better visibility.

Vertex Creation

The only direct reference for creating vertices is with the Create/Vertex command. With this command, you can add vertices only to an existing object, because they do not start out as objects of their own. This is actually convenient because it would be cumbersome to isolate the newly created vertices if they were all independent objects. This way, you can isolate the object receiving them and select them more easily later.

After selecting the object to receive the new vertices, you simply pick points on the screen. Each point you pick defines two coordinates. Figure 10.4 shows how the third coordinate—its height in relation to your pick point—is determined by the construction plane placement for that viewport. After you begin to pick new vertex points, you are not restricted to staying in a single viewport and can freely move between any nonperspective viewport (see Chapter 5, "Building Models in the 3D Editor," for information on placing construction planes).

This is one command where displaying the construction's planes (with Display/Const/Show) is extremely helpful. Their presence can make sense of difficult to determine point locations.

If you are creating an exact model and know precise point values, you can specify vertex locations with the keyboard by entering each of their X, Y, and Z coordinates.

Figure 10.4
Vertice placement
in accordance
with construction
planes.

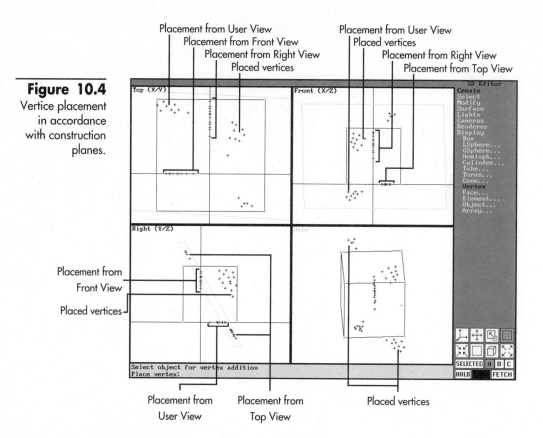

Using Existing Meshes for Vertices

Your greatest source for creating vertices is existing meshes. You either can "strip" the faces off a mesh by deleting them and leaving the vertex "cloud," or select their vertices and clone them with a Modify/Vertex command. A cloned selection of vertices becomes a single object with no mesh. The faces that shared the cloned vertices are left behind.

Commonly, you might need to duplicate an existing mesh's vertices in place so that these vertices can become the building blocks for another mesh that relates to the first. If you are going to add vertices to an object and want the vertices to correlate to existing vertices, you should clone them in place, or to the side, for use as a source. You can use any Modify/Vertex command to clone with, although pressing ⇧Shift while moving vertices might be the most commonly used method. This method is usually easier and more accurate than carefully placing the construction planes for each level of vertices.

> **Note**
>
> To clone a selection of vertices in place—or any selection—simply activate the selection with the (Spacebar), use a Modify command, and pick the same point twice on the screen. This can be done faster and without concern if Snap is activated. If Snap is off, the selection may move, and the new vertices will no longer correspond exactly to the originals.

The important thing to remember is that you are not cloning faces—only vertices. This creates an object without form. If you need to clone the mesh, use a Modify/Face branch command instead.

Modifying Vertices

Editing meshes at the vertex level actually is quite powerful. As you manipulate vertex positions, you stretch, pull, and scale the faces that share them. Much of the secret to manipulating vertices effectively comes in selecting the correct vertices to be edited and leaving the others alone.

The effect that modifying vertices has on the parent mesh often is dramatic, but sometimes is surprising and undesirable. It is good practice to Hold or Save before issuing Modify/Vertex commands. Many modelers prefer to clone the original mesh and save it for comparison and as a source for future iterations.

Although you can edit vertices one-by-one, most of your vertex editing is done with selections. In fact, only the Move, Rotate, Align, Weld, and Delete commands are relevant to a single vertex. The others require a selection to make sense of the operation.

Selecting Multiple Vertices

Vertices can be selected under the Select branch one-by-one (with Single), by a rectangle (with Quad), by an irregular closed polygon (with Fence), or by a circle (with Circle). Because vertices are solitary, crossing or window options do not apply. As always, you deselect by holding the (Alt) key while selecting. When you use a Modify/Vertex command, you also can select or deselect single vertices by pressing the (Ctrl) key or using (Alt)+(W) to give you a Quad selection.

When elements and objects are selected, all their vertices are selected as well. This does not occur with face selection, as faces are selected independent of their vertices. (Notice that when selecting faces, the vertices are left "white" and thus not selected.) Knowing this, you quickly can select an entire element's vertices and then deselect those you do not want. Similarly, you can use a quick vertex Quad selection to deselect those of an unwanted object or element by selecting it twice.

The Material/Show and Smoothing/Show commands only create selections of faces—*not* vertices. To select vertices with these commands, use the Select/ Invert option after "showing" the faces.

Moving Vertices

Move is the most basic vertex editing command and the most often used to clone. When you move vertices, you actually are stretching the faces of the mesh, as shown in figure 10.5. A mesh's appearance can thus be tweaked by pushing and pulling its vertex locations. This is especially useful in character animation. You might want to use this command on selections of vertices, dragging them back and forth, to become comfortable with the impact they have on the mesh. You might notice that moving all the vertices of an object's side is much like using the Skew command.

Figure 10.5
The stretching effect of moving a mesh's vertices.

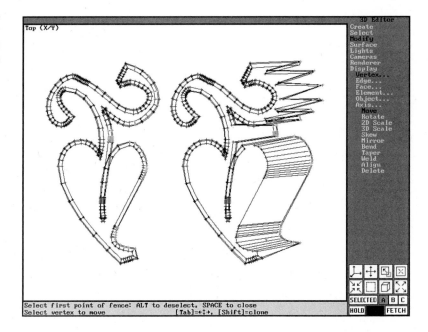

AutoCAD users can relate the moving of vertices to the effect the Stretch command has on polylines and polymeshes.

Rotating Vertices

Vertex/Rotate bases its effect on the use of the local axis or the location of the global axis. When you manipulate selections of vertices, the local axis is always a temporary one relating to that selection. This bounding box has nothing to do with the element or object of which the vertices may be a part. Because the temporary bounding box is always square to the world axes, it might be at a different angle than the mesh's bounding box if the parent has been rotated.

 If you are rotating a single vertex, you must use the global axis because rotating about the local axis is irrelevant and returns the message:

`Invalid rotate—single vertex can't use local axis.`

The act of rotating vertices is just like using Rotate/Object, but its results are much different. When noncontiguous selections of vertices are rotated, the effect on the parent mesh can be quite dramatic, as shown in figure 10.6. Figure 10.7 shows how rotating a selection of vertices about the local axis can have a "teeter-totter" effect on the mesh. Rotating the top of an object is much like using the Lofter's Twist deformation.

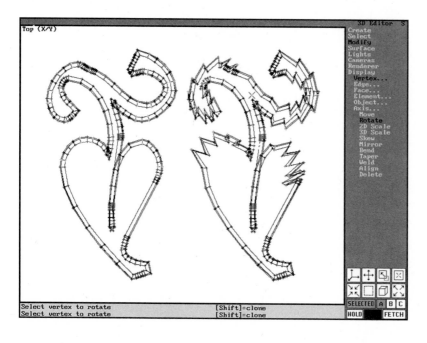

Figure 10.6

The effect of rotating every other segment's vertex group about the global axis.

III

Advanced Modeling

Figure 10.7
Rotating a
selection of
vertices about the
local axis in both
the Front and
Right viewports.

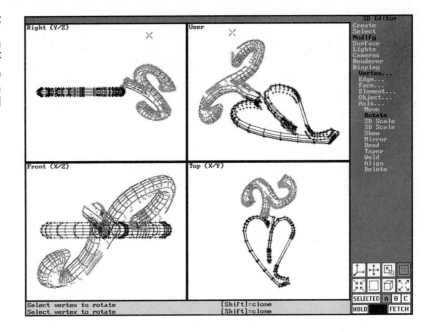

Rotating Vertices

You do not need a complicated model to investigate the powerful effects that vertex manipulation can have, as shown in the basic L-Sphere created in the following exercise.

Create a 16-sided, faceted L-Sphere in an Orthogonal viewport

While in that viewport, select every other "longitude"
of vertices with the Fence *option (see fig. 10.8)*

Click on the HOLD *button*

With the local axis on, choose the Modify/Vertex/Rotate *command and rotate the selection back and forth*	Changes the object from a 16-sided to an 8-sided sphere

Even though the pole vertices are selected, they have no effect on the mesh when rotated. This is because they are coincidental with the local axis and spin in place without affecting anything.

Click on the FETCH *button, then choose Yes*	Restores hold buffer
Switch to a perpendicular viewport and click on the B selection icon	Turns off the original selection

Select every other horizontal row of vertices
on the sphere with a quad selection

New Riders Publishing
INSIDE
SERIES

Return to the first viewport and rotate the selection

The sides of the sphere are twisted in a chevron pattern, as seen in figure 10.9.

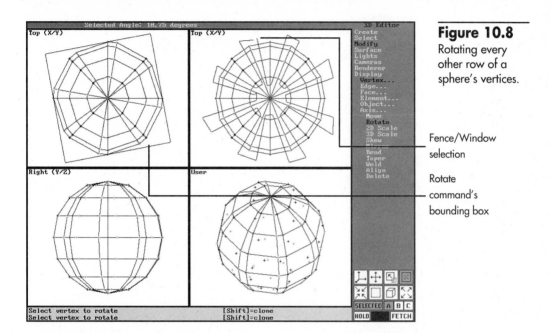

Figure 10.8

Rotating every other row of a sphere's vertices.

Fence/Window selection

Rotate command's bounding box

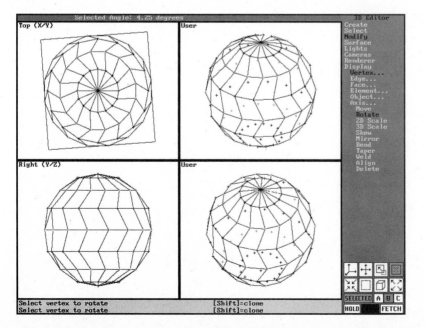

Figure 10.9

Rotating every other horizontal band of vertices.

III

Advanced Modeling

Scaling Vertices

The 2D and 3D Vertex Scale commands are often used to pinch or expand portions of a mesh. Both of these commands are based on the current axis location. Because of these commands' impact, the axis location should be carefully considered. Remember that the local axis is not for the object, but for the selection set of vertices.

Vertices do not have any "scale" to themselves. The Scale commands scale only the position of vertices in relation to the axis. Because of this, scaling single vertices about the local axis is not allowed. Using the global axis with a single vertex has the effect of "moving" it.

The act of scaling vertices is just like using Object/Scale, but the effect is quite different. When you scale a mesh, it shrinks or grows. When you scale its vertices, portions of the mesh pinch or expand. Just as in scaling objects, using 2D Scale affects the vertices in that plane only, whereas 3D Scale affects them in all planes. Figure 10.10 shows how selecting the appropriate vertices of an item to be scaled is the key to the Scale command's usefulness. You might find similarities between scaling vertices and using the Lofter's Scale deformation. The following exercise demonstrates how vertex scaling can affect portions of the model as if they were part of a loft.

Figure 10.10
The effects of scaling a mesh's vertices locally in several areas and in a larger area.

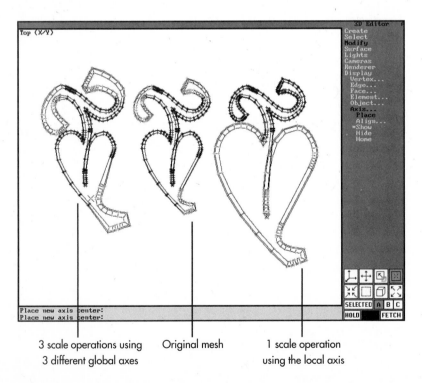

3 scale operations using   Original mesh   1 scale operation
3 different global axes   using the local axis

Scaling a Cylinder into a Dumbbell

*Create a smooth cylinder with 20 sides and
6 segments in an Orthogonal viewport*

Select the middle three cross-sections of vertices

Choose Vertex/3D Scale *and scale the
selection using the local axis*

Shrinks the center section of the cylinder
and becomes a "handle," as in figure 10.11

The 3D SCALE command has the same effect from within any viewport. The inside ends of this
"dumbbell" are quite flared and would be better if they were only slightly chamfered.

*Deselect the inner row of vertices by pressing
the* Alt *key and using a Quad selection*

Choose Vertex/2D Scale *and press* Tab⁕
*to get a direction that points along the length
of the cylinder*

Scale the vertices using the local axis

The vertices are pushed out equally to either
side, as shown in figure 10.12

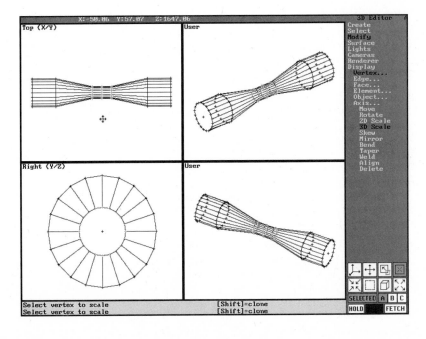

Figure 10.11
Pinching a
cylinder with a 3D
vertex scale about
the local axis.

Figure 10.12
The final dumbbell mesh after an additional 2D Scale command.

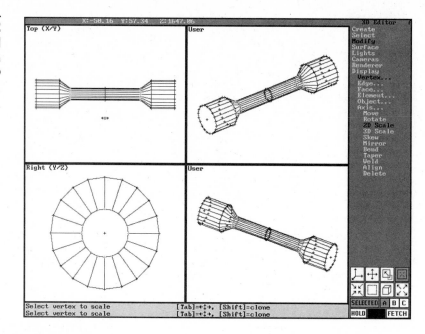

Skewing Vertices

Using Vertex/Skew is similar to using Object/Skew because both commands move the vertices in relation to the axis. With Vertex/Skew, you can be much more selective of what portion of the mesh the operation is going to affect. The important concept to understand about vertex skewing is that all vertices that rest on the same plane maintain their relationship to one another; only their distance to the axis changes. The greater the distance a plane of vertices is from the axis, the farther it moves away. These effects can be seen in figure 10.13. When used with the local axis, Skew's effect is very similar to moving the opposing ends in opposite directions.

The Skew command affects different planes of vertices. An invalid skew results if your selection defines only one plane in regard to your directional Tab arrow. A single vertex cannot have multiple planes, and therefore is never a valid skew.

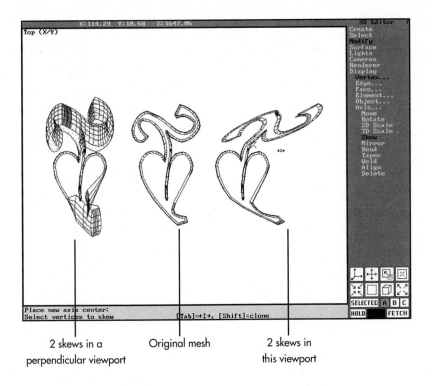

Figure 10.13
The effects of the Skew command when used in different viewports with placed global axes.

2 skews in a perpendicular viewport

Original mesh

2 skews in this viewport

Mirroring Vertices

The Vertex/Mirror command flips the position of the vertices 180 degrees about a line determined by your pick point and multidirectional Tab arrow. Figure 10.14 shows how as vertices are flipped, they pull their faces with them. This has an effect similar to turning the mesh "inside out." Mirroring a single vertex is the same as moving it as it is not changing position with another.

If the effect of the mirror is not what you want, perform the mirror again by quickly selecting the same point, and the effect of the mirror will be nearly reversed. You now can pick another mirror point to try to get a better result.

III

Advanced Modeling

Figure 10.14
The effects of mirroring a selection of a mesh's vertices in the three directions.

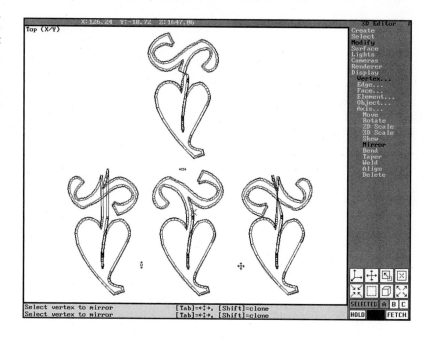

Bending Vertices

The Vertex/Bend command is often used to create bends or kinks in objects. Notice that bending is different from rotating because the vertices' relationships to each other change. As in Object/Bend, this command bases its effect on the selection's bounding box. The direction of the bend's "top" is pointed to by your directional Tab cursor, as shown in figure 10.15. (Figure 10.15 is a composite image of two different bend commands.)

The number of segments that go into making the bending portion is the real determination for whether the result reads as a kinked or bent object. When creating objects, your need to bend the mesh is the greatest determining factor for how many segments an object should have.

The following exercise shows how using Bend several times on different selections within the same object can create a dramatic object.

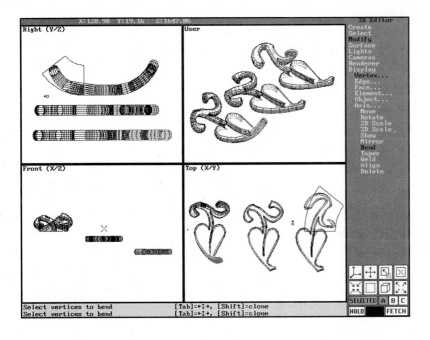

Figure 10.15
Different effects of bending a vertice selection in the Right and the Top viewports.

Repeated Bends on Varying Selections

Begin by creating a smooth cylinder having 16 sides and 24 segments in the Top *viewport*

Copy the cylinder to the side for reference and future use — Creates a copy for reference

In the Top *viewport, select all the vertices except for the row on the edge closest to the copy*

Switch to the Front *viewport and choose the* Vertex/Bend *command*

Click on the HOLD *button or press* Ctrl+H

Press Tab⇥ *until the cursor points up, and turn on angle snap by pressing* A

Perform a 15-degree bend — Bends the selected vertices

Switch to the Top *viewport and deselect the row of vertices to either side of the stationary row* — Bends all but three rows of vertices

continues

continued

Switch back to the Front *viewport and do another 15-degree bend*	Bends all but three rows of vertices

Repeat the last two steps two more times

The cylinder now has a flared, sharp top, as shown in figure 10.16.

Figure 10.16
The completed sharp-edged and flared cylinder.

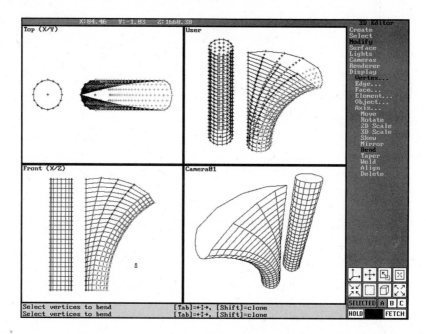

After performing a bend, you should analyze the object's smoothing groups and determine if they are still appropriate. This is especially important for morph objects where the smoothing actually should be analyzed before the bend. It is possible that the original smoothing characteristics were compromised and that new ones might need to be assigned. The correct use of smoothing groups has a significant influence on the believability of the bend in a rendering.

Be aware that after you bend a selection, the relationship vertices have with their temporary bounding box changes. Performing a subsequent, "reverse" bend may not result in the original geometry, and performing a Hold is usually prudent. (See Chapter 5, "Building Models in the 3D Editor," for more information on this.)

Tapering Vertices

The Vertex/Taper command, as described for objects in Chapter 5, acts somewhat like a cross between the 2D-Scale and Skew commands. Like the Bend command, Taper bases its effects on your selection's bounding box and has different effects depending on which viewport and in which plane you use it. Figure 10.17 shows the effects that Vertex/Taper had on the same two selection sets, but performed in differing viewports.

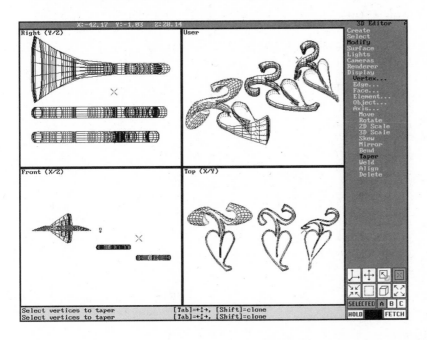

Figure 10.17

Different effects of tapering vertices in the Right and the Top viewports.

Be aware that after you taper a selection, the relationship the vertices have with the bounding box changes. Performing a subsequent, "reverse" taper does not necessarily result in the original geometry. This deformation, as in all deformations, can be used as a modeling technique if you are aware of its outcome.

The following exercise purposefully overextends the retrievable limits of the Skew command as a tool to create several useful shapes. (If you were to make a clone of each iteration, it would make an interesting morph animation.)

Deforming Vertices with Skew

Begin by creating a smooth cylinder with 16 sides and 24 segments in the Top *viewport*

In a side viewport, select all but the bottom row of vertices (use Alt+W *to access quad selection quickly)*

Choose Modify Vertex/2D Scale *and scale the selection vertically, about the local axis, until the vertices are close together*	Scales the vertices so that they are now close to one end of the shaft

Clone the cylinder to the side for reference and backup in case something goes wrong

Deselect the lowest row of vertices from the current selection set (you can use Alt+W *with the* Alt *key as well)*

Choose Modify/Vertex/Taper *and taper the selection to 1 percent about its local axis*	Pinches the vertices to a chisel point
Switch to an adjacent side viewport and taper the selection again by 1 percent	Pinches the vertices to a point like that of a sharp pencil
Now taper the selection by 200 percent	Rounds point in that viewport, as shown in figure 10.18

Return to the Front *viewport and taper the selection by 20 percent*

The tip now has a uniform round and pointed tip.

If you want, clone the object at this point for future reference, or proceed and modify its tip even more.

Taper the selection to 1 percent in both viewports again	Flares the tip inward to a very sharp point, as seen in figure 10.19
Taper the selection to 400 percent in both viewports	Flares the tip outward like an onion dome, as shown in figure 10.20.

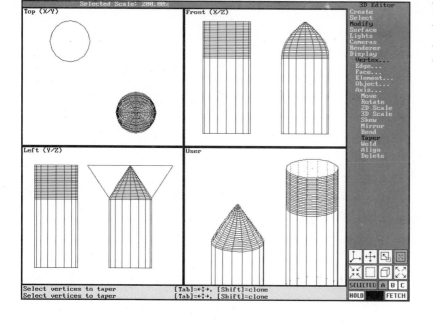

Figure 10.18
Tapering the
cylinder into
a bullet.

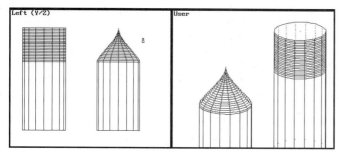

Figure 10.19
Tapering the
cylinder to a
watercolor
brush point.

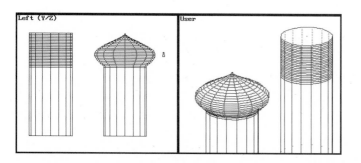

Figure 10.20
Tapering the
cylinder into an
onion dome.

III

Advanced Modeling

Aligning Vertices

The results of the Modify/Vertex/Align command might not be completely obvious. It is good advice to HOLD before using it. The Vertex/Align command aligns your selection by moving vertices perpendicular to your current viewport until they lie on its construction plane. (Construction planes are positioned with the Display/Const/Place command.)

Although the vertices' positions appear unchanged in your current viewport, they actually have been made coplanar. Figure 10.21 shows how this has the effect of "squashing" the vertices against the plane's wall. Subsequent uses of the command in the same viewport have no effect if the construction planes are not repositioned.

Figure 10.21
The effects of aligning some of a mesh's vertices.

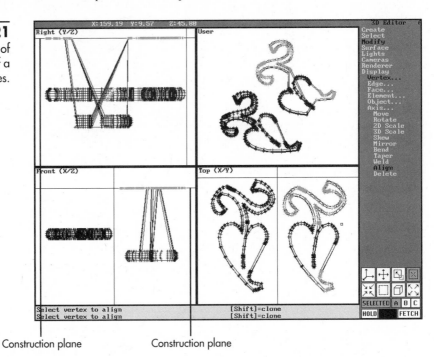

Construction plane   Construction plane

Note   The Vertex/Align command is the *only* Modify branch command that references the construction planes for any purpose.

Aligning vertices is most useful when the selection of vertices is already coplanar and only needs to be aligned at an angle. The Vertex/Align command also can be used to quickly make any mesh coplanar—an effect that might be desired for some animations.

Deleting Vertices

When you delete a vertex, you also delete any faces that share it. Some might find this surprising, but remember that the criteria for making a crossing selection of faces is to enclose any of their vertices. Consequently, deleting vertices can be a fast method for deleting faces, not just vertices. In addition, 3D Studio will not prompt you about deleting or not deleting the object's isolated vertices.

As always when using a Delete command in the 3D Editor, remember that there is no Undo command available. Check to see that no elements or objects, and thus their vertices, are selected before you delete. Remember to examine meshes that have been recently unhidden—it is quite possible to forget about an earlier selection that is now active.

Selected vertices can be difficult to see, especially in a complex model. Consider using (Alt)+(N) to deselect everything before building your selection set as a safety precaution against affecting unwanted vertices.

Vertex Accuracy

Although 3D Studio is not a program that depends on accuracy—or even promotes it— accurately aligning vertices is an important concept to master. *Welded vertices* (those shared by more than one face) "knit" an element together and define its extents. Although mapping coordinates can extend over unwelded faces, smoothing groups cannot. Without being properly smoothed, a mesh will never look quite right. Figure 10.22 shows how a smoothed surface has an apparent ridge or seam where the faces are no longer welded, and the smoothing group's effect stops.

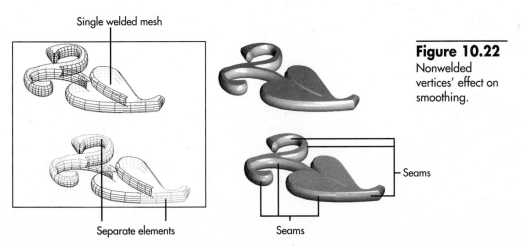

Single welded mesh

Separate elements

Seams

Seams

Figure 10.22
Nonwelded vertices' effect on smoothing.

III

Advanced Modeling

It is common for DXF mesh files that are imported into 3D Studio to not seem to render "right." This is usually a result of adjacent, or even coincidental, vertices within meshes not being welded, and should be one of the first things you check. This is not a limitation of 3D Studio, but rather of the method the original modeling program used to create the mesh.

Using the Weld Threshold

When Modify/Vertex/Weld is used on a *selection* of vertices, 3D Studio determines which are coincidental by the value set for the *weld threshold.* This is the round-off or "fuzz" factor used when comparing groups of vertices. The weld threshold value is expressed in units and checks the actual distance between vertices. Welding vertex selections is thus independent of any viewport resolution. The higher the value, the more vertices fall within each other's distance range and are welded to one another.

The weld threshold is not used for single vertex welds. When welding vertices one by one, the size of your *pick box* is the determining factor of what is considered a coincidental vertex (as is with Vertex Snap).

The default value for the weld threshold is set in your 3DS.SET file, but also can be changed as you need from within the System Options dialog box. This value is easy to edit because the Weld Threshold edit box is highlighted upon calling it up.

Welding Vertices

The Modify/Vertex/Weld command is one of the most commonly used commands in the Vertex branch. This command enables you to weld vertices one by one or by entire selection sets.

When welding an individual vertex, you drag the selected vertex to the position of another. After confirming that you want to weld the two vertices, one vertex is deleted. Any faces that become co-linear as a result of the new placement are deleted as well, while the remaining faces now share the common vertex. You thus can use Weld to join or simplify meshes.

You might find the Weld command somewhat finicky about selecting the second vertex for welding. Enlarging your pick box increases the proximity for a recognized weld. The pick box is set with Configure and can be quickly accessed with the ⁺ key.

Welding is often needed for modeling operations that are not quite right or a little sloppy. Selecting an entire mesh and performing a weld may decrease the mesh's size, and ensures that all the faces that appear to have shared vertices actually do have shared vertices. Before

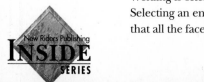

performing an object or element weld, check your weld threshold and make sure that its size will not eliminate vertices that you do not want welded.

When welding a selection of vertices, you are presented with the warning message: `Mapping coordinates will be removed`. This occurs if the weld succeeds in welding even one vertex. (If the operation finds none to weld, the mapping coordinates are kept.) If you need to maintain the mesh's original mapping, you should acquire it from the object before the weld so that it is ready to be applied immediately after the operation. This technique does not work for objects that contain more than one set of mapping coordinates for their elements. For these, only the first mapping coordinates applied to the object can ever be acquired.

Tip

To maintain a mesh's mapping information while welding, you must weld the vertices one by one. This results in somewhat distorted mapping for the affected faces, but the remainder of the object maintains its original mapping information. This is the *only* method for preserving lofted mapping coordinates while welding.

Understanding Face Editing in the 3D Editor

Editing faces is extremely similar to editing vertices, and you will probably find that you often use these two command branches interchangeably. The choice of which branch to use usually comes down to whatever works best for the particular application or selection you may be working on at the time.

Working with faces is much like working with vertices in sets of three. Unlike a vertex, a face defines a mesh and a face normal, and brings with it material, smoothing, and mapping information that can make their editing somewhat different.

III

Advanced Modeling

Modifying Edges

Edges are strictly a by-product of faces and represent their outline or sides. They are the sides of faces and cannot exist without them. Although they are not a piece of geometry unto themselves, they can be used to manipulate the faces of which they are a part and form the basis by which additional faces can be created.

Edge Visibility

You can only manipulate edges that you can actually see. Because of this, you should always turn on their visibility with the Display/Geometry/All Lines command before manipulating them. With the All Lines option active, previously invisible edges appear dashed or "hidden."

The 3D Studio Reference Manual sometimes refers to displayed, invisible edges as *construction lines*.

You can change the visibility of edges individually with Modify/Edge/Visible or Modify/Edge/Invisible by selecting edges one at a time. Although you can always make an edge invisible, you must use the All Lines display option before you can select hidden edges to become visible.

3D Studio includes the capability to automatically affect the visibility of an object's edges with the Modify/Edge/AutoEdge function. AutoEdge essentially operates on the same principal as the AutoSmooth function. With it, you specify the *angle* threshold formed by projecting one face forward as the maximum angle for a visible edge. Figure 10.23 shows how this included angle is easily seen by comparing the projected planes of adjacent faces. Basically, the higher the angle threshold, the more acute faces can be to one another and still appear smooth.

Figure 10.23

Angle threshold determination between welded faces.

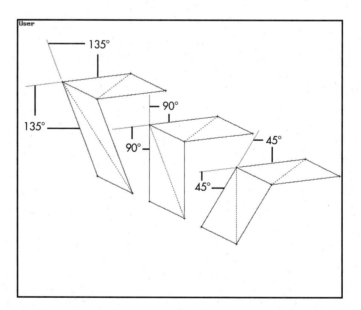

3D Studio treats the 0 degree and 180 degree angle threshold values as special cases. Planes that are coplanar to one another are said to have a 0 degree angle, whereas 180 degrees is considered the angle that all others fall below.

After entering an angle, the AutoEdge command checks all edges shared between faces and makes invisible the ones that fall below that threshold. Using a value of 0 degrees displays all edges, and 180 degrees makes all edges invisible. Figure 10.24 shows how AutoEdge affects meshes having varying angles or different degrees of "roundness."

For the most part, the only difference between visible and invisible edges is organization and visual clarity. Edge display does not generally influence the line weight of an object or its renderability. The only time edges do have an influence on a rendered image is when the mesh is rendered in wireframe. When the scene is rendered in Force Wire mode, or a mesh is assigned a wireframe material and rendered, only the visible edges of the mesh will appear in the image. Figure 10.25 shows the meshes of figure 10.24 rendered with a wireframe material.

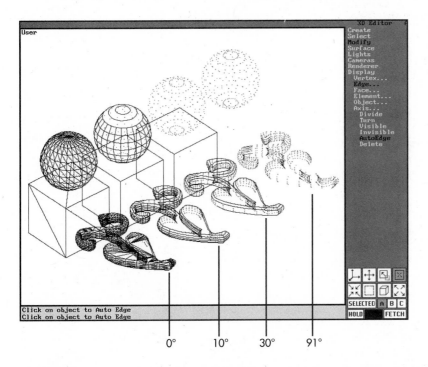

0°   10°   30°   91°

Figure 10.24

Examples of AutoEdge used with values of 0, 10, 30, and 91 degrees.

III

Advanced Modeling

Because AutoEdge only accepts integer values, a bit of a round-off error can occur when the threshold angle you specify is exactly that formed by the mesh. For example, using AutoEdge on a box with a threshold of 90 degrees results in a random order of visible edges, whereas 1 degree to 89 degrees displays them correctly, and 91 degrees to 180 degrees hides all edges.

Figure 10.25
The geometry of
figure 10.24
rendered with a
wireframe
material.

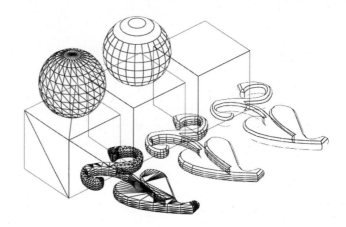

Dividing Edges

The Modify/Edge/Divide command affects a single edge by actually inserting a vertex at its midpoint and splitting the original face into two faces. If the edge is shared between two faces, both are split, resulting in four faces. The edges that intersect the new vertex are always created as invisible (construction lines). This is the only Modify branch command that actually creates geometry. Regardless of its positioning, Divide should definitely be remembered as a Create option because its ability to create a vertex and face at a key location can be quite valuable.

Diving edges is a very convenient way to introduce a vertex and add a face at mesh areas that need to be welded. Many models are improperly meshed, having dissimilar vertex counts at transition points (three dimensional fillets, for example). To make these meshes smooth properly, vertices need to be created within the portion with the lower count and welded to the other mesh section. The Edge/Divide command is a very useful tool for this operation. The following exercise demonstrates just some of the uses for Edge/Divide.

Modeling with Divided Edges

*Begin by creating a cube in an orthogonal
viewpoint with* Create/Box *while holding*
Ctrl

Change your display to show Vert Ticks/   Makes editing much easier
All Lines/See Thru

Switch to the User *viewport*

Choose Modify/Edge/Divide *and diagonal*   Adds a vertex in the center of each
(dashed) edges on all six of the cube's sides   side, and creates a pair of faces

*Check the model for adequate lighting and render
the User view*

The cube appears unchanged. Because all the faces are still coplanar, the sides of the cube render exactly the same. This is the case regardless of how many divisions are made. To see the effect, the faces must be moved.

Select the six new center vertices (use the User
viewport or Perpendicular *viewports)*

Choose Modify/Vertex/3D Scale *and
scale the selected vertices 50 percent about
the local axis*

The cube collapses inwardly, as seen
in figure 10.26

Render the User view

The cube rendered the same because 3D Studio assigns a smoothing group to all faces when an object is created. The Renderer is trying to make the crushed cube appear smooth. To see the effects of the scale, you must remove the smoothing effect.

Choose Surface/Smoothing/Object/
Clear All *and select the cube*

The smoothing groups are removed
from the cube

Render the User view

The cube renders correctly

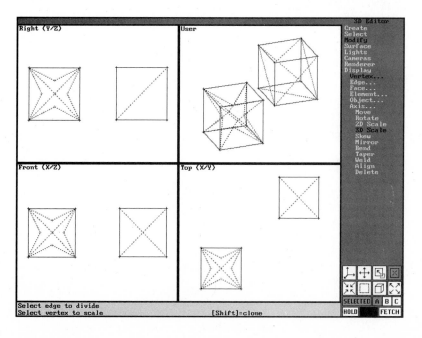

Figure 10.26
Scaling the
vertices created
with Edge/Divide.

III

Advanced Modeling

As seen in the earlier exercises, faces created with Modify/Edge/Divide assume the smoothing groups of their parents. Equally convenient is that the new faces assume the material and mapping assignments of the parent face as well. While the automatic material assignment is useful, the existence of mapping does not mean that the coordinates are oriented correctly. Figure 10.27 shows how the direction and scale of the mapping coordinates are almost always distorted for the newly created faces.

Figure 10.27
Mapping distortions due to edge dividing.

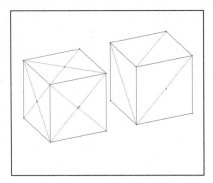
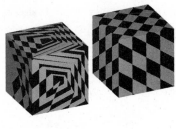

After you are finished dividing edges, you will probably need to acquire the mapping coordinates from the object and reapply them so the newly created faces' mapping is oriented correctly.

Once you are comfortable with the map-turning effects of dividing edges, you may find it a unique way to introduce interesting variations within your object's mapping. When combined with Edge/Turn, Edge/Divide can add considerable variation to key areas of your mesh that would be impossible to achieve with conventional mapping.

Turning Edges

The Modify/Edge/Turn command works on single shared edges by redirecting the edge to the faces' other two vertices. Remarkably, this does not alter most mapping assignments. Mapping coordinates are not turned with the face, but rather maintain their original direction with the rest of the mesh.

The turning of an edge can change the profile of your geometry by making a face coincidental with another or flipping the face and its normal the other direction. Figure 10.28 shows how the profile, smoothing, and highlight characteristics change as edges are turned. The "safest" edges to turn are those between coplanar faces. These edges continue to turn and have no effect on the profile of the mesh.

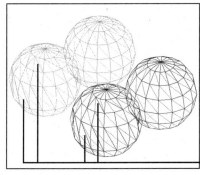

Figure 10.28
The effects of turned edges on a spherical mesh.

Rows of turned edges

With all those potential problems, why use Edge/Turn? Turning an edge is a subtle modeling tool. It is a readjustment that does not make the mesh any more complex because it simply reorients what already exists. If a mesh's area needs to be roughed up or smoothed out a little, turning an edge can help. If a Boolean operation is not working, turning an edge on coplanar faces might readjust the geometry enough for it to work without otherwise changing the object's position or complexity.

The direction of an edge does change the way face-mapped materials render and can be a critical tool in adjusting their appearance. See Chapter 6, "Introduction to the Materials Editor," for information on using turned edges with face maps.

Deleting Edges

When you delete an edge, you delete the face(s) belonging to that edge as well. If a shared edge is deleted, both faces that share the edge are deleted. You can delete edges to surgically eliminate faces in a complex mesh because it can be easier and quicker to select an edge than a face.

Unlike the Modify/Face/Collapse command, deleting an edge does not affect adjacent faces, and thus leaves a hole where the delete faces were.

Creating Faces

Faces usually are created as parts of objects. On occasion, you will likely need to create faces individually to net together holes and gaps within and between meshes of an object.

III

Advanced Modeling

Face editing depends on vertices; faces simply do not exist without them. Because of this, you should already be comfortable with vertex manipulation before you try editing faces. So many similarities exist between the two forms of editing that it becomes a judicious decision as to which to use.

Selecting Single Faces

Selecting a single face is not the easiest action to perform in 3D Studio. You will need to select single faces quite often, so it pays to get comfortable with the procedure. To select a single face, you must first select one of its vertices—not an edge. The first face found at that vertex is highlighted in blue. (This color changes according to your display colors and the colors of the object.) If the vertex is not shared by another face, the desired face is highlighted, and you can select it. If the vertex is shared, you must cycle through all the faces that share that vertex by moving your cursor. Each individual face is highlighted in turn. When the correct face is highlighted, click again to finally select it.

A single vertex can be shared by a very large number of faces, such as at the poles of a sphere. If this is the case, consider selecting the face by one of its less "popular" vertices. Coincidental vertices can cause a significant problem for selecting single faces. The oldest object present has its vertex selected, so only its faces can be cycled through. If you need to select a single face by a coincidental vertex, you must first hide the interfering element or object.

Selecting Multiple Faces

Multiple faces are much easier to select. They can be selected under the Select branch by a rectangle (with Quad), an irregular closed polygon (with Fence), or a circle (with Circle). Each option then can be coupled with either a Window (all three vertices must be enclosed) or Crossing (any one vertex can be enclosed) method. You might want to use these methods for selecting single faces if the standard method is inconvenient for your situation.

Faces can be selected by other methods outside the Selection branch, and should always be kept in mind as options when building sets. Faces can be selected by their assigned Smoothing groups through the Surface/Smoothing/Show command, and by their assigned material through the Surface/Material/Show command. Only faces are selected with these methods, however, not the vertices or object definition—regardless of whether the entire object happens to share the same material or smoothing group.

When you use the Modify/Face or Create/Face command, you also have the option of selecting or deselecting single faces (by holding the [Ctrl] key) or Quad selections (by using [Alt]+[W]). The selection method used by Quad is the last specified under the Select/Face branch.

By selecting elements and objects, you select all their faces at once. Remembering this, you can quickly select all of an element's faces, and then deselect those you do not want. Similarly, you can select faces quickly with Quad Crossing and deselect those belonging to an unwanted object by selecting it twice.

It is common to work interchangeably between the Modify/Face and Modify/Vertex branches. In doing so, remember that when you select faces, you do not select their vertices.

Detaching Faces

The Create/Face/Detach command strips the faces off one mesh to become an independent object. Although you can detach faces one by one, the Detach command is used primarily with a selection of faces. Detached faces stay in place and are not initially moved.

Detaching faces also can be considered a method for "unwelding" vertices. When detaching faces that share vertices (that is, they are welded), the new faces gain the vertices that once were welded as they become a new object.

You commonly need to peel back a face or hinge a section of a mesh from the rest. This cannot be done directly if the mesh is a welded entity because the other faces peel and hinge as well. The simple cube in the following exercise shows the technique used to hinge a mesh.

Opening the Top of a Box

Begin by creating a box in an orthogonal viewport

Select the faces of one of its sides using a quad window

Choose Create/Face/Detach, *press the* (Spacebar), *and pick the active viewport*

Enter a name for the new object

Notice that the appearance of the box has not changed.

Select the last object (use Ctrl+N) *and activate the selection by pressing the* (Spacebar)

Place the global axis at the hinge point by choosing Modify/Axis/Align/Object *where you see the selected faces on edge, and then click in a viewport*

Choose the Align *command* Left *option and make sure that the local axis is off*

Because the lid is perpendicular to the viewport plane, the Left, Upper Left, and Lower Left options also place the axis in the same location.

continues

continued

Press the (Spacebar) *to activate selection*

Choose Face/Rotate *and rotate the*
lid to the desired angle

The lid is now open, as shown
in the Top viewports of figure 10.29

Figure 10.29
A box with
an open lid.

Global axis ——

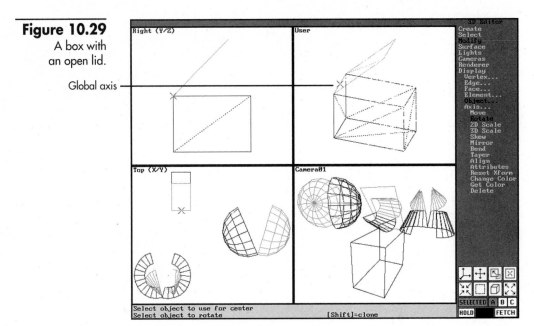

Using Object/Rotate or Vertex/Rotate would have the same result, whereas Element/Rotate
could not have used the selection. At this point, it might be advantageous to attach the lid back
to the box.

Choose Create/Object/Attach, *select*
the lid, and then select the box

Attaches the lid to the box object

Select the object, turn on Selected *and choose*
Modify/Vertex/Weld

Attaching eliminated the first selection.

Weld the selection

The lid and box now share the same two vertices.

Although the previous exercise is a simple demonstration, the same technique holds true for any mesh regardless of its complexity, as seen in the lower viewports of figure 10.29.

Copying/Cloning Faces

Your greatest source of faces is existing meshes. You likely will need to steal, or copy, a portion of a mesh to be its own object. You then are free to make multiple copies and edit numerous permutations.

The Create/Face/Copy command copies a selection of faces to a new location. This is identical to cloning the faces with Shift+Modify/Face/Move. Either operation creates an object independent of the copied mesh, which in turn can be copied or cloned again.

The Create/Face/Copy command and clone option can be thought of as an alternative to the Create/Face/Detach command because the original faces remain selected and can be deleted quickly.

Building Faces

At times, simply copying faces will not serve your purposes, as you need to connect meshes or add additional faces to them. The Create/Face/Build command is the only procedure available for doing this. With this command, you create or "build" faces with a "connect-the-dot" method between three vertices that determine the new face. The only caveat is that all the vertices used to build faces must belong to the same object. If you build faces on the vertices of existing faces, they share the same vertices and are automatically welded. Newly built faces inherit none of the parent mesh's material, smoothing, or mapping information, and are assigned the default material with no smoothing or mapping information.

The normal of a newly created face is determined by the order in which you connect its vertices when building it. A counterclockwise pick order creates the face with its normal facing you. A clockwise pick order orients the normal away from you. If you are using the Backface display mode in the latter case, the new face may not appear to have been created since you cannot see it.

Most modelers feel that it is easier to build faces while using See Thru mode, and then switch to Backface mode once finished, to flip the normals of the newly built faces as needed.

The Build command is similar to Weld with regard to vertex selection and the size of your pick box. You can increase the pick box size to make choosing vertices, and thus building faces, easier. To do this, access the Configure dialog box with the ⌗ key.

Selecting the last vertex of long, tapered faces still can be somewhat difficult because the rubber-band triangle drawing aid often converges before the actual pick box. In building such faces, you will find it easier to select the longest sides first, thus reducing the acuteness of the rubber-band triangle. It is very likely that you may need to zoom close and edge pan as you choose vertices because you unfortunately cannot switch between viewports while building faces.

Tessellating Faces

The Create/Face/Tessellate command is a tool for refining meshes by splitting each selected face into three. This adds two faces and one vertex to each face tessellated with all newly formed edges being visible. The new edges actually bisect the angle of the original face, and the new vertex is thus the face's centroid. The new set of faces are coplanar with the original and conveniently assume the material and mapping of the parent face.

The Face/Tessellate command can be used selectively—face by face—to increase detail where needed, or on an entire selection set to create new geometric patterns, as seen in figure 10.30.

Normally, the simple act of tessellating faces does not have an immediate effect on the mesh since the new faces are coplanar with the original. Unlike divided edges, tessellated faces inherit the material and the correct mapping orientation of the parent face. The only time that there is a noticeable change is when the mesh is assigned a face map material, as shown in figure 10.31.

Figure 10.30

Examples of standard segments and tessellated face patterns.

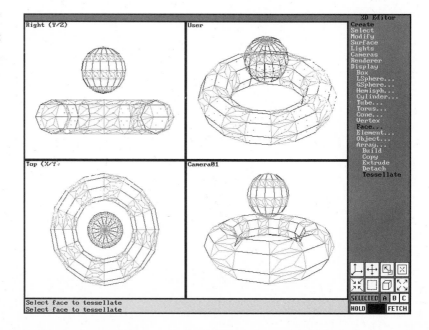

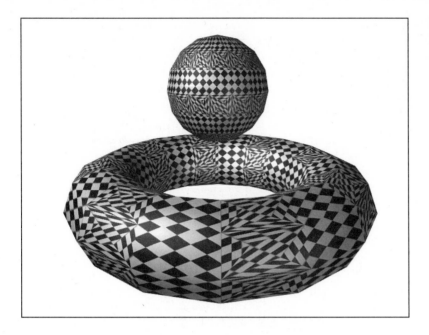

Figure 10.31
The tessellated faces of figure 10.30 rendered with a face map material.

Tessellating Objects and Elements

The various tessellation commands only add to a mesh's face count and never create a new mesh or object as their locations in the menu's Create branch might suggest. You can increase an element or object's complexity by tessellating it. You should do so, however, only for a particular reason. The most common situation is a need to create more vertices with which to modify the mesh. A mesh might not contain enough faces to "dent" or "bend" correctly, for example. Another common use is to increase the object's complexity enough for failing Boolean operations to work properly. The DISPLACE Plug-In from the Yost Group is a classic example of how tessellation allows a mesh to be deformed more accurately (in this case, by an applied bitmap).

 Cloning is not available while using any Tessellate command. If you do need a copy of the original, clone the mesh before the tessellation.

Quite a difference exists between tessellating objects and elements, and you should choose which one based upon the model's needs. In general, tessellating elements is the same as tessellating faces—the mesh's profile remains constant. Tessellating objects, however, provides you with an additional tessellation technique and the ability to have the new faces bulge in or out.

The Create/Element/Tessellate command works exactly as Create/Face/Tessellate except that it affects every face contained within the element. This is a quick operation to triple the complexity of a mesh. More vertices and faces mean more opportunities to distort and model the mesh. Because all tessellated faces are coplanar, this command does nothing to refine the initial appearance of the element. If you are not going to deform the mesh in a later operation, you have no reason to use the Tessellate command.

It can be effective to tessellate an element assigned a face-mapped material. This can serve to "randomize" a texture bit map, which is only somewhat random to begin with. Tileable materials, such as granite, sand, or grass, can benefit from having more faces to stretch their bit maps across.

The Create/Object/Tessellate command gives you several more options and the capability to significantly change the object's geometry. This is the only Tessellate command that can change the mesh's geometry immediately. After you select an object for the Object/Tessellate command, the Tessellation Controls dialog box appears (see fig. 10.32).

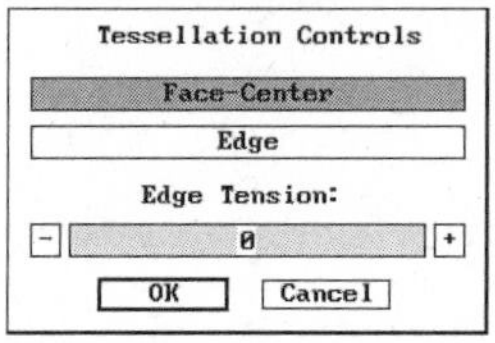

Figure 10.32
The Tessellation Controls dialog box for Create/Object/Tessellate.

> Tessellation Controls
> Face-Center
> Edge
> Edge Tension:
> – | 0 | +
> OK   Cancel

Two face creation options exist at the object level. The standard method of tessellation, common to both Face/Tessellate and Element/Tessellate is called *Face-Center*. A variation that divides each face into four by connecting the midpoints of each edge is called *Edge*. Although the Edge option creates an additional face and two more vertices, it works well for changing orthogonal geometry.

The "squared-off" Edge tessellation option unfortunately is available only at the object level. To use this tool at the face level, you need to select the faces, detach them, tessellate the new object, reattach it to the original object, and weld if necessary.

You also have control over the placement of an object's tessellated faces with the Edge Tension value slider. A value of zero produces coplanar faces, just as with Face or Element Tessellation, with no deformation. Increasing the tension has the effect of "inflating" the mesh, placing the new vertices farther and farther from the object's local axis. A negative tension "deflates" the object by placing the new vertices closer to the local axis.

The positive values represent the object's bounding box distance, with the maximum value of 100 displacing the faces a distance equal to the object's overall length. Negative tension is most effective with lower values (below 50) because higher values can cause faces to cross themselves as they pull in. The exact effect that tension has on an object can be a bit unpredictable, especially at extreme values.

When tessellating meshes, any vertices selected before a tessellation remain selected afterward and can be used for subsequent manipulation. (Faces do not because they have been replaced.) As a result, you can select an object, tessellate it with a tension of zero, and control its contortions with the Modify/Vertex commands. This technique cannot duplicate the effects of tension, but deforms the mesh in its own manner. The reference manuals give an example of creating a spiked ball with this technique. With a little control, it can be used as a modeling tool for many other effects as well.

As tessellation creates faces and vertices, it gives you an interesting opportunity to manipulate a complex vertice selection. The following exercise explores a few of the possibilities.

Modifying Selections after Tessellation

Begin by creating a short, faceted cylinder with 16 sides and 1 segment in the Top *viewport*

Copy the cylinder to the side for future use

Choose Create/Object/Tessellate *and*   Selects the cylinder
select the cylinder while holding Ctrl

Release the Ctrl *key, activate the selection with the* Spacebar, *and click in the viewport*

Click on OK *in the dialog box that appears*

Choose the Edge *option, a tension of 0,*   Tessellates the cylinder, and the
and click on OK   faces are deselected

Choose Modify/Vertex/2D-Scale *and press the* Spacebar

Scale the selection up about 125 percent   Scales the vertices and becomes
in both directions while using the   a gear with a pinch in the center of
local axis   the teeth, as in figure 10.33

The cylinder is now a more complicated, albeit a fairly predictable shape. If it was the goal of an animation to have this gear work its way through steel, the result could be as follows.

Copy the object to the side for possible use as a future morph shape

continues

III

Advanced Modeling

continued

Figure 10.33

Deforming a
cylinder into a
starburst "gear."

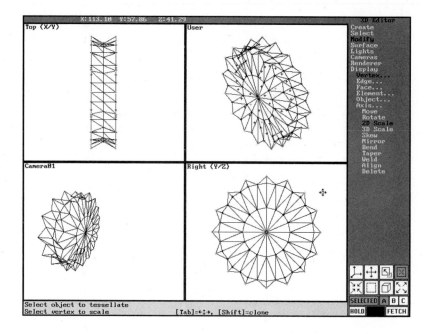

Deselect the gear's center vertices

Choose HOLD

Choose Modify/Vertex Bend

Cycle the unidirectional arrow with the ⸢Tab⸥ *key to point up and bend the vertices over 30 percent or so*	The teeth of the gear are twisted over itself, as in figure 10.34

You can have an equally dramatic effect on the original cylinder if you invert the selection before modifying the vertices. This makes the tessellation's vertices the selection and leaves the original selection alone.

Hide the tessellated cylinders and zoom extents to zero on the original cylinder	
Tessellate the selected cylinder, as you did earlier	The cylinder is tessellated, and the original faces are deselected
Choose Select/Invert	Selects the cylinder except for the original vertices

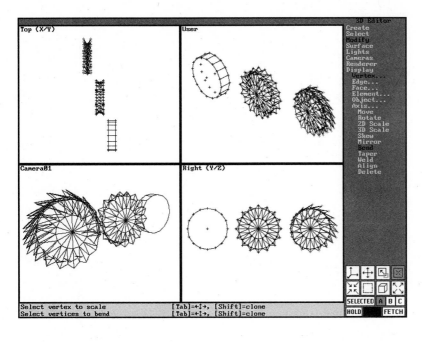

Figure 10.34
Bending the "teeth" of the gear.

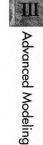

Choose Modify/Vertex/2D Scale, *and scale down the selection to about 90 percent in both directions*	Makes the cylinder become somewhat star-shaped
Switch to the Front *viewport, turn on the local axes, and scale the vertices up about 120 percent in the direction of the star's height*	
Switch back to the Top *viewport, choose* Modify/Vertex/Rotate, *and rotate the selection about 10 degrees*	Rotates the vertices and turns the object into a rotary blade of sorts, as seen in figure 10.35

By scaling an inverted vertex selection, you are approximating the effects of tessellation tension. Although the effects are not identical (because scale is linear, and tension is based on face normals), the effects can be similar, but much more controllable.

Tessellated faces assume the smoothing group of their parent. You always need to examine the smoothing effect on an object deformed by tension. More than likely you will need to use AutoSmooth on the object to assign the correct smoothing groups and achieve an appropriate effect for the new geometry. Remember that when you are creating morph targets, you can morph the smoothing as well.

Figure 10.35
Manipulating an inverted selection set of vertices.

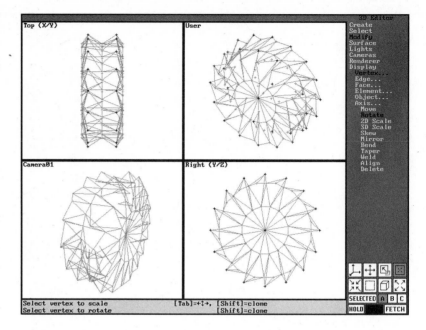

 Tip The newly created edges of tessellated faces always are displayed regardless of the parent's visibility. Using AutoEdge with a value of 1 cleans the mesh's appearance by turning coplanar faces invisible.

As always, tessellated faces have a dramatic effect on face map materials, except that the effect is now across the entire object. See Chapter 6 for a detailed description of these effects. What might be surprising is that the Edge option does not create uniform face maps because the faces were not created in the correct order.

Extruding Faces

The Create/Face/Extrude command is useful in giving "thickness" or "depth" to a selection of faces. The Extrude command creates a set of faces along a vector perpendicular to the composited, averaged normal of all the selected faces. This command works best when all the faces are coplanar, and the extrusion vector is thus perpendicular to the selected faces.

Extruding the faces out "pulls" the selection in the direction of its normal and faces its sides outward like a closed box. The In option "pushes" the selection backward from its normal and faces its sides inward like an open box. In both cases, the original faces maintain their normals, and the new faces inherit the parents' material and mapping. Note that this command only creates the sides of the extrusion and does not cap the other side.

Note For AutoCAD users, Face/Extrude is one method to give thickness to imported 3D polylines that cannot normally be given thickness.

Extrusion is useful in giving depth to coplanar objects and pulling details of elements outward. Extrusion also is used to give depth to meshes that either have lost their extrusion or were created coplanar. Figure 10.36 shows an example of text brought directly from the Shaper into the 3D Editor and extruded with the Create/Face/Extrude command.

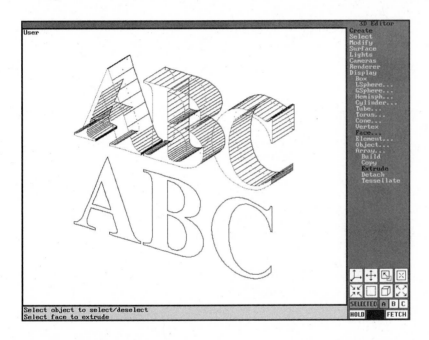

Figure 10.36
Extruding the faces of a coplanar object.

III

Advanced Modeling

Exploding Elements

The Create/Element/Explode command is best thought of as a tool for dissecting meshes. When performing an explode operation, you are given the option to order the new meshes as elements or objects. Which option to choose depends on what you plan to do with the mesh. If you are separating an object for modeling purposes, you probably want to keep the meshes as elements; if you are animating the meshes, however, you should usually make them objects.

A convenient way to renumber consecutive series of objects is to detach all the object's faces into a single object, and then use Explode with an angle threshold of 180 degrees. This will create an object for each discreet element, thus renaming and renumbering the original objects. This is very convenient when some objects in a series have been deleted and the objects' consecutive numbering is critical (as with the Yost Groups SKIN Animated Plug-In).

The critical component of an Explode operation is the determination of the correct angle threshold. The angle determination between faces calculation improved in Release 3 (Release 2 had a problem with exploding coplanar faces). The angle threshold is specified in the dialog box shown in figure 10.37. The basis for this angle is the same as that for AutoEdge and AutoSmooth—it is the included angle formed by projecting one plane forward (see fig. 10.23 for an example of this). An angle of 0 degrees explodes all faces, and 180 degrees does nothing.

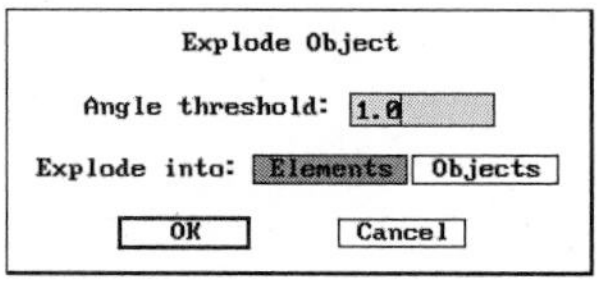

Figure 10.37
The Explode
Object dialog box
(the Element/
Explode
command).

The Explode command does not do a thorough job of checking for duplicate names when creating new objects. If a sequentially numbered name already exists, the command creates a duplicate name anyway. This can be confusing because only one of the duplicate names can be selected. (3D Studio deletes one of the names upon the next file load.) This can easily happen when you perform multiple explosions on the same object, and you continue to accept the default name. Specify a unique starting name for each operation to avoid this problem.

When you are comfortable with analyzing this angle, you can use Explode to separate portions of your model quickly or geometric primitives for use as pieces elsewhere, as shown in the following exercise.

Using Explode to Dissect Objects

*Begin by creating a box of any size
and array into five objects*

Creates several boxes to
"play" with

Choose Create/Element/Explode *and
select the box*

Choose the Elements option and specify
any angle between 180 degrees and 90 degrees
in the Angle Threshold edit box, and select a box

Nothing happens because 90 degrees is not greater than the cube's right angles.

Explode another box, but with a value between 1 and 90	Separates the box into six elements—one for each side
Now explode another box, but with a value of 0 degrees	Separates the box into 12 elements—one for each face

Although this exercise uses a simple box, the concept holds true for all coplanar faces.

Press F12 *to access the PXP Loader*	Displays the PXP Selector dialog box
Choose Grids *and click on* OK	Displays the Grids dialog box
Enter a value of 5 for each of the Grids values and click on OK	Creates a cube that has a 5 by 5 grid on each side
Explode the grid with a 90 degree angle threshold	Separates the grid into six elements—one for each side
Explode one of the new side objects with a 0 degree threshold	Separates each side into 50 elements—one for each face

This concept can be applied to more complex geometry as well.

Create a 16-sided L Sphere

Explode the sphere using a 25 degree threshold

None of the sphere's faces are separated.

Explode the sphere again, but lower the threshold to 22.5 degrees	Separates the faces having the greatest angle threshold, the poles separate into two new objects
Explode the midsection of the sphere, but lower the threshold to 22.1 degrees	Separates all the latitudinal sections as separate rings, except for the equator, as shown in figure 10.38
Explode the equator section again, but lower the threshold to 22 degrees	Separates all the facets because the angle between the last two rings is less than the facets' angle

The angle threshold for a sphere, or any round object, decreases as the number of sides increases. A 24-sided L Sphere, for example, explodes into rings with a threshold a little below 15 degrees; and a 100-sided L Sphere at just below 4 degrees. For circles, this threshold can be determined by dividing 360 degrees with the number of segments. A 100-sided cylinder does not separate until a 3.6 degrees threshold is given. This number is more of a ballpark for spheres because they possess angles in more than one direction.

III

Advanced Modeling

Figure 10.38
Selecting the new ring of elements after exploding L-Spheres.

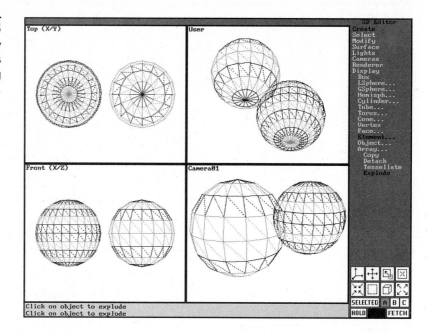

Modifying Faces

Working with Modify/Face commands is very similar to using Modify/Vertex commands. After you make your face selection, you are, in effect, modifying their vertices and not the faces themselves. Because of this, many Modify/Face commands work exactly like their corresponding Modify/Vertex commands.

Move

Move is an obvious command and can be used to visualize the results that moving faces has on the rest of the mesh. When you move faces, you are actually moving their vertices—the face definition simply comes along with them. Any faces that share these vertices are stretched with the selection over the move's displacement. Move is often used to clone faces off of objects, similar to the Create/Face/Copy command.

Rotate, Scale, Skew, Mirror, Bend, and Taper

The Rotate, Scale, Skew, Mirror, Bend, and Taper commands work identically to their Modify/Vertex cousins. For information and tips on using these commands, refer to the appropriate Vertex commands in this chapter and their Object branch commands in Chapter 5, "Building Models in the 3D Editor."

Delete

The Modify/Face/Delete command deletes only the selected faces and not any faces that might share vertices or edges. Deleting at the face level is much more predictable than deleting vertices because no "additional" geometry exists that can be eliminated. When deleting faces, you can analyze your selection and be confident before you delete it.

If vertices are left isolated when you delete a selection of faces, you are prompted as to whether you want to delete these vertices as well. Normally, the only use for isolated vertices is to build new faces. Unless you intend to reuse these vertices with the Create/Face/Build command or as targets for vertex alignment, answer Yes to this prompt.

Although selecting an object with a face select command does not select the entire object, deleting an object's faces and answering yes to delete their vertices will delete the object reference. Face selections that include an object's entire mesh, very common when using Material/Show and Smoothing/Show, will delete the object without a specific warning.

Collapse

The Modify/Face/Collapse command simplifies a mesh by using a unique method of deleting faces. The selected face is deleted and replaced by a centered vertex (the same location as from a tessellated face). Any faces that share an edge with the collapsed face are also deleted. Collapse can thus delete a maximum of four faces at one time—the collapsed face and three with shared edges. The only drawback to the Collapse command is that you can use it on only one face at a time, and you must select it by way of the single face selection method.

Adjacent faces that share vertices with deleted ones have their vertex locations stretched (and welded) to the newly created vertex. Because three faces with shared edges can be deleted, nine faces can be stretched to fill the void, as shown in figure 10.39. Mapping coordinates applied to the mesh are preserved to a fairly high degree. You will need to examine the resulting mapping and might need to acquire and reapply it. This is especially true after collapsing multiple faces within the same mesh area.

Depending on how a mesh was created, it is possible for Collapse to not treat adjacent faces as sharing an edge. This is common at mesh corners and results in a hole where the mesh should have stretched (as seen on the front corner of the illustrated cube in fig. 10.39). If there are not adjacent faces to fill in the space, the deleted faces remain as isolated vertices.

In practice, Collapse is most often used as a sculpting tool; it is somewhat like a chisel in the way that it "chips" away at a mesh's profile and face count. Collapse is best used on meshes that contain a considerable amount of faces with which to work. The command can prove very useful when used on fractally generated landscape and organic meshes that you need to refine, give variation, and leave your mark. When used on a mesh with a regular surface, the Collapse command provides pinched points where the new vertex is located. The cube in figure 10.39 can be further kinked by selecting the new vertices on the coplanar collapses and scaling them inward.

Figure 10.39
"Chiseling" a mesh by collapsing select faces.

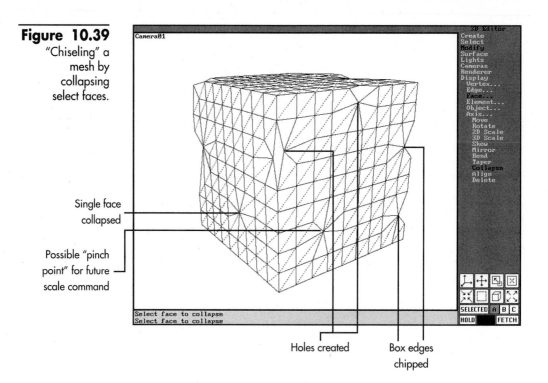

Single face collapsed

Possible "pinch point" for future scale command

Holes created

Box edges chipped

Align

The Face/Align command aligns a single face to that viewport's construction plane. This operation moves and reorients the face, pulling all welded faces with it. It is a good practice to issue the Hold command before using Align because correcting the resulting displacement is difficult.

If you need to align more than one face, select the vertices belonging to the faces and use Modify/Vertex/Align rather than Modify/Face/Align.

Understanding Surface Properties at the Face Level

The face level contains much of the information that defines how a mesh renders. Each face contains information telling 3D Studio in which direction is the front of the face (its normal) and how round it should appear (its smoothing group). As Chapter 6 detailed, the face level

also contains material assignments and the orientation and type of mapping applied. As faces and vertices are manipulated, so too are the effects of these properties.

Smoothing Faces

The careful assignment of smoothing groups to select faces within a mesh can create very realistic images and economical models. The basics of smoothing described in Chapter 5 hold especially true when applied at the face level.

Remember that smoothing is an illusion and always attempts to approximate the shading of the same form—a sphere. No "degrees" of smoothness exist. Faces are either smooth or they are not.

When 3D Studio creates an object, it assigns a smoothing group to every face within that object. Flat or faceted ends that are coplanar are assigned the same group. This does not have an immediate effect on rendering, but does show an effect when faces on these sides are later distorted so they are no longer coplanar. Instead of appearing as a crease or a bend, the fold renders smooth. This can be either exactly what you desire or an unwanted surprise—just remember that it's the default.

Understanding Smoothing

Smoothing can occur only between welded faces. When assigned the same smoothing group, the faces of shared vertices are smoothed. The Smoothing function always tries to approximate the effect of a spherical form. Figure 10.40 shows how smoothing faces that meet at angles more acute than 60 degrees—especially 90 degrees—can result in unrealistic effects as the program attempts to smooth the corners in a spherical fashion.

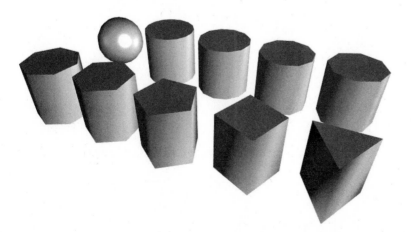

Figure 10.40
The effect of smoothing the sides of various angled meshes (tops and bottoms have no smoothing assigned).

III

Advanced Modeling

As you can see figure 10.40, the shading effect of smoothing is pulled diagonally across the mesh's sides. As a mesh gains more sides, and those sides become progressively smaller, the diagonal highlight sharpens in angle and approaches a vertical. When smoothing is used on faces having acute angles, the rendered effect is more of bright and dark diagonal streaks than an illusion of roundness.

Faces assigned a smoothing group check each shared vertex to see if the adjacent, welded face has a matching group. If they match, the two faces are smoothed with one another. Multiple combinations of smoothing groups have no effect because the amount of smoothing cannot be increased. Assigning a face more than one smoothing group means only that more groups will be considered when comparing adjacent faces.

Since a face can have a maximum of 6 adjacent faces, assigning more than six smoothing groups per face does not serve a purpose for smoothing. You can, however, use additional smoothing groups as a tool for storing specific face level selections. This type of permanent "hidden" face selection can be very convenient for mesh manipulation during the life of the model.

Auto Smoothing

The easiest way to assign smoothing groups is with the AutoSmooth command. This command works on either the element or object level and assigns smoothing groups to their faces based upon their angle to one another. This angle is determined in a similar manner to Modify/ Edge/AutoEdge and Create/Element/Explode, as illustrated in figure 10.41.

Figure 10.41

The smoothing angle thresholds of the geometry in figure 10.40.

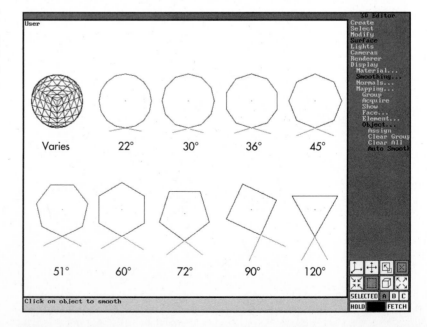

The AutoSmooth function is a great time-saver for large meshes, but it does have an idiosyncrasy for coplanar faces. Coplanar faces are interpreted as having a 0 degree, not 180 degree, relationship. This is why all coplanar faces are assigned a smoothing group when the angle threshold is greater than 0. Using a cube as an example, entering a 1 degree to 89 degree value results in six smoothing groups—one for each side. Entering 90 degrees or higher gives one smoothing group to all faces, and 0 degrees removes all smoothing.

AutoSmooth is only of use if the mesh's faces form angles that are consistent with their smoothing needs. A mesh that has many 45 degree chamfers—some of which need to be smoothed, while others need to stay sharp—is an example of a poor candidate for AutoSmooth.

If you want an entire mesh to be smooth, simply assign the element one smoothing group. If you want particular sections of a mesh smoothed and the mesh is fairly consistent at its corners, assigning smoothing groups by hand is more accurate and will result in a minimum of groups being applied. (AutoSmooth has a tendency to assign redundant smoothing groups.) If an object is not supposed to be smoothed, such as a box or most buildings, you should remove all smoothing groups rather than use AutoSmooth to assign one group to each plane.

Choosing, Showing, and Acquiring Smoothing Groups

The choice of which smoothing group number to use is arbitrary. The 32 group numbers are only a means to make smoothing assignments more obvious and possibly effective. A common modeling technique is to use one smoothing group constantly for objects that are rounded, and have only one group. If this is group 1, then the other 31 are for specific smoothing occurrences. Another technique is to use sequential groups for each object. (ObjectK7, for example, might use groups 2, 3, and 4; ObjectA4 uses 5 and 6; ObjectM3 uses 7–12.) The order just happens to be the sequence in which they were picked for smoothing. Giving specific smoothing groups in this manner enables you to isolate those regions of the mesh easily with Surface/Smoothing/Show.

Because smoothing groups have such a dramatic impact on the rendered image, it becomes very important to know where these groups are assigned. The Surface/Smoothing/Show command creates a selection of all faces that contain the groups that you specify to "show." This is a face selection only, and neither the object definition nor its vertices are selected.

The AutoSmooth function is a great time saver for large meshes, but its Odd streaks and overly darkened edges are often signs of incorrect smoothing assignments. If an object does not seem to be rendering correctly, check to see that its smoothing group assignments are appropriate.

Smoothing/Acquire can be used to check the smoothing group assignments for a specific face. After you select a single face, the smoothing groups assigned to it are displayed. You can click on one of the groups to choose it as the current smoothing group.

Smoothing Group Strategies

Assigning smoothing groups really can be a study in face selection. Getting the selections required for certain effects can involve multiple select, deselect, invert, freeze, and hide procedures. Keep in mind the capability to select faces by their smoothing group with Surface/Smoothing/Show, the Invert Selection option, hiding faces or elements, and selecting twice to deselect.

The number of smoothing groups you need for an element varies, but it rarely will exceed three. Do not be overwhelmed by the fact that 32 groups exist and that 3D Studio uses most, if not all of them when it assigns smoothing. Remember that the program assigns smoothing to all faces, even if they are flat and not smoothed. To keep them flat, 3D Studio cycles through many group assignments so that similar groups do not have a chance of touching and becoming smoothed. Because you know what is planned for the mesh, you do not have to assign nearly so many groups. If part of a mesh is going to be flat, then you do not have to waste any time assigning smoothing to it. When performing custom smoothing, it is usually best to start fresh by clearing all smoothing groups from the object, element, or faces.

It is easy to assign or clear the wrong smoothing group. It pays to always check which group is current before acting. An easy mistake is to think that the smoothing group you just showed with the Surface/Smoothing/Show command is now current—it is not. The current smoothing group is set only by selecting it with the Surface/Smoothing/Group command or acquiring it from a face with Surface/Smoothing/Acquire.

You also can easily get confused as to what groups already are assigned. The three selection groups are good organizers for this information. Use Surface/Smoothing/Show to select a respective group and store this selection for reference as you assign groups.

Note If the smoothing for your mesh does not render properly, check for adjacent faces that might have non-welded, coincidental vertices.

Assigning Smoothing Groups for Effect

You can create many different effects on the same mesh when series of faces are assigned different smoothing groups. The following exercise demonstrates how using smoothing can dramatically change the rendered appearance of the same meshes.

Varying a Geometry's Appearance with Smoothing

*Begin by creating a 24-segment smooth L-Sphere in
the Top viewport and name it Ball01*

Choose Surface/Material/Show	Displays Show Material dialog box with only one group assigned
Select the assigned smoothing group and click on OK	Selects all the sphere's faces
Copy the sphere to the side as a reference as Ball02	
Choose Surface/Smoothing/Object/Clear All *and select Ball01*	Discards the object's smoothing groups, although nothing visually occurs
Switch to the Front *viewport and deselect every other horizontal row of faces on Ball01*	

The sphere now has stripes of selected and deselected faces, as in figure 10.42.

Choose Surface/Smoothing/Group *and click on group 9*	Makes group 9 smoothing current
Choose Surface/Smoothing/Face/Assign, *press* (Spacebar)*, and click in the current viewport*	Assigns smoothing to group 9 to the selection
Check for adequate lighting and render the view	

Ball02 is smooth, but only every other ring within Ball01 is smooth.

Copy Ball01 to the side as Ball03 and freeze both the new sphere and Ball02	Prevents Balls 2 and 3 from being affected by the following exercise step
Invert the selection, set the current smoothing group to 10, and assign it to the face selection	
Render the view again	

Ball02 now has smooth rings that connect with ridges, as shown in figure 10.43.

Although these effects are interesting, more can be created when the faces are selected radially as well.

Copy/Clone Ball01 to the side as Ball04 and freeze the new sphere	Preserves the sphere as Ball01 continues to be manipulated
Remove Ball01's smoothing by using Remove All	
Switch to the Top *viewport and select every other wedge of faces using a* Fence/Window *in a radial "bow tie" fashion*	

continues

Figure 10.42
The selection of
every other ring
on a sphere.

Group 10

Group 9

Group 1

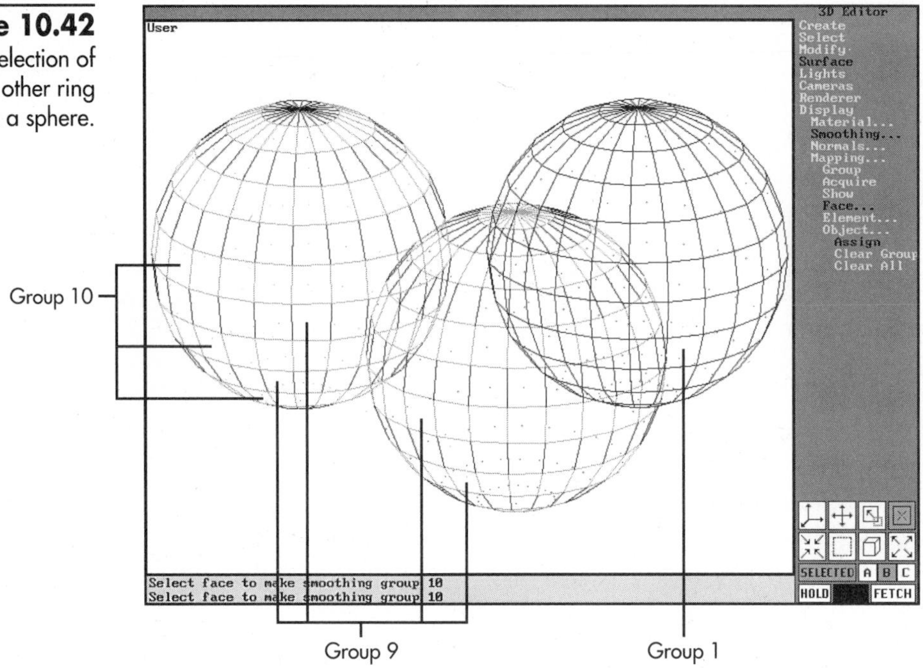

Figure 10.43
The rendered
effect of
smoothing every
other ring on
a sphere.

continued

*Set the current smoothing group to 17 and
assign it to the selection of faces*

Render the view

Every other "hoop" of faces is rendered smoothed.

Copy/Clone Ball01 to the side as Ball05 and freeze the new sphere	As always, Ball01 stays to be worked on
Use Select/Invert to select the other faces, choose smoothing group 18, and assign it to the selection	Every face now has a smoothing group, as shown in figure 10.44

Render the view

Ball01 now has vertical ridges separating its smoothed faces, as shown in figure 10.45.

So far, only one smoothing group at a time has been acting on the faces. By assigning additional groups, smoothing gets broadened and nonsmoothed areas more suspect.

*Copy/Clone Ball01 to the side as Ball06
and freeze the new sphere*

*Click on a different selection button to
clear the selection*

Show smoothing group 18	Selects the faces of smoothing group 18

Choose Surface/Smoothing/Face/Clear All

Press Alt+N	Deselects all faces

*Switch to the Front viewport and select every
other horizontal row*

Set smoothing group 19 current and assign it to the selection of faces	The horizontal bands are assigned the selection

Render the view

Ball01 renders smooth with square "flat spots" where no smoothing was assigned
(see fig. 10.46).

Two smoothing groups actually are acting on the facets where the sphere's smoothing group rings overlap. This has no effect other than telling the faces to smooth. The rendered effect of the sphere would have been the same if the smoothed faces would only have been assigned group 18, for example.

Figure 10.44
More smoothing
variations for
the spheres.

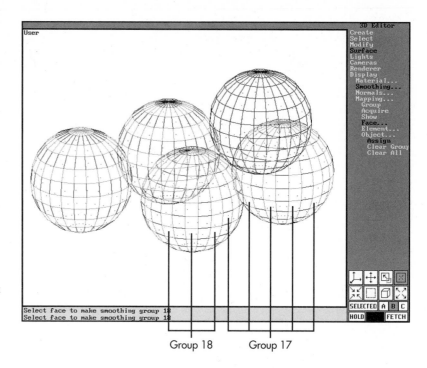

Group 18   Group 17

Figure 10.45
The rendered
effect of smoothing
every other
"wedge" on
a sphere.

Figure 10.46
The final selection of consistent smoothing variations.

The effect on smoothing is most dramatic with metal materials and especially those that use reflection maps. Figure 10.47 shows the effect on the spheres in the previous exercise with the CHROME GIFMAP material assigned to them.

Figure 10.47
The rendered effect of spheres with selected nonsmoothed areas.

III

Advanced Modeling

The process of careful smoothing group assignments could keep on going. Imagine a sphere that had its facets diagonally smoothed. Although a difficult face selection, the result would be spirals. Proper smoothing group assignments cannot be overemphasized. The most carefully prepared model will not look convincing unless it has been properly smoothed.

The deliberate application of smoothing can obviously have a powerful modeling effect. The preceding example showed how simply assigning different smoothing groups makes the same meshes appear radically different. Keep this in mind whenever creating a model and especially when assigning its smoothing groups. Also remember that smoothing can only occur across a contiguous mesh—an element. The ability to smooth should be a primary concern when detaching faces' form meshes to become separate objects/elements. While these new discrete meshes now have the ability to have independent mapping assignments, they will not be capable of being smoothed with the mesh from which they were detached.

Eased Edges

Most real-world objects do not have severe right angles. It is difficult to manufacture such items and keep them square thereafter, and generally is considered unpleasant from a tactile sense. To make objects appear real, you can round their edges slightly—often referred to as an *eased* or *chamfered edge.*

Applying smoothing to right-angled elements has quite a different result, however, as 3D Studio attempts to make the corners spherical. If faces of a square-edged element appear to have extreme dark and light bands, check to make sure that a smoothing group has not been assigned by accident. Because you cannot control the degree of smoothing, you must model an eased edge and carefully assign its smoothing.

To simulate an eased edge, you must model a small chamfer (see fig. 10.48). The larger the chamfer, the more pronounced the round edge. Chapter 5 showed methods for using a Boolean subtraction to create a quick chamfer on the side of a right-angled object. If this chamfer is relatively small, and it and the adjacent two sides are assigned common smoothing groups, the result is an eased edge, as shown in figure 10.49.

Chamfering is just one example of when additional faces are needed for a mesh to render with the correct smoothness. Whenever faces meet at an acute angle, the effect of smoothing is radical. An airplane wing is a good example of this. Figure 10.51 shows the effects of the plane's wing having a chamfered or knife edge. The left wing renders correctly, whereas the right wing is trying to curve below itself to complete the acute angle's smoothing. Figure 10.50 shows a close-up of the two wing tips and illustrates how the simple addition of a bevel in the mesh makes all the difference in the finished image.

Chamfered edges

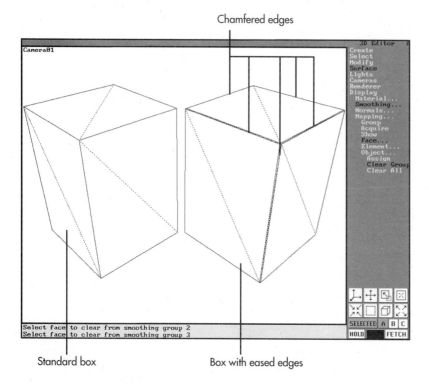

Standard box   Box with eased edges

Figure 10.48
A box that was given small chamfers at its corners.

Figure 10.49
The rendered effect of eased edges versus square edges.

III

Advanced Modeling

Figure 10.50
Detail of the left and right airplane wing tip meshes.

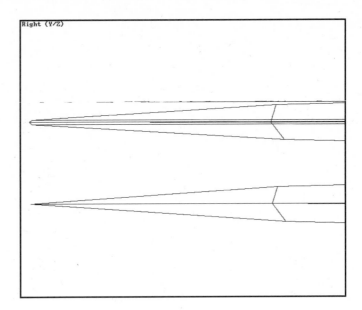

Figure 10.51
The effects of smoothing on acute angled meshes.

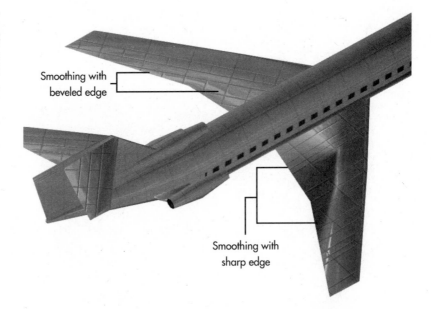

Smoothing with beveled edge

Smoothing with sharp edge

Face Normals

Face normals determine which side of a face can be seen. In doing so, face normals are used by several functions both during rendering and modeling as references for basing the commands' operations. Normals determine too much within 3D Studio to be ignored by always resorting to the Two-Sided rendering mode as a supposed "shortcut."

Face normals also are consulted by some modeling commands for their controlling vectors. These are most notably the Create/Object/Boolean and Create/Face/Extrude commands. Both of these base their results on the directions the normals are facing.

Some SXP textures are also dependent on correct normals. These textures might seem to render erratically if a mesh's normals are inconsistent. Many procedural and animated Plug-Ins (PXPs and AXPs) base their effects on the normals of the mesh. To have these routines operate correctly, the mesh must have unified normals.

Face normals are read by the program several times during the rendering process. Face normals determine the visibility of the face for the view, and their visibility to each shadow casting light and auto reflecting surface.

Unifying Normals Versus Two-Sided Materials

Objects created within 3D Studio are characterized by having correctly faced normals. The program assumes that anything created is to be looked at from outside the object, not from its inside. Infinitely thin meshes that render in one direction are not always what you need, however.

At times, you might want to enter an object, such as going into a room. At other times, you can see the interior of an object through holes or windows within it. Other modeling programs that create DXF files (such as AutoCAD) have no method for facing normals, and their meshes might need correcting. You then must weigh the time it would take to model the inside of the objects, and/or flip their normals correctly, against the speed lost in rendering and the need to perform Boolean operations on them.

It is easy to make the conclusion that a 2-Sided material only takes twice the resources to render as a one-sided material, and is thus not too much of an expense. Reality shows, however, that closer to four times more faces are calculated by the Renderer, by each shadow casting light and by each reflecting surface within the scene. This is a result of rendering both sides of what is facing you (2×), and then both sides of what is not facing you (perhaps an additional 2×, but possibly more).

You always have the 2-Sided option to render both sides of a face, and thus skip the time required to correct face normals. This can be done by the property of a material, or the Renderer can be forced to treat the entire scene as two-sided. This modeling "shortcut" does cost rendering time since each face is calculated in both directions. The memory requirements of the two sided option will have an increasing impact if your rendering is casting shadows or calculating reflections.

2-Sided materials do have many applications that are needed. Certain materials' natural properties, most notably glass, require a 2-Sided material to be believable. Meshes visible on both sides and not close enough in the scene to be perceived as infinitely thin (such as leaves, flags, paper, cloth, and bags) are also good candidates for two-sided materials. The backs of objects that reflect into mirrors are often given 2-Sided materials to make up for their one-sidedness. Finally, you can assign 2-Sided materials to specific, troublesome objects that refuse to render correctly without having to render the entire scene in Force 2-Sided mode.

Unifying Normals

The Surface/Normals/Object Unify command is used to reset an object's normals according to 3D Studio's default—reorienting the normals to face out from the object's center. For this procedure to work correctly, an object's faces and vertices must already be ordered properly. Within each element, every face that shares an edge with an adjacent face must also share two vertices. A misleading situation is when adjacent faces have coincidental vertices and appear to be welded. If an apparently correctly built mesh is having problems with normal unification, ensure that its vertices are actually welded. If this principle rule is not followed, 3D Studio finds it difficult to locate a common centroid and determine which way is "out."

Objects that have disjointed elements, or elements facing different directions, might have trouble being unified. Many times it pays to Detach the elements, Unify, and then Attach them again. It is possible that the result of Object Unify orients a mesh's normals in the wrong direction. When this happens, you must flip the face normals at either the element or face level.

Strategies for Flipping Normals

Although the term *flipping normals* may sound like a game, it can be a frustrating and somewhat time-consuming endeavor. Applying and combining several face selections techniques and display options is the usual method for attacking this chore. As a rule, the Backface display mode should be on when flipping normals. Not only do you need to see the directions of the faces, the program will only flip the normals you tell it to while displaying in Backface mode.

Begin by isolating your object and examining it to determine which way it should face. If the majority of the mesh is facing the wrong direction, then flip all the faces with either Surface/Normals/Element Flip or Surface/Normals/Object Flip. Select the incorrectly oriented faces by whatever means is most expedient for you. After using the Face Flip command to flip your selection, it is common to miss a few faces or flip some the wrong way—you are at least narrowing it down. As your mesh's direction becomes more cohesive, you might find it easier to flip faces that are facing you rather than away from you. Switching your view to see the object's backside can aid in this. (If, for example, you are flipping the normals of a flat plane in a Top view, switch to a Bottom view to see the remaining ones.)

 A visualization aid for face flipping is to perform an Object or Element Flip so that you are working "backward"—flipping faces you can see rather than those you cannot. After you flip all visible faces, simply flip the entire object or element back again.

Modeling with Procedural Plug-Ins

External processes, or Plug-Ins, provide extremely powerful modeling tools. The procedural modeling tools—those that affect the physical geometry of the mesh—make up the PXP branch of the external processes. These programs work within the 3D Editor and either affect the geometry of existing objects, create iterations based on existing objects, or create iterations for use as morph objects. Just because these routines are intended to create meshes for morphing animations does not mean they should not be used as a means to create the mesh outright—many procedural Plug-Ins make superb modeling tools.

Geometry Creation

Two basic *Procedural eXternal Processes* (PXPs) Plug-Ins are included in 3D Studio that actually create an object from scratch, without an object reference—GRIDS_I.PXP and GEARS_I.PXP. Although you might have limited use for creating gears, the cubes and planes created with Grids are often useful as the starting point for other meshes. The Grids routine is so useful that it is questionable why it was not included in the core code as an extension to the Box command.

You can use Grids to create a planar mesh by giving it a zero value for one of its axis grid numbers. Generic planes of sufficient complexity created in this manner can be transformed into unique objects with the vertex and editing commands discussed in this chapter.

Many other Plug-Ins exist that create meshes parametrically, but you must purchase them separately from third-party developers. Ones currently on the market include the capability of creating trees, shrubs, chains, fractal terrain, and fractal grids. Such routines often can assign mapping and materials at the time of object creation, which can be an enormous time saver.

The attention to detail and true character of the procedural meshes rely, of course, on the program's creators. Many routines have a feel about them that make their meshes identifiable. The correct one to use is based on the needs of your application.

Figure 10.52 shows just a few examples of what is possible with the Yost Group's Silicon Garden suite of procedurally created meshes. Other companies, most notably Schreiber Instruments' Imagine Nursery, provide other resources for creating trees and shrubs.

Figure 10.52
Landscape
vegetation
created with
Silicon Garden.

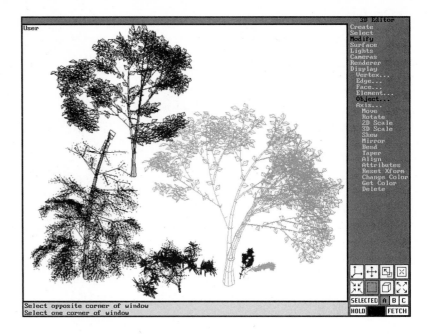

Morphing Objects as an Editing Tool

Other PXP Plug-Ins included with 3D Studio create morphs of an original object, which can become quite valuable as meshes in their own right. Release 3 and 4 include three useful PXP's: JUMBLE, WAVES, and RIPPLE. The effects of these commands vary considerably, depending upon the parameters you assign to them. The possible results are so diverse that you should experiment with them at length to master their capabilities. Figure 10.53 shows how the lower object was transformed into a random assortment by using JUMBLE.PXP and the box at the top of the screen as a reference object.

Numerous routines are available to melt, twist, stretch, and crumple any given mesh. If you create meshes that rely heavily on curved meshes, you should seriously consider purchasing these additional routines. Figure 10.54 shows how using the Yost Group's STRETCH.PXP can transform a simple torus into more sophisticated shapes with different parameters and template objects. As with most PXP's, you can create a number of meshes stretched to various degrees for use as morph objects.

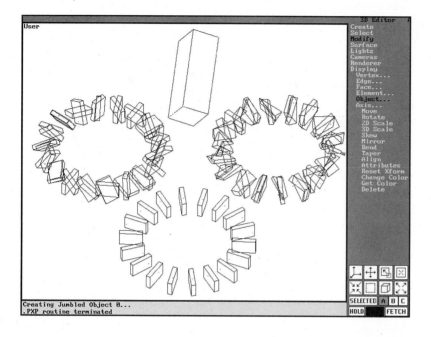

Figure 10.53
Some effects of
using JUMBLE.PXP.

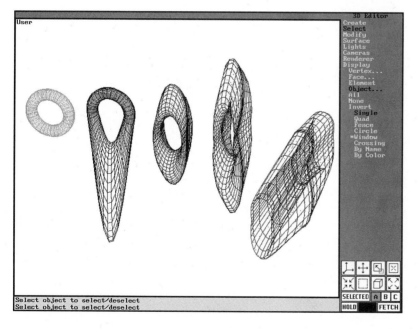

Figure 10.54
Using
STRETCH.PXP
as a modeling
deformation tool.

III

Advanced Modeling

Summary

The similarity between 3D Studio's modification commands sometimes hides the subtleties possible when the same commands are used at different mesh levels. This chapter explored those differences and pointed to a theme that runs through all 3D Studio commands. No matter how basic the command, complex the mesh, or intricate the selection, you always are manipulating vertices. As vertices are manipulated, the faces welded to them are affected. Keeping this in mind when performing any manipulation, at any level, aids in determining which command is best and at what level it should be performed.

A good working knowledge of face and vertex commands is essential when bringing in models from other programs. These meshes behave differently from those created within 3D Studio. Knowing the basics of how entities function helps you to build these models while in other programs, as well as correct them after they are imported. Chapter 11, "Integrating AutoCAD with 3D Studio," explores the use of AutoCAD as a 3D Studio modeling tool, and the basics you learned in this chapter go a long way toward making those models successful.

The intricacies of basic face and vertex modification are critical in perfecting the effects of materials and catching the correct character of light. These concepts are explored in Chapter 12, "Materials and Mapping," and Chapter 13, "Lighting and Camera Special Effects."

Chapter Snapshot

This chapter includes the following detailed information that is critical to the successful integration of AutoCAD and 3D Studio:

✔ Understanding how the AutoCAD environment relates to 3D Studio

✔ Understanding how AutoCAD DXF entities are translated by 3D Studio's various modules

✔ Learning the differences between DXF interpretation and AutoCAD's 3DSOUT function, and when to use which

✔ Examining AutoCAD modeling techniques to ensure proper face normals in 3D Studio

✔ Organizing AutoCAD DWGs and diverse ongoing projects for 3D Studio models

✔ Using AutoVision for additional 3D Studio integration and understanding what information is interpreted by the two programs

CHAPTER

Integrating AutoCAD with 3D Studio

Although 3D Studio has an impressive modeler of its own, times might arise when you would like to coordinate model building with AutoCAD or perhaps import models created in AutoCAD. This chapter explores how these two programs work together and shows how 3D Studio can significantly increase the model-building capability of AutoCAD itself. This chapter also investigates some of the abilities and entities new to AutoCAD Release 13. It should be noted, however, that this information is in regard to the earliest shipping version of Release 13 and subsequent versions may differ somewhat.

As programs evolve, so do their conventions and abilities. AutoCAD has a long-established history within the CAD world, and includes quite different capabilities depending upon its release. The majority of this chapter concerns itself with the capabilities common to AutoCAD Release 11 and 12. This information is still accurate for Release 13, with the exception of semantics. To reflect its new (internal) method for storing data, AutoCAD Release 13's interface and documentation now refer to what were entities as "objects." This chapter continues to refer to AutoCAD geometry as "entities" because the term "object" conflicts with 3D Studio's and is a departure from earlier convention.

Understanding Why You Should Use AutoCAD

With all the modeling capabilities inherent to 3D Studio, you might wonder: Why coordinate with a CAD program? Several potential reasons lie in waiting, but the real decision is based on each program's capabilities and strengths.

If you already are comfortable with AutoCAD and familiar with its 3D commands, you should build on this knowledge for use with 3D Studio. Just because the 2D Shaper and 3D Lofter exist in 3D Studio does not mean you have to use them. Countless models have been rendered and animated in 3D Studio without ever being lofted.

If you are a veteran AutoCAD user, you might want to continue using it as your principle modeling tool and learn 3D Studio's capabilities piece meal. Nothing is wrong with an approach that enables you to work as quickly as possible. If AutoCAD is more expedient for your work, use it.

Wealth of Information

There is no denying that the use of AutoCAD is extremely widespread. Therefore, it is likely that useful information already exists for the model on which you are working. Many projects progress from the design stages straight to preliminary CAD documents. The early stages are when a visualization is often required and where you need 3D Studio to integrate and expand the existing information so that you can create the visualization.

The database of available information goes far beyond the project at hand. Numerous third-party vendors offer models for AutoCAD incorporation, and many manufacturers provide models of their entire product line free of charge. Governments and municipalities are beginning to record everything around us—from street systems and land contours to demographics and agriculture. You can extract all this information for use in 3D Studio by taking the necessary steps in AutoCAD first.

Third-Party Tools

AutoCAD is an *open-ended* environment that enables you to customize its many capabilities by yourself (with its AutoLISP language) or with the help of third-party packages designed with your application in mind. You will find no real limits to this, as a perusal of available catalogs readily shows. As AutoCAD usage continues to grow, third-party programs developed for AutoCAD modeling are sure to become more and more applicable to your specific needs.

Precision

Despite all 3D Studio's capabilities, it does lack precision. After all, 3D Studio was designed as an animation program, not a CAD package. With video animations, a credo often heard is "If it looks right, it is right." True enough for animations, but unacceptable when exact precision is required. This is especially true for high resolution images where a static printed image is subject to considerable viewer scrutiny. Animation lets you get away with much that would fall apart as a stand-alone image.

There is little debate that AutoCAD is superior in all forms of accuracy. The capability to key enter coordinates, displacements, and angles relative to the world or a point obtained from object snap makes modeling in AutoCAD very precise.

As 3D Studio imports geometry, the values will be somewhat rounded off because the same level of precision is not maintained between the two programs. This should not present too much of a problem since it is consistent and will not vary between the various methods of importing or exporting.

Proper Coordination with 3D Studio

One of AutoCAD's strongest assets is its capability to coordinate with the 3D Studio coordinate system exactly, every time, and without error. The world origin is always 0,0,0 for both programs, and a DXF export always arrives in the same location during a load or merge. This enables the AutoCAD model to evolve, undergo revisions, export changes, and incorporate them seamlessly into the 3DS model. This coordination of extensive material is not easily accomplished in the 2D Shaper due to its vertex limitation and alignment difficulties with the 3D Editor.

3D Studio's implementation of units and scale *will* effect the units and scale of imported models. It is important that the units being used in 3D Studio correspond to those defined in the AutoCAD drawing. In AutoCAD, you draw in generic units, and distances are reported back according to how you want to interpret them (a unit could be an inch or a meter, for example—it's all relative). In 3D Studio, the Units Setup (accessed with Ctrl+U) is a global interpretation and will scale imported files accordingly.

Creating 3D Studio Information within AutoCAD

Besides modeling geometry, AutoCAD Release 13 includes the capability to create lights and cameras, and define simple materials for export to 3D Studio with the new 3DSOUT command. Autodesk's AutoCAD rendering program AutoVision (Releases 1.0 and 2.0) expand this ability by allowing the definition of more complex materials and the placing of mapping coordinates. An earlier Autodesk product, Visual Link, also included the ability to organize the AutoCAD drawing according to 3D Studio Keyframer hierarchies. These options enable AutoCAD users to create much of the 3D Studio environment within AutoCAD, using tools of accuracy such as object snap and custom AutoLISP routines to accomplish difficult or tiresome tasks (arraying 100 lights at radiating angles, for example). As always, the "correct" choice of where to create items for 3D Studio is where it is most convenient for you as a user.

III

Advanced Modeling

Comparing the AutoCAD Environment and 3D Studio

Many similarities exist between AutoCAD and 3D Studio, although you might need to look for them. These similarities occur more because the two programs are based on vectors and faces than the fact they happen to be distributed from the same company. AutoCAD and 3D Studio are created by separate groups of people having different goals for decidedly diverse users having vastly different needs.

Working with AutoCAD

AutoCAD has many of the same geometrical forms used in 3D Studio, but the programs use different names. These differences begin in the way each program stores its information. Whereas 3D Studio has several file extensions (for shapes, lofts, meshes, projects, libraries, and so on), AutoCAD has only one—the DWG (drawing) format. Although AutoCAD can read and write DXF (drawing interchange format) and *International Graphics Exchange Specification* (IGES) files, they are secondary, much larger, and prone to more errors. If you are working in AutoCAD, then you are working in a drawing file.

While the 3DS file format of 3D Studio is available for others to write to (with Autodesk's "3D Studio File Toolkit"), AutoCAD's DWG format has always been proprietary. Because of this, information from within AutoCAD drawings must be converted to another format before it is usable in 3D Studio. The traditional method for this exchange has been through DXF files. AutoCAD Release 13 now includes the ability to read and write 3D Studio's 3DS format directly (the 3DS export/import ability began with Visual Link and continues with AutoVision). This chapter refers to the read and write conversion of files as *exporting* and *importing*.

The manner in which AutoCAD entities are converted varies significantly upon the procedure chosen. There are three methods to export AutoCAD information to 3D Studio (3D Studio's DXF import, the DXF3DS shareware utility, and AutoCAD/AutoVision's 3DS export feature), all of which have different capabilities and meshing results. To understand the differences, refer to the appropriate sections in this chapter on DXF output, DXF3DS, and 3DSOUT.

Understanding AutoCAD Terminology

AutoCAD creates much of the same geometry that you find in 3D Studio, but because it is a different program, refers to them by different names. Knowing the basics of these definitions and how they relate to 3D Studio is important for extracting exactly what you need from the AutoCAD database.

Entities

Every piece of geometry in the AutoCAD environment that you can independently affect is termed an *entity*. An entity can be as basic as a simple point or as complex as a block. The basic modeling entities are points, lines, arcs, circles and 3D faces, and it is from these basic entities that more complex ones are formed. Release 13 includes several new types of entities, listed at the end of this section.

Polylines

Polylines actually come in several varieties. A *2D polyline* is a series of line and arc segments in a two-dimensional plane—much like a polygon in the 2D Shaper. You can give 2D polylines width to make them appear wider on-screen and to plot bolder. You also can give them curve information with Curve-fit and Spline-fit options, which actually create a series of intermediate vertices that control the angle of the curve.

3D polylines are a series of linear line segments that can trace a path anywhere in three-dimensional space, and are not restricted to a single plane as 2D polylines are. While they can be "splined" to approximate curves, they cannot contain true arcs. They also do not have width capabilities, and cannot be given thicknesses without the use of a LISP routine.

Meshes

Entities that form a three-dimensional skin are called *meshes* in AutoCAD. Mesh entities include 3D faces (a single, rectilinear 3D face is equivalent to two 3D Studio faces), polygon meshes, and polyface meshes.

Polygon meshes are actually a form of polyline created by using one of AutoCAD's 3D surface commands. *Polyface meshes* usually are not directly created by the user directly, but rather are the product of routines and programs. 3D Studio exports its mesh to a DXF file in the form of polyface meshes.

Blocks

Blocks, XREFs (externally referenced blocks), and hatches (anonymous blocks) are drawings within drawings. Blocks are used extensively in AutoCAD to conserve disk space. This is done by defining the block once and using it repeatedly, which makes blocks similar to instances in the Keyframer. A key advantage to using blocks is the ability to modify their contents and update all of their insertions.

Entities New to Release 13

Possibly the most significant addition for 3D Studio users is the *3D Solid* (also known as *ACIS* solids). These entities define three-dimensional forms and can be edited with fillet, chamfer, and Boolean operations. These entities always exist in a parametric state while within AutoCAD, and are only converted to mesh form when exported to 3D Studio (with Release 13's 3DSOUT command).

III

Advanced Modeling

Release 13's two-dimensional cousins to 3D Solids are *regions*. These entities define a two-dimensional area and are similar in appearance to 2D polylines. Regions are not created in and of themselves, but rather are the products of simpler geometry (such as polylines and circles). They are important because their boundary represents a mesh for 3D Studio export.

The *ellipse* entity is a true ellipse and replaces the AutoCAD tradition of approximating them with polyline arcs.

The *spline* entity is a fully three-dimensional quadratic or cubic spline (also known as a *NURB*) that understands curvature and continuity and can be manipulated with control points.

The *multiline* entity (also known as *mlines*) consists of parallel lines, which are often used to represent walls, but do not possess any three-dimensional abilities.

Entity Properties

You can give entities certain properties that affect the way they are organized within the database and treated in three dimensions. AutoCAD has many properties that you can assign, but only a few are relevant for export to 3D Studio.

Color

You can assign entities individual color integers from 1 to 255 that correspond to the standard 255 AutoCAD display colors. You also can assign them the By-Layer option (the default), which allows them to accept whatever color is currently defined for the layer on which they reside. The latter is the standard and default method, whereas the former requires you to use the CHANGEPROP command or alter the COLOR variable.

Layers

All entities reside on layers. Although layer names can be quite long, 3D Studio keeps only the first eight characters during conversion. Unlike 3D Studio, AutoCAD is not a case-sensitive environment, and its layer names will be converted to uppercase upon import into 3D Studio.

Layers affect the display of entities within AutoCAD and their export to 3D Studio. Layers that are Off or Frozen are not interpreted during the DXF conversion—entities on such layers are simply skipped by 3D Studio.

Thickness

Many entities are allowed to have a defined thickness. Lines, arcs, circles, and 2D polylines are all eligible for a thickness property. The thickness makes the entity behave in AutoCAD as if it were a mesh, as shown in figure 11.1. This property allows the entity to hide lines in AutoCAD. If an entity's thickness is zero or unassigned, it is considered to be flat. If an entity's thickness property is nonzero (any positive or negative value), the entity is considered by 3D Studio as a three-dimensional mesh.

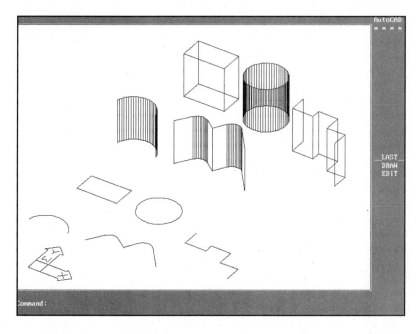

Figure 11.1
AutoCAD entities with and without thickness properties.

Giving an entity thickness has often been termed *extrusion* by users and texts alike. Release 13, however, contains an explicit EXTRUDE command that converts closed entities to 3D Solids. Because this significantly modifies the word's meaning, this chapter reserves the term "extrude" for describing the EXTRUDE command's function.

Color Versus Layers Organization

Two principal methods are widely used to organize information in AutoCAD—by color and by layer. For most AutoCAD users, the primary goal of a drawing is a two-dimensional, hard copy plot. Organizational techniques have thus evolved to coordinate this output according to the pen weights, fills, and colors required of the plots. The organization of the information as a three-dimensional database unfortunately often is ignored in the quest for presentable hard copies.

AutoCAD coordinates plotting by assigning pen numbers to display color numbers. AutoCAD is an 8-bit display environment, so 255 colors are available (because one is the screen background color). You can assign colors directly to entities or to the layer they are on and change the layer's color as needed. When these two methods are mixed, the result can be a very confusing database.

For modeling use, it is highly recommended that you organize drawings according to layer, which enables you to give explicit names to the layers and efficiently control display. If you inherit a drawing based on a color organization, you probably will find that the time spent changing it to a layered organization is made up for in efficiency and ease of use.

Using DXF Files for 3D Studio Import

The principal method for exchanging information between AutoCAD and 3D Studio has traditionally been by converting the native format into a DXF file and letting the other program's DXF translator perform the conversion. There are many translation subtleties and modeling shortcuts that occur at this time. To ensure minimal corrective editing in 3D Studio and maximize the modeling opportunities available, a firm grasp of AutoCAD entities and exactly how 3D Studio interprets its DXF descriptions is essential.

While both AutoVision and Release 13 include the ability to write a 3DS file directly, there are many times when this is *not* the optimal method for conversion. It is still important to understand DXF file transfer to optimize your modeling.

Using AutoCAD's DXFOUT

AutoCAD uses the DXFOUT command to write a drawing's information to a DXF file. The file can be in an ASCII or compiled binary format. The ASCII format is often used because it can be edited manually or created externally by many third-party programs. The DXF file is broken into various sections entitled TABLES, BLOCKS, and ENTITIES.

The DXFOUT command produces the following prompt:

```
Enter decimal places of accuracy (0 to 16)/Entities/Binary <6>:
```

Very different DXF files are produced, depending on which of the following options you select:

✔ The Entities option prompts you to select which entities to write to a DXF file, and then prompts you for the precision of the written file (either binary or a number of decimal places). Doing this creates a file that has only the ENTITIES section, and lists them in the order you select them. Blocks cannot be exported with this option.

✔ If you do not select Entities and only choose an accuracy option (a decimal of accuracy or binary), AutoCAD writes all sections for all entities in the drawing, regardless of whether their layers are frozen or turned off. You must use this method to export block information. The ENTITIES section is listed in the order of creation.

✔ The decimal places of accuracy option parameter refers to how many decimal places are written for every point indication within the database (for example, the point defined with six places as 1.143761,10.37452,100.43981 would become 1,10,100 with zero places). This option creates an editable ASCII file.

✔ The Binary option makes things much easier because it always writes the DXF file to AutoCAD's full precision of 16 places. This file is smaller and can be read quicker, but cannot be conventionally edited.

Although Release 13 has modified the DXFOUT prompt by renaming the "Entities" option as "Objects," it performs as it has traditionally.

For DXF export to 3D Studio, the only question you need to answer for yourself is whether you need to export blocks. If you are not exporting blocks, the optimum choice for DXFOUT is Entities, followed by Binary. This exports only what you need and the entities' order is guaranteed. If you need to export blocks, the optimum choice is Binary. It is unlikely that you will need to edit the DXF file, and the Binary option is quicker to write, faster to read, and takes much less disk space than the ASCII alternative.

3D Studio ignores all entities on frozen and turned off layers at the time of the DXFOUT command, while the locked status of layers has no effect. AutoCAD does not check to see if a previous DXF file with the same name exists when you use the DXFOUT command, so it does not warn you if it is overwriting an existing file.

 Blocks residing on layers that are off at the time of a DXF export will not be interpreted, even if all of their components are on layers that are on.

Entities Incapable of DXF Import

3D Studio's first four modules have varying capabilities as to which DXF entities they can import. Regardless of the module, the following entities can never be directly imported into 3D Studio:

✔ **Release 13's 3D Solids.** These must be written directly to the 3DS format with AutoCAD's 3DSOUT command. Note that this is the only way to physically mesh a 3D Solid.

✔ **Release 13's Regions.** These must either be exploded and made into traditional polylines or exported with AutoCAD's 3DSOUT command.

✔ **Release 13's Ellipses, Splines, and MLines.** These must be either converted to Regions for use by the 3DSOUT command, or saved to disk as a Release 12 drawing (thus converting them to traditional 2d or 3d polylines), brought back into AutoCAD, and exported via DXF.

✔ **XREF entities.** These are externally referenced blocks, which means they are actually separate files. Before 3D Studio can import XREFs, you must insert them into the drawing using the XBIND command.

✔ **Text and Shape entities.** If you absolutely need to import AutoCAD Text or Shapes, you can plot to a DXB file and use the DXBIN command to import the file back into AutoCAD as straight line segments.

✔ **Point entities.** Although points are the equivalent of 3D Studio vertices, they cannot be converted. If you need raw vertex information, you must create a polyline or line(s) and import their vertices instead.

DXF Versions

3D Studio can read any version of the DXF file format that has applicable information. The DXF file written by 3D Studio is in the AutoCAD version 11 ASCII file format and contains only the ENTITIES section. Before you can read a DXF file written by 3D Studio, you must use AutoCAD version 11 or higher.

AutoCAD Release 13's DXF format is significantly different than its previous versions. None of the entities introduced with Release 13 can be read by 3D Studio when written to the DXF format directly.

Loading DXF Files into 3D Studio

When you load or merge a DXF file into a model into 3D Studio Release 3 or 4, you are presented with several options that make a great impact on how the file is converted by 3D Studio (see fig. 11.2).

Figure 11.2
3D Studio's DXF
File Load
dialog box.

DXF Object Definitions

You can organize DXF entities into 3D Studio objects according to layer, color, or entity. *Layer* gives you the most control when you are trying to coordinate 3D Studio with AutoCAD. All entities that reside on a layer are assigned to the same object. The name of the object is the first eight letters of the layer name with 01 added at the end. If the layer name already ends with a numeral, the numeral portion is truncated and replaced with 01.

The truncating of numeric layer names can lead to organizational problems that you should keep in mind when you name layers for informational purposes (for example, the layers PANEL60, PANEL48, STREET42, and PANEL72 are renamed by 3D Studio as PANEL01, PANEL02, STREET01, and PANEL03).

The color option should be the choice only if the model is clearly organized according to color properties rather than layers. Here, the 255 layer colors are made into objects that possess corresponding names (for example, entities that have colors 1, 45, and 252 become objects Color01, Color45, and Color252). The disadvantage inherent in this system is that the object names are not very descriptive of the meshes and provide no assistance for tagging. Cloned objects can further complicate the system by filling in the numeric gaps in the names (for example, a clone element of Color45 would be Color02).

You should use the entity option only with the knowledge that every AutoCAD entity becomes a separate object that begins with the name Entity01. If you are not careful, or not aware of this, you can find yourself faced with an unmanageable number of objects, especially if the model is composed primarily of 3D faces or lines with thickness.

Block entities inherit the block's name as the basis for the object name in the same manner as Layer names. The peculiarity is that all blocks of the same name are considered one entity and thus become one object when imported. Blocks containing multiple layers will create individual objects for each layer.

An undocumented 3DS.SET option forces 3D Studio to sort object names according to case, and then alphabetically. If you add the line SORT-CASE-SENSITIVE = YES to the 3DS.SET file, uppercase letters are sorted before lowercase letters. Because AutoCAD objects always begin in uppercase, this segregates DXF imported objects until you have a chance to check normals, apply materials, mapping coordinates, and signify the update by renaming them to a lowercase name.

DXF Surface Options

You might take the Weld Vertices option for granted, but you should use it with care. It is quite common to stack entities, such as polylines with thickness, on top of one another. Doing so creates many coincidental vertices within the object that will be welded. This can destroy the integrity and cause erratic face normals that would normally face correctly. Unless you know your model does not have such conditions (such as one composed entirely of 3D Faces), you actually should leave this option set to No and weld the vertices selectively at the object or entity level on your own. Choosing the weld option on import does take extra time, especially if the resulting objects are quite large. If models seem to importing very slowly, you might try turning off the Weld Vertices option.

III

Advanced Modeling

The Unify Normals option should always be set to Yes unless you are importing solid models. Setting the option to Yes takes virtually no time at all and can make things much quicker for you when you begin to adjust face normals. Solid models tend to build their faces with correctly facing normals (usually for their own Boolean functions), and they may be incorrectly reset if unified.

The Auto-smooth function works similar to 3D Studio's Surface/Smoothing/Object/Auto Smooth command. Generally, however, it does not do as good a job as you would on your own. Auto-smooth also has the habit of assigning a great number of smoothing groups when few might actually be necessary. Accordingly, it is not recommended to Auto-smooth the DXF file, but you can do so selectively on your own. Oddly enough, choosing No does not prevent 3D Studio from assigning smoothing group information (at least one is always assigned). To prevent 3D Studio from assigning any smoothing, you must choose Yes and reduce the smoothing angle to 0.

Maximum Object Size

Although models in 3D Studio are unlimited as to size, there is a 64 KB (65,536) limit for vertices and faces that any *one* object cannot exceed. (As a rule, meshes usually have far more faces than vertices, so this limit is often termed the 64 KB face limit.) This is rarely a problem within the program, but it can be when you import DXF files whose entities reside on few layers or use few colors. If you exceed this limit during conversion, an error message appears and no part of that object will load. To import overly large objects, you must either divide the object into smaller pieces in AutoCAD before creating the DXF file or use a different DXF importing option (by color if by layer was too large, for example).

Modeling Effects of Entity Conversion

As entities are exported and interpreted by 3D Studio (through the DXF file), they can undergo several transformations. This is not a bad thing because this evolution makes the drawing model more usable and can relieve you of much AutoCAD modeling. The actual way AutoCAD entities convert depends on which of 3D Studio's modules you import them to.

Two primary differences exist between the AutoCAD and 3D Studio modeling environments: 3D Studio categorizes the stages of a model within its various modules, whereas AutoCAD allows all entities to coexist. AutoCAD supports true curves, while 3D Studio must eventually segment them.

It's a good modeling practice to maintain Arc and Circle entities within the AutoCAD model to allow for future modeling and additional DXF exports with varying arc segmentation. The DXF conversions of these arcs can thus have their arc-step segmentations increased or decreased in a manner similar to the shape steps in the 2D Shaper.

Single Polyline Import with the 3D Lofter and Keyframer

The 3D Lofter's Path/Get/Disk and the Keyframer's Paths/Get/Disk commands enable you to load a single polyline from a DXF file. This allows you to import a path to loft along or assign to an object as a motion path. An important concept to grasp is that the coordinate system and orientation of the 3D Lofter, 3D Editor, and AutoCAD are the same. This means that polyline paths, exported from AutoCAD, will create lofted meshes that will align precisely with the remainder of the imported AutoCAD model. You should realize, however, that a path exported from the 3D Lofter to the 2D Shaper will be translated into that environment and will no longer correspond to the rest of the model.

The polyline imported from the DXF file is the last one listed in its ENTITIES section. This is either the last entity created when making a complete DXF export, or the last polyline selected when using DXFOUT's Entity option. In the former situation, the status of frozen and turned-off layers affects which polyline is determined to be last.

If you need to import circles, lines, or arc entities as paths, you must use AutoCAD's PEDIT command to turn them into polylines before you write the DXF file.

The polyline can be either a 2D or 3D polyline. Any thickness, layer, or color information the polyline might contain is ignored. Each of the polyline's vertices convert as a vertex, while any arc or spline-fit information is preserved but converted into steps.

Although the 2D Shaper and Keyframer ignore the intermediate vertices created by Spline-fit, they do create the intermediate vertices defined by Curve-fit.

The 3D Lofter interprets a polyline's arc information in the same way it interprets polygon arcs from the 2D Shaper—by placing steps along the arc according to the Path/Steps setting. The polyline's intermediate vertices are thus converted into path steps, and a Steps setting of 0 makes the path straight.

The Keyframer inserts keys to define the arc according to the total number of frames in the current segment. You place a key at each vertex and any intermediate vertices defined by curve-fit information. If the Keyframer is transforming a curvilinear polyline into straight segments, it is because there are not enough frames available to define the curve. When you import a DXF path to the Keyframer, at least as many frames in the current time segment as there are vertices within the polyline are required. Too few frames results in the error message `Not enough frames in current segment for this path`. To import such a polyline simply increases the number of frames.

Polylines that have been curved with Curve-fit have one intermediate vertex for every vertex over two, which is not evident when you are in AutoCAD. Unlike intermediate spline-fit vertices, curve-fit vertices are always created.

The number of path steps and frames have a great impact on how curvilinear the resulting DXF polyline path is. Figure 11.3 shows the differences the number of frames makes on imported paths. As can be seen, increasing the number of frames makes the imported paths progressively smoother.

Figure 11.3
The resulting paths in the Keyframer with various time segment lengths.

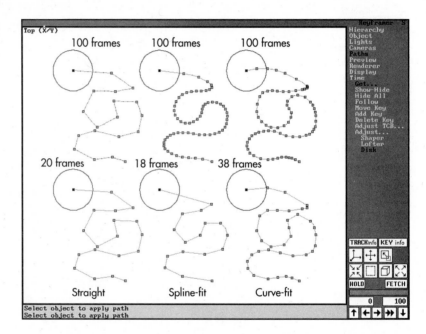

The three paths previously illustrated were created from the same polyline that was spline-fit and curve-fit within AutoCAD. The Spline-fit option actually reduced the minimum number of vertices, while the Curve-fit option doubled it. This also points to an anomaly in 3D Studio Release 3's translator—it always inserted an extra step into the DXF path. This has been corrected in Release 4—DXF paths now import with the correct number of corresponding vertices.

2D DXF Import with the 2D Shaper

The 2D Shaper imports all polygons within a DXF file and converts them into appropriately straight or curved segments. The X and Y coordinates of the 2D Shaper relate directly to those found in AutoCAD's World Coordinate System. When you're in a plan view of AutoCAD's WCS, you are effectively looking at how the DXF information will be interpreted by the 2D

Shaper. Any three-dimensional information, be it thickness or placement, is ignored, and the entity is flattened according to AutoCAD's X- and Y-axis plane.

Circle entities are the exception to the flattening rule, as a true circular polygon is created based on the center and radius every time (they are *not* projected to become "ellipses"). Arcs stretch in the conversion, but as they become linear, they still retain a certain amount of bulge. Figure 11.5 shows the 2D Shaper's transformation of the imported AutoCAD geometry shown in figure 11.4.

For undistorted import into the 2D Shaper, any entities that are not parallel to AutoCAD's World Coordinate System should be rotated to conform before DXF export.

Unequally scaled blocks that contain arc entities will have their arcs interpreted by the 2D Shaper in unexpected ways. To get such entities into the 2D Shaper, first use AutoCAD Release 13's Explode command to return them to simple entities (arcs become splines). Next, use the SAVEASR12 command to convert the splines to polylines. Finally, import the new drawing and create a DXF file of the polylines as usual. Note that this procedure works for converting other Release 13 entities as well.

The eligible entities for DXF import into the 2D Shaper are lines, circles, arcs, 2D polylines, and 3D polylines. The 3D Face, polygon mesh, and polyface mesh entities are considered 3D entities and do not load. Entities new to Release 13 are also incapable of being directly imported (see the preceding Tip). If the 2D Shaper does not find a polygon to import, it issues the error message `Invalid file`. This does not mean the DXF file is corrupt, just that it contains only mesh entities.

You can import block definitions composed of the entities listed in the preceding paragraph if all DXF sections were written to the file. Ineligible entities within the block's definition encountered during the conversion are skipped.

You *can* import the two-dimensional "image" of mesh entities into the 2D Shaper if you convert them to two-dimensional lines before DXF export. This is accomplished by plotting to a DXB file, and then using DXBIN to bring the file back in as lines (note that the imported file will need to be scaled to an appropriate size).

III

Advanced Modeling

Figure 11.4
The original
AutoCAD entities.

Figure 11.5
The Shaper's
translation of
objects that are
not parallel to
AutoCAD's
X-Y plane.

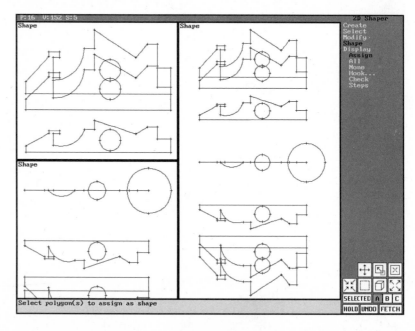

Polylines that have Curve-fit or Spline-fit segments will have their intermediate vertices created. Polyline arc segments are defined by their beginning and ending vertices only (the

RYB

Color Wheel

CYM

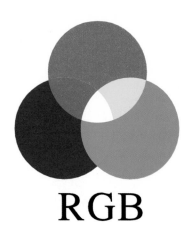

RGB

Top Left: The RYB pigment color model.
Top Right: The traditional RYB color wheel.
Bottom Left: The CYM color model.
Bottom Right: The RGB color model.

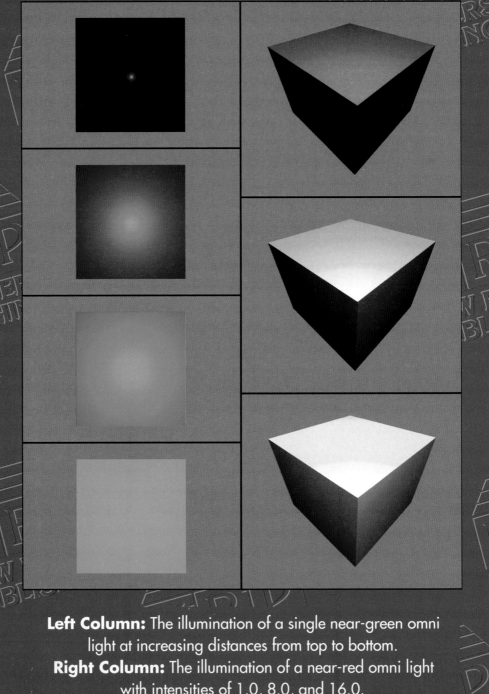

Left Column: The illumination of a single near-green omni light at increasing distances from top to bottom.
Right Column: The illumination of a near-red omni light with intensities of 1.0, 8.0, and 16.0.

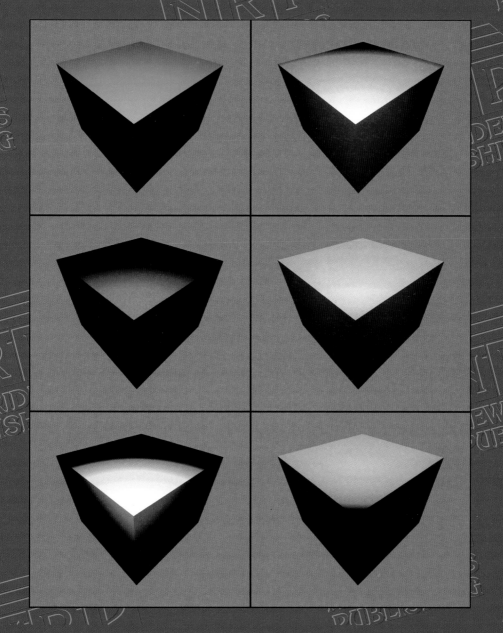

Left Column: The resulting illumination of a white omni light shining next to a near-red omni light with a -1.0 multiplier. The illumination of a closely placed attenuated near-red omni light. The illumination of the same near-red omni light given a 16.0 multiplier.

Right Column: The illumination of a near-red spotlight with an 8.0 intensity whose target is placed at the front corner, middle, and rear corner of the cube's top surface.

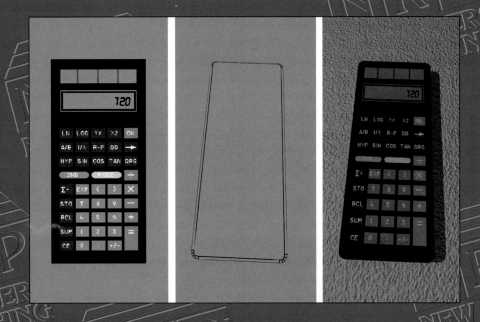

Left: The Animator Pro map with button detail.
Middle: The wire frame model in the 3D Editor.
Right: The rendered object with map applied.

Rendering of the ghost painter model with animated
brush from Chapters 8 and 19.

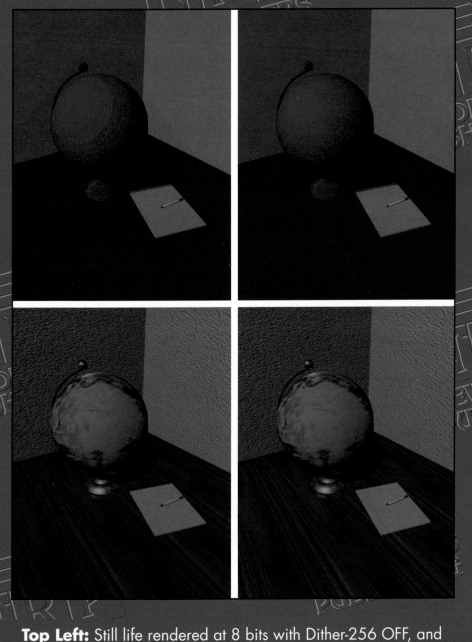

Top Left: Still life rendered at 8 bits with Dither-256 OFF, and no maps. Notice banding on globe and wall surfaces.

Top Right: Still life rendered at 8 bits with Dither-256 ON and no maps. Banding is still evident but dithering softens the edges.

Bottom Left: Still life rendered at 8 bits with Dither-256 OFF and maps applied. The maps hide almost all of the banding; only a little banding is noticeable in the globe base.

Bottom Right: Still life rendered at 24-bit true color.

Sequence of frames showing the "morph" of the duck model
into the vase model from the exercise in Chapter 20.

A simple AutoCAD model instanced in the Keyframer
and rendered with a uniform material.

By: Phillip Miller

The cover for the Executive Summary of the Greater
Rockford Airport Authority's Military Relocation Plan.

By: Phillip Miller (image courtesy of Larson and Darby, Inc.)

The cover for the Greater Rockford Airport
Authority's Regional Transportation Study.

By: Phillip Miller (image courtesy of Larson and Darby, Inc.)

A remote banking facility for the First Bank
of America in Rockford, Illinois.

By: Phillip Miller (image courtesy of Larson and Darby, Inc.)

Magda Pietrasiak's architectural thesis project created while attending the Warsaw University of Technology's School of Architecture.

A visualization study of proposed addition for Rockford Memorial Hospital.

By: Phillip Miller (Image courtesy of Larson and Darby, Inc.)

A landscape rendered by VistaPro and used as a background
image for the balloon model in 3D Studio.

By: Steven Elliott

A Martian landscape created by VistaPro and exported to 3D Studio as a
DXF file. The DXF landscape was used for positioning the robot
walker and for receiving shadows. The robot walker and its shadow were
then composited with the VistaPro rendering of the landscape.

By: Steven Elliott

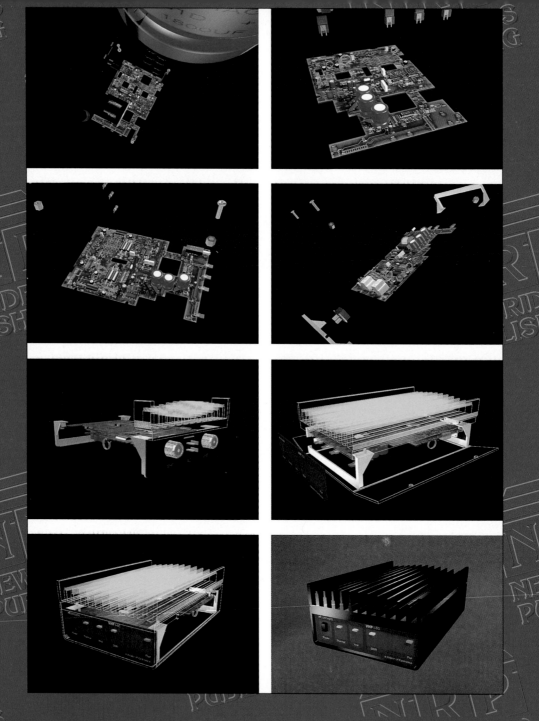

A sequence of 8 frames from an animated assembly of a radio frequency amplifier prototype from its component parts. The animation uses a combination of high-resolution textures and "morphed" materials to blend the heat sink and case from a wire frame to opaque anodized aluminum.

By: Copyright Forcade & Associates

This image uses illuminated mapping and projector spotlights
to create a lighted monument sign at dusk.

By: Copyright Forcade & Associates

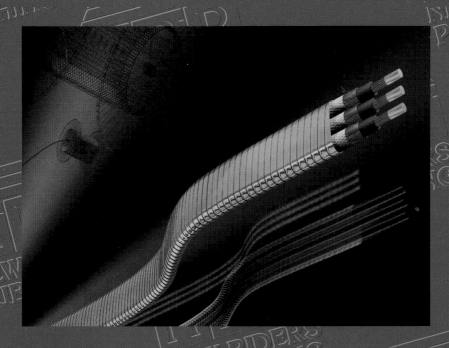

Created for the cover on an 11"x17" promotional piece, this image and
two dozen additional cutaway models were produced for use in print,
multimedia, and video animation.

By: Copyright Forcade & Associates

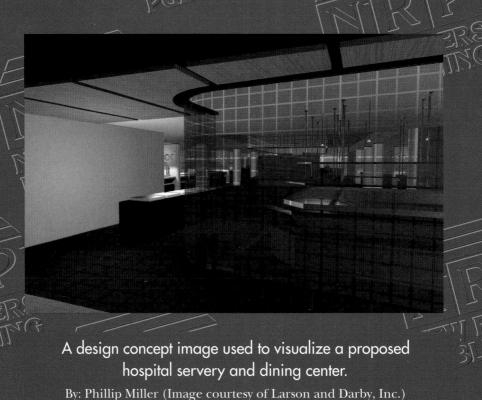

A design concept image used to visualize a proposed
hospital servery and dining center.

By: Phillip Miller (Image courtesy of Larson and Darby, Inc.)

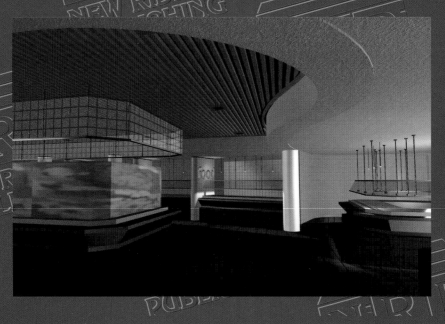

A design concept image used to visualize a proposed
hospital servery and dining center.

By: Phillip Miller (Image courtesy of Larson and Darby, Inc.)

curve information is read directly from the vertex's bulge factor). Any width information contained by the polyline is discarded. Figure 11.6 shows how various polylines are converted by the 2D Shaper.

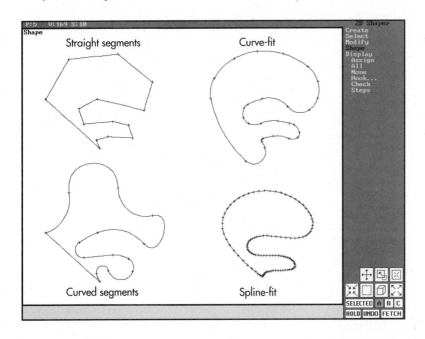

Figure 11.6
The conversion of polyline arc and curve information.

Arcs and circles are converted to polygons that have the additional vertices that would have been included if the 2D Shaper had created them in the first place (that is, each now has four vertices). All curved segments retain the correct relationship to one another and define their curves according to the Shape steps setting.

Polygon definition is determined by what the entity was in AutoCAD. Polylines and circles are imported as polygons. Arcs and lines are imported as individual polygons, regardless of whether they share vertices, are created consecutively, or are the result of an exploded polyline. Blocks that were created by the HATCH command actually are a series of line segments and import as straight, individual polygons.

3D DXF Import in the 3D Editor

The 3D Editor has the greatest capability to convert DXF information since it is converting the data into three dimensions. DXF files can be imported with either the Load File or Merge File command. Since the Keyframer contains the same commands, it imports DXF files in the same manner as the 3D Editor. Because the DXF conversion is identical in either module, the 3D Editor is referenced as the module for three-dimensional DXF import throughout this chapter.

III

Advanced Modeling

The 3D Editor treats the information within a DXF file much differently than the 2D Shaper or 3D Lofter does. AutoCAD's World origin of 0,0,0 is always aligned with 3D Studio's 0,0,0 origin, and AutoCAD's X-Y plane is always equivalent to 3D Studio's Top viewport. Entities always import as they relate to AutoCAD's World Coordinate System and not as they relate to any User Coordinate System that might have been active at the time the DXF file was written. The labeling of 3D Studio's axes has no impact on the DXF file's conversion.

If you intend to integrate AutoCAD with 3D Studio often, you will probably want to relabel 3D Studio's X and Z coordinates to correspond with AutoCAD's. This can be done easily in the 3DS.SET file with impact only on the appearance of the coordinates, not the placement of existing or future models.

The 3D Editor only interprets entities that define a mesh. 3D Studio's definition of what is a mesh is much broader than AutoCAD's since it interprets *any* closed entity as defining a mesh. This means that all closed 2D polylines and circles are loaded as a coplanar mesh as defined by their perimeter. This is equivalent to using Create/Object/Get Shape to import a valid (closed) shape from the 2D Shaper.

Unlike shapes in the 2D Shaper, a closed AutoCAD entity can overlap itself and still be imported as a mesh. 3D Studio does its best to determine what the defining perimeter is, but the result is usually not desirable. As figure 11.7 shows, importing an overlapping closed entity leads to a quick understanding of why the 2D Shaper does not allow this.

Figure 11.7
Importing an overlapping closed entity.

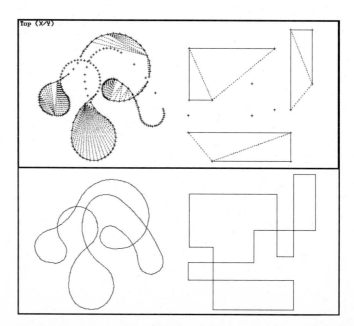

The results of importing AutoCAD entities can be seen in figures 11.8 and 11.9. The technical aspects of the DXF conversion follow:

- ✔ Closed and flat 2D polylines, 3D polylines, and circles import as a coplanar mesh as determined by their perimeter. Polyline arc segments and circles are segmented.

- ✔ 3D Faces import as rectilinear meshes and respect the edge visibility assigned to them in AutoCAD.

- ✔ Solids and traces import as rectilinear meshes having an invisible diagonal edge.

- ✔ Lines, arcs, and open 2D polylines with thickness import as an extruded mesh. The entity appears as in AutoCAD except it now has top and bottom vertices where before it only had one vertex level and a thickness property. The diagonal edge connecting the vertices is always invisible. Polyline arc segments and circles are segmented.

- ✔ Closed 2D polylines and circles with thickness import as an extruded mesh with their top and bottom ends capped as a coplanar mesh. Polyline arc segments and circles are segmented.

- ✔ Traces and solids with thickness properties are extruded and capped top and bottom.

- ✔ 2D polylines with width properties, closed or open, are imported with their widths defining the extents of the mesh. If the polyline has a thickness in addition to a width property, it is widened and extruded along its length.

- ✔ Blocks that have the entities previously listed import their entities as described. Blocks created by using the HATCH command are always composed of separate line segments, so they cannot be imported into the 3D Editor. Such entities could, however, be brought into the 2D Shaper and the 3D Editor.

There are two 3DS.SET parameters that dramatically affect how the preceding DXF entities are imported. The FILL-PLINES parameter dictates whether closed entities are capped. This parameter should always be set to ON so that closed entities, with or without extrusion, can cap. Note that while undesired capping can be quickly deleted, building faces over noncapped sections can be very tedious.

The other parameter is DXF-ARC-DEGREES, which controls the number of segments, or steps, that arcs and circles contain. This parameter has a default of 10 degrees, which means a full circle is imported as a 36-sided polygon. Unfortunately, you can only control this critical parameter by editing the 3DS.SET file prior to your 3D Studio session. This is one reason you might not want to use 3D Studio's built-in DXF translator (see the use of the DXF3DS.EXE utility later in this chapter).

III

Advanced Modeling

Figure 11.8
The basic AutoCAD entities.

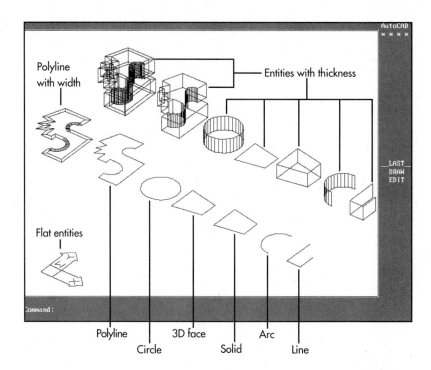

Figure 11.9
The resulting 3D Studio meshes from figure 11.8.

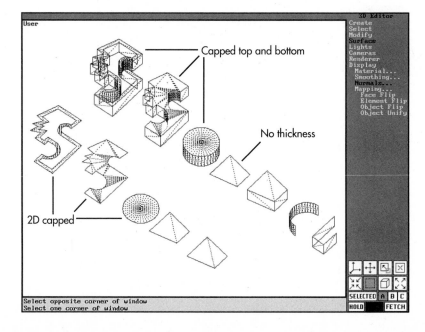

If you save an AutoCAD model to the 3DS format with either AutoVision or AutoCAD Release 13, the arc-step segmentation is a fixed value that cannot be adjusted by the user.

Automatic Material Assignments by Color

When DXF files are converted, 3D Studio looks for materials in the current materials library that begin with the key name COLOR. If such materials exist, the imported entities are assigned the corresponding material based on their color property or layer color. The materials are assigned at the entity level and the process works regardless of the import option chosen.

3D Studio provides a specific library entitled ACADCLR.MLI for this automatic material assignment, which contains 255 materials for the 255 possible AutoCAD display and entity colors. The materials in this library correspond directly to the AutoCAD display colors (for example, COLOR01 is bright red and COLOR07 is white). All materials in this library are Phong and two-sided, but vary in shininess values. Although 3D Studio is making it convenient for AutoCAD models to take on two-sided materials, you should accept the two-sided option only if absolutely necessary. Creating the model correctly, and spending the time to unify normals is usually far wiser than using the quick fix of applying two-sided materials.

You do not need to use the ACADCLR.MLI to assign materials automatically. The key COLOR names work in any current materials library and can actually define any possible material—COLOR01 might represent brick, COLOR03 grass, and COLOR07 plaster, for example. Although using such a library assigns materials automatically on import, it also has the drawback of creating material names without much meaning to others not familiar with your AutoCAD coloring standards.

Unifying Face Normals of DXF Imports

The face normals determined in the conversion process are often considered the bane of using DXF files. You can conquer them quite easily, however, with a knowledge of how they are determined and forethought in the AutoCAD modeling.

Face Normal Determination

The direction of a face's normal is determined in the order in which its vertices are created. Selecting the vertices clockwise is the opposite of a face built counterclockwise. There is no need to consider this while modeling in AutoCAD. When you are modeling, the last thing you need to think about is the order in which you are indicating vertices. It is much more important to create a model that welds properly. Figure 11.10 shows the differences between a correctly and incorrectly modeled opening.

III

Advanced Modeling

Figure 11.10
Correct and incorrect 3D face building methods.

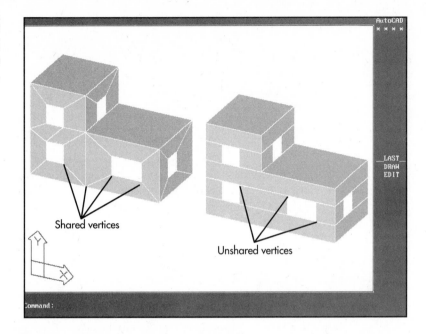

The primary rule of face building is that adjacent faces must share two vertices (that is, an edge) for it to be able to be consistently welded. Only a welded object can have its normals unified automatically, and only adjacent faces that share a vertex can be smoothed across. Remember also that entities must be on the same layer or color to be imported as parts of the same object, and thus be eligible for welding.

Care should be taken if you are using a third-party "automatic" AutoCAD modeler. Many of these modelers give default thickness properties, and create 3D faces or polyface meshes without regard to their rendering ability. You should look carefully at how automatic routines build adjacent faces, making sure that they share two vertices, before investing too much effort with them. It is always faster to build a model correctly, rather than correct the poor modeling practices of an "automatic" modeler. An example of a program that *does* build models correctly for 3D Studio export is FACADE from Eclipse software.

Entities that Import with Uniform Normals

The following entities consistently import with uniformly faced normals (assuming they do not self-intersect):

✔ Coplanar entities that are capped have their mesh faced uniformly. The direction the element faces is nearly random, however, and will need to be adjusted with Surfaces/Normals/Element Flip.

✔ Entities with thickness have their normals facing out in a box-like fashion.

✔ Polygon mesh and polyface mesh entities come in with uniform normals facing outward. This can be a problem for objects created using AutoCAD's REVSURF command.

✔ Solid models usually import with correctly faced normals. This inherent trait could be compromised if 3D Studio's Unify Normals option is chosen.

The troublesome entities then are limited to 3D faces and lines and arcs having thickness. Unfortunately, these entities can make up the bulk of many models. An arc with thickness will have its normals facing away from its center, whereas lines with thickness and 3D faces are seemingly random if they do not join with others to form a resolvable element. The only way to ensure that these entities' normals unify correctly is to build them accurately with aligned vertices following the ordering principals of shared vertices, as described earlier.

For DXF export, the workhorse within AutoCAD often becomes the somewhat humble polyline. Polylines are extremely versatile entities that efficiently define capped meshes and convert with consistent normals. Figure 11.11 shows this technique in the modeling of a building's window openings.

Even when you don't need to cap a polyline, you should really consider closing the entity and allowing it to cap anyway. Doing so ensures that its face normals are uniform and directed out. Selecting and deleting capped faces is much easier than correcting their normals.

Flipping Normals

You almost inevitably need to flip normals when you work with complex DXF files. When objects are derived by layer or color, the direction and extents of all the included entities can become quite diverse and unfocused. This can cause imported models to have initially erratic normals. If the model is built correctly for 3DS import, these normals should be consistent on an entity-by-entity basis and are not difficult to correct.

See Chapter 10, "Creating and Editing Faces and Vertices in the 3D Editor," for face normal flipping strategies.

When flat, closed entities are imported as planar meshes, the direction they face is nearly random. Objects composed of these elements almost always need to be flipped at the element level.

Figure 11.11
Using closed
polylines with
thickness as
building blocks.

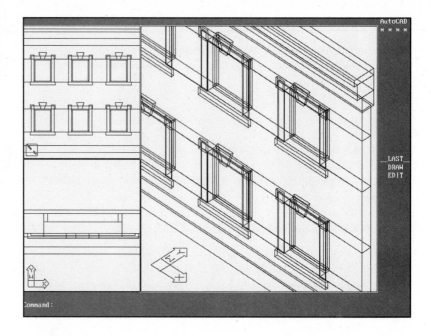

Welding Entities

Only an object that is properly welded can have its normals unified correctly with the Normals/Object Unify command. A standard procedure is to select the appropriate elements or objects and use Modify/Vertex/Weld to weld any coincidental vertices.

You can correct for modeling inaccuracies during a weld by increasing the Weld Threshold value located in the System Options. Analyze the model to determine the maximum value usable without affecting closely and correctly spaced vertices.

AutoCAD Versus 3D Studio Precision

AutoCAD offers much greater precision than 3D Studio, both in its internal database structure and in the tools available for accurate modeling. AutoCAD bases all its real-number calculations on double-precision floating-point values, whereas 3D Studio is single-precision. This is actually only a minor difference because the increased accuracy eventually is rounded off by 3D Studio.

The real advantage of AutoCAD is its capability for exact and relative point placement. If you model in AutoCAD, there is no reason not to do so accurately. The object snap capabilities with OSNAP should ensure that all vertices are aligned and that all faces meet at exact points. The capability to pick points and define command displacements to existing points ensures the proper placement and exact alignment of entities.

Many modelers find AutoCAD a more difficult three-dimensional modeling environment to master than 3D Studio. Its strength is in creating accurate simple geometry, whereas 3D Studio's strength is in creating complex "close-enough" geometry. The strategy often used in AutoCAD is to build the model from many accurately placed "building block" pieces. These are often closed polylines stacked and aligned with one another, or frequently repeated three-dimensional blocks. It should be noted that Release 13's new collection of solid modeling commands could easily make it a robust modeling counterpart to 3D Studio.

Appropriate Arc Steps Using DXF3DS.EXE

3D Studio Release 1 contained a bug that did not let it convert DXF files properly. As a remedy, Autodesk and the Yost Group produced the DXF3DS.EXE utility to convert DXF files to 3DS files from the DOS prompt, which solved the problems the program was having with DXF conversion and gave the user much more latitude as to precision, arc steps, and smoothing. 3D Studio Release 2 fixed the original import bug, but without incorporating all the capabilities found in the DXF3DS.EXE utility. Oddly enough, Release 3 and 4 have not included them either. Because of its capabilities, you might want to use this routine as an additional conduit between AutoCAD and 3D Studio.

 The DXF3DS.EXE utility is shareware, and the latest version is always available on CompuServe's ASOFT forum. The program ships with a comprehensive instructional document that should make its use self-explanatory.

The primary feature contained with DXF3DS to justify its separate use is the capability to define the arc segmentation of each DXF conversion at the command line. This enables you to convert DXF geometry according to the need of its arc step interpretation. This is very useful for making small arc entities coarse (20 degrees to 30 degrees, for example), and large arc entities quite fine (possibly 1 degree or 2 degrees). Getting 3D Studio to do the same requires editing the 3DS.SET file's perimeter and restarting the program for each DXF conversion.

All the standard capabilities of 3D Studio's DXF translator are available and react the same—you just have more control. The DXF3DS routine thus becomes a much used intermediate step between the AutoCAD's DXFOUT and 3D Studio's load or merge.

III

Advanced Modeling

Note DXF3DS works properly within a 3D Studio DOS shell, thus enabling you to make many conversions with varying settings without needing to quit and restart 3D Studio.

Using AutoCAD's 3DSOUT for 3D Studio Import

AutoCAD Release 13 brings with it the ability to import and export 3DS files without having to resort to DXF files for intermediate conversion. While this is a welcome ability, there are significant differences between the two methods that must be realized before one is chosen as the default export option.

How 3DSOUT Differs from DXF Conversion

AutoCAD Release 13 bases its 3DS translator on the same one initially introduced by Visual Link, and then modified by AutoVision. The 3DS conversion capabilities of AutoVision 2.0 are identical to those of Release 13's core code for mesh interpretation (AutoVision enables material and mapping information to be written to the 3DS file as well).

Things are exported by Release 13 in the manner that they render within AutoCAD. If you perform a Hide, Shade, or especially a Render within AutoCAD, you will see how those entities will be exported by the 3DSOUT command. Conversions that are specifically different include the following:

✔ Closed entities (polylines, ellipses, splines, and mlines) are not capped, regardless of thickness property. Closed 2D entities can be meshed if they are converted to Regions. Polylines with thickness must be extruded to form 3D Solids instead.

✔ Circles are capped, but have a "fan-like" mesh rather than a center vertex, as they do by DXF conversion.

✔ Circle and arc segmentation is based on the VIEWRES variable, with a maximum arc-step of 10 degrees.

✔ ACIS entities (3D Solids and Regions) are converted to meshes, but with limited control over their density (see the following).

✔ Edges are always displayed (DXF conversion retains the original edge visibility seen within AutoCAD).

To be somewhat consistent with traditional 3D Studio import, you might find yourself converting many entities to Regions and/or extruding them into 3D Solids. Two new AutoCAD variables will influence your success in doing so.

The first variable to be aware of is *OBJDEL* (for "Object Delete"). When **OBJDEL** is set to 1, entities are deleted when they are transformed into Regions and 3D Solids. This is not always desirable, since it's very convenient to keep both versions of the entity—one for editing and the other for exporting. Setting **OBJDEL** to 0 will preserve the original entity during a Region or Extrude operation.

The second variable, critical to mesh density, is *FACETRES* (for "Face Tessellation Resolution"). The FACETRES variable is stored within the drawing and is referred to whenever Regions and 3D Solids are called upon to be meshed. This occurs at rendering time and, more importantly, when writing 3DS files.

There is no need to mesh the Release 13 wireframe models before export as there was with the older AME models. The 3DSOUT command does the meshing for you. While this process is easy, you do not have a tremendous amount of control over the resulting mesh density. The governing FACETRES variable has a range of 0.01 to 10.0. The resulting mesh density will vary somewhat within this range and is influenced to some extent by the viewport's resolution of the mesh. Typical mesh densities resulting from various FACETRES settings are shown in table 11.1.

Table 11.1
Mesh Results from FACETRES Settings

FACETRES Values	Typical Arc Step per 90° of Arc	Resulting Circle Mesh
0.01–1.0	1 segment	4 sides
1.01–2.0	2 segments	8 sides
2.01–3.0	4 segments	16 sides
3.01–4.0	8 segments	32 sides
4.01–8.0	16 segments	64 sides
8.01–10.0	32 segments	128 sides

While these values are approximations, the resulting arc step increment for 90-degree segments is always in powers of 2.

It's extremely prudent to confirm the FACETRES value before using the 3DSOUT command. The following AutoLISP routine examines the current FACETRES value, enables you to change it, and executes the 3DSOUT command:

```
(defun c:3dso (/ orig new ask)

    (setq orig (getvar "FACETRES")
```

III

Advanced Modeling

```
                              ask  (strcat "\nNew FacetRes Value <" (rtos orig 2
        ➥2) ">: "))

            (while (/= orig "end")

                  (setq new (getreal ask))

                  (if (not new) (setq new orig))

                  (if (or(> new 10.0)(< new 0.01))

                        (prompt "\nFacetRes range is 0.01 - 10.0")

                        (setq orig "end")))

            (setvar "FACETRES" new)

            (princ"\nBegining 3DSOUT")

            (c:3DSOUT)

            (prin1)

      )
```

When to Use 3SDOUT Instead of DXF

Although Release 13's 3DSOUT feature has some accuracy limitations that DXF conversion does not, it definitely is useful, if not essential, for exporting certain AutoCAD information, as described in the following points:

✔ 3DSOUT is currently the only method to create a mesh of a Region or 3D Solid. Once you understand the nuances of the FACETRES variable, this 3D modeling ability is extremely valuable. Modeling with 3D Solids can make quick work of tasks that are nearly impossible in 3D Studio (filleting an angled cylinder with a cone, for example).

✔ 3DSOUT is the only way to export lights and cameras. AutoCAD Point Lights and Spotlights correspond to 3D Studio Omni Lights and Spotlights. AutoCAD's Distant Light is converted to a 3D Studio spotlight as well. Cameras are defined in AutoCAD as any saved view created by the DVIEW command.

✔ If your model does not depend on capping or accurate arc segmentation, the 3DSOUT command is a definite shortcut to the two-step DXF approach and will deliver the same results.

When to use DXF rather than 3DSOUT

Several situations arise when you may prefer to use the traditional DXF method of exchanging information with 3D Studio, as follows:

✔ **Arc segmentation.** If you have arcs in your model and want control over their smoothness then DXF export is your only choice (with the DXF3DS utility providing maximum flexibility).

✔ **Capping.** If your model depends on 3D Studios traditional method of capping closed entities, then you must use DXF export. Since Release 13's new entities are not currently read by 3D Studio, it may be necessary to convert them to Release 12 entity equivalents with the SAVEASR12 command (if you wanted to cap a Release 13 ellipse, for example).

✔ **Shape and Path export.** Currently, DXF remains your only tool for exporting geometry to the 2D Shaper and paths to the 3D Lofter or Keyframer. The new Spline or Ellipse entities can be used as paths or shapes if they are first converted to their Release 12 entity equivalents, as mentioned previously. Splines convert fairly accurately to 3D polylines, which can then be "splined" for even smoother curvature.

Understanding AutoCAD and 3D Studio Coordination

The successful coordination of evolving AutoCAD drawings with corresponding 3D Studio meshes is a matter of modeling organization and using consistent procedures. As projects and their models evolve, a great number of interrelated files—all with different purposes—can be produced. Some organizational forethought is therefore necessary to ensure the proper integration of information.

Layer Organization

When you coordinate 3D Studio and AutoCAD, the most effective method of organization is to do so by layer. The object level in 3D Studio is very important for defining mapping coordinates that relate to the assigned material. Because of this, it makes the most sense to organize AutoCAD layers according to their eventual material assignments. Although this might not be your standard layer organization method, it does break down the model into applicable components quite well.

Project Organization

AutoCAD and 3D Studio work very well together as the drawing database evolves and becomes more refined. The AutoCAD model can continue to change, be modeled, exported with DXFOUT, modeled in 3D Studio, imported with DXFIN, modeled more, exported again with DXFOUT, and so on. The alignment between their coordinate systems is constantly maintained, allowing the AutoCAD database to grow to whatever size is needed—something the 2D Shaper could never do.

As AutoCAD projects become more and more complex, it is useful to save parts of the model that require more detail as separate drawings with the WBLOCK command. As long as the WBLOCK command is given 0,0,0 (the default) for the new drawing's insertion point, the two drawings and the 3DS file align.

Using this multiple file technique, it is quite common to have multiple AutoCAD drawings that correspond to the same 3D Studio model. The following is a sample list of one possible project organization that is designed to evolve with inevitable changes:

✔ **Master Design/Drafting/Engineering Documents.** Used to produce the "product" and in a constant state of evolution and refinement as they near the project's completion.

✔ **Presentation Drawings.** Copies of the master drawings that have been stripped of construction information, such as dimensions and notes, and organized to effectively present the design.

✔ **3D Master/Working Drawings.** Copies of the presentation (or master) drawings that have been stripped of all nonreal items, meaning that all text, dimension, and notational blocks have been eliminated. All entities capable of being made into a polyline with PEDIT are usually done so at this time. Models are constructed accurately, and often assembled in a "building block" fashion.

✔ **3D Detail Drawings.** Drawings that have been extracted from the Working 3D Drawing with the WBLOCK command. These are usually areas or elements of high detail that warrant an independent drawing for speed and ease of modeling.

✔ **Master 3D Studio Project.** The Master 3D drawing is initially imported and becomes the true model of the design. This is where all lights and cameras are placed and materials assigned. As long as the model does not move in 3D Studio or AutoCAD, you can pass the modeling information back and forth continuously with consistent alignment.

✔ **Temporary 3D Studio Meshes.** It is quite common to load DXF files from the 3D Detail drawings as new 3DS meshes. This enables you to weld vertices and unify normals without being encumbered by the size of the overall project. After the mesh is consistent, you can save and merge it into the master project file.

All these drawings and meshes usually are in a constant state of flux. Keeping backups, saving files as evolutions (very convenient with the ⊞ button from 3D Studio's Save commands), and keeping an up-to-date file record are essential for making the design and visualization process work.

A consistently updated notebook dedicated to the project is often considered a necessity by professional modelers working on teams. This allows others to continue work on the project when the original people may be unavailable.

Exporting 3D Studio Meshes to AutoCAD

You often need to export meshes from 3D Studio to AutoCAD, for alignment purposes if nothing else. To export a 3D Studio mesh, save it as a DXF file and use AutoCAD's DXFIN command to import it to the working 3D drawing file.

 3D Studio is used by many modelers as an AutoCAD modeling tool because it caps closed entities in a way that is difficult to achieve using just AutoCAD.

Results of Writing the DXF File

When you save a 3D Studio mesh to the DXF format, you are presented with the options shown in figure 11.12. The DXF file written by 3D Studio has only one AutoCAD entity type—the polyface mesh. The size and layer names of these objects depend on which option you choose.

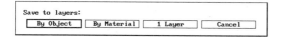

Figure 11.12
The 3D Studio DXF file writing options.

Choosing the By Object option exports a single entity for each defined object on a layer that has the object's name. Choosing By Material exports a single entity composed of all the faces that are assigned the same material on a layer that uses the material's name. Choosing 1 Layer simply exports the entire model as one entity on one layer.

The resulting elements are very different than any element created in AutoCAD proper. Any of these methods will more than likely create single entities of disconnected meshes. 3D Studio elements are not written as individual polyfaces, but rather disconnected pieces of the same object mesh. This is only possible in AutoCAD with the polyface mesh entity and can be a bit surprising since it's unlike any other entity type in the program. All edges that were invisible remain invisible in the AutoCAD mesh.

You can stretch, rotate, scale, and move, but not edit, polyface meshes by using the standard PEDIT command. If you need to separate pieces of the polyface mesh, you must use the EXPLODE command to break it into individual 3D Face entities (much like the 3D Editor's Element/Explode command).

Using AutoCAD's DXFIN

AutoCAD imports DXF files using the DXFIN command. If you use DXFIN in an existing drawing, you are prompted with the warning: Not a new drawing, only entities section `will be imported`. For 3D Studio's DXF files, this is completely acceptable because only the ENTITY section was written originally. Objects import as independent layers, always have the color 0, and are named with either the object or material name.

Using Release 13's 3DSIN

The 3DSIN function in Release 13 definitely makes the process of importing 3DS files easier, but it should not be used blindly. When you import a 3DS file, AutoCAD assumes that you will eventually want to render it. To help you in this effort, it converts any materials assigned within the file. In the process of converting textured materials, it averages the referenced bitmaps to derive an averaged base color for the resulting AutoCAD material. This process can take additional time, especially if there are many materials. If you only want to import the 3DS mesh to AutoCAD, and you're not concerned about losing material assignments, you should consider using the traditional DXF process. Although larger in file size, the DXF equivalent will more than likely load faster into AutoCAD.

If you do intend to render the original 3DS model in AutoCAD, or more likely with AutoVision, then the 3DSIN command is extremely helpful. See the end of this chapter for the particular conversions that occur in the conversion.

Examining Additional AutoCAD Tools

Several additional tools are available for coordinating AutoCAD and 3D Studio. Although many of those mentioned are Autodesk products, it should be noted that there are several third-party programs that provide worthwhile modeling tools.

Customizing with AutoLISP

You can automate many modeling procedures, or at least assist them, by using customized AutoLISP routines. These can be for personal preferences or purchased procedures. A wealth of LISP routines are available from third-party developers and as freeware or shareware on CompuServe's ACAD forum. Although you might not find the exact routine for your needs, the AutoLISP language is fairly easy and other routines can point to methods for writing your own.

More advanced programs are available as ADS programs. These integrate with AutoCAD in much the same way Plug-In works with 3D Studio. These advanced programs are compiled C programs that work in the AutoCAD interface and can provide whatever options the programmers chose to include. Such programs are almost always purchased programs and are rarely freely distributed.

3D Solids in AutoCAD Release 13

Release 13's implementation of 3D Solids makes it a very good companion to 3D Studio. While there is only marginal control over the resulting mesh density, you can create complex models rather quickly. The Boolean tools available are much the same as 3D Studio's, but are more accurate and flexible.

Release 13 also contains certain modeling functions that 3D Studio simply does not have. The ability to perform three-dimensional fillets and chamfers are features that make modeling certain objects quite easy (integrated the spout and handle on a tea pot, for example). The seemingly basic Extrude command enables you to taper as you extrude, and includes the option to "extrude along a path." This last option is somewhat similar to lofting a shape, with one exception—the Extrude command scales the entity as it follows bends in the path to ensure a constant cross-section (something that has to be done by hand for each corner transition in the 3D Lofter).

Autodesk's Designer and AutoSurf

Designer and AutoSurf are AutoCAD software tools designed primarily for the mechanical and industrial design trades that can provide some valuable modeling abilities for creating models for 3D Studio. As of this printing, Designer and AutoSurf have only been released for AutoCAD Release 12, but it is very likely that improvements will be made and additional abilities included for their Release 13 versions.

Designer is a *feature-based, parametric, solid modeler* that enables you to define three-dimensional models through conventional dimensioning and orthographic views. Designer models can then be meshed and exported to 3D Studio for rendering. AutoSurf is different in that it's a *surface modeler* that can literally model "anything." Its results, however, are intended for CAM Tool paths and not for mesh models. Because of this, the meshes outputted from AutoSurf reflect independent surfaces that do not necessarily knit together to form render-ready models. Considering the robustness of these programs initial introductions, their Release 13 versions should definitely be investigated (when available) for 3D Studio integration.

Autodesk's AutoVision

Release 13 includes the new AutoVision 2.0 release in its shipping version. AutoVision is essentially a ray-trace renderer for creating realistic models within AutoCAD. This section concerns itself with what its capabilities hold for a 3D Studio user. Although not the required conduit to 3D Studio that it once was, there are situations when a 3D Studio user may want make use of its abilities.

III

Advanced Modeling

Advantage of AutoVision 2.0

Release 13 included much of the functionality that was before the sole territory of AutoVision. The following features are those that AutoVision has and AutoCAD Release 13's core does not:

✔ Sun location (for a distant light) determined by your placement in the world, date, and the time of day. Accurately placed distant lights can be exported to 3D Studio as spotlights, thus providing a method to approximate a relevant solar shadow.

✔ Precise controls over mapping coordinates using the same three mapping types as 3D Studio.

✔ Mapping at the entity level with the capability to recall previous mapping coordinates.

While 3D Studio's renderer is faster, AutoVision's ray-trace renderer does provide some functions worthy of note that could be used in conjunction with 3D Studio for certain effects, as follows:

✔ The ability to render Release 13's 3D Solids and Regions without meshing them. This ability can make considerably complex solid models manageable.

✔ True ray-trace renderer capable of true multiple ray-traced reflections (AutoVision 2.0's renderer is significantly faster than the original version).

✔ Shadows that respect the color of transparent objects.

✔ Light refraction within transparent materials can be approximated.

Considerations When Using AutoVision

AutoVision's 3DS translator works well, but should only be used in a one-directional situation. Importing 3DS models to AutoCAD for an AutoVision rendering or exporting an AutoVision model to 3D Studio for an animation both work well. Returning the model back to the respective programs as part of a "round trip" is not advised. While the data used by one program is converted fairly well into the other's, there is no attempt at saving what the other program does not use.

When exchanging models between 3D Studio and AutoVision, the original model should not be discarded, but rather should be saved—one program's information is not kept in the others. Returning a previously exported model to the original program will obviously result in the loss of program-specific information.

Before exporting models to AutoVision, you should take into account the abilities that you may take for granted in 3D Studio, which are either impossible within the AutoCAD database or simply not features within AutoVision, as follows:

✔ There is no method for interpreting information at the face and vertex level. Materials and mapping assigned at less than the object level will need to be split into separate objects if their qualities are to be maintained.

✔ All Plug-In APPDATA (such as IK joint parameters and embeded scripts) are discarded upon import into AutoCAD. Though not normally a problem, it could be if you count on them being there for a return trip to 3D Studio.

✔ All Keyframer information is discarded. The model is imported according to its state in the 3D Editor.

✔ All object attributes are discarded (AXP assignments, matte object, and shadow-casting attributes).

✔ Only the properties inherent to AutoVision are kept for imported lights and cameras. Multipliers, exclusion, attenuation, ranges, exclusion, projected images, overshoot, and square cone options are thus discarded for lights, as are ranges for cameras. Again, these properties are not used by AutoVision and will only cause a problem if you are depending upon their existence for a round trip back to 3D Studio.

Summary

The AutoCAD environment is quite different from that of 3D Studio. Each brings with it capabilities the other lacks. AutoCAD is an accurate modeler designed to handle organizations of great complexity that contain numerous types of relative information. 3D Studio is a robust modeler capable of making complex forms easily and animating them. Using these two programs in conjunction provides impressive modeling capabilities, and the capability to connect to countless databases makes dual use very advantageous.

III

Advanced Modeling

Chapter Snapshot

The goal of this chapter is to show you some of the ways of combining the many alternatives now available within the Materials Editor. Specifically, this chapter covers the following concepts:

✔ Using the new texture, shininess, self-illuminated, and specular maps

✔ Understanding Alpha channels and incorporating them within materials

✔ Understanding how masks are interpreted by the seven map types and how they are best utilized

✔ Exploring the many options for reflective materials and for what applications they are best used

✔ Combining IPAS SXP materials for maximum effect

✔ Examining issues to consider and pitfalls to avoid when creating materials for realism

✔ Examining issues of true-color editing and how to use paint programs to coordinate background images and edit bitmaps for proper tiling

CHAPTER

Materials and Mapping

3D Studio Release 3 brought with it several new map types and countless possibilities for combining them. This chapter investigates maps, their use, and the materials that combine several mapping types to create complex and realistic effects. The more advanced features available with masks, Alpha channels, automatic reflection maps, and box mapping also are reviewed. Woven into the discussions of the various mapping types is the inclusion of Plug-In solid-surface procedural textures. As materials incorporate these routines, their effects can be non-repetitive, yet consistent and quite believable.

This chapter shows you some ways to combine the many features now available within the Materials Editor, and hopefully will lead you to an understanding of how to create your own rich, diverse materials.

Understanding the Capabilities of Fully Mapped Materials

The materials described and created in Chapter 6, "Introduction to the Materials Editor," are convincing and quite usable. Because of their newness and special applications, several map types were reserved for this advanced discussion. The use of these advanced map types gives you effects that were extremely difficult, if not impossible, to create in previous releases.

As was discussed in Chapter 6, this book defines a fully mapped material to be one that incorporates the mapping and masking techniques first available with Release 3. The term *fully mapped* implies that a standard mapped material is not complete. After learning about all the additional capabilities in the Materials Editor, it is possible that you might regard this as a true observation. The difference between a "mapped" and a "fully mapped" material comes down to a matter of sophistication.

As you learn the new capabilities now available with maps, the difference between the new and old types will probably become blurred and irrelevant. This is how it should be. Materials used within 3D Studio are in a period of readjustment. Those that worked fine for years can be improved immensely by incorporating newer techniques, and the use of other materials that never before were available will soon be commonplace.

Additional Mapping Types

Release 3 brought with it four completely new map types. Texture was doubled into two maps with numerous combination possibilities. You can now tile and decal within the same material. A shininess map was added to control the amount and location of highlight and shine. A specular map was included to create the illusion of an image reflected in a highlight. And finally, the addition of the self-illuminated map made it possible to control the effects of signage and patterned glass.

Texture 1 and 2 Combinations

The Texture 1 and Texture 2 map types both apply texture maps to the material. If only one is active, their effects are identical. The real purpose of Texture 1 and 2 maps is to be used together, at which point their effects are quite different.

To make sense of the numbering, think of Texture 1 as being applied *first*, and Texture 2 *second*. This means that Texture 2's bitmap always covers any bitmap indicated in Texture 1. If Texture 2's value slider is less than 100, Texture 1 blends with the remaining proportion. (Texture 2 at 60 percent, for example, mixes with 40 percent of a Texture 1 applied at 100 percent.)

The combination of texture maps is very effective when Texture 2 is a single or tiled decal. In this case, Texture 2 sits on the bitmap field defined in Texture 1. The use of these two map types is shown in the following exercise.

Exploring the Use of Two Textures

Begin in the Materials Editor by getting **WHITE PLASTIC** *from the 3DS.MLI*	Renders shiny, white Phong sphere in the first sample window (see fig. 12.1)
Click on the Texture 1 Map *file slot, choose* **ASHSEN.GIF** *at 100 percent, and then press the* (Spacebar) *to render the sample*	Renders the sphere as very shiny wood

This wood looks far too shiny to be real.

Decrease the shininess to 20 and the shininess strength to 40, click on the Soften parameter, and render the sample	Renders the wood much more realistically
Click in the Texture 2 *map file slot, select* **ADESK2.TGA** *at 100 percent, and render the sample*	Renders a black-on-gray Autodesk logo replacing the wood texture

Remember that Texture 1 is applied first, and Texture 2 is applied second. To see Texture 1, you need to see through Texture 2. In addition, the logo seems very large for the material.

Access Texture 2's parameters by clicking on its (S) *button, change it to be a decal, lower its U and V scales to 0.5, and render*	Renders the logo smaller and places it on top of the wood texture as a decal

Although the logo is now on the wood, it does not seem to be a part of it. Cold gray paint is not most people's first choice for applying on wood.

Access the logo's parameters again, and change its source to Luma Tint	Changes the map source to RGB Luma Tint and two color swatches appear, representing the darkest and lightest values
Make the right swatch pure red, the left swatch a very dark red, move up the logo a little by giving it a -0.1 V offset, and render	Renders the logo a little higher on the sphere in a deep red color

Figure 12.1
Six steps in creating a two-textured material from scratch.

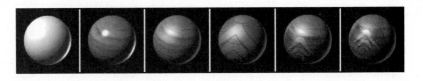

Reducing Texture 2 over Texture 1 has the effect of a transparent wrap over a material. This can be useful for simulating packages wrapped with translucent film or paper. This technique also can be used to blend two bitmaps to form a hybrid variation, as shown in the following exercise.

Blending Texture Maps

This exercise returns to the wood material created in the preceding exercise.

Drag Texture 1's file slot of ASHSEN.GIF *to Texture 2*	Resets the values for Texture 2
Change Texture 2's bitmap to BUBINGA.GIF *and render*	Renders the sphere in a deep red wood grain
Slide Texture 2's strength slider down to 50 and render	Merges the two woods into a new form of wood

If you put this to a scene and examine it closely, you will notice that many of the wood grains clash.

Drag each texture's map file label in turn to View Image	Displays each bitmap file

It is clear that ASHSEN has its grain primarily at the bottom, whereas BUBINGA's is at the top of the bitmap.

Change the Texture 2 (BUBINGA) V Scale *parameter to -1.0*	Mirrors the bitmap in place
Render the sample	Blends the wood's bitmaps together

You could continue this adjustment and mixing for some time—adjusting the strength sliders, tinting each map's source, and allowing some of the material's base color to show through are just some of the possibilities in creating custom wood.

Shininess Maps

Shininess maps are a new and subtle mapping capability. These maps use intensity maps as a guide to which areas of the materials are shiny and to what extent. Black values are matte, whereas white values retain their original shininess. Shininess maps affect the shine already defined by the highlight curve. Using one does *not* make the material any more shiny than it already is—it defines where that shine will be. A material must already be producing a highlight for the map to have a visible effect. If the shininess curve is dead flat, a vertical line, or if the specular color is black, no or very little highlight exists for the shininess map to block.

The map's value slider is the control for how much shine is removed. This is a common need, as intensity maps often are composed with black, and these areas make the material completely matte. Depending on the material, this might not be a realistic situation because in reality, most materials have at least some shine. Throttling back the slider to even 98 or 95 allows a little gleam across the surface.

> Shininess maps have a much greater impact on metal-shaded materials because the material's color is calculated from the shininess properties. Because of this, metal materials show the effects of a shininess map across their entire surface and not just in their highlights.

Shininess maps are extremely useful in adding realism to materials. As a material simulates different effects across its surface, you usually need to vary the shininess for the various parts. Many modelers have ignored this need because the capability was previously just not available. Now that the capability is available, you must understand and use it well.

When used without any other map types, a shininess map makes some areas of the object look shinier than others. Only a few situations exist in which you might want to do this, because you are actually defining shine patterns for a perfectly smooth and consistently colored material. Using the shininess map alone can simulate scraped, scratched, stained, and dusty areas on an otherwise shiny material, or burnished, polished, gilded, and wet areas on an otherwise matte surface. Using the map as both a tile and a decal mode might provide the best results for these special situations.

> Be careful when you use shininess maps as decals at full strength. In such a case, only the area defined by the mapping coordinates receives any shininess values, and the rest remains matte.

A shininess map's greatest use is in conjunction with other map types. It can combine with texture maps to make different areas of the map more or less shiny. The brass dividers in a wood parquet, the gold in a logo decal, chromed fasteners on brushed metal, the polished dots on a watch's matte face, or the glass within a frame are all shinier than the rest of the material.

When combined with bump maps, the shininess map can make raised areas more or less polished, and recessed areas matte. The shininess qualities of a material relate quite often to its recesses and projections. The grooves between metal panels, joints between glazed brick, and cracks in a pot all are matte in comparison to the rest of the material. A shimmer across these areas would spoil the illusion, and reusing the bump map as a shininess map prevents this from happening.

During the life of an object, high spots are subject to daily abrasion. This has different effects on different types of materials. In general, the higher areas of polished materials grow duller, whereas those on rough materials start to wear smooth and become more polished. Rivets on rough metal, raised areas of old wood, and high points on a sculpture become shinier; whereas the treads of a tire, grips on a racquet, and ridges on glass become duller.

Shininess maps can make reflective materials look especially real when combined with a reflection map. The different shiny values cause the reflection to "dance" across the surface as the object is rotated. When representing materials in which everything is not perfectly smooth, such as with old metal plating, shininess maps can be used to chart the course of the irregularity and give play to a subtle, low-strength reflection. This is much more effective than merely varying the colors of the texture maps themselves.

When an object is made transparent by an opacity map, the transparent areas are treated as if they are actually clear glass and will still catch highlights. It is very common for an opacity map to represent cutouts and profiles within an object, and highlights in these areas destroy the effect. To keep these areas free of highlights, copy the opacity bitmap for use as the shininess map. Perfecting the illusion of opacity with shininess maps is demonstrated in the following exercise.

Using Shininess to Perfect Opacity

Begin a new material with WHITE PLASTIC, *make it two-sided, and choose* LATTIC1.CEL *as an opacity map*	Renders the sphere as a partitioned sphere
Increase the number of repetitions and correct for distortion by decreasing the U Scale to 0.125 and the V Scale to 0.25, and then render the sphere	Renders the sphere as an open "basket" of sorts

Pay attention to the highlights and you will notice a gleam over the transparent areas of the sphere's basket, as shown in the left sphere of figure 12.2.

Increase the highlight curve by lowering the shininess to 10 and increasing the strength to 70, and then render

It is now very obvious that the highlight is going over the holes.

Copy the opacity map file slot to the shininess map and render

Removes the highlight from the holes, and the sphere looks like a real basket

Perfecting this material did not take any additional memory because the bitmap was already referenced.

Figure 12.2
Transparency without and with a shininess map.

Bullet holes are another good use for combined maps. The base texture map is pierced by a bullet hole opacity map. To cancel the reflections and truly make the holes appear real, copy the bitmap as a shininess map. To finalize the effect, copy the bitmap again as a bump map. This results in a convincing bullet hole. If you wanted the bullets shot from the other side, simply reverse the bump map.

Self-Illuminated Maps

By using *self-illuminated maps*, you can isolate the simulation of light emission. Intensity maps are used to control the location and strength of self-illumination. Black has no effect, whereas white is the equivalent of the Self Illum property slider at 100. Just as the Transparency property slider is ignored in the presence of an opacity map, the Self Illum property slider is ignored when a self-illuminated map is included.

Remember that self-illumination is simulated in 3D Studio by replacing the ambient color with the diffuse color—replacing all aspects of shade. The material's true diffuse component is thus the color shown by the white areas of a self-illuminated map. It might be difficult to get an intense self-illuminated effect when the material is monolithically colored. Matching texture maps are thus often included to give added contrast to the self-illuminated areas.

When used as decals, self-illuminated maps provide an excellent method for simulating the light effects of a lamp's etched glass or even glow-in-the-dark paint. Although this effect can be used in an attempt to simulate neon, most find it somewhat unrewarding because the map has no depth and no actual light is produced. (See Chapter 13, "Lighting and Camera Special Effects," for some techniques for using neon.) A quick investigation into self-illuminated maps follows.

Using Self-Illuminated Maps

Begin by getting the BLACK MATTE *material from the 3DS.MLI*

Renders a matte black sphere

Click on the Self Illum *map file slot, choose* GHOSTS.JPG, *and render*

Figure 12.3 shows how there seems to be no effect

Figure 12.3
Steps in making a controllable self-illuminated material.

Self-illumination always bases itself on the diffuse color of the material. Because both the ambient and diffuse colors are black, there is very little color to replace.

Increase the diffuse color's luminance and render at various levels of luminance

Renders the self-illuminated letters brighter as the diffuse color gets brighter

This increases the appearance of the self-illuminated map, but lightens the color of the entire material.

Copy the Self Illum's *map file slot to* Texture1 *map, turn off the* Self Illum *map, and render*

Renders the texture map, as shown in the second illustrated sphere

Reactivate the Self Illum *map and render*

The text is now very bright against the black field, as shown in the third sphere.

The texture map has replaced the diffuse and ambient colors, and now gives you control over the color emitted by the Self Illum setting.

Change the texture map's source to Luma Tint, *make the right swatch a bright yellow, and render*	Renders the letters of the bitmap very bright and uniform yellow

The fuzzy "glow" that was characteristic of the bitmap has been lost. To get it back requires the use of a mask. (The full use of masks is discussed later in this chapter.)

Change the texture map's source back to RGB, *copy its map file slot to the right as its mask, and render*	There seems to be little effect because the mask matches the texture map
Click on the mask's parameter box, change it to Negative, *and render*	Renders the text with the self-illuminated property of the black diffuse material, as shown in the fourth sphere

This is actually an interesting quality unto itself. What is important is that the texture map defines the surface, whereas the diffuse color controls the text's color.

Change the diffuse color to a bright yellow and render

The text is now glowing yellow against a black background, as shown in the last sphere.

The material created in the previous exercise uses the same map three times, yet only uses memory for one. In its final form, the color of the text is completely controlled by the diffuse color, whereas the field is governed by the texture map. Because the latter can have as its source a luma tint, the colors are endless. Adjusting the texture map's left RGB Luma Tint swatch to deep blue places the self-illuminated yellow letters on a deep blue field.

Self-illuminated maps also prove quite useful in tailoring the effects of illuminated signage. Commonly, signs are painted on glass or pressed from plastic. The opacity of the paint and thickness of the plastic affects the amount of light emitted. You can reinforce this effect by using the material's texture or bump bitmap as a self-illuminated map and adjusting its effects accordingly.

Specular Maps

Specular maps are included as an option for the very special purpose of being able to see an image or varying color in the highlight of an object. With them, you can simulate subtle reflections that occur only when a light's highlight passes over the surface. You also have complete control over where this "reflection" occurs, unlike with reflection maps, since specular maps respect the surface's mapping coordinates.

Specular maps are the only map type that affect the coloring of specular base color.

Specular maps replace the material's specular base color when used with a strength of 100. When below 100, the specular map mixes proportionally with the specular color in the same manner texture maps blend with the diffuse and ambient colors. As the specular color blends with the diffuse, so does the specular map. The material's diffuse color, be it from a texture map or diffuse component, has a significant impact on the coloring of specular image.

Because metal materials do not have a specular component, they cannot render a specular map. Specular maps are primarily used with phong-shaded materials only.

The specular map is the only color map besides texture that has editable parameters. With specular maps, you can control the scale, placement, and color of the specular image. This is important because the presence of a specular image implies what lies elsewhere in the scene.

The primary use for specular maps is to place an image of the scene's light source on the object. Since this image is simulating a reflection, the bitmap should be a representative of what you want the area around the highlight-causing light source to be. A patterned window with curtains, an ornate street lamp, or a blazing sun are just a few examples. This addition can add considerable realism, and is often seen on curved, shiny objects in daily life. When you see the shape of a window in the highlight of a balloon, you are seeing the equivalent of a specular map.

Creating a CUB for an object (with Renderer/Setup/Make CUB in the 3D Editor) is an easy way to capture what the object "sees" in its reflections. Using one of the six bitmaps generated by Make CUB as a specular map for that object is both accurate and realistic.

Specular maps are especially convincing when used in conjunction with reflection maps. The reflection enforces the illusion that the material is shiny. Seeing the specular reflection of a nearby neon sign, for example, in the reflection bitmap's highlight can be a very realistic touch.

The specular bitmap is only seen in the specular area of the material, so the prominence of the map is directly related to its highlight curve. Specular maps have the greatest success when applied to smooth, curvilinear meshes because they have the greatest capability to form a constant highlight. Note that the more lights you have in the scene, the more chances there will be for highlights to be created on the surface.

If a specular map's bitmap is grayscale, its effect is nearly identical to using the same bitmap as a shininess map. This is because the color of the specular map is combined with the material's diffuse color in an additive or light-based manner. When a color is added that has no hue (for example, gray) the luminance of the diffuse material increases in a linear fashion. If the added color is black, no color change occurs. Specular maps are thus most effective when they contain hue. If the bitmap is grayscale, tint it with Luma or RGB tint so that the shine still appears to go over the specular map's surface.

Because shininess maps mask the presence of a highlight, their use can affect a specular map. Be careful when combining these two map types.

The Alpha Channel Option

An *Alpha channel* essentially is a grayscale image that represents opacity. White is completely opaque, black is totally transparent, and shades of gray vary in transparency according to their luminance. The resulting Alpha channel has 256 levels (or 8 bits) of transparency. An Alpha channel is thus the same in color depth and purpose as a grayscale opacity map. The difference is in how it is created and the accuracy its effect can have.

When in use, a bitmap image with an Alpha channel is placed over another bitmap and the original seems to overlay perfectly, without any evidence of an edge. Anything that was transparent in the original image will allow the underlying image to show through appropriately. As shown in figure 12.4, a car rendered with an Alpha channel could be placed over the image of a landscape, for example. Not only does the outline of the car blend seamlessly with the landscape, you can see through its windshield as if the car was always against that landscape. Although very effective within 3D Studio itself (as used in materials and especially within Video Post), images with Alpha channels are extremely useful when brought into true color paint packages for compositing still images.

After learning all the possibilities now open to Alpha channel use (and especially 32-bit files), you might find yourself slowly replacing your map library with Alpha channel options. It is very possible that Alpha channel inclusion will become the professional standard for 3D Studio bitmaps and textures to follow in the future.

III

Advanced Modeling

Figure 12.4
Compositing
one image on
top of another
using alpha
transparency.

3D Studio rendering

The included Alpha channel mask

Original image

The result with 32-bit image pasted on

Alpha Channel Creation and Use

When 3D Studio renders a mesh, it calculates an Alpha channel for its profile and applies this transparency against the remainder of the scene to create anti-aliased edges. It is this 8 bits of transparency information that anti-aliases the edges of objects against their background and enables you to look through transparent portions. This information usually is calculated by the renderer, composited to create the image, and discarded at the end. By setting the Render Alpha option to Yes in the Render Options dialog box, you can save this valuable anti-aliasing and transparency information in the form of an Alpha channel.

Alpha channel information is created only for meshes—never for backgrounds—and only for materials that have transparency information. Figure 12.5 shows an image of airplanes rendered against a sky background, and their corresponding Alpha channel information next to it.

The Alpha channel is grayscale and represents 8 bits of transparency information. A true-color TGA or TIF file that contains an Alpha channel in addition to its RGB channels is referred to as a *32-bit* or *RGBA* file. Many image editing programs cannot read a 32-bit file or will discard the extra 8 bits of alpha upon loading it. If you want the capability to edit the 24-bit file and still keep the alpha information, turn the Alpha Split option (located just below Render

Alpha) to Yes. This creates a separate 8-bit, grayscale TGA image with a file name proceeded with "A_". Although the separate file gives you editing flexibility, it requires more memory to use than the imbedded Alpha channel.

Figure 12.5
Original image of objects rendered against a background image and the corresponding alpha information.

 3D Studio will create a split alpha image *only* if you are rendering to the TGA format.

3D Studio saves the scene's Alpha channel information within an image file only if you are writing to a true color TGA or TIF. These are the only files 3D Studio writes that are capable of being 32-bit. Using the option on other file types will have no effect.

Transparency and Anti-aliasing

In 3D Studio Release 2, the only use for the Alpha channel was in Video Post. Although useful, its benefit was basically limited to compositing images on top of one another. The use of Alpha channel information is now possible within the Materials Editor for all map and mask types that have a settings (S) button. You always have the option of using either the bitmap's color or alpha information for each reference. This gives you many opportunities for combining effects with the parent color image, its Alpha channel, and any other bitmaps within the material.

III

Advanced Modeling

When 32-bit TGA or TIF bitmaps are used, they are loaded into memory only once at a cost of 3 bytes per pixel—regardless of whether the Alpha channel is referenced. Referencing the Alpha channel as an intensity map requires no extra memory and is thus "free."

The easiest and most effective use of 32-bit images is as decals. Whenever a color map is used in a Decal mode, the program checks to see if an Alpha channel is present. If one is found, it is used for the bitmap's transparency rather than keying on its upper left pixel color. This is a much more effective technique because you now have 256 levels of transparency instead of two and do not run the risk of duplicating the upper left's color in the image by mistake.

When using a 32-bit image as an intensity map, you have the option of having its color/RGB information converted to a grayscale or using its Alpha channel directly. To use the alpha instead, simply change the source from RGB to Alpha.

When you use a 32-bit image as a Texture map, 3D Studio assumes that you want to use it as a decal. A 32-bit image used in Tile mode will always render as a decal, regardless of the Ignore Alpha button. Because of this anamoly, 32-bit images should only be used as textures if they have a black background.

The Alpha channel gives you much more insight into the anti-aliasing properties of an image than a standard opacity map can. For this reason, an Alpha channel is the ideal opacity map for images that have nonrectilinear edges (because rectilinear edges gain the least from anti-aliasing information).

Materials that represent cutouts, such as trees and people, are most realistic and memory efficient when made with 32-bit bitmaps. The texture map reads the 24-bit RGB channel and both the opacity and shininess maps read the Alpha channel. Using all three maps still only uses three bytes per pixel.

The Map Mask Option

The inclusion of map masks was introduced with Release 3 and is based on a simple yet very useful concept. Masks screen the effects of their associated map type. Since they are masking, they can never intensify the map's effect, only limit it. Masks are much like an airbrush artist's frisket, a watercolorist's rubber resist, a painter's masking tape, or the crayon a child uses to repel watercolor paints. The various mediums applied over these resists are analogous to the mask's accompanying map.

How Masks Are Used with Maps

Basically, *map masks* are intensity maps that act in an opacity map fashion for any given map type. This gives you complete control of each map's effect because the mask directs and limits it to specific areas of the material.

Each of the eight map types has a corresponding mask slot for its own map mask and contains all the parameter options of a standard intensity map. Because each mask type only affects the map to its left, they are meant for use in combination with it. Masks do not have an effect without an accompanying map—they must have something to mask.

The bitmaps used for map masks are often copies of other map types. This is especially true of opacity and bump maps. These maps usually represent a different effect within the material that might need to be coupled with, or excluded from, another map in the form of a mask.

Although mask bitmaps are interpreted in the same fashion as intensity maps, the effect each has on the map to its left is quite different. Do not assume that a bitmap that works one way for a texture mask will work the same way for a bump or specular mask. The effect each is masking is quite different, and the results are equally so.

Alpha Channels Versus Intensity Maps

Files with Alpha channels (split or embedded) can be used in lieu of a standard intensity map. Alpha channels have the inherent capability to create soft, anti-aliased edges that can be quite difficult to produce for any bitmap whose subject is not rectilinear.

Texture Masks

Masks can be used with textures to control where the image is seen. This is very effective when two texture maps are used in combination. When a material needs to isolate pieces of the images, it is usually important to use the maps at full strength (otherwise their images begin to be washed out by the material's base color or that of other maps). Texture masks enable you to isolate pieces of the images.

The primary method for allowing Texture 1 to show through areas of Texture 2 is to give the latter a mask. If Texture 1 also has a mask, the material's base color shows through the areas common to both masks. This ability is easier to see than describe, and is shown in the following exercise.

Using Texture Map Masks

Create a wood material that has a white highlight, uses ASHSEN.GIF *as 100 percent Texture 1, and* BUBINGA.GIF *as 100 percent Texture 2*

Render the sample	Renders the deep brown bubinga over the ashen map
Click in the Texture 2's mask file slot, choose LATTIC1.CEL, *and render*	The ashen texture shows through the "holes" of Texture 2's mask, as in the left sphere of figure 12.6

continues

III

Advanced Modeling

continued

Figure 12.6
Using a Texture 1 mask and reusing it as a bump map and shininess map.

The materials have been separated, but they still share the same surface for reflection, shine, and smoothness. They appear as if one has been airbrushed on or applied as an infinitely thin veneer. Some materials, such as wood inlays, cloisonné, and print, are like this. Others are not so perfectly made and require a bit more mapping to be believable.

Copy Texture 2's mask file slot to the | Renders the dark, bubinga areas shiny,
shininess map file slot, and then render | and the ashsen areas are totally matte

Assume that the desired effect is raised squares and not a standard lattice. This effect is quite easy to do.

Give the shininess map a negative value, | Renders the squares shiny, and the
reduce its strength slider to about 80, | darker lattice with a slight gleam
and render

Copy the shininess map file slot up to the
bump map file slot, reduce its strength slider
to about a 50, and render

The ashen squares now project in front of a Bubinga field, as shown in the right sphere of figure 12.6.

An equally interesting material could be made if another lattice CEL was included that was only black-on-white linework. Used as a bump map, it would create grooves or joints between the two wood types instead.

You probably will find masks a welcome addition to older material types as well. One material that has been around as long as any other is floor tile. In the following exercise, this basic material is made much richer with masks.

Using Masks with Marble Tile

The following exercise uses a common tile intensity map named TILEBUMP.TIF, which is a white square with a thin black border and a one-pixel-wide gray inner border.

Begin by getting MARBLE GREEN *from the 3DS.MLI*

Renders a green marble sample that uses MARBTEAL.GIF as a 100 percent texture map

Click in the bump map file slot, select TILEBUMP.TIF *as the map, slide the strength slider down to about 50, and render*

Renders the tile grooved, but too shiny for a well-trafficked floor

Decrease the shininess to about 30, the Shine Strength to about 65, and render

Renders the material grooved, as in the left cube picture in figure 12.7

Figure 12.7
Combining map types to make a superior tile material.

This is the point where many materials in the past would stop. Masks and the new maps provide more opportunities, however.

Copy the bump map file slot over to the texture's mask file slot and render

Shows the black of the material's base color through the grooves

Make the material's diffuse color more of a white cream, copy it to the ambient *swatch, darken it, and render*

The tile now has cream lines in the grooves, which is beginning to look more like grout. This improves the tile's look considerably, but grout usually is not shiny.

Copy the bump map to the shininess map and render

Renders the grout lines matte

This might be a good stopping point, unless you plan to get especially close to the grout lines. In that case, the solid cream grout does not look very realistic.

continues

continued

Copy Texture 1's map and mask to Texture 2

Select GRAVEL1.CEL *as Texture 1, and copy a*
NONE *mask file slot to be its mask*

The mapping assignments should now look like figure 12.7.

Lower Texture 1's strength to 50	Allows the gravel texture to blend with the material's base color
Render the sample	Renders the tile very realistically, as shown in the right cube of figure 12.7

Figure 12.8 shows the final material in the previous exercise. Here Texture 2 is a tileable marble bitmap. The bump map is a white square with a black edge on the top and left sides, allowing it to tile in both directions and be scaled as needed. This bitmap is used as Texture 2's map mask, with the black grout line allowing Texture 1 to show through. Texture 1 is a small, tileable sand texture used at a much smaller scale than Texture 2. Because the grout is not polished, the bump map's tile is copied for use as a shininess map. The tile is now complete, with the original bump bitmap serving in three slots.

Figure 12.8
The final mapping
assignments for
grouted marble tile.

Map Type	Amount	Map		Mask	
Texture 1	50	GRAVEL1.CEL	S	NONE	S
Texture 2	100	MARBTEAL.GIF	S	TILEBUMP.TIF	S
Opacity	100	NONE	S	NONE	S
Bump	50	TILEBUMP.TIF	S	NONE	S
Specular	100	NONE	S	NONE	S
Shininess	100	TILEBUMP.TIF	S	NONE	S
Self Illum	100	NONE	S	NONE	S
Reflection	100	NONE	A	NONE	S

Interesting effects also can be made when only one texture map and mask are used. This allows the material color to show through. Examples of this might be writing a message in the condensation of a wet table or fogged mirror.

Opacity Masks

With *opacity masks*, the transparency values between the map and mask are added and cannot be subtracted. You thus can make an area more transparent with a mask, but never more opaque. This stems from the fact that when an opacity map is active, the entire material is considered transparent except where the map tells it to be opaque. The mask is thus restoring the transparency by blocking the opaque influences of the map. A mask never can make the material more opaque than the opacity map will allow.

Opacity masks are most useful when the map does not allow too much of the material to be 100-percent transparent. Possible uses for these masks are on a sign or on areas of glass that are more transparent than the field. Scratches on the opaque paint of a store window's glass is only one example.

Bump Masks

To predict the effects of *bump masks*, it is important to understand how the bump illusion is actually created. Bumped areas appear to be recessed or projected because of the highlights and shades caught by simulated ridges and valleys. This is the bump effect—not the fields of color, but their edges. Bump maps do not affect the shading properties of the different "terraces," "levels," or "steps" that appear to be formed on the surface. These areas all are rendered as if they were one smooth surface—it's their bumped edges that give the illusion of depth.

Because a bump mask only masks the bump map's effect, only the edges within the bitmap can be masked. The following exercise investigates how masks affect a bump map application.

Working with Bump Masks

Begin by getting the material GOLD (LIGHT) *from the* 3DS.MLI	Renders a gold sample sphere with a subtle reflection map
Choose GRANITE.CEL *as a 100-percent-strength bump map and render*	Renders the gold sphere crinkled and bumpy like crushed foil
Choose CHECKER.CEL *as its mask and render*	Masks the crinkled areas and allows the reflection map to cast across the smooth spots, as seen in the left sphere of figure 12.9

This was a fairly predictable result, but to see the true impact the mask has on the bump map, you must reverse the use of the two bitmaps. You might conclude that the granite has an effect on the entire checkerboard, but the result is much different.

Copy the bump mask file slot up to another mask file slot	Stores the bitmap information
Copy the bump map file slot as the mask and the stored mask as the bump map, and then render	Renders the ragged ridges of an alternating checkerboard, as shown in the right sphere pictured in figure 12.9

The effect of the granite mask is extremely hard to predict. If you use it in a scene and render it large enough, you will see that it "ripples" the ridges of the checks. This demonstrates that the ridges are the bump, and the projection of the alternating checks is just an illusion created by the ridge's highlight and shadow.

The reason the first mask assignment in the previous exercise works well is because the granite created so many bumped edges that masking them defines a recognizable area.

III

Advanced Modeling

Figure 12.9
The effects of using the same bitmaps in alternating roles of map and mask.

Bump masks thus work best if the bump bitmap creates a considerable number of ridges and valleys to be masked. Random patterns controlled by regular masks are the most common uses of bump masks. Examples in which this effect can work well are etched glass, rough cut wood signs, burnished metal, and fabric.

Specular Masks

Specular masks define which areas of the specular map show the material's specular color. Only in using a mask can the base specular color have an effect. The amount of the material's specular color that shows through is determined by the luminance of the mask. Black areas allow all the specular color to show through, white areas block all of it, and gray areas mix the two colors accordingly.

If the material's specular color is black, the mask has a darkening effect on the specular mask, in effect decreasing all the colors' luminance sliders. This is useful in creating specks of dirt or streaks on an image.

When the material's specular color is white, the mask acts as a luminance intensifier. This has the appearance of having a reverse effect because black areas of the mask allow all the color through and increase them to white, whereas white allows none through. If you are using the mask to "tint up" the map, you might want to activate its negative parameter to make the effect more predictable.

Using masks with specular maps is an important step in making them more realistic. It is very common for a specular image to appear on an object, but it is usually in conjunction with the material's specular color. If the bitmap contains the images or at least the colors of the scene, its effect is more believable. It is very common, however, to use stock bitmaps, such as windows and lamps, for the image and tinting does not have quite the right effect. The obvious choice might seem to be to make the specular map a decal, but doing this replaces the entire specular color with the upper left pixel's color. (For 32-bit images, the color of the Alpha channel is used.) To see the material's specular color when using a specular map as a decal, you need to use a specular mask. Copying the specular map as a mask often does the trick. (Make sure that you change the source to "Use alpha" when using a 32-bit bitmap.)

New Riders Publishing
INSIDE
SERIES

Shininess Masks

Because the shininess map determines how much of the highlight is displayed, a *shininess mask* is somewhat of a "mask's mask." As with the shininess map, its mask cannot make a material any more shiny than its highlight curve already makes it. The main purpose of shininess masks is to restore shine to the areas already masked by the shininess map.

 Tip
Shininess masks are nearly a necessity when you use the shininess map as a decal. Only by masking the decal's effects can you restore the shine settings to the remainder of the material.

Because the shininess mask can restore only highlights taken away by the map, its primary use lies in constraining those effects or creating new and more complicated combinations. In this respect, the mask can be thought of as a polishing rag for the dullness created by the map.

The most interesting effects occur when the shininess map is widespread and possibly random. In this respect, its use is very similar to bump masks. The use of the shininess mask as a randomizing element can create the effect of rain drops, stains, or dust. The mask in effect "cleans" these areas by restoring the material's highlight. Some examples of its use might be water spots and streaks, letters written in scattered dust or on a fogged glass, and joints in metal panels.

Self-Illumination Masks

Self-illuminated masks simply block out the effects created by the self-illuminated map. In this respect, the purpose of self-illuminated masks is to restore the material's ambient color and shade. They cannot produce any additional effect of self-illumination—only remove it.

Masks are used with self-illumination primarily to temper the effects of the self-illuminated map. This can be useful if the material simulates a "texture of light"—possibly the effects of spattered paint on a lamp or sign. If you want to make an illuminated area appear dirty, assign a random bitmap mask to it.

Reflection Masks

Reflection masks should be used with the understanding that they affect the mesh differently than the reflection map does. A reflection mask reacts as any other mask and requires standard mapping coordinates, unlike the automatically applied reflection maps. These masks represent areas of the mesh and not areas of the scene.

Reflection masks are invaluable in controlling where a reflection occurs on the applied mesh. A material that uses a combination of many maps is a good example in which to study the effects of reflection masks. The goal of the following exercise is to create a material with the illusion of a gold sphere held within an iron grid. This material uses a simple black cross on a white field called CROSSBMP.TIF for several assignments.

Combining Multiple Maps and Masks

Begin by getting the GOLD (LIGHT) *material*

Apply CROSSBMP.TIF *as a mask to the reflection map and render again*	Renders a sphere without reflection in the grid area
Copy the reflection mask as a texture map and render	Covers up the material's gold color and renders as a black grid on a white field
Copy the texture map to the right as a texture mask and render	Renders gold bands on a reflective white field because the texture map's grid image is masked
Activate the texture mask's negative parameter and render	Renders the bands black against the reflective gold field
Copy the texture mask to the bump map file slot, lower its strength slider to 50, and render	Causes the black grid to protrude from the face of the reflective gold sphere, as in the third sphere of figure 12.10

Figure 12.10
Steps in making a
gold material
within an iron grid.

The material now looks fairly convincing, as shown on the left sphere in figure 12.11, but a very rough iron enclosure is needed for the gold. The material currently shows the iron as a shiny, black metal. This surface is too shiny, black, and smooth for ancient iron.

Figure 12.11
Smooth and
corroded gold
materials held
within metal
bands.

Copy the bump map to the right as a bump mask, choose GRANITE.CEL *as the new bump map, and render*	Renders with very coarse edges that catch considerable highlights, as shown in the fourth sphere of figure 12.10
Change the texture map's source to RGB Luma Tint *and change the left swatch to a deep, slate gray*	
Copy the reflection mask over to the shininess map, lower its slider strength to about 80, and render	Renders the reflective gold sphere encased in a grid of dull, corroded iron, as seen in figure 12.11

As figure 12.12 shows, the same map was used repeatedly throughout the material definition, thus saving considerable memory.

Figure 12.12
The mapping assignments for the second gold and iron material.

Reflection masks also are good tools for blocking areas of a flat mirror. This enables you to create a pattern on the surface of your mirror and alleviates some restrictions of not being able to extend a flat mirror beyond an element's extents. Some examples are picture frames, tiles, and etched mirror glass. It is a natural to reuse the mirror mask as bump, texture, and shininess masks and maps.

III

Advanced Modeling

Smoothing a Bitmap's Effect with Blur

By their very nature, bitmaps are not perfect. No matter how evenly shaded or complex in color depth, bitmaps are just an arrangement of colored squares. Squares are fine when you look at them straight on, as when viewing a bitmap in a paint program or with View File in the Materials Editor. The pixels' squareness becomes a liability, however, when you see them on a tilted surface, at an angle, and in perspective. The square edges of the pixels become more pronounced, and you have the jaggies, scintillation, or aliasing. This is where 3D Studio's filter maps comes into play.

Actually, the effects of not using blur are easier to identify. Compare figure 12.13 (which does not use filter maps) with figure 12.14 (which does use filter maps). These figures point out how blur's primary effect is to eliminate *scintillation*—those extremely annoying lines of "dancing" pixels and moiré patterns. These are especially noticeable as fine lines begin to converge in perspective (as in the distance) or come close together (as in the sides of the cubes). Examine the left cube within both figures, and you can also see how the diagonal lines appear "jagged" without blur, but render smooth with it. Also notice that the appearance of the marble texture is nearly identical in both figures. In actuality, there is a slight but subtle difference, as figure 12.14's marble is a bit "softer" in appearance. Of all the map types, blur has the most profound effect on bump maps. In fact, bump maps don't render correctly without Filter Maps turned on.

Figure 12.13
A tile floor material rendered with Filter Maps Off (no blur).

Figure 12.14
The same tile floor material rendered with Filter Maps On (using blur).

Pyramidal Filtering

Filter maps are the Renderer's mechanism for smoothing the edges of bitmaps. In earlier releases, bitmaps were anti-aliased as if they were geometry. Although this worked, it was painfully slow. Because 3D Studio's mission combines quality with speed, this method was abandoned for a quick technique of interpolating a bitmap's pixels called *pyramidal texture filtering* (also known as *mip mapping*). Pyramidal texture filtering is activated when the rendering parameter, Filter Maps, is turned on. The additional memory cost for using pyramidal filter maps is one byte per pixel, but is minimal compared to its effectiveness. Bitmaps thus require four bytes per pixel rather than three when filter maps are used.

> SXPs are unaffected by blur because they are mathematically determined and have no need for it. No blur sliders are within their parameters. This is some concession for their additional calculation time.

The bitmap's blur setting determines the amount that an image is filtered. Blur actually should be thought of as the *filter slider* because its strength determines the filter map's effect. Blur settings have no effect unless filter maps are turned on during a render. A blur setting of zero allows the filter map to perform its minimal pixel interpolation. Higher settings cause more and more pixels to be sampled and averaged, thus creating more "blur" in the bitmap.

> Bump map effects are not rendered correctly unless the Renderer's Filter Maps option is *On*. Thus, when using bump mapped materials, you should calculate 4 bytes of memory usage per pixel for all material bitmaps that are using standard pyramidal filtering.

Pyramidal Versus Summed Area Filtering

Your big option when using filter maps is which one to use—pyramidal or summed area filtering. The summed area filter is superior in quality, but costs an *additional* 12 bytes per pixel. This can add up very quickly for bitmaps because they consume nearly four times more memory than pyramidal filtering when using this option (15 bits per pixel versus 4 bits). This summed area thus becomes a very expensive button to turn on and might be thought of as "$ummed Area" instead. But are the memory requirements worth the effect? For some materials it is; for others, high memory requirements might not even be noticeable.

Summed area filtering has the greatest effect on materials having closely spaced lines that diminish into perspective, or those that use a heavy blur setting to gain a "fuzzy" effect. Figure 12.15 compares pyramidal filtering on the left with summed area filtering on the right. Both of these use 100 percent Texture 1 maps with a 15 percent blur setting. The greatest effect can be seen in analyzing the lines that are getting closer in spacing to one another in perspective rather than those that are converging. Pyramidal renders these lines with the same intensity,

III

Advanced Modeling

whereas summed area lightens them according to their proximity. The latter is the more correct method, since the lines should become thinner as their position progresses down the depth of the cubes. This is most evident on the cubes' sides. With pyramidal filtering, the vertical lines are pronounced, whereas summed area diminishes the verticals to the point that they are barely visible—you are only seeing the converging, horizontal lines. Using summed area filtering can thus alleviate the "overtexturing" that can occur when very regular patterns are applied to surfaces seen at oblique angles.

Figure 12.15
Pyramidal (left) versus summed area filtering (right).

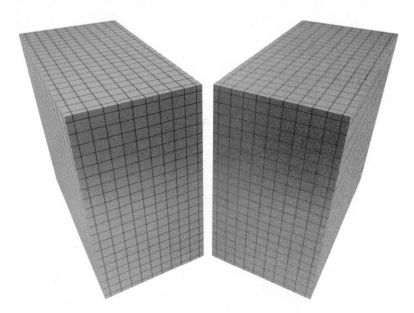

The best strategy for using summed area filtering is for bitmaps being used repeatedly in material definitions, thus gaining the most quality for the extra memory expended. For most purposes, you should choose pyramidal filtering as your first choice, and switch to summed area only as a last resort on the road to perfecting a material's rendered appearance.

Use of Blur

When does a material's bitmap need more blur? This is a subjective call and needs to be made by seeing the material's effect within the scene. (Render Last and Auto Put are great tools for this.) If the bitmap is scintillating or showing irregular edges, increase its blur setting. Blur is not magical and cannot make an aliased source image anti-aliased. Blur only can correct the aliasing of the bitmap as it is cast in perspective. If the bitmap is inherently jaggy, you need to smooth it with a paint program before assigning it. You would not want 3D Studio to correct the inherent quality of a bitmap because doing so would smooth images that were supposed to be jaggy.

In practice, most bitmaps require blur settings of 0 to 20, whereas bump maps require the most blur. By creating areas of highlight and shadow that simulate bumps and ridges, bump maps create images that naturally scintillate. Unfortunately, bump maps, which need summed area filtering the most, do not have it available. You need to increase blur for bump maps accordingly, and it is not uncommon to use ranges of 20 to 60. Remember that the quality of your bump map effect improves as the bitmap's scale of detail, in pixel width, increases. (Lines that are 6 pixels wide will create a much crisper bump effect than that created by 1 pixel-wide lines.)

Blur also can be used to create special effects besides correcting the overall bitmap quality. When the blur setting is very high, for example 70 to 100, you can create smudge stick, airbrush, and spray paint effects. This works well for high contrast images, such as text or patterns on a solid background. At very high settings, you can see the greatest difference between pyramidal or summed area filters. As figure 12.16 shows, pyramidal blur filtering dissipates the image and makes it streak in a rectilinear manner, whereas summed area blur keeps the image together and heavily blurs the edges. In figure 12.16 the upper cubes all use pyramidal filtering, and the lower cubes use summed area filtering. The center cubes have a standard blur of 10, the left cubes 70, and the right cubes are maximized at 100.

Figure 12.16
Effects gained by using very high blur settings.

Duplicating these effects within the bitmap requires a much larger image to produce the broad, soft, and fuzzy edges. The cost for a 200-line bitmap with summed area filtering (200 × 200 × 15=600 KB) is equal to the memory of a 388-line bitmap with pyramidal filtering (388 × 388 × 4=602 KB), and it requires at least a 600-line image and a considerable amount of time in a paint program to create the same soft-focus effect. Used in this way, summed area filters are actually memory savers.

Using Complex Materials

Complex materials represent the last material classification used in this book. These materials require additional—and possibly substantial—computations and bitmap loadings at the time of rendering. Because of their cost, they should be used judiciously within the scene and placed in areas of the greatest importance.

Reflection Map Options

Several methods of creating reflections also are available other than faking them with a reflection map. At your disposal are flat mirror and automatic reflections (which calculate the mirror's bitmap at rendering time), and cubic reflections (which load previously created images of the scene). The choice of which method to use depends primarily on the form of geometry it is being applied to and whether the scene is static or stationary.

Flat Mirror Reflections

The *flat mirror* option creates a direct mirror image of the scene. This is the effect that most often comes to mind when people are asked to define a reflection. The operative word in this map's title is *flat*, as this mapping type only works properly with coplanar meshes.

When you assign a flat mirror material at the object level, 3D Studio issues a warning that flat mirrors should only be applied to a 2D set of faces. This warning is displayed regardless of whether the object actually is coplanar. Conversely, no warning is issued if you assign the material at the face or element level—regardless of how many non-coplanar faces are assigned. It is completely up to you to analyze the mesh and determine whether it is truly "flat."

Flat mirrors are calculated for each object that contains faces assigned a flat mirror material. Only one map is ever calculated per object, regardless of how many planes or elements are assigned a flat mirror or if multiple flat mirror materials exist within the object. The first face encountered by the Renderer that has a flat mirror material defines the plane of the mirror.

Release 3 improved the speed of mirror calculations by calculating only what could be seen by that mirror, rather than the entire scene. Flat mirror reflection maps are not calculated if the mirror faces face away from the camera.

Reflections base much of their effect on your angle of view, and are only calculated properly when rendered in Camera viewports. This is important to remember when making quick previews of your scene for material judgments.

Each flat mirror occurrence generates its own reflection map of the scene as viewed from the plane of the mesh. The size of the reflection map needs to be at least the size that the reflective surface will be in the rendered image. Each flat mirror map created will use the map size times itself times 3 bytes (for example, a 500-line map requires $500 \times 500 \times 3 = 750$ KB).

If multiple flat mirror planes are in a scene, you can save memory by assigning materials with varying sized reflection maps to meshes, based on the planes' prominence in the scene.

The color of the scene that a flat mirror reflects is based primarily on its specular and diffuse colors. Of these, the specular is the most influential because it determines the overall tint of the reflected image. This is done in a subtractive, pigment-like manner with a white value changing nothing, gray values toning down the image's luminance, black eliminating the reflection, and hues darkening and tinting the image accordingly. The specular color actually can be considered an extension of the Reflection Amount slider. A mid-gray specular value is equivalent to a reflection strength of 50.

The diffuse color works in an opposite manner by mixing with the image in an additive, light-like manner. This results in white heavily tinting or washing out the image, grays lightening the luminance, black affecting nothing, and hues tinting the image and increasing the luminance accordingly. The diffuse color casts an overall deep-base hue to the mirror surface. Knowing this, a perfect reflecting mirror will have black ambient and diffuse colors and a white specular color.

Because automatic maps are not created until rendering time, you cannot see their effects while within the Materials Editor. Using Renderer/Render Last of a Renderer/Render Region is very useful for seeing the effects as they relate to your scene.

Mirrors create an image on their normal side only and do not render both sides if made into a two-sided material, or if forced to render two-sided in the Renderer. This is rarely a problem, but if you are rotating ultra-thin mirrors, it can be. In this case, you need to create the mirror as a very thin box and detach either side's faces into new objects. These detached planes can then be assigned a flat mirror map and work best if they are linked together in the Keyframer. (Do not attach the separate mirror plane objects in the 3D Editor or they will lose their independent flat mirror capability.)

Flat mirrors cannot reflect bitmapped or gradient backgrounds. This makes sense because doing so can create an oddly distorted or glancing image. If you need to reflect a background, you must create an object to act as a "billboard" and assign it a material that uses the appropriate bitmap as a texture map.

A background billboard mesh works best if the material assigned to it is self-illuminated and without shine so that the material is not affected by the lighting conditions within the scene.

If objects in the scene are not being properly reflected, you should start by examining their normals and making sure that they are facing in that direction. Remember that mirrors can reflect only objects that face them and will react properly only when viewed within a perspective viewport.

You cannot see recursive reflections within flat mirrors—only Automatic Reflections (the six map type) have the ability to see another's reflection in 3D Studio. This is why the 3DS.SET variable controlling multiple reflections is named NONFLAT-AUTOREFLECT-LEVELS.

The reflection map's mask file slot is extremely useful for modifying the effects of a flat mirror and makes even the simplest form a complex material.

The sample mesh CAFETABL.3DS is used in the following exercise to demonstrate a flat mirror. To make the scene more applicable, the material assignments and lighting will need to be modified. In addition, the scene has a fog atmosphere that will need to be removed to properly see the effects of a mirror.

Using Flat Mirror Masks

Begin by loading CAFETABL.3DS from the meshes directory

Choose Surface Material/Acquire *and select the floor slab*

Displays the Material Selector and informs you that the floor used the CEMENT material

Switch to the Materials Editor and get CEMENT *from the scene by pressing* 🄵 *and choosing the* CEMENT *material from the list*	Renders a sample using CEMENT.CEL as a 100-percent-strength texture map
Click on the texture's file map slot, change the map to CHECKER.CEL, *and render*	Renders the sample with a black-and-white checker pattern
Increase the repeat of the map by changing its U and V scale parameters to 0.25, and then render	Covers the sample sphere with a checkered pattern
Put this material to the scene by pressing 🄸, *return to the 3D Editor, and render the Camera01 view*	The furniture now sits on a checkered floor

Note that doing a render region of the area in which the chair and table meet the floor will speed the rendering times when perfecting materials.

Return to the Materials Editor; click on the reflection map's A button	The file slot changes from NONE to AUTOMATIC
Click on the map file slot (now labeled AUTOMATIC)	The Automatic Map dialog box appears, as shown in figure 12.17

Figure 12.17
The Automatic Reflection Map dialog box in the Materials Editor.

Choose Yes *for* Flat Mirror, *and leave the map size at 100 (small map sizes are best for sample renders)*

Render the sample

There is no effect because the Materials Editor cannot represent a flat mirror.

Click on Auto Put *and choose* Render Last	Renders the previous scene, but the floor's reflection is very faint

Flat mirrors, like all reflections, base the color of their image on the material's specular color. Because the cement started out dark gray, very little reflection exists.

continues

continued

Increase the specular luminance to white by dragging the Luminance slider all the way to the right, then choose Render Last	The checkered floor now reflects the furniture
Copy the texture's map file slot over to reflection mask and choose Render Last	Only the white squares of the floor have a reflection
Give the reflection mask a Negative parameter and choose Render Last	Now only the black checks in the floor reflect the furniture, as shown in figure 12.18

Figure 12.18
A scene with a reflective floor of alternating matte and polished tiles.

Automatic Reflections

If a spherical reflection map is not realistic enough, your next choice should be an automatic reflection map. This works similarly to the flat mirror except it creates a map for six directions rather than one. This reflection cube can be thought of as the object's bounding box. The program stands at the object's local axis and takes a mirror map "snapshot" of the scene in

each direction. The object now is surrounded by a cubic reflection globe much as with a stretched spherical reflection map. The effect on each face is traced from the object's center to the edges of this reflection cube.

Unlike flat mirror maps, the Materials Editor does supply a CUB file of six simple images to give you a rough idea of how the material will reflect. This file is named MEDIT.CUB and can be changed with any ASCII editor to refer to whichever six files you prefer to see while within the Materials Editor. Alternatively, you can create your own CUB file for a specific object and base your material editing on it (temporarily using a cubic reflection map while in the Materials Editor and changing to an automatic reflection before assigning the updated version to the scene).

As with spherical reflection maps, automatic reflection maps work best when assigned to curvilinear objects because the flat sides of rectilinear objects can have problems capturing enough of the scene to read as a reflection. A cube that sits on a textured floor reflects only a blurred portion because its face "sees" only a small piece of the reflection cube's image. If you need this reflection, you either can increase the reflection map's size significantly, or detach the object's coplanar faces as an object and assign it a flat mirror material.

Increasing the map size is a very costly option because six maps are made for every object assigned an automatic reflection map. A material that uses a 300-line map costs 300 lines × 300 lines × 6 maps × 3 bytes = 1.62 MB for every object to which it is assigned. Detaching the flat faces as flat mirrors is both more realistic and memory efficient. Note that a mirrored cube, made of six-sided objects with six flat mirror maps, costs no more memory than one automatic reflection map and is much more accurate.

Mirrored text is a good example of when the front faces should be detached as an object with a flat mirror map, and the remaining object assigned an automatic reflection.

Automatic reflection maps do have an advantage over flat mirror maps in being able to reflect a bitmapped or gradient background. Because the background is being wrapped around the object, it is important to choose one that is tileable from left to right to avoid an annoying seam. In addition, automatic reflections can see another's reflection, whereas flat mirrors cannot.

In some situations, mirrored surfaces reflect each other's reflection. In 3D Studio, you can control the number of times these reflections occur, whereas true ray-tracing programs do so infinitely. 3D Studio's reason for limiting reflection bounces concerns speed. The more reflections calculated, the longer it takes. The default is to reflect a mirror's reflection once. Although you can increase this up to 10 times by changing the NONFLAT-AUTOREFLECT-LEVELS parameter in the 3DS.SET file, setting it above three or four has little effect in most scenes.

Although these reflections take in much of the scene, they cannot see themselves because the object's bounding box determines the mirror's clipping plane. This is true even if other elements within the object have different materials. If you require an object to see its own reflection, you need to detach elements or faces as their own auto-reflecting objects. Be aware that doing this requires that the Renderer create six more maps and that they do not share the same central point as the parent object. If this causes too much of a distraction within your object, you need to use a cubic reflection map and adjust the bitmaps as necessary.

 To get a good idea of what an object will actually reflect, you might want to make a small set of CUB images (see the following section on cubic reflection maps) and examine the results with View Image or in a paint program side by side.

As with flat mirror reflections, only one automatic reflection map can be assigned per object. If more than one automatic or flat mirror map material is assigned, the first face found in an object's definition defines the material used and reflection map type calculated.

Cubic Reflection Maps

Cubic reflection maps can be thought of as either a static version of automatic reflection maps or as a six-sided spherical map. Cubic reflections use six bitmaps to create what automatic reflections do at rendering time. The reflection is thus fixed and does not change as the scene changes.

So why use cubic reflection maps? Rendering speed is one reason. If your viewing position is static and only the mirrored object is animated in the same general area, the reflection map for each frame will be very much the same. Similarly, if the mirrored object is static, and you are doing a walk- or fly-around with a camera, the reflection might not need to be updated—the illusion of a reflection is many times all that is needed. Loading the six bitmaps into memory once is much less costly, and quicker, than calculating a new set of six for each frame.

The second reason to use cubic reflections is realism for high-resolution images. Because the reflection is using six bitmaps, you can edit these as much as you want in a 24-bit paint program. This can be essential for editing details, correcting backgrounds, placing emphasis on particular items, or using filters to affect the images in artful ways (using an Aldus Gallery Effects watercolor filter, for example). If you are rendering a high-resolution static scene, you might prefer this method to conserve rendering time because loading six images is much quicker than rendering them.

The third reason to use cubic reflection maps is that you can assign multiple cubic reflections within the same object. These also can be used in combination with spherical, automatic, and flat mirror reflection maps as well. By using them in combination, you can get the right look for each area of an object and tailor-make it if necessary.

Tip

You can make an object "see itself" in a reflection by assigning it a cubic reflection. The trick is in rendering the CUB about a small stand-in object placed at the center area of the object that needs to be seen. Assign this CUB to these faces and another CUB or automatic reflection to the other areas. (Although the first reflection saw the object, it could not see past it.) Mirrored text is a good example of an object that occasionally needs to see evidence of itself to be photo-realistic.

Cubic reflection maps are easier made than described. Use the Renderer/Setup/Make CUB command and select the object that defines the center of the views. Figure 12.19 shows the special, smaller rendering dialog box presented that enables you to choose the level of rendering, the use of shadows, maps, anti-aliasing, hiding geometry, and most important, the size for the six bitmaps.

```
                Generate Cubic Environment Map
    Shading Limit:   Flat   Gouraud   Phong   Metal
    Anti-aliasing:    On    Off
         Shadows:    On    Off   Mapping:   On    Off
        Hidden Geometry:   Show   Hide
       Object:  chairscafe   Resolution: 100
                    Generate     Cancel
```

Figure 12.19
The 3D Editor's Renderer/Setup/ Make CUB dialog box.

After making the rendering choices, you are prompted with a file dialog box to choose the name of the CUB file. The CUB file is a simple ASCII file that lists the six bitmap names to be used. You can change the bitmaps used by editing the CUB file (with Release 4's Script Editor, if you want). The program initially creates images that are compressed TGAs, and their names are based on the first six letters of the CUB's. The MEDIT.CUB included with Release 4 is as follows:

```
UP    = MEDITUP.JPG
DOWN  = MEDITDN.JPG
LEFT  = MEDITLF.JPG
RIGHT = MEDITRT.JPG
FRONT = MEDITFT.JPG
BACK  = MEDITBK.JPG
```

Making a CUB file and examining the six images side-by-side in a paint program can prove to be an education in how 3D Studio calculates not just CUB files, but automatic reflections as well.

III

Advanced Modeling

If you have many reflecting objects and your goal for them is not ultra realism, you can save considerable time and memory by making one larger set of cubic reflections. The center for this CUB file should either be the center of the scene or the object that requires the most realism. By using a material that accesses this CUB and assigning it often, you save the cost of creating or loading multiple automatic maps.

Box Mapping

Box mapping is a material capability that can be described only as a cross between cubic reflection maps and face maps. With the 3D Editor's Surface/Material/Box/Assign command, you can assign six different materials in a manner reminiscent of the sides of a CUB file. These materials can be anything you want—mapped or unmapped—as long as they are in the current materials library. (Materials with reflections have their automatic reflection property ignored, however.) Objects assigned a box material do not need mapping coordinates for mapped materials because the bitmap is stretched across the entire length of the object.

The size and orientation of the box material are based on the object's bounding box. The larger the object, the more the material is stretched to fit it. Faces of the object are assigned the material based upon the direction they are facing. This works fine for rectilinear geometry, but is fairly useless for objects that curve. There is no blending of the material types across faces, and a face is determined to be facing a certain direction as soon as it crosses the bordering 45-degree angle.

Although the concept of box mapping has some appeal, its usefulness is definitely limited. Problems with box materials include getting objects to face the correct way for the six material assignments; stretching of the bitmaps is controlled only by the size of the object and the map's scale parameters. Each different-sized object will have the materials stretched to a respectively different size and proportion. Because of this, box materials work best with unmapped materials or on objects with consistently dimensioned sides.

Another disadvantage box materials have is that they do not define a material for the faces. You can adjust the box mapping recipe with Surface/Material/Box/Acquire and Surface/Material/Box/Modify, but you cannot select or show faces based upon their material assignments. These materials technically do not exist in the scene and cannot be retrieved by the Materials Editor for adjustment. You must know the object has a box material assignment, get the material, modify it, and put it back into the library for it to affect the scene.

With all the shortcomings and caveats, some objects are perfect for box materials. Dice are the ultimate users of box mapping. These could be scores of objects, all with the same size ratios and all needing six different maps. A series of square, wooden spindles within a banister might be another candidate for box mapping (as long as you correct for the bitmap stretch in the map's V Scale parameter). Boxes, packages, presents, and file cabinets are other possibilities for box mapping.

Plug-In Material Options

The SXP type of Plug-Ins is the final, and potentially the most powerful, material map option. As the term *Solid Pattern External Process* (SXP) implies, these materials are cast through the entire mesh. This is done entirely with programmed equations—therefore, no pixel edges can be caught at odd angles and streak. The SXP is calculated about the object's geometry, and the resulting material is cast completely through it. Materials that only use SXP maps do not require any mapping coordinates. SXPs are also known as *procedural shaders* because they use mathematical procedures to shade the mesh's surface. The SXPs can be used in place of a bitmap in any map or mask file slot except for reflection maps and masks.

A feature of SXPs is that they are resolution independent because they are created by formulas rather than bitmaps. This means that you can get as close to a mesh's surface as you want, and the material remains smooth and without pixelation. The following exercise shows how useful these textures can be.

Experimenting with Solid Surface Plug-Ins

Create two intersecting spheres in the 3D Editor

The detail and type are not that important.

Perform a Boolean subtraction between the spheres	One sphere "takes a bite" out of the other
Enter the Materials Editor and create a material that uses MARBLE_I.SXP *as a 100-percent-strength texture map and make it current in the scene by pressing* C *and giving it a name*	Accept the SXP's default values for now
Assign the current material to the carved object, add some lights, and render	The veins of the marble material course through the object, as shown in figure 12.20

Figure 12.20
Marble applied to a sphere before and after Boolean operations.

No mapping coordinates are ever applied to the object and the material runs naturally and somewhat randomly through the object's entire depth. There are no right or wrong sides for an SXP material.

Using SXPs

For all their possibilities, SXPs do have drawbacks. The first disadvantage is that SXPs take a considerable amount of additional rendering time. You can show yourself how much additional time they require by comparing the rendering time of the previous exercise to the rendering time for the same object with a 320×200 texture map—the new rendering time for the texture map is probably only half that of the SXPs. Other drawbacks are that the orientation, angle, and scale of the Plug-In material are controlled by the orientation of the object's bounding box and the SXP's parameters only control the color, scale, and variation of the material.

The speed of calculating SXP materials has increased significantly with Release 4.

The amount an SXP can be manipulated depends on the parameters its programmers included. Each SXP replaces the standard bitmap parameters with its own custom parameter box. Some SXPs, such as VARY, have many options, whereas others have few or none. (CCUBE.SXP has no parameters because it was included as an example of what can be done.)

The direction in which a Plug-In material applies its effect is dependent on an object's bounding box orientation. For random SXPs, such as VARY, DENTS, NOISE, and STUCCO, the direction does not matter much because the pattern is applied equally in all directions. For those that create oriented patterns, such as MARBLE and WOOD, however, it matters a great deal. Figure 12.21 shows the disturbing effects of when these materials run contrary to the integrity of the object.

To change the direction of the marble veins and wood grain in the columns in figure 12.21 requires that you reset their bounding boxes, which can be accomplished by following these steps:

1. Rotate the object (using angle snap about the local axis makes this easy) so that it is facing the world axes correctly.

2. Use Modify/Object/Reset Xform to realign the bounding box.

3. Rotate the object back to its original position—it should now be correct.

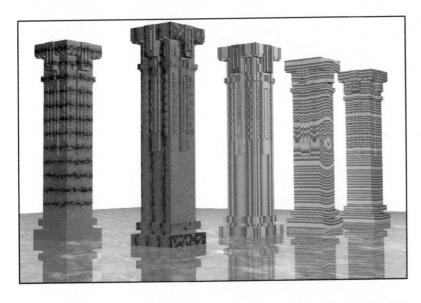

Figure 12.21
The effect of SXP materials with various bounding box orientations.

This might not seem too critical with a sphere, but it is paramount with objects built according to a material's orientation. Wood objects, for example, are cut with the grain. Seeing the grain of a chair leg going sideways, or worse yet showing the end grain, gives the impression that the chair will soon crack. Marble objects tend to have their veins running lengthwise as well. A formal column with horizontally striped marble is an odd sight.

After determining how the material runs in real life, you can reset an object's bounding box correctly. The WOOD.SXP, for example, places its end grain parallel to the front viewport's orientation. If you want the wood grain projected at an angle, rotate the object at an angle to the front viewport before resetting the bounding box.

SXPs as Bump Maps

Only certain SXPs work well when used as bump maps, including DENTS, STUCCO, and NOISE. These three also can be used as masks on one another to create even more variations, intensities, and iterations.

Other SXPs create subtle color variations across very small mathematical areas. Because bumps create their effect by showing a highlight or shadow at the transition of intensity, the result with these SXPs is minimal to nonexistent.

Using SXPs repeatedly within a material can deliver very convincing results. The following exercise shows how STUCCO.SXP is a good example of this.

III

Advanced Modeling

Repeating the Use of SXP Materials

Begin by creating a lustrous Phong material that uses STUCCO_I.SXP as a 100-percent-strength bump map

Renders the sample sphere, but the stucco dents are too large to see

Access the Stucco's parameter box, lower its size to 20, and render

Renders the sample sphere with stucco-like fissures, as in the left objects of figure 12.22

Figure 12.22
Using STUCCO.SXP once and then multiple times within a material.

The stucco's bumps are realistic, but the material is more like eroded plastic than anything else. To make it more lifelike requires additional maps.

Copy the bump map file slot to the shininess map file slot and render

The sphere is matted, but its fissures remain shiny

Access the shininess map's parameter box, and change the Color1 (black) color swatch to white and the Color2 (colored) swatch to black

This is the same as activating the Negative parameter for a standard intensity map

Render the sample

The sample is now shiny with dull fissures

This is beginning to look realistic, but it would be even more so if dust or sand were resting in the stucco's dents.

Click on a texture map file slot, choose GRANITE.CEL as a 55-percent-strength map, and render

The entire surface is covered with a light granite texture

Copy the bump map's file slot to the texture's mask file slot and render (see fig. 12.23)

Sand now rests in the fissures of the material, as shown in the right objects of figure 12.22

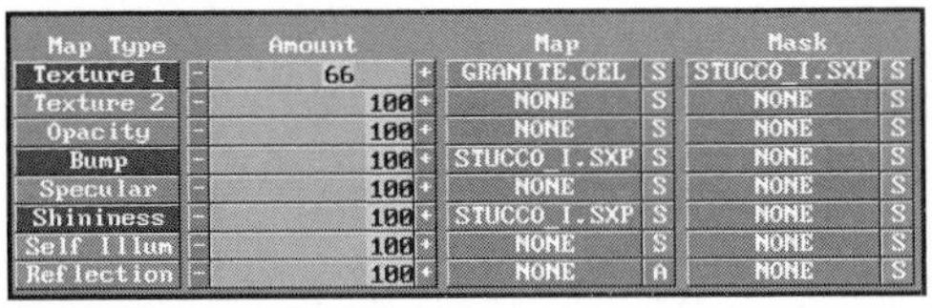

Map Type	Amount	Map		Mask	
Texture 1	66	GRANITE.CEL	S	STUCCO_I.SXP	S
Texture 2	100	NONE	S	NONE	S
Opacity	100	NONE	S	NONE	S
Bump	100	STUCCO_I.SXP	S	NONE	S
Specular	100	NONE	S	NONE	S
Shininess	100	STUCCO_I.SXP	S	NONE	S
Self Illum	100	NONE	S	NONE	S
Reflection	100	NONE	A	NONE	S

Figure 12.23
The final mapping assignments for the sand-filled stucco material.

Because a standard bitmap was added as a map, the material now requires mapping coordinates. The gravel's effect could have been accomplished by using another SXP, but would have made the material that much more costly in terms of rendering time.

New Life for SXPs

Most SXPs are limited to using two or three base colors from which they shade the material. This is fairly limiting and does not produce very realistic results. Some basic SXPs (wood and marble being the most notable) do not create enough variations to be very convincing. (The MARBLE.SXP has even been referred to as a "watermelon" texture because of its all too consistent veining.) This now can be overcome with the mapping capabilities first introduced with Release 3.

When the same SXP is used with scale variations as both the Texture 1 and Texture 2 maps, the results are much more convincing. Marble and wood veins and grain now run small and large. By changing the colors of the marble and wood, they produce even more realistic effects. By copying the file slots to isolate the shine or to bump one out more than the other is another method to add life to the material.

Combining these double textures with SXP bump and specular maps can have very convincing effects. Remember that standard bitmaps can be used as well, as long as mapping coordinates are applied to the mesh. These work well for adding more elements of randomness to the material mix.

Using SXPs to Create Bitmaps

When SXPs are used in combination, they can create wonderfully varied results, but the time constraints can be a problem. What many users forget is that SXPs also can be used to create, or at least start, your own random bitmaps.

This can be done simply by rendering a mesh with the material in a viewport that is square to the object's plane. Make sure that the lighting is smooth, or use no lights, increase the ambient light level to white, and render the view to a file. The result is a bitmap ready to be applied as a texture or modified in a paint program.

III

Advanced Modeling

Examining Material Pitfalls

Completed objects can be lit correctly, follow all the rules of perspective, be rendered smoothly and flawlessly by 3D Studio, and still look "wrong." You might see the effect yourself or it might be pointed out by a colleague—or worse—by a client. It is quite possible to work so much with a model and see its materials rendered so often, that you become anesthetized to the effect the materials actually are having. The reasons for a flawed effect are many; this section covers the most common and influential of them.

Artists often examine a work in progress by looking at it in a mirror (often a hand mirror over the shoulder). This trick of flipping the image shocks your visual senses and makes you analyze the image unbiasedly.

Correct Scaling

A very annoying effect is to have the incorrect scaling for a material that has a real-world size and proportion. Brick is a common example of this. Architects and builders know these proportions intuitively and base the size of details on the number of bricks required. If these sizes and proportions are off, or are different for various areas of the model, the believability of the image or animation is shattered.

Real-scale materials always must be applied with the correct mapping scale to not look "wrong." Getting the mapping scale right once and reusing it often is the key to being productive with these materials. In the case of bricks, three courses equals eight inches in height. If the bitmap represents 12 courses in a tileable manner, the mapping icon must be 32 inches in height—always. The bitmap also should be drawn to the correct proportions. In brick's case, bricks usually are three times as wide as they are tall. If the 12-course bitmap is square, it should be four bricks in width. This is the correct proportion as long as you are square to the face that receives it. If you use the common technique of applying the map at a 45-degree angle, the width of the map stretches by the length of the hypotenuse. (See Chapter 6, "Introduction to the Materials Editor," for scaling methods to correct this.)

Assigning materials and mapping to simple box objects, and saving them as an "acquirable material mesh library" that can be merged when needed, is very efficient for real-world materials whose scales are critical.

Correcting for the stretched-width effect is even trickier when using cylindrical mapping. If the brick texture is assigned to a silo, the width of the bricks is defined by the silo's radius. As discussed in Chapter 6, the brick's height-to-width ratio must equal the silo's circumference-to-icon height ratio to come out with the correct proportions. Because the height of the bricks and the radius of the silo are fixed, you can determine the bitmap's width scale factor. If a

32-inch–tall brick texture is assigned to the a silo with a radius of 15 feet (which has a circumference of 94.2 feet), the bitmap is stretched by the ratio of 1:35.325. To reverse the effect, you need to reduce the bitmap's U Scale parameter to 0.028308 (the inverse of 35.325) to correct for distortion and have correctly scaled bricks. (See Chapter 6 for a more in-depth discussion.)

The Need for Randomness

As materials are used repeatedly throughout a model, their effects can be taken for granted and become ineffective. This is the *wallpaper* effect, with which the same pattern is repeated so often and so regularly that it reads as a tone rather than a texture. Most real-world materials that have a repeat to them do not do so with such regularity. Materials like stone, tile, and brick have variation, and seeing a defined pattern destroys their believability. Applying them as basic tiled textures creates the effect of wallpaper and not, for example, brick.

Materials need variation and require a bit of randomness. In earlier releases of 3D Studio, this meant that you had to make larger and larger bitmaps to create enough internal variation to minimize the effects of tiling. The current capability to overlay maps and masks at different scales, offsets, and rotations can provide limitless variations with only a few, often-repeated bitmaps.

Making Materials Look Real

If there is one quality in an image or animation that signals its computer-generated origins, it is that things tend to look *too good* to be real. Although somewhat humorous, and possibly meant as a back-handed compliment, this is a very valid criticism.

Real-world objects have a life to them. They become scratched and stained, wear unevenly, or are not constructed perfectly to begin with. When materials meet, they tend to have a seam or gap and are rarely perfectly flush. Objects are rarely arranged in perfect order and doing so is viewed by many as obsessive. Yet these are qualities common to computer models and mapping. If you are striving for true realism, you will need to take the extra time to vary and give life to the materials.

Simulating Grime, Dirt, Wear, and Age

The key to simulating real-world materials is to represent their inconsistencies and faults. Objects are not perfectly smooth and completely clean in daily life. The best method for adding these elements of grit to your materials is to create a collection of tileable, random bitmaps that represent smears, streaks, dust, cracks, droplets, and stains. After these are created, use the same bitmaps throughout your "real world" materials library. By designing effective maps, you can reuse them repeatedly in subtle ways without them getting old.

When the same collection of randomizing maps is used for materials, the memory costs are not overly prohibitive. These maps should be as low in strength as shininess, Texture 1, and bump maps, as well as in the form of masks to add scars and inclusions to other maps. Creating truly realistic materials is not easy, but then again neither is painting them.

Editing True Color

Editing a true-color, 24-bit image sounds intimidating but should not be. In fact, many people find it easier and more intuitive to work in true color than with 8-bit color. The reason is that you are working in a WYSIWYG (pronounced "Whizee Wig," it stands for "What-You-See-Is What-You-Get") environment. You don't have to think about color palettes—all you have to do is paint.

With a 24-bit color paint program, you see an image as it is, in true color. This used to be a luxury that came at a premium price and with limited options. The recent arrival of low-cost, high-color graphics cards and option-packed paint programs, however, makes true color affordable to the point that it should be considered standard equipment. If you are using 3D Studio, you definitely should be viewing its output on a 24-bit color card and have access to a true-color paint program.

True-Color Image Sources

3D Studio's World Creating Toolkit is a great resource of high-quality images. Other images can be purchased from third-party suppliers and most often come on CD-ROM (due primarily to their inherent size). Some of the best and most appropriate images might, however, come from you.

Color Scanners

Scanners come in hand-held, drum, and flatbed varieties. Although affordable, *hand-held* scanners have a tendency to stretch and curve the image as your hand speed varies and shifts. *Drum* scanners are the highest quality, but require a flat, bendable image and are quite expensive. *Flatbed* color scanners have come down significantly in price and offer the most latitude in what items can be scanned.

A scanner copies any opaque item that can be placed on its glass. Scanners are great for scanning photographs, sketches, or actual samples of physical materials.

Most color scanners have an input resolution of at least 300 dpi. This makes even a standard 3 ½-inch × 5-inch photo a 1050 × 1500 true-color image, which is very suitable for most purposes.

Photo CDs

An alternative to scanning is 35mm photography. You can always take photographs, make prints, and have them scanned, but this is only the beginning.

Kodak introduced its Photo CD format in 1993 and opened up an entirely new option for computer artists and photo retouchers. A Kodak-certified lab can place an image from any 35mm negative or transparency on a CD at a resolution of 3072 × 2048 for a reasonable price (usually much less than two dollars per image). Up to 100 images can fit on a single CD, and you can append images to an existing Photo CD.

For a CD player to read appended images to a Kodak Photo CD, it must have a multisession capability. All players should be able to read the first series of images put to the CD, however.

A good technique for creating Photo CD libraries is to always shoot slide film. This enables you to pick, choose, and organize the images to be put to the CD while having a "thumbnail" slide of it for reference.

Transparencies are never color-corrected by a processing lab, whereas prints from negatives often are. Processing can eliminate effects you strove to capture, such as contrast and colored filters. If you want the purest representation of what you photograph, always shoot slide film.

Copyright Issues with Images

It is very important to realize that any published image is, by default, copyrighted. Whenever you scan a published image, you are walking a tightrope of legal ambiguity. The capability to capture, reshape, and reuse images is so new that the legal system has not kept up with it. The thing to remember is that an image is the property of the artist or photographer and possibly the publisher.

It is generally acceptable to use an image if you "make it your own." This does not mean that recropping, stretching, or sending it through a quick filter makes it yours. You must spend sufficient time to transform the image into a personal statement. A subjective gray area? Definitely, and it is one that should be handled carefully.

You are probably safe in extracting a portion of a photo for use as a texture or effect, as long as it is not in itself the photo's original composition. As a rule, you should never use published photos for backgrounds because this is a direct copy of the original.

When you purchase images from third parties, make sure that party has waived all copyrights as to the images' use. You might be surprised to find out that most have not waived their rights and are simply selling you "pretty pictures"—not images to be used at will. Note that the World Creating Toolkit is sold to you without any restrictions, but you are not entitled to turn around and resell the images.

Many items are copyrighted outright. Cartoon characters and company logos are common examples of things that cannot be reproduced without permission. This situation can even extend into buildings and places. The Walt Disney company, for example, considers anything within its theme parks to be copyrighted and does not allow the commercial reproduction of any photo taken without direct permission. The best rule to follow is: "If you're not sure, don't use it."

III

Advanced Modeling

To be secure in the ownership of your product, use your own artwork and photographs or those from commissioned photographers and artists. Keep in mind, also, that *you* have ownership of these images and that a market for useful and high-quality images does exist.

True-Color Options

Nearly as many image file types exist as do programs to edit them. Deciding which file type to use often is determined by which format can be accessed by the programs and service bureaus you plan to use. Many true-color paint programs are designed around the concepts of photo retouching, four-color separations, and the needs of the graphic and printing industry. Eight-bit programs, such as Animator Pro, are geared toward computer imaging and video game design and might work better for creating smaller decals and textures.

The native image file format for 3D Studio is the 24- and 32-bit compressed TGA and, all other things being equal, should be your first choice for output. This is the only file format that enables you to place comments and record Gamma information. Note that the TGA format is primarily a DOS standard and you might have difficulty porting it to other platforms, such as the Macintosh (whose native format is TIFF).

Most true-color paint programs on the DOS platform work within the Windows operating system (notable exceptions to this are QFX and Lumena). Most of these programs can read and write many image formats, but might vary as to their "flavors" or version of writing and compression algorithm. Things to watch out for are formats that cannot be written in compressed format and especially those that discard or corrupt alpha information within 32-bit images. Although the native image format for Windows is .BMP, it cannot be compressed and few other platforms support it. It is not uncommon to have to open up programs just to read an image file and save it to another format.

Many programs can read uncompressed files more quickly than compressed ones. If disk space is not at a premium, you might want to consider saving working files in uncompressed TGA or TIFF formats.

When you use a true-color paint program, you always are drawing and editing in true color, even if your display is not capable of displaying all 16.7 million colors. For this reason, many users work in 16- or 15-bit color, sacrificing color depth for a larger display resolution. When working at these color resolutions (65 KB and 32 KB colors), you can see some banding and color differences in what are actually smooth and even transitions. The file has not changed, only your ability to see the colors. Although 24-bit color is preferred, this depth of color is often acceptable. Working on true-color images in 8-bit (256-color) is inaccurate to the point of being dangerous and should not be considered an option.

When to Edit in True Color

The question of whether to edit a file in true color or in 8-bit color (as with Animator Pro) comes down to the simple question of "do you need the image in true color?" This might sound absolutely obvious, but you actually should consider the following points:

✔ True-color files obviously require more disk space and take more time to load, but as far as 3D Studio is concerned, all files take the same amount of memory at rendering time—three bytes per pixel.

✔ True color is not always needed. Bitmaps are often small and may not even contain 256 colors. If the bitmap does not require a higher color count, you do not need to use a format that allows for high color. This is especially true of intensity maps for which the optimal format is actually 8-bit grayscale.

✔ Will the image be seen at a size in which true color becomes an issue? Material bitmaps might start out as low color but are affected by perspective, have all the effects of light, shade, and shadow placed upon them, and the result rendered in true color. If the object is not very pronounced in the final image, it probably will be difficult to tell whether its material's bitmap began as an 8-bit or 24-bit image.

✔ The higher the output resolution, the more true-color maps you should use. As images are rendered larger, their quantity of base colors becomes more important. Your eye has more time and area in which to inspect the image, and low-color bitmaps can cause an image to look flat or pixelated. In most cases, if an image starts out as true color, it should be kept that way until disk space no longer allows it.

✔ If the image is to be used as a background, it almost has to be true color. If the background sky is 8-bit, only the original 256 shades of color are present in the sky at the completion of the rendering. 3D Studio only affects a background image if an atmosphere is active. Otherwise, the rendered result is the same as rendering the scene on a solid color, and then pasting the rendered image on the background bitmap in a paint program (except that 3D Studio provides the anti-aliasing for the scene against the background).

You *can* affect a background image through the use of the Keyframer's Video Post and possibly IXP processes.

✔ If you are editing a final scene image, true color is really your only choice (unless your final copy is intended to be low color). It is quite common to need to edit or at least proof a final image. True-color paint programs give you the opportunity to make final adjustments, add highlights, tweak modeling errors, and so on. Some modelers find it easier to add an entourage of trees, cars, and people at this stage than to do so earlier. (Note, however, that these added pieces might not be in the same perspective, lighting, or atmosphere as the rendered scene.)

Adjusting Background Images

Background images make up an important part of many 3D Studio images. The trick is using the appropriate background image in the correct place and at the needed scale. As with standard bitmaps, background images require three bytes per pixel to use. An additional three bytes per pixel are required if the bitmap needs to be rescaled to fit the scene at rendering time. This is what the manuals mean by "not requiring any additional memory." Backgrounds require the three bytes per pixel regardless of the actual file type or size.

The Background Rescale option (located in the Renderer's dialog box) thus becomes an expensive tool and should never be used with a model, if possible. If you find the need to rescale an image while you are within 3D Studio, render a blank screen and resize the image to a new file. This newly resized image should be the background image you use from then on.

Simply rescaling an image might not be the right answer for a background. In this book, it is assumed that the bitmap for the background is an unretouched true-color image. An image can handle only so much distortion before it becomes obvious and disturbing. When scaling an image, you want to make sure that its height-to-width ratio stays constant. Ideally, you want to scale an image down—not up. As an image gets larger, it does not gain any more detail—it just gets fuzzier. This might be acceptable for soft images like clouds but can be distracting for definitive images such as street scenes. Decreasing image size is fine (the detail is averaged), but do not make the mistake of discarding the original because it contains the better-quality image.

After you know your output resolution, you can resize your background image to fit it. This is best done in a paint program because tools are available to ensure the correct proportions.

Qualities of a Background Image

A background image sets the overall mood and coloring for the scene. It's very possible that the direction and color of the light source are indicated by shadows and highlights within the background image as well. If your scene's characteristics contradict those of the background, it can easily ruin the effect. Your goal should be to make the background image appear as an extension of the scene—not as a backdrop photo for a model. You must either make the scene fit the background, or the background fit the scene.

Paint programs are very good at quickly flipping or rotating images. This is helpful in casting their shadows in the right direction. The higher-end programs (for example, Photoshop, PhotoStyler, and QFX) are very good at changing color balances, contrasts, and highlights.

Backgrounds and Horizons

It is very common for a background image to show the horizon. This reinforces the illusion of distance and gives greater depth to your images. These effects are ruined, however, if the image's horizon does not match the scene's!

Placing a stock background image indiscriminately can make the viewer feel that the scene is in a hole when the horizon is too high, or on a hilltop if the horizon is too low. When the final camera position and angle of view are determined, it is time to locate the scene's horizon.

One method for locating the horizon in a rendering is to place a single plane, or the side of a box, at the height of the camera. Scale the object about this point until it fills the screen—this is the horizon for that camera. Rendering this camera view with just the object in wireframe mode produces an image with the proper resolution and a line at the exact pixel location of the horizon, which can then be referenced from within your paint program.

Remember that the horizon is always parallel to the ground plane, and its height is determined solely by the height of the view's camera from the ground plane. It does not matter at what angle the target is or if the camera has been rolled. (See Chapter 2, "Concepts and Theories," for further discussion on a scene's horizon.)

Release 4 enables you to see a camera's horizon line and its relationship to an 8-bit color background image with Camera Control.

After the horizon is located in the scene, the background must be positioned to match it. Unfortunately, no mechanism exists for placing the background image itself. 3D Studio starts the image in the upper left corner and tiles the image from that point onward, if necessary, as shown in figure 12.24.

You have three pieces of information on which to base the size of the background image: the output resolution, your background image's resolution, and the height in pixels of the scene's horizon. Figure 12.25 shows how the image must be cropped if the top of the image is higher than the horizon distance. If the image is too short, it needs to be enlarged to match the height proportionally about the horizon line.

Figure 12.24
3D Studio's background tiling.

Figure 12.25
Cropping decisions for a horizon image.

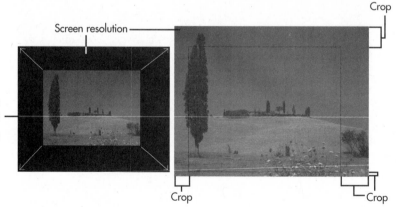

 If a horizon image is too short for the current rendering resolution, you can scale or stretch just the sky portion of the image (in a paint program) to create the required output size. This type of edit is rarely noticeable and leaves other areas of the image undistorted.

Often, you do not need much of the image below the horizon. The modeled scene's mid- and foreground take up much of this real estate, and cropping the image at this point will save memory.

An alternate method to compositing the scene within 3D Studio is to do it in a true-color paint program that respects Alpha channels. Rendering your scene in 32-bit enables you to bring that image into the paint program and simply slide it around over another image until it is in the desired position. Your rendered image's alpha information provides the transparency information for a perfect, anti-aliased composite.

Making a Background Tileable

The most useful background images are those that tile from left to right. This background trait allows the image to wrap seamlessly in reflections and can be tiled for larger images. The problem is that photographs and stock images do not naturally tile. This situation requires editing, and is a major reason for needing a true-color paint program.

Making an image tileable requires patience, skill, and trickery. You will need to use most of the painting, editing, and selection tools available within your true-color paint program. This section assumes that you are already comfortable with your paint program's use and capabilities.

Selecting an Appropriate Image

A big part of making an image tile successfully is selecting the right image and the right place for the seam. The image should have interest, but not any extremely identifiable elements or landmarks that will be obvious when repeated. Images that include the sun are obviously poor choices if the image is going to repeat. The image also should indicate depth and distance without indicating perspective. Shots that include diminishing streets, walks, or lined buildings can conflict with the scene's perspective and cause it to look "out of square" with the world.

Making the Image Tile

The image pictured in figures 12.24 and 12.25 is TUSCANY.JPG—included in 3D Studio's MAPS directory. This image has many of the elements that go into making a good tileable background. The following exercise manipulates this image.

As figure 12.22 shows, the TUSCANY.JPG image cannot tile from left to right. After a few steps in a paint program, it will be able to tile without a problem. The following exercise steps are generic instructions that can be applied to numerous true-color paint programs.

Making a Tileable Background

Begin by opening the image and determining its dimensions	The bitmap is 640 × 480 in size
Start a new image the same height, but twice as wide	The new (blank) image is 1280 × 480

continues

continued

Copy TUSCANY *to the new image and paste it side by side*	The image looks similar to figure 12.26

Figure 12.26
The beginning step in creating a tileable background image.

Seam area to be blended

Figure 12.26 shows the area of the seam where all the editing occurs. Now it is just a matter of blending the two sides of the image together with whatever paint and selection tools are at hand. Begin with any landmarks cut by the seam.

Tip

A common problem occurs when the seam cuts through a significant feature and there is nothing comparable to blend with on the other side. One way of fixing this is to copy the portion of the image with the feature and flip/mirror it horizontally. Now paste this image next to the original's edge and the feature is mirrored to completion. The only drawback is that you now have two seams to blend. Note that it is important to record the width of this filler piece.

Select sections of the shrub and flip them horizontally	Creates a matching mirror image
Paste several of these sections and use blur, smudge, and soften tools to work them into the scene	The pasted images can, and should, overlap
Below this area, copy irregular horizontal portions of the grass from one side, paste them over the seam, and blend as usual	

Soften, blur, and smudge are some of the most useful tools. The goal is not to leave a visible seam. An aid in doing this is to grab small selections of the image and paste or pull them over the seam during the editing process. This prevents the area from looking like a vertical smear. Feel free to extend your blends and blurs horizontally, far to either side of the seam. Doing this will minimize the vertical seam.

The horizon line presents a different problem. Here you need to create a sloping hill to merge the left and right horizons.

Copy a portion of ground from the darker right-hand portion over the seam	Try to align the highlights in the sand
Emphasize the color difference between the two hills	This makes the second hill appear farther in the distance
Blur a highlight onto the ridge of the left hill and soften the new hill against the sky	Again, try to emphasize depth of field

Now all that is left is the sky, which is usually the easy part. Skies change color from the horizon to the azimuth, therefore you must be careful to make all selection pastes and paint blurs horizontally and never vertically or at an angle.

Make several free-form–shaped selections and paste them from the left and the right over the seam	
Use softening tools to blur the sky from left to right	The seam and the image are now complete (see fig. 12.27)

Valid area for selecting final image

Figure 12.27
The working image with a completed seam.

Sky copied in free-form pieces and blurred

Hill crested by pasting and blending

Shrub mirrored and blended

Grass pasted from either side

When a convincing match is made at the seam, the image only needs to be recropped. As long as no filler pieces are placed between the sides, the tileable image is the same size as the original.

continues

III

Advanced Modeling

continued

Crop an area of the scene that has the seam in its middle third	The newly cropped image will be full height and needs to be exactly 640 pixels wide
Save the new 640 × 480 image	The image is now complete and tileable, as shown in figure 12.28

Figure 12.28
The finished, tileable background image.

The final image should capture all the blending and modifying you did to either side. You do not need to be concerned with composition at this point. After the image has been cropped, you can tile/fill it across a new file and crop again. Examine the tile seams to see if more work needs to be done. (They should be invisible.) After you have the image tiled in a new file, you can crop it again to form the intended composition. This can be cropped anywhere along the length of the tiled image as long as it remains the exact size of the tiling image.

If a filler piece was used, add its width to that of the original image. Adding pieces always adds to the overall width of the finished tileable image.

Other Tiling Backgrounds

Skies are the easiest backgrounds to create tiles with. Skies can be flipped, blurred, and stretched without looking "wrong"—who's to say what a cloud can or cannot look like? Make sure that the sky does not change color from the horizon to the azimuth. Blurs and copies should be made horizontally, or the sky's gradation will be incorrect.

After a sky is made horizontally tileable, it becomes very useful as a spherical reflection map because no seam is at the rear. As with all spherical bitmaps, the image should be exactly twice as wide as it is tall to minimize the distortion.

Two-Way Tiling Images

Images that tile in both directions are primarily used as texture maps. Texture maps are the most valuable bitmaps in your collection because they are the most flexible and require the least amount of memory for the greatest effect.

Tileable, true-color maps are a rare commodity, and you usually need to create your own. The sample .TGA and .JPG textures on the World Creating Toolkit can make excellent tiles, but they also require a fair amount of your time to make them work. After they are made, however, they will be a valuable addition to your map library and of use for a very long time.

Making Tileable Wood

If an image is not tileable it must be mapped at full size to not show a seam. Although the World Creating Toolkit's sample wood textures are rich in color, they lose their appeal when they tile and show seams or are stretched far beyond the size of any naturally occurring grain. By making these tile, you can assign the wood texture at the proper scale for your object. This is extremely important for realism in an image.

 When an image is edited to properly tile, it inevitably loses some detail and much of its randomness. For this reason, the original should never be discarded, but rather used in association with the tileable image(s) for objects that require richer detail at a smaller scale.

The procedure for making a two-way tile is the same as a one-way tile—you just have to do it twice. The easiest method is to make the image tile correctly in one direction, and then make it tileable in the other. Remember that the tiling image always is the same size as the original bitmap. Figure 12.29 shows the bitmap ASHSEN.GIF, supplied in 3D Studio's MAPS directory, after it has been tiled. Because ASHSEN.GIF cannot tile in either direction, it has been renamed ASHEN0 to distinguish it from its tiling cousins.

With a definitive material like wood, it is very important to maintain the integrity and characteristics of the grain. Examine which way the grain runs and what might be the next natural progression to either side. This is what you need to approximate across the seam. Blending and blurring on a wood texture only makes for a smeared connection. The key with definable materials is copying numerous, irregularly shaped pieces and rotating, flipping, and stretching them until they form the connecting grain. After the defining grain is established, you blend the surrounding fields together. This job is easier with ASHSEN0 because several of the seam

Figure 12.29
The original
ASHSEN0, and
the effect of it
being tiled.

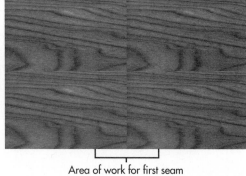

Area of work for first seam

Figure 12.30
The impression of
ASHSEN1 after it
has been made to
tile like horizontal
planking.

Area of work for second seam

grains are already very close. Completing the tip of the left swirl and patching the other side's connections does the trick and delivers ASHSEN1, as shown in figure 12.30.

 It often is useful to keep the single direction tiling image as its own bitmap in your map collection. This enables you to tile in one direction when you need to (planks of wood or rows of marble, for example).

When the image is tileable in one direction, the working image needs to be enlarged to allow for another copy to the top or bottom. A good starting point for the blend is often the intersecting cross of the four images, going an equal distance to either side. The starting and ending points really do not matter as long as the blend extends the width of the original image. With ASHEN1, several pieces of grain were mirrored to complete the dominant swirl pattern.

Figure 12.31
The impression of ASHSEN2 after it has been made to tile like a repeating veneer.

After the second seam blend is made, crop the image to the original size anywhere that includes the new blend. You now can tile the image, check, make corrections, and crop again. As long as you maintain the original image size, you always can crop and edit anywhere across the tiled image. Figure 12.31 shows the completed ASHSEN2 bitmap and the effects of its tile.

The choice of the bitmap's final composition is completely up to you. Examine the tiled effect, and you will see that you can place a 320×200 cropping window anywhere along the image, and it will tile correctly. This applies to any tiling image—even ones that are purchased. If the bitmap's single composition is not to your liking, tile it and crop it until you are satisfied with it. As long as the cropped bitmap maintains the original size, it will tile seamlessly again.

 If color depth is not critical, converting the image to an 8-bit dithered GIF or JPEG can be a final step in making the image more seamless. This reduction of color smooths seamed areas that might be difficult to make convincing.

Summary

The subject of materials and mapping and relating them to those within the world can never be fully discussed. The Materials Editor provides the tools you need to create nearly any imaginable texture or illusion. Time spent learning these techniques goes a long way toward making even the simplest model rich with variety and interest.

Chapter Snapshot

In this chapter, the following topics are presented:

✔ Simulating the sun and its shadows

✔ Modeling common interior lighting effects

✔ Creating the appearance of various types of illuminated signage

✔ Using projector lights

✔ Simulating light beams

✔ Correcting perspectives for wide-angled camera lenses

✔ Using atmospheres in scenes

✔ Using Fast Preview and Camera Control to align background images

Lighting and Camera Special Effects

This chapter utilizes and combines the capabilities of lighting and cameras first described in Chapter 7, "Lights, Cameras, and Basic Rendering Options." This chapter is about applications and combining effects to create the appropriate mood or condition. Because of this, very little new material is covered and it is assumed you have become comfortable with the commands and techniques illustrated previously.

Few photo-realistic effects in 3D Studio are automatic or *canned*. To create the proper effect requires the correct combination of all its elements: modeling, materials, lighting, and viewing. Proper lighting and viewing require that all other elements are developed. The final placement of those elements depends on the decisions that are previously made.

Examining Lighting Techniques

The many parameters, settings, options, and attributes for lights and shadows combine to give you a great deal of flexibility in achieving specific and special effects. This section explores ways to use these settings to create realistic lighting simulations and possibly reduce overall rendering times.

Maximizing Shadow Control

You might be surprised, but this chapter does not heavily discuss the use of shadows. After you learn the balancing of shadow parameters, the effects are fairly automatic, although time intensive for rendering. The majority of lighting effects rely on light positioning, exclusion, projected images, and attenuation rather than shadows. This can require more spotlights, but the time required to calculate them is far less than that of shadows.

But shadows do have their place, and for bitmapped shadows the quality depends immensely on the correct balance of the three parameters. Because these vary greatly according to each model, it is assumed that the optimal settings have been discovered and are being used.

The darkness of a shadow is compromised by all the light that can strike the same surface. This means ambient light, all omni lights, and non-shadow casting spotlights will reduce a shadow's effect. Careful placement of auxiliary lights and using them with attenuation are the keys to maximizing the depth of shadows.

The one light that is always present and which you can never reduce is ambient light. A shadow can never be any darker than the light level produced by this setting. As a result, many modelers leave this light quite dim (an RGB of 10,10,10 for example) to intensify shadows and rely on other lights for general illumination. Because ambient light is always present, you can use it to tint the color of your shadows. If the ambient light's RGB color is 15,5,10, the color found in the shadows is purple-based.

The ambient light level can be reduced by the definition and use of an atmosphere (described at the end of this chapter).

Simulating the Sun

The sun is the most commonly needed light source for a model, yet it is not directly available in 3D Studio. To simulate the effects of the sun requires correct spotlight placement and basic understanding of how sunlight strikes the earth.

Shadow Flare

The sun possesses several unique qualities, but the most noticeable is the type of shadows it casts on the earth.

For a static scene, the most noticeable impact sunlight has is its shadows. Standard forms of light create shadows whose edges flare in perspective towards the vanishing point defined by the light source. A common lighting position might be fairly close, as shown in figure 13.1, which results in the highly flared shadows shown in figure 13.2. A shadow location is traced along a vector stretched from the light source to the object's edge—the closer the light, the greater the flare.

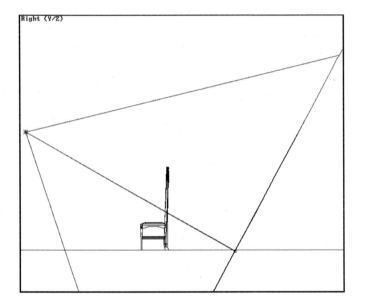

Figure 13.1
A closely placed spotlight.

Flared shadows can add considerable drama to your scene, especially because they can make the object appear much larger and foreboding. Sometimes, however, flared lights aren't your best option, especially when you're talking about outdoor scenes and architectural models. Shadows cast from a building's overhangs and balconies that do not parallel each other can create a disturbing effect. The effect is of a miniature model illuminated with a studio lamp—which is exactly what 3D Studio is doing.

Parallel Shadows

The sun observes the rules of cast shadows as well, but its great distance from the earth places the traced vectors so close in angle to one another that they are considered parallel. This is the definition of a parallel light source and must be approximated in 3D Studio.

III

Advanced Modeling

Figure 13.2
The resulting shadow flare of the closely placed spotlight.

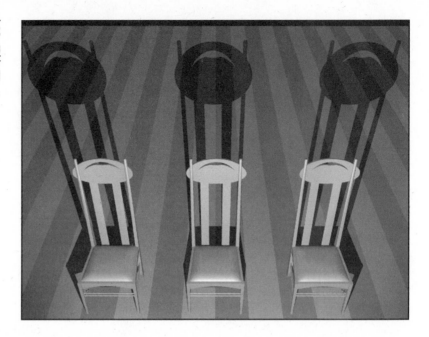

The key to creating near-parallel shadows is to place the spotlight as *far away* as possible so that the traced vectors' angles are as *close* as possible to one another. The extent to which you can move a spotlight is tied to its minimum falloff angle. In Release 4, this angle is 1 degree with a 0.5 degree hotspot. After you change a spotlight's parameter to these minimum angles, it's just a matter of moving the light out to a point at which the minimum cone fills the scene. The Lights/Spot/Dolly command makes this procedure quite easy. After you achieve the correct lighting angle for the sun, you can use the Dolly command to move it to the furthest possible position without disturbing its angle of incidence. Once at the maximum position, the lines of the spotlight's cone appear to be nearly parallel, as shown in figure 13.3. Figure 13.4 shows how the shadows cast from this extreme light are nearly parallel (as parallel as they get with the current release).

You should couple the placement of such a spotlight with a parameter setting strategy. For best results, the sun spotlight should always cast ray-traced shadows, and its falloff cone should be as small as possible for the model. Exclude as many objects as possible from casting shadows (especially the ground plane). Activate the sun spotlight's Overshoot parameter so its tight cone isn't noticeable. Figure 13.5 shows many of the characteristics common for solar definition.

Because this light is so far away, it has a very even angle of incidence to the model's objects and should not be given an RGB color channel much greater than 180. Higher color values wash out too many of the surfaces perpendicular to the sun.

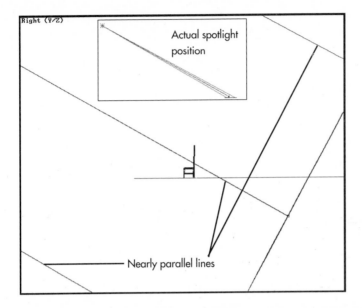

Figure 13.3
The near parallel lines of an extreme spotlight.

Figure 13.4
The near parallel shadows resulting from an extreme spotlight.

III

Advanced Modeling

Figure 13.5
Possible sun-like parameters for a spotlight definition.

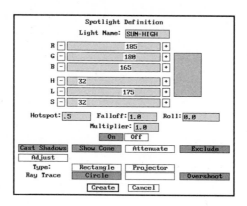

The Color of Sunlight

Parallel shadows are only the first attribute of sunlight. The color of sunlight varies considerably with the time of day, its position in the sky, and the purity of the atmosphere. The color you choose can vary considerably and still be "correct" because the quality of the sun's light changes day to day. The only rule to keep in mind is that sunlight is whitest when the sun is highest in the sky. When the sun is lower in the sky, it penetrates much more atmosphere, which makes for the often spectacular sunrises and sunsets.

 You can simulate the varied light of a sunset or sunrise by making the sun spotlight a projector that uses a vibrant, random, and very softly focused image.

Solar Positioning

The position of the sun in the sky depends on the latitude of the scene's location on earth, the time of year, and the time of day. Knowing this information, you can derive the sun's angle by consulting a solar path diagram. These are available for various latitudes and can be found in numerous references (Architectural Graphic Standards, for example).

 AutoVision, Autodesk's rendering program for use within AutoCAD, includes a sun locator for its parallel light source. When writing to a 3DS file, this light is converted to a 3D Studio spotlight at the correct angle for the time and location previously chosen.

This procedure delivers one solar angle and position for one time of the day. It's common, however, to need to chart the sun's shadows across the length of a day in a time-lapse fashion. You can make a rough approximation of this by creating an inclined arc in the 2D Shaper and applying it as a Spotlight path in the Keyframer. This can create the illusion you want if accuracy is not paramount, and if you have the time.

Animating the Sun

If you need to animate the sun for a particular time and place, the SOLARTRACK Plug-In (available from the Pyros Partnership) can be invaluable. The SOLARTRACK Plug-In charts a path for the sun's position (or any of the planets' position) in relationship to a selected object for the specified date, location, and duration. If you apply this path to the spotlight in the Keyframer, the result is an arced path (see figs. 13.6 and 13.7).

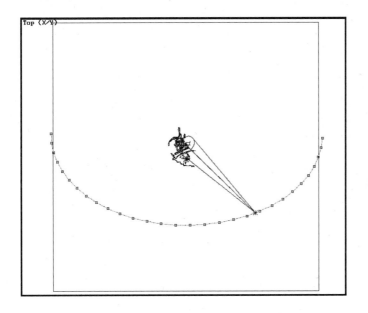

Figure 13.6
A solar path, as seen from the top.

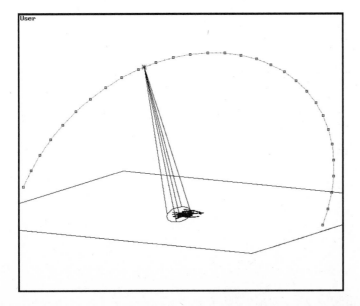

Figure 13.7
The same solar path, as seen from an angle.

Advanced Modeling

Examining these correct solar paths can give you some insight into a sun's basic path. Figure 13.7 shows that the path is actually an even arc that is at an incline to the ground plane. As the time of year approaches summer, or the location nears the equator, the arc becomes closer to perpendicular to the earth's surface.

You can create a circular path motion for a spotlight quite easily by linking the spotlight to a correctly positioned dummy object and rotating it to form the arced path.

Simulating Artificial Lighting

When you try to approximate real-life lighting situations, you should pay careful attention to how lamps actually cast light. Overdramatizing a lighting effect and casting very harsh-edged light is a common mistake. Most light does not occur in this fashion, and is much more diffused, soft, and without definite light pools. Lighting designers and architects go to great lengths to place and space fixtures so that they do not create hotspots, scallops, or solitary pools. Lighting manufacturers try to manufacture lights that distribute light evenly and without pattern. Both of these practices are difficult in the real world, and you might find them equally difficult to simulate in 3D Studio.

Simulating Interior Lighting

Most lighting designers strive for even illumination in most areas and reserve dramatic lighting to call attention to architectural details or artwork, or to act as a patterned light design on its own. Overemphasizing light sources and their impact is unfortunately all too common in computer renderings. Just because a light source is present does not mean that its effect is blatantly obvious.

Can lights are a typical example of this tendency. Many modelers feel that they must show the effects of each light—after all, they are there and they have been positioned and possibly even modeled. To make their presence clear, their light is often strong and their hotspots sharp. The result is *pools of light*—a characteristic that has its uses for highlighting certain objects, but that is generally considered poor lighting design. The correct way to illuminate the scene is to use broad soft lights that gently overlap and whose light pools are not particularly discernible.

Sconces and Light Scallops

Wall sconces are elements of lighting design that require emphasis of their effects. These indirect lights are often used to create scalloped light pools on the wall as they illuminate the ceiling—the intent being to light that area of the room indirectly by bouncing their light off of the ceiling. Because 3D Studio lights do not do this automatically (only a radiosity renderer can), their effect must be simulated.

The following exercise uses the SCONCES.3DS room model, with meshes already developed for the fixtures and a low omni light for general ambient lighting effect. If you simply want to see the final lighting effects, you can merge the lights from the LIGHTS_1.3DS file.

Simulating Wall Sconce Illumination

Load the SCONCES.3DS *file*

Begin by placing a spotlight in the center of the middle sconce, just in front of the wall

Point the target at the ceiling and flare the falloff until it meets the edge of the fixture, and then render

There is a strong light pool on the ceiling, but the wall is barely illuminated

Light from a sconce does not actually go straight up, but radiates from the point source. To get this effect right, the spotlight must aim at the wall and not the ceiling.

Move the target into and past the wall plane and flare the falloff again until it is just behind the lip of the fixture

The angle of the target and falloff to the fixture should appear as shown in figure 13.8

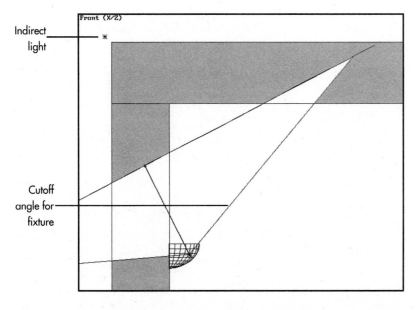

Figure 13.8
Constraining the falloff to form the fixture's critical cutoff.

Adjust the hotspot so that it is about half the diameter of the falloff

The hotspot should be similar to the middle fixture of figure 13.9

continues

III

Advanced Modeling

continued

Figure 13.9
Different hotspot
ratios for cloned
spotlights.

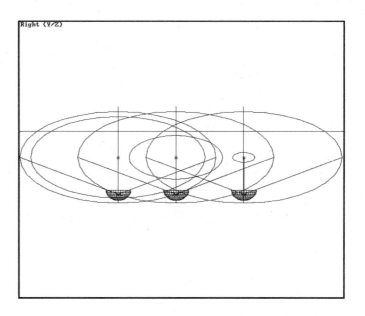

Render the scene

A scalloped light pool is formed, as shown
in the middle fixture of figure 13.10

Figure 13.10
Light scallops from
spotlights with
varying hotspots.

Copy the spotlight to the left sconce, move the hotspot close to the falloff's edge, and render	The light scallop now has a very crisp edge in the left fixture
Copy the spotlight to the right sconce, reduce the hotspot, and render	The light is now very soft, and a scallop is barely discernible in the right fixture

The quality of the light scallop is controlled by the hotspot's size, not the spotlight's intensity. These effects did not require the use of shadows or even attenuation. A common misconception is that to get these effects requires the falloff to exceed the size of the fixture and cast a shadow to form the cutoff. This produces a very crisp edge and takes considerably longer to render. In actuality, you only need to do this when the lighting fixtures are transparent or translucent, and you need to cast the shadows of their enclosure.

The preceding example produced a scalloped pattern on the ceiling and wall, but did nothing to illuminate the space around it—light cannot be reflected in 3D Studio. To simulate bounced light (radiosity) requires an additional light source, as shown in the following exercise.

Simulating Bounce Light

Create an omni light and place it behind the ceiling and wall plane corner (see upper left corner of fig. 13.8)	The location should be similar to figure 13.8
Choose Lights/Omni/Adjust	
Adjust the omni light to no more than half the intensity of the sconce lights	The desired effect is a soft, evenly spread light
Exclude the sconce(s), wall, and ceiling from the omni light	This helps increase rendering speed
Render the scene to show the floor	There is now a soft glow of "indirectly" cast light

III

Advanced Modeling

Simulating Linear Light Sources

Linear light sources are not directly supported by 3D Studio, but with some effort and the use of rectangular spotlights and possibly projected bitmaps, you can simulate their illumination effects.

Linear Tube Lights

A rectangular spotlight can be made to seem linear if its aspect ratio is maximized. You can create a linear light pattern by increasing the spotlight to a maximum falloff (175 degrees), and then adjusting the aspect ratio until it is a long, thin rectangle.

This might seem like a simple solution, but rectangular spotlights must be used knowing one caveat—the focus point remains circular. The result from such a spotlight is an illuminated rectangle that has a circular center hotspot—not usually the desired result. You can overcome this problem by moving the spotlight much farther away from the apparent source than would be expected. Instead of placing the spotlight within the fixture, you place it below the fixture, near the floor, so that its light distribution is even across the ceiling.

The next exercise uses TUBELITE.3DS, a room with modeled, linear light tubes that now require the proper illumination to prove realistic. It also contains two omni lights for ambient lighting. If you simply want to see the lighting effects, the LIGHTS_2.3DS, LIGHTS_3.3DS, and LIGHTS_4.3DS files contain the lighting for each of the three following exercises.

Linear Light Tubes

Load the TUBELITE.3DS *file*

Create a spotlight at floor level in the Front *viewport that has its target pointing directly up at the center tube (using Snap makes this easier)*

Make the spotlight rectangular and turn on Show Cone

Switch to the Right *viewport and move the light to the tube's midpoint while holding the* Ctrl *key*

This will move the source and target together

Increase its falloff until it encompasses the ceiling plane

The spotlight will look similar to figure 13.11

Switch to the User *viewport, adjust the spotlight's aspect to slightly less than the spacing between light tubes, and render in the* Camera1 *viewport*

Creates a rectangular light pattern on the ceiling, but the bottom of the fixture is bright

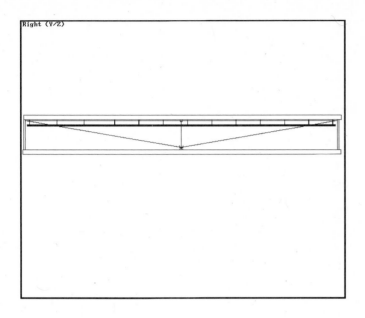

Figure 13.11
The spotlight placement for an indirect lighting tube.

Choose Lights/Spot/Adjust *and exclude the tube fixture (you may also exclude the floor, walls, and any other items below the tube light's level to speed rendering)*

Render the scene The light pattern now seems correct

The spotlight's hotspot is controlling the intensity of the cast light. Adjust the angle to match figure 13.12 to achieve the effect shown in figure 13.13.

Once perfected, the light can be copied for subsequent fixtures.

Switch to the User *viewport and move the spotlight to the center of the next fixture while holding down the* Ctrl *and* Shift *keys* Copies a clone of the spotlight with the same target angle

Copy the light again to the next light tube The spotlight arrangement is similar to figure 13.12

Render the view The light pattern is rendered, as shown in figure 13.13

continues

III

Advanced Modeling

continued

Figure 13.12
Cloned spotlights that have slightly different spotlight angles.

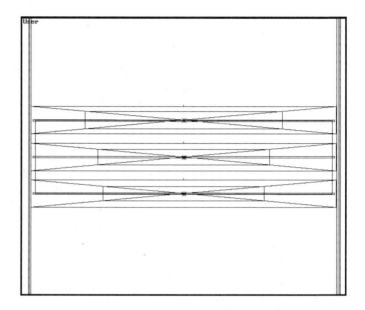

Figure 13.13
The resulting three rectangular light pools.

The effect on the ceiling is correct for a lighting tube that has a well-designed, closed end-cap, which does not create wall scallops. It is often desirable to include the scallops as a design feature, but doing so requires a little more spotlight modeling.

Adding Wall Scallops and Reflected Light

While in the User *viewport, clone a spotlight over to the end of the fixture*

Switch to the Right *viewport and move the spotlight up into the fixture while holding the* Ctrl *key*

Moves the target with the light to keep the light's aspect constant

Zoom in and adjust its position and falloff so it is barely cut off by the tube's end

The angle should be similar to figure 13.14

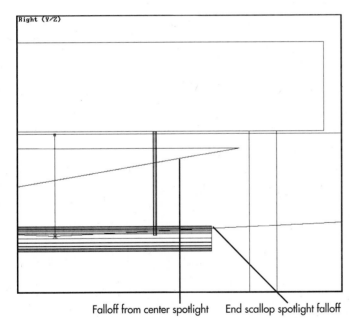

Falloff from center spotlight   End scallop spotlight falloff

Figure 13.14
Spotlight placement for an end scallop.

Exclude the ceiling, but not the wall

Avoids redundant light on the ceiling

Render the view and enlarge the hotspot until the desired effect is achieved

Enlarges the hotspot, for a sharper scalloped edge

Clone the end spotlight to the other tubes

Creates spotlight arrangement, as in figure 13.15

continues

continued

Figure 13.15
Final spotlight
placement with
cloned end
spotlights.

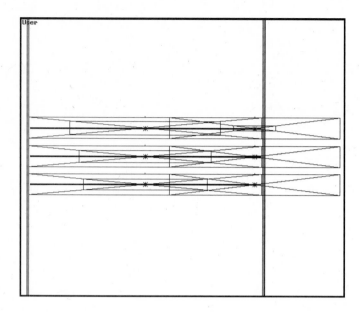

The effect on the ceiling and wall is quite convincing, but there is no indirect light being reflected back to the floor. Because this is the primary purpose for the lighting tubes, its effect must be simulated as well.

While in the User *viewport, move the middle spotlight slightly to the side while holding the* ⬦Shift *and* Ctrl *keys*	Copies a clone of the spotlight
Switch to the Right *viewport, zoom out, and move the new spotlight up past the ceiling and aim it at the floor*	Creates the "indirect" light
Adjust the Aspect and Falloff to cover the floor, exclude everything else, and render	An indirect light pool is created on the floor, but it is fairly bright

Adjust the light's intensity to half that of the tubes (you can reduce the multiplier to 0.5 or lower the luminance), and reduce the hotspot angle to half that of the falloff.

Render the scene	A soft rectangular glow is placed on the ground, as shown in figure 13.16

Figure 13.16
The completed lighting design with an additional indirect light.

This technique of creating light pools does have the drawback of not being able to create a soft edge for the light pool. As you reduce the hotspot, the edges get softer but the full intensity light pulls away from the walls at a fast rate (due to the extreme aspect ratio). If you want full control over the quality of the light edge, you need to project a bitmap. The effect will now be done with one light source covering the ceiling, masked by a bitmap.

Projecting a Bitmap to Create Soft Edges

Delete the center upward spotlights from two of the tubes

Set the spotlights falloff to 60 degrees and move the remaining center spotlight down until it fills the ceiling

The Right viewpoint will look similar to figure 13.17

Switch to the User *viewport and adjust the aspect ratio to cover the area previously lit by the three tubes*

Press $\boxed{\$}$ *to create a spotlight viewport for the low spot*

Enables you to trace the effects of the light

continues

continued

Figure 13.17
The position for
the spotlight
projector.

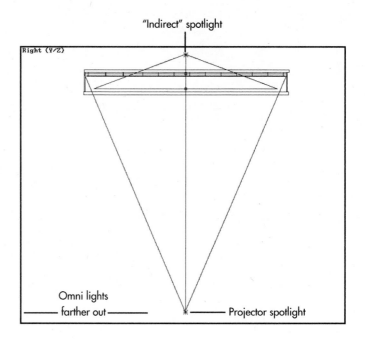

If you want to skip the following bitmap creation, you can use the LIGHTBM3.TIF file from the 13D disk.

Render this view at the desired resolution and bring it into an external paint program (the example used a 600 × 400 sized bitmap)	
In the paint program, using one tube's position as a guide, create a rectangle with a gradient white-to-black edge and copy this portion to the other tube light locations (the size of the edge gradient will determine the softness of the light pool's edge)	Creates a bitmap similar to figure 13.18
Save as a grayscale bitmap and return to 3D Studio	
Choose Lights/Spot/Adjust *and change the lower spotlight's type to* Projector, *click on the empty tile below Projector to select the file name, and select the bitmap file as the image*	
Render the scene	Creates a very realistic lighting effect as shown in figure 13.19

Figure 13.18
The spotlight projector's bitmap "mask."

Figure 13.19
The effect of projecting a custom bitmap to approximate linear light.

III

Advanced Modeling

Some lighting tubes have a lens along their bottom to cast a diffuse light downward instead of upward. For these tubes, the lights used above, in either technique, could be copied upward and projected down. By adjusting the hotspot, the illumination could be softened to achieve the desired effect. You may also want to reduce the end scallops, as fluorescent tubes often have greater falloff at their ends.

You can extract and use both of these techniques for numerous other lighting situations. Light troughs and linear strips of neon are just a couple of possibilities.

Fluorescent Lighting Grids

One of the most common interiors found is the 2 × 4 or 2 × 2 lay-in grid ceiling with fluorescent fixtures. Simulating the effect of an array of lights was previously impractical, if not impossible. Rectangular spotlights make it quite easy to simulate the effects of a single fluorescent fixture. As the number of fixtures and spotlights grow, this capability is harder and its effect loses considerable realism. Lighting grids overlap and pool their illumination in very subtle ways. The light level is generally uniform and hotspots are rare.

This makes modeling the true lighting effect quite easy. Just because there are 24 fixtures on the ceiling does not mean that 24 spotlights are necessary to simulate the illumination. One spotlight produces an illumination level that is closer to reality than 24 individual spotlights.

Figure 13.20 shows the position of one such light. A self-illuminated material is assigned to the lights, which poke through the single ceiling plane. The Top viewport shows how this rectangular spotlight corresponds to the room's dimensions and has a maximum hotspot. The spotlight is positioned high so that the angle of incidence is fairly even throughout the ground plane. This sharp angle cuts off illumination to the walls and provides no illumination for the ceiling. The standard use of omni fill lights is continued, but their placement is made below the floor plane so as not to add to the spotlight's effect.

Figure 13.20
Lighting setup for a lighting grid.

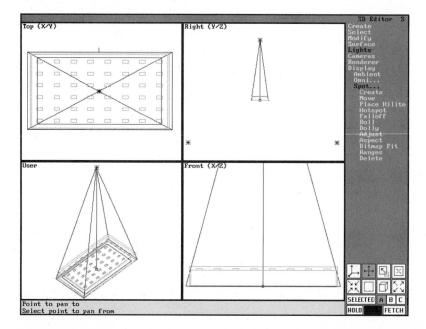

Rendering the Bottom viewport to a file provides the starting point for creating the lighting pattern. This image is brought into a paint program and heavily blurred and softened to produce the bitmap shown in figure 13.21.

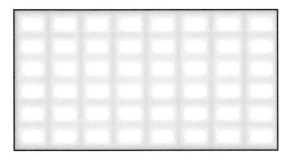

Figure 13.21
The projected bitmap to simulate a lighting grid's illumination.

This bitmap is then assigned to the top spotlight as a projected image and the result is a diffuse pattern of square lighting pools as shown in figure 13.22. A light pool pattern this distinct might be too much for many lighting designers, but then the fixtures are spaced farther in the grid than normal.

Figure 13.22
The illuminated interior using one overhead projector spotlight and three below-floor omni lights.

III

Advanced Modeling

You can transfer this concept for interior lighting to any lighting pattern, even if the grid is random, contains can (recessed) lights, or even has strip fluorescent fixtures. The time spent in a paint program is far less than you would spend setting up and rendering a "correctly" positioned array of spotlights.

Simulating Signage Illumination

Glowing signs are objects that users often need to simulate. But before modeling the mesh and placing the lights, take a good look at how the sign is really supposed to illuminate the scene.

Most signage is meant to be read, and the primary characteristic of making a sign readable is contrast. Contrast is created from color and illumination, which is why most signs do not illuminate the wall on which they are placed, but rather cast light forward. The edges or side walls of most signs are opaque and the backside of neon is painted black. This prevents them from casting light onto their field and lowering, if not eliminating, their contrast.

Considering its needs, the self-illuminated material type actually works well for signage. The object appears to glow because it has no ambient shading and does not cast light onto its surrounding area. If the sign is freestanding or isolated on a wall's face, it is complete—there is no need for it to actually cast light if there is nothing to receive it. If the sign is close to another plane, it requires the creation of additional light sources to complete the illusion of self-illumination.

Self-Illuminated Signage

The most common form of lit signage is the *self-illuminated sign*. The self-illuminated sign usually takes the form of isolated letters with translucent faces that project colored light.

The following exercise uses the SIGNSELF.3DS file, in which a signage object already exists in an environment where its light can be cast. The file also includes two omni lights for ambient lighting. A quick sign like this can be created simply by lofting a string of text along a straight path to the 3D Editor (with Optimize on).

Creating a Red Self-Illuminated Sign

Load the SIGNSELF.3DS file

In the Materials Editor, *get* Green Neon *for adjustment*	Provides material to be used as a starting point
Lock the ambient and diffuse values and change one of them to a light red of R225,G35,B35	Self-illuminated material should have the same diffuse and ambient values
Reduce the Self-Illum value to about 82	Signs are more realistic when allowed to shade a little
Check a sample render	Puts the material to the scene as current
Press [C] *and rename it* "RED SIGN"	The sphere is now a bright, rose red that has a very even appearance

New Riders Publishing
INSIDE
SERIES

The material now needs to be assigned to the text object. Most signs do not cast light to their sides, so only the front plane of the text should receive the new RED SIGN material.

Return to the 3D Editor, *select only the front faces of the text object, choose* Surface/Material/Assign/Face, *and assign the current material to the selection*

The front of the sign is now self-illuminated red

Render the Camera *view*

The front of the sign is bright red against the shaded environment

Create a rectangular spotlight with colors 225, 35, 35 (same as the sign), Show Cone on, and place it just behind the face of the sign, with its target just in front of the sign

Flare the spotlight's falloff to its maximum or set Falloff to 175 (see fig. 13.23)

Move the target and adjust aspect ratio to frame the sign, as shown in figure 13.23

The light is now the same proportion as the text

Render the Camera *view*

The sign lights the room

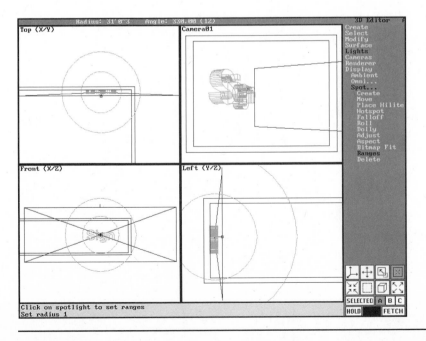

Figure 13.23
Positioning the sign's spotlight and its ranges.

III

Advanced Modeling

This creates the effect that the sign is emitting light, but the amount is far too great for standard signage. Using attenuation with the spotlight creates a more realistic effect. Figure 13.23 shows the correct ranges for the three orthogonal viewports.

Also, if the sign is to comprise a major portion of the scene, you might want to add one more touch of realism. Most signs, especially glossy plastic ones, have an amount of reflection or ripple in their surface. To simulate this play of light, the addition of a reflection is needed in the face of the sign. Because reflection maps only work correctly with curvilinear objects, a texture map is the best solution. The approximation of signage illumination is demonstrated in the following exercise.

Attenuating the Spotlight and Simulating Reflection

Set the ranges for the spotlight so the inner circle slightly intersects the room's planes, and the outer circle has at least twice the radius (refer to fig. 13.23)

This localizes the intensity of the light and allows for a broad diffusion

Turn on the spotlight's Attenuate parameter and render the Camera view again

The sign casts an even halo of light into the room

In the Materials Editor, change RED SIGN's definition to include REFMAP.GIF as a map with Amount (texture strength) set to 15

The low setting simulates a reflection in a self-illuminated material

Press T

Puts the material to the scene

In the 3D Editor, choose Surface/Mapping/Adjust/Scale and hold down Alt *while picking the sign in the Front viewport*

The low setting simulates a reflection in a self-illuminated material

Automatically fits the map to the exact size of the sign

Render the finished sign

The sign appears as shown in figure 13.24

Figure 13.24
The simulation of self-illuminated signage with one spotlight.

Back-Lit Signage

One form of signage that illuminates its mounting plane is back-lit signage. *Back-lit signage* casts light from the back of the letters onto a plane, putting the text in a bright silhouette. This is actually an easy effect to create by using the spotlight's exclude option.

The SIGNBACK.3DS file contains signage in an environment ready for the following exercise, which illustrates one technique for approximating this type of signage. For added contrast, the face of the text is BLACK PLSTC (plastic), its sides are GRAY PLASTIC, and the wall GREEN MATTE, to create enough natural contrast for the letters (a reflection map is another alternative).

Creating Back-Lit Signage

Load the SIGNBACK.3DS *file*

Create a rectangular spotlight with Show Cone on and a neutral gray color of 130 luminance, and then place it squarely in front of the sign

The perpendicular spotlight keeps the light consistent

continues

continued

*Focus the spotlight's aspect and falloff to
the proportions of the sign (see the* Front
viewport of fig. 13.25)

Figure 13.25
Spotlight setup for
back-lit signage.

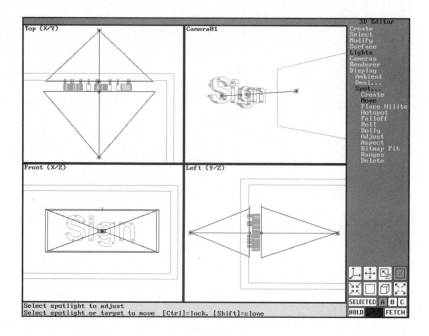

The front spotlight is not very bright because it is directly perpendicular to the wall's surface.

Adjust the spotlight's Exclude parameter to exclude the sign	The sign needs to be silhouetted, so it cannot receive this light
Minimize the spotlight's hotspot by reducing it to 1.0 in the dialog box	Increasing the distance between hotspot and falloff creates a softer light edge
Render the scene	The sign is silhouetted by a soft glow

Although the amount of light seems correct, the sign "floats" and does not seem to be part of the scene because it lacks reflected light from the bright green wall. Add an additional spotlight to simulate this bounce light.

Move the spotlight directly to the rear of the wall while holding the Ctrl *and* ⇧Shift *keys*	Clones the spotlight to a rear position
Move the rear light while pressing the Ctrl *key, as shown in the* Top *and* Left *viewports of figure 13.25*	Separates the two targets

Adjust the color of the new light to match the wall (R:0, G:127, B:0), lower the multiplier to 0.5, and exclude the wall but not the sign

Using the true color of the wall and lowering its light is easier than approximating the lower color and luminance of reflected light

Render the final scene

The sides of the sign pick up the "reflected" light of the wall, as shown in figure 13.26

The spotlights used for this exercise did not need to cast shadows for the effect to work.

Figure 13.26
The simulation of back-lit signage with two spotlights.

Simulating Neon Signage

One of the most interesting lighting forms is neon. The curves and shapes that are possible, and the intense colors that are emitted, make it a popular effect to simulate. It also is one that puzzles many modelers. Look closely at a neon sign, and you will notice that it casts very little illumination of its own. The letters themselves are quite bright, but the light given off can only be described as a saturated glow, which actually makes it easier to simulate in 3D Studio.

The following exercise shows that the trick to simulating neon is to give just enough of an effect to make it *appear* to glow. This exercise uses the NEONSQR.3DS FILE, which contains a signage object created by lofting a string of text to the 3D Editor. To minimize faces, Optimize is on and Cap End is off.

Creating a Neon Sign

Load the NEONSQR.3DS *file*	The text object is placed against a brick wall
In the Materials Editor, get Green Neon *for adjustment*	Provides material to be used as a starting point
Lock the ambient and diffuse values and change one of them to a light red of R225, G35,B35	Self-illuminated material should have the same diffuse and ambient values
Reduce the Self-Illum value to about 82	Signs are more realistic when allowed to shade slightly
Render the sample	The sphere is now a bright, rose red, but a little too "frosted"
Make the material shinier by increasing the shininess to about 20 and the shininess strength to about 55	Although neon is an intense color, it is still glass and tends to have white specular highlights
Render a sample	The red neon material is now closer in appearance to real-world, glass-enclosed neon
Press C *and rename it as* "Red Neon"	Puts the material to the scene as current
Choose Surface/Material/Assign/By Name, *select* neon-sign *and choose* OK, *then render the Camera scene*	Assigns the current material to the sign; the sign is bright against the dark background, but its effect seems detached

If you only want to see the lighting effects and skip the rest of the exercise, you can merge the LIGHTS_7.3DS file and render.

Create an omni light the color of the red neon material (R225, G35, B35), then place it in the center of the sign and render	The wall and floor are flooded with red light

The omni light casts too much light. Attenuate the omni light to reduce it. (Lowering its multiplier or luminance would not cast an intense enough color to simulate neon.)

Choose Lights/Omni/Ranges, *pick the omni light, set the inner range to half of the sign's width, and set the outer range to just enclose the sign*	Localizes the illumination, but keeps it very circular
Choose Adjust, *pick the omni light, turn on Attenuation, and then render*	

Clone the omni light to either side and set the ranges so they define the sign overlap	Creates overlapping ranges that look like figure 13.27

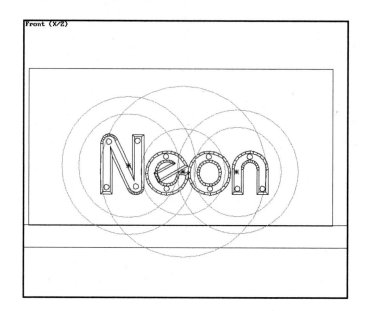

Figure 13.27
A composite illustration showing overlapping attenuation ranges.

Render the scene	The light is now very convincing on the wall, but the floor is receiving only a strip of illumination
Create a rectangular spotlight of the same color as the neon, Attenuation, and with Show Cone on, and place it behind the wall	Throws light forward from the sign
Adjust the falloff and aspect to frame the sign (see fig. 13.28), then set its ranges to enclose the sign and wall	
Choose Adjust and exclude all objects for the spotlight except the floor	This will make the new light the least expansive
Render the scene	The neon sign glows against the wall and casts a subtle light onto the floor (see fig. 13.29)

continues

III

Advanced Modeling

continued

Figure 13.28
The addition of a
special back light
for added
projection.

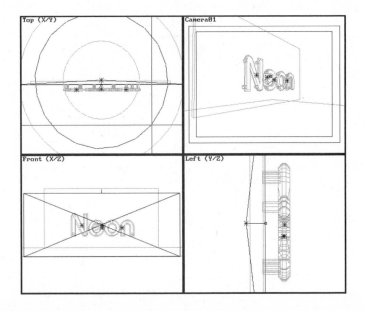

Figure 13.29
The simulation of
neon signage
using omni lights.

Free-Form and Strip Neon

The previous exercise demonstrates a technique that is adequate for closely spaced neon signage, but not very good for neon that is diverse in its form. Strip and free-form artistic neon are now possible with the use of projector lights.

Simulating Free-Form Neon Illumination

The following builds on placements and techniques from the previous exercise. The neon mesh in the NEONFREE.3DS file was created by lofting a circle along a curvilinear path using Tween and Contour. The red neon material created in the previous exercise was assigned to the neon mesh. The three omni lights were deleted and the rear spotlight moved to the front of the wall to create a clone of the original centered, rectangular rear spotlight. The rear spotlight's cone has been slightly adjusted; this exercise will modify the new front spotlight, named neon_front.

Load the NEONFREE.3DS *file*

Choose Lights/Spot/Adjust, *pick the rear spotlight, and turn off Show Cone*	Makes editing the front spotlight easier
Click in the Lower Left *viewport, press* $, *select the neon-front spotlight, and click on* OK	A Spotlight view is created, looking at the neon in perspective
Use Move, Aspect, Hotspot, Falloff, *and* Dolly *to frame the view until it just encloses the mesh, as shown in figure 13.30*	

If you want to skip the following bitmap creation steps, you can use the NEONMAP1.TIF file from the I3D disk.

Choose Display/Hide/By Name, *hide all but the neon-strip mesh, and render it to a bitmap file*	Renders against a black background to form the basis for the projector's bitmap
Bring the bitmap into a paint program, make it a grayscale, and increase the contrast until the image is white on black	
Create outlines of successively darker and wider grays, apply a heavy softening tool, and save the bitmap to a file	Creates a spotlight bitmap, as shown in figure 13.31
Return to 3D Studio and choose Display/Unhide/All, *and then* Unhide/Lights	

continues

continued

Figure 13.30
Using a Spotlight
viewport to
coordinate the
projection.

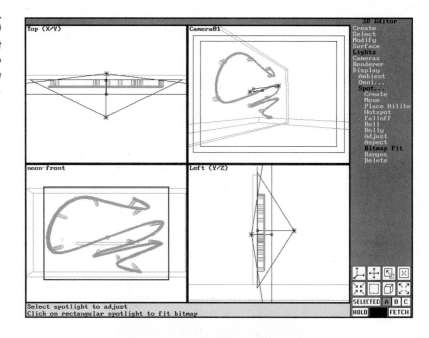

Figure 13.31
The resulting
graduated
bitmap used in
the spotlight
projection.

Choose Lights/Spot/Adjust, *change the neon-front spotlight's type to* Projector, *click on the empty tile below Projector, and select the bitmap file as the image*	Assigns the new bitmap to the front spotlight for projection
Choose Spot/Bitmap Fit, *click on the front spotlight, and then select the bitmap file*	Sets the spotlight's falloff to the same ratio as the bitmap
Scale the falloff to include the boundaries of the new bitmap	Increases falloff slightly, due to the offset gradations

Increase the hotspot to 1/2 degree less than the falloff angle

Exclude the floor and neon-strip mesh from the spotlight and render

The neon glows with a curvilinear effect and the rear spotlight still casts a soft pool of light forward, as shown in figure 13.32

Figure 13.32
Simulating neon lighting with a custom projected image.

Unlike most spotlights, the front projector spotlight should have a maximum hotspot. Its edges will remain soft because the light grays of the projected bitmap soften the edges for you.

Using Projector Lights

Projector lights have many uses beyond simply projecting an image like a 35mm slide. One traditional use for these lights is to project a silhouette image to cast simulated shadows. Used in this manner, spotlights are referred to as *gobo lights* and the "shadowed" light they cast is often called *textured light*.

Gobo Projections

Any bitmap can become a gobo cutout, but the best ones are made with slightly grayed edges, which cast softer images. This is, or at least is the equivalent of, an *Alpha channel*. Rendering objects with the Alpha Channel and Alpha Split options turned on produces white-on-black silhouettes and the anti-alias information is built into the gray edges. Remember, however,

III

Advanced Modeling

that an Alpha channel makes opaque areas white and transparent areas black—the opposite of what you need for a projector light. To make it useful for a gobo cutout, you will need to bring it into a paint program (any will do since the Alpha channel is 8-bit) and make it negative.

If you do not have a paint program, or do not want to exit 3D Studio, you can make a negative version of the Alpha channel by creating a self-illuminated material that uses it as a texture map with its negative parameter activated. Assign this material to an appropriately proportioned rectangle and render.

Figure 13.33 shows this technique as it was used on a tree created with Silicon Garden. The tree mesh itself was much simpler than its silhouette because the leaf outlines are created by opacity maps. Figure 13.34 shows the effect of textured light on a simple scene.

Figure 13.33
A "gobo" bitmap for use with a spotlight projector (created by making a negative of a split Alpha channel).

For a projector spotlight to properly simulate cast shadows, you should have its overshoot parameter on. If you use it in this manner, the chosen bitmap must have at least a one-pixel wide white border or you get an aliased edge on the projected image.

The gobo creates a definite illusion of shadow and you might have to look twice to discern that the furniture in figure 13.34 is not casting any shadows of its own. The mind's eye tends to accept that there are shadows without there really being any. This can be a great aid in animations where the look of shadowed light is desired, but the rendering time constraints are prohibitive.

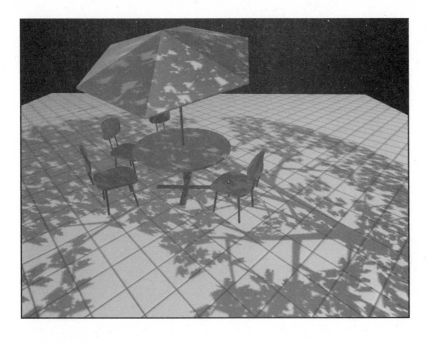

Figure 13.34
Textured light created by casting "shadows" with a projector light.

Casting Colored Shadows

Projector spotlights have the unique capability of being able to cast the color of their bitmap. Ray-traced shadows respect transparency, but do not interpret the material's color. The work-around for casting a colored shadow is thus to use a projector light with the appropriate image and align it with the object to simulate the effect. This is not as hard as it might sound because the light is projecting the image in the same manner as it casts a shadow. The key is in aligning the spotlight precisely with the color shadow casting object(s).

The color of the spotlight mixes with the color of the bitmap additively. If you want the true color of the bitmap to come through, you must give the spotlight saturation a 0 value, which allows you to dim the spotlight's effect without creating a color shift in your image.

A striking effect quite worth the modeling effort is colored light filtered through a stained glass window. This exercise uses the ROSEWNDW.3DS file, in which a substantial model has been created that houses such a window, as well as indirect cove lighting.

The Stained Glass Window Effect

Load the ROSEWNDW.3DS *file—make sure the* WALLROCK.TGA *and* STONEWL.TGA *files (from the World Creating Toolkit CD) are on your map paths*

continues

III

Advanced Modeling

continued

Create a spotlight named RoseWindow, with colors R237, G237, B237 and Show Cone on, and place it perpendicular to and centered on the window

Click in the Lower Left *viewport, press* $, *and select* RoseWindow

Activates a spotlight viewport and fills it with the window

Switch to the Right *viewport, move the light upwards, and target down to match figure 13.35*

Keep an eye on the effect in the Spotlight viewport

Figure 13.35
Setting up a projector spotlight for a rose window.

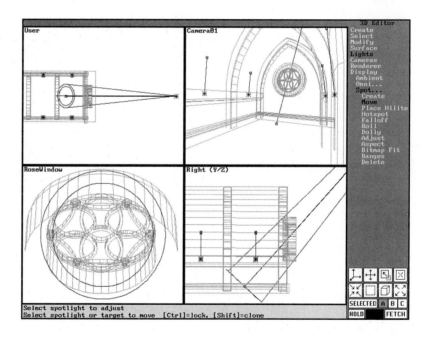

Adjust the falloff, choose Render Object, *and select the floor plane; readjust until the pool is at a satisfactory position and proportion similar to figure 13.36*

Render Object enables you to quickly judge the spotlight pool

Choose Lights/Spot/Adjust *and pick the RoseWindows spotlight, then turn on Projector, click on the blank tile below Projector, and select the* ROSEWNDW.TIF *file; set Hotspot to 1.5 less than Falloff*

Adjusts the spotlight to project the bitmap, and increases hotspot to near maximum because images cast from sunlight do not normally have a blurred edge

Figure 13.36
The projected bitmap.

Render the scene

The projected image falls through the wall onto the floor, as shown in figure 13.37

Figure 13.37
Projecting a colored bitmap to simulate a stained glass shadow.

The choice of where to acquire the stained glass image varies with the model. If you're lucky, you might have a photograph that you can scan, or you might need to draw it from scratch or as a collage in a paint program. If the window is being modeled in 3D Studio, you might be able to render it. If you have a bitmap of the stained glass artwork, you can use it as both the glass object's texture map and the projector's bitmap. In this particular model, the window was modeled (using the Shaper's Boolean tools heavily) to illustrate the depth of the window's framing so the projector's bitmap was created from the scene itself (refer to fig. 13.33).

Simulating Light Beams

An effect needed frequently is the beam of light cast by a spotlight and reflected by dust or fog in the air. This can be the headlights of a car, the light surrounding a street lamp, or the rays of sunlight streaking through a window.

Streaking Sunbeams

In the previous exercise, the indirect cove lighting pictured on the sides was created by using elongated rectangular spotlights with attenuation. They give a fairly good illusion of light, but point to a weakness in the projected image. The light boxes are casting what seem to be rays of light because they are illuminating the beams and walls next to them. The light coming through the stained glass on the other hand seems detached, not part of the scene. What is needed is a beam of light to connect the window with its cast image. Because light must strike a surface to cause illumination, the beam of light must be modeled.

Modeling the sunlight that casts through a window requires care to simulate correctly. The light cast by the sun is parallel, which means that the beam of light the sun casts through the round window should be in the form of a cylinder rather than a cone. Although this is technically correct, it is fairly impractical because a 3D Studio spotlight must be a cone. For the best approximation of sunlight, then, you must begin with a minimum degree spotlight.

Simulating a Sun's Light Beam

Continue from the previous exercise, or load ROSEWNDW.3DS, merge the light from LIGHTS_9.3DS, and press $ in the Lower left viewport to create a RoseWindow spotlight viewport.

Move the RoseWindow spotlight target and camera to match the target and angle shown in figure 13.38 (check the spotlight view to be sure the spotlight is still centered on the opening)

Adjust the RoseWindow spotlight to have a 1.5 degree falloff and a 1.0 degree hotspot   Makes the spotlight's cone very small

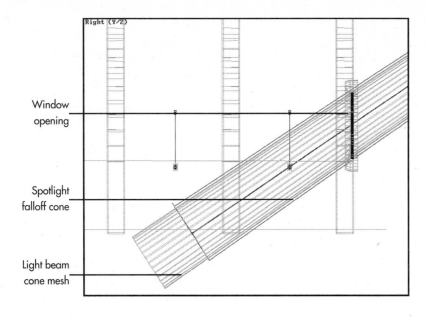

Figure 13.38
The angle of the light beam cone to the spotlight's falloff cone.

Window opening

Spotlight falloff cone

Light beam cone mesh

Choose Lights/Spot/Dolly *and dolly the spotlight until its cone once again fills the window opening*

The light is moved out many times farther than it was before

Create a 32-sided smooth cone centered on the spotlight's target, with radius 1 equal to the light's falloff and radius 2 as small as possible, and make it at least half as long as the spotlight's cone

Simulates a light beam, which should have at least 32 sides with a very sharp tip

Move the bottom center of the cone to the spotlight's target point

Choose Modify/Axis/Align/Object *and position the world axis on the cone's bottom, center the vertex, and then rotate the cone to align with the spotlight*

Move and adjust the alignment until it matches figures 13.38 and 13.39; after final alignment, increase the spotlight's falloff by a slight amount

Ensures that the projected image barely exceeds the light beam's edge and eliminates any cropped appearance

continues

III

Advanced Modeling

continued

Figure 13.39
The arrangement of the light beam cone in the scene.

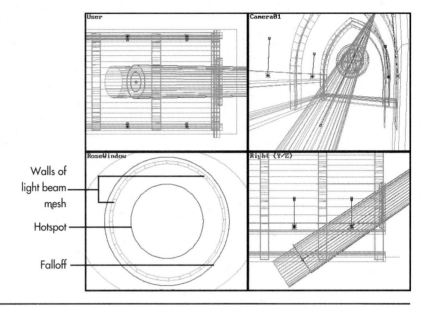

Walls of light beam mesh

Hotspot

Falloff

Performing this operation illustrates the difficulty 3D Studio has with precise rotations. You are limited to a 0.25 degree rotation increment. This is not nearly accurate enough to align entities pivoting from such a distant point—you need to get the light beam as close as possible and then move the spotlight to align with it. The spotlight viewport is invaluable for judging the light beam's alignment. When it is perfectly aligned, the light beam's inner and outer ring should be concentric with the spotlight's hotspot and falloff circles. The spotlight is looking down the throat of the light beam cone. With it correctly positioned, only its material needs perfecting. This is explored in the next exercise.

When you adjust placement of a light beam's cone, you might find locating the global axis at the center of the stationary end very convenient. By selecting the other end's vertices and 3D Scaling them about this axis, the beam slides up and down the length of the spotlight vector without losing alignment.

Adding a Light Beam Material

In the Materials Editor create a 2-sided, 60–70% additive transparent, very light dust-colored Phong material that has a 100% Outward Transparency Falloff

This is a good starting point for a light beam material

Put to the scene as current, name it
SMOKE, *return to the 3D Editor, and*
assign it to the light beam cone

Choose Render Region *and window the*
spotlight's impact area

Adjust the cone and the spotlight, and
then test render until they align on the
floor

Render the final scene after the
projected image and light beam cone
are aligned

The completed effect is similar to
that shown in figure 13.40

Figure 13.40
Simulating a
suncast light beam
and stained-glass
projection.

You can intensify the light beam's material by making it slightly self-illuminated. You can
change the quality of the cone dramatically by assigning an animated opacity or texture map
to the cone (the Yost Group's SMOKE.SXP is quite useful for this). Note that doing so does
not create colored light along a hollow cone. Even though SXPs treat the mesh in a solid
manner, only their surfaces are actually mapped. The projected light is traveling down the
throat and not striking any mesh.

The previous exercise illustrated the most difficult form of light beam—one cast by the sun
that you must align with a projected image. Most light beams are not this difficult. The

procedure is the same, but the critical nature of exact alignment is not. Note that the shape of the light beam mesh must be the same as the spotlight's projected image (for example, if it is a square projection, it is a prism).

Glowing Light Fixtures

Creating light beams in the way shown in the previous section is fine as long as you don't want the light beam to attenuate. The light cast by many light sources, especially those outside, is in the form of a localized halo. This glow is strong at the source and quickly dims as it continues along what would be the light beam.

To simulate this type of lighting effect requires a slightly different application. Figure 13.41 shows the modeling and lighting setup for such an effect. Here, the glow of each lamp is modeled in the form of a drooping sack of light. The mesh is formed by creating a hemisphere, deleting the end cap, and then scaling it downward with the global axis at the lamp shade's center. The flare is created by tapering the stretched dome outward in two viewports.

Figure 13.41
Modeling a lamp's glowing halo.

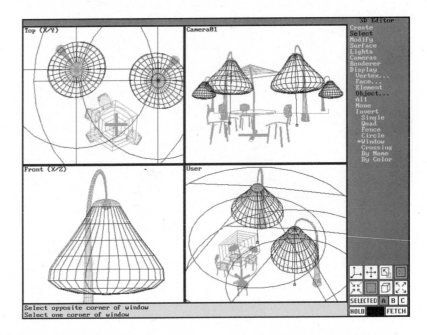

The material used for the halo is similar to the previous exercise's, but less intense. The base color should have a luminosity between 180 and 220. It needs to have 100-percent outward transparency falloff and use additive transparency. If you leave the material at this point, it creates a glow, but the effect begins at the center of the object and is transparent at the edges. This is fine if the light source is a globe and the light cast is a sphere, but this is a downward lamp and the glow must fall off as it descends. The opacity map shown in figure 13.42 is used to accomplish this effect, and the meshes are given cylindrical mapping.

Figure 13.42
Opacity bitmap used for halo falloff.

The effects of this material on the scene are shown in figure 13.43. The two distant street lamps do not have spotlights. These are omitted to show that the lamp halo's effect can be convincing without adding additional spotlights.

Figure 13.43
The simulation of lamp halos using meshes having an opacity-mapped material.

Exploring Advanced Camera Techniques

Several of the special effects possible in 3D Studio are created by manipulating cameras and the Camera viewport. Releases 3 and 4 added several new features that make the lowly 35mm camera a very impressive instrument.

The mood and character of a scene are largely determined by the composition created with the camera. Using a camera in 3D Studio is no different than using one in the real world (except you are not constrained to the limits of your environment). You need to constantly take into account the impact of your composition. Is it implying motion? Direction? Is it emphasizing a certain object or setting in the scene? Is it balanced? Is it distorted? Is the perspective implying size and magnitude? All these questions should be in your mind as you position cameras for the best effect. Many modelers end up studying traditional photography and applying techniques they learn to their computer modeling. At its simplest, the camera view *is* the composition.

Parallax and Perspective Correction

As discussed in Chapter 2, "Concepts and Theories," the upward convergence of lines in a level composition is a phenomenon associated with three-point perspective. This is termed *parallax*, and happens whenever the camera and its target are not perfectly level with the ground plane. As soon as the camera looks up or down, the view is turned into a three-point perspective and the vertical lines of buildings, rooms, and furniture begin to flare. This can lead to dramatic compositions, but it also implies the viewer's size relationship to the scene. Figure 13.44 shows the effects of parallax by looking down a street and looking up to see the flag of a tall building—the building's vertical lines flare to a vanishing point in the sky.

Figure 13.44
Parallax caused by looking up in a scene.

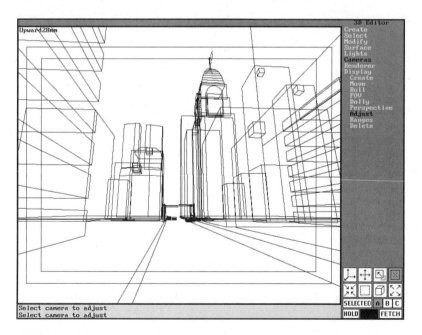

You often do not want the effects of parallax. Architectural photographers go to great lengths to avoid or correct its apparent distortion. For standard compositions, this means that the camera to target line of sight vector must be parallel to the ground plane. Figure 13.45 shows how the vertical lines of the buildings are straightened as the camera is made level. The problem is that the composition is no longer the same—you can no longer see the tops of the buildings.

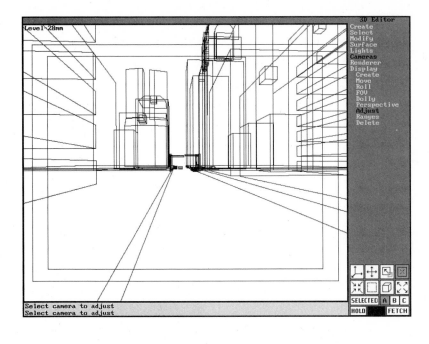

Figure 13.45

The same scene viewed with a level camera.

Perspective Correction with Render Blowup

You can correct the effects of parallax in the real world by using a large format camera or a 35mm with a *perspective control* (PC) lens. In 3D Studio, you can correct it by using the Render Blowup option first introduced in Release 3.

Perspective control lenses are not magical—they do not change the way perspective works, they just expand the camera's composition to allow for perspective correction. You do this by leveling the camera as shown in figure 13.45. You then expand the camera's field of view to encompass the desired area of the scene. In this example, the goal is to capture the flag on the top of the building. The original camera lens was already a 28mm wide angle. Figure 13.46 shows the scene as the lens is zoomed out to a 16mm lens.

The effect of using such a wide-angled lens is an exaggeration of converging lines, but this distortion occurs at edges of the composition. Perspective is controlled by the camera's distance and angle to the scene, while the FOV is determining how much of the scene is viewed. As a camera's FOV widens, the effects of perspective remain the same for the center composition—only the newly included edges show signs of exaggerated convergence. The center composition shown in figure 13.46 is the same as that of figure 13.45.

The problem with using such a wide-angled lens is the inclusion of side areas not intended for the final composition; because these show exaggerated perspective, however, they are ideal to crop. The Render Blowup feature enables you to specify any area of the viewport to be rendered at the current rendering resolution. Unlike Render Region, the rectangular region of Render Blowup that you draw has a fixed aspect ratio equal to your output image's aspect ratio. The area that you crop therefore will fill the rendered image completely. Figure 13.46 shows how an area is cropped to match that of the original view seen in figure 13.44. A view rendered with Render Blowup is shown in figure 13.47.

Figure 13.46
The same camera position using a very wide angle view.

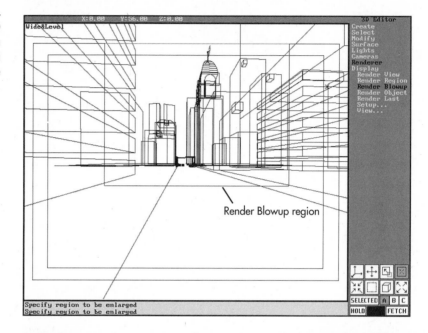

Figure 13.47
The corrected view as created by Render Blowup.

In examining figure 13.47, you will notice that all the vertical lines remain parallel because no three-point perspective is applied to the view. The camera has remained in a constant position throughout the procedure. The same technique can be accomplished by dollying out the camera and using a telephoto lens, but there are times when this is not practical or the resulting flattening of perspective is not desired.

Correcting Distortions of Interior Photography

Interior photography is a very good example of when dollying out is not possible because the photographer soon backs into a wall. Although this might not be a limitation in 3D Studio (because you can photograph through the wall by hiding it), it might cause problems as the missing wall is no longer blocking light and cannot be seen in reflections.

Such a situation is illustrated in figure 13.48. Here the camera, and thus the observer, is at the extreme corner of the room. Moving back any farther would place the camera outside the room. The focus of the room is the skylight, so it is essential that the composition include it. Tilting the camera up (with a 28mm lens) creates parallax, however, and the side walls tilt inward in a disturbing fashion.

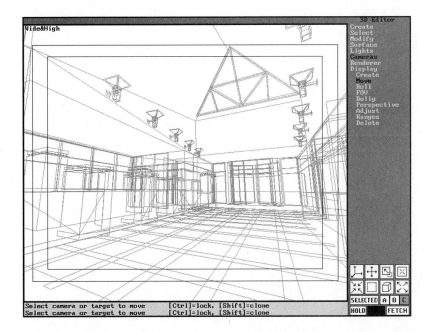

Figure 13.48

An interior composition distorted by parallax.

III

Advanced Modeling

Figure 13.49 shows the same view as the camera is leveled and zoomed out using a 16mm lens. The perspective is very exaggerated at the edges, as evidenced by the irregular square floor grid. The inner rectangle shows the region to be rendered by Render Blowup that corresponds to what could be seen with the upward pointing 28mm lens. The walls and furniture are now perfectly vertical, while the extremely flared regions are cropped out.

Figure 13.49

The same camera position using Render Blowup for perspective correction.

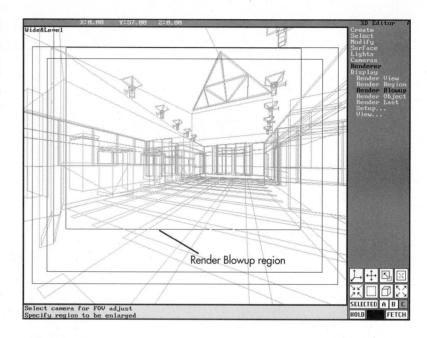

The disadvantage of using Render Blowup is that you must reindicate the region each time you render. Render Last delivers your previous region accurately, but does not provide the ability to write to a file. You can, however, use Render Blowup in the Keyframer. By leveling the camera and using Render Blowup, you can create a perspectively corrected walk-through. This is a unique capability that cannot be reproduced with real-world cameras, and can be a significant asset to architectural and interior simulations.

Using Atmospheres

3D Studio has the capability to fade the scene either in relation to your viewing point, with distance cue and fog, or as a defined strata in your model, with layered fog. These techniques, termed *atmospheres* in 3D Studio, are available only in Camera viewports and act only on Phong or Metal materials.

Atmospheres are controlled with the Renderer/Setup/Atmosphere command. Accessing this command brings up the Atmosphere Definition dialog box (see fig. 13.50). Each of the three atmospheres has its respective dialog box.

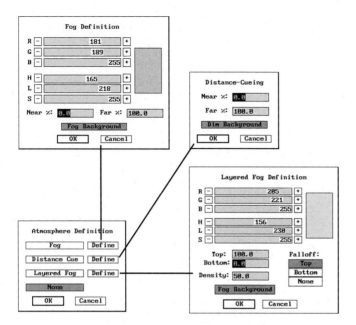

Figure 13.50
The atmosphere control dialog boxes.

Fading Out a Scene with Distance Cue and Fog

The atmospheres of fog and distance cue produce similar results. Both of these atmospheres fade out the scene based on your viewing position—the camera. You control the distance for this fadeout by using the Cameras/Ranges command. Ranges for cameras work much the same way as attenuation ranges for lights. Accessing the command displays two concentric circles: the inner circle defines the range at which there is no atmospheric effect, while the outer circle determines where the ultimate fadeout occurs. The area between the two circles is a gradation zone, in which the effects of the atmosphere diminish in a linear fashion.

Beginning with Release 3, the range settings are specific to each camera, unlike the global settings of previous releases.

Distance cue dims the scene by the Near and Far percentage settings found in its dialog box. The default settings are 0 and 100 percent, respectively, which deliver a fade to black effect, as shown in figure 13.51. Lower percentages dim the scene accordingly.

Figure 13.51
Fading a scene
to black with
distance cue.

This technique is very useful for quickly attenuating a scene's light level without requiring a change to any lighting parameters. The effect is very appropriate for stage and studio lighting whereby you want the light to have a definite cutoff. This enables you to be very loose with your lighting setup because you can control its spill with distance cue.

Note   The use of atmospheres is the only way to lower a scene's light level below that of the ambient light.

The Dim Background option applies the Far percentage to whatever background you define, be it color, gradient, or bitmap. Note that you are actually tinting the background by a gray level defined by the same percentage as lowering the color's luminance. A 50-percent Far setting reduces the background's luminance by 50 percent—white becomes mid-gray and red becomes dark red.

Fog works in the same manner as distance cue except you can define the color to which the scene fades. An RGB color value of 100,120,140 would fade the scene to a blue-gray, as shown in figure 13.52. The fog colors the scene and background in a subtractive, pigment-like manner—the darker the fog, the darker the resulting scene, which is why black fog is the same as distance cue. The Fog Background option should always be used because its absence makes any background image appear totally detached from the scene.

Figure 13.52
Using fog to fade
out a scene to
a cool gray.

Atmospheres do not have the capability to cause light sources to have halos or to streak. The glowing light effects illustrated in this chapter use the technique demonstrated previously in this chapter. They are included to show the effects that additive transparency has on atmospheres—the material adds its color value to that of the atmosphere, thereby illuminating it.

III

Advanced Modeling

The fadeout effects of these two atmospheres remain at a constant distance from the camera. As the camera moves, so does the effect. When animated, this gives distance cue the impression of a floodlight that tracks the camera as it moves through the scene. When animating a camera through fog, the effect is that the fog seems to be cleared around the camera as it moves. Because you have complete control over the dimming color of fog, you might want to think of fog as "distance cue to color" rather than fog.

Creating True Atmosphere with Layered Fog

A layered fog atmosphere enables you to define a floating slab of fog that is fixed in place, independent of your camera placement. The slab is always parallel to your Top viewport, but you have complete control over its vertical start and stop points with the Top and Bottom parameters (located in the Layered Fog Definition dialog box, shown in fig. 13.50). These values refer to unit distances along the vertical axis and position, and are fixed for the scene.

Although the layered fog's position is fixed, you can animate the effect of lifting fog by moving the entire model upward in the Keyframer. In the same manner, you can create a wall of fog by rotating your model 90 degrees, enabling you to animate advancing fog by moving the rotated model horizontally in the Keyframer against this wall.

The direction of the fog's opacity is controlled by the Top and Bottom falloff options. The effect of layered fog is a linear zero to full effect gradation between the Top and Bottom locations. Choosing Bottom puts the zero effect at the bottom location, as shown in figure 13.53, and Top at the top location, as shown in figure 13.54. Choosing None negates the gradation and delivers a constant opacity.

You can never see the fog's "edge" because the slab of fog is infinite—you are either in the fog or looking up or down at it. If you are in the fog, the entire scene is tinted by the strata your eye level is at. The fog in figure 13.53 is fading from 0 percent at the ground to 80 percent at the street lamp's top. The floor looks fogged because the camera's eye level is just above the table and is looking through about a 25-percent fog effect. If you view the same scene using Top falloff (as shown in fig. 13.54), the street lamp bottoms are barely visible because you are looking through a layer of about 60-percent opaque fog.

Figure 13.53
Layered fog fading down to its bottom location.

Figure 13.54
Layered fog fading up to its top location.

III

Advanced Modeling

Understanding Rendered Camera Control with Release 4

New to Release 4 is the ability to manipulate a camera from within a rendered viewport, as shown in figure 13.55. Not only does this command provide an intuitive method with which to manipulate cameras, it also includes precise controls and tools not available anywhere within the traditional Camera command branch. For these reasons, it is quite possible that users will begin to use Camera Control as the default method for adjusting camera movement in general.

Figure 13.55
Release 4's Camera Control and Match Perspective Interface.

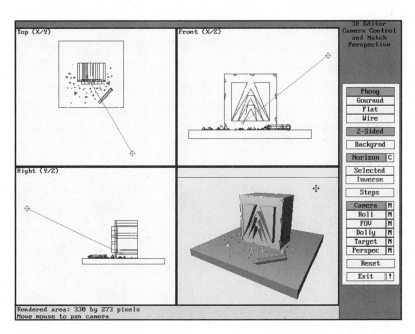

The FPREVIEW.VLM Plug-In

Release 4's Camera Control and Fast Preview functions are both controlled by the FPREVIEW.VLM file. As with all VLMs, it must be located in your 3D Studio root directory. Because it is not an IPAS Plug-In, the FPREVIEW.VLM can only be accessed if it's included as one of your User Programs in your 3DS.SET file. Release 4 by default assigns FPREVIEW to the F7 key with the following 3DS.SET statement:

```
USER-PROG2 = "$VIBRANT$FAST-PREVIEW","FAST PREVIEW"
```

Pressing ⌧F7⌧ in either the 3D Editor or Keyframer will invoke Camera Control or Fast Preview respectively. As with all user programs, you can assign FPREVIEW to other function keys by simply changing the PROG# in the preceding statement.

 As with all Release 4 Plug-Ins, FPREVIEW will not run unless you are using a Release 4 version of the executable or later.

Because of their similarity, this section often describes the capabilities of both Camera Control and Fast Preview. When the description is particular to the 3D Editor, the command is referred to as *Camera Control*, when referring to the Keyframer, it is called *Fast Preview*, and when it is a trait of both commands, it is referred to as *FPREVIEW*.

Capabilities of Camera Control

You will notice that Camera Control also includes within its title "and Match Perspective." This string points to how Camera Control came into being. High on the 3D Studio user wish list was the ability to match a Camera view's composition and perspective with that of a background image. To do this first requires the ability to see the background image clearly, and at the correct aspect ratio. Next, you need very fine control over your camera adjustments to achieve an alignment. Finally, you need to constantly see your model's mass and colors correctly to ensure proper adjustments. These requirements are what created Release 4's Camera Control, and in so doing established a new, interactive, and very accurate method for positioning a camera.

The Camera Control dialog box temporarily replaces the 3D Editor's sidebar menu and is organized as shown in figure 13.56. The top section of buttons refers to the rendered quality of the model, the middle section concerns various display options, and the bottom section contains the actual camera control options. What is important to realize is that every function has a keyboard equivalent so that the mouse is not even required (see table 13.1).

III

Advanced Modeling

Table 13.1
Corresponding Camera Control Hot Keys

Keyboard Alternate	Camera Control Function
P	*Phong*
G	*Gouraud*
F	*Flat*
W	*Wire*
2	*2-Sided*
B	*Background*
H	*Horizon*
S	*Selected* (objects)
I	*Inverse* (objects not selected)
E	*Steps* (increments for keyboard arrows)
C & Ctrl+C	*Camera* and its Numeric
R & Ctrl+R	*Roll* and its Numeric
V & Ctrl+V	*FOV* and its Numeric
D & Ctrl+C	*Dolly* and its Numeric
T & Ctrl+D	*Target* and its Numeric
K & Ctrl+K	*Perspective* and its Numeric
Alt+L	Hide/Unhide Lights
Ctrl+Z	Reset camera and target to original position
←↑→↓	Alternate to mouse movement for camera/target adjustment commands
↵Enter	Accepts the current positioning (same as second mouse click)
Ctrl+	Camera and Target moved together in commands
Spacebar	Activate Camera Viewport (same as left-mouse click)
←Backspace	Undoes the action of the Camera viewport and keeps it active
Esc	Cancels Camera Viewport action (same as right-mouse click)
Tab⇄	Cycles the directional mouse cursor and changes between keyboard fields when in dialog boxes

Figure 13.56
The Camera Control and Match Perspective side menu control.

Rendering Modes

Each rendering mode respects the material assignments at the face level, while Gouraud and Phong modes respect their smoothing groups as well. The rendered effects of the various modes can be seen in the composite figure 13.57. When looking at the materials, the display only concerns itself with the base colors (ambient, diffuse, specular), shininess values, 2-Sided option, self-illumination option, and transparency option. The Wire property is respected, but is always held to a one-pixel width. Transparency falloff properties are ignored. In the interest of speed and usability, no mapping is considered in the displayed materials.

FPREVIEW uses a box dithering technique to maintain speed. Although this is unlike 3D Studios diffusion dither, it still produces a very understandable image. After all, these commands are for previewing—not for final output.

The Phong rendering mode is actually Gouraud with Phong-like highlights. FPREVIEW's Phong setting is the only mode in which specular highlights are displayed. If you want to see how shiny a material is and where highlights are occurring, you need to use the Phong rendering mode. Gouraud and Flat are very similar in speed, but differ in display. Flat displays all planes faceted, while Gouraud respects smoothing groups at the face level and performs proper smoothing. Wire mode is quite useful since it is the fastest and allows more of a possible background image to show through for alignment purposes. Note, however, that Wire mode always respects mesh's edge display—there is no option to see "All Lines" as there is in the 3D Editor.

Figure 13.57
FPREVIEW's four rendering modes.

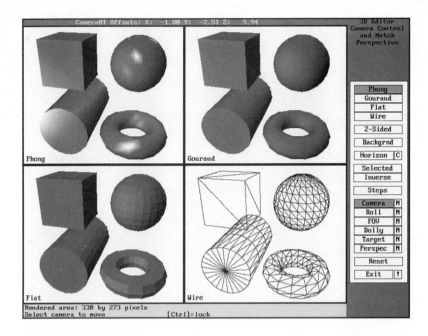

When FPREVIEW renders mapped materials, it defers to their base colors. Previous releases of 3D Studio's 3DS.MLI (as well as the shipping sample files) had the practice of making the ambient and diffuse colors black for 100-strength texture-mapped materials. FPREVIEW looks for this occurrence of a pure black diffuse color and replaces it with white. This is important because when rendering in Wire mode, FPREVIEW displays all materials solely according to their diffuse base color.

 The texture mapped materials of Release 4's 3DS.MLI now include corresponding base colors, enabling those materials to render in FPREVIEW with more applicable color.

Rendering Speed in FPREVIEW

The speed at which FPREVIEW updates its interactive Camera Control view, or displays a new frame in Fast Preview, is dependent upon several things. In order of importance, these are as follows:

✔ The speed of your processor

✔ The speed of your graphics card

✔ The throughput of your system's bus

✔ The size of your rendered scene

✔ The rendering mode chosen

✔ The number of lights within the scene

Because the first three requirements are hardware-based and somewhat fixed, your real control over rendering speed is the amount of geometry being rendered and the rendering mode. Manipulating the minimum amount of geometry is almost always your best choice for performance (the unhidden portion of your scene).

Selecting key objects before entering Camera Control and using the Selected option to position your camera are techniques that greatly increase performance. Once the camera seems to be aligned, turn off the Selected option and view the model in its entirety.

Lighting within FPREVIEW

FPREVIEW takes into account every light within the scene when rendering its image, including the Ambient light level. While respecting each light's color and multiplier, it treats all lights as omni lights and does not respect attenuation.

The lighting effects you see in your image are thus fairly close, but could be too bright. Keep in mind that spotlights that are aiming in a direction opposite of your view will still cast illumination because they are now omni lights.

When Phong mode is active, highlights are calculated for your model based upon your view and light placement. As can be seen in figure 13.58, there is a significant difference between the size and shape of the highlights created by FPREVIEW and the Renderer. Although noticeably different, the important thing to realize is that the *placement* of the highlights is correct. FPREVIEW can thus be quite useful for determining highlight locations from varying views.

Background Options

You can have either a solid color or bitmap background. User-defined background colors are mapped to their own color registry and accurately reflect the user-selected color. Loaded bitmaps are dithered to FPREVIEW's 200 color space, and all require an image buffer to process and another to resize (if necessary). This can be memory-intensive for large images. Loading an image requires three bytes per pixel to load, three bytes per pixel to resize, and approximately another byte for the dithering.

You can make loading background images much faster and require half the RAM if the bitmap's critical dimension matches that of your display viewport.

Figure 13.58
Highlights created
by the Renderer
versus FPREVIEW.

When initializing Camera Control, the pixel size of your active viewport is listed on the bottom line of your screen by the prompt `Rendered Area: X# by Y# pixels`. Similarly, when you load a background image, Camera Control returns an *updated* Rendered Area size. This is the display size resulting from that particularly proportioned bitmap. By noting these values, you can use the Renderer to resize a background image to a proportional size for use by FPREVIEW. This technique of using adjusted bitmaps is critical when matching to high-resolution background images where the memory overhead of resizing could be burdensome.

 The Render Area pixel sizes are only valid for that image's proportion and that viewport's size—changing either will result in different values for the quick loading bitmaps size.

Loading Presets

You FPREVIEW choices are saved between uses, but are not saved between 3D Studio sessions. When exiting FPREVIEW, pause and think if you want those rendering options upon startup the next time you initialize it. If you are working with a large scene, you may want to ensure that the Wire and Selected buttons are active to allow the fastest subsequent load. If you are using a background, decide whether you really want it loaded, and possibly resized, the next time.

 If you initialize FPREVIEW and a previous background image begins to load that you do not want, you can cancel the background by pressing (Esc).

You do have control over most of the modes FPREVIEW begins with in a session. The 3DS.SET file contains several parameters which adjust the shading mode, 2-Sided option, Step distance, Step angle, default wire frame color, background color, and even a background image. Setting this to Wire mode ensures the fastest load. Setting the step rates can be important if the majority of scenes you create are of a certain size.

Camera Control Differences

The various Camera Control commands work identically to those of the Camera branch with the notable exception of Camera movement. The readout display is identical to the corresponding Camera branch command as well, except that the FOV command displays its output in Lens MM as well as FOV degrees.

Moving the Camera is significantly different in that it is done orbitally about the targets location, as shown in figure 13.59. This is identical to using Camera/Move and moving the target from within a Camera viewport (where the target orbits about your camera's position). Camera Control is using the same paradigm and rotates the camera about the target's location. This can take some time getting used to because it is completely different than any Camera branch method for moving the camera. In Camera Control, when you move your camera "up," you are actually moving it "up and over." Continue to move "up" and you will eventually be on the other side of your model, looking back at where you started.

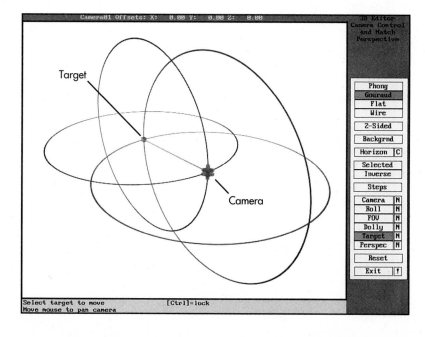

Figure 13.59
Camera and target adjustment with Camera Control.

It may be necessary to move the camera in relation to the viewing plane. This would be the equivalent of side-stepping or moving vertically, while keeping your camera trained on the same point. Although this is somewhat possible by conventional camera move commands (by moving the camera in an orthogonal viewport), it is not directly supported in Camera Control. You can make a vertical move by simply changing the Camera's vertical numeric field. To make a lateral move, you need to press the ⌈Ctrl⌋ key, move both the camera and target, and then move the target back to its original position. Noting the target's actual position before doing this will aid in returning it to its original location.

Using Camera Control

Working within Camera Control can be very intuitive, but sometimes it's easy to forget that you are maneuvering for a view—not manipulating objects. You are looking through a camera's viewfinder and the scene changes position in the opposite relation of what you do. To get an object to "move" to the left, you pan your target right. To place an object overhead, you move your camera down. To make an object more prominent, you dolly the camera toward it or decrease your FOV to zoom in on it.

Matching a Background Image

Aligning a view to a bitmap background can take time. A photographed composition is a balance of five variables: the photographer's position (Camera), where the camera was aimed (Target), the lens size used (FOV), the photographer's distance from the scene (Dolly), and the angle the camera was held at (Roll). Luckily, the Roll angle is usually easy to determine, leaving you with four variables to juggle.

There is no specific "trick" to aligning a scene to a background image. It is simply a matter of using conventional camera adjustments to match the five variables listed previously. There are, however, elements within a background to key in on, as follows:

✔ Horizon lines (described in detail later) are your biggest clue in aligning to an image. The *horizon line* is the relationship of your target to your camera. Getting it correct gives you the angle at which the camera was held (camera roll) and pointed (target location). A correct horizon line position thus solves for two variables.

✔ The camera's height can be derived from what is visible in the scene, and if elements diminish in perspective at the correct rate. How much of the roof can be seen? How level does the sidewalk appear? Do the curbs or wall edges angle to the horizon as much as they should?

✔ The required FOV can be derived from the image's perspective flare. Quickly diminishing lines have a wide FOV (small mm lens), while nearly parallel lines have a very small FOV (large mm lens).

✔ The distance your camera is from the scene may actually be the most difficult variable to determine. Distance and FOV produce very similar compositional effects. You need to carefully analyze the scene's diminishing lines (its perspective flare) to determine which to modify—if the perspective seems correct, then dolly the camera.

A camera's lens can perform distortion that a 3D Studio camera cannot duplicate. Extremely wide-angled lenses curve and bend the extremities of the images they capture. The wider the lens, the greater the distortion. Knowing that you cannot match such distortion will help you filter out images inappropriate for background matching.

Using Horizon Lines

The ability to see the camera's horizon line is a very useful addition for manipulating cameras and critical for aligning them with bitmaps. As illustrated in Chapter 2, "Concepts and Theories," the horizon line is simply the height of your camera above the ground plane.

The ground plane is always considered to be the plane of the Top viewport, and Camera Control's horizon line will always be in relationship to it. If your model is not built with the Top viewport's plane being the "ground," the Horizon feature will not be of use and you might consider rotating your model accordingly.

As shown in figure 13.60, when the target is level with the camera, the horizon bisects the composition. As the camera points up (its target is moved upward), the horizon line lowers. As the camera points down (the target is moved downward), the horizon line raises. When the camera's roll angle is 0, the horizon line is perfectly horizontal. As the camera rotates (the roll angle changes), the horizon line rotates as well. Panning the camera from side to side (moving the target left to right) has no effect on the horizon line's position, regardless of roll angle. Moving the camera and target together (with the Ctrl key) has no effect on the horizon line's position.

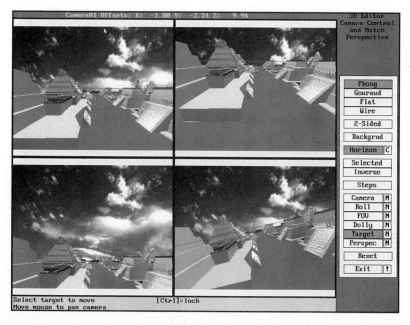

Figure 13.60
Horizon line alignments resulting from Target placement and Roll angle.

III

Advanced Modeling

Aligning your camera's horizon with the bitmap's is often the first step in matching an image. With the horizon line aligned, use either the Camera or Target command with the (Ctrl) key to perform a transitional movement up or down. The horizon line is "fixed" during this operation so you can concentrate on maneuvering the angle of your viewed scene to match the bitmap's perspective.

It is quite possible that your image does not contain a horizon line (a very common situation for interior shots). If this is the case, you should take the time to mentally locate where the horizon line would be. As shown in Chapter 2, lines that are parallel to the ground plane (the Top viewport) can all be extended back to vanishing points on the horizon. You can locate the resulting horizon line by tracing two (non-parallel) sets of lines backward to determine two points. When exact alignment with images is critical, it is probably worth the extra time spent in a paint program to physically draw the image's horizon line for subsequent use in Camera Control.

Keyboard and Mouse Control

Although using the mouse is a very interactive method, it is far from exact. It is very possible that the display cannot keep up with your mouse movements, and your reference image is delayed. It is also difficult to make minor adjustments—you have it nearly correct, and then a seemingly small mouse adjustment disturbs the composition. The keyboard alternatives within Camera Control thus become critical to accurate adjustment.

Every function within Camera Control is duplicated by the keyboard. In fact, you do not need to perform a single mouse click the entire time you are working within it.

When composing the scene in relation to a background image, keyboard control is nearly essential. When aligning with bitmaps, users often abandon the mouse in favor of the keyboard all together. Performing a bitmap match entails scores of adjustments, and the fastest method for switching between the options is usually the winner. The keyboard also gives you the ability to step back and undo a step. Pressing the arrow key a number of times to back up on an incorrect adjustment is quite easy when compared to moving the mouse back an unknown distance in a possibly uncertain direction.

The keyboard strokes to remember begin with your four *arrow* keys—these represent distance and angle adjustment for all commands. The (⇧Shift) key reduces an arrow key movement to 10 percent. The *Settings* option sets the keyboard rate and is mapped to the (E) key. As with any of the control dialog boxes, you can cycle between any text fields with the (Tab⇆) key.

In addition to the arrow keys, the (Spacebar) initializes the viewport without clicking in it. Pressing the (↵Enter) key accepts an adjustment and ends that command. The (⬅Backspace) key undoes an operation while keeping the command active. The (Ctrl) key moves the Camera and Target together. All of these keys can be used in conjunction. You could, for example, use (Ctrl)+(⇧Shift)+(↑) to move both the camera and target up a 10-percent increment.

Aligning with Two-Point Perspectives

As explained earlier in this chapter (see the section on "Parallax and Perspective Correction"), a two-point perspective does not contain convergence for vertical elements. This is the preferred result for many professional photographers—especially those creating architectural and interior compositions. Images without vertical convergence (two-point perspectives) are created in 3D Studio by maintaining the camera and target level to the Top viewport (the ground plane). This results in a composition in which the horizon bisects the viewport. If your image's horizon line is in the exact middle, you are in luck—Camera Control will do a good job of matching it. You may find, however, that using such compositions may not be so common.

As a rule, professionals seek to avoid placing the horizon at an image's center because doing so makes the composition static and pat. To avoid this, the image is either cropped when it is taken (by using a large format or PC lens) or cropped afterward (in the darkroom or at paste up). Either way, the result is a two-point perspective with a horizon line that is not in the images center. These images *cannot* be matched directly with Camera Control, and trying to do so is sure to generate frustration.

In order to correct for this situation in Camera Control, you need the ability to slide the image up and down to align its horizon with the center of the viewport. Although this is not possible in 3D Studio directly, you can accomplish the task with the help of a paint program. 3D Studio ships with an image that is a good example of a cropped two-point perspective. The left of figure 13.61 shows the bitmap 2992FNL.JPG as it is found in 3D Studio's IMAGES directory.

Original image

Area added to center horizon

Figure 13.61
Locating a horizon line and compensating for the cropped portion.

III

Advanced Modeling

The image's horizon line is located by tracing converging lines to their vanishing point. This locates the horizon and shows what should be the center of the image. You then determine the distance the horizon is to the farthest side and enlarge the opposite side by an equal amount. The right image of figure 13.61 shows the gray swatch added to the image's bottom, thus returning the horizon to the image's center. This second image can then be taken into Camera Control for proper alignment.

Rendering the Final Composition

Aligning your camera's view of the scene to match a bitmap's perspective is obviously only of use if your final rendering matches as well. This means that when you render, the rendering resolution must match the background image's.

Camera Control has no way of reading your current rendering resolution, and thus does not respect your current Safe Frame. The viewport's proportion will only change if you load a background bitmap. It is then assumed your rendering output will match the proportion of the bitmap, but *it is up to you* to manually reset the rendering resolution.

Camera Control respects the height to width proportion *and* embedded aspect ratio of your selected background bitmap. This is why your camera viewport active area changes proportion upon selecting a bitmap—it is having the same effect on the view's proportion that a conventional Safe Frame would with that rendering resolution proportion. Camera Control assumes that you intend to use that image as a background and is matching the camera viewport resolution to it.

Your camera's composition will seem to shift or be cropped upon exiting Camera Control if your selected bitmap does not fit your viewport's extents exactly (a fairly rare occurrence). This discontinuity will be corrected the moment you activate that viewport's Safe Frame and your rendering resolution matches the proportion of your background bitmap.

Summary

The lighting and camera techniques demonstrated in this chapter employ all of 3D Studio's capabilities to produce the highest level of quality possible for still images. Using the correct lighting, camera angles, and materials on an optimally created model is essential for high-resolution image work—the next chapter's topic.

This chapter's techniques are only the beginning for 3D Studio—all the examples have been static and are not composited with other images or effects. Although 3D Studio is quite capable of creating exceedingly impressive images, it is designed to produce animations. Only when objects, lights, cameras, and even materials begin to move, does the true power of 3D Studio become evident. This is the world that will be explored starting with Chapter 15, "Introduction to the Keyframer."

Chapter Snapshot

True color, or 24-bit rendering, might sound complicated or a
little intimidating, but actually it is much easier than 8-bit color
rendering. As discussed in Chapter 8, "8-Bit Still Imaging,"
reducing an image's color palette to 256 colors and producing a
quality image is not automatic. It takes forethought and a good
deal of understanding of how color distribution, banding, and
dithering work. With 24-bit rendering, there's none of that—it
always produces the top-quality image and enables you to spend
your time compositing materials and lighting the model to the
best possible degree.

With the lure of true-color images often comes the requirement
to reproduce them at larger and larger sizes. This translates into
output resolution and the need to understand memory
allocations, file sizes, output options, image overlays, and
bitmap quality. These are the issues that pertain to producing
high-resolution, true-color images and are discussed in this
chapter. Many modeling and mapping decisions are based on
which production method will be used for final output. This
chapter will analyze the following issues that are critical to
successful high-resolution production:

✔ Determining output media types and their limitations

✔ Determining image clarity and crispness

✔ Determining optimum output resolutions

✔ Examining model complexity and accuracy

✔ Using background images with high resolutions

✔ Incorporating text and image overlays

✔ Examining memory requirements for rendered images

✔ Understanding service bureaus

CHAPTER

24-Bit High Resolution Imaging

It is critical to determine the project's ultimate goals as early as possible in the modeling process—preferably before you begin to model. Several questions should be asked, and the answers should be used to determine the direction that the modeling takes. These questions are important for all models and animations, but are critical for high-resolution work because they dictate model complexity and detail, memory requirements, and file-exchange issues. Answer the following questions before you begin to model:

- ✔ What size will the printed image be?

- ✔ What media will the final image use?

- ✔ How crisp does the image need to appear?

- ✔ What resolution will be used for printing?

- ✔ Where is the visual focus within the model?

- ✔ How close will the viewer get to the various parts of the model?

These questions should be discussed as the project is being conceived and planned, and should be asked even if the project is for in-house use, has no client, or is an independent venture. The answers will give vital direction to what could otherwise be an overly large model that is not accurate enough or cannot be rendered or printed.

Determining Output Resolution and Selecting Media

The resolution of the output image is determined from the print media chosen, the desired crispness of the printed image, and the printed size. You need to make decisions on all of these issues before you can determine what is needed for your final output image.

Impact of Media Selection

The most important issue when selecting the type of output media is deciding if you want to produce a continuous tone or screened print. The choice made will have a significant impact on the required resolution. In general, a *screened print* is one produced by dithering the image, while a *continuous tone print* resembles a photograph.

Continuous Tone Prints

When any bitmap image is printed, the pixels that form the composition must be translated to a format understandable by the printing device. A continuous tone process places the pixels immediately next to one another without any space between them to allow the white of the paper to show through. The tones of the print are thus blended together, and no isolated dots exist. This is the easiest print type to understand because it produces an image very similar to how it appears on your monitor. A continuous tone print is also the easiest to print because the sole determining factor of the image's quality is the resolution you supply in the image.

The most common type of continuous tone print is the standard photographic print. Outputting to photographic film involves using a film recorder to expose the image on conventional 35mm film or 4" × 5" large format film. You can use any standard 100 ASA photographic print or transparency film (although transparency is recommended to ensure proper color reproduction). Film recorders usually are capable of 4,000 to 8,000 lines of resolution.

A film recorder's lines of resolution refers to the number of scan lines through which an image is interpreted. Because each pixel must have at least one scan line, a 4,000 pixel wide image is the maximum size for a 4,000 line recorder. Even though film recorders have this high capability, this does not mean that the image you supply needs to be that large. All images are shot to fill the

frame, regardless of their original resolution. Convincing images are quite possible with resolutions of 1200 × 800, and those as low as 600 × 400 can be worth presenting.

Dye sublimation printers are another common form of continuous tone printing available for computer images. These can be desktop or E-size production printers and typically range from 100 to 400 *dots per inch* (dpi) of resolution. The look of a dye sublimation print is similar to a color glossy print—both cover the entire paper and perform no dithering of their own. In actuality, the dye sublimation printers deliver an explosion of molecules so that the dots run into each other, giving the appearance of continuous tone from a dot process.

The quality of the final continuous tone image is determined by the density of pixels per printed inch. This is subjective and will vary between images. Images with text and fine detail require more pixels per printed inch, whereas abstract images can get by with fewer pixels per printed inch. If you are outputting to 35mm film, you should consider the size of the prints and not the size of the film. For photo-retouching or high-end reproduction, you should use the lowest pixel to scan-line ratio possible. The standard resolution for photographic reproduction is 3072 × 2048 resolution because of the introduction of Kodak's Photo CD. This translates to approximately 2200 pixels per inch on 35mm film. File sizes for an image of this resolution are 18.69 MB each and require large storage and transfer considerations.

Screened Prints

A *screened print* is one that takes the original image and dithers it to achieve true color. Screens are essential for many processes because the inks would bleed and blend together in pools of mottled color. The screens place the color components (cyan, yellow, magenta, and usually black) onto separate areas of the printed page. The pattern of the dispersed color dots is created by the screen used. Examine most printed material closely and you will see the separated dots that, at a distance, appear to be true color.

Screened images are commonly used for mass production purposes, such as magazines, marketing brochures, or advertisements. Screened images also are used with noncontinuous tone printers. The latter includes most varieties of laser, inkjet, electrostatic plotters, thermal wax, and thermal dye transfer printers. All of these devices require that the image be screened for printing.

When printing to any of these devices, the image first is dithered by a halftone screen. Screens come in many shapes and sizes, including dot, line, and diffusion. The size of the halftone screen is expressed in *lines per inch* (lpi) and often is referred to as its *screen frequency*. This is an expression of how many screen lines per printed inch are on the final document—the larger the lpi, the finer the screen. Printing houses will vary their standard lpi use depending on the application. Coarse printing, such as for newspapers, might use an 85-line screen, whereas magazines typically use a 133- or 150-line screen for images. The size of the screen used determines how many pixels per printed inch are required in your images.

It is easy to confuse the terms *dots per inch* (dpi) and *pixels per inch* (ppi). *Pixels per inch* refers to the number of pixels displayed per inch on your monitor, whereas *dots per inch* refers to the number of ink dots that the printer can print per inch. When creating computer images, you are interested in a third ratio: the number of pixels in the final printed inch. This often is termed *pixels per printed inch* and will govern the size of your final image.

Many desktop publishing applications and some printers enable you to specify the type of screen used for printing images. (Often a default screen is applied to an image by the printer itself.) Converting images to screens takes time and can take an enormous amount of memory for large images. It is not uncommon to wait hours for a high-resolution image to process on an average desktop printer, whereas commercial machines and film recorders can process in minutes. Image quality is determined by the sophistication and alignment of a screen. In general, screens found in desktop printers are not as high quality as those typically found in commercial, high-quality printing.

The shape, density, and angle of screens used by commercial printers are often considered proprietary information. Because of this, each printer has individual rules of thumb for the best dpi-to-lpi ratio. It is best to discuss image-clarity requirements with your printer early. You will find that most printers prefer to work with images that have between 200 to 400 pixels per printed inch. The number of pixels per printed inch makes a dramatic impact on your file sizes and memory requirements. Increasing your image from 200 to 400 pixels per printed inch requires four times more processing memory and file disk space.

Issues of Image Clarity

As images are reproduced beyond their optimum resolution, they begin to get blurred, fuzzy, or pixelated. The extent and distraction of these effects vary with the print media selected.

Pixelation

The larger an image is printed, the more obvious the square pixels from which it is composed become. This is known as *pixelation* and usually is something that should be avoided. Pixelation destroys the photo-realistic illusion of computer rendered images. Making an image pixelate is the easy part. Making it appear photo-realistic takes a bit more effort and considerably more memory. Pixelation is reduced by rendering the image at a higher resolution.

There are situations when pixelation is desired. Some very dramatic images have been produced that pixelate the foreground and lead the viewer into a high-resolution center focus. This actually is an overlay of two or more images, or the entire image was made at high resolution but employed an undersized bitmap to cause the close-up pixelation. Pixelation also can be used to disguise an area or reinforce the fact that the image is computer-generated.

Crispness of Screened Images

The crispness and clarity of a screened image is determined by the number of image pixels per screen line (or the pixels per printed inch to screen lines per printed inch). This is discussed in terms of the ratio of pixels per screen line and often is termed the *screen ruling* ratio. To avoid poor-quality images, never use a ratio less than 1:1. For optimum quality, use a *ratio* of 2:1. Increasing the number of pixels beyond 2:1 has diminishing, if not imperceptible, returns of image quality. Avoid creating images larger than 2:1 as it requires substantially more memory to render, disk space to store, time to print, and does not return a higher quality print.

If your printer is using a 150-line screen, then you provide an image that has between 150 and 300 pixels per printed inch. The needs of various screens, presses, and printers vary, so it is important to discuss this ratio with your printer before determining the final output resolution for the project.

Printed Size and Output Resolution

The print size of the image has the biggest impact on the required image resolution and what your model needs in the way of detail to make it convincing. After the media is selected and the pixels per inch ratio is determined for the desired clarity, the image's resolution is simply a matter of arithmetic:

(ppi) × (Print Width) = Width Resolution

(ppi) × (Print Height) = Height Resolution

The memory required to store an image on disk and a printer to process in RAM is the following:

$(ppi)^2 \times$(printed width in inches)×(printed height in inches)×(3 bytes per pixel) = memory required in bytes

The data size of a 24-bit color pixel (8 bits of color per channel × 3 channels) is 3 bytes. The size of the print multiplies its impact against the needs of crispness and the resulting dpi. Every printed inch requires more memory.

Many times the media will dictate the size, or at least the maximum size of your output. Desktop printers typically are limited to 4" × 5" or 8" × 10" prints, while dye sublimation printers are available in E-Size (36" × 48"). As an example, a 4" × 5" print using a 150-line screen will print best if the supplied image is sized to print as follows:

(150 lpi) × (2.0 pixels per line) = 300 ppi

This in turn means that the image's resolution needs to be 4" × 300 ppi = 1,200 × 5" × 300 ppi = 1,500 or 1,550 × 1,200. Such an image will require 1,500 × 1,200 × 3 = 5.4 MB of printer processing RAM.

III

Advanced Modeling

Printing with Less than True Color

You might be forced to print with equipment that is not capable of printing in 24-bit, true color. It is common for most plotters and many desktop printers to have a maximum capability of 15- or 16-bit color.

When you send a 24-bit image directly to an output device, you are relying on its programming to interpolate the differences in the color depths. This usually will not produce the best results, as most drivers rely on basic algorithms that average the differences. Typical results are banding, streaking, and moiré patterns. You can avoid much of this by having 3D Studio write a 16-bit color TGA file with dither true color on.

Calculating Screens for Existing Images

Many times you will have an image that you need your printer to print the best it can. Doing so is quite easy if you know the following information:

- ✔ Resolution in pixels
- ✔ Screen lines per inch
- ✔ Printed dots per printed inch

The optimum screen size (lpi) to print an image is half the image's pixel-per-printed-inch resolution. If you have a 1024×768 image to print and the finest screen available is 150-line, the image should be printed at 300 pixels per printed inch, which results in a final image of $3.41" \times 2.56"$. If you want to use the same image to fill a $4" \times 3"$ space on the page, you need a 256 pixel-per-printed-inch ratio and a 128-line screen. Although coarser line screens enable you to use smaller resolutions, they also minimize the amount of detail printable in any given inch.

Examining Model Complexity and Accuracy

The accuracy and detail of the model need to be balanced with that of the intended final output. Determining an object's detail is twofold: how close will the observer get to any particular object and what will be the final output resolution?

When producing animations, the speed at which an object will pass across the screen creates a third accuracy factor to take into account.

This information is necessary when building a model so that the proper amount of detail can be included at the critical locations. An object that looks acceptable at a video resolution of 512×486 could easily fall apart or look foolish when printed as a color glossy photo with a resolution of 3072×2048.

Model Focus Detail Hierarchy

Most scenes have a focus. This could be a specific object, group of objects, or area. As your model begins to take shape, you should have a rough idea as to the final composition and how prominent the focus objects will be in the final images. This object or area obviously will require the most detail and attention. For an efficient and manageable model, you should consider sketching out a list of areas as they fit into a "detail hierarchy."

Such an organization can be traced to traditional illustration as well. Architectural and design drawings make common use of suggestive figures and loose brush or pen strokes. This gives the illusion of detail without overwhelming the rendering's focus. Artists term this *vignetting*, and it is often used on entourage, backgrounds, and even extension foreground materials.

A detail hierarchy clarifies which objects will be made detailed and which will be minimized. Detail comes in two forms—geometry and mapping. As the object occupies more pixels in the final output, modeling techniques that worked at one resolution might become coarse or cartoon-like at higher resolutions.

Geometry Detail

Arcs and curves need special attention as they begin to occupy more pixels in the final output. Distant arcs might be capable of getting by with as little as 15 degree arc steps, whereas objects that arc through the entire scene might require 0.1 degree steps. Seeing the segmented outlines of round and curved objects is the best way to destroy their believability. Your model will be most efficient if high arc steps are concentrated at the focus of the scene and reduced in distant or less-focused areas. Just because the foreground spheres have 80 segments does not mean the background spheres cannot use 10.

Maps that were convincing as modeled textures can be much less convincing when enlarged. This is especially true of bump maps. The dents or grooves that were once faked might now need to be modeled. Close-up, seams and grooves are much more convincing if you take the time to model them. Taking the time often is much less trouble than making larger bitmaps and adjusting their blur until they appear acceptable. Bump maps cannot truly be anti-aliased, while the modeled joints can be done automatically by the Renderer's anti-aliasing engine and with much less memory overhead.

You should not be afraid to add faces for detail when the alternative is to use larger bitmaps. Adding appropriate geometry detail requires more modeling time than it does rendering resources. Eight thousand faces, for example, can be added to a model for less than the cost of rendering one 640×480 bitmap.

Bitmap Detail

Bitmaps will need to be used in most renderings. You should follow these two rules of thumb:

- ✔ Use a bitmap with as high a level of color detail as possible
- ✔ Try not to exceed the original bitmap's size in the rendering

Materials that use SXP's will not require nearly as much adjustment because their effects are based on algorithms and are independent of resolution.

Because you are paying the memory to load every bitmap as a true-color image, there is no reason why you should not try to use 24-bit files as often as possible. Of course, the bitmap must have more than 256 colors to warrant being in a 24-bit file format. Bitmaps that are designed for use as intensity maps could always remain in an 8-bit grayscale format because no further information is gained from higher color.

The size of the bitmap can become a problem as its presence in the scene increases. When bitmaps are rendered in excess of their original size, they begin to show signs of pixelation and square patching. The ability to notice this effect depends on the image's subject. Bitmaps that are portraying square, block, and rectilinear images will not experience much, if any degradation as they are increased beyond their original bitmap size. A bitmap of a checker pattern, for example, could be enlarged to 10 times its size and look fine as long as it isn't being used as a bump map. If the same bitmap was an image of a hummingbird, however, its pixelation would be very obvious. (See Chapter 6, "Introduction to the Materials Editor," for the minimum bitmap limits.)

3D Studio does a good job of anti-aliasing the edges of rotated bitmaps. If you need a rotated bitmap pattern, you should create it as parallel to the UV coordinates as possible, then rotate the mapping icon or the material's mapping parameters. This causes the Renderer to calculate the appearance of rotated edges. This is far superior to relying on the bitmap's fixed resolution for edges.

Background Image Issues

Unlike bitmaps, there is very little leeway in the selection of a background image for high-resolution output. Background bitmaps should always be 24-bit color (without JPEG compression) and should not be stretched much beyond their original dimensions.

If a background is enlarged, it appears in the rendered image that the foreground has been pasted on the background. The discrepancies between the two resolutions are very apparent, although a layman might not be able to identify why it looks wrong. When images are enlarged, they are inevitably blurred. Enlarging a black square on a white field does not produce just a larger black square—a soft gray gradation is also formed at the square's edges.

You always should try to use images that don't need to be enlarged. Ideally, you should use images that require reducing. Images in Kodak CD-ROM format are convenient for this purpose because they have a 3072×2048 resolution. Extremely high-resolution images require background bitmaps to be scanned from original, high-quality photographs.

If you must use an existing, smaller bitmap as a background image, you should bring it into a true-color paint program for conversion. This enables you to enlarge the image to exact dimensions and use soften or sharpen tools as needed to disguise the effects of the enlargement. (See Chapter 12, "Materials and Mapping," for correct horizon positioning.)

Some images lend themselves to enlargement much better than others. Images of skies, smoke, water, and other free-form objects do not suffer as much as street scenes, forests, and interiors. If your smaller bitmap contains such elements, you might consider concentrating its enlargement specifically to those areas.

Using Background Objects

Several more opportunities present themselves when the background is made a backdrop object with a texture map material. When used in this way, the bitmap can be accessed by other materials without loading it again. This is especially useful for reflection maps that approximate the surrounding scene. This also is the only way that flat mirror materials can reflect a background.

The object that contains the background image is acting as a billboard and should be thought of as such. It will take some time to align the object's plane parallel with that of the Camera viewport, but the results can be worth it. With a backdrop object, you can position the image as you want and make it larger or smaller by using placement, mapping coordinates, or mapping parameters without the memory overhead of resizing a background image.

Background image objects in a scene will be rendered in perspective along with everything else. Because the object is placed parallel to the viewing plane, there are no horizontal perspective effects. Those elements that are vertical will be affected by perspective. This can be especially important for backgrounds that contain architecture, tall straight trees, flag poles, or any objects with very definite vertical lines.

The recipe for such an image is simple. You do not want it affected by lighting conditions within the scene, so it should be 100-percent self-illuminating and dead flat with a black specular color. In addition, the billboard object should have its shadow casting and receiving attributes turned off. The mapping coordinates for the material should be placed using the Mapping/Adjust/Bitmap Fit command to ensure the proper proportions for the image.

Using the See Background Image Preview

The See Background command ([Alt]+[G]) can be useful for positioning objects in the scene in relationship to a background image only if you know its caveats. The See Background command creates a proxy image of the background by splitting its colors into three shades of contrast (the middle is the display's color), as shown in figure 14.1. You can adjust the threshold of these partitions with the Adj Backgrnd command found in the Views pull-down menu shown in figure 14.2. Adj Backgrnd has its own, smaller preview window to show changes you make in the settings.

Figure 14.1
The See Background function as used on TUSCANY.JPG.

Figure 14.2
The Adj Backgrnd dialog box.

The proxy image will always fill the viewport to the extent of the current safe frame, regardless of whether it is too large and cropped or smaller and tiled. Your only control over its display is the Bgrnd Preserve Ratio option located in the Systems Options dialog box from the Info pull-down menu. When this option is on, the image fills the screen while preserving its aspect

ratio and leaves the remaining horizontal or vertical strip clear. When Bgrnd Preserve Ratio is off, the proxy image is resized to fit the safe frame's proportions. This option and the appearance of the background proxy image have no effect on the way the background bitmap will be rendered by the Renderer.

The proxy image is useful only if the background image is actually the same size as one of the output image's dimensions. If it is tiling from top to bottom, only the top of the image shows, whereas only the left of the image shows when tiling horizontally.

Although useful, the proxy image is memory-intensive and can take a very long time for large images to display. The background preview uses a separate scaling buffer and a separate background buffer to keep the image in memory as screen sizes change and modules are switched. This requires approximately 8 bytes of memory per image pixel and will quickly cause you to page to disk if you use it with a high-resolution image (unless you have a lot of RAM).

Background preview is not a good choice for large images, yet its function is quite useful. As a work-around, you should reduce your background image proportionally and use it as a thumbnail of your true image. No advantage is gained by using an image with a resolution greater than 640×480; resolutions as low as 160×120 are quite adequate. Remember to turn off See Background before you switch back to your true background image so that memory is not expended to load the large bitmap.

Another reason to keep the bitmap small for See Background is that the proxy image is recalculated each time your display is reinitialized. This means the first time you toggle between normal size and full-screen (there is a second buffer used), and each time you return from the Materials Editor, view an image, or view the results of a rendering, the proxy image is recalculated. To keep this recalculation time to a minimum, you should always use a thumbnail bitmap of the larger background image.

Incorporating Text Overlay

A very common need is to position text on top of a final image. This might be in the form of a logo, title, signature, or diagrammatic text. All paint programs provide some capability to create text for overlay; some even have the capability to create anti-aliased text. No paint programs, however, have the anti-aliasing capability built into 3D Studio Release 4. 3D Studio actually is the best text compositor available on the desktop. If you want to have complete control over final text placement, you should composite it before you send it to the printer.

Issues Concerning Text Objects

Text is acutely sensitive to the effects of resolution. The resolution of the final image must be large enough to render the text sharply, with full definition and no fuzzy edges. Bold sans serif fonts are the most tolerant of lower resolutions, but might not be appropriate. Curves and fine lines of light serif fonts require the highest resolution to preserve their edges' fine detail.

The text can be created quite easily in the Shaper with PostScript Type 1 fonts. These fonts should be examined carefully because large curves may need extra vertices to define more arc steps (by using the Modify/Segment/Refine command). To conserve faces, you should always loft text with Optimization on, even if the text is flat, because you cannot use Optimize directly from the 2D Shaper to the 3D Editor.

After the text is created, it can be composed against the proxy image and rendered against the background bitmap for final output. For nondistorted text, you should render in an orthogonal viewport. For three-dimensional text, you must render in a Camera viewport.

The Cameras/Perspective command is very useful in controlling the perspective flare of overlaid text.

The Video Post Option for Compositing Images

The Keyframer's Video Post suite provides options for queuing bitmaps for overlay and underlay. Video Post can create multilayer effects by accessing Alpha channels and overlapping images. Video Post also provides control over a bitmap's placement, alignment, and scale. If the bitmap is smaller than the output size, it does not tile but rather floats against a black or colored bitmap image background.

If you need to compose the scene's geometry with more than one image, Video Post is the way to go. If you are only overlaying the geometry onto a single image, then Video Post will require much more memory than the background image method. You also will not be able to align the text with a background proxy image.

See Chapter 21, "Special Keyframer Techniques," for uses, applications, and operation of the Keyframer's Video Post option.

Compositing with Alpha Channels

It is common to have a "signature" credit text or logo inserted at the bottom of an image. This is most easily done by modeling your logo text in 3D Studio and rendering it to a 32-bit file. Once you are satisfied with the final appearance and resolution of the text or logo, you can use perfected 32-bit image to stamp or sign many images. The Keyframer's Video Post function can perform this application quite well and has no problem overlaying multiple images. If you select a sequence of files as the underlay, Video Post will composite each in turn as if they were an animation.

The problem that may arise with high-resolution images is that Video Post requires an extra framebuffer of its own. This means that the final image will require three times the standard images buffer—one for the output image, a second for the background image, and a third for Video Post. If the images are large, this could exceed the limits of your system.

If you run into a memory shortage on your system, you can map the logo text bitmap onto an object as a decal texture map and reuse its Alpha channel as an opacity map. Doing so enables you to place and compose the logo object as needed against the background image. You can render the original logo mesh against the background image as long as you have maintained the proper resolution and spacing for your standard imprint. As a final option, you can bring the background image into a paint program that supports Alpha channels and manually place the logo image in that application.

Using the Keyframer for Multiple Still Images

Even with still images, the Keyframer can be a very valuable tool used to access camera angles, determine the best lighting configuration, and render multiple final static images.

The Keyframer uses frames that represent moments in time. The organization for the entire scene's composition is contained within each frame, and the positions of all objects, lights, and cameras can be individually adjusted. This enables the Keyframer to hold multiple setups for various renderings.

See Chapter 15, "Introduction to the Keyframer," for detailed information on the Keyframer.

The important concept to understand about using the Keyframer is when modeling components are altered, the effects are interpolated across any frames that exist between defined changes. This effect is what you want for animations, but it can be an obstacle for multiple still images. To keep things static between key transformations, change the governing tension or copy the same tracks so no transformation occurs.

The Keyframer's frame 0 is a special case in that it represents the object's status in the 3D Editor. If you make a change on frame 0, you affect frame 0 in the 3D Editor as well. Making a transition on any other frame, however, will not affect that frame's positioning or status in the 3D Editor.

If you link a light or a camera to an object, the 3D Editor will mimic adjustments made to the current frame in the Keyframer. This occurs with any adjustments made to the lights and cameras and to their parents.

Framing Multiple Camera Compositions

You can render several views of a model as sequential 24-bit files by adjusting a camera in various frames. This enables you to compose several different frames and let them render over lunch, overnight, or even over the weekend.

When setting up several compositions over multiple frames, pay attention to any transitions that are occurring over time. Cameras have separate keys for their position, roll, and field of view. It is easy to concentrate on the camera's position and not realize that its FOV is being interpolated over time.

Creating Multiple Lighting Setups

Manipulating lights involves many of the issues of adjusting cameras but adds more opportunities. Lights have separate keys for their position, color, hotspot, falloff, and roll. It is often convenient to adjust lights to create lighting setups specific to each frame that has a different camera composition. This is easier than making adjustments in the 3D Editor as you can recall what worked or did not work and copy settings (tracks) from one light to another. The color of the ambient light also can be adjusted for each frame to complement the current frame's lighting conditions properly.

One technique used by some modelers is to render the same camera view with various lighting transitions. The lights are allowed to gradate between frames and the results can be viewed in the rendered images. These are usually low-resolution images so that the lighting "test" can be made rather quickly. If you want to see the varying effects that red light has on the scene, set the light's color at frame 1 to RGB 255,0,0 and RGB 127,0,0 on frame 30. The resulting 30 frames then can be compared, and the desired intensity of red selected for the final lighting setup.

Shadow Usage Within the Keyframer

A benefit of rendering successive frames is that the shadows calculated for the first frame are reused and only calculated again if an object moves or the shadow-casting light is adjusted. This is true for both shadow maps and ray-traced shadows. This means that you can set up lights with accurate shadows and only calculate the shadows once as various frames are rendered. Although this has the greatest benefit for animated walk-through, it does speed the total rendering time of disjointed static frames as well.

Understanding the Memory Requirements for Large Images

When creating high-resolution images, it is critical to understand the memory requirements of 3D Studio because each rendering and mapping decision will make a significant impact on your systems resources. When rendering to video, or even computer monitor resolutions, the memory requirements may be significant, but they usually are manageable. Exceeding your system's RAM capacity causes 3D Studio to page to disk. This causes slower rendering, but does work. When you create a high-resolution image, you place a burden on your system that is much greater than that caused for a low-resolution image. If the proper system preparations are not made for the added memory requirements, the image might take many hours to render or not render at all.

The current memory available and in use by 3D Studio can be displayed with the Current Status command, as shown in figure 14.3. This command is located in the Info pull-down menu or can be accessed with the ? key.

The Current Status command is inaccurate when using 3D Studio under Windows.

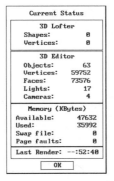

Figure 14.3
The current status of a typical high-resolution model.

III

Advanced Modeling

Specific Rendering Memory Issues

Many items in 3D Studio require memory allocations. Some of these are fixed, such as the size of ADI drivers, anti-aliasing, render-band height, and IPAS routines. For most 3D Studio systems, between 3 MB and 4 MB of RAM is required for the program, ADI drivers, and other necessities. This amount of RAM should be subtracted from your system's total RAM to show

how much RAM actually is available for the Renderer. For large images, these basic requirements are not worth calculating and should be considered givens. The memory-intensive options of which you do have control are as follows:

✔ **Output Image Size.** This usually is the single biggest memory factor because it affects an increase in all other memory-intensive areas as well. The memory required for the image buffer is 3 bytes per pixel (width × height × 3 bytes). Rendering a 3072 × 2048 image will require 18.432 MB of RAM before it looks at the model. If you choose to render the Alpha channel, an additional 1 byte per pixel is required.

✔ **Shadow Maps.** As the scene gets larger, so do its shadow maps. Shadow maps are as large as the shadow-casting geometry in the scene and can get quite large for high resolutions. (See Chapter 13, "Lighting and Camera Special Effects," for information on shadow clarity and model size.) The memory each shadow map requires is its size multiplied by itself multiplied by 4 bytes. Therefore, each 1000-line shadow requires 4 MB (1000 × 1000 × 4=4 MB). To conserve memory, specify where you need shadows in a large image, use exclusion to maximize their quality, and consider using overshoot to allow the shadow casting spot to have a smaller falloff. Note that ray-traced shadows do not require RAM but rather extensive calculation times.

✔ **Background Images.** If you choose to use a background image, it will require 3 bytes per pixel in the image. It does not require additional memory if it is smaller than the image buffer and tiles. If you choose to resize the image with the Renderer (not recommended), a significant amount of memory is used. The 3D Studio documentation states that this requires an additional 3 bytes per output pixel. Memory tests show it close to 6 additional bytes per pixel. If you need to resize an image, render it to a blank scene and save it as a resized image for future use.

✔ **Material Bitmaps.** Each bitmap that you use will require 3 bytes per pixel or 4 bytes per pixel if you are using filter maps. Because bump maps only render properly with filter maps turned on, you should always budget 4 bytes per pixel. You cannot turn off filter maps for a single map—either all bitmaps are affected or none are. The only individual control you do have over filter maps is in choosing summed area filtering. This always should be used with the knowledge that it requires 12 times the memory of pyramidal filtering, so a summed area bitmap will cost a total of 15 bytes per pixel. Because bitmaps are only loaded into memory once, it is beneficial to select several good maps and use them often throughout the scene's materials.

✔ **Mirror Maps and Projected Images.** These both require 3 bytes per pixel, but unlike materials, they cannot be reused by other parts of the program without using additional resources. Flat mirrors work a little differently in that they will only use what they need of the full-reflection map. Flat mirrors' memory requirements vary as flat mirrors change position and size in the scene.

✔ **Mesh Components.** When creating high-resolution images, the model usually is the least expensive of all memory requirements. Each vertex requires 34 bytes and each face 60 bytes. A solitary face thus requires 162 bytes, while 4 faces welded together require 444 bytes. Although instances in the Keyframer are a great way to conserve disk space, the geometry takes the same amount of memory to render.

Adding the preceding memory requirements together does not deliver an exact calculation of memory usage but does offer one that is close enough for most purposes. Several portions of the Renderer use memory on an as-needed basis, so their usage is difficult to predict. These deviations usually are small, but are the reason some RAM requirement calculations do not add up correctly.

When system requirements are fixed (that is, you cannot afford any more), you might need to reverse engineer the memory requirements to arrive at the maximum combination for your system. You might have to reduce the size of the image, reduce or eliminate the shadow maps, convert the summed area filtering to pyramidal filtering, and shrink bitmap sizes to trim the Renderer's requirements to fit your situation.

Swap Files

As soon as the Renderer runs out of RAM while creating an image, it begins to create a swap file. When this happens, 3D Studio's calculations are reduced from the speed of your RAM to that of your hard drive. If you are paging to disk and time is important to you, there are only two alternatives. You can buy more RAM or reduce the memory requirements of the rendering. The latter can be done by down-sizing your output image and reducing memory-intensive elements within it, such as shadow maps.

When a swap file is created, 3D Studio will continue to use it even though it might not need to. The only way to prevent its continued use is to quit 3D Studio and restart.

The disk space you need for a large image can be considerable, and the swap files created while rendering it can be doubly so. When creating large files, it is important to make sure you have enough disk space available for the render. If the Renderer finishes but runs out of disk space before the file is written, it simply stops the file-write and might or might not issue an error message. The resulting partial image file is not in the correct format and cannot be read. You might not realize that file-write has stopped because swap files will be returned to free disk space after exiting 3D Studio, and it will appear that you have plenty of space.

If you are running 3D Studio under Windows 3.1, the memory usage returned by Current Status will not accurately reflect disk swapping because of Window's use of virtual memory.

If you are swapping to disk, you should have at least three times the size of your uncompressed output image available for a swap file. To speed disk access, the free space on the drive also should be made contiguous by using a disk optimizing program before an intensive rendering session. This will only help a little, but it is all that you can do to speed the swapping and file-writes.

The use of RAM disk caches does not assist 3D Studio and deprives it of RAM with which it could use to render.

Image Output Parameters

Several factors are important to your final output decisions. The first are the size and proportions of the image. These should be the true proportions of the final print and should never need to use anything but a 1.0 Aspect Ratio. The Aspect Ratio is intended for converting images between different display devices and resolutions. Doing so for hard copy will only stretch the image.

The use of output gamma should be carefully considered. Many output devices, such as film recorders, do not need gamma to produce a correct image. Many of these devices work best with a gamma of 1.0 (that is, it's off) and will deliver exactly what you see on your preview monitor. It is important to coordinate your output with your printer's requirements, and you always should run a series of tests with and without gamma to ensure the proper color interpretation. If aspect ratios are in question, renderings of true circles provide a good test for image distortion. This test should be run early in the process so that time is not wasted and deadlines are not looming.

Final Image Considerations

Before making final renderings, you should consider who will be using them and what is needed or preferred in the way of formats. If the printing facilities are in-house, you should know these requirements and count yourself lucky. The majority of 3D Studio users require the use of service bureaus and printers. You should contact these bureaus and printers so that the correct form of data storage medium and the preferred image format (TGA/TIF/PCX, compressed/uncompressed, gamma, and so on) is used. Making incorrect assumptions can cost both time and money. These businesses also should be contacted before making substantial storage device purchases as local device compatibility is highly desirable.

Summary

Even though 3D Studio was designed as an animation program, it can produce superb high-resolution still images. The animation capabilities it has enable you to explore changing lighting options and capture multiple-camera compositions at the same time. Creating high-resolution images usually involves pushing your system's resources to the maximum. In addition, it demands a full understanding of the requirements and how the most can be made of what is at hand.

Part IV

Basic Animation Techniques

Chapter Snapshot

This chapter introduces the Keyframer module of 3D Studio. Specifically, this chapter discusses the following basic concepts:

✔ Understanding Keyframer terminology

✔ Understanding the process of keyframing

✔ Working with frames as a measure of time

✔ Editing objects over time

✔ Using hierarchical linking

✔ Introducing the reader to morphing

✔ Using the new Release 4 Fast Preview feature

Introduction to the Keyframer

The Keyframer is where you make your models come alive. You can only go so far with drawings and still renderings, which is why physical models are so popular. You can hold a physical model in your hand, turn it over, and examine it from all sides. The Keyframer goes beyond the physical model by enabling you to see the model in motion, and go inside and view the model as if it had already been built. Animation has great power—don't underestimate it.

To understand how the Keyframer works, you might find it enlightening to look at the way traditional animation studios operate. After the story boards are approved and the test animations and character studies are complete, the arduous task of drawing each individual frame of film begins. The master animators draw only the most important scenes and special character expressions. The scenes or frames that the master animator draws are called *keys*. The keys are then handed to the junior animators, who draw the frames that occur between the keys. This task is called *in-betweening*.

3D Studio makes you the master animator, and the Keyframer serves as your workshop full of eager junior animators. You position your objects at the key frames, and 3D Studio takes care of the rest. Part of becoming a master animator is learning what you must key and what you can pass on to others. This chapter introduces the Keyframer and starts you on the road to understanding how to key an animation.

Understanding Keyframer Terminology

Just like the other modules of 3D Studio, the Keyframer uses terminology that is unique unto itself. Understanding these terms and how they relate to each other is required if you want to get the most out of 3D Studio.

Frames

The term *frame* is a carryover from traditional movie film. Take a look at the strips of camera film you get back from the photo-processor, or unroll someone's old super-8 home movies, and you can see the physical frames on the film. Each frame has one complete picture; when the pictures are projected fast enough, they appear to be in motion.

3D Studio does not use sprocketed film, but still uses the term frame to represent each individual image rendered for an animation. In the Keyframer, you specify how many frames are in the total animation, how many of those frames to render, and the frame with which you are currently working.

Keys

Whenever you adjust something in the Keyframer, you create a key at the frame where you made the adjustment. You can think of keys as place holders that say, "Attention, the master animator has made a mark here!" 3D Studio then checks all your keys and calculates the positions and effects on all of the objects in the scene for all of the frames between the keys.

Remember that 3D Studio adjusts only for frames between the keys. Whatever you set at a key frame is permanent—only you can change it.

Links

The term *link* describes the invisible connection that 3D Studio enables you to create between objects. You must keep in mind, however, that 3D Studio links objects in only one direction. For example, if you link a ball to a box, the ball becomes a child of the box. The direction of the link is always from parent to child, and nothing ever travels from the child to the parent. Anything that happens to the parent (the box) is passed along the link and also affects the child (the ball). However, anything that happens to the child has no bearing on the parent.

Release 4 of 3D Studio introduced a Plug-In module for *inverse kinematics* (IK). The IK module enables you to manipulate a child object and pass the effects back up through its linked parent objects. See Chapter 20, "Advanced Linking and Inverse Kinematics," for more information.

Understanding Time

Time is a dimension. The 3D Editor uses three dimensions: length, width, and height. The Keyframer adds the fourth dimension of time. The unit that you use to measure time in the Keyframer is the frame. Unfortunately, the frame is a variable unit of measure that is dependent upon your intended output media. Traditional film is played at 24 frames per second, video at 30 frames per second, and Saturday morning cartoons at about 12 to 15 frames per second. The more frames per second, the smoother the animation appears.

Before you can properly set up a final animation in the Keyframer, you must decide the type of output to use, as well as determine the appropriate frame rate. The two most typical outputs for 3D Studio are frame-accurate videotape and real-time flic playback on the PC. If you are going with frame-accurate videotape, you are most often dealing with 30 frames per second. With videotape, you also have the issue of fields to consider, which is discussed in Chapter 23, "Animation for Field/Frame-Accurate Recording." If you are rendering to a flic file for playback in Animator Pro or AAPLAYHI, then hardware considerations limit you to about 12 frames per second depending upon the resolution. A discussion of hardware limitations and flic playback speeds is presented in Chapter 19, "Animation for Flic-Based Presentation and Recording."

Keyframing

Keyframing involves positioning objects at critical frames and allowing someone—or in the case of 3D Studio, something—to fill in all the frames between the keys. The decision about which frames to key and which frames to allow 3D Studio to in-between is something of an art itself. If you place a key on every single frame, you are probably working too hard and ignoring powerful tools built into 3D Studio. If you provide too few keys, 3D Studio does not get enough direction, and you don't create the intended illusion.

A good way to drive this point home is to imagine two extremes. The first involves keyframing to excess. Suppose that you want to animate a ball falling off a table. You are wasting your time if you manually position the ball on every frame from the tabletop to the floor. 3D Studio can do that for you. All you need to do is indicate that at this frame, the ball is just off the edge of the table, and at that frame, the ball hits the floor. 3D Studio calculates all the positions for all the frames between your two keys.

The second extreme involves using too few key frames—most 3D Studio users are frequently guilty of doing this. 3D Studio is a very powerful program, but it is not magic. Imagine what would have happened in the Disney studios if the master animator had walked into the production shop with only two drawings. "Here is Pinocchio as a wooden boy and here is Pinocchio as a real boy. Now draw the in-betweens!"

So how do you decide how many keys to use? It is a matter of aesthetics, taste, and personal preference, but here are some points to consider:

✔ Mechanical motion and motions governed by the laws of physics require few keys. Robots, engines, and other appliances operate (normally) in a very rigid and consistent manner. Projectiles and objects that are falling or rolling follow predictable paths. 3D Studio excels at this type of motion and needs very few keys to animate it properly.

✔ Human and animal motion, and motion caused by the forces of nature, is very erratic and unpredictable. 3D Studio needs much help with this kind of motion; if the animation is to be believable, it requires many keys.

✔ In traditional animation studios, the junior animator was only expected to draw a maximum of three frames between each pair of key frames. For typical film work, where each frame was shot twice, that translates into one key for every eight frames. One key for every eight frames is a good rule-of-thumb. Simple motions may require fewer frames; complex motions will certainly require more.

Creating Time

You create time in your animations by adding more frames. The primary command for accomplishing this is the Time/Total Frames command, or you can click on the total frames icon in the lower right corner of the screen. Either way, a dialog box appears, as shown in figure 15.1, in which you enter a new value for the total number of frames in the animation. The new frames are added to the end of the animation.

Figure 15.1
The Set Number
of Frames
dialog box.

You can also add frames in an animation by scaling a segment. This technique is described in the section, "Scaling Time."

Although you can add frames to an animation whenever and wherever you want, you should do it carefully. If you plan out your story board and script as described in Chapter 3, "Universal Modeling Techniques," you should know how many frames you need right from the beginning. Rescale segments to fine-tune your timing, not to make up for bad planning.

Moving Through Time

Many ways exist to move from one frame to the next in 3D Studio. You will develop a personal preference for one or the other, but they all have advantages. Figure 15.2 shows the location of most of the current frame controls. The following list describes the methods for moving from frame to frame:

✔ Clicking on the arrow icons at the lower right corner of the screen is a great way to precisely move forward or back a few frames. It is not suitable for moving over a large number of frames.

✔ Press the comma (,) and period (.) keys on the keyboard to move backward and forward. For those who prefer the mouse, this is the same as clicking on the arrow icons.

✔ Holding down the Alt key while performing either of the two preceding options moves you forward or backward to the next key frame. This is a very useful command once you begin manipulating objects in the Keyframer.

✔ Choosing Time/Go to Frame or clicking on the current frame icon displays a dialog box, asking to which frame you want to go. This is the best command for quickly jumping to a specific frame from anywhere in the animation.

✔ Clicking on the up and down arrow icons or pressing Shift+, (comma) or Shift+. (period) takes you to the first or last frame respectively.

✔ Moving the cursor to the bottom of the screen displays the frame slider. You can click in this area to jump to a frame, or you can press and drag to dynamically move to a frame. The press-and-drag technique is particularly useful because you also see a box mode preview of the animation as you drag the slider. This is similar to the traditional animator's technique of picking up a stack of drawings and flipping through them to check the motion.

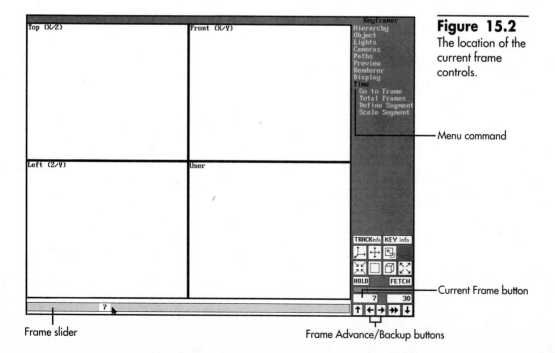

Figure 15.2
The location of the current frame controls.

— Menu command

— Current Frame button

Frame slider

Frame Advance/Backup buttons

Partitioning Time

Sometimes you have a large animation and you want to work with only a small part of it. The command Time/Define Segment or clicking on the segment icon displays a dialog box that enables you to set a range of frames to be the current segment (see fig. 15.3). After a segment is defined, you can work only with the frames within the segment. You must define a new segment or set the segment back to All to access the other frames.

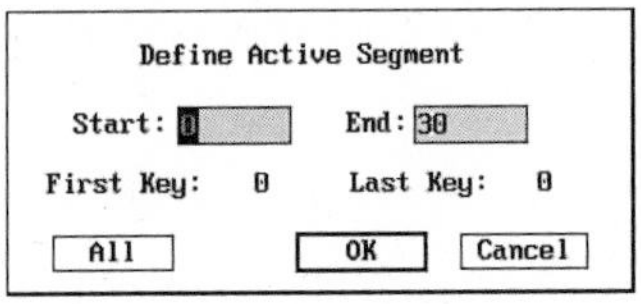

Figure 15.3
The Define Active Segment dialog box.

```
        Define Active Segment

    Start: 0         End: 30

    First Key:   0   Last Key:   0

    [ All ]      [ OK ]   [ Cancel ]
```

Scaling Time

Choosing the Time/Scale Segment enables you to increase or decrease the total number of frames within a segment. This command displays a dialog box telling you how many frames are currently within the segment and enabling you to enter the number of frames that you want in the segment (see fig. 15.4). Any keys within the segment are also scaled to fit the new segment length.

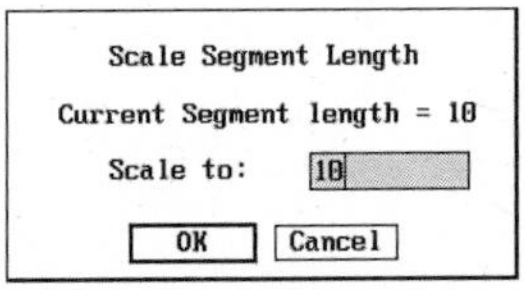

Figure 15.4
The Scale Segment Length dialog box.

```
        Scale Segment Length

   Current Segment length = 10

       Scale to:    10

         [ OK ]  [ Cancel ]
```

Understanding Object Transformations

You create animation by manipulating objects over multiple frames. The primary commands for doing this are Move, Rotate, Scale, and Squash. Although it may seem that this is not much of a selection, you can accomplish just about anything you can imagine by using these commands.

You should also note the absence of the Local Axis icon in the lower right corner of the screen. All object transformations in the Keyframer occur about an object's pivot point. By default, an object's pivot point is located at the object's local axis origin. Later in this chapter, you learn how to specify your own pivot point for any object.

A final point is that all motion and transformation occurs at the object level. You cannot keyframe vertices, faces, or elements. This is an important distinction to keep in mind as you build your model. If something must move on its own, it must be a separate object. If something always moves as part of another object and never moves on its own, then consider permanently attaching it to that object.

Get in the habit of checking what frame you are in before performing any command in the Keyframer (even though this may seem obvious). Remember that you are manipulating objects over time and that every change you make sets up a motion. Many people have been burned by falsely assuming that they were repositioning an object when they were really setting up a motion over multiple frames.

Local Coordinates Versus World Coordinates

Chapters 3 and 10 both discussed the issues of the local axis, global axis, bounding box, and transformation matrix. While these concepts are useful in the 2D Shaper and 3D Editor, they take on much more significance when you enter the Keyframer.

All transformations in the Keyframer (such as Rotate and Scale) and hierarchical linking are performed with respect to an object's local coordinate system. What often confuses users of 3D Studio is the fact that an object's local coordinate system rarely matches the world coordinate system. The 3D Studio Reference Manual describes the local coordinate system with the example that the local Z axis of a torus runs through the center of the hole in the torus. You can define a more general rule as the following:

> The local Z axis of any object created using the first eight primitives in the Create/Object branch of the 3D Editor is oriented perpendicular to the viewport in which that object was created, and the Z axis of any lofted object is oriented parallel with the path rotation, as defined by the Paths/Rotate Path command in the 3D Lofter.

Now that you know how an object's local coordinate system is oriented, why do you care? Understanding local coordinate systems is critical to understanding how objects behave in the Keyframer. Also, if you use the Keyscript programming language, all scripting functions operate through an object's local coordinate system. See Chapter 22 for details about writing and using keyscripts.

You should never use the Modify/Object/Reset Xform command, in the 3D Editor, after you have linked or altered objects in the Keyframer. Since all Keyframer effects are dependent upon an object's local coordinate system, resetting the transformation matrix can cause profound (and usually undesirable) side effects.

The Special Case of Frame 0

Before you manipulate anything in the Keyframer, it is important to understand the special situation at frame 0. Unlike the other modules of 3D Studio, the 3D Editor and the Keyframer share a single file. The connection between these two modules occurs at frame 0. Anything modeled in the 3D Editor shows up at frame 0 in the Keyframer. Any manipulation performed at frame 0 in the Keyframer is telegraphed back to the objects in the 3D Editor.

IV

Basic Animation Techniques

There are some exceptions to the frame 0 situation, particularly in dealing with linked objects. These exceptions are described in the 3D Studio Reference Manual. Also, it is actually the first key frame that affects the connection between the Keyframer and the 3D Editor. By default, the first key frame is always at frame 0 unless you move it—you should not move it, however.

Move

The Move command works the same way it does in the 3D Editor except that now it occurs over time. Move is the most basic of the Keyframer manipulations, but it is sometimes the most frustrating as well. When you set up a move over multiple frames, 3D Studio always takes the most direct path from one key frame to the next—it does not know or care about obstacles. Other settings in the Keyframer can cause the object to overshoot the key position early and then back in to your specified position.

Move is a deceptively simple command, but getting it to do what you want can take some finesse. Check out Chapter 19 for help on adjusting the Tension, Continuity, and Bias settings and how to make objects follow a path.

Rotate and Rotate Absolute

Many people get confused when using Rotate in the Keyframer because it works so much differently from its namesake in the 3D Editor. In the 3D Editor, your rotation axis is fixed perpendicular to the active viewport. You also have the choice of rotating about the object's local axis or the global axis. In the Keyframer, your rotation axis is variable, and pressing the Tab key cycles you through the object's local X, Y, and Z axes of rotation. Also, there is only one choice for center of rotation in the Keyframer—the object's pivot point.

Rotate Absolute is a variation on the Rotate command. It still uses the defined pivot point of the object as the center of rotation, but the three rotational axes are "squared up" with the current viewport. Figure 15.5 shows an object with the two sets of rotational axes indicated. This is an excellent command to use when you must rotate an object about an oblique angle. Simply set a User viewport perpendicular to the axis of rotation and use Rotate Absolute.

Because of the way rotations are calculated, you can get unexpected results if you rotate objects about more than one axis. With some work—and luck—you can often get rotations about two axes to work. Attempting a rotation about a third axis almost always cancels out all or some of the rotation on one of the other two axes. If you need an object to rotate about multiple axes, you are much better off to use Dummy Objects and Links. This technique is described in the section on dummy objects covered later in this chapter.

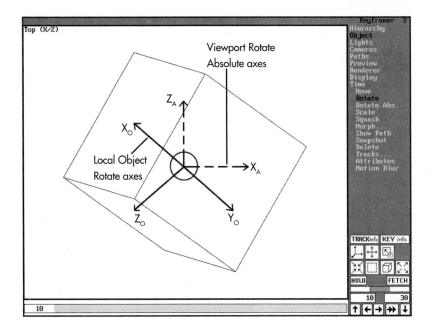

Figure 15.5
The Object Rotate axes versus the Rotate Absolute axes.

Scale

The Keyframer has only one Scale command, and it is a workhorse that does everything. The center of scale is always about the object's pivot point, and you select a scale axis by pressing the Tab key. There are four settings that the Tab key cycles through: X axis only, Z axis only, Y axis only, and full 3D scale.

You may ask, "What about 2D Scaling?" It is possible to scale about any two axes while leaving the third untouched, just like 2D Scale in the 3D Editor. This technique requires the use of Key Info and the setting of axis locks. Key Info is discussed in Chapter 16, "Manipulating Tracks and Keys."

Squash

The Squash command is a unique scale function that takes into account the properties of Squash and Stretch described in Chapter 2, "Concepts and Theories." Pressing the Tab key cycles you through scaling about each of the three axes. The important issue to remember about Squash is that the scale factor you apply to one axis is also applied in the opposite direction to the other two axes. The net effect is that the object deforms while appearing to maintain a constant volume. Figure 15.6 demonstrates how Squash works.

Figure 15.6
Squashing a
sphere along
the Z axis.

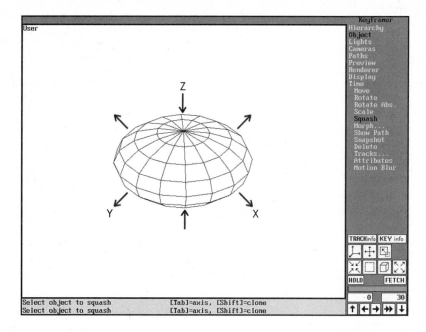

 Although it is easy to mistake the Squash command as a 2D Scale, all three axes are always being scaled.

Examining Hierarchical Linking

The Hierarchy branch in the Keyframer contains the commands for creating and manipulating links between objects. *Linking* is a very powerful technique that can save you much time and effort if used properly.

Linking has two primary functions. The first is to enable you to simulate the real world by linking objects together in some sort of jointed assembly. A good example of this is a machine or a human figure. If you move the figure's upper arm, you want the lower arm, hand, and fingers all to move with it. Manually moving all the pieces throughout an animation is nearly impossible. Linking takes care of all that work and makes it easy.

The other use for linking is to assist in the definition of complex motion. Imagine that you want to animate a block tumbling down a slope. Manually moving and rotating the block is quite difficult. Linking enables you to easily rotate the block, and then drag it down the slope by linking it to an invisible object. These invisible objects are called *dummy objects*, and they are the key to many complex motion solutions.

Parent Objects

Any object that has another object linked to it is a *parent object*. A parent can have any number of other objects linked to it, and these other objects are called its *children*. Parent objects can also be linked as a child to some other parent object. Any translation that affects a parent also affects the children attached to that parent.

Child Objects

Child objects are one of any number of objects linked to a parent. Although a parent can have any number of children, a child can have one and only one parent. If you try to link a child object to a second parent, the link to the first parent is destroyed and replaced with the link to the new parent.

Hierarchical Tree

As you create links between objects, they are arranged in a tree structure. This tree structure takes the form of a list, where the names of the child objects are indented below and to the right of their parent objects. You can view this list by choosing the Hierarchy/Show Tree command (see fig. 15.7).

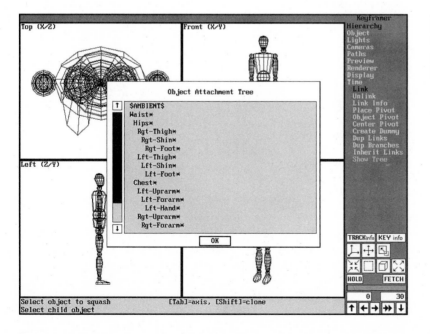

Figure 15.7

The tree structure for MANEQUIN.3DS.

Links

The command Hierarchy/Link is the way you actually specify which objects are linked to other objects. Pay careful attention to the prompt at the bottom of the screen. You always select the child first and then the parent. It is easy to get this backward.

When you specify links, it is very easy to select the wrong object, especially if your model is even the slightest bit complex. Use the Click on Object by Name feature by pressing Ⓗ when you are prompted to select a child or parent object.

Unlink

The Hierarchy/Unlink command severs the link between a child and its parent. Again, it is a good idea to press Ⓗ on the keyboard and use the Click on Object by Name dialog box to avoid choosing the wrong object.

Pivots

The three pivot commands are used to set the pivot point for an object. Even though the pivot commands are under the Hierarchy branch, they can be used with all objects, not just those that are linked. The *pivot point* is the point about which all object rotation, and scaling, is centered.

Changing the pivot point of an object after you have specified any translations after frame 0 can lead to unexpected side effects. Make any changes to your pivot points before you start animating your objects.

Place Pivot

The Place Pivot command displays a small X on the screen that indicates where the object's current pivot point is located. You reposition the pivot point by picking new points on the screen. Figure 15.8 shows the MANEQUIN.3DS file with the pivot point for the Chest object displayed. When you pick a new pivot point, keep in mind that it takes at least two picks to fully reposition the pivot. A single pick in any viewport only adjusts for the two axes parallel to that viewport. A second pick in another viewport is required to adjust for the third axis.

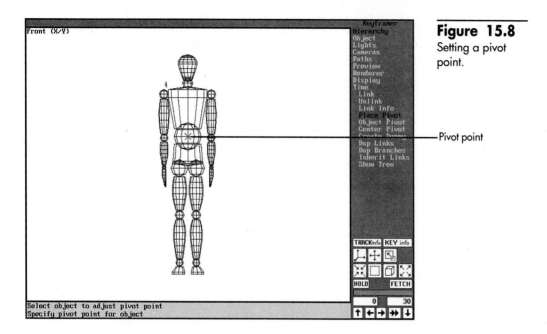

Figure 15.8

Setting a pivot point.

Pivot point

The Place Pivot command also continues to accept input for the new pivot location until you explicitly end the command. You must right-click in the active viewport or choose another command to finish placing the pivot point.

Object Pivot

The Object Pivot command works just like the Place Pivot command, except that it temporarily hides all the objects in the scene except for the selected object and its parent. It also displays the object according to its own internal local coordinate system, rather than the world coordinate system. This command has two particular advantages, as follows:

✔ It makes it easier to adjust pivot points in complex scenes.

✔ It is useful for checking the local axis orientation of an object.

Figure 15.9 shows one of the upper arms after selection during the Object Pivot command. Notice that only the arm object and its parent, the chest, are visible on the screen.

Basic Animation Techniques

Figure 15.9
The upper-arm object selected for the Object Pivot command.

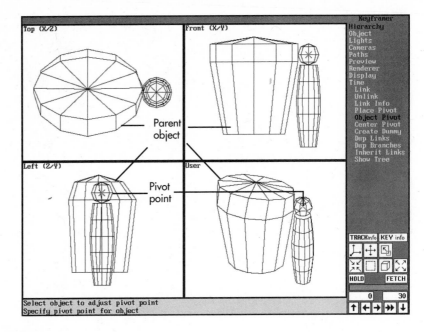

Center Pivot

The Center Pivot command realigns the pivot point with the object's local coordinate system. Another name for this command could be Default Pivot.

A Walking Mannequin

This exercise shows you how to link part of a mannequin model together and specify its pivot points. Careful analysis and placement of pivot points is critical for successfully animating linked models. You then create a typical cartoon walk cycle for your mannequin model.

Start or reset 3D Studio, and then load the file I3DWALK.3DS *into the 3D Editor*	Loads the mesh model of a wooden mannequin
Press F4 *to enter the Keyframer and choose* Hierarchy/Show Tree	Displays the current link status of the entire model in the Keyframer (see fig. 15.10)

As you can tell from the tree structure, this model is not yet fully linked. You must complete the links and place the pivots for the left arm.

In general, when you create links, you want to start with the child objects out at the extremities of a model and work your way back in until the master parent object is at the center of the model. Another good way to decide on the appropriate hierarchy is to look for the object to which most of the other objects connect and that has the least amount of independent motion. Remember that any movement of the parent is passed on to the children. You want to choose a parent that does not move too often, and when it does move, is appropriate for all the children attached to it. The mannequin model uses the large sphere named Waist as its master parent object.

Choose Hierarchy/Link *and select the* L-Hand *object as the child and the* L-Forarm *object as the parent*

Links the hand as a child of the forearm

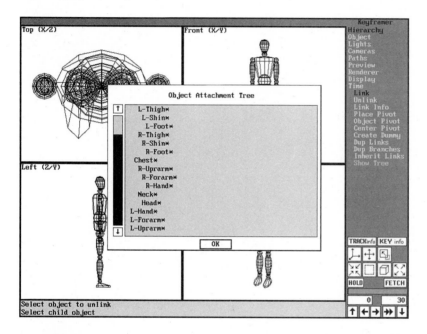

Figure 15.10
The link tree structure for the mannequin model.

Pressing H to display the Select Object by Name dialog box makes it easy to select L-Hand and L-Forarm.

Continue linking the rest of the arm—select L-Forarm *as a child of* L-Uprarm, *and select* L-Uprarm *as a child of* Chest

Completes the linking of the mannequin model

Choose Hierarchy/Object Pivot *and select the* L-Hand *object, specify the pivot point shown in figure 15.11, then right-click in the active viewport to complete the command*

Displays the L-hand object with the parent object in four viewports

Repeat the preceding technique to specify pivot point for the L-Forarm and L-Uprarm objects, as indicated in figure 15.12.

Figure 15.11
Specifying the pivot point for L-Hand.

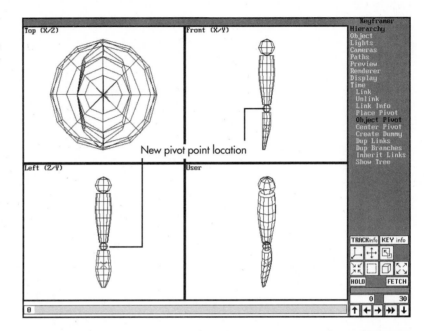

Figure 15.12
Pivot points for the remaining arm objects.

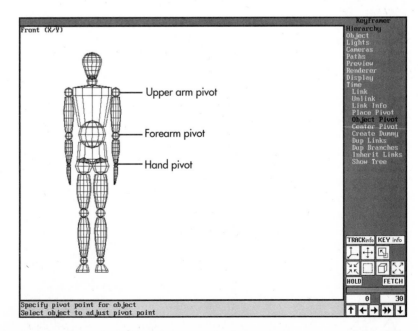

You are now ready to establish a walk cycle for the mannequin. A *walk cycle* is a sequence of key positions that can be looped over and over to create the illusion of a character walking in place. If you then link this character to a moving object or pan the background behind the character, it appears to walk around the scene. This is also a good time to talk about the general aspects of walk cycles and character animation.

The 3D Studio CD-ROM ships with some sample models and walk cycles in the vendor's directory. Other books are also available that describe the process of creating walk cycles. A few examples of such books are: *The Human Figure in Motion* by Eadweard Muybridge, *The Animator's Workbook* by Tony White, and *Animation from Script to Screen* by Shamus Culhane. You should study and use all these references in your own work. The main rule for animating a realistic walk is to not use the same walk cycle too often!

Imagine animating a character walking down a street. You create a walk cycle for this character and put it in motion. After about the third time through the cycle (and this occurs in as little as two seconds of animation), your eye picks up on the repeating cycle. As soon as the cycle is recognized, interest drops off and the illusion of life breaks down. Real creatures do not walk in repeating cycles—there are always slight differences from one step to the next. Walk cycles are a convenient shortcut, but you need to be aware that you are sacrificing realism for convenience.

The basic stereotypical walk cycle consists of eight different positions spaced over 17 frames. This creates a medium-fast, adult walk. Figure 15.13 shows the eight positions and the frame number on which they occur. The first four positions appear to be the same as the last four positions, and they nearly are. The main difference is that the right leg is forward in the first four positions and the left leg is forward in the last four positions.

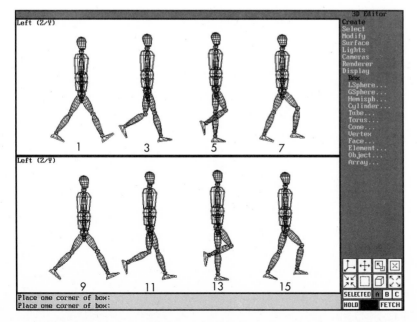

Figure 15.13
The eight basic walk positions.

Basic Animation Techniques

There are two approaches for setting up these positions. One approach is called the *straight-ahead* method—just as its name implies, you start at the first frame and position objects continuing straight ahead until you reach the last frame. The other technique is called *pose-to-pose*—it involves setting up a start pose and an end pose, and then repeatedly positioning the pose between any other two poses until the sequence is complete.

Straight-ahead animation produces the most lifelike and artistic motion, but is very hard to control. Pose-to-pose animation has a tendency to produce more mechanical-looking motion, but it is easier to produce and control. The following exercise uses the pose-to-pose technique. You set the standard walk positions at the following frames in this order: 1, 17, 9, 5, 13, 3, 7, 11, and 15.

Setting Up the Walk Positions

In the Keyframer, choose Time/Total Frames *and set the frame count at 17*	Sets the total number of frames from 0 to 17
Go to frame one and position the mannequin in the position indicated in figure 15.13	Positions the figure at the start of the walk

You have to perform rotations on all of the leg objects, and then move the waist object down until the mannequin's feet touch the floor.

Note that figure 15.13 shows the mannequin moved horizontally so that you can see the different positions. You should not move the waist object horizontally, only up and down. This results in the mannequin walking in place.

Go to frame 17 and click on the Track Info *button. Select the* Waist *object, then click on the button* Sub-Tree, *click on the* Add *button, and click on the* Top All Tracks *row in the highlighted column of frame 17 (see fig. 15.14)*	Creates keys at frame 17 to duplicate the position of the mannequin at frame 1

Figure 15.14
Using Track Info to duplicate keys at frame 17.

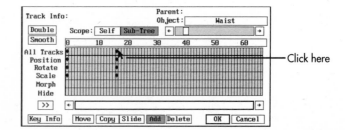

Click on OK

Details on the use of the Track Info dialog box are presented in Chapter 16, "Manipulating Tracks and Keys."

Go to frame 9 and position the mannequin as indicated, then do the same for frames 5, 13, 3, 7, 11, and 15	Positions the mannequin for the remaining frames

Every time you change the mannequin's position, you should explicitly alter all the leg objects and the waist—everything changes at each position.

Drag the frame slider back and forth to check the motion or click on the double-arrow playback icon	Plays the animation in Box mode or Wireframe mode

You should look for errors in the motion, such as the feet passing through the floor. Errors are likely to occur on the even-numbered frames where there are no keys. If you spot an error, go to the odd-numbered key frames and adjust the objects to correct the error. It is very tempting to try to fix the error on the actual frame where it occurred, but this is a poor technique to be avoided in order to prevent an overabundance of keys. Tweaking the animation on nearly every frame makes it very difficult to edit motion later and often causes other errors in the frames that follow the tweaked motion.

After checking and correcting the motion, you would probably like to render a quick animation. Try using Preview/Make and render with lines only. This makes a quick flic preview that does not require you to set up lights first.

Where do you go from here? This exercise only animated the legs of the mannequin—a proper walk still requires some body lean, swinging arms, and shifting of weight from side to side. Try adding these features to your walk cycle.

Dummy Objects

The Create Dummy command creates an invisible, nonrendering object whose sole reason for existence is to be linked to other objects. Dummy objects are used as place holders or support structures for other objects that must perform complex motions.

Earlier in this chapter, an example for the use of a dummy object described a box tumbling down a hill. Another example is an atomic structure. Imagine modeling the motion of electrons as they travel around the nucleus of an atom. Manually specifying the various rotational and positional keys for the electrons would be a daunting task. The following exercise shows you how to do the same thing with linked dummy objects.

This exercise also demonstrates how to model electrons orbiting the nucleus of an atom. The exercise uses dummy objects hidden inside the atom with the electrons linked to the dummies.

A Linked Atomic Structure

Start or reset 3D Studio, then load
the file ATOM.3DS

Loads a model of an atom into the
3D Editor

Figure 15.15 identifies the objects in the model.

Figure 15.15
The model of
ATOM.3DS.

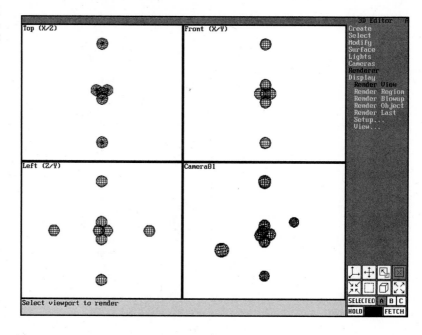

Press F4 *to enter the Keyframer*

Choose Hierarchy/Create Dummy *and*
make four dummy objects at the center of the
nucleus, naming the dummy objects
Dummy01, Dummy02, Dummy03,
and Dummy04

Creates four invisible cubes around the
center of the nucleus (the cubes display
with dotted lines, but do not render)

Choose Hierarchy/Link *and link*
Elect01 as a child of Dummy01, Elect02
as a child of Dummy 02, Elect03 as a
child of Dummy03, Elect04 as a child
of Dummy04, and then choose
Hierarchy/Show Tree

Links the electrons to the dummy
objects at the center of the nucleus
(the tree structure should appear as in
fig. 15.16)

The next step is to put the electrons into orbit. The links to the dummy objects make this
quite easy. Rotating any dummy 360 degrees causes its linked electron to complete one full
orbit around the nucleus. You use the Rotate command for two of the orbits and Rotate
Absolute for the other two orbits.

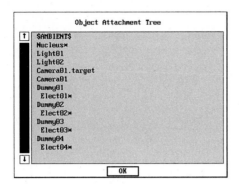

Figure 15.16
The atomic
structure
hierarchy.

Move to frame 30 and choose Objects/Rotate, *then press* H *and select* Dummy01, *press* Tab⇄ *until the X axis is the active rotation axis, and specify a rotation of 360 degrees*	Causes Elect01 to orbit the nucleus vertically
Press H *again and select* Dummy02, *press* Tab⇄ *until the Y axis is the active rotation axis, and specify a rotation of 360 degrees*	Causes Elect02 to orbit the nucleus horizontally
With the Top *viewport active, press* U, *then* ↵Enter *without moving the cursor, and then press the right arrow key on your keyboard six times*	Converts the Top view into a User view and then rotates the view about the Y axis 60 degrees
Choose Object/Rotate Abs, *then press* H *and select* Dummy03, *press* Tab⇄ *until the X axis is the active rotation axis, and specify a rotation of 360 degrees*	Causes Elect03 to orbit the nucleus
Press H *again and select* Dummy04, *press* Tab⇄ *until the Y axis is the active rotation axis, and specify a rotation of 360 degrees*	Causes Elect04 to orbit the nucleus
Click in the Camera *viewport to make it active, and click on the play icon at the lower right corner of the screen*	Plays a wire frame of your animation
Choose Preview/Make *and accept all the defaults, then click in the* Camera *viewport*	Renders and plays a low-resolution preview of the orbiting electrons

IV

Basic Animation Techniques

This exercise demonstrated how simple it is to set up complex motion with a few dummy objects. You could argue that this same exercise could have been completed without using dummy objects by placing each electron's pivot point at the center of the nucleus—you would be correct. The drawback to that approach occurs if you later decide to map a texture to the electrons and show them spinning about their own centers. The offset pivot point is now a problem. The linked dummy objects are easier to understand, easier to manipulate, and leave more options open for other effects.

This model already has lights and materials set up. If you want, go ahead and render it to a flic file. If you need help, rendering of flic files is discussed in Chapter 19.

Using Simple Morphing

The effect known as *morphing* is a technique in which one object gradually turns into something else. This technique has become incredibly popular in film, television, and advertising, almost to the point of excess. However, morphing is still a valuable technique and one with which you should be familiar.

Another drawback to the popularity of morphing is that it tends to overshadow the more mundane but highly useful effects for which morphing is suitable. Most people immediately connect morphing with the fantastic and imagination-stretching visuals used in the popular media, but consider these other possibilities, as follows:

✔ Morphing is a good choice to simulate natural phenomena. Plants bending in the wind, waves washing up on shore, and the flowing of thick viscous liquids like honey or lava are easily accomplished with a morph.

✔ Animating living tissue such as facial characteristics and the motion of the body must often be performed by morphing. Linking and animating separate objects works well in many situations, but linked objects always show seams where they meet. Morphing allows motion to move across surfaces without revealing seams.

✔ Mechanical functions such as rolling shutters, telescoping parts, and bellows are often easier to simulate with a morph rather than to slavishly duplicate the real function of the object.

Try to remember that morphing is a technique that does not always have to be obvious to be effective. If you write it off as just a flashy gimmick, you are missing out on a powerful tool.

The actual process of setting up a morph involves creating a master object and multiple morph targets. The master object is the only one that is actually rendered. The morph targets are usually hidden and serve only as templates into which the master object must fit.

The only technical restriction regarding what constitutes a valid morph target is that the master object and all its morph targets must have the same number of vertices. In practical application, you should also make sure that the master object and its targets have the same vertex order and are derived from a similar source.

New Riders Publishing
INSIDE
SERIES

There are two predictable methods for creating morph objects. The first uses the Shaper/Lofter combination to loft various shapes with the same number of vertices along paths with the same number of vertices. The second technique is to use the 3D Editor to create copies of a master object, and then edit those copies into morph targets. Using the 3D Editor technique to manually edit objects can be quite tedious. Fortunately, there are many IPAS routines available that automate the process of creating morph targets.

Shaper Considerations

Creating shapes in the Shaper that will be lofted into morph targets involves two considerations. All the shapes must have the same number of vertices and the first vertex of all the shapes should be aligned. If the number of vertices is not the same, the object is rejected as a morph target. If the first points do not match up, the morph effect may not be smooth.

Number of Vertices

The Shaper command of Modify/Segment/Refine makes it simple to match up the vertex count on any kind of shape. Simply count the vertices on each shape and use Refine to add vertices to the shape that has fewer.

Other techniques involve using N-Gon/Circular when you need a circle shape with any number of vertices, or using the various Modify/Vertex commands. You can copy a shape and then use Modify/Vertex to move, scale, and adjust its vertices into another form.

Setting the First Point

Always use Display/First/Show and Display/First/Choose to match up the first vertices on shapes intended to be morph targets. Just as the Lofter links up the first vertex of multiple shapes on the path, the Keyframer links up the first vertex of targets in a morph. If the first vertices are not in similar positions on the morph targets, the transition effect is not smooth or very controllable.

Lofter Considerations

The primary consideration for lofting morph objects is that the paths used for the various morph targets must have the same number of vertices and the same Path Steps setting, and the Optimization button must be turned off.

3D Editor Objects

The easiest way to make morph targets in the 3D Editor is to make copies of the original object, and then edit the copies. This technique has a couple of advantages. First, it ensures that all your morph objects have the same number of vertices and that the vertices are in the same order. This is no small feat if you are trying to build morph targets from scratch. Second, if you mess up one of the targets, you can always go back to the master object and make another copy to start fresh.

The Process of Assigning Morphs

After you create your morph targets, you must assign them in the Keyframer using the Object/ Morph/Assign command. The process involves moving to the frame where you want a morph transformation to be complete, choosing the Morph/Assign command, selecting the object to morph, and then choosing from a list of valid morph targets. Figure 15.17 shows the Select Morph Object dialog box with sample morph targets listed. You know immediately if you fail to create valid morph targets because only objects that have the same number of vertices appear in the dialog box. Appearance in the dialog box does not mean that the target creates a good morph, only that a morph to that shape is possible.

Figure 15.17
The Select Morph Object dialog box.

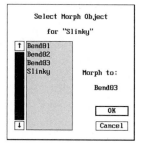

A common mistake when assigning morphs is not to include a sufficient number of morph targets. 3D Studio always takes the most direct route when morphing from one shape to the next. Usually the direct route is not the artistic or the realistic choice. It is up to you to provide 3D Studio with enough information to produce a believable effect.

Figure 15.18 shows the result of specifying too few morph targets. The upper part of the figure displays the two original morph objects—a straight cylinder, and a copy bent over 180 degrees. Two targets are not enough information and 3D Studio makes the most direct transition from one to the other. The result is the odd collection of objects copied from the Keyframer in the bottom half of the figure.

Figure 15.19 shows the same morph after adding two more intermediate morph targets. All the morph objects are shown in the upper half of the figure. Now there is enough information, and 3D Studio produces a smooth morph of the cylinder bending over. The result of the morph is displayed in the lower half of the figure.

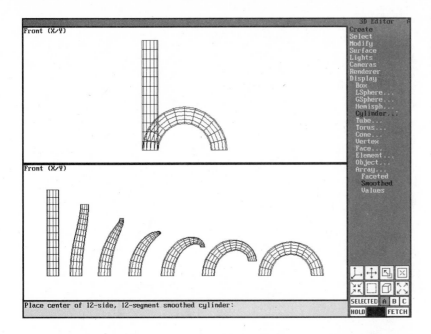

Figure 15.18
The result of too few morph targets.

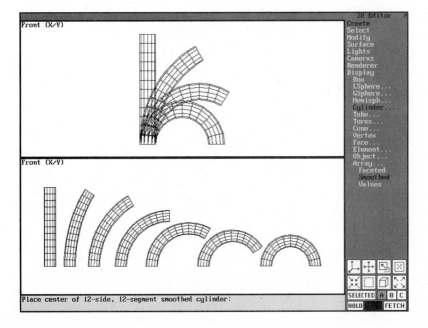

Figure 15.19
The result of a morph that has a sufficient number of targets.

IV

Basic Animation Techniques

Boxing the World

A popular challenge that almost everyone eventually tries is morphing a sphere into a cube. This is actually a fairly easy task once you approach it from the right direction. You create a sphere, and then use the vertex editing commands in the 3D Editor to modify a copy of the sphere into a cube. Because this is such an uncomplicated transition, only two objects are needed to create the morph.

Start or reset 3D Studio

In the 3D Editor, press $\boxed{S}$ *and create a 24-segment L-Sphere with a radius of 200 units at an angle of 0 degrees in the* Top *viewport—name the object* World	Turns on Snap and creates a sphere aligned with the global axis system
Choose Modify/Object/Move *and select the world while pressing* $\boxed{\text{⇧Shift}}$, *then click to place the copy in the same location and name it* Bizarro	Creates a copy of the world in the exact same position
Choose Display/Hide/By Name *and select* World	Hides the world, leaving only the Bizarro object

You are now ready to flatten the sides of the Bizarro object to turn it into a cube. The technique involves selecting groups of vertices, positioning the global axis, and performing a 2D Scale on the vertices to flatten them into a plane. (By the way, ask a fan of the Superman comic series why the boxed world is called Bizarro.)

Choose Modify/Axis/Place *and locate the global axis at the 0 degree point on the third ring of latitude from the top (see fig. 15.20)*	Positions the global axis
Choose Select/Vertex/Quad *and select the vertices on the right side of the sphere from the third ring of latitude and beyond (see fig. 15.20 again)*	Selects the vertices to flatten
Choose Modify/Vertex/2D Scale, *press* $\boxed{\text{Spacebar}}$ *to activate the selection set, press* $\boxed{\text{Tab ⇋}}$ *until horizontal constraints are active, and scale the selected vertices down to one percent*	Scales the vertices toward the side of the sphere, creating a flat surface
Reposition the global axis and select and scale the vertices for the other three sides, using the same procedure as described previously	Flattens the remaining three sides of the sphere

Activate the Front *viewport and flatten the top and bottom of the sphere using the same technique that you used on the sides*

Flattens the top and bottom of the sphere (it now looks almost like a cube—see fig. 15.21)

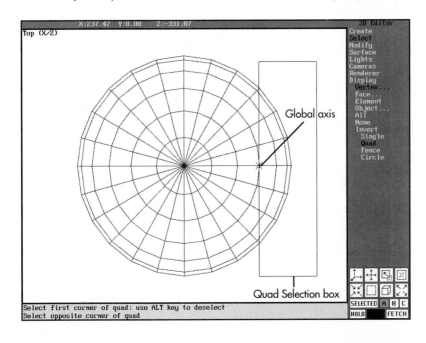

Figure 15.20
Placing the global axis and selecting the right side vertices.

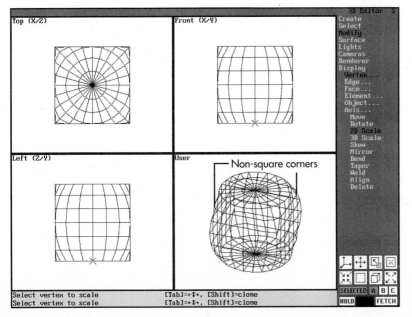

Figure 15.21
The Bizarro object with flat sides, top, and bottom.

IV

Basic Animation Techniques

continues

continued

The editing of the sphere is almost complete. Carefully examining the object reveals that the corners still need to be squared up. You can accomplish this by using the Modify/Vertex/Move command. By working in the Top viewport, you can pick vertices at both the top and bottom of the object and move them into position. You must, however, move each vertex one at a time. After you move a vertex, always redraw your screen to display the vertex at the other side, and then move that vertex as well.

In the Top *viewport, choose* Select/Vertex/Circle, *select the vertices indicated in figure 15.22, and move them to the positions on the edge of the box*	Moves the indicated vertices to square up the corners

Figure 15.22
The vertices to move to square up the corners.

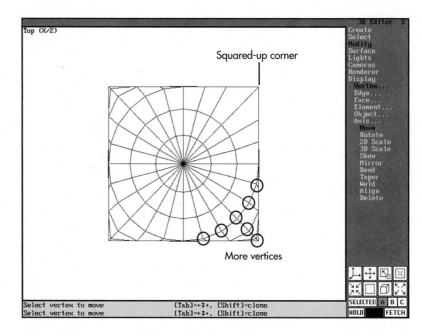

Repeat the procedure for the other three corners in the Top *viewport*	The Bizarro object is now a cube
Choose Display/Unhide/All, *then choose* Display/Hide/By Name *and hide the* Bizarro *object*	Displays the spherical world and hides the Bizarro cube

Press F4 *to enter the Keyframer, choose* Display/Hide/By Name, *and again hide the* Bizarro *object*	Hides the Bizarro cube in the Keyframer as well
Go to frame 15, choose Object/Morph/Assign, *select the* World *object, and then select* Bizarro *from the dialog box*	Assigns a morph at frame 15, causing the world to take on the shape of Bizarro
Go to frame 30, choose Object/Morph/Assign, *select the* World *object, and then select* World *from the dialog box*	Assigns another morph, causing the world to return to its original spherical shape
Click on the Play *icon*	Plays the animation in Wireframe mode

You now have an animation of a sphere morphing into a cube. If you wanted to go all out with this effect, you could use advanced morphing techniques to morph materials and animate smoothing groups—these techniques are discussed in Chapter 21, "Special Keyframer Techniques." Consider applying a texture map of the Earth and creating a morphing moon to orbit your world. Have fun.

Exploring Fast Preview

The Fast Preview Plug-In is the second half of the module that also provides the Camera Control/Match Perspective functions in the 3D Editor. If necessary, you can review the Camera Control functions in Chapter 13, "Lighting and Camera Special Effects."

This section will describe those portions of Fast Preview that differ from Camera Control and provide some insights on the use of Fast Preview.

You start Fast Preview by choosing CAMERA/PREVU from the Program pull-down menu, or by pressing F7. Unlike Camera Control in the 3D Editor, Fast Preview works in any viewport.

Shading Controls

The Fast Preview control panel appears on top of the standard Keyframer screen menu, as shown in figure 15.23. The shading limits and background options at the top of this panel are the same as those for Camera Control, as described in Chapter 13.

IV

Basic Animation Techniques

Figure 15.23
The Fast Preview
Control Panel.

Frame Controls

The middle of the control panel is filled with the frame controls for playback and navigation through your animation.

The first control is the Frame Rate slider. The slider has a range from 0 to 30, and you use it to set your desired playback speed in *frames per second* (fps). A Frame Rate of 0 instructs 3D Studio to play the animation as fast as possible for your hardware configuration. A Frame Rate greater than 0 instructs 3D Studio to attempt to play the animation at the specified FPS. The Actual tile just underneath of the Frame Rate slider reports exactly how fast the animation is actually playing.

There are two options for controlling playback speed. One option is to leave 3D Studio in its default configuration and let it attempt to play at the specified speed. You can squeeze better performance out of the playback by specifying wire frame shading and configuring your screen for the smallest possible viewport—the smaller the viewport, the faster the playback. Unless you have a very fast machine with accelerated graphics, you probably will not get near 15 FPS.

A second, and probably preferable, option is to change 3D Studio's configuration in the 3DS.SET file. If the line PREVIEW-PLAY-MODE = SKIP is activated, 3D Studio will simulate the specified playback rate by dropping frames. This means that 3D Studio will skip the display of as many frames as necessary in order to maintain the specified playback speed. Your animation will not appear very smooth, but you will get a good feel for the speed of the animation when it is played at the proper rate.

Fast Preview is not intended to create final-quality output. It is meant to provide a reasonably accurate and convenient motion check of your animation. To that end, most users of 3D Studio should set their 3DS.SET file to PREVIEW-PLAY-MODE = SKIP, and keep the shading limit set at Wire or Flat.

The last two rows of frame controls duplicate the bottom two rows of icons in the standard Keyframer screen. These are the Current Frame button on the left and the Total Frames tile on the right, with the five standard navigational buttons below. These buttons work exactly as their Keyframer counterparts described earlier, except that the Total Frames tile is informational only in the Fast Preview control panel and cannot be used to change the total frames in the animation.

Make FL?

Clicking on the Make FL? button near the bottom of the panel displays the Make FLI/FLC dialog box, shown in figure 15.24. This dialog box is described in the 3D Studio Release 4 New Features Manual, and it provides control over the shading limits, resolution, and number of frames rendered by Fast Preview. Once the flic has been created, you can view it using either Renderer/View/Flic or Preview/View Flic.

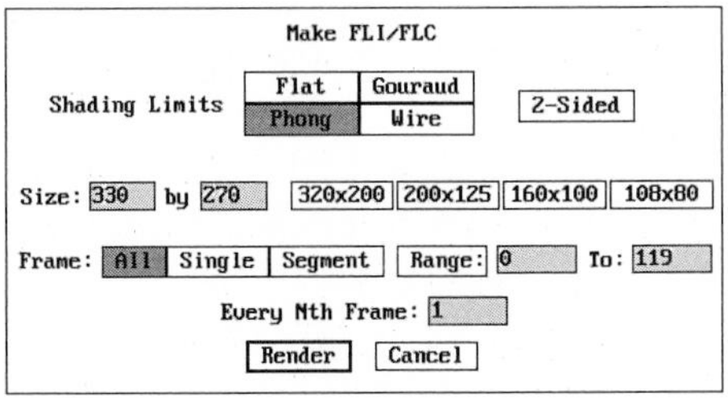

Figure 15.24
The Make FLI/FLC dialog box.

Since Fast Preview renders a more realistic image than the regular preview command, most people will choose the Make FL? option of Fast Preview for creating animation tests.

Summary

This chapter introduced you to some of the techniques and strategies behind basic animation with 3D Studio. Pay special attention to the techniques of linking and morphing because they are powerful tools in your animator's toolbox. The next chapter extends your basic knowledge of animation by showing you how to fine-tune your animations by manipulating tracks and keys.

IV

Basic Animation Techniques

Chapter Snapshot

In this chapter, you will read about the following issues:

✔ Understanding the commands in the Track Info dialog box

✔ Organizing and adjusting an animation through manipulating keys in the Track Info dialog box

✔ Copying tracks between objects

✔ Inserting tracks from external files

✔ Manipulating objects with the Key Info dialog box

✔ Understanding the Tension, Continuity, and Bias sliders

CHAPTER

Manipulating Tracks and Keys

The last chapter examined setting up animation using the simplest of the Keyframer's tools. Namely, you picked an object and then visually moved, scaled, or rotated it on a particular frame. This chapter shows you how to fine-tune your rough work by using tracks and keys. If you look at this as a manufacturing or woodworking process, the last chapter was about making rough cuts, and now you are about to explore finishing techniques.

Using Track Info

Clicking on the Track Info button and selecting an object displays the Track Info dialog box, which shows the frame location and type of all keys for all objects in the animation (see fig. 16.1). The Track Info dialog box is not only a useful chart of what is going on in your animation, but also a powerful editing tool.

Tip

The object name in the upper right corner is now a button that brings up a select by name dialog box.

Figure 16.1
The Track Info dialog box.

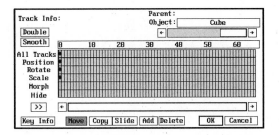

The Tracks

Each horizontal track represents a type of keyframable attribute for the selected object. Each type of object, such as meshes, cameras, and lights, has a different set of controlling tracks. Knowing which tracks are available for which objects is not that critical. The important issue to understand is that the tracks show you exactly when key actions are set in your animation.

A well-planned animation displays a Track Info dialog box that shows a clean, well-ordered set of keys. Animations that you approach in a haphazard and unplanned fashion frequently exhibit a Track Info dialog box that looks like it was hit with a shotgun blast. Figures 16.2 and 16.3 demonstrate this point. Figure 16.2 shows the Track Info dialog box for a bouncing ball animation that was quickly keyed with little thought or planning as to how to specify the motion. The only criterion was getting the motion to "look right." Figure 16.3 produces the same animation, but it was planned and organized around major key poses.

You might ask, "If both sets of keys produce the same animation, what's the difference?" The difference is apparent when your client comes in and asks you to make the ball bounce faster, or fall faster and rise more slowly. Which set of keys would you rather edit? The key sequence in figure 16.3 is easy to adjust. Any changes to the sequence in figure 16.2 requires that you adjust keys on almost every frame.

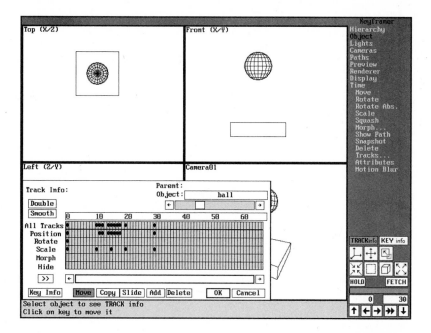

Figure 16.2
A haphazard motion organization for a bouncing ball.

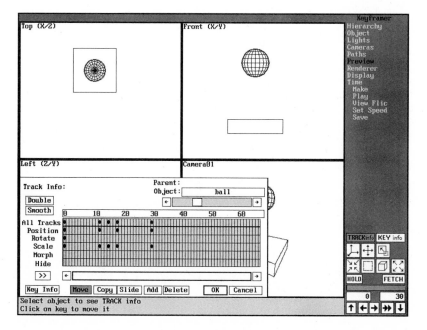

Figure 16.3
An organized approach to a bouncing ball.

Scope

The two scope buttons are vitally important for adjusting the keys of linked objects. If the scope is set for Self, then the key display is for the selected object only. If the scope is set for Sub-Tree, then the keys are displayed for the selected object and all other objects linked to it. Setting the scope to Sub-Tree enables you to view and modify all the keys for all the objects in a linked structure. This can be an immense time-saver and troubleshooter.

Adding Keys

The Add button inserts a key for the track type and at the frame number of the cell in which you click. Adding a key using the Add button does not adjust anything at that particular frame—instead, it records and "locks in" the current animation effect at that frame. The Add button is most often used to freeze an object at a particular frame.

Assume that you have keyed an animation effect that occurs from frame 1 to frame 20. Later you decide that another effect needs to occur between frame 15 and 20. You can preserve the motion that occurs between frame 1 and 15 by using Track Info to add a key to the object at frame 15. 3D Studio then takes the information for the object at that frame and keys it. This ensures that regardless of what you do on other frames, the object maintains its current value at frame 15.

Adding keys to a master parent object is particularly valuable when the scope is set for Sub-Tree. You can use this technique to freeze the settings of all the objects linked to a parent at a particular frame.

Copying Keys

Copying keys takes the animation value of an object at one frame and copies it to another. This is useful when you modify an object at one frame and at a later frame you want it to return to an earlier position. Simply use Track Info to copy the appropriate key from the earlier frame to the current frame.

Moving Keys

Moving keys is one of those incredibly useful commands that is not immediately obvious, and is really a matter of adjusting timing. As you first set up an animation, it usually is easiest to specify key frames in fairly even, regularly spaced intervals. After you get basic animation down, it might appear a little flat or lifeless. Playing with the timing is how you add spark and interest to an animation.

Moving two keys closer together makes the action between them occur faster. Moving keys apart makes the motion appear slower. This is an especially useful technique if you combine it with turning on the Sub-Tree scope.

The following is a short exercise that demonstrates moving keys in the Track Info dialog box. You adjust the walk cycle from the exercise in Chapter 15 to make it a little more interesting.

Moving Keys in the Track Info Dialog Box

Start or reset 3D Studio and load the walk cycle that you created in Chapter 15; if you didn't save that file, you can load I3DWALK2.3DS

Loads a mesh and animation of a walking mannequin

Enter the Keyframer and click on the Play *icon*

Plays the animation in wire frame; the walk is very stiff and repetitious

Click on the Track Info *button, select the* Waist *object, and then turn on the* Sub-Tree *scope button*

Displays the Track Info dialog box with all the keys for the Waist object and its linked children (see fig. 16.4)

Make sure that the Move *button is active, then click on the top* All Tracks *key in frame 3 and move it one frame to the left to frame 2; move the keys at frames 5, 7, and 9 so that all the keys are side-by-side*

Compresses the motion of the first step from 9 frames down to 5; this part of the walk appears faster

Move the keys at frames 11, 13, and 15 so that they are spread out with two blank frames between each key position (see fig.16.5)

Expands the motion of the second step from a total of 8 frames to twelve; this motion appears slower

Click on the Play *button in the* Track Info *dialog box*

Plays the animation in wireframe before you accept the new key positions

If you like the motion, click on OK *or try moving more keys*

Accepts the new key positions and permanently changes the animation

Choose Preview/Make, *set the buttons for* Lines only *and a range of* 1 to 17 *frames, then click on the* Preview *button*

Renders a quick preview of the walk cycle

The mannequin now seems to favor one leg, or limp. This was a simple example of adjusting the timing of the animation, but the same technique applies to more sophisticated animations to randomize the motion and make it appear more lifelike.

The most important step in the exercise was turning on the Sub-Tree button to affect the keys of all the linked objects simultaneously.

IV

Basic Animation Techniques

Figure 16.4
The motion
keys for
I3DWALK2.3DS.

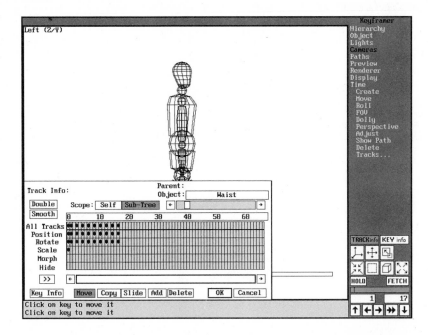

Figure 16.4
The motion
keys for
I3DWALK2.3DS.

Figure 16.5
The new keys for
the walk cycle.

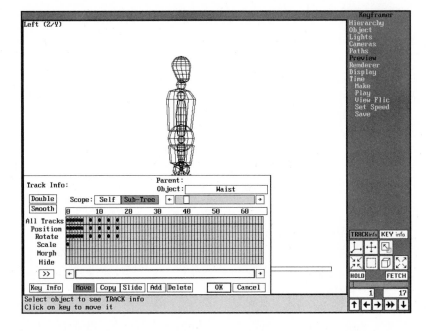

New Riders Publishing
INSIDE
SERIES

Sliding Keys

Sliding keys is similar to moving keys, except that all the keys that follow the selected key move, or slide, along with it. In other words, if you have the Slide button active, and then select a key and move it four frames to the right, all the keys that come after the key you select move four frames to the right as well. Do not worry about losing any keys that slide past the end of the animation. You can add more frames to the animation or slide another key back the opposite direction to gain access to them.

Deleting Keys

The Delete button does just what you would expect. It is particularly useful for wiping out a motion assignment that does not work out the way you want. Just delete the offending key or keys, and everything returns to the way it was before.

You should avoid deleting any keys at frame 0. If you delete a key at frame 0, the geometry in the 3D Editor changes to match the conditions of the next key to the right.

Double

Clicking on the Double button duplicates all of the frames and key settings in the current segment and adds the copies onto the end of the segment. This command has the result of increasing the total length of your animation by the number of frames doubled.

An example of using Double would be if you wanted to create a 30-frame animation where a ball bounced twice and then did something else. You would perform the following steps:

✔ Manually key the first bounce. Assume you used frames 0 through 5.

✔ Specify a segment from frame 0 through 5.

✔ Click on Track Info and select the bouncing ball.

✔ Click on the Double button.

The result is that the ball bounces twice and your segment is expanded to include frames 0 through 10. Your total animation is now 35 frames long. This is because the five frames in the active segment were duplicated and tacked onto the end of the segment at frame 5.

Smooth

The Smooth button takes all of the keys in the Position track only and adjusts their position such that the current object maintains a constant velocity through the entire segment. This command is useful after you manually keyframe an animation and want 3D Studio to adjust the motion.

Be careful with the Smooth command if you set other key frames or object motions that depend on the position keys of the object you select. Smooth changes all the position keys for the current segment of the selected object, which could lead to a big mess.

Using the Commands in the Object/Tracks Branch

Four commands in the Object/Tracks branch expand on the functions in the Track Info dialog box. One of the commands, Loop, is little more than a shortcut for a manual procedure in the Track Info dialog box, but the other three are unique and powerful options you can use to manipulate the objects in your animation.

Looping Tracks

The Object/Tracks/Loop command asks you to select an object, and then copies all the key settings at frame 0 to the last frame in the animation. You also can optionally copy all the keys for linked children of the selected object. The purpose of this command is to enable you to match up positions at the beginning and the end of the animations to create a smoothly looping motion. This is functionally equivalent to using the Track Info dialog box and copying the All Tracks key from frame 0 to the last frame in the animation.

Reversing Tracks

Choosing Object/Tracks/Reverse takes the motion currently assigned to the selected object within the current segment and keys it backward, which is extremely useful for creating assembly animations. This type of animation usually starts with many objects scattered around the screen and then they come to life and assemble themselves into a finished product. The problem is that it is a lot easier to model the product in its assembled form. A solution is to model the object in an assembled state and then animate it as the various parts are taken away. The last step is to apply the Object/Tracks/Reverse command to each object so that the product starts out in pieces and then reassembles itself.

Copying Tracks

The Copy Tracks command enables you to pick up the keys from one object and apply them to another—a very useful command when you have multiple objects that all have to be doing the same thing, such as planes flying in formation or cars driving down a highway. When you apply the keys to the new object, you can apply the keys in relative mode or absolute mode. *Relative mode* applies the motion as an offset from the object's current location, while *absolute mode* relocates the object to the same position as the object from which keys were copied.

This command is particularly powerful if you combine it with Track Info options and the Paths/Get command. Check the exercise in Chapter 21 for an example of combining various Path commands with Tracks/Copy.

Inserting Tracks from a File

The final command under the Tracks branch is the File Insert command. File Insert enables you to apply the motion from any object in any file to any similar object in the current file. Similar object means that, for example, light motion can be applied only to lights, mesh object motion can be applied only to mesh objects, and so on.

The 3D Studio Reference Manual and Tutorials mention that when you use Tracks/File Insert with linked objects, you should check that their hierarchies are the same. If the source object and destination objects do not have the same link hierarchy, the motion keys are not applied predictably. But what does this mean? It means that if you want the inserted motion to work properly, the receiving object must be linked to the same type of structure and that structure must be linked in the same order as the object from the source file.

The following exercise demonstrates the importance of proper link structure for the success of the Tracks/File Insert command. Not only must you link the source object and the destination object to the same type of structure, but you must create the structure in the same order.

Walking the Walk

Start or reset 3D Studio and then load the file BUDWALK.3DS	Loads the Bud simplified mesh object, which is similar to the mannequin model
Enter the Keyframer *and drag the frame slider back and forth*	Plays the animation in Box mode and Bud appears to walk (see fig. 16.6)

The simplified model (Bud) consists of a body to which are linked two legs, two arms, and a neck. Assume that you have created a brother for Bud and you want to insert Bud's walking motion into the brother.

Load the file BUD2.3DS, *drag the frame slider back and forth, then return the slider to frame 0*	Loads BUD2, but dragging the slider does nothing—BUD2 has no motion assigned to him

continues

continued

Choose Object/Tracks/File Insert *and select the object* Body; *then select the file* BUDWALK.3DS *and select the object* Body *from the dialog box*	Selects the Body object in the current file to receive the tracks from the Body object in BUDWALK.3DS
Turn on the buttons for Sub-Tree *and* Relative, *if needed, and click on* OK	Inserts the tracks and extra frames from BUDWALK.3DS into the current file
Drag the frame slider back and forth and observe the motion	Plays the motion, except now Bud swings his arms strangely rather than walks (see fig. 16.7)

What went wrong? The mesh models looked the same. They were even linked to the same number of objects with the exact same names. The problem lies with the fact that they were linked in a different order. The file BUDWALK.3DS was linked in the following order: first the left thigh, then the right thigh, then the left arm, and finally the right arm. The file BUD2.3DS had the arms linked first and then the legs. 3D Studio can only rely on the tree structure and the order in which the tree was assembled. Here, the motion of the first two children of BUDWALK (the legs) was assigned to the first two children of BUD2 (the arms).

Figure 16.6
Bud walking.

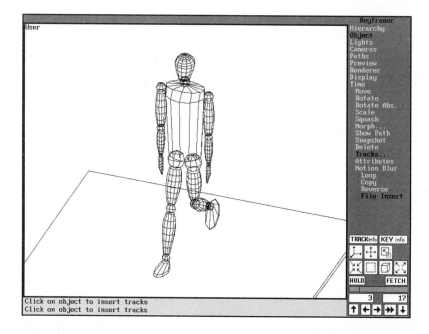

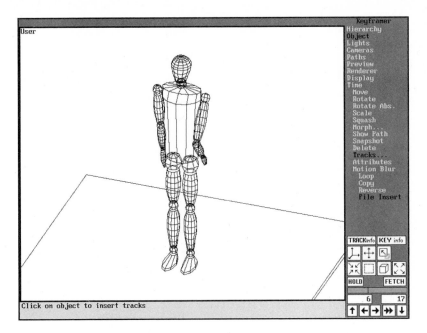

Figure 16.7
Bud with messed-up arms.

Using Key Info

Accessing the Key Info dialog box takes you even deeper into the fine-tuning of your animation. Key Info might at first seem cryptic and intimidating, and full of strange fields, such as Bias, Tension, Ease To, and Rotational Vector coordinates. The reality is that after you spend some time looking at the Key Info dialog box, you discover that it is really useful.

You access Key Info by clicking on the Key Info button and then selecting an object or key to display. Key Info buttons are found at the lower right corner of the screen, in the Track Info dialog box. A typical Key Info dialog box for a mesh object is shown in figure 16.8.

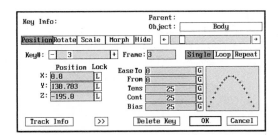

Figure 16.8
A typical Key Info dialog box.

Setting Key Types

The Key Info dialog box has a series of buttons in the upper left corner that you use to determine which of the available key tracks is being used. The number and name of the buttons change according to the type of object you select and the types of transformations that you perform on it. You must click on the button that corresponds to the type of key you want to manipulate.

The following sections look at the three key types that you use most often—Position, Scale, and Rotation. They are always present for every mesh object in the scene, and the Position key also is common for cameras and lights.

Position Settings

If the Position button is active, you can see a series of three fields to the left of the dialog box. These fields specify the distance from the local axis center of the selected object to the pivot point of that object's parent, or to the world origin if the object is not linked to anything. You can reposition the object by typing in new values for the X, Y, and Z fields (see fig. 16.9).

Figure 16.9
Editing the position fields.

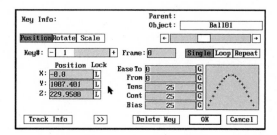

One advantage of using the position fields is that they enable very precise entry of coordinates, up to 8 decimal places. If you are having trouble positioning something, consider editing its position fields in the Key Info dialog box. It's a rare day when you need to position something quite so precisely, but it's nice to have the option when you need it.

Altering the Position, Scale, or Rotation fields on frame 0 (key #1) is exactly like editing an object on frame 0. The new position is reflected in both the Keyframer and the 3D Editor.

Scale Settings

The Scale fields specify the percentage scale factor applied to the object where the center of scaling is always at the local axis origin for the object (see fig. 16.10). Again, the main advantage here is precision. Some people are frustrated by scaling limits in the 3D Editor and

Keyframer. The 3D Editor limits scale precision to 0.25 percent and maximum scale amount to 400 percent, and the Keyframer limits scale precision to 1 percent. The Key Info dialog box has no such limits, and enables you to enter scale factors with up to 8 decimal places.

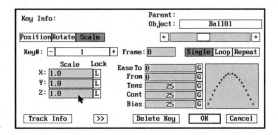

Figure 16.10
Editing the scale fields.

Rotation Settings

The rotation fields have four entries instead of just the three that position and scale have (see fig. 16.11). The first three fields specify the direction of the rotational vector as it leaves the local axis origin of the object. You probably will not manually enter values in these fields very often; it is much easier to set the rotation axis graphically. The fourth field is simply the amount of rotation about that vector expressed in degrees. This fourth field is the valuable one. Again, it is a matter of precision—the 3D Editor enables you to specify rotation angles only to the nearest 0.25 degree and the Keyframer limits you to rotations of full degrees only. The Angle field in the Key Info dialog box enables you to enter almost any angle up to eight places.

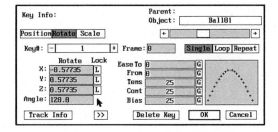

Figure 16.11
Editing the rotation fields.

Setting Locks

Next to each axis field is a small button emblazoned with the letter L. This is the Lock button, and even though you are accessing it at a specific key, the effect is global throughout all frames. Turning on a Lock button for a specific field prevents the object from being transformed along a particular axis. Locking the X axis under rotation, for example, prevents the object from rotating about the X axis; locking the Z axis under scale prevents the object from scaling along the Z axis.

IV

Basic Animation Techniques

An important observation about locks is that they do not affect transformations caused by links. Suppose that you link a box as the child of a ball. You enter the Key Info dialog box and lock Z axis rotation for the box. Now, if you rotate the ball about the Z axis, you might reasonably expect the box to remain still. The box is locked against Z axis rotation, is it not? In this situation, the lock has no effect. The box has no rotation key applied to it, it is only along for the ride, and it is the ball that rotates. A separate dialog box, called Link Info, addresses this issue and is discussed in Chapter 21, "Special Keyframer Techniques."

You use locks in the Key Info dialog box to get a true 2D Scale in the Keyframer. If you want to scale an object along the X and Y axes but not the Z axis, you must enter Key Info and lock Z axis scaling. Then when you perform a 3D Scale on the object, its size along the Z axis will remain unchanged.

Key Spline Adjustments

To the right of the Key Info dialog box are the various Key Spline adjustments. These adjustments are represented as sliders, and they control the motion curve as it passes through the key point. The controls affect the nature of the motion curve between key frames only. This means that the spline controls have the greatest effect and are most noticeable when there are a lot of frames between key frames. The fewer frames between key frames, the weaker the effect of the spline controls. If key frames follow one right after the other, with no unkeyed frame between them, the values of the spline controls are completely ineffectual.

The Ease To Slider

The Ease To slider affects the speed at which the object approaches the key position. Use Ease To to set whether the object slows down as it approaches the key position. The higher the Ease To setting, the more the object slows down. You can see that deceleration is being applied by the marks along the curve. The closer the marks to each other, the slower the motion at that point on the curve (see fig. 16.12).

Slider

Figure 16.12
The Ease To slider
set for maximum
deceleration.

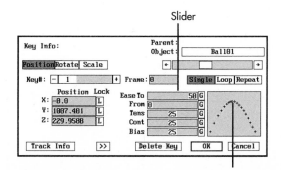

Marks clustered near key

Most objects in the real world must slow down to change direction. This deceleration is the result of expending energy to overcome the inertia of the current motion. Examples of objects that would not display this effect are as follows:

✔ Mechanical or robotic systems

✔ Extremely lightweight objects

✔ Objects suddenly acted upon by an overwhelming force

The Ease From Slider

The Ease From slider involves the same concepts as the Ease To slider, but now you are dealing with acceleration. If your object has been at rest or has slowed down to change direction, Ease From enables you to simulate the effect of coming back up to speed. Increasing the value of the Ease From slider causes the object to begin slowly and then accelerate to its keyed velocity (see fig. 16.13).

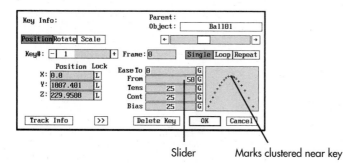

Slider — Marks clustered near key

Figure 16.13
The Ease From slider set for maximum slow start.

Tension

The Tension slider sets the amount of curvature present in the motion. As tension increases, the motion curve approaches a flat line segment; as tension decreases, the curve becomes more pronounced and rounded. Tension also has a side effect. As tension increases, the marks on the motion curve cluster together around the key point, which indicates that increasing tension also contributes a slight Ease To and Ease From effect (see fig. 16.14).

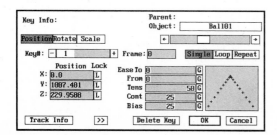

Figure 16.14
The Tension slider set for maximum tension.

IV

Basic Animation Techniques

Continuity

The Continuity slider controls the tangency of the curve at the key point. The default setting of 25 provides a smooth curve passing through the key point where the curve segments are tangent to each other on either side of the point. As continuity decreases, the curves drop away from the point and flatten out. Continuities below 25 always produce a pointed curve. As continuity increases, the curve overshoots the point and must come back to it. This produces very rounded curves to either side of the point with a kink or depression at the key point (see fig. 16.15). Adjusting the continuity does not alter the spacing of the marks on the curve, so it lacks the Ease To and Ease From side effect of the Tension slider.

Figure 16.15
The Continuity slider set at maximum.

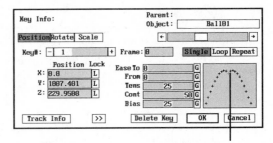

Motion overshoots key

Bias

The Bias slider controls when the motion will occur in respect to the key frame. If the Bias slider is set at 25, the motion is centered on the key frame. Decreasing the slider causes the motion to occur before the key, while increasing the slider causes the motion to occur after the key (see fig. 16.16).

Figure 16.16
The Bias slider set at maximum pushing the motion past the key.

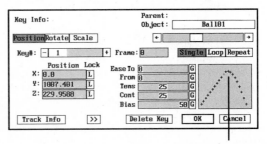

Motion pushed beyond key

Global

When you adjust the Key Spline Controls, you affect the motion at that single key. If you click on the G button to the right of the slider, your adjustments affect all keys for the object. You do not even have to adjust the slider to apply its values globally. If you adjust the slider first and then decide that you want to apply its setting globally, just click on the G (global) button. The current setting for the key instantly is applied to all the other keys, even if you make no more adjustments on the slider.

The following exercise demonstrates the effect that the various sliders have on an object's motion. You adjust the Key Spline Control sliders for a series of bouncing balls and examine the changes in motion.

Adjusting TCB and Easing

Start or reset 3D Studio, then enter the Keyframer and load the file TCB.3DS

Loads a file with four balls that bounce off a wall; the motion paths of the balls are also visible (see fig. 16.17)

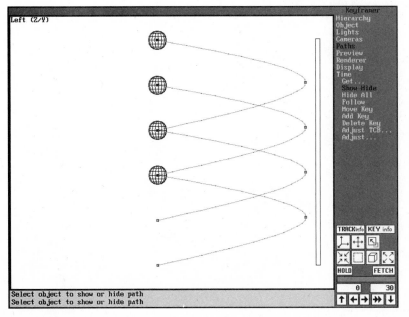

Figure 16.17
The default arrangement of TCB.3DS.

continues

continued

Drag the key slider back and forth	Moves all four balls along their motion path; the paths and movement of the balls are identical
Choose System Options *from the* File *pull-down menu and turn on the* Modal KF Buttons *button*	Sets the Key Info button to remain on after it is selected
Click on the Key Info *button and select the second ball from the top* (Ball02), *click to activate the* Position *button, then set the* Ease To *slider to 50*	Sets all the keys for Ball02 to use maximum Ease To
Select the third ball from the top (Ball03) *and set both the* Ease To *and* Ease From *sliders to 50, then turn on the* G *button to the right of both sliders*	Sets all the keys for Ball03 to use maximum Ease To and Ease From
Select the fourth ball from the top (Ball04) *and set the* Ease From *slider to 50, then turn on the* G *button to the right of that slider*	Sets all the keys for Ball04 to use maximum Ease From
Drag the frame slider back and forth	Moves all four balls along their motion paths (see fig. 16.18)

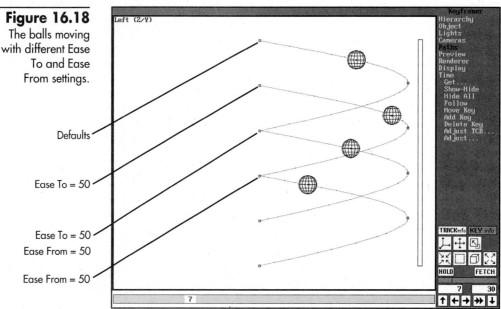

Figure 16.18
The balls moving with different Ease To and Ease From settings.

Defaults

Ease To = 50

Ease To = 50
Ease From = 50

Ease From = 50

Animated Materials

I f you haven't read or reviewed Chapter 6, "Introduction to the Materials Editor," and Chapter 12, "Materials and Mapping," you might want to do so before reading this chapter. Animated materials are designed and applied to objects in exactly the same manner as standard materials.

Understanding Basic Concepts

The use of animated materials is a very common technique in computer animation. The section on modeling complexity in Chapter 3, "Universal Modeling Techniques," mentioned a rule that stated, "Never model with geometry what can be represented with a map." Animated materials take this rule one step further by using maps to represent motion effects. A common use of animated materials is to create the illusion that the surface of an object is moving without having to model the geometry to accomplish the effect. This technique can lead to tremendous savings of time and effort in modeling, keyframing, and rendering.

When using animated materials, 3D Studio applies a different map for each frame of the animation. As each frame is rendered, 3D Studio automatically advances to the next image in the animated map. These maps can be in many different formats, from lists of images captured through a rotoscoping process to animations previously created with 3D Studio or Animator Pro.

Uses for Animated Materials

You can use animated materials to simulate many different real-world effects, as well as to create special effects. As with regular materials mapping, you must carefully consider whether any specific effect can be simulated with an animated map or whether the requirements of your project demand that you explicitly model the effect. After reading this chapter, you will realize that, more often than not, your decision will be "map it."

The following are just a few examples of the many uses for animated materials:

✔ Assume that you need to have a live image playing on a television screen. Applying an animated texture map to the front of the television set gives the viewer the sense that the television set is turned on. The flame from a fire is another excellent use for this type of an animated material.

✔ A very useful procedure is to use a material with animated opacity and shininess maps to dissolve the outer skin of an object, enabling you to view what occurs within the body of the object.

✔ An animated background map often is used to combine live action with computer animation. You can use a rotoscoping process to capture a series of images from a live action video source and use them as an animated map.

✔ It is sometimes more efficient to render all the background portions of a scene in one pass, and then use the resulting animation as an animated background for the final rendering. This is particularly useful if your client approves the background, but continues to request changes to the foreground objects.

✔ Another use of animated materials is to produce a moving reflection, often used in the letters of gold or chrome titles. The animated images are then used as a reflection map for the material assigned to the letters.

✔ Animated materials can also be used for other special effects, such as explosions, smoke, and lightning.

Creating Animated Materials

You can create animated materials in several ways. The most common method uses animated bitmaps, of which there are two types—flics and cels. Another way to create animated materials is to use an *Image File List* (IFL) of any 3D Studio-supported still file types. You also can create animated materials by using a sequence of incrementally numbered bitmaps, as well as solid texture external mapping processes (SXPs). Any of these types can be used as any of the mapping types, such as texture, bump, opacity, and so on.

In addition, you can use animated maps (except for SXPs) anywhere that 3D Studio can use bitmap images, such as in backgrounds and projector lights.

Flics and Cels

Flics and cels are two very similar animated file types supported by 3D Studio. These file formats were first used in Autodesk's Animator, so both types are limited to a maximum of 256 colors. A *flic* is an animated file type and uses an FLC or FLI extension. The two file types are identical except for the fact that an FLC can be any resolution, whereas an FLI is limited to 320×200 pixels. A *cel* can have any resolution. When used in Animator Pro, a cel also contains the location on-screen where it was originally used. 3D Studio ignores this information.

Flics and cels range from 1 to 4,000 frames in length. If a flic is one frame long, it is treated the same as a static GIF file. Frame 0 in the Keyframer uses the first frame of your flic, Frame 1 in the Keyframer uses the second frame, and so on. This can be confusing because Animator Pro numbers its frames beginning at 1. Animated bitmaps match up with the frames rendered in the Keyframer, so if you are rendering with the Nth frame setting greater than 1, you will also skip over N frames in the animated map. If the animated map has fewer frames than the Keyframer animation, 3D Studio will go back to the first frame of the map and loop through as many times as needed to complete the Keyframer animation.

If you render to 24-bit color files, don't worry about using flics and cels, even though they are limited to only 256 colors. 3D Studio uses the colors in the file as the base colors, but then adds lighting, shadows, highlights, reflections, and so on in the rendering, which makes the 256-color map look much better and have richer colors than you might originally predict.

Flics and cels do suffer from one major drawback when they are used as animated maps—they store their images using a method called *delta compression*. This means that only the first frame of the animation is stored in its entirety; all other frames are stored as the changes that occur from the previous frame. In other words, for 3D Studio to apply an animated map to an object on the fourth frame, it must start reading at the beginning of the flic file and read all of the changes until it gets to the fourth frame. 3D Studio must go back to the beginning of the flic to read the fifth frame, the sixth frame, and so on. It is easy to see how this could consume a lot of time, especially when using flics with many frames.

If you are using a flic or cel with many frames as an animated map, you might want to consider converting it to a collection of sequential bitmap files. Such files may take up more disk space, but 3D Studio can read them much faster. The next section describes how to use sequential bitmaps.

Sequences of Bitmaps

You can utilize any of the bitmap file types supported as a file sequence in 3D Studio. These include TGA, TIF, BMP, JPG, and GIF. GIF files are limited to only 256 colors, but the other file types can use as many as 16.7 million colors.

A sequence of bitmaps consists of any supported file types that have incrementally increasing file names. TEST0000.TGA, TEST0001.TGA, and TEST0002.TGA, for example, is a valid sequence of files for this purpose. Like any map, all of these files must be stored in a directory in your map paths.

To specify a sequence of bitmaps in the Materials Editor, enter the base file name using a wild card, such as TEST*.TGA, in the file selector box. 3D Studio then automatically inserts the properly numbered file for each frame rendered. If there are fewer numbered files than frames in the Keyframer, 3D Studio will loop through the list just as it does with flics and cels.

To avoid the flic reading penalty described previously, you might want to consider converting a flic or cel file to a sequence of GIFs. There are two easy ways of doing this, as follows:

1. **Load the flic or cel into Animator Pro and run the NumPic Poco program.** One of the options is to save the current flic as pics. This will save your animation as a sequence of GIF files using the proper sequential number naming technique.

2. **Specify the flic or cel as a background bitmap and render an empty viewport in the Keyframer.** You should set the total number of frames equal to the number of frames in the flic, and configure the renderer for GIF output and the same resolution as the flic file. The rendering process will save each frame of the flic as a separate GIF file using the proper sequential number naming technique.

Image File Lists

An *Image File List* (IFL) is the most controllable method for creating animated materials. An IFL is a simple ASCII text list of all the files you want to use in the animation, along with the number of frames in which they are to be repeated (the default is one).

The directory that contains the bitmaps must be specified in your map paths—not in the IFL. If a flic or cel is included in the IFL, only the first frame of the flic or cel is used.

A typical Image File List looks like the following:

```
; comments may be inserted by starting the line with a semicolon
; this IFL is for an animation of 50 frames, filename OCEAN.IFL
; it is good practice to use the top line to give info on the project
➥pinetree.gif 35
; note that the pinetree.gif above is to be repeated for 35 frames
➥sunrise.tga
; with no number listed, sunrise will only be used for 1 frame
➥highnoon.flc
; any flic or cel will only have the first frame used
➥sunset.jpg 10
; end of file OCEAN.IFL - not required, just good practice
```

You can easily adjust an image file list to make the number of images coincide with the number of frames in your animation by changing the number of times an image repeats, or by adding or deleting a few animation frames. If you use a bitmap file sequence instead of an IFL, it is very difficult to adjust if a client makes a change to the animation.

Many methods can be used to automate the creation of an IFL file. Each has advantages and speed benefits. Using DOS 5.0 and higher, if you have a series of files named TREE0000.TGA through TREE0300.TGA in a directory, enter the following:

DIR TREE*.JPG /on /b > PLANTS.IFL [rt]

To add another series of bitmaps to this file, instead of the DOS "create file" character (>), enter the "append to file" characters (>>), as follows:

DIR BUSH*.GIF /on /b >> PLANTS.IFL [rt]

Another method you can use to create an IFL is to build the file in a spreadsheet program, using the addition function to quickly build the list and print it out to a text file.

Autodesk includes a utility program with 3D Studio called MAKEIFL.EXE, which you also can use to automate the process. The syntax is as follows:

MAKEIFL *<file name>* *<prefix>* *<start frame#>* *<end Frame#>* *[suffix]* *[rt]*

<file name> specifies the name of the IFL file you want to create.

<prefix> specifies the first four (base) letters of the file name.

<start frame#> and *<end frame#>* specify the beginning and end of the range of numbers for the file names. If the range is given from highest to lowest, the range is built in descending order.

The preceding parameters are required. MAKEIFL defaults to a TGA extension, but you can change it by using the optional *[suffix]* parameter.

To use this program to create the preceding file, enter the following:

```
MAKEIFL PLANTS TREE 0 300 JPG [rt]
```

If you need to add another group of files, create a second list and use the DOS COPY command to join them together as a third file, as follows:

```
COPY PLANTS.IFL + PLANTS2.IFL PLANTS3.IFL
```

Make sure that your IFL file, as well as the listed maps, are on a network map path if you render on a network.

Rotoscoping

Rotoscoping is the process of capturing live images one frame at a time from video to use as an animated map. After you capture the files and place them on your computer's hard disk, you can use them as you would any animated map by specifying a file sequence or an IFL in the Materials Editor.

See Chapter 23, "Animation for Field/Frame-Accurate Recording," for details on rotoscoping.

If you use only one computer, there is an alternative to rotoscoping in hundreds of frames and having them take up space on your hard disk. This option is based on the fact that 3D Studio always loops an animated map when it finds that there are no more images in the sequence. If you only have one map, BIRD0000.TGA for instance, and you use the full name of the file as a map, it is treated as a static map. 3D Studio only loads the file once, on the first frame, and continues rendering with that file for the entire animation. If, however, you use the wild card option BIRD*.TGA, for example, 3D Studio reloads the same file for each frame of the animation. Since BIRD0000.TGA is the only map matching the wild card in this example, 3D Studio will continuously reload BIRD0000.TGA.

Now if you change this file to a different image for each frame and keep the same name, 3D Studio reads the new file each time, without taking up additional space on your hard disk. You accomplish this by using Video Post. Video Post, in addition to its other features, can also run an external program or batch file. You can use this capability to run a batch file that automatically captures a frame from videotape and stores it to the file name you choose. Run the batch file in the first line of Video Post.

See Chapter 21, "Special Keyframer Techniques," for more details on using Video Post.

Every video controller operates slightly differently, so you have to customize the routine, depending on which one you have. If you have a DiaQuest controller, a simple two-line batch file such as the following works:

```
@DIGITIZE        Tells the DiaQuest TSR to capture a frame of video
@VSAVE c:\3ds3\maps\bird0000.tga              Writes the file to disk
```

Use the @ character to tell DOS not to echo the commands to your screen as it executes them. After the batch file is executed, control is returned to Video Post to continue the process.

The DiaQuest controller keeps the digitizing and editing frame numbers in separate buffers, and each is incremented automatically. This enables you to digitize from one section of tape, render to your frame buffer, and then record to another section of the same tape. This in turn enables you to accomplish two extremely disk storage-intensive tasks, using no extra disk space whatsoever, if you are rendering on only one computer.

Animated IPAS SXP Programs

Solid pattern external process (SXP) routines can create animated solid maps for your objects in such a way that they appear to be created out of an actual 3D material. In addition, you can animate some SXP materials over time. Refer to Chapter 12, "Materials and Mapping," for general SXP information and application.

Sample animated SXP routines that ship with 3D Studio include BALL.SXP, NOISE.SXP, and VARY.SXP. You can use each of these to change properties of a material over time. BALL.SXP creates round "polka dots" on the surface of an object. If the object is cut, you can see that the dots actually are spheres that follow the surface of the object. You can set the colors of the balls to change over time.

NOISE_I.SXP adds realism to a scene by applying a random texture over the surface of an object that changes over time. Depending on the colors chosen, it can appear as anything from grass to water to smoke. Using routines such as this can help remove some of the computer-generated feel to your animations. Real-life objects are not perfect, and striations and randomness are inherent in all of them to some extent.

VARY_I.SXP has many uses. In addition to changing colors over time, it can change many other properties, such as dissolving the surface of an object to examine the interior by using VARY as an opacity map. You can make entire objects appear or disappear using VARY.

IV

Basic Animation Techniques

Using Animated Maps

The most common use of animated materials is as texture maps. Do not forget that bump maps, opacity maps, shininess maps, and reflection maps also can use the same animated maps in the same way for different effects. If you use an animated map for one purpose, such as a fire burning in a fireplace, you can use the same map for the opacity map, and also for a projector light to have the glow flicker with the fire. Setting up an animated map in this manner does not cost you additional time for loading the bitmap or additional RAM for storage.

Animated Texture Maps

Animated texture maps are by far the most commonly used type of animated map —as many uses for these maps exist as there are animations. Whenever you want to save modeling and keyframing time, use maps. They are used everywhere—from moving eyeballs in character animation to creating fire in a fireplace. Water in fountains, waterfalls, and flowing rivers also can make good use of animated texture maps. You can apply entire animations to a mesh that appears behind a curtain so that when the curtain is opened, you are looking at a movie screen. You also can make clouds blow across the sky, or colors change over time. It is much easier to animate gauges, blinking lights, or digital readouts with an animated texture map than it is to model them. Lightning flashing across the sky is another situation for a map. Maps are so versatile that it is difficult to think of an animation that would not benefit from them.

The Ghost Painting exercise in Chapter 19, "Animation for Flic-Based Presentation and Recording," uses an animated texture map to simulate a brush laying paint on the surface of a canvas.

Animated Bump Materials

You can animate bump maps to show everything from waves to cracks spreading across a wall. Anything that would benefit from a rippling effect, such as textured skin, quicksand, or footprints of an invisible monster, can be created using animated bump maps.

The following exercise shows one method of using NOISE.SXP, which ships with 3D Studio as both a texture map and a bump map, to create animated water.

Animating SXP Water

Start or Reset 3D Studio

Choose Load Project *from the* File *menu and select* WATER.PRJ *from the CD-ROM*

Loads a ready-made model of a pool that needs a water material applied

Your screen should look like figure 17.1.

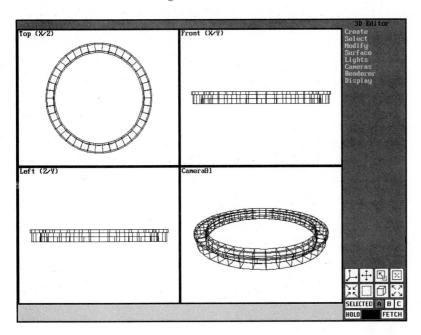

Figure 17.1
The WATER project in the 3D Editor.

Press F5	Switches to the Materials Editor
Press G *to get a material from the Materials Library*	Displays the Get Material dialog box
Select the BLUE PLASTIC *material*	Gets the material and renders a sample sphere
Click on the Texture 1 *map file slot*	Displays the Select Texture Map dialog box
Click on the *.SXP *button, then double-click on* NOISE2_I.SXP	Loads the NOISE2_I.SXP as a texture map
Click on the S *button next to the* Texture 1 *map file slot*	Displays the Noise dialog box
Enter 30 *in the Size edit box and enter* 5 *in all of the* End Offset *edit boxes*	Specifies a smaller (finer) pattern and sets up the motion effects (offset)
Click on and hold the NOISE2_I.SXP *texture map file slot, then drag it to the bump map file slot and release the mouse button*	Creates a copy of the texture map for a bump map

IV

Basic Animation Techniques

continues

continued

Drag the Texture 1 *slider to 50*

Drag the Bump *slider to 30, then press*
Spacebar   Render a sample sphere

Your Materials Editor screen should look similar to figure 17.2.

Figure 17.2
Material set-up
for the WATER
material.

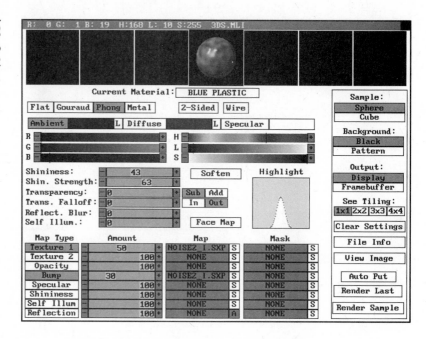

Click on the S *button next to the*   Displays the Noise dialog box again
Texture 1 *map file slot*

Click on the Color 1 *button, then drag*   Changes the black color box
the B *slider to 128*   to blue

Your NOISE.SXP setup screen should now look like figure 17.3.

Click on OK *twice to accept all changes*

Press C *and change the name of the*   Puts the material into the scene
material to WATER-MAP, *then choose* OK   as the current material in the
                                                 3D Editor

Press F3   Returns to the Materials Editor

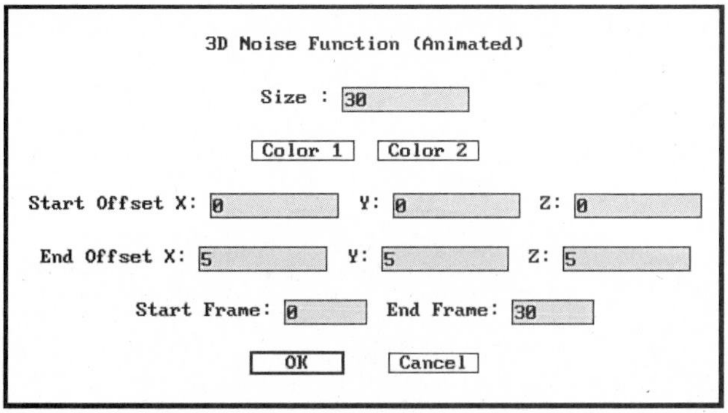

```
                3D Noise Function (Animated)

                      Size : 30

                  [Color 1]  [Color 2]

   Start Offset X: 0          Y: 0        Z: 0

   End Offset X: 5         Y: 5        Z: 5

            Start Frame: 0    End Frame: 30

                     [  OK  ]   [Cancel]
```

Figure 17.3
Parameters for
the NOISE.SXP
texture.

Choose Surface/Material/Assign/Object, *click on the* WATER *object in any viewport, then choose* OK *in the dialog box that appears*	Assigns the new WATER-MAP material to the WATER object
Press F4	Takes you to the Keyframer module
Make the User *viewport current, then press* C	Changes the User viewport to the Camera01 viewport
Choose Renderer/Setup/Configure, *set* File Output *to* Flic, *click on the* 320 × 200 *button, and then click on the* OK *button*	Configures the renderer to produce a 320 × 200 flic
Choose Renderer/Render View, *then click in the* Camera01 *viewport*	Displays the Render Animation dialog box
Set Shading Limit *to* Phong, *turn on* Mapping *and* Anti-aliasing, *set* Frames *to* All, Display, *and* Disk, *and then click on* Render	Sets rendering parameters
Enter the file name WATER *in the* Filename *field, and then click on* OK	Produces a flic file named WATER.FLI
When the rendering is done, choose Renderer/View/Flic *and double-click on the file name of the flic you just rendered*	Plays the animation
Press Esc	Returns you to the Keyframer

Figure 17.4 shows a sample frame from the exercise. Other options that you might explore are changing the End Offset values—the higher the value, the more the water moves—and adjusting transparency. A completed example of the exercise flic, with some transparency added, is available on the CD-ROM as WATER-EX.FLC.

IV

Basic Animation Techniques

continued

Press and drag the NEON-OP.FLC *map file slot to the* VIEW IMAGE *button and release*	Plays the NEON-OP flic

The NEON-OP flic is a simple black-to-white transition that fills the screen from left to right with over 30 frames, and also holds ten more frames of white, for a total of 40 frames. Remember that with opacity maps, white areas are opaque and black areas are transparent.

The neon sign was lofted with mapping coordinates (see Chapter 9, "Lofting Complex Objects," for more details on this technique). Lofted mapping coordinates apply the map with its horizontal dimension wrapped around the shape and the map's vertical dimension stretched along the length of the path. You will need to rotate the flic before it will work properly.

Press Esc *to return to the Materials Editor*

Click on the S *button next to the* Opacity *file slot and set the rotation angle to 90 degrees, and drag the blur slider to 0*	Rotates the map
Press and drag the NEON-OP.FLC *map file slot to the* Shininess *map file slot and release*	Copies the map and all of its settings to the Shininess map file slot
Choose Put To Scene *from the Materials menu, and respond* OK *to the warning dialog*	Updates the material on the sign

Press F4 *to enter the Keyframer*

Choose Renderer/Render View *and click in the* Camera *viewport, then turn off* Filter Maps, *turn on* Disk, *render* All *frames, and click on* Render

Enter LIQUID *as the name of the flic file to save*

It is important to turn off Filter Maps for this effect. If Filter Maps was left on, 3D Studio would blur the leading edge of the opacity map. Instead of appearing as the sharp edge of liquid neon flowing into the sign, it would appear more like a glow. You may want to experiment with this setting.

When rendering is complete, choose Renderer/View/Flic *and select the flic that you just rendered*

An example of the completed flic can also be found on the CD-ROM as LIQUD-EX.FLC. Figure 17.6 shows a sample frame from the exercise.

Figure 17.6
A sample frame from the Liquid Neon exercise.

Animated Reflection Materials

Animated reflection maps have long been used on titles and logos to give a shiny metallic look to the geometry. This is especially effective with beveled text.

Reflections are most effective when you see some movement in the reflected image. You can animate the object using a static reflection map to get this effect, but sometimes you can't move the object or you need a stronger motion effect. This is where animated reflection maps come in handy. In general, animated reflection maps with large, irregular areas of color and broad, sweeping motion effects work best.

Animated Projector Lights

Projector lights also can use any of the animated bitmap methods previously described. You can simulate clouds passing in front of the sun shining through a stained glass window, for example, by using an animated image of the window fading in and out in a projector light. You also can simulate a fire glowing, branches of trees casting shadows, or even the light from a movie screen reflecting onto an audience.

Basic Animation Techniques

See Chapter 18, "Animating Lights and Cameras," for more information on projector lights.

Animated Masks

Animated masks are used to vary the placement and strength of a map. As you remember from Chapter 12, "Materials and Mapping," masks are used to block the effect of their associated map. Animating a mask provides added flexibility to static maps by enabling you to cause the map to appear or disappear, or move the map effect around the surface of the object.

The following exercise uses VARY_I.SXP as an animated mask to slowly reveal a static bump map. The effect is similar to a smooth lake bed drying up and cracking in the sun.

Animated Cracks

Start or reset 3D Studio

Choose Load Project *from the* File *menu and select the file* CRACKED.PRJ *from the CD-ROM*

Loads a project with a simple flat slab object named Mud, as seen in figure 17.7

Figure 17.7
The CRACKED project.

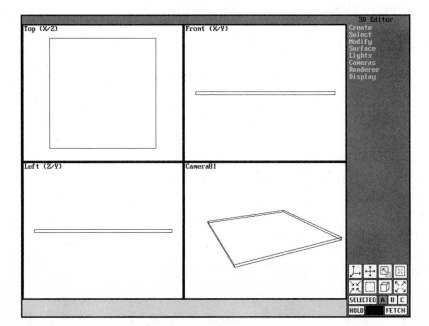

Press F5 *to enter the Materials Editor*

Choose Get Material *from the* Materials *menu and select* BEIGE MATTE

A sample sphere renders with the **BEIGE MATTE** material

Click on the Bump *map file slot and choose the map* CRACKS.TIF *from the* NRPMAPS *directory of the CD-ROM*

Assigns a static bump map

Click on OK *for the Map-Path warning, then choose* Configure *from the* Info *menu, and add the* NRPMAPS *directory to your Map-Paths*

Add the map-path so 3D Studio can find CRACKS.TIF at render time

Drag the Bump *amount slider to 20, then click on* Render Sample

Sets the amount of bump and renders the sample sphere with cracks all over its surface, as shown in figure 17.8

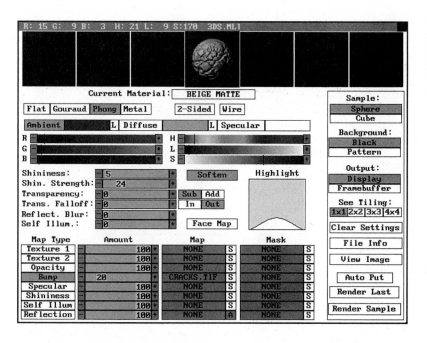

Figure 17.8
The Materials Editor setting for the CRACKED-MUD material.

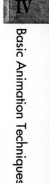

Click on the Bump *mask slot and choose* VARY.SXP *from the* 3DS\MAPS *directory*

Sets a mask for the bump map

continues

continued

Click on the $\boxed{\text{S}}$ *button next to the mask file slot and set the* start color *at* Luminance 255, *set the* end color *at* Luminance 0, *set the* start frame *at* 5, *and set the* end frame *at* 35	Sets the mask to start at pure white, completely masking the bumps, and to gradually fade to black, revealing the bumps
Click on Render Sample *again*	Renders the sample sphere with no bumps; they are masked by VARY.SXP
Press $\boxed{\text{C}}$ *for* Current *and change the name of the material to* CRACKED-MUD	Names the new material as CRACKED-MUD and makes it the current material in the 3D Editor
Press $\boxed{\text{F3}}$ *to enter the 3D Editor*	
Choose Surface/Materials/Assign/Object *and select the* Mud *object in any viewport*	Assigns CRACKED-MUD to the Mud object
Press $\boxed{\text{F4}}$ *to enter the Keyframer*	
Choose Renderer/Render View *and click in the* Camera viewport	
Accept the default rendering settings, render All *frames, make sure* Disk *is turned on, then click on* Render	Renders the 40 frame animation
Save the animation as CRACKED.FLI	
When rendering is complete, choose Renderer/View/Flic *and select the flic that you just rendered*	Plays the flic file

The resulting flic should start out as a smooth flat surface, and then develop cracks in its surface as if it had dried up in the sun. Figure 17.9 shows a frame from the exercise after the mud has cracked. A sample flic is on the CD-ROM as CRACK-EX.FLI.

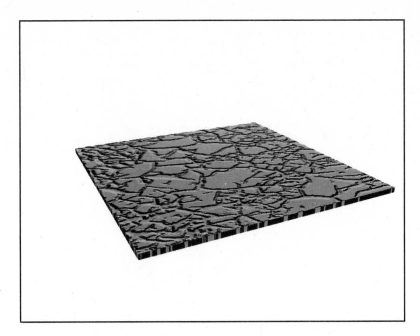

Figure 17.9
A sample frame from the Cracked Mud exercise.

Summary

Animated materials can be used to your advantage in many ways, from adding realism in scenes to saving modeling and rendering time. Remember, don't model with geometry what you can simulate with a map.

Chapter Snapshot

In this chapter, the following concepts and procedures for using cameras and lights in the Keyframer are discussed:

✔ Understanding the basic concepts of light and camera adjustments in the Keyframer

✔ Creating realistic and useful camera movements

✔ Using paths in conjunction with cameras and lights

✔ Linking cameras and lights for added capabilities and smooth motion

✔ Understanding the issues of animating lights and when they calculate shadows

CHAPTER

18

Animating Lights and Cameras

T he previous two chapters discussed basic methods for animating and linking objects in the Keyframer. This chapter shows how you can animate lights and cameras in much the same way. Likewise, you can set the majority of parameters and all the positions determinable in the 3D Editor for each frame in the Keyframer.

Lights and cameras are extremely simple entities in the 3D Studio environment, yet their most basic movements can enliven an animation considerably. Many eye-catching animations manipulate only lights and cameras—moving the audience through the scene, shifting shadows, and changing the qualities of light.

Exploring Common Concepts for Lights and Cameras

Light and camera entities do not have quite as many animation options as objects, but share many of the same capabilities and exclusions. It is important to remember what is possible when you plan animations and create your model.

Cloning without Instances

Unlike objects, you cannot create instances of lights and cameras in the Keyframer. If you hold the Shift key during an operation, a clone of the light or camera will be created in both the Keyframer and the 3D Editor.

Clones created in the Keyframer inherit all the track and key information from the parent, as well as any assigned hierarchy. This is very different from cloning a light or camera in the 3D Editor because those entities contain Keyframer information for frame 0 only. The Snapshot feature also is unavailable for lights and cameras, even if they are linked to an object that is in turn selected for the snapshot command.

Linking Limitations

You can control and orchestrate the animation of lights and cameras by linking them to objects and dummy objects. You can link lights, cameras, and their targets to objects and they behave like any other linked children.

Although they can become children, lights and cameras *cannot* be parents. The only exception to this rule is when cameras are allowed to be parents, but of lights *only* (not their targets).

Non-Keyframeable Features

The following characteristics of lights and cameras do not have keys and cannot be animated:

✔ On and off status for lights

✔ The multiplier value for lights

✔ Shadow-casting parameters, including whether it casts shadows, the type cast, and any shadow parameter

✔ The Exclusion and Attenuation options for lights

✔ The Overshoot option for spotlights

✔ The Aspect Ratio of rectangular spotlights

✔ Ranges for lights and cameras

✔ Atmosphere color and layered fog position

✔ The output size and resulting Camera viewport aspect ratio

Although the preceding list might seem long, lights and cameras have many more basic options than objects. The good news is that you can manipulate every other parameter over time.

3D Editor Correspondence

Unlike objects, you can transfer the current frame position of cameras and lights to the 3D Editor. When lights and cameras are moved or adjusted independently without being linked, only their frame 0 position correlates to the 3D Editor, just as objects behave. This respect to the 3D Editor changes whenever a light or camera is linked to an object (dummy or otherwise) in the Keyframer.

The position of targets and all parameters of lights and cameras is transferred to the 3D Editor as they are in the current Keyframer frame. If only the target is linked, the parent camera or spotlight status does not transfer. Parameters that are in transition between keys have their interpolated value transfer. Because you cannot link ambient light, the 3D Editor always respects its frame 0 status. Although this transfer of light and camera Keyframer status is an exception to the rule, it does have its advantages. Commands, such as Ranges, Aspect, and Bitmap Fit, are not keyframeable, so you cannot access them from within the Keyframer. Transferring the current camera and light status enables you to adjust these fixed parameters for critical locations in an animation.

Examining Realistic Camera Movement

Because cameras represent the observer's eye, it is extremely important to relate what the camera sees to how the observer would perceive it in the scene. People have a strong sense of what speed looks like and interpret your animations by relating them to their own experience. Most observers inherently know what a stroll, a run, or a car race is, and whether the speed of the camera turn would have hurt their necks.

Because reduced playback speed means additional frames and increased rendering time, computer animations have a tendency to run and fly through scenes. As an animator, you need to consider carefully what feeling of speed the observer should experience and whether it is appropriate for your animation.

Implications of Camera Speed

The speed at which a camera moves through a scene implies how fast the observer feels. *Speed* is the relation of the number of frames that it takes to cover a given distance—the fewer the frames, the quicker the animation plays back and the faster the audience feels they are moving.

IV

Basic Animation Techniques

If your scene has objects that have real-world scale, your audience has a very good feel for the speed of the camera. You also should spend some time and plot out how quickly a person would travel in a given situation just to see what they see.

For scenes of an abstract nature, you are freed from this constraint and need only concern yourself with creating an effective animation. Animations of atomic structures, solar systems, and machine parts are just a few examples of when the distance covered per frame has little to do with how fast the observer feels he or she is going. If the human mind does not have human-scale objects to which to relate, it simply accepts the animation as fact and enjoys the show. But when an animation does have elements of scale, such as buildings, furniture, and cars, the observer has a keen sense of relative speed and the animation automatically assumes a certain atmosphere of motion.

It's easy to overestimate the abilities of the average pedestrian. Table 18.1 gives a rough approximation of some common gaits.

Table 18.1
Pedestrian Gaits

Type	Miles Per Hour	Feet Per Second
Casual stroll	1.5–2.0	2.2–3.0
Average walk	2.5–3.5	3.6–5
Brisk walk	4–5	6–8
Average jog	6–8	9–12
Average run	8–10	12–15
All out sprint	12–16	18–24

The number of feet the camera progresses in any given frame is a factor of your output, for example 12, 24, or 30 frames per second. Dividing feet per second by frames per second delivers feet per frame for that form of playback. If the camera was moving at one foot per frame and was being output to standard NTSC (30 frames per second), the observer would be moving at 30 feet per second—the speed of a world class sprinter, a horse trot, or a slow moving vehicle.

It usually is acceptable to move the camera somewhat faster than the gait at which you would normally take in the scene. The thing to remember is that the viewer can only digest so much information and this is a factor of the camera's speed. Many animations are looped to play back repeatedly for the primary reason that the animation was too fast for the audience to comprehend what was in the model with only one viewing.

Camera Pans and Head Turns

The speed at which you turn a camera (move its target) relates directly to how fast the observer feels his head is turning. In reality, you can turn your head quite fast—for example, 90 degrees in a fraction of a second—but you have almost no recollection of what you saw in the turn. Figure 18.1 shows a common camera pan.

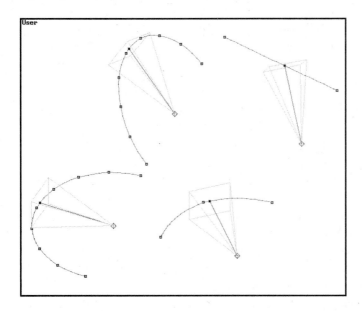

Figure 18.1
Head turns from camera target paths.

For most people, a comfortable pan begins at about one second for every 45 degrees of turn. Panning faster becomes more of a blur. A careful observation takes about one second for every 15 or 20 degrees.

Some of the easiest and smoothest head turns can be accomplished by linking the target, and possibly the camera, to a rotating parent object. This will be discussed later in this chapter under "Using Dummy Objects."

The effect of a fast pan is even more uncomfortable with a computer camera. A video or motion picture camera shows blur as objects pass too quickly in front, while the computer renders each object perfectly in place. If the camera pan is too quick for the computer to display, the clearly defined objects appear to jump and slice across the screen in a phenomenon known as *screen tear* (see Chapter 19, "Animation for Flic-Based Presentation and Recording," for issues dealing with screen tear). Screen tear generally is something to avoid unless you truly want to emphasize a head spin, and then you should seriously consider using scene blur.

3D Studio Release 4 includes the capability to assign motion blur to objects or the entire scene. *Object blur* suggests fast moving objects, whereas *scene blur* is equivalent of a fast head turn. The latter is a Video Post rendering option and is quite realistic for reducing screen tear while inferring motion (see Chapter 21, "Special Keyframer Techniques").

Careful pans can require many frames. If the observer is looking up, down, and around during the pan (that is, the target is scanning while the camera is moving and rotating), even more frames are required for the animation to convey all the model's animation. If you want to indicate action, startlement, or sudden change of direction, simply reduce the number of frames for a pan.

In long walk-throughs, casual head turns are essential for reducing monotony and making the event appear more natural. This takes more work because you must choreograph the target's movement as well as the camera's, but if you neglect them, you can end up with a very mechanical (and uninteresting) animation.

Planning Camera Transitions

Telling your animation's story through camera movement can be very effective, but it also can be quite boring if you don't give enough thought to the script. Even if the animation is a walk-through of a shopping mall, you don't have to limit the camera to a correctly and evenly paced movement.

When you experience a place, the impression recorded by your mind's eye is not simply a stroll down the halls looking from side-to-side. As you walk, you might pause and look at details or situations. Monotonous stretches often are forgotten as you concentrate on more interesting destinations. The result is a memory of sequential events, movement, and images that do not replay in your mind as a continuous (and possibly monotonous) walk-through. Re-creating this impression is what creates interesting animations. The observers are not in the space and cannot decide what is worth looking at—you make that decision for them. This means you need to plan pauses, breaks, and transitions.

Just because you animate a camera does not mean you have to show your entire script through a continuous pan or progression. Imagine, for example, the act of walking the viewer to an atrium's railing to view a plaza below. This is a very appropriate transition point where you can key the camera on an area of the scene, fade out, and bring the observer to the point viewed—looking back at where the camera was once viewing from. This is much easier and more natural than having the camera proceed over the edge in a "death dive" to arrive at the same location. It also keeps the animation's tempo moving, especially when compared to walking the viewer down the stairs, elevator, or ramp.

Using Animated Camera Adjustments

Moving a camera in time can produce one of the easiest and most often created animations in 3D Studio. To do so effectively requires an understanding of the effects that basic commands have on perception, and how to relate this to what has already been discussed about head turns, speed, and transitions.

Smooth Moves and Pans

Moving cameras usually are a study in fluid motion. The camera represents the audience and targets their point of interest. Because of this, it is important to make movements and pans at natural speeds, with comfortable arcs and fluid transitions.

Cameras are different from other objects in that their movements always define time and speed. Objects often are moved and positioned for effect—sometimes for very subtle effects. Whereas object motion might go unnoticed, camera motion rarely does.

A common mistake is to insert too many keys in an effort to correct the camera's display at specific frames. Although those frames now display what you want, their transitions tend to be choppy, jerky, or mechanical. A common animation error is the *bob,* where the camera moves from what was a smooth path. This is caused by the addition of extraneous keys. For fluid movement, you should specify the minimum number of essential keys and let 3D Studio create the smooth splines to connect them.

The spline motion curve formed between keyed positions is much more of a fixed commodity than splines in the Shaper or Lofter. After defining a few camera positions, it is beneficial to display its path so that further adjustments can be made in reference to it. This can be done with either the Cameras/Show Path command or the Paths/Show-Hide command. The desired path for most camera movements is smooth with adjacent portions of the path being tangent to one another. On paths that are kinked or sharply angled, overshoot should be avoided.

Figure 18.2 shows how you can affect the bulge and tangent of the curve by adjusting the keys' Tension, Continuity, and Bias settings. This is the only method available for adjusting the curve's actual shape, and you can do this in the Key Info dialog box or visually on the path with the Paths/Adjust options (see Chapter 21 for detailed uses of this command branch).

The effects of the TCB and Ease settings can have a great impact on the shape of a path. It is important to be comfortable with these effects while they are still graphically portrayed by the path. The spline paths pertaining to a camera's roll and FOV or a light's color, falloff, and hotspot follow a similar concept, but are not visible.

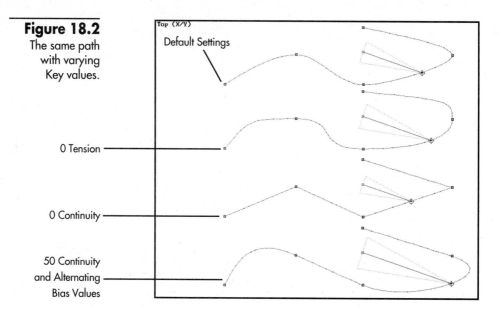

Figure 18.2
The same path
with varying
Key values.

Rolling

Rolling a camera gives the impression that the audience is tilting their heads or spinning. A camera roll animation usually is combined with a twisting or swerving path to give the feeling of a banking movement. Coordinating roll within an animation is discussed later in this chapter under "Follow and Bank Options for Paths."

Zooming

The effect of zooming is simply a matter of adjusting the camera's FOV. The camera and target remain constant as the lens size (and resulting FOV) is shifted, much like sliding a zoom lens. The 35mm lens equivalents used in the 3D Editor are still available in the Cameras/Adjust dialog box, but are not available when you manually edit tracks and keys.

An unsmooth FOV path creates an effect that is similar to moving your head in and out. Although you cannot see the path directly, you can get a feel for its smoothness by using the Play button and examining the wire frame.

Walk-throughs and Dolly

The Dolly command always moves the camera along the vector traced to its target. Because of this, it is quite easy to elevate the camera accidentally, and care should be taken in using this command to create a walk-through. If the camera and target are level to the ground plane, the command works quite well since Dolly will not change the camera's elevation. If the target points even slightly up or down, the result is a vertical movement that usually is not desirable. In such situations, the camera must always be moved within the Top (or an equally parallel) viewport.

Attempting Vertigo

This is the effect made famous by several notable films. It involves dollying a camera while simultaneously adjusting its FOV to maintain a constant picture frame. The result is a flaring perspective that is unlike any natural observation, but one that can be excellent for special effects.

The vertigo effect is somewhat possible if you use the Cameras/Perspective command, but it is not automatic. Keeping a stable frame while dollying a camera and sliding its zoom lens is no small feat in the real world, and it's not so easy in 3D Studio, either. Although the Perspective command maintains a fairly constant picture frame as it slides the position and FOV, it is only correct for that frame.

The problem is that the relationship between FOV and distance is not linear. The Keyframer's Perspective command makes no allowances for this discrepancy and creates keys with default values. You can correct this, but it takes quite a bit of time using the Key Info dialog box or creating additional keys. If you don't correct it, the frame in the middle of the transition has a FOV that is much too broad, which causes the animation to zoom back and then zoom in to its original place when it reaches the final frame.

To achieve a smooth vertigo effect, you might want to adjust only the two key settings. As a starting point, you will want to begin (assuming the keys are beginning with their defaults) with a Continuity of 0 for FOV and Position, an Ease From of 50 for Position, an Ease To of 50 for the first FOV key, and a Tension of 50 for the first FOV and the second Position. The variables to work with are the first Position's Tension and Bias and the second FOV's Ease To and Tension. This helps you to achieve a nearly smooth effect, but it is not perfect.

Adding additional keys only creates additional FOV discrepancies that you then have to overcome. The only sure way to achieve a smooth transition is to manually place an FOV key for every frame.

Depth of Field Approximation

A real-world camera has focus, and the range over which the scene is in focus is termed *depth of field*. The amount of the scene in focus depends on the size of the aperture—the smaller the aperture, the more that will be in clear focus. Because 3D Studio's camera renders everything in sharp focus, you might consider it the world's smallest pinhole camera. You can approximate depth of field in 3D Studio, but never with ease and speed, so you should reserve it for special projects.

The Keyframer's Video Post suite enables you to create a depth of field approximation by compositing layers of the scene in sequential queue entries. The concept is to independently render areas of the scene as they relate to the camera's position (for example, foreground,

IV

Basic Animation Techniques

middle ground, background) in the standard Renderer with alpha on. These rendered images are placed in the Video Post Queue to be composited, accessing their Alpha channel and possibly incorporating additional effects.

The last step is the tricky and rendering-intensive part. If you use only basic 3D Studio techniques, you have to render each scene section with a corresponding Scene Motion Blur setting. If background images are used, they will need to be blurred in a true-color paint program because scene motion blur ignores them. If your paint program uses Alpha channels, you can skip the time-intensive scene motion blur, apply the effect directly on the rendered image, and composite the images there. The BLUR.IXP is an alternative to paint programs and scene motion blur in that it can blur bitmaps in the Video Post queue and does so much quicker than scene motion blur (there also is no chance for strobing). When using BLUR.IXP, however, you will still need to split the scene into different images to apply varying levels of focus/blur.

BLUR.IXP is part of the *image processing* suite of IPAS routines available from the Yost Group.

Using Paths for Cameras

An alternative to moving and coordinating keys for lights, especially cameras, is to draw the path elsewhere and import it. This can be done as a two-dimensional polygon in the Shaper, a three-dimensional path in the Lofter, or a polyline from AutoCAD. The advantage is that you now have complete control over the path's curvature and do not have to rely on the key settings to adjust the spline.

Assigning Paths

Paths are assigned in the keyframer with the Paths/Get command. After you select the object to receive the path, you can get the defined shape from the Shaper, the current path from the Lofter, or a LFT or DXF file from the disk. After you determine the path's origination, several options are presented, as shown in figure 18.3.

Figure 18.3
The Get Path
dialog box.

The `Relocate object to path start` does just that—it deletes the object's first position key and replaces it with the first vertex's position key. If you answer No, the object maintains its first key position and the path's later positions are displaced accordingly.

The `Reverse path direction` switches which path's end vertices are read first.

The `Adjust keys for constant speed` option places the total number of frames evenly across the path's total length (see bottom path in fig. 18.4). The vertices remain as keys in the same position, but the number of frames between each key varies proportionally with the intermediate distance. (Note that it is important to say *yes* to this option for smooth camera paths.) When this option is not selected, a like number of frames are placed between each pair of vertices regardless of the distance (see top path in fig. 18.4), and the path is inevitably uneven over time.

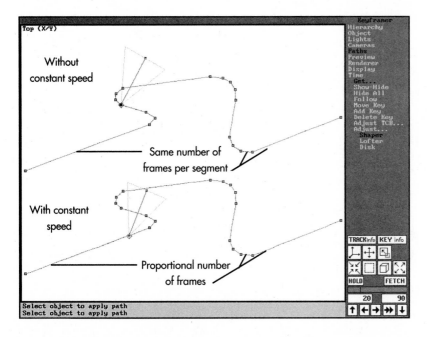

Figure 18.4
Path steps with and without constant speed.

Drawing Paths with the 2D Shaper

The 2D Shaper has many of the tools you need to create accurate and fluid paths. Using the 2D Shaper's 3D Display option to produce an underlay of the scene's geometry is quite useful for creating proper paths.

Keep the following points in mind when you use the 2D Shaper for creating paths:

✔ The paths are always two-dimensional.

✔ The path is imported parallel to the Top viewport.

IV

Basic Animation Techniques

✔ The path is placed on the construction plane parallel to the Top viewport.

✔ You must have at least as many frames in the animation as vertices in the path. Excess frames are distributed along the length of the path.

✔ The shape steps setting has nothing to do with roundness of a path's curves. This is solely a function of how many frames exist in the current segment to determine the path. If a path needs to be linear, you should make it out of polygon linear segments.

A City Walk-through

Begin by loading OLDCITY.3DS and make the Top *viewport current*	Loads the Release 1 City mesh
Go to the Shaper and choose Display/3D Display/Choose	Displays a list of the objects in the scene
Click on All *and deselect the detailed items by entering* **C*** *and clicking on* Untag, *and then entering* **D*** *and clicking on* Untag	Selects all the objects but those starting with C and D
Click on OK *to the selection list and choose* 3D Display/On	Displays the 3D Editor's Top viewport mesh
Choose Create/Line *and draw a series of lines that trace a path around the central building (see fig. 18.5)*	Draws a series of connected lines
Choose Modify/Polygon/Curve *and select the polygon you just drew*	Makes the polygon a continuous curve
Modify the polygon using Vertex/Adjust *and* Segment/Adjust *until it creates the desired path*	Changes the bulge and tangencies of the spline to something like figure 18.6
Switch back to the Keyframer, choose Paths/Get/Shaper, *and select the camera*	Displays the Get Path dialog box (refer back to fig. 18.3)
Answer Yes *to Relocate Object,* No *to Reverse Path, and* Yes *to Constant Speed options*	Moves the camera to the beginning of the path
Choose Paths/Show-Hide *and select the camera*	Displays the path drawn in the Shaper that is now assigned to the camera

The imported path is not very smooth because the Keyframer is still set to the default 30 frames. This tells us that there aren't nearly enough frames to make the path smooth.

Increase the total number of frames to 90 (or higher)

Choose Path/Get/Shaper *and reassign the path again*	Replaces the old path with a much smoother version, as shown in figure 18.7
Make the Camera *viewport active and click on the double arrow play button*	Plays the animation full screen for the camera view

The camera is quite low, and the animation is more of a worm's eye. This is because the path was imported at the height of the construction plane, which for this model was at the street level.

Enter the Front *viewport, choose* Cameras/Move, *press* Alt *,and move the camera up a little above the cars*	
Make the Camera *viewport active and play the animation*	Moves the camera and the entire path upward to eye level

The playback looks much better, but the camera is always fixed on the building's peak. As the camera gets close to the building, it seems unnatural and makes you feel as if you are straining your neck.

Advance to the frame that first has the camera at its closest, make the Camera *viewport active, and press* Alt+E	
Make sure your Tab↹ *arrow is vertical, and pan the camera down until the building's base is clear*	
Advance to the last frame and pan up until the top of the building is visible	Displays the Camera viewport's safe frame
Cycle through the animation with the Frame slider to locate points where the camera still needs to pan and pan the camera as needed	Moves the camera target straight down to reorient the view
Choose Cameras/Show Path *and select the target*	Displays the scene in box mode for each frame as quickly as you slide through the frames
Play or render the final walk-through animation	Displays the target's vertical path, as shown in figure 18.8

The walk-through animation now is complete and should be fairly convincing. Given the amount of ground that was covered, the animation is most likely playing too fast. Try using Time/Scale Segment to increase the number of frames to 1000, for example. This places extra frames between the keys so all of your adjustments are still relevant and lengthens the video animation from 3 to 30 seconds.

Figure 18.5
Drawing a straight
path in the
Shaper.

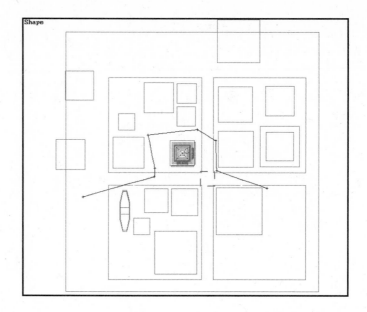

Figure 18.6
Modifying the path
to be a smooth
curve that respects
the city's grid.

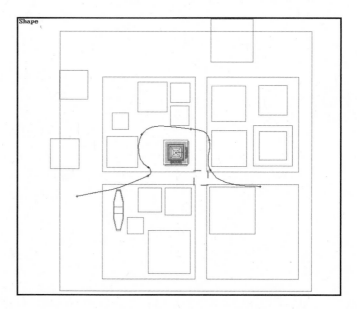

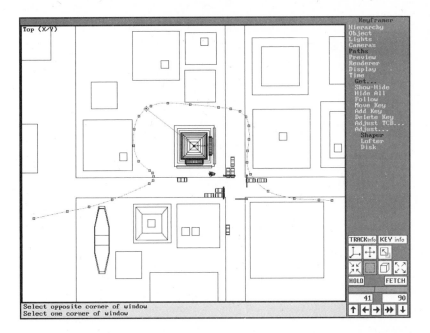

Figure 18.7
The imported path in the Keyframer.

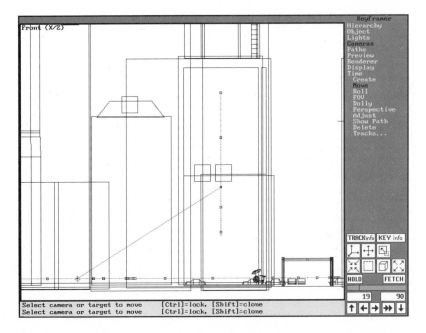

Figure 18.8
The camera target's vertical path.

Drawing Paths in the Lofter

The Lofter enables you to align the path and position its vertices in three dimensions while using its 3D display of the scene as a guide. Although you can construct a path vertex by vertex within the Lofter, it usually is more efficient to draw it as a polygon in the Shaper first, import the path, and then adjust its vertical positioning.

The following exercise builds on the path that was created in the previous exercise, "A City Walk-through."

A City Fly-Thru

Enter the Lofter, choose Paths/Get/Shaper, *and answer* Yes *to Replace Current Path*	Imports the Shaper's two-dimensional path
Choose 3D Display/Choose, *select the* Flagball *object, and turn on the 3D Display*	Displays the 3D Editor's mesh of the central tower building
Reduce the path's steps to 0	Straightens the path to emphasize the vertex positions
Move the first vertex higher than the building and move the intermediate vertices up as needed	Stretches the path vertically, as shown at the left of figure 18.9
Increase the path steps to 10 and use Move Vertex *to smooth the curve*	Changes the path to a spline, as shown in the right of figure 18.9

You should adjust the path until it is smooth and defines a fluid motion. Remember that you can adjust the spline's bulge by holding down the mouse key while moving a vertex.

Switch back to the Lofter, choose Paths/Get/Lofter, *select the camera, and assign the path as before*	Changes the camera's path to be that of the Lofter's, as shown in figure 18.10
Choose Cameras/Tracks/Copy, *select a building, then the target, click on* Position & Relative, *and answer* Yes	Copies the building's tracks to the target and effectively resets its path
Cycle through the animation and adjust the target as necessary	

You now have a fly-thru that is constantly looking at the city's tower. This usually is the result you want for an illustrative animation. If you were portraying a chase, the effect would be much different because you would want the Camera view to show the direction of the vehicle. You can do this by assigning the target a similar path.

Assign the Lofter's path to the target and allow it to be relocated	Aligns the target with the camera's path
Click on the Tracks *button and select the target*	Displays the Tracks dialog box for the target's path
Click on Slide *and slide the second key to the left, back in time one frame*	Moves all the target's tracks one to the left

Play the animation

The animation has changed from a stable helicopter to a fast-moving plane or bird. You had to move the target's keys forward one so that it was always looking ahead. If you slid the keys back one instead, the camera would look behind itself during the fly-thru. By sliding the tracks back and forth during the animation, you can make the camera look over its shoulder, so to speak.

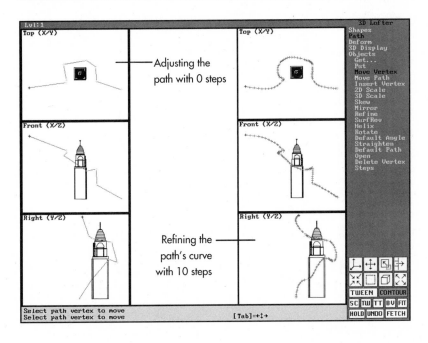

Figure 18.9
Adjusting a three-dimensional path in the Lofter.

Figure 18.10

Assigning the
Lofter's path to
the camera.

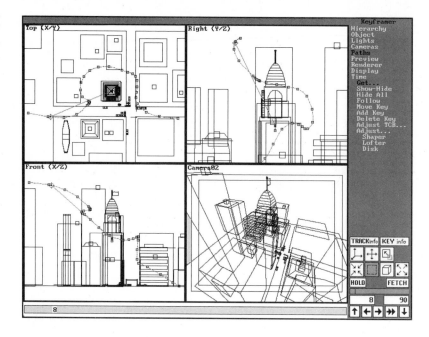

Using AutoCAD DXF Paths

If you load a DXF file as a path, the last polyline listed in its Entities section will be used. This is either the last polyline drawn in the database (when exporting the entire DWG) or the last one selected (when you export a selection set of entities). DXF import is described at length in Chapter 11, "Integrating AutoCAD with 3D Studio." Of particular note is the number of intermediate vertices created for Curve-fit polylines that are not created for naturally curvilinear or Spline-fit polylines.

A limitation in the Lofter's DXF and polygon translation requires that the animation have one more frame than the path has vertices. This extra frame is placed in the middle of the path and can cause some problems for carefully orchestrated path movements (such as robotic and forensic animations). To work around this, import the path with the required frames (vertices plus one) and slide the tracks over the rogue, interpolated frame.

Linking Cameras and Their Targets

Assigning the path directly to the camera is quite easy, but does have its limitations. The camera, and possibly its target, are rigidly assigned to the path, and there is very little room for adjustment without disturbing the fluidity of the movement. You will have more opportunities for realistic movement if you link the camera and/or target to a moving object.

Target Linking Considerations

Camera targets are often linked to moving objects to follow their motion, which can be very effective. You should consider the effect the animation is trying to achieve, however. Linking the target to a fast-moving, acrobatic plane could give the viewer an intense feeling of interaction if the plane comes close to the camera. The motion's effect is maximized because of the plane's changing size. If the plane stays at a distance, the impact of its acrobatics is significantly reduced because there is nothing nearby with which to gauge distances—the plane appears to be held in space at a fixed point and twirled. Not linking the target would allow the plane to climb in the scene and maneuver from right to left. When you link it, the plane is constantly centered.

The same is true of objects that move through a scene. Locking the camera's target on a bouncing ball makes the ball appear stationary as the world comes up to meet it—not an effect usually sought after.

The parents of camera targets directly effect how the audience feels their head is turning. If you rotate the parent object during the animation, the target pans and creates a smooth head turn.

Camera Linking Considerations

A camera is often linked to an object to show the "cockpit view" of the traveled path. A parent object has the capability to rotate the camera's position during or in lieu of the path. An object's rotation never has an impact on the camera's Roll setting—only its position. It is possible to make the conclusion that the camera is rolling with the rotation when its target is linked to the object as well. In reality, this usually means that the camera is off-center with the effect caused by the resulting eccentricity.

Using Dummy Objects

You cannot realize the full benefits of paths without using dummy objects. The preceding exercises assigned the path directly to the camera. This works well, but has its limitations—if the camera or target wants to divert from the path or use a path of its own at the same time, it cannot.

Linking both the target and camera to the same dummy enables you to manipulate both entities by adjusting only the dummy's path. The camera and target are still free to diverge from the shared path by adjusting their own keys.

The primary capability gained by linking cameras and targets to dummy objects is the use of the dummy's rotation keys. This might sound trivial, but you have no other way to simply rotate a camera. If the camera is off-center of the dummy object, it rotates around its axis. If it is located at the axis, the icon rotation is not displayed but its target could be if it were linked to the same dummy. This is how you get cameras to pan and spin using simple rotate commands. It is the only way to rotate a camera (or spotlight) about a defined point.

The ideal position for a linked camera is the parent's centroid, with the target placed in front. This allows the camera to follow the parent without being thrown from side-to-side during a rotation, while still guiding its viewing angle correctly along the path.

Creating Smooth Velocity

Imported paths are best for animations that have consistent movement with no acceleration or deceleration. The Paths/Get Constant Speed option smoothes time along the path. Importing the path without constant speed will vary a velocity according to the vertex placement. Either option creates extra keys to properly define the curve. Importing a circle from the Shaper requires at least five frames (four vertices plus one), yet it continues to refine the curve by creating up to 16 keys if the total number of frames allows.

The extra keys make it quite difficult to adjust the transitions and still maintain smooth motion. The Paths/Adjust/Key Time command helps out in this by enabling you to slide interpolated frames from one side of a position key to the other. Although this enables you to adjust the number of frames given to each segment, it can take some time to coordinate the key settings that produce the right effect.

If you need to throttle the velocity, you should consider *not* using a polygon-generated path. In such situations, it can be much more convenient to link the camera or light to a dummy object and control movement through rotation. This enables you to control its velocity by using Key Info or the Path/Adjust command options.

A Walk-Around with Velocity

Begin by loading CAFETBLE.3DS from the Meshes directory and move the camera up so you can see the top of the table clearly

While in the Top *viewport of the Keyframer, create a dummy object near the camera's target and link the camera to it*

Links the camera to the dummy's movements

Go to frame 30, rotate the dummy 360 degrees, and show the camera's path

Displays a circular path, as shown in figure 18.11

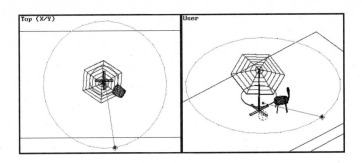

Figure 18.11
A circular walk-around from a 360 degree dummy object rotation.

Make the Camera *viewport active and preview the animation*	Animates a smooth, consistent walk-around

This shows a very easy way to create a circular path that does not rely on any position keys. The effect becomes more interesting when the speed is made less consistent.

Click on the Key Info *button and select the dummy object*	Displays the Key Info dialog box for the dummy
Move to the first Rotation key, set the From value to 50, decrease the Continuity to 0, and click on its global button	Straightens the preview curve
Move to the second Rotation key, set its Ease to value to 50, and click on OK	Changes the path's geometry by moving frame locations (see fig. 18.12)

Preview the animation and let it cycle

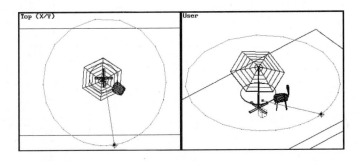

Figure 18.12
The same path with varying Ease To and From values.

The resulting animation is moving slowly at frame 0 and very quickly at frame 15, creating a centrifugal amusement ride effect. Although this is perceptible in a circular path, it becomes much more noticeable when the path grows in size over time.

While in the Top *viewport, create another dummy object near the umbrella's top edge and link Dummy01 to it*

continues

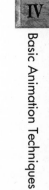

IV

Basic Animation Techniques

continued

*Create a third dummy (above the second) near the
floor's edge and link Dummy02 to it*

If you access the Hierarchy/Show Tree command at this point, the Object Attachment Tree
should look something like the following:

Dummy03

Dummy02

Dummy01

Camera01

*Increase the total frames to 90, go to frame 60, and rotate
Dummy02 360 degrees*

Forms the camera's path into a
double loop

Go to frame 90 and rotate Dummy03 360 degrees

Forms the camera's path into a
triple loop, as shown in figure 18.13

Preview the animation

Figure 18.13
The unrefined
effect of linking
three rotating
dummy objects.

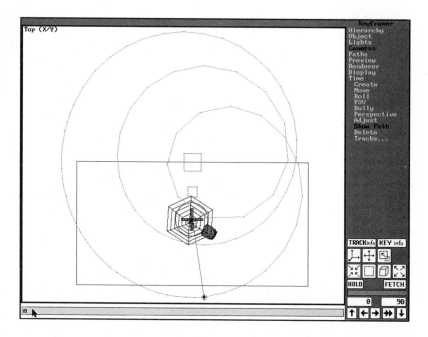

The animation loops through the scene in a very uncontrolled manner—possibly through the table itself. This is a result of the three paths influencing each other over the entire 90 frames. The easiest way to make the correction is to make the adjustments on the keys themselves.

Click on the Key Info *button, select Dummy03, and move to the first Rotation key (frame 0)*	Displays the Key Info dialog box for Dummy03
Reduce the Continuity to 0, and do the same for Dummy02	Straightens the sample curve
Click on the Track Info *button for Dummy02 and copy frame 0's Rotation key to frame 60*	Displays Dummy02's track Info
Move to Dummy03, copy its frame 0 Rotation track to frame 60, and click on OK	

The camera's path is now three circles that are nearly tangent at the frame 0 location.

The animation is no longer erratic and creates a walk-around of the table that takes progressively larger circles. When the last two dummy object's paths are adjusted for speed, the effect of the increasing distance is accentuated.

Access the Key Info for dummies 02 and 03 and
increase their last Rotation key's Ease to setting to 50
and their previous Rotation key's From setting to 50

Preview the animation

The frame spacing on the path's circles becomes very coarse at the top, as shown in figure 18.14.

This exercise just touched on the possibilities of what is really a simple technique. The cycle's speed moves to the path's bottom if you reverse the Rotation key settings for Ease To and From for the three dummy objects. You can also push the speed from side-to-side by using the Bias values, and you might want to place different velocities at different points on each circle.

IV

Basic Animation Techniques

Figure 18.14
The resulting camera path with changing velocities.

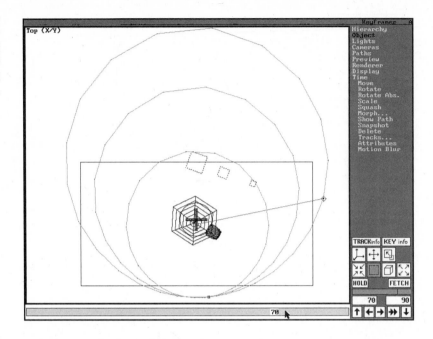

Follow and Bank Options for Paths

If you assign an object a path, it progresses along it in a rigid manner. The Paths/Follow command is provided to guide the object along the path by inserting additional rotation keys and modifying existing ones. After selecting the object, or its path, you are presented with the option of whether to *bank* or not (see fig. 18.15). Real-world examples of banking include an acrobatic plane that tilts its wings from the horizontal to make turns and a person running an obstacle course who leans into turns and extends his/her arms for balance. The results of using Follow and Bank are shown in figure 18.16.

Figure 18.15
The Follow Path dialog box.

The Follow command applies only to objects, but is presented here because of its importance to dummy objects, to which lights and cameras are so often linked. The Follow command itself will not let you select a camera, light, target, or their paths.

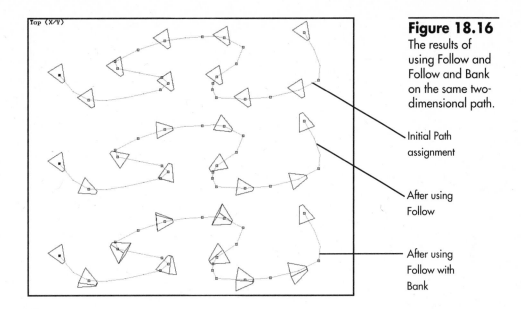

Figure 18.16
The results of using Follow and Follow and Bank on the same two-dimensional path.

Initial Path assignment

After using Follow

After using Follow with Bank

Banking is not often useful with lights and cameras because these entities do not observe any banking rotations assigned to a parent dummy object. Cameras and spotlights respect a linked object's rotation only as it applies to its primary direction axis (the way it is facing) and not its minor axis (the way it is leaning). If you want a camera roll to simulate a banking curve, you need to insert Roll keys manually.

A Turbulent Tunnel Ride

Because this exercise uses a project file, the model's components are located in all five program modules: the Shaper contains the original tunnel shape and two-dimensional path, the Lofter holds the same path adjusted for height and the shapes along the path, the 3D Editor contains the resulting tunnel mesh, and the Materials Editor contains various materials for application to the tunnel. The Keyframer does not have any animation at this point—that's what happens next.

Begin by entering the Keyframer and loading TUNLRIDE.PRJ

Resets all program modules to those in the PRJ file

Create a dummy object anywhere in the scene, choose Paths/Get/Lofter, *select the dummy, and answer* Yes *to relocate and constant speed but* No *to reverse direction*

Relocates the new dummy object to the mouth of the tunnel, near the camera

continues

continued

Because the Lofter's path was used to create the TunnelForm object, it is the perfect path with which to guide a camera. The ideal position for a linked camera is the dummy's centroid, but it can be difficult to place it there manually. The following two steps show a Keyframer trick to do it quickly.

Choose Cameras/Tracks/Copy, *select the dummy object and then the camera, and choose* Absolute	Assigns the dummy object's path to the camera and moves it to the exact same position
Choose Tracks/Copy *again, select the tunnel object and then the camera, and choose* Relative	Assigns TunnelForm's keys to the camera (which are empty) and effectively resets the camera's animation
Move the camera's target so that it is centered on the leading face of the dummy object	Reorients the camera view to see down the tunnel, as shown in figure 18.17
Choose Paths/Show-Hide *and select the dummy object*	Displays Dummy01's snaking path through the tunnel

Figure 18.17
The camera and target's relationship to the dummy object.

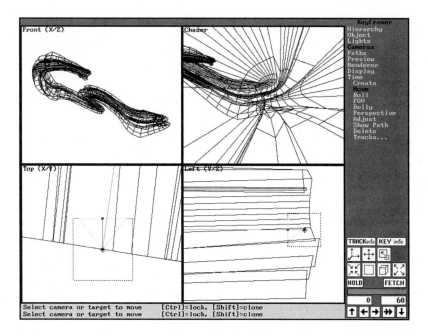

The camera is now at the correct position to follow the direction of the dummy object.

Choose Hierarchy/Link *and link both the camera and its target to the dummy object*	Allows Dummy01 to guide the camera along its path
Advance the frames and examine the positions and resulting camera view	

The camera view is erratic because the dummy object is not rotating with the direction of the path. This is quickly corrected with the Follow command.

Choose Path/Follow *and select the dummy object*	Displays the Bank Option dialog box
Choose No *to Bank, and preview the animation*	The camera follows the dummy though all the tunnel's twists and turns

The Lofter's path started directly at the mesh's beginning. It gives the animation context if the camera starts out in front of the tunnel so the audience sees what they are getting into.

Increase the total number of frames from 60 to 65 and return to frame 0	Adds 5 frames onto the end of the animation
Choose Track Info, *select the dummy object, and slide all of its tracks forward 5 frames*	Moves the five new frames to the front of the animation
Move the dummy object along a straight path, out in front of the opening, and use Rotate-Absolute *to align it with the path*	Recomposes the animation's beginning to include an entry sequence of the tunnel, as shown in figure 18.18

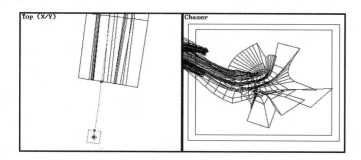

Figure 18.18
Adding five frames to the beginning of the animation.

You could easily stop here and have an eye-catching animation, but you can add more drama to the ride if the camera were to bank with the turns.

continues

continued

Choose Path/Follow *again, select the dummy object, accept the default 30° Max. Bank Angle, and answer* Yes *to Bank*	Adjusts Dummy01's Rotate keys to bank for the turns
Cycle through the animation and examine the dummy object's rotation and the resulting camera view	

You might be surprised that the camera and target are unaffected by Dummy01's new banking rotation. Because the camera is centered on the dummy object, the added rotation is along the same axis as the camera-to-target vector, similar to an arrow that follows a path through the air with a slight rotational spin. Even though the arrow rotates along the axis, the direction it points is the same—as with the camera. It takes manual adjustment to make the camera roll. The easiest way to do this is to hang another object in front of the traveling camera as a guide against which to make roll adjustments.

Create a dummy object, smaller than the first, and copy Dummy01's tracks to it absolutely	Centers the Dummy02 on Dummy01's starting position
Copy TunnelForm's tracks to Dummy01 relatively and return to frame 0	Clears Dummy02's keys, but keeps its track 1 relationship with Dummy01
While in the Top *viewport, move the dummy upward until it is clearly visible within the* Camera *viewport*	Places an alignment target for the roll calculations
Link Dummy02 to Dummy01 and examine the banking animation of the newly linked dummy object in the Camera *viewport*	Shows the effect of banking, as shown in the upper right (Camera) viewport of figure 18.19

Now it's just a matter of using Camera/Roll to align the camera with the rotation of Dummy02. The goal is for Dummy02 to remain fairly stable and square throughout the ride. To do this, you need to advance to the frames that have the most extreme banking and counter them with a camera roll. After one time through, you almost always need to do it again, adding more keys, and then again in an effort to smooth out the rolls. After concentrating on the leading dummy object, it might seem as if you're straightening the camera rather than banking it. It might help if you hide Dummy02 so you can analyze the camera's travel without being distracted.

Here, you might want to render a full animation. The tunnel object was lofted with mapping coordinates and assigned a texture-mapped material whose parameters correct the mesh's length and circumference. A mapped material reinforces the feeling of speed by giving the observer something by which to gauge distance. The Materials Editor has two additional materials (with the same name) that you can put to the scene for different effects. There also are corresponding materials in the right sample boxes with 1.0 scale factors to enable you to gauge their effects from within the Materials Editor. The exit of the tunnel is shown in figure 18.20 with textured and opacity maps.

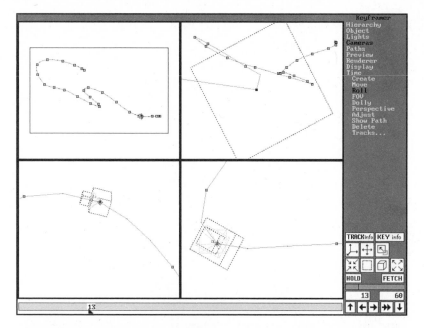

Figure 18.19
Using a forward-
placed dummy
object to calculate
camera roll.

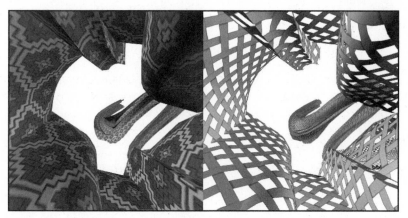

Figure 18.20
View of the
tunnel's exit with
textured and
transparent net
materials.

Animating Light Adjustments

After you understand the principles of animating cameras, you know how to move, pan, and
roll lights. Lights and cameras have the same capabilities and limitations (only cameras can be
parents of lights, although not their targets). Lights do have more natural capabilities than
cameras, and several of these (such as color, falloff, and hotspot) cannot be fully realized until
the scene is rendered, so it is important to understand the effects keys have on what is an
unviewable path.

Moving, Dollying, and Panning Lights

Lights do not need to obey any of the laws of physics, time, or smooth motion to be believable—you can move light as quickly or as slowly as necessary. You move lights solely to create effects, and it is the success of lighting that becomes the sole criteria by which an audience judges whether they are correct.

When lights move, their angle of incidence to surfaces changes. Moving a 3D Studio light closer causes the surfaces to become dimmer and more unevenly lit (assuming the light is not using attenuation). If you want a surface to become brighter from a light's movement, you need to position it close and dolly it back, so its angle to the entire surface approaches the perpendicular. This is more effective than throttling the light's color value as the already bright areas stay consistent and there is no chance of a color shift in the cast light.

Hotspot, Falloff, and Roll

The spotlight's hotspot and falloff settings are somewhat analogous to the camera's FOV settings, whereas a spotlight's roll is exactly the same as a camera's. As with cameras, spotlights cannot directly inherit banking information from a parent unless the light is off-center and affected by the other axes.

Changing Color

Animating a light's color is very easy to define but can be difficult to visualize. A light, for example, that is pure red (RGB 255,0,0) on frame 0 and pure blue (RGB 0,0,255) on frame 30 is purple on frame 15 (RGB 117,0,117). Unfortunately, you cannot visualize color transition over time without rendering it. If you are changing a light's color over time, you might want to use the Adjust command to monitor its transitioning color swatch as you cycle through frames.

Turning Off Lights

You cannot turn lights on and off using a key the way you can hide objects. The only way to turn "off" a light is to reduce its color to a true black (RGB 0,0,0). This only eliminates the light's illumination and does not prevent the Renderer from calculating its presence or its shadows (if it is casting any).

Ambient Light Transitions

3D Studio Release 4 has the capability to animate the ambient light's color. This can add a subtle touch to an animation that includes changing light colors and values. An example would be a scene that animates a sunrise. At twilight, before the sun rises, the ambient light could be a very cool gray. As the sun rises with a deep red color, the ambient light might shift to a dark blue. As the sun rises, becomes brighter and yellow, the ambient light might shift to a subtle blue or violet. When the sun is high enough to be a warm white, the ambient light could slip back to a neutral or cool gray.

Animated Projectors

When projectors are assigned a flic, sequential bitmaps, or a FLI file, the spotlight projects each image frame by frame. The spotlight projects the image that is sequentially the same as the frame's, regardless of what segment of the animation is being rendered. A 15-frame flic, for example, begins on frame 0, plays to frame 14, and begins over on frame 15. If an animation begins past frame 0, the flic is advanced to that proper point. The status of the current segment has no effect on the order of projected images.

Animated projectors have a multitude of possible uses beyond the obvious of projecting images like a film strip. When the images are primarily black and white, similar to gobos, the projection appears as an animated shadow. Instead of assigning an animation as a reflection map, or having the object calculate automatic reflections for each frame, you can project an animation across several objects to simulate a shared reflection. The effect of this technique with a low-intensity spotlight can be quite convincing.

What often is forgotten is that the spotlight's color tints the projected image. When this color is animated over a static image, the effect can increase the single bitmap's impact or change the entire appearance of an animated sequence.

Shadows Within an Animation

Shadows are calculated within a scene whenever the model has object animation or the shadow-casting light is adjusted. The Renderer searches the keyframes for all objects. If it finds a single key in any track for any object (hidden or unhidden) in any frame, it calculates shadows. The only way to prevent a moving object from causing a shadow calculation is to turn off its shadow-casting attribute (and possibly turn it on again if it moves into a position that requires cast shadows). Shadows also are calculated if the shadow-casting light has anything but its color changed over time.

Because of the time and memory required for shadow calculations (especially ray-traced ones), you need to know what you can animate that does not cause shadow calculation. The following adjustments do not cause shadows to be calculated after the first frame of an animation:

- ✔ Shadow-casting light color values

- ✔ Any adjustments to omni lights, ambient light, nonshadow-casting spotlights and their targets

- ✔ Any camera and camera target adjustments

- ✔ Dummy object adjustments of any type (that do not cause a child to make a shadow-casting adjustment)

- ✔ Any adjustments for objects that have their Cast Shadows attribute turned off

IV

Basic Animation Techniques

Understanding Linked Light Movement

You often need to move a light with an object. This can be a following light when you link a spotlight's target, or a moving light source where you link the light and possibly the target.

Linking to Cameras

Cameras can be parents of lights, but it is extremely doubtful that you would want to do this. If you need a light to track a camera, linking the camera to a dummy object and then linking the light and possibly the target to it generally is more effective. This allows greater movement flexibility for all the entities.

Spotlights do not respect a camera's Roll keys, nor can it inherit its Roll tracks. If you require a spotlight to roll with a camera or bank with an object, you need to manually adjust its Roll keys, as discussed previously with cameras under "Follow and Bank Options."

You can see what keys a child will inherit from a parent by using Copy Tracks. A linked entity inherits only tracks that you can copy.

Maintaining a Highlight

You always should use the Place Hilight command with the knowledge that it is going to move the light to a point perpendicular to the areas of the face you select. This creates a highlight, but one valid only for that specific frame. If you move the highlighted object, the light needs to move with it to maintain a constant highlight.

If you require a specific location on an object to be in bright light constantly, use Place Hilight at frame 0 and link the light (and possibly target) to the object.

Linking Lights

Linking lights to moving objects has many applicable situations: the headlights of a car, a panning searchlight, the flashlight held at one's side, a miner's cap, or even a flaming arrow. The concept is simple—you just link the light to the moving object or controlling dummy object. With a spotlight, you need to link its target as well, but might consider adding its own movement to indicate sway.

The following exercise shows the effectiveness of linking a spotlight.

Making Headlights for the Tunnel Ride

This exercise builds on the results of the previous exercise.

*While at frame 0, create a circular spotlight and
position it at the rear of Dummy01, pointing forward*

*Link the spotlight and target to Dummy01 and cycle
through the animation*

Because you cannot see a spotlight's cone through a camera viewport, you need to examine
the animation in the Top and side viewports. Adjust the spotlight's cone and falloff until you
are comfortable with the spotlight's relationship to the ride.

Give each of the three omni lights a 0.4 multiplier and reduce the ambient light to RGB 5,5,5	Reduces the scene's general illumination to show the effects of the spotlight

Multipliers are convenient when you need to adjust a light's illumination across all its tracks.
Because it is has no key, you can adjust it at any time without worrying about unwanted
transitions.

At frame 0 and while in the Top *viewport, move the spotlight to the side of the dummy object while holding the* Ctrl *key*	Moves both the spotlight and target together
Move the spotlight to the other side of Dummy01 while holding the Ctrl + ⇧Shift *keys*	Clones the spotlight to the other side, as shown in figure 18.21, and maintains its linkage to Dummy01

Cycle through the animation and render it if you like

As you can see in the rendered still to the right of figure 18.21, the animation takes on a
completely different feeling if you add two spotlights. Played as a rendered animation, it's easy
to come away with the impression that the ride actually was in a vehicle. If you replace
Dummy02 with an object that forms a framing cockpit, the impression of being in a vehicle is
solidly reinforced.

You also can try to attenuate the spotlights to give the impression that the tunnel is deep and
murky.

Figure 18.21
Linking two
spotlights to a
traveling object.

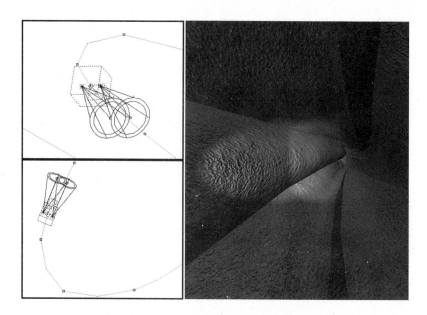

Exploring Animated Lighting Effects

Several animation forms rely on light movement for all action. Typical examples are time-lapse shadow studies and light pans.

Creating Gleam and Glimmer

The shifting gleam from a light pan is a subtle but eye-catching technique that can be very basic or quite involved, depending on what your animation needs. No set rules are written for producing this effect, but some methods do work better than others. The path of the moving light needs to be as fluid as any other animated object, yet dancing lights placed for highlighting purposes can be as erratic as you want.

Gleam from a Light Pan

Enter the Keyframer and begin by loading LIGHTPAN.3DS   Resets the Keyframer and 3D Editor with the new file

The file has two distant omni lights and one central spotlight. The spotlight is not aimed directly at the text object because doing so creates a disturbing hotspot. For the same reason, the spotlight has a minimum hotspot angle.

While in the Top *viewport at frame 0, create a dummy object centered on the spotlight's target*

Link the spotlight to the dummy object and show the light's path	Displays a red dot because there is no path yet
Go to frame 30 and rotate the dummy object until the spotlight has made a symmetrical arc about the text object	Forms a true arc segment for the spotlight's path

If you render the animation at this point, the light glides across the surface, but does not quite appear natural.

Enter the Front *viewport, go to frame 15, and move the spotlight up about half the distance of the path*	Changes the path to an upward curve from frame 1 to 15 and straight from 15 to 30
Click on Track Info, *select the path, copy track 0's position key to frame 30, and click on* OK *to exit*	Changes the path to a gentle arc, as seen in figure 18.22

This is you all you have to do to make sweeping gleams across a surface. If the animation is long (over 3 or 4 seconds), you might want to add additional light movement to maintain interest. Closely placed omni lights that fly around near the object's surface are very good for this. Remember that unattenuated lights do not get any brighter as they get closer—the illumination becomes much less regular and the total impact actually is dimmer because the angle of incidence is shallower.

Go to frame 0 and move the distant omni lights close to the front of the text object and show both of their paths	
Go to frame 15 and move the omni lights toward one another's frame 0 position and then up or down again	Displays a linear path for the omni lights
Go to frame 30 and move the lights back toward their frame 0 position	Changes the path to a tight curve
Choose Paths/Move Key *and continue to adjust the paths until they are smooth*	Forms the paths into "boomerang" shapes, as shown in figure 18.23

The goal of these omni lights is to relate a little to the panning spotlight while creating a diverse effect close to the surface. No rule is set for the number of flying omni lights to use—if it produces the desired effect, then it's the right amount.

A final technique for panning light play is the inclusion of a projector spotlight. Such a light links to the same rotating dummy object, but you can place it at a different vertical position, as shown in figure 18.24. This spot has a falloff that focuses on the object and is quite a bit dimmer. The idea is to add just a touch of a moving reflection. This has some advantage over a reflection map in that the images are projected over flat and curved surfaces in a fairly even manner.

IV

Basic Animation Techniques

Figure 18.22

The path of a panning spotlight for creating a gleam.

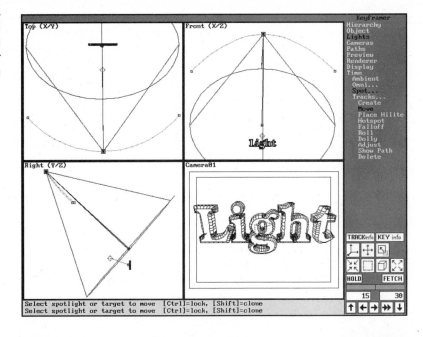

Figure 18.23

Animating closely spaced omni lights for added light play.

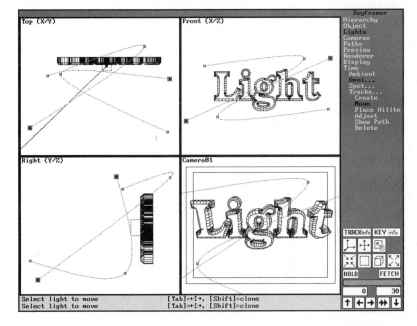

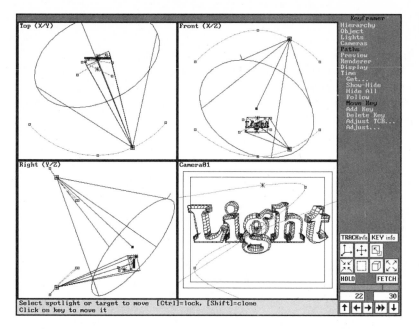

Figure 18.24
The final addition of a projector spotlight to simulate a glancing reflection.

IPAS Lighting Options

Several IPAS routines are available for special animated lighting effects. Of these, three have been around since the beginning of IPAS development, and their use has become nearly standard in many production facilities. As with all IXP's, these routines work within Video Post and effect the queues that are placed before them.

The FLARE.IXP routine is a lens flare filter that produces the spotty, ringed, and ray-streak artifacts that you receive when a direct light source strikes your camera lens. Although photographers strive to avoid this effect, it can convey an intense light or a merciless sun and add a very realistic touch.

The HILITE.IXP routine produces cross-shaped sparkles on key colors in the scene. These glints can be stars of numerous points and their size varies with that of the key color. Placing stand-in objects with unique colors enables you to pinpoint the location and size of the sparkles. Although you can approximate this effect with an animated material (self-illuminated with texture and opacity maps), you might find the results less than rewarding and difficult to make realistic.

The GLOW.IXP does exactly what its name implies—it makes the queue above it glow and is best used for objects that you render as separate images and composite with their Alpha channels.

Basic Animation Techniques

Chapter Snapshot

This chapter looks at the issues involved in creating 8-bit flics with 3D Studio and in creating scripts for real-time playback and video recording of your scripts. Some of the issues that you read about are the following:

✔ Understanding Flic playback restrictions

✔ Managing color palettes

✔ Planning for timing issues with 8-bit flics

✔ Designing transitions

✔ Creating playback scripts for AAPLAYHI

✔ Exploring real-time recording techniques

CHAPTER

Animation for Flic-Based Presentation and Recording

3D Studio is a true professional-quality rendering and animation program. What often gets left behind in the excitement and pursuit of state-of-the-art animation is the realization that professional work is possible at the 8-bit level. Granted, you are not likely to sell an 8-bit flic to a major network or lay it to video for a board presentation at a Fortune 500 company. Many clients, however, such as architects, engineers, city councils, school boards, and local television networks, are receptive to well-produced, low-cost animations provided in an 8-bit format.

This chapter looks at 3D Studio's capability to produce 8-bit animation in the Animator Pro .FLC format. If you create animation for 8-bit presentation, you are faced with a wide variety of constraints and limitations. Some of the issues that you must address include the following:

✔ Normalizing the color palette over multiple frames

✔ Avoiding playback anomalies such as video tearing

✔ Keeping file sizes low for more efficient playback

✔ Planning cut and other transitions as a technique of implementing the previous point

✔ Optimizing your presentation to fit the chosen delivery method, on a computer system or capturing to video

Understanding Flic Playback Restrictions

Animator Pro is the program for which the FLC file format was developed. Recently, Microsoft adopted the FLC format as a standard for Windows-based multimedia presentations, so you will soon see many other programs that work with FLC files as well. This chapter focuses on Animator Pro—more specifically, the player program AAPLAYHI.EXE—for the playback, presentation, and recording of 8-bit animation.

To use 8-bit animation successfully, you must understand how to avoid some of the limitations inherent in the format.

Palette Problems

The first problem that you must address is the issue of working with an 8-bit color palette. If you haven't already, go back to Chapter 8, "8-Bit Still Imaging," and review the issues of 8-bit color palettes for still rendering. The two most important issues to remember from Chapter 8 are the design of the color scheme and the avoidance of dithering.

You must plan the colors and materials selection of your 8-bit images very carefully. Only 256 colors are available in the 8-bit color palette, so you need to get as much as you can out of each color selection. You do this by keeping most of your color and material selections within the same family of colors. This restriction is not as limiting as you might think, especially when you're talking in terms of warm earth tones, cool blue-greens, and subtle grays. Indeed, you might find that working with these limitations improves your eye for color. Most good color designs work with a limited palette.

Not only do you have to worry about color limitations within a single image—now you have to worry about colors expressed over time. What objects move in and out of the scene? Does the position or color of the lights change? Does your animation move to a different scene with its own color requirements? All these questions complicate the selection of a good color palette. You can handle the first two issues by using 3D Studio to help you build a color palette. The last issue is best handled by creating multiple flics and designing a transition between them.

Creating the Color Palette

When you render 8-bit animations, 3D Studio presents you with four palette choices, which you can access by selecting Renderer/Setup/Configure. The Device Configuration dialog box appears, offering the palette choices of Low, Medium, High, and Custom (see fig. 19.1).

```
         Device Configuration
    File Output:      Flic
                      Gif
                      Targa
                      Color Tiff
                      Mono Tiff
                      BMP True
                      BMP 256
                      JPEG
             Image File Comments
             Display:   RDPADI
    Palette:  Low  Medium  High  Custom:
    Resolution:  Width: 0      Height: 0
             Aspect Ratio: 0.0
       320X200   256X243   512X486   640X480
                   Default
                 OK    Cancel
```

Figure 19.1
Choosing palette
modes in
the Device
Configuration
dialog box.

✔ **Low.** This palette setting calculates the colors for the first frame of the animation and then uses that fixed set of colors for all subsequent frames. It's very fast, but leads to a few problems. First and foremost, if any objects are out of the scene on the first frame, their color requirements are not taken into account. Imagine animating a backyard scene. You have bright green grass, dark green trees and bushes, brown tree trunks, and a blazing blue sky. After a few frames, a child's red ball bounces into view. Where do the red colors come from? If you render using the Low palette setting, you have no reds. Maybe a few warm tones are associated with the colors for the tree trunks, but the chances are that the ball is anything but red.

✔ **Medium.** This palette mode renders each frame with its own 256-color palette. After you finish rendering the animation, 3D Studio looks at all the individual color palettes and builds a single palette to serve all frames. This option works extremely well and provides you with almost the best possible palette for the animation. The main drawback is that it's slow. After 3D Studio renders the flic file with a separate palette for each frame, it must rewrite each frame using the new color palette that it has created. This process can take a considerable amount of time.

✔ **High.** The third option is the High palette setting. This option works much like Medium, except that instead of rendering each frame with its own 256-color palette, it renders each frame as a separate 24-bit TARGA file. After you render all the frames in 24-bit format, 3D Studio examines the colors used by all frames and designs a 256-color palette from the composite 24-bit color range. The final step is to convert all the TARGA files into a flic file using the new palette. This option has major drawbacks in time and disk space. The temporary TARGA files take up considerable disk space, and the color conversion process is slow. Also, while the High palette mode is technically superior to the Medium mode, the difference in visual quality probably goes unnoticed by the typical observer.

IV

Basic Animation Techniques

✔ **Custom.** The final and most widely used option is the Custom palette option. This option requires that you provide 3D Studio with a predefined color palette from either a GIF, FLC, or COL file. Fortunately, 3D Studio provides you with the tools to easily create this color palette. The trick involves rendering a representative sample set of frames at Medium mode and then having 3D Studio render the whole animation with a custom palette taken from the sample frames.

You create the sample set by using the Every Nth Field field in the Render Animation dialog box (see fig. 19.2). The value that you enter here should be sufficient to render anywhere from 10 percent to 25 percent of the total frames in your animation. The more frames in your animation, the larger the number you want to enter in the Every Nth Field field.

Figure 19.2
Setting the Every Nth Field field in the Render Animation dialog box.

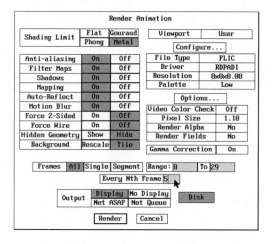

Be sure to save this sample flic file to disk, and also save the file to the directory from which you loaded the current 3DS file or one of the directories in your Map Path settings. The reason for this is that when you render the final animation, you choose Custom palette and assign the sample flic as the custom palette file. If the sample flic is not in the directory from which you loaded the 3DS file or a Map Path directory, then it can't be found during rendering, and 3D Studio displays the warning dialog box shown in figure 19.3.

Figure 19.3
The warning dialog box displayed if the color palette is not found.

WARNING: That palette is in not in your
MAP-PATH directory.
Palette must be placed in this directory
to be found at rendering time.

OK

Using Multiple Palettes

Sometimes, your animation has scenes that change drastically in both lighting and color. An example might be a walk-through animation in which you move from the warm and neutral tones of a living room to a bright and colorful patio. When this happens, you are advised to render each part as a separate segment with its own color palette. Trying to fit the wide ranges of colors from both scenes into a single palette leaves neither scene with sufficient colors to produce acceptable results.

The key to making this work for later presentation and playback is to stage a transition effect at the time that the scenes are switched. The transition effect should be something that would naturally cause a break in the motion or distract the viewer. During this break, you would employ one of the techniques described later in this chapter to switch from one flic file to another.

Avoiding Dithering

You are generally better off if you can avoid using the 256-Dither button. Dithering reduces banding in solid color objects, but does little else to improve the realism of the image, and greatly increases the file size. Use various mapping techniques to add realism to the scene because maps generally prevent banding better than dithering and usually without creating such large files.

Another reason to avoid dithering when you render flic files is that it is very difficult to make the dither patterns stand still. As objects move around the scene and lighting patterns change, the dithering pattern also changes. Sometimes the changes in the dither pattern are harmonious with the animation and are hardly noticeable, but other times the dither patterns seem to take on a life of their own, causing colors and shadows to look as if they are crawling around on the surface of your objects. The Custom palette technique described earlier helps to minimize this effect, but does not completely eliminate it. Your best results come from using a custom palette in conjunction with using realistic mapped materials and avoiding dithering altogether.

Video Tearing

Video tearing refers to the inability of your display hardware to keep up with the playback speed of an animation. Figure 19.4 shows a frame of an animation captured during playback that exhibits video tearing. The phenomenon occurs when your graphics card cannot pump information through your system fast enough to keep up with the motion of objects in the animation. What you see is the display of two frames at the same time. The top part of the screen shows the next incoming frame, while the bottom part of the screen shows the previous outgoing frame.

Figure 19.4
An animation
demonstrating
video tearing.

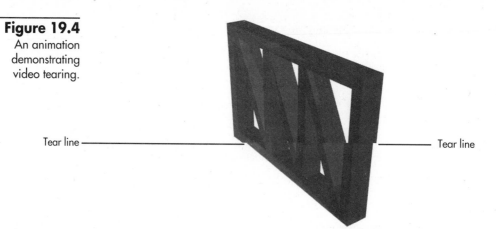

Tear line ———————————————————   ——————— Tear line

Hard-and-fast rules that tell you under exactly what circumstances video tearing occurs don't exist. A fast 486 DX/2 with a local bus video system is highly resistant to video tear. An older 486 that has an ISA bus and an 8-bit SuperVGA card tends to be considerably plagued by video tearing. The best that you can do is plan for the lowest typical system on which your animation is played and design according to that playback quality.

A few rules of thumb exist that you can observe to help reduce the likelihood of video tearing. The degree to which the rules are effective depends highly upon understanding the hardware on which the animation is played.

✔ **Avoid fast-moving objects.** Video tearing is a direct result of the speed at which the computer displays a single image. The faster an object moves, the more likely it is to tear apart.

✔ **Avoid motion of vertical edges.** The mechanics of video information transmission (left to right, then top to bottom) means that large vertical edges that move horizontally across the screen represent the worst-case scenario for video tearing. If moving vertical edges are unavoidable, such as in architectural walk-throughs, try to attract attention away from the area that may exhibit tearing.

✔ **Use the smallest acceptable screen size for the project.** The more pixels in the image, the more data to send, and thus, the more likely the system can't keep up. In other words, if 320×200 satisfies the client, don't push for 1024×768.

✔ **Experiment with motion blur effects.** A little bit of motion blur can enhance the realism of the motion and help mask video tearing. See Chapter 21, "Special Keyframer Techniques," for more information on motion blur.

File Size

You waste all your efforts to produce realistic images and avoid video tearing if you force the playback system to play the animation from disk. Disk access slows everything down so much that you might as well be viewing an old-fashioned slide show. You must know the system on which you plan to play the animation, and then size your animated segments to fit within the memory limitations of that system.

If you render for playback on another system, you must decide what the minimum memory requirements are for running your presentation. The typical home and small business PC probably has no more than 4 MB of RAM, and some systems are likely to have only 2 MB, with a few possibly having 8 MB. How much memory is actually available for holding your flic file depends on the player program, the type of memory manager, and whether the system has device drivers loaded high. The only way you can make an educated guess is by experimenting with a system configured the same as your target audience machine. Of course, if you are rendering for real-time playback on your system only, this task is much easier.

The goal is to design your animation so that you can break it up into segments that fit the available memory. This allows each segment to run as smooth and as fast as possible without the frequent pauses typical when you play animations from a hard drive.

Examining Timing Considerations

The previous section mentioned designing your animation so that it could be broken into segments that fit into available RAM. The key word is design. You don't just slice up an animation to make it fit. If you want your animation to be successful, you must plan where the segment breaks occur and stage those breaks around a sequence in the animation where a break makes sense.

The following paragraphs discuss timing considerations for real-time playback of flic files and how to plan for transitions and segment breaks. This information ties in closely with the issues on animating cameras and planning visual transitions covered in Chapter 18, "Animating Lights and Cameras." If you have not read that chapter, it would be a good idea to go back and look it over before continuing.

Determining Playback Speeds

Before you can plan your transitions and break points for your animation, you must determine the final playback speed. Typically, flic files are not played at 30 *frames per second* (fps). The hardware to play flics that fast is not widely available yet. A more typical playback speed is 14 fps, which is the default speed that 3D Studio uses when it creates a flic file. When you play your animations using AAPLAYHI or Animator Pro, a play speed of 5 is roughly equal to 14 fps.

Planning for Break Points

Chapter 18 mentioned the need to plan camera moves and changes of scene every few seconds. In today's fast-paced world, it is hard to hold someone's attention for more than five seconds. If you watch television and track how often a scene changes, you will notice that a change occurs every three to five seconds. If you watch music videos, the scene changes occur even faster. It's not uncommon for a music video or commercial to have a scene change every one to two seconds.

Although consideration of scene changes and the length of a shot are important for all well-designed animations, they are absolutely critical for animations you intend to use for real-time recording and playback. Every time you change a scene in your animation, you have the opportunity to break the animation into separate segments. These scene changes are called *transitions*.

Using Transitions

The term *transition* refers to any change from one scene to another. Many different types of transitions are common in film and video, but only two are important for flic playback. These two transition types are *cuts* and *fades*.

Cuts

A *cut* is an abrupt change from one scene to the next. Cuts take no time at all and are typified by the feeling that you changed position in the "blink of an eye." The most common use for a cut is when you want to change your point of view within the same scene or you want to change to a scene that is set up by the current scene. Two typical examples of these types of cuts are as follows:

✔ Two people are talking. The view frequently cuts from one person to the other, usually looking over the shoulder of the person who is not talking. This kind of cut keeps the viewer interested during the dialogue, and the over-the-shoulder angle makes it seem as if the actor is speaking to the viewer.

✔ You are standing in a dining room as your eyes pan around the room. The pan stops with you gazing into the kitchen where you see a pot boiling over. The scene cuts to the kitchen where you see a hand reach out and remove the pot from the burner. In this case, the cut to the kitchen was set up or anticipated by the previous scene.

Both of these techniques are useful for maintaining interest in your animation and for identifying break points where you can separate the flic files into segments. Cuts are not as useful as fades, however, because the rapid change from one scene to the next defies the capabilities of most systems. In general, for a cut to work properly during flic playback, both segments must be in memory and both must use the same color palette.

Fades

A *fade* occurs when a scene gradually disappears, leaving only a solid color on the screen. This is called a *fade-out*. The reverse, or a *fade-in*, occurs when you start with a solid color and slowly reveal the scene.

A useful side effect of a fade is that it gives the system time to adjust colors if the two segments on either side of the fade are not using the same color palette. You have probably noticed that if flic files are played in a script with straight cuts, you see a strange flash of colors just as one flic ends and the next one starts. This flash occurs because the color palette for the incoming animation is being loaded before the outgoing animation is completely cleared from the screen. A fade avoids this problem entirely. In fact, you can set up a fade for as little as 1/10th of a second—long enough for the system to change color palettes and short enough that you can often use it instead of a cut.

Pauses

Cuts and fades are the way you join animated segments together. A *pause* is where you sneak the segments in and out of memory. Unless you are animating a music video or a fast-paced commercial, you need to plan for various pauses in your animation. The pause enables your viewer to read text on the screen, examine a scene more closely, or just catch up and digest the last segment of animation before moving on to the next.

The hidden benefit of a pause is that it gives you a chance to release previous animation segments from memory and load the next segments. The number of pauses required for loading and unloading animations has a direct relationship to the amount of memory available on the playback system. The less memory available, the more pauses required to move segments in and out of RAM, which is why you need to know what type of system your animation plays on before you start keyframing and rendering the flics.

Understanding Scripting

How do you actually implement the flic playback and transitions? Many programs can support flic playback and have numerous options for transitions and programmability. This section focuses on how to play back your animations using the AAPLAYHI program from Autodesk.

The key to using AAPLAYHI is to use a playback script. The script tells the program which flics to play, in what order, and how to transition between them. The AAPLAYHI script language also has commands for loading flic files in and out of memory. The following section demonstrates some of the functions and options available with the AAPLAYHI program. You should check the file AAPLAYHI.DOC for details on specific commands and syntax.

IV

Basic Animation Techniques

A Simple Script

The following example is a simple script that you could use to display a collection of animations:

```
loadflic myflic01.flc
loadflic myflic02.flc
myflic01.flc -t fadein 1.0
myflic02.flc -t fadein 0.1
freeflic myflic01.flc
freeflic myflic02.flc
loadflic myflic03.flc
loadflic myflic04.flc
loadflic myflic05.flc
loop (forever)
 myflic03.flc -t fadein 0.1 color(128,128,128)
 keychoice
 choice 1
  myflic04.flc -l 4 -t fadeout 2.0 color(128,128,128)
 choice 2
  myflic05.flc -p 2.0 -t fadeout 2.0 color(128,128,128)
 choice 3
  exittodos
 endchoice
endloop
```

The preceding script displays five animations. It starts out by loading MYFLIC01.FLC and MYFLIC02.FLC into memory. The script then plays these two animations, using a long fade-in from black to start the whole sequence and a short fade-in from black between the two flics. MYFLIC02 should be designed for a pause at the end because its final frame is held on the screen for as long as it takes to load flics 03, 04, and 05. Immediately before loading the new flics, the previously played animations are released from memory.

Right after flics 03 through 05 are loaded, the script enters a loop statement. This loop displays flic 03, which should end with some kind of menu screen where user input determines whether to play MYFLIC04, MYFLIC05, or to exit out to DOS. After playing flic 04 or 05, the loop repeats and goes back to MYFLIC03 again.

Loading Flics In and Out of RAM

Loading flic files in and out of memory is a critical facet of designing useful playback scripts. The command to load a flic into memory is LOADFLIC, followed by the name of the flic file that you want to load. The companion command to LOADFLIC is FREEFLIC, and it releases a loaded flic from memory, making room for loading another flic. The FREEFLIC command also requires that the name of the flic to be released follows the command. The use of

LOADFLIC and FREEFLIC follow a few simple rules:

✔ You can load a flic at anytime in a playback script.

✔ Every flic that you load must be played sometime during the script.

✔ FREEFLIC is used only to clear out memory for loading other flics. There is no requirement that loaded flics must be freed.

✔ LOADFLIC freezes the last image displayed on the screen while it loads. It is important that you plan your load sequences and pauses so that you can load flics into memory with minimum disturbance to the flow of the animation.

Fades

Fades are handled by using the script command -T. The statement -T following a flic name indicates a transition effect when the flic is played. There are three transition effects, but only two need to be referenced with the -T option. The first transition is a cut that really means no transition effect and is the default if you specify nothing at all. The remaining two transitions are FADEIN and FADEOUT. Both FADEIN and FADEOUT accept two optional parameters— length of the effect and fade color.

A line from the preceding script uses the following transition syntax:

```
MYFLIC05.FLC -p 2.0 -t fadeout 2.0 color(128,128,128)
```

The fade-out effect lasts for 2.0 seconds and the fade color is medium gray, Red:128, Green:128, and Blue:128. Remember that a fade effect can be as short as 0.1 seconds, and at that speed, it is almost a cut. The -p 2.0 parameter specifies a pause of 2.0 seconds on the last frame of the flic before starting the fade effect.

Looping

You can loop animations in a playback script in two ways. The first technique involves using an -L option following a flic name and specifying the number of times that the flic should repeat. This command works best for flics where you want to play the animation multiple times with a fade effect only at the beginning or the end of the entire sequence.

The following is a statement from the sample script using the -L option:

```
MYFLIC04.FLC -l 4 -t fadeout 2.0 color(128,128,128)
```

This statement plays the flic MYFLIC04 four times, and at the end of the fourth play, it adds a fade-out to medium gray that is 2.0 seconds long. Contrast this with the second method of looping, which uses the LOOP (*number*)... ENDLOOP sequence, as follows:

```
loop 4
MYFLIC04.FLC -t fadeout 2.0 color(128,128,128)
endloop
```

IV

Basic Animation Techniques

This statement repeats four times where each time it plays the flic MYFLIC04 once, followed by a 2.0-second fade-out to medium gray. You use LOOP (number)... ENDLOOP command primarily when you want to repeat a sequence of multiple statements or when you want to keep returning to a menu from which the viewer can select which animation to play. You can specify the exact number of times that you want the loop to repeat, or you can use the special case of (forever) to cause the loop to repeat continuously until something else breaks the script out of the loop. This second technique is employed in the sample script to keep returning to a menu using the KEYCHOICE command.

Viewer Control

Only one command in the AAPLAYHI scripting language is available for getting user input. This command is the KEYCHOICE command. The KEYCHOICE command freezes the screen on the last displayed image and waits for a key to be pressed. Because the command freezes the screen on the last displayed image, KEYCHOICE requires that a display command immediately precede it. This means that no command such as LOADFLIC, FREEFLIC, or LOOP can immediately precede a keychoice command. Also, you want to be sure that the last image that you display before a KEYCHOICE command includes a menu or some other instruction that tells the viewer how to proceed. After a key is pressed, the player checks that key against the available options and proceeds with the commands under that option or waits for another key press.

The following section of the sample script uses this technique:

```
loop (forever)
 MYFLIC03.FLC -t fadein 0.1 color(128,128,128)
 keychoice
 choice 1
  MYFLIC04.FLC -l 4 -t fadeout 2.0 color(128,128,128)
 choice 2
  MYFLIC05.FLC -p 2.0 -t fadeout 2.0 color(128,128,128)
 choice 3
  exittodos
 endchoice
endloop
```

The loop statement was included in this example because you rarely want to present a viewer with a choice of options without providing some method for returning to the menu screen and choosing something else. The KEYCHOICE and ENDCHOICE statements indicate the start and finish of the entire control sequence. In between these statements are the various choice statements. A CHOICE statement is followed by any single character from 0–9, a–z, or the special case of escape. Pressing the key listed after the CHOICE statement executes any commands on the following lines until another choice statement is encountered. The characters a–z are not case-sensitive, so A is equal to a for the KEYCHOICE command.

In the preceding example, the viewer has three options:

✔ Press 1 to play MYFLIC04 and return to the menu

✔ Press 2 to play MYFLIC05 and return to the menu

✔ Press 3 to break out of the loop and return to DOS

Exploring Hardware Set Up and Recording Techniques

Now that you are familiar with how to design your flic for real-time playback and create scripts to control playback, it is time to consider capturing the playback sequence to videotape. Remember that this technique does not provide the quality of a frame-accurate system, but it also does not require the same investment.

This section assumes that you use the same system to record your animations as you use for creating them. This works extremely well because your modeling and rendering system should have a large amount of RAM, preferably a minimum of 16 MB, which facilitates loading and freeing flics from memory.

Video Configuration

How do you get the picture from your computer screen to videotape? You need the following three basic components:

✔ A video encoder that converts the computer's video signal into a valid video signal for your videotape recorder

✔ A videotape recorder to put that signal on tape

✔ A preview video monitor so you can see what is really being recorded

You can spend anywhere from several hundred dollars to several thousand dollars on each of these pieces of equipment. It is up to you to balance your desire for low cost with your quality requirements. Appendix B, "Rendering and Output Equipment," describes the various types of equipment available and their associated costs.

Hands-Free Recording

Hands-free recording is just that—start the script, start the recorder, and turn it off when you are done. The key is to design an animation and write a playback script that runs from start to finish without operator assistance.

This means that you must debug your script to eliminate any error messages, such as `insufficient memory for a LOADFLIC operation` or `file not found`. It also means that your script is completely devoid of any KEYCHOICE statements. If you can watch your script run without thinking, "Gee, that pause is way too long," or, "Oops, that segment is in the wrong place!," you are ready to record.

The technique involved is quite simple, as follows:

1. Set up your tape deck to record the images on your screen and, of course, insert a tape.

2. Press the Record button on the deck and immediately press Pause. This positions the record head and the tape for immediate recording as soon as you release the Pause button.

3. Enter the command line that starts your playback script. As soon as any startup messages and command prompts disappear from the screen, release the Pause button on your record deck.

4. Sit back and wait for the script to finish, and then shut everything off.

You can use two small tricks to make this technique even easier. The first trick is to use the LOADFLIC command to load your first animation segment as the first line in the script. Depending on the size of the segment, this gives you a few seconds of solid black screen to reach over and release the Pause button on the tape deck. If you need more time or just want a longer lead before the animation starts, use the following as the first line of your script:

```
BLACK.GIF -p 10
```

This statement assumes that you have a blank GIF file named BLACK.GIF. The command gives you 10 seconds of black screen to start your tape deck and record a little bit of blank screen before the animation starts.

The second technique is to include another command like the preceding one as the last line of your script, usually with a much longer pause. Assuming everything else goes well, the last thing you want popping up after your animation is the old DOS prompt. Displaying a blank GIF file with a pause of 100 seconds gives you plenty of time to stop recording before the DOS prompt appears.

Manual Techniques

Sometimes, no matter how hard you try, you just cannot get a script to run right all by itself. This is usually the result of a long animation segment that you just cannot split and that takes a long time to load. The solution is to resort to manual recording techniques, but your playback script is still an important part of the solution.

What you need to do is write a script that plays the entire animation from beginning to end, but with break points where you can stop the recording. Create these break points by using

the KEYCHOICE command. KEYCHOICE freezes the last image on the screen and waits for you to press the appropriate key. During this time, you can stop the recorder, rewind the tape to the appropriate spot, and prepare to record again. The following code segment shows one way you might accomplish this:

```
LOADING.GIF
freeflic MYFLIC01.FLC
loadflic MYFLIC02.FLC
SET-UP.GIF
keychoice
 choice 1
endchoice
BLACK.GIF
keychoice
 choice 1
endchoice
MYFLIC02.FLC
```

Some GIF files appear as part of this sequence, and there are two KEYCHOICE commands. The files LOADING.GIF and SET-UP.GIF are informational screens that tell you what is going on. It is always a good idea to program prompts, even for yourself. You never know when you are going to be distracted from the playback; when you look back at the screen, you don't want to see a blank screen that has no indication of what is happening. Figures 19.5 and 19.6 show examples of how your informational screens can look.

**Loading a flic
stop the recorder
and wait for
Set-up Screen**

Figure 19.5
The LOADING.GIF screen.

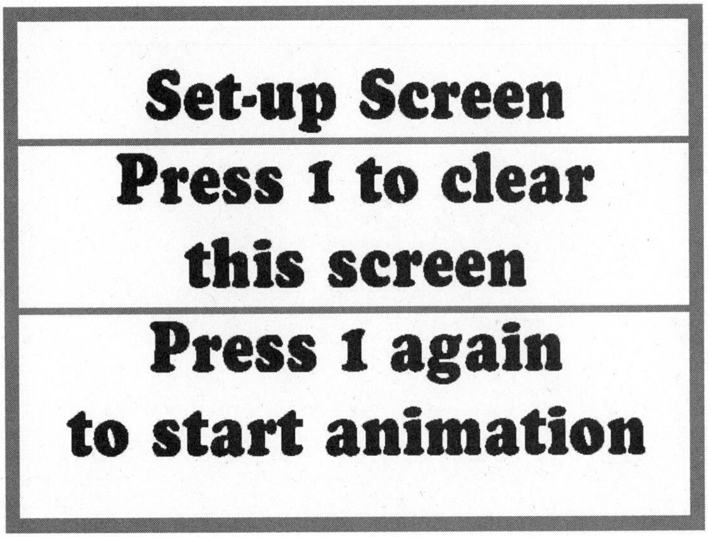

Figure 19.6
The SET-UP.GIF
screen

Set-up Screen

Press 1 to clear
this screen

Press 1 again
to start animation

The LOADING.GIF screen appears while the flic file MYFLIC02 is being loaded. The assumption is that this file takes some time to load, and that is why you must stop the recording here. When you see this screen, press Stop on the tape recorder. Then rewind the tape a few seconds and play back until the end of the last flic but before the LOADING.GIF image. Prepare the tape machine for recording again with the Pause button active, and wait for the SET-UP.GIF screen to appear. The first KEYCHOICE command removes the setup message from the screen and replaces it with plain black. Release the Pause button on the tape recorder and press the appropriate key for the second KEYCHOICE command at the same time. This initiates the recording and starts the animation simultaneously.

Tip   The technique described in the preceding paragraph can be used to create a true cut as well. This way you can avoid the 0.1 second fade-in.

The following exercise puts to use some of the many skills that you have read about in the preceding chapters. The exercise is divided into two parts so that you can focus on just one part if you prefer.

The first part draws on the skills from previous chapters to set up a "ghost painting" animation. You start with the PAINTING.3DS file that you created in Chapter 8. The goal is to bring the brush to life as if it were controlled by a ghostly hand, and cause it to paint on the canvas. The skills that you will employ include timing and motion considerations, keyframing, morphing, and using Animator Pro to create a texture map that is synchronized with the movement of the brush.

New Riders Publishing
INSIDE
SERIES

The second part of the exercise focuses on the issue of creating a custom color palette and rendering an 8-bit flic.

The first step for any good animation is to create a story board and plan out the script, which has already been done for this exercise. The following exercise assumes a frame rate of 15 fps on which to base all timing. The following is a description of the script:

✔ The brush stands up on its own and moves over to the black paint blob on the palette (10 frames).

✔ The brush then wiggles around in the paint (5 frames).

✔ The brush moves over to the upper left corner of the canvas (10 frames).

✔ The brush presses down on the canvas, spreading its bristles, and prepares to write (5 frames).

✔ The brush travels across the canvas in a zigzag fashion, pivoting as it turns corners, and painting a curve on the canvas (45 frames).

✔ The brush lifts up from the canvas and is deposited in the water can (15 frames).

This animation lasts 90 frames, and at 15 fps, that comes to only six seconds. Even though the animation is short, you should be fairly pleased with the final result.

Animating a "Ghost Painting"

Start or reset 3D Studio, then load the file PAINTING.3DS *that you created in Chapter 8, or load the file* GHOST.3DS *if you did not do the exercises in Chapter 8*	Loads the file with a brush, palette, and canvas
Choose Merge *from the* File *pull-down menu, turn off all the buttons except* Mesh Objects, *select the file* BRUSHTIP.3DS, *and then select the object* Brush01 *to merge*	Merges the mesh object Brush01 into the file (the mesh represents the brush tip when it is pressed against the canvas, and is used as a morph target)
Choose Display/Hide/By Name *and select* Brush01, *then go to the Keyframer and hide* Brush01 *there as well*	Hides the brush object
Select Time/Total Frames *and set the animation length to 90 frames*	Displays the Total Frames dialog box
Choose Hierarchy/Link *and link the parts of the brush in the following order:* Shaft *as a child of* Ferrule, Ferrule *as a child of* Brush	Links the objects together with the bristles as the master parent

continues

IV

Basic Animation Techniques

continued

Choose Hierarchy/Object Pivot *and select the* Brush
object, then place the pivot point as indicated in figure 19.7

Figure 19.7
Placing the
pivot point for
the brush.

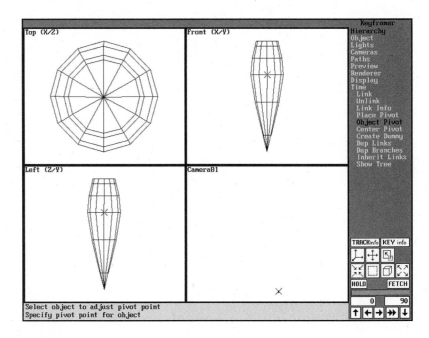

Normally, the logical choice for the pivot point would be the tip of the brush. However, this brush morphs, and when the bristles are spread out, the tip moves up and to the left. The pivot point does not follow. This part of the exercise places the pivot in the center of the brush just above where the morph target bends.

Go to frame 3 and choose Object/Rotate *and rotate the*   Raises the brush on frame 3
brush up in the air about 60 degrees around the X axis,
then move the brush up so that its point no longer pierces
the canvas

Go to frame 10 and move the brush over to the palette about   Places the tip of the brush into
where you think the black spot of paint is located   the paint

You can only guess where the paint is located on the first try, but then you can zero in on it by using the Render Region command.

Make the Top *view active and choose* Renderer/Render   Quickly renders the view and shows
Region, *then specify the region just around the palette*   how close you placed the brush to
                                                                  the paint location

When the Render Animation *dialog box displays, turn off anti-aliasing and shadows, turn on* Single, *and render to display only*

Move the brush closer to the center of where the paint is and render again to check your results   Fine-tunes the position of the brush

Repeat the preceding step until you are satisfied with the location in the top view

In the Left *view, move the brush down so that the tip pierces the palette a little bit*   Pushes the brush into the paint

Choose Track Info, *select the brush, turn on the* Add *button and the* Sub-Tree *button, then click on frame 10 of* All Tracks   Locks down all keys associated with the brush at frame 10 so that no other adjustments throw off its position

Drag the Frame Slider *back and forth and note the motion of the brush, then go to frame 5 and raise the brush up in the air a couple of units*   Plays the motion in box mode and reveals the brush as it moves through the canvas on its way to the palette

Raising the brush on frame 5 gives it a more natural trajectory. Figure 19.8 shows the brush in its position at frame 10.

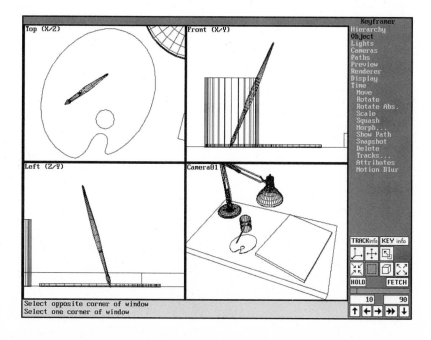

Figure 19.8
Position of the brush at frame 10.

IV

Basic Animation Techniques

continues

continued

Go to frame 15, click on Track Info, *select the brush, turn on* Add, *then click on* All Tracks *of frame 15*	Locks down the position of the Brush at frame 15
Click on Key Info, *select the brush, and set the* Continuity *slider for the position keys at frames 10 and 15 to 0*	Prevents the brush from moving position between frames 10 and 15
Go to frame 12, make the top view active and choose Object/Rotate Abs, *then select the brush and rotate it about -30 degrees around the Y axis*	Swirls the brush around in the paint
Go to frame 14 and use Rotate Abs *to rotate the brush about 60 degrees in the opposite direction*	Swirls the brush around the other way
Go to frame 27 and move the brush so that its tip is just inside the upper left corner of the canvas, then enter Track Info *and add a key for the brush in* All Tracks *at frame 27*	Positions the brush on the canvas and locks in its position
Go to frame 21 and move the brush up in the air a couple of units	Causes the brush to move up and down as it travels to the corner of the canvas, resulting in a more natural motion
Return to frame 27 and use Track Info *to add a morph key for the brush at that frame*	Prevents the shape of the brush from morphing between frames 0 to 27
Go to frame 30 and choose Object/Morph/Assign, *select the brush object, and choose* Brush01 *from the* Morph Assign *dialog box*	Morphs the brush into a flattened, bent shape
Move the brush down so that the tip is again in contact with the canvas, then use Key Info *to set the* Cont *slider of the position keys at frames 27 and 30 to 0*	Makes the morph appear to be the result of pushing the brush into the canvas, and prevents the brush from wandering from side to side between keys 27 and 30
Use Rotate Abs *in the* Top *viewport to rotate the brush -30 degrees around the Y axis*	Aims the brush in the direction of the paint stroke

Figure 19.9 shows the brush in position at frame 30.

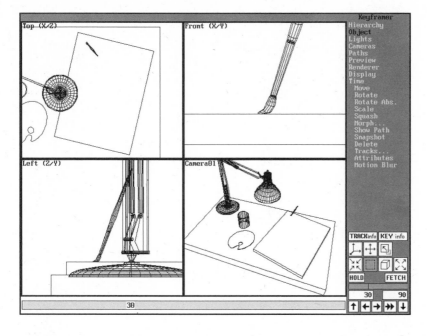

Figure 19.9
The brush at
frame 30.

Using figure 19.10 as a guide, move the brush to position 1 at frame 45, position 2 at frame 60, and position 3 at frame 75

Moves the brush in a zigzag curve across the canvas

Go to frame 45, choose Track Info *and select the brush, then add a* Rotation *key at frame 42, and use* Rotate Abs *to rotate the brush at frame 45 so that it points towards position 2*

Holds the rotation of the brush between frames 30 and 42, and then rotates it around for the stroke between frames 45 and 60

Go to frame 60, choose Track Info, *select the brush, then add a* Rotation *key at frame 57, and use* Rotate Abs *to rotate the brush at frame 60 so that it points towards position 3*

Holds the rotation of the brush between frames 45 and 57, and then rotates it around for the stroke between frames 60 and 75

Go to frame 75, click on Track Info, *select the brush, then add a key in* All Tracks *at frame 75*

Locks down the position, rotation, and morph values for the brush at frame 75

Figure 19.10 shows the important positions of the brush between frames 30 and 75.

continues

IV

Basic Animation Techniques

continued

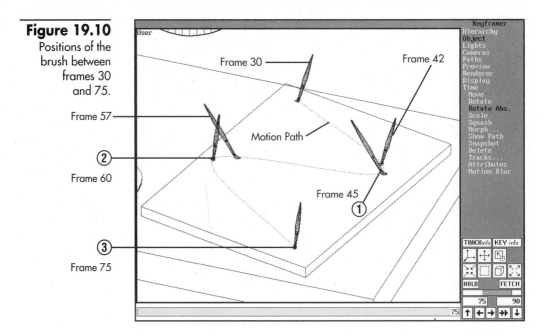

Figure 19.10
Positions of the brush between frames 30 and 75.

Go to frame 76, choose Object/Morph/Assign, *select the brush, then choose* Brush *from the morph assign dialog box, and move the brush up until its tip touches the surface of the canvas*	Quickly morphs the brush back to its original shape
Go to frame 90 and move the brush into the water can, rotate and move the brush as needed to give the appearance that it is leaning against the edge of the can (see fig. 19.11)	Moves the brush into the water can
Go to frame 84 and move the brush up a few units so that its motion drops into the water can, rather than passing through the side of the can	Provides a more realistic curved motion and avoids penetrating the can

Your efforts to position the brush at frame 90 require you to perform some test renders to check that the brush is leaning against the edge of the can and not piercing it.

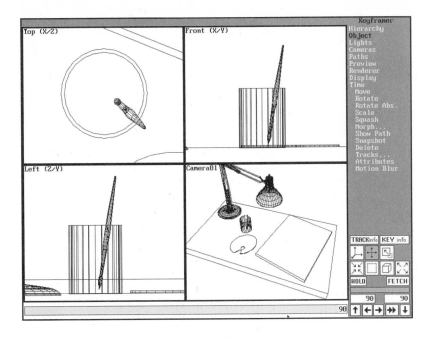

Figure 19.11
Final position of the brush on frame 90.

You have now set the keys for the motion of the brush, and it is time to render and create the texture map for the ghost writing. There are many techniques for performing this next step, and everyone has a preferred method. This part of the exercise shows you how to create an animated texture map that displays the line on the canvas as the brush moves. The key to this technique is not to try to make the brush follow the map, but rather to use the brush itself to help create the map.

Choose Save *from the* File *pull-down menu and save your file as* GHOSTPTR.3DS	Saves the file
Go to frame 30 and make the Top *viewport active, then click on the* Full Screen *icon*	Makes frame 30 the current frame and fills the screen with the Top view
Press ⎡U⎤ *and then* ⎡↵Enter⎤ *to convert the view to a user view, then rotate the view with the left- and right-arrow keys until the canvas is oriented as close to 90 degrees as possible*	Rotates the user view
Choose Display/Hide/All, *then choose* Display/Unhide /By Name *and unhide the objects* canvas *and* brush	Hides all objects except the canvas and the brush

continues

IV

Basic Animation Techniques

continued

Enter the 3D Editor and use the commands Lights/Omni /Adjust *to turn off omni light* Omni01, *and* Lights/ Spotlight/Adjust *to turn off spotlight* Spot01, *then set ambient light to* Luminance 255	Turns off all shading lights and floods the scene with flat even illumination
Return to the Keyframer and use the Zoom Window *icon to zoom in close to the canvas in the* User *viewport, choose* Renderer/Render View *and click in the* User *viewport, then configure the renderer for flic output, 320×200 resolution, flat shading, all options off, and render a range from frames 30 to 75*	Renders an animation that forms the basis of your texture map

Save the flic file as WRITING.FLI

Figure 19.12 shows the settings of the Render Animation dialog box prior to rendering.

Figure 19.12
The settings of the Render Animation dialog box.

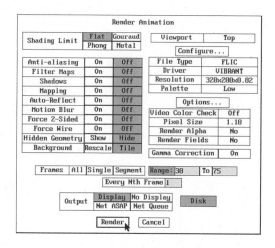

The next step involves using the Next Blue command of the Trace menu in Animator Pro to paint the track of the brush using the brush object itself. For each frame of the flic, you fill the brush and the previous track with black ink, then use Next Blue to copy the track to the next frame.

Quit 3D Studio without changing the recent changes	Exits 3D Studio without saving the changes to the lights or viewports
Start Animator Pro *and load the flic* WRITING.FLI, *click on the* Play *icon and right-click, then click on the* Up Arrow *icon to return to frame 1*	

The flic loads showing the brush on the canvas. Playing the animation shows the brush move around the canvas, but it leaves no trail.

Right-click on the Fill *tool on the left side of the* Home *panel and choose the tool* Fill To *to take its place, then press* ⸨Spacebar⸩ *to return to the* Home *panel*	Puts the Fill To tool in the current tool slot
Click on the black key color slot to the far left on the mini-palette to make black the active ink color, then using the Fill To *tool, pick a point on the canvas and fill in the body of the brush*	Makes black the active ink color and fills in all pixels of the brush until the color of the canvas is encountered

The entire brush shape turns black; this is the start of your ghost ink trail.

Choose Next Blue *from the* Trace *pull-down menu and advance one frame*	Displays the next frame with the beginning of the ink trail in the bluing color

The bluing color is the color in the mini-palette slot immediately to the right of the key color slot.

Use the Fill To *tool to fill in both the previous trail and the brush shape with black ink, then use the* Line *tool to draw connecting lines between the two shapes and fill in the gap with the* Fill To *tool*	Connects the two shapes to extend the trail (see fig. 19.13)

Figure 19.13 shows an example of drawing the lines between the two shapes.

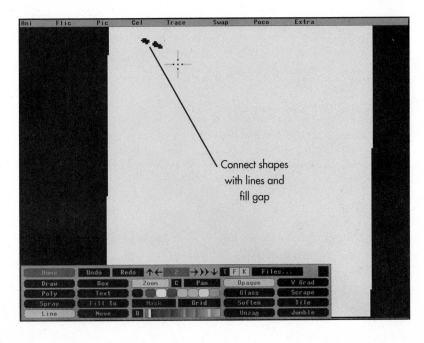

Figure 19.13
Connecting the shapes with the Line tool.

continues

IV

Basic Animation Techniques

continued

Repeat the last two steps for each frame of the animation	Draws the trail that becomes the ghost writing in your animation

After you repeat the preceding steps for every frame, you have an animation that accurately tracks the brush path and leaves a trail behind it. All that is left is to clean up the animation and clip it out as a CEL.

Click on the Play *icon, then stop playback and return to frame 1*	Plays the animation of a curve being drawn across the canvas
Right-click on any slot in the mini-palette and click on the canvas, then click on the mini-palette slot again	Puts the canvas color in the selected mini-palette slot and makes it the current ink color
Use the Line *tool to straighten up the edges of the canvas on frame 1, then choose* Clip Changes *from the* Trace *menu*	Straightens the edges of the canvas, and then puts only the changes you have made into the CEL buffer
Turn on the T *button near the upper right corner of the* Home *panel, then choose* Paste *from the* Cel *pull-down menu, right-click and then click on the* Render *button*	Turns on time and pastes the clean-up changes to every frame in the animation
On frame 1, click on the Frame Number *icon and then click on* INSERT	Enters the Frames panel and inserts one frame after frame 1
Return to the Home *panel, turn the* T *button off, and use the* Fill To *tool with the canvas color to wipe out the brush mark on frame 1 only*	Creates a clean blank canvas on frame one
Click on the Frame Number *icon again and right-click on the* INSERT *button, then set the dialog to insert 29 frames after the current frame*	Inserts 29 more blank canvas frames to cover frames 0 through 29 of the 3D Studio animation where the brush has not started painting yet
Click on the down arrow *and right-click on the* Total Frames Number *icon and specify that the animation should have a total of 91 frames*	Adds frame to the end of the animation to cover when the brush leaves the canvas and moves to the water can
Return to the Home *panel and frame 1, then turn on the* T *button and choose* Clip *from the* Cel *pull-down menu and click on the* Render *button*	Clips out the canvas from the black background for every frame and stores it in the Cel buffer
Choose Files *from the* Cel *pull-down menu and save the Cel as the file* WRITING.CEL *in the* \MAPS *directory of 3D Studio*	Saves the file for use as a texture map

Choose Quit *from the* Ani *pull-down menu and abandon Animator Pro*	Quits Animator Pro without saving all of its temporary files

You are now ready to return to 3D Studio and use the WRITING.CEL file as a texture map. If you have trouble creating this file or do not own Animator Pro, the file GHOSTPTR.CEL is provided for you. Use the file GHOSTPTR.CEL wherever the exercise calls for WRITING.CEL.

Using the animated texture is easy because the canvas is already mapped with its own material. All you have to do is add the WRITING.CEL texture to the material specification.

Start 3D Studio and load the file GHOSTPTR.3DS, *then enter the Materials Editor*

Choose Get From Scene *from the* Materials *pull-down menu and select the* WHITE CANVAS *material*	Renders a sample sphere of WHITE CANVAS and displays its settings
Click in the map slot for Texture 1 and select the file WRITING.CEL, *then check that the map slider is at 100 percent*	Assigns WRITING.CEL as the Texture 1 map
Choose Put To Scene *from the* Materials *pull-down menu and click on* Yes	Updates the WHITE CANVAS material in your scene

Enter the 3D Editor and save the file as GHOSTPTR.3DS

You are ready to render the ghost painting animation. The last few steps involve creating a low-resolution flic to create a custom color palette. This technique ensures that colors for all objects in the entire animation are accounted for when you render the final flic file.

Rendering the Animation

Turn Light01 *and* Light02 *back on and then change the ambient light back to H:170, L:8, s:255; unhide everything except* Brush01

Enter the Keyframer and go to frame 35	Advances to a frame where all objects, including the paint track, are visible
Choose Render *or* Render View *and click in the* Camera *viewport, then configure the renderer for 320×200 resolution, anti-aliasing off, Frames All, Every Nth Frame at 10, and render to disk; specify a file name of* COLORS.FLI *and place it in the* \MAPS *directory of 3D Studio*	Renders a low resolution flic that has all the colors you need for the animation

continues

continued

Choose Renderer/Setup/Configure *and specify a custom palette using* COLORS.FLC, *and click on the button for a render resolution of 640×480*	Sets the rendering parameters
Choose Renderer/Setup/Options *and make sure that* Dither 256 *is* Off	Prevents the flic from being dithered
Choose Renderer *or* Render View *and render the camera viewport for all frames and save the flic to disk as* GHOSTPTR.FLC *(see fig. 19.14)*	Renders the flic file

Figure 19.14
The settings in the Render Animation dialog box.

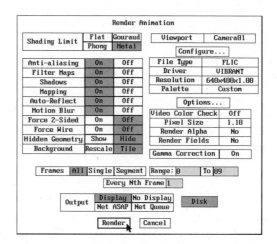

Depending on the speed of your system, this rendering could take several hours. The resulting 91-frame flic, however, is less than 500 KB, which makes it easy to load and play in AAPLAYHI. If you are impatient and want to view the flic now, you can load and play the flic GHOSTFIN.FLC provided on the *Inside 3D Studio* CD-ROM (see fig. 19.15).

As an extra exercise, you could set up an AAPLAYHI script to play this animation with an opening title screen, a fade-in effect, and a pause with fade-out out at the end. This would create an impressive demonstration flic that you could transport on a single disk.

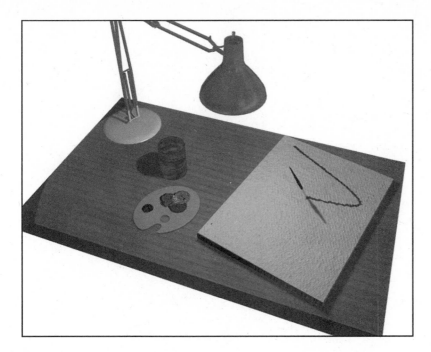

Figure 19.15
A frame from
GHOSTFIN.FLC.

Summary

This chapter has shown you some of the techniques that lead to successful flic format animations. These animations are suitable for disk-based presentations and real-time recording to video. Produced properly, flic-based presentations can satisfy many professional presentation requirements.

IV

Basic Animation Techniques

Part V

Advanced Animation

Chapter Snapshot

The Keyframer provides many methods for creating and animating the joints of connected objects. This chapter continues on from the basic linking concepts presented in Chapter 15, "Introduction to the Keyframer," and presents advanced linking techniques. The chapter ends with the new Release 4 feature called *inverse kinematics*.

The following is a list of some of the new topics discussed in this chapter:

✔ Modeling with instances in the Keyframer instead of geometry in the 3D Editor

✔ Using the new Release 4 inverse kinematics Plug-In to simplify complex joint keyframing for character or mechanical movement

CHAPTER

Advanced Linking and Inverse Kinematics

C hapter 15 introduced you to the use of hierarchical linking, which is very useful for the simulation of jointed objects and complex motions. This chapter explores some of the more advanced commands for manipulating hierarchical links and introduces you to a new feature of 3D Studio Release 4—the concept of inverse kinematics.

Understanding Instances

No command in 3D Studio actually creates instance objects. *Instances* are copies of your mesh objects that exist only in the Keyframer and are always the product of another command.

The simplest way to create an instance object is to hold down the Shift key while performing an Object command in the Keyframer. The prompt at the bottom of the screen states that holding down Shift creates a clone, but this can be misleading. A clone in the 3D Editor is simply a copy of the original object. After you create the clone, it is independent—it's just like any other object in the 3D Editor. Cloning in the Keyframer creates an instance object that is partially dependent on the master object that created it.

An instance object is dependent upon the object that created it for its shape, material, and mapping. Any change that you make to the master object in the 3D Editor also is transmitted to all the instance objects in the Keyframer, including materials and mapping. Instance objects have the same material and mapping assignments as their master object. If the mapping and materials of the master object change after the creation of an instance, the materials and mapping on the instance will also change.

Instance objects can, however, behave independently with respect to animation. You can move, squash, link, and otherwise manipulate an instance object that exists in the Keyframer independently of the master object if you use only Keyframer commands. Instance objects do not exist in the 3D Editor, and anything done to the master object in the 3D Editor is transmitted to the instances. The exception to this rule involves deletion of the master object. Object/Delete in the Keyframer is really a 3D Editor command that snuck into the Keyframer. Anything deleted on any frame in the Keyframer also is deleted from the 3D Editor, so if you delete the master object in the Keyframer, it is also deleted from the 3D Editor, and all of its instances are deleted from the Keyframer as well.

When you create instance objects, it is important that you know whether you have created any keys for the master object (other than that created automatically at frame 0). If you have not created any keys for the master object, the instance has no keys and the two are animated completely independently of each other. If the master object already has keys, the instance inherits all of those keys in a fashion similar to Copy Tracks/Relative. The instance object duplicates the motions of the master object, but you can independently change its keys after the fact.

If you want instance objects to be completely independent of each other, create the instances before you create any keys. If you want instance objects that duplicate the motion of the master, create the instances after you create keys for the master object.

Examining Advanced Linking

This section takes a look at four more features of hierarchical linking. Two of these commands are really modeling commands, while the remaining two provide ways to manipulate links.

The Duplicate Links and Duplicate Branches commands create new instance objects that are automatically linked into the selected hierarchical tree. This is a very fast and efficient way to model linked structures that follow a repetitive pattern.

The commands Inherit Links and Link Info enable you to adjust existing links by passing link values down through the tree structure or by limiting the scope of individual links.

Duplicate Links

The Duplicate Links command travels down the tree structure of your selected object until it gets to the last item in the link structure. After the last item (or items) is discovered, it is copied, which creates a new instance object. This new object is then connected to the tree structure using the same link information that connected the former last object to its parent. This link information includes any changes in rotation or scale between the parent and its child. Figure 20.1 shows a pair of linked beads in which the child is 20 percent smaller than its parent. Figure 20.2 shows the effect of performing the Duplicate Link command four times on the parent bead.

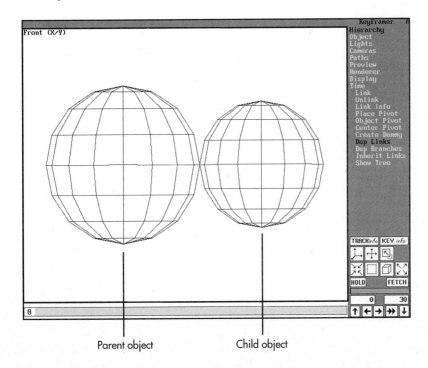

Parent object   Child object

Figure 20.1
Two linked beads.

V

Advanced Animation

Figure 20.2
The result of four
Duplicate Link
commands on
the beads.

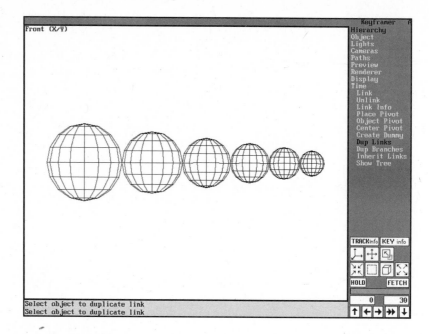

Figure 20.2
The result of four
Duplicate Link
commands on
the beads.

Duplicate Branches

Duplicate Branches is similar to Duplicate Links, except for where it takes the link information. In the Duplicate Branches command, after the last object is found, 3D Studio backs up one level and examines the parent object. All of the links coming out of the parent object are then duplicated on the child objects. If the parent object has only one child, the effect is the same as the Duplicate Link command. If the parent has more than one child, then each child receives the same number of children as its parent.

Figure 20.3 shows a model in which the parent object is linked to three children. Compare the results of performing the Duplicate Links command twice, shown in figure 20.4, to performing the Duplicate Branches command twice, shown in figure 20.5.

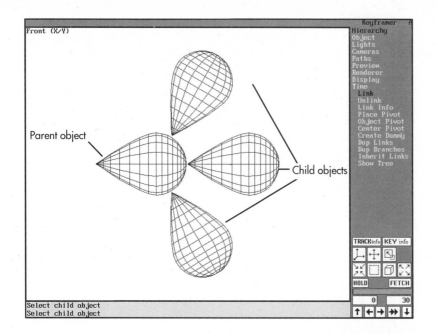

Figure 20.3
The original linked model.

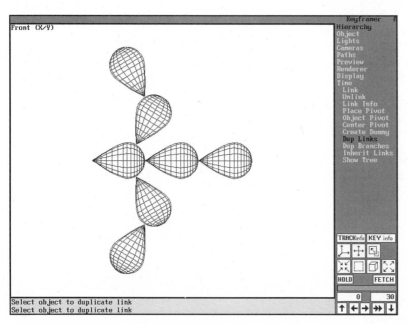

Figure 20.4
The model after two Duplicate Link commands.

Figure 20.5
The model after two Duplicate Branches commands.

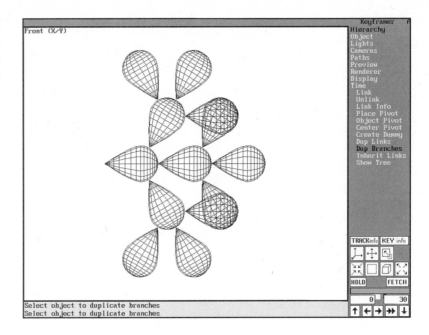

 The Duplicate Links command and the Duplicate Branches command both create instance objects, and instance objects pick up any animation keys assigned to the master object at the time they are created. Unless you are trying a special motion effect, you generally want to use the Duplicate Links and Duplicate Branches commands before you assign keys to the objects.

The following exercise shows you how fast and easy you can model a chain by using the Duplicate Links command.

Creating a Chain with Duplicate Links

Start or reset 3D Studio and load the file CHAIN.3DS *into the 3D Editor*

Loads the file that has a single mesh object called Chain (see fig. 20.6)

Go to the Keyframer, choose Object/Move, *and hold down the* ⧉Shift *key while selecting the* Chain *object in the* Top *viewport, then move the object 200 units to the right, and accept the default name of* CHAIN.COPY01

Creates an instance object in the Keyframer of the original chain object

Choose Object/Rotate *and select the instance object* CHAIN.COPY01, *then rotate it 90 degrees about its X axis*

Rotates the instance object so that it passes through the Chain object like a link in a chain

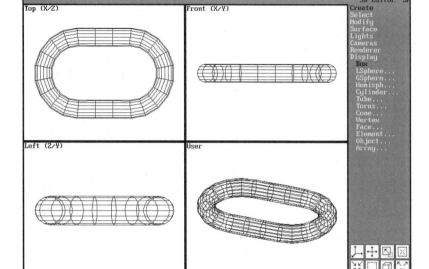

Figure 20.6
The Chain mesh object.

Choose Hierarchy/Link *and link the object* CHAIN.COPY01 *as a child of the object* Chain, *and then right-click on the* Zoom Extents *icon*

Links the instance to the original object and zooms to extents in all views (see fig. 20.7)

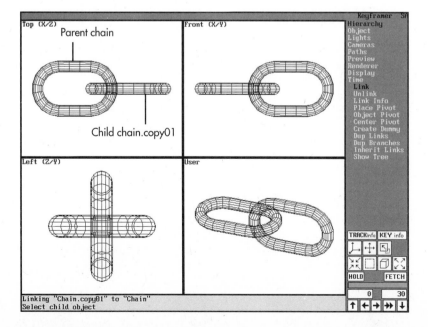

Figure 20.7
Two links in the chain.

You can now use the Duplicate Links command to create a chain of any length. This is much faster than trying to build the chain in the 3D Editor because the links are automatically positioned properly and hierarchically linked together.

Choose Hierarchy/Duplicate Links *and select the parent object* Chain, *select the same object four or more times, then right-click on the* Zoom Extents *icon*

Creates a new link in the chain every time you select the object Chain—figure 20.8 shows the result of six duplications

Save the file as MYCHAIN.3DS

Figure 20.8
The completed chain.

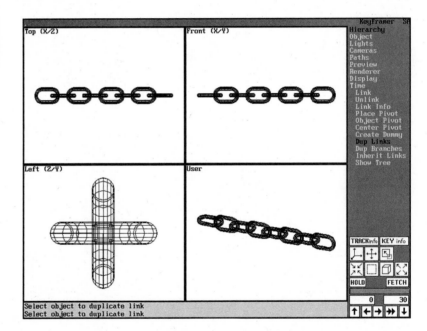

The preceding exercise demonstrates how quickly the Duplicate Links command can help you build a seemingly complex model. If you don't use Duplicate Links, you have to use many more commands in the 3D Editor, and then laboriously link everything together in the Keyframer.

Inherit Links

Inherit Links doesn't build instance objects. Instead, it passes link information along the hierarchical tree to objects already linked together. The 3D Studio Reference Manual

provides a good example of using the Inherit Links command to make a linked object bend over gradually. What is not shown is how using this command multiple times can result in very interesting and organic-looking motion.

The Inherit Links command wipes out any link information beyond the selected object, so the key to using the command is to always work outward from the root of the hierarchical tree. The following exercise demonstrates this concept.

This exercise shows you how to apply Inherit Links multiple times to achieve interesting animated effects. You begin by loading a model of a linked string of beads, and then you animate the beads in a whip-like motion. The setup file BEADS.3DS is shown in figure 20.9.

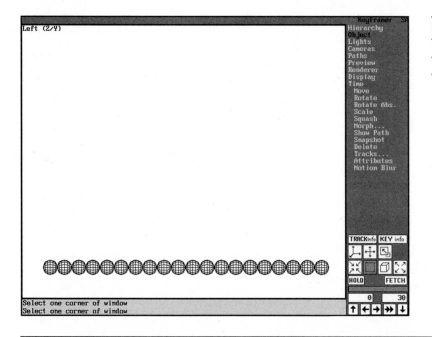

Figure 20.9
The linked beads with no animation applied.

V

Advanced Animation

Cracking the Whip with Hierarchical Links

Start or reset 3D Studio and then load the file BEADS.3DS *into the Keyframer*

Go to frame 15 and choose Object/Rotate, *then rotate the second bead from the left (Bead.copy01) 10 degrees about the X axis*	Rotates the bead, and all the beads linked to it rise up in a straight line
Go to frame 30 and rotate the same bead back down -10 degrees about the X axis	Rotates the bead back to its original position along with all the beads linked to it

continues

continued

Choose Hierarchy/Inherit Links *and*
select the first bead on the left
(Bead), then click on the Play *icon*

Plays the animation in wire frame—the
beads bend up and back down again
(see fig. 20.10)

Figure 20.10
The bending
beads on
frame 12.

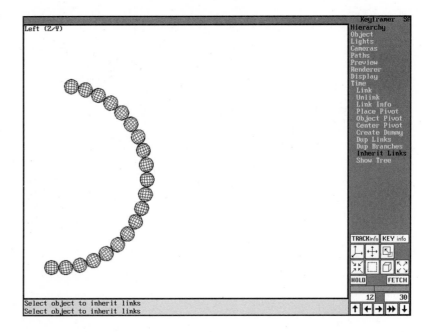

Using Inherit Links passes the 10 degree rotation along the hierarchical tree and the effect
builds on itself as it moves down the tree. The result so far is a smooth, bending animation and
is still similar to the example in the 3D Studio Reference Manual. The motion, however, is still
rather stiff. You now apply more effects further down the hierarchical tree to create a more
realistic motion.

 You might want to Hold frequently during the next steps. Selecting the wrong
bead during an Inherit Links command can wipe out the animation effect you
just specified.

Go to frame 5 and choose Object/Rotate,
select a bead near the middle of
the structure (Bead.copy10), and
then rotate it -10 degrees about the
X axis

Rotates the bead back -10 degrees,
displaying a noticeable kink in
the middle of the string

Choose Hierarchy/Inherit Links *and select the parent of the bead that you just rotated (Bead.copy09)*	Passes the rotation information to all the beads linked after Bead.copy10, which results in a smooth curve that bends backward in the middle
Go to frame 10 and choose Object/Rotate *then select a bead near the three-quarters point of the structure (Bead.copy15) and rotate it -20 degrees about the X axis*	Rotates the bead back -20 degrees, displaying a noticeable kink in the string
Choose Hierarchy/Inherit Links *and select the parent of the bead that you just rotated (Bead.copy14)*	Passes the rotation information to all the beads linked after Bead.copy15, resulting in a smooth curve that bends backward at the end of the string (see fig. 20.11)

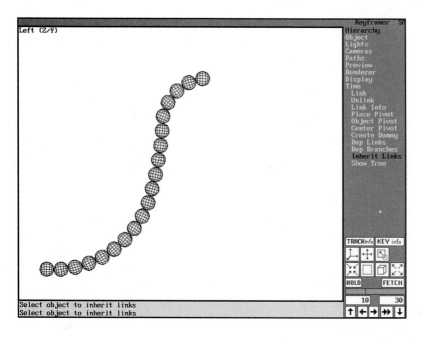

Figure 20.11
The result of two more inherent Links commands.

Click on the Play *icon*	Plays the animation—the beads now move in a realistic whip-like fashion

The key to successfully completing this exercise was that you started at the root object, Bead, and worked the animation forward from there. If you ever tried to manipulate the Bead object after setting the rotations for Bead.copy10 or Bead.copy15, the Inherit Links command would wipe out those rotations and you would have to start over.

Link Info

The Link Info command enables you to display the Define Link Type dialog box, which has information about the link between an object and its parent. This dialog box also provides a series of buttons that enable you to selectively release the link for certain rotational or scale axes (see fig. 20.12). This capability is particularly useful when you model mechanical linkages. Often an object is linked to something where it is constrained on one axis, yet free to rotate about another. Examples of such linkages are connecting rods in an engine and buckets on a conveyor belt.

In figure 20.12, link buttons that are highlighted are active. The axes represented by the active buttons pass information from the parent to the child, constraining the child's motion. Inactive buttons release the child on those axes so the child is no longer constrained by the parent.

Figure 20.12
The Define Link
Type dialog box.

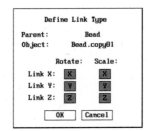

Understanding Inverse Kinematics

As pointed out in Chapter 15, hierarchical linking is a one-way effect. Objects are linked from parent to child and animation effects applied to a parent are also passed along to its children. Effects applied to a child do not pass up the chain to parent objects.

This type of linking is very useful, but it does not accurately reflect jointed objects in the real world. As you know, when real objects are linked together, manipulating either end of the chain affects all of the linked objects. 3D Studio provides this type of effect through a Plug-In called *inverse kinematics* (IK). IK enables you to manipulate an entire linked chain by working with one object at any point in the chain.

Modeling and Setup Issues

Before you jump into the inverse kinematics Plug-In, there are a few preliminary concepts that will help ensure success. Understanding how IK interacts with the objects in your scene will help you to avoid problems later on.

Coordinate Systems

The first issue is actually an old issue that has been discussed repeatedly throughout this book. That issue is an object's local coordinate system and how it relates to the world coordinate system. Just as with linking, everything that you specify in IK is in relation to each object's local coordinate system.

The world coordinate system never changes, and you can think of it as the base reference point for your entire scene. Local coordinate systems are carried within each individual object. It is the local coordinate system that you see when you access position, and rotation values when working with Key Info, hierarchical linking, and inverse kinematics. Many of the animations that you create will rely on various objects having their local coordinate systems aligned in a very specific way. It is very easy to alter the local coordinate system in the 3D Editor and ruin this critical alignment.

For example, imagine that you are modeling a laser cannon as part of a science fiction animation. The cannon will fire bolts of energy from its tip and recoil in a telescoping fashion. Figure 20.13 shows two views of a simple cannon model. The first view shows the mesh objects. The second view shows the model in box mode with the local coordinate axes labeled.

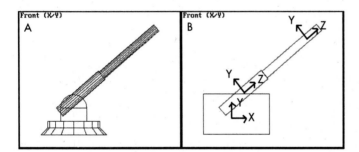

Figure 20.13
Two views of a cannon model. A: Viewed as a mesh. B: Viewed in box mode with local coordinate axes labeled.

As you can see from figure 20.13, the local coordinate systems of the two barrel objects are aligned with each other along the axis of the barrel. This coordinate alignment would happen quite naturally if you used the Create/Cylinder command to make the barrels, and then used the Modify/Object command to rotate and move the barrel objects into position. Animating the recoil is a simple matter of sliding one barrel back and forth along its Z axis. In IK, this situation could easily be defined as a sliding joint.

It is very easy to alter an object's local coordinate system during the course of building a model, and end up with something that is very difficult to animate. Returning to the laser cannon example, you might feel that the cannon model looks too conventional for a futuristic weapon. You decide to place a sphere at the end of the barrel that will act as the energy bolt emitter. You create a sphere in the top viewport, move it to the end of the barrel, and attach the barrel and sphere together by using Create/Object/Attach, then selecting the barrel first and the sphere second. Figure 20.14 shows the model before and after the Attach command.

Figure 20.14
The cannon model before and after attaching the emitter sphere to the barrel.

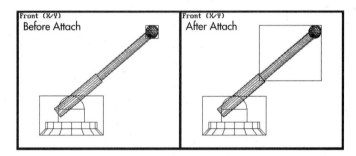

Attaching the barrel to the sphere caused the barrel to give up its local coordinate system and become part of the sphere using the sphere's local coordinate system. Since the sphere was created in the top viewport, its local coordinate system was square to the world coordinate system and not aligned with the barrel of the cannon. It will now be very difficult to animate the recoil because the motion does not occur along a single axis; instead, the recoil is now a complex motion occurring along all three axes.

This problem could have been avoided by selecting the sphere first when using the Attach command, causing the sphere to give up its coordinate system in favor of the barrel, or by not attaching the objects at all and using linking in the Keyframer. The important concept to remember from this example is that certain 3D Editor commands alter the orientation of an object's local coordinate system, and you may need to preserve a specific orientation for certain animation effects.

You should be aware of how various commands alter the local coordinate system and plan for how those changes will affect your animation. In general, the following is true:

✔ Modifying objects at the object level modifies the local coordinate system the same amount. For example, rotating an object 30 degrees about its X axis also rotates the coordinate system 30 degrees about the X axis.

✔ Modifying objects at the element, face, or vertex level will not reorient the local coordinate system. For example, rotating all of the faces of an object 30 degrees about its X axis does not affect the orientation of the local coordinate system (see fig. 20.15).

✔ Attaching objects always sacrifices the coordinate system of the first object selected, and uses the local coordinate system of the second object selected.

✔ Boolean commands always reset the local coordinate system of the new object to be aligned with the world coordinate system.

✔ Reset Xform always aligns an object's local coordinate system with the world coordinate system.

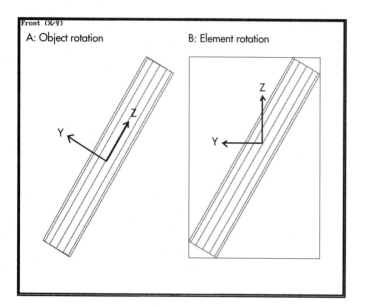

Figure 20.15
The effects of rotating a cylinder at the object level and at the element level. A: Rotation at the object level. B: Rotation at the element level.

Gimble Lock

The term *gimble lock* refers to a condition in which the orientation of an axis becomes indeterminate. A good way to visualize the problem is to think of the age-old question, "When you are standing at the North Pole, which way is north?" Gimble lock occurs in IK when the orientation of an object's local coordinate system is parallel, but rotated 90 degrees to the coordinate system of its parent object.

Figure 20.16 shows a model that exhibits gimble lock. Notice that the coordinate systems of both objects have parallel axes; however, the X axis of one object is rotated 90 degrees to the X axis of the other object. The same is true for the Y axes and the Z axes. When these two objects are linked together, they will experience gimble lock in the IK Plug-In.

An easy way to check for gimble lock is when you are specifying rotational joint parameters in IK. (Specifying joint parameters is described later in this chapter.) If changing the values of two axes causes the same rotation, or if changing the value of one axis causes no rotation at all, you have a gimble lock condition.

Figure 20.16
A gimble lock
condition.

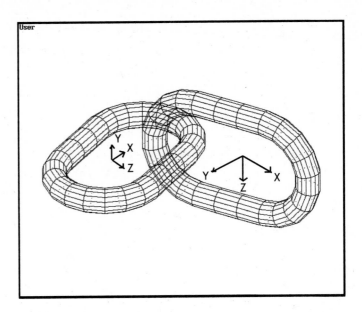

The solution is to reorient the local coordinate system of one or both objects to remove the gimble lock condition. You can do this by unlinking the objects, performing a Reset Xform command on one or both objects, and then linking them together again. Be sure that before you use the Reset Xform command, you consider all of the other side effects this might have, as described in the previous section.

Frame 0

A final point to consider is how to preserve your model in the Keyframer. The IK module manipulates your model on all frames in the active segment, including frame 0. As mentioned in Chapter 15, "Introduction to the Keyframer," changes that occur on frame 0 are telegraphed back to the 3D Editor. More often than not, you want to preserve the orientation of your model in the 3D Editor and prevent changes from being telegraphed back from the Keyframer.

The safest way to do this is to use the Track Info command in the Keyframer and copy the All Tracks key for the World object from frame 0 to frame 1. This duplicates the starting (frame 0) position of everything in your scene at frame 1. Finally, define the active segment as beginning at frame 1 and continuing to the end of the animation. This helps to protect frame 0 from inadvertent keyframing, but you still need to check the Time Segment values in the IK dialog as well.

Many people like to use this technique even when they are not using IK. It is a convenient safety tip to protect your model in the 3D Editor. Be aware that many commands, including IK, enable you to override the current segment setting. This tip helps make sure that you must make an explicit choice to modify objects on frame 0.

Chains and Joints

Once you have linked your objects together, you can begin specifying their behavior in the IK Plug-In. The heart of the IK Plug-In is the definition of which objects are part of the current chain and how the links between the objects (their joints) are constrained.

Before you can do any of this, you must start the IK Plug-In and select the hierarchically linked model with which you want to work. Choosing IK from the Program menu in the Keyframer (or pressing F8) displays the IK Plug-in dialog box, shown in figure 20.17.

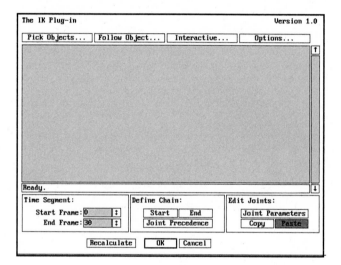

Figure 20.17
The IK Plug-in dialog box.

Your next step is to select a hierarchy to animate. Click on the Pick Objects button to temporarily hide the dialog box and redisplay the Keyframer viewports. Click on any object in your scene to display its names and the names of all the objects sharing the same hierarchy in the IK dialog. Figure 20.18 shows the IK dialog box with the hierarchy of the MANEQUIN.3DS model from the CD-ROM loaded.

Defining the Chain

Once you have loaded a hierarchy into the IK Plug-In, you must further narrow your scope of work. A single hierarchical tree can have many branches, but the IK Plug-In can only work with one branch at a time.

Figure 20.18

The mannequin hierarchy in the IK dialog box.

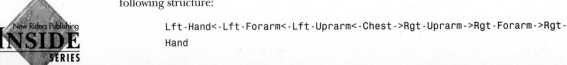

```
The IK Plug-in                                              Version 1.0
 ┌─────────────┐ ┌──────────────┐ ┌─────────────┐ ┌────────────┐
 │ Pick Objects...│ │ Follow Object...│ │ Interactive...│ │ Options...│
 └─────────────┘ └──────────────┘ └─────────────┘ └────────────┘
 Waist                                                            ↑
  Hips
   Rgt-Thigh
    Rgt-Shin
     Rgt-Foot
   Lft-Thigh
    Lft-Shin
     Lft-Foot
  Chest
   Lft-Uprarm
    Lft-Forarm
     Lft-Hand
   Rgt-Uprarm
    Rgt-Forarm
     Rgt-Hand
   Neck
    Head                                                          ↓
 Pick an object to paste clipboard joint parameters to.
 ┌─Time Segment:──┐ ┌─Define Chain:──┐ ┌─Edit Joints:──────┐
 │ Start Frame:0  │ │ Start │ End   │ │ Joint Parameters  │
 │ End Frame:30   │ │ Joint Precedence│ │ Copy │ Paste     │
 └────────────────┘ └────────────────┘ └───────────────────┘
        ┌──────────┐  ┌────┐ ┌──────┐
        │ Recalculate│ │ OK │ │ Cancel│
        └──────────┘  └────┘ └──────┘
```

Looking back at the hierarchy of the mannequin model from figure 20.18, you can see that the root object of the hierarchy is the waist. Branches run out from the waist connecting objects until they reach a leaf object at the far end of the hierarchical tree. For the mannequin, these leaf objects are the hands, the feet, and the head. You can work with any single branch, or part of a branch, running from the root object to a leaf object. You identify the branch with which you want to work by defining a chain.

The Define Chain controls are located at the bottom-center portion of the IK dialog box. Defining the chain is as simple as clicking on the Start button and selecting the object to be the start of the chain, and then clicking on the End button and selecting the object to be the end of the chain.

You must respect the following constraints when specifying the chain:

✔ The start of the chain must be closer to the root of the hierarchical tree than the end of the chain. This is easy to identify visually by looking at the list in the IK dialog box. The higher-level parents are to the left, while the children are indented to the right. Therefore, the start of the chain must always be to the left of the end of the chain.

✔ The entire chain must exist within a single branch of the hierarchical tree. Another way to look at this is that no two objects in the chain can share the same parent.

Using the mannequin model for another example, you can see that a chain from the Chest to the Rgt-Hand is a valid chain. It has the following structure:

```
Chest->Rgt-Uprarm->Rgt-Forarm->Rgt-Hand
```

Trying to specify a chain from the Lft-Hand to the Rgt-Hand, however, is not valid. It has the following structure:

```
Lft-Hand<-Lft-Forarm<-Lft-Uprarm<-Chest->Rgt-Uprarm->Rgt-Forarm->Rgt-
Hand
```

The problem is that both the Lft-Uprarm and the Rgt-Uprarm share the Chest as their parent. What you have here are two branches rooted at the chest and an invalid IK chain.

Setting Joint Parameters

When a chain is first defined, all of the joints, by default, are free to rotate in all directions. If you want a controllable, realistic effect, you must specify constraints on how the joints operate. There are two types of joints available in IK—rotating joints and sliding joints. Any joint can be a rotating joint, a sliding joint, or both, and you have independent control over how much the joint rotates or slides about all three axes of the local coordinate system.

Clicking on the Joint Parameters button in the lower right portion of the IK dialog will prompt you to "Pick an object to edit joint parameters." Click on any object in the hierarchy to display the joint parameters dialog box, as shown in figure 20.19. The button at the top left of this dialog box is a toggle to switch between specifying the parameters for a revolving joint versus a sliding joint.

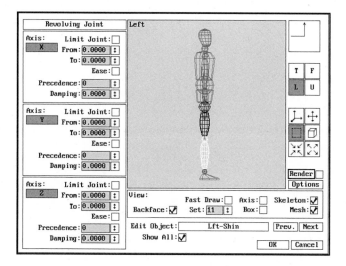

Figure 20.19

The joint parameters dialog box.

The meaning of the various buttons and fields in the joint parameters dialog box are well-documented in the New Features manual of 3D Studio Release 4. However, it is worth discussing some of the main issues related to this dialog box.

The axis button must be activated (red) if the object is to rotate about, or slide along, that axis. If the axis button is deactivated (gray), all of the other settings for that axis are ignored.

It is also important to note that the axis orientation for a joint is dependent upon the type of joint. *Revolving joints* are specified about the object's local coordinate axes. *Sliding joints* are specified along the local coordinate axes of the object's parent. This means that you must pay close attention when setting joint parameters.

After specifying the limits of a joint for a particular axis, you must activate the Limit Joint check box for the settings to take effect. If the Limit Joint box is not checked, the From: and To: settings are ignored for that axis.

Activating the Ease check box for an axis causes resistance to motion on that axis to increase as the joint approaches its limit. The more resistance there is at a joint, the more other joints in the chain must contribute to the solution. Think of Ease as being similar to trying to move your arm or leg through its maximum range of motion. Most of the range is easy to move, but as you approach your limits, there is greater resistance and the motion becomes more difficult.

Setting a value in the Damping field applies resistance across the entire range of motion. A Damping value of 0.0000 applies no resistance, while a maximum Damping value of 1.0000 cancels all motion for that axis. Think of damping as being similar to a rusted, or very tight joint. The damped joint resists all motion and lets other joints in the chain do most of the work. Damped joints begin to move as the other joints in the chain approach their limits.

Joint Precedence

The setting of *joint precedence* controls how motion is distributed between the joints in a chain. Joints with a high precedence absorb a greater share of the overall motion than joints with a low precedence.

Joint precedence can be set in two places. You can manually set the precedence for each axis of each joint by entering a value in the Precedence fields of the joint preferences dialog box. This method gives you very precise control over motion distribution along the chain, but it is very tedious. Most of your need will probably be handled with the presets.

Automatic joint precedence is set at the main IK dialog. Clicking on the Joint Precedence button, just beneath the Start and End buttons for Define Chain, displays the dialog box shown in figure 20.20. You have three choices: End to Start, Start to End, and Reset to 0.

Figure 20.20
The Joint
Precedence
Presets
dialog box.

```
Joint Precedence Presets:

[ End to Start ] [ Start to End ] [ Reset to 0 ] [ Cancel ]
```

End to Start is the first choice, both visually as the first button in the list, and conceptually as the typical solution for most situations. Remember that the start of the chain must be closer to the root of the hierarchical tree than the end of the chain. In most linked systems, the root of the hierarchical tree is placed at the object representing the center of mass or the anchor point for the system. The leaves of the tree represent the free ends of the linked system and are at the end of the chain. Joints near the end of the chain, where the motion is applied, naturally flex sooner and to a greater amount than joints near the start of the chain, which are farther from where the motion is applied. End to Start simulates this natural effect.

Start to End reverses the precedence causing the joints of the root objects to flex more than the end objects.

Reset to 0 gives all joints an equal precedence of zero and joint calculation proceeds in the order described in the New Features manual. The end result is that equal joint precedence is similar to a very weak End to Start effect.

Animating with Inverse Kinematics

Once you have completed the setup steps of loading a hierarchy, defining a chain, and setting joint parameters, you are ready to begin animating with IK. Animation in IK is always specified by moving the end object in the current IK chain. Since it is possible to specify the end of the chain virtually anywhere in the hierarchical tree, it would not make sense to refer to this object as a leaf. IK calls the last object in the chain the *end effector*. Manipulating the end effector causes motion throughout the entire chain.

There are two main forms of IK animation—following an object (which can be relative or absolute) and interactive animation.

The *follow object* method is what you use when you want your hierarchy to mimic the motion of another object in the scene. This method is actually the most flexible because you can quickly change the animation by choosing different follow objects or by changing the path of a single follow object and recalculating.

The *interactive* method is similar to modifying the hierarchy with the standard object commands in the Keyframer. The difference is that interactive mode in IK enables you to manipulate the entire chain by moving a child object. This method gives you much more freedom and artistic control when specifying the original motion, but it is more difficult to go back and change later.

Follow Object Relative

Click on the Follow Object button to display the Pick Follow Object dialog box, shown in figure 20.21. The end object of the current chain is pre-selected as the end effector, and will be forced to follow the motions of the object that you select from the dialog box.

Activating the "Follow object motion is relative:" check box causes the end effector to mimic the motion of the follow object without actually trying to point at or reach the follow object itself. This option is very useful for animating gestures and secondary motions.

The following exercise shows you how to use the follow object relative technique to simulate the recoil of the cannon model described earlier. This model is already linked and has joint parameters specified with End to Start precedence. It is ready to be animated.

A follow object named Recoil is provided as a follow object to simulate the back and forth motion of a recoil effect. The cannon does not need to point at the Recoil object, only mimic its back and forth motion, so Follow Object Relative will be used.

Figure 20.21
The Pick Follow
Object dialog box.

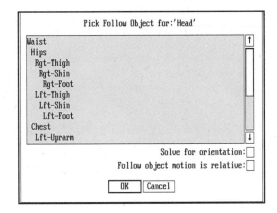

IK Cannon Recoil

*Start or Reset 3D Studio, then
load the model* RECOIL.3DS *from
the CD-ROM*

Loads the RECOIL.3DS model, as shown
in figure 20.22

Figure 20.22
The RECOIL.3DS
model from the
CD-ROM.

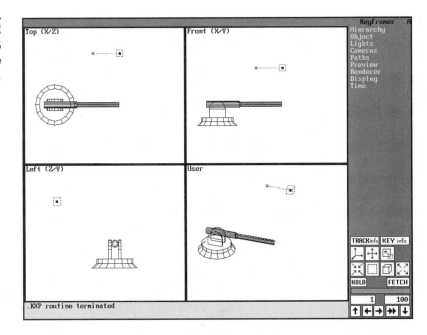

Choose Keyframer *from the* Program *pull-down menu, activate the* User *viewport, then click on the* Play *icon*	Plays the animation, showing the Recoil object moving back and forth while the cannon remains still
Press ⎡Esc⎤ *to return to the* Keyframer	
Choose IK *from the* Program *pull-down menu, then click on the* Pick Objects *button and select any part of the cannon*	Loads the cannon hierarchy into the IK Plug-In—a default chain from the Turret to the Barrel is already defined
Click on the Follow Object *button and select* Recoil *from the list of objects, then activate the* Follow object motion is relative *check box and click on* OK	Instructs 3D Studio to make the Barrel end effector mimic the motion of the recoil object
Click on OK *in the main IK dialog box*	Places the appropriate motion keys in the Keyframer
Click on the Play *icon*	Shows the cannon barrel moving similar to the Recoil object
Press ⎡Esc⎤ *to return to the* Keyframer	
Save the model to your working directory as RECOIL.3DS	

Follow Object Absolute

Use Follow Object Absolute when you need the end effector to point at or even touch the follow object. When using the absolute mode of follow object, 3D Studio attempts to make the pivot point of the end effector match the location of the pivot point of the follow object. The chain is still constrained by the settings of the joint parameters, so it may not be possible for the end effector to actually reach the follow object. In that case, 3D Studio places the end effector as close as possible to the follow object.

The following exercise uses Follow Object Absolute to make the cannon track a target around the scene. Since the Barrel object has already been animated by following the Recoil object, it cannot be used again for tracking. If you used Barrel as your end effector again, the new joint calculations would wipe out the recoil effect that you created earlier. A dummy object named Aim has been created and placed between the Barrel and the Breach objects in the hierarchy to serve as the aiming end effector.

IK Cannon Targeting

Continue with the RECOIL.3DS model that you saved in the previous exercise, or load the file TARGET.3DS *from the CD-ROM.*

Loads the cannon model with a recoil animation

Choose Keyframer *from the* Program *pull-down menu*

Ensures that you are in the Keyframer module

Choose Display/Unhide/By Name, *then select* Target *from the list*

Displays the Target dummy object at which you want the cannon to track and fire (see fig. 20.23)

Figure 20.23
The cannon model with the Target displayed.

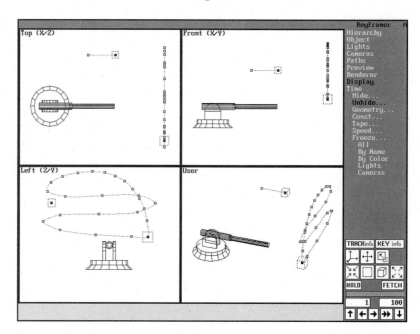

Choose IK *from the* Program *pull-down menu*

Displays the IK main dialog box

If necessary, click on the Pick Objects *button and select any part of the cannon*

If you are continuing from the previous exercise, the hierarchy is already loaded; otherwise, load the cannon hierarchy into the IK module

Click on the End *button under* Define Chain, *then select* Aim *from the list*

Redefines the IK chain to exclude the Barrel object; the Aim object is now the end effector

Click on the Follow Object *button and select* Target *from the list of objects, deactivate the* Follow object motion is relative *check box, then click on* OK	Instructs 3D Studio to make the Aim end effector precisely follow the Target object
Click on OK *in the main IK dialog box*	Places the appropriate motion keys in the Keyframer
Click on the Play *icon*	Shows the cannon tracking and firing at the target object
Press Esc *to return to the Keyframer*	

The keys to this exercise are excluding the Barrel object from the chain and having the Aim dummy object available to handle tracking of the follow object.

Dummy objects take on a new significance with IK. Many types of complex joint conditions and complex animation effects can be simulated through the use of dummy objects.

 Modeling complex joints with dummy objects often requires exactly matching pivot point locations between the dummy objects and other objects in your scene. This is a prefect task for custom scripts. See Chapter 22, "Keyframer Scripting," for information on creating scripts.

Recalculation

The New Features manual that ships with 3D Studio Release 4 demonstrates the use of the Recalculate button. In that tutorial, you set up a walking animation with IK, and then apply a new motion to the root object of the hierarchy (the Egret-Body object). Re-entering IK and clicking on the Recalculate button quickly fixed the walking animation to account for the changes in the Egret-Body.

While the Recalculate button is a great tool, you must be careful that you do not use it indiscriminately. For example, the cannon exercise that you just completed would be ruined if you clicked on the Recalculate button. This is because both of the end effector objects (Aim and Barrel) are in the same branch of the hierarchy. Recalculation is global and the keys of all end effector objects for all chains are adjusted. In the case of the cannon, the keys for the first end effector (Barrel) are wiped out when the keys for the second end effector (Aim) are recalculated.

The following general rules will help you to determine when Recalculate can be used:

✔ Recalculate only works with follow objects. If you have no follow objects assigned, Recalculate displays an error dialog box.

✔ Recalculate can be used when you have only one following end effector in any branch of the hierarchy. You are allowed to have more than one end effector in the same branch, but Recalculate will throw away all extra end effectors except the one closest to the root of the hierarchy.

✔ The follow relative or absolute setting is global and the current setting will be applied to all end effectors during a recalculation. You should not use Recalculate if you have mixed relative and absolute follow objects.

Interactive

The Interactive method of IK animation enables you to manually position your end effectors, while viewing the results of your changes in a real-time display. After loading your hierarchy and setting joint parameters, you can click on the Interactive button to display the hierarchy in the interactive dialog box. Figure 20.24 shows the interactive dialog box with a chain of beads loaded.

Figure 20.24

The interactive IK dialog box.

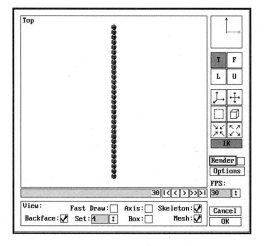

Details about the use of the interactive dialog box are presented in the New Features manual of 3D Studio Release 4. An important point to keep in mind is that you do not need to define a chain when using the interactive dialog box. When you select an object, a valid chain is automatically traced back to the root of the hierarchical tree and your selected object becomes the end effector.

You can move to different frames, define chains, and move end effectors at will until you have set up your desired animation. At any time, you can preview the animation by using the play-back and rendering controls on the right side of the dialog box.

Summary

This chapter demonstrated some of the many realistic and complex animations that are possible through the combination of hierarchical linking and inverse kinematics. Remember that inverse kinematics is just another tool in your animation kit. Try to resist the temptation to always use this new tool. Other linking and Keyframer techniques still have their uses and IK introduces a whole new set of restrictions and planning considerations. The information in this chapter will help you decide when and how to make use of IK.

Advanced Animation

Chapter Snapshot

This chapter delves more deeply into Keyframer topics to which you have already been introduced, and lifts the shroud of "Terra Incognita" from some of the other selections on the screen menu. The following is a list of topics that you have already seen, but can explore more fully in this chapter:

- ✔ Creating and using instances

- ✔ Working with duplicated and inherited links, and adjusting link information

- ✔ Morphing between dissimilar shapes and materials

- ✔ Creating paths in the 2D Shaper and 3D Lofter modules

- ✔ Manipulating and adjusting paths in the Keyframer

21
CHAPTER

Special Keyframer Techniques

The Keyframer has a variety of powerful tools, some of which seem too advanced for all but the most experienced users. In reality, many of the more advanced Keyframer tools are not that hard to grasp, and as you learn them, they become a valuable part of your arsenal of professional animation tools.

The following is a list of some of the topics explored in this chapter:

✔ Using Video Post as a tool for compositing your animations—building an animation up by layers can improve productivity and provide many new effects

✔ Using motion blur to simulate speed effects at the object level and within Video Post

✔ Using Snapshot to send copies of your model back to the 3D Editor

Understanding Advanced Morphing

This section examines some more morphing techniques that go beyond the simple bending and shape changing covered in Chapter 15, "Introduction to the Keyframer." The concepts in that chapter cover most of the important morphing issues, and this chapter just takes those same concepts a little bit further.

Morphing Materials

It used to be difficult to morph materials in 3D Studio. The introduction of 3D Studio Release 3 changed that, and now morphing materials is as simple as setting an option in a dialog box. After you assign a morph to an object using the Object/Morph/Assign command, you can use the Object/Morph/Options command. When you select a morph object using the Object/ Morph/Options command, the Morph Options dialog box appears (see fig. 21.1).

Figure 21.1
The Morph
Options
dialog box.

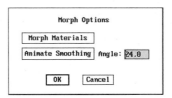

The Morph Options dialog box has buttons for two options. The first button (Morph Materials) tells 3D Studio whether to morph materials for the object—if you turn it on, an object not only changes its shape to match a morph target, but it also picks up the materials assignment of the morph target as well. You need to remember that you are still dealing with the original object, not one of the morph targets. The original object changes its shape and its material assignment to look like the target object, but it does not actually become the target object. Along with the restrictions described in the Reference Manual for morphed materials, it also is helpful to observe the following techniques:

✔ If Morph Materials is turned on, the materials assignments of all morph targets are used, even those with the default material. If many targets are used, they must all be assigned appropriate materials.

✔ Mapping coordinates are not morphed. If the materials used require mapping coordinates, they must work with the mapping coordinates applied to the original object.

✔ If any target uses a mapped material, you must apply mapping coordinates to the original object. You must apply the mapping coordinates even if the original object does not use a mapped material.

The second button (Animate Smoothing) enables 3D Studio to compensate for changing face angles in smoothed objects. 3D Studio can reapply smoothing groups to the morphing object on every frame of the animation, if you so desire. Animate Smoothing is useful for objects that morph from curved surfaces to flat-sided objects. If Animate Smoothing is not turned on, 3D Studio might smooth over the corners and edges of the object, which can produce strange results.

Complex Morph Editing

The main issue with morphing is that the technique is vertex-based. The single absolute requirement of a successful morph is that all objects involved have the same number of vertices. The best way to ensure that all morph targets have the same number of vertices is always to edit the original object. You can do this in many ways, such as the following:

✔ Loft different shapes with the same number of vertices along the same path, with Optimize turned off

✔ Loft the same shape along different paths that have the same number of vertices, again with Optimize turned off

✔ Copy objects in the 3D Editor and edit the copies

If you use the last option—editing copies of an object in the 3D Editor—you must decide whether to edit the object at the Object, Element, Face, or Vertex level. In general, because morphing is vertex-based, you get more predictable results by thinking about how your changes affect the object at the vertex level. The key is to understand how editing affects the transformation matrix.

The Transformation Matrix

The bounding box and transformation matrix have been discussed in Chapters 5, "Building Models in the 3D Editor," and 10, "Creating and Editing Faces and Vertices in the 3D Editor." This section takes a look at how the transformation matrix affects morphing. *Morphing* is a vertex-based technique. The transformation matrix comes into play because all the vertices in an object are located relative to the object's local axis origin, or the origin of the transformation matrix.

There are two things to consider about how 3D Studio handles the transformation matrix. The first is how the transformation matrix is affected by various modify commands. The second is how you manipulate the matrix.

Modify Commands and the Transformation Matrix

Some modify commands in the 3D Editor alter the position of the transformation matrix and others do not. If you are editing an object to use as a morph target, the location of its transformation matrix is critically important. Some commands in the Modify/Object branch recalculate and reposition the transformation matrix, but commands under Modify/Element, Face, and Vertex do not. A good example of this difference is to examine the effects of the 2D Scale command applied at the Object and Face levels. Figure 21.2 shows three cylinders and their respective transformation matrix origins. The first cylinder is the original object. The second cylinder is a copy of the original that was scaled using the Modify/Object/2D Scale command. The third cylinder also is a copy of the original, but it was scaled using Modify/Vertex/2D Scale. All three cylinders are valid morph targets for each other.

Figure 21.2
Three cylinders.

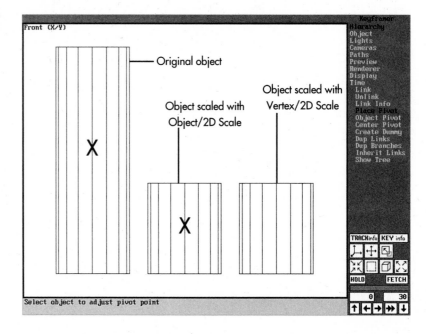

Notice the location of the transformation matrix origin for each cylinder. The original cylinder has its origin at its center. The second cylinder, scaled at the object level, has had its transformation matrix recalculated and the origin placed at the center of the scaled cylinder. The third cylinder, scaled at the vertex level, has not had its origin relocated—it remains at the same location as before the cylinder was scaled.

What does this have to do with morphing? When an object is morphed, the transformation matrix origin of the morph targets is aligned with the origin of the original object. The vertices of the original object then are moved to match up with the vertices of the target objects. The way that the vertices move depends on the way the origins of the targets match up with the original object. Figure 21.3 shows the result of using the cylinders from figure 21.2 as morph targets. The first cylinder is the original with no morphing applied. The second cylinder shows the result of morphing the original cylinder into the second. When the origin of the second cylinder was aligned with the first, it rose up into the air, causing both ends of the original cylinder to morph toward the middle. The third cylinder shows the result of morphing the original cylinder into the third. Because the third cylinder was scaled at the vertex level, its origin location did not change. When the origins are aligned, the bases of both the original cylinder and the morph target match up—now only the top of the cylinder moves as it morphs toward its base.

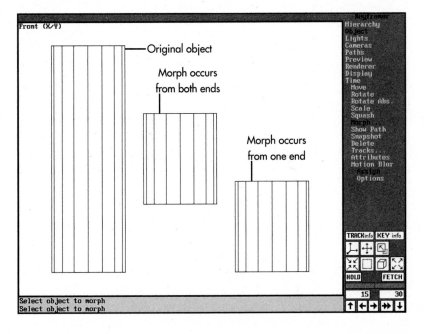

Figure 21.3
The cylinders after morph assignments.

Using Attach to Manipulate the Transformation Matrix

Another technique involves using the Create/Object/Attach command. If you attach one object to another, the attached object relinquishes its transformation matrix and uses the transformation matrix and origin of the base object. The order in which objects are attached becomes important for morphing because the second object selected provides the origin for the composite object. Figure 21.4 demonstrates the result of attaching a lofted object to a sphere. Part A of the figure shows the two objects before they are attached. The origin of the lofted object is centered with its bounding box and the origin of the sphere is centered on the sphere. Part B of the figure shows the result after attaching the lofted object to the sphere. The new composite object uses the same origin as the sphere.

Figure 21.4
A) The objects before attaching.
B) The objects after attaching.

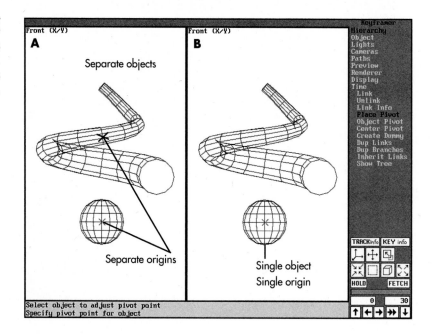

 Tip

Create/Object/Attach is a handy command for placing the transformation matrix origin wherever you want. Make a small sphere and place the center of the sphere wherever you want to put the origin of a complex object. Then use Create/Object/Attach and attach the complex object to the sphere. The new object now has its origin at the center of the sphere. You can then use Modify/Element/Delete to get rid of the sphere without altering the origin location.

In Chapter 15, "Introduction to the Keyframer," you followed an exercise where you morphed a sphere into a cube and back again. This was accomplished by editing the vertices on a copy of the sphere. What do you do if you want to morph between two extremely different objects—especially if the objects do not have the same number of vertices?

The solution involves sleight of hand. You first create morphs for both objects that turn them into some generic object; then you swap one object for the other using the hide keys in the Keyframer. The following exercise shows you how to morph between two files that ship with 3D Studio Release 3. You morph the Duck model into the Vase3 model by morphing both objects into a cube and swapping cubes in the middle of the animation.

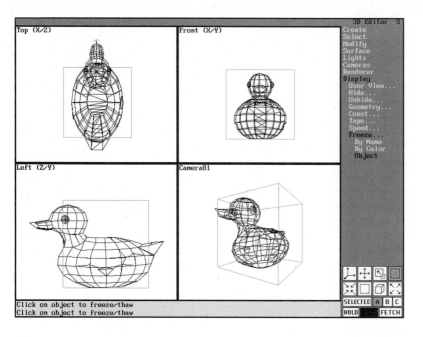

Figure 21.6
The Boundary cube and Duck01, ready for editing.

Selection box

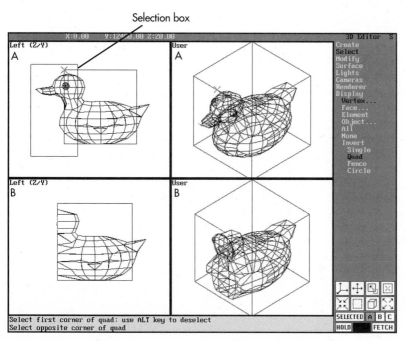

Figure 21.7
A) Selecting the vertices to scale. B) Duck01 after scaling.

continues

continued

Repeat the previous steps for all sides of the cube

Scales out the faces of Duck01 until it starts to approximate a cube (see fig. 21.8)

Figure 21.8
Duck01 with all sides scaled.

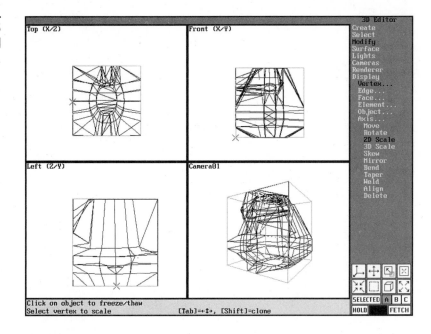

As you can see from figure 21.8, much vertex editing remains to be done before Duck01 fills out the volume of the boundary cube. After you complete the vertex editing for Duck01, you must do the same for Vase01. If you have time, this is good practice for vertex editing and the manipulation of the global axis. If you want to proceed to the morphing part of this exercise, the following steps instruct you to merge the file TARGETS.3DS into your current file. This file has morph targets for the Duck and the Vase, as shown in figure 21.9.

Choose Merge *from the* File *pull-down menu and make sure that all the buttons except* Mesh Objects *are off; select the file* TARGETS.3DS, *choose all the objects for merging, and then click on the* Delete Old *button in the dialog box that asks you whether to delete the old Duck01 and Vase01*

Merges in the new morph targets for the Duck and Vase

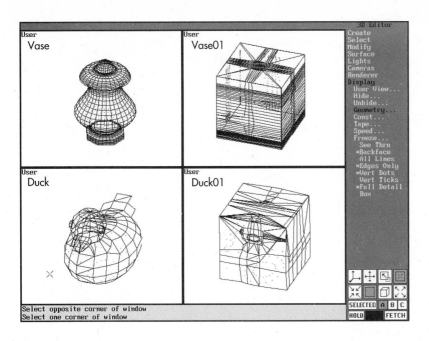

Figure 21.9
The original objects and their morph targets.

Choose Surface/Material/Choose *and choose* Yellow Plastic *as the current material, then choose* Surface/Material/Assign/Object *and assign* Yellow Plastic *to both Duck01 and Vase01*	Assigns Yellow Plastic to both morph targets, enabling you to morph materials between the Duck and the Vase
Choose Display/Unhide/All, *then choose* Display/Hide/By Name *and select* Boundary	Displays all the objects except Boundary
Go to the Keyframer and choose Display/Hide/By Name *and select everything except the Duck and Vase01*	Hides all unnecessary objects
Go to frame 15 and choose Object/Morph/Assign *and select the Duck, then choose* Duck01 *as the morph target*	Causes the Duck to morph into the cube shape of Duck01 by frame 15

continues

continued

The Morph/Assign *command is still active, so select* Vase01 *and choose* Vase01 *as the morph target*	Forces Vase01 to hold its shape until frame 15
Choose Object/Move *and select* Vase01, *then move it so that it matches up with the cube-shaped Duck01*	Positions Vase01 to match
Go to frame 30 and choose Object/Morph/Assign *and select* Vase01, *then choose* Vase *as the morph target*	Causes Vase01 to change to the shape of Vase by frame 30
Choose Object/Morph/Options *and select* Vase01, *then turn on the* Morph Materials *button—do the same for Duck*	Causes the materials to morph, as well as the shape
Click on Track Info *and select the* Duck, *then click on the* Add *button, add a key in the Hide track at frame 15, then click on* OK	Causes the Duck to disappear at frame 15 when rendered
Click on Track Info *again and select* Vase01, *then Move the Position key at frame 15 to frame 0, and Add Hide keys at frames 0 and 15, then click on* OK	Causes the position adjust that you made at frame 15 to occur at frame 0, transmits back to the geometry in the 3D Editor, and also causes Vase01 to be hidden from frames 0 through 14 and suddenly appear on frame 15
Choose Preview/Make *and click in the* Camera *viewport, then click on* Render	Creates and then plays a preview of the morphing animation—figure 21.10 shows some of the intermediate morphs for the two objects

If you want, you can now render the final animation. Other options that you might want to try include going to the 3D Editor and scaling Duck01 and Vase01 to 50 percent, and adjusting the keys in the 3D Editor to provide pauses on the Duck and the Vase before and after the morph transitions. Scaling the morph targets to 50 percent sometimes produces a more pleasing effect because the objects seem to shrink into and grow out of the intermediate cube object.

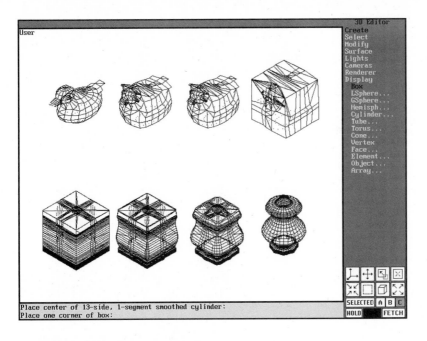

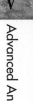

Figure 21.10
Some intermediate morph steps between the Duck and the Vase.

IPAS Morph Objects

Many IPAS procedural modeling programs are available, and nearly all are designed to create morph objects. Two such routines that ship with 3D Studio are RIPPLE and WAVE, which produce morph targets of objects that have concentric ripples or linear waves passing through them.

Other IPAS routines are available that melt and twist objects and seem to grow plants. Of these routines, one simulates the process you went through in the preceding exercise: SPHERIFY. The SPHERIFY routine takes any object and creates intermediate morph targets that turn it into a sphere. You could then use the same Hide technique you used in the preceding exercise to swap the first sphere for another that morphed back into a different object.

Exploring Snapshot Modeling

The Object/Snapshot command in the Keyframer enables you to capture geometry at any frame in the animation and copy it back into the 3D Editor. This capability is of great significance when you think about how you might use it to position objects and capture intermediate morph objects.

Many of the illustrations in this book, such as figure 21.10, were created by using Snapshot. The Snapshot command is an excellent way to capture multiple copies of an object as it goes through a transformation.

Using Snapshot with Modified Objects

Using the Snapshot command is handy for generating multiple copies of an object at different points in your animation. Probably the best example of this technique is the Robot Arm exercise in the 3D Studio Tutorials Manual. Combining Snapshot with Hide keys is a powerful technique for simulating objects that other objects in the scene pick up and put down.

You also can use Snapshot to model geometry that repeats itself along a path. Imagine modeling a spiral staircase. Creating all the treads and properly positioning them is quite tedious in the 3D Editor. Figure 21.11 shows a mesh model in the 3D Editor of a center pole and a single tread for a spiral staircase. The following steps convert that model into a full spiral staircase. This particular stair has 13 treads, 14 risers, rotates 360 degrees, and rises 8'10" to the floor above.

Figure 21.11

Beginning geometry for a spiral stair.

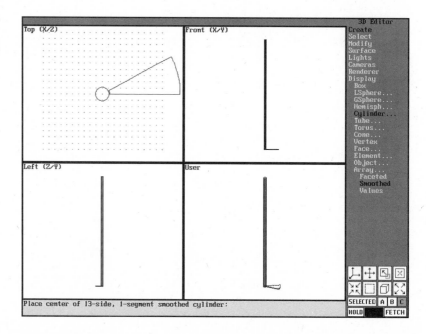

1. In the Keyframer, set the total frames to 12. This actually gives you 13 frames as 0 through 12 equals 13 (one frame for each tread).

2. On frame 12, raise the tread to the proper height and rotate it 360 degrees about the Z axis. This places a tread at its proper place on each frame, but you want all the treads in the 3D Editor.

3. Use Object/Snapshot and select the tread. Turn on the buttons in the Snapshot dialog box for Range from 0 to 12, and 13 copies (see fig. 21.12).

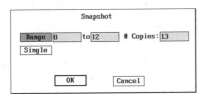

Figure 21.12
The Snapshot dialog box.

After the command is done, you have 13 stair treads in the 3D Editor, all correctly arranged around the center pole. Figure 21.13 shows the completed stair. The Snapshot command can be used as a variation of the Array command in the 3D Editor, effectively converting the Keyframer into a modeling tool.

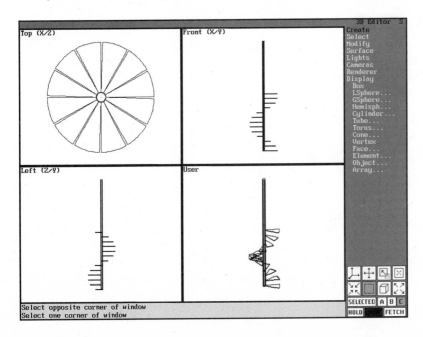

Figure 21.13
The completed spiral stair.

V

Advanced Animation

Using Snapshot with Hierarchical Links

Another use for the Snapshot command is to copy hierarchically linked objects after they are positioned in the Keyframer. Imagine using the 3D Editor to place a model like 50PMAN.3DS or MANEQUIN.3DS in a seated position. But, once again, what is tedious and difficult in the 3D Editor is quite simple in the Keyframer if you use hierarchical linkage.

The Snapshot command enables you to send a copy of the positioned figure back to the 3D Editor. When you make a snapshot of a linked object, the Subtree button appears in the Snapshot dialog box. Figure 21.14 shows the Snapshot dialog box with the Subtree button highlighted. When the Subtree button is on, Snapshot makes a copy of the object and all objects linked below it. The only drawback is that the copied figure loses its linking in the process.

Figure 21.14
The Subtree button in the Snapshot dialog box.

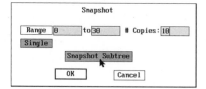

Using Snapshot with Morphs

A last way to use Snapshot is to capture intermediate morph objects. You often need to provide multiple morph targets for the animation to look right. It is no trouble to model both the start and finished shape of the morph, but what about the shapes in between? This is where Snapshot modeling can be useful.

The following is an example of how you might use Snapshot to copy an intermediate morph object back to the 3D Editor:

1. Set up the morph with only the start and finish morph targets specified.

2. Drag the Frame Slider back and forth, stopping frequently to examine the morphed object on various frames.

3. Determine at which frames you want to create intermediate morph targets, and Snapshot the object on those frames.

You now have copies of 3D Studio's version of the intermediate morph objects in the 3D Editor. Chances are that these objects are close, but not quite correct for the effect you want. You can edit these objects or just use them as guides for creating new objects.

Examining Motion Blur

Motion blur is an effect that exists in two variations in 3D Studio. The first version is Object Motion Blur in the Keyframer, which enables you to specify a motion blurring effect for individual objects. The second version is Scene Motion Blur in Video Post, which applies the effect to the entire scene. The technique that you use, or how you combine both techniques, depends on the effect that you are trying to achieve.

The 3D Studio Reference Manual describes Object Motion Blur as a form of anti-aliasing over time and Scene Motion Blur as an applied special effect. The manual goes on to state that you get the best results if you combine Object Motion Blur and Scene Motion Blur. This section describes both types of motion blur and how they work together. The discussion of Scene Motion Blur in Video Post address Video Post issues only to the extent necessary for the motion blur explanations. You should check the section, "What is Video Post," later in this chapter for details on the use of Video Post.

Concepts

Most people think of motion blur in conjunction with "bad" or special effects photography. If an object is moving fast enough when a picture is taken, it appears blurred on the film. What is recorded on the film is the result of the object being in one position when the camera shutter opens and another position when the camera shutter closes. The blur effect is the result of an infinite number of copies of the object, each exposed for an infinitely small fraction of the total exposure time. The copies are exposed as the object moves from one position at the start of the exposure to a second position by the end of the exposure.

3D Studio is not an analog device, so it has a small problem dealing with infinity. The solution is to divide time into discrete segments and render one motion blur copy for each specified time segment. You control the size of the time segments and the number of motion blur copies created through various dialog settings in 3D Studio.

The technique that 3D Studio employs is mathematically and technically correct, but unfortunately is visually wrong. The top blurred ball in figure 21.15 shows the default way that 3D Studio renders motion blur. This is technically correct, but it doesn't look right. The multiple copies used to create the blur effect cause the appearance of greater density at the middle of the blur than at the ends. Most observers would consider this to be an image of something vibrating rapidly rather than moving forward. Even if this were part of an animation, the error would be detected subconsciously and the animation would seem a "little off." Because of the way you perceive moving objects, you expect the leading edges of the object to be sharply focused while only the trailing edges blur back along the line of motion. That is why you draw "speed lines" behind objects in motion and why traditional animators are taught to draw motion blur with only the trailing edges blurred. The bottom ball in figure 21.15 shows the result of simulating this technique in 3D Studio.

Figure 21.15
Two moving balls rendered with motion blur effects.

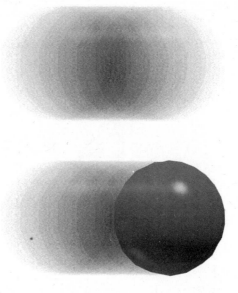

Tip

Creating the effect shown for the bottom ball in figure 21.15 requires that you composite a nonblurred version of the object behind the blurred object. Compositing images is done in Video Post and is described later in this chapter. The trick involved here is to get the nonblurred object to lead the blurred object. The amount of lead required depends on the type of motion blur and the settings for each type.

Object Motion Blur

To apply Object Motion Blur to individual objects, use the Object/Motion Blur command in the Keyframer (see fig. 21.16). This command specifies that 3D Studio render multiple copies of an object on each frame and dither the copies. You must apply Object Motion Blur to each object that you want blurred, and the object must move for the command to have any effect. Apparent movement caused by camera motion is not taken into account by Object Motion Blur.

Figure 21.16
The Motion Blur dialog box.

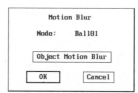

The settings that control the effect of Object Motion Blur are found in the Renderer/Setup/ Options dialog box (see fig 21.17): Number, Samples, and Duration.

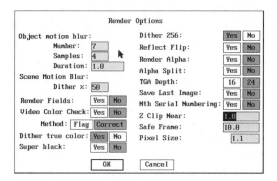

Figure 21.17
The Object Motion Blur settings in the Render Options dialog box.

Number

The value in the Number field represents the number of copies to be rendered for each frame. The number that you enter in this field is critical for a successful effect. If the number is too small, the copies are completely separate—this is an effect called *strobing*. If the number is too large, the copies pile up on top of each other, and the result looks more like a solid smudge than a motion blur. Also, rendering motion blur copies takes time. Rendering more copies than you need can waste a considerable amount of time for a long animation.

3D Studio imposes a maximum value of eight copies. You can calculate a good starting number by using the following formula:

$$Number > (distance \div size) \div overlap$$

✔ *distance* is the distance the object travels over the Duration setting. In general, if duration is set to 1.0, distance equals the distance traveled over one frame. If duration is set to 0.5, distance equals the distance traveled over half a frame.

✔ *size* is the length of the object along the line of motion. You can usually use the average of width×height×depth.

✔ *overlap* is a value between 0 and 1 that controls how much the copies overlap each other. The smaller the overlap value, the more the copies overlap one another. The overlap value should usually be less than 0.5; anything greater causes the objects to appear to separate.

Figure 21.18 shows a motion-blurred ball exhibiting strobing because of too small a value in the Number field.

Figure 21.18
A motion-blurred ball exhibiting strobing.

Samples

Samples controls the amount of dithering that occurs between the copies. The lower the value, the more dither. The lowest valid value of 1 provides maximum dithering. The highest valid value is equal to the Number value and produces copies that appear semitransparent.

Duration

Duration controls the amount of motion applied to the rendering on each frame. The 3D Studio Reference Manual describes this as similar to the amount of time that the shutter on the camera is open. Refer back to the Number section for the description of calculating distance traveled under the Number field. The number of copies specified by the Number field is spread out over the distance covered in the number of frames specified in the Duration field. The Duration value also can be less than one, which means that the copies are compressed into a distance less than what is covered by one frame.

An interesting point about Object Motion Blur concerns where the copies are placed. The copies are spread out over the distance specified by the Duration value, and then the copies are centered on the actual position of the object on that frame. This means that when you look at a blurred image in 3D Studio that was produced with Object Motion Blur, the true position of the object is in the center of the blur effect. Figure 21.19 shows a nonblurred ball composited over its motion-blurred image.

Figure 21.19
A nonblurred ball composited over its motion-blurred image.

Scene Motion Blur

Scene Motion Blur applies an effect similar to Object Motion Blur, except that it is applied to all objects that move between frames and it considers camera motion. Object Motion Blur and Scene Motion Blur can be applied at the same time. This is suggested in the Reference Manual for producing the best-looking motion blur effects.

Scene Motion Blur Settings

You have to apply Scene Motion Blur in Video Post. You also have only two entries by which to control it—one entry in Video Post and one entry in the Render Options dialog box. Figure 21.20 shows the Video Post field for motion blur: a single button that sets whether Scene Motion Blur is on or off and a field that specifies the number of copies to render. The number of copies value works exactly the same for Scene Motion Blur as it does for Object Motion Blur, with the default for Duration always set at 1.0.

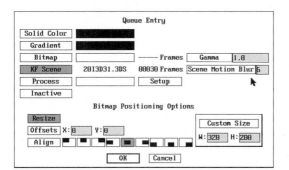

Figure 21.20
The entry in Video Post for Scene Motion Blur.

The other field, called Scene Motion Blur Dither %, is found in the Render Options dialog box, and it sets the percentage of dither applied to the copies created by Scene Motion Blur. A value of 0 produces semitransparent copies, while a value of 100 fully dithers the copies.

Scene Motion Blur Copies

Where are the copies placed? Scene Motion Blur uses a different technique for placing its copies than Object Motion Blur. Scene Motion Blur always uses a Duration of 1.0. The copies are spread out over the distance traveled in a single frame and placed starting at the current position of the object and extending forward to the position of the object on the next frame. In other words, the true position of the object is at the trailing edge of the blur effect, and the blur itself extends forward in time to the next frame. Figure 21.21 shows a nonblurred ball composited over its Scene Motion Blurred image.

Figure 21.21
A nonblurred ball composited over an image blurred using Scene Motion Blur.

You can have Scene Motion Blur Duration of less than 1.0 by using the Nth frame option when you render. Scaling an animation to use 60 frames, and then rendering with Scene Motion Blur and Nth frame set at 2, is similar to rendering the same animation at 30 frames and using Object Motion Blur with a Duration of 0.5.

Combining Object and Scene Motion Blur

You get the best results if you combine Object Motion Blur with Scene Motion Blur. You use Scene Motion Blur to provide the general blur effect and Object Motion Blur to provide extra dithering between the Scene Motion Blur copies.

Something to keep in mind when you combine Object Motion Blur and Scene Motion Blur is the effect that it has on the Duration value. When you combine Object Motion Blur with Scene Motion Blur, the Duration value is applied to the distance between Scene Motion Blur copies rather than the distance between frames, so the Number value for Object Motion Blur should be low and the Duration value usually 1.0 or less.

Using Paths

The Paths branch in the Keyframer has two main functions. One is to import paths from sources outside of the Keyframer. The other is to manipulate the paths of objects graphically. Manipulating paths with commands in the Paths branches duplicates most of the commands found in the Track Info and Key Info dialog boxes, but rather than working with fields and sliders, you can manipulate the path as a graphical object.

The commands for editing paths under the Paths branch only affect keys for the position track. You cannot use these commands to affect keys for other tracks.

Much of the information relevant to importing paths from other sources was presented in Chapter 18, "Animating Lights and Cameras," which covers making cameras and lights follow paths—the same issues apply to making objects follow paths. This section reviews the path editing commands available in the Paths branch and concludes with an exercise for making multiple objects follow the same path in sequence.

Showing Paths

The Paths/Show-Hide command prompts you to select an object. Once selected, the object's path appears as a spline curve (see fig 21.22). The large vertices on the path represent key frames, and the small dots between each key represent intermediate frames.

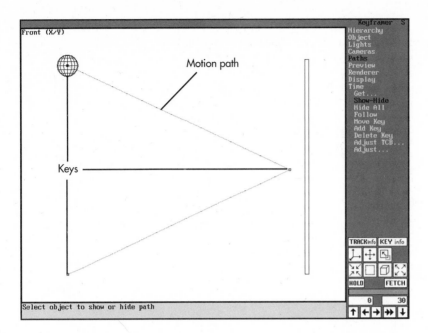

Figure 21.22
Displaying an object's path in the Keyframer.

After you display one or more paths, you can hide them all by choosing Paths/Hide All. You can hide the path of a single object by choosing Paths/Show-Hide and selecting an object with its path already displayed.

Editing Paths

The commands to edit the visible paths fall under two general categories. The first category represents those commands that affect the placement of a key. The commands in the first category are the following:

✔ **Move Key.** Enables you to position a key anywhere in space, just like entering new values in the Position Axis fields of the Key Info dialog box. The command does not alter the frame on which the key occurs.

✔ **Add Key.** Inserts a new key into the Position Track at the frame selected on the path. You must select one of the intermediate frame dots on the displayed paths. The added key does not necessarily occur on the current frame. This is like using Add in the Track Info dialog box.

✔ **Delete Key.** Removes the selected key from the path. The only key removed is the key in the Position Track. Keys in other tracks at the frame are not affected. This is like using Delete in Track Info for the Position Track only.

The second category represents commands that adjust the values of a key as they are presented in the Key Info dialog box. These are the commands found under Paths/Adjust and Paths/Adjust TCB. The exception is the Paths/Adjust/Time command, which enables you to move the key to any frame between the keys that come before and after the selected key. The Paths/Adjust/Time command is similar to Move in the Track Info dialog box.

Using Paths/Follow

The Paths/Follow command was presented in Chapter 18. The main difference between using Follow with a camera and using it with an object concerns the setting for Bank. Unlike cameras, many objects bank as they corner. Selecting Bank Yes and specifying a maximum bank angle helps you simulate that effect.

Be aware, however, that banking is not precise and requires manual adjustment to attain a high degree of accuracy. This is most evident if you examine banking on a path that has a combination of very tight curves and wide sweeping curves. An object always reaches the maximum bank angle quickly and holds that angle through most of the curve, for all the curves on the path. In the real world, an object reaches the maximum bank angle only on the tightest curves and banks, much less on the wide sweeping curves. Bank is a good shortcut, but you must not take it for granted.

A common animation problem involves how to model a series of objects that must accurately follow each other around a path. Examples of this situation are a train engine with its cars, links in a bicycle chain, or objects on a conveyor belt. You quickly discover that hierarchical linking does not suffice. As soon as the parent object heads into a curve, all the children turn too, appearing to jump off the path. Even releasing rotation in Link Info does not help because the positions of the children still wander off the path.

The solution is to have each object follow the path individually. The trick lies in properly designing the path for the objects that will follow it. The important points are as follows:

✔ All the objects must be of the same size and evenly spaced.

✔ The length of the path must be evenly divided by the length of one object, plus the space between it and the next object. For example—if a single object is 25 units long with a spacing of 5 units between objects, the path must be long enough to divide by 30 with no remainder. Paths of 600, 990, and 1500 units would be valid; a path of 1250 units would not.

✔ The path must be at least as long as all the objects combined.

✔ The number of frames in the original animation is equal to the path length divided by the object plus spacing length.

The following exercise begins with a simplified model of a train that is 10 cars long. Each car is 25 units long with a 5 unit spacing, making a total car length of 30 units. You create a path for the train to follow and animate the cars to properly travel the path.

New Riders Publishing
INSIDE SERIES

Using Paths in the Keyframer: A Train on a Track

Start or reset 3D Studio and load the file TRAIN.3DS

Loads the train model into the 3D Editor; the objects are named Engine, and Car01 through Car09

Go to the Lofter and create a path in the Top *viewport that is 4500 units long*

Creates a path for the train to follow; 4500 units divides evenly by a total car length of 30 units (see fig. 21.23)

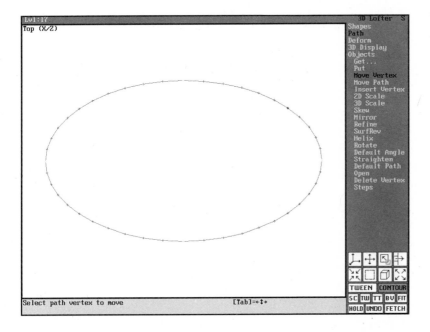

Figure 21.23
The path in the Lofter.

The advantage to using the Lofter is that it always reports the total length of the path. Another option would be to create the path in AutoCAD, where you can easily determine the total length of a polyline. The following tips are meant to help you create a successful path:

✔ Use as few vertices as possible. Using too many vertices makes it difficult for 3D Studio to evenly space the frames.

✔ Space the vertices as evenly as possible.

✔ Locate the first vertex of the path near a flat or shallow curved section. This makes it easier to match up the rotation angle of the objects with the path.

If you are in a hurry, the path shown in figure 21.23 is provided as the file TRACK.LFT. You can load that file into the Lofter to proceed with the next steps.

continues

continued

Go to the Keyframer and set the total number of frames to 150	Sets the required number of frames, path length ÷ car length = frames
Choose Paths/Get/Lofter *and select the* Engine; *the buttons in the dialog box should read as follows:*	
Relocate to start: Yes	
Reverse Direction: No	
Constant Speed: Yes, *then click on* OK	Relocates the Engine to the start of the path and adjusts the keys for constant speed

If you create your own path rather than use TRACK.LFT, you might need to address one or both of the following conditions:

✔   Drag the Frame Slider back and forth. If your train runs backward, choose Paths/Get/Lofter again and turn on the Reverse Direction button.

✔   If the orientation of the Engine is not parallel with the path, use Object/ Rotate to align it with the path before using Paths/Follow in the next step.

Choose Paths/Show-Hide *and select the* Engine, *then choose* Paths/Follow *and select the* Engine *again, set Banking to off, then click on* OK	Causes the Engine to follow the path, properly turning around corners (see fig. 21.24)
Choose Object/Tracks/Copy *and select the* Engine, *press* ⒣ *and select all the cars in the list, then set the Tracks dialog box to copy the Position and Rotation keys with the* Absolute *button on and click on* OK	Copies the Position and Rotation keys of the Engine to all the cars; turning on the Absolute button causes all the cars to stack up in the same spot as the Engine

Right now you have a horrible train wreck, but you are about to fix it. Here is where the importance of setting the number of frames properly is evident. Because the number of frames is equal to the path length divided by the car length, each frame advances the objects one car length down the path. Straightening out the train is now simply a matter of sliding keys.

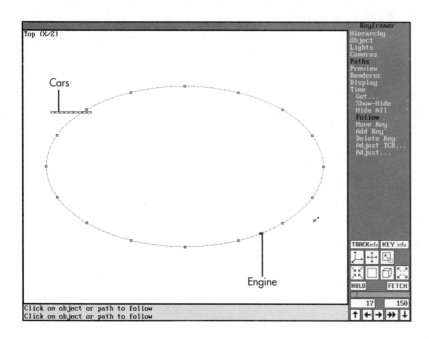

Figure 21.24
The Engine
following the path
before the Copy
Tracks command.

V

Advanced Animation

Choose Track Info *and select* Car01, *then click on* Slide, *select the* All Tracks *key at frame 0, and slide forward one frame*	Slides the keys for Car01 forward one frame; because Loop was turned on automatically when the closed path was imported, the car slides backward to line up behind the engine
Repeat the preceding step for all the other cars, sliding their keys one frame beyond the previous car— Car02 slides 2 frames, Car03 slides 3 frames, and so on	Positions all the cars one behind the other
Drag the Frame Slider back and forth	Moves the cars around the path—the motion looks just like a train (see fig. 21.25)

If you watch the train closely, you can still see some discrepancies in the motion. Occasionally, the cars crowd together or spread out a little. If you followed the general tips on path creation earlier in this exercise, your discrepancies should be minor.

Figure 21.25
The train running
around its track.

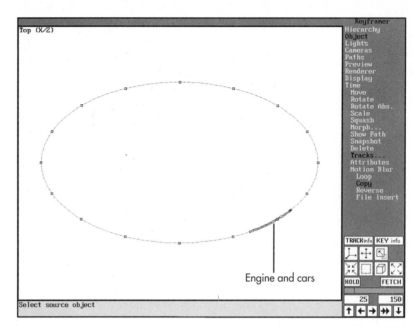

Engine and cars

Understanding Video Post

Video Post is derived from the term *post-production*, the final stage of film-making. Post-production occurs after the shooting of the film and the actual production work is complete. In this final stage, each of the elements are edited into a finished form. An editor, along with the director, decides how, when, and where transitions take place. Special effects, if any, are often inserted at this point. Usually, the transition is a *cut*, simply switching to the new scene on the very next frame without any effect. In some situations, however, a more dramatic transition is called for, such as slowly fading in one image while fading out another, or revealing an image with a wipe from left to right across the screen. In the past, these transitions, along with special effects, were possible only in a post-production facility that had a professional editor and paint-box artist. Video Post enables you to be the director, editor, and artist, and has a variety of effects and transitions from which to choose.

Think of the Video Post dialog box, as shown in figure 21.26, as a box of glass panes (see fig. 21.27). Each pane represents a different entry in the queue and affects the visibility, or look, of all the panes behind it. If you were to place an opaque pane in the third slot, for example, you couldn't see the first and second panes. Therefore, the order in which you place the effects in the queue is very important. The queue consists of the three columns on the left side of the dialog box. The grid on the right is a timeline. You can turn the effects on and off at specific frames in your animation by using the timeline.

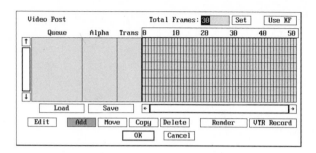

Figure 21.26
The Video Post
dialog box.

Figure 21.27
Video Post entries
are like panes
of glass.

The Add button at the bottom of the dialog box places a new entry in the queue list. The new entry defaults to KF Scene, which is the currently loaded 3DS file. To change to another effect, click on the Edit button, and then click on the entry you want to change. The Queue Entry dialog box appears, as shown in figure 21.28. Here you choose the type of effect from one of the six radio buttons in the top left corner of the dialog box. The six options are described later.

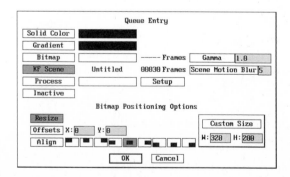

Figure 21.28
The Queue Entry
dialog box.

When Video Post is active, the Set Background settings in the Editor and Keyframer have no effect on the scene. If you want to set the background to a specific bitmap, color, or gradient, you have to use Video Post. Typically, you place your background choice in the first (top) position in the queue, and layer your other effects over it.

You create Solid Color by clicking to the right of the Solid Color button. In the dialog box that appears, you can select the RGB values from slider bars to create a solid color.

Gradient works much like solid color, except that you have three colors to set for a gradient effect. A simple way to get a two-color ramp from dark at the top to light at the bottom is to leave the top color box set to black, set the middle color box to white, and then click in the Gradient preview box to move the arrow all the way to the bottom (see fig. 21.29). The third color box is not used in this example.

Figure 21.29

Creating a two-color gradation in the Define Gradient Colors dialog box.

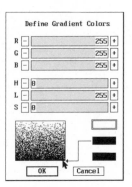

A bitmap can be any image file supported by 3D Studio, including flic files, IFL files, sequentially numbered bitmap files, and any file format supported by installed BXP IPAS processes. All files must reside in a directory in your map path settings. To use a series of numbered image files, enter the first few letters of the name of the file series, followed by an asterisk. If you use a numbered file series, flic file, or IFL, the number of frames in the animation appears in the Queue Entry dialog box.

The number of frames in an animation listed in the queue does not appear immediately. When you click on OK, the program checks to see whether the file is in a valid map path. If so, the length of the animation is represented by a black line in the timeline (under the red line), and the number of frames is shown in the Queue Entry dialog box the next time you access it.

Leave Gamma off unless you want to set a specific gamma value for the bitmap image. By leaving the button turned off, the gamma value for the image is determined by one of two factors, as follows:

✔ **The gamma values contained in the image.** You typically find gamma values only in TGA files.

✔ **The Input File Gamma settings in the 3DS.SET file.** You also adjust these settings in the Gamma Control dialog box. If no gamma values are found in the image file, the program uses the global settings, provided Gamma Correction is on in the global Gamma Control dialog box.

Bitmaps also are affected by the Bitmap Positioning options at the bottom of the Queue Entry dialog box: Resize, Offsets, and Align. Resize scales the image to fit the current output device. Offsets positions the upper left corner of the image at a specified distance from the upper left corner of the screen. Align aligns the image to the screen according to the icon selected.

If you render an animation to disk with Render Fields set to Yes, it might not have a correct field order when you display it on some frame buffer devices. This can cause the fields to be laid to tape in the wrong order, resulting in objects that appear to shake as they move. Usually this occurs when animations are rendered to disk on one system, and then brought to a service bureau to be transferred to tape on another. If you notice this problem with your field-rendered animation, you can use the Offsets option in the Queue Entry dialog box in Video Post as compensation. Simply create a Bitmap Video Post entry of the image files you are transferring to tape. Select Offsets in the Queue Entry dialog box, and enter 0 and 1 in the X and Y offset fields respectively. This has the effect of switching the field order of the rendered files by shifting the image down one pixel row, the equivalent of one field. You can then use VTR Record in Video Post to record the images to tape.

KF Scene is the active viewport of the currently loaded 3DS file. You can only use the 3DS file that is active. If you want to use different 3DS files in the same Video Post queue, you can render one 3DS file to disk, and then use Bitmap to composite the rendered files in Video Post. If no KF Scene entry is listed in the Queue, the current scene is ignored by Video Post.

You can use KF Scene more than once in the Queue to generate special effects, such as staggered motion. You could animate an ant walking across the screen, for example, and then use Video Post and add several KF Scene entries to the queue. You then could stagger the point at which each KF Scene begins by using the timeline on the right side of the Video Post dialog box (discussed later). The result is a parade of ants marching across the screen.

The "I" in IPAS stands for IXP or Image External Process. IXPs are used in Video Post to produce specialized photographic effects, such as lens flares, motion blur, posterization (reducing the number of colors in an image), glows, and other special effects. For IXPs, Video Post renders all the effects to a temporary image file, and then calls the IPAS program, enabling it to process each pixel in the temporary image according to the parameters you set.

You can also use your own EXE or BAT files in Video Post. Typically, this is how you rotoscope in 3D Studio. Put simply, *rotoscoping* is grabbing a frame of video from a source, such as video tape, manipulating it, and placing it back onto tape, usually not in the same place from which it is grabbed. To rotoscope in Video Post, you need hardware capable of digitizing video from an external source, such as a TARGA or ATVista frame buffer board. You also need frame-accurate control over your video source. Usually this means a Diaquest VTR controller or similar device. Finally, you need a program that can save the captured image to disk and increment the frame number of the source VTR. This type of software usually is supplied with your VTR controller; check with your manufacturer to find out what's available. A typical Video Post rotoscoping setup might be the following:

1. First Entry: Call the external VTR software to digitize a frame of video, save it to disk (for example, GRAB0000.TGA), and increment the in-point of the source VTR.

2. Second Entry: KF Scene that uses the file GRAB0000.TGA as a texture map somewhere in the scene.

3. Record the image to a blank location on the source tape.

4. Repeat the process.

GRAB0000.TGA is written over with each successive grab from the source VTR. In addition, GRAB0000.TGA must be saved to a directory in your map path.

To get a strong motion trail effect, use a very fast moving object and two KF Scene entries in Video Post. Set the Total Frames option at the top of the Video Post dialog box to 1 frame higher than the total number of frames in the scene. Turn on Scene Motion Blur in the first entry, and shift the start and end points of the entry to the right square in the timeline. To do this, ⟨Shift⟩+click on the dot at the left end of the line, then move it one frame to the right. Because Motion Blur receives its data from subsequent, rather than previous, frames, this delay in the first entry's start time allows the second entry to render a solid object at the apparent head of the motion trail. By leaving Motion Blur turned off in the second KF Scene entry, the final image is a solid object with a motion blur trailing behind it, as in figure 21.30.

Figure 21.30
A solid object with motion blur.

True-color image files, such as TGA files, come in a variety of bit depths, such as 8, 16, 24, and 32 bits per pixel. In a 32-bit true-color file, each pixel on the screen has four channels that describe it. You probably already know about three of the channels—Red, Green, and Blue. The fourth, Alpha, is something of a mystery to many people. In a 24-bit file, the Red, Green, and Blue channels each use 8 bits of memory to describe the color of every pixel in the image (3×8=24 bits per pixel). A pure green pixel, for example, has RGB values of 0,255,0 because 8 bits represent the numbers 0 to 255 in binary.

Alpha, in its simplest form, can be thought of as just another channel. It represents the level of transparency, using another 8 bits of memory, for every pixel in the image. Suppose that you render a flat white circle over a black background using a material on the circle that is 50-percent transparent. When the Renderer encounters a pixel that falls inside the circle, it writes the values 255,255,255,128 to a 32-bit image file for that pixel. These values tell the program to display the pixel as a mixture of full intensity red, full intensity green, and full intensity blue (white), and to allow any image beneath that pixel to be 50-percent visible (that is, the black background showing through the white circle, producing gray). The benefit of all this is that you can now composite the 50-percent transparent circle over any image in Video Post, such as a cloud-filled sky, and you see the clouds through the circle.

To get 3D Studio to create 32-bit RGBA images, you must have Render-Alpha turned on, Alpha-Split turned off, and TGA-Depth set to 24 in the Render Options dialog box.

Alpha entries enable you to specify how to composite the current over previous entries in the queue. If you recall the panes of glass, you can think of alpha as the opacity of the images on the glass. Some images are totally opaque, others are translucent, but clouded, and yet others are totally transparent.

If you click in the Alpha column, the Alpha dialog box appears (see fig. 21.31). Here you specify how the image or effect is to be composited with the others in the queue. Not all images have alpha information—only 32-bit true-color files have this capability. For that reason, you are given a variety of methods to create alpha information for your Video Post effects.

Queue Alpha Channel uses the alpha information contained in the bitmap image. If no alpha information is found in the image, then a pseudo-Alpha channel is created, using the RGB values of the image. This is also how Queue RGB obtains its transparency information when the Intensity option is active. Darker colors (lower values) are given higher levels of transparency; therefore, black is assigned a totally transparent alpha value and white is assigned a totally opaque alpha value.

Figure 21.31

The Alpha
dialog box.

```
┌─────────────────────────────┐
│            Alpha            │
│ ┌─────────────────────────┐ │
│ │   Queue Alpha Channel   │ │
│ ├─────────────────────────┤ │
│ │        Queue RGB        │ │
│ ├──────────┬──────────────┤ │
│ │ RGB Mask │              │ │
│ ├──────────┤              │ │
│ │Alpha Mask│              │ │
│ ├──────────┴──────────────┤ │
│ │      None (Opaque)      │ │
│ └─────────────────────────┘ │
│       RGB Transparency       │
│ ┌──────────┬──┬───────────┐ │
│ │Key Color │▓▓│Blur Edges │ │
│ ├──────────┴──┴───────────┤ │
│ │        Intensity        │ │
│ └─────────────────────────┘ │
│          Modifiers          │
│ ┌─────────────────────────┐ │
│ │        Negative         │ │
│ └─────────────────────────┘ │
│       Opacity Threshold      │
│ ┌─┬─────────────────┬───┐   │
│ │-│             255 │ + │   │
│ └─┴─────────────────┴───┘   │
│     ┌────┐   ┌──────┐       │
│     │ OK │   │Cancel│       │
│     └────┘   └──────┘       │
└─────────────────────────────┘
```

RGB Mask and Alpha Mask enable you to define a bitmap to use as a source for alpha
information. When you click in the box to the right of these options, a file selection box
appears, prompting you for the name of a bitmap image. If Alpha Mask is selected, the alpha
information from the selected image file is used. Likewise, if RGB Mask is selected, the RGB
values from the selected image are used, with black (0,0,0) being completely transparent and
white (255,255,255) completely opaque. Suppose, for example, that you have an image of a
wood grain, like WHITEASH.GIF, as the first entry in the Queue. For the second entry, you
have another wood grain, like ASHEN.GIF. You could use RGB Mask to allow only certain
parts of the first entry to show through. Figures 21.32 and 21.33 show what the image used for
the RGB Mask and what the final composite image might look like.

Figure 21.32

A mask image
created in
3D Studio.

Figure 21.33
The final composite of ASHEN.GIF over WHITASH.GIF using RGB Mask for transparency information.

Queue RGB has a second option, Key Color, that enables you to choose a color to make totally transparent. This is similar to the Decal option in the Materials Editor in that wherever the chosen color appears in the image, the underlying image shows through. The Blur Edges option is useful for smoothing the edges on objects in images that do not contain alpha information.

There are two modifiers in the Alpha dialog box. The first is the Negative button. When active, it works much as you would expect, reversing the alpha or RGB transparency information for the selected entry. This means that for RGB Mask images, light areas become dark and dark areas become light. For Alpha Mask, opaque areas become transparent and transparent areas become opaque.

The second modifier is Opacity Threshold. This slider sets the level at which all pixels are considered opaque for both Alpha and RGB channels of transparency. At 255, all levels are available, allowing full variation of the transparency level. At 100, only values 1 to 100 are used; values above 100 are completely opaque. This modifier can be helpful when you use Queue RGB to composite images that have many dark areas. If, for example, you use Queue RGB to composite the image of a dark-haired person over a gradient background, you might find that the gradient shows through the person's hair. Opacity Threshold enables you to set a level at which even the dark areas of the figure appear opaque. This can often save you from having to create an all-white matte image by hand in a paint program.

The third column in the Queue is the Transition column. When you click in this column, the Transition dialog box appears (see fig. 21.34). The Fade In and Fade Out radio buttons enable you to dissolve an image in or out of view over a specified length of time. The Image button enables you to specify a file to use for the transition effect, such as a flic file. To create a one-second wipe from left to right, you create a 30 frame flic of a totally white polygon filling the screen. You start the polygon off-screen to the left of the screen, and then move it to the right to completely fill the screen by the 30th frame. You could then use this flic as an image transition in the Transition column of Video Post.

Figure 21.34

The Transition dialog box.

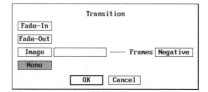

The timeline on the right side of the Video Post dialog box controls the start and stop points for all the effects in the Queue. Different queue entries default to different in and out points in the timeline. Each entry in the timeline consists of 2 lines, one on top of the other. The top red line represents the actual usage of the effect. Under the red line is a black line that represents the physical length of the effect, and that cannot be shortened or lengthened the way you can the red line.

 The Edit button under the Queue column must be on before you can change any settings in the timeline.

If you have a 30-frame flic file as an entry in the queue, but only want to use frames 10 through 20, set the first red dot to frame 10 and the second red dot to frame 20 by clicking on the dot, sliding it to a new position, and clicking again to set it. The underlying black line remains with a starting point at frame 0 and an end point at frame 30. You cannot move the black line prior to frame 0 or past the last active frame in the timeline. If the length of an animation used in an entry is longer than the specified length of Video Post, however, the black line extends past the end of the timeline.

Suppose that you want your 30-frame animation to loop twice during a 90-frame animation, starting at frame 15. You would first set the Total Frames at the top of the dialog box to 90 and click on Set. Then move the beginning of the red line so it matches the beginning of the black line at frame 0. Now move the end of the red line to frame 60. You will notice that as you move the end of the red line past the end of the black line, the word "looping" appears at the top of the screen, followed by a number. This helps confirm the fact that the flic will indeed be repeating itself, and the number represents how many times it will repeat. Now hold down the Shift key and move the beginning of the red line to frame 15. Notice that the Shift key causes the red and black lines to move together. This setup will produce an entry that comes into view on frame 15, plays twice until frame 75, and then disappears until the end of the animation.

Whenever there are two red lines overlapping in the timeline (see fig. 21.35), the effects they represent are composited together using any alpha or transition information provided. KF Scene and IPAS routines do not use alpha or transition information. Any transparency you want to assign to a KF Scene is done with the Materials Editor. IPAS routines get their transparency information from themselves.

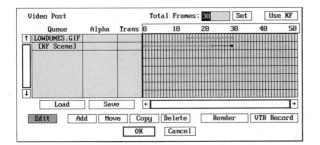

Figure 21.35
The Video Post dialog box, showing overlapping effects in the timeline.

Sometimes, the only way to achieve an effect is through Video Post. For example, if you have ever mapped a two-dimensional polygon with a two-sided texture mapped material in 3D Studio, you may have discovered that a mirror image of the bitmap appears on the back side of the polygon. While many times this can be overcome with a three-dimensional object or two 2D objects back to back, there are occasions when it is more desirable to use a single two-dimensional object, such as modeling the pages of a book turning. In this example, you will render two animations, compositing the second over the first using Video Post.

Create a rectangle in the 2D Shaper and assign it (see fig. 21.36). Switch to the 3D Editor and select Create/Object/Get Shape and name it Page. Assign planar mapping coordinates to the polygon and assign the material APE. Add some lights and a camera to the scene, like those in figure 21.37.

Now that you have created the page, it's time to animate it. Go to the Keyframer, right-click on Zoom Extents, and turn the lower right viewport into a camera viewport if it isn't already. Click on Hierarchy...Place Pivot and click on the polygon in the front viewport. Place the pivot point along the left edge of the polygon, as seen in figure 21.38. Move the frame slider at the bottom of the screen to frame 30. Click on Object...Rotate and in the top viewport, rotate the polygon 180 degrees clockwise around the Y axis.

You are now ready to render the first of your two flics. Set up your configuration to render the Camera View to a 320 × 200 flic file, and make sure the output file will be in one of your map paths since you will be using it later in Video Post. Call the animation FRONTPGE.FLI.

Figure 21.36

A rectangle representing a book's page created in the 2D Shaper.

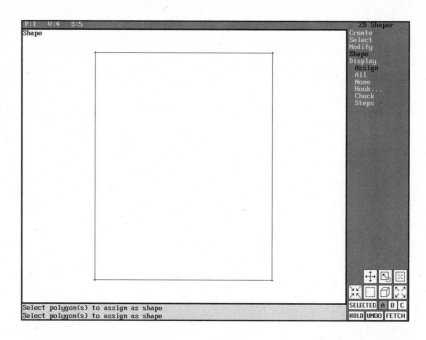

Figure 21.37

The page model with lights and camera placed.

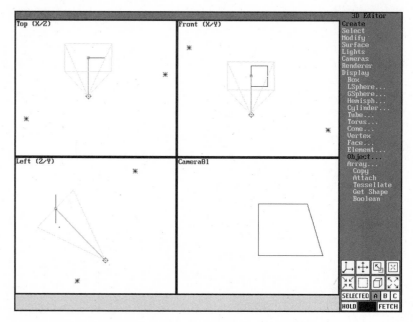

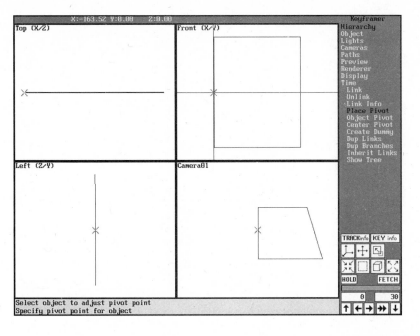

Figure 21.38
Placing the pivot point on the page in the Front viewport.

After the animation has finished rendering, go back to the 3D Editor, click on Surface/ Normals/Flip, and then click on the polygon. Make one of the viewports a back viewport and assign mapping coordinates again so the image will not be reversed on the polygon when it is rendered. Assign the material 3D CEL to the polygon—this will give you a different, right-reading image on each side of the polygon.

In the Keyframer, click on Video Post, and then click in the camera viewport. Click on Add in the resulting dialog box, and place three entries in the queue list. Click on Edit, and then click on the first queue entry. Click on gradient and set the sliders to a gradient setting of your liking, then click on OK. Now click on the second queue entry. Click on bitmap, select frontpge.fli from the file list, and then click OK. The third entry will stay a KF Scene. It's a good idea to save your work in Video Post with a name similar to the mesh/animation file related to it.

Now you are ready to render the final composite animation. Click on render in the Video Post dialog box, and use the same settings you used for the first animation—that way, the two animations will fit precisely together. Figure 21.39 shows a sample frame from the finished animation.

Try creating pages that bend as they turn, or using animated flic files for texture maps on the pages. Page turns are a great segue between topics in a video.

Figure 21.39
The final
composited
animation.

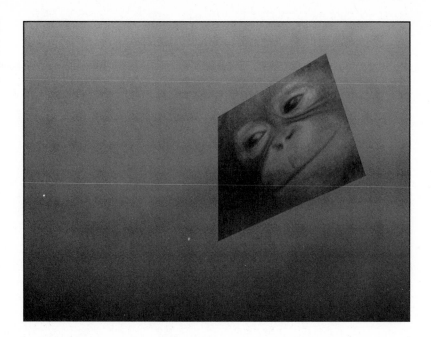

The uses for Video Post are countless. Many users find its biggest benefit is in reducing render time. Background areas that never change throughout a portion of your animation can be rendered once to a still frame, then composited as a background into Video Post. It also provides an easy-to-use interface for .IXP and external files for creating special effects. The best way to learn about Video Post is to use it. Once you feel comfortable using the tools it provides, you will discover hundreds of uses of your own.

Summary

This chapter demonstrates some of the advanced techniques that you can use in the Keyframer. Careful experimentation with features such as Snapshot, Linking, and Motion Blur can open the door to many interesting and powerful techniques.

Chapter Snapshot

This chapter explores 3D Studio Release 4's new Keyscript Plug-In. In doing so, it describes what you need to know about 3D Studio's underlying architecture in order to script operations within it. Some of the key topics explained in this chapter are the following:

✔ Understanding what Keyscript is and how scripting can be used to manipulate the Keyframer environment

✔ Using scripts and 3DE files created by others

✔ Learning Keyscript's functions and capabilities and understanding what it can and cannot do

✔ Understanding how 3D Studio stores its data and interprets objects in three-dimensional space

✔ Learning about the sample utilities included on the *Inside 3D Studio* CD-ROM and how they were created

Keyframer Scripting

3 D Studio Release 4 contains a robust programming language with which you can manipulate your model in the Keyframer environment. Essentially, anything you can animate, you can script. The language that gives you this ability is termed *Keyscript* and is accessible with Release 4's SCRIPT_I.KXP Plug-In. The term "script" is deceivingly modest since a Keyscript is actually a BASIC program that utilizes unique programming functions that closely parallel those of the Plug-In KXP programming language. Although you need to understand the essentials of BASIC programming and 3D Studio's database techniques before being proficient at creating your own scripts, you can utilize scripts written by others without any knowledge of programming at all.

3D Studio does not know anything about the scripting language by itself. The entire KScript language—the functions, their functionality, and their relationship to the Keyframer environment—is contained entirely within the SCRIPT_I.KXP Plug-In.

Understanding Keyscript

The concept behind Keyscript is actually quite interesting. Keyscript is a *Plug-In* (a compiled C program) working within 3D Studio's Keyframer environment to produce its own BASIC-like scripting language. When you execute a script, you are actually instructing a Plug-In how to manipulate Keyframer keys and hierarchies. In other words, you are running a program to tell a program to tell a program what to do! When you compose a script within Keyscript, you are writing raw ASCII code within a running Plug-In that is checked and interpreted by that Plug-In, and then relayed back to the 3D Studio executable for action. Unlike C programming, there is never a need to compile a script before execution—it's always ready to run.

Although scripts cannot run as quickly as an equivalent Plug-In KXP, the development time for creating them is assured to be much faster and less painful. 3D Studio's IPAS language for Plug-In development is C-based. To write a Plug-In, you must have a fairly high end C compiler (either the MetaWare High C™ or WATCOM™ C) *and* a Phar Lap™ DOS linker. This C code must be compiled and linked before a test can be made within 3D Studio. Scripting makes writing code much easier and faster since you can compose it on-the-fly and see the results of your program all within 3D Studio. This simplicity will most likely make scripting a prototyping tool for Plug-In programmers since they can get their code to work satisfactorily as a script, and then turn it into a Plug-In program once they are satisfied with it. This also means that users such as yourself can create scripts, and then contract with seasoned Plug-In programmers to transform the scripts into marketable Plug-Ins.

The Keyscript Environment

As figure 22.1 shows, Keyscript's interface will look familiar to anyone who has worked with the Text Editor introduced with Release 3 (accessed with F11). All the abilities of this internal ASCII editor are paralleled within Keyscript. The fact that the Text Editor's many prompts have always contained the terms "script" and "scripting" hints that the concept of scripting was being developed for some time.

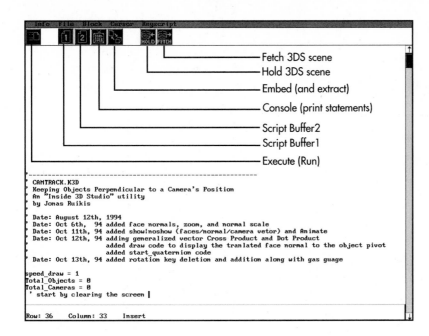

Figure 22.1
The Keyscript
Plug-In interface.

Fetch 3DS scene
Hold 3DS scene
Embed (and extract)
Console (print statements)
Script Buffer2
Script Buffer1
Execute (Run)

```
' CAMTRACK.K3D
' Keeping Objects Perpendicular to a Camera's Position
' An "Inside 3D Studio" utility
' by Jonas Ruikis
'
' Date: August 12th, 1994
' Date: Oct 6th,   94 added face normals, zoom, and normal scale
' Date: Oct 11th,  94 added show|noshow (faces/normal/camera vetor) and Animate
' Date: Oct 12th,  94 adding generalized vector Cross Product and Dot Product
'                     added draw code to display the tranlated face normal to the object pivot
'                     added start_quaternion code
' Date: Oct 13th,  94 added rotation key deletion and addition along with gas guage

speed_draw = 1
Total_Objects = 0
Total_Cameras = 0
' start by clearing the screen |
```

Row: 36   Column: 33   Insert

You may want to use the keyboard equivalents in the Keyscript pull-down menu to provide the fastest writing, navigating, and executing of scripts, as well as review the optional 3DS.SET parameters controlling keyboard editing conventions.

Interface

Keyscript's interface parallels that of the Text Editor. The 3DS.SET variables controlling the Text Editor affect Keyscript's interface in precisely the same manner—text editing keyboard equivalents in one will always match the other. Keyscript's first four pull-down menus are also identical to the Text Editor. Its new abilities are located in the Keyscript pull-down and duplicate Keyscript's icon functions.

The Text Editor and Keyscript are completely independent environments, even though they look and perform much the same. Text written within one, or copied to their Clipboards, is not available to the other. If you want to exchange information between the two, you must save the text to disk and load it within the other module.

Script Buffers Versus Scene Buffers

Keyscript contains two script *buffers*, enabling you to have two scripts open at the same time. This is especially useful for loading sample or library function scripts that can be cut and pasted into the one being composed. It also enables you to load two different scripts, running whichever you want as you need it.

Keyscript's Hold and Fetch options do *not* hold and fetch the script buffer contents. They are actually the standard 3D Studio commands for the Keyframer and 3D Editor's buffer and will reset your scene accordingly. The Fetch command's warning of `Restore old buffer?` reflects the prompt of the standard 3D Studio Fetch command and does *not* mean the restoring of just the script "buffer."

Keyscript Backups

Whenever you execute a script or quit 3D Studio, Keyscript performs a backup of the running script or the entire environment. The actual contents of the script buffers and Console are stored in temporary files in the PROCESS directory and may be restored directly in the case of a fatal mistake (accidentally over writing your current script, for example). The files $KSCR1$.DAT, $KSCR2$.DAT, and $KSCR3$.DAT are ASCII files that contain the Buffer1, Buffer2, and Console contents respectively and can be reloaded as a standard script. Note, however, that Keyscript overwrites the first line with compiled information, and this line must be either deleted or commented out for the restored script to execute.

It is very prudent to include a single character or space as a script's first line, given that the buffer's first line is overwritten within its temporary backup. Remember, these files were not intended to be manually restored.

Console Display

The Console window displays the results of print statements that a script may create while it executes. As a rule, print statements are used while developing and debugging a script, although they can serve as primitive user feedback for final scripts. The print statements are meant to track a script's execution so the programmer can analyze the returned values as progressive steps are made through the script. The Console represents whichever script was last executed. If you execute a script from within the Console window, the last script executed will be run. Unlike the script buffers, the Console's contents are not saved with Hold and Fetch.

Embedding Scripts

Embedding scripts within objects, lights, and cameras (known in scripting as *nodes*) is an interesting concept, but it is of somewhat limited use in regards to actual scripting. An embedded script is most useful when you exchange 3DS files and a node's proper behavior is dependent upon a particular script. Embedding the script into that node will ensure that a relevant copy exists with that mesh file. The embedded script still needs to be extracted in order to be run—it cannot run "automatically." When compared to a K3D file stored on disk, however, an embedded script could be comparatively difficult to access and update.

Embedding a script does not embed any corresponding 3DE files that may be required for the script's execution.

Because 3DE files are in ASCII, they could conceivably be loaded as a script and subsequently embedded into a node. This embedded 3DE file could then be retrieved and saved to disk for proper referencing.

An alternate application exists for script embedding that can be very useful for all 3D Studio users. Instead of embedding program scripts, you can embed important information about that node, the scene, or the project. Embedded "scripts" can thus become a valuable log of your actions and intentions—*this* object's purpose is to do *this* in relation to *this*; *this* light represents *this* and is highlighting *that* part of the scene; *this* camera target is tracking *this* object, and the camera represents the user standing at *that* location; *this* model was edited by Karen on *this* date and made to do *this*; *this* model relates to the following AutoCAD drawings; job hours to date have been *this* total; *this* dummy object is an IK follow object that does *this*, and so on.

This technique makes for another use of the two script buffers: the first to hold running scripts and the second to hold project comments. You can embed as many scripts (or text notations) within an object as you want. Figure 22.2 shows that each script within a particular object must have unique name. This does not mean that each object cannot have the same script name ("UPDATE," for example). Also note that Keyscript allows periods to be included as part of names. This enables you to further classify what that embedded "script" actually may be.

Figure 22.2
Keyscript's dialog
box for script
embedding.

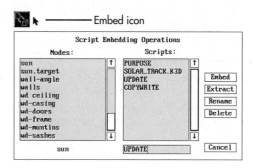

Embed icon

Using 3D Studio's New command with the "Keep Mesh" option destroys all embedded scripts for all nodes within the current scene.

Using Scripts Created by Others

As stated before, you do not need to know anything about programming to use a script that was created and supplied by someone else—you simply enter the Keyscript Plug-In, load the script, and click on the execute icon. Although this seems straightforward enough, there may be situations when you need to edit the script to get it to perform properly.

3DE Files

While Keyscript provides several basic dialog boxes, many programmers find it necessary to create custom ones to convey critical information and retrieve corresponding input (a custom dialog box is needed to display more than one button or option, for example). This is accomplished by creating and using 3DE files. A *3DE file* contains all the data structures and graphical information necessary to display and receive feedback from the script that calls it. 3DE files are not compiled—the 3DE format is in ASCII and is both editable and executable.

The 3DE files themselves are created and edited with the *3D Script Dialog Editor* shareware program. The editor is accessed by the 3DE.EXE executable and is most often referred to simply as *"3DE."* This utility was originally created by the Yost Group for their own use. It was later extended to IPAS programmers so that they could design dialog boxes quickly and easily for inclusion in their Plug-In applications. The 3DE program itself does not ship with 3D Studio, but is available courtesy of the Yost Group on CompuServe's ASOFT forum, and is included on the *Inside 3D Studio* CD-ROM for your use in script development (see later in this chapter for information on using 3DE.EXE).

Making Sure Scripts Find Their 3DE Files

If a script uses an accompanying 3DE file, it must know where that 3DE file is located in order to load it. By default, Keyscript looks for the 3DE file in 3D Studio's most current directory path. Since this path can change during many 3D Studio operations, it is always safest to indicate exactly where the 3DE file should be within the script. (This is often referred to as *hard coding* the path.) Keyscript provides the `GetPaths` function to retrieve 3D Studio's current path structure. Accessing this function is prudent because you do not know where another user may be locating files. Scripts that employ 3DE files contain a line similar to that found within the NODEINFO.K3D sample script, as follows:

```
GetPaths GFX PROCESS PATH
Dlg_Load3DE PathName$+"\NODEINFO.3DE"
If RC = 0 then GFX_Continue "NODEINFO.3DE Must be in your PROCESS
➥directory" : End
```

The first line's `GetPaths` function sets the reserved variable `PathName$` to where 3D Studio's current PROCESS directory is located (the SCRIPTS directory location is not defined within the 3DS.SET file and cannot be retrieved). The second line's Dlg_Load3DE function combines the returned path location with the name of the 3DE file. If Keyscript fails to find NODEINFO.3DE at this location, the *return code* (RC) is returned with a value of 0. The second line checks for this failure by analyzing the return code with an *IF* statement. If RC equates to 0, it will post a warning message that tells the user where it was looking for the 3DE file (using a *GFX* function) and terminates the script with *END*.

It is critical for scripts to test for the presence of all required 3DE files that they load. Without a check for failure, Keyscript may request its next user input within an infinite loop and effectively lock up 3D Studio.

Keyscript uses Ctrl+Alt+⇧Shift as an Escape key combination to terminate an infinitely looping script.

If the script you are using cannot find an accompanying 3DE file, you must either move the 3DE file to the correct disk location or edit the name of the 3DE file to include the proper path. It is usually easiest to use Search (accessed from the Cursor pull-down menu or with Alt+S) for the keyword "3DE" to locate the critical line that tells the script where to find the 3DE file.

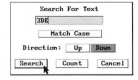

Figure 22.3
Using Alt+S to search for the string case "3DE" in a script.

Keyscript Conventions and Terminology

Keyscript and its Release 4 documentation use specific terminology when referring to the various pieces of the 3D Studio environment and the Keyscript language. It is important to become familiar with these terms before editing existing scripts or creating those of your own, because confusion could easily result.

Node	A 3D Studio entity that has a unique set of track keys. There are seven types of nodes in 3D Studio: *objects*, *cameras*, *targets* (for camera and spotlight), *lights* (omni light), *spotlights*, *ambient light*, and *dummy objects*.
NodeType	The corresponding ID number (or reserved variable) that identifies what node type is being referenced for certain functions. These are respectively 1–7 for the node types listed in the preceding.
Key	An event in time represented by a black key dot within Track Info, containing all the information found in Key Info. A key is always for one frame only.
Track	All of the keys that lie along a single row within Track Info (Rotation, for example). There are nine unique tracks in 3D Studio: *Position, Scale, Rotation, Morph, Hide, Roll, FOV, Color, Hotspot,* and *Falloff.*
TrackType	The corresponding ID number (or reserved variable) that identifies what type of track is being referenced for certain functions. These are respectively 1–9 for the track types listed in the preceding.
Track Flag	The parameters that influence an entire track's behavior (locked axes and looping, for example).
Function	Any built-in function within Keyscript (note that these are referred to as "commands" in the Autodesk documentation). Functions are *never* case-sensitive—you may capitalize them as you wish. Any reserved variables a function uses *are* case-sensitive, however.
GFX function	A family of Keyscript functions that draw on the Command screen and interact with the mouse and keyboard.

DLG function	A family of Keyscript functions that interact with 3DE (3D Script Dialog Editor) dialog box files and track user interaction within them.
Variable	A generic term for a name that represents a value. Variables are defined by assigning them a value. Variable names are *always* case-sensitive.
String Variable	A variable that is assigned a string of text. A string variable name *always* has a trailing $ and can never be used in numeric calculations. String variables can be assigned numbers, but they are treated as if they were text. String variables are assigned values encased within quotes and can be strung together with the + sign (`string1$ + "this is note" + string2$`, for example).
Numeric Variable	Any variable assigned an integer or real (floating point), positive or negative number. There are not separate numeric variable types for integers and reals.
Reserved Variable	A variable specifically used by Keyscript functions that either returns a function's evaluation or influences the behavior of a function. As a rule, reserved variables should never be reassigned by the user directly.
Return Code	The returned value by a Keyscript function, set to the reserved variable `RC.` This variable represents either the success of the function (whether it was able to perform the requested action) or the requested information (the number of objects picked in *PickObjects* is set to `RC`, for example). Because nearly every Keyscript function resets `RC`, it is customary to check its value immediately after the function and set it equal to another, user-defined variable for later use.
Array	A logical "grid" of values that can be one-, two-, or three-dimensional in nature. (Note that single strings are one-dimensional in nature, and that a two-dimensional string array is essentially a list of strings.)

Data Structure	A storage organization for large numbers of variables that enables related pieces of information to be kept together (the various Key Info values for a given track key, for example).
Label	A string of characters or name that defines a point in a script for GoTo and GoSub functions. An @ precedes the name at the actual location, while the name without the @ identifies which label to go to. Labels are case-sensitive—just like variables.
Subroutine	A self-contained segment of a script, which performs a specific operation that can be used by other sections of the script. Subroutines are preceded by a label and terminate with a *Return* function. Subroutines essentially perform a task and return to the spot in the script that called it. Variables are not implicitly "passed" to a subroutine—all variables are global.
XForm	A data structure containing the transformation matrix (often referred to as the "TM") for a given node on a given frame. This is a 4×3 matrix that contains the rotation, scale, and translation adjustments for the node and is the key in converting location data between object and world space.
Pivot	The point about which that object rotates and scales at a distance from the node's centroid.

Keyscript Capabilities

Although Keyscript is unquestionably quite powerful, it does help to understand the basics of what you can and cannot do with it so you do not waste time struggling to do the impossible. It's also important to know what capabilities a Plug-In has that a script does not when using scripts as a prototyping tool for an eventual Plug-In.

What Keyscript Can Do

Keyscript can essentially do anything within the reach of the Track Info and Key Info dialog boxes, and then some. Table 22.1 lists Keyscript's basic abilities and all the various programming functions associated with them. These functions are the building blocks upon which all Keyscripts are created, and are your tools for constructing your own.

Table 22.1
Keyscript Abilities and Related Functions

Programming Task to be Accomplished	Related Functions
Get the number and name of nodes in the current scene	*GetNodeCount* *GetNodeName* *GetNodeNumber*
Get, create, and delete any type of key and associated value present in Key Info	*GetKey* *GetKeyByNumber* *GetKeyCount* *GetNextKey* *CreateKey* *DeleteKey*
Delete every key along a track for a node	*DeleteTrack* *DeleteAllTracks*
Get and affect the values within Hierarchy/Link Info and Key Info's Loop, Repeat, and lock options	*GetTrackFlags* *SetTrackFlags*
Get the interpolated value between keys	*InterpolateKey* *FracInterpolateKey*
Get the scene's frame and segment information	*GetCurrentFrame* *GetSegment* *NumFrames*
Set the scene's current frame and segment length	*SetCurrentFrame* *SetNumFrames* *SetSegment*
Read, link, and unlink scene hierarchies	*GetChild* *GetNumChildren* *GetParent* *SetParent*
Get an object's size, orientation, and internal transformation matrix	*GetBoundBox* *GetXForm*
Get and set object pivot points	*GetPivot* *SetPivot*
Read from, and write to, ASCII files on disk	*Open* *Close* *Write*

continues

Table 22.1, Continued
Keyscript Abilities and Related Functions

Programming Task to be Accomplished	Related Functions
Hold and Fetch the 3DS scene	*HoldScene* *FetchScene*
Get 3D Studio's current directory paths	*GetPaths*
Check for valid morph targets	*Morphtest*
Check for collision between objects	*Collision* *DefCollide*
Get an object's vertex and face information	*GetVerts* *GetFaces* *GetFVCount*
Use a built-in dialog for simple user input	*Input*
Use a dialog for selecting multiple nodes	*PickObjects*
Use a dialog for selecting a single node with a displayed hierarchy	*ChooseNode*
Use built-in dialogs for choosing colors and selecting files	*SelectColor* *SelectFile*
Print to the Console window for program feedback	*Print* *Pwindow* *ClosePWindow*
Programmatical loops, conditional statements, Go To, and Subroutine functions	*For/Next* *If/Then* *Goto/@label* *Gosub/@label/Return* *On/GoTo & On/GoSub* *Pop*
Basic relational and logical conditional statements	*=, <, >, <=, >=, <>* *AND, &, OR, |* *NOT, !, XOR, ~*
Basic math, trigonometric, and logarithmic functions	*+, -, /, *, %* *Sqr, X^n* *Sin, Cos, Tan* *Asin, Acos, Atn* *Log, Log10, Exp*

Advanced Animation

V

Programming Task to be Accomplished	Related Functions
Basic number testing and manipulation	*Abs, Even, Odd, Int, Rnd, Sgn*
Basic string manipulation functions	*Asc, Chr$, Left$, Len$, Mid$, Right$, Str$, Time, Val*
Use standard 3D Studio data structures for keys common to all nodes	*DefTrackFlags DefPosition*
Use standard 3D Studio data structures for objects, and dummy object keys	*DefRotate DefScale DefMorph DefHide*
Use standard 3D Studio data structures for Light nodes	*DefColor DeffFallOff DefHotSpot*
Use standard 3D Studio data structures for Camera nodes	*DefRoll DefFOV*
Use standard 3D Studio data structures for geometric information (transformation matrices, bounding boxes, pivot points, faces, and vertices)	*DefXForm DefBoundBox DefPivot DefFace DefVertex*
Create user-defined data structures and arrays/matrices	*Define Def Dim*
End the script	*End*
Graphically blank the Keyscript environment and possibly redraw the Keyframer's interface	*GFX_ClearScreen GFX_ClearScr GFX_Clear GFX_Redraw*
Use common dialog boxes for Yes/No input, continuing, and pausing	*GFX_YesNo GFX_Continue GFX_Continue2 GFX_StandBy*

continues

Table 22.1, Continued
Keyscript Abilities and Related Functions

Programming Task to be Accomplished	Related Functions
Use built-in gas gauge display to show progress	*GFX_SetGas* *GFX_ShowGas* *GFX_PutHole*
Color draw with pixels	*GFX_PutDot*
Color draw with lines	*GFX_Line* *GFX_XORLine* *GFX_HLine* *GFX_Vline* *GFX_XORHLine* *GFX_XORVLine*
Color draw with solid boxes and hollow frames	*GFX_CBlock* *GFX_XORCBlock* *GFX_XORTBlk* *GFX_Frame* *GFX_XORFrame*
Line draw within clipped regions	*GFX_SetClip* *GFX_ClipFrame* *GFX_ClipLine* *GFX_ClipDLine*
Display colored text	*GFX_ColorText* *GFX_PlainText*
Track the position and button clicking of the user's mouse	*GFX_ButUP* *GFX_LButUP* *GFX_RButUP* *GFX_WaitClick* *GFX_WaitInput* *GFX_PollMouse* *GFX_MouseXY*
Track the actions and state of the user's keyboard	*GFX_KeyWait* *GFX_KeyHit* *GFX_GetKey* *GFX_GetKeyboard* *GFX_KState*

Programming Task to be Accomplished	Related Functions
Load and control 3DE dialog boxes	*DefDLGItem*
	DLG_Load3DE
	DLG_DoDialog
	DLG_Active
	DLG_Draw
	DLG_GetSize
	DLG_SetSize
	DLG_End
Write and retrieve text to and from 3DE dialogs elements	*DLG_SetText*
	DLG_GetText
Interact with 3DE dialog buttons	*DLG_SetButton*
	DLG_GetButton
	DLG_PushButton
	DLG_Radio
Interact with 3DE dialog sliders	*DLG_Slider*
	DLG_NumSlider
	DLG_SetSlider
	DLG_GetSlider
Have 3DE dialog elements call subroutines	*DLG_Feel*
	DLG_See
Get 3D Studio's current display size, font size, and palette colors.	*GFX_SCWIDTH*
	GFX_SCHEIGHT
	GFX_CHWIDTH
	GFX_CHHEIGHT
	GFX_COLORS
	GFX_PALETTED

What Keyscript Can't Do

Although the preceding section shows that Keyscript has a tremendous number of abilities, it does not encompass everything. The following list of its inabilities is good to remember so you do not waste time trying to figure out what is not possible:

✔ Do anything you cannot normally do within the standard Keyframer. This includes affecting a mesh at the vertex, face, or element level, and animating atmosphere definitions.

✔ Access a traditional Keyframer command for use within a script. (You must script what the 3D Studio command is actually doing to the database with Keyscript functions instead.)

✔ Interact with the Renderer or affect motion blur settings.

✔ Create any new node or copy an existing one (including Keyframer instances).

✔ Delete an existing node (including Keyframer instances).

✔ Change object attributes or rename any node.

✔ Interact with the standard Keyframer display directly or interactively. (This ability is available to Plug-Ins.)

✔ Get any information about your current 3D Studio session other than 3DS.SET directory paths. (Plug-Ins have additional access to the environment.)

✔ Get updated information of the scene as the script manipulates it—you are not able to get the bounding box that results from a scripted scale operation while the script is active, for example. (This ability is available to Plug-Ins.)

✔ Perform fast *bit-blitting* operations. (This is what makes rendered viewports possible, and popular, for Plug-Ins.) Although scripts can draw on the screen with GFX functions, the redraws will never be close to the speed available to a Plug-In.

Although the preceding list does outline limitations, it is more important to realize what it does *not* contain—*anything* else that you can normally do within the Keyframer's standard interface, you *can* do with Keyscript!

Function Syntax and Variables

Syntax within Keyscript is consistent, but of course varies depending on the function. The initial function title is never followed by a comma, while every entry after that point must be delineated by a comma. You can place multiple functions on the same line, but each must be separated from the other by a : (colon).

Table 22.2 lists all of the Keyscript functions alphabetically, and gives their generic syntax and any returned variables. Brackets indicate optional parameters for the function (note that the delineating comma is within the brackets). If parentheses are shown, they are required syntax for the given entry. String variables are indicated with a trailing $ and labels with a preceding @. If a variable is not otherwise indicated, then it is numeric.

Table 22.2
Keyscript Functions, Syntax, Returned Variables, and Success Checking

Keyscript Functions	Function Syntax	Returned Variable or Action	Success Checking
Abs	(Number)	evaluates	
Acos	(Number)	evaluates	
Asc	(String$)	evaluates	
Asin	(Number)	evaluates	
Atn	(Number)	evaluates	
ChooseNode	Prompt$ [, *Filter*]	*NodeName$*	*RC*
Chr$	(String$)	evaluates	
Close	[@Handle]	closes	*RC*
ClosePWindow		clears	
Collision	Obj$,Obj$,Time, Time,ColStruct	*Collision*	*RC*
Cos	(Number)	evaluates	
CreateKey	Node$,KeyStruct	redefines	*RC*
Def [UserStructName]	UserStructName [(Size)]	*UserStruct*	
DefBoundBox	StructName	*3DS_Structure*	
DefCollide	StructName	*3DS_Structure*	
DefColor	StructName	*3DS_Structure*	
DefDlgItem	DlgName	*3DS_Structure*	
DefFace	StructName	*3DS_Structure*	
DeffFallOff	StructName	*3DS_Structure*	
DefFOV	StructName	*3DS_Structure*	
DefHide	StructName	*3DS_Structure*	

continues

V

Advanced Animation

Table 22.2, Continued
Keyscript Functions, Syntax, Returned Variables, and Success Checking

Keyscript Functions	Function Syntax	Returned *Variable* or <u>Action</u>	Success Checking
Define	StructName (Var [,Var])	*3DS_Structure*	
DefMorph	StructName	*3DS_Structure*	
DefRoll	StructName	*3DS_Structure*	
DefPivot	StructName	*3DS_Structure*	
DefPosition	StructName	*3DS_Structure*	
DefRotate	StructName	*3DS_Structure*	
DefScale	StructName	*3DS_Structure*	
DefTrackFlags	StructName	*3DS_Structure*	
DefVertex	StructName	*3DS_Structure*	
DefXForm	StructName	*3DS_Structure*	
DeleteAllTracks	Node$	<u>redefines</u>	*RC*
DeleteKey	Node$,TrackID,Number	<u>redefines</u>	*RC*
DeleteTrack	Node$,TrackID	<u>redefines</u>	*RC*
Dim	Var ,(Length [,Length])	*ArrayDefin*	
Dlg_Active	Dialog$,EntryField	<u>activates</u>	*RC*
Dlg_DoDialog	Dialog$,Initial EditElement$	<u>dialog_box</u>	*RC*
Dlg_Draw	Dialog$,Element$	<u>draws</u>	*RC*
Dlg_End	Dialog$,Value		*RC*
Dlg_Feel	Dialog$,Element$, @Label	<u>calls @Label</u>	*RC*
Dlg_GetButton	Dialog$,Element$ [,Value]	<u>defines</u>	*RC*

Keyscript Functions	Function Syntax	Returned *Variable* or <u>Action</u>	Success Checking
Dlg_GetSize	Dialog$,Element$, DlgStruct	*DlgStruct*	*RC*
Dlg_GetSlider	Dialog$,UpEl$,DnEl$, TrackEl$,@Label	<u>defines</u>	*RC*
Dlg_GetText	Dialog$,Element$,Var$	*Variable$*	*RC*
Dlg_Load3DE	3DE_Filename$	<u>loads</u>	*RC*
Dlg_NumSlider	Dialog$,UpEl$,DnEl$, TrackEl$,@Label	<u>defines</u>	*RC*
Dlg_PushButton	Dialog$,Element$	*RC*	*RC*
Dlg_Radio	Dialog$,Element$, Var,Value	<u>defines</u>	*RC*
Dlg_See	Dialog$,Element$, @Label	<u>calls subr.</u>	*RC*
Dlg_SetButton	Dialog$,Element$,Value	<u>defines</u>	*RC*
Dlg_SetSize	Dialog$,Element$, DlgStruct	<u>defines</u>	*RC*
Dlg_SetSlider	Dialog$,TrackElement$, Min,Max,Value	<u>defines</u>	*RC*
Dlg_SetText	Dialog$,Element$, String$	<u>types</u>	*RC*
Dlg_Slider	Dialog$,TrackElement$	<u>defines</u>	*RC*
End		<u>ends</u>	
Even	(Number)	<u>evaluates</u>	
Exp	(Number)	<u>evaluates</u>	
FetchScene		<u>fetches</u>	*RC*
FracInterpolateKey	Node$,FrameFract, KeyStruct	*KeyStruct*	*RC*
GetBoundBox	Obj$,Frame,Coord Type,BBoxStruct		*RC*

continues

Table 22.2, Continued
Keyscript Functions, Syntax, Returned Variables, and Success Checking

Keyscript Functions	Function Syntax	Returned *Variable* or <u>Action</u>	Success Checking
GetChild	Node$,ChildNumber	*NodeNumber/ NodeName$/ NodeType*	*RC*
GetCurrentFrame		*Time*	*RC*
GetFaces	Obj$,Start,Count, FaceStruct	*FaceStruct*	*RC*
GetFVCount	Obj$	*Verts/Faces*	*RC*
GetKey	Node$,TrackID,Frame	*KeyNumber / NodeType*	*RC*
GetKeyByNumber	Node$,Key,KeyStruct	*KeyStruct*	*RC*
GetKeyCount	Node$,TrackID	*KeyCount*	*RC*
GetNextKey	Node$,TrckID,Frame	*KeyNumber*	*RC*
GetNodeCount		*NodeCount*	*RC*
GetNodeName	NodeNumber	*NodeName$ /*	*RC*
GetNodeNumber	Node$	*NodeNumber*	*RC*
GetNumChildren	Node$	*NodeChildren*	*RC*
GetParent	Node$	*NodeName$ NodeType*	*RC*
GetPaths	Type [,Number]	*PathName$*	
GetPivot	Obj$,PivotStruct	*PivotStruct*	*RC*
GetPrevKey	Node$,TrackID,Frame	*KeyNumber*	*RC*
GetSegment		*SegStart / SegEnd*	*RC*
GetTrackFlags	Node$,Track,TrackStruct	*TrackStruct*	*RC*
GetVerts	Obj$,Start,Count,Frame, AbsFlag,VStruct	*VStruct*	*RC*

Keyscript Functions	Function Syntax	Returned *Variable* or <u>Action</u>	Success Checking
GetXForm	Node$,Frame,TMStruct	*TMStruct*	*RC*
Gfx_CBlock	XPos,YPos,XSize,Ysize, ColorNum	<u>draws</u>	
Gfx_ClearScreen		<u>clears</u>	
Gfx_ClearScr		<u>clears</u>	
Gfx_Clear		<u>clears</u>	
Gfx_ClipFrame	X1,Y1,X2,Y2,ColorNum	<u>draws</u>	
Gfx_ClipLine	X1,Y1,X2,Y2,ColorNum	<u>draws</u>	
Gfx_ClipDLine	X1,Y1,X2,Y2,ColorNum	<u>draws</u>	
Gfx_ColorText	Text$,X,Y,ColorNum, ColorNum	<u>types</u>	
Gfx_Continue	Text$	<u>dialog</u>	
Gfx_Continue2	Text$,Text$	<u>dialog</u>	
Gfx_Frame	XPos,YPos,XSize,Ysize, Color	<u>draws</u>	
Gfx_HLine	Y1,X1,X2,Color	<u>draws</u>	
Gfx_GetKey			*RC*
Gfx_GetKeyboard			*RC*
Gfx_KeyHit			*RC*
Gfx_KState		**	
Gfx_KeyWait			*RC*
Gfx_LButUP		*	
Gfx_Line	X1,Y1,X2,Y2,Color	<u>draws</u>	
Gfx_MouseXY	X,Y		
Gfx_PlainText	Text$,X,Y,Color	<u>types</u>	
Gfx_PollMouse		*	

V

Advanced Animation

continues

Table 22.2, Continued
Keyscript Functions, Syntax, Returned Variables, and Success Checking

Keyscript Functions	Function Syntax	Returned *Variable* or <u>Action</u>	Success Checking
Gfx_PutHole		<u>dialog</u>	
Gfx_PutDot	X,Y,Color	<u>draws</u>	
Gfx_RButUP		*	
Gfx_Redraw		<u>redraws</u>	
Gfx_SetClip	XPos,YPos,XSize,YSize	<u>defines</u>	
Gfx_SetGas	Text$,Fraction,Total	<u>dialog</u>	
Gfx_ShowGas	Text$	<u>dialog</u>	
Gfx_StandBy	Text$	<u>dialog</u>	
Gfx_Vline	X1,Y1,Y2,Color	<u>draws</u>	
Gfx_WaitClick		*	
Gfx_WaitInput		*	
Gfx_XORCBlock	XPos,YPos,XSize,Ysize, Color	<u>draws</u>	
Gfx_XORFrame	XPos,YPos,XSize,Ysize, Color	<u>draws</u>	
Gfx_XORHLine	Y1,X1,X2,Color	<u>draws</u>	
Gfx_XORLine	X1,Y1,X2,Y2,Color	<u>draws</u>	
Gfx_XORTBlk	X,Y,NumChars, ColorNum	<u>highlites</u>	
Gfx_XORVLine	X1,Y1,Y2,ColorNum	<u>draws</u>	
GfX_YesNo	Text$		*RC*
Goto	/@*labels*	<u>goes to</u>	
Gosub	/@*label/Return*	<u>goes to</u>	
HoldScene		<u>holds</u>	*RC*

Keyscript Functions	Function Syntax	Returned *Variable* or <u>Action</u>	Success Checking
Input	Prompt\$,UserVar [,Default]	*UserVar*	*RC*
Int	(Number)	<u>evaluates</u>	
InterpolateKey	Node\$,Frame,KeyStruct	*KeyStruct*	*RC*
Left\$	(String\$)	<u>evaluates</u>	
Len\$	(String\$)	<u>evaluates</u>	
Log	(Number)	<u>evaluates</u>	
Log10	(Number)	<u>evaluates</u>	
Mid\$	(String\$)	<u>evaluates</u>	
Morphtest	Obj\$,Obj\$		*RC*
NumFrames		*Time*	*RC*
Odd	(number)	<u>evaluates</u>	
Open	Filename, Mode, @Handle	<u>opens</u>	*RC*
PWindow	XPos,YPos,Xsize,YSize	<u>sizes</u>	
Print	[String\$] [,Var] [,@Handle]	<u>prints</u>	
PickObjects	Prompt\$, Array\$ [,Filter]	*Array\$/RC*	*RC*
Pop		<u>frees @call</u>	
Right\$	(String\$)	<u>evaluates</u>	
Rnd	(Number)	<u>evaluates</u>	
SelectColor		*Red/Green/Blue*	*RC*
SelectFile	Prompt\$,Path\$,File\$ [Ext\$]	*FileName\$*	*RC*
SetCurrentFrame	Frame	<u>redefines</u>	*RC*
SetNumFrames	Frames	<u>redefines</u>	*RC*

continues

V

Advanced Animation

Table 22.2, Continued
Keyscript Functions, Syntax, Returned Variables, and Success Checking

Keyscript Functions	Function Syntax	Returned *Variable* or Action	Success Checking
SetParent	Node$,Node$ [fixup]	redefines	*RC*
SetPivot	Obj$,PivStruct	redefines	*RC*
SetSegment	FrameStart,FrameEnd	redefines	*RC*
SetTrackFlags	Node$,Track, TrackStruct	redefines	*RC*
Sin	(Number)	evaluates	
Sgn	(Number)	evaluates	
Sqr	(Number)	evaluates	
Str$	(String$)	evaluates	
Tan	(Number)	evaluates	
Time	(Number or String$)	evaluates	
Val	(String$)	evaluates	
Write	@Handle,Var,[,Var]	writes	*RC*
For/Next		loops	
If/Then		loops	
On/GoTo & On/GoSub		goes to @	
+, -, /, *, %		result	
X^n		result	
=, <, >, <=, >=, <>		result	
AND, &, *OR*,			result	
NOT, !, XO, ~		result	

* Returns six reserved variables for GFX mouse polling functions, as follows:
GFX_MOUSEX, GFX_MOUSEY, GFX_UMOUSEX, GFX_UMOUSEY, GFX_MBUTTON,
and **GFX_MMOVED**

New Riders Publishing
INSIDE
SERIES

** Returns eight reserved variables for the Gfx_KState function, as follows:
GFX_RightShift, GFX_LeftShift, GFX_Ctrl, GFX_Alt, GFX_ScrollLock,
GFX_NumLock, GFX_CapsLock, and *GFX_Ins*

Affecting the Scene with Keyscript

When you examine the list of Keyscript functions, you will notice that there are only ten functions that physically affect the scene. The rest are all information gathering, data manipulation, and user interaction tools.

Your primary tool for affecting the scene is the *CreateKey* function. Keys relate directly to how you would manipulate the node with a standard Keyframer command. Creating a key on the same track and frame as an existing key effectively replaces the old one—you do not have to delete it first. The *SetTrackFlags* function works in conjunction with the CreatKey function to manipulate track behavior and/or clear user-defined flags that may adversely affect the script's success.

While you may use transformation matrices to locate points and angles relative to an object, you *never* modify a transformation matrix directly. Instead, you create appropriate position, scale, and rotation keys. The adjustments reflected in these keys are transformed into the matrix by 3D Studio.

Keyscript's deletion functions (*DeleteKey, DeleteTrack,* and *DeleteAllTracks*) are used primarily to clear the way for your own keys. For example, if you wanted an object to rotate a specific way between frames 0 and 60, you might delete its rotation track to ensure your two keys were unaffected by any stray keys that may be on frames 1 to 59.

The time functions (*SetCurrentFrame, SetNumFrames,* and *SetSegment*) are usually used to expand the scenes segment and frame upon exiting the script. You do *not* need to expand the current segment to create keys. Keys can be created and deleted for any frame, regardless of the scene's current segment.

Hierarchies are manipulated with the *SetParent* function. Setting a parent for a node will unlink it from any current parent while linking it to the new parent. You cannot create a hierarchy that you could not otherwise form in 3D Studio. Closed loops, multiple parents, and light or target parents are all impossibilities.

The *SetPivot* function influences the point about which all transformations (position, rotation, and scale keys) are performed. This is the one operation that requires the most script interaction for it to be consistent with 3D Studio's standard method of operation (see "The Importance of Pivot Points" later in this chapter).

Simple Scripts

Because Keyscript follows the practices of BASIC, it actually has a fairly loose structure. Besides the need to define data structures and arrays before use, you can assign variables as needed, and they can be reused as is convenient. Subroutines are simply denoted by a label, and GoTo statements can happen wherever you want them. You are only limited by the principles of creating a logical decision process—the basic foundation of all programming languages.

In examining figure 22.4, you will see LINKPICK.K3D—a very short script that performs a useful task. This script asks for a selection of nodes and then links them together alphabetically. This illustrates the bare essentials of all a script needs to have. As can be read in the side comments, the script starts by defining a required structure, asks for a selection of nodes, and then performs a loop to link the selection from beginning to end. There was no need for string searching because 3D Studio returns the selection already sorted. (LINKPICK.K3D can be found on the *Inside 3D Studio* CD-ROM.)

Figure 22.4
The LINKPICK.K3D
sample script.

```
Info  File  Block  Cursor  Keyscript

 [≡]   [1][2][COL] [≡]
                   HOLD FETCH

;--------------------------------------------------------------
; LINKPICK.K3D
; Links objects in a cascading ladder according to 3D Studio's
; standard alphabetic sorting method.
;
; An "Inside 3D Studio" sample utility
; by Phillip Miller

     Dim child$(99,18)                    :; establish an array for 100 strings of 18 characters.

                                          :; get the objects, filtering for objects and dummies.

     PickObjects "Objects for Alphabetic Linking:", child$, 65

     k2=(RC-2) : k=1 : k1=0 : k$=""       :;set some counting variables.
     For count=0 to k2                    :;do the loop for each object in turn!
        SetParent child$(k), child$(k1),1 :;link the object.
        print k$+child$(k)+" linked to "+child$(k1) :;optional printing statement.
        k=k+1 : k1=k1+1 : k$=k$+" "       :;increase the counts.
     Next count                           :;get next object to link.
     ClosePWindow                         :;get rid of the print window.
End                                       :;end the routine.




Row: 1     Column: 1      Insert
```

Many scripts are written just to get a certain job done. Sometimes these evolve into more and more elaborate programs, while other times they serve their initial purpose and are discarded. Other scripts serve as building blocks for others. Figure 22.5 illustrates a script that built on the Release 4 sample script PIVOT.K3D to perform a somewhat unique operation, but does not perfect it. The scene that prompted its creation contained nearly a hundred identical objects that all needed to have the same pivot point placement. Rather than use the Object Pivot command on each one, a script was created to do it automatically.

```
  Info  File  Block  Cursor  Keyscript
 ┌─┐ ┌─┐ ┌─┐ ┌─┐ ┌─┐ ┌─┐       ┌─┐┌─┐
 │◄│ │►│ │1│ │2│ │   │        │HOLD│FETCH│
 └─┘ └─┘ └─┘ └─┘ └─┘ └─┘       └─┘└─┘
; PIVTCOPY.K3D                                                        ↑
; *** Currently only updates Frame 0 Position Key! ***

DefPivot piv,piv1,piv2                    :;define 3 pivot data structures.
DefXForm TM                               :;define a transformation matrix struct.
DefPosition pos                           :;define a position key structure.
Define POINT (x,y,z) : DefPOINT PT,pt1,pt2 :;define a User Structure called "POINT"
Dim changes$(99,20)                       :;define some "POINT" structures.
ChooseNode "Object w/ Desired Pivot Point:", 65 :;get the correct object.
GetPivot NodeName$, piv1                  :;get the pivot point.
PickObjects  "REDFINE Pivot Points For:", changes$, 65 :;get the objects to change.
k=0                                       :;define a count variable.
For count=1 to RC                         :;do the loop for each object!
   getkeybynumber changes$(k), 0, pos     :;  get the first position key.
   GetPivot changes$(k), piv2             :;  get the pivot for the object.
   GetXForm changes$(k),0,TM              :;  get the TM for the object.
       PT.x=piv2.x : PT.y=piv2.y : PT.z=piv2.z :;     get ready for subroutine.
   Gosub RotatePT : pt1=PT                :;  transform first pivot point.
       PT.x=piv1.x : PT.y=piv1.y : PT.z=piv1.z :;     get ready for subroutine.
   Gosub RotatePT : pt2=PT                :;  transform new pivot point.
       pos.x=(pos.x+(pt2.x-pt1.x))        :;  compensate for the translation
       pos.y=(pos.y+(pt2.y-pt1.y))        :;  "   "              "    "
       pos.z=(pos.z+(pt2.z-pt1.z))        :;  "   "              "    "
   CreateKey changes$(k), pos             :;  change the position key.
   SetPivot changes$(k), piv1             :;  change the pivot point.
   print "New Pivot for: "+changes$(k)    :;  optional print statement.
   k=k+1                                  :;  increase the count.
Next count                                :;get the next object.
ClosePWindow    : End                     :;end the routine.

:RotatePT                                 :;subroutine to transform the point.
    xnew=PT.x*TM.tm(0,0)+PT.y*TM.tm(1,0)+PT.z*TM.tm(2,0)  :;from world to object space.
    ynew=PT.x*TM.tm(0,1)+PT.y*TM.tm(1,1)+PT.z*TM.tm(2,1)
    znew=PT.x*TM.tm(0,2)+PT.y*TM.tm(1,2)+PT.z*TM.tm(2,2)
    PT.x=xnew:PT.y=ynew:PT.z=znew
Return

Row: 44    Column: 1     Insert                                       ↓
```

Figure 22.5

The PIVTCOPY.K3D sample script.

V

Advanced Animation

This script prompts the user for an object that has a correct pivot point, and then for a selection of objects to which to copy that pivot point placement. The dialog boxes shown in figure 22.6 are standard to Keyscript, and are displayed with just one call. As the side comments show, the pivot point location is copied to each object. The displacement caused by the pivot movement is only compensated for the first position key. It's assumed that the objects have not been animated yet. The result is a 32-line script that saves a considerable amount of work. (PIVTCOPY.K3D can be found on the *Inside 3D Studio* CD-ROM.)

This shows a script that was a natural to build upon and embellish. Also on the CD-ROM is the COPYPIVT.K3D script, which improved on the original. This version checks for and changes all position keys, and enables you to copy the pivot point relatively or absolutely. The absolute option is presented as a GFX_YesNo function and will make every object's pivot point the exact same world space position.

Figure 22.6
Using Keyscript's
built-in dialog boxes
for user input.

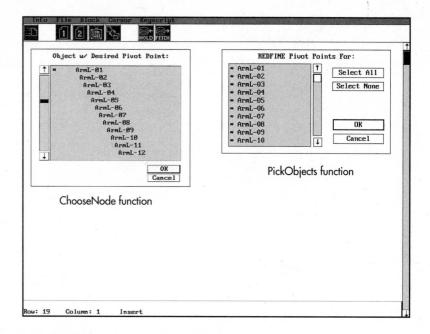

ChooseNode function

PickObjects function

Using the 3DE Resource Editor

Although Keyscript contains several built-in dialog boxes to request user input, it soon becomes necessary to expand the interface with custom dialog boxes. Traditionally, creating dialog boxes for use within IPAS was limited and somewhat painful. The IPAS Resource Editor *3DE* was developed to make this task much easier, and is the tool required to create custom dialog boxes for use with scripts (see fig. 22.7). Because it becomes a near necessity to develop your own dialog boxes for anything but the simplest scripts, 3DE is included for your use on the *Inside 3D Studio* CD-ROM.

3DE is a shareware program with the sole purpose of making dialog creation and editing an easy task for 3D Studio programmers. Because it is shareware, it is presented "as is" for your use. Please note that the 3DE program is *not* supported by Autodesk, the Yost Group, or New Riders Publishing. Although this may seem like an ominous warning, 3DE has, and is, being used by hundreds of Plug-In developers on a daily basis (all of IK's dialogs were created in 3DE, for example). 3DE has traditionally been located on CompuServe's ASOFT forum, and the latest version of the editor can always be downloaded from there.

The 3DE.TXT and 3DENOTES.TXT files contain much of the necessary information to use 3DE. It is strongly advised that you load several of Release 4's 3DE files, examine how they are defined, and learn how their various pieces work with their respective scripts before doing extensive dialog creation of your own. What follows is a brief overview of 3DE, with additional tips on its usage that are not included in the TXT files.

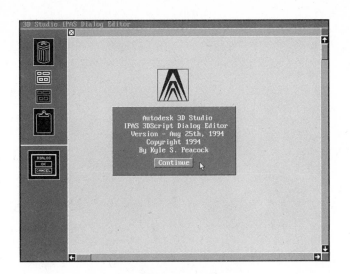

V

Advanced Animation

Figure 22.7
3DE—The IPAS
Resource Editor.

The 3DE Interface

When starting 3DE, you begin in the *dialog overview* work area. Here, dialog boxes are represented by simple icons (regardless of their actual complexity), as shown in figure 22.8. A new, blank dialog box is created by dragging the dialog icon from the side bar menu over to the work area. You are prompted for a name when first creating a dialog box. This case-sensitive name is what you will need to refer to within your script for every DLG function. If you want to rename an existing dialog box, simply double right-click on its icon.

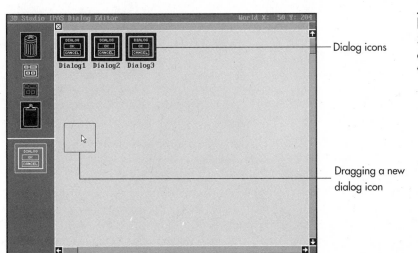

Figure 22.8
3DE's dialog
overview
work area.

Dialog icons

Dragging a new
dialog icon

Double left-clicking on the icon brings the selected dialog into the *dialog edit* work area, as shown in figure 22.9. This is the mode in which the real dialog box creation and editing occurs. There are seven types of *elements* within 3DE: *Buttons, Edit fields, Strings, Boxes, Frames, Icons,* and *Boxed characters.* Each of these is created by dragging the respective side menu icon over to the work area.

Figure 22.9
3DE's dialog edit work area.

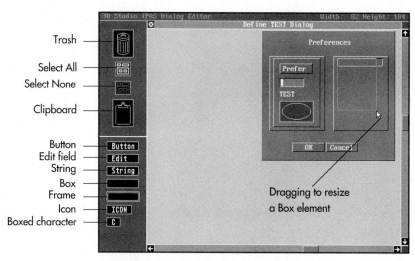

Editing Dialog Boxes in 3DE

Once in position, elements can be resized by clicking on the element's lower right corner and dragging downward to the desired size (as shown in the top right of fig. 22.9). Elements are moved by simply clicking within their boundary and dragging them into position.

 Tip

3DE includes separate snap functions for horizontal and vertical movement and scaling that make accurate element alignment and sizing much easier.

You can also move selections of elements. Right-clicking on an element selects it, while right-clicking again deselects it. A quad selection is performed by clicking on an area not within an element and then dragging the selection window to the desired size. Selections of elements move as a group whenever one is clicked on to be moved, and can be pasted to the Clipboard together. The Clipboard enables you to exchange elements between different dialog boxes and/or place a selection temporarily to the side to make additional element movements and resizing easier.

You can clone elements and selections of elements within 3DE by holding down the ⇧Shift key during a movement. A direct copy of the selection is made with similar parent-child relationships, but with blank identifier fields.

When elements are placed on top of one another, the newly moved element becomes a child and the lower element a parent. When you move a parent, its children move as well. An operation that places one element over another triggers the prompt: Continue with new Parent/Child links?. Answering Yes completes the move, making the moved element a child, while answering No cancels the operation and no move takes place.

Parent-child relationships exist for dialog box manipulation only. They do not have an impact on how the dialog element functions within a script (although they do affect the order in which they are displayed).

A dialog element's contents are edited by double left-clicking on the element. This brings up the appropriate definition dialog box, as shown in the four examples of figure 22.10. Each of the seven element types have different controlling parameters and thus have different dialog boxes (icons have an icon editor as well). Of all the fields within the element definitions, the most important one is the *Identifier*. This is the name, or label, of the dialog element that is referenced within scripts. Identifiers are always uppercase and must be unique for the given dialog box.

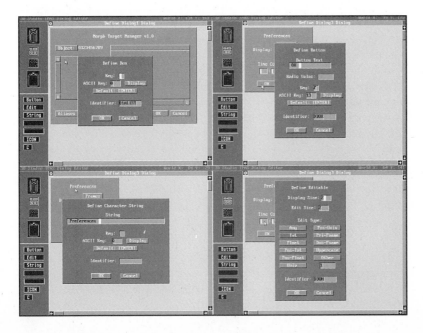

Figure 22.10
Definition dialog boxes for various element types within 3DE.

(right margin) V

Advanced Animation

Commas and C-programming delineators (such as (), [], {}, and <>) *cannot* be included within labels and strings. These characters conflict with Keyscript's string parser and can corrupt the dialog box, or even worse, crash your system.

Referencing 3DE Dialogs in Scripts

Once a dialog box is created in 3DE and saved to disk, it is ready for scripts to access. The "DLG" family of functions all control how dialog boxes operate and display. It is also quite common to combine them with GFX functions for drawing within the dialog box (Release 4's MORPH.K3D and LIGHTMAN.K3D are good examples of this). Once your script displays a dialog box with the Dlg_DoDialog function, you are completing within its method of operation.

It is essential that you include an escape function for at least one element within your dialog box, or the user will not be able to exit! Many programmers include an OK/Cancel button combination within all of their initial dialog boxes.

If you accidentally put your dialog box into an unending loop, you can cancel it by pressing Ctrl+Alt+⇧Shift.

The components within the dialog box communicate with the user through subroutines the script assigns them. Each element begins with default *see* and *feel* functions. These can be redefined in a script with Dlg_Feel and Dlg_See functions so each dialog element can react appropriately for a user action—they simply call a subroutine defined elsewhere in the script. Dialog functions in scripting are fairly tolerant. If a referenced subroutine or 3DE identifier does not exist, the script will still run and the dialog will still display—the requested action is simply not performed because it cannot be found.

The 3DE dialog files you create for scripts are the same format used for inclusion in traditional 3D Studio Plug-Ins. Scripting thus provides a flexible prototyping environment for perfecting dialog behavior for Plug-Ins as well.

It can prove very convenient to run 3D Studio under Microsoft Windows when scripting and creating 3DE files. In this environment, you never have to leave the Keyscript Plug-In and can simply switch between the 3DE resource editor and 3D Studio with Alt+Tab↹.

Understanding How 3D Studio Treats 3D Space

Although you may consider yourself a strong 3D Studio user who knows the interface thoroughly, you will probably discover some surprising revelations about its underlying architecture through scripting. As you know, 3D Studio gives you the power to animate objects, lights, cameras, and their hierarchies, and enables you to adjust, scale, and rotate them as desired while they are animating. Any program that provides such flexibility is going to be doing a fair amount of calculations and transformations behind the scene to accomplish the task.

Through its user interface, 3D Studio shields you from all that is "under the hood"—its data structures, procedures, and transforms are simplified to object names, commands, and keys. Scripting, however, brings you face-to-face with much of 3D Studio's underlying architecture and process. While some of it may take a while to fully grasp, you will undoubtedly comprehend the true workings of 3D Studio much better through scripting.

You can create many varieties of scripts that manipulate the Keyframer without having to know a tremendous amount of math or three-dimensional relationships. When you begin to manipulate a node's position, rotation, and scale, a basic understanding of geometry and three-dimensional translation is definitely helpful. Depending upon the complexity of your script, you may need to reference traditional texts on geometry, trigonometry, and analytical geometry. The most relevant text can be found in books and papers dedicated to computer animation programming (see the end of this chapter for recommended reading).

3D Studio's Internal Coordinate System

Position information for nodes is stored by 3D Studio in a fixed Cartesian coordinate system. While 3D Studio's convention is to label the Top viewport as X and Z, the program's internal code actually understands the Top viewport as being X and Y (this labeling will be referred to in this chapter as *world space*). This axes labeling convention is also known as the *right hand rule* and should be familiar to AutoCAD users. When IPAS programs access the 3D Studio database, points and direction are always returned to their programs as they are stored internally—with the Top viewport being X and Y. It is important to understand that this is the same orientation that will be returned to a script since Keyscript is essentially an IPAS relay to 3D Studio's internal data base.

The 3DS.SET's axis labeling control has no effect on the axis labels returned to you within Keyscript. The display's viewport axis labeling will correspond if you modify the 3DS.SET parameters to be H-LABEL=Z and D-LABEL=Y.

When writing scripts, it is very important to take into account how the user may be interpreting the Y and Z axes labels. It's often safer to request user data in generic terms (such as "up"), rather than assume the users will be displaying their axes labels the same as you are.

Object Space Versus World Space

When an object is created, it has an internal understanding of which way is "up," or more accurately, which way it sees the X, Y, and Z axes as facing. This understanding is said to be its *object space* (see fig. 22.11). The subsequent placement, orientation, and scale of the node is stored as adjustments to the original object space. These adjustments are known as *transforms*, and are recorded within the object's *transformation matrix*. An object's actual (world) position and rotation are always calculated in relation to its internal transformation matrix.

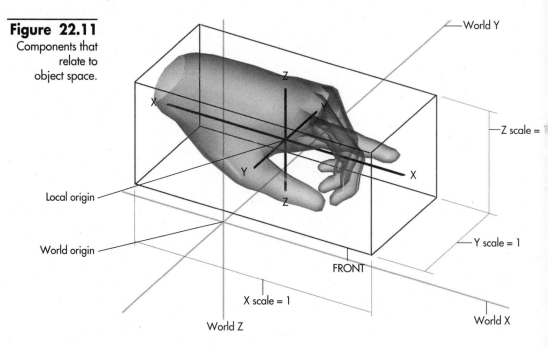

Figure 22.11
Components that relate to object space.

When modeling in the 3D Editor, only the rotation and position of the object is updated in its transformation matrix. Scale operations are recorded at the vertex level. The Keyframer uses the same transformation matrix as the 3D Editor, but includes scale as an expression of the object's overall size, as shown in figure 22.11. An X scale of 2.0 means that the object is scaled 200 percent along its internal X axis, for example. This is the fundamental reason why you cannot affect objects at the vertex level in the Keyframer—the transformation matrix has no way of recording it. The Keyframer updates an object's transformation matrix on every frame that a translation (movement), rotation, and/or scale occurs.

As figure 22.12 shows, the transformation matrix itself is a 4×3 array with the first three rows representing rotation and scale about the three internal axes, and the last row representing its translation (distance from the world origin). The translation's X, Y, and Z values represent the centroid of the object's bounding box in world space at the time it is created. This is known as the object's *local origin* and is what 3D Studio uses to store the object's location in relation to the world (see fig. 22.13). (Note that attaching objects and performing non-object level deformations in the 3D Editor will change the relationship of this value from the object's apparent "centroid.")

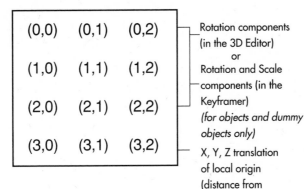

Figure 22.12
The elements of the transformation matrix.

Although the transformation matrix may seem intimidating, it doesn't need to be. It may help to think of the matrix as more of a "translator" that is given points by a script for converting between object and world space (see "The Importance of Pivot Points" later in this chapter for more information). Understanding how its values are actually derived is not what's important since you never alter it directly. The scale and rotation key values you create are converted by 3D Studio to form the first 9 numbers of the matrix, while position keys and the pivot point translate into the last 3 numbers. (Note that this is far superior to manipulating the matrix directly. Doing so would involve solving for quaternion equations, which is a foreign concept to most nonprofessional programmers.)

An object's bounding box is a valuable visual cue to its internal orientation. The three axes defined by the transformation matrix are always parallel to the sides of the bounding box, as shown in figure 22.14. By examining its orientation, you can determine the poles about which the object is allowed to rotate. The bounding box structure itself is stored as two points representing the minimum and maximum X, Y, and Z corner positions in relation to the local origin. When bounding box data is retrieved in object space, the points are often complements to one another (their sum is zero) because they are equidistant from the local origin. (Note that this relationship can change due to 3D Editor modifications.)

Figure 22.13
Locating an object
in world space.

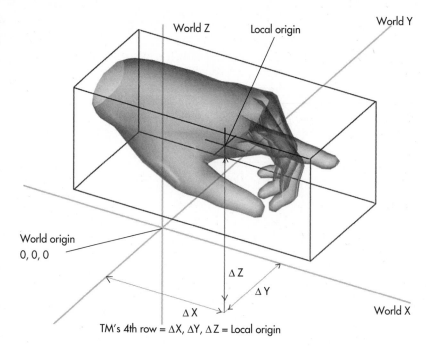

TM's 4th row = ΔX, ΔY, ΔZ = Local origin

Figure 22.14
A rotated object
displaying its
bounding box,
internal axes, and
minimum and
maximum corners.

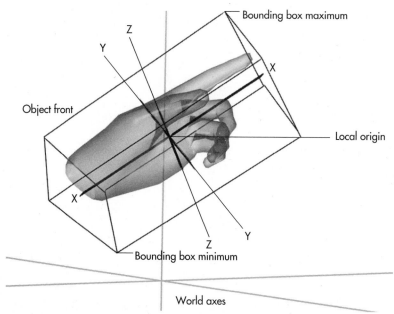

Understanding the Internal Axes of Object Space

While the bounding box shows you the object's overall orientation, it does not inform you of
which axis is which. The Keyframer's Hierarchy/Object Pivot command is your tool to see this

relationship. When an object is selected with Object Pivot, it is displayed in the orthogonal viewports according to its internal axes, without any additional rotation or scale. This is how that object "sees" its surroundings—this is its *object space* (also known as its *local coordinate system*). Object Pivot becomes essential in understanding which direction the object will move, rotate, or scale in regards to scripting (and inverse kinematics).

Adjusting joint parameters in Release 4's IK module illustrates and reinforces the concept of internal axes (see Chapter 20, "Advanced Linking and Inverse Kinematics"). As you adjust different axes and examine their effect on the model, the "real world" direction that various objects rotate or slide can easily seem different. Sliding Object01 along its X axis may slide it "up," while the same operation on Object02 may slide it "back." They are both sliding along the X axis as far as the objects are concerned. They only *seem* to be different because they are rotated from their point of creation in relation to the world.

What may not be immediately obvious is that similar objects *always* begin with the same transformation matrix, and thus the same internal axes orientation. 3D Studio creates its objects with their home orientation being the *Front* viewport, regardless of creation method. Another way to think of this is that an object's height is always projected along its positive Z axis. No matter what viewport you create a primitive in, which way a Lofter path is positioned, or how an object is oriented after creation, the objects will always display in Object Pivot with their "top" (or plan view) being the object space's Front viewport. Figure 22.15 shows six of the primitives and their default orientation. No matter how these objects are created or later animated, they will always use these internal axes for transformations. Cones, for example, will always consider their tip to be along the positive Y axis. (Note that the viewports are labeled in the manner Keyscript understands them to be.)

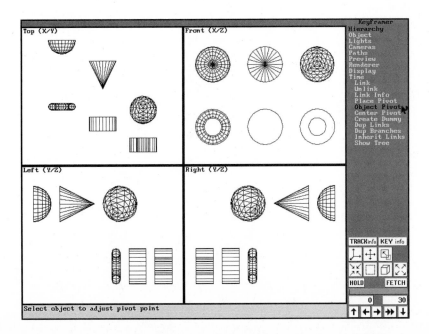

Figure 22.15
3D Studio primitives and their default orientations returned by Hierarchy/Object Pivot.

Of course, figure 22.15 only shows what the objects originally regard as their internal axes. You can always use the 3D Editor's Reset XForm command to reset an object's transformation matrix according to how it is currently oriented in the 3D Editor.

In understanding the default home position of object creation, the intention of 3D Studio's *traditional* axes labeling becomes clear—objects are actually created in the X and Y of the Front viewport, with Z representing the height. (This is the same paradigm as the right hand rule, where objects are created in the X and Y of the Top viewport with Z representing height.)

The Importance of Pivot Points

Until now, you might easily have thought of an object's pivot point as being the Keyframer's version of its local axis. After all, a pivot point is used in much the same way as the local axis is in the 3D Editor. In reality, its behavior is much different.

The 3D Studio database always considers the centroid of the object to be its true origin and locates the object in the world according to this point (this is equivalent to the 3D Editor's concept of the local axis). This local origin is maintained as the fourth row of the object's transformation matrix in world space coordinates. In contrast, the object's pivot point is stored in object space as an offset to the local origin (in other words, it's expressed as an offset from the object's centroid). The pivot point can be located in world space by passing it through the object's transformation matrix. Figure 22.16 shows the resulting vectors used to locate the pivot's local XYZ offset in terms of object space (as was done by PIVTCOPY earlier in this chapter and in Release 4's PIVOT.K3D example).

Figure 22.16

Locating an object's pivot point in relation to object space.

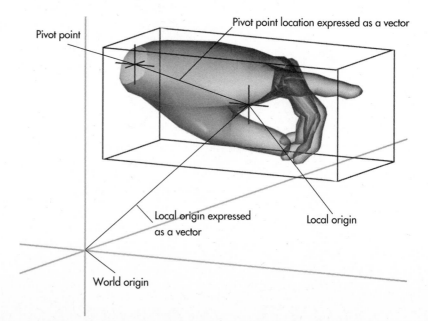

The pivot point is important because all transformations (position, rotation, and scale keys) base their effect on its location. When the pivot point is moved, rotations revolve around and scales expand and shrink towards the new point. In reality, position transformations do as well, although it is not obvious in Keyframer's interface. 3D Studio convention presumes that if you move an object's pivot point, you do not want the object to move with it. In reality, however, position keys base their location upon pivot points as well. When a pivot point is moved, their results change in relation to the world. To compensate for this displacement, 3D Studio automatically adjusts every position key to negate the unwanted translation (this is why objects, and any children, get redrawn when you adjust their pivot points in the Keyframer). A script that places a pivot point will need to adjust position keys if the object is to remain stationary.

While this may at first seem to be a chore, it does give you an ability that is missing in the Keyframer. If only the object's pivot point is set (with SetPivot), then the pivot point remains stationary in regards to the world, and the object moves instead. This is because the pivot point is stored in object space as an offset to the local origin, as shown in figure 22.16. Thus, when the pivot point moves up and to the right, the object is actually moving down and to the left. This is an important ability when the pivot point location is critical, but you want to move the object. Note, however, that pivot points are static in nature—they cannot be animated, and their adjustment affects all frames.

Two Release 4 scripts (PIVOT.K3D and PIVOT2.K3D) provide the essentials for pivot point placement and position key translation. While they do provide a good example of pivot point adjustment, they also contain essential codes for using the transformation matrix. These scripts use three small, but extremely useful, subroutines that perform the basic transformations necessary to convert points from world to object space. The following subroutines are excerpts from PIVOT2.K3D and PIVOT.K3D and are examples of "building block" subroutines, which need to be in nearly any program that locates positions in world or object space. These subroutines essentially perform a matrix math operation on the supplied point components to return the translated point.

```
; Subroutine to rotate translation PT thru transformation matrix TM
; thus locating point PT in world space.
; Note that TMs 4th column (translation) is ignored since this is just
➥rotation.
; (extracted from Tom Hudson's PIVOT.K3D example)
      @RotatePT
             xt=PT.x*TM.tm(0,0)+PT.y*TM.tm(1,0)+PT.z*TM.tm(2,0)
             yt=PT.x*TM.tm(0,1)+PT.y*TM.tm(1,1)+PT.z*TM.tm(2,1)
             zt=PT.x*TM.tm(0,2)+PT.y*TM.tm(1,2)+PT.z*TM.tm(2,2)
             PT.x=xt:PT.y=yt:PT.z=zt
      Return
;
; Subroutine to transform point PT thru transformation matrix TM
; thus translating point PT from object to world space.
; (extracted from Tom Hudson's PIVOT2.K3D example)
      @TransformPT
```

```
              xt = PT.x*TM.tm(0,0) + PT.y*TM.tm(1,0) + PT.z*TM.tm(2,0)
➡+ TM.tm(3,0)
              yt = PT.x*TM.tm(0,1) + PT.y*TM.tm(1,1) + PT.z*TM.tm(2,1)
➡+ TM.tm(3,1)
              zt = PT.x*TM.tm(0,2) + PT.y*TM.tm(1,2) + PT.z*TM.tm(2,2)
➡+ TM.tm(3,2)
              PT.x = xt  :  PT.y = yt  :  PT.z = zt
      Return
;
; Subroutine to inverse-transform point PT thru transformation matrix
➡TM
; thus translating point PT from world to object space.
; (extracted from Tom Hudson's PIVOT2.K3D example)
      @InvTransformPT
              xt = PT.x - TM.tm(3,0)
              yt = PT.y - TM.tm(3,1)
              zt = PT.z - TM.tm(3,2)
              PT.x = xt*TM.tm(0,0) + yt*TM.tm(0,1) + zt*TM.tm(0,2)
              PT.y = xt*TM.tm(1,0) + yt*TM.tm(1,1) + zt*TM.tm(1,2)
              PT.z = xt*TM.tm(2,0) + yt*TM.tm(2,1) + zt*TM.tm(2,2)
      Return
```

While PIVOT.K3D and PIVOT2.K3D are very useful, they do not adjust any children of the affected object. See this chapter's PIVOTBBX.K3D for an example of how this can be done.

Using the NODEINFO and VIEWER Utilities

The preceding sections covered several concepts describing pivot points, bounding boxes, transformation matrices, and the differences between object and world space. Admittedly, this can be somewhat confusing. The concepts are much clearer when you can visualize all the data at once at see how it relates to one another. The NODEINFO.K3D script is included on the *Inside 3D Studio* CD-ROM for this purpose. As figure 22.17 and 22.18 show, the accompanying NODEINFO.3DE resource file presents an interface that displays the critical information for a given node.

While the numbers reported by NODEINFO are informative, a visual representation is usually more immediate and relevant. A definite barrier exists, however, since Keyscript cannot interact with the Keyframer interface. The sample utility VIEWER.K3D (located on the CD-ROM) was developed to lessen this limitation. As figure 22.19 shows, VIEWER draws the basic representation of an object within its own viewport. Displayable are the object's bounding box, pivot point, internal axes, vertices, and faces. The object can be rotated about its three axes and displayed in orthographic views according to its internal axes (much like the Object Pivot command does). Because it is a script, the display speed is not remarkable, but the fact it is working within a script at all somewhat is.

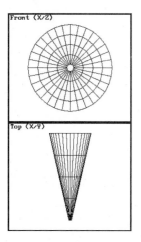

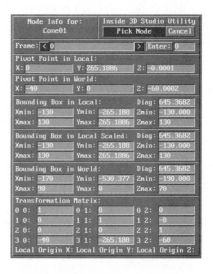

Figure 22.17

The NODEINFO interface for Cone01 at Frame 0.

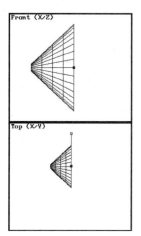

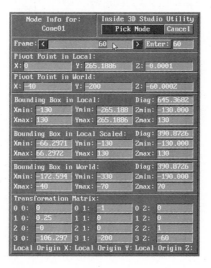

Figure 22.18

The NODEINFO interface for Cone01 at Frame 60 with a 90-degree rotation, a 200-unit translation, and a 2-axis scaling.

Figure 22.19
The VIEWER script
graphically
showing object
information.

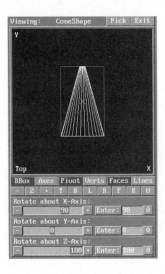

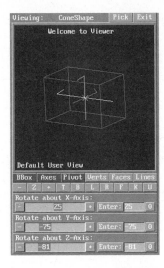

While VIEWER displays some valuable information that the Keyframer interface does not (like the orientation of the internal axes), it was not intended to be an end to itself. The intent of VIEWER is to provide you with the building block code for incorporating a display viewport within your own scripts. Much of the internal code is a series of subroutines that can be clipped and used as needed—or added onto.

Keyframer Versus 3D Editor Operations

In the Keyframer, you manipulate objects about a point that is particular to that object—its pivot point. Any adjustment you make to an object (Move, Rotate, or Scale) can be reversed by reversing the operation or adjusting the appropriate key's value. An adjustment such as this is often referred to as an *affine* operation, or as a *single-matrix deformation*. All of these operations are occurring in object space. Scale, rotation, and pivot placement are all in relation to the object's extents and have no bearing on where the object may actually be in the world. All Keyframer commands are affine operations and are recorded within the 12 numbers of the object's transformation matrix.

In the 3D Editor, you manipulate objects about a certain point in space (either the world axis or the selections local axis). You also have the ability to modify an object in a way that cannot be reversed (with Bend or Taper, for example). A modification such as this is known as a *non-affine* operation or a *multimatrix deformation*. Because you can manipulate vertices in the 3D Editor, their positions are recorded in the object's vertex list and not in its transformation matrix. The Keyframer's frame 0 (original) scale key is never affected by scale operations that occur in the 3D Editor.

Examining Sample Scripts

The *Inside 3D Studio* CD-ROM contains several scripts to illustrate some of the more advanced elements of Keyscript. While the scripts themselves can be located anywhere on your computer, they assume their accompanying 3DE files are located in 3D Studio's current PROCESS directory.

Most of the example scripts included on the *Inside 3D Studio* CD-ROM (and as Release 4 samples) are heavily commented so they can be followed and learned from. You can improve their performance significantly by eliminating all comments, tabs, and extra spaces within the code. Many programmers keep their commented and formatted code for reference and make a stripped version for final execution.

Scripts for Command Improvement

It is a common desire to improve an existing command so it performs the way *you* believe it should have done from the start. The following section provides examples of such a command improvement.

Improved Pivot Placement

While a properly placed pivot point is critical to animation, 3D Studio's tool for placing them is far from perfect. By default, an object begins with its pivot point located at its local origin. Using either Hierarchy/Place Pivot or Hierarchy/Object Pivot only enables you to locate the point by eye—getting exact locations can be quite difficult. The Center Pivot command is the only tool provided to locate the pivot point in relation to geometry, and then only at its default, centroidal position.

A natural desire would be to have this command operate more like the 3D Editor's Modify/ Axis/Align command, which places the global axis according to the extents of an object's bounding box. PIVOTBBX.K3D (short for "Pivot by Bounding Box") was developed with this goal in mind.

PIVOTBBX—Pivot Point Placement by Bounding Box

The PIVOTBBX script begins by asking for a selection of objects and/or dummy objects for pivot point alteration. After a selection has been made, the `mainDlg` is presented, as shown in figure 22.20. In keeping with the script's goal, it is necessary to somehow relate user input to the edges of the bounding box. This is accomplished with a custom dialog box created in 3DE. The navigation of 27 possible pivot locations is reduced to two mouse picks. The object's top plane (the direction it sees as "top" with Object Pivot) is displayed as nine icon choices. The height of the point is derived from three side icons. Together they define the correct point in relation to the object's bounding box. The labels of both icon groups are updated to reinforce the user's choices. Clicking on OK quickly redefines the pivot points for the entire selection set chosen.

Figure 22.20
The PIVOTBBX Interface.

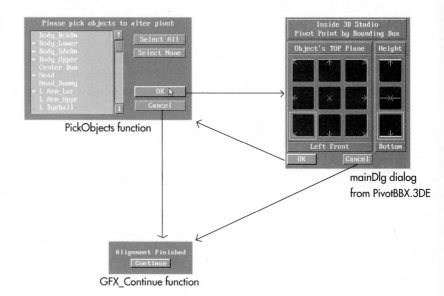

PickObjects function

mainDlg dialog
from PivotBBX.3DE

GFX_Continue function

The PIVOTBBX script can be broken down into the required programming steps with the following pseudo code:

```
; The script begins by requesting user information:
    Define required data structures variables
    Define Feel and See functions for dialog elements
    Get a list of objects for pivot placement (with PickObjects)
    Put up the mainDlg dialog (from PIVOTBBX.3DE)
        Evaluate user dialog interaction (see fig. 22.21)
        Get the icon positions for the Top and Height icons
        Update the dialog's labels with user choices
    End dialog
; Once the script has the required user input, the real work begins:
        For each object:
            Get and store a list of the object's children (with
➥GetParent)
            Unlink the object's children (with SetParent)
            Get object's pivot point (with GetPivot)
            Get object's transformation matrix (with GetXForm)
```

```
              Get object's bounding box in object space (with GetBoundBox)
              Locate the pivot point according to bounding box extents
              Determine the distance form old to new pivot point
              Get the number of position keys (with GetKeyCount)
              Create position keys to negate translation (with CreateKey)
              Assign the pivot point (with SetPivot)
              Relink any children back to the object (with SetParent)
          Do next object
      End script
  ; Required subroutines are placed at the end-
      Transformation matrix subroutines
      Dlg_Feel subroutines (for dialog buttons)
      Dlg_See subroutines (for dialog frames)
      Gfx_Demo
```

Tip

PIVOTBBX is most useful when you understand the true orientation of the objects' internal axes. As mentioned throughout this chapter, the Keyframer's Object Pivot command is your primary tool for understanding this relationship. You will have the most success if you use the Object Pivot command to understand which direction the object sees as its "top" before using the PIVOTBBX script.

The PIVOTBBX script is a good programming example of using a fairly simple 3DE dialog box and using icons and frames to indicate user picks. It also demonstrates an alternative method for pivot point redefinition when children are concerned. Instead of altering every position key the children may have, the script unlinks them, redefines the parent's pivot point, and links them back again (thus saving what could be a considerable amount of key creation).

Scripts for Animation Automation

One of the great abilities of scripting is to alleviate the tedium that arises from doing the same operation over and over. Not only can multiple operations be tiresome, they may be impossible to do accurately by conventional methods. The following section investigates a script that makes a previously unthinkable task very practical.

Camera Tracking Script

A common practice, or trick, in computer animation is to use simple planes to represent more complex geometry. These planes are assigned texture and opacity maps so they simulate entourage objects, such as trees, people, and cars. While initially convincing, their illusion is shattered when your viewing angle becomes oblique to their surface and they appear as knife edges. The desire then is to place these decal objects so their surface is perpendicular to the camera's. While this could be accomplished fairly easily for a single image, the task becomes nearly impossible for an animation. After all, every decal object would have to rotate to stay perpendicular for every frame that the camera is moving. A script can automate the process and make the result rock solid.

CAMTRACK—Staying Perpendicular to a Camera

CAMTRACK.K3D and CAMTRACK.3DE are included on the *Inside 3D Studio* CD-ROM for your use. CAMTRACK's purpose is to rotate a selection of objects so they remain perpendicular to a camera (see fig. 22.21). The script is written so that the objects will remain perpendicular, regardless of camera and/or object movement. Because the script checks for proper face normal orientation, the planes can be oriented in any manner, and two-sided rendering is not required.

Figure 22.21
The CAMTRACK interface.

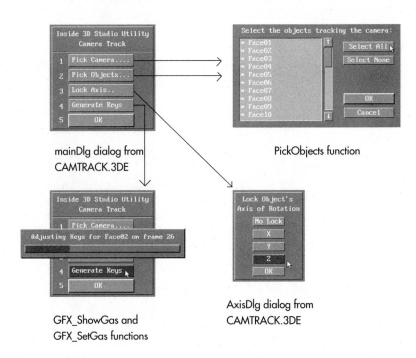

mainDlg dialog from
CAMTRACK.3DE

PickObjects function

GFX_ShowGas and
GFX_SetGas functions

AxisDlg dialog from
CAMTRACK.3DE

This script performs several tasks that illustrate essential elements of computer animation programming. The script is heavily commented and includes descriptions of useful mathematical and programming concepts. Examine CAMTRACKs subroutines and feel free to cut and paste applicable ones into your own scripts if you find them valuable. Operations that are of particular interest might be *face normal determination*, *vector calculations*, a *quaternion rotation calculation*, and *axis locking*.

The script begins by requesting user information, as follows:

```
; The script begins by requesting user information:
  Define required data structures variables
  Define Feel and See functions for Dialog elements
  Put up the mainDlg dialog from CAMTRACK.3DE
      Evaluate user dialog interaction (see fig. 22.21)
          Get a Camera to track (with ChooseNode)
          Get a list of objects to rotate (with PickObjects)
          Get locking directives (with AxisDlg for CAMTRACK.3DE)
          Rotate the objects!
; Once the script has the user input, the real work begins:
        For each object:
            For each frame:
                Get face, vertex, pivot point and TM data for the
➡object
                Calculate the direction of the first face's
➡normal
                Calculate the vector from the pivot to the camera
                Calculate the angle to be normal to the vector
            Create a rotation key to form a perpendicular
          Display gas gauge increment and advance to next frame
        Do next object
      End dialog
  End script
; Required subroutines are placed at the end:
  Find_Normal_and_Angle
  Find_Normal
  Transform_Camera
  Transform_Point
  Transform_Pivot
  Transformation matrix subroutines
  Dlg_Feel subroutines (for dialog buttons)
  Feel_Animate (main subroutine for rotation calculations)
```

Figure 22.22 shows a scene with a camera path meandering through a "forest" of planar objects. The material assigned to the planes has a texture and opacity map, as shown in the rendered viewport. Currently, the scene is less than convincing since most of the planes are oblique to the camera's viewpoint.

Figure 22.23 shows the same scene after executing CAMTRACK. The objects are now all perpendicular to the camera, regardless of where they are in the scene. When viewed in the Top viewport, the camera's position now seems like the center of a wheel, with all of the planes revolving about it. What's interesting is that this appearance of being the "hub of a wheel" will carry over on every frame, even if the planes are moving. The scene depicted in figure 22.22 (and its texture map) can be found on the *Inside 3D Studio* CD-ROM as CAMTRACK.3DS and TARGET.TGA for your experimentation.

Figure 22.22
The scene before running the CAMTRACK script (all planes are in rows).

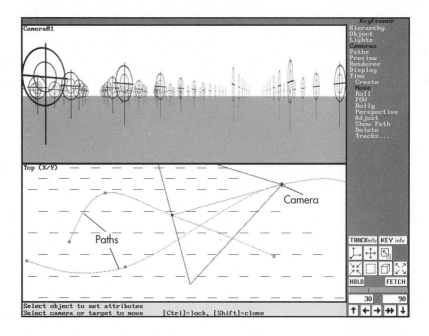

Figure 22.23
The scene after running the CAMTRACK script (all planes are perpendicular to the camera).

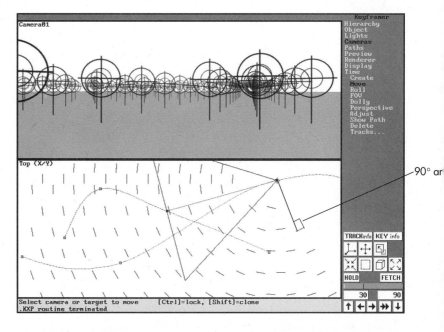

What should be obvious is that the plane's pivot point should be coincidental with the portion of texture that needs to appear stationary (the trunk of a tree, for example). If the pivot point is off-center, the texture maps will appear to twirl or swing rather than stay perpendicular to the camera. Other possibilities for this script are falling leaves and snowflakes, asteroids, dirt particles, and even birds as animated materials. Now that there's an easy way to keep objects facing your camera, you are free to include animation complexities, at a very low modeling cost, that were previously very difficult, if not impossible, to incorporate.

Scripts for Special Effects

Possibly the most advanced form of script is one that performs a special effect. The desire is to do something that by its very nature is normally considered beyond the realm of 3D Studio. This can prove to be a significant challenge for the script programmer as the envelope begins to be pushed.

SKIN Slice Scaling

The animated Plug-In SKIN has become an extremely popular AXP. At render time, SKIN creates a Bézier stand-in patch that meshes over Bézier curve control points. The control points are actually the vertices of "slices." The slices are created when SKIN's sister product, SLICE.PXP, slices the lofted object into appropriate cross sections that define the original mesh's surface. When rendered, these slices are "skinned" with a perfectly smooth mesh by the AXP; the original mesh is then no longer needed. The advantage of using SKIN is that the individual slices can be animated without fear of exposing a joint. The disadvantage is that it is very difficult to get a successful result from scaling individual slices, and scaling groups of slices over time is essentially impossible. The difficulty lies in the fact that the slices represent control points—not exact mesh positions. Getting even one slice out of alignment might strangely deform the rendered mesh.

An obvious thing to model with SKIN is the human form. Inverse Kinematics has made animating such models much easier. The convention quite often used now is to link the series of slices to an underlying bone structure. The bones are given IK joint parameters, while the slices are totally constrained. When the bones are animated, the linked slices come along. Muscles flex, strain, and bulge, however. These are characteristics that must be reflected in scaling the various groups of slices—this is where a script can be invaluable.

BULGE.K3D was created with the goal of flexing muscles. It is assumed that the model is composed of SKIN slices and linked as described previously. It is also assumed that you have already animated the model by conventional methods (more than likely with IK). You are given control of how much the various slices are allowed to bulge through the use of a DAT file—this file contains your model, its slices, how far each slice can bulge, and what axes to respect. When the BULGE script is run, you load the DAT file that pertains to your model. BULGE then examines your scene's animation and calculates the angle being formed between adjacent bones. As the angle becomes acute, the limb is contracting and the appropriates slices will bulge out accordingly.

But bulging is only the first step—slices have, by default, a centered pivot point that is rarely changed. When the slices are scaled, they will do so uniformly—that is unlike most muscles (a bicep only bulges "up," for example). To compensate for this, BULGE keeps a record of each slice's original bounding box and transformation matrix. Execute BULGE again, solve for position, and the result will be a constrained and realistic muscle bulge!

BULGE—Getting Muscles to Bulge

BULGE.K3D and BULGE.3DE are included on the *Inside 3D Studio* CD-ROM for your use. BULGE's purpose is to scale skin slices attached to an underlying bone structure. The position of the underlying bone structure is analyzed, and the slices belonging to the bones(s) are bulged as the angle(s) between the bones becomes more acute.

The BULGE script requires that the user predetermine the scaling characteristics of the model. This is done in a *.DAT file that BULGE aids the user in creating with its "Create BULGE.DAT file" option (see fig. 22.24). This DAT file must then be modified by hand in an ASCII editor to reflect the model's muscle bulging characteristics. (3DS's Text Editor or the other Script Buffer works well for this.) This enables you to have one DAT file that controls the muscle bulging of an entire model—from head to toe.

Figure 22.24
The BULGE
Script interface.

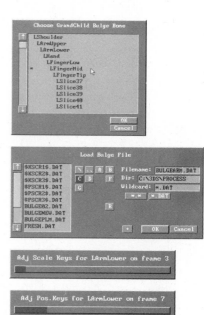

The format for the DAT files used by BULGE is as follows:

```
"EffectingBoneName", "SlicePrefixName", XMinScale, XMaxScale,
➥YMinScale, YMaxScale, BeginSlice#, EndSlice#
Slice#, ScaleType, Alignment (repeated as a new line for each slice)
```

Codes for the slice lines that follow each bone are as follows:

```
ScaleType: LOCKED = 0 CENTERED = 1 ALIGNED = 2
Alignment: No_Align = 0 R_Align = 1 L_Align = 2 B_Align = 3
                        T_Align = 4 K_Align = 5 F_Align = 6
```

The Scaletype code informs BULGE of whether the slice is scaled, and if so, whether to align it or not. The following Alignment code is examined when the Scaletype is set to 2. The Alignment code's value declares the side of the slice that is anchored (the bottom of a bulging bicep, for example). Note that this is in relation to the slice's internal understanding of which way is up—it's in object space according to the internal axes.

BULGE solves for all bones/slice groupings within a given DAT file at once. While each bone segment has a given scale range, the middle slice receives the maximum scale and others are scaled proportionally less. It is usually only necessary to scale the middle 1–3 slices of a given bone segment to generate a convincing bulge.

Once the governing DAT file is created, you are ready to start bulging muscles for that model. (Note—you only need to create the DAT file once for each model, and it should probably be named accordingly.)

This version of BULGE requires executing the script twice. After a proper DAT file is created, the first execution is the following:

```
"Load Bulge.DAT File," "SCALE Bulge Slices," and Exit
```

The slices are resized, but are currently scaled uniformally about their pivot points. To align them, run the script again. The second execution thus involves the following:

```
"Load Bulge.DAT File," "ALIGN Slice Edges," and Exit
```

This requirement of two executions results from not being able to read the modified slice's bounding box values in world coordinates immediately after creating a new scale key. BULGE's work-around for this is to save the prescaled transformation matrix, along with the bounding box data of each affected slice, within a temporary file during scale executions. During the second execution, and prior to creating the modified alignment position keys, the temporary file of prescaled data is read in. Note that this Keyscript limitation could be overcome if the script did the calculations itself (instead of relying on Keyscript's GetBoundBox function), and the process could be reduced to a single loop, and even a single button option.

Included on the *Inside 3D Studio* CD-ROM is BULGEARM.PRJ, which demonstrates the use of the BULGE script. Figure 22.25 shows the model after it was initially animated with the IK module. The right portion of figure 22.25 is the same mesh after being rendered, showing what SKIN.AXP actually does.

The governing DAT file (BULGEARM.DAT) is included so you can run BULGE on the same model. When the script is run, BULGEARM.DAT is loaded and the scale keys are generated. Figure 22.26 shows the model after this first BULGE execution.

Figure 22.25
The original model after standard animation.

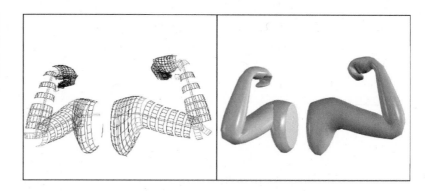

Figure 22.26
The model after initially running BULGE to scale the Slices.

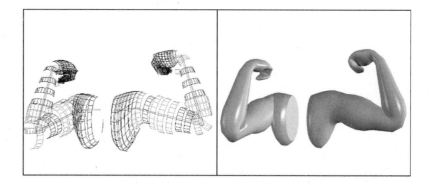

Once the scale keys are written, the BULGE script is run again (there's actually no need to ever leave Keyscript). The same BULGEARM.DAT is loaded and the ALIGN Slice Edges button is pressed. The temporary file that was written during the first execution is read back in, and the slices are aligned according to their new bounding box sizes. The result is a convincing muscle bulge, as shown in figure 22.27.

Figure 22.27
The model after running BULGE again to equalize the slice positions.

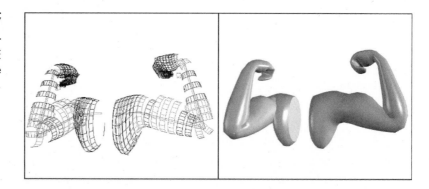

New Riders Publishing
INSIDE SERIES

Summary

Scripting gives you control of 3D Studio by letting you affect the scene at the code level, in much the same way as a Plug-In can. You are limited only by what you can code. There is great potential with this newfound ability that has only begun to be explored. There is much in the way of physical data that can now be fed into the Keyframer via Keyscript. Many animations can be the product of natural and fractal algorithms (gravity, collision, scattering, and flocking are just some possibilities).

While CompuServe's ASOFT Forum is the definitive place for 3D Studio discussion in general, there is now a new section dedicated to scripting. While always being a place to ask questions and learn, this section also promises to host many user supplied scripts that should prove both useful as utilities and as examples.

The programmers that created Keyscript have also developed the equivalent environment for every variety of 3D Studio Plug-In (except BXPs). KUB Software (pronounced "cube") markets the *Script Extension*—a set of four integrated Plug-In modules for 3D Studio scripting. This suite of Plug-Ins should be seriously considered by anyone that finds Keyscript in the least bit useful. The Script Extension is available from Schreiber Instruments.

The Script Extension includes SCRIPT.PXP, SCRIPT.AXP, SCRIPT.IXP, and SCRIPT SXP. The PXP is universal, and can be used to control both the 3D Editor and Keyframer environments. It also can execute scripts created with conventional Keyscript (Keyscript actually becomes somewhat unnecessary once you have the Script Extension). All four Script modules share the same core code, interface, and basic syntax. If you have learned the essentials of Keyscript, you're in good shape to learn their equivalent for the other Plug-In formats. The Script modules can even pass information to one another. (An animation script could affect a procedural script and then interact with a particle system script, for example!). The Script Extension should give users maximum control of 3D Studio's inner workings.

If you are enthusiastic about scripting, taking control of 3D Studio, and computer animation programming in general, you are strongly encouraged to investigate the following texts:

Vince, John. *3-D Computer Animation*. Addison-Wesley Publishing Company.

Feiner, Foley, Hughes, and VanDam. *Computer Graphics: Principles and Practice (Second Edition)*. Addison-Wesley Publishing Company.

Autodesk, Inc. *IPAS 4 Toolkit*.

Autodesk, Inc. *3D Studio File Toolkit*.

Chapter Snapshot

The only method of achieving smooth full-color playback of your animations is to record them on video. This chapter discusses the theories of frame-accurate animation and different methods of recording single frame animations. The following topics are presented:

- ✔ Rendering frames versus fields
- ✔ Rendering directly to videotape
- ✔ Rendering to a hard disk
- ✔ Rotoscoping

Animation for Field/Frame-Accurate Recording

C reating animations for video is very different from creating animations intended for computer playback. You should know the final format for your project long before your preliminary storyboards are created, because the differences between computer and video playback have a bearing on almost every decision you make during the course of your project—both creative and technical.

This chapter discusses the differences between computer and video playback, and covers the details of frame-accurate recording to videotape.

Appendix C contains a discussion of some newer hardware technologies in frame-accurate recording, such as laser disc recorders, *digital disk recorders* (DDRs), and real-time RAM playback units.

Understanding Real-Time Recording of Computer-Based Animations

The simplest method of recording your animations on videotape is to play them back on your computer through 3D Studio or Animator Pro and record them on videotape "live." Because of the different formats of computer and video, there must be a hardware link to translate, or encode, the computer's RGB output to that of video. A few different methods for accomplishing this translation are available. One method is to have a graphics board in your computer that has dual outputs—one for RGB for your computer monitor, and also a standard VHS or SVHS output.

Another method is to have a second card in your computer. The video signal is looped through the second board from your VGA card and out to video from there. This method enables you to upgrade your graphics board to a newer or faster one when available without having to spend more for a video card that includes recordable video output.

Even better than this method is to have an external unit to accomplish the translation. This provides the greatest flexibility in moving from computer to computer. Also, laptop computers typically have no slots to make use of an internal board, which limits their use in on-site presentations. Computer playback of animations has many drawbacks, whether the animations are played back on computer or recorded live to videotape.

Playback Speed and Accuracy

The best animation quality is achieved when high-resolution images are played back as fast as or slightly faster than your eye/brain combination can distinguish individual images in full color. This is the goal, but certain physical factors make this difficult to achieve.

A single frame of 24-bit color (16.7 million colors) at video resolution is almost a full megabyte uncompressed. Compressed images are approximately half a megabyte in size. Playing back these images at the speed of videotape—30 frames per second—means reading 15 MB of data from your hard disk and transferring that data onto your graphics card every second. Keeping a sustained transfer rate of that magnitude is not possible with today's PC technology.

First, the speed drops far below what is necessary to sustain the illusion of motion. Even more disconcerting is that the speed is constantly changing—frames that compress smaller play faster, and frames that do not compress as far slow down the animation even more.

Any animations that require extremely accurate playback speed should not depend on computer playback. The differences in computers, graphics boards, and even the amount of memory available affect the speed of playback.

Colors Available

3D Studio's computer built-in playback depends on a 256-color maximum and a compression scheme for animation. 256 colors (8 bits) produces a much smaller file size than 24-bit images. In addition, the animations are stored in a single compressed file. The method of storage is based on the idea that the only information necessary to store is the entire first frame, and the differences (or delta) in the pixels between the first frame and subsequent frames. If a small change occurs between the first frame and the second frame, only a small amount of data is necessary, and the animation plays back quickly. This occurs in a flying logo animation, for example.

If a large delta occurs between the frames—which occurs, for example, when a camera is moved through an architectural animation—the file size grows larger, and a large amount of individual pixels on the screen needs to be updated for each frame. This can cause a tearing effect in the animation as it tries to update faster than the hardware allows.

Smooth Motion

The way to solve all these problems is through frame-by-frame recording of the animation. Each frame is stored on the computer as a separate file; therefore, the full 16.7 million colors are available at high resolution. Also, when copied to videotape one frame at a time, you can depend on all your animations to play back extremely smoothly at 30 frames per second at exactly the same speed. When rendering to videotape, you have the option of field rendering. This type of rendering, discussed later in this chapter, plays back on your video system at 60 fields per second, for the absolute smoothest animations possible.

If you are working on forensic animation for accident reconstruction, or any other type of animation in which timing is an issue, plan on using frame-by-frame recording.

VCR Availability

Another advantage of videotape recording is that you can depend on your clients having a VCR player available, either at their office or at home. The VCR playback always is the same speed and shows your animation the way you intended it. With computer playback, you can't be sure whether your client can use the computer disk you mail him, whether his graphics board is capable of displaying enough colors at the proper resolution, or at what speed his equipment can play back your animation without tearing and jerking.

Configuring for Frame-Accurate Tape Recording

Some general rules apply to any type of frame-accurate recording, no matter what particular brand or model of tape deck you have. For more detailed information on a particular deck, see the manuals that came with your controller and the *videotape recorder* (VTR).

The theory of frame-accurate recording is that the computer loads a frame into the framebuffer, and then "tells" the controller to back up the tape deck three to five seconds. This is done to make sure that the heads and tape have a chance to come up to speed before the recording actually takes place. This is called a *pre-roll*. Next, the deck is put into play mode, and at the exact moment the tape is on the proper frame, the Record command is given for exactly 1/30th of a second. The tape then stops after another second of forward motion. Another frame is loaded into the framebuffer, and the entire process is repeated again—30 times for one second of animation or 1,800 times for a minute of animation.

A few controller companies have just come out with a new method of recording animations to tape that is faster and causes less wear and tear on the mechanism. They determine how fast frames can be loaded into the framebuffer, and then start a pass of numerous frames without a pre-roll. If, for example, a particular animation's frames can be loaded in two seconds, the system pre-rolls and starts recording frames 0, 60, 120, 180, and so on. The system rewinds the tape and starts again, recording frames 1, 61, 121, 181, and so on until the entire animation is on tape. Depending on how many frames are to be recorded on tape, a tremendous reduction in time can occur. More time is saved as the animations get longer. This method, however, does not work with all decks.

Time Code

The computer keeps track of where on tape the individual frames go through a system called *time code*. A home VCR does not use time code; it works with a system of pulses, all identical, called a *control track*. The control track works adequately for a home system, and even for minor editing, but it is erratic and not exact enough for frame-by-frame animation.

Time code (also referred to as *SMPTE time code*, for the Society of Motion Picture and Television Engineers) is a system whereby a separate track is recorded on the tape that holds the frame information in an hours:minutes:seconds:frames format—for example, 01:22:35:03. The format is stored on the tape similar to the way audio information is stored on tape, and in fact, some tape decks that do not have a separate time code track work very well by storing the time code information on an audio track.

The information is stored in 80 bits per frame. The actual time code information is only 48 bits; the other 32 bits are referred to as *user bits*, which are available to the user. Information that can be stored in the user bits includes control commands, roll numbers, character information, and so on.

The two types of time code are *Longitudinal Time Code* (LTC) and *Vertical Interval Time Code* (VITC). No practical difference exists between the two; each stores the same information, just in a different way. LTC is stored on a third audio track, whereas VITC is superimposed onto the vertical blanking interval.

Drop Frame Versus Non-Drop Frame Time Code

National Television Standards Committee (NTSC) video, the standard in the United States, is not exactly 30 frames per second; it is actually 29.97 frames per second. For most purposes, this is close enough. Over a longer period, however, enough of a discrepancy exists to cause a problem in a time-critical application—such as a network television broadcast show or commercial. To alleviate the timing issues, a system called *Drop Frame* (DF) time code is used. In this method, a frame is dropped from the count every few frames to make up for the difference. This is not a problem in editing because the editor can take this into account. In single-frame animation, however, the system cannot account for the lost frame, and 3D Studio cannot record with the frame number "missing." If you need your final output to be on DF time code, you must first record your animation on a *Non-Drop Frame* (NDF) tape, and then only re-record the time code track with a DF time code, or dub it onto a tape with a DF time code.

Blacking a Tape Before Use

A tape must be prepared to accept data before it is first used in single frame animation. This is analogous to formatting a floppy disk before using it in a computer. This process is sometimes referred to as *blacking* or *striping* a tape.

The tape is placed in the machine where it is to be used. A stable black signal is then fed into the video input. The time code generator is turned on and set for Non-Drop Frame output, and the entire tape is recorded with this information. The tape now is ready to be used for single-frame animation. Check your VTR—some VTRs have alternative methods to stripe the tape.

VTR Formats

Many different types of formats of frame-accurate decks exist. They are much more expensive than your home VCR because they must be capable of recording one single frame in an absolutely perfect position thousands of times per day, without missing a frame or laying it down in the wrong location. How well they do this depends on the overall quality of the mechanism in the deck, which is directly related to the price. Do not expect a $3,000 SVHS deck to compare with a $15,000 BetaSP deck in mechanical quality, performance, or image quality.

The four major categories of video equipment are consumer, prosumer, industrial, and professional (sometimes referred to as broadcast). *Consumer* decks are not capable of frame-accurate work. *Prosumer* decks are the next level up and include both SVHS and Hi-8 decks. Prosumer decks are the cheapest decks that can be used for frame-accurate animation.

The *industrial* category offers better quality images, in addition to a higher quality deck. Into this area fall the 3/4-inch decks—both 3/4 inch and 3/4 inch SP (Superior Performance).

The *professional* decks include Beta and BetaSP, recordable laser disc, M-II, 1 inch, and the digital formats D1, D2, and D3. Professional-level decks keep the video signal separated into its component parts for higher quality images. These formats can be edited numerous times without the signal degradation that accompanies copying one tape onto another. If, for example, you lay your animation onto one tape, edit it into a video, and then make dubs of the copy to distribute, you take your master down three generations. Each generation degrades the quality of the video. Professional level decks minimize or eliminate generational loss of quality.

Hardware Configuration of Typical VTRs

You must understand that you seldom control a tape deck directly. 3D Studio gives commands to a controller, which then controls the deck. A few different controllers are on the market today, and they can be divided into two types: software only or a combination of hardware and software.

Two sets of cables connect a frame-accurate deck to your computer. One set carries the video signal. Depending on the deck, it can be (in order of preference) RGB, component, SVHS, or composite. The other set of cables is the controller cable. This can be one of three types, depending on the deck: parallel, serial RS422, or serial RS232. A considerable difference exists between the different types; although when each is set up, the user sees no practical difference.

Many older decks use a parallel interface. Although similar in concept to a computer parallel port, it is a very different interface, and must have a hardware controller to operate.

Most newer decks use a 9-pin serial RS422 interface. This is the standard Sony protocol and is emulated by almost all new decks. Serial RS422 is very different from a computer serial communications port. Serial RS422 is the control interface used if the deck is utilized as part of an edit suite.

Some decks now can be controlled by a 25-pin Serial 232 interface, the standard computer serial interface. These decks usually are the easiest to control from a computer for that reason. 3D Studio Release 4 includes ADI drivers licensed from the Pyros Partnership, Inc. for the Sony EVO-9650, a Hi-8 serial deck, and the Sony CRV Recordable laser disc series of products. These are the only frame-accurate decks for which 3D Studio has included drivers. For almost all other devices, you must not only purchase the deck, but also a controller card or software.

Sync Sources

The video signal coming from your computer must be synchronized with the tape deck. If it is not, you cannot place the frames in the proper location on the tape, and you might end up with half a frame. This is the equivalent of the image rolling either horizontally or vertically on your television screen.

There are three methods that you can use to synchronize the computer output with the deck. They depend on which device is used as a master sync source. You can use your framebuffer as the master, the deck, or a separate sync generator. If both your deck and framebuffer have a sync in and a sync out, you can use any of the three methods. If you have a device that has only a sync out or only a sync in, you are more limited in your choice.

The preferred method is an external sync generator, or *house sync*. This method synchronizes not only your computer, but also an entire edit suite. The result is that all your equipment can be perfectly synchronized, enabling you to use any piece without rewiring.

Rendering Frames Versus Fields

Knowing the difference between frame rendering and field rendering and when t) use each can make the difference between a good animation and a great one. The increased smoothness of a field-rendered animation over one rendered by frames is like night and day.

Understanding Frames and Fields

Frame rendering is the default method for creating animations in 3D Studio. Each rendered frame is placed on one frame of videotape, and each one is displayed for 1/30th of a second. If an object moves through your scene quickly or the camera is panning quickly, the animation appears to move in a series of jerks across the screen. Your eye can distinguish movement at more than 1/30th of a second, and an animation rendered at this speed does not appear very smooth.

If all video is shown at 30 frames per second, what can you do to make it smoother? The answer to this lies surprisingly in a technology, which the industry strives to avoid in computer monitors, called *interlacing*. This feature now is used in recording to video. A computer monitor displays every scan line in succession, starting with the top one and working down in a method called *non-interlaced*, or *progressive scan*.

A television set, on the other hand, starts with the top line, but displays every other line to the bottom, and then comes back to pick up the lines it missed. This is called an *interlaced display*. Each separate set of scan lines is called a *field*. A video camera records images in the same manner using two fields. Refer to figure 23.1 to see the relationship between fields and frames.

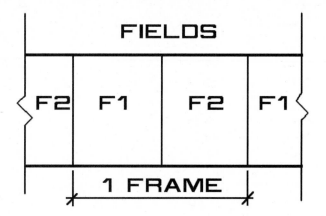

Figure 23.1
The relationship between fields and frames.

If you use a video camera to record an image of a basketball moving quickly, and then play it back and pause on a single frame with a high-quality deck, you will see that the basketball moves between the time the camera records the first field and the second one. The basketball actually appears to be in two places at once; the image appears to be jittering back and forth. This is a demonstration of *field recording*.

To demonstrate this effect while in 3D Studio, create a sphere approximately one-third the size of your camera view and aim a light at it. Now, in the Keyframer, set the number of frames to two, and place the sphere at the left edge of the camera view in frame 0, and at the right edge of the viewport in frame 2 (see fig. 23.2).

Render frame 1 and observe that the sphere is in the center of your viewport (see fig. 23.3).

Figure 23.2
The camera view of the image to render in fields and frames.

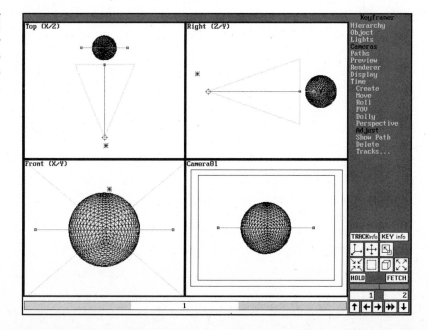

Figure 23.3
The rendered image without fields.

Prepare to render the same scene, but before starting the Renderer, change the Render Fields option in the Render Options dialog box from No to Yes. Now render the sphere again. The Renderer now renders the scene twice, but only renders every other line each time, calculates the location of the sphere based on fields instead of frames, and renders both fields on the same file (see fig. 23.4).

Figure 23.4
The rendered image with fields.

Depending on the animation, field rendering can take almost no more time than frame rendering. This is because only half the image is rendered in each pass. The time to render fields increases if shadows or automatic reflections are used. Both of these must be recalculated for each field, and this can be the most time-consuming portion of the rendering.

When to Render Frames

In certain situations, frame rendering should be used. Use frame rendering, for example, when you render still images. Field rendering is not a substitute for motion blur. Never use fields if you will utilize computer playback of your animation because fields are not used in progressive scan devices. The same holds true if you are rendering to film. Film projectors play back one frame at a time.

Another use for frame rendering is when you anticipate many holds, or when your animation is to be used for slow playback, such as courtroom animations. If you want the viewer to be able to pause on any frame to review the video, render to frames.

When to Render Fields

Render to fields whenever smooth motion is required, and the project will be output to videotape. If the first or last frame will be held on the tape, it is a good idea not to render these two frames with fields so that no jitter occurs during the hold.

If you hold the first or last frame when recording to videotape, it is especially important to have an ease from or an ease to on these frames for a smooth start and end to your animation. If not, your animation has a noticeable jump when the action starts or stops.

Setting Up Fields

Preparing for field rendering is a very simple procedure. Verify that your FIELD-ORDER parameter in the 3DS.SET file is set to 1. Unless you know for a fact that your service bureau has specific requirements otherwise, this is the standard for 99 percent of all renderings.

Now load your animation and access the Render Options dialog box by choosing Renderer/ Setup/Options, then set the Render Fields option to Yes (see fig. 23.5). Any renderings you do after these preparations are properly field-rendered.

Figure 23.5
The Render Options dialog box showing field rendering.

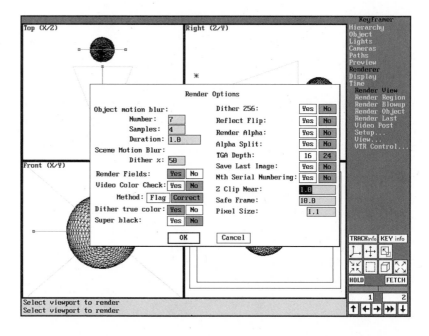

Rendering Directly to Videotape

Two methods of laying your animations on videotape are available. You either can render them directly to your tape deck, or render to disk first and then lay them on tape all at the same time.

Advantages of Rendering to Tape

The single largest advantage of rendering directly to tape is that you never have to worry about running out of disk storage space. As your animations are completed, they are recorded directly to tape before proceeding to the next frame of your animation.

This enables you to watch the animations as they render, not only as stills, but also as animations as the VTR does a pre-roll and record. If you render the animation to files on disk, you cannot see an animation problem until the entire animation is finished rendering and then recorded to tape.

Problems of Rendering to Tape

The main problem of rendering directly to tape is that you cannot use the network-rendering features of 3D Studio Release 4. Only the computer that has the VTR attached to it can record frames directly to videotape. Another disadvantage of rendering to tape is that the files are not on disk. If a problem occurs that could easily be fixed by compositing an additional layer in Video Post, the entire project has to be re-rendered. Generally speaking, you want to render to disk unless you just don't have the disk space.

Using VTR Control

After your VTR and controller are properly configured, you have full control over its operation from within 3D Studio. The commands to control a VTR, such as Play, Go To, Rewind, and Fast Forward, can be found in Keyframer's Renderer/VTR Control menu branch. These commands are identical whether you are rendering directly to tape, to disk and then to VTR, with the exception of the last two menu items, which determine the method of laying to tape.

VTR Setup

VTR Setup, as the name implies, is the first menu item to pick any time you want to do any recording to tape, either directly or disk-to-VTR (see fig. 23.6). The Frame Repeat option determines the number of times each frame is recorded on tape. Normally, this is always left at 1. For quick tests, you can set it to 2 to render every other frame for rough motion and timing tests. This is referred to as 'shooting on twos,' and often is used for cartoon animation.

Figure 23.6
The VTR Setup
dialog box.

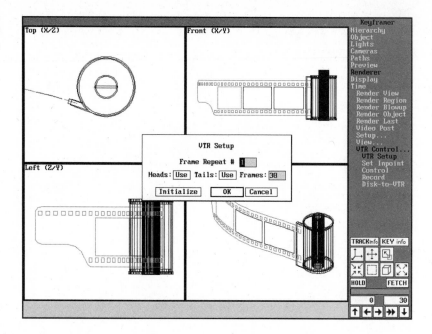

The Heads and Tails boxes provide a *handle* on your animations for easier editing and enable viewers to see what is happening before the animation is over. If either Heads or Tails is used, make sure that there is no movement if field rendering is being utilized. The Frames option determines the length of the hold.

Initialize is the most important button in this dialog box. The Initialize command tests the connection, initializes the VTR and controller, and prepares everything to start recording. You must select Initialize each time the system is used to output files to the VTR. Some ADI drivers, such as the Sony CRV laser disc driver that ships with 3D Studio Release 4, set a flag to verify that this command has been run if any VTR menu item is chosen, and if not, runs it automatically. You cannot assume, however, that all drivers were written with this in mind.

Set Inpoint

The Renderer/VTR Control/Set Inpoint command enables you to specify exactly on which frame your animation begins on the tape. Enter the explicit hour, minute, second, and frame here, or select Current Frame to begin at whatever point you are currently (see fig. 23.7).

The Set VTR Inpoint box dialog box is updated automatically after each frame is rendered to keep track of where the next frame is to be placed. If you use a new tape, make sure that you are at least 30 seconds or more past the beginning before laying an animation to allow for pre-roll and to make sure that you have a good start into the tape.

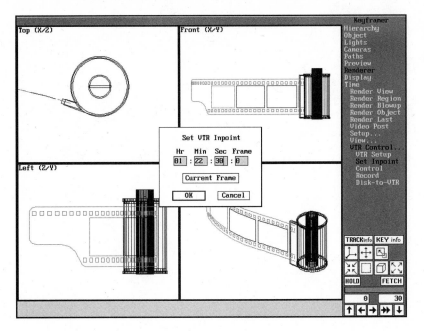

V

Advanced Animation

Figure 23.7
The Set VTR Inpoint
dialog box.

Control

The VTR Control dialog box (see fig. 23.8) enables you to use your computer as a remote control for your VTR. You can see the current location on the tape and input any point in hours:minutes:seconds:frames format prior to selecting the Go To button to move quickly to a specified point.

The arrow buttons duplicate the major controls on the deck. The single arrows move you one frame at a time in either direction. The triple arrows select Fast Forward or Rewind, and the double arrow designates Play. The Stop button immediately puts the VTR into Pause mode, stopping the movement of the tape.

Record

Choosing Record displays the standard Renderer/Render View dialog box. Choose the Render button after verifying the configuration to place a frame on the tape as soon as it is rendered.

Figure 23.8
The VTR Control
dialog box.

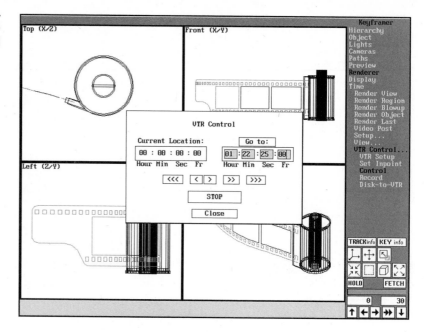

Figure 23.8
The VTR Control
dialog box.

Rendering to a Hard Disk

Most 3D Studio video renderings are first rendered to files on a hard disk, and then recorded to a VTR system. The most common file format for this rendering is compressed TARGA files. If space is at a premium, it is possible to save to a JPEG file, which has a user-definable compression ratio. The main difference to remember is that a compressed TARGA file uses *loss-less compression*, meaning that what you get out is exactly what you put into the file. JPEG is a lossy compression scheme, and higher compression ratio results can be noticeable. TARGA, therefore, is recommended for higher quality results.

Sequential Files

3D Studio saves each frame as a consecutively numbered file. Up to four of the characters you give it are used as the first four characters of the file name, and the last four characters are numbers (for example, TEST0000.TGA, TEST0001.TGA, and so on). Be careful in naming your output because the last four characters are overwritten. A file name of SEASHORE, for example, overwrites SEASHELL, giving you SEAS0000.TGA in both cases.

It also is recommended that the last character of the file name characters is a letter, rather than a number. If you use the name of GP14, 3D Studio adds its number sequence to it. Suddenly, instead of starting at 0000, your animation numbering sequence starts at 140000!

Advantages of Rendering to Disk

The reasons for rendering to disk before laying animation to tape are numerous, but the main reason is support for network rendering. If you have two or more systems rendering, the files must be rendered to disk, and then laid off to a VTR from one system all at the same time.

Rendering to files on disk allows much more control over the final output than rendering directly to tape. If the images are too dark or too light, you can run them through Video Post to change them. If an object has an error, you can re-render just that object and composite it back into your scene with Video Post. Also, if there was a problem while recording the animation on your VTR—such as a dropped frame, dropout, or random glitch—you only need to lay the frames to tape again, which is much faster than re-rendering the entire project.

Problems of Rendering to Disk

The main disadvantage of rendering to disk is the disk space required for the files. 3D Studio will stop rendering if the disk fills to capacity. This is covered in detail in the following section.

Other problems in rendering to disk are that you probably will render using NULL-DISPLAY, and cannot see the frames as they are rendering. You can never see the progress of any animation until it is completed. It might take a few days to see the results of your work.

Disk Space Considerations

Each file can be between 500 KB and 1 MB. This can add up quickly, especially if you are rendering on a network. Rotoscoped maps and textures used in the project add further to disk space requirements.

Different file formats have different disk space requirements. GIF files have only 8 bits per pixel, or 256 colors. The file size, therefore, is much smaller than a 24-bit (16.7 million color) TARGA. A compromise is to render to a 16-bit (64,000 color) TARGA files. When dithered from 24 bits to 16 bits, there might be little or no difference in the final output, and the disk space required is much less.

If you are rendering the Alpha channel, either as Alpha-Split or as a 32-bit TARGA file (the resulting disk space is identical), remember that this takes twice as much disk space as a 16-bit TARGA.

Disk to VTR

After all your frames are rendered to disk, you can lay them on videotape. 3D Studio has the capability of doing this in two ways, each of which has advantages.

The normal method is to go through the Disk-to-VTR dialog box in the Keyframer. The other method is to go through Video Post. The only difference is that Video Post enables you to make some adjustments in the brightness and contrast of the image or move it on the screen.

Be careful of moving vertically if you rendered to fields. You only can move the image an even number of pixels or your fields render backward.

Running the Disk-to-VTR option is a straightforward procedure. First, make sure that the directory where the files are stored is in your map path. Choose Renderer/VTR Control/Disk-To-VTR from the screen menus, and the standard 3D Studio sequential file to record dialog box appears (see fig. 23.9).

Figure 23.9
The sequential file to record dialog box.

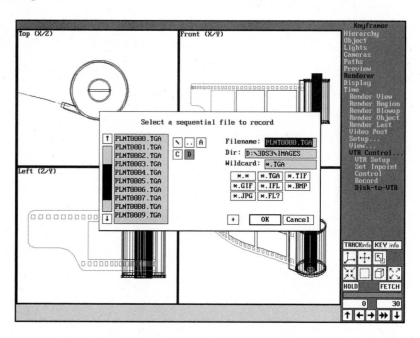

The Disk-to-VTR option enables you to output a series of files to a VTR. They can be a series of TARGA, GIF, JPEG, BMP, or TIF files, a flic file, or an ASCII *Image File List* (IFL) file.

In the file selector dialog box, choose the first file in the sequence to output to tape. Normally, this is file 0000. If, however, you previously have taken out the first group of frames, simply select the file name to begin processing.

An IFL gives you much more control over how files are recorded on tape. You can easily create an IFL through DOS by using the following command:

```
DIR TEST*.TGA /ON /B > MY-FILES.IFL
```

This DOS command creates a directory of all the files beginning with TEST and having a TGA extension (TEST*.TGA); orders them by name (ON); keeps only the brief information (B), which means no file size, date, and so on; and writes it out to a file called MY-FILES.IFL in the same directory.

If no number is after a bitmap file in the IFL, 3D Studio outputs the file the number of times specified by the VTR Setup dialog box Frame Repeat parameter. If there is a number after the file, the frame is recorded that number of times in succession.

After choosing the starting file in the sequential file to record dialog box, another dialog box appears that enables you to control how many times the images are to be looped on the tape (see fig. 23.10). If a number other than the default of 1 is specified, the animation will be recorded to tape with the Head specified in the VTR Setup dialog box, the animation is repeated this number of times, and then the Tail is specified. The Head and Tail are not used for each individual loop, only for the overall animation.

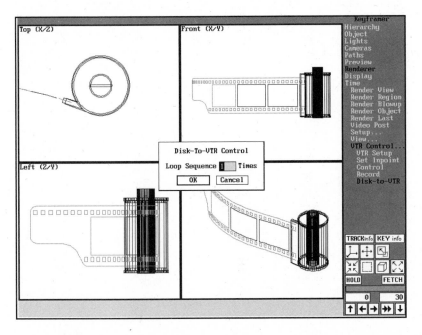

Figure 23.10
The Disk-to-VTR Control dialog box.

After looping sequence information is specified, 3D Studio goes out to your map paths directories and verifies the lowest and the highest number in the sequence. It does not verify if any files are missing from the sequence. A final dialog box appears, asking you to verify the full number of frames to record (see fig. 23.11).

Figure 23.11
The Record
frames 0-150?
dialog box.

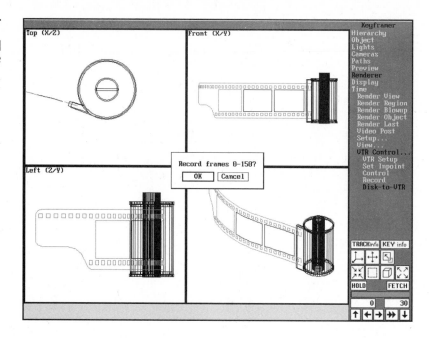

At this point, the actual recording process begins. Depending on the type of VTR, pre-roll requirements, and the speed of your hard disk, framebuffer, and network, the process takes anywhere from 3 seconds per frame to 25 seconds per frame.

Understanding Rotoscoping

Rotoscoping is discussed in this chapter because of its similarities to frame-by-frame output. *Rotoscoping*, as the term is used today in computer graphics, is the process of taking live video from a videotape and bringing it into the computer, a frame at a time, for use as a background or texture map. The older definition of rotoscope was bringing a frame of film to trace for a traditional cel animation.

3D Studio does not, in itself, do rotoscoping. You should either bring all the frames at once onto your hard disk, or bring them in as needed as a batch file entry in Video Post.

Capturing Live Images

The theory of rotoscoping is exactly the same as the theory of the Disk-to-VTR operation, but in reverse. The VTR is pre-rolled and put into Play mode. At the proper time, the framebuffer is told to capture a frame and store it on disk with a sequential file name. The VTR is then pre-rolled again, and the process is repeated until the files are all stored on disk.

New Riders Publishing
INSIDE
SERIES

The directory in which the files are stored must be specified in your map paths. When creating a material, background, or projector light using rotoscoped bitmaps, specify the first four letters and an asterisk with the extension in the Maps File dialog box (for example, FIRE*.TGA). 3D Studio then assigns FIRE0000.TGA to frame 0, FIRE0001.TGA to frame 1, and so on. If not enough files are on disk for all frames of the animation, the files are looped back to the beginning.

Disk Space Considerations

Files rotoscoped from tape are extremely large because they do not compress well. This is because every pixel has a different color value. Compression schemes depend on adjacent pixels being identical, and this does not happen often with live video capture.

Plan on keeping a large amount of disk space available for rotoscoped files. If you plan as if you had uncompressed files, you will not be very far off when predicting the amount of free disk space required to store the files. A 512×486×24-bit file is almost 3/4 of a megabyte, and 756×486×24-bit images are just over 1.1 MB each.

Capture Methods

Aside from the standard VTR rotoscoping method outlined earlier, a few other methods are gaining popularity. They are similar to the newer frame-by-frame output technologies gaining popularity. One method of rotoscoping and outputting files quickly is the recordable laser disc. The video to be rotoscoped is simply dubbed onto the laser, and each frame is brought into the computer. Because the laser disc needs no pre-roll, transfer occurs very quickly.

Digital disk recorders capture the frames directly to a hard disk in their own proprietary format using hardware compression schemes to save the files quickly. Use the software that comes with the board to transfer the files to a series of standard TARGA files.

When to Remove Fields

The files rotoscoped from live video appear to have been captured by fields. This is not a problem if the images are to be used as a background because the animation actually looks smoother because of it. If you will be mapping the images onto an object, however, the fields might be a problem. The way to solve this problem is to remove the fields. This is accomplished in two ways. The simplest one is to have a program copy every other scan line down one line. This removes all the field effect, and is a relatively quick procedure, cutting the resolution of your bitmap in half. If the object onto which the material is mapped is taking up a small portion of the screen, this might be all that is needed.

If the object is prominent in your animation, however, you might want to clean up the rotoscoped map some more. This can be accomplished by running the files through a program that not only copies each line of pixels down, but also interpolates between the two lines that remain to have a smooth image. When done properly, the image looks much better than if the fields are just copied down. An IPAS routine called DEFIELD.IXP does exactly this, and has an option to either copy the line or interpolate. The routine is part of the Utilities Library of the Action IPAS routines. See Appendix D for more information on this and other IPAS utilities for manipulating rotoscoped images.

Using IFLs

For more control over when each image is used, an IFL can be created as described earlier in the Disk-to-VTR description. This enables you to control exactly when each image is used, and to avoid wasting images. If, for example, you rotoscoped a video of fire to use in the fireplace of your animation, and the fireplace is only visible on frames 100 through 150, you could have your IFL tell the program to use the same image for the first 100 frames, use the sequence, and then just keep the last image for the rest of the animation. This prevents the program from having to re-load bit maps not being used in the animation.

Summary

This chapter discussed the theories of frame-accurate animation and different methods of recording single-frame animations. Specifically, rendering frames versus fields, rendering directly to videotape, rendering to a hard disk, and rotoscoping were discussed.

Part VI

Appendixes

APPENDIX

System Requirements

3D Studio has very specific minimum system requirements. Attempting to run without meeting them will result in the program either not running or being so slow that you would not want to use it.

This appendix covers the minimum physical requirements for running 3D Studio, and also provides recommendations on minimum practical requirements where they differ.

Using the Main System Hardware

3D Studio is extremely demanding on system resources, and you might not be able to use a computer system that will run a word processor or a spreadsheet with 3D Studio.

PharLap DOS-Extender and Virtual Memory Manager

DOS supports only 1 MB of main memory directly, of which 640 KB is usable by standard programs and 360 KB is reserved for system ROM, hardware board addresses, and so on. 3D Studio needs much more than the base 640 KB to run, so Autodesk licenses two technologies from a company called PharLap. The first is a DOS-extender, which allows a program to utilize memory above 640 KB. The process is a bit more complicated than it sounds, even though it is totally transparent to the user when it is running.

When you boot your computer, DOS takes over and enables you to do your normal operations, such as disk access, printing, mouse drivers, and so on from your first megabyte of main memory. This is all done in what is called *real mode*, which is the default mode for the computer. To access all the extra memory on the computer and run programs such as 3D Studio from this additional memory, PharLap created a DOS-extender technology. When your CPU chip is switched into protected mode, although it now has access to all this additional memory, it cannot communicate with the real-mode programs and processes on your computer, and vice versa. Part of the DOS-extender technology is used for switching the CPU back to real mode for accessing the myriad of functions necessary for the computer to operate and communicate with peripherals, and then switching back to protected mode to continue operations there. This is very different from memory-paging schemes where small chunks of memory are swapped in and out from this extra memory and actually used in real mode by the program.

In addition to the DOS-extender, Autodesk also licenses the Virtual Memory Manager (VMM/386) from PharLap. This technology allows 3D Studio to access much more memory than the RAM that is physically present in your machine. If you need more memory than you have, the VMM takes a portion of data that is currently in RAM and places it on your disk, making room for more data in RAM. It keeps track of exactly what is in memory, what is on disk, and where it is located so that if data currently out on disk is needed, it can take a different area of memory, place it on disk, and bring back the needed data. The process of writing data to and reading data from disk is called *swapping*.

Swapping is transparent to the user. Swapping data to disk increases the time it takes to render because disk access is incredibly slow compared to RAM access. A rendering can easily double or triple in time if swapping is required.

You can verify exactly how much swapping is occurring by pressing the ? key while in 3D Studio, or from the Current Status menu item in the Info pull-down menu. The dialog box shows you the total amount of memory available to 3D Studio, the amount you have used, the amount of swapping you have done since the beginning of your current 3D Studio session, and the number of page faults, which is the number of times 3D Studio has needed to use the disk swap file. The memory-available and memory-used settings are not accurate if you are running under Windows.

The biggest drawback with the PharLap VMM/386 technology is that once memory has been used by 3D Studio, it cannot be released. This usually poses no problems when all your rendering is done in RAM. If your rendering causes you to swap to disk, however, every rendering from that point on in that rendering session will continue to swap to disk, even if it would easily fit into RAM. Whenever you find yourself swapping, the best thing to do is exit 3D Studio and start up again. If you are rendering a series of different mesh files in the Network Queue, reorder the queue so that the files that do not require swapping render first, and the ones that swap will start last to minimize rendering time.

CPU Speed and Type

3D Studio Release 4 runs only on the Intel line of 80386 and later processors and requires a math coprocessor to operate, either an external 80×87 matched to your main processor or a chip with the coprocessor built into it, such as the 80486DX or DX2. 3D Studio Release 1 and 2 could utilize an external math coprocessor from Weitek; however, this is not supported in Release 3 and 4 due to incompatibilities with the compiler and the DOS-extender.

The main *Central Processing Unit* (CPU) of your system is one of the most important factors in determining the difference between a system that runs 3D Studio and one that you will be happy with. Luckily, the prices of computers are coming down so fast that excellent systems today are less expensive than basic systems from only a year or two ago.

The minimum CPU required for 3D Studio is an 80386 with an 80387 coprocessor. Some of the first 80386 chips had a problem in accessing some functions and paging. If you have an early 16 MHz 80386, make sure it is a Step D0 or later. There are no problems with the faster chips manufactured after that time.

You should get the fastest computer available for running 3D Studio. Not only will it make your renderings go much faster, but it will make working with 3D Studio much more enjoyable. The amount of tests and experimentation required for even the most simple animation will go much faster, thus enabling you to spend more time perfecting the animation and lighting, rather than waiting for test renderings.

Now that Pentium chips are readily available, the costs will go down even further, and the cost of a 486/66 chip will drop fast. The 486/66 is a double-speed 486/33 chip that operates in a 486/33 motherboard to keep costs down. This double-speed chip renders faster than a true 486/50. Intel will soon start shipping the 486/99, a triple-speed chip that also will work in a 486/33 motherboard, and should provide an excellent upgrade path.

VI

Appendixes

RAM Requirements

The minimum RAM needed to run 3D Studio is 8 MB, but you probably will want more than this as soon as you start dealing with more complicated models, texture maps, shadows, and reflections. 16 MB is a practical minimum for operating the program. One of the biggest advantages in dealing with memory is that you can easily add more in the future. As you get a feel for the amount of memory required for your particular type of models, add just enough to keep them from swapping. Get in the habit of knowing how much memory each model takes to render by hitting the question mark key periodically.

Disk Space

The amount of space required for loading 3D Studio is nothing compared to the amount of space required for storing graphics files and animations. This section is broken into three parts: disk space required for stand-alone systems, networked systems, and network servers.

Stand-alone Systems

3D Studio Release 4 requires approximately 20 MB of disk space to load and run. Try to keep the amount of available free space at a minimum of 20 MB to 40 MB. If you are rendering stills, find out the size of a single still and multiply it by the number of frames in your animation. Many people prefer to have a 500 MB to 1 gigabyte hard disk on their systems for graphics files. Add to that the space required for output, the swap file, any temporary files, and if you have enabled it in the 3DS.SET file, the LAST-IMAGE-HOLD file. To render a 3000 × 2000 image requires a LAST-IMAGE-HOLD file of 18 MB if you are rendering with alpha off, and a 24 MB file if alpha is on. This is in addition to the output file and swap files if you don't have enough memory in your system to render in RAM.

Networked Systems

Individual workstations on a network need much less space. All the maps can be loaded on the server, as can the meshes and project files. All that is needed on a station is the contents of the main 3D Studio directory, the process directory, and the temporary directory. Make sure that all the swap space is pointed to the individual stations and not to the server.

Networked systems could have as little as 20 MB free if you are certain that the renderings will fit into memory and not swap to the disk, and if all the output files will be stored on the server. In addition, if you are rendering flics with High palette, the temporary TARGA files can get very large and are always stored locally in the TEMP directory. It is not advised to use High palette unless you absolutely need to.

Network Server

The network server needs to have disk space proportional to the number of stations rendering, in addition to the space required for projects, maps, rotoscoped files, and other storage. A network with 10 to 15 systems rendering can generate more than a gigabyte of data overnight.

Input Devices

Most users utilize a Microsoft-compatible mouse for input. This is the default for 3D Studio, as well as for most other programs. Many options are available, however, depending on your personal preference. Aside from the trackball, which is basically an upside-down mouse, digitizing tablets are available. 3D Studio has internal support for the Summagraphics line of tablets. Other tablets can be used with either their mouse-emulation mode or their native mode with an ADI driver (DGPADI). Set this in the 3DS.SET file under INPUT-DEVICE, and also set the port to which the device is attached (COM-PORT).

Some digitizers have the option of using absolute or relative mode. If you plan on using a digitizer to trace images into the 2D Shaper, make sure that it supports absolute mode. *Absolute mode* refers to an absolute point on the digitizing tablet, so it can be used for tracing. *Relative mode,* which is how a mouse works, means that the system only looks for the relative distance between one point and the next. The easiest way to tell if you are in absolute or relative mode is to point to an area on the screen, pick up the pointing device, and put it down somewhere else. If the cursor moved, you are probably in absolute mode. If it did not, it is relative. A mouse would not move the cursor in this test, which is one reason why you cannot utilize a mouse for tracing.

Using a digitizer can give the added benefit of having your choice of using a puck or a stylus. If you go this route, look into the pressure-sensitive stylus options available. 3D Studio does not support pressure-sensitive digitizers, but they will come in handy for creating maps in paint programs.

MOUSE-SPEED controls the speed of moving the mouse as it relates to the amount the cursor moves on the screen. Another handy option is to switch the function of the two buttons for left-handed people in MOUSE-BUTTON-SWITCH. These settings are found in the 3DS.SET file.

CD-ROM Drives

You should have access to a CD-ROM player while you are working. It is not an absolute requirement, but 3D Studio comes with a CD-ROM of over 500 MB of data, including meshes, fonts, textures, and samples — it is a shame if you cannot access them. CD-ROM players are available for under $300. In addition, many companies are producing CD-ROMs with data specifically for 3D Studio, as well as generic textures and backgrounds that can be utilized in 3D Studio.

It is not necessary to get the latest, fastest, and most expensive CD-ROM drive available if all you do is retrieve 3D Studio data. If you just use it to access a texture or a mesh to work with, you don't need fast or real-time playback of animations. It is beneficial to have multisession Kodak photo-CD capability, but it is not a requirement.

If you have a CD-ROM drive always accessible to you while you are within 3D Studio, and use many of the maps available on the CD, you can go into the 3DS.SET file and remove the semicolons from the Disk Paths section for the MAP-PATH parameters. Change the "Z:" to whatever the CD-ROM drive letter is on your system to have automatic access to all the maps available and render all the meshes included on the CD-ROM with no additional work.

Scanners

A color scanner is not a requirement, but it is needed for any serious work. Many times you will need a particular texture, wallpaper, or carpet, and you only have the actual item or manufacturer's catalog, but you need to get it into your computer for use in a rendering. Perhaps you have taken a photograph of the site for a building and want to use it for a background. If an item is too large or too bulky to place directly on your scanner, you can photograph it and scan the photograph.

Color scanners come in many sizes, shapes, and price ranges. Most come bundled with software that offers advanced editing features as well. Others use the TWAIN interface, which is rapidly becoming a standard. Any image-manipulation program that supports TWAIN can be used with any complying scanner. Most scanners today will support a minimum of 300 dpi resolution when scanning, with many supporting 600 dpi and above.

Video Input Devices

Another handy item for acquiring textures and backgrounds is a video camera. These can range from a simple camcorder with a video-out capability to a full RGB camera that can be plugged directly into your TARGA or AT-Vista graphics board for extremely high-quality results. This will enable you to quickly digitize items that are too large to place on your scanner when you do not have the time to photograph them and reduce them down to size.

Video input is extremely fast—you can capture an image in 1/30 of a second, compared to many minutes for a color scanner. The main disadvantage for video input is the resolution. While a scanner set for 300 dpi on a 4" × 5" photo will give you a file of 1,200 by 1,500 pixels, the maximum available with video capture is the resolution of the graphics board, typically 512 × 486 or 756 × 486. This usually is not a problem, however, because video output is limited to the same low resolutions. Often your scan will be made as a texture map on an object covering a small percentage of the screen so that even with a high-resolution print it will not be noticeable. Care must be taken to create even lighting when using video input. Color scanners do not have this problem.

Understanding Graphics Displays

Three types of graphics displays are available that you should understand to work in 3D Studio—main display, rendering display, and television display. The term *display* includes both the graphics board and the monitor that works with it.

A professional workstation will utilize all three displays while being used with 3D Studio for video animation. If your only output is printed stills, there is no need for a television display. Some users can work with a single monitor for 3D Studio, but it is highly recommended to have separate displays for modeling and rendering. With a single display, you cannot see the rendered output while you are modeling or working in the Materials Editor, adding to the overall time required to complete a project.

It is a tremendous time-saver to render a camera view, adjust the geometry or materials of an object, render a region, and have the rectangle you have chosen render perfectly over the rest of the previously rendered camera view.

Main Display

The Main Display is the screen where you interact with 3D Studio. Literally hundreds of different solutions are available for your Main Display graphics card and a monitor to work with it. This display is used for all the modules of 3D Studio. The 2D Shaper, the 3D Lofter, the 3D Editor, and the Keyframer will be considered in one group, and the Materials Editor will be considered separately. For a listing of various graphics cards on the market, run 3DSvibcfg.

The 2D Shaper, 3D Lofter, 3D Editor, and Keyframer Displays

The best graphics board available for these modules will have a high resolution, 1024×768 or higher, and be capable of supporting 256 colors at that resolution. If it does not support 256 colors, you will lose the ability to have different colors available for different objects in the 3D Editor and Keyframer. Another thing to look for in a graphics board is speed. Some boards are optimized for DOS, others for Windows. If you work on large models, a fast board is a must.

Materials Display

The Materials Editor in 3D Studio Release 4 supports 24-bit color. There is no need to have a higher resolution than 640×480, and going higher will only slow down the rendering of the sample spheres in the program. If your graphics board will not support 24-bit color at this resolution, try 15- or 16-bit color.

If your graphics board will not run at a higher number of colors, you can run the Materials Editor with 256 colors, but there are some disadvantages to doing so. You can only see the current sample sphere in color at a time; all the other sample spheres are converted to grayscale. If you cannot support the minimum of 640×480 with 8-bit color, you will not be able to access the Materials Editor.

Rendering Display

The Rendering Display can be a totally different graphics system than the Main Display. 3D Studio will run at anything from pure VGA at 320×200 with 256 colors, up to whatever your graphics board will support. If you are rendering to NTSC video resolution, make sure you have a board that will run at that resolution so that you can see exactly what your clients will see. Low-end video is considered 512×486 (TARGA resolution), while high-end video is 756×486 (Vista resolution). If you render high-resolution still images, get the highest resolution display you can afford.

The rendering display has three options. It can be run from the same board as the Main Display, it can be run as a separate graphics board but looped through to the same monitor as the main display, or it can be a separate board and second monitor, which is the best solution for most uses. The most important purpose of a rendering card and monitor is to produce a true representation of the final output.

There are two more options available in this category—using a framebuffer or using a standard graphics card. A framebuffer usually is defined as a 16- or 32-bit graphics card that will genlock to an outside sync source. This means that it is capable of running video resolutions and timing. Some framebuffers have an encoder and decoder built into them. An NTSC *encoder* takes an interlaced RGB and sync signal and encodes it into composite video so it can be recorded. A decoder takes a video signal and breaks it apart into RGB and sync components. Most encoder/decoders also will convert to and from a Y/C signal, which is the SVHS standard. If your framebuffer does not have an encoder/decoder built in, you might need an external unit to change your RGB signal into an NTSC video signal, unless you are using an output device that accepts an RGB signal. Targa plus cards have an onboard encoder. AT Vista does not.

Because NTSC video is interlaced, your framebuffer monitor needs to accept this signal. A standard VGA signal is 35 kilohertz, and higher resolutions take this up to 64 or higher. NTSC, however, is 15 kilohertz, and most computer monitors will not "sync" down this low. In addition, because this signal is interlaced, there will be quite a bit of flicker in the image. If you are only viewing the images with this monitor, that should not be a problem. If, however, you have an image-manipulation program that runs on your framebuffer (which is highly recommended), you will want to get a long-persistence phosphor monitor to make it workable. This type of monitor takes longer for the image to fade out on each scan line so that the negative effects of the interlacing are harder to notice. This is the only way to work on a TV-resolution monitor without losing your eyesight quickly.

Television Display

If you are rendering animations to video, as opposed to computer playback, a television display is a requirement. This is the only way to see what the final output of your work will look like. The best configuration is to have a broadcast TV monitor properly calibrated to check the quality of the image, in addition to a cheap TV set to see exactly what it is your clients will see when they view your tape or see it broadcasted. A standard TV shows you how much your colors will bleed and how the small details and text will actually look to your client.

Everything on TV looks better on a small set. If you want to take a critical look at your work, have a 19" or 26" TV placed near your workstation.

Examining the Operating System

3D Studio Release 4 must be run under standard MS or PC-DOS version 3.3 or later on an Intel-based personal computer. It is possible to run it as a full-screen application under Windows 3.1, but at a reduced speed. It can be run under OS/2, and some of the proponents of this operating system swear by it, but with the special drivers required and only a few graphics cards supported, it is not for the casual user. It will not run under Windows NT or any version of UNIX.

 DOS versions 5.0 and later include utilities and memory managers that are very helpful in running 3D Studio, and are highly recommended.

Memory Managers

The first thing to say about memory managers is that if one is not needed by other programs on your computer, do not use one. 3D Studio includes full memory management capabilities with its *Virtual Control Program Interface* (VCPI) technology and will manage all the memory in your computer within the program itself.

If you need a memory manager to run other programs, such as Windows, there are some that have been tested to work with 3D Studio. Quarterdeck QEMM386, Qualitas 386Max, Microsoft MS-DOS 5.0, EMM386 version 5.0 or later, or Compaq CEMM 4.01 or later will all work. Earlier versions of these programs did not support VCPI, and will either not work or will not allow 3D Studio access to the memory it needs.

The version of HIMEM.SYS that shipped with DOS 5.0 will only support a maximum of 16 MB of memory. If you have more than that amount, 3D Studio cannot use any of it while using this memory manager. The version of HIMEM.SYS that shipped with Windows 3.1 supports over 16 MB of memory and is recommended.

Disk Managers and Compression

Disk compression software works by compressing software from all the programs and data on your hard disk and uncompressing it transparently to the user as the disk is being accessed. This can almost double the amount of storage space on your hard disk. The negative side to this is that it takes longer to read and write to the disk because of this compression and decompression. Also, if there is a disk crash or problem, normally all of the data on the compressed drive is lost. If you decide to run disk compression software, it is recommended that you keep your programs on a compressed disk, and have all your disk swapping and temporary files directed to an uncompressed disk or partition. Common compression software includes Stacker and Doublespace from DOS 6.0.

Using Storage Tools and Devices

Graphics files take up more disk space than any other types. No matter how much disk space you have, the data generated by 3D Studio will fill it and leave you wanting more. Data management becomes a major issue, especially if you send your files to an outside firm to be put on tape.

There are two types of files that you will need to store. One is the mesh file, with all of its associated maps. On a large project with many custom textures, this can total 10 to 50 MB. The other type of file will be your rendered files. For larger projects, these types of files can total gigabytes.

Archiving Software

3D Studio comes with a facility for archiving a mesh with all of its associated maps. 3D Studio enables you to use an external archiving program to create these archives. Place the name of the program and any parameters it needs in your 3DS.SET file in the parameter ZIP-COMMAND. The default is the shareware program PKZIP, which compresses a series of files into one. This program does not come with 3D Studio, but it is readily available on computer bulletin boards and CompuServe.

Tape Backup

The standard method of storing large amounts of data has always been a tape backup system. Tapes come in many flavors, from QIC 40 and QIC 80 to 1/4" and 8mm, and now DAT storage and many proprietary formats. They have been used for many years and are relatively easy to use and trouble-free.

The most important consideration in choosing a format is whether your format must be compatible with another company's (or service bureau's) in order for them to lay files on tape or print them at high resolution. If that is the case, your decision is an easy one: get the same device as that of the company with which you are exchanging files.

A recent development is taking your rendered output and copying it to a *Digital Disk Recorder* (DDR) for real-time output onto a high-quality format, such as D-1 for broadcast work. One of the most popular DDRs is made by Abekas, which supports an 8mm tape made by a company called Exabyte. The Exabyte drives can be used for general backup purposes, as well as transferring files to service bureaus.

Removable Media

Another type of archiving is a removable mass storage device. These have advantages in access speed because they are non-linear, whereas a tape drive must fast forward past all the other files to get to the one desired. The SyQuest drive has long been the standard in print work for service bureaus. These drives also are interchangeable between different computers, so if your slide service bureau runs on an Apple computer, you can store a bitmap on the SyQuest from your PC and they can read it on their Macintosh. Two models are available that will hold from 44 MB to 270 MB of data on each cartridge. The cartridges can appear expensive, but no more so than buying individual floppy disks, and they are much easier to store.

A Bernoulli drive basically is a very large floppy drive. They have different models that can store from 44 MB to 150 MB each. Bernoulli Transportable 150's are very popular among 3D Studio users. They are interchangeable among MAC, SUN, and IBM PC.

Optical Storage

The newest type of storage medium is optical. These drives can hold between 500 MB and 1 gigabyte on a single cartridge. Some are write-once, while others can erase and write again on the same disc. Optical jukeboxes are available that can hold 6 or more discs and switch the one you need into the reader for many gigabytes of online storage. The Kodak CD-ROM is a type of optical storage in which you can send a negative or slide out and have it digitized at different resolutions and stored on a disc.

Understanding Network Rendering

The requirements for successful network rendering are actually very simple. You need a method of linking two or more computers so that they can share data located on a common hard disk. In addition, there should be a method of file locking so that more than one computer cannot open the same file for writing at the same time. If you want to use the timeout checking option in 3D Studio, the only other requirement is that there be a method of synchronizing the clocks on the machines within a few seconds of each other. Almost all networks have this capability. See Chapter 1, "Configuring and Preparation," for more information.

Networks Supported

3D Studio does not require any particular network to run. It has been tested with Sun Microsystem's PC-NFS, Novell NetWare, and LANtastic, to name a few. Mixed networks, such as using a UNIX server for a number of PC workstations, also work very well with 3D Studio, as long as the file system on the UNIX server appears transparently as a standard DOS device, which most of them do. Peer-to-peer networks will work with networks of up to about five systems. Above five systems, it is recommended to use a dedicated server and a full networking system.

Storage Requirements

The storage requirements on a network vary greatly with the type of animations that you create. Plan on having room for all your maps, meshes, and other input files, as well as room for all the rendered output.

The network server is the best location for storage devices, such as tape drives and optical storage devices. If your network supports it, this is also the best location for a CD-ROM player so that all your machines can have access to the meshes and maps on it.

Speed Considerations

The network should be as fast as possible, but it is not necessary to spend a lot of money on a small speed increase. When 3D Studio begins rendering, it must load all the maps across the network that are required for that animation. Unless you use many animated maps, that is the only information that is pulled onto the individual workstation from the network.

The main network load occurs when the workstations each finish a frame and store it across the network to the server. If a single frame of your animations takes 15 minutes to render, the difference between storing a frame in a fast 4 seconds or a slow 8 seconds is negligible in the overall rendering time.

Network robustness is much more important than speed. The last thing you need when the deadline approaches for a major project is to have to worry about whether your network can handle the strain of many computers working on it. A rugged UNIX server system, such as a Sun SparcStation or a 486/66 dedicated server running Novell/386, is highly recommended for larger networks.

Load Considerations

More important than speed (although the two are interrelated) is the network bandwidth required when all the slaves are communicating with the server and checking the *Master Control Script* (MCS) file. Autodesk recommends that no more than 20 slave systems share an MCS file at once, although many more than that number can share texture maps.

If you have more than 20 systems, set up two directories for the MCS and other network information files, and have half of the systems look to each one. It also is a good idea to keep both of these on physically different hard disks on the server. When you start a rendering, have the first half of the systems render the first half of the frames, and the second group of systems render the rest. This means you have to start the rendering twice (once for each group of computers), but the overall rendering time will decrease.

APPENDIX

Rendering and Output Equipment

This appendix concentrates on the hardware required to both render your animations on a network and record them so they can be played back on videotape. There is a detailed discussion of tape formats and alternatives to using tape for frame-accurate recording.

Understanding Video Recording: Tape Formats

This section is broken into four sections to coincide with the four different levels of quality of tape formats: Consumer, Prosumer, Industrial, and Professional/Broadcast. Each has its place in the overall tape market—you will have to determine which level is required for each of your projects.

The differences are not always that apparent in viewing a tape, but become very important depending on where your animations will be shown. If your animations will be shown for internal use for a client only, they will have a different requirement than if they are going out to a city planning department for homeowner's review or for a network broadcast.

The most important concept in dealing with video is *generation loss*. This refers to the loss of quality as a tape goes through many editing or dubbing passes. For example, your first generation tape may look beautiful when played back, but by the time the tape gets edited into the final piece (second or third generation), dubbed out for duplication, and then copied for distribution, it may not look as good by the time your client sees the final piece because you are into the fourth or fifth generation.

Therefore, a format such as SVHS, which looks very good in the first generation, quickly loses its appeal when compared with 3/4"SP, which holds an image much better through repeated dubs.

The general rule is to always start with the highest quality format you possibly can. You can always dub down, but dubbing up cannot replace the information that is not on the tape.

Consumer Quality

Consumer quality refers to the tape decks that make their way into the average household. These are characterized by low quality (even the first generation has noticeable loss of quality) in both video and audio. These decks have standard RCA connections for both audio and video. They cannot be used for any type of frame-by-frame recording.

VHS

The VHS decks are by far the most popular format in use today, and the lowest quality. With only 200 lines of horizontal resolution, even the best of these decks is limited by the format itself. The construction is also poor, being made specifically for the mass market. However, no matter what type of recording and editing systems you have, you should always have a VHS deck onto which you can copy the animation for quick, low-cost reviews.

VHS decks can record and playback only a composite signal. They use a 1/2" tape.

Prosumer Quality

Prosumer (PROfessional conSUMER) quality is a big step above consumer quality, although it is far below the professional decks. These decks have 400 lines of horizontal resolution, although the tapes quickly lose their quality with even a few generations of editing. They still have standard RCA jacks for their unbalanced audio system, but the video connections are usually made through higher-quality BNC connectors for composite.

In addition to the composite video inputs and outputs, the decks in this category have a Y/C input and output, sometimes referred to as an SVHS connector. The Y/C connector splits the signal into its luminance and chrominance components, and records the signals separated in this manner for a much higher-quality recording.

The better decks in this group are capable of frame-by-frame recording and are built to much tighter tolerances than the consumer decks. This group ranges from a basic $500 SVHS deck to the $3,000 through $9,000 single-frame-accurate editing decks.

Hi-8

The Hi-8 format was originally created as an acquisition format so that a news team could go out into the field, record a story, and bring it back to the television station where it would be immediately dubbed up to the station's editing format. The format became popular and systems are currently being sold to do editing and single-frame-recording to these tapes.

The biggest complaint of the people using these decks for computer animation is the relatively large percentage of dropouts on the tapes. This stems largely from the diminutive size of the tape cassette. The tape is simply not wide enough to hold enough information, and any minor imperfection is immediately apparent.

SVHS

The other format in the prosumer category is SVHS. These decks use a cassette that appears to be identical to a standard VHS cassette, with a single additional hole in the shell for the sensing mechanism. SVHS is recommended over the Hi-8 format because of the better consistency in the recordings.

A VHS tape recorded on a VHS system can be played back on an SVHS system, although the reverse is not true. The SVHS tape uses a finer magnetic particle and holds a charge better than standard VHS tape. If a VHS tape is recorded on an SVHS system, it can be played back on a VHS deck. This feature also enables the SVHS decks to do double-duty as VHS decks.

Sanyo has come out with a $3,000 single-frame-accurate deck, although most of the SVHS decks are in the $5,000 to $8,000 range.

Industrial Quality

Those decks we now refer to as *industrial quality* had been the broadcast standard up to a few years ago, and many cable stations still use 3/4" decks exclusively. It is probably the most popular higher-end format for demo reels and transfers. Because this format is still in a period of transition, there are many used decks of this type available.

3/4" and 3/4"SP

3/4" U-Matic has been the workhorse of the video-editing profession for many years. It has recently been upgraded to 3/4"SP, for Superior Performance. The SP decks are a higher quality, with better horizontal resolution and audio capabilities. They can be used for editing without a noticeable loss for a few generations.

An interesting feature of these two formats is that they are both forward and backward compatible. A 3/4"SP tape recorded on a 3/4"SP deck can be played back on a standard 3/4" deck. These decks are known for their excellent construction, and they last for many years.

The 3/4" formats have two different physical sizes of cassettes. The "small load" cassette can hold up to 30 minutes of tape, and is the usual purchase for animation purposes. The "large load" is simply a larger plastic shell which can hold more tape. Either size cassette fits into the deck. The small load is not that much larger in size than a standard VHS tape, although it is thicker.

Professional/Broadcast Quality

The professional/broadcast quality decks are definitely a step above the industrials. The signal is separated even further than the Y/C of SVHS—usually into three parts. This is either Y, R-Y and B-Y, or a RGB separation, even though the actual recording is Y, R-Y, and B-Y. The luminance and chrominance are recorded with separate video heads on separate tracks.

M-II

M-II and BetaSP are very similar formats. M-II was conceived by Panasonic as an answer to Sony's BetaSP. M-II stores the signal in a related manner, separating out the Y, R-Y and B-Y signals, but the levels are higher and the signal is stored differently. There is a modification to the M-II decks to allow them to both input and output Beta signals.

This format is not as popular as Beta, and it is more difficult to find a post-production house that utilizes it. However, those who have the format are extremely impressed with its construction, reliability, and features.

Beta and BetaSP

Sony's Beta and the newer BetaSP formats are today's standard professional tape. They are extremely high-quality and can go almost 10 generations without noticeable loss. Most higher-end clients require this format for their deliveries.

Sony has started shipping a low-end BetaSP deck capable of single-frame-accurate recording for below $9,500. This will put BetaSP quality within the reach of many computer animators, and the format should become even more popular. The decks range from this low-end product up through $40,000 studio editors.

Recordable Video Laser Disc

The Sony *Component Recordable Video* (CRV) Laser Disc is a very popular format for frame-by-frame animation. Because there is no pre-roll required, it is extremely fast and flexible for this application. Because this is technically not a tape format, it is discussed in detail in the next section "Examining Video Recording: Alternatives to Tape."

1" Tape

1" tape is a reel-to-reel format that is extensively used in high-end post-production houses today. Many people are surprised to find that it is a composite format. The 1" tape can hold so much information through repeated dubs that it belongs in this location on our list. The decks are in the $50,000 price range.

Digital BetaCam

Digital BetaCam is the newest format to be released. It is a full-component digital format, with decks in the $55,000 range. The cassettes are the same size as the standard Beta tapes.

This appears to be a better price/performance solution than D1 tape, and may replace it as it becomes better known.

D1 and D2

These are the digital formats. D1, the highest quality format, is full-component digital, with decks in the $115,000 neighborhood. With this format, you can make an unlimited number of generations with no loss. The information is stored in a binary form on the tape and is passed from one deck to another digitally.

D2 was made as a replacement for the 1" tape decks and uses composite input and output, even though it stores the information in digital format. These decks carry a suggested list price from $37,000 through $52,000.

Examining Video Recording: Alternatives to Tape

Some of the most interesting advances recently are in the areas of tape alternatives. Tape is a *linear* system, which means that to go from one area on the tape to another, the tape deck must go into a fast-forward or reverse mode, and you have to pass by all the material in between. This takes time; it is not an extremely fast process. This is the traditional method of working with video. Tape always requires a pre-roll before recording or playing back, which is another disadvantage in increasing the time required.

Non-Linear Recording and Edit Systems

Non-linear will be the wave of the future. *Non-linear* means that all the video is stored in a manner where there is immediate access to any frame. Editing systems can preview many different cuts immediately. Animation can be immediately stored at any location, with no pre-roll required for either recording or playback. This is similar to the difference between retrieving a file from a hard disk versus restoring from a tape backup; the disk head can be positioned immediately over the area and the information retrieved.

Recordable Video Laser Disc Systems

The recordable laser disc has proven itself to be an excellent alternative to recording to videotape. The video is burned into the disc with an optical laser. Sony supplies a unit with composite, component, Y/C (SVHS), and RGB input and output for around $16,000. The quality is approximately the same as BetaSP, but it has many advantages. There is no pre-roll required, and the unit can record a frame as fast as a file can be input into your framebuffer. Another advantage is that the laser disc unit has an RS-232 input for computer control in addition to a standard RS-422 control to be integrated into an edit suite. 3D Studio Release 4 includes an ADI driver for controlling this unit.

Another advantage with this type of unit is that a laser disc will hold a still and generate sync for as long as power is supplied to the unit! Contrast this with a tape in pause mode. This can be used to your advantage in that you only need to render any non-moving frame once and can tell the unit through computer control to hold as long as you need. This can also be used to play back segments of the animation in different orders.

There are a few disadvantages to the unit. The biggest one is that the discs are not the standard discs used by home laser disc players. Although more and more units are being sold into post-production houses, there are still many that do not have this format in-house.

The other disadvantage is that the units are write-once. Once a frame is recorded, it cannot be changed. If an error is made, that section of the animation must be copied out again to another portion of the disc. Because the recording goes so quickly, that is not usually a problem.

Each disc can hold 88,000 frames, or more than 48 minutes of video. The price of a disc may initially seem high at $400, but that translates to only 0.4 cents per frame. A typical five-second animation (150 frames) would therefore be 60 cents worth of material—a very reasonable rate.

This is one of the best methods of frame-by-frame animation to video. There is no stretched tape, dropped frames, or wear and tear on the unit. Except for the disc spinning, the head is the only other moving part. The head itself never touches the disc, so the media will not wear out or degrade with use.

CAV Laser Discs

There are two methods of storing images on a laser disc. These methods are just as applicable to home units as to office equipment. If you have ever wondered why some laser discs sold in stores can be used for holding a still or stepping one frame at a time through a movie, whereas some laser discs cannot, here is the reason—most home players can play back both types, although dedicated recorder units may not be able to do so.

The discs on which we can record images frame-by-frame are called *Constant Angular Velocity* (CAV), or standard play. A CAV disc consists of a series of tracks, starting at the center of the disc and progressing to the outer edge. Imagine that the disc has a line drawn down the middle, with the left side being the first field, and the right side being the second field. One full revolution of the disk under the head is one full frame. Therefore, if the head does not move across the disc, the system would play back a single frame, or a still image.

The name *Constant Angular Velocity* comes from the fact that if you look at a disc from the top, the images always take up the same angle for storage, which is 360 degrees per frame—a full revolution. The images in the center of the disc have their information packed much more tightly than the information at the outer edge. Because the space required at the center of the disc is all that is required, these discs hold less information than they could. However, they make up for it by enabling the user to hold a still and step through the disc frame-by-frame.

The Sony unit mentioned earlier uses a CAV storage scheme to record frames.

CLV Laser Discs

The other type of disc is called *Constant Linear Velocity* (CLV). This is sometimes referred to as Extended Play in a home unit. The video information is stored on the disc in a manner that ensures that the video image is stored in the same amount of space wherever it is on the disc.

The center of the disc is similar to a CAV disc in that one frame may extend for almost a full 360 degrees. However, at the edge of the disc, there may be three frames stored per revolution.

The advantage of the CLV method is that the disc can hold up to twice as much data as a CAV disc. The disadvantage is that you cannot hold a still unless your player has a memory system built-in, and you cannot move step-by-step through the disc to review images or record frame-by-frame animations.

Digital Disk Recorders

Another non-linear device is the *Digital Disk Recorder* (DDR). These devices are capable of copying your frames to its hard disk and then playing them back in real time for recording onto videotape.

The Abekas A60 and A66 are extremely high-quality devices of this type. Abekas has been providing these decks for years, and they are considered the standard in the industry. They can input full D-1 quality images without compression and play them back at 60 fields per second. There is absolutely no generation loss due to the totally digital format. The original Abekas decks were over $60,000, but the newer generations are less than $20,000. They can accept input from either a built-in EtherNet network connection or by adding a SCSI Exabyte 8mm tape drive. The Abekas decks can hold 50 seconds of video for playback. The way this is handled on longer projects is to control the Abekas through a standard RS-422 Sony protocol and edit the output onto a high-quality tape format. After the next 50 seconds is copied onto the disk, it is edited to the tape immediately after the first, and the process continues.

There is a new generation of DDRs that have just started shipping. They are similar in concept to the Abekas line, but the major difference is that they store their data in a compressed format. A good example of these systems is the *Personal Animation Recorder* (PAR) from *Digital Processing Systems* (DPS) out of Canada. DPS has a very popular system for the Amiga computer, and has just ported the hardware and software to the PC. The PAR consists of a single board for the PC, with either one or two dedicated hard disks. Each disk can hold either 500 megabytes or 1 gigabyte of data, which is equivalent to 5 or 10 minutes of full-color, 60-field-per-second video. They use a motion JPEG algorithm for storing the video with a user-defined compression ratio. At higher compressions, the disks will hold more data, but at a lower quality. This unit has component, Y/C, BetaSP, or M-II composite out. There is an optional second time base corrector board that works along with the main board for real-time capture of live video for rotoscoping. The main board sells for $1,995; the TBC board is $995, plus the IDE hard disk.

This is an excellent cost-effective method of taking your animations out to video. The quality is extremely high and can be used for final output for many clients. For those who require even higher quality, the unit is excellent for previewing your animations before sending them to a more costly format, especially for those who do not have any other type of single-frame output in-house and send their work out to a service bureau.

RAM Playback Systems

RAM playback systems closely parallel the hard disk systems described in the preceding sections. Instead of using a hard disk, these systems use RAM to store the files for playback. As you can imagine, this takes a tremendous amount of memory and can only store a small amount of graphic information. There are systems made for large workstations, which cost a proportionately large amount of money, as well as those for the PC. The Bandit from Fast Forward Video utilizes 32 megabytes of RAM for playback in real-time. The compression schemes are very similar to the DPS-PAR described previously. The Bandit is an entire computer that is attached to your computer through a SCSI cable, and controlled from the host computer. They will be adding a SCSI disk to their computer system to increase the video time stored. The base system starts at $5,900 without disk or memory.

Exploring Video Recording: Real-Time

Real-time video recording is based on running a flic file on your computer and recording it as it plays, as opposed to frame-by-frame recording. The limitations of this system will soon become apparent. The flics are limited to 256 colors, and because they are playing back on a computer system, they are also limited in size and pixel updates. The way flic files are stored is that the first frame is stored as a whole, and the subsequent frames are only stored as the differences between that new frame and the one before. This change is often referred to as the *delta* between frames. This method leads to a very compressed file format that plays back well when there are only small changes. However, when there are large deltas, such as moving the camera through an architectural project, every pixel gets updated on every frame. The video card often cannot keep up with the processor, and the image starts to tear as it updates.

Another problem with this method of playback is that the speed is dependent on the individual computer on which it is being viewed, the central processor, the amount of memory available, and the speed of the graphics card itself.

Equipment Required

There are a few methods of getting these computer graphics out to video. The simplest is an external "black box" that has an input from your computer graphics card and an output for your computer monitor as well as video. These units are very flexible and can easily be moved from machine to machine.

Another similar method is to use an NTSC video card that fits inside your computer and encodes the video for television viewing, and also has an output for a monitor. These work in the same way as the external systems, but have no power supply or case to bring the price up. They are also not as flexible.

A third method is to use a graphics card that has a video output, such as a Truevision Targa card. The Targa can be used as either a one-or two-monitor system by looping the video from your VGA card through the Targa card on the way to the monitor. Although the system works well like this, it is recommended that you use the Targa as a two-monitor system, and not utilize the loop-through. You will then always be able to view the images at the same time you are working on the model.

These systems are a good method of previewing animations, and getting clients to approve them before sending them out to a frame-by-frame animation system.

Video Output

The outputs from any of these systems can be dubbed to any of the tape formats discussed in the preceding sections. Depending on how careful you have been in choosing your colors for NTSC compliance, these tapes can be used for broadcast if copied to one of the broadcast formats and you are careful with the speed of the playback.

These units commonly have a composite output, as well as a Y/C (SVHS) output for much higher quality.

Video Compression

Video compression is what allows the computer to play back video images in real time. Without some methods of compression, this would be prohibitively expensive. Compression methods are generally broken into two groups: software only and hardware/software. Software compression usually consists of removing colors and only storing the differences between frames as one large file (flic compression). There are a few programs that are attempting to utilize this method of storage for 15-bit (32,000 color) animations, taking advantage of the faster processors and graphics systems available today. As computers get more powerful, these systems will gain in popularity.

Hardware compression/decompression is the fastest growing segment of the video market. Dedicated processors can take live video, use an algorithm like JPEG, Motion JPEG, or MPEG scheme to compress it into a single large file, and store it on a hard disk. It can then be modified on the computer system and played back through the decompression circuitry in real time.

Understanding Video Recording: Single-Frame-Accurate

Single-frame-accurate tape decks can range from $3,000 to well over $100,000. Which you will need depends both on your budget as well as what your clients require.

A broadcast client will need a much higher quality format than a client using the animation for a quick design review. This is the single most important consideration in choosing equipment.

Equipment Required

The tape format should be the first item chosen. Once a format is selected, the other decisions will fall into place. This will also establish a quality level for the equipment purchases.

Video Controllers

The video controller is the link between the computer and the tape deck. Your choice of VTR will limit your choice of controllers, because not all controllers will work with all tape decks. The simplest decks to control are those with RS-232 serial capability. These can plug directly into your computer's serial port, and a software-only controller can handle them. Many of these units have ADI drivers that fulfill the function of a controller.

Parallel controllers are still used in decks such as the Sony 3/4" VO-5850 and some of the decks from JVC and Panasonic. A parallel VTR requires a hardware controller.

Some controllers are software-based. The most popular of these is SoftVTR, from Moonlight Productions. They are made to control decks with a serial RS-422 or RS-232 connection.

Framebuffers and Encoders

All tape decks that can take their video input from a video signal need a framebuffer to generate that signal. There may be a need for an encoder to translate the signal from your framebuffer to the VTR. Most VTR systems do not accept RGB input, with a few exceptions, such as the Sony CRV Laser Disc system. The most popular framebuffers are the Truevision Targa and AT-Vista. The Targa will generate an image of 512×486 at 32 bits, while the AT-Vista will give you over $1008 \times 486 \times 32$ bit resolution for video.

See Appendix A, "System Requirements," for more information on framebuffers.

Using Animation/Tape Service Bureaus

Service bureaus can be utilized to take much of the load off your own resources. They can be used in different ways, depending on your requirements and in-house equipment. If you only have a few machines and land a big animation project, they will assist you in the logistics of rendering thousands of frames and getting them out on video. They can also do video editing and add sound to your work.

These two functions of a service bureau are discussed separately in this section, although a good service bureau dedicated to assisting computer animators will have both. Rendering is the biggest bottleneck in computer animation. Having the assistance of a service bureau will enable you to take on a project that you might otherwise have to turn down.

If you are creating a 5-minute animation, you have to deal with 9,000 individual frames. If you figure it takes 10 minutes per frame on average, that comes to 1,500 hours of pure rendering on one machine, or over 62 days! A service bureau with a 15-system network will finish this in just over 4 days—and you can get some sleep at night. Let the service bureau worry about the wear and tear on their machines and keeping the network running properly. Another advantage is in letting someone else deal with the problem of fast obsolescence of computer hardware.

The same goes for purchases of high-end video editing gear. Unless you can justify the outlay on the basis of constant use, a BetaSP deck or recordable laser disc system may be out of the question. Very few animation houses have or want their own Abekas or D1 equipment.

What you do need to have, though, is a method of previewing your animations. An in-house system like the Personal Animation Recorder is a perfect compromise. You can render portions of the animation to check on the motion and color, and then send it to your client for approvals. After you are comfortable with the way it looks, you can send it out for final rendering and out to tape.

Information Required

You need to be able to discuss the mechanics of your project with the service bureau. These include the rendering quality (Phong or Metal), resolution required, final tape output format, pixel size, and all the other variables that need to be set. Frame order will have to be set by whomever does the rendering. If this is you, make sure you find out what setting the service bureau recommends.

In addition, be prepared to answer a few questions about the file. Letting the service bureau know how long it takes to render on your machine with the amount of memory required at the final resolution will give them a good indication of how long it will take for their own equipment to render, and also will assist in their planning.

Transfer Equipment

To send files to a service bureau, you will need to find out what formats of backup devices they have. Most service bureaus have QIC-40 and QIC-80 tape backup (Colorado), SyQuest drives, and Exabyte tape-backup units.

Many users will want to render their own files. However, the best method of sending your work for rendering is to create an archive file, which includes all the maps, the mesh, and saves all the current settings as a Project file in a compressed format. These files can get large! By the time you gather all your maps and the mesh itself, a 20- to 50-megabyte backup is possible.

Costs

There is a full range of costs involved in working with a service bureau. They will usually charge you by the hour of rendering time, as reported by the *.DAT file created by the 3D Studio network renderer. The price per hour will vary depending on the turnaround required, holidays, and whether it can be done only at night or has to be rendered during the day as well.

Quantity discounts usually apply to these services, either by hour or by the number of frames. Many service bureaus initially tried to charge by the frame, until someone sent them a file with 20 shadow-casting spotlights and a number of automatic flat-reflection maps.

Depending on this information, expect an hourly rate of between $20 and $50 for rush services.

After the project is rendered, the service needs to give you a price for laying to tape. This ranges from $0.25 to $1.50 a frame, again depending on the format and the turnaround time. There are some service bureaus that charge by the hour for their layoff instead of by the frame, so ask them how many frames they anticipate per hour.

Examining File Types and Industry Standards

When using any rendering software application, such as Autodesk's 3D Studio, the final product is rarely the rendered image on your video display. In most cases, some format of hardcopy output is required, even with animation where single-frame stills are popular in storyboarding sequences. However, before a rendering can be converted into hardcopy output, it must be stored in a format that allows easy retrieval, printing, and display.

Many popular formats for storing images exist in the computer graphics industry. Most of these formats only allow storing of raster data. However, a few formats, like PostScript and CGM, can store other graphic primitives such as lines, arcs, and text.

Perhaps the most important aspect of any image format is the level of the color it can store. Most formats store data with *Red, Green,* and *Blue* (RGB) intensities. The variations of intensity range with the number of bits used to store the image data. The intensity range can be expressed as 2^n-1, where n is the number of bits used to store each color component. If a format stores the data as 24-bit RGB, there are 8 bits used for each component of red, green, and blue. Therefore, the intensity range for the color components of a 24-bit RGB image is 2^8-1, or 0 to 255. Typically, this means that the more bits an image format uses to store the color components, the wider the range of colors.

Another aspect of image formatting to consider is which compression algorithm to employ. Compression is important when you consider the amount of space required to store a rendering. For example, consider an image rendered in 3D Studio at a resolution of 2048 × 1280 pixels and stored as 24-bit RGB data. There are 2,621,440 pixels, each one requiring 3 bytes of memory to store its color components. This means that 7,864,320 bytes of space are required to store this image in an uncompressed format.

Using a *lookup table* (LUT) is the simplest form of compression. A LUT can reduce a 24-bit image to an 8-bit image by building a palette of the 256 most-prevalent colors. Indexes into the LUT are then used to represent each pixel in the image. Any time an algorithm achieves its compression by reducing the images color range, it is referred to as *lossy* compression. This means that when the image is uncompressed, it does not match the original image in color content.

Most other forms of compression utilize some method of *run length encoding* (RLE) or *run length compression* (RLC). In RLE formats, repeating byte patterns are encoded into a LUT. In RLC compression techniques, repeated bytes are compressed as a count and a value, and non-repeating byte patterns are simply compressed as a count followed by the literal data.

The following list of image formats represents some of the more popular image formats:

Type: TGA (TARGA)
Color Space: RGB
Data: 16-, 24-, or 32- bit
Compressions: Uncompressed, LUT, RLC, or Huffman
Maximum Gamut: 16,777,216 colors using 24 bits
Information:
AT&T
Electronic Photography and Imaging Center
2002 Wellely Ave.
Indianapolis, IN 42629

Type: TIF (TIFF-Tagged Image File Format)
Color Space: RGB, CMYK, or custom
Data: 1–24-bit (depends on compression)
Compressions: Uncompressed, Macintosh pack bits, Modified Huffman, LZW,
CCITT fax, others
Maximum Gamut: 16,777,216 colors using 24 bits
Information:
Aldus Corp.
411 First Avenue South
Seattle, WA 98104

Type: GIF (GIF-Graphics Interchange Format)
Color Space: RGB
Data: 24-bit
Compressions: LUT
Maximum Gamut: 256 indexed colors
Information:
CompuServe, Inc.
5000 Arlington Center Blvd.
Colombus, OH 43220

Type: PCX
Color Space: RGB
Data: 1-,4-,8-, or 24-bit
Compressions: LUT, RLC
Maximum Gamut: 16,777,216 colors using 24 bits
Information:
ZSoft Corp.
450 Franklin Road
Suite 100
Marietta, GA 30067

Type: JPG (JPEG-Joint Photographic Experts Group)
Color Space: RGB
Data: 24-bit
Compressions: Proprietary lossy
Maximum Gamut: 16,777,216 colors using 24 bits and dependent of compression
Information:
Joint Photographic Experts Group

PostScript

Since PostScript was introduced in 1985, it has become one of the most widely used file formats in the graphics industry today. This page description language was developed by Adobe Systems, Inc. in an effort to standardize the format used to drive printers and plotters. Although PostScript is not a particularly good format for the storage and retrieval of images, it cannot be ignored in its importance in producing hardcopy output. The current implementation of PostScript (Level 2) allows the easy reproduction of color images on a wide range of devices. Images can be stored as RGB, CMYK, or CIE color models and can utilize a number of compression techniques.

One of the most important aspects of PostScript is to the printing industry. PostScript uses the same screened dithering to reproduce images that the printing industry has used for years in offset printing. With PostScript, an application can control every aspect of screened printing, including the spot function, frequency, angle, black generation, and under-color removal. In addition, scaling, translation, and rotation of images can be achieved when using PostScript as an output format. It is because of these powerful capabilities that PostScript has emerged as an output standard for the computer graphics industry.

Understanding Continuous Tone Printing

The term *continuous tone* refers to a device's capability to reproduce the complete gamut of colors in an image by the capability to vary the intensity of each pixel or dot placed on the output media. Continuous tone devices can reproduce an image without the aid of any dithering. Film recorders and dye sublimation printers are two examples of continuous tone output devices.

Film Recorders

A film recorder can automatically image your rendering onto a film-based media. The output can be either a slide or a photographic negative. Because the image is reproduced on film, there is not a lack of color associated with most printer devices. Also, because the output is in the form of a slide or film, creating large-format color output is easily accomplished using photographic enlargement.

Dye Sublimation Printers

The dye sublimation (dyesub) printers use a transfer sheet to apply ink to the output media. This process is also known as *dye diffusion* or *dye transfer*. The ink from the transfer sheet is released from heat applied by the print head elements. Because the temperature of each of these elements can be modulated in both intensity and duration, the ink can be gradually diffused on the output media. This process allows a wide variation of color saturations that produce a photographic quality print.

For more information regarding continuous tone printing, please refer to Chapter 14, "24-Bit High Resolution Imaging."

Understanding Dithered Printing

Reproducing an image on any output device is a complicated matter because most images are stored using 24-bit RGB (16,777,216 possible colors), and most output devices have a fixed palette of colors that are usually much more limited. For example, on a CMYK printer, each pixel can be only one of seven colors:

> Cyan
>
> Magenta
>
> Yellow
>
> Red (Magenta+Yellow)
>
> Green (Cyan+Yellow)
>
> Blue (Cyan+Magenta)
>
> Black

Most video displays have a fixed range of 16 or 256 colors, with a few achieving 65,536 or more. It is these fixed intensities that make these devices unsuitable for reproducing an image without dithering. Because the majority of graphic output devices in the market have a limited number of colors they can reproduce, it is often necessary to dither images for reproduction.

The term *dithering* describes the technique of arranging pixels to create the appearance of a much wider gamut of colors on a device with a limited range of displayable colors. Dithering takes advantage of an optical illusion that makes the human eye perceive a group of closely arranged dots as a single color. For example, if a 50-percent red is to be produced, the pixels on the output device are arranged in such a way that 50 percent of the output is covered with red pixels and the other 50 percent is left white. Because the individual pixels have such a fine resolution, their close proximity to each other makes them indistinguishable from each other without looking very closely or using a magnifying glass. The arrangement of the pixels have the appearance of a 50-percent red, even though there is actually no variation in the intensity of the individual pixels. Two methods of dithering that are primarily used in the graphics industry are *error dispersion* and *screening*.

Error Dispersion

Dithering an image using error dispersion means that the pixels are dispersed using an error accumulation algorithm. A simple error dispersion algorithm will accumulate intensities until the maximum intensity of the color space is reached. It is at this point that the corresponding pixel would be set. For example, an image has a maximum intensity of 255, and the following pixel values are to be output using error dispersion:

> 64 128 96 128 32 128

The dithering algorithm will accumulate these values until the intensity reaches 255.

> 64+128=192
> 192+96=288

The accumulator now exceeds the maximum intensity of 255 and causes the third pixel on the output device to be set. Now the accumulator must be adjusted to represent that the pixel was set, as follows:

> 288-255=33

The accumulator is now 33, and the process proceeds with the fourth pixel:

> 33+128=161
> 161+32=193
> 193+128=321

Again the accumulator has exceeded the maximum value of 255, thus causing the sixth pixel on the output device to be set.

This is a very simple example of error dispersion. Most error dispersion algorithms distribute the value of a pixel over several pixels both horizontally and vertically. This is done to reduce the possibility of producing unwanted patterns or artifacts.

Screening and Halftoning

The second method of dithering is *screening* or *halftoning*. This is the method commonly used in the printing industry. Screening utilizes uniform dots of varying size distributed on a fixed grid commonly called *cells*. The spacing of the grid is known as its *frequency* and is typically measured in *lines per inch* (lpi). If a frequency of 72 lpi is specified on a 300 dpi printer, this means that the size of the cell is 300dpi/72lpi, or approximately 4.2 pixels.

The shape of the dot used is referred to as a *spot function*. Many different spot functions can be used when printing an image, but the most common spot functions are the circle, ellipse, square, and rhombus functions.

The size of the dot or the amount of the cell filled is proportional to the intensity of the image pixel to be reproduced. If the range of intensities is from 0 to 255, a pixel value of 255 would cause a cell to be completely filled by the spot function. Likewise, if the pixel only has a level of 127, then approximately 50 percent of the cell would be filled by the spot function.

Besides the capability to control the frequency and spot function, the angle at which the cells are rendered can be controlled while screening. Adjusting the screen angles for overlaid color planes provides a method by which to avoid moiré patterns from being created at certain frequencies. The best combination of frequency and angle vary between devices and are usually preset in the device by the manufacturer.

Exploring Popular Color Image Devices

There are many devices that require dithered raster data in order to render an image. The more popular color image devices are explained in the following sections.

Electrostatic Plotter

An electrostatic plotter uses a specially coated (dielectric) medium. This medium is coated with a uniform negative charge. An imaging head with nibs, either PCB or wire, applies a positive charge to each pixel to be plotted on the medium. Next, electrostatic toner is applied to the medium, usually from a toner fountain. The liquid toner contains solid toner particles that are also negatively charged, thus the particles are attracted and adhere to the positive charges and are repelled from the dielectrically coated medium itself. Electrostatic plotters are excellent devices for producing large-format color output quickly. These plotters currently range in size up to 54 inches in width.

Thermal Wax Printers

Thermal wax printers use a transfer sheet with colored wax to apply color to an output medium. The wax is melted using heat produced by an imaging head. This is similar to the dye sublimation process with a major difference: dye sublimation printers can vary the intensity of the heat used to apply ink, whereas thermal wax printers apply wax with a uniform consistency. Thermal wax printers are an excellent choice for commercial graphics because of their ability to produce vibrant colors.

Ink Jet Devices

The name *ink jet* clearly explains how these printers and plotters produce their images. A small jet of ink is used to apply the individual pixels to the output media. Ink jet devices typically use toner cartridges that not only contain the inks, but also the jets that apply them. This produces one major disadvantage in that the cost of ink jet cartridges can be high. Ink jet technology

has been used in a wide range of devices from small monochrome printers to large-format color plotters. Ink jet devices have the advantages of being inexpensive, fast, and printing on plain media.

Laser Devices

Laser printers and plotters have been used for a long time to produce high-quality monochrome output quickly and inexpensively. These devices utilize a laser and dry toner to image data. The toner is fixed to the output media using heat. Although this technology has been used in color copiers for some time, it has just recently been applied in desktop color printers. These new color printers are bringing the high speed and quality of laser printing into the color graphics market. The major drawback of color laser printers, however, is their high cost.

Understanding Printing Terminology

This section is a glossary of terms commonly used in the printing industry.

anti-aliasing   A technique used to smooth the staircase effect produced when rasterizing lines or images with hard edges. Most anti-aliasing techniques average pixels along the edge of the hard edge with the background to produce the appearance of a smooth edge.

BCMY   Black, Cyan, Magenta, Yellow.

bleed   The amount of the output medium that can actually be used to print on. A full-bleed device can use the entire medium for printing without any borders.

choke   See trapping.

CIE   Commission Internationale de l'Eclairage. An international standard for color specification that is independent of any output device characteristics.

Color Management System (CMS)   Every device in a color graphics system (scanner, video display, printer, etc.) utilizes its own color space and gamut. This means that the colors produced on them are device-specific. A color management system uses profiles to compensate when translating colors in between these devices, thereby creating accurate color matching.

Color Rendering Dictionary (CRD)   This term is specific to PostScript devices. A color rendering dictionary provides the definition used to translate colors from one color space to another on a PostScript device.

CMYK   Cyan, Magenta, Yellow, Black.

dithering   The technique of arranging pixels to produce the illusion of a wider range of colors on a device with a limited gamut.

dpi Dots per inch. Used to describe the output resolution of a device. A 300 dpi printer is capable of producing 300 pixels in a row one inch in length. Some devices can have a different resolution for its horizontal dimension than its vertical dimension.

error diffusion A dithering technique where the arrangement of pixels is produced by dispersing the error produced from an unplotted pixel to adjacent pixels.

error dispersion See *error diffusion.*

gamut The range of producible colors for an image or a device.

halftoning See *screening.*

lpi Lines per inch. This term describes the frequency of a screened dither pattern. A 72 lpi screen has 72 halftoned cells along one inch in the direction of the screen angle. The screen angle can vary for each output color. This is different from dots per inch, which are measured horizontally and vertically.

prepress The practice of checking a document prior to sending it out for offset printing. This is usually accomplished by printing the document on a high resolution printer that is capable of the same size as the required output.

proofing See *prepress.*

resolution The number of pixels that an output device can produce in one unit of length either horizontally or vertically. Also used to describe the width and height of an image in pixels.

RGB Red, Green, Blue.

RIP Raster image processor. A RIP is a method of rasterizing data containing higher-level graphic primitives. This term is most commonly used in conjunction with PostScript processors.

screening A dithering technique where dot patterns are produced on a grid. The pattern for the dot is referred to as its spot function and the grid spacing is referred to as its frequency. The dot size is varied according to the intensity of the image.

separations When printing on an offset press, the colors used to produce the document must be separated into individual raster images. Color separations are printed as monochrome images on clear film.

spread See *trapping.*

trapping In order to adjust for misregistration on a press, overlapping colors need to be adjusted. This involves either enlarging (spread) or reducing (choke) lighter colors into darker colors.

Other Software Tools

In many ways, 3D Studio is a very open-ended program. It can read 3D models in the DXF format that is supported by many other programs. It can read 2D vector data in both DXF and AI format, which covers most 2D drawing programs, and the Materials Editor can use any one of seven standard file formats as a map. With this much flexibility, it's only natural that other programs are pressed into service in support of 3D Studio.

The following collection of programs is by no means a definitive list. These programs are just a few of the more interesting and popular programs employed by many 3D Studio users.

Adobe Illustrator

This is a popular program for 2D drawing and illustration. It is used with 3D Studio primarily for the creation of shapes to be imported into the Shaper. The 3D Studio Shaper can read Illustrator's native AI format files, and Illustrator can export in DXF format as well.

Illustrator also creates full-color, 24-bit images that can be exported in both BMP and TIFF formats. This capability makes Illustrator suitable for map creation as well, although it does not have the bitmap editing capabilities of a true image processing program.

 For more information, contact Adobe Systems Inc., 1-800-833-6687.

Altamira Composer

Altamira Composer is a new and exciting image-processing program that brings new techniques to bitmap editing, most notably its treatment of layers and transparency. Imported bitmaps, clippings, and masks are floated on their own layers with varying degrees of transparency. You can slide these layers around much like a collage to compose your image. When you are completely finished with the image, you flatten it into a standard bitmap.

Altamira Composer is suitable for creating 24-bit maps, masks, and backgrounds for 3D Studio. Although it is a new program, it has generated much discussion and interest on the ASOFT forum on CompuServe.

 For more information, contact Altamira Software Corp., (415) 332-5801.

Animator Pro

Animator Pro is Autodesk's 8-bit paint and 2D animation program. Some uses for Animator Pro are discussed further in Chapters 6, 8, and 19. A great need still exists for 8-bit support in 3D Studio, and Animator Pro is tough to beat for creating 8-bit color maps, any type of intensity map or mask, or for processing flic output from 3D Studio.

For more information, contact Autodesk Inc., 1-800-525-2763.

Chaos

Chaos, also from Autodesk, is a fractal image generator with an easy-to-use graphical interface. The program saves fractal images in an 8-bit, 320 × 200 GIF format only. These images can then be used as maps in the Materials Editor for many types of random and organic effects.

Another use for fractal images is to process them with a program call GIFDXF, described later in this appendix. The end result of this process is a 3D mesh that can be used as a landscape or other surface in 3D Studio.

CorelDRAW!

CorelDRAW! is similar to Adobe Illustrator in purpose and features. CorelDRAW! has more special effect commands and is bundled with a collection of utility programs, a CD-ROM of more than 200 Adobe Type 1 fonts, and 10,000 clip art images. CorelDRAW! is a native PC application, whereas Adobe Illustrator originated on the Macintosh. For that reason, PC users are frequently more familiar with CorelDRAW!

CorelDRAW! can export drawings in both Adobe's AI format and Autodesk's DXF for use with 3D Studio. Its bitmap file support includes BMP, TGA, and TIFF, so it also can be used to create 24-bit maps for the Materials Editor.

 For more information, contact Corel Systems Corp., 1-800-836-3729.

Fractal Design Painter

Fractal Design Painter is a unique 24-bit paint program that simulates traditional artists' tools and media. This is an exceptionally creative and flexible tool for creating images that require a handmade or traditional look.

Using Computer Images or Simulations

It often makes more sense to create a computer visualization than a live video shoot. Although computer animation is relatively expensive and time-consuming to create, in many cases it is much more economical than the alternatives. All the factors, however, must be taken into account when deciding on whether to use a computer animation.

Another option to consider is a combination of computer animation and live footage. This can be utilized as separate scenes on the final video, or the computer animation can be combined with the live footage on the same frames.

Creating Non-Existent Subjects

Many times the subject of an animation, whether an architectural visualization still in design stages or the re-creation of an item damaged by fire, simply does not exist. It might be easier and simpler to build a realistic computer representation of the model than to actually build or rebuild it.

Designing Inexpensive Mock-Up Models

Often, the cost of creating a mock-up for design review is much more expensive than creating a computer model. When a project will go through many design iterations in either form or color, it is cheaper to build it electronically than to keep making changes to the actual model.

If the object is a product that requires molding or tooling, this also will raise the budget. Moving parts are animated very easily on computer, but cannot be physically modeled without hinges, pivots, and tubes. If you need to see how an object works on the inside, or if it is too large or small to view at normal scale, a computer model is much more practical than an actual model.

Replacing destructive testing with computer animation is another cost-saving technique when the object in question is too expensive to destroy.

Simulating Dangerous or Difficult Effects

In many situations, it would be far too difficult or dangerous to create a live event for filming. How would you film a nuclear bomb demolishing a city, for example? Opting for a computer animation of the event definitely has its advantages.

Many other situations exist where computer animation is safer than live filming. Product testing might simply be too dangerous to repeat over and over when a computer simulation will accomplish the same goals. Aircraft simulators for dogfighting are another example of using the capabilities of the computer to make training safer.

Saving Construction Time

When an event is created on the computer, you have full control of the time element for completion. A building can be built much faster on a computer than in real life. Showing the full rotation of the earth around the sun takes a year, but the rotation can be studied on a computer visualization in a few minutes. Other heavenly phenomena, such as eclipses and the creation of the solar system, can be observed accurately and in a reasonable amount of time.

Creating Physically Impossible Events and Effects

Another reason for creating computer visualizations is for animating events that are not physically possible. If you cannot create the event live, such as a space battle or an underwater city, a computer animation might be the only solution.

Other events, such as 3D morphing one object into another, cannot occur in real life, but can be created on a computer. Changing the transparency of an object's skin to dissolve it and see inside is another example. Creating a company logo in which fireworks explode is easy with 3D Studio and some of the add-on IPAS routines, but it can't be done in real life.

Presenting Events Accurately

Many situations exist where you need a very accurate representation of an event, and a live shoot will not give you that needed accuracy. Something that requires duplicating perfectly each time also is a good candidate for computer animation.

Examining Anthropology

The field of anthropology benefits greatly from computer animations and visualizations. Re-creating items, such as houses, temples, pottery, and hunting implements, from long-dead civilizations is made possible by using small scraps and samples.

Site/Architectural Re-Creation

Entire cities have been re-created on the computer from the remains of foundations and drawings. Animations of how the pyramids of Egypt and the surrounding temples looked when they were built have been aired on national television, showing how the Nile flowed into a canal to bring the floating barges to the base of the pyramids. The Sphinx has been modeled and animated in great detail, showing the original form. The temple collapsed by Samson in the Bible has been modeled and analyzed to see how it could be possible for one man to perform such a feat. All of these projects could only have been created on a computer.

Artifact Re-Creation

Artifacts of which only portions remain can be reassembled in the computer to show the entire object. The computer also can make extrapolations from small remains to show what an object would have looked like. These studies can help answer questions about the people of ancient civilizations, and show us how they lived and worked.

Event Re-Creation

Computers can show how events took place. A volcanic eruption can be created on the computer to match the evidence uncovered on an archeological dig, showing the speed of the lava flow and the destruction of a town.

Exploring Architectural Visualizations

Architectural visualizations are one of the most popular uses of computer animations. They are used in all phases of an architectural project, including site studies, analysis, massing studies, design studies, and building proposals, through interior design, furniture, and color studies.

Computer animations are used in the architect's office to help design the project, and later to present the proposal to the client. More and more governing agencies are requiring a visualization to show planning commissions, city councils, and homeowner's associations what impact the design will have on the community. It is far easier to illustrate to financing institutions and investors what a project will look like through a computer animation than an artist's renderings.

Studies showing view impairment are becoming more popular in communities where much of the value of the properties lies in the view from the lot. The computer can show what a new building or addition looks like from adjoining properties, and what portions of the view will be blocked by the structure. Computer models of buildings are much more accurate than renderings. This provides more credibility when showing the results of a design decision than a sketch or rendering, which many people perceive as too easy to fake to get the result desired by the artist.

Concept Models

Preliminary concept models can be rough animations, showing mainly the block massing of the project. These generally are created for approval of the design concept so that you don't spend too much time progressing in the wrong direction. Different scenarios can be examined quickly and changed as required, as opposed to creating a scale model that might be difficult to change. Preliminary concept models are even more valuable when the adjoining buildings are roughed out on the model, showing the building in its proper context.

Walk-through Animations

Architectural walk-throughs and fly-bys usually are created after most of the design work has been completed. They can be as simple or as complicated as the budget will allow. Design elements can be added, as well as furniture and fixtures.

This often will be the first time the client can appreciate what the design really looks like. Most clients cannot read blueprints well, and have problems relating color chips and fabrics to final room sizes with furniture and wallpaper. If done soon enough, these visualizations can be powerful design and communication tools. The danger is in waiting until it's too late to make changes—when the client sees the animation, and is frustrated with what he sees.

Image and Concept Stills

Image and concept stills are created to show the client or investors the feel of the project. They usually are created before design work has progressed to the point of showing much detail. A concept still might show similar furniture, with floor coverings, fixtures, colors, and plants as a basic design statement, even though the exact elements in the image may not be a part of the project.

Assemblies

Visualizations of assemblies often are used to communicate a complicated construction concept. They sometimes are used for depicting details of construction, such as how a window design might be integrated into a specific type of wall or how an anchor detail is to be built.

High-Resolution Images

High-resolution still images are used often in architectural work. Many clients require a 2'× 3' or larger framed image of their building to display in a sales office or corporate boardroom.

Examining Cartoon Animation

Computer animations are starting to be used in more and more of the traditional cel animation areas. Full-length computer animations are starting to appear on Saturday morning cartoons, as well. But even more important are the inroads that 3D computer animations are making into the high-end theater animations.

Complex Animation

Classic cel animations, such as Walt Disney's *Beauty and the Beast*, have started to incorporate 3D computer-generated images into the scenes. One of the more notable scenes was the Beauty and the Beast ballroom scene, where all the backgrounds for the dance scene were created on computer. It would have been very difficult to draw this moving background by hand.

In Disney's *Aladdin*, the magic carpet was computer generated. This is one of the first instances of an actual character being done on the computer. One of the main reasons for going with computer animation in this instance was that the intricate pattern on the carpet would have been almost impossible to draw by hand with all its movements and gyrations, whereas the computer could apply the texture map perfectly every time.

Stop-Motion Animation

Stop-motion animation animates characters that are often made by shooting one frame at a time, then moving the character into the next position, and shooting again. This process is incredibly tedious because every single frame must be set up by hand and filmed. 3D computer graphics are being used more and more for this type of animation because the computer only requires the important, or key, frames to be defined, and the computer fills in all the intermediate steps. This can be a tremendous time savings, even though the rendering step can add some extra time.

Character Animation

Character animation has always been difficult to create in computer graphics. Using many of the same tools as traditional cel animators to plan out the animation makes this type of animation much easier.

Many computer animators today have a computer background and do not understand the fundamentals of animation. This is unfortunate in that many people view the computer animations, see them as cold and flat, and get a negative impression of computer animation in general.

Exploring Commercial Art

The commercial art category includes product brochures, advertisements, and training materials. There is a tremendous need for presentation graphics for these uses, and computer imagery fits into many of them.

Three-Dimensional Text

Creating 3D text in 3D Studio is considered by many to be extremely easy to do, and is one of the more sought-after effects for everything from magazine ads to book covers. The effect can make an ad, and therefore the product, look much more interesting than flat printed letters. Looking at a perspective view of the letters provides a very different effect than a normal typeface can give.

Three-Dimensional Product Illustration

Almost every brochure or pamphlet can benefit from having a 3D representation of the product. With 3D representation, users can better understand the proper use of a product because of the increased comprehension gained through viewing a realistic 3D image over a typical 2D line drawing. This is especially true for safety features and warnings about improper product usage.

Lighting Variations on 2D Flat Artwork

3D graphics provide much more control over lighting than 2D graphics. By moving lights to the desired locations, the computer automatically figures out how the light would hit the objects, giving you an opportunity to create very dramatic lighting without having to re-do your entire image each time you change it.

Understanding Forensic Graphics

Forensic graphics refer to graphics and animations for the entire legal industry—from simple plan drawings to detailed visualizations. Computer animation enables you to show how an accident occurred, how a part failed, how pollution spread, or the nature of an injury.

Courtroom Evidence

The most difficult part of working with graphics for courtroom exhibits is showing *foundation*, or the basis for admitting a particular graphic into evidence. It is difficult to get an animation admitted into evidence because often there are many interpretations of an event. If, however, an expert witness uses an animation to depict how he thinks an event might have occurred, it is much easier to get the animation admitted. It can appear to be a small technicality, but it also can be the difference between admissibility and expensive pictures that no one ever gets to see.

It took some time to get preliminary approval of computer graphics into the legal system. Currently, however, more and more courts are admitting computer graphics during trials. In many cases, the animator must testify as to how the animation was made and how the data was input. Even if a case does not get to trial, a good animation used during the discovery phase might convince an opponent to settle quickly.

Accident Re-Creation

Accident re-creation is what most people think of whenever they hear of forensic graphics. These animations must be done very carefully, with special attention given to every phase of the modeling—especially the keyframing. If even a small portion of the scene or keyframing is incorrect, the entire animation is thrown out.

Showing how an accident occurred can be incredibly valuable in a trial. Instead of trying to describe the location and circumstances, the jury can see them. The animation can be rendered from any perspective, including the perspective of the people involved, so that the judge and jury can see what those involved saw and understand why they did what they did.

Ballistics

Ballistics is the study of firearms and their firing characteristics. Animations can show the process of firing and the location of a weapon when it was fired based on the locations and entry angles of bullets fired.

In a major murder case in northern California, 3D Studio animations were used in court to show the sequence of events leading up to the murder, the location of the participants, and the trajectory of the bullets. This was matched to an audio-tape recording of a neighbor's 911 call that recorded the sound of each shot.

What-If Scenarios

Computers have always been excellent at depicting many different scenarios dependent on a few key events. Each scenario can be shown quickly based on information that is not questioned.

Understanding Industrial Design

Industrial design is the design of almost anything other than buildings. The packaging of products, as well as the design of the products, fall into this category.

Product Design and Exploration

Product design benefits greatly from computer visualization. From initial design studies, to movement analysis, to color review, 3D computer simulations can save a tremendous amount of money and time spent building conventional prototypes. In field markets where timeliness can be the difference between a leader and a "me too" company, it is imperative that the company use all the modern methods available to design their products to be as interactive as possible.

Product Demonstrations

Products can be shown within a company for review, as well as to prospective clients and financing sources. How a product works, what it looks like in operation, and its options can be shown quickly and easily.

Packaging Design and Presentation

Quickly mocking up product packaging can lead to great time-savings over creating mock packages, printing, and review time. Imagine trying to design a new ketchup bottle and showing how it would look on a grocer's shelves in five different sizes in a few hours. This method also makes product labels on the package easy to review. A similar label can be scanned and altered, or a new label can be created and applied to the computer model quickly.

Concept Illustration

Concepts are the hardest things to convey to others without a lot of work, and are at a stage where there will be many changes before the product is even approved enough to spend money creating prototypes. If a concept can be shown quickly and economically to others, there will be a tremendous time and money savings at this all-important phase of the project.

Assembly Techniques

3D computer animations are excellent for showing the assembly of a product. Intricacies of construction methods, as well as how something goes together, can be shown. Having the pieces "fly" together cleanly without the clumsiness of someone's hands getting in the way is a major advantage.

Examining Motion Picture and Broadcast TV

The motion picture and broadcast TV industries have used 3D computer graphics for many years. These systems are workstation-based, however, and out of reach to most animators or would-be animators. Now that the PC is getting powerful enough to compete with these systems, and the software is available to compete with the quality of the output, you will see even more 3D animation incorporated into what you watch every day.

With the prices and the ease-of-use factor going down, more and more people are getting involved in this field every day. In the beginning, PCs were only used as tests for the big workstations, but a lot of final work is being done on PC systems today, and the percentage is steadily increasing.

Story Boarding

Story boards are created as the first step after the rough script is written to show the flow of the program. They are extremely rough, and often not animated, but merely a series of stills. Showing the flow of a story often can lead to finding faults quickly before money is spent developing an idea that will not work.

Pre-Visualizations

After the story board is complete, difficult-to-visualize portions of a scene are modeled and animated. This is happening increasingly with complex stunt sequences. The action is animated in a very rough manner, with attention paid more to the timing than to the smoothness of the movement or detail in the scene. Many times the animation is played back as flics, recorded in real-time, and edited into a rough cut for review.

Stage and Site Composition

Computer animation has been a great tool for showing the way the sets will look to the camera or audience. Different colors can be studied, with emphasis on the lighting and camera locations. Modeling the building in which the sets will be built first helps eliminate problems with the size of the final set or layout when you construct it.

Special Effects

The area of special effects already has been noted as one of the best places to incorporate 3D computer graphics. Major motion pictures such as *Star Wars, Total Recall, Lawnmower Man, Terminator 2, Death Becomes Her,* and *Jurassic Park* have all used extensive 3D computer graphics sequences.

Explosions, Glows, Ripples, SXPs

The capability of exploding a building realistically on the computer without expensive and dangerous pyrotechnics is a boon to the movie industry. Also, having the capability of creating a glow around objects or changing their physical properties by using other computer effects available with IPAS, such as ripples, melt, and reshape, provides the entertainment industry with the capability to create a fantastic range of effects without the necessity of custom programming each routine.

Vehicle and Model Animation

Making a vehicle or model—such as a car, truck, airplane, or spaceship—move, crash, or explode in real life is a major expense. Often human life is at risk, and the effect might not work properly, requiring a retake of the shot with a new vehicle. Creating these effects on a computer and overlaying them onto live backgrounds is an effective and economical way of creating effects at a much more reasonable cost.

Replacing Motion Models

For a long period of time, the entertainment industry relied on shooting miniatures either with a live camera or by exposing a single frame, moving the model, and exposing the next frame. These tedious methods can almost be eliminated with 3D computer animations.

Rotoscoping Scene Insets

Portions of live footage can be rotoscoped into the computer, processed, and sent back out to the original medium. This processing can include making changes to the footage, adding computer-generated overlays, or running through some image-processing algorithms.

Windows on Models and Films within Films

Rotoscoped scenes also are used for application to objects within the overall live scene. Applying an animation to a mirror or a window can make viewers think they are seeing something totally different than what is actually occurring. This effect also can be used to have computer-generated images seen as the display in a television set or a movie screen within the scene.

Television Commercials

Many television commercials use 3D computer animations, and more commercials will use 3D computer animations as the price drops and the quality goes up. This is another area that was once the domain of workstations with high-end, expensive programs; television commercials now are being targeted by PC animators.

Flying Logos and Text

Flying logos and text probably were the first, and still are the most common, use of computer animation in commercials. Most computer animators have worked extensively on flying logos and text at one time or another.

Product and Mascot Animation

Animating advertised products not only shows the product in the best possible light, but also leaves a lasting impression on the audience. Whether it is an animated mouthwash bottle fighting germs or a tub that comes to life when cleaned with a certain cleaner, commercials such as this are not soon forgotten.

3D computer graphics also are used for animating the company mascot. This is a heavily used technique, and makes good use of computer graphics.

New and different effects are always sought for these purposes, and companies will spare no expense for a commercial that works.

Rotoscoping

Rotoscoping for commercials can be used extensively for the same reasons rotoscoping is used in the entertainment field. An added advantage for commercials is that the entire commercial usually is only 30 seconds of video. The entire animation can be kept on a hard disk without the logistics of trying to store several minutes of high-resolution film in digital format.

VI

Appendixes

Exploring Photography

The computer is being used more and more in still photography to augment the photographer's work. In addition to 2D touchups that are now rather common, 3D objects can be easily incorporated into the image. By rendering with the photograph as a background, an object will appear on it perfectly anti-aliased. Photographs also can be used as texture maps on objects for other desired effects.

Compositing Real-World and Computer-Generated Objects

Composite objects, either real or computer generated, can be used as background or foreground objects. If a real-world object is to be used as a foreground object, it might first be necessary to bring the photo into a paint program to cut out the background and add an alpha channel to the image.

Complex or Impossible Compositions and Lighting

Situations exist where the photographer wants a certain effect that might not be possible, such as two objects that do not appear together (the Egyptian pyramids and the Empire State Building, for example) or objects flying in space. Problems might be associated with lighting certain scenes in real life. Often these scenes are easy to produce on a computer.

Examining Scientific Illustration

Many scientific phenomena cannot be seen or photographed. They do, however, lend themselves extremely well to 3D visualization. The data can either be input directly to the program through an IPAS routine or modeled and animated normally.

Molecular Illustration

Molecular images are easy to understand when modeled on a 3D computer system. Atomic relationships can be easily portrayed, and even movement can be animated.

Outer-Space Simulations

Scientific visualizations of outer-space events can best be completed on a 3D computer animation system. Computer control of spaceships can be studied and fine-tuned with this type of visual feedback. Observations of events that are only received on radio waves can be visually interpreted by the computer.

Physical Representations

Physical representation of things that cannot be seen, such as the earth's magnetic pull or ozone layer, can be shown on the computer and analyzed. Effects of global warming and deep ocean currents are other areas in which the computer can translate data into visualizations for us.

Theoretical Concept and Theorem Animations and Illustrations

Most of the results of theoretical science are not comprehended by others. A theory that is shown in a 3D animation can be understood by many people. Scientists who illustrate their concepts by building 3D models of the data sets and animating them have better chances of communicating their theorems to scientists and laymen alike.

Using Visualization in Theater

The theater has many uses for 3D visualization. If the theater and stage are first modeled accurately, the sets then can be created in 3D Studio for every scene and checked not only for visual interest, but also for sight lines from any seat in the house.

Set Construction and Experimentation

All of the sets made on a computer can be verified and experimented with before the actual costly construction begins. Changes can be made in advance, and problems in moving and striking the sets can be foreseen.

Staging Options

Many different staging options can be reviewed and studied before actors even arrive on the set for rehearsals. Like many other professions, the better the initial planning, the smoother the entire process will be.

Lighting Simulations

After the sets are modeled on computer, the stage lights can be input in their actual locations. They can be colored and focused on the computer in the same manner that the actual lights operate, and their effects analyzed before the lights have to be installed and then moved. Lights can even be animated, with a follow-spot illuminating a model of a person to give the best effect, with other lights turned on and off as the director requires.

Exploring Action IPAS Libraries

Pyros Partnership, Inc. has authored many routines for creating special effects within 3D Studio. They also publish many 3D Studio-related utilities. Their SunPath IPAS routine has become the standard method of animating shadow studies. Their image-processing effects add a softness and surrealism to any animation. In addition, they write many custom routines on contract, and drivers and utilities for various hardware companies. These programs are available through your 3D Studio dealer or direct from Pyros Partnership, Inc.

All of the following IPAS routines from the Pyros Partnership are included on the *Inside 3D Studio* CD-ROM in evaluation form.

SUNPATH Library

SUNPATH.PXP calculates and animates the Sun's path throughout the course of a day. This routine is absolutely required for architectural shadow studies. Optionally, it can animate the moon or any other planet in the solar system. This routine has already withstood a court of law for accuracy.

Transitions Library

These programs can be used as transitions and special effects. They can be used to start a transition with one image—either an animation or a still—create an effect with it, and come out of the effect with another image.

PGFLIP.IXP duplicates the expensive *Digital Video Effects* (DVE) found in major post production houses. You can flip an image into the distance and then continue the flip with either another or the same animated image. QUATRO.IXP divides the screen into any given number of rectangles up to 64 by 64, each having a copy of the original image. Animate this one for lots of effects.

ROTATE.IXP takes the entire image and rotates it the specified number of degrees, animating as it goes. SQUASH.IXP takes an image and reduces it by the specified percentages, in either the X or Y dimension, or both. Also, you can start with a small image and enlarge it to fill the entire screen.

SWIRL.IXP turns any image into an animated whirlpool—it spins either from the inside or the outside, clockwise or counterclockwise, with either a fixed border attached to the edges of the frame or one that breaks free and starts rotating. Combine it with ROTATE and SQUASH for a spectacular effect.

Effects Library

This group of programs was created to be used as a special effect for either computer animations or rotoscoped live video. The LINE program has some fantastic effects with live images.

BRICK.IXP applies a three-dimensional brick pattern under an image. It looks as if you are projecting a movie of your scene on a brick wall. CRACK.IXP applies a cracking or peeling three-dimensional pattern under the entire image or parts of it controlled by the Alpha channel. It looks as if you are projecting a movie of your scene on an old plaster wall.

DRIP.IXP takes individual pixels and drips them down or across the screen. Your whole image, or parts of it controlled by the Alpha channel, will appear to soften and shimmer. LINE.IXP creates an "auto trace" line drawing of selected parts of an image controlled by the Alpha channel. The program uses a user-defined color for the background or a randomized background where random parts of the background image show through between the lines.

PLAQUE.IXP places a mosaic of user-controllable animated black-bordered plaques on the image in areas determined by the Alpha channel. It looks as if the image was created with individual tiles.

Medias Library

The programs in this group have been written to make your images look as if they were created with other media. OLDMV.IXP turns your still or animation into what looks like an old-time movie—complete with random scratches, dust particles, fungus, color loss, and sepia. You also can wobble the image both vertically and horizontally. Look out Charlie Chaplin!

BMASK.IXP highlights or stresses the contribution made to the total image appearance by specific color bits. The results can range from the look of an infrared photograph to wild psychedelic colors. It affects either the entire image or portions of it constrained by the Alpha channel.

GRAYS.IXP takes an image, or an Alpha controlled portion of it, and transforms it into a user definable grayscale palette. Optionally, it can animate the number of grays in the image over time. NEGAT.IXP creates a color negative of an image or parts of an image controlled by the Alpha channel for an otherworldly effect. PIXEL.IXP pixelizes an image in areas controlled by the Alpha channel and animates the pixel size as it works. This routine has already withstood a court of law for accuracy!

Film Library

FILM.IXP is a much-requested program that makes a video image look as if it was originally shot on film and transferred to video. It adds a user-definable amount of film grain to an image. It can help remove that computer-generated feel of your images, and is absolutely essential when mixing live images with computer animation on film, print, or videotape.

Utilities Library

The following are indispensable utilities for 3D Studio animators. They do everything from assisting with the manipulation of your rotoscoped maps to verifying images before laying them on tape.

HBLUR.IXP adds a user-defined amount of softening through horizontal blur to selected portions of your image. It is excellent for blending pixels that might scintillate in maps or in detailed geometry. This program is the only such program to work with field rendering.

THERMO.IXP adjusts the overall color temperature of your image. This takes the whole image, or selected portions of it based on the Alpha channel, and makes it appear "warmer" or "cooler."

BRTCON.IXP adjusts the brightness and contrast of your images or those rotoscoped from live video. It is an absolutely indispensable utility for serious 3DS users.

DEFIELD.IXP takes images that were brought in live or rendered with fields and totally removes the fields. It not only removes the fields, but it optionally blends in new lines to avoid reducing the resolution of the image. DEFIELD.IXP is required for using images with fields as maps or before rescaling the images.

LEGAL.IXP automatically makes sure that all your colors are legal for video. This avoids the over-saturation and bleeding that are normally associated with computer images. It also can mark the offending colors with any color you choose so that you can see where the problems are. LEGAL.IXP is similar to the Release 4 capability, but enables you to specify the color for easier adjusting.

JPEG.IXP saves all of your rendered images as standard JPEG compressed files instead of TARGAs or GIFs to greatly reduce your disk space storage requirements. WHATTGA.EXE and WHATJPEG.EXE verify all your TARGA or JPEG image files in a directory for consistency, format, size, aspect ratio, and more before you lay them out on tape—a true lifesaver. The program automatically shows them on your TARGA display card as it works to verify them visually, also.

Paints Library

The Paints library consists totally of animated paint effects. OIL.IXP turns any image, or portions constrained by the Alpha channel, into an oil painting, complete with brush size control and amount of paint application.

PUNTI.IXP creates a "Puntilinea" or "Pointillism" oil painting out of your image or parts of it controlled by the Alpha channel. ROUGH.IXP roughs out an entire image, or parts of it controlled by the Alpha channel, and turns it into what looks like a painting that had a dry brush applied with perpendicular strokes. You can control the amount and size of brush strokes.

SMUDGE.IXP adds a diagonal smudge to your image, or portions of it controlled by the Alpha channel, at a user-defined average size. SMUDEGE.IXP creates a very painterly look. It is a great softening effect for live video also. VANGO.IXP makes a Van Gogh painting out of any image or parts of one constrained by the Alpha channel.

SONY RS-232 Single Frame Controllers

These programs and drivers are each sold separately. They avoid the need for complicated and expensive hardware controllers for those decks that do not absolutely require them.

SONY RECORDABLE LASERDISC DOS DRIVER records your animation automatically and controls your laser disc. It runs directly from DOS, and is incredibly fast. The program has a low overhead, but maintains full error checking. This driver is a required accessory for the professional production studio.

SONY RECORDABLE LASERDISC ADI DRIVER controls your laser disc recorder's functions through 3D Studio. It includes full support for all of 3D Studio's functions, and is licensed by Autodesk.

SONY EVO-9650 HI-8 ADI DRIVER records and controls the Sony Hi-8 single frame accurate deck from within 3D Studio. This driver provides full support for all of 3D Studio's functions, and is licensed by Autodesk.

For more information on these products, contact:

Pyros Partnership, Inc.
1201 Dove Street, Suite 550
Newport Beach, CA 92660
(714) 833-0334 FAX (714) 833-8655
CompuServe: 73027,3632 INTERNET: gpyros@pyros.com

Using Schreiber Instruments Imagine

Schreiber Instruments has been creating high-quality add-on programs for AutoCAD for many years. Its programs for 3D Studio contain everything from IPAS explosion routines to AutoCAD to 3D Studio translators. These programs are sold separately through Autodesk MultiMedia dealers or direct from Schreiber.

Imagine Nursery

This program creates fully detailed, three-dimensional shadow casting trees by type, time of year, and height. It includes 58 different tree types each with correct seasonal foliage color including: flowers in the spring, vibrant fall colors, dead-of-winter foliage, or bare branches in winter months. This IPAS routine generates the trees directly in 3D Studio. A stand-alone version of the program is included to generate trees from the DOS prompt or through a batch file. An ADS program also is included for operation inside the AutoCAD model. Materials are included with mapping and smoothing assigned for render-ready trees.

Imagine 3DSURF

3DSURF creates a TIN, or grid mesh, from ASCII input files or from the built-in random terrain generator. It can import survey data directly for a fast and accurate terrain model. The program includes several different surface materials from asphalt to grass. An extract AutoLISP routine is included to create an ASCII data file from your AutoCAD entities. The rolling grid features continuous slope and curvature across the surface while it honors the data for the best possible surface. The program enables the user to control the grid density.

Imagine INTERFACE

INTERFACE provides complete 3D Studio editing capabilities in AutoCAD Release 11 and 12 (DOS extended). With INTERFACE, you can develop complete 3D Studio files with objects, materials, lighting, cameras, and paths; convert AutoCAD entities into 3D Studio objects and assign your materials inside AutoCAD; open or merge existing 3D Studio files to add entities from AutoCAD as objects; and retrieve all objects back to AutoCAD and perform editing. INTERFACE enables you to use the modeling capabilities of AutoCAD, and leaves the rendering and animation to 3D Studio.

Imagine DETAILOR

DETAILOR generates over 100 different fences and walls automatically. Combined with a multi-megabyte materials library (such as stone, brick, weathered, and unweathered woods), the DETAILOR program enables you to create virtually any fence or wall. DETAILOR creates full three-dimensional models instantly. DETAILOR provides the finishing touch to your architectural renderings that cannot be duplicated anywhere.

Imagine SUN

SUN is a program that automatically positions a light source for proper sunlight shadow casting in your 3D Studio file. Imagine SUN operates from the DOS prompt and asks only for the required information (latitude, time of day, day of year). The program then calculates the closest position for a light source for proper shadow casting—a must for architectural renderings where the position of the SUN is critical.

Imagine CIVIL DETAILOR

CIVIL DETAILOR is a parametric civil engineering-related geometry generator. Generate three-dimensional geometry effortlessly along a 3D path. You can automate generator guard rails and road details. It uses output from the 3D Studio Shaper and produces full geometry for all common barriers, guard rails, and striping. CIVIL DETAILOR also produces railroad and monorail lines.

Imagine FX

Imagine FX is an animated special effects package of routines containing lightning, comet, starburst, rings, particle cloud, and explode volume. Lightning provides a weather-realistic effect for your animation or you can simply add a comet for another interesting sky type effect. Starburst and rings can be used to simulate several space conditions—for example, you could start with an expanding universe to the view just after a sun explodes. Finish off a scene with a volume explosion without gravity settings and a large bounding area for your exploding star system. Complete the sequence with a particle cloud of the residue after you have completely blown up the solar system.

Yost Group—IPAS Boutique

The Yost Group is under contract to Autodesk as the creators and programmers of 3D Studio. This is a listing of its IPAS programs, broken into the same groups under which they are sold. They are available through your authorized 3D Studio dealer.

IXP (Image Processing External Process)

IPAS set #1 is a collection of six IXP external processes by Tom Hudson. Each is a flexible tool for simulating photo-realistic "optical" image processing effects within the Video Post interface of 3D Studio.

BLUR FILTER enables you to defocus all or parts of an image in 3D Studio automatically. This IPAS routine works on still images or animations with options including the following:

- ✔ Blur only above (specified) brightness threshold (for "blowing out" only the highlights)

- ✔ Start and end frame control for simulating cinematic "racked focus" effects

- ✔ Different blur algorithms for global blurs or subtle blur "halos"

BLUR FILTER is very useful for creating multilevel focusing effects and dramatic transitions within Video Post.

LENS FLARE FILTER creates film-quality lens flare—simulates the optical physics of a multi-element zoom lens. There are 25 different options available, including: number of lens elements, flare color, amount of chromatic aberration, core flare size, "ring" quality, ray size, flare density, plus control over automatic brightening of the scene during flare peaks. This program adds a tremendous amount of realism to outdoor imagery.

GLOW FILTER enables you to add colored auras, halos, and neon effects. GLOW FILTER options include the following:

- ✔ Capability to glow the entire image or just those regions in or out of the Alpha channel

✔ Capability to control the glow through brightness threshold, hue, or Alpha channel (for creating neon silhouettes)

The size and "feathered" quality of the glow can be set separately. This IXP is essential for getting away from the hard-edged quality of typical computer graphics.

HILIGHT FILTER creates twinkles, sparkles, and "cat's eye" effects using optical cross-star highlights. HILIGHT FILTER options include the following:

✔ Capability to create highlights on specific Video Post layers with Alpha channel control

✔ Highlight generation based on brightness threshold or hue

The number of cross-star points is selectable, as are the angle and per-frame increment for rotating animated highlights. Both the size and falloff softness of the highlights can be controlled separately.

MONO FILTER tints and posterizes images. MONO FILTER also is useful for modifying the color of other image processing effects within Video Post. MONO FILTER options include the following:

✔ Tinting based on a brightness threshold

✔ Tint color control

✔ Capability to select the number of shades to use in the final image and the posterization threshold

STARS II enhanced version of the starfield generator originally came with 3D Studio Release 2. It supports both field/frame modes, and you can set the size of the stars. STARS II includes a "streaking" effect for creating motion-blurred star trails as you move the camera through the starfield. Try this with HILITE.IXP for starfields with rotating cross-stars on the head of each star.

Special Effects Toolkit: IXP, PXP, AXP, SXP Mix

IPAS set #2 covers the IPAS spectrum and provides a wide array of procedural textures, image-processing effects, and parametric object deformation tools by Dan Silva and Tom Hudson.

NOISE II (SXP) is similar to the animated noise function that shipped originally with 3D Studio Release 2, except that this new version is completely non-periodic (you can't see any pattern or repeats across infinite-sized objects). Use this solid texture to create natural random surface effects.

Need a planet for your next project? PLANET (SXP) is a procedural texture function that creates the appearance of planet surfaces from fractal equations including continents, islands, and oceans. PLANET (SXP) options include the following:

✔ Capability to specify both the size and how "rugged" you want the terrain to be

✔ Capability to blend the water/land boundaries

You also can use an Autodesk Animator palette file to control the colors of the land/water masses. (This does not actually produce geometry; see the FRACTALIZE PXP on Disk 5 for that.)

SMOKE (SXP) creates milky or smoky effects inside objects with this versatile solid texture. Originally created to make smoky beams of light, this animated fractal turbulence function readily simulates cloudy/smoky/murky appearances. It can be used as either an opacity, texture, or bump map. Options include the following:

- ✔ Scaling
- ✔ Fractal iterations
- ✔ Motion start and end frames

WATER (SXP) is perfect for those recipes that call for you to "just add water." This IPAS routine provides for very realistic animated water textures (based on the sensual movement of the Perlin wave-distribution algorithm). It can be used as either an opacity, texture, or bump map. WATER (SXP) options include the following:

- ✔ 2D or 3D wave distribution
- ✔ Number of wave sets
- ✔ Wave radius
- ✔ Wave length
- ✔ Wave amplitude
- ✔ Wave speed
- ✔ Color blending
- ✔ Motion start and end frames

SPECKLE (SXP) is ideal for creating speckled or mottled appearances. This routine is simple, but comes in handy when you need that perfect random speckled look for simulating granite, eggshells, and other natural surfaces.

CRUMPLE (PXP) is a procedural modeling tool that "crumples" any object to make it look like it's been trashed. This function preserves your original object and produces a less-than-perfect morph target. Mangle options include the following:

- ✔ Crumple axis
- ✔ Minimum and maximum crumple amounts

XMAS (PXP) is a procedural modeling tool that lays down icosohedrons along the surface of any object. You can then eliminate the original object and you will have a new object, which appears to be made out of Christmas lights. XMAS enables you to assign up to four different materials from your Materials Library and enables you to create an unusual new type of beaded "particulate" object out of virtually anything.

XMAS options include the following:

- ✔ Light spacing

- ✔ Light size

SPHERIFY (PXP) is a procedural modeling tool that converts any object into a sphere. SPHERIFY (PXP) is very useful for making objects look as if they're getting pumped up with air. SPHERIFY (PXP) preserves your original geometry and creates a perfect spherical morph target for it. You also can use this IPAS routine to pseudo-morph from one dissimilar object to another. Just morph each object to a sphere and then use Video Post to dissolve between the two spheres.

PLASMA (AXP) is an animated procedural model builder that creates electric "plasma orbs" similar to the lightning spheres you see advertised in the "expensive toys for grownups" catalogs. PLASMA (AXP) produces nice special effects, especially when used with the GLOW.IXP image processing routine from Disk 1. PLASMA (AXP) options include the following:

- ✔ Number of lightning arcs

- ✔ Brownian variation

- ✔ Maximum degrees per frame "walk" of each lightning arc per frame

FLIP (IXP) is a useful Video Post image processing utility for flipping entire images either left-to-right, top-to-bottom, or both ways.

CLAMP (IXP) is a contrast "clamping" utility for Video Post. CLAMP (IXP) enables you to set a "ceiling" and a "floor" for max/min contrast values. By inverting these values, you can achieve excellent negative-images for special effects. CLAMP (IXP) is great for video and print applications in which harsh blacks and whites need to be muted.

PXP (Procedural Modeling External Process)

IPAS set #3 is a collection of six PXP external processes by Darrel Anderson. Each is a flexible procedural modeling tool for creating animated deformations and organic object effects within 3D Studio.

MELT melts any object toward a "floor" with gravity simulation. It can be used in reverse to animate an object forming from a puddle. (Remember that movie?) MELT options include the following:

- ✔ Melt percentage

- ✔ Crumple percentage

- ✔ Edge sagging amount

✔ Sagging acceleration

✔ Spreading amount

MANTA WAVE sends a nice undulating ripple or wave through any object. It provides an extremely useful damped sine wave deformation, with mirror control for producing realistic manta ray motion. This gradient sine wave is much more natural than the linear wave function that first shipped with 3D Studio Release 2. MANTA WAVE options include the following:

✔ Positionable amplitude center

✔ Control over amplitude curve

✔ Fine control over exact position of the wave function relative to the object

✔ Wave period

RESHAPE gives you a handy reshaping tool that does a spline-fit to any object. It enables you to pull vertices or faces from an object, and then refits the object to blend smoothly between the original object and the version with the pulled faces (similar to a taffy-pull effect). RESHAPE is great for morphing animated characters, mountains out of flat plains, and so on. RESHAPE options include the following:

✔ Curve tension setting

✔ Vertex range control

✔ Magnitude

SKLINE is a skewed spline-fitting tool used to make bending and wavy objects. SKLINE allows up to 10-point bending of any object along three axes simultaneously. It also generates a template based on your object that enables you to set the characteristics of the spline customized for each object. SKLINE is great for character animation and for simulating wind and rubbery effects. SKLINE options include the following:

✔ Skline extent settings

✔ Curve tension control

STRETCH provides you with a new non-linear scaling tool. It works by fitting any object inside a deformable "scaling" box. STRETCH is excellent for making an object appear to bow, morphing tear-drop shapes, and other nonlinear types of deformations. STRETCH options include the following:

✔ Stretch axis

✔ Stretch anchor

✔ Resistance

VI

Appendixes

Everyone's been asking for a generalized twist/torque tool. TWIST is a flexible IPAS routine that enables you to twist any object on any axis for "screwy" types of effects. TWIST nicely complements 3D Studio's built-in commands. (The 3D Lofter only allows twisting along the path of extrusion.) TWIST options include the following:

✔ Twist extent settings

✔ Twist direction

✔ Number of full twists

✔ Twist bias

AXP (Animated Stand-In External Processes)

IPAS set #4 is a collection of six AXP external processes by Darrel Anderson. Each provides a unique parametric particle system for the creation of animations that simulate natural phenomena with real-life physics.

RAIN is a rain-making process that fills a cubic volume with a 3D downpour. Texture maps can be projected onto the front of the rain so that the rainstorm reveals a pattern. RAIN options include the following:

✔ Number of rain particles

✔ Raindrop size

✔ Raindrop splash diameter (drops splash into little puddles when they hit the "ground")

✔ Rainfall time "envelope" controls (with eases for gradual effects)

✔ Cycling or continuous rain

✔ Wind direction vector

✔ Chaos factor

SNOW is a snow-making process that fills a cubic volume with a 3D blizzard. SNOW includes turbulence functions for realistic swirling snow effects. Texture maps can be projected onto the front of the snow so that the snowstorm reveals a pattern. SNOW options include the following:

✔ Number of particles

✔ Snowflake diameter

✔ Snowflake spiral control

✔ Snowfall time "envelope" controls (with eases for gradual effects)

✔ Snowflake shape (triangular or 6-sided)

✔ Wind direction vector

✔ Chaos factor

FIREWORKS creates particle-system fireworks in the shape of any 3D object. No more flying logos... now they can burst! FIREWORKS comes with sets of texture maps that provide animated color over time and animated shading over the spark's trail. Or use your own maps for even more custom effects. FIREWORKS options include the following:

✔ Number of particles

✔ Spark size

✔ Spark velocity

✔ Spark "trail" size

✔ Gravity constant

✔ Time "envelope" controls

✔ Initial velocity

✔ Deceleration

✔ Chaos factor

Imagine turning any object into thousands of spheres that then fall and bounce on the ground. DISINTEGRATE is a particle-system disintegrator that automatically places spheroid particles on the surface of any object and then explodes, drifts, or "gravitizes" them. The myriad of options include the following:

✔ Density factor

✔ Particle size

✔ Bounce factor (when particles hit the ground plane, they can bounce up to four times)

✔ "Wobble factor"

✔ Gravity constant

✔ Time "envelope" controls

✔ Blast center positioning

✔ Velocity falloff

✔ Minimum and maximum chaos factors

In addition, full texture-mapping is supported—even in the "spheroid" state.

VI

Appendixes

EXPLODE shatters objects and makes their fragments fall with gravity. It's a surface-geometry demolition tool that takes any object and simulates what would happen if you exploded dynamite inside of it (with accurate physics, of course). If the object is texture-mapped, the individual pieces retain both their smoothing groups and mapping coordinates perfectly during the explosion. EXPLODE options include the following:

- ✔ Gravity constant
- ✔ Bounce factor (object pieces can hit the "ground" and bounce up to four times)
- ✔ Time "envelope" controls
- ✔ Face fragmentation factors (for minimum piece size and maximum piece size)
- ✔ Blast center (pieces nearer the center will be fragmented into smaller pieces than pieces at the periphery)
- ✔ Initial velocity
- ✔ Velocity falloff
- ✔ Deceleration
- ✔ Chaos factor

SPURT is a general-purpose particle-system generator for spurting and streaming effects. It's very good for creating sparklers, fountains, laser beam blasts, lawn sprinklers, and similar erupting phenomena. In addition, the stream of particles can trace the shape of any object. Animated particle texture mapping also is supported. SPURT options include the following:

- ✔ Number of particles
- ✔ Gravity constant
- ✔ Particle size and trail ratio
- ✔ Particle life span
- ✔ Time "envelope" controls
- ✔ Radial or parallel particle flow
- ✔ Custom object shaping constraints
- ✔ Chaos factor

PXP—Silicon Garden

IPAS set #5 contains a set of PXP external processes by Hayes Haugen and Rolf Berteig that generate an extensive variety of trees, plants, flowers, terrain, rocks, and other natural objects using fractal "L-System" mathematics.

SILICON GARDEN is four procedural flora generators within one user interface (which conveniently enables you to use only one PXP slot in your 3D Studio Program drop-down menu). The flora models are all extremely size-efficient; a typical Maple tree has less than 1,500 faces.

TREES creates eight general categories of trees, including Willow, Cherry, Maple, Birch, Pine, Redwood, forest, and tropical. The forest setting produces groups of low-detail trees (deciduous, evergreen, or mixed), which are extremely useful as distant elements in outdoor scenes. TREES options include the following:

✔ Season setting (for leaf density and color)

✔ Leaf texture-mapping

✔ Wind and gravity strength

✔ Age

✔ Width

✔ Branching angle

✔ Low/medium/high detail settings

✔ Optimized or morphable geometry state

FLOWERS includes five types of flowers: Campion, Mycelis, Rose, Sunflower, and a "generic" flowering plant. FLOWERS' options include the following:

✔ Petal color

✔ Size

✔ Low/high detail settings

✔ Petal texture mapping

✔ Age

✔ Wind and gravity strength

✔ Optimized or morphable geometry state

SHRUBS includes six types of shrubs: Palm, Fern, Reed, Grass, Rhododendron, and a "generic" shrub. SHRUBS' options include the following:

✔ Frond bend/orientation/twist/regularity

✔ Size

✔ Low/medium/high detail

✔ Shape

✔ Leaf texture mapping

✔ Wind and gravity strength

✔ Optimized or morphable geometry state

STRUCTURES has nine basic categories of beautiful and unusual space-filling fractal objects including: Gosper Hex, Koch Circle, Koch Lattice, Koch Quilt, Hilbert Curve, 3D Chain, 3D Fence, Spirals, and Cylinders. STRUCTURES' options include the following:

✔ "Seed" object

✔ Divergence

✔ Length

✔ Height

✔ Detail

✔ Size

✔ Complexity

FRACTALIZE is a fractalizing procedural modeling tool that enables you to build morphable terrains out of any object. It retains texture coordinates so that you can fractalize pretextured objects and not lose their textures. In addition to an all-purpose terrain-generator, it's also very useful for making objects appear wrinkled, blistery, or rock-like. FRACTALIZE options include the following:

✔ Fractal iterations

✔ Slope

✔ Smoothness

✔ Randomness

✔ Fractal growth direction

TERRA MATERIALS LIBRARY is a disk full of texture maps that includes a materials library, which is both integrated into the Silicon Garden and also an invaluable resource for your own modeling. The library includes dozens of texture maps for bark, leaves, grass, ground, rocks, and so on.

PLACE-ING TOOL is handy for aligning any object on a complex surface, such as planting a tree on a fractal terrain.

More IPAS Coming Up

As Autodesk 3D Studio increases in popularity, more and more IPAS routines become available. The Autodesk Multimedia Division has announced a strategic development agreement with Xaos (pronounced "chaos") to develop high-end image processing and special effects tools for 3D Studio. Many of these tools will be IPAS routines.

VI

Appendixes

The Inside 3D Studio CD-ROM

The *Inside 3D Studio* CD-ROM contains 3D Studio files for the exercises and examples in this book, a collection of programs useful to 3D Studio users, IPAS routines from Pyros Partnership, Inc., and over 200 MB of original images that you can use as maps with 3D Studio. This appendix shows you how to use the files on CD-ROM and how to install the programs.

Many of the programs on this CD-ROM were collected from CompuServe. CompuServe is one of the greatest sources of information and programs for 3D Studio users. The ASOFT forum on CompuServe has an extremely active message section dedicated to 3D Studio. Many of the world's greatest and most successful 3D Studio animators exchange information and generally hang out on the ASOFT forum. In addition, the ASOFT forum has a file library loaded with 3D Studio goodies including IPAS routines, meshes, and maps. The graphics forums on CompuServe also contain valuable information and programs for 3D Studio users.

Using the Exercise Files

The files for the exercises are located in the \I3D subdirectory on the *Inside 3D Studio* CD-ROM. The exercise files can be used directly from the CD-ROM; you do not need to install the files onto your hard drive. This saves your valuable hard drive space for more important things, such as storing animation output.

Saving Exercises to Your Hard Drive

You cannot save your work on the CD-ROM because it is a read-only device. If you want to save an exercise as a work in progress or for posterity, you must save it on your hard drive. When you do this, you also must take precautions to ensure that 3D Studio can find associated map files in the future.

You can use two different methods to ensure that 3D Studio finds the exercise map files. Each has its advantages and disadvantages.

The first way is to add the subdirectory that contains the files to 3D Studio's map paths. This can be done in two ways. You can temporarily assign the CD-ROM's subdirectory as the map path by choosing Info, Configure, and then clicking on the Map Paths button in the Program Configuration dialog box. After the Specify Map Paths dialog box appears, click in the list box and enter the full path (including drive letter) of the exercise maps. If your CD-ROM drive is D, the map path should look like the following:

        D:\I3D

This method for specifying map paths only works for one 3D Studio work session. If you quit and start up 3D Studio again, you will need to respecify the map path to the CD-ROM.

To make sure the map files are on the map path every time you start 3D Studio, add the following line to the MAP-PATH section of the 3DS.SET file:

        MAP-PATH = "D:\I3D"

If your CD-ROM drive is something other than D, substitute your drive letter. See Chapter 1, "Configuring and Preparation," for more information on map paths and editing the 3DS.SET file.

The second way to make sure 3D Studio can find the map files is to copy the necessary maps from the *Inside 3D Studio* CD-ROM to the subdirectory on your hard drive that contains the saved 3DS file. 3D Studio automatically looks in the subdirectory of the 3DS file for maps. Copying the map files to the hard drive has the added benefit of increasing access speed to the maps, and ensures that the maps are available even if the *Inside 3D Studio* CD-ROM is not in your CD-ROM drive or if the CD-ROM drive is not available to the operating system.

Copying the Exercise Files to Your Hard Drive

If you do not have permanent access to a CD-ROM drive, you will need to copy the *Inside 3D Studio* exercise files from the *Inside 3D Studio* CD-ROM to your hard drive. Storing the exercise files on your hard drive has the added advantage of speeding up access to the files; CD-ROM drives are many times slower than a hard drive. In addition, you will always have access to all the maps required for the exercises automatically.

The following exercise outlines the steps for copying the exercise files from the CD-ROM to your hard drive. The exercise assumes that your CD-ROM drive is drive D and you want to put the exercise files on drive C. If your system is different, substitute your drive letters wherever you see C or D.

Copying the Exercise Files

Start from the DOS prompt. Make sure you are at the root directory of drive C (or the drive onto which you want to put the exercise files).

`C:\> MD I3D ↵`	Makes the \I3D subdirectory
`C:\> CD I3D ↵`	Makes the \I3D subdirectory current
`C:\I3D> COPY D:\I3D\*.* ↵`	Copies the exercise files from the CD-ROM to the C:\I3D subdirectory
`C:\I3D> CD\ ↵`	Makes the root directory current again
`C:\`	

That's all there is to it! Now, when you want to perform an exercise in the book, start 3D Studio as you normally do, and load the exercise files from and save to the C:\I3D subdirectory.

If you do not have permanent access to a CD-ROM drive, you might want to copy the program files and selected map files to your hard drive in addition to the exercise files. Put them into subdirectories with the same names as the ones on the CD-ROM.

Using Paint Shop Pro 2.01

Paint Shop Pro is a Windows program that enables you to work with multiple bitmap images at one time. You can display, convert, alter, scan, and print images in the following file formats: BMP, CLP, CUT, DIB, EPS, GIF, IFF, IMG, JAS, JIF, JPG (JPEG), LBM, MAC, MSP, PCD

(Kodak Photo CD), PIC, PCX, RAS, RLE, TGA, TIFF, WMF, and WPG. Paint Shop Pro performs batch conversion for those large conversion jobs.

With Paint Shop Pro, you can flip, mirror, rotate in one-degree increments, resize, resample, crop, add a border, and use 19 standard filters to alter bitmap images. Paint Shop Pro also supports user-defined filters to enable you to create and apply your own filters. You can adjust brightness, contrast, highlight, shadow, gamma correction, and *red, green, blue* (RGB) values of an image. You can also grayscale and solarize the colors of an image. Paint Shop Pro also enables you to increase or decrease color depth.

Installing Paint Shop Pro

Before you can use Paint Shop Pro, you have to run the installation program from Windows so it will work properly on your computer. You cannot just copy the files from the CD-ROM to your hard disk, nor can you run Paint Shop Pro from the CD-ROM. The files on the CD-ROM are compressed to save space. The installation program decompresses the program files, copies them onto your hard drive, and sets up Paint Shop Pro in Windows.

The following exercise describes how to install Paint Shop Pro from the *Inside 3D Studio* CD-ROM. The exercise assumes that your CD-ROM drive is drive D and you want to install Paint Shop Pro on drive C. If your system is different, substitute your drive letters wherever you see C or D.

Installing Paint Shop Pro

Start Windows, make Program Manager *the active window, and place the* Inside 3D Studio CD-ROM *in your CD-ROM drive*

Choose File, *then* Run	Opens the Run dialog box
Type **D:\PSP\SETUP** *in the* Command Line *text box*	Specifies the name and location of the installation program
Leave the Run Minimized *check box off, and choose* OK	Executes the installation program
Choose OK *to accept the default installation subdirectory or specify an alternate drive and subdirectory for the Paint Shop Pro program files, and then choose* OK	

The installation program creates any necessary subdirectories, decompresses the necessary files, and places them onto your hard drive. The status of the installation process is displayed as each file is installed.

*When the program files have been copied
to your hard drive, choose* Yes, *then
select a program group from the
drop-down list, and choose* OK

Adds the Paint Shop Pro icon
to a Program Manager group
automatically

The setup program will notify you when the installation is complete.

Be sure to read Paint Shop Pro's online documentation. It is full of useful information for
working with bitmap images.

Registering Paint Shop Pro

Paint Shop Pro is published by JASC, Inc. and is distributed as shareware. You can use the
shareware version of Paint Shop Pro for a 30-day trial period. If you would like to continue to
use Paint Shop Pro after the 30-day trial period, you are required to purchase the licensed
version of Paint Shop Pro. You are not released from purchasing the licensed version of Paint
Shop Pro by purchasing *Inside 3D Studio* and the *Inside 3D Studio* CD-ROM.

When you purchase the licensed version of Paint Shop Pro, you will receive a disk with the
licensed version and the printed user's guide. Technical support for Paint Shop Pro is
provided by JASC, Inc. to registered users. JASC can be reached at (612)930-9171. Paint Shop
Pro can be purchased from a number of sources. To obtain the listing of vendors and print an
order form, follow the steps in the next exercise.

Obtaining a Paint Shop Pro Vendor List

Double-click on the Paint Shop Pro *icon*

Starts Paint Shop Pro

Choose the Help *button in the* Paint
Shop Pro Shareware Notice *dialog box*

Accesses the Windows help system

Click on the vendor of your choice

Displays ordering information

Choose File, *then* Print Topic

Prints the order form

Using Graphic Workshop 7.0

Graphic Workshop is a DOS program to view, print, and alter bitmap images. It has many
features that are similar to Paint Shop Pro. Graphic Workshop has the added advantage of
being accessible from within 3D Studio. Just set up Graphic Workshop as an external program
in the 3DS.SET file. See Chapter 1 for more information on the 3DS.SET file.

VI

Appendixes

With Graphic Workshop, you can dither and threshold the color images to black and white, reverse, rotate and flip, scale, reduce the number of colors and do color dithering, sharpen, soften, apply special effects, crop, create catalogs of a collection of images, and adjust the brightness, contrast, and color balance of bitmap images. Graphic Workshop also has a scripting language.

Installing Graphic Workshop

Before you can use Graphic Workshop, you have to run the installation program so that it will work properly on your computer. You cannot just copy the files from the CD-ROM to your hard disk, nor can you run Graphic Workshop from the CD-ROM. The files on the CD-ROM are compressed to save space. The installation program decompresses the program files, copies them onto your hard drive, and sets up Graphic Workshop.

The following exercise shows you how to install Graphic Workshop from the *Inside 3D Studio* CD-ROM. The exercise assumes that your CD-ROM drive is drive D and you want to install Graphic Workshop on drive C. If your system is different, substitute your drive letters wherever you see C or D.

Installing Graphic Workshop

Place the *Inside 3D Studio* CD-ROM into your CD-ROM drive. Start from the DOS prompt and log in to your CD-ROM drive. Make sure you are at the root directory.

`D:\> CD\GWSDOS` ↵	Changes to the subdirectory that contains the installation files
`D:\GWSDOS> SETUP` ↵	Starts the installation program
Press ↵Enter *to accept the default installation drive and subdirectory, or enter an alternate drive and subdirectory*	Specifies the subdirectory for installation

The installation program creates any necessary subdirectories, decompresses the files, and places them onto your hard drive. The status of the installation process is displayed as each file is installed.

Press any key to continue after the files have been copied to your hard drive	
Press Y *and read the configuration section of the documentation*	Displays the documentation
Press Esc *when you are done reading*	Exits the documentation and starts the configuration program

Configure Graphic Workshop according to the documentation. It is not necessary to completely configure Graphic Workshop; it will work with all default settings.

Press F10	Saves the configuration and returns to the DOS prompt
C:\GWSDOS> **GWS** ↵	Starts Graphic Workshop
Press Esc, *then* Y	Exits Graphic Workshop

 Add the Graphic Workshop subdirectory to your DOS path in your AUTOEXEC.BAT file so that you can easily access Graphic Workshop from the DOS prompt at any time.

The Graphic Workshop documentation contains important information for working with the various types of bitmap file formats, detailed instructions for configuring and using Graphic Workshop, and a list of books for graphics programming.

Registering Graphic Workshop

Graphic Workshop is published by Alchemy Mindworks and is distributed as shareware. You can use the shareware version of Graphics Workshop for a 30-day trial period. If you would like to continue to use Graphic Workshop after the 30-day trial period, you are required to purchase the licensed version of Graphic Workshop. You are not released from purchasing the licensed version of Graphic Workshop by purchasing *Inside 3D Studio* and the *Inside 3D Studio* CD-ROM.

You can register Graphic Workshop by calling 1-800-263-1138 in the United States and Canada or 1-905-729-4969 outside North America. You can pay the registration fee with American Express or Visa. CompuServe users can register Graphic Workshop by typing **GO GWREG** at any CompuServe prompt. Alchemy Mindworks can be contacted on CompuServe at 70451,2734.

Technical support for Graphic Workshop is provided only by Alchemy Mindworks. Alchemy Mindworks provides technical support to registered users only. In addition to technical support, registered users of Graphic Workshop will receive the Graphic Workshop accessory disk and the Graphic Workshop screen-capture utility at no additional cost.

Using the Autodesk Animator Pro Player

The Autodesk Animator Pro Player is a flic-playing program that lets you play animations and display pictures. Animations and pictures can be displayed one at a time or automatically following a text script file. You can prepare and present complex animated presentations, complete with variable screen resolutions and keyboard-controlled menus. The Autodesk Animator Pro Player can display flic, animated cel, and image files from Autodesk Animator Pro, Autodesk 3D Studio, Autodesk Animator, and any other application that generates compatible files.

The Autodesk Animator Pro Player and its support files can be freely distributed by you. It is designed to let you deliver your presentations independently of Autodesk Animator Pro and 3D Studio.

Installing the Autodesk Animator Pro Player

The following exercise shows you how to install the Autodesk Animator Pro Player from the *Inside 3D Studio* CD-ROM. The exercise assumes that your CD-ROM drive is drive D and you want to install the Autodesk Animator Pro Player on drive C. If your system is different, substitute your drive letters wherever you see C or D. The exercise also assumes that you want to install the Autodesk Animator Pro Player into a subdirectory named \ AAPLAYHI. If you want to install into another subdirectory, you will have to change the XCOPY command to reflect your desired installation subdirectory. The installation files are located in the \AAPLAYHI subdirectory on the CD-ROM.

Installing the Autodesk Animator Pro Player

Start from the DOS prompt.

`C:\> XCOPY D:\AAPLAYHI\*.* C:\AAPLAYHI\*.* /S` ↵

The XCOPY command creates the necessary subdirectories and copies all the program files from the CD-ROM to your hard drive.

`C:\> CD\AAPLAYHI` ↵

`C:\AAPLAYHI> PLAY` ↵   Starts the demonstration script

Press Esc   Ends the presentation

Consult the AAPLAYHI.DOC file for instructions on how to use the Autodesk Animator Pro Player. Technical support for the Autodesk Animator Pro Player is only provided by Autodesk on the ASOFT forum on CompuServe.

Examining New Riders Publishing Map Files

The CD-ROM contains over 200 MB of TIFF bitmapped files. Most of the files are 24-bit color, some are 8-bit color, a few are tileable, and some have Alpha channel information. You are free to use them in your animations without restriction. You cannot, however, give the files to anyone else.

The map files are located in the \NRPMAPS subdirectory on the CD-ROM. Also in the \NRPMAPS subdirectory are two files to help you keep track of all the images. The first file is a flic that has thumbnail snapshots of all the images. The name of the flic file is CATALOG.FLC. You can load the file in the Autodesk Animator Pro Player, 3D Studio, or any other program that can play FLC files to view the thumbnails. The second file is a text file with a list of all the file names and descriptions of the image, image size, and color depth. This file is named CATALOG.TXT and can be loaded by the 3D Studio Text Editor. After the file is loaded in the Text Editor, you can search it for keywords to help you find the image you need.

Using the Map Files

The map files can be used directly from the CD-ROM. You do not need to copy them to your hard drive. If you do not have full-time access to a CD-ROM drive, you can copy the images you need to a subdirectory on 3D Studio's map paths. The usual location for maps is in the \3DS3\MAPS subdirectory.

If you want to use the files directly from the CD-ROM, you will have to make sure that 3D Studio can find the files at render time. You must add the location of the NRP maps to 3D Studio's map paths. This can be done in two ways. You can temporarily assign the CD-ROM's subdirectory as the map path by choosing Info, Configure, and then clicking on the Map Paths button in the Program Configuration dialog box. After the Specify Map Paths dialog box appears, click in the list box and enter the full path (including drive letter) of the NRP maps. If your CD-ROM drive is D, the map path should look like the following:

```
D:\NRPMAPS
```

This method for specifying map paths only works for one 3D Studio work session. If you quit and start up 3D Studio again, you will need to respecify the map path to the CD-ROM.

To make sure the NRP map files are on the map path every time you start 3D Studio, add the following line to the MAP-PATH section of the 3DS.SET file:

```
MAP-PATH = "D:\NRPMAPS"
```

If your CD-ROM drive is something other than D, substitute your drive letter. See Chapter 1 for more information on map paths and editing the 3DS.SET file.

Exploring Vistapro

Vistapro is a program for quickly creating realistic landscape images. The images can be used as maps or background images in 3D Studio. You can use *U.S. Geological Survey* (USGS) *digital elevation model* (DEM) data or fractal patterns as input for creating landscapes.

Included in the back of this book is an offer from Virtual Reality Laboratories, Inc. for an upgrade to the CD-ROM version of Vistapro 3.0. This version of Vistapro has many additional features including DXF output of terrain models, and a CD-ROM full of DEM data from all over the United States and the planet Mars. There is a demo version of Vistapro 3.0 on the *Inside 3D Studio* CD-ROM. You do not need to install the demo to run it. Just change to the \VISTADMO subdirectory and run the VPDEMO program.

Installing Vistapro 1.0

Before you can use Vistapro, you have to run the installation program so it will work properly on your computer. You cannot just copy the files from the CD-ROM to your hard disk, nor can you run Vistapro from the CD-ROM. The files on the CD-ROM are compressed to save space. The installation program decompresses the program files, copies them onto your hard drive, and sets up Vistapro.

The following exercise shows you how to install Vistapro from the *Inside 3D Studio* CD-ROM. The exercise assumes that your CD-ROM drive is drive D and you want to install Vistapro on drive C. If your system is different, substitute your drive letters wherever you see C or D.

Installing Vistapro

Place the *Inside 3D Studio* CD-ROM in your CD-ROM drive, start from the DOS prompt, and log in to the CD-ROM drive.

`D:\> CD\VISTAPRO ⏎`	Changes to the subdirectory that contains the installation files
`D:\VISTAPRO> INSTALL ⏎`	Starts the installation program
Click on the Start Installation *button*	
Specify the letter of your CD-ROM drive in the CD-ROM Source *edit box*	
If you want a different destination subdirectory, specify an alternate location in the Destination *edit box*	Specifies the subdirectory for installation
Click on the Start Installation *button*	

The installation program creates any necessary subdirectories, decompresses the files, and places them into your hard drive. The status of the installation process is displayed as each file is installed. The setup program will notify you when the installation is complete.

Click on OK *in the* Installation Complete *dialog box*

The installation program gives instructions for starting Vistapro. The documentation for Vistapro is contained in several text files in the destination subdirectory. Vistapro is only supported by Virtual Reality Laboratories, Inc.

Using Scripts

There are several custom Keyscript programs in the \KEYSCRPT directory on the *Inside 3D Studio* CD-ROM. You are free to use them to produce your animations and create your own Keyscript programs. You can share your programs based on the code in these programs with others as well. You cannot, however, charge for any programs that use code from these programs. You also must acknowledge New Riders Publishing's copyright to the borrowed sections of code. Chapter 22, "Keyframer Scripting," contains information about programming in Keyscript and how to use these programs.

Using 3DE

3DE is a utility for creating dialog boxes for your Keyscript programs. You can build dialog boxes for IPAS Plug-In applications as well. 3DE is freeware and is presented "as is." It is not supported by Autodesk, the Yost Group, or New Riders Publishing. You can get your questions about 3DE answered on CompuServe in the ASOFT forum.

To install 3DE, copy the contents of the \3DE directory to your \3DS4\PROCESS subdirectory. There are several text files included in the \3DE directory that explain how to use 3DE in detail. Chapter 22 contains information on how to use 3DE to create dialog boxes for your Keyscript programs.

INDEX

Symbols

INDEX

INDEX

INDEX

INDEX

INDEX

INDEX

INDEX

INDEX

INDEX

INDEX

INDEX

INDEX

INDEX

INDEX

INDEX

H

INDEX

INDEX

INDEX

INDEX

INDEX

INDEX

INDEX

INDEX

INDEX

INDEX

INDEX

INDEX

INDEX

INDEX

INDEX

INDEX

INDEX

REGISTRATION CARD

Fill out this card to receive information about future 3D Studio books and other New Riders titles!

Name _____ **Title** _____

Company _____

Address _____

City/State/ZIP _____

I bought this book because: _____

_____

I purchased this book from:

☐ A bookstore (Name _____)

☐ A software or electronics store (Name _____)

☐ A mail order (Name of Catalog _____)

I purchase this many computer books each year:

☐ 1–5   ☐ 6 or more

I currently use these applications: _____

_____

_____

_____

I found these chapters to be the most informative: _____

_____

I found these chapters to be the least informative: _____

_____

Additional comments: _____

_____

☐ I would like to see my name in print! You may use my name and quote me in future New Riders products and promotions. My daytime phone number is: _____

New Riders Publishing 201 West 103rd Street • Indianapolis, Indiana 46290 USA

Fold Here

- -

PLACE
STAMP
HERE

New Riders Publishing
201 West 103rd Street
Indianapolis, Indiana 46290
USA

Fold Here

PLACE
STAMP
HERE

New Riders Publishing
201 West 103rd Street
Indianapolis, Indiana 46290
USA

GET CONNECTED
to the ultimate source of computer information!

The MCP Forum on CompuServe

Go online with the world's leading computer book publisher!
Macmillan Computer Publishing offers everything
you need for computer success!

Find the books that are right for you!

A complete online catalog,
plus sample chapters and tables of contents
give you an in-depth look at all our books.
The best way to shop or browse!

➤ Get fast answers and technical support for
   MCP books and software

➤ Join discussion groups on major computer
   subjects

➤ Interact with our expert authors via e-mail
   and conferences

➤ Download software from our immense
   library:

  ▷ Source code from books
  ▷ Demos of hot software
  ▷ The best shareware and freeware
  ▷ Graphics files

Join now and get a free CompuServe Starter Kit!

To receive your free CompuServe Introductory Membership, call **1-800-848-8199** and ask for representative #597.

The Starter Kit includes:

➤ Personal ID number and password
➤ $15 credit on the system
➤ Subscription to *CompuServe Magazine*

Once on the CompuServe System, type:

GO MACMILLAN

for the most computer information anywhere!

MACMILLAN
COMPUTER
PUBLISHING

CompuServe

PLUG YOURSELF INTO...

The MCP Internet Site

Free information and vast computer resources from the world's leading computer book publisher—online!

Find the books that are right for you!
A complete online catalog, plus sample chapters and tables of contents give you an in-depth look at *all* our books.

- ✦ **Stay informed** with the latest computer industry news through discussion groups, an online newsletter, and customized subscription news.

- ✦ **Get fast answers** to your questions about MCP books and software.

- ✦ **Visit** our online bookstore for the latest information and editions!

- ✦ **Communicate** with our expert authors through e-mail and conferences.

- ✦ **Play** in the BradyGame Room with info, demos, and shareware!

- ✦ **Download software** from the immense MCP library

Drop by the new Internet site of Macmillan Computer Publishing!

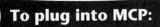

GRAPHICS TITLES

INSIDE CORELDRAW! 4.0, SPECIAL EDITION

DANIEL GRAY

An updated version of the #1 best-selling tutorial on CorelDRAW!

CorelDRAW! 4.0
ISBN: 1-56205-164-4
$34.95 USA

CORELDRAW! SPECIAL EFFECTS

NEW RIDERS PUBLISHING

An inside look at award-winning techniques from professional CorelDRAW! designers!

CorelDRAW! 4.0
ISBN: 1-56205-123-7
$39.95 USA

CORELDRAW! NOW!

RICHARD FELDMAN

The hands-on tutorial for users who want practical information now!
CorelDRAW! 4.0
ISBN: 1-56205-131-8
$21.95 USA

INSIDE CORELDRAW! FOURTH EDITION

DANIEL GRAY

The popular tutorial approach to learning CorelDRAW!…with complete coverage of version 3.0!
CorelDRAW! 3.0
ISBN: 1-56205-106-7
$24.95 USA

NETWORKING TITLES

#1 Bestseller!

INSIDE NOVELL NETWARE, THIRD EDITION

DEBRA NIEDERMILLER-CHAFFINS & DREW HEYWOOD

This best-selling tutorial and reference has been updated and made even better!

NetWare 2.2, 3.11, & 3.12
ISBN: 1-56205-257-8
$34.95 USA

MAXIMIZING NOVELL NETWARE

JOHN JERNEY & ELNA TYMES

Complete coverage of Novell's flagship product...for NetWare system administrators!

NetWare 3.11
ISBN: 1-56205-095-8
$39.95 USA

NETWARE: THE PROFESSIONAL REFERENCE, SECOND EDITION

KARANJIT SIYAN

This updated version for professional NetWare administrators and technicians provides the most comprehensive reference available for this phenomenal network system.

NetWare 2.x & 3.x
ISBN: 1-56205-158-X
$42.95 USA

NETWARE 4: PLANNING AND IMPLEMENTATION

SUNIL PADIYAR

A guide to planning, installing, and managing a NetWare 4.0 network that best serves your company's objectives.

NetWare 4.0
ISBN: 1-56205-159-8
$27.95 USA

To Order, Call 1-800-428-5331